HANDBOOK OF EVIDENCE-BASED PRACTICE IN CLINICAL PSYCHOLOGY VOLUME 1

HANDBOOK OF EVIDENCE-BASED PRACTICE IN CLINICAL PSYCHOLOGY VOLUME 1

Child and Adolescent Disorders

Edited by

PETER STURMEY
AND
MICHEL HERSEN

WILEY

John Wiley & Sons, Inc.

Library of Congress Cataloging-in-Publication Data

Handbook of evidence-based practice in clinical psychology / edited by Peter Sturmey and Michel Hersen.
  v. ; cm.
Includes bibliographical references and index.
Contents: v. 1. Child and adolescent disorders – v. 2. Adult disorders.
ISBNs for Vol. 1: 978-0-470-33544-4 (cloth: alk. paper); 978-1-118-14471-8 (ebk); 978-1-118-14472-5 (ebk); 978-1-118-14470-1 (ebk)
ISBNs for Vol. 2: 978-0-470-33546-8 (cloth: alk. paper); 978-1-118-14476-3 (ebk); 978-1-118-14475-6 (ebk); 978-1-118-14474-9 (ebk)
ISBN 978-1-118-15639-1 (eMRW)
ISBN 978-0-470-33542-0 (set)
    1. Clinical psychology–Practice.   2. Evidence-based psychotherapy.   I. Sturmey, Peter.   II. Hersen, Michel.
[DNLM: 1. Mental Disorders–therapy.   2. Evidence-Based Practice.   3. Psychology, Clinical–methods.   WM 400]
  RC467.95.H36 2012
  616.89—dc22

                                                                                          2011012039

Contents

124990

Preface

Eysenck (1957) concluded that "the figures fail to support the hypothesis that psychotherapy facilitates recovery from neurotic disorder" (p. 322), but by 1977 Smith and Glass could conclude, after reviewing 375 studies, that "findings showed psychotherapy to be effective" (p. 752). Over the next 35 years interest in psychotherapy outcomes research flourished and is no mere idle academic question, but an issue for public policy, and now directs the expenditures of public health monies on a national scale in some countries. Currently, professional organizations, such as the American Psychological Association, and national organizations, such as the United Kingdom's National Institute of Clinical Excellence (NICE), periodically publish lists of therapies that meet standards for evidence-based practice; the NICE goes further and influences national spending and professional training in disseminating and evaluating evidence-based practices in large-scale routine service settings. Psychotherapy outcome research has come a long way since Eysenck's dystopic conclusion.

This first volume of *Handbook of Evidence-Based Practice in Clinical Psychology* shows that in the area of child and adolescent disorders there has been much progress in identifying and disseminating evidence-based practices. Each chapter documents the large amount of research that now identifies evidence-based practices for most disorders. To be sure, some disorders have very large evidence bases that permit greater confidence in conclusions and answers to more specific questions, such as which of several treatments might be most effective; others have more modest databases, permitting only modest and less certain conclusions.

Various forms of cognitive behavior therapy predominate as evidence-based practices, although in other areas—such as intellectual disabilities, autism spectrum disorders, and pica—behavioral treatments alone are at the forefront. For some disorders, certain forms of psychotherapy, such as interpersonal psychotherapy, meet the criteria for evidence-based practice. As evidence continues to accumulate these conclusions may change.

This volume is in two parts. Part I of this volume addresses general issues such as what the standards of evidence are, professional issues, and economics of evidence-based practice. Part II addresses many specific disorders of childhood and adolescence.

We believe that this volume presents a snapshot of an ever-developing field. It provides therapists, teachers, students, and other practitioners a starting point to become familiar with evidence-based practice in clinical psychology. It challenges psychology teachers to see if they teach evidence-based psychotherapies and also challenges service providers and finders to examine their own practices to see if they provide evidence-based practice.

REFERENCES

Eysenck, H. J. (1957). The effects of psychotherapy: An evaluation. *Journal of Consulting Psychology, 16*, 319–324.

Smith, M. L., & Glass, G. V. (1977). Meta-analysis of psychotherapy outcome studies. *American Psychologist, 32*, 372–360.

Acknowledgments

We would first like to thank our authors. Many of them undertook an enormous task of summarizing sometimes hundreds of articles, systematic literature reviews, and consensus panels and at times reviewing the outcome literature for many different forms of treatment for one disorder. They faced the challenge of being accurate and fair in identifying those practices that the literature support, those that researchers have little convincing evidence to support, and those that research has shown to be ineffective or harmful. We believe they all succeeded in doing so. We would both like to express our unending thanks to Carole Londeree's persistent and cheerful technical assistance throughout this project. Finally, we would like to express our thanks to the editorial staff at John Wiley & Sons who worked so hard to make this project a success.

Contributors

Nancy D. Berkman, PhD, is a Senior Health Policy Research Analyst at RTI, International. She has led the development of four systematic reviews of the literature for the Agency for Healthcare Research and Policy's Evidence-based Practice Center Program (EPC) including management of eating disorders. Dr. Berkman is currently the Project Director for an EPC-sponsored project developing, refining, and coordinating qualitative methods research related to conducting systematic and comparative evidence reviews of the literature.

Jonathan Breidbord is a graduate student at the University of Cambridge and has interest in childhood developmental conditions, critical appraisal, and metric meaningfulness.

Kimberly A. Brownley is Assistant Professor of Psychiatry at the University of North Carolina at Chapel Hill with a broad background in cardiovascular and neuroendocrine stress research. Her current and most recent work focuses on the psychobiology of appetite regulation and its application to understanding the etiology and consequences of eating disorders, psychotropic medication-induced weight gain, functional dyspepsia, and ethnic disparities in obesity.

Jennifer L. Bruzek, PhD, is a Postdoctoral Fellow in the Kennedy Center at Vanderbilt University. She has published several scholarly papers on intellectual disabilities, child-parent interactions, and behavior analysis.

Cynthia M. Bulik is the Jordan Distinguished Professor of Eating Disorders in the Department of Psychiatry in the University of North Carolina School of Medicine, Professor of Nutrition in the Gillings School of Global Public Health, and Director of the University of North Carolina Eating Disorders Program.

J. Gerard Byrne is a Consultant Child and Adolescent Psychiatrist at the Lucena Clinic, Dublin, Eire. He specializes in attachment theory in children and adolescents.

Mark J. Chaffin is a Professor of Pediatrics at the University of Oklahoma Health Sciences Center, and director of research for Developmental and Behavioral Pediatrics and the Center on Child Abuse and Neglect. His research interests include development and implementation of prevention and intervention models in child abuse and child welfare settings. Dr. Chaffin serves on the advisory board of the California Evidence Based Clearinghouse for Child Welfare.

Jane E. Cole is an Assistant Professor of Special Education at Miami, Ohio University. She received her PhD from the University of Virginia in 2007. Her research interest is primarily in the area of mathematics assessment and intervention for students with high incidence disabilities.

Christine A. Conelea received her MS in Clinical Psychology from the University of Wisconsin-Milwaukee and is currently completing her predoctoral internship at the Alpert Medical School of Brown University. Ms. Conelea has authored or coauthored 18 papers or chapters on tic disorders, trichotillomania, obsessive-compulsive disorder, and other repetitive behavior problems, and has clinical and research interests in the phenomenology, maintenance, impact, and treatment of these disorders.

Joshua Cooper is a CUNY Graduate Center doctoral student in the Queens College Learning Processes and Behavior Analysis program. He is currently involved in research investigating equivalence classes and procedures to induce joint stimulus control.

Felicity Cowdrey completed her undergraduate degree in Psychology and Cognitive Neuroscience at the University of Nottingham. She is currently a DPhil candidate at the Department of Psychiatry, University of Oxford. Her current research interests include the cognitive and emotional processes that maintain eating disorders, especially anorexia nervosa.

Angie Dahl is a doctoral student in the Clinical, Counseling and School Psychology PhD Program at Utah State University in Logan, Utah. Her research focuses on factors related to optimal developmental outcomes in child and adolescent populations and she is employed as a school psychologist.

Amy L. Damashek is an Assistant Professor of Clinical Psychology at Western Michigan University. She teaches and provides clinical supervision in Western Michigan University's clinical psychology doctoral program. She received her PhD from the University of Missouri and completed a postdoctoral fellowship at the University of Oklahoma Health Sciences Center, Center on Child Abuse and Neglect. Her research interests include prevention of unintentional child injuries and child maltreatment. Her recent research has focused on the role of caregiver supervision in children's unintentional injuries. She is also interested in research on dissemination of evidence-based child maltreatment interventions.

Robert Didden is Professor of Intellectual Disabilities, Learning and Behavior at the Behavioural Science Institute of the Radboud University Nijmegen, the Netherlands. He also is head of Trajectum Center of Expertise and a psychologist at Trajectum Hanzeborg, a center for the care and treatment of individuals with mild intellectual disability. His research and clinical interests include behavioral and psychiatric disorders in intellectual disability and/or autism spectrum disorders.

Klaus Drieschner is senior research psychologist at Trajectum, a treatment center for individuals with mild intellectual disabilities and serious problem behavior or offending behavior. His research interests include the effectiveness of correctional treatment, treatment motivation, and test construction.

Paul M. G. Emmelkamp is a licensed psychotherapist and clinical psychologist and full professor of clinical psychology at the University of Amsterdam. Over the years, he has published widely on the etiology and treatment of anxiety disorders. He is involved in therapy-outcome studies on adults with work-related distress, substance abuse disorders, personality disorders, depression, and anxiety disorders; on youth with ADHD, conduct disorder, and anxiety disorders; and on the elderly with anxiety disorders. He has written and coedited many books, and has over 350 publications in peer-reviewed journals or books. He has received a number of honors and awards, including a distinguished professorship ("Academy Professor") by the Royal Academy of Arts and Sciences.

Gregory A. Fabiano is an Associate Professor in the Department of Counseling, School and Educational Psychology at the University at Buffalo–SUNY. His research focuses on evidenced-based practices for children and adolescents with attention-deficit/hyperactivity disorder (ADHD).

Clint Field is an Assistant Professor of Psychology at Utah State University in Logan, Utah. He conducts research related to applied behavior analysis, parent-child interaction patterns (particularly as they relate to the treatment of childhood disorders), and the early intervention and primary prevention of children's conduct problems.

Peter Fonagy is Freud Memorial Professor of Psychoanalysis, Head of the Research Department of Clinical, Educational and Health Psychology at University College London and Chief Executive at the Anna Freud Centre, London. He is a clinical psychologist and training and supervising analyst in the British Psycho-Analytical Society in child and adult analysis. His clinical interests center around issues of borderline psychopathology, violence, and early attachment relationships. His work attempts to integrate empirical research with psychoanalytic theory. He chaired the guideline development group for the National Institute for Health and Clinical Excellence's clinical guideline on childhood depression.

E. Michael Foster is professor at the Gillings School of Global Public Health, University of North Carolina at Chapel Hill. His research focuses on the statistical methods of causal inference and the economic evaluation of programs and interventions for at-risk children and youth.

Kurt A. Freeman is an Associate Professor of Pediatrics and Psychiatry at Oregon Health and Science University of Portland, Oregon. He has published on behavioral assessment and intervention strategies for common to severe child rearing challenges including bedtime/sleep problems, parenting practices, conduct problems, and aberrant behavior in individuals with developmental disorders.

Sarah Gebhardt is currently a doctoral student in the school psychology program at Lehigh University. She received her master's degree from Miami, Ohio University in 2009. Her research interests include applied behavior analysis and pediatric psychology.

Ata Ghaderi's research focuses on eating disorders, including identifying risk and protective factors in the development of eating disorders among young women in the general population, the prevalence and incidence of eating disorders and interventions for eating disorders including refinement of cognitive behavioral treatment (CBT) as well as CBT-based self-help for bulimia nervosa, binge eating disorder, and other eating disorders not otherwise specified.

Tamlynn D. Graupner is cofounder and Chief Executive Officer of the Wisconsin early Autism project. She is currently completing a doctoral degree in pediatric neuropsychology and conducting a study of brain structure and functioning using fMRI neuroimaging with adolescents who received intensive behavioral therapy as toddlers.

Alan M. Gross is Professor of Psychology and Director of Clinical Training at the University of Mississippi. His research interests are in the area of behavior problems in children and sexual assault.

Rebecca J. Hamblin is a graduate student in Clinical Psychology at the University of Mississippi. Her research interests are in internalizing and externalizing disorders in children and implementation of effective treatments in school settings.

Michael Handwerk, PhD, is a Clinical Psychologist at Harrisburg Medical Center in southern Illinois. He conducts research on the assessment and treatment of disruptive behavior disorders, variables relating to the development of antisocial and aggressive behavior, and the effectiveness of residential care.

Marianne Jackson received her master's and doctoral degrees in Behavior Analysis from the University of Nevada, Reno. She is currently an Assistant Professor at California State University, Fresno, where she also serves as codirector of the Central California Autism Center and continues to pursue her research interests in the development of derived relational responding, the role of derived responding complex human behavior, and the processes of verbal motivation. Areas of clinical interest include problem behavior, teaching the basic processes of verbal behavior, verbal processes in health and fitness, and the development of complex social skills.

Anthony James is Honorary Senior Lecturer, University of Oxford, and Consultant Child and Adolescent Psychiatrist. His research interests include early-onset psychoses and anxiety disorder.

Christine James studied biomedical sciences at University College London and is currently doing an MSc at Kings College, London.

Mark Jones is a biostatistician for the Centre for Healthcare Related Infection Surveillance and Prevention, Queensland Health, and is also an Adjunct Senior Lecturer with the School of Population Health, the University of Queensland. He has a strong interest in stuttering treatment research, clinical trials, and biostatistics. He leads the team at the

Australian Stuttering Research Centre with the design of clinical trials, and has led the team in developing new outcome measures for clinical trials of stuttering treatments.

Craig H. Kennedy is Associate Dean for Research and Professor of Special Education and Pediatrics at Peabody College of Vanderbilt University. He has published over 180 scholarly papers and books on intellectual disabilities, autism, instructional methods, and behavior analysis.

Russell Lang is Assistant Professor of Special Education at Texas State University, San Marcos, Texas. His research has involved the use of applied behavior analysis in the treatment of problem behavior and in the instruction of communication, academics, and self-help skills for individuals with developmental disabilities.

Giulio E. Lancioni is a professor in the Department of Psychology at the University of Bari, Italy. His research interests include the development and evaluation of assistive technology, social and adaptive skills training, and strategies for examining and teaching choice with individuals with severe or profound and multiple disabilities.

Michelle Levine graduated from the University of Rochester in 2009 with a BA in Brain and Cognitive Sciences. She is currently a research assistant at the Yale Child Study Center and plans to pursue a PhD in clinical psychology in the near future.

Scott O. Lilienfeld is a faculty member in the Department of Psychology at Emory University, Atlanta, since 1994. His research interests include the causes and assessment of personality disorders and personality traits, personality assessment psychiatric classification and diagnosis, pseudoscience and clinical psychology, evidence-based clinical practice, scientific thinking and its application to psychology, and philosophical psychology.

Maya S. Madzharova is doctoral student at the Learning Processes and Behavioral Analysis program at the Graduate Center and Queens College, City University of New York.

Her current research focuses on developing effective strategies to train staff and parents and to increase peer-to-peer interactions among individuals diagnosed with ASD.

Lindsay Maffei-Almodovar is a doctoral student in the Learning Processes and Behavior Analysis subprogram of the Psychology Department at the CUNY Graduate Center. Her research focuses on training caregivers to use evidence-based behavior analytic practices in teaching children with developmental disabilities.

Jessica Malmberg is a doctoral student in the Clinical, Counseling, and School Psychology PhD Program at Utah State University in Logan, Utah. Central to her research interests are variables related to the development, display, and modification of disruptive behavior problems exhibited by children. She has particular interest in studying associated risk factors and in establishing primary prevention strategies for such problems of childhood.

William Martinez is a graduate student in the Clinical-Child Psychology doctoral program at DePaul University in Chicago. In 2010, he was awarded a Mental Health and Substance Abuse Services Fellowship through the American Psychological Association's Minority Fellowship Program. His research interests include the development, implementation, and dissemination of evidence-based treatment programs for urban, ethnic minority youth with a particular emphasis on treatments for anxiety and trauma in Latino youth populations. In addition, he is interested in the assessment of internalizing symptoms, including evaluating the psychometric properties and measurement equivalence of instruments used with ethnic minority populations.

Michael E. May is Assistant Professor of Special Education at Southern Illinois University. He has published several scholarly papers on intellectual disabilities, gene-brain-behavior, aggression, and behavior analysis.

Michael W. Mellon is a pediatric psychologist in the Department of Pediatrics at

Cincinnati Children's Hospital Medical Center with prior appointments at Arkansas Children's Hospital and the Mayo Clinic. Dr. Mellon earned his PhD from the University of Memphis and completed an internship at the University of Mississippi Medical Center. He currently provides psychotherapy to children with inflammatory bowel disease. He has published and presented papers in the areas of behavioral treatments for enuresis and encopresis and attention-deficit/hyperactivity disorder. Current research activities include developing and validating efforts to adapt acceptance and commitment therapy to patients with irritable bowel syndrome.

Glenn A. Melvin is a psychologist and lecturer at the Centre for Developmental Psychiatry and Psychology, School of Psychology and Psychiatry, Monash University, Melbourne, Australia. After completing a PhD in the treatment of adolescent depression at Monash University, he spent 2 years working as research scientist in the Division of Child and Adolescent Psychiatry at the New York State Psychiatric Institute. He is currently an investigator on a National Health and Medical Research Council funded clinical trial investigating psychosocial and pharmacological approaches to school refusal. Glenn's other research and clinical interests include assessment and treatment of pediatric internalizing disorders, irritability, responses to trauma, and suicide risk.

Ross Menzies works at the Australian Stuttering Research Centre, Faculty of Health Sciences, the University of Sydney. He a clinical psychologist with an interest in the origins and management of anxiety, and has a private practice in Sydney. He has developed cognitive behavior therapy packages for the treatment of obsessive-compulsive disorders and published theories of the origins of phobias. He led the Australian Stuttering Research Centre team in clarifying the role of anxiety in stuttering and its deleterious effects on speech rehabilitation

David B. McAdam is an Assistant Professor of Pediatrics at the University of Rochester School of Medicine and Dentistry. His research interests include the functional analysis and assessment of problem behavior, pica, and applied behavioral analytic interventions for persons with autism.

Kimberly McCombs-Thornton has worked with numerous nonprofits serving young children and families. Most recently, she and E. Michael Foster developed a plan for conducting an economic evaluation of a system-wide early childhood initiative for First 5 Los Angeles. She also has done extensive data analysis with large secondary data sets including the Fragile Families and Child Wellbeing Study, the National Study of Child and Adolescent Wellbeing, the National Longitudinal Survey of Youth, and the National Longitudinal Transition Study-2.

Rob McNeill is a Lecturer in the School of Population Health at the University of Auckland. His primary research interests are in the area of health services research and evaluation and he has taught research methods for over 10 years.

Oliver C. Mudford is Senior Lecturer in Psychology and Director of the Applied Behavior Analysis Program at the University of Auckland, New Zealand. His research and publications are on interventions, particularly with intellectual disabilities and/or developmental disorders, and applied behavior analysis methods. He is a member of the editorial boards of six scientific journals in those fields.

Maaike H. Nauta is an Assistent Professor at the Department of Clinical Psychology of the University of Groningen, the Netherlands. In addition, she works as a clinical psychologist and behavioral therapist at the outpatient clinic for child and adolescent psychiatry of the University Medical Center. Her main research interests include treatment outcome research in youth, treatment response, assessment, etiology, and intergenerational factors in the field of anxiety, mood, and emotional disorders in youth.

Susan O'Brian works at the Australian Stuttering Research Centre, Faculty of Health

Sciences, the University of Sydney. She has extensive experience in the field of stuttering treatment and research. Her major research interest is the effectiveness of early stuttering intervention in community settings. She also has published extensively in the area of adult stuttering treatment and stuttering measurement, and has developed mathematical methods for analysis of stuttering data for clinical trials.

Thomas G. O'Connor is Professor of Psychiatry and of Psychology and is Director of the Wynne Center for Family Research at the University of Rochester Medical Center. His research focuses on the mechanisms by which early stress exposure, both pre- and postnatal, alters bio-behavioral development in the child. He has been recipient of numerous research grants in the United States and United Kingdom and has received distinguished awards for his research. He also serves as an editor for the *Journal of Child Psychology and Psychiatry*.

William T. O'Donohue is widely recognized in the field for his proposed innovations in mental health service delivery, in treatment design and evaluation, and in knowledge of empirically supported cognitive behavior therapies. He is a member of the Association for the Advancement for Behavior. He has edited over 20 books, and written 35 book chapters and more than 75 articles in scholarly journals.

Mark O'Reilly is Mollie Villeret Davis Professor of Learning Disabilities at the University of Texas at Austin. His research focuses primarily on the assessment and treatment of challenging behavior, social skills training, and the design of assistive technology with persons with developmental disabilities.

Mark Onslow is the Foundation Director of the Australian Stuttering Research Centre, Faculty of Health Sciences, the University of Sydney. His background is speech pathology. He is a Principal Research Fellow of the National Health and Medical Research Council of Australia. His research interests are the epidemiology of early stuttering in preschoolers, mental health of those who stutter, measurement of stuttering, and the nature and treatment of stuttering.

Ann Packman works at the Australian Stuttering Research Centre, Faculty of Health Sciences, the University of Sydney. She has worked for more than 30 years in the area of stuttering as a clinician, teacher, and researcher. One of her current interests is theory of the cause of stuttering. She has cowritten a textbook on that topic, and has developed a theory of the cause of stuttering. She is the only Australian scientist to serve editorships of journals of the American Speech-Hearing Association.

Tonya M. Palermo is Professor of Anesthesiology and Pain Medicine at University of Washington School of Medicine and Seattle Children's Hospital. She has published widely on sleep in youth with medical conditions, pediatric chronic pain management, and behavioral treatments for pain and sleep disturbances.

William E. Pelham Jr. is a Professor in the Department of Psychology at Florida International University and Director of the Center for Children and Families. He is also a Professor Emeritus in the Department of Psychology at the University at Buffalo–SUNY. His research focuses on developing and evaluating evidence-based practices for children and adolescents with attention-deficit/hyperactivity disorder (ADHD), especially psychosocial interventions.

Katrina J. Phillips is a senior tutor in the Department of Psychology, the University of Auckland, New Zealand. She has copublished on staff training and developmental and intellectual disabilities.

Cathleen C. Piazza received her PhD from Tulane University. She is Professor of Pediatrics and Director of the Pediatric Feeding Disorders Program at the University of Nebraska Medical Center in Omaha, and she previously directed similar programs at the Marcus Institute in Atlanta and at the Johns Hopkins University School of Medicine in

Baltimore. Her research in the area of pediatric feeding disorders has been among the most systematic in the field and has firmly established behavioral approaches as preferred methods for assessment and treatment. Highly regarded for her general expertise in research methodology, Dr. Piazza just finished her tenure as editor of the *Journal of Applied Behavior Analysis*.

Stephen Pilling is Professor of Clinical Psychology and Clinical Effectiveness in the Research Department of Clinical, Health and Educational Psychology, University College London. He is the director of the National Collaborating Centre for Mental Health, which develops clinical practice guidelines for the National Institute for Health and Clinical Excellence. His research focuses on the evaluation of complex interventions for the treatment of severe mental illness, the development and evaluation of psychological treatments for depression, and the competences required to provide them effectively.

Antonio J. Polo is an Assistant Professor in the Department of Psychology at DePaul University in Chicago. Dr. Polo has been involved in school-based research for the past 15 years, primarily working with urban youth of African American and Latino backgrounds. His interests include understanding the social and cultural factors involved in the manifestation of youth internalizing and externalizing problems, particularly in immigrant and linguistic minority populations. His research also focuses on the delivery of evidence-based treatments for youth depression in community and practice settings and the retention and engagement of youth and their families in mental health care.

Glen O. Sallows is a Clinical Psychologist and Board Certified Behavior Analyst and president and cofounder of the Wisconsin Early Autism Project. He has taught at the University of Wisconsin and published and presented nationally and internationally in the areas of child treatment and treatment of autism spectrum disorders.

Megan Scott is a postdoctoral fellow in pediatric neuropsychology at Rainbow Babies and Children's Hospital, University Hospitals of Cleveland, Ohio. Dr. Scott's training background is in clinical assessment and treatment of children.

Jennifer R. Shapiro is a licensed clinical psychologist specializing in the treatment of eating disorders and obesity. She is currently the Scientific Director at Santech, Inc. in La Jolla, California, in which she applies for and directs research projects for the purpose of using the Internet and mobile technologies to enhance health conditions, particularly obesity. She has published numerous papers in the fields of eating disorders and obesity and annually presents at conferences.

Jeff Sigafoos is Professor of Educational Psychology at Victoria University of Wellington in New Zealand. He has published widely in the areas of special education provision, communication intervention, and evidence-based practice in the rehabilitation of individuals with developmental disabilities.

Mary Spagnola is a postdoctoral fellow in the Wynne Center for Family Research in the Department of Psychiatry, University of Rochester Medical Center. Her research focuses on family factors associated with behavioral adjustment and asthma symptoms.

Roger E. Thomas is Professor of Family Medicine, University of Calgary. He has published Cochrane systematic reviews on adolescent smoking and influenza vaccine. Other research interests are palliative care and child development problems.

Bruce J. Tonge is Professor of Psychological Medicine and Head of the Centre for Developmental Psychiatry and Psychology, School of Psychology and Psychiatry, Monash University, Australia. He has researched and published widely on mental health and intellectual disability, autism spectrum disorders, parent education and skills training, and the psychological and pharmacological treatment of anxiety and depression in children. He is coauthor of the *Developmental Behaviour Checklist*, a parent completed assessment of emotional and behavioral disorders in children, adolescents, and adults with Intellectual Disability.

Benjamin T. P. Tucker received his BA from St. Olaf College in 2007 with a major in psychology and a concentration in statistics. He completed his MS in clinical psychology at the University of Wisconsin-Milwaukee in the spring of 2010. He has coauthored several journal articles, book chapters, and presentations in these areas. He currently works as a behavior specialist for Tucci Learning Solutions in San Jose, California.

Valerie M. Volkert is an Assistant Professor and Director of the Pediatric Feeding Disorders Outpatient Program at the University of Nebraska Medical Center. She received a Bachelor's of Science from the University of Florida, and her PhD in School Psychology from Louisiana State University in 2007. She has authored two book chapters and published 10 peer-reviewed research studies and she currently serves on the board of editors for the *Journal of Applied Behavior Analysis*.

Lisa Walton is an emerging researcher in health services based at the University of Auckland, School of Population Health, Auckland, New Zealand. She is completing a PhD in supportive care in gynecologic cancer and has an interest in evidence-based psychosocial interventions for people living with cancer.

Daniel A. Waschbusch is a Professor in the Center for Children and Families and in the Department of Psychology at Florida International University. His research focuses on developing and evaluating empirically based practices for children with conduct problems, attention-deficit/hyperactivity disorder (ADHD), and callous-unemotional traits.

T. Steuart Watson is Professor of Educational Psychology at Miami, Ohio University. His primary research interests include applied behavior analysis, direct behavioral consultation, and designing efficient, empirical treatments for academic and behavior problems in young children. He is coeditor of the *Journal of*

Evidence-Based Practices for Schools and author of numerous refereed publications, book chapters, and books.

Tonya S. Watson is a Clinical Professor in Family Studies at Miami Ohio University. She is a licensed school psychologist and has worked extensively with families at risk for emotional/behavioral and academic problems. Her primary research and teaching interests include application of behavioral principles when working with children and their families and pediatric psychology.

Don E. Williams is a Behavioral Consultant in private practice at Richmond Behavioral Consulting in Richmond, Texas. He has published numerous articles on self-injurious behavior and other severe behavior disorders.

W. Larry Williams is the Director of the Behavior Analysis Program at the University of Nevada, Reno. After gaining his PhD from the University of Manitoba, he cofounded and directed the first graduate program in Special Education in Latin America, teaching over an 8-year period. He subsequently directed several clinical programs for persons with Intellectual Disabilities in Toronto, Canada, over a 10-year period. Having published several books and over 60 journal articles, he maintains a lab group with interests in conditional discrimination processes, relational framing, verbal behavior, clinical assessment, and interventions staff training and management systems.

Douglas W. Woods received his MS in Clinical Psychology from North Dakota State University and a PhD in Clinical Psychology from Western Michigan University. After completing an internship at the Nebraska Internship Consortium in 1999, Dr. Woods was hired on the faculty of the Clinical Psychology PhD program at the University of Wisconsin-Milwaukee, where he is now a Professor and Director of Clinical Training. Dr. Woods sits on the editorial board of six psychology journals. He is also a founding member of the Tourette Syndrome Association's (TSA) Behavioral Sciences Consortium, is a member of TSA's

Medical Advisory Board, serves on the Scientific Advisory Board of the Trichotillomania Learning Center, and is an advisor to the Obsessive Compulsive-spectrum workgroup for *DSM-5*. He has authored or coauthored 130 papers or chapters, and authored or coauthored seven books on tic disorders, trichotillomania, and other repetitive behavior problems, and one on behavior analytic accounts of psychopathology. Dr. Woods has received over $2.5 million in extramural funding from the NIMH, TSA Grants program, Trichotillomania Learning Center Grants program.

Kristen Zychinski is a graduate student in the Clinical-Child Psychology doctoral program at DePaul University in Chicago. Her research interests include the development and treatment of internalizing problems in urban, ethnic minority youth. In particular, she studies the relationship between school factors, specifically academic achievement, and mental health in children and adolescents. Additionally, she is interested in developing and investigating evidence-based treatments designed to be effective for and accessible to underserved populations.

PART I

Overview and Foundational Issues

1

Rationale and Standards of Evidence in Evidence-Based Practice

OLIVER C. MUDFORD, ROB MCNEILL, LISA WALTON, AND KATRINA J. PHILLIPS

What is the purpose of collecting evidence to inform clinical practice in psychology concerning the effects of psychological or other interventions? To quote Paul's (1967) article that has been cited 330 times before November 4, 2008, it is to determine the answer to the question: "*What* treatment, by *whom*, is most effective for *this* individual with *that* specific problem, under *which* set of circumstances?" (p. 111). Another answer is pitched at a systemic level, rather than concerning individuals. That is, research evidence can inform health-care professionals and consumers about psychological and behavioral interventions that are more effective than pharmacological treatments, and to improve the overall quality and cost-effectiveness of psychological health service provision (American Psychological Association [APA] Presidential Task Force on Evidence-Based Practice, 2006). The most general answer is that research evidence can be used to improve outcomes for clients, service providers, and society in general.

The debate about what counts as evidence of effectiveness in answering this question has attracted considerable controversy (Goodheart, Kazdin, & Sternberg, 2006; Norcross, Beutler, & Levant, 2005). At one end of a spectrum, evidence from research on

psychological treatments can be emphasized. Research-oriented psychologists have promoted the importance of scientific evidence in the concept of empirically supported treatment. Empirically supported treatments (ESTs) are those that have been sufficiently subjected to scientific research and have been shown to produce beneficial effects in well-controlled studies (i.e., efficacious), in more natural clinical environments (i.e., effective), and are the most cost-effective (i.e., efficient) (Chambless & Hollon, 1998). The effective and efficient criteria of Chambless and Hollon (1998) have been amalgamated under the term "clinical utility" (APA Presidential Task Force on Evidence-Based Practice, 2006; Barlow, Levitt, & Bufka, 1999). At the other end of the spectrum are psychologists who value clinical expertise as the source of evidence more highly, and they can rate subjective impressions and skills acquired in practice as providing personal evidence for guiding treatment (Hunsberger, 2007). Kazdin (2008) has asserted that the schism between clinical researchers and practitioners on the issue of evidence is deepening. Part of the problem, which suggests at least part of the solution, is that research had concentrated on empirical evidence of treatment efficacy, but more needs to be conducted to elucidate the relevant parameters of clinical experience.

In a separate dimension from the evidence–experience spectrum have been concerns about designing interventions that take into account the uniqueness of the individual client. Each of us can be seen as a unique mix of levels of variables such as sex, age, socioeconomic and social status, race, nationality, language, spiritual beliefs or personal philosophies, values, preferences, level of education, as well as number of symptoms, diagnoses (comorbidities), or problem behavior excesses and deficits that may bring us into professional contact with clinical psychologists. The extent to which there can be prior evidence from research or clinical experience to guide individual's interventions when these variables are taken into account is questionable, and so these individual differences add to the mix of factors when psychologists deliberate on treatment recommendations with an individual client.

Recognizing each of these three factors as necessary considerations in intervention selection, the APA Presidential Task Force on Evidence-Based Practice (2006, p. 273) provided its definition: "*Evidence-based practice in psychology* (EBPP) is the integration of the best available research with clinical expertise in the context of patient characteristics, culture, and preferences." The task force acknowledged the similarity of its definition to that of Sackett, Straus, Richardson, Rosenberg, and Haynes (2000) when they defined evidence-based practice in medicine as "the integration of best research evidence with clinical expertise and patient values" (p. 1).

Available research evidence is the base or starting point for EBPP. So, in recommending a particular intervention from a number of available ESTs, the psychologist, using clinical expertise with collaboration from the client, weighs up the options so that the best treatment for that client can be selected. As we understand it, clinical expertise is not to be considered as an equal consideration to

research evidence, as some psychologists have implied (Hunsberger, 2007). Like client preferences, the psychologist's expertise plays an essential part in sifting among ESTs the clinician has located from searching the evidence.

Best research evidence is operationalized as ESTs. Treatment guidelines can be developed following review of ESTs for particular populations and diagnoses or problem behaviors. According to the APA (APA, 2002; Reed, McLaughlin, & Newman, 2002), treatment guidelines should be developed to educate consumers (e.g., clients and health-care systems) and professionals (e.g., clinical psychologists) about the existence and benefits of choosing ESTs for specific disorders over alternative interventions with unknown or adverse effects. Treatment guidelines are intended to recommend ESTs, but not make their use mandatory as enforceable professional standards (Reed et al., 2002). The declared status, implications, misunderstanding, and misuse of treatment guidelines based on ESTs continue to be sources of controversy (Reed et al., 2002; Reed & Eisman, 2006).

Our chapter examines the issues just raised in more detail. We start with a review of the history and methods of determining evidence-based practice in medicine because the evidence-based practice movement started in that discipline, and has led the way for other human services. Psychologists, especially those working for children and young people, tend to work collaboratively with other professionals and paraprofessionals. Many of these groups of colleagues subscribe to the evidence-based practice movement through their professional organizations. We sample those organizations' views. The generalizability to psychology of methods for evidence-based decision making in medicine is questionable, and questioned. Next we examine criteria for determining the strength of evidence for interventions in psychology. These criteria are notably different to those employed in medicine, particularly concerning the relative value to the evidence base of research in psychology that has employed methods distinct from medicine (e.g., small-N design research). The controversies concerning treatment guidelines derived from ESTs are outlined briefly. The extent to which special considerations exist regarding treatment selection for children and adolescents is then discussed. Finally, we highlight some of the aspects of EBPP that require further work by researchers and clinicians.

EVIDENCE-BASED MEDICINE

Evidence-based practice can be perceived as both a philosophy and a set of problem-solving steps, using current best research evidence to make clinical decisions. In medicine, the rationale for clinicians to search for best evidence when making diagnostic and treatment decisions is the desire or duty, through the Hippocratic Oath, to use the optimal method to prevent or cure physical, mental, or social ailments and promote optimal health in individuals and populations (Jenicek, 2003). This section of the chapter provides an overview of the history of evidence-based practice in medicine (EBM), as well as a description of the current methodology of EBM. A critical reflection on the process and evidence used for EBM is also provided, leading to an introduction of the relevance of evidence-based practice (EBP) to other disciplines, including psychological interventions.

History of Evidence-Based Practice in Medicine

The earliest origins of EBM can be found in 19th-century Paris, with Pierre Louis (1787–1872). Louis sought truth and medical certainty through systematic observation of patients and the statistical analysis of observed phenomena; however, its modern origins and popularity are found much more recently in the advances in epidemiological methods in the 1970s and 1980s (Jenicek, 2003). One of

the key people responsible for the emergence and growth of EBM, the epidemiologist Archie Cochrane, proposed that nothing should be introduced into clinical practice until it was proven effective by research centers, and preferably through double-blind randomized controlled trials (RCTs). Cochrane criticized the medical profession for its lack of rigorous reviews of the evidence to guide decision making. In 1972, Cochrane reported the results of the first systematic review, his landmark method for systematically evaluating the quality and quantity of RCT evidence for treatment approaches in clinical practice. In an early demonstration of the value of this methodology, Cochrane demonstrated that corticosteroid therapy, given to halt premature labor in high-risk women, could substantially reduce the risk of infant death (Reynolds, 2000).

Over the past three decades, the methods and evidence used for EBM have been extended, refined, and reformulated many times. From the mid-1980s, a proliferation of articles has instructed clinicians about the process of accessing, evaluating, and interpreting medical evidence; however, it was not until 1992 that the term *evidence-based medicine* was formally coined by Gordon Guyatt and the Evidence-Based Working Group at McMaster University in Canada. Secondary publication clinical journals also started to emerge in the early to mid-1990s, with the aim of summarizing original articles deemed to be of high clinical relevance and methodological rigor (e.g., *Evidence-Based Medicine, ACP Journal Club, Evidence-Based Nursing, Evidence-Based Mental Health*).

Various guidelines for EBM have been published, including those from Evidence-Based Working Group (Guyatt et al., 2000), the Cochrane Collaboration, the National Institute for Clinical Excellence (NICE), and the British Medical Journal Clinical Evidence group, to name but a few. David Sackett, one of the strong proponents and authors in EBM, describes it as an active clinical decision-making process involving five sequential steps: (1) convert the patient's problem into an answerable clinical question; (2) track down the best evidence to answer that question; (3) critically appraise the evidence for its *validity*—closeness to truth; *impact*—size of the effect; and *applicability*—usefulness in clinical practice; (4) integrate the appraisal with the practitioner's clinical expertise and the patient's unique characteristics, values, and circumstances; and (5) evaluate the change resulting from implementing the evidence in practice, and seek ways to improve (Sackett et al., 2000, pp. 3–4). The guidelines for EBM are generally characterized by this sort of systematic process for determining the level of evidence for treatment choices available to clinicians, while at the same time recognizing the unique characteristics of the individual's characteristics, situation, and context.

It is not difficult to see the inherent benefits of EBM, and health professionals have been quick to recognize the potential benefit of adopting it as standard practice. Citing a 1998 survey of UK general practitioners (GPs), Sackett and colleagues (2000) wrote that most reported using search techniques, with 74% accessing evidence-based summaries generated by others, and 84% seeking evidence-based practice guidelines or protocols. The process of engaging in EBM requires some considerable understanding of research and research methods, and there is evidence that health professionals struggle to use EBM in their actual practice. For example, Sackett et al. (2000) found that GPs had trouble using the rules of evidence to interpret the literature, with only 20% to 35% reporting that they understood appraising tools described in the guidelines. Clinicians' ability to practice EBM also may be limited by lack of time to master new skills and inadequate access to instant technologies (Sackett et al., 2000). In addition to these practical difficulties, there have also been some criticisms of EBM's dominant methodology.

An early criticism of EBM, and nearly all EBP approaches, is that it appears to give greatest weight to science with little attention to the "art" that also underlies the practice of medicine, nursing, and other allied health professions. For example, Guyatt and colleagues cited attention to patients' humanistic needs as a requirement for EBM (Evidence-Based Medicine Working Group, 1992). Nursing and other health-care disciplines note that EBP must be delivered within a context of caring to achieve safe, effective, and holistic care that meets the needs of patients (DiCenso, Cullum, Ciliska, & Guyatt, 2004).

Evidence-based practice is also criticized as being "cookbook care" that does not take the individual into account. Yet a requirement of EBP is that incorporating research evidence into practice should consistently take account of the patient's unique circumstances, preferences, and values. As noted by Sackett et al. (2000), when these three elements are integrated to inform clinical decision making, "clinicians and patients form a diagnostic and therapeutic alliance which optimizes clinical outcomes and quality of life" (p. 1).

One of the key issues in the use of EBM is the debate around what constitutes best evidence from the findings of previous studies and how these various types of evidence are weighted, or even excluded, in the decision-making process. The following section first outlines the way in which evidence currently tends to be judged and then provides a more in-depth analysis of each type of evidence.

Levels and Types of Evidence

Partly through the work of Archie Cochrane, the quality of health care has come to be judged in relation to a number of criteria: efficacy (especially in relation to effectiveness), efficiency, and equity. Along with acceptability, access, and relevance, these criteria have been called the "Maxwell Six" and have formed the foundation of decision making around service provision and funding in the United Kingdom's National Health Service (Maxwell, 1992). Other health systems around the world have also adopted these criteria to aid in policy decision making, in both publicly and privately funded settings. Despite this there has been a tendency for evidence relating to effectiveness to dominate the decision-making process in EBM and, in particular, effectiveness demonstrated through RCTs.

There has been considerable debate about the ethical problems arising from clinicians focusing too much on efficacy and not enough on efficiency when making decisions about treatment (Maynard, 1997). In any health system with limited resources, the decision to use the most effective treatment rather than the most efficient one has the potential to impact on the likelihood of having sufficient resources to deliver that treatment, or any other, in the future. By treating one person with the most effective treatment the clinician may be taking away the opportunity to treat others, especially if that treatment is very expensive in relation to its effectiveness compared to less expensive treatment options.

According to current EBM methods, the weight that a piece of evidence brings to the balance of information used to make a decision about whether a treatment is supported by evidence can be summarized in Table 1.1. Although there are subtle variations in this hierarchy between different EBM guidelines and other publications, they all typically start with systematic reviews of RCTs at the top and end with expert opinion at the bottom.

Before discussing systematic reviews, meta-analyses, and clinical guidelines, it is important to understand the type of study that these sources of evidence are typically based on: the RCT. RCTs are a research design in which the participants are randomly assigned to treatment or control groups. RCTs are really a family of designs, with different components such as blinding (participants and experimenter), different randomization methods, and other differences in design. Analysis of RCTs is quantitative, involving estimation of the statistical significance or probability of the difference in outcomes

TABLE 1.1   Typical Hierarchy of Evidence for EBM

Level of Evidence	Type of Evidence
1 (High)	Systematic reviews or meta-analysis of randomized controlled trials (RCTs) OR Evidence-based clinical practice guidelines based on systematic reviews of RCTs
2	At least one well-designed RCT
3	Well-designed quasi-experimental studies
4	Well-designed case control and cohort studies
5	Systematic reviews of descriptive and qualitative studies
6	A single descriptive or qualitative study
7 (Low)	The opinion of authorities and/or expert committees

Source: Adapted from Melnyk and Fineout-Overholt (2005, p. 10)

observed between the treatment and control groups in the study. The probabilities obtained are an estimate of the likelihood of that size difference, or something larger, existing in the population.

There are a number of international databases that store and provide information from RCTs, including the Cochrane Central Register of Controlled Trials (CENTRAL; mrw.interscience.wiley.com/cochrane/cochrane_clcentral_articles_fs.html), OTseeker (www.otseeker.com), PEDro (www.pedro.fhs.usyd.edu.au), and the Turning Research Into Practice (TRIP; www.tripdatabase.com) database. Another effort to increase the ease with which clinicians can access and use evidence from RCTs has come through efforts to standardize the way in which they are reported, such as the CONSORT Statement and other efforts from the CONSORT Group (www.consort-statement.org).

The major strength of well-designed RCTs and other experimental designs is that the researcher has control over the treatment given to the experimental groups, and also has control over or the ability to control for any confounding factors. The result of this control is the ability, arguably above all other designs, to infer causation—and therefore efficacy—from the differences in outcomes between the treatment and control groups.

RCTs, and other purely experimental designs, are often criticized for having poor ecological validity, where the conditions of the experiment do not match the conditions or populations in which the treatment might be delivered in the real world. Low ecological validity can, although does not necessarily, lead to low external validity where the findings of the study are not generalizable to other situations, including the real world. Another issue with RCTs is that they are relatively resource intensive and this leads to increased pressure to get desired results or to suppress any results that do not fit the desired outcome (Gluud, 2006; Simes, 1986).

In social sciences, RCTs are not always possible or advisable, so many systematic reviews and meta-analyses in these areas have less restrictive inclusion criteria. Commonly, these include studies that compare a treated clinical group with an untreated or attention control group (Kazdin & Weisz, 1998; Rosenthal, 1984). In these situations, a quasi-experimental design is often adopted. There is also evidence that RCTs are not necessarily any more accurate at estimating the effect of a given treatment than quasi-experimental and observational designs, such as cohort and case control studies (Concato, Shah, & Horwitz, 2008).

Systematic reviews provide a summary of evidence from studies on a particular topic. For EBM this typically involves the formation of an expert committee or panel, followed by the systematic identification, appraisal, and synthesis of evidence from relevant RCTs relating to the topic (Melnyk & Fineout-Overholt, 2005). The result of the review is usually some recommendation around the level of empirical support from RCTs for a given diagnostic tool or treatment. The RCT, therefore, is seen as the gold standard of evidence in EBM.

Systematic review and meta-analysis are closely related EBP methods to evaluate evidence from a body of sometimes contradictory research to assess treatment quality. There is a great deal of overlap between methods, stemming in part from their different origins. The systematic review arises from EBM and the early work of Cochrane and more recently Sackett and colleagues (2000). Meta-analysis originated in the 1970s, with the contributions of Glass (1976) in education and Rosenthal (1984) in psychology being central. Meta-analyses are a particular type of systematic review. In a meta-analysis, measures of the size of treatment effects are obtained from individual studies. The effect sizes from multiple studies are then combined using a variety of techniques to provide a measure of the overall effect of the treatment across all of the participants in all of the studies included in the analysis.

Both approaches use explicit methods to systematically search, critically appraise for quality and validity, and synthesize the literature on a given issue. Thus, a key aspect is the quality of the individual studies and the journals in which they appear. Searches ideally include unpublished reports as well as published reports to counteract the "file drawer" phenomenon: Published findings as a group may be less reliable than they seem because studies with statistically nonsignificant findings are less likely to be published (Rosenthal, 1984; Sackett et al., 2000).

The principal difference between systematic review and meta-analysis is the latter includes a statistical method for combining results of individual studies that produces a larger sample size, reduces random error, and has greater power to determine the true size of the intervention effect. Not only do these methods compensate for the limited power of individual studies resulting in a Type I error, the failure to detect an actual effect when one is present, they can also reconcile conflicting results (Rosenthal, 1984; Sackett et al., 2000).

The criticisms of meta-analysis mostly relate to the methodological decisions made during the process of conducting a meta-analysis, often reducing the reliability of findings. This can result in meta-analyses of the same topic yielding different effect sizes (i.e., summary statistic), with these differences stemming from differences in the meta-analytic method and not just differences in study findings (Flather, Farkouh, Pogue, & Yusuf, 1997). Methodological decisions that can influence the reliability of the summary statistic produced from a meta-analysis include the coding system used to analyze studies, how inclusive the study selection process was, the outcome measures used or accepted, and the use of raw effect sizes or adjusted sample sizes (Flather et al., 1997). Some meta-analyses are conducted without using a rigorous systematic review approach, and this is much more likely to produce a mathematically valid but clinically invalid conclusion (Kazdin & Weisz, 1998; Rosenthal, 1984).

There are also some criticisms of the meta-analysis approach, specifically from child and adolescent psychology literature. Meta-analyses can obscure qualitative differences in treatment execution such as investigator allegiance (Chambless & Hollon, 1998; Kazdin & Weisz, 1998) and are limited by confounding among independent variables such as target problems, which tend to be more evident with certain treatment methods (Kazdin & Weisz, 1998).

Evidence-based clinical practice guidelines are also included in this top level of evidence, with the caveat that they must be primarily based on systematic reviews of RCTs. The purpose of these practice guidelines is to provide an easy-to-follow tool to assist clinicians in making decisions about the treatment that is most appropriate for their patients (Straus, Richardson, Glasziou, & Haynes, 2005).

There are some issues with the publication and use of evidence-based clinical practice guidelines. One problem is that different groups of experts can review the same data and arrive at different conclusions and recommendations (Hadorn, Baker, Hodges, & Hicks, 1996). Some guidelines are also criticized for

not being translated into tools for everyday use. One of the major drawbacks of clinical guidelines is that they are often not updated frequently to consider new evidence (Lohr, Eleazer, & Mauskopf, 1998).

In addition to individual researchers and groups of researchers, there are a large number of organizations that conduct systematic reviews, publish clinical practice guidelines, and publish their findings in journals and in databases on the Internet, including the Cochrane Collaboration (www.cochrane.org/), the National Institute for Clinical Evidence (NICE; www.nice.org.uk/), the Joanna Briggs Institute (www.joannabriggs.edu.au/about /home.php), and the TRIP database (www .tripdatabase.com/index.html). For example, the Cochrane Collaboration, an organization named after Archie Cochrane, is an international network of researchers who conduct systematic reviews and meta-analyses and provide the results of these to the research, practice, and policy community via the Cochrane Library.

The overall strengths of systematic reviews, meta-analyses, and clinical practice guidelines relate partly to the nature of the methods used and partly to the nature of RCTs, which were discussed earlier. The ultimate goal of scientific research is to contribute toward a body of knowledge about a topic (Bowling, 1997). Systematic reviews and clinical practice guidelines are essentially trying to summarize the body of knowledge around a particular treatment, which is something that would otherwise take a clinician a very long time to do on their own, so it is easy to see the value in a process that does this in a rigorous and systematic way.

There are a number of overall weaknesses for this top level of evidence for EBM. For example, the reliability of findings from systematic reviews has been found to be sensitive to many factors, including the intercoder reliability procedures adopted by the reviewers (Yeaton & Wortman, 1993). It is possible for different people using the same coding system to come up with different conclusions about the research evidence for a particular treatment. The selection of comparable studies is also a major issue, and especially in matching comparison groups and populations. The control and treatment groups in RCTs and other studies are usually not identical and this raises issues, particularly in the use of meta-analyses, where the treatment effects are being combined (Eysenck, 1994). The mixing of populations can also cause problems, where the treatment may only be effective in one or more specific populations but the review has included studies from other populations where the treatment is not effective. The overall effect of mixing these populations is to diminish the apparent effectiveness of the treatment under review (Eysenck, 1994).

Other issues with this top level of evidence relate to the information not included. Once a review or guideline is completed it must be constantly updated to check for new evidence that may change the conclusions. There are also issues around the information not included in the review process, including non-RCT studies, gray literature, such as technical reports and commissioned reports, and unpublished studies. Studies that do not get into peer-reviewed journals, and therefore usually get excluded from the review process, are often those that did not have significant results. The effect of this is that reviews will often exaggerate the effectiveness of a treatment through the exclusion of studies where the treatment in question was found to be ineffective. For this reason there has been a recent move to introduce what is called the "failsafe N" statistic. This is the hypothetical number of unpublished (or hidden) studies showing, on average, no effect that would be required to overturn the statistically significant effects found from review of the published (or located) studies results (Becker, 2006).

Quasi-experimental designs are the same as RCTs but the groups are not randomly assigned, there is no control group, or they lack one or more of the other characteristics of an RCT. In many situations randomization of participants or having a control group is not practically and/or ethically possible. The strengths of quasi-experimental designs come from the degree of control that the research has over the groups in the study, and over possible confounding variables. A well-designed quasi-experimental design has the important characteristic of being able to infer some degree of causation from differences in outcomes between study groups.

Case control studies identify a population with the outcome of interest (cases) and a population without that outcome (controls), then collects retrospective data to try to determine their relative exposure to factors of interest (Grimes & Schulz, 2002). There are numerous strengths of case control studies. They have more ecological validity than experimental studies and they are good for health conditions that are very uncommon (Grimes & Schulz, 2002). There is a relatively clear temporal sequence, compared to lower level evidence, which allows some degree of causality to be inferred (Grimes & Schulz, 2002). They are also relatively quick to do, relatively inexpensive, and can look at multiple potential causes at one time (Grimes & Schulz, 2002). The weaknesses of case control studies include the inability to control potentially confounding variables except through statistical manipulations and the reliance on participants to recall information or retrospectively collating information from existing data; the choice of control participants is also difficult (Grimes & Schulz, 2002; Wacholder, McLaughlin, Silverman, & Mandel, 1992). All of this often leads to a lot of difficulty in correctly interpreting the results of case control studies (Grimes & Schulz, 2002).

Cohort studies are longitudinal studies where groups are divided in terms of whether they receive or do not receive a treatment or exposure of interest, and are followed over time to assess the outcomes of interest (Roberts & Yeager, 2006). The strengths of cohort studies include the relatively clear temporal sequence that can be established between the introduction of an intervention and any subsequent changes in outcome variables, making the establishment of causation possible, at least to some degree. The limitations of cohort studies include the difficulty in controlling extraneous variables, leading to a relatively limited ability to infer causality. They are also extremely resource intensive and are not good where there is a large gap between treatment and outcome (Grimes & Schulz, 2002).

Descriptive studies involve the description of data obtained relating to the characteristics of phenomena or variables of interest in a particular sample from a population of interest (Melnyk & Fineout-Overholt, 2005). Correlational studies are descriptive studies where the relationship between variables is explored. Qualitative studies collect nonnumeric data, such as interviews and focus groups, with the analysis usually involving some attempt at describing or summarizing certain phenomena in a sample from a population of interest (Melnyk & Fineout-Overholt, 2005). Descriptive studies in general sit low down on the ladder of evidence quality due to their lack of control by the researcher and therefore their inability to infer causation between treatment and effect. On the other hand, much research is only feasible to conduct using this methodology.

Qualitative research in health services mostly arose from a desire to get a deeper understanding of what the quantitative research finding meant for the patient and provider (Mays & Pope, 1996). It asks questions such as "How do patients perceive . . . ?" and "How do patients value the options that are offered?"

Expert opinion is material written by recognized authorities on a particular topic. Evidence from these sources has the least weight in EBM, although to many clinicians the views of experts in the field may hold more weight than the higher level evidence outlined above.

Despite its criticisms and methodological complexity, EBM is seen by most clinicians as a valid and novel way of reasoning and decision making. Its methods are widely disseminated through current clinical education programs at all levels throughout the world. As proposed by Gordon Guyatt and colleagues in 1992, EBM has led to a paradigm shift in clinical practice (Sackett et al., 2000).

CURRENT STATUS OF EBP MOVEMENTS ACROSS HEALTH AND EDUCATION PROFESSIONS

Evidence-based practice was initially in the domain of medicine, but now most human service disciplines subscribe to the principles of EBP. For example, EBP or the use of empirically supported treatment is recommended by the APA, Behavior Analyst Certification Board (BACB), American Psychiatric Association, National Association of Social Workers, and General Teaching Council for England. For U.S. education professionals, EBP has been mandated by law. The No Child Left Behind Act of 2001 (NCLB; U.S. Department of Education, 2002) was designed to make the states, school districts, principals, and teachers more answerable for the performances shown by the students for whom they were providing education services. Along with an increase in accountability, the NCLB requires "schoolwide reform and ensuring the access of children to effective, scientifically based instructional strategies and challenging academic content" (p. 1440). The advent of the NCLB and the resulting move toward EBP occurred because, despite there being research conducted on effective and efficient teaching techniques (e.g., Project Follow Through: Bereiter & Kurland, 1981; Gersten, 1984) and a growing push for accountability from the public (Hess, 2006), this seldom was translated into actual practice. Education appears to have been particularly susceptible to implementing programs that were fads, based on little more than personal ideologies and good marketing. Much money and time has been lost by school districts adopting programs that have no empirical support for their effectiveness, such as the adoption of known ineffective substance abuse prevention programs (Ringwalt et al., 2002) or programs that are harmful for some students and their families, such as facilitated communication (Jacobson, Mulick, & Schwartz, 1995). This leads not only to resource wastage, but an even greater cost in lost opportunities for the students involved.

It seems like common sense for EBP to be adopted by other disciplines, as it is difficult to understand why reputable practitioners, service providers, and organizations would not want to provide interventions that have been shown to be the most effective and efficient. Yet, despite this commonsense feeling, the codes of conduct and ethical requirements, and mandated laws, many disciplines (including medicine) have found it difficult to bridge the gap between traditional knowledge-based practice and the EBP framework (Greenhalgh, 2001; Stout & Hayes, 2004). Professions such as social work (Roberts & Yeager, 2006; Zlotnick & Solt, 2006), speech language therapy (Enderby & Emerson, 1995, 1996), occupational therapy (Bennett & Bennett, 2000), and education (Shavelson & Towne, 2002; Thomas & Pring, 2004) have all attempted to overcome the difficulties that have arisen as they try to move EBP from a theoretical concept to an actual usable tool for everyday practitioners. Although some of these disciplines have unique challenges to face, many are common to all.

Many human services disciplines have reported that one of the major barriers to the implementation of EBP is the lack of sound research. For example, speech language therapy reports difficulties with regard to the quality and dissemination of research. A review of the status of speech language therapy literature by Enderby and Emerson (1995, 1996) found that there was insufficient quality research available in most areas of speech language therapy; however, they did find that those areas of speech therapy that were associated with the medical profession (e.g., dysphasia and cleft palate) were more likely to have research conducted than those associated with education (e.g., children with speech and language disorders and populations with learning disabilities). There continues to be a lack of agreement on speech language therapies effectiveness (Almost & Rosenbaum, 1998; Glogowska, Roulstone, Enderby, & Peters, 2000; Robertson & Weismer, 1999).

In addition to the lack of research, Enderby and Emerson were also concerned about the manner in which health resources were being allocated for speech language therapists. They found that of the resources allocated to speech language therapy approximately 70% were being used with children with language impairments, despite there being limited quality evidence of the effectiveness of speech language therapy with the population at that time. They also identified that dysarthria was the most commonly acquired disorder, but had very little research outside of the Parkinson's disease population. So, again, many resources have been allocated to programs that have no evidence of effectiveness. This questionable allocation of resources is seen in other fields also. For example, a number of studies have found that people seeking mental health treatments are unlikely to receive an intervention that would be classified as EBP and many will receive interventions that are ineffective (Addis & Krasnow, 2000; Goisman, Warshaw, & Keller, 1999).

A number of organizations and government agencies within a variety of fields try to facilitate the much-needed research. Examples in education include the United States Department for Children, Schools, and Families (previously Department for Education and Skills), the National Research Council (United Kingdom), and National Teacher Research Panel (United Kingdom). Similarly, in social work the National Association of Social Workers (United States) and the Society for Social Work and Research (United States) both facilitate the gathering of evidence to support the use of EBP within their field;

however, even if these organizations generate and gather research demonstrating the effectiveness of interventions, this does not always translate into the implementation of EBP. As mentioned previously, resource allocation does not necessarily go to those treatments with evidence to support them due to a lack of effective dissemination on the relevant topics. Despite medicine being the profession with the longest history of EBP, Guyatt et al. (2000) stated that many clinicians did not want to use original research or they fail to do so because of time constraints and/or lack of understanding on how to interpret the information. Rosen, Proctor, Morrow-Howell, and Staudt (1995) found that social workers also fail to consider empirical research when making research decisions. They found that less than 1% of the practice decisions were justified by research.

Although the lack of research-based decision making is concerning, many professions are attempting to disseminate information in a manner that is more user friendly to its practitioners. Practice or treatment guidelines have been created to disseminate research in a manner that will facilitate EBP. These guidelines draw on the empirical evidence and expert opinion to provide specific best-practice recommendations on what interventions or practices are the most effective/efficient for specific populations (Stout & Hayes, 2004). There are a number of guideline clearinghouses (National Guidelines Clearinghouse [www.guideline.gov/] and What Works Clearinghouse [ies.ed.gov/ncee/wwc/]). Associations and organizations may also offer practice guidelines (e.g., American Psychiatric Association).

Although there appears to have been emphasis placed on EBP, there is still much work to be done in most human service fields, including medicine, to ensure that there is appropriate research being conducted, that this research is disseminated to the appropriate people, and that the practitioners then put it into practice. Reilly, Oates, and Douglas (2004) outlined a number of areas that the

National Health Service Research and Development Center for Evidence-Based Medicine had identified for future development. They suggest that there is a need for a better understanding of how practitioners seek information to inform their decisions, what factors influence the inclusion of this evidence into their practice, and the value placed, both by patients and practitioners, on EBP. In addition, there is a need to develop information systems that facilitate the integration of evidence into the decision-making processes for practitioners and patients. They also suggest that there is a need to provide effective and efficient training for frontline professionals in evidence-based patient care. Finally, they suggest that there is simply a need for more research.

EVIDENCE IN PSYCHOLOGY

Although RCT research is still held up as the gold standard of evidence in medical science, in other clinical sciences, especially psychology, best research evidence has been less focused on RCTs as being the only scientifically valid approach. Randomized controlled trials are still held in high regard in clinical psychology, but it has long been recognized that alternative designs may be preferred and still provide strong evidence, depending on the type of intervention, population studied, and patient characteristics (APA Presidential Task Force on Evidence-Based Practice, 2006; Chambless & Hollon, 1998).

Research Methods Contributing to Evidence-Based Practice in Psychology

We have described and discussed RCTs in the previous section on EBM. The issues concerning RCTs and their contribution to the clinical psychology evidence base are similar. The inclusion of evidence of treatment efficacy and utility from research paradigms other than RCT methods and approximations thereto has been recommended for clinical psychology since the EBPP movement commenced (Chambless & Hollon, 1998). The APA Presidential Task Force on Evidence-Based Practice (2006) findings support the use of qualitative studies, single-case or small-N experimental designs, and process-outcome studies or evaluations, in addition to the RCT and systematic review techniques employed in EBM. A more in-depth discussion of some of these methods will be provided.

Psychologists and members of other professions that are more influenced by social science research methods than medicine may consider that findings from qualitative research add to their EBP database. Although qualitative research is not accepted as legitimate scientific study by many psychologists, and not usually taught to clinical psychologists in training, it may well have its place in assessing variables regarding clinical expertise and client preferences (Kazdin, 2008). Research questions addressable through qualitative research relevant to EBPP are similar to those mentioned for EBM.

Another important source of scientific evidence for psychologists, educators, and other nonmedical professionals is that derived from small-N research designs, also known as single-case, single-subject, or $N = 1$ designs. These alternative labels can confuse, especially since some single-case designs include more than one subject (e.g., multiple baseline across subjects usually include three or more participants). The most familiar small-N designs are ABAB, multiple baseline, alternating treatments, and changing criterion (Barlow & Hersen, 1984; Hayes, Barlow, & Nelson-Gray, 1999; Kazdin, 1982). Data from small-N studies have been included as sources of evidence, sometimes apparently equivalent to RCTs (Chambless & Hollon, 1998), or at a somewhat lower level of strength than RCTs (APA, 2002).

Strength of evidence from small-N designs. Small-N designs can be robust in terms of controlling threats to internal validity; however, external validity has often been viewed as problematic. This is because participants in small-N studies are not a randomly selected sample from the whole population of interest. The generality of findings from small-N studies is established by replication across more and more members of the population of interest in further small-N studies. A hypothetical example of the process of determining the generality of an intervention goes like this: (a) A researcher shows that a treatment works for a single individual with a particular type of diagnosis or problem; (b) Either the same or another researcher finds the same beneficial effects with three further individuals; (c) Another researcher reports the same findings with another small set of individuals; and so on. At some point, sufficient numbers of individuals have been successfully treated using the intervention that generality can be claimed. Within a field such as a particular treatment for a particular disorder, small-N studies can be designed so results can be pooled to contribute to an evidence base larger than $N = 1$ to 3 or 4 (Lord et al., 2005).

Even if there is an evidence base for an intervention from a series of small-N studies, every time another individual receives the same treatment, the clinician in scientist-practitioner role evaluates the effects of the intervention using small-N design methods. Thus, every new case is clinical research to determine the efficacy and effectiveness of *this* treatment for *that* individual.

Clinical psychologists can be cautioned that physicians and medical researchers have a similar-sounding name for an experimental design with their "N of 1 trials." The definition of N of 1 trials can vary somewhat but typically they are described as "randomised, double blind multiple crossover comparisons of an active drug against placebo in a single patient" (Mahon, Laupacis, Donner, & Wood, 1996, p. 1069). These N of 1 trials are continued until the intervention, usually a drug, in question shows consistently better effects than its comparison treatment or control condition.

Then the intervention is continued, or discontinued if there were insufficient beneficial effects. The N of 1 trials can be considered top of the hierarchy of evidence in judging strength of evidence for individual clinical decisions, higher even than systematic reviews of RCTs (Guyatt et al., 2000). This is because clinicians do not have to generalize findings of beneficial effects of the treatment to *this* patient from previous researched patients. Consistent beneficial findings from many N of 1 trials add up to an "N of many" RCT, thus providing evidence of the generality of findings. An N of 1 trial is quite similar to the alternating treatments small-N design employed in clinical psychology, especially applied behavior analysis; however, they are not identical and the differences may be overcome for some psychosocial interventions only with careful planning, but many interventions could not be assessed by fitting them into an N of 1 trial format. Further details are beyond the scope of this chapter; however, close study of the methodological requirements of both N of 1 designs and small-N designs can show the similarities and differences (Barlow & Hersen, 1984; Guyatt et al., 2000; Hayes et al., 1999; Kazdin, 1982; Mahon et al., 1996).

Some state that small-N designs may be most suitable for evaluating new treatments (Lord et al., 2005), others that single-case studies are most suitable for determining treatment effects for individuals (APA Presidential Task Force on Evidence-Based Practice, 2006). We do not disagree with either, except to point out that it has been argued that small-N studies can contribute much more to EBPP than these two advantages. In the following section, we review how ESTs can be determined from an evidence base consisting entirely of small-N studies.

Criteria for Assessing Efficacy

Lonigan, Elbert, and Johnson (1998) tabulated criteria for determining whether an intervention

for childhood disorders could be considered well-established (i.e., efficacious) or probably efficacious (i.e., promising). For the former, they recommended at least two well-conducted RCT standard studies by independent research teams or a series of independent well-designed small-N studies with at least nine participants carefully classified to the diagnostic category of interest showing that the intervention was better than alternative interventions. The availability of treatment manuals was recommended. For "promising" treatments, the criteria were relaxed to allow nonindependent RCTs, comparing treatment to no treatment, or a minimum of three small-N studies. These criteria followed those established at the time for psychological therapies in general (Chambless & Hollon, 1998).

We have discussed the determination of empirical support from RCTs already. The next sections will examine how evidence is derived from small-N studies: First, how evidence is assessed from individual research reports; and second, how the evidence can be combined from a group of research articles addressing the same topic of interest.

Evaluating Evidence From Small-N Research Designs

How do those assessing the efficacy of a treatment from small-N designs measure the strength of the design for the research purpose and whether, or to what extent, a beneficial effect has been demonstrated? Chambless and Hollon (1998) recommended reviewers to rate single-case studies on the stability of their baselines, use of acceptable experimental designs, such as ABAB or multiple baseline designs, and visually estimated effects. Baselines need not always be stable to provide an adequate control phase; there are other valid designs (e.g., changing criterion, multielement experimental designs); and visual estimates of effects are not necessarily reliable (Cooper, Heron, & Heward, 2007). Validity and, probably, reliability of reviews using only Chambless and Hollon's (1998) criteria could not be assured.

Attempts to improve reliability and validity of judgments about the value of small-N design studies have included establishing more well-defined criteria. Quite detailed methods for evaluating small-N studies have been published. For example, Kratochwill and Stoiber (2002) describe the basis of a method endorsed by the National Association of School Psychologists (NASP) designed for evaluating multiple research reports that used single-case designs for establishing evidence-based recommendations for interventions in educational settings. The system is more inclusive of design variations beyond those recommended by Chambless and Hollon (1998), and reviewers are instructed to code multiple variables, including calculating effects sizes from graphical data. The coding form extended over 28 pages. Shernoff, Kratochwill, and Stoiber (2002) illustrated the assessment procedure and reported that, following extensive training and familiarity with the coding manual, they achieved acceptable agreement among themselves. They stated that the process took 2 hours for a single study, although, so our own graduate students report, it takes much longer if multiple dependent and independent variables or hundreds of data points had been features of the research article with which they chose to illustrate the NASP procedure. The NASP method was constructively criticized by Levin (2002), and is apparently being revised and expanded further (Kratochwill, 2005).

Meanwhile, others have developed what appear to be even more labor intensive methods for attempting to evaluate objectively the strength of evidence from a series of small-N designs. As an example of a more detailed method, Campbell (2003) measured every data point shown on published graphs from 117 research articles on procedures to reduce problem behaviors among persons with autism. Each point was measured by using

dividers to determine the distance between the point and zero on the vertical axis. Campbell calculated effect sizes for three variables: mean baseline reduction, percentage of zero data points, and percentage of nonoverlapping data points. Use of these statistical methods may have been appropriate considering the types of data Campbell examined; nonzero baselines of levels of problem behavior followed by intervention phases in which the researchers' goal was to produce reduction to zero (see Jensen, Clark, Kircher, & Kristjansson, 2007, for critical review of meta-analytic tools for small-N designs). Nevertheless, the seemingly arduous nature of the task and the lack of generalizability of the computational methods to reviewing interventions designed to increase behaviors are likely to mitigate wider acceptance of Campbell's (2003) method.

A final example of methods to evaluate the strength of an evidence base for interventions is that outlined by Wilczynski and Christian (2008). They describe the National Standards Project (NSP), which was designed to determine the benefits or lack thereof of a wide range of approaches for changing the behaviors of people with autism spectrum disorders (ASD) aged up to 21 years. Their methods of quantitative review enabled the evidence from group and small-N studies to be integrated. Briefly, and to describe their method for evaluating small-N studies only, their review rated research articles based on their scientific merit first. Articles were assessed to determine whether they were sufficiently well-designed in terms of experimental design, measurement of the dependent variables, assessment of treatment fidelity, the ability to detect generalization and maintenance effects, and the quality of the ASD classification of participants. If the article exceeded minimum criteria on scientific merit, the treatment effects were assessed as being beneficial, ineffective, adverse, or that the data were not sufficiently interpretable to decide on effects. Experienced trained reviewers were able to complete a review for a research article in 1 hour or less with interreviewer agreement of 80% or more.

Inevitable problems for all these systems for review of single case designs arise from the necessity of creating "one size fits all" rules. For example, the evaluative methods of both the NASP (Kratochwill & Stoiber, 2002) and NSP projects (Wilczynski & Christian, 2008) include consideration of level of interobserver agreement for determining partly the quality of measurement of the dependent variables. The minimum acceptable level of agreement is specified at, say, 70% or 80%, which makes it relatively convenient for reviewers to determine from reading the published research article that they are rating; however, it has been known for more than 30 years that an agreement percentage is rather meaningless without examination of how behaviors were measured, what interobserver agreement algorithm was employed, and the relative frequency or duration of the behaviors measured (Hawkins & Dotson, 1975). Another example concerns coding rules for evaluating the adequacy of baseline measures of behavior. Whether the criterion for a baseline phase of highest scientific merit is a minimum of 3 points (NASP) or 5 points (NSP), there will be occasions when the rule should be inapplicable. For example, in Najdowski, Wallace, Ellsworth, MacAleese, and Cleveland (2008), after more than 20 observational sessions during intervention showing zero severe problem behavior, a return to baseline in an ABAB design raised the rate of problem behavior to more than four per minute, which was higher than any points in the first A-phase. To continue with the baseline to meet NASP or NSP evaluative criteria would have been unnecessary to show experimental control and dangerous for the participant.

These examples indicate why more detailed and codified methods for reviewing small-N studies quantitatively are, as yet, not firmly established. Although there may be satisfactory methods for fitting RCTs' scientific merit and size of effects into databases for meta-analyses, that appears to be more problematic with small-N designs, given their flexibility in use (Hayes et al., 1999).

Volume of Evidence From Small-N Studies Required to Claim That an Intervention Is Evidence Based

Having rated the strength of evidence from individual research articles, the next step is to determine whether a group of studies on the same topic between them constitute sufficient evidence to declare that an intervention is an empirically supported treatment or a promising or emerging intervention. We discuss only empirically supported treatment criteria here. Consensus on what minimum criterion should apply has yet to be reached. Chambless and Hollon (1998) originally recommended a minimum of two independent studies with three or more participants ($N \geq 3$) showing good effects for a total of $N \geq 6$ participants. Lonigan et al. (1998) required three studies with $N \geq 3$; that is, beneficial effects shown for $N \geq 9$ participants. Since then, the bar has been raised. For instance, Horner et al. (2005) proposed that the criteria for determining that an intervention is evidence-based included a minimum of five small-N studies, from three or more separate research groups, with at least 20 participants in total. Wilczynski and Christian (2008) used similar criteria with ≥ 6 studies of strongest scientific merit totaling $N \geq 18$ participants with no conflicting results from other studies of adequate design. Others have recommended similar standards: Reichow, Volkmar, and Cicchetti (2008) described a method for evaluating research evidence from both group and small-N designs, as had Wilczynski and Christian (2008). Finally, Reichow et al. (2008) set the criterion for an established EBP at ≥ 10 small-N studies of at least "adequate report strength" across three different locations and three different research teams with a total of 30 participants, or, if at least five studies of "strong report strength" with a total of 15 or more participants existed, that could substitute for the 10-study criterion.

The rationale for selecting the numerical criteria is usually not stated. Thus, all we can state is that some systems (e.g., Reichow et al., 2008) are more conservative than others (e.g., Lonigan et al., 1998). Sometimes conservative criteria may be appropriate, for example, when the costs of treatment are high, and/or the intervention is exceedingly complex requiring highly skilled intervention agents, and/or the benefits for the intervention are less than ideal (i.e., it reduces problems to a more manageable level, but does not eliminate them), and/or some negative side effects have been observed. On the other hand, if relatively few resources are required to implement an effective and rapid intervention without unwanted side effects, fewer well-conducted studies may be needed to persuade consumers that the intervention is empirically supported, and therefore worth evaluating with the individual patient. This brief discussion should advise readers to examine and consider criteria carefully when reviewers claim that a particular intervention is an empirically supported treatment for a particular disorder or problem for a particular population.

The discussions on evidence from small-N designs have left much out. For instance, Reichow et al. (2008) and Wilczynski and Christian (2008) developed algorithms for assessing the strength of evidence at different levels, although we have outlined only the highest levels. Both groups have also reported algorithms for determining ESTs from mixed methods (e.g., RCTs and small-Ns). Wilczynski and Christian (2008) report rules for incorporating conflicting results into the decision-making process about overall strength of evidence (De Los Reyes & Kazdin, 2008).

Level of Specificity of Empirically Supported Treatments

The issue to be discussed next concerns the unit of analysis of the research evidence. We illustrate by examining an example provided by Horner et al. (2005) in which they assessed the level of support for functional communication training (FCT; Carr & Durand, 1985). Functional communication training is an approach to reducing problem behaviors that teaches an appropriate nonproblematic way for individuals to access reinforcers for the problem behavior that have been identified through functional assessment. Horner and colleagues cited eight published research reports that included 42 participants who had benefited in FCT studies across five research groups. The evidence was sufficient in quantity for it to be concluded that FCT is an empirically supported treatment, exceeding all criteria reviewed earlier except that two more studies would have been needed to reach the number of studies ≥ 10 by the criteria of Reichow et al. (2008).

It might reasonably be asked: "For which population is FCT beneficial?" Perusal of the original papers cited by Horner et al. (2005) shows that 21/42 participants' data were reported in one of the eight cited studies (Hagopian, Fisher, Sullivan, Acquisto, & LeBlanc, 1998), with the oldest participant being 16 years old, and none reported to have a diagnosis of autism. Thus, applying Horner et al.'s criteria, it cannot be concluded from the studies cited that FCT is an empirically supported treatment for participants with autism or for participants older than 16, regardless of diagnosis. As an aside, eight participants across the other seven studies were reported to have autism, and three participants in total were aged over 20 years; however, the literature on FCT that Horner et al. (2005) included did not appear to have been obtained from a systematic search, so it is possible that there has been sufficient research to show that FCT is an empirically supported treatment for subgroups, and perhaps autism and adults are two of those.

TREATMENT GUIDELINES

Treatment guidelines specifically recommend ESTs to practitioners and consumers. Alternative descriptors are clinical practice and best practices guidelines (Barlow, Levitt, & Bufka, 1999). The view of APA was that guidelines are

> not intended to be mandatory, exhaustive, or definitive . . . and are not intended to take precedence over the judgment of psychologists. APA's official approach to guidelines strongly emphasizes professional judgment in individual patient encounters and is therefore at variance with that of more ardent adherents to evidence-based practice. (Reed et al., 2002, p. 1042)

It is apparent that many health-care organizations, insurance companies, and states in the United States interpret the purpose of lists of ESTs and treatment guidelines differently (Gotham, 2006; Reed & Eisman, 2006). They can interpret guidelines as defining what treatments can be offered to patients and, via manualization, exactly how treatment is to be administered, by whom, and for how long. The requirement for manualization allows funders of treatment to specify a standard reimbursement for the treatment provider. Thus, the empirically supported treatment movement was embraced by governments and health-care companies as it was anticipated to be a major contributor to controlling escalating health-care costs.

Many practicing psychologists were less enthusiastic about the empirically supported treatment and EBPP movements (see contributions by clinicians in Goodheart et al., 2006; Norcross et al., 2005). General concerns included that requirements to use only ESTs restrict professionalism by reframing psychologists as technicians going by the book mechanically; restricting client choice to effective interventions that have been granted empirically supported treatment status higher than others, only because they, like drugs, are relatively easy to evaluate in the RCT format. Prescription of one-size-fits-all ESTs may further disadvantage minorities, and people with severe and multiple disorders for whom there is scant evidence available. There were also concerns that the acknowledged

importance of clinical expertise, such as interpersonal skills to engage the client (child) and significant others (family) in a therapeutic relationship, would be ignored.

Contrary to the pronouncements from the APA (2002, 2006), guidelines have been interpreted or developed that "assume the force of law" in prescribing some interventions and proscribing others (Barlow et al., 1999, p. 155). Compulsion of psychologists in practice to follow treatment guidelines has been reported to occur in the United States by giving immunity from malpractice lawsuits to those who use only ESTs, and increasing the vulnerability of those who do not to litigation and increased professional indemnity insurance (Barlow et al., 1999; Reed et al., 2002). Some guidelines, especially those produced by agencies or companies employing psychologists, have been viewed as thinly veiled cost-cutting devices justified with a scientistic gloss.

Ethical Requirements

For many human service professional organizations, EBP and ESTs have become an ethical requirement. The APA's *Ethical Principles of Psychologists and Code of Conduct* document mentions the obligation to use some elements of EBPP; for example, "Psychologists' work is based upon established scientific and professional knowledge of the discipline" (American Psychological Association, 2010, p. 5). Other professional groups appear to be more prescriptive with regard to EBP. The BACB's Code for Responsible Conduct, for example, recommends EBP with statements such as, "Behavior analysts rely on scientifically and professionally derived knowledge when making scientific or professional judgments in human service provision" (Behavior Analyst Certification Board, 2004, p. 1). The BACB also require the use of ESTs:

> a. The behavior analyst always has the responsibility to recommend scientifically

supported most effective treatment procedures. Effective treatment procedures have been validated as having both long-term and short-term benefits to clients and society. b. Clients have a right to effective treatment (i.e., based on the research literature and adapted to the individual client). c. Behavior analysts are responsible for review and appraisal of likely effects of all alternative treatments, including those provided by other disciplines and no intervention. (Behavior Analyst Certification Board, 2004, p. 4)

As shown by the previous examples, each of these organizations have variations in how they have included EBP and empirically supported treatment into their codes of conduct and ethical statements; however, they both include the basic tenets of EBP: combining the best research information with clinical knowledge and the preferences of the individuals involved.

CHILDREN, ADOLESCENTS, AND EVIDENCE-BASED PRACTICE IN PSYCHOLOGY

Despite there being ESTs for a number of disorders and problem behaviors manifesting in children and adolescents, there are more than 500 treatments in use with children (Kazdin, 2008), most of which are unresearched. Chambless and Ollendick (2001) listed 108 ESTs for adults, compared with 37 for children, suggesting that research on therapies for young people is lacking relative to adults. Further research with child and adolescent populations has been prioritized by APA (APA Presidential Task Force on Evidence-Based Practice, 2006). Researching the effects of treatments for children brings special difficulties (Kazdin & Weisz, 1998). Regarding practice, children do not typically self-refer for mental, psychological, or behavioral disorders, nor are they active seekers of ESTs or preferred interventions. Parents

or guardians tend to take those roles, either independently or following recommendations from family, or health or education professionals. Children and youth cannot legally provide informed consent for treatments or for participation in research studies. These are among the developmental, ethical, and legal factors that affect consideration of EBPP with children.

Lord et al. (2005) discussed the challenges of acquiring rigorous evidence regarding efficacy of treatments for children with complex, potentially chronic behavioral/psychological disorders. Contributors to the article were researchers from multiple disciplines assembled by the National Institutes of Health in 2002. They wrote about autism spectrum disorders specifically, but acknowledged that the issues may have relevance to other child and youth problems.

Parents may be unwilling to consent to randomization studies in case their child is assigned to what parents perceive to be a less preferred treatment alternative, particularly when the intervention is long term and early intervention is, or is perceived to be, critical, such as early intensive behavioral intervention for pervasive developmental disorders. Lord et al. (2005) noted that ethical concerns may prohibit RCTs of promising interventions when randomization to no treatment or treatment of unknown effects is required by the evaluation protocol. Additional factors that reduce the internal validity of group comparison studies of psychosocial interventions include that parental blindness to the intervention allocated to their children is nigh on impossible, diffusion of treatment through parent support groups is likely, parents may choose to withdraw their children from no treatment or treatment as usual groups and obtain the experimental intervention or an approximation to it from outside the study, and children with severe disorders will often be subjected to multiple interventions of unknown benefit, provided with varying fidelity that may interact with one another to produce uninterpretable beneficial, neutral, or adverse effects (Smith & Antolovich, 2000).

Parents seek out information on their child's disorder and intervention recommendations through Internet or parent organizations, sometimes accepting advice from professionals. Mackintosh, Meyers, and Goin-Kochel (2006) received 498 responses to a Web-based survey of parents with children with autism spectrum disorders and found that the most oft-cited sources of information were books (88%), Web pages (86%), other parents (72%), and autism newsletters (69%). Lagging somewhat as sources of advice were professionals other than educators or physicians (57%). Physicians, education professionals, and family members were cited as sources of information by fewer than half the parents who responded to the survey.

Multiple fad treatments have been recommended for childhood onset disorders, and their adoption by families and some professionals, including psychologists, wastes resources and time that could have been spent profitably by employing ESTs (Jacobson, Foxx, & Mulick, 2005). Although some of our examples of supported and unsupported treatments have related to children with autism spectrum disorders (Romanczyk, Arnstein, Soorya, & Gillis, 2003), the problem of treatment selection uninformed by research affects children with other difficulties and their families. Some interventions for children with developmental and other disabilities have been found ineffective or harmful (Jacobson et al., 2005), and the same occurs for children with ADHD (Waschbusch & Hill, 2003). (See also Chapter 2 of this volume for a further discussion of this point by Waschbush, Fabiano, and Pelham.) We believe that clinical psychologists working with young people ought to have a professional ethical obligation to inform themselves and others about empirically unsupportable treatments as well as ESTs for their clients.

LIMITATIONS OF THE EVIDENCE BASE REGARDING EVIDENCE-BASED PRACTICE IN PSYCHOLOGY

There is a relatively large body of evidence concerning efficacy of treatments (Kazdin & Weisz, 1998, 2003), but far less on treatment utility, effectiveness, and efficiency. There is evidence that the utility of some efficacious treatments has been demonstrated, but further study is needed before the general statements can be made about the similarity or difference between outcomes from controlled research and clinical practice (Barlow et al., 1999; Hunsley, 2007).

There is less evidence concerning dimensions of clinical expertise and client characteristics, culture, and preferences that are relevant to beneficial treatment outcomes (Kazdin, 2008). Employment of qualitative research methods may help us to understand clients' experiences of psychological treatments. The APA Task Force has suggested that clinical expertise is made up of at least eight components, including assessment and treatment planning, delivery, interpersonal skills, self-reflection, scientific skills in evaluating research, awareness of individual and social factors, the ability to seek additional resources where necessary, and having a convincing rationale for treatment strategies (APA Presidential Task Force on Evidence-Based Practice, 2006). Qualitative methods may provide evidence regarding clinical expertise also. Improvement of two-way communication between psychologists who are primarily researchers and those who identify more as practitioners would assist dissemination of ESTs, collaboration in clinical utility studies of efficacious treatments, and facilitate research into clinical expertise and barriers to the adoption of ESTs by clinicians (Kazdin, 2008).

Lilienfeld (2005) and McLennan, Wathen, MacMillan, and Lavis (2006) recommended further research on interventions in child psychopathology on two fronts: (1) increased research on promising or new but plausible interventions; and (2) on research to combat questionable, but potentially harmful, interventions. Attention is needed to increase training of clinical psychologists in ESTs and cessation of training to use treatments that have been shown to be harmful, ineffective, or less effective. Decreasing the demand and use of treatments that have not been evaluated scientifically or have been found ineffective or harmful may be another strategy for helping clinical psychologists orient more to treatments that do work (i.e., ESTs).

Woody, Weisz, and McLean (2005) report that APA accredited clinical psychologist training programs taught and supervised interns in fewer ESTs in 2003 than they had in 1993. The training of clinical psychologists should include sufficient study of research methodology so that career-long learning, and contribution to research in practice concerning ESTs can be enhanced (Bauer, 2007; Kazdin, 2008). Considering the APA definition of EBPP, trainees need supervised practice in incorporating clients' preferences, values, and cultural considerations as well as to develop clinical expertise (Collins, Leffingwell, & Belar, 2007). Further training for university-based psychologist training faculty should be studied.

Psychologists in practice may wish or feel forced to adapt to employing EBPP, but willingness or compulsion to do so is not the same as becoming immediately competent to use an empirically supported treatment effectively. The typical workshop format for introducing new techniques is as ineffective for professionals (Gotham, 2006), as it is for direct care staff (Reid, 2004). Skill-based training can be effective when trainees practice an intervention method in the natural clinical environment with differential feedback from the trainer on their performance of the skill. This should occur after workshops that introduce the rationale and method, and include in vivo or videotaped demonstration of the skill by the trainer (i.e., modeling). Frequent follow-up observations by the trainer, again with objective feedback to the trainee, can facilitate maintenance of the newly acquired skills (Reid, 2004). Gotham (2006) identified barriers to implementation of EBPP, and provided an example of how to implement an empirically supported treatment statewide despite obstacles. McCabe (2004) wrote quite optimistically for clinicians about the challenges of EBPP, offering advice in a step-by-step form to psychologists. Reorienting and training clinicians is an area for further clinician-researcher collaboration that requires emphasis.

We have not included discussion of an area of EBPP that has, to date, received less attention than evidence-based treatment, which is "evidence-based assessment" (Kazdin, 2005; Mash & Hunsley, 2005). An initial assessment with clinical utility will identify what is the disorder or problem behavior so that it points the psychologist in the right direction for identifying the range of available ESTs for this client. Evidence-based assessment includes identifying reliable and valid ongoing measures that show the effects of an intervention with the individual client (Kazdin, 2005). Typically, empirically supported treatment reviews identify treatments for *DSM*-type classifications, the nosological approach; however, an idiographic functional approach to assessment may lead to better problem-EST match (Sturmey, 2007).

It was mentioned earlier that some professional groups are concerned at the lack of research on the outcomes of their assessment and treatment methods. Because clinical and other psychologists have extensive training in research methods, we can assist other professions to assess the evidence for their intervention methods. Interdisciplinary collaborations also may help elucidate the interaction effects of behavioral or psychological ESTs with interventions with presently unknown effects delivered by other professions.

CONCLUDING REMARKS

The issues concerning evidence-based clinical practice of psychology for children and adolescents are arguably even more complex than for adult clients. All readers would welcome the day when, for any referred psychological, behavioral, or mental problem, psychologists with clinical expertise were able to offer a wide range of effective and safe interventions. Then the young person, with more or less help from those who care for them, could select the effective treatment that suited their culture, preferences, and resources. The literature reviewed for this chapter suggests that, generally speaking, the health care, including clinical psychology, and education professions are starting on the road to addressing the aspirational targets of the EBP movement. The lack of unanimous agreement within professions that the evidence-based practice movement is desirable and what constitutes evidence for beneficial interventions is unsurprising; however, with more evidence for safe, acceptable, and effective interventions such as contained in the present volume and more education for consumers, professionals, and the public, eventually the naysayers and peddlers of unsupportable treatments may find they have no raison d'être (and also no income!).

REFERENCES

Addis, M. E., & Krasnow, A. D. (2000). A national survey of practicing psychologists' attitudes toward psychotherapy treatment manuals. *Journal of Consulting and Clinical Psychology, 68,* 331–339.

Almost, D., & Rosenbaum, P. (1998). Effectiveness of speech intervention for phonological disorders: A randomized controlled trial. *Developmental Medicine and Child Neurology, 40,* 319–325.

American Psychological Association. (2002). Criteria for evaluating treatment guidelines. *American Psychologist, 57,* 1052–1059.

American Psychological Association. (2010). *Ethical principles of psychologists and code of conduct.* Retrieved from www.apa.org/ethics/code/index.aspx#

American Psychological Association Presidential Task Force on Evidence-Based Practice. (2006). Evidence-based practice in psychology. *American Psychologist, 61,* 271–285.

Barlow, D. H., & Hersen, M. (1984). *Single case experimental designs: Strategies for studying behavior change* (2nd ed.). New York, NY: Pergamon.

Barlow, D. H., Levitt, J. T., & Bufka, L. F. (1999). The dissemination of empirically supported treatments: A view to the future. *Behaviour Research and Therapy, 37,* 147–162.

Bauer, R. M. (2007). Evidence-based practice in psychology: Implications for research and research training. *Journal of Clinical Psychology, 63,* 683–694.

Becker, B. J. (2006). Failsafe *N* or file-drawer number. In H. Rothstein, A. Sutton, & M. Borenstein (Eds.), *Publication bias in meta-analysis: Prevention, assessment and adjustments* (pp. 111–125). Hoboken, NJ: Wiley.

Behavior Analyst Certification Board. (2004). *Behavior Analyst Certification Board guidelines for responsible conduct for behavior analysts.* Retrieved from www.bacb.com/Downloadfiles/BACBguidelines/40809_ BACB_Guidelines.pdf.

Bennett, S. A., & Bennett, J. W. (2000). The process of evidence based practice in occupational therapy: Informing clinical decisions. *Australian Occupational Therapy Journal, 47,* 171–180.

Bereiter, C., & Kurland, M. (1981). A constructive look at Follow Through results. *Interchange, 12,* 1–22.

Bowling, A. (1997). *Research methods in health: Investigating health and health services.* Philadelphia, PA: Open University Press.

Campbell, J. M. (2003). Efficacy of behavioral interventions for reducing problem behavior in persons with autism: A quantitative synthesis of single-subject research. *Research in Developmental Disabilities, 24,* 120–138.

Carr, E. G., & Durand, V. M. (1985). Reducing behavior problems through functional communication training. *Journal of Applied Behavior Analysis, 18,* 111–126.

Chambless, D. L., & Hollon, S. D. (1998). Defining empirically supported therapies. *Journal of Consulting and Clinical Psychology, 66,* 7–18.

Chambless, D. L., & Ollendick, T. H. (2001). Empirically supported psychological interventions: Controversies and evidence. *Annual Review of Psychology, 52,* 685–716.

Collins, F. L., Leffingwell, T. R., & Belar, C. D. (2007). Teaching evidence-based practice: Implications for psychology. *Journal of Clinical Psychology, 63,* 657–670.

Concato, J., Shah, N., & Horwitz, R. (2008). Randomized, controlled trials, observational studies, and the hierarchy of research designs. *New England Journal of Medicine, 342*, 1887–1892.

Cooper, J. O., Heron, T. E., & Heward, W. L. (2007). *Applied behavior analysis* (2nd ed.). Upper Saddle River, NJ: Pearson.

De Los Reyes, A., & Kazdin, A. E. (2008). When the evidence says, "Yes, No, and Maybe So": Attending to and interpreting inconsistent findings among evidence-based interventions. *Current Directions in Psychological Science, 17*, 47–51.

DiCenso, A., Cullum, N., Ciliska, D., & Guyatt, G. (2004). Introduction to evidence-based nursing. In A. DiCenso, N. Cullum, D. Ciliska, & G. Guyatt (Eds.), *Evidence-based nursing: A guide to clinical practice*. Philadelphia, PA: Elsevier.

Enderby, P., & Emerson, J. (1995). *Does speech and language therapy work? Review of the literature*. London, England: Whurr.

Enderby, P., & Emerson, J. (1996). Speech and language therapy: Does it work? *British Medical Journal, 312*, 1655–1658.

Evidence-Based Medicine Working Group. (1992). A new approach to teaching the practice of medicine. *Journal of the American Medical Association, 268*, 2420–2425.

Eysenck, H. (1994). Meta-analysis and its problems. *British Medical Journal, 309*, 789–793.

Flather, M., Farkouh, M., Pogue, J., & Yusuf, S. (1997). Strengths and limitations of meta-analysis: Larger studies may be more reliable. *Controlled Clinical Trials, 18*, 568–579.

Gersten, R. M. (1984). Follow Through revisited: Reflections of the site variability issue. *Educational Evaluation and Policy Analysis, 6*, 411–423.

Glass, G. (1976). Primary, secondary, and meta-analysis of research. *Educational Researcher, 5*, 3–8.

Glogowska, M., Roulstone, S., Enderby, P., & Peters, T. J. (2000). Randomised controlled trial of community based speech and language therapy in preschool children. *British Medical Journal, 231*, 923–927.

Gluud, L. (2006). Bias in clinical intervention research. *American Journal of Epidemiology, 163*, 493–501.

Goisman, R. M., Warshaw, M. G., & Keller, M. B. (1999). Psychosocial treatment prescriptions for generalized anxiety disorder, panic disorders and social phobia, 1991–1996. *American Journal of Psychiatry, 156*, 1819–1821.

Goodheart, C. D., Kazdin, A. E., & Sternberg, R. J. (Eds.). (2006). *Evidence-based psychotherapy: Where practice and research meet*. Washington, DC: American Psychological Association.

Gotham, H. J. (2006). Advancing the implementation of evidence-based practices into clinical practice: How do we get there from here? *Professional Psychology: Research and Practice, 37*, 606–613.

Greenhalgh, T. (2001). *How to read a paper: The basics of evidence based medicine*. London, UK: BMJ Publishing Group.

Grimes, D. A., & Schulz, K. F. (2002). Cohort studies: Marching towards outcomes. *The Lancet, 359*, 341–345.

Guyatt, G. H., Haynes, R. B., Jaeschke, R. Z., Cook, D. J., Naylor, C. D., & Wilson, W. S. (2000). Users' guides to the medical literature: XXV. Evidence-based medicine: Principles for applying the users' guides to patient care. *Journal of the American Medical Association, 284*, 1290–1296.

Hadorn, D., Baker, D., Hodges, J., & Hicks, N. (1996). Rating the quality of evidence for clinical practice guidelines. *Journal of Clinical Epidemiology, 49*, 749–754.

Hagopian, L. P., Fisher, W. W., Sullivan, M. T., Acquisto, J., & LeBlanc, L. A. (1998). Effectiveness of functional communication training with and without extinction and punishment: A summary of 21 inpatient cases. *Journal of Applied Behavior Analysis, 31*, 211–235.

Hawkins, R. P., & Dotson, V. A. (1975). Reliability scores that delude: An Alice in Wonderland trip through the misleading characteristics of interobserver agreement scores in interval recording. In E. Ramp & G. Semb (Eds.), *Behavior analysis: Areas of research and application* (pp. 359–376). Englewood Cliffs, NJ: Prentice Hall.

Hayes, S. C., Barlow, D. H., & Nelson-Gray, R. O. (1999). *The scientist-practitioner: Research and accountability in the age of managed care* (2nd ed.). Boston, MA: Allyn & Bacon.

Hess, F. M. (2006). Accountability without angst? Public opinion and No Child Left Behind. *Harvard Educational Review, 76*, 587–610.

Horner, R. H., Carr, E. G., Halle, J., McGee, G., Odom, S., & Wolery, M. (2005). The use of single-subject research to identify evidence-based practice in special education. *Exceptional Children, 71*, 165–179.

Hunsberger, P. H. (2007). Reestablishing Clinical Psychology's subjective core. *American Psychologist, 62*, 614–615.

Hunsley, J. (2007). Addressing key challenges in evidence-based practice in psychology. *Professional Psychology: Research and Practice, 38*, 113–121.

Jacobson, J. W., Foxx, R. M., & Mulick, J. A. (Eds.). (2005). *Controversial therapies for developmental disabilities: Fad, fashion, and science in professional practice*. Mahwah, NJ: Erlbaum.

Jacobson, J. W., Mulick, J. A., & Schwartz, A. A. (1995). A history of facilitated communication: Science, pseudoscience and antiscience. *American Psychologist, 50*, 750–765.

Jenicek, M. (2003). *Foundations of evidence-based medicine*. New York, NY: Parthenon.

Jensen, W. R., Clark, E., Kircher, J. C., & Kristjansson, S. D. (2007). Statistical reform: Evidence-based practice, meta-analyses, and single subject designs. *Psychology in the Schools, 44*, 483–493.

Kazdin, A. E. (1982). *Single-case research designs: Methods for clinical and applied settings*. New York, NY: Oxford University Press.

Kazdin, A. E. (2005). Evidence-based assessment for children and adolescents: Issues in measurement development and clinical application. *Journal of Clinical Child and Adolescent Psychology, 34*, 548–558.

Kazdin, A. E. (2008). Evidence-based treatment and practice: New opportunities to bridge clinical research and practice, enhance the knowledge base, and improve patient care. *American Psychologist, 63*, 146–159.

Kazdin, A. E., & Weisz, J. R. (1998). Identifying and developing empirically supported child and adolescent treatments. *Journal of Consulting and Clinical Psychology, 66*, 19–36.

Kazdin, A. E., & Weisz, J. R. (Eds.). (2003). *Evidence-based psychotherapies for children and adolescents*. New York, NY: Guilford Press.

Kratochwill, T. R. (2005). Evidence-based interventions in school psychology: Thoughts on a thoughtful commentary. *School Psychology Quarterly, 17*, 518–532.

Kratochwill, T. R., & Stoiber, K. C. (2002). Evidence-based interventions in school psychology: Conceptual foundations of the *Procedural and Coding Manual* of Division 16 and the Society for the Study of School Psychology Task Force. *School Psychology Quarterly, 17*, 341–389.

Levin, J. R. (2002). How to evaluate the evidence of evidence-based interventions? *School Psychology Quarterly, 17*, 483–492.

Lilienfeld, S. O. (2005). Scientifically unsupported and supported interventions for child psychopathology: A summary. *Pediatrics, 115*, 761–764.

Lohr, K. N., Eleazer, K., & Mauskopf, J. (1998). Health policy issues and applications for evidence-based medicine and clinical practice guidelines. *Health Policy, 46*, 1–19.

Lonigan, C. J., Elbert, J. C., & Johnson, S. B. (1998). Empirically supported psychosocial interventions for children: An overview. *Journal of Clinical Child Psychology, 27*, 138–145.

Lord, C., Wagner, A., Rogers, S., Szatmari, P., Aman, M., Charman, T., . . . Yoder, P. (2005). Challenges in evaluating psychosocial interventions for Autistic Spectrum Disorders. *Journal of Autism and Developmental Disorders, 35*, 695–708.

Mackintosh, V. H., Meyers, B. J., & Goin-Kochel, R. P. (2006). Sources of information and support used by parents of children with autism spectrum disorders. *Journal on Developmental Disabilities, 12*, 41–51.

Mahon, J., Laupacis, A., Donner, A., & Wood, T. (1996). Randomised study of n of 1 trials versus standard practice. *British Medical Journal, 312*, 1069–1074.

Mash, E. J., & Hunsley, J. (2005). Evidence-based assessment of child and adolescent disorders: Issues and challenges. *Journal of Clinical Child and Adolescent Psychology, 34*, 362–379.

Maxwell, R. (1992). Dimensions of quality revisited: From thought to action. *Quality in Health Care, 1*, 171–177.

Maynard, A. (1997). Evidence-based medicine: An incomplete method for informing treatment choices. *The Lancet, 349*, 126–128.

Mays, N., & Pope, C. (Eds.). (1996). *Qualitative research in health care*. London, England: BMJ Publishing Group.

McCabe, O. L. (2004). Crossing the quality chasm in behavioral health care: The role of evidence-based practice. *Professional Psychology: Research and Practice, 35*, 571–579.

McLennan, J. D., Wathen, C. N., MacMillan, H. L., & Lavis, J. N. (2006). Research-practice gaps in child mental health. *Journal of the American Academy of Child and Adolescent Psychiatry, 45*, 658–665.

Melnyk, B. M., & Fineout-Overholt, E. (Eds.). (2005). *Evidence-based practice in nursing and healthcare: A guide to best practice*. Philadelphia, PA: Lippincott Williams & Wilkins.

Najdowski, A. C., Wallace, M. D., Ellsworth, C. L., MacAleese, A. N., & Cleveland, J. M. (2008). Functional analysis and treatment of precursor behavior. *Journal of Applied Behavior Analysis, 41*, 97–105.

Norcross, J. C., Beutler, L. E., & Levant, R. F. (Eds.). (2005). *Evidence based practices in mental health: Debate and dialogue on the fundamental questions*. Washington, DC: American Psychological Association.

Paul, G. L. (1967). Strategy of outcome research in psychotherapy. *Journal of Consulting Psychology, 31*, 109–118.

Reed, G. M., & Eisman, E. J. (2006). Uses and misuses of evidence: Managed care, treatment guidelines, and outcomes measurement in professional practice. In C. D. Goodheart, A. E. Kazdin, & R. J. Sternberg (Eds.), *Evidence-based psychotherapy: Where practice and research meet* (pp. 13–35). Washington, DC: American Psychological Association.

Reed, G. M., McLaughlin, C. J., & Newman, R. (2002). American Psychological Association policy in context: The development and evaluation of guidelines for professional practice. *American Psychologist, 57*, 1041–1047.

Reichow, B., Volkmar, F. R., & Ciccetti, D. V. (2008). Development of the evaluative method for evaluating and determining evidence-based practices in autism. *Journal of Autism and Developmental Disorders, 38*, 1311–1319.

Reid, D. H. (2004). Training and supervising direct care support personnel to carry out behavioral procedures. In J. L. Matson, R. Laud, & M. Matson (Eds.), *Behavior modification for persons with developmental disabilities: Treatments and supports, Volume 1* (pp. 101–129). Kingston, NY: NADD Press.

Reilly, S., Oates, J., & Douglas, J. (2004). *Evidence based practice in speech pathology.* London, England: Whurr.

Reynolds, S. (2000). The anatomy of evidence-based practice: Principles and methods. In L. Trinder & S. Reynolds (Eds.), *Evidence-based practice: A critical appraisal* (pp. 17–34). Oxford, England: Blackwell.

Ringwalt, C. L., Ennett, S., Vincus, A., Thorne, J., Rohrbach, L. A., & Simons-Rudolph, A. (2002). The prevalence of effective substance use prevention curricula in U.S. middle schools. *Prevention Science, 3*, 257–265.

Roberts, A. R., & Yeager, K. R. (2006). *Foundations of evidence based social work practice.* New York, NY: Oxford University Press.

Robertson, S. B., & Weismer, S. E. (1999). Effects of treatment on linguistic and social skills in toddlers with delayed language development. *Journal of Speech, Language, and Hearing Research, 42*, 1234–1247.

Romanczyk, R. G., Arnstein, L., Soorya, L. V., & Gillis, J. (2003). The myriad of controversial treatments for autism: A critical evaluation of efficacy. In S. O. Lillienfeld, S. J. Levin, & J. R. Lohr (Eds.), *Science and pseudoscience in clinical psychology* (pp. 363–395). New York, NY: Guilford Press.

Rosen, A., Proctor, E. E., Morrow-Howell, N., & Staudt, M. (1995). Rationales for practice decisions: Variations in knowledge use by decision task and social work service. *Research on Social Work Practice, 5*, 501–523.

Rosenthal, R. (1984). *Meta-analytic procedures for social research.* Beverly Hills, CA: Sage Publications.

Sackett, D. L., Straus, S. E., Richardson, W. S., Rosenberg, W., & Haynes, R. B. (2000). *Evidence-based medicine: How to practice and teach EBM* (2nd ed.). Edinburgh, Scotland: Churchill Livingstone.

Shavelson, R. J., & Towne, L. (2002). *Scientific research in education.* Washington, DC: National Academy Press.

Shernoff, E. S., Kratochwill, T. R., & Stoiber, K. C. (2002). Evidence-based interventions in school psychology: An illustration of task force coding criteria using single-participant research design. *School Psychology Quarterly, 17*, 390–422.

Simes, J. (1986). Publication bias: The case for an international registry of clinical trials. *Journal of Clinical Oncology, 4*, 1529–1541.

Smith, T., & Antolovich, A. (2000). Parental perceptions of supplemental interventions received by young children with autism in intensive behavior analytic treatment. *Behavioral Interventions, 15*, 83–97.

Stout, C. E., & Hayes, R. A. (2004). *Evidence-based practice: Methods, models, and tools for mental health professionals.* Hoboken, NJ: Wiley.

Straus, S. E., Richardson, W. S., Glasziou, P., & Haynes, R. B. (2005). *Evidence-based medicine: How to practice and teach EBM* (2nd ed.). Edinburgh, Scotland: Elsevier.

Sturmey, P. (Ed.). (2007). *Functional assessment in clinical treatment.* Burlington, MA: Academic Press.

Thomas, G., & Pring, R. (2004). *Evidence-based practice in education.* Maidenhead, England: McGraw-Hill Education.

U.S. Department of Education. (2002). No Child Left Behind Act of 2001. Public Law 107-110. Retrieved from www.ed.gov/policy/elsec/leg/esea02/107-110.pdf

Wacholder, S., McLaughlin, J., Silverman, D., & Mandel, J. (1992). Selection of controls in case-control studies. *American Journal of Epidemiology, 135*, 1019–1028.

Waschbusch, D. A., & Hill, G. P. (2003). Empirically supported, promising, and unsupported treatments for children with attention-deficit/hyperactivity disorder. In S. O. Lillienfeld, S. J. Levin, & J. R. Lohr (Eds.), *Science and pseudoscience in clinical psychology* (pp. 333–362). New York, NY: Guilford Press.

Wilczynski, S. M., & Christian, L. (2008). The National Standards Project: Promoting evidence-based practice in autism spectrum disorders. In J. K. Luiselli, D. C. Russo, W. P. Christian, & S. M. Wilcyznski (Eds.), *Effective practices for children with Autism: Educational and behavior support interventions that work* (pp. 37–60). New York, NY: Oxford University Press.

Woody, S. R., Weisz, J., & McLean, C. (2005). Empirically supported treatments: 10 years later. *The Clinical Psychologist, 58*, 5–11.

Yeaton, W., & Wortman, P. (1993). On the reliability of meta-analytic reviews: The role of intercoder agreement. *Evaluation Review, 17*, 292–309.

Zlotnick, J. L., & Solt, B. E. (2006). The institute for the advancement of social work research: Working to increase our practice and policy evidence base. *Research on Social Work Practice, 16*, 534–539.

2

Evidence-Based Practice in Child and Adolescent Disorders

DANIEL A. WASCHBUSCH, GREGORY A. FABIANO, AND WILLIAM E. PELHAM JR.

The purpose of this chapter is to provide an overview of evidence-based practices (EBPs) for use with children and adolescents. We seek to address big picture issues about the use and implementation of EBPs with children and adolescents, with a special emphasis on key challenges that remain to be addressed. We will not address specific disorders or treatments; these will be the topic of subsequent chapters. We begin with a brief summary of the development of EBPs in youth.

A BRIEF HISTORY OF IDENTIFYING EVIDENCE-BASED PRACTICES FOR YOUTH

Over the past two decades, there has been a concerted effort to identify evidence-based practices (EBPs) for use with children and adolescents. The origins of this work has a long history but seems to have gained increased momentum in the early 1990s for several reasons (Lonigan, Elbert, & Johnson, 1998). First, the American Psychological Association (APA) produced a report that, among other things, listed several empirically supported psychosocial treatments (Task Force on Promotion and Dissemination Psychological Procedures,

1995). Although some of the interventions described in the report targeted children and adolescents, the report did not compile a comprehensive list of such interventions. Second, both traditional (Kazdin, 1991) and meta-analytic reviews (Weisz, Weiss, & Donenberg, 1992; Weisz, Weiss, Han, Granger, & Morton, 1995) found that interventions for children and youth with mental health problems were generally effective; however, these reviews were rather global, evaluating interventions as a whole rather than seeking to identify specific interventions that were effective for specific types of problems. Third, health insurance companies were moving toward managed care. As part of this process, services were scrutinized more carefully before being approved for coverage or reimbursement. Fourth, professional organizations and government agencies began developing practice guidelines for psychological interventions (American Academy of Child and Adolescent Psychiatry, 1997, 2007; American Psychological Association Working Group on Psychoactive Medications for Children and Adolescents, 2006), much the same way that practice guidelines have been developed for other professions.

One outcome of these factors was that the Clinical Child Psychology section of the

Clinical Psychology division of the APA formed a task force to identify empirically supported interventions for children and adolescents (Lonigan et al., 1998). The task force developed criteria for evaluating the evidence base (see Mudford, McNeill, Walton, & Phillips, Chapter 1 of this book), and these were published in 1998 in a special issue of the *Journal of Clinical Child Psychology*, which has since been renamed the *Journal of Clinical Child and Adolescent Psychology*. Included in the special issue were articles that applied the EBP criteria to select disorders of childhood and adolescence, including depression (Kaslow & Thompson, 1998), anxiety and phobias (Ollendick & King, 1998), autism (Rogers, 1998), conduct problems (Brestan & Eyberg, 1998), and attention-deficit/hyperactivity disorder (Pelham, Wheeler, & Chronis, 1998), along with articles that talked more conceptually about the application of EBPs to youth (Kazdin & Kendall, 1998; Weisz & Hawley, 1998).

The original articles were recently updated to incorporate research conducted in the decade since the original reviews and the resulting manuscripts were published in a special issue of the *Journal of Clinical Child and Adolescent Psychology* (David-Ferdon & Kaslow, 2008; Eyberg, Nelson, & Boggs, 2008; Pelham & Fabiano, 2008; Rogers & Vismara, 2008; Silverman, Pina, & Viswesvaran, 2008). Also included in the 2008 special edition were reviews of treatments for disorders not included in the 1998 special edition. These included reviews of treatments for eating disorders and eating problems (Keel & Haedt, 2008), obsessive-compulsive disorder (Barrett, Farrell, Pina, Peris, & Piacentini, 2008), exposure to traumatic events (Silverman, Pina et al., 2008), and adolescent substance abuse (Waldron & Turner, 2008), as well as a chapter reviewing EBPs for minority youth (Huey & Polo, 2008).

These special issues represent a remarkable achievement. The considerable financial costs invested by the APA and personal efforts expended by the authors have effectively consolidated a large body of research into a useable format. The efforts seem to have had considerable impact as evidenced by the fact that the original articles were cited more than 1,100 times in less than a decade (Silverman & Hinshaw, 2008). Likewise, school psychology (Kratochwill & Shernoff, 2003; Kratochwill & Stoiber, 2002) and pediatric psychology (Holden, Deichmann, & Levy, 1999; Janicke & Finnev, 1999; Jelalian & Saelens, 1999; Kerwin, 1999; Powers, 1999; Walco, Sterling, Conte, & Engel, 1999) seem to have followed the lead of clinical psychology and begun their own efforts to identify EBPs. It is clear that considerable progress has been made toward identifying EBPs for child and adolescent mental health problems. This progress provides a solid foundation for future efforts at improving EBPs for children and adolescents.

WHAT DO WE KNOW ABOUT EBPs FOR YOUTH?

Evidence-based practices have typically been organized and evaluated according to diagnosis, as shown in the subsequent chapters of this book. However, when examined across diagnoses it becomes clear that there are several common features of EBPs (Pelham & Burrows-MacLean, 2005). The first common feature of EBPs for youth is that they are extensively studied, procedures are described in treatment manuals, and the treatments or treatment components are often included in intervention guidelines published by professional organizations. This may seem obvious considering that these features are in some sense part of the definition of EBPs, but it is a useful point to highlight because these features are part of the advantages of EBPs. The importance of these features becomes clear when one considers their alternative—interventions without systematic or clearly defined procedures, lacking an evidence base, and without expert guidance or recommendation.

Second, all current EBPs for youth rely on reinforcement programs to strengthen children's appropriate behavior (Pelham & Burrows-MacLean, 2005). Reinforcement is used both during treatment sessions in which children are being taught new skills and in the home and school settings where the new skills are designed to be used. Even when the EBP is a child-based intervention, such as treatment for depression or anxiety or OCD, reinforcement programs are employed to motivate behavior during the treatment session and afterward in the child's natural environment.

Third, unlike more traditional forms of therapy, EBPs for youth typically involve parents, teachers, or both as the agents of change. For instance, all EBPs for youth include a component in which parents are taught skills that, if used, would help reduce or eliminate their child's problems and would help promote their child's positive, adaptive skills. The reason parents and teachers are included in EBPs for youth is because they are collectively in the child's environment almost all the time and this is the setting where the behaviors that result in referrals for treatment occur. In contrast, a therapist typically sees the child about 50 minutes once a week.

Fourth, all current EBPs for mental health problems in youth are behavioral or cognitive-behavioral interventions with components that are directly tied to targeted behaviors or goals of treatment. More specifically, current EBPs for youth typically employ a functional analytic framework to develop, monitor, and modify the treatment in which the therapist and parents or teachers carefully defines the child's treatment goals (target behaviors). Data are collected to evaluate progress toward achieving the treatment goals, and treatment is modified as necessary on the basis of the data collected.

The final common component of EBPs for youth is that they typically include specific procedures designed to faciiitate generalization across settings and maintenance across time of any gains the youth has made as the result of treatment. For example, if treatment has resulted in a child with oppositional defiant disorder having higher compliance with parental commands, then therapists in collaboration with the parents may begin to work on teaching other adults in the child's life (e.g., teachers, grandparents, coaches, babysitters, day care workers, etc.) to employ the same strategies. Therapists and parents may also develop procedures for continuing to systematically monitor the child's behavior and their own behavior to ensure that neither party begins to regress once treatment is stopped, and to plan steps that will be taken if regression does occur. For example, if a child has improved at school as a result of treatment, the parent, teacher, and therapist may plan to meet at the end of the school year to develop a plan for establishing the same effective procedures with the next year's teacher.

WHAT DO WE STILL NEED TO KNOW ABOUT EBPs FOR YOUTH?

The list of potential factors that could influence EBPs is long and research that systematically examines these factors is relatively modest. It is not surprising, then, that numerous important questions about EBPs for youth remain largely unaddressed. We do not intend to produce a comprehensive list of key issues that could be addressed to better understand EBPs for youth; it would be nearly impossible to do so. Instead, we discuss issues that we feel are among the most important.

First, the scope of potential treatments to be evaluated is large, and one important issue is determining which treatments should be among those that are next examined. Currently, the treatments that are examined are, largely, those that individual researchers or teams of researchers have elected to evaluate. More recently, larger scale projects, consisting of multisite teams of researchers, have been developed to evaluate prevention and treatment approaches (Conduct Problems

Prevention Research Group, 2002; Kendall, 2008; MTA Cooperative Group, 1999a; Treatment for Adolescents with Depression Study [TADS] Team, 2004). Collectively, these approaches have produced a high volume of quality research that has answered very important questions; however, an important drawback of this approach is that the treatments selected for evaluation have largely been those developed in carefully controlled settings, typically university or medical school settings. Further, these interventions are typically implemented as an intensive treatment package, with all children receiving the entire package regardless of reasons for referral so that the combination of treatments evaluated in research may differ from the treatments that are used in clinical practice. In fact, both quantitative and qualitative reviews suggest that researchers have focused on evaluating behavioral and cognitive behavioral treatments, whereas surveys of clinicians in practice show that they tend to use other treatments with equal or greater frequency as behavioral and cognitive behavioral treatments (Kazdin, Bass, Ayers, & Rodgers, 1990; Kazdin, Siegel, & Bass, 1990; Weisz, Jensen-Doss, & Hawley, 2006; Weisz, Jensen, & McLeod, 2005). As a result, many of the treatments that are routinely used in clinical practice have not been subjected to empirical evaluation. Thus, one key task for furthering knowledge of EBPs is to broaden the scope of research to include an evaluation of the treatments that are actually being used in clinical practice.

In the same vein, a second key issue is to broaden how treatments are described with respect to their evidence base. Considerable efforts have been made toward elucidating criteria for evaluating when a treatment is effective or probably effective (Lonigan et al., 1998). Criteria have also been suggested for evaluating possibly efficacious and experimental treatments (Silverman, Ortiz et al., 2008). However, these efforts focus on using evidence to decide that a treatment works; little effort has been made toward using

evidence to determine that a treatment does not work. As a number of authors have noted, describing a treatment as evidenced based does not imply that other treatments are ineffective (Kazdin & Kendall, 1998; Lonigan et al., 1998). In fact it is likely, perhaps inevitable, that many treatments that are not currently on the list of EBPs will eventually make their way onto the list as the research base builds up. On the other hand, some treatments are not likely to be effective regardless of how much research evaluates them. One important question about EBPs, then, is whether greater distinction should be made among those treatments that do not meet criteria for being evidenced based. Specifically, it seems necessary to distinguish treatments that have been evaluated and shown to be ineffective—that is, invalid treatments—and treatments that have never been evaluated. Distinguishing examined from unexamined treatments and treatments that have been examined and shown to be invalid is important because the ethics of delivering treatments that have not been evaluated is unclear, whereas it is clearly unethical to deliver treatments that have shown to be invalid (Kinscherff, 1999; Ollendick & Davis, 2004; Rae & Fournier, 2008). Further, if one goal of the EBP movement is to promote use of effective strategies for improving mental health in children and adolescents, then identifying treatments that are shown to be invalid, based on methodologically sound, replicable research, would provide parents, teachers, and policymakers clear information for making informed decisions about treatment (Hoagwood, Burns, Kiser, Ringseisen, & Schoenwald, 2001; Weisz & Hawley, 1998). Making this distinction among non-EBP treatments is feasible. As an example, Waschbusch and Hill (2003) reviewed alternative treatments of ADHD by classifying them into empirically supported, promising, ineffective, and not researched. Likewise, in a comprehensive review of the efficacy and effectiveness of the most common child and adolescent mental health problems, the Hawaii Empirical Basis to Service Task Force classified interventions as well-established, probably efficacious, possibly efficacious, unsupported, and possibly harmful (Chorpita et al., 2002). These examples show that it is feasible to further distinguish among treatments that do not meet criteria as an EBP, and it seems important to do so.

Third, much more needs to be learned about the influence of developmental factors on EBPs (Vernberg, 1998). Considering the effects of development processes when evaluating psychopathology is one of the hallmarks of modern research on mental health in children, as evidenced by the rise of developmental psychopathology as a field of study (Cicchetti & Richters, 1997; Sroufe, 1990; Sroufe & Rutter, 1984). Applying a developmental frame to EBPs suggests that practices that are supported at one age may not be supported at another. For instance, an evidence-based assessment or intervention for depression in adolescents may not be appropriate for assessing and treating depression in children (Hoagwood et al., 2001). Surprisingly little is currently known about developmental effects in EBPs. This may be, in part, because treatments for children and adolescents have historically been adapted from treatments used with adults, with little attention paid to developmental differences within childhood or within adolescence (American Psychological Association Working Group on Psychoactive Medications for Children and Adolescents, 2006). The research that has been done on developmental differences in EBPs provides inconsistent findings. For example, most research suggests that parent interventions produce statistically significant positive gains in preschool, elementary school, and adolescent age youth (Eyberg et al., 2008), but this is somewhat qualified by other research suggesting that parents of younger children may be less likely to drop out of treatment early than older youth (Dishion & Patterson, 1992) and that older youth may be less likely to

make clinically significant improvements in response to parent interventions (Ruma, Burke, & Thompson, 1996). Mixed evidence has also emerged about the role of age in cognitive behavior therapies, with some evidence suggesting that older children show more benefit to cognitive behavioral treatment (Durlak, Fuhrman, & Lampman, 1991) and other evidence finding the opposite pattern (Southam-Gerow, Kendall, & Weersing, 2001).

Applying a developmental framework to understand EBPs means more than simply evaluating whether EBPs differ as a function of age. Rather, one must also consider the context of childhood and adolescence. Unlike providing EBPs to adults, where an individual is typically the sole target of intervention, providing EBPs to children and adolescents almost certainly will involve both the individual child/adolescent as well as their family and often their school (Hoagwood et al., 2001). In fact, the majority of mental health services for children are provided by schools (Burns et al., 1995). Likewise, nearly all aspects of treatment provided to children will require some parental involvement—parents typically identify and refer children for treatment, assessments typically rely heavily on the parent's perception (e.g., through a clinical interview or rating scale about the child), and treatment is often delivered through the parent (e.g., parent training). Family context also likely interacts with age in terms of their impact on EBPs. For instance, research suggesting that adolescents may have lower rates of clinically significant improvement in response to parent training for antisocial behavior (Ruma et al., 1996) could be at least partly due to the fact that parents of adolescents are typically less likely or less able to monitor them. Gaining a better understanding how development and EBPs interact is fundamental to understanding how to best serve children and adolescents.

Fourth, more needs to be learned about the role of gender in EBPs. As with age, evidence published to date provides mixed evidence about gender differences in response to EBPs. In one meta-analytic review of treatment studies targeting youth, Weisz, Weiss et al. (1995) found higher effect sizes (more positive response to treatment) in studies that used primarily female samples as compared to studies that used primarily male samples. There was also an interaction with age that suggested adolescent females showed the most positive response to treatment; however, these results contradicted findings of an earlier meta-analysis conducted by the same investigators that found no difference in treatment outcome between boys and girls (Weisz, Weiss, Alicke, & Klotz, 1987). More work to resolve these discrepant findings is needed.

Fifth, there is limited information about the processes that mediate EBPs. Nearly all research on EBPs has focused on outcomes, while little attention has been paid to the processes that produce those outcomes. Much more is known about what the treatments do (outcomes) than how the treatments work (the mediators). One likely reason is that theories supporting EBPs are often disconnected from research evaluating EBPs. As described by Kazdin (2001, p. 59),

> there is little in the way of theory that underlies current therapies for children and adolescents. We are in an odd position of having no clear understanding of therapeutic change, no clear set of studies that advance our understanding of why treatment works, and scores of outcome studies that are at the same time wonderfully but also crassly empirical.

Procedures for testing mediation have been clearly described (Baron & Kenny, 1986; Holmbeck, 1997), including procedures for doing so in treatment outcome studies (Kraemer, Stice, Kazdin, Offord, & Kupfer, 2001; Kraemer, Wilson, Fairburn, & Agras, 2002). Applying these methods to evaluating EBPs will help to identify the "active ingredient" in treatments, which in turn will provide greater insight into why treatments do and do not work. In turn, this will help develop and refine EBPs to make them more effective (Weisz et al., 2005).

Sixth, the role of comorbidity on EBPs is under-studied (Shirk & McMakin, 2008). It has long been demonstrated that comorbidity is often the rule rather than the exception in samples of children with mental health problems, and this is especially true in samples of children referred for treatment (Angold, Costello, & Erkanli, 1999). Despite this established finding, relatively little research has examined the role of comorbidity in prevention or treatment efforts (Weisz et al., 2005). In fact, it is widely believed that researchers sometimes exclude children with comorbid disorders from intervention research in an effort to produce a homogeneous sample and this produces a mismatch between children seen in community treatment settings— who typically have high rates of comorbidity— and children included in clinical treatment research. Bickman (2002), for example, suggests that approximately 50% of children identified in and treated in community clinics have comorbid disorders, whereas almost all EBPs are designed for specific disorders without regard to comorbid conditions. Because comorbidity is often associated with more severe forms of psychopathology (Brady & Kendall, 1992; Loeber & Keenan, 1994; Seligman & Ollendick, 1998; Waschbusch, 2002), it is tempting to assume that comorbid conditions are likely associated with a diminished response to EBPs; however, research suggests a more complex pattern (Hinshaw, 2007). In fact, some research suggests that the presence of a second disorder may potentiate the response to treatment. For instance, some evidence suggests that children with ADHD and comorbid conduct problems show a less positive response to medication treatment than do children with ADHD who do not have conduct problems (Barkley, McMurray, Edelbrock, & Robbins, 1989), whereas other research shows the opposite pattern—that children with both ADHD and conduct problems show a better treatment outcome in response to behavioral parent training (Hartman, Stage, & Webster-Stratton,

2003). Still other research suggests no impact of comorbid conduct problems for either medication or behavior therapy treatment (e.g., MTA Cooperative Group, 1999b; Pelham et al., 1993). These contrasting findings illustrate that the impact of comorbidity on EBPs is likely to be complex and influenced by factors such as the nature of the primary disorder and the comorbid disorder, as well as the type of EBP.

Seventh, little is known about the sequencing and integration of EBPs. There is almost no research guidance about which treatments should be used when there is more than one EBP available, and there is almost no research guidance on how to proceed when more than one mental health problem is present and therefore more than one EBP may be needed (Chorpita et al., 2002; Pelham & Fabiano, 2008). Gaining a better understanding of how to sequence and integrate EBPs is important for at least three reasons. First, EBPs tend to be specific to one particular problem area, but children and adolescents who present for treatment often do not present with just one problem. For children and adolescents with more than one mental health problem, it is left to the clinician to determine which problem should be prioritized and therefore how EBPs should be sequenced, or if problems should be tackled simultaneously and the EBPs should be integrated. Regardless of what route the clinician chooses, there is almost no research on how to proceed (i.e., which EBP should come first or how to integrate two different EBPs). Second, integrating and sequencing EBPs is common practice in clinical settings. One survey of practitioners found that eclectic therapy, which can be defined as treatment that uses techniques drawn from different therapeutic orientations, was the most widely used treatment approach by both psychologist and psychiatrists in clinical practice (Kazdin, Siegel et al., 1990). Third, evidence suggests that how treatments are sequenced and integrated can change the nature of the treatments. It is often assumed that combining two treatments

will result in additive effects in that the effects of one treatment will be added to the effects of the other treatment; however, this is just one possible way treatments could combine (Pelham & Murphy, 1986; Schroeder, Lewis, & Lipton, 1983). Treatments could also combine to potentiate one another, yielding a combined effect greater than the total of the two component effects, or they could inhibit one another, yielding an effect that is less than the effect of either component. Reciprocation can also occur in which combining two treatments results in the same outcome as either treatment alone. Likewise, sequencing may also alter treatment outcomes. For example, some treatment guidelines published by professional organizations recommend stimulant medication as the first-line treatment for children with ADHD, with behavior therapy implemented later if needed (American Academy of Child and Adolescent Psychiatry, 2007; American Academy of Pediatrics, 2001). Yet the only published study that has systematically examined the sequence of implementing these two evidence-based treatments for ADHD—stimulant medication and behavior therapy—found that 82% of children who were started on stimulant medication were later judged to need additional behavior therapy, whereas only 26% of children who were started on behavior therapy were later judged to need stimulant medication (Dopfner et al., 2004). Likewise, research we recently completed showed that parents of children with ADHD were much less likely to attend parent training if their child was first treated with stimulant medication as compared to if their child was first treated with behavior therapy (Pelham, Fabiano, & Waschbusch, 2009). Clearly, gaining further knowledge of sequencing and integrating treatments has the potential for improving knowledge of how to effectively implement EBPs.

Finally, and perhaps most importantly, much more needs to be learned about how to implement EBPs in real life settings. Researchers have long distinguished between efficacy and effectiveness research. Briefly, efficacy studies are those that seek to evaluate internal validity by examining intervention effects under ideal conditions, whereas effectiveness studies seek to examine clinical utility by examining intervention effects under typical treatment conditions (Chorpita, Barlow, Albano, & Daleiden, 1998; Hoagwood, Hibbs, Brent, & Jensen, 1995). Currently, efficacy research forms the backbone of efforts to evaluate the evidence base of child and adolescent interventions (Lonigan et al., 1998). There are numerous differences between efficacy and effectiveness studies. Prototypically, efficacy studies examine treatment effects on clients who are carefully selected to meet a specific profile and using carefully selected therapists who are trained to implement treatment in a carefully defined and controlled manner. In contrast, the prototypical effectiveness study examines treatment effects on clients who present for services using a treatment as implemented by therapists who work at the service agency and who implement the protocol in variable ways.

Given these differences, it is no wonder that treatment effects often vary considerably when implemented under ideal conditions (in efficacy studies) as compared to when implemented in clinical practice (in effectiveness studies). Several reviews, including meta-analyses, have examined the effects of interventions for children and adolescents as evaluated using efficacy studies and these reviews consistently report moderate to large positive effects (Hoag & Burlingame, 1997; Kazdin, 1991; Weisz et al., 1987; Weisz, Weiss et al., 1995). In contrast, meta-analytic reviews of treatment as delivered in typical clinical practice (effectiveness studies) suggests that they are no more effective than control conditions (Weisz & Hawley, 1998; Weisz et al., 2006; Weisz, Weiss, et al., 1995). More recent evidence is consistent with these findings. For instance, one recent randomized clinical trial showed that traditional psychotherapy as delivered in clinical practice was no more effective than a nontreatment control

condition both immediately after treatment (B. Weiss, Catron, Harris, & Phung, 1999) and 2 years later (B. Weiss et al., 1999). Likewise, a recent meta-analysis reviewed studies in which youth were randomly assigned to treatment with an EBP or to treatment with typical clinical practice and found that the EBP outcomes were superior to outcomes associated with typical clinical practice both immediately after treatment as well as at follow-up (Weisz et al., 2006). The effect sizes comparing EBP and typical clinical treatment were 0.30 at posttreatment and 0.38 at follow-up, indicating that, on average, 62% of youth treated with EBPs were better off than youth who were treated with usual clinical care. These findings suggest that EBPs produce more positive outcomes than usual clinical practice. As one author stated, "the literature on effectiveness of treatment as usual in the community for children and adolescents is depressingly consistent in its poor outcomes" (Bickman, 2002, p. 195). It should be noted that this and other conclusions about the seeming ineffectiveness of community-based treatment are based on average outcomes computed across studies. By their nature averages hide the considerable variation that was apparent from study to study. In fact, some studies show that EBPs have large advantages over typical clinical care, other studies show no differences, and still other studies find that usual care has advantages over EBPs. It would therefore be incorrect to conclude that all typical clinical practices are inferior to all EBPs; instead, the results suggests that, on average, EBPs seem to have advantages over typical clinical care.

It should also be emphasized that there are many differences between EBPs and usual clinical care. Treatments delivered as part of research typically have careful evaluation of the fidelity of the implementation, whereas treatments delivered in usual practice typically do not. Fidelity evaluations have been shown to be an important determinant of treatment effects (Cordray & Pion, 2006). Further, research on treatment of mental health problems for youth often use samples selected to be homogenous and use carefully controlled treatment conditions (e.g., low caseloads for therapists who specialize in a particular disorder), whereas treatments delivered in community settings serve heterogeneous populations and treatment conditions are not carefully controlled (e.g., patients with highly diverse presenting problems, clinicians with high caseloads and varying levels of education and expertise, treatment provided in various settings) (Weisz, Donenberg, Han, & Kauneckis, 1995). The fact that researchers are apparently evaluating different treatments, clients, and therapists than what is found in typical clinical settings (Kazdin, Bass et al., 1990), and using more rigorous methods of determining whether treatment is being implemented as designed (i.e., conducting fidelity evaluations), raises an important question: To what extent are mental health professionals using EBPs in real life settings?

USE OF EBPs IN REAL LIFE SETTINGS

It should be obvious that EBPs will not have a meaningful, positive impact on children with mental health problems if they are not used by practitioners that provide treatment (Gonzales, 2002). As Hoagwood and colleagues wrote, "Treatments that fail to reach those who stand to benefit from them cannot be said to be effective" (Hoagwood et al., 2001, p. 1182). An important question, then, concerns the extent to which EBPs are actually used in real life settings. The general consensus among researchers seems to be that EBPs are not widely used in clinical practice. As stated in one recent book chapter, "Despite the outpouring of research on psychotherapy over the past half century, by and large, the clinical activities of most psychotherapists remain largely untouched by findings of empirical research" (Nathan & Gorman, 2002, p. 643). What evidence supports this assertion?

One line of evidence comes from work by Kazdin and colleagues. In one study, these researchers surveyed over 1,100 practitioners providing services to children with mental health problems about the services they provide, their attitudes toward different treatments, and their priorities about treatment research (Kazdin, Siegel, et al., 1990). In a second study, the authors evaluated the characteristics of research on the treatment of child and adolescent mental health (Kazdin, Bass, et al., 1990). Comparing the two studies suggests that there are important differences between what researchers are studying and what practitioners are encountering and doing in practice. Results of the survey of practitioners showed that eclectic treatments were rated by 72.6% of respondents as effective most of the time or all of the time, whereas behavior modification was rated as effective by 55.1% of respondents and cognitive treatments were rated as effective by 49.2% of respondents. In contrast, the survey of treatment research showed that the majority of studies have examined behavior treatments (49.5%) or cognitive behavioral techniques (22.1%); only 3.6% of research has examined eclectic treatments. Likewise, adjustment disorder was the fourth most common problem that professionals reported treating, whereas virtually no treatment research has examined adjustment disorders. O'Connor and Cartwright's chapter on adjustment disorders in adults in Volume 2 of this handbook confirms that impression. Taken together, these findings suggest an important disconnect between treatment research and treatment use.

More recently, Plante, Andersen, and Boccacini (1999) surveyed 211 clinical psychologists about their attitudes toward and use of EBPs. Most of the respondents described themselves as employed in independent practice and as spending the majority of their professional time providing psychotherapy services. Sixty-five percent of respondents held a generally positive view about EBPs but only 46% routinely used EPBs in their own practice. Further, correlations showed that those who spent the most time delivering services were least likely to use EBPs.

Surveys of parents and teachers of children with mental health problems also suggest that use of EBPs is not necessarily the norm. Two recent surveys of parents of children with autism spectrum disorders found that parents were using an average of four to seven different treatments for their child and that EBPs and non-EBPs were equally likely to be used (Goin-Kochel, Myers, & Mackintosh, 2007; Green et al., 2006). Likewise, a nationally representative sample of public and private schools whose principals were surveyed about activities for preventing and treating discipline problems showed that only about two thirds of schools were using evidence-based practices (behavioral approaches) for reducing conduct problems in schools (D. C. Gottfredson & Gottfredson, 2002; G. D. Gottfredson & Gottfredson, 2001). By comparison, the same percentage of elementary school principals reported using packaged or "off-the-shelf" programs to prevent conduct problems, almost none which have been evaluated. For instance, the Drug Abuse Resistance Education (DARE) program was used by about half of elementary schools, despite the fact that there is evidence that it is ineffective (Lynam et al., 1999). Overall, these surveys, along with data from mental health service providers, support the assertion that EBPs are not widely used in real life settings—at least relative to treatments without empirical support.

On the other hand, more recent data provides optimism. One recent survey queried 616 individuals about their attitudes toward and use of EBPs (Sheehan, Walrath, & Holden, 2007). The majority of participants (90%) described themselves as direct providers of mental health services and 80% of respondents noted that they used at least one EBP in the course of their work. About one third to one half of employers required service providers to use EBPs, suggesting that the use of EBPs may be increasing in recent years since this survey reported rates

of EBP use that were nearly double those reported by Plante et al. almost a decade earlier. Further, this increase may be due to the practitioners electing to use EBPs rather than due to mandates imposed by the employer.

WHAT DETERMINES WHETHER CLINICIANS USE EBPs?

The relatively low usage of EBPs in clinical practice raises an important question: Why are EBPs not used more often in mental health service settings? One factor that may be relevant is clinician attitudes toward EBPs (Higa & Chorpita, 2008). Theory and research suggest that attitudes can be a significant factor in the decision about whether to pursue or accept innovative change. For example, motivational interviewing seeks to address ambivalence about change in clients seeking treatment and has been shown to be effective for treatment of alcohol and other substance use problems (Rubak, Sandbaek, Lauritzen, & Christiansen, 2005). One recent survey of mental health professionals found considerable variation across the sample on their openness to EBPs and that interns still in training were more open to adopting EBPs than were those already in practice (Aarons, 2004). A related study surveyed practicing clinicians about their use of treatment manuals in clinical practice (Addis & Krasnow, 2000). Because treatment manuals are part of the definition of a well-established EBP (Lonigan et al., 1998; Silverman & Hinshaw, 2008) but seldom used in typical clinical practice (Weisz et al., 2006), clinician attitudes toward treatment manuals are arguably a proxy for their attitudes toward EBPs. Twenty-three percent of clinicians had never heard of a treatment manual. Of those who had, only 6% reported using a treatment manual often or almost always. In contrast, 46% reported never using one. Those who viewed treatment manuals more negatively did so because they conceptualized them as cookbooks and as imposed on them for bureaucratic reasons, suggesting that lack of flexibility in applying treatments is a barrier to implementing EBPs. This same theme emerged in other recent studies of practicing clinicians (Nelson, Steele, & Mize, 2006; Pagato et al., 2007). None of these studies directly evaluated whether those clinicians with more negative attitudes toward EBPs are less likely to use EBPs, but they are consistent in suggesting that there is wide variation in attitudes and that at least some clinicians view EBPs as unhelpful largely because they believe EBPs consist of a rigid set of treatment rules imposed on them by bureaucrats.

Another, more tangible, reason that EBPs are not more widely used in clinical practice is that they are not required to be used. In contrast to medications, which cannot be prescribed without approval by the Food and Drug Administration, psychosocial treatments are not regulated by governments or by professional organizations. Currently, there is no requirement that clinicians can only provide psychosocial treatments that have an evidence base, nor are their sanctions against providing psychosocial treatments that are untested or that have been shown to be ineffective. The same has been historically true regarding payment for services, though this may be changing. That is, mental health providers have been paid for providing any manner of psychosocial interventions regardless of evidence base; there has been little difference in compensation for services with an empirical base or services without an empirical base. There are many reasons for this, such as lack of agreement as to what constitutes an EBP as well as political considerations within professional organizations, but the likely result of lack of regulation and lack of differential compensation is that there is little incentive for mental health professionals to offer EBPs as compared to other treatments. Further, this lack of a central oversight agency means that consumers have no easily identifiable source for obtaining information on best psychological practices.

Along with a lack of incentive to begin using EBPs, there is also a significant disincentive

for clinicians to seek out EBPs (Weisz et al., 2005). When considering the amount of education that is required of most mental health professionals, even those clinicians who are relatively new in the field have invested considerable time, energy, and often money toward learning and using their current intervention approach. In some cases, adopting an EBP intervention would mean that the payoff for this investment would be diminished. In addition, many clinicians would need to make additional investments in their training if they are to provide EBPs, both in terms of finances to invest in training and in terms of lost revenue while receiving training (Higa & Chorpita, 2008). Further, given the considerable variation observed in treatment outcome research, it is likely that many clinicians have seen at least some success using their current approach. Even if these successful outcomes are more rare than they are common they may act as intermittent reinforcement that serves to maintain the therapists' behaviors (Shirk, 2004). Further, attribution theory and research shows that healthy individuals tend to remember successes more readily than failures (Taylor & Brown, 1988), suggesting that many clinicians will have a positively skewed judgment of their own efforts. This may be especially likely if clinicians do not systematically track their clients' progress or do so using subjective measures (treatment progress notes) rather than objective measures of treatment response (e.g., psychometrically sound rating scales). The net result is that asking clinicians to move toward providing EBPs may essentially equate to asking clinicians to set aside their firsthand experience of successful outcomes in favor of secondhand evidence from a scientific study, and to spend their own time and money to do so.

Another factor that may influence whether professionals use EBPs is consumer demand (Pagato et al., 2007). It has probably always been true that parents who are seeking help for their child or adolescent have difficulty differentiating sound advice from poor advice, but this is likely increased substantially in the information age. For every professional organization that provides sound information on evidence-based practices there are likely hundreds of websites that post poor information that has little or no evidence base. An Internet search on ADHD treatment, for example, provides over 470,000 Web sites including the second ranked page that decries both EBPs for ADHD (stimulant medication and behavior therapy) while touting treatments (megavitamin and dietary restrictions) that have no empirical support, are costly, and may be dangerous. Further, unlike the medication interventions that are required to have a certain level of empirical support (as regulated by the Food and Drug Administration) and are then marketed (often aggressively) to consumers, there is no industry that is committed to "whipping up demand" for empirically supported psychosocial interventions (Weisz, 2000a, 2000b). The pharmaceutical industry has been very effective at connecting research-based interventions to practitioners and to consumers; no such mechanism is in place for psychosocial interventions.

Finally, many clinicians are skeptical of the foundation and nature of EBPs (Addis, Wade, & Hatgis, 1999; Levant, 2004). One review of studies examining the efficacy and effectiveness of EBPs for children and adolescents concluded that "clinician reluctance remained a primary obstacle to dissemination" (Chorpita et al., 2002, p. 167). Others have endorsed this same conclusion (Kendall, 2002). As noted earlier, many therapists are skeptical of manualized treatments in general and EBPs in particular, viewing them as imposing a "one-size-fits-all" approach onto situations in which individualization and adaptation are necessary strategies (Addis et al., 1999). Others view the research foundation of EBPs with skepticism, criticizing the methodology of the studies (Ablon & Marci, 2004; Goldfried & Eubanks-Carter, 2004; Westen, Novotny, & Thompson-Brenner, 2004) and suggesting that research on EBPs is not generalizable to the setting or clients that the practitioner encounters (Shirk, 2004; Westen et al., 2004). Other concerns

raised are that more evidence is needed before treatments can be widely disseminated, apparently implying that definition of EBPs may be too lax (Kettlewell, 2004).

These concerns are not without merit. For instance, one study compared children with anxiety disorders and their families served in research settings to those served in a community outpatient clinic and found that those from the community setting were more likely to evidence comorbid externalizing problems and were more likely to come from low-income and single-parent homes (Southam-Gerow, Weisz, & Kendall, 2003). As others have noted, these and similar findings reinforce that the concerns of mental health professionals about EBPs have some validity (American Psychological Association Task Force on Evidence-Based Practice for Children and Adolescents, 2008; Hoagwood et al., 2001; Weisz et al., 2005).

In sum, it is not surprising that clinicians are reluctant to use EBPs when one considers how they likely view the situation: (a) There is little tangible benefit and may be a considerable cost to providing them; (b) they have likely seen at least some success with the approach they are currently using; (c) there is no requirement from government, insurance, or professional organizations to provide EBPs; (d) there are few parents and no corporations advocating for EBPs; (e) research suggesting that EBPs are more effective than usual care seems irrelevant in that it uses treatment conditions that may not replicate actual practice and is evaluated using clients that are not like clients in community settings; and (f) the nature of EBPs seems overly restrictive and does not allow for adaptation to meet real life concerns.

HOW SHOULD EBPs BE TRANSPORTED TO CLINICAL SETTINGS?

Given these barriers, how can EBPs be successfully transported beyond university and medical school settings and into clinical practice? This question concerns dissemination, which can be defined as the process of systematically deploying EBPs into typical practice settings. It is not an exaggeration to assert that this is currently the biggest, most salient challenge facing the EBP movement (American Psychological Association Task Force on Evidence-Based Practice for Children and Adolescents, 2008; Schoenwald & Hoagwood, 2001). Research focusing on implementation and dissemination of EPBs is currently a priority research area for the National Institute of Mental Health with respect to children and adolescents (Hoagwood & Olin, 2002). Despite this priority and the importance of the topic, relatively little research has examined how to disseminate EBPs. Using a search of PsycINFO, Herschell, McNeil, and McNeil (2004) found that only 23% of studies relevant to EBPs that were published between 1995 and 1999 focused on dissemination of treatments. They also reviewed selected journals that focus on treatment studies and found that the number of articles devoted to evaluating and disseminating adult treatments were double the number devoted to child and adolescent treatments.

In contrast to the paucity of research, much has been written on the theory and process of disseminating EBPs (Fixen, Naoom, Blase, Friedman, & Wallace, 2005; Herschell et al., 2004; Schoenwald & Hoagwood, 2001; Weisz et al., 2005). One approach that has been proposed is the Deployment Focused Model (Weisz et al., 2005). The rationale behind the Deployment Focused Model is to

> bring treatments into the crucible of clinical practice early in their development and then treat testing in the practice setting as a sequential process . . . to break down the long-standing distinction between clinical trials research and mental health services research. (Weisz et al., 2005, p. 27)

This is accomplished through several steps of treatment development research:

(1) theoretically and clinically guided construction, refinement, and manualizing the intervention protocol; (2) initial efficacy trial under controlled conditions to establish evidence of benefit; (3) single-case applications in practice settings, with progressive adaptations to the protocol; (4) partial effectiveness tests; (5) full tests of effectiveness and dissemination; and (6) tests of sustainability in practice contexts. As is apparent from this description, the goal of the Deployment Focused Model is to conduct the majority of research in community/practice settings. This includes research designed to evaluate: (a) necessary and sufficient components of treatment; (b) moderators and mediators of outcomes; (c) costs and benefits; (d) the impact of organizational factors on treatment outcomes; and (e) variations in treatment procedures, packaging, training, and delivery that are intended to improve the fit with the settings in which it is employed.

An alternative to Weisz's Deployment Focused Model model is offered by Schoenwald and Hoagwood (2001). In a cogent discussion of theoretical and practical issues about moving treatment research into practice settings, these authors argue that there are important distinctions between diffusion, dissemination, and transportability. Diffusion is conceptualized as the natural, unplanned, spontaneous movement of EBPs from research settings into clinical practice. In contrast, dissemination is conceptualized as the directed, planned, organized movement of EBPs from research to practice. Transportability is conceptualized as a precursor to dissemination that focuses on understanding factors associated with successfully moving EBPs from research to practice. Schoenwald and Hoagwood suggest that transportability research is critical to successful dissemination. Thus, Schoenwald and Hoagwood seem to recommend taking more time to understand the EBP before moving toward implementing it in practice settings. This contrast with Weisz's DFM model that seems to recommend moving quickly toward implementing treatments in practice settings and researching them in that context. Currently, there is no research that compares these two different dissemination models.

These dissemination models provide a useful framework for furthering dissemination research with the ultimate goal of moving EBPs into real life settings; however, a serious drawback for each of these models is that they may take years to produce a knowledge base with sufficient breadth and depth to be helpful. In the absence of this research base, it may be helpful to speculate about factors that may positively impact the uptake of EBPs in clinical practice settings.

First, consumer demand would likely increase uptake of EBPs. If parents, schools, and others who make decision about children's service use were to begin taking their business only to practitioners who provide evidence-based services, the market would likely ensure that evidence-based methods predominate. Toward this end, educating mental health users about what treatments are and are not evidence-based is a crucial component of disseminating EBPs. Currently, many parents likely assume that all treatments are evidence based. When asked whether they felt it is important that the treatment offered to their child have scientific evidence to support its use, one parent we worked with replied, "You mean there are treatments given to kids that don't have scientific support?" This is borne out in sophisticated marketing surveys that show parents clearly prefer clinical information that is based on research evidence (Cunningham et al., 1998).

Second, EBPs would become widely used if they were more appealing to consumers as compared to their non-EBP counterparts. Likewise, practitioners would be more likely to deliver EBPs if they were formulated in ways that they found highly acceptable and even satisfying. Thus, we need to know what treatments are acceptable to clinicians, parents, and children as a step toward increasing the use of EBPs (Bickman, 2002). Treatment acceptability has long been of interest to

mental health researchers (Lebow, 1983) and has traditionally been studied using surveys in which parents or teachers complete questionnaires that ask them to rate various treatments or treatment characteristics (dosReis et al., 2003; Reimers, Wacker, & Koeppl, 1987). Studies of this type are useful, but they share several methodological limitations. One limitation is that most questionnaires evaluate treatment as a single package by asking parents or teachers how they feel about the treatment as a whole. However, treatments are complex, with some positive aspects and some negative aspects. More could be learned about parental opinions of treatment by asking them to separately evaluate different aspects of treatments. Another limitation is that respondents are not forced to make difficult choices that are inherent in any decision to pursue a treatment. In a typical paper-and-pencil survey about treatment options, for example, a parent is allowed to answer that she or he would prefer a treatment that is cheap, easy, effective, and carries a low risk for side effects. Such a treatment is indeed highly desirable, but is also not typical of most or any available treatment that has yet been developed. More realistic would be to require parents to make meaningful trade-offs when evaluating treatment options such that they cannot pick all the benefits and none of the drawbacks. In other words, just as a consumer seeking to purchase a television is likely to make trade-offs of factors such as size, cost, quality of picture, and other features, so too are parents likely to make trade-offs of positive and negative treatment factors when deciding what treatment to "buy" for their child or adolescent.

Because of these and other limitations, recent research has turned to methods used by marketing researchers to gain a better understanding of what characteristics of treatment are preferred by parents seeking help for their child. Considering that market researchers have spent literally millions of dollars perfecting methods for measuring consumer preferences and then turning that data into actions (i.e., getting consumers to buy a product), applying market research methods seems a natural fit for measuring parental preferences for EBPs and turning that data into actions (i.e., getting them to seek EBPs for their child). More specifically, marketing research methods known as discrete choice conjoint experiments (DCE) provide a means of evaluating parental preferences about treatment that: (a) asks about specific aspects of treatment, rather than evaluating treatment as a unitary construct; (b) forces parents to choose among treatment characteristics, just as they do when making other complex choices; and (c) allows for the evaluation of individual differences among respondents (Orme, 2006). In applying DCEs to examine treatment preferences, parents make a series of choices between different treatment attributes presented in context of each other, thereby requiring them to consider the trade-offs associated with competing alternatives. This limits superficial decision making, reduces halo effects, and reduces social desirability biases, thereby providing a better understanding of underlying preferences (Phillips, Johnson, & Maddala, 2002). In other words, by requiring respondents to trade off some treatment characteristics against others, DCEs offer a proxy of how parents make real-world decisions (Payne, Bettman, & Johnson, 1993) and results in data that better predicts actual behavior (Phillips et al., 2002). Although these methods were developed by mathematical psychologists (Luce & Tukey, 1964), marketing researchers adopted them to involve consumers in product and service design (Orme, 2006). These methods have recently been extended to involve patients in health service design (Oudhoff, Timmermans, Knol, Bijnen, & Van der Wal, 2007; Ryan & Farrar, 2000; Ryan & Gerard, 2003; Spoth & Redmond, 1993), explore treatment preferences (Ahmed, Blamires, & Smith, 2008; Dwight-Johnson, Lagomasino, Aisenberg, & Hay, 2004; Fraenkel, Gulanski, & Wittink, 2006; Singh, Cuttler, Shin, Silvers, & Neuhauser, 1998),

model health outcome choices (Ryan, 1999; Stanek, Oates, McGhan, Denofrio, & Loh, 2000), study clinical decisions (McGregor, Harris, Furuno, Bradham, & Perencevich, 2007), and involve students in design of medical education programs (Cunningham, Deal, Neville, Rimas, & Lohfeld, 2006).

There is also evidence that they may be useful in understanding parental preferences for treatment of children's mental health. A recent study used a DCE to examine the preferences of parents seeking mental health services for children ages 6 to 18 years old (Cunningham et al., 2008). Nearly 1,200 parents who were self-referred to outpatient mental health clinics for their child's problems completed choice tasks designed to evaluate their opinions about the content and method of treatment, and about the importance of different outcomes with respect to their child's treatment. Latent class analyses of their responses showed that parents could be divided into three categories. Parents in the Action group, which represented about 43% of respondents, preferred treatment materials that provided step-by-step solutions for their child's mental health problems, along with weekly meetings with other parents and coaching calls from a therapist. Parents in the Information group, which represented 41% of respondents, preferred treatment materials that provided them information about their child's mental health problem, but they were not interested in materials that would help them solve their child's problem. These parents were also more likely to state that logistical factors were important, such as where treatment was held, the time required to participate in treatment, and how treatment would be delivered (with other parents in a group, through a book, with a therapist, etc.). Parents in the Overwhelmed group, which represented 16% of respondents, reported higher conduct problems in their children, were more depressed themselves, and felt their child had a worse impact on their family. Even so, they were less interested in receiving information about their child's problem or about solving their child's problems.

This study indicates that there are important differences between parents who seek help in outpatient settings. It may be possible to deliver EBPs in different ways depending on the parents' opinions about their child's treatment, thereby making their child's treatment more acceptable to them. For instance, parent training is consistently demonstrated to be an empirically supported treatment in research settings (Chorpita et al., 2002; Eyberg et al., 2008), but most parents in community settings drop out before completing treatment (Kazdin, 1996). It may be that parents in the Action group are ready, willing, and eager to receive parent training as traditionally delivered in EBP efficacy studies, whereas parents in the Information group are willing to listen but need a motivational interviewing type intervention first, and parents in the Overwhelmed group need therapy for their own depression before they are ready to even consider addressing their child's difficulties. These possibilities are simply speculations based on one study, but they illustrate the potential for using marketing research techniques to help tailor EBPs to be delivered in maximally effective ways.

A third factor that is likely to be important in disseminating EBPs is ease of access. Currently, less than one-quarter of children and adolescents with behavior problems see a mental health specialist and most interventions are delivered in schools (Burns et al., 1995). In addition, the majority of mental health services are delivered by social workers rather than by psychologists (Weisz, Chu, & Polo, 2004). Thus, it is imperative that delivery of EBPs move beyond the traditional model where treatments are delivered in outpatient settings. Several investigators have done innovative work toward furthering this agenda, including delivering treatment in schools and in school-based mental health clinics (Atkins et al., 1998; Cunningham et al., 1998; Santor, Kususmakar, Poulin, & Leblanc, 2007), community-based group parent education (Cunningham, Davis,

Bremner, Dunn, & Rzasa, 1993), distance treatment delivered by phone and Internet (Lingley-Pottie & McGrath, 2006, 2007; Santor, Poulin, Leblanc, & Kususmakar, 2007), and treatment delivered in recreational settings (Pelham, Fabiano, Gnagy, Greiner, & Hoza, 2005; Reitman, Hupp, O'Callaghan, Gulley, & Northup, 2001; Waschbusch, Pelham, Gnagy, Greiner, & Fabiano, 2008).

Fourth, EBPs would be immediately disseminated if clinicians were ethically, legally, and monetarily required to provide them. In the reviews of EBPs published by the clinical child and adolescent psychology division of APA, it was explicitly stated that the purpose of developing an EBP list was not to prescribe mandated treatments (Chambless et al., 1996; Silverman & Hinshaw, 2008). The state of the science is not sufficient that mandated treatments are a realistic option; however, if sufficient evidence does accumulate to demonstrate beyond a reasonable doubt that a treatment is superior to others, or that a treatment is demonstrably ineffective, then it is not unreasonable to put in place policies that are consistent with this evidence. As one recent author noted,

> it is a sorry state of affairs that lawsuits all too often are necessary to get individuals and systems to consider what needs to be done to improve the quality of services in general, and in services to children, adolescents, and families, specifically. (Roberts, 2002, pp. 217–218)

Interestingly, the move toward EBPs has been embraced by leading government officials. In an editorial published in the *New York Times*, Newt Gingrich and John Kerry (along with Billy Beane, a former baseball player and current baseball executive who is renowned for successfully using evidence to make high stakes baseball decisions) wrote:

> Studies have shown that most health care is not based on clinical studies of what works best and what does not—be it a test, treatment, drug or technology. Instead, most care is based on informed opinion, personal observation

or tradition . . . a health care system that is driven by robust comparative clinical evidence will save lives and money. . . . To deliver better health care, we should learn from the successful teams that have adopted baseball's new evidence-based methods. The best way to start improving quality and lower costs is to study the stats. (Beane, Gingrich, & Kerry, 2008, p. A31)

This is not to suggest that simply making it public policy that treatments must be empirically based will solve all dissemination problems; there is evidence from education settings that it will not (C. H. Weiss, Murphy-Graham, Petrosino, & Gandhi, 2008). Rather, policies that further the dissemination of EBPs will help doctors make informed decisions based on established research:

> Evidence-based health care would not strip doctors of their decision-making authority nor replace their expertise. Instead, data and evidence should complement a lifetime of experience, so that doctors can deliver the best quality care at the lowest possible cost. (Beane et al., 2008, p. A31)

Even so, policies that restrict practitioners from using treatments shown not to work and requiring them to produce rationale if they elect not to use an EBP if one is available seem like common sense regulations. Such policies would likely be accepted and even expected by consumers and practitioners alike when considering treatment for a medical condition; if so, then the same standard should be applied to psychological conditions.

Finally, introducing EBPs into continuing education and graduate education programs may further dissemination efforts (Herschell et al., 2004). One of the barriers to disseminating EBPs is that many clinicians lack the knowledge or training to conduct them. Providing this training during graduate education, internship, or both seems a logical step toward overcoming this barrier. Recommendations for achieving this goal have been provided (Leffingwell & Collins, 2008). In addition,

program directors in graduate training programs should emphasize training in EBP, and practica or internship students should be first vetted for adequate training, experience, and supervision in EBP. Using continuing education to provide training in EBPs presents more difficulties. Many people who deliver mental health services are not licensed and therefore are not required to take continuing education, and staff turnover in practice settings is often high, suggesting that employers who seek to train employees in EBPs would have to do so continually (Higa & Chorpita, 2008). In fact, one could imagine that employers who send their employees to continuing education for EBPs would provide them with new skills that would make them more marketable and thus allow them to find a better job. In addition, continuing education programs are often expensive, suggesting that it would be a considerable cost for either the employer or the employee. Such challenges emphasize the importance of integrating training in EBPs into graduate work and internships.

SUMMARY

The movement toward evidence-based practices for use with children and adolescents with mental health problems presents numerous challenges, many of which seem quite significant. These challenges should not be minimized, but should also not be viewed as insurmountable. Successful development and dissemination of EBPs would likely lead to more effective treatments for more youth at lower cost. Such an outcome is in the best interests of both the children and adolescents who seek treatment and in the society that cares for them.

REFERENCES

Aarons, G. A. (2004). Mental health provider attitudes toward adoption of evidenced-based practice: The Evidence-Based Practice Attitude Scale (EBPAS). *Mental Health Services Research, 6,* 61–74.

Ablon, J. S., & Marci, C. (2004). Psychotherapy process: The missing link: Comment on Westen, Novotny, and Thompson-Brenner (2004). *Psychological Bulletin, 130,* 664–668.

Addis, M. E., & Krasnow, A. D. (2000). A national survey of practicing psychologists' attitudes toward psychotherapy treatment manuals. *Journal of Consulting and Clinical Psychology, 68,* 331–339.

Addis, M. E., Wade, W. A., & Hatgis, C. (1999). Barriers to dissemination of evidence-based practices: Addressing practitioners' concerns about manual-based psychotherapies. *Clinical Psychology: Science and Practice, 6,* 430–441.

Ahmed, S. F., Blamires, C., & Smith, W. (2008). Facilitating and understanding the family's choice of injection device for growth hormone therapy by using conjoint analysis. *Archives of Disease in Childhood, 93,* 95–97.

American Academy of Child and Adolescent Psychiatry. (1997). Practice parameters for the assessment and treatment of children, adolescents and adults with Attention-Deficit/Hyperactivity Disorder. *Journal of the American Academy of Child and Adolescent Psychiatry, 26,* 85s–121s.

American Academy of Child and Adolescent Psychiatry. (2007). Practice parameters for the assessment and treatment of children and adolescents with Attention-Deficit/Hyperactivity Disorder. *Journal of the American Academy of Child and Adolescent Psychiatry, 46,* 894–921.

American Academy of Pediatrics. (2001). Clinical practice guideline: Treatment of the school-aged child with attention-deficit/hyperactivity disorder. *Pediatrics, 105,* 1033–1044.

American Psychological Association Task Force on Evidence-Based Practice for Children and Adolescents. (2008). *Disseminating evidence-based practice for children and adolescents: A systems approach to enhancing care.* Washington, DC: American Psychological Association.

American Psychological Association Working Group on Psychoactive Medications for Children and Adolescents. (2006). *Report of the working group on psychoactive medications for children and adolescents. Psychopharmacological, psychosocial, and combined interventions for childhood disorders: Evidence base, contextual factors, and future directions.* Washington, DC: American Psychological Association.

Angold, A., Costello, E. J., & Erkanli, A. (1999). Comorbidity. *Journal of Child Psychology and Psychiatry, 40,* 57–87.

Atkins, M. S., McKay, M. M., Arvanitis, P., London, L., Madison, S., Costigan, C., . . . Webster, D. (1998). An ecological model for school-based mental health services for urban low-income aggressive children. *Journal of Behavioral Health Services and Research, 5,* 64–75.

Barkley, R. A., McMurray, M. B., Edelbrock, C. S., & Robbins, K. (1989). The response of aggressive and nonaggressive ADHD children to two doses of methylphenidate. *Journal of the American Academy of Child and Adolescent Psychiatry, 28,* 873–881.

Baron, R. M., & Kenny, D. A. (1986). The moderator-mediator variable distinction in social psychological research: Conceptual, strategic, and statistical considerations. *Journal of Personality and Social Psychology, 51,* 1173–1182.

Barrett, P. M., Farrell, L., Pina, A. A., Peris, T. S., & Piacentini, J. (2008). Evidence-based psychosocial treatments for child and adolescent obsessive-compulsive disorder. *Journal of Clinical Child and Adolescent Psychology, 37,* 131–155.

Beane, B., Gingrich, N., & Kerry, J. (2008, October 24). How to take American health care from worst to first. *New York Times.*

Bickman, L. (2002). The death of treatment as usual: An excellent first step on a long road. *Clinical Psychology: Science and Practice, 9,* 195–199.

Brady, E. U., & Kendall, P. C. (1992). Comorbidity of anxiety and depression in children and adolescents. *Psychological Bulletin, 111,* 244–255.

Brestan, E. V., & Eyberg, S. M. (1998). Effective psychosocial treatments of conduct-disordered children and adolescents: 29 years, 82 studies, and 5,272 kids. *Journal of Clinical Child Psychology, 27,* 180–189.

Burns, B. J., Costello, E. J., Angold, A., Tweed, D., Stangl, D., Farmer, E. M. Z., & Erkanil, A. (1995). Children's mental health service use across service sectors. *Health Affairs, 14,* 147–159.

Chambless, D. L., Sanderson, W. C., Shoham, V., Johnson, S. B., Pope, K. S., Crits-Christoph, P., . . . McCurry, S. (1996). An update on empirically validated therapies. *The Clinical Psychologist, 49,* 5–18.

Chorpita, B. F., Barlow, D. H., Albano, A. M., & Daleiden, E. L. (1998). Methodological strategies in child clinical trials: Advancing efficacy and effectiveness of psychosocial treatments. *Journal of Abnormal Child Psychology, 26,* 7–15.

Chorpita, B. F., Yim, L. M., Donkervoet, J. C., Arensdorf, A., Amundsen, M. J., McGee, C., . . . Morelli, P. (2002). Toward large-scale implementation of empirically supported treatments for children: A review and observations by the Hawaii Empirical Basis to Services Task Force. *Clinical Psychology: Science and Practice, 9,* 165–190.

Cicchetti, D., & Richters, J. E. (1997). Examining the conceptual and scientific underpinnings of research in developmental psychopathology. *Development and Psychopathology, 9,* 189–191.

Conduct Problems Prevention Research Group. (2002). The implementation of the Fast Track program: An example of a large-scale prevention science efficacy trial. *Journal of Abnormal Child Psychology, 30,* 1–18.

Cordray, D. S., & Pion, G. M. (2006). Treatment strength and integrity: Models and methods. In R. R. Bootzin & P. E. McKnight (Eds.), *Strengthening research methodology: Psychological measurement and evaluation* (pp. 103–124). Washington, DC: American Psychological Association.

Cunningham, C. E., Cunningham, L. J., Martorelli, V., Tran, A., Young, J., & Zacharias, R. (1998). The effects of primary division, student-mediated conflict resolution programs on playground aggression. *Journal of Child Psychology and Psychiatry, 39*, 653–662.

Cunningham, C. E., Davis, J. R., Bremner, R., Dunn, K. W., & Rzasa, T. (1993). Coping modeling problems solving versus master modeling: Effects on adherence, in-session process, and skill acquisition in a residential treatment parent-training program. *Journal of Consulting and Clinical Psychology, 61*, 871–877.

Cunningham, C. E., Deal, K., Neville, A., Rimas, H., & Lohfeld, L. (2006). Modeling the problem-based learning preferences of McMaster University's undergraduate medical students using a discrete conjoint experiment. *Advances in Health Sciences Education: Theory and Practice, 11*, 245–266.

Cunningham, C. E., Deal, K., Rimas, H., Buchanan, D. H., Gold, M., Sdao-Jarvic, K., & Boyle, M. (2008). Modeling the information preferences of parents of children with mental health problems: A discrete choice conjoint experiment. *Journal of Abnormal Child Psychology, 36*, 1123–1138.

David-Ferdon, C., & Kaslow, N. J. (2008). Evidence-based psychosocial treatments for child and adolescent depression. *Journal of Clinical Child and Adolescent Psychology, 37*, 62–104.

Dishion, T. J., & Patterson, G. R. (1992). Age effects in parent training outcome. *Behavior Therapy, 23*, 719–729.

dosReis, S., Zito, J. M., Safer, D. J., Soeken, K. L., Mitchell, J. W. J., & Ellwood, L. C. (2003). Parental perceptions and satisfaction with stimulant medication for attention-deficit hyperactivity disorder. *Journal of Developmental and Behavioral Pediatrics, 24*, 155–162.

Durlak, J. A., Fuhrman, T., & Lampman, C. (1991). Effectiveness of cognitive-behavior therapy for maladapting children: A meta-analysis. *Psychological Bulletin, 110*, 204–214.

Dwight-Johnson, M., Lagomasino, I. T., Aisenberg, E., & Hay, J. (2004). Using conjoint analysis to assess depression treatment preferences among low-income Latinos. *Psychiatric Services, 55*, 934–936.

Eyberg, S. M., Nelson, M. M., & Boggs, S. R. (2008). Evidence-based psychosocial treatments for children and adolescents with disruptive behavior. *Journal of Clinical Child and Adolescent Psychology, 37*, 215–237.

Fixen, D. L., Naoom, S. F., Blase, K. A., Friedman, R. M., & Wallace, F. (2005). *Implementation research: A synthesis of the literature.* Tampa, FL: University of South Florida, Louis de la Parte Florida Mental Health Institute, the National Implementation Research Network (FMHI Publication #231).

Fraenkel, L., Gulanski, B., & Wittink, D. (2006). Patient treatment preferences for osteoporosis. *Arthritis and Rheumatism, 55*, 729–735.

Goin-Kochel, R. P., Myers, B. J., & Mackintosh, V. H. (2007). Parental reports on the use of treatments and therapies for children with autism spectrum disorders. *Research in Autism Spectrum Disorders, 1*, 195–209.

Goldfried, M. R., & Eubanks-Carter, C. (2004). On the need for a new psychotherapy research paradigm: Comment on Westen, Novotny, and Thompson-Brenner (2004). *Psychological Bulletin, 130*, 631–663.

Gonzales, J. J. (2002). The tangled and thorny path of science to practice: Tensions in interpreting and applying "evidence." *Clinical Psychology: Science and Practice, 9*, 204–209.

Gottfredson, D. C., & Gottfredson, G. D. (2002). Quality of school-based prevention programs: Results from a national survey. *Journal of Research in Crime and Delinquency, 39*, 3–35.

Gottfredson, G. D., & Gottfredson, D. C. (2001). What schools do to prevent problem behavior and promote safe environments. *Journal of Educational and Psychological Consultation, 12*, 313–344.

Green, V. A., Pituch, K. A., Itchon, J., Choi, A., O'Reilly, M., & Sigafood, J. (2006). Internet survey of treatments used by parents of children with autism. *Research in Developmental Disabilities, 27*, 70–84.

Hartman, R. R., Stage, S. A., & Webster-Stratton, C. (2003). A growth curve analysis of parent training outcomes: Examining the influence of child risk factors (inattention, impulsivity, and hyperactivity problems), parent and family risk factors. *Journal of Child Psychology and Psychiatry, 44*, 388–398.

Herschell, A. D., McNeil, C. B., & McNeil, D. W. (2004). Clinical child psychology's progress in disseminating empirically supported treatments. *Clinical Psychology: Science and Practice, 11*, 267–288.

Higa, C. K., & Chorpita, B. F. (2008). Evidence-based therapies: Translating research into practice. In R. G. Steele, D. Elkin, & M. C. Roberts (Eds.), *Handbook of evidence-based therapies for children and adolescents* (pp. 45–61). New York, NY: Springer.

Hinshaw, S. P. (2007). Moderators and mediators of treatment outcome for youth with ADHD: Understanding for whom and how interventions work. *Ambulatory Pediatrics, 7*, 91–100.

Hoag, M. J., & Burlingame, G. M. (1997). Evaluating the effectiveness of child and adolescent group treatment: A meta-analytic review. *Journal of Clinical Child Psychology, 26*, 234–246.

Hoagwood, K., Burns, B. J., Kiser, L., Ringseisen, H., & Schoenwald, S. K. (2001). Evidence-based practice in child and adolescent mental health services. *Psychiatric Services, 52*, 1179–1189.

Hoagwood, K., Hibbs, E. D., Brent, D., & Jensen, P. S. (1995). Introduction to special section: Efficacy and effectiveness in studies of child and adolescent psychotherapy. *Journal of Consulting and Clinical Psychology, 63*, 683–687.

Hoagwood, K., & Olin, S. S. (2002). The NIMH Blueprint for Change report: Research priorities in child and adolescent mental health. *Journal of the American Academy of Child and Adolescent Psychiatry, 41*, 760–767.

Holden, E. W., Deichmann, M. M., & Levy, J. D. (1999). Empirically supported treatments in pediatric psychology: Recurrent pediatric headache. *Journal of Pediatric Psychology, 24*, 91–109.

Holmbeck, G. N. (1997). Toward terminological, conceptual, and statistical clarity in the study of mediators and moderators: Examples from the child-clinical and pediatric psychology literatures. *Journal of Consulting and Clinical Psychology, 65*, 599–600.

Huey, S. J., & Polo, A. J. (2008). Evidence-based psychosocial treatments for ethnic minority youth. *Journal of Clinical Child and Adolescent Psychology, 37*, 262–301.

Janicke, D. M., & Finney, J. W. (1999). Empirically supported treatments in pediatric psychology: Recurrent abdominal pain. *Journal of Pediatric Psychology, 24*, 115–127.

Jelalian, E., & Saelens, B. E. (1999). Empirically supported treatments in pediatric psychology: Pediatric obesity. *Journal of Pediatric Psychology, 24*, 223–248.

Kaslow, N. J., & Thompson, M. P. (1998). Applying criteria for empirically supported treatments to studies of psychosocial interventions for child and adolescent depression. *Journal of Clinical Child Psychology, 27*, 146–155.

Kazdin, A. E. (1991). Effectiveness of psychotherapy with children and adolescents. *Journal of Consulting and Clinical Psychology, 59*, 785–798.

Kazdin, A. E. (1996). Dropping out of child psychotherapy: Issues for research and implications for practice. *Clinical Child Psychology and Psychiatry, 1*, 133–136.

Kazdin, A. E. (2001). Bridging the enormous gaps of theory with therapy research and practice. *Journal of Clinical Child Psychology, 30*, 59–66.

Kazdin, A. E., Bass, D., Ayers, W. A., & Rodgers, A. (1990). Empirical and clinical focus of child and adolescent psychotherapy research. *Journal of Consulting and Clinical Psychology, 58*, 729–740.

Kazdin, A. E., & Kendall, P. C. (1998). Current progress and future plans for developing effective treatments: Comments and perspectives. *Journal of Clinical Child Psychology, 27*, 217–226.

Kazdin, A. E., Siegel, T. C., & Bass, D. (1990). Drawing on clinical practice to inform research on child and adolescent psychotherapy: Survey of practitioners. *Professional Psychology: Research and Practice, 21*, 189–198.

Keel, P. K., & Haedt, A. (2008). Evidence-based psychosocial treatments for eating problems and eating disorders. *Journal of Clinical Child and Adolescent Psychology, 37*, 39–61.

Kendall, P. C. (2002). Toward a research-practice-community partnership: Goin' fishing and showing slides. *Clinical Psychology: Science and Practice, 9*, 214–216.

Kendall, P. C. (2008, October). *Findings and clinical implications from the Multisite Child/Adolescent Anxiety Multimodal Treatment Study (CAMS).* Paper presented at the Kansas Conference in Clinical Child and Adolescent Psychology: Translating research into practice, Lawrence, KS.

Kerwin, M. E. (1999). Empirically supported treatments in pediatric psychology: Severe feeding problems. *Journal of Pediatric Psychology, 24*, 193–214.

Kettlewell, P. W. (2004). Development, dissemination, and implementation of evidence-based treatments: Commentary. *Clinical Psychology: Science and Practice, 11*, 190–195.

Kinscherff, R. (1999). Empirically supported treatments: What to do until the data arrive (or now that they have)? *Clinical Child Psychology Newsletter, 14*, 4–6.

Kraemer, H. C., Stice, E., Kazdin, A., Offord, D. R., & Kupfer, D. J. (2001). How do risk factors work together? Mediators, moderators, and independent, overlapping, and proxy risk factors. *American Journal of Psychiatry, 158*, 848–856.

Kratochwill, T. R., & Shernoff, E. S. (2003). Evidence-based practice: Promoting evidence-based interventions in school psychology. *School Psychology Quarterly, 18*, 389–408.

Kratochwill, T. R., & Stoiber, K. C. (2002). Evidence-based interventions in school psychology: Conceptual foundations in the procedural coding manual of division 16 and the Society for the Study of School Psychology Task Force. *School Psychology Quarterly, 17*, 341–389.

Lebow, J. L. (1983). Client satisfaction with mental health treatment. *Evaluation Review, 7*, 729–752.

Leffingwell, T. R., & Collins, F. L. (2008). Graduate training in evidence-based practice in psychology. In R. G. Steele, D. Elkin, & M. C. Roberts (Eds.), *Handbook of evidence-based therapies for children and adolescents* (pp. 551–575). New York, NY: Springer.

Levant, R. F. (2004). The empirically validated treatments movement: A practitioner/educator perspective. *Clinical Psychology: Science and Practice, 11*, 219–224.

Lingley-Pottie, P., & McGrath, P. J. (2006). A therapeutic alliance can exist without face-to-face contact. *Journal of Telemedicine and Telecare, 12*, 396–399.

Lingley-Pottie, P., & McGrath, P. J. (2007). Distance therapeutic alliance: The participant's experience. *Advances in Nursing Science, 30*, 353–366.

Loeber, R., & Keenan, K. (1994). Interaction between conduct disorder and its comorbid conditions: Effects of age and gender. *Clinical Psychology Review, 14*, 497–523.

Lonigan, C., Elbert, J. C., & Johnson, S. B. (1998). Empirically supported psychosocial interventions for children: An overview. *Journal of Clinical Child Psychology, 27*, 138–145.

Luce, R. D., & Tukey, J. W. (1964). Simultaneous conjoint measurement: A new type of fundamental measurement. *Journal of Mathematical Psychology, 1,* 1–27.

Lynam, D. R., Milich, R., Zimmerman, R., Novak, S. P., Logan, T. K., Martin, C., . . . Clayton, R. (1999). Project DARE: No effects at 10-year follow up. *Journal of Consulting and Clinical Psychology, 67,* 590–593.

McGregor, J. C., Harris, A. D., Furuno, J. P., Bradham, D. D., & Perencevich, E. N. (2007). Relative influence of antibiotic therapy attributes on physician choice in treating acute uncomplicated pyelonephritis. *Medical Decision Making, 27,* 387–394.

MTA Cooperative Group. (1999a). A 14-month randomized clinical trial of treatment strategies for attention-deficit/hyperactivity disorder. *Archives of General Psychiatry, 56,* 1073–1086.

MTA Cooperative Group. (1999b). Moderators and mediators of treatment response for children with attention-deficit/hyperactivity disorder. *Archives of General Psychiatry, 56,* 1088–1096.

Nathan, P. E., & Gorman, J. M. (2002). Efficacy, effectiveness, and the clinical utility of psychotherapy research. In P. E. Nathan & J. M. Gorman (Eds.), *A guide to treatments that work* (2nd ed., pp. 643–654). New York, NY: Oxford University Press.

Nelson, T. D., Steele, R. G., & Mize, J. A. (2006). Practitioner attitudes toward evidence-based practice: Themes and challenges. *Administration and Policy in Mental Health Services Research, 33,* 398–409.

Ollendick, T. H., & Davis, T. E. (2004). Empirically supported treatments for children and adolescents: Where to from here? *Clinical Psychology: Science and Practice, 11,* 289–294.

Ollendick, T. H., & King, N. J. (1998). Empirically supported treatments for children with phobic and anxiety disorders: Current status. *Journal of Clinical Child Psychology, 27,* 156–167.

Orme, B. K. (2006). *Getting started with conjoint analysis: Strategies for product design and pricing research.* Madison, WI: Research Publishers.

Oudhoff, J. P., Timmermans, D. R., Knol, D. L., Bijnen, A. B., & Van der Wal, G. (2007). Prioritising patients on surgical waiting lists: A conjoint analysis study on the priority judgments of patients, surgeons, occupational physicians, and general practitioners. *Social Science and Medicine, 64,* 1863–1875.

Pagato, S. L., Spring, B., Coups, E. J., Mulvaney, S., Coutu, M. F., & Ozakinci, G. (2007). Barriers and facilitators of evidence-based practice perceived by behavioral science health professionals. *Journal of Clinical Psychology, 63,* 695–705.

Payne, J. W., Bettman, J. R., & Johnson, E. J. (1993). *The use of multiple strategies in judgment and choice.* Hillsdale, NJ: Erlbaum.

Pelham, W. E., & Burrows-MacLean, L. D. (2005). Mental health interventions: Evidence-based approaches. In

L. M. Osborn, T. G. DwWitt, L. R. First, & J. A. Zenel (Eds.), *Pediatrics* (pp. 1940–1948). Philadelphia, PA: Elesevier Mosby.

Pelham, W. E., Carlson, C., Sams, S. E., Vallano, G., Dixon, M. J., & Hoza, B. (1993). Separate and combined effects of methylphenidate and behavior modification on boys with attention deficit-hyperactivity disorder in the classroom. *Journal of Consulting and Clinical Psychology, 61,* 506–515.

Pelham, W. E., & Fabiano, G. A. (2008). Evidence-based psychosocial treatment for attention-deficit/hyperactivity disorder: An update. *Journal of Clinical Child and Adolescent Psychology, 37,* 184–214.

Pelham, W. E., Fabiano, G. A., Gnagy, E. M., Greiner, A. R., & Hoza, B. (2005). The role of summer treatment programs in the context of comprehensive treatment for attention-deficit/hyperactivity disorder. In E. D. Hibbs & P. S. Jensen (Eds.), *Psychosocial treatment for child and adolescent disorders: Empirically based strategies for clinical practice* (2nd ed., pp. 377–409). Washington, DC: American Psychological Association.

Pelham, W. E., Fabiano, G. A., & Waschbusch, D. A. (2009, June). *Tailoring treatments for ADHD using functional deficits.* Paper presented at the annual conference of the International Society for Research on Child and Adolescent Psychopathology, Seattle, WA.

Pelham, W. E., & Murphy, A. (1986). Attention deficit and conduct disorders. In M. Hersen (Ed.), *Pharmacological and behavioral treatment: An integrative approach* (pp. 108–148). New York, NY: Wiley.

Pelham, W. E., Wheeler, T., & Chronis, A. M. (1998). Empirically supported psychosocial treatment for attention deficit hyperactivity disorder. *Journal of Clinical Child Psychology, 27,* 190–205.

Phillips, K. A., Johnson, R., & Maddala, T. (2002). Measuring what people value: A comparison of "attitudes" and "preference" surveys. *Journal of Health Services Research, 37,* 1659–1679.

Plante, T. G., Andersen, E. N., & Boccaccini, M. T. (1999). Empirically supported treatments and related contemporary changes in psychotherapy practice: What do clinical ABPPs think? *The Clinical Psychologist, 52,* 23–31.

Powers, S. W. (1999). Empirically supported treatments in pediatric psychology: Procedure-related pain. *Journal of Pediatric Psychology, 24,* 131–145.

Rae, W. A., & Fournier, C. J. (2008). Evidence-based therapy and ethical practice. In R. G. Steele, D. Elkin, & M. C. Roberts (Eds.), *Handbook of evidence-based therapies for children and adolescents* (pp. 505–519). New York, NY: Springer.

Reimers, T. M., Wacker, D. P., & Koeppl, G. (1987). Acceptability of behavioral interventions: A review of the literature. *School Psychology Review, 16,* 212–227.

Reitman, D., Hupp, S. D. A., O'Callaghan, P. M., Gulley, V., & Northup, J. (2001). The influence of a token economy and methylphenidate on attentive and disruptive behavior during sports with ADHD-diagnosed children. *Behavior Modification, 25,* 305–323.

Roberts, M. C. (2002). The process and product of the Felix Decree review of empirically supported treatments: Prospects for change. *Clinical Psychology: Science and Practice, 9,* 217–219.

Rogers, S. J. (1998). Empirically supported comprehensive treatments for young children with autism. *Journal of Clinical Child Psychology, 27,* 168–179.

Rogers, S. J., & Vismara, L. A. (2008). Evidence-based comprehensive treatment for early autism. *Journal of Clinical Child and Adolescent Psychology, 37,* 8–38.

Rubak, S., Sandbaek, A., Lauritzen, T., & Christiansen, B. (2005). Motivational interviewing: A systematic review and meta-analysis. *British Journal of General Practice, 55,* 305–312.

Ruma, P. R., Burke, R. V., & Thompson, R. W. (1996). Group parent training: Is it effective for all ages? *Behavior Therapy, 27,* 159–169.

Ryan, M. (1999). Using conjoint analysis to take account of patient preferences and go beyond health outcomes: An application to in vitro fertilization. *Social Science and Medicine, 48,* 535–546.

Ryan, M., & Farrar, S. (2000). Using conjoint analysis to elicit preferences for health care. *British Medical Journal, 320,* 1530–1533.

Ryan, M., & Gerard, K. (2003). Using discrete choice experiments to value health care programmes: Current practice and future research reflections. *Applied Health Economics and Health Policy, 2,* 55–64.

Santor, D. A., Kususmakar, V., Poulin, C., & Leblanc, J. (2007). Facilitating help seeking behavior and referrals for mental health difficulties in school aged boys and girls: A school-based intervention. *Journal of Youth and Adolescence, 36,* 741–752.

Santor, D. A., Poulin, C., Leblanc, J., & Kususmakar, V. (2007). Adolescent help seeking behavior on the Internet: Opportunities for health promotion and early identification of difficulties. *Journal of the American Academy of Child and Adolescent Psychiatry, 46,* 50–59.

Schoenwald, S. K., & Hoagwood, K. (2001). Effectiveness, transportability, and dissemination of interventions: What matters when? *Psychiatric Services, 52,* 1190–1197.

Schroeder, S. R., Lewis, M. H., & Lipton, M. A. (1983). Interactions of pharmacotherapy and behavior therapy among children with learning and behavioral disorders. *Advances in Learning and Behavioral Disabilities, 2,* 179–225.

Seligman, L. D., & Ollendick, T. H. (1998). Comorbidity of anxiety and depression in children and adolescents: An integrative review. *Clinical Child and Family Psychology Review, 1,* 125–144.

Sheehan, A. K., Walrath, C. M., & Holden, E. W. (2007). Evidence-based practice use, training, and implementation in the community-based service setting: A survey of children's mental health service providers. *Journal of Child and Family Studies, 16,* 169–182.

Shirk, S. R. (2004). Dissemination of youth ESTs: Ready for prime time? *Clinical Psychology: Science and Practice, 11,* 308–312.

Shirk, S. R., & McMakin, D. (2008). Client, therapist, and treatment characteristics in EBTs for children and adolescents. In R. G. Steele, D. Elkin, & M. C. Roberts (Eds.), *Handbook of evidence-based therapies for children and adolescents* (pp. 471–486). New York, NY: Springer.

Silverman, W. K., & Hinshaw, S. P. (2008). The second special issue on evidence-based psychosocial treatments for children and adolescents: A 10-year update. *Journal of Clinical Child and Adolescent Psychology, 37,* 1–7.

Silverman, W. K., Ortiz, C. D., Viswesvaran, C., Burns, B. J., Kolko, D. J., Putnam, F. J., & Amaya-Jackson, L. (2008). Evidence-based psychosocial treatments for children and adolescents exposed to traumatic events. *Journal of Clinical Child and Adolescent Psychology, 37,* 156–183.

Silverman, W. K., Pina, A. A., & Viswesvaran, C. (2008). Evidence-based psychosocial treatments for phobic and anxiety disorders in children and adolescents. *Journal of Clinical Child and Adolescent Psychology, 37,* 105–130.

Singh, J., Cuttler, L., Shin, M., Silvers, J. B., & Neuhauser, D. (1998). Medical decision-making and the patient: Understanding preference patterns for growth hormone therapy using conjoint analysis. *Medical Care Research and Review, 36,* AS31–45.

Southam-Gerow, M. A., Kendall, P. C., & Weersing, R. V. (2001). Examining outcome variability: Correlates of treatment response in a child and adolescent anxiety clinic. *Journal of Consulting and Clinical Psychology, 30,* 422–436.

Southam-Gerow, M. A., Weisz, J. R., & Kendall, P. C. (2003). Youth with anxiety disorders in research and service clinics: Examining client differences and similarities. *Journal of the American Academy of Child and Adolescent Psychiatry, 32,* 375–385.

Spoth, R., & Redmond, C. (1993). Identifying program preferences through conjoint analysis: Illustrative results from a parent sample. *American Journal of Health Promotion, 8,* 124–133.

Sroufe, L. A. (1990). Considering normal and abnormal together: The essence of developmental psychopathology. *Development and Psychopathology, 2,* 335–347.

Sroufe, L. A., & Rutter, M. (1984). The domain of developmental psychopathology. *Child Development, 55,* 17–29.

Stanek, E. J., Oates, M. B., McGhan, W. F., Denofrio, D., & Loh, E. (2000). Preferences for treatment outcomes in patients with heart failure: Symptoms versus survival. *Journal of Cardiac Failure, 6,* 225–232.

Task Force on Promotion and Dissemination Psychological Procedures. (1995). Training in and dissemination of empirically validated treatments: Report and recommendations. *The Clinical Psychologist, 48*, 3–23.

Taylor, S. E., & Brown, J. D. (1988). Illusion and well-being: A social psychological perspective on mental health. *Psychological Bulletin, 103*, 193–210.

Treatment for Adolescents with Depression Study (TADS) Team. (2004). Fluoxetine, cognitive-behavioral therapy, and their combination for adolescents with depression: Treatment for adolescents with depression study (TADS) randomized-controlled trial. *Journal of the American Medical Association, 297*, 807–820.

Vernberg, E. M. (1998). Developmentally based psychotherapies: Comments and observations. *Journal of Clinical Child Psychology, 27*, 46–48.

Walco, G. A., Sterling, C. M., Conte, P. M., & Engel, R. G. (1999). Empirically supported treatments in pediatric psychology: Disease-related pain. *Journal of Pediatric Psychology, 24*, 155–167.

Waldron, H. B., & Turner, C. W. (2008). Evidence-based psychosocial treatments for adolescent substance abuse. *Journal of Clinical Child and Adolescent Psychology, 37*, 238–261.

Waschbusch, D. A. (2002). A meta-analytic examination of comorbid hyperactive/impulsive/inattention problems and conduct problems. *Psychological Bulletin, 128*, 118–150.

Waschbusch, D. A., & Hill, G. P. (2003). Empirically supported, promising, and unsupported treatments for attention-deficit/hyperactivity disorder. In S. O. Lilienfeld, J. M. Lohr, & S. J. Lynn (Eds.), *Science and pseudoscience in contemporary clinical psychology* (pp. 333–362). New York, NY: Guilford Press.

Waschbusch, D. A., Pelham, W. E., Gnagy, E. M., Greiner, A. R., & Fabiano, G. A. (2008). Summer treatment programs for children with ADHD. In K. McBurnett & L. J. Pfiffner (Eds.), *Attention-Deficit/Hyperactivity Disorder: Concepts, controversies, new directions* (pp. 199–210). New York, NY: Informa Healthcare.

Weiss, B., Catron, T., Harris, V., & Phung, T. M. (1999). The effectiveness of traditional child psychotherapy. *Journal of Consulting and Clinical Psychology, 67*, 82–94.

Weiss, C. H., Murphy-Graham, E., Petrosino, A., & Gandhi, A. G. (2008). The fairy godmother and her warts: Making the dream of evidence-based policy come true. *American Journal of Evaluation, 29*, 29–47.

Weisz, J. R. (2000a, Summer). Lab-clinic differences and what we can do about them: II. Linking research and practice to enhance public impact. *Clinical Child Psychology Newsletter, 15*(1–4), 9.

Weisz, J. R. (2000b, Fall). Lab-clinic differences and what we can do about them: III. National policy matters. *Clinical Child Psychology Newsletter, 15*(1–4), 6.

Weisz, J. R., Chu, B. C., & Polo, A. J. (2004). Treatment dissemination and evidence-based practice: Strengthening intervention through clinician-researcher collaboration. *Clinical Psychology: Science and Practice, 11*, 300–307.

Weisz, J. R., Donenberg, G. R., Han, S. S., & Kauneckis, D. (1995). Child and adolescent psychotherapy outcomes in experiments versus clinics: Why the disparity? *Journal of Abnormal Child Psychology, 23*, 83–106.

Weisz, J. R., & Hawley, K. M. (1998). Finding, evaluating, refining, and applying empirically supported treatments for children and adolescents. *Journal of Clinical Child Psychology, 27*, 206–216.

Weisz, J. R., Jensen-Doss, A., & Hawley, K. M. (2006). Evidence-based youth psychotherapies versus usual clinical care: A meta-analysis of direct comparisons. *American Psychologist, 61*, 671–689.

Weisz, J. R., Jensen, A. L., & McLeod, B. D. (2005). Development and dissemination of child and adolescent psychotherapies: Milestones, methods, and a new development-focused model. In E. D. Hibbs & P. S. Jensen (Eds.), *Psychosocial treatments for child and adolescent disorders: Empirically based strategies for clinical practice* (pp. 9–39). Washington, DC: American Psychological Association.

Weisz, J. R., Weiss, B., Alicke, M. D., & Klotz, M. L. (1987). Effectiveness of psychotherapy with children and adolescents: A meta-analysis for clinicians. *Journal of Consulting and Clinical Psychology, 55*, 542–549.

Weisz, J. R., Weiss, B., & Donenberg, G. R. (1992). The lab versus the clinic: Effects of child and adolescent psychotherapy. *American Psychologist, 47*, 1578–1585.

Weisz, J. R., Weiss, B., Han, S. S., Granger, D. A., & Morton, T. (1995). Effects of psychotherapy with children and adolescents revisited: A meta-analysis of treatment outcome studies. *Psychological Bulletin, 117*, 450–468.

Westen, D., Novotny, C. M., & Thompson-Brenner, H. (2004). The empirical status of empirically supported psychotherapies: Assumptions, findings, and reporting in controlled clinical trials. *Psychological Bulletin, 130*, 631–663.

3

Professional Issues and Evidence-Based Practice

The Quality Problem in Behavioral Health Care

WILLIAM T. O'DONOHUE AND SCOTT O. LILIENFELD

As a field, we know little about which variables influence behavioral health professionals' behavior. We know that educational degree is somewhat predictive; for example, psychiatrists are much more likely to recommend medication than are nonmedically trained mental health professionals (Meredith, Wells, & Camp, 1994). We also know that theoretical allegiance is relevant. Psychodynamically inclined professionals tend to see more pathology and are more influenced by a stigmatizing label of an interaction than are behavioral psychologists (Langer & Abelson, 1974). Krasner and Houts (1984) also showed that clients may come to adopt the terminology and world views of their therapists. Although interesting, such results overlook the central problem plaguing our field: a systematic lack of quality in our professional practice.

This problem permeates all of our endeavors, from assessment, such as problems in quality in custody evaluations (Emery, Otto, & O'Donohue, 2005; O'Donohue & Bradley, 1999), to therapy (Dawes, 1994; Lilienfeld, Lynn, & Lohr, 2003); to undergraduate and graduate education in mental health

(O'Donohue & Boland, 2011); and perhaps, though insufficiently investigated, even our research efforts (Lykken, 1991; Meehl, 1978). We define quality along the lines of the Quality Improvement literature (Walton, 1986), that is, an orientation toward continuous improvement; exceeding customers' expectations; and impressive performance at an acceptable price. In health care, the Joint Commission defined quality in medical services along nine dimensions: (1) efficacy, (2) appropriateness, (3) efficiency, (4) respect and caring, (5) safety, (6) continuity, (7) effectiveness, (8) timeliness, and (9) availability. Other useful definitions of quality are found in Table 3.1. These views of quality stand in stark contrast to less systematic and more static definitions of quality as psychology's licensing laws or ethical boards use; namely, health care that simply exceeds standards of minimal competence. We as a profession can and should set the bar considerably higher. We see the evidence-based practice movement as an important component of a wider vision: the systematic use of quality improvement in behavioral health care.

TABLE 3.1   Definitions of Quality

1. ISO 9000: "Degree to which a set of inherent characteristic fulfills requirements."The standard defines requirement as need or expectation.

2. Six Sigma: "Number of defects per million opportunities." The metric is tied in with a methodology and a management system.

3. Philip B. Crosby: "Conformance to requirements." The difficulty with this is that the requirements may not fully represent customer expectations; Crosby treats this as a separate problem.

4. Joseph M. Juran: "Fitness for use." Fitness is defined by the customer.

5. Noriaki Kano and others, presenting a two-dimensional model of quality: "must-be quality" and "attractive quality." The former is near to the "fitness for use" and the latter is what the customer would love, but has not yet thought about. Supporters characterize this model more succinctly as: "Products and services that meet or exceed customers' expectations."

6. Robert Pirsig: "The result of care."

7. Genichi Taguchi offered two definitions: (a) "Uniformity around a target value." The idea is to lower the standard deviation in outcomes, and to keep the range of outcomes to a certain number of standard deviations, with rare exceptions. (b) The loss a product imposes on society after it is shipped." This definition of quality is based on a more comprehensive view of the production system.

8. American Society for Quality: "A subjective term for which each person has his or her own definition. In technical usage, quality can have two meanings: (a) the characteristics of a product or service that bear on its ability to satisfy stated or implied needs; and (b) a product or service free of deficiencies."

9. Peter Drucker: "Quality in a product or service is not what the supplier puts in. It is what the customer gets out and is willing to pay for."

EVIDENCE-BASED PRACTICE AND EMPIRICALLY SUPPORTED TREATMENTS: USE, NONUSE, AND MISUSE

Up until the 1990s, there were few, if any, formal guidelines for clinical practice in psychotherapy; even as of this writing, there are no such guidelines for clinical assessment. Consequently, behavioral health care has been plagued by serious problems with quality control. In the psychotherapy domain, this state of affairs finally changed in 1993, when a task force appointed by the Society for Clinical Psychology (Division 12) within the American Psychological Association (APA) developed a set of criteria for, and provisional list of, what were then called "empirically validated treatments," later termed "empirically supported treatments" (ESTs). Empirically supported treatments are therapies that have demonstrated: (a) Superiority to a placebo treatment in two or more methodologically sound randomized controlled trials (RCTs) conducted by at least two independent research groups, (b) equivalence to a well-established treatment in several methodologically sound RCTs, or (c) efficacy in at least three single-subject controlled designs conducted by at least two independent research groups with at least nine participants (Chambless & Hollon, 1998). According to the Division 12 task force, the studies must be conducted with treatment manuals that specify a reasonably clear procedure for conducting the intervention.

Despite the importance of developing quality control guidelines in psychotherapy, there is intense resistance to ESTs in many quarters of the clinical community, as borne out by several survey studies. In one early survey of training practices in doctoral clinical psychology programs, Crits-Christoph, Frank, Chambless, Brody, and Karp (1995) found that more than 20% of programs did not include training in more than three fourths of ESTs. Horan and Blanchard (2001) similarly found that most internships provided training in less than half of 72 ESTs surveyed. More recently, in a survey of APA-accredited clinical internship sites, Hays et al. (2002) found that only 28% of sites provided more than 15 hours of training in ESTs. The variability in EST training was especially pronounced at university counseling centers. Among the major obstacles to training in ESTs cited by training directors were their lack of flexibility in the number of allowable sessions (16.6%) and their failure to address clients' genuine presenting problems (12.3%).

In a large national survey of psychology, psychiatry, and social work training programs, Weissman et al. (2006) found that large percentages did not require training in ESTs, which overlapped with, but were not identical to, ESTs. Among PhD programs, for example, 90% and 97% offered training in behavioral and cognitive behavior therapy, respectively, but only 34% and 53%, respectively, required such training. The corresponding figures for social work programs were 64% and 66%, respectively, and 13% and 21%, respectively. Among the major obstacles to EST training cited were lack of trainee interest (25.9% in PhD programs), an absence of qualified faculty to teach ESTs (11.4% in PhD programs), and the fact that ESTs can be difficult to teach (9.7% in PhD programs). Karekla, Lundgren, and Forsyth (2004) similarly reported that 31.8% of students in APA-accredited doctoral clinical, counseling and school psychology reported having never taken any courses in ESTs, and 51% reported no coursework in EST training manuals.

At least some of the resistance to ESTs among mental health professionals is understandable (Arkowitz & Lilienfeld, 2006). In particular, there are legitimate concerns that the EST list may become ossified; that is, regarded as an inflexible and permanent list of efficacious treatments. Nevertheless, we should remember the logical principle of "abusis non tollit usum": The abuse of an idea does not invalidate it. An ossification of the EST list would be a gross misuse of the concept of evidence-based practice, as by definition any list based on solid scientific evidence should be self-correcting and amenable to change in response to new data.

Another legitimate criticism is that the EST list is based on a simplistic "all-or-none" model of efficacy: A treatment is either empirically supported or it is not. The true state of affairs, of course, is likely to be far more complicated, because some treatments for a given disorder are probably effective for certain symptoms or in certain settings, but relatively ineffective for others (De Los Reyes & Kazdin, 2008). As a result, some researchers have recently proposed more sophisticated alternatives to the EST list that depict each treatment's effectiveness in a more multidimensional fashion that takes into account such factors as the domains of change, the amount of change within each domain, and the quality of research evidence for these changes (Miller & Wilbourne, 2002).

Still other critics have pointed out that many ESTs differ only in their superficial features, and that a number of seemingly different treatments may be working for the same underlying reasons. They have argued that a list of empirically supported principles of change, such as exposure to feared stimuli in many effective treatments for anxiety disorders and restoration of hope in many effective treatments for depression, may prove more fruitful than a list of ESTs (Rosen & Davison, 2003). There may be merit to this suggestion, although it will need to await stronger consensus among clinical scientists regarding the underlying mechanisms of change that cut across many therapies. Nevertheless, at least some of the resistance to ESTs appears to be premised largely on misconstruals of the EST list or its rationale. Here we address eight widespread misconceptions concerning ESTs (Chambless & Ollendick, 2001; Weisz, Weersing, & Henggeler, 2005).

Randomized Controlled Trials, on Which the EST List Is Based, Are Fallible and No More Informative Than Other Sources of Evidence

This claim is problematic on two fronts. First, as noted earlier, the EST list does not require treatments to be tested using RCTs, as a series of rigorous single-case designs. Second, the assertion that RCTs are no more informative than other sources of evidence is false, because RCTs control for a host of sources of error, such as placebo effects (improvement resulting from the mere expectation of improvement), spontaneous remission (the tendency for some psychological problems to improve on their own accord), regression to the mean (the tendency for more extreme scores to become less extreme over time), and demand characteristics (the tendency of psychotherapy clients to tell therapists what they want to hear).

The EST List Is Biased Against Psychodynamic Therapies

To some degree this accusation is true, although that is only because most psychodynamic therapies have been inadequately researched and therefore have yet to accumulate a sufficient research base. Admittedly, some grant panels may be unduly biased against such treatments and therefore be reluctant to fund research on their efficacy. Nevertheless, this is a criticism of researchers' biases, not of the EST list itself. A more accurate assertion may be that given the vagueness and complexity of their constructs and the length of time of many of their treatments, some of the traditional properties of psychodynamic therapies may be viewed biased against ESTs.

The EST Criteria Are Unfair, Because Some Treatments Not Yet Studied May Turn Out to Be Efficacious

The second part of the sentence is correct, but the first part of the sentence does not follow from it. It is indeed true that one must distinguish *unvalidated* treatments—those that have yet to be adequately researched—from *invalidated* treatments—those that have been tested and shown not to work (Arkowitz & Lilienfeld, 2006; Persons & Silberschatz, 1998). The EST list does not imply that unstudied treatments or treatments that initially have negative outcome data might not become empirically supported eventually with sufficient research; it implies only that such treatments have yet to prove their mettle. Nevertheless, it is crucial to recall that the burden of proof falls on proponents of treatments to show that they work, not on critics to show that they do not work. We must also entertain the possibility that some unevaluated treatments may be less effective than available standard treatments, ineffective, or even harmful. Hence, the argument that it is unfair to exclude unvalidated treatments from the EST list violates one of the most crucial standards of science: namely, that one should not accept claims without adequate evidence. In addition, it is always possible that with thorough informed consent, a client may consent to undergo therapy with a practitioner; however, we would not recommend that third parties pay for this treatment.

The EST List Is Unnecessary, Because Research Shows That All Psychotherapies Work Equally Well

In criticizing the EST list, some researchers have invoked the "Dodo Bird" verdict, named after the Dodo Bird in *Alice in Wonderland*, which said (following a race) that "Everybody has won and all must have prizes" (Wampold, 2001). According to the Dodo Bird verdict, all therapies work equally well, so the EST list is based on an erroneous premise, namely, that some therapies work better for certain disorders than others. Nevertheless, the Dodo Bird verdict is false (Hunsley & DiGuilio, 2002). For example, studies show that behavioral and cognitive behavioral treatments are more effective than other treatments for childhood disorders, and that exposure-based treatments—those that expose people to the stimuli that provoke their fears—are more effective than other treatments for obsessive-compulsive disorder, phobias, and several other anxiety disorders (Chambless & Ollendick, 2001). In addition, it is difficult to define the entire universe of therapies as psychotherapies are continually being invented and combined. In any case, the Dodo Bird hypothesis suffers from a logical problem. If a study finds no difference between two therapies, this lack of difference may merely be due to the lack of experimental power of the study or omission of dependent variables that would have shown a change. Thus, the claim of equivalencies among hundreds of different therapies and combinations makes this claim clearly unsupported by currently available data and is arguably illogical.

There is a related, and arguably more sophisticated, argument against the EST list. Some argue that, even if the Dodo Bird verdict is false, the amount of variance in therapy outcomes accounted for by nonspecific factors shared by most or all therapies, like therapists' warmth, empathy, and capacity to instill hope is greater than the amount of variance accounted for by specific factors unique to particular therapies, like exposure to anxiety-provoking imagery in behavioral therapies and dream interpretation in psychoanalytic therapies. Nevertheless, this argument too is flawed. Here is why. Imagine that one were to conduct a study of baseball teams and found that the quality of one's hitters accounted for more variance in success than the quality of one's pitchers. Would that mean that one should ignore the quality of one's pitchers? Of course not, because pitching also accounts for a nontrivial amount of variance in baseball success. Still, if these nonspecifics do account for most of the variance, then this fact has huge implications for graduate selection, graduate education, our claims of expertise, and subsequent payment rates. That is, we would need to

select graduate students largely on their "nonspecifics" or their ability to develop these skills, or claims of expertise would be oriented toward the nonspecifics (we are warm rather than more "technically skilled," and payment would be for this service rather than for delivery of specific techniques—with the scarcity of this service determining price).

Some Studies on Which the EST List Is Based Are Flawed

This claim is almost certainly true (Westen, Novotny, & Thompson-Brenner, 2004); indeed, all studies are flawed in certain respects (Dawes, 1994). The goal of the EST list, like that of all developments in science, is to reduce uncertainty—or in the phrasing of the quality improvement literature—to reduce variability (McFall, 1991). Without this list, there is little or no explicit guidance to clinicians regarding which treatments to administer, and, hence, no quality control. With this list, there is at least some scientifically informed guidance, which is better than none. Imperfect but informative evidence is virtually always superior to no evidence at all.

ESTs Are Generalizable to the Real World

Some critics have charged that research on "efficacy"—how well treatments perform in carefully controlled settings—does not generalize to research on "effectiveness"—how well they perform in real-world settings (Persons & Silberschatz, 1998). In part, these critics suggest, that it is because the efficacy studies on which ESTs are based often exclude severely disordered patients or patients with comorbid conditions. There may be some merit to this criticism, but this possibility must be tested with evidence: In fact, many recent efficacy studies have begun to include patients with conditions more closely resembling those in real-world settings (Chambless & Ollendick, 2001) and have often found that treatments with high efficacy also display high effectiveness (Gaston, Abbott, Rapee, & Neary, 2006; Hahlweg, Fiegenbaum, Frank, Schroeder, & Witzleben, 2001; Wade, Treat, & Stuart, 1998).

Because ESTs Are Manualized, They Necessarily Constrain Clinical Creativity

To some extent, this criticism is based on a caricature of manualized therapies. Treatment manuals do not necessarily mandate extremely rigid responses to patient behavior in therapy. Instead, most manuals provide flexible guidelines for how to proceed at different stages of treatment or what Kendall, Gosch, Furr, and Sodd (2008) termed "flexibility within fidelity" (p. 1). Moreover, increasing numbers of treatment manuals are affording therapists leeway during treatment to respond flexibly to differing patient trajectories.

The EST List Is Fixed Over Time and Cannot Change in Response to New Evidence

As noted earlier, the EST list is not permanent: It is a work in progress, subject to continual updating and revision in light of new data. In particular, one decided advantage of this list is that allows previously underresearched treatments to be listed as empirically supported as new positive evidence becomes available.

In sum, the EST movement is not a panacea; however, it is an important and necessary step in the direction of improved quality control. Many of the previous criticisms suffer from the "panacea fallacy"; if the solution is not perfect, then it is no good at all. To date, critics have not offered a better alternative to the EST movement as means of reducing poor quality care in psychotherapy.

QUALITY IMPROVEMENT

A crucial question is not merely what influences professional behavior, but also what

ought to influence such behavior. The typical view is that the only major problem related to professional behavior is the lack of adherence to EBP, such as ESTs. Clearly, this problem needs to be addressed. Nevertheless, we argue that there are actually *three* additional and crucial problems: (1) the lack of leadership regarding serious quality problems in assessment and psychotherapy, (2) the crisis of a lack of quality management, and (3) the lack of quality entrepreneurship with its attendant "creative destruction." We discuss each of these problems further on.

Evidence-based practice, as typically construed, is a necessary but not a sufficient condition for quality. In his classic *Manifesto for a Science of Clinical Psychology*, McFall (1991) was one of the first to note the intimate connection between clinical science and quality improvement. As he noted,

> "Excellence," "accountability," "competence," and "quality" are key concepts nowadays in education, government, business, and health care. It is ironic that psychologists, with their expertise in measurement and evaluation, have played a major role in promoting such concepts in other areas of society while ignoring them in their own backyard: Are psychologists guilty of "nimbyism"? The failure to assure the quality of services in clinical psychology—whatever its causes—cannot continue (p. 78).

We also argue that traditional EBP is best seen as an integral component of a wider total quality improvement system, but only one component. A systematic quality improvement system generates not only evidence for the larger questions addressed by the traditional academic EBP movement, namely, what therapies produce change for Problem X, but also allows for the generation of additional evidence for important subproblems not typically addressed by the EBP movement. For example, even when using evidence-based guidelines, how can we reduce the variance of outcomes across therapists in the treatment of depressed clients? How can we reduce the cost of effective treatment, thereby giving our consumers improved value and making our services more accessible to individuals with lower incomes? How can we increase the timeliness of our services? How can we exceed customer expectations, that is, what can be our "wow" factor? Moreover, just because a certain therapy is known to be the most effective intervention for a certain problem does not mean that a particular therapist, who claims some knowledge of that therapy, can actually deliver it effectively. The medical quality improvement literature demonstrates that not only must the practitioner deliver an EST, but that his or her experience with implementing the technique hundreds or even thousands of times is necessary for high-quality treatment (Gawande, 2003). Professionals have learning curves for particular treatments, although admittedly the relation between years of experience and therapeutic efficacy is typically weak (Dawes, 1994). More research is needed regarding the learning curves for ESTs to determine under what conditions competence and excellence are generally obtained.

A BRIEF HISTORY OF THE PROBLEM OF QUALITY

The current generation of graduate students in the mental health professions may be too young to possess intimate knowledge of the quality revolution that occurred in Japanese industry that eventually spread to many countries, particularly those in Asia, and the resultant competitive pressures that have dramatically impacted U.S. industry. In the 1960s, when the chapter authors were young, the appellation "made in Japan" was synonymous with junk. Indeed, a common way of teasing or insulting playmates was to tell them that their toys were made in Japan. The Japanese, devastated by the effects of World War II on their homeland and population, then made cheap trinkets that frequently broke within hours or even minutes of use. In contrast, American goods, from cars, to TVs, to steel, to furniture, were some of the best quality in the world. How times have changed!

Beginning in the 1970s, the world economy shifted dramatically. Japan went from a poor country recovering from the destruction of World War II with few exports to become the second largest economy in the world, due largely to exporting high-quality goods, from steel to cars to electronics. It often exported these high-quality products to the United States and as a result drove some large and powerful U.S. companies out of business, such as U.S. Steel, dramatically reduced the size of others, such as General Motors, and through competition improved the quality of others, such as Caterpillar Tractor. Toyota now sells more cars than any other car company (*Fortune*, May 7, 2007); huge companies like U.S. Steel went into bankruptcy as Japanese steel companies produced higher quality steel at lower prices. Electronics produced by such companies as Sony and Mitsubishi competed with what were giant U.S. companies such as RCA and Motorola. Apple and Nokia are produced by Japan as well as by other Asian countries that also were influenced by their model, such as South Korea and more recently, China. It is generally agreed that China will become the economic dynamo of the 21st century.

What happened? We believe the answers are critical for understanding what could happen—and what ought to happen—in the behavioral health sector. It is commonly recognized that one of the major factors that caused this change in Japan and the rest of world was the adoption of quality improvement philosophy and technology, based primarily on the work of W. Edwards Deming (Walton, 1986). Deming was hired by the Japanese in the 1950s and taught Japanese management and industrial leaders his methods for producing quality. They embraced it, transformed their industries, and became the industrial powerhouse we know today. One of the most coveted prizes in the business world is now the Deming Application Prize, awarded in Japan.

American industries have varied in the rate and consistency with which they have embraced systematic quality improvement methods. Nordstrom has done a better job than Kresge, which is now bankrupt; Starbucks a better job than the International House of Pancakes; and Toyota a better job than Chrysler. Some sectors of the economy have not really touched quality improvement at all—unfortunately, public education is one of them (Greene, 2005)—whereas others, such as the auto industry, are just now making significant strides toward the use of quality improvement methods.

Quality Improvement and the Health-Care Sector

One of the most important leaders in the movement for quality improvement in health care, Daniel Berwick (Berwick & Nolan, 1998), suggested that there are two major approaches to quality improvement in con-temporary American health care. The first and major one may be called "the theory of bad apples," which views quality as best achieved by detecting, punishing or removing defective practitioners. The "bad apple" approach attempts to improve quality by after-the-fact inspection, and includes such procedures as licensing and adjudication of complaints, the establishment of thresholds for acceptability, and focuses on better tools for inspection, such as the Examination for Professional Practice in Psychology (EPPP) and state licensing exams. These approaches have problems that we will briefly describe (Dawes, 1994; O'Donohue & Buchanan, 2003). Essential to the "bad apple" approach is the search for outliers by, for example, examination of mortality or mor-bidity data, or complaints by licensing or eth-ical boards. In this approach, one uses fear as a deterrent to improve quality and punishment or the threat of punishment to control health-care workers who do not care enough or whose work does not meet basic standards of quality. This approach leads to a defensive and fearful workforce that attempts to hide its perceived

mistakes or weaknesses. In addition, this approach may catch only the most egregious quality problems, such as sex with clients, while leaving other serious quality problems, such as the use of energy therapies to treat trauma-related conditions (Lilienfeld et al., 2003) or the use of the Rorschach Inkblot Test in child custody evaluations (Emery et al., 2005) untouched. Behavioral health has relied almost exclusively on the bad apples approach to quality control.

The second approach to quality is the "theory of continuous improvement." This approach holds that problems, which are viewed as opportunities to improve quality, are built into production processes. This approach only rarely attributes defects in quality to specific individuals' lack of will, skill, or intention. Even when individuals lie at the root of the defect, the problem is generally not one of motivation or effort, but rather of poor job design, poor tools and support, failure of leadership or management, or unclear purpose. According to this view, genuine improvement in quality depends on understanding and con-tinually revising the production processes on the basis of systematic and usually ongoing data about the processes themselves. Continual improvement is sought throughout the organ-ization through a constant effort to reduce waste, errors, rework, and complexity. The focus is on the average producer, not the out-lier, and on learning, not on being defensive. In Deming's terminology, the focus is on decreasing variation due to "common causes" rather than variation due to "special causes." The focus is not on the few instances in which psychologists have sex with their clients, but the many instances in which psychologists administer tests or treatments that are not evidence-based, ineffective, or harmful. The approach never rests, but continually strives to improve average performance along multiple dimensions, such as cost, size of effects, decreased variability, speed, and ease of use.

Unfortunately, behavioral health services have focused almost exclusively on the bad apple approach, in which a wide amount of variance is tolerated until thresholds of ethicality are breached. Thus, therapists who sleep with their clients, or injure or even kill their clients, (such as the now notorious Denver rebirthing tragedy involving 10-year-old Candace Newmaker [Mercer, Sarner, & Rosa, 2006]), are at least sometimes detected and punished; however, much of therapy and assessment that does not fall outside these ethical boundaries is tolerated and never improved. But how much of the therapy currently delivered is quality therapy? Has there been a systematic improvement in the quality of therapy delivered today over that delivered 5 years ago? Remarkably, given the paucity of systematic survey data on clinicians' practices, it is difficult or impossible to know. If not, is that lack of improvement part of the problem in the market's perception of our value, as evidenced by our decreasing salaries?

The Lemon Problem and Our Pay Rates

Cummings and O'Donohue (2008) argued that a quality gap is driving lower wages in our field. They pointed out that our consumers face what economists call "the lemon problem." Lemons—poor quality products—drastically drive down the prices consumers are willing to pay. Suppose you currently pay $5.00 for a gallon of milk and that nearly all (99.99%) of the milk you buy is of good quality. You would like to pay less, but the quality of the milk leaves you relatively satisfied. Now suppose something happens with the quality of milk and 50% of it is unacceptable because half is sour, contaminated, or discolored. Now, you need, on average, to buy two gallons to find one gallon that is drinkable. The question becomes: What price are you now willing to pay for milk? Economists suggest that the answer is half or less due to "opportunity costs," namely the hassles and negative experience with the bad milk, because if you pay $2.50 each for two gallons, you have a good chance of still paying on average $5.00 for an acceptable gallon of milk.

The implications of this analogy for behavioral health practice are clear, but largely unaddressed by leadership in our field. Currently, consumers, such as third-party payers, may be willing to pay, for example, $90 for an hour of psychotherapy, but how many lemons are they paying for? To what extent do these lemons artificially depress the price of our product? Leadership in our professional organizations, such as the APA, has not addressed this problem. Instead, the APA has instead simply attempted to demonize third-party payers by, for example, suing managed care organizations (Holloway, 2004). Cummings and O'Donohue (2008) argued a better tack is to strive to improve the quality of our services and products.

The Institute of Medicine's Crossing the Quality Chasm Report

There has been recent attention to the problem of quality in health-care practice, although most of the focus has been on physical medicine. In December 1999, the Institute of Medicine (IOM) released a report estimating that 98,000 people die every year in the United States from mistakes made by health-care professionals. If accurate, this would mean that more people die from medical errors than from breast cancer, AIDS, or motor vehicle accidents. Leape (2004) showed that health-care encounters result in a higher risk of fatalities than mountain climbing, bungee jumping, or driving. In *Crossing the Quality Chasm*, the IOM identified six aims for improvement in health care. First, health care should be *safe* by avoiding injuries to patients from care that is intended to help them. Second, it should be *effective* by providing services based on scientific knowledge to all who could benefit, refrain from providing services to those unlikely to benefit by avoiding under- and overuse). Third, it should be *patient-centered* and provide care that is respectful of and responsive to individual patient preferences, needs, and values and ensure that patient values play an appropriate role in clinical decisions. Fourth, it should be *timely*—services should reduce waits and sometimes harmful delays for both those who receive and give care. Fifth, services should be *efficient*, avoid waste, such as unneeded equipment, supplies, ideas, and energy, and maximize use of available resources. Sixth, services should be *equitable* by providing care that does not differ in quality because of such personal characteristics as gender, ethnicity, geographic location, and socioeconomic status. Shuster, McGlynn, and Brook (1998) showed that approximately only 50% of Americans received recommended preventative care. Among patients with acute illnesses, approximately only 70% received recommended treatment and approximately 30% received contraindicated treatments. Among patients with chronic illnesses, approximately 60% received recommended care and approximately 20% received contraindicated treatments. The report also suggested that cost of these errors could be as high as $29 billion a year in the United States, and listed medical mistakes as the fifth leading cause of death in this country. The IOM's report concluded that "between the healthcare

we have and the healthcare we could have lies not just a gap but a chasm" (p. 1).

Brent James, at Intermountain Health in Utah, has been one of the leaders in creatively applying quality improvement practices to physical health and measuring the results of these practices. He has concentrated on analyzing processes, developing information management systems to track outcomes, providing incentives to key players, and integrating administrative and clinical support into quality improvement efforts. The model involves dividing savings from improvements among the providers, the health-care organization, and the health plan. The savings due to increased quality can be regarded as "gold left in the mine." For example, Intermountain Health Care Services, savings in overall costs from just a few dozen quality improvement initiatives have run into the tens of millions of dollars. Table 3.2 illustrates this.

Quality Problems in Behavioral Health

There are several serious problems with quality in behavioral health, all of which receive far

TABLE 3.2   Cost Savings from Practice Guidelines and Protocols at Intermountain Health Care

50% reduction in pneumonia costs

At Intermountain Health Care, the use of practice guidelines and protocols has reduced mortality rates, saved considerable amounts of money, shortened lengths of stay, and reduced medical complications.

Community-acquired pneumonia

	Both inpatient and outpatient care	
	1994 without guideline	1995 with guideline
Percent patients admitted	39%	29%
Average length of stay	6.4 days	4.3 days
Time to antibiotic	2.1 hours	1.5 hours
Average cost per case	$2,752	$1,424

	Inpatient care only			
	Without protocol	With protocol	Percent change	P
"Outlier" (complication) DRG at discharge	15.3%	11.6%	↓24.7	< 0.001
In-hospital mortality	7.2%	5.3%	↓26.3	0.015
Relative resource units (RRUs) per case	55.9	49.0	↓12.3	< 0.001
Cost per case	$5,211	$4,729	↓9.3	0.002

Source: Intermountain Health Care (www.managedcaremag.com/archives/0412/0412.james.html)

too little attention: (1) There is too much common cause variation in the kinds of assessment and therapies delivered by behavioral health professionals for the same problem. (2) There is too much common cause variation in the outcomes of the assessment and treatments delivered by mental health professionals. (3) There is too little understanding of the variables that contribute to (1) and (2). (4) There is a crisis in management and leadership in behavioral health. Deming (2000) conjectured that 80% of the problems are caused by bad management. Yet, there is little emphasis on systematic quality improvement technology in behavioral health management. As long as management and leadership are of poor quality, the point of service quality will be low. (5) There is a lack of knowledge regarding what our various consumers (clients, families, payers, employers) expect and how they define quality. (6) There is a lack of knowledge of common cause variation in our production systems. To what extent are failures due to personnel problems, graduate education problems, lack of proper tools, lack of measurement and benchmarking, lack of leadership, and so on? Benchmarking is the process of defining standards and outcomes. So, a benchmark can be something like "the average weight loss for children in an 8-week obesity treatment is 10 lbs." (7) There is a lack of knowledge regarding costs and value propositions and how to reduce the former and increase the latter. Successful industries attempt to offer better value to consumers. An example of this principle is Moore's law; namely, that every 2 years the power of the computer doubles while its price is reduced in half. Our industry has nothing remotely like Moore's Law. We do little to reduce our price through innovation or to improve what we are selling. A century later, it would be difficult to prove that we are any more productive or efficient than Freud. Most of us still see one patient an hour, often with little effect. (8) There are access problems to our services. Behavioral health services are

not ideally distributed geographically and are not readily available in the locations our customers want. The primary care medical system is the de facto mental health system in the United States. The primary care physician treats more depression, sleep problems, sexual dysfunction, and (increasingly) psychosis than the mental health professional (Katon, 1987). (9) There is a lack of benchmarks for our effects and a lack of standardization of treatment pathways or protocols. (10) There are "orphaned problems" such as exhibitionism, narcissistic personality disorder, and hypoactive sexual desire, which for the past several decades have received little to no treatment outcome research.

The field of mental or behavioral health is a fascinating mess marked by a host of unsettled basic issues. Do we know how to define mental disorder, or whether this is even the right term (Lilienfeld & Marino, 1995)? Do clinicians even agree on meta-issues, such as the proper role of science in these debates, what is ethically permissible, and the role of broad philosophical or political beliefs in clinical decisions (O'Donohue & Dyslin, 2005; Wright & Cummings, 2005)? Assuming conceptually we know how to define a clinically relevant construct, such as intelligence or posttraumatic stress disorder, how validly can we measure it? To what extent will clinicians develop the same case formulation; that is, pick out the same kinds of information as important, look at similar mitigating factors, diagnose comorbidity similarly, and so on (Garb, 1998)? If these clinicians disagree on these crucial questions, how far are they apart? Can these differences be resolved are they incommensurable? To what extent do clinicians recommend the same treatments for the same problems? Again, how much disagreement is there? To what extent do clinicians competently execute a particular assessment or treatment? That is, even if they recommend "cognitive therapy for depression," is their execution of this treatment excellent or at least competent? There are surprisingly few if any answers to these basic questions, or standards of practice.

WHAT IS QUALITY IMPROVEMENT?: A PRIMER

Assuming that we have established that there is a quality problem in our field and that there are systematic tools for its remediation, we next want to provide the reader with a glimpse of what these tools might look like. Quality improvement is a meta-system—a set of principles that set the stage for other principles, such as evidence-based practice. We believe that ultimately Quality Improvement (QI) systems need to show their worth empirically. To date, there are no tests comparing a behavioral health delivery system utilizing QI with a system that does not. This would be a critical set of data, which we would argue is a priority. To be consistent with the goal of evidence-based practice, we need demonstration projects evaluating the worth of QI as a meta-system for enhancing such practice.

However, first we must understand what such a system would look like. It is not simply adopting an attitude that quality is important. It is a system—a means of structuring clinical practice to maximize such quality. Thus, in this section, we briefly view the work of two key figures in the development of QI: Malcolm Baldrige and W. Edwards Deming. This review should provide a basic grounding so the reader can see the possibilities in behavioral health—Deming's "gold left in the mine." Quality improvement has come a long way since the work of these groundbreaking theorists, but psychology's need for such improvement may be so basic that these simple approaches may be sufficient for now.

Malcolm Baldrige

Malcolm Baldrige, a secretary of commerce under former President Ronald Reagan, was one of the first theorists in quality improvement. The Baldrige program identifies seven key action areas or categories for quality improvement efforts. These include: (1) *Leadership*, which involves efforts by senior leadership and management leading by example to integrate quality improvement into the strategic planning process and throughout the entire organization, and to promote quality values and QI techniques in work practices. We are missing this leadership in behavioral health care. (2) *Information and Analysis*, which concerns managing and using the data needed for effective QI. Because quality improvement is based on management by data, information and analyses are critical to QI success. (3) *Strategic Quality Planning*, involving three major components: (a) developing short-term and long-term organizational objectives for quality standards; (b) identifying ways to achieve those objectives, and (c) measuring the effectiveness of the system in achieving quality standards. (4) *Human Resource Development and Management Process Management* concerns the creation and maintenance of high-quality services. Within the context of QI, process management refers to the improvement of work activities and work flow across functional or departmental boundaries. (6) *System Results* involves assessing the quality results achieved and examining the organization's success at achieving quality improvement. (7) *Satisfaction of Patients and Other Stakeholders* involves ensuring ongoing satisfaction by those internal and external to the behavioral health-care system with the services provided (Heaphy & Bruska, 1995).

Implications of Baldrige's View for Behavioral Health

First, we must recognize that there has been a crisis of competent management in behavioral health. Managers, whether found in group private practice, psychology departments, or mental health institutions, are usually amateurs who have been promoted to administration. Management in other industries has been professionalized and the manager is systematically trained in strategic planning, quality improvement, financial management, human resources, and marketing, among other skills. We, in contrast, have not usually experienced the benefits of professional managers. Thus, the quality problem in behavioral health is reflexive: There is a problem in the quality of management in behavioral health that must be addressed. With the informal, amateurish approach taken by mental health management that largely ignores most of the basic knowledge that management professionals now possess, one wonders if the first problem that needs to be addressed is the professionalization of management in behavioral health so managers are systematically trained in quality improvement technologies.

Competent managers manage by using formal management information systems. Ideally, these systems provide data to continually monitor key variables thought to be relevant to such questions as productivity, quality, costs, demand, and satisfaction. Such systems are much more consistent with science than informal management by anecdote and informal impressions used by many managers in mental health today; however, most mental health systems are run with no or inadequate management information systems. A key part of this problem is the lack of Electronic Medical Records (EMR). There is a saying in physical health that "paper kills": Paper records result in medical errors due to lack of legibility, incompleteness, timeliness, integration with knowledge systems, and so on. There is a tremendous movement in physical medicine to move away from paper records to electronic records, which can be accessed anytime, anywhere, and that are complete and integrated with systems that flag such potential problems as allergies and drug interactions. The V.A. system has been a leader in this movement (see, for example, www1.va.gov/opa/pressrel/pressrelease.cfm?id=1114). Again, behavioral health is decades behind these efforts, posing a tremendous quality problem.

Finally, we offer a few quick statements regarding some of Baldrige's other points. Regarding his third point, it is rare for any organization in behavioral health to have a systematic plan to improve quality; for example, what is the APA's plan to improve the use of ESTs? Regarding the fourth point, we rarely give our workers good tools so they can do the job better; a key question is what tools are needed, such as web-based practice guidelines and stepped care tools, and how can we develop them (O'Donohue & Draper, 2011)? Instead, we rely on continuing education, which itself suffers from huge quality problems and is largely devoid of evidence for efficacy (Wood, Garb, Lilienfeld, & Nezworski, 2002). Lastly, we rarely measure consumer satisfaction or probe our consumers for what they expect. Instead, as mentioned earlier, the APA sues our consumers—managed care organizations (Holloway, 2004).

W. Edwards Deming

Deming argued that certain key pieces of knowledge underpin all improvements in a system. He gave these elements of knowledge the name "System of Profound Knowledge" (Deming, 2000). "Profound," for Deming, denotes the deep insight that this knowledge yields in making changes that will result in sizable improvements. "System" denotes the emphasis on the interaction of all the components of the larger organization. According to Deming, to comprehend the workings of a system and thus be able to improve it, one must have an appreciation of the system as an entity onto itself. For example, one must have an understanding of its variability, a theory of knowledge of how to bring about changes in this variability, and an understanding of variables that impact personnel. Appreciation of a system helps us to understand the interdependencies and interrelationships among all components of a system and, thus, increases the accuracy of our predictions about the impact of changes throughout the system.

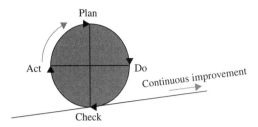

Figure 3.1   The Deming Cycle

Understanding of variation helps us to understand that all systems, including behavioral health care, constantly exhibit variation.

The pursuit of improvement relies on cycles of learning. Figure 3.1 illustrates these cycles and also illustrates McFall's points (1991) that QI efforts are similar to the scientific method in its incorporation of self-correction and improvement; however, it is not sufficient to show in a test that a change is an improvement. Change must be fully integrated into the functioning system. This takes some planning and usually some additional learning in matters of dealing with those whom the change will affect, who will implement the change, and who will make these changes sustainable.

Deming developed his famous 14 points to transform management practices.

1. *A behavioral health organization's highest priority is to provide the best quality care at the lowest cost possible.* How many behavioral health organizations are trying to drive down costs to improve the value proposition to consumers? Higher education is not doing this: Tuition is rising much higher than the rate of inflation. The APA is trying to increase prices, assuming this is what the guild wants (Cummings & O'Donohue, 2008). But of course the most basic economic principle of supply and demand predicts that as prices rise, demand decreases. Contrast this with much more successful industries such as computers, electronics, and automobiles.

2. *Everyone must adopt the new philosophy.* Everyone working in the organization can find ways to promote quality and efficiency, to improve all aspects of the system, and to promote excellence and personal accountability. Pride of workmanship must be emphasized from recruitment to retirement. By their behavior, leaders set the standard for all workers.

3. *Cease dependence on inspection to achieve quality.* Reliance on routine inspection to improve quality, such as a search for errors, problems, or deficiencies by licensing or ethics boards, assumes that human performance error or machine failure is highly likely. Deming points out that "Inspection (as the sole means) to improve quality is too late!" Lasting quality comes not from inspection, but from systematic innovations and improvements in the system. A key question becomes: What are common causes of unwanted variation built into the system, and how can we use cycles of learning to reduce them?

4. *Do not purchase on the basis of price tag alone.* Purchasers must account for the quality of the item being purchased, as well as the cost. There is a saying, "Buy quality and you only cry once." High-quality organizations tend to think of their suppliers as partners in their operation. Successful partnerships require clear and specific performance standards and feedback on whether those standards are being met. Supplier performance can also be improved through: (a) an understanding of supplier QI efforts, (b) longer-term contracts that include explicit milestones for improvement in key features, (c) joint planning for improvement, and (d) joint improvement activities. There is a saying in the legal profession, "There is nothing so expensive as a cheap lawyer." We believe there is a corresponding adage in our profession: "There is nothing so expensive as a cheap behavioral health professional."

5. *Constantly improve the system of production and service.* Quality can be built

into all health delivery activities and services and can be continually evaluated to identify potential improvements. This process requires close cooperation between those who provide services and those who consume them. Currently, we understand little about our clients' satisfaction with our services, and how they value different features or possible innovations, such as eHealth, or group versus individual treatment. Improved efficiency and service can result from focusing not only on achieving present performance targets, but more important, by breaking through existing performance levels to new and higher levels. Often the effect sizes for our psychotherapies are only modest. For example, using meta-analytic methods, Weisz, Donenberg, Han, and Kauneckis (1995) reported disappointing and often negligible effect sizes for childhood and adolescent treatments in community settings. We need to work constantly to improve the effectiveness of our treatments in the real world.

6. *Institute QI training on the job.* On-the-job QI training ensures that every worker has a thorough understanding of: (a) the needs of those who use and/or pay for behavioral services, (b) how to meet those needs, and (c) how to improve the system's ability to meet those needs. Incorporating QI into the fabric of each job can accelerate learning.

7. *Institute effective leadership.* The job of management is leadership. Effective leaders are thoroughly knowledgeable about the work being done and understand the environment and complexities with which their workers must contend. Leaders create the opportunity for workers to suggest improvements and act quickly to make needed changes in the production process. Leaders are concerned with success as much as with failure and focus not only on

understanding substandard, but also super-standard performance. The effective leader also creates opportunities for below and above average performers to interact and identify opportunities for improvement. There has been little leadership for quality in academia, in institutions, or in private practices.

8. *Drive out fear.* The Japanese have a saying, "Every defect is a treasure," meaning that errors and failures are opportunities for improvement. Errors or problems can help identify more fundamental or systemic root causes and ways to improve the system. Yet fear of identifying problems or needed changes can kill QI programs. Also, some may feel that the idea of making improvements is an admission that the current way of doing things is flawed or that those responsible are poor performers. Improved performance cannot occur unless workers feel comfortable that they can speak truthfully and are confident that their suggestions will be taken seriously. For example, case conferences could be oriented toward difficult clients and treatment failures instead of alleged displays of super-competence that might feed narcissist needs (see Meehl, 1973, for a hilarious and devastating critique of the typical clinical case conference).

9. *Break down barriers among departments.* Barriers among organizations or among departments within one organization are obstacles to effective QI. Interdepartmental or intraorganizational friction or lack of cooperation, result in waste, errors, delay, and unnecessary duplication of effort. A continuous and lasting QI program requires teamwork that crosses traditional organizational lines. The QI requires that all workforce members, departments, and units share a unified purpose, direction, and commitment to improve the organization. For example, we have huge barriers among

educational institutions that produce our professionals, the marketplace that hires them, and the payors that pay them.

10. *Eliminate slogans, exhortations, and targets for the workforce for zero defects and new levels of productivity.* The problem with such exhortations is that they place the burden for quality on worker performance instead of poor system design. The QI program requires that the organization focus on improving its work processes. In so doing, service quality will increase, productivity and efficiency will rise, and waste will diminish.

11. *Eliminate management by numbers and objective—substitute leadership!* For Deming, work production standards and rates, tied to incentive pay, are inappropriate because they burn out the workforce in the long run. Alternatively, a team effort should be marshaled to increase quality, which will lead to increased profits/savings that can then be translated to, for example, higher salaries or better benefits. Improvement efforts should emphasize improving processes; the outcome numbers will change as a consequence.

12. *Remove barriers to pride of workmanship.* The workforce is the most important component of a behavioral health delivery system. The behavioral health delivery system cannot function properly without workers who are proud of their work and who feel respected as individuals and professionals. Managers can help workers be successful by making sure that job responsibilities and performance standards are clearly understood; building strong relationships between management and the workforce; and providing workers with the best tools, instruments, supplies, and information possible. A key question in our field is: What tools are needed or wanted by workers? For the past century with little change the answer has been books, manuals, workshops, and case conferences. Excellent performance

is usually unrecognized and unrewarded. This state of affairs needs to change. In medicine there have been attempts to establish Centers of Excellence that serve as hubs to improve the quality in allied delivery systems (DeBakey, 1993); we would be wise to follow their lead.

13. *Institute a vigorous program of education and self-improvement.* Behavioral healthcare workers can improve their lives through education and ever-broadening career and life opportunities. The field needs not just good people; it needs people who are growing through education and life experiences. Management, as well as members of the workforce, must continue to experience new learning and growth. A key subissue is to develop and implement quality continuing education, as opposed to much that is currently available. See Glenn Hutchinson's Psyc.TV Web site at www.psyc.tv for a refreshing attempt to base continuing education on solid clinical science.

14. *Put everybody to work to accomplish the transformation.* The essence of QI is an organization-wide focus on meeting the needs of those who use and/or pay for behavioral health services. Effective quality management programs go beyond emphasizing one or two efforts or areas to improve performance. Every activity, every process, and every job in behavioral health care can be improved. Everyone within the organization can be given an opportunity to understand the QI program and their individual role within that effort.

EXAMPLES OF CONCRETE STEPS TO IMPROVE QUALITY IN BEHAVIORAL HEALTH

Institute Strategic Quality Planning

Every entity in behavioral health should develop and implement a strategic quality plan. Achieving ever higher levels of service performance requires that behavioral health managers develop a strategic quality plan that integrates QI into their system. The Strategic Quality Plan should: (a) identify clear goals that define the expected outcome of the QI effort; (b) be databased and use indicators to measure progress; (c) include systematic cycles of planning, execution, and evaluation (see Figure 3.1); (d) concentrate on key processes based on the System of Profound Knowledge, described before, as the route to better results; and (e) focus on patients and other stakeholders such as employers and payors.

Improve Management Information Systems and Analysis

The efficient collection and management of data and its transformation into useful information are fundamental to a successful QI program. Data are necessary to describe customer needs, evaluate performance, establish goals for improvement, and monitor progress. (a) Are services timely? Quality can also be partly determined by the timeliness of services. It is not helpful to deliver an empirically based treatment months after the client needs it. (b) Do providers adhere to prescribed evidence-based protocols? If not, are acceptable variance reports used to understand and incorporate needed variability? (c) What is the level of patient/stakeholder satisfaction? What are the trends in this satisfaction? (d) How does performance compare with similar systems, such as the development and use of benchmarks? (e) Are data and information used in planning and operations? (f) Do all workforce members understand and use available data? (g) Have QI efforts been successful at improving performance? (h) Are changes in one critical performance indicator affecting other areas? Stakeholder data, such as information from insurance companies, employers, and managed-care companies, are used to determine the types of behavioral health-care services needed or desired. Such information

can be obtained and updated periodically by questionnaire or interview. For example, employers, who are the ultimate payers for a large percentage of health care, might be interested in programs that decrease their disability costs and increase the productivity of their workers. But if these stakeholders are not brought to the table to solicit their needs and expectations, programs may ignore them.

The Development and Implementation of Behavioral Health Electronic Medical Records

A serious problem in our field is the lack of quality, complete, and timely patient records. The accepted norm seems to be incomplete, scattered, illegible records that are received many weeks, if at all, after a release of information is sent. Generally, this means that the current treating clinician is treating the patient largely blind to the patient's treatment history and perhaps many current problems. This situation is unacceptable. The vision is to have an integrated, complete, legible, electronic, perhaps Web-based, record that can be accessed immediately with the patient's permission. This change of course requires leadership to find solutions so that the disparate records systems can communicate with one another; however, we worry that insufficient attention is being spent on this effort and that patient care is being compromised as a result. If it is true that "paper kills" (Merritt, 2007), it may be equally true that "illegible paper slaughters." There can be important bells and whistles in electronic medical records, such as Web-based practice standards, benchmarks, and patient handouts. For example, when a clinician enters a diagnosis, practice guidelines can be programmed to appear for the clinician's use.

Practice Standards and Benchmarks

Although there have been noteworthy developments such as the APA Division 12's Task

Force on ESTs (Chambless & Ollendick, 2001), there has been little adoption of these standards in practice. Again, this is not just a philosophical commitment but rather a commitment to actual implementation. It is interesting to pose the question of how much of care behavioral health payers are paying that is wasteful, non-evidence-based versus efficient, evidence-based treatments. Our conjecture is that the majority of costs currently being accrued are for non-evidence-based care. This ratio should be a metric that is monitored constantly for improvement. As we noted earlier, benchmarks are standards by which performance can be evaluated. There can be benchmarks for magnitude of change, for example, the mean Beck Depression Inventory score decrease from pre- to posttreatment in our practice is 8; benchmarks for number of sessions used to produce this change; benchmarks for total cost; benchmarks from initial call to date services are provided; and benchmarks for mean satisfaction for patients. We need to develop and implement these industry standards. Currently, we appear to be in a sad state in which our industry has few, if any, systematic standards.

Transparent Report Cards

Increasingly in physical health, organizations are posting their report cards. One can go to hospitalscompare.hhs.gov, enter in one's zip code, and look at audits on practice standards for major illnesses. This system allows consumers to make better decisions regarding their health care and incentivizes health-care organizations to care about quality. Currently, there is little movement in this area for behavioral health, and again we need leadership to change this situation.

Continuity of Care

Behavioral health care is fractionated. It is a cluster of fairly independent providers who focus, unsurprisingly, on their own niche; however, this means that there is little continuity of care. Inpatient settings often do not communicate with outpatient settings, and vice versa, and specialty care such as drug and alcohol abuse treatments rarely communicate with other service providers. Patients are discharged from inpatient settings and are often left on their own to seek aftercare. Providers in one geographical setting often do not communicate efficiently with providers in other geographical settings due to lack of EMRs. We need to measure and improve the continuity of care.

Plans to Improve Access

The de facto mental health system in the United States is the primary care medical clinic. Patients have better access to primary care medicine than they do specialty care mental health; however, we know that individuals living in rural and frontier areas, especially the poor and elderly, have problematic access. We need to systematically measure access problems and seek innovations to improve this state of affairs.

Systematic Plans to Decrease Our Customers' Expense and Improve the Value Proposition We Offer

Most industries are driven by the idea of driving down costs to keep competitive. Paradoxically, we are driven by attempts to drive *up* our costs in complete ignorance of the economic law of supply and demand (APA, 2004). As costs increase, demand decreases. Somehow we want to be exempt from this law. We want to raise prices and serve the poor. Innovations need to be prioritized to decrease the costs of behavioral health care given its high need. We need to see many of these problems as public health problems, not just clinical problems. How can we treat depression more cost-effectively (quality Web-based programs?); how can we best treat child obesity (books or school-based programs?); how can we get the elderly the behavioral health care they need (creating paraprofessionals for geriatric services?); how can we get the quality behavioral health to the poor (colocated master's-level therapists in the convenience health-care delivery sites that are evolving, such as in Wal-Mart and in the large workplace?). We need to be more innovative and not merely think in terms of developing new one-on-one therapies delivered individually by doctorally trained providers in specialty offices.

Quality Campaigns Such as Zero Missed Enuresis Screens

There have been campaigns of various sizes and impact regarding quality improvement; for example, there have been campaigns to reduce prescription errors. In behavioral health, we can do the same. We can have a national campaign for 100% functional enuresis screens in first graders; or no obese 4-year-old child left untreated, or no nursing home resident unscreened or untreated for depression or bereavement. We should look at what seem to be the most solvable problems and the ones that are generating the most human and financial costs and develop quality campaigns for them. Currently, again, our national organizations have provided little if any leadership in this regard.

Providers' Incentive Pay for Performance

Currently, behavioral health providers receive payment based on time spent instead of the results achieved creating perverse incentives. If one spends more time, regardless of outcomes, one receives more payment. This is a fixed interval schedule of reinforcement and we know that fixed interval schedules are associated with low rates of responding. In contrast, ratio schedules, especially variable ratio schedules, are associated with high rates of responding. Physical care organizations are experimenting with other payment systems that more clearly link payment to outcomes and thereby provide better incentives. First, in

these systems, there is a focus on measurable outcomes, not just on measurable time spent or services billed. Second, the incentive system is constructed so that the provider is incentivized to provide effective care, rather than just time spent. A first step in this process can be to identify desired performance. Examples include: (a) use of an electronic medical record, (b) appropriate screening, (c) use of an evidence-based practice guideline, and (d) producing changes according to a benchmark (e.g., an 8-point reduction in Beck Depression Inventory scores in the treatment of depression). This approach uses financial incentives to reward desired behavior instead of just exhortations. There is a movement in medicine called "pay for performance" that contrasts with "pay for services rendered." Pay for performance is an attempt to tie payment to both service and positive outcomes.

Integrated Care

We need to understand where and how patients want care. There is evidence that they prefer one-stop shopping and receive much of their behavioral health care where they receive their physical health care, namely in their primary care physician's office. Cummings and O'Donohue (2008) measured patient satisfaction in these settings and found that colocating a trained, integrated care psychologist in a primary care medical office can reduce overall medical costs, increase physician efficiency, and improve patient health and satisfaction. Specialty behavioral health care is still needed, such as for problems like autism and schizophrenia, but many problems, such as treatment noncompliance, chronic pain, lifestyle changes, depression, and anxiety, can be treated in primary care medical settings.

A Movement Away From the "Bad Apples" Approach

Our professional organizations and licensing boards need to adopt a new philosophy by moving away from the "bad apples" approach to quality and in its stead embrace a systematic approach to QI. Of course, our field needs to detect and investigate the rare bad apples, but an almost exclusive focus on this approach implies that we need not set the typical clinician bar for treatment effectiveness any higher. O'Donohue and Fisher (2006) suggested that the APA's ethical statement be changed from loose references to "professional knowledge" and instead be replaced by something like "All professional services must be implemented with a systematic quality improvement process."

The Crisis of Missing Entrepreneurship

There is little innovation in our field compared with physical medicine, the computer industry, and even the car industry. Why? One reason may be what Meehl (1978) called "the slow progress of soft psychology" (p. 806). Because our field is complicated, we have few breakthroughs in which important nomothetic principles are discovered, but another reason is that we do not have a tradition of entrepreneurship. We have an antibusiness mentality, which may make us insensitive to what the market thinks of us and wants from us. We hold myths, such as the notion that business is just about the greedy who want to make money and miss all the paychecks that feed families, or the needs and wants met by the business's products, or the taxes that support social programs or government. To the contrary, entrepreneurship is also about seeing needs and opportunities in the marketplace, which can be read as what consumers want and are willing to pay for with their hard-earned dollars and taking risks to attempt to actualize these opportunities.

The Austrian economist Joseph Schumpeter (1952) argued that entrepreneurship is useful because its process is one of "creative destruction." Innovations drive out the old—they have a clean-up function—and replace it with the new. We have an endemic problem in our field of driving out the old. Just look, for example, at the continued widespread use of many projective techniques, such as the Rorschach Inkblot Test and human figure drawings, despite decades of research showing that these techniques have marginal validity for most clinical purposes (Lilienfeld, Wood, & Garb, 2000). We also have a problem of a lack of significant innovations. To address this problem, we need to encourage more entrepreneurship. The innovations in the computer industry are driven partly by basic computer science, but also by individuals with other talents. Think, for example, of the business talents of a Bill Gates or the aesthetic and marketing talents of a Steve Jobs. We are not arguing for flim-flam business products, but high-quality products that are designed by behavioral health professionals along with astute business individuals to better satisfy unmet needs of the marketplace at a good value.

The behavioral health-care space is about 5% of the total expenditures on health care in the United States and approximately 17% of the GDP of the United States, and is growing faster than the general rate of inflation (Cummings & O'Donohue, 2008). Thus, there is a significant amount of economic activity in the areas of behavioral health care—around $100 billion annually. We hope entrepreneurs will see the need for quality products in the assessment and treatment of depression, anxiety, obesity, treatment compliance, bereavement, Alzheimer's disease, and other commonplace clinical problems and partner with more business friendly behavioral scientists to "destroy"—to use Schumpeter's term—the poor value services and products currently available and replace them with improvements. It may be insufficient for academics and clinicians alone to produce this "creative destruction."

REFERENCES

American Psychological Association. (2004). Psychology joins class action lawsuit against managed care. *Monitor on Psychology, 35*, 1.

Arkowitz, H., & Lilienfeld, S. O. (2006, April/May). Psychotherapy on trial. *Scientific American Mind, 2,* 42–49.

Berwick, D., & Nolan, T. (1998). Physicians as leaders in improving healthcare: A new series in the Annals of Internal Medicine. *Annals of Internal Medicine, 128,* 289–292.

Chambless, D. L., & Hollon, S. D. (1998). Defining empirically supported therapies. *Journal of Consulting and Clinical Psychology, 66,* 7–18.

Chambless, D. L., & Ollendick, T. H. (2001). Empirically supported psychological interventions: Controversies and evidence. *Annual Review of Psychology, 52,* 685–716.

Crits-Christoph, P., Frank, E., Chambless, D. L., Brody, C., & Karp, J. F. (1995). Training in empirically validated treatments: What are clinical psychology students learning? *Professional Psychology: Research and Practice, 26,* 514–522.

Cummings, N. A., & O'Donohue, W. T. (2008). *Eleven blunders that have crippled psychology.* New York, NY: Routledge.

Dawes, R. M. (1994). *A house of cards: Psychology and psychotherapy built on myth.* New York, NY: The Free Press.

DeBakey, M. E. (1993). Medical Centers of Excellence and health reform. *Science, 252,* 523–525.

De Los Reyes, A., & Kazdin, A. E. (2008). When the evidence says, "Yes, no, and maybe so." *Current Directions in Psychological Science, 17,* 47–51.

Deming, W. E. (2000). *Out of the crisis.* Cambridge: MIT Press.

Emery, R. E., Otto, R. K., & O'Donohue, W. (2005). A critical assessment of child custody evaluations. *Psychological Science in the Public Interest, 6,* 1–29.

Garb, H. N. (1998). *Studying the clinician: Judgment research and psychological assessment.* Washington, DC: American Psychological Association.

Gaston, J. E., Abbott, M. J., Rapee, R. M., & Neary, S. (2006). Do empirically supported treatments generalise to private practice? A benchmark study of a cognitive-behavioural group treatment program for social phobia. *British Journal of Clinical Psychology, 45,* 33–48.

Gawande, A. (2003). *Complications: A surgeon's notes on an imperfect science.* New York, NY: Picador.

Greene, J. P. (2005). *Education myths: What special interest groups want you to believe about our schools—and why it isn't so.* New York, NY: Rowman & Littlefield.

Hahlweg, K., Fiegenbaum, W., Frank, M., Schroeder, B., & van Witzleben, I. (2001). Short- and long-term effectiveness of an empirically supported treatment for agoraphobia. *Journal of Consulting and Clinical Psychology, 69,* 375–382.

Hays, K. A., Rardin, D. K., Jarvis, P. A., Taylor, N. M., Moorman, A. S., & Armstead, C. D. (2002). An exploratory survey on empirically supported treatments: Implications for internship training. *Professional Psychology: Research and Practice, 33,* 207–211.

Heaphy, M. S., & Bruska, G. F. (1995). *The Malcolm Baldrige National Quality Award.* New York, NY: Addison-Wesley.

Holloway, J. D. (2004). Psychology joins class action lawsuit against managed care. *APA Monitor in Psychology.* Retrieved from www.apa.org/monitor/nov04/lawsuit.html.

Horan, W. P., & Blanchard, J. J. (2001). Training opportunities in empirically supported treatments and their relationship to intern recruitment and post-internship placement: A survey of directors of internship training. *Clinical Science* (Winter), 1–10.

Hunsley, J., & DiGiulio, G. (2002). Dodo bird, phoenix, or urban legend? *Scientific Review of Mental Health Practice, 1,* 11–22.

Institute of Medicine. (2001). *Crossing the quality chasm: A new health system for the 21st century.* Washington, DC: National Academies Press.

Karekla, M., Lundgren, J. D., & Forsyth, J. P. (2004). A survey of graduate training in empirically supported and manualized treatments: A preliminary report. *Cognitive and Behavioral Practice, 11,* 230–242.

Katon, W. (1987). The epidemiology of depression in primary care. *International Journal of Psychiatric Medicine, 17,* 93–112.

Kendall, P. C., Gosch, E., Furr, J. M., & Sood, E. (2008). Flexibility within fidelity. *Journal of the American Academy of Child and Adolescent Psychiatry, 47,* 987–993.

Krasner, L., & Houts, A. C. (1984). A study of the value systems of behavioral scientists. *American Psychologist, 39,* 840–849.

Langer, E. J., & Abelson, R. P. (1974). A patient by any other name . . . Clinical group differences in labeling bias. *Journal of Consulting and Clinical Psychology, 42,* 4–9.

Leape, M. (2004). *Patient safety: The new accountability.* CDC Quality Institute. Retrieved from www.phppo.cdc.gov/mlp/qiconference/presentations/leape%20cdc%20talk.pdf

Lilienfeld, S. O., Lynn, S. J., & Lohr, J. M. (2003). *Science and pseudoscience in clinical psychology.* New York, NY: Guilford Press.

Lilienfeld, S. O., & Marino, L. (1995). Mental disorder as a Roschian concept: A critique of Wakefield's "harmful dysfunction" analysis. *Journal of Abnormal Psychology, 104,* 411–420.

Lilienfeld, S. O., Wood, J. M., & Garb, H. N. (2000). The scientific status of projective techniques. *Psychological Science in the Public Interest, 1,* 27–66.

Lykken, D. T. (1991). What's wrong with psychology anyway? In D. Cicchetti & W. M. Grove (Eds.), *Thinking clearly about psychology, vol. 1: Matters of public interest* (pp. 3–39). Minneapolis: University of Minnesota Press.

Meehl, P. E. (1973). Why I do not attend case conferences. In P. E. Meehl (Ed.), *Psychodiagnosis: Selected papers* (pp. 265–302). Minneapolis: University of Minnesota Press.

Meehl, P. E. (1978). Theoretical risks and tabular asterisks: Sir Karl, Sir Ronald, and the slow progress of soft psychology. *Journal of Consulting and Clinical Psychology, 46,* 806–834.

McFall, R. M. (1991). Manifesto for a science of clinical psychology. *The Clinical Psychologist, 44,* 75–88.

Mercer, J., Sarner, L., & Rosa, L. (2006). *Attachment therapy on trial: The torture and death of Candace Newmaker.* Westport, CT: Praeger Publishers.

Meredith, L. S., Wells, K. B., & Camp, P. (1994). *Clinician specialty and treatment style for depressive outpatients with and without medical comorbidities.* Rand Report. Agency for Healthcare Policy and Research.

Merritt, D. (2007). *Paper kills.* Washington, DC: CHT Press.

Miller, W. R., & Wilbourne, P. L. (2002). Mesa Grande: A methodological analysis of clinical trials of treatments for alcohol use disorders. *Addiction, 97,* 265–277.

O'Donohue, W., & Boland, M. (in press). *Beyond the Rube Goldberg model of clinical training: Reforms in graduate education in clinical psychology.* Manuscript in preparation.

O'Donohue, W., & Bradley, A. R. (1999). Conceptual and empirical issues in child custody evaluations. *Clinical Psychology: Science and Practice, 6,* 310–322.

O'Donohue, W., & Buchanan, J. A. (2003). The mismeasure of psychologists: A review of the psychometric properties of licensing requirements. In W. O'Donohue & K. Ferguson (Eds.), *Handbook of professional ethics for psychologists* (pp. 81–200). Thousand Oaks, CA: Sage.

O'Donohue, W., & Draper, C. (Eds.). (2011). *Stepped care and e-health. Practical applications to psychology.* New York, NY: Springer.

O'Donohue, W., & Dyslin, C. (2005). Abortion, boxing and Zionism: Politics and the APA. In R. Wright & N. A. Cummings (Eds.), *Destructive trends in mental health* (pp. 235–252). New York, NY: Routledge.

O'Donohue, W., & Fisher, J. E. (2006). The role of practice guidelines in systematic quality improvement. In J. Fisher & W. O'Donohue (Eds.), *Practitioner's guide to evidence-based psychotherapy* (pp. 1–23). New York, NY: Springer.

Persons, J. B., & Silberschatz, G. (1998). Are results of randomized controlled trials useful to psychotherapists? *Journal of Consulting and Clinical Psychology, 66,* 126–135.

Rosen, G. M., & Davison, G. C. (2003). Psychology should identify empirically supported principles of change (ESPs) and not credential trademarked therapies or other treatment packages. *Behavior Modification, 27,* 300–312.

Schumpeter, J. A. (1952). *Ten great economists from Marx to Keynes.* London, England: Allen & Unwin.

Schuster, M. A., McGlynn, E. A., & Brook, R. (1998). How good is the quality of health care in the United States? *Milbank Quarterly, 76,* 517–563.

Wade, W. A., Treat, T. A., & Stuart, G. L. (1998). Transporting an empirically supported treatment for panic disorder to a service clinic setting: A benchmarking strategy. *Journal of Consulting and Clinical Psychology, 66,* 231–239.

Walton, M. (1986). *The Deming Management method.* New York, NY: Perigee.

Wampold, B. E. (2001). *The great psychotherapy debate: Models, methods, and findings.* Hillsdale, NJ: Erlbaum.

Weissman, M. M., Verdeli, H., Gameroff, M. J., Bledsoe, S. E., Betts, K., Mufson, L., . . . Wickramaratne, P. (2006). National survey of psychotherapy training in psychiatry, psychology, and social work. *Archives of General Psychiatry, 63,* 925–934.

Weisz, J. R., Donenberg, G., Han, S., & Kauneckis, D. (1995). Child and adolescent psychotherapy outcomes in experiments versus clinics: Why the disparity? *Journal of Abnormal Child Psychology, 23,* 83–106.

Weisz, J. R., Weersing, V. R., & Henggeler, S. W. (2005). Jousting with straw men: Comment on Westen, Novotny, and Thompson-Brenner (2004). *Psychological Bulletin, 131,* 418–426.

Westen, D., Novotny, C. M., & Thompson-Brenner, H. (2004). The empirical status of empirically supported psychotherapies: Assumptions, findings, and reporting in controlled clinical trials. *Psychological Bulletin, 130,* 631–663.

Wood, J. M., Garb, H. N., Lilienfeld, S. O., & Nezworski, M. T. (2002). Clinical assessment of personality. *Annual Review of Psychology, 53,* 519–543.

Wright, R., & Cummings, N. A. (Eds.). (2005). *Destructive trends in mental health.* New York, NY: Routledge.

4

Developing Clinical Guidelines for Children and Adolescents

Experience From the National Institute for Health and Clinical Excellence

STEPHEN PILLING AND PETER FONAGY

The National Institute for Health and Clinical Excellence (NICE) was established in 1999 to develop guidance for the National Health Service in England and Wales. It operates as an independent body within the state funded health-care system, known as the National Health Service (NHS), but its funding and the remit for its work comes from the government. The NICE's central role is to provide recommendations on the best practice in health care and thereby set standards by which health care and health outcomes can be improved. It produces guidance in four areas: (1) *Clinical Practice*, which are clinical guidelines, such as guidance focused primarily on a disorder or condition, such as depression in children or type I diabetes. (2) *Technology Appraisals*, which are cost-effectiveness reviews of health technologies that are usually, but not limited to, drugs; for example, mental health technology appraisals have covered novel hypnotics, ECT, drugs for the treatment of ADHD, and parent training in conduct disorder. (3) *Interventional Procedures*, which are concerned primarily with the efficacy and safety of surgical procedures, but do on occasion move outside this field to consider nonsurgical interventions; for example, trans-magnetic stimulation for the treatment of depression. (4) *Public Health Guidance*, which is concerned with public health interventions, where its brief extends beyond health care to involve social care, education, and the wider environment; for example, guidance has been developed on social and emotional well-being in primary education and school-based interventions for alcohol-related problems. These four elements constitute the largest single program for development of clinical guidance in the world. This chapter will provide an introduction to the work of NICE in mental health, concentrating primarily on the clinical guidelines program for children and adolescents and its impact on development of psychological treatments in the United Kingdom, but it will also refer to other elements of the NICE program. Some guidelines cover both adults and children; for example, eating disorders. (See Volume 2, Chapter 2, by Pilling for a more detailed account of NICE's work on adult mental health.)

Although NICE is probably the largest guideline development organization, it is not alone. The past 20 years have seen a major expansion in guidance development across the world. Some measure of the rate of expansion can be obtained from the following figures. Parry, Cape, and Pilling (2003) reported that the total number of guidelines concerned with the treatment of depression on the National Guidelines Clearinghouse, an international register of completed guidelines (www.guide line.gov), was 170. As of December 31, 2008, this figure had reached 487; however, if a search of the same register is conducted for child or adolescent depression, fewer guidelines are identified, the vast majority of which focus specifically neither on children nor adolescents, nor depression. A review of identified guidelines revealed only three focused specifically on child and adolescent depression. (Note this did not include the NICE guideline on childhood depression [NICE, 2005a].)

Very few guidelines have explicitly focused on psychological therapies. An exception to this is the guideline on *Treatment Choice in Psychological Therapies and Counselling* (Department of Health, 2001). Despite this lack of explicit focus, psychological interventions have assumed an increasingly important role in a number of mental health guidelines, in particular the NICE mental health guidelines, where psychological interventions have been identified as key recommendations for implementation in 13 out of the 16 mental health guidelines so far produced (www.nccmh.org .uk). Indeed, the location of psychological interventions within broadly based diagnostic- or condition-based guidelines has been important in establishing psychological therapies as mainstream treatment options.

DEVELOPING CLINICAL GUIDELINES

The focus of this chapter is on the development of clinical guidelines, particularly as they apply to psychological therapies for children and adolescents and mental health more generally. It will first consider the rationale for their development; briefly review the methods by which they are produced, reviewing some particular problems in their development; consider evidence for their effective implementation; briefly describe some major implementation initiatives in the NHS; and, briefly, consider future developments in clinical guidelines in mental health and psychological therapies. The chapter draws on the first author's (henceforth identified as "SP") experience as the joint director of the National Collaborating Centre for Mental Health, a British Psychological Society and Royal College of Psychiatrists joint initiative that develops clinical practice guidelines in mental health for NICE and in the case of the second author (henceforth identified as "PF") as the chair of a NICE guideline on depression in children and young people (NICE, 2005a).

One important consideration in development of clinical guidelines for children and adolescents is that comorbidity is commonplace in mental disorders in childhood and adolescence. For example, conduct disorder is the most common mental health problem in childhood, with 6% of 5- to 16-year-olds diagnosed with a conduct disorder in the United Kingdom (Green, McGinnity, Meltzer, Ford, & Goodman, 2005). However, 90% of children with conduct disorder also have other disorders (Moffitt, Caspi, Rutter, & Silva, 2001) with much higher rates of depression and substance misuse; for example, ADHD is more than 10 times more common in those with conduct disorder (Angold, Costello, & Erkanli, 1999). Looking beyond conduct problems to antisocial problems in adolescence, we also find that the vast majority of youths present with two or more disorders in addition to delinquency (Lader, Singleton, & Meltzer, 2003). Beyond this comorbidity with conduct disorder, there are important associations with callous and unemotional personality traits, psychopathic traits, problems on the autism spectrum (Howlin, 1998), substance misuse (Lader et al.,

2003), early onset psychosis (Chitsabesan et al., 2006), and depression and anxiety (Wood, Harrington, & Moore, 1996). Comorbidities in children and adolescents are of considerable importance for clinical guidelines and clinical management in general, because of the association with accessibility to treatment. For example, individuals with more marked psychopathic characteristics may be particularly hard to treat (O'Brien & Frick, 1996). By contrast, comorbidity with anxiety tends to be an indicator of relatively favorable treatment outcome (Fonagy & Target, 1994). In many instances, psychiatric comorbidity may also yield important moderators of outcome; however, most guideline development programs take a disorder- or condition-based approach to development of clinical guidelines. Even where this is acknowledged, for example, in NICE guidelines on ADHD (NICE, 2008), it presents some challenges when developing recommendations. This issue will be revisited at key points in the rest of the chapter.

Rationale for Clinical Guidelines

Clinical guidelines are defined as "systematically developed statements to assist practitioner and patient decisions about appropriate health care for specific clinical circumstances" (Field & Lohr, 1990, p. 8). This definition, developed in the 1990 Institute of Medicine report, is the one adopted by the UK health-care system (Department of Health, 1996). Clinical guidelines differ from standard literature reviews and textbooks in the explicit methods used in their construction, which usually involve a representative guideline development group of professionals who use a systematic approach to identify and evaluate the evidence. Increasingly, patients and caregivers also participate in the development of guidelines. Evidence from secondary research, usually in the form of systematic reviews, is used in combination with the expertise and knowledge of the guideline development group to arrive at a set of recommendations for clinical

practice. Guideline development groups increasingly follow standard methods for development of recommendations including, where appropriate, formal and informal consensus methods (NICE, 2007). An important characteristic of high-quality clinical guidelines is that the method is transparent and well described so that the evidence supporting each recommendation is clearly identifiable.

A primary aim of clinical guidelines is to promote clinically and cost-effective care, and in order to achieve this they need to be based on the best available evidence. In seeking to achieve this aim, guidelines set standards for interventions by health-care professionals that should guide professional behavior; however, they are not a substitute for the clinical judgment exercised by a health-care professional when determining the most effective care for an individual (NICE, 2007). Because clinical guidelines are based on the needs of hypothetical typical patients and patient needs inevitably vary from the average, recommendations may require adaptation to suit the individual. For example, this might mean varying the duration or intensity of recommended treatment for patients with comorbid disorders, such as treatment of ADHD with comorbid conduct disorder (NICE, 2008). Typically, it might be expected that recommendations contained in a guideline would apply to about 80% of individuals with the condition or disorder covered by that particular guideline (Eddy, 1990). Clinical guidelines should also be distinguished from protocols. Protocols specify precisely what a health-care professional should do in a certain set of circumstances. They should be based on good quality evidence with a high degree of certainty about the benefits and/or risks of the intervention; for example, the means of administration of certain cytotoxic drugs and opinions/options where a synthesis of evidence sets out a range of possible interventions and evidence for their effectiveness without necessarily specifying in detail the circumstances in which they might be used, such as the empirically supported treatment approach adopted by the American Psychological Association (Chambless, 1993). Clinical guidelines can be particularly important when considerable uncertainty exists about correct intervention for a particular disorder or problem, as is often the case in child and adolescent mental health; however, given the added complexity of comorbidity in child and adolescent mental health, it is particularly important to remember that clinical guidelines are aids to and not substitutes for clinical judgment.

The focus in clinical guidelines on setting standards for and improving patient outcomes has a number of direct and indirect consequences. In addition to improved quality of care, these include the allocation of resources toward more effective treatments and away from less effective treatments and improved access to effective care, particularly if the guidelines also make recommendations about the nature of service delivery systems. Clinical guidelines are also increasingly used to inform patients more effectively about the type of care they may expect. This requires that guidance be presented in forms accessible to patients. The NICE produces publications for all its guidance that specifically aims to inform patients and their carers about guidance it has issued (NICE, 2007). This means that guidelines can not only help patients in making informed decisions about their care, but may also improve communication between patients and professionals. Guidelines may also be used by health-care commissioners and managers to guide the purchasing of services, to: (a) develop the service structures needed to deliver effective health care, (b) develop systems for the effective monitoring of services, and (c) evaluate services. Finally, guidelines can also have a role in the education and training of health-care professionals and may assume an increasing prominence in the curricula of the undergraduate and postgraduate training of health-care professionals. The aim of clinical guidelines is to reduce existing uncertainties about which interventions are most likely to bring benefit for patients and generate greater cost-effectiveness in the health-care system, thereby ensuring that unacceptable variation in both clinical practice and the distribution of resources is reduced.

As can be seen from the previous discussion, NICE and other developers of clinical guidelines are increasingly drawn into discussions about the allocation of resources. This represents an engagement with issues beyond the simple identification of effective interventions and is a challenge that faces all health-care systems where the demand for health-care outstrips the system's capacity and resources to deliver, including those in the United States (Peterson, 2008; Steinbrook, 2008). While it is not the role of clinical guidelines or their developers to decide on what resources should be allocated by a community for the health care of its citizens, guidelines have a role to play in determining the means by which those agreed resources are allocated. Therefore, it is important that methods by which this is achieved are seen to be fair and transparent. This is particularly important if guidelines are to retain the support of professional and patient communities whose practice and care is directly impacted by them. Inevitably this requires that the values on which the guidelines are based are made explicit, together with the methods by which the guidelines are produced.

While guideline development methods have become increasingly transparent (Grilli, Magrini, Penna, Mura, & Liberati, 2000), there are few guideline development organizations that make explicit the values that underpin their work. NICE is one of the few guideline development organizations that has an explicit statement of its social value judgments (NICE, 2005c). These values include: (a) statements on recommending interventions where good evidence is available, but not doing so where it is not available; (b) considering cost-effectiveness in the evaluation of interventions; (c) considering age, race, or gender only where it is an indicator of likely effectiveness of an intervention that cannot be accounted for by any other means; and, (d) not denying interventions because the condition that they aim to ameliorate may, in part, be self-inflicted (NICE, 2005c). This approach recognizes that it is extraordinarily difficult, if not impossible, to develop an agreed-upon set of rules that could allow allocation of health-care resources, on which all citizens could agree (Daniels & Sabin, 2002), but that it may be possible to obtain agreement on the process by which the decisions are reached. This approach, known as procedural justice (Daniels & Sabin, 2002), underpins the NICE program and requires a transparent and fair process in which all relevant stakeholders are actively involved. Guideline developers are not expected to satisfy everyone since this may well not be achievable, but they can be held to account for the reasonableness of their decision-making process (Rawlins & Dillon, 2005).

Methods for Developing Clinical Guidelines

There are a number of methods for the synthesis of evidence to support clinical decision making and development of clinical guidelines. These include systematic reviews (Egger, Davey Smith, & Altmann, 2001), meta-analysis or other methods of aggregating multiple data sets on the effects of an intervention (Egger et al., 2001), evidence briefings (see www.nta.nhs.uk for examples from the field of substance misuse), reviews of the cost or cost-effectiveness of health interventions (Whitten et al., 2002), and formal and informal consensus methods (Black et al., 1999). As will be seen from the following discussion, these approaches are not mutually exclusive. Systematic reviews are the building blocks of almost all high-quality evidence reviews and methods for doing this, while not always followed, are the best developed. See Moher et al. (1999) for a statement on methods to be adopted for high-quality systematic reviews.

In most cases clinical guidelines, including those from NICE, are condition- or problem-based. Thus, they may address diagnoses, such as depression or diabetes, or problems, such as violence in psychiatric settings. They focus on what should be done and rather less on how treatments might be delivered (Parry et al., 2003). The consequences of this approach for clinical guidelines in mental health and psychological therapies will be revisited later in this chapter; however, in most health-care systems, the clinical guideline remains the most complete manifestation of evidence-based medicine and one that may also include advice on the care pathways and service structures to support effective delivery of care.

Initially, most clinical guidelines were developed by specialist uniprofessional groups; for example, groups of specialist physicians, such as cardiologists or neurologists. In a systematic review of specialist guidelines developed by uniprofessional groups, Grilli et al. (2000) focused on three areas of guideline development: (1) professional and stakeholder involvement, (2) identification of primary evidence, and (3) appropriate grading of recommendations. They highlighted some of the potential problems with this specialist uniprofessional approach. For example, of the 431 speciality guidelines they reviewed, only 5% were rated as adequate in terms of search strategies used, structure of the guideline development groups, and recommendation grading. Grilli et al. argued that this demonstrated the need for a multidisciplinary approach with explicit and transparent methods based on international standards of good practice. Recent trends in guideline development have supported this view and the recent significant international expansion of evidence-based medicine has often been based in multiprofessional development programs, such as NICE in England and Wales, the Scottish Intercollegiate Guidelines Network, and the Agency for Healthcare Research and Quality in the United States (Parry et al., 2003). In addition, there have been recent and important advances in the methods for evaluation of the quality of clinical guidelines. Perhaps the best developed, reliable, and most widely used method is the AGREE instrument (www .agreecollaboration.org) produced by an international group of guideline developers and methodologists (AGREE, 2003) to assess the quality of guideline development. It includes ratings of the scope and purpose of the guideline, extent of stakeholder involvement, rigor of development, clarity and presentation, applicability of the guideline, and degree of editorial independence of the developers. For an example of its use in an international review of the quality of clinical guidelines in schizophrenia, see Gaebel, Weinman, Sartorius, Rutz, and McIntyre (2005).

Clinical guidelines typically rely on two main methods for identification and aggregation of data from primary research: systematic review and meta-analysis. Thus, the quality of these activities is central to the development of high-quality clinical guidelines. Systematic reviews usually summarize large bodies of evidence, synthesizing the results of multiple primary investigations by using strategies designed to reduce bias and random error (Egger et al., 2001). In well-conducted systematic reviews, these methods are predefined and presented in a reliable, transparent, and reproducible manner (Egger et al., 2001). They clearly specify the means by which studies will be identified, selected for inclusion, appraised, and their results aggregated, and include steps to minimize bias at each of these stages. In most systematic reviews of the efficacy of a clinical intervention, the randomized controlled trial (RCT)—regardless of results— is the preferred building block (Starr & Chalmers, 2003). A systematic review usually, but not always, contains a quantitative synthesis of results—a meta-analysis—but this might not always be possible; for example, when study designs included in the analysis are too different from each other for an average of their results to be appropriate. This may occur when: (a) combining data from individual or cluster randomized trials without data

available to allow for adjustments to take into account the effects of clustering, (b) if outcomes are not adequately reported, or (c) where the difference in the nature of the outcome measures is too great to allow for a direct comparison. A meta-analysis can also be performed without a systematic review, simply by combining results from more than one study, but considerable caution is often needed in the interpretation of the results.

One major difficulty that arises in the interpretation and use of systematic reviews in support of clinical decision making derives from methods used to identify, select, and critically appraise the relevant studies. For most well-conducted systematic reviews, a well-designed electronically based search strategy is required, which includes clearly specified search terms relevant to the subject under review and that searches relevant databases such as Medline, EMBASE, and PsycINFO. The development of these strategies is well described in a number of publications (Egger et al., 2001) and any well-conducted review should report the number of relevant studies identified at each stage of the search and appraisal process (Moher et al., 1999). However, even the best-designed search strategies have their limitations. In relation to efficacy studies, these include the inability of the search strategies to compensate fully for the consequences of bias in publication. These biases include presence or absence in the review of unpublished studies or selective reporting of outcomes, limitations of the Medical Subject Headings terms used in descriptions of some studies, and delay in entering recently published studies onto relevant databases. Solutions to the latter two problems can be addressed to an extent by hand-searching of references of identified studies and regular updating of searches during the course of a review, but the problem of publication bias presents a much greater challenge.

The extent of problems presented by unpublished studies is illustrated in the systematic review by Whittington et al. (2004), which compared clinical recommendations that could be made about use of selective serotonin reuptake inhibitors (SSRIs) for children and adolescents with depression, based on published and unpublished clinical trials of these drugs. The analysis was performed in support of the NICE clinical guideline on depression in children (NICE, 2005a). They demonstrated that if published studies alone had been used, a systematic review would have supported the widespread use of these drugs with few concerns being raised about the potential increased incidence of suicidal ideation in this very vulnerable group. The addition of unpublished studies led to a very different outcome, with all but one SSRI—fluoxetine—being identified as having an unacceptable harm/benefit ratio. This problem of selective reporting of trial outcomes has been confirmed in a number of studies, which have demonstrated that inclusion of previously unpublished data may significantly alter the outcomes of a systematic review. For example, Melander, Ahlqvist-Rastad, Meijer, and Beermann (2003), in a review of trials of SSRIs submitted to the Swedish medicines regulatory authority, demonstrated that studies with significant results were more likely to be published than those with nonsignificant results.

Another source of bias may arise from investigator allegiance. This can be seen in a number of studies of pharmaceutical industry sponsorship, including Perlis et al. (2005) and Lexchin, Bero, Djulbegovic, and Clark (2003). Perlis et al. (2005) reported that company-sponsored trials were 4.9 times more likely to report a positive outcome for a particular drug than non–industry-sponsored studies. Lexchin et al. reported evidence of a systematic bias in favor of products produced by the company funding the research and suggested that this may in part be accounted for by use of inappropriate comparators and publication bias. Much of the focus of this work has been on bias introduced into clinical research by commercial interests of the pharmaceutical

industry. Non-industry-sponsored trials, including trials of psychological or service interventions, are also not free from publication bias. Jacobson and Hollon (1996), in a discussion of Elkin et al.'s (1989) trial of pharmacological and psychological treatment for depression, also raised the possibility of investigator allegiance as a factor that may have influenced the outcome of the trial. In a well-conducted review, Chan, Hrobjartsson, Haahr, Gøtzsche, and Altman (2004) also demonstrated how final trial report outcomes often differed from those set out in original protocols, including many nonpharmacological trials, which resulted in a bias toward publication of significant results. They suggested that this problem could be addressed by registration of trial protocols when the trial is established and that subsequent publication of the trial outcomes be assessed against the original protocol. A more immediate solution to the problem of publication bias commonly used in systematic reviews where quantitative synthesis of data is undertaken, is to use a funnel plot (Egger, Davey-Smith, Schneider, & Minder, 1997). A funnel plot is a scatter plot of the effects of the intervention from individual studies against a measure of each study's size or precision. The term arises from the fact that precision of the estimated effects increases as the size of the study increases. Effect estimates from small studies will therefore scatter more widely at the bottom of the graph, with the spread narrowing among larger studies. Where no bias has occurred the funnel plot should approximate to a symmetrical, inverted funnel. Where bias has occurred, for example, because of small nonsignificant unpublished studies, this will result in an asymmetrical plot. Such plots tend to be associated with an overestimation of intervention effects. Most often asymmetry is assessed visually, but there are doubts about researchers' capacity to do this and a number of statistics are now available to guide assessment of asymmetry (Higgins & Green, 2008).

THE NATIONAL COLLABORATING CENTRE FOR MENTAL HEALTH

The National Collaborating Centre for Mental Health (NCCMH) is one of seven National Collaborating Centres (NCCs). Originally established by NICE in April 2001, the NCCMH has a specific, but not exclusive brief—to generate evidence-based guidelines in mental health. In establishing the NCCs, NICE made an explicit decision to locate the groups outside of NICE and closely allied to the main health professional groups. Other NCCs originally covered primary care, nursing and supportive care, cancer, acute care, care of chronic conditions, and women and child health. In 2008, four centers—primary care, nursing and supportive care, acute care, and care of chronic conditions—merged into a single center, leaving four NCCs. Most of the NCCs are based in or have very strong links with the leading professional bodies in England and Wales, such as the medical Royal Colleges. The NCCMH is a collaboration between the Royal College of Psychiatrists and the British Psychological Society, supported by a management board with representatives from relevant professional bodies, social care organizations, patient organizations, and health services managers. The NCCMH has a joint university (University College London) and professional base (the Research Unit of the Royal College of Psychiatrists). It has currently just under 20 staff, including two part-time directors, who are both practicing clinicians, one center manager, two project managers, four systematic reviewers, one information scientist, three health economists, one editor, and five research assistants, and has capacity to develop six guidelines at any one time.

Topics selected for mental health guidelines are identified by a consideration panel, which in turn advises the Department of Health with whom the final decision rests about which guidelines are to be developed. Suggestions for development of new guidance can be made to NICE by professional bodies, the Department of Health, patients' organizations and, through the NICE Web site, by individual health professionals or patients. Once a topic has been agreed upon, a remit is sent to the NCC, who uses it to develop a scope, which sets out the specific aspects of the condition or disorder to be reviewed and identifies the key clinical questions to be addressed. In keeping with emphasis on consultation and transparency a scoping meeting is held, to which all registered stakeholders are invited, and at which the scope is further developed, before undergoing a period of formal public consultation. Registered stakeholders include professional bodies, patient and caregiver organizations, the Department of Health, the pharmaceutical industry, health and social care provider organizations, and invited experts. There are few restrictions on registering, but individual professionals are encouraged to submit comments via relevant professional bodies (NICE, 2007). During this time the NCCMH, in conjunction with NICE, have appointed an independent chair of the guideline development group, who will usually be a respected senior clinician who may or may not have specific topic of expertise. Key qualifications are an understanding of the process of evidence-based medicine, the process of clinical guideline development, and an ability to chair a large multiprofessional group. In turn the chair and the NCCMH then appoint a Guideline Development Group (GDG). These groups typically comprise 10 to 12 individuals drawn from relevant professions such as physicians, nurses, psychologists, social workers, and patient and caregiver organizations. Professionals, however, do not represent their professions. There are typically two patient representatives and one caregiver representative, chosen for their knowledge and experience of the specific topic under consideration, as well as an understanding of evidence-based medicine, guideline development, and ability to function in a multidisciplinary setting. They are supported by a technical team from the NCCMH comprising one of the joint directors, a systematic reviewer, a health economist, the information scientist, a project manager, and a research assistant. All individuals function as full members of the GDG, contributing to evidence identification, synthesis, and interpretation, which in turn leads to development of clinical recommendations. The full method is set out in detail in the NICE Technical Manual (NICE, 2007). The GDG also is provided with specific training in guideline development by the NCCMH, with patients and caregiver representatives in receipt of additional support from a specialist unit within NICE, the Patient and Public Involvement Unit, which supports patient and caregiver members throughout the development process.

The first major task of the GDG is agreeing and/or refining clinical questions. The majority of the questions are questions of efficacy. These questions are answered using a problem, intervention, comparator, outcome approach and often draw on RCTs as the basis for the evidence. NICE and the NCCMH do not rely solely on RCTs for evidence of efficacy; rather, the emphasis is on identifying best available evidence, which might most simply be defined as that which is "fit for purpose." NICE has explicitly moved away from evidence hierarchies (Rawlins, 2008) and lays considerable emphasis on the GDG, exercising its judgment on what kind of evidence is best placed to answer the important clinical questions facing the group. In this way, NICE has developed a different approach from that set out by authorities in the United States (e.g., Chambless & Hollon, 1998). There are a number of reasons for this. Principal among them are the major gaps in the coverage of the research literature, which is a particular concern with certain, particularly uncommon childhood mental health problems (Weisz, Jensen-Doss, & Hawley, 2006). For example, there are few high-quality RCTs of anorexia in children and none of bulimia, yet the annual mortality is 12 times above expected rates for

15- to 24-year-olds. Bulik, Berkman, Brownley, Sedway, and Lohr (2007) reviewed 32 studies of anorexia and reported that 13 were too poor in design, 8 were of medication, 7 of family therapy, 3 of CBT, 1 of Cognitive Analytic Therapy, 1 of psychoanalytic psychotherapy, and 1 of supportive therapy, but mostly for adults. But there are similar gaps in the literature for more common conditions such as substance abuse in youths, particularly concerning the use of harder drugs, and, interestingly, ADHD in adolescence. There are 150 *DSM* diagnoses that can be applied to youths; and it is to be expected that strong evidence bases drawn from large-scale high-quality RCTs will only ever cover a small selection of these. This means that questions such as when anorexia nervosa may require inpatient care will be better answered by well-designed cohort studies, small N experimental designs, or case series. This has to be acknowledged in development of clinical guidelines.

In addition, guideline development groups may use correlational data that is "fit for purpose." One possible example of this concerns the observations of possible impact of macro initiatives undertaken by national and international drug regulatory bodies in relation to pediatric use of SSRIs for depression. Epidemiological investigations have highlighted how reducing access to SSRIs may have served to increase suicidality in both the United States and Europe following the crisis of confidence in drug trials (Gibbons et al., 2007). The NICE guideline on childhood depression (NICE, 2005a) played an important role in raising concerns about risks and benefits of SSRIs based on a careful analysis of published and unpublished data. Analysis of trial data subsequent to the publication of the guideline may not have much changed the guideline recommendation, but a review of observational data referred to earlier may lead to a review of the recommendation. Perhaps there are no obvious desirable steps that could be taken to slow implementation of emerging evidence. Any such steps would probably be both unethical and undesirable; however, this example serves to highlight the problems that may arise where the evidence base is relatively limited and conclusions drawn from it are potentially subject to significant change by the emergence of new data.

Another example is where case series have unequivocally established effectiveness of an intervention, such as the use of acetylcysteine in the treatment of acetaminophen (also called paracetamol in the United Kingdom) overdose (Prescott et al., 1979). The RCTs in mental health often provide relatively little information on possible harms, and cohort studies or data mining studies are potentially better sources for such evidence. The NICE guidelines are also concerned with other types of questions, including: (a) prognostic indicators, in which case cohort studies would usually be the best source of evidence; (b) problems evaluating harm, where data mining studies may be the best source; and (c) patient experience, where evidence from qualitative studies is of real value. For questions concerned with service design a GDG may draw on all of the aforementioned. In addition, NICE recommendations often draw simultaneously on different sources of evidence; for example, for efficacy drawn from RCTs and harm from cohort studies, thus privileging of one kind of evidence over another in a predetermined hierarchy begins to make little sense. Nevertheless, when determining intervention efficacy, NICE continues to draw on the RCTs or meta-analyses of RCTs.

The NICE guidelines are also concerned with matters of cost-effectiveness, recognizing that all health decisions have cost implications and that all health-care systems face cost constraints (Steinbrook, 2008). The preferred NICE approach to health economics is the Quality Adjusted Life Year (QALY), which is widely accepted as the best developed metric for assessing cost-effectiveness (Drummond, Sculpher, Torrance, O'Brien, & Stoddart, 2005). The QALY is an incremental cost-effectiveness ratio that provides information on the relative cost of an additional quality life year achieved by one treatment compared to another treatment. The NICE currently sets an acceptable QALY at between £20,000 (approximately $32,000 in 2009 dollars) to £30,000 (approximately $49,000 in 2009 dollars) with costs beyond that usually seen as not cost-effective. A GDG's ability to make use of such methods in child and adolescent mental health is often limited by absence of supporting data on the utilities for child and adolescent disorders. In addition, recent developments at NICE suggest that for certain end-of-life treatments these thresholds may be varied to reflect the different value that is placed on the quality of life when a person has a terminal illness and only a few months to live. This threshold, which is often more problematic for the NICE Technology Appraisal program than for the clinical guidelines program, has been the subject of considerable controversy (Appleby, Devlin, & Parkin, 2007), but a detailed discussion is beyond the scope of this chapter.

Just as evidence of clinical efficacy alone does not determine clinical recommendations, neither does cost-effectiveness. Both, along with other sources of evidence relevant to the clinical question, are considered alongside contextual evidence such as their potential impact or feasibility in the UK NHS. Examples of how contextual factors may modify recommendations include evidence for the efficacy of individual supported employment schemes in schizophrenia. A number of well-conducted RCTs were identified during the development of the NICE schizophrenia guidelines; however, all trials were conducted in the United States and, although the evidence was strong, the GDG was concerned about the transferability of the model from the United States to the United Kingdom. Consequently, the recommendation was couched in suitably cautious terms. Similar considerations applied to recommendations concerning the literature on multisystemic therapy (MST) for delinquent youths in the recent guidelines for antisocial personality disorder (ASPD) (NICE, 2009). Again, a number of good-quality RCTs of this approach suggested that this was the most effective treatment for delinquent adolescents in reducing recidivism and improving individual and family pathology (Borduin, 1999; Henggeler, Cunningham, Pickrel, Schoenwald, & Brondino, 1996; Henggeler, Melton, & Smith, 1992; Henggeler, Melton, Smith, Schoenwald, & Hanley, 1993). It certainly appeared to be substantially more effective than individual treatment even for quite troubled and disorganized families (Borduin et al., 1995). Multisystemic therapy shares a particular strength with other systemic family approaches in reducing attrition rates in this highly volatile group (Henggeler, Pickrel, Brondino, & Crouch, 1996). Success of this program was noted to be quite striking: At an average 4-year follow-up, recidivism in those who completed MST was significantly reduced (22.1%) relative to recipients of individual therapy (71.4%); however, the NICE systematic review undertaken for development of guidelines for ASPD (NICE, 2009) also highlighted some of the limitations of evidence for transportability outside the U.S. context. One major trial, the Ontario study (Leschied & Cunningham, 2002) showed no treatment effects and, although a Norwegian study (Ogden & Hagen, 2006) showed strong effects, it also presented major transportability issues since children under 15 in Norway are not charged with criminal offenses and antisocial behavior is dealt with by the child welfare system, offering no objective treatment indicators of criminal offending.

In conjunction with NICE, the NCCMH typically produces a number of publications from any guideline development group. These products include: (a) a full guideline produced by the NCC; (b) the NICE guideline, available only in electronic form; (c) the Quick Reference Guide, a digest sent out to the NHS; and (d) a patient guide. In addition to consultation on the scope of questions to be answered,

these publications are also subject to a formal public consultation in which all registered stakeholders plus specialist methodological reviewers comments (NICE, 2007). Guideline developers are required to respond to all comments and have to satisfy NICE that responses are of a sufficient standard. This can lead to significant improvements in guidelines; helpful comments often center on interpretation of evidence and drafting of recommendations.

Another distinctive feature of NICE guidelines is abandonment of a formal grading system of the strength of recommendations. These systems were originally developed in the United States (Agency for Health Care Policy and Research, 1993) and were intended to inform the clinician on the strength of recommendations and therefore the confidence with which the clinician should act. They were supported by a system for grading the strength of the evidence that was based on a hierarchy with large-scale RCTs and meta-analyses at the top and case series at the bottom (Hadorn, Baker, Hodges, & Hicks, 1996). There are a number of significant limitations to this approach: (a) it does not take account of contextual issues such as the transferability of complex interventions between different health-care systems; (b) recommendations are often based on multiple sources of evidence, not all of which can easily fit within the evidence hierarchy; (c) it does not consider the offset between patient choice and treatment risk; for example, the decision to take anticoagulants following a deep venous thrombosis (DVT), where strong evidence of reduced recurrence of a DVT has to be offset against the increased risk of bleeding; (d) important recommendations, such as use of acetylcysteine in acetaminophen overdose, which are not supported by RCTs inevitably receive lower grade recommendations, which can lead to such recommendations being ignored. For example, in the United Kingdom one leading professional body would typically only evaluate or endorse to their members recommendations that were graded at level A or B.

The NICE has arrived at a twofold solution to these problems: First, exploration of the adoption of the Grading of Recommendations Assessment, Development and Evaluation (GRADE) system (Guyatt et al., 2008) for assessment of evidence, and second, a move away from any grading of recommendations. The GRADE system aims to improve both the rating of the quality of the evidence and strength of recommendations by first introducing some rigorous and explicit criteria for rating of evidence, including any study design limitations, the inconsistency of results, the indirectness of evidence, the imprecision of results, and any evidence of reporting bias. The advantage of such a system is that it helps to make both explicit and transparent the move from evidence to recommendations. Also, the GRADE system separates the assessment of evidence from the grading of recommendations and allows for factors such as the quality of the evidence, uncertainty about the balance of positive and negative consequences of treatment, patient values and preferences, and uncertainty about effective resource use. The GRADE, then, proposes that recommendations be classified as "strong" or "weak"; "conditional" or "discretionary" are also offered as alternative terms. While the NCCMH and NICE have explored the adoption of the GRADE system for assessing evidence, they have so far not adopted the strong/weak approach to grading recommendations. Currently, the NCCMH prefers to deal with this issue in the wording of the recommendations, reflecting the strength of the recommendation in the language used. For example, a strong recommendation could be worded as: "Teachers who have received training about ADHD and its management should provide behavioural interventions in the classroom to help children and young people with ADHD" (NICE, 2008, p. 27). A recommendation where there is less certainty might be worded as follows: "Therapies to be considered for the psychological treatment of anorexia nervosa include cognitive analytic therapy, cognitive behavior therapy (CBT), interpersonal psychotherapy, focal psychodynamic therapy and family interventions focused explicitly on eating disorders" (NICE, 2009, p. 11).

There is also considerable interest from the NCCMH in writing recommendations that reflect as far as possible the decisions clinicians and patients have to make in everyday practice. This inevitably leads to more complex recommendations where clinicians are asked to consider a range of options depending on a range of patient factors. This can be seen in the two sequential recommendations taken from the guideline for depression in children and young people.

> If moderate to severe depression in a child or young person is unresponsive to combined treatment with a specific psychological therapy and fluoxetine after a further six sessions, or the patient and/or their parent(s) or carer(s) have declined the offer of fluoxetine, the multidisciplinary team should make a full needs and risk assessment. This should include a review of the diagnosis, examination of the possibility of comorbid diagnoses, reassessment of the possible individual, family and social causes of depression, consideration of whether there has been a fair trial of treatment, and assessment for further psychological therapy for the patient and/or additional help for the family.

This is succeeded by:

> Following multidisciplinary review, the following should be considered: an alternative psychological therapy which has not been tried previously (individual CBT, interpersonal therapy or shorter-term family therapy, of at least 3 months' duration), or systemic family therapy (at least 15 fortnightly sessions), or individual child psychotherapy (approximately 30 weekly sessions)" (NICE, 2005a, p. 28)

A particular methodological challenge facing NICE is that of updating guidelines.

Currently, NICE reviews all guidelines 2 years after publication to see if significant new evidence has emerged that would require some form of update and commits to an update at 4 years. To date this has not yet arisen for guidelines produced by the NCCMH. Experience from the updates of the schizophrenia and depression guidelines suggests that this process can be as time consuming as their original production. This in part reflects methodological advances in the development of guidelines and to a lesser extent available new evidence, but the most significant challenge comes from disentangling the interrelated nature of many recommendations in the guideline. One solution to this problem is to distinguish: (a) what to do for recommendations, for example, which type of treatment; (b) how to do recommendations, for example, what duration/intensity of treatment); and (c) where to do recommendations, for example, what place in a stepped care system should the treatment occupy. The adoption of such a system could make the process of updating somewhat more efficient.

THE NICE MENTAL HEALTH GUIDELINES

The NICE mental health clinical guideline program has so far produced 16 guidelines, with a further four in production and two currently being updated. A full list of the published guidelines is set out in Table 4.1. To date, only one has focused exclusively on children (NICE, 2005a), although the ADHD guideline (NICE, 2008) is focused primarily on children with a small section on treatment and management of adults with ADHD. Five guidelines cover both adults and children and nine are concerned solely with adult disorders. These choices reflect the remit that that the NCCMH received from the Department of Health. In some cases, it could be argued that combining guidelines for adults and children makes good sense; for example, with eating

TABLE 4.1   NICE Guidance in Child and Adolescent Mental Health

Guidance	Date Published
Clinical Guidelines	
Eating disorders[1]	January 2004
Posttraumatic stress disorder[1]	March 2005
Depression in children[2]	September 2005
Obsessive-compulsive disorder[1]	November 2005
Bipolar disorder[1]	July 2006
Attention-deficit/hyperactivity disorder[1]	February 2008
Personality disorder–antisocial[1]	January 2009
Public Health Guidance	
Interventions to reduce substance misuse among vulnerable young people[3]	March 2007
School-based interventions on alcohol[2]	November 2007
Social and emotional well-being in primary education[2]	March 2008
Technology Appraisals	
Attention-deficit/hyperactivity disorder—methylphenidate, atomoxetine, and dexamfetamine[2]	March 2006
Conduct disorder in children—parent-training/education programs (NICE, 2006)[2]	July 2006

[1] Adults and children
[2] Children only
[3] Age range up to 25 years

disorders, where a peak age of onset in the midteens makes the traditional adult/child distinction unhelpful, or in ASPD, where evidence for prevention through intervention in childhood and adolescence is a good deal more compelling than for interventions with adults. For a number of disorders combined guidelines make less sense for several reasons. In many instances the therapeutic approach recommended is substantially different. The most obvious case is childhood depression where the treatment that is a first-line option in the case of adult depression (SSRIs) is currently only cautiously recommended for young people (NICE, 2005a). In some instances likening child and adult recommendations within a single guideline may have the unintended consequence of confirming a diagnosis as being developmentally homologous. This is certainly the case with bipolar disorder, where the diagnosis—in the UK at least—is highly controversial in childhood and where symptoms that evidence the diagnosis are different from those that suggest the adult condition (Carlson & Meyerson, 2006). In other disorders the context of treatment delivery, even with the same disorder, may be so different that it may be hard to bring together a GDG with all relevant expertise. For example, PTSD in children often occurs in a complex family situation that requires addressing alongside if not ahead of the child's anxiety symptoms (King et al., 2003), and this might require knowledge and expertise in the GDG beyond the treatment of PTSD alone. In many childhood and adolescent disorders, services need to be provided in very different settings, and comorbidity of disorders common in childhood and adolescence require a broader approach to care than one focused on a specific disorder.

In addition to clinical guidelines on child and adolescent mental health produced by the NCCMH, the Centre for Public Health Excellence at NICE has produced three guidelines directly relevant to childhood mental health. These are again detailed in Table 4.1 and have a stronger emphasis on the prevention rather than the treatment of the disorder. Finally, there are two technology appraisals for children on drug treatments for ADHD, which was incorporated into the NICE guideline on ADHD (2008) and parent training (NICE, 2006) for conduct disorder.

The remainder of this chapter will focus largely on childhood disorders and will address three key issues in relation to NICE mental health guidelines. First, it will set out some of the key recommendations, particularly in relation to psychological therapies. Second, it will address some of the commonly made criticisms. Third, it will highlight some of the challenges and successes of the implementation program.

KEY ASPECTS OF NICE RECOMMENDATIONS

The number of recommendations in a NICE guideline can vary considerably, and rarely falls below 50 but can exceed 100. Thus, clinicians and service mangers face a challenge in deciding what to implement. NICE assists in this process by identifying key recommendations for implementation—usually between five and eight per guideline. The means by which these are chosen in the NCCMH essentially comes down to two key criteria: (1) the likelihood that implementation will significantly reduce variation in practice across the NHS, and that (2) implementation will have a significant impact on clinical outcome. A major consequence of the application of these two criteria has been to see a significant number of psychological interventions feature in key recommendations for implementation. Table 4.2 gives examples of some of these recommendations. Table 4.2 is not exhaustive but the emphasis on psychological interventions that can be seen in Table 4.2 had a significant impact on the NHS, where historically the availability of psychological therapies, particularly outside metropolitan areas, had been relatively limited (Lovell & Richards, 2000; Perera, Gupta, Samuel, & Berg, 2007).

In addition to providing a higher profile for evidence-based psychological therapies, NICE guidelines for both children and adolescents and for adults promoted a stepped care model for their delivery. This model, which originally developed in the field of addiction (Davidson, 2000), was also broadly in line with the tiered approach to the delivery of mental health care for children and adolescents that had developed in the United Kingdom (Department of Health, 2004; NHS Health Advisory Service, 2005; www.childrensmapping.co.uk; www.everychildmatters.gov.uk/health/camhs). Within child and adolescent mental health, stepped care does not translate to increased worker experience or skill with each step in line

TABLE 4.2   Some Examples of NICE Child and Adolescent Mental Health Guidance That Have Recommended Psychological Treatments

Guidance	Treatment
Eating disorders[1]	Family and psychological interventions for anorexia nervosa Cognitive behavior therapy for bulimia nervosa and binge eating disorders
PTSD[1]	Trauma-focused cognitive behavior therapy
Depression[1]	Individual cognitive behavior therapy, interpersonal therapy, or shorter-term family therapy
OCD[1]	Individual or group-based cognitive behavior therapy (including exposure and response prevention) with family involvement
ADHD[1]	Parent training program, on its own or with a group treatment program (cognitive behavior therapy and/or social skills training) for ADHD with moderate levels of impairment
ASPD[1,2]	Parent training programs, functional family therapy, cognitive problem-solving skills training, and multisystemic therapy
Substance misuse[1,3]	Family support programs and group-based behavioral programs

[1] Clinical guideline
[2] Includes interventions for conduct disorder to prevent development of ASPD
[3] Public health guidance

with complexity of presenting problems, as in the adult sphere, but rather to the context or complexity of the service in which the intervention is delivered.

An example of a stepped care model for children and adolescents, in which psychological and other interventions are integrated, can be seen in Figure 4.1, which is taken from the NICE depression in children and young people guideline (NICE, 2005a). The increased emphasis on psychological interventions in the guidelines also shifted treatment focus away from medications such as SSRIs. For example, NICE (2005a) had an explicit recommendation that cautioned against the routine use of antidepressants in mild depression:

"Antidepressant medication should not be used for the initial treatment of children and young people with mild depression" (NICE, 2005a, p. 25). In the NICE (2005b) guideline on the treatment of PTSD, caution about the use of medication extended beyond the use of antidepressants: "Drug treatments should not be routinely prescribed for children and young people with PTSD" (NICE, 2005b, p. 23).

Across the wider NHS recommendations were generally welcomed, but there were a number of criticisms. Family doctors were very concerned about an increased demand for psychological interventions, since in the United Kingdom 90% of common mental disorders are treated in primary care (Lovell & Richards, 2000). Hodes and Garralda (2007) echoed this, suggesting that offering support or screening in a primary care setting for adolescents experiencing disruptive life events might be impractical. In addition, there was an increasing concern on the part of some psychopharmacologists that the importance of psychological interventions had been overplayed (Nutt & Sharpe, 2008). The first of these criticisms has real substance and it was not until the development of the Improving Access to Psychological Treatments program (IAPT) program that it could be properly addressed, at least for adults. The IAPT program is described in some detail here, in part because of its importance in implementation of NICE guidelines, but also because current discussions are under way for a parallel program to be rolled out for children and adolescent services (Layard, 2008; Layard & Dunn, 2009). The second criticism is unfortunate. Although the discussion has spilled out into the academic and professional press (Nutt, 2008; Nutt & Sharpe, 2008; Pilling, 2008a), it might be best seen as a simple misrepresentation of the NICE guidelines, where medication and its use in combination with psychological intervention is given a prominent position. (See, for example, the NICE guideline on ADHD, [NICE, 2008]). Some of the most strident criticism of the

Focus	Action	Responsibility
Detection	Risk profiling	Tier 1
Recognition	Identification in presenting children or young people	Tiers 2–4
Mild depression (including dysthymia)	Watchful waiting	Tier 1
	Nondirective supportive therapy/group cognitive behavioral therapy/guided self-help	Tier 1 or 2
Moderate to severe depression	Brief psychological therapy +/− fluoxetine	Tier 2 or 3
Depression unresponsive to treatment/ recurrent depression/psychotic depression	Intensive psychological therapy +/− fluoxetine, sertraline, citalopram, augmentation with an antipsychotic	Tier 3 or 4

Figure 4.1   The Stepped-Care Model for the Depression in Children and Young People

Note: The guidance follows these five steps: (1) detection and recognition of depression and risk profiling in primary care and community settings; (2) recognition of depression in children and young people referred to Child and Adolescent Mental Health Services (CAMHS, 2007); (3) managing recognized depression in primary care and community settings— mild depression; (4) managing recognized depression in tier 2 or 3 CAMHS—moderate to severe depression; and (5) managing recognized depression in tier 3 or 4 CAMHS—unresponsive, recurrent, and psychotic depression, including depression needing inpatient care.

Source: Guideline (NICE, 2005a)

NICE program is that it has significant methodological limitations and as a result has overemphasized certain psychological interventions, especially CBT, at the expense of others. This response can be seen as a reawakening of the "Dodo bird hypothesis" (Beutler, 2002; Luborsky, Singer, & Luborsky, 1975; Wampold et al., 1997). This criticism is dealt with in some more detail later, as it comes most prominently from other psychologists.

Limitations of Clinical Guidelines

One of the most common criticisms of clinical guidelines is that they draw their evidence base from populations that are unrepresentative of those encountered in routine clinical practice. This criticism will be considered in the following text. Before addressing this criticism, it should be pointed out that the expectation is that NICE guidelines apply to about 80% to 85% of the patients with the disorder (Eddy, 1990); that is, about 15% to 20% of patients seen in routine practice may be outside the recommendations of the guideline. If this is the case then recommendations may require some adaptation if they are to be of value in helping determine a treatment plan for a particular patient. (It should be noted that, along

with similar procedural advice developed in guideline production it draws largely on an adult framework, and given the comorbidity and more limited evidence base in children and adolescent populations we might expect this number to be nearer 70%.) Further criticism has focused on outcomes definition, for example, symptoms rather than quality of life. Although there has been considerable criticism of the lack of recognition of common factors in driving therapeutic change (see discussion of the "Dodo bird hypothesis"), surprisingly little mention has been made of therapist competence, which is also a very significant factor in determining treatment outcome (Brown, Lambert, Jones, & Minami, 2005). These problems and a response to them have been discussed by Pilling (2008b) and Pilling and Price (2006); they are briefly summarized further on.

Patient Population

RCTs, particularly efficacy studies that constitute the vast majority of psychological RCTs, require high internal validity and therefore may include precisely specified populations. Many now consider that some childhood diagnostic clinical entities such as major depressive disorder are in many respects unsatisfactory. Major depressive disorder probably represents a heterogeneous group of disorders that are likely to respond differentially to specific treatments. The NICE guidelines have tended to underscore the problem of variable responses to the treatment by different individuals (NICE, 2005a, 2008); nevertheless, objections are most frequently made about the diagnosis issue. The heterogeneity of diagnostic groups in trials can undoubtedly lead to frequent partial replication of findings, moderate effect sizes, and an unusually large range of treatments that have been tried to address childhood disorders (Roth & Fonagy, 2005). The heterogeneity of conditions like major depressive disorder are also underscored by etiologic studies, which, for example, show that life events are likely to be associated with depression as an outcome only in those who have one particular polymorphism of a serotonin receptor gene (Caspi et al., 2003).

For its logic the RCT depends on addressing restriction to a well-defined clinical group. The high level of comorbidity associated with depression is thought by many to jeopardize the claim of clinical homogeneity (Kessler et al., 2003). RCTs must be internally valid (i.e., design and conduct must keep to a minimum the possibility of bias) and to be clinically useful the result must also be relevant to a definable group of patients with limited comorbidity in a particular clinical setting. This may lead to trial participants unlike those encountered in routine practice. The proportion of patients with a particular disorder in the local community served by a participating center who are considered for recruitment into a trial will often be well below 1% (Weisz et al., 2006).

For example, in child and adolescent mental health disorders comorbidity of disorders is common, with over approximately 50% of people with a depressive disorder also having significant comorbid anxiety (Goldberg et al., 2005) and approximately 40% of people with PTSD are also diagnosed with a depressive

disorder (NICE, 2004). The criteria for exclusion often also work to exclude patients with family adversity who are more severely disturbed, likely to miss appointments, drop out of treatment, have families characterized by parental psychopathology, family life event stressors, and child maltreatment. This means that exclusion rates in child RCTs can be high. This difference between trial and routine care populations is often cited as a reason by clinicians for the lack of uptake of evidence-based medicine (Sackett, Rosenberg, Gray, & Haynes, 1996); however, there are a number of reasons why differences in patient populations may not limit extrapolation to the extent that is often assumed. First, it must be remembered that the comparisons are relative since both experimental and comparator groups are from the same population with or without associated comorbidities. In addition, comorbidities do not necessarily prevent patients from benefiting from particular interventions. For example, young people with comorbid ADHD and conduct disorder can benefit from essentially the same psychological interventions—parent training (NICE, 2008)—even if it may require some extension and augmentation of the intervention, such as the addition of cognitive problem-solving skills training (Kazdin, Siegel, & Bass, 1992; NICE, 2008).

A number of examples from the adult literature suggest that exclusion from trials does not imply an exaggeration of treatment effects. Franklin, Abramowitz, Kozak, Levitt, and Foa (2000), in a study of obsessive-compulsive disorder, demonstrated that those patients who had been excluded from RCTs because of comorbidities and related problems, benefited as much, if not more, than those in the original trials. Gillespie, Duffy, Hackmann, and Clark (2002) reported a study of adults with PTSD following the Omagh bombing in Northern Ireland, which demonstrated that the provision of the same treatment as delivered in clinical trials produced comparable results in non-selected populations. A similar study of child and adolescent survivors of the 2004 Bam earthquake in Iran (Shooshtary, Panaghi, & Moghadam, 2008) again showed positive results in an unselected sample in line with those from RCTs.

Outcomes Used and Duration Follow-Up

Current reporting of outcomes in RCTs presents several problems for guideline developers. One major concern is reliance on symptomatic measures as primary outcome measures; often with little follow-up beyond the end of treatment. Related to this point is the claim that the lack of evidence of functional recovery following most treatments for mental disorder in childhood and wide use of surrogate measures of therapeutic outcome means that outcome is assessed on an arbitrary metric (De Los Reyes & Kazdin, 2005, 2006). Given the broad impact on social, interpersonal, and educational functioning of many chronic mental disorders on children and adolescents, there is a strong argument that measures of these areas of functioning should be given much more prominence as primary outcomes, but this is not often the case (Pilling & Price, 2006). For example, a survey (Chitsabesan et al., 2006) demonstrated that between a third and a half of a representative young offenders sample had health, educational, or work and social relationship needs that were commonly not recognized by agencies. A quarter of the sample had intellectual disabilities (mental retardation) and presented with major educational difficulties. The existence of this significant subgroup with mild intellectual disabilities highlights the importance of tailoring treatment programs to the subject's level of development and cognitive ability. These considerations imply that a narrow focus on forensic outcome may not be adequate to the evaluation of benefit from interventions for this population, particularly from complex multifaceted approaches such as MST. Complex cases, which MST was designed to address, may be referred from a range of service settings, but require a similar intensive

family-preserving intervention. The absence of long-term follow-up can also lead to an overestimation of treatment effects. For example, the meta-analysis by Westen and Morrison (2001) reviewed short- and long-term outcomes of psychological treatments for panic disorder, generalized anxiety disorder, and depression. They found that while good results were obtained in both the short- and long-term for panic disorder, this was often not the case for depression or generalized anxiety disorder.

Comparators Used in Trials

Assessing the efficacy of any intervention depends crucially on an understanding of the comparator condition. In some cases this can be straightforward, such as where the comparator is an alternative drug; however, in many trials the comparators are often inadequately described. Terms such as *treatment as usual* or *usual care* are often assumed to be equivalent, but such assumptions may mean that important differences are missed with a consequent misinterpretation of results. For example, in the Elkin et al. (1989) NIMH trial of psychological and pharmacological interventions for depression, the antidepressant arm consisted of both antidepressants and *clinical management*, which consisted initially of weekly sessions with a psychiatrist lasting 20 minutes and the availability of 7-day-a-week, 24-hour-a-day crisis interventions. Such an intervention is very different from that routinely provided in either the United States or the United Kingdom and it is possible that regular psychiatrist contact and access to crisis services would have a therapeutic benefit over and above that of antidepressants. Problems can also arise when the comparator is usual care in the evaluation of a complex intervention. For example, Henggeler, Schoenwald, Rowland, and Cunningham (2002) suggested that there was real benefit in a number of trials of MST for the intervention, but the majority of the trials have been in the United

States. When trials of MST are conducted outside of the United States—for example, in Canada (Littell, Popa, & Forsythe, 2005)—then results appears less certain, raising the question as to whether the lack of benefit identified in the Canadian study may have arisen from the general higher quality of the usual care services.

Therapist Competence

This issue is often not referred to in discussion of the interpretation of clinical trials, but recent research suggests that it may be one of the most significant factors in accounting for variance in outcome. It is well illustrated by a series of studies from Lambert's group in the United States, who analyzed outcome data on large cohorts of individuals in psychological treatment and, importantly, also on a large number of therapists. For example, Brown et al. (2005) in a study of over 10,000 patients and 281 therapists, demonstrated that the most effective 25% therapists had overall 53% greater improvement, which could not be explained by diagnosis, age, sex, severity, prior treatment history, length of treatment, or therapist training and experience. In a similar study, of over 7,500 patients and 149 therapists, Okiishi, Lambert, Eggert, Nilesen, and Dayton (2006) showed that the most effective 25% of therapists had over 100% better recovery rates (22.40% vs. 10.61%), and perhaps more worryingly over 100% less deterioration (5.20% vs. 10.56%) than the least effective 25% of therapists. This has led to an increasing focus on therapist competence (Roth & Pilling, 2008), an issue that has yet to be properly addressed in clinical guidelines. As evidence of what constitutes competent practice becomes clearer, the evidence base on which guideline developers can draw will be expanded. Roth and Pilling (2009) examined the relationship of certain therapist competences and behaviors to outcomes, drawing largely on the psychotherapy process–outcome literature. Although data in this area are

limited, a number of relevant findings have emerged. For example, a focus on the concrete aspects of CBT for depression, such as agenda setting, homework, or a focus on negative thoughts (McGlinchey & Dobson, 2003), may be associated with improved efficacy. This research begins to point to the kind of recommendations that might bridge the gap between what should be done and how it might be done in clinical guidelines, an important distinction when the skill of the therapist is a key determinant in the outcome of an intervention.

Differences Between Therapeutic Modalities

Clinical guidelines have also been criticized for promoting certain treatments at the expense of others. One oft repeated phrase is "the absence of evidence does not mean the absence of effect"; however, it is not possible in a guideline development program to recommend treatments for which no evidence can be found, when good evidence for other interventions exists. A more substantial objection is that the supposed differences between treatments simply do not exist (Wampold et al, 1997). This objection, referred to as the "Dodo Bird" Hypothesis (Luborksy et al., 1975), holds that there are really no important differences between psychotherapies and that variables, such as common therapeutic factors or therapist competence, account for far more of the variance than do differences in treatment model. A number of authors have responded critically to this assertion (Beutler, 2002). A review by Benish, Imel, and Wampold (2008) has extended this work and focused on the comparison of bona fide treatments. Bona fide treatments are treatments delivered by a competent therapist; delivered face to face, individualized; and containing psychologically valid components (Wampold et al., 1997). Benish et al. (2008) argued that all bona fide treatments for PTSD were equally effective, including not only eye movement desensitization retraining and trauma-focused CBT (NICE, 2005b), but also hypnotherapy and psychodynamic therapy, which they claimed were as effective as eye movement desensitization retraining and trauma-focused CBT. This contrasts with Bisson et al.'s (2007) review, which formed the basis of the recommendations for the NICE PTSD guidelines (NICE, 2005b) and that reported clinically significant differences between a number of different treatments, including between different forms of CBT for PTSD. They concluded that trauma-focused CBT was clinically and statistically significantly more effective that nontrauma-focused CBT. A review of the two papers reveals that they had different aims: Benish et al. sought to demonstrate the equal effectiveness of bona fide treatments and Bisson et al. sought to support recommendations for a clinical guideline. Of course, a finding of no difference between treatments does not mean they are equivalent. The trials performed on Benish et al.'s analyses were efficacy trials and not equivalence trials. As such, they were neither designed nor powered to establish equivalence; see Piaggio, Elbourne, Altman, Pocock, and Evans (2006) for a fuller discussion of these issues. Consequently, Benish et al. were concerned with the relative effectiveness of treatments, a task in which they are hampered by the small number of studies, resulting in a number of their comparisons being based on just two studies. Bisson et al. were concerned, not just with effectiveness, but also with the robustness of the findings. For example, they investigated whether the intervention had been tested in a number of different studies, by different investigators in different settings, and if the outcome is of clinical significance. In addition, clinical guidelines are also concerned with cost-effectiveness and this can lead to recommendations based on differences in cost-effectiveness where no differences in clinical effectiveness are identified (see Simon, Pilling, Burbeck, & Goldberg, 2006).

WHAT IMPACT HAS NICE HAD ON MENTAL HEALTH PRACTICE?

The impact of NICE guidelines on mental health practice has been considerable. This will be illustrated with a number of examples, which, while primarily focused on psychological interventions, show the range of methods that have been used across the NHS to support guideline implementation. Three examples from national programs have been chosen: (1) the IAPT program of the Department of Health, (2) the Child and Adolescent Mental Health Services (CAMHS) Evidence-Based Practice Unit, and (3) the role of the Health Care Commission (HCC) in the audit of NICE Schizophrenia Guidelines. Of these, the first has a focus on adult and child mental health, the second is exclusively concerned with children, and the third is an example of a national audit of adult services but that has straightforward parallels with work with children and adolescents.

Before reviewing each of these areas, general evidence for clinical guideline implementation will be briefly reviewed, which is an area that has undergone considerable evaluation (Grimshaw et al., 2004; Grol & Jones, 2000). Perhaps the most important message to emerge from this literature is that the majority of interventions to support implementation have only small to moderate effect sizes. Grimshaw et al. (2004), in a comprehensive review of 235 guideline implementation studies, identified improvements in the desired direction in 86% of studies, but effects on improvements in care were modest, falling broadly within the range of 6% to 14% improvement in experimental versus comparator groups, although a small number of projects have reported larger effects between 30% to 60% improvement in care (Grol & Jones, 2000). Reminders to clinicians were consistently observed to be most effective with more limited effects reported for educational outreach, and variable but sometimes important effects for dissemination of educational materials. Multifaceted approaches, such as those associated with the chronic care model (Von Korff & Goldberg, 2001), were not necessarily more effective than single interventions. Audit and feedback, and use of opinion leaders, were usually less successful in bringing about positive change. One discouraging aspect of implementation research on clinical guidelines is that the overall improvement is often much the same for poorly performing clinicians as clinicians who performed well, with the result that guideline implementation programs may do little to reduce variation in practice.

Grol and Grimshaw (2003) reviewed a number of organizational interventions designed to improve patient care, including leadership, process redesign, organizational culture, and organizational learning interventions. They concluded that there was no consistent evidence that supported the use of any one intervention over any other, but that all potentially could bring about positive benefits in patient care; however, they raised questions about sustainability of benefit if interventions were not maintained. The guideline implementation literature indicated that organizational interventions, such as clinician-specific reminders or educational interventions, may be effective, as might the development of leadership programs and new professional roles and multidisciplinary teams; however, uncertainty about the sustainability, long-term benefits, and cost effectiveness of the interventions remained. Multifaceted approaches and use of quality management programs look less promising and this may arise from a lack of specificity or targeting of the change interventions in these programs, or the failure to develop effective quality management technology so far.

A number of authors, including Wensing, Wollersheim, and Grol (2006), have argued that the lack of an agreed taxonomy for organizational interventions, including implementation of guidelines, presents significant problems in both developing and evaluating them. Development of such a taxonomy requires not only effective descriptions of interventions, but also ways of characterizing the environment in which the interventions are set. The importance of this can be seen in a UK-based evaluation of the implementation of NICE clinical guidance—the Technology Appraisal program (Sheldon et al., 2004). They reported variable uptake of a range of health technologies, primary pharmaceuticals and some surgical procedures, with the guidance more often being followed for pharmaceuticals, in particular drugs for cancer and obesity, but with a lower uptake for a range of surgical procedures. Organizational factors associated with successful implementation included strong professional support, effective professional management structures, and good financial and clinical monitoring systems.

The lack of a taxonomy for characterizing change in organizational behavior referred to by Wensing and colleagues (2006) is also mirrored in the lack of a taxonomy for changing health professionals' behavior, despite the fact that many service improvement strategies focus on this area. Michie et al. (2005) argued that this lack of a typology of health professionals' behavior has significantly held back the development of effective strategies to support implementation. They have developed a typology of health behaviors based on a systematic review of psychological theories of behavior change, which, they argued, should form the basis of a typology of future studies to change behavior. These behaviors included knowledge, skills, social/professional role and identity, beliefs about capabilities, beliefs about consequences, motivation and goals, memory, attention and decision processes, environmental context and resources, social influences, emotion regulation, behavioral regulation, and the nature of the behavior. This approach has been used in a number of pilot studies, including work on the style in which clinical guidelines are written (Michie & Johnston, 2004; Michie & Lester, 2005) and also on clinicians' attitudes and intentions regarding implementation of specific guidance (Michie et al., 2007). In their 2007 study, Michie et al. used the framework to examine the implementation of specific recommendations in the NICE schizophrenia guideline (NICE, 2002). The study demonstrated that the model can not only serve as a framework for developing an intervention but can also lead to a more precise directing of resources onto the skill or support needs identified by staff who are required to implement the intervention.

Understanding what constitute effective elements of a complex organizational intervention is not only handicapped by lack of appropriate typologies at the individual or organizational level, but also by absence of an overarching theoretical framework in which to integrate them. Ferlie and Shortell (2001) provided a multilevel framework in which it may be possible to begin to integrate the different levels of approach. They specified four levels: the individual health professional, the health-care team, the organization providing health care, and the larger health-care system, such as the NHS. They argued that change at any one level may require change at another level or, at a minimum, awareness of the change; therefore, adoption of the framework can guide selection of appropriate interventions at each level. Such a framework may indeed prove helpful, but to date few studies have focused on these wider organizational issues, preferring to focus on individual health professional behavior (Grimshaw et al., 2004).

The Improving Access to Psychological Therapies Program

The IAPT program, launched by the Department of Health in 2007, is the single largest psychological therapies implementation program in the world. Currently, the program is focused on adults but it is described here because it is a major example of the impact of NICE guidance on adults and also because proposals are under development for a parallel program to be rolled out for children and adolescent services (Layard, 2008; Layard & Dunn, 2009). This child and adolescent program can be expected to follow much the same approach, with a strong emphasis on training and implementation of evidence-based interventions identified in relevant NICE guidelines. The IAPT program aims, over the course of 6 years, to train an additional 7,200 psychological therapists in addition to those already completing clinical and counseling psychology training programs, who will treat an additional 1,800,000 patients at a cost of £346 million (approximately $560 million in 2009 dollars). The program owes much to the work of Richard Layard, a noted labor economist, who with support from David Clark, a leading psychological treatment developer and evaluator, set out a series of arguments (Centre for Economic Performance, 2006) which made a powerful case for a significant expansion of psychological therapies. A central tenet of their argument was that the NICE guidelines for depression and anxiety disorders had made a strong, evidence-based case for increased psychological treatment, but lack of resources meant that this was being denied to people with consequent significant health and social care costs. This argument was accepted and, after the evaluation of two successful pilots in Doncaster and Newham (Clark, Layard, & Smithies, 2008), the UK government launched the program in 2007. Full details of the IAPT program can be found on www.iapt.nhs.uk. The program is delivered at a local level with specialist treatment centers being developed for populations of around 250,000. These services provide NICE-supported treatments within a stepped care framework with so-called low-intensity interventions, such as guided self-help, computerized cognitive behavior therapy, and psychoeducational groups, provided by a group of specifically trained and recruited paraprofessional staff and high-intensity interventions, such as formal psychological therapies—predominantly CBT but also including interpersonal therapy, eye movement desensitization retraining, and couples therapy—provided by trained psychological therapists at master's and doctoral levels. In addition to the new resources made available, a significant number of the psychological therapy staff are provided by existing local services. Typically, a service comprises about 40% low-intensity and 60% high-intensity staff. Working within the stepped care framework, about 60% of the patients are treated by low-intensity staff and about 40% by high-intensity staff. The stepped care framework operates such that the majority of patients are first seen by the low-intensity worker; patients may then be treated or referred on for high-intensity treatment. This initial assessment process is closely monitored and supervised and referral is determined by a number of factors including the nature of the disorder. For example, there are currently no evidence-based low-intensity interventions for PTSD. Failure to respond to a brief intervention will result in referral to high-intensity intervention. Current practice suggests that about 20% of patients may be stepped up and about 20% to 30% are referred directly for high-intensity interventions, but a clearer picture will emerge as the IAPT system becomes established. National guidance on the appropriate treatments for specific disorders has been issued by the IAPT program and can be found on the IAPT Web site (www.iapt.nhs.uk). It is expected that this will be reflected in local protocols.

For both high- and low-intensity staff, there are also specifically designed training courses conducted at a regional level and typically covering five to eight treatment centers with around 50 trainees on any one course. The courses are both of 1-year duration with 1 day at the training institution for the low-intensity staff and 2 days for the high-intensity staff. There is also a strong emphasis on careful supervision in the workplace. There are nationally agreed curricula specifically developed for the IAPT program based on a competency framework for CBT developed specifically for the IAPT program (Roth & Pilling, 2008). A competency

framework for the delivery of psychological interventions in child and adolescent mental health services is under development. See again www.iapt.nhs.uk and www.ucl.ac.uk/CORE for further details.

The IAPT program has a number of other features that are not typical of what is currently provided in the NHS. These include the use of session-by-session outcome monitoring. The pilot sites demonstrated a very high completion rate of sessional monitoring through the use of specially designed software. The IAPT also includes the possibility of self-referral; most referrals in the NHS to psychological treatment services are made by family doctors. This is important, as evidence from the pilot sites showed that self-referrals had similar levels of morbidity to professional referrals, but a higher proportion of people from minority ethic groups. The outcome monitoring is essential as the aim of the programs is to obtain outcomes for patients, equivalent to those in the NICE guidelines; that is, those typically obtained in well-conducted clinical trials.

The program is now well under way. The first 34 centers have opened and over 750 staff are in training. The program is under close scrutiny but the early indications are that it has been well received. Other countries are developing similar models with Scotland rolling out a similar training model and a pilot of low-intensity interventions being developed across the province of British Columbia in Canada.

THE CHILD AND ADOLESCENT MENTAL HEALTH SERVICES EVIDENCE-BASED PRACTICE UNIT

The CAHMS Evidence-Based Practice Unit was established in 2006 with the explicit aim of developing and disseminating information about the latest research and guidance about child and adolescent mental health. In addition, the unit actively promotes outcomes-based practice through use of routine outcome measurement and provides educational programs for clinical leaders in the field of child mental health. The unit is closely linked to the Children and Adolescent Mental Health Outcomes Research Consortium (CORC; www.corc.uk .net), a membership-based organization with a broad membership across the United Kingdom. The CORC provides advice on the use of outcome measures, support in developing reports, and benchmarking data. This means that the EPBU is well placed to support the dissemination and implementation of clinical guidance and, through its link with CORC, to monitor their impact.

The Evidence-Based Practice Unit has produced two publications in recent years that have supported the implementation of NICE guidance: first, a compendium of all key recommendations from NICE guidance (Wolpert et al., 2006) and second, a companion document designed for young people and their families (CAMHS Evidence-Based Practice Unit, 2007). Wolpert et al. (2006) provided fairly comprehensive coverage of child and adolescent mental disorders, which in a number of disorders goes beyond those covered in NICE guidance. Where this is the case evidence is drawn from other authoritative sources (Fonagy, Target, Cottrell, Phillips, & Kurtz, 2005). Both publications have proved extremely popular and have been widely used throughout the United Kingdom with over 10,000 copies of Wolpert et al. (2006) and 23,000 copies of "Choosing What's Best For You" having been sold.

HEALTH CARE COMMISSION AUDIT OF NICE SCHIZOPHRENIA GUIDELINES

Both examples described so far have been nationally led initiatives that have had considerable resources devoted to them. An alternative approach that has supported the implementation of NICE guidance has been via the use of national audit programs. The HCC (www.healthcarecommission.org.uk) is the body in the NHS in England charged with monitoring service standards. Among its activities are a series of thematic service reviews. So far it has conducted two reviews of community mental health services. Community mental health services are specialist mental health services for those with severe mental illness. In both of these reviews, the HCC adopted audit criteria from NICE schizophrenia guidelines and focused specially on provision of psychological interventions and use of atypical antipsychotic medication. In the second review in 2007–2008, focus was explicitly on NICE schizophrenia guidelines. The consequence of this was to force providers of services to place greater emphasis on provision of psychological interventions for schizophrenia, as future funding of any healthcare provider will be significantly influenced by their HCC evaluation. It is increasingly likely that this form of audit will play a key part in supporting implementation of NICE guidelines. The HCC role has recently been redefined and a new body, the National Audit Governance Group, with increased resources for audit, has been established (www.nagg .nhs.uk).

The examples given previously all draw on national implementation programs and it is one of the benefits of a national system of health care that this is possible; however, much of the implementation of NICE guidance happens at a local level and all health-care providers now have systems in place to support local implementation. They are helped in this task by a clear requirement from national government and local commissioners to see NICE guidance implemented. There is also an increasing focus within NICE on influencing commissioning decisions. For example, NICE has recently produced guidance specifically for commissioners on CBT for common mental disorders in adults, based on recommendations in existing NICE guidance (www.nice.nhs.uk). Changing the pattern of health-care resources allocation and health-care professionals practice takes time, but NICE guidelines have set out a compelling case for change driven by a strong evidence base. This has been achieved by working with the key professional bodies, patients' organizations, and health-care managers. For example, the NCCMH has produced joint information sheets on NICE guidance with patients' groups. Effective implementation requires support of a broad constituency, and it takes time.

FUTURE DEVELOPMENTS IN NICE CLINICAL GUIDELINES

The process and methods for developing guidelines are constantly evolving. Some of the more imminent challenges for NICE and NCCMH include developing novel methods of guideline development to support more effective and efficient updating, improving methods of decision making in GDGs, and development of service or clinical pathway related guidance. There is considerable demand for this kind of guidance from the NHS, but it presents a real challenge as the evidence base for organizational development, such as care pathways, is generally weak and political and policy changes ensure the wider service context will change, often independently of the evidence to support such change. In addition, limited evidence on treatments for childhood mental disorders presents further challenges; however, because they represent a definitive statement of the current state of knowledge, NICE guidelines are well placed to provide research recommendations that, if implemented, are likely to provide vital input into clinical practice recommendations for the next iteration of a guide. For example, the NICE guideline on depression in children and young people (NICE, 2005a) recognized that there was insufficient information to guide clinicians as alternative forms of psychological treatment and research recommendation led to funding of a large multicenter trial of psychological treatments.

The achievements of the NICE mental health program to date have been considerable and are most obviously seen in the massive expansion in the availability of evidence-based psychological interventions for adults in the NHS. Despite this, much remains to be done. Standards achieved need not only to be met but improved; continuing support of professions and patients needs to be further nurtured and encouraged and there is a need for more careful scrutiny of the benefits that accrue to patients and their families from the program.

REFERENCES

Agency for Health Care Policy and Research. (1993). *Acute pain management: operative or medical procedures and trauma.* Rockville, MD: United States Department of Health and Human Services.

AGREE Collaboration. (2003). Development and validation of an international appraisal instrument for assessing the quality of clinical practice guidelines: The AGREE project. *Quality and Safety in Health Care, 12*, 18–23.

Angold, A., Costello, E. J., & Erkanli, A. (1999). Comorbidity. *Journal of Child Psychology & Psychiatry, 40*, 57–97.

Appleby, J., Devlin, N., & Parkin, D. (2007). NICE's cost effectiveness threshold. *British Medical Journal, 335*, 358–359.

Benish, S., Imel, Z., & Wampold, B. (2008). The relative efficacy of bona fide psychotherapies for treating posttraumatic stress disorder: A meta-analysis of direct comparisons. *Clinical Psychology Review, 28*, 746–758.

Beutler, L. (2002). The Dodo bird is extinct. *Clinical Psychology: Science and Practice, 9*, 30–34.

Bisson, J., Elhers, A., Matthews, R., Pilling, S., Richards, D., & Turner, S. (2007). Psychological interventions for PTSD: A meta-analysis. *British Journal of Psychiatry, 190*, 97–104.

Black, N., Murphy, M., Lamping, D., McKee, M., Sanderson, C., Askham, J., & Marteau, T. (1999). Consensus development methods: A review of best practice in creating clinical guidelines. *Journal of Health Services Research and Policy, 4*, 236–248.

Borduin, C. M. (1999). Multisystemic treatment of criminality and violence in adolescents. *Journal of the American Academy for Child and Adolescent Psychiatry, 38*, 242–249.

Borduin, C. M., Mann, B. J., Cone, L. T., Henggeler, S. W., Fucci, B. R., Blaske, D. M., & Williams, R. A. (1995). Multisystemic treatment of serious juvenile offenders: Long-term prevention of criminality and violence. *Journal of Consulting and Clinical Psychology, 63*, 569–578.

Brown, G. S., Lambert, M. J., Jones, E. R., & Minami, T. (2005). Identifying highly effective psychotherapists in a managed care environment. *American Journal of Managed Care, 11*, 513–520.

Bulik, C. M., Berkman, N. D., Brownley, K. A., Sedway, J. A., & Lohr, K. N. (2007). Anorexia nervosa treatment: A systematic review of randomized controlled trials. *International Journal of Eating Disorders, 40*, 310–320.

Carlson, G., & Meyerson, S. (2006). Phenomenology and diagnosis of bipolar disorder in children, adolescents, and adults: Complexities and developmental issues. *Development and Psychology, 18*, 939–969.

Caspi, A., Sugden, K., Moffitt, T. E., Taylor, A., Craig, I. W., Harrington, H., . . . Poulton, R. (2003). Influence of life stress on depression: Moderation by a polymorphism in the 5-HTT gene. *Science, 301* (5631), 386–389.

Centre for Economic Performance. (2006). *The depression report: A new deal for depression and anxiety disorders*. London, England: London School of Economics.

Chambless, D. L. (1993). *Task force on promotion and dissemination of psychological procedures*. A report adopted by the Division 12 Board, October 1993. Washington, DC: American Psychological Association.

Chambless, D. L., & Hollon, S. D. (1998). Defining empirically supported therapies. *Journal of Consulting and Clinical Psychology, 66*, 7–18.

Chan, A. W., Hrobjartsson, A., Haahr, M. T., Gøtzsche, P. C., & Altman, D. G. (2004). Empirical evidence for selective reporting of outcomes in randomized trials: Comparison of protocols to published articles. *Journal of the American Medical Association, 291*, 2457–2465.

Child and Adolescent Mental Health Services (CAMHS) Evidence-Based Practice Unit. (2007). *Choosing what's best for you: What scientists have found helps children and young people who are sad, worried, or troubled*. London, England: CAMHS Publications.

Chitsabesan, P., Kroll, L., Bailey, S., Kenning, C., Sneider, S., MacDonald, W., & Theodosiou, L. (2006). Mental health needs of young offenders in custody and in the community. *British Journal of Psychiatry, 188*, 534–540.

Clark, D. M., Layard, R., & Smithies, R. (2008). *Improving access to psychological therapy: Initial evaluation of the two demonstration sites*. Centre for Economic Performance Working Paper No. 1648. London, England: London School of Economics.

Daniels, N., & Sabin, J. E. (2002). *Setting limits fairly: Can we learn to share medical resources?* New York, NY: Oxford University Press.

Davidson, G. C. (2000). Stepped care: Doing more with less? *Journal of Consulting and Clinical Psychology, 68*, 580–585.

De Los Reyes, A., & Kazdin, A. E. (2005). Informant discrepancies in the assessment of childhood psychopathology: A critical review, theoretical framework, and recommendations for further study. *Psychological Bulletin, 131*, 483–509.

De Los Reyes, A., & Kazdin, A. E. (2006). Conceptualizing changes in behavior in intervention research: the range of possible changes model. *Psychological Review, 113*, 554–583.

Department of Health. (1996). *Clinical guidelines: Using clinical guidelines to improve patient care within the NHS*. Leeds, England: NHS Executive.

Department of Health. (2001). *Treatment choice in psychological therapies and counselling: Evidence-based clinical guideline*. London, England: Author.

Department of Health. (2004). *National service framework for children, young people and maternity services: The mental health and psychological wellbeing of children and young people*. London, England: Author.

Drummond, M. F., Sculpher, M. J., Torrance, G. W., O'Brien, B. J., & Stoddart, G. L. (2005). *Methods for the economic evaluation of health care programmes* (3rd ed.). Oxford, England: Oxford University Press.

Eddy, D. M. (1990). Clinical decision making: From theory to practice. Resolving conflicts in practice policies. *Journal of the American Medical Association, 264*, 389–391.

Egger, M., Davey Smith, G., & Altman, D. G. (2001). *Systematic reviews in health care: Meta-analysis in context. Second edition of systematic reviews*. London, England: BMJ Books.

Egger, M., Davey Smith, G., Schneider, M., & Minder, C. (1997). Bias in meta-analysis detected by a simple, graphical test. *British Medical Journal, 315*, 629–634.

Elkin, I., Shea, M. T., Watkins, J. T., Imber, S. D., Sotsky, S. M., Collins, J. F., . . . Parloff, M. B. (1989). National Institute of Mental Health treatment of depression collaborative research programme. General effectiveness of treatments. *Archives of General Psychiatry, 46*, 971–982.

Ferlie, E. B., & Shortell, S. M. (2001). Improving the quality of health care in the United Kingdom and the United States: A framework for change. *The Milbank Quarterly, 79*, 281–315.

Field, M. J., & Lohr, K. N. (Eds.). (1990). *Clinical practice guidelines: Direction for a new program*. Washington, DC: National Academies Press.

Franklin, M. E., Abramowitz, J. S., Kozak, M. J., Levitt, J. T., & Foa, E. B. (2000). Effectiveness of exposure and ritual prevention for obsessive-compulsive disorder: Randomized compared with nonrandomized samples. *Journal of Consulting and Clinical Psychology, 68*, 594–602.

Fonagy, P., & Target, M. (1994). The efficacy of psychoanalysis for children with disruptive disorders.

Journal of the American Academy of Child and Adolescent Psychiatry, 33, 45–55.

Fonagy, P., Target, M., Cottrell, D., Phillips, J., & Kurtz, Z. (2005). *What works for whom: A critical review of treatments for children and adolescents* (2nd ed.). New York, NY: Guilford Press.

Gaebel, W., Weinmann, S., Sartorius, N., Rutz, W., & McIntyre, J. S. (2005). Schizophrenia practice guidelines: International survey and comparison. *British Journal of Psychiatry, 187,* 248–255.

Gibbons, R. D., Brown, C. H., Hur, K., Marcus, S. M., Bhaumik, D. K., Erkens, J. A., . . . Mann, J. J. (2007). Early evidence on the effects of regulators' suicidality warnings on SSRI prescriptions and suicide in children and adolescents. *American Journal of Psychiatry, 164,* 1356–1363.

Gillespie, K., Duffy, M., Hackmann, A., & Clark, D. M. (2002). Community based cognitive therapy in the treatment of posttraumatic stress disorder following the Omagh bomb. *Behaviour Research and Therapy, 40,* 345–357.

Goldberg, D., Pilling, S., Kendall, T., Ferrier, N., Foster, T., Gates, J., . . . Tylee, A. (2005). *Management of depression in primary and secondary care.* London, England: Gaskell.

Green, H., McGinnity, A., Meltzer, H., Ford, T., & Goodman, R. (2005). *Mental health of children and young people in Great Britain.* London, England: Office for National Statistics.

Grilli, R., Magrini, N., Penna, A., Mura, G., & Liberati, A. (2000). Practice guidelines developed by specialty societies: The need for critical appraisal. *The Lancet, 355,* 103–106.

Grimshaw, J. M., Thomas, R. E., MacLennan, G. S., Fraser, C., Ramsay, C. R., Vale, L. D., . . . Donaldson, C. (2004). Effectiveness and efficiency of guideline dissemination and implementation strategies. *Health Technology Assessment, 8,* 1–352.

Grol, R., & Grimshaw, J. (2003). From best evidence to best practice: Effective implementation of change in patients' care. *The Lancet, 362,* 1225–1230.

Grol, R., & Jones, R. (2000). Twenty years of implementation research. *Family Practice, 17,* S32–S35.

Guyatt, G. H., Oxman, A. D., Kunz, R., Falck-Ytter, Y., Vist, G. E., Liberati, A., & Schunemann, H. J. (2008). Rating quality of evidence and strength of recommendations. Going from evidence to recommendations. *British Medical Journal, 336,* 1049–1051.

Hadorn, D., Baker, D., Hodges, J., & Hicks, N. (1996). Rating the quality of evidence for clinical practice guidelines, *Journal of Clinical Epidemiology, 49,* 749–754.

Henggeler, S. W., Cunningham, P. B., Pickrel, S. G., Schoenwald, S. K., & Brondino, M. J. (1996). Multisystemic therapy: An effective violence prevention approach for serious juvenile offenders. *Journal of Adolescence, 19,* 47–61.

Henggeler, S. W., Melton, G. B., & Smith, L. A. (1992). Family preservation using multisystemic therapy: An effective alternative to incarcerating serious juvenile offenders. *Journal of Consulting and Clinical Psychology, 60,* 953–961.

Henggeler, S. W., Melton, G. B., Smith, L. A., Schoenwald, S. K., & Hanley, J. H. (1993). Family preservation using multisystemic treatment: Long-term follow-up to a clinical trial with serious juvenile offenders. *Journal of Child and Family Studies, 2,* 283–293.

Henggeler, S. W., Pickrel, S. G., Brondino, M. J., & Crouch, J. L. (1996). Eliminating (almost) treatment dropout of substance abusing or dependent delinquents through home-based multisystemic therapy. *American Journal of Psychiatry, 153,* 427–428.

Henggeler, S. W., Schoenwald, S. K., Rowland, M. D., & Cunningham, P. B. (2002). *Serious emotional disturbance in children and adolescents: Multisystemic Therapy.* New York, NY: Guilford Press.

Higgins, J. P. T., & Green, S. (Eds.). (2008). Cochrane handbook for systematic reviews of interventions version 5.0.1 [updated September 2008]. *The Cochrane Collaboration, 2.* Retrieved from www .cochrane-handbook.org

Hodes, M., & Garralda, E. (2007). NICE guidelines on depression in children and young people: Not always following the evidence. *Psychiatric Bulletin, 31,* 361–362.

Howlin, P. (1998). *Treatment of autistic children.* Chichester, England: Wiley.

Jacobson, N. S., & Hollon, S. D. (1996). Cognitive-behavior therapy versus pharmacotherapy: Now that the jury's returned its verdict, it's time to present the rest of the evidence. *Journal of Consulting and Clinical Psychology, 64,* 74–80.

Kazdin, A. E., Siegel, T. C., & Bass, D. (1992). Cognitive problem-solving skills training and parent management training in the treatment of antisocial behavior in children. *Journal of Consulting and Clinical Psychology, 60,* 733–747.

Kessler, R. C., Berglund, P., Demler, O., Jin, R., Koretz, D., Merikangas, K. R., . . . Wang, P. S. (2003). The epidemiology of major depressive disorder: Results from the National Comorbidity Survey Replication (NCS-R). *Journal of the American Medical Association, 289,* 3095–3105.

King, N., Heyne, D., Tonge, B., Mullen, P., Myerson, N., Rollings, S., & Ollendick, T. (2003). Sexually abused children suffering from Post-traumatic Stress Disorder: Assessment and treatment strategies. *Cognitive Behavior Therapy, 32,* 2–12.

Lader, D., Singleton, N., & Meltzer, H. (2003). Psychiatric morbidity among young offenders in England and Wales. *International Review of Psychiatry, 15,* 144–147.

Layard, R. (2008). *Child mental health: Key to a healthier society*. Retrieved from cep.lse.ac.uk/textonly /_new/staff/layard/pdf/RL502A_ChildMentalHealth _15082008.pdf

Layard, R., & Dunn, J. (2009). *A good childhood: Searching for values in a competitive age*. New York, NY: Penguin.

Leschied, A. W., & Cunningham, A. (2002). *Seeking effectiveinterventions for serious young offenders: Interim results of a four-year randomized study of multisystemic therapy in Ontario, Canada*. London, Ontario: Centre for Children and Families in the Justice System.

Lexchin, J., Bero, L. A., Djulbegovic, B., & Clark, O. (2003). Pharmaceutical industry sponsorship and research outcome and quality: Systematic review. *British Medical Journal, 326*, 1167–1170.

Littell, J. H., Popa, M., & Forsythe, B. (2005). Multi-systemic therapy for social, emotional, and behavioral problems in youth aged 10–17. *Cochrane Database of Systematic Reviews* (4), Art. No.: CD004797. doi: 004710.001002/14651858.CD14004797.pub14651854

Lovell, K., & Richards, D. (2000). Multiple Access Points and Levels of Entry (MAPLE): Ensuring choice, accessibility and equity for CBT services. *Behavioural and Cognitive Psychotherapy, 28*, 379–391.

Luborsky, L., Singer, B., & Luborsky, E. (1975). Comparative studies of psychotherapies: Is it true that "Everybody has won and all must have prizes"? *Archives of General Psychiatry, 32*, 995–1008.

McGlinchey, J. B., & Dobson, K. S. (2003). Treatment integrity concerns in cognitive therapy for depression. *Journal of Cognitive Psychotherapy, 17*, 299–319.

Melander, H., Ahlqvist-Rastad, J., Meijer, G., & Beermann, B. (2003). Evidence b(i)ased medicine—selective reporting from studies sponsored by pharmaceutical industry: Review of studies in new drug applications. *British Medical Journal, 326*, 1171–1173.

Michie, S., & Johnston, M. (2004). Changing clinical behaviour by making guidelines specific. *British Medical Journal, 328*, 343–345.

Michie, S., Johnston, M., Abraham, C., Lawton, R., Parker, D., & Walker, A. (2005). Making psychological theory useful for implementing evidence based practice: A consensus approach. *Quality and Safety in Healthcare, 14*, 26–33.

Michie, S., & Lester, K. (2005). Words matter: Increasing the implementation of clinical guidelines. *Quality and Safety in Health Care, 14*, 367–370.

Michie, S., Pilling, S., Garety, P., Whitty, P., Eccles, M., Johnston, M., & Simmons, J. (2007). Factors influencing the implementation of a mental health guideline: An exploratory investigation using psychological theory. *Implementation Science, 1*, 2–8.

Moffitt, T. E., Caspi, A., Rutter, M., & Silva, P. A. (2001). *Sex differences In antisocial behavior: Conduct disorder, delinquency, and violence in the Dunedin Longitudinal Study*. Cambridge, England: Cambridge University Press.

Moher, D., Cook, D. J., Eastwood, S., Olkin, I., Rennie, D., & Stroup, D. F. (1999). Improving the quality of reports of meta-analyses of RCTs: The QUOROM statement. *The Lancet, 354*, 1896–1900.

National Institute for Health and Clinical Excellence (NICE). (2002). *Core Interventions in the treatment and management of Schizophrenia in primary and secondary care. Clinical guideline 1*. Retrieved from www.nice.org.uk

National Institute for Health and Clinical Excellence (NICE). (2004). *Depression guideline management of depression in primary and secondary care. Clinical guideline 23*. Retrieved from www.nice.org.uk

National Institute for Health and Clinical Excellence (NICE). (2005a). *Depression in children and young people: Identification and management in primary, community and secondary care. Clinical guideline 28*. London, England: National Institute for Health and Clinical Excellence.

National Institute for Health and Clinical Excellence (NICE). (2005b). *Management of PTSD in adults in primary, secondary and community care*. Retrieved from www.nice.org.uk

National Institute for Health and Clinical Excellence (NICE). (2005c). *Social value judgments: Principles for the development of NICE's guidance*. Retrieved from www.nice.org.uk

National Institute for Health and Clinical Excellence (NICE). (2006). *Conduct disorder in children— Parent-training/education programmes: Guidance TA102*. Retrieved from www.nice.org.uk

National Institute for Health and Clinical Excellence (NICE). (2007). *The guidelines manual*. Retrieved from www.nice.org.uk

National Institute for Health and Clinical Excellence (NICE). (2008). *Attention Deficit and Hyperactivity Disorder: Clinical guideline 72*. London, England: NICE. Retrieved from www.nice.org.uk

National Institute for Health and Clinical Excellence (NICE). (2009). *Antisocial Personality Disorder guideline: Clinical guideline 77*. London, England: NICE. Retrieved from www.nice.org.uk

NHS Health Advisory Service. (2005). *Child and adolescent mental health services together we stand: The commissioning, role and management of child and adolescent mental health services*. London, England: Stationary Office Books.

Nutt, D. (2008, April). "Have psychotherapies been overhyped?" *Pulse 20*. Retrieved from www.pulse today.co.uk/story.asp?storycode=4118734

Nutt, D. J., & Sharpe, M. (2008). Uncritical positive regard? Issues in the efficacy and safety of psychotherapy. *Journal of Psychopharmacology, 22*, 3–6.

O'Brien, B. S., & Frick, P. J. (1996). Reward dominance: Associations with anxiety, conduct problems, and psychopathy in children. *Journal of Abnormal Child Psychology, 24,* 223–240.

Ogden, T., & Hagen, K. A. (2006). Multisystemic treatment of serious behavior problems in youth: Sustainability of effectiveness two years after intake. *Child and Adolescent Mental Health, 11,* 142–149

Okiishi, J. C., Lambert, M. J., Eggert, D., Nilesen, L., & Dayton, D. D. (2006). An analysis of therapist treatment effects: Toward providing feedback to individual therapists on their clients' psychotherapy outcome. *Journal of Clinical Psychology, 62,* 1157–1172.

Parry, G., Cape, J., & Pilling, S. (2003). Clinical practice guidelines in clinical psychology and psychotherapy. *Clinical Psychology and Psychotherapy, 10,* 337–351.

Perlis, R. H., Perlis, C. S., Wu, Y., Hwang, C., Joseph, M., &. Nierenberg, A. A. (2005). Industry sponsorship and financial conflict of interest in the reporting of clinical trials in psychiatry. *The American Journal of Psychiatry, 162,* 1957–1960.

Perera, A., Gupta, P., Samuel, R., & Berg, B. (2007). A survey of anti-depressant prescribing practice and the provision of psychological therapies in a South London CAMHS from 2003–2006. *Child and Adolescent Mental Health, 12,* 70–72.

Peterson, M. A. (2008). The truth about health care: Why reform is not working in America; The health care mess: How we got into it and what it will take to get out; The health care mess: How we got into it and how we'll get out of it. *Journal of Health Politics, Policy and Law, 33,* 343–357

Piaggio, G., Elbourne, D. R., Altman, D., Pocock, S. J., & Evans, S. J. W. (2006). Reporting of non-inferiority and equivalence randomized trials: An extension of the CONSORT Statement. *Journal of the American Medical Association, 295,* 1152–1160.

Pilling, S. (2008a, April). "Have psychotherapies been overhyped?" *Pulse 20.* Retrieved from www.pulse today.co.uk/story.asp?storycode=4118734

Pilling, S. (2008b). History, context, process and rationale for the development of clinical guidelines. *Psychology and Psychotherapy: Theory, Research and Practice, 81,* 331–350.

Pilling, S., & Price, K. (2006). Developing and implementing clinical guidelines: Lessons from the NICE schizophrenia guideline. *Epidemiologia e Psichiatria Sociale, 15,* 109–116.

Prescott, L. F., Illingworth, R. N., Critchley, J. A., Stewart, M. J., Adam, R. D., & Proudfoot, A. T. (1979). Intravenous N-acetylcystine: The treatment of choice for paracetamol poisoning. *British Medical Journal, 6198,* 1097–1100.

Rawlins, M. (2008). *DE TESTIMONIO: On the evidence for decisions about the use of therapeutic interventions.* The Harveian Oration: Royal College of Physicians, London.

Rawlins, M., & Dillon, A. (2005). NICE discrimination. *Journal of Medical Ethics, 31,* 683–684.

Roth, A., & Fonagy, P. (2005). *What works for whom? A critical review of psychotherapy research* (2nd ed.). New York, NY: Guilford Press.

Roth, A. D., & Pilling, S. (2008). Using an evidence-based methodology to identify the competences required to deliver effective cognitive and behavioural therapy for depression and anxiety disorders. *Behavioural and Cognitive Psychotherapy, 36,* 129–147.

Roth, A. D., & Pilling, S. (2009). *The impact of adherence and competence on outcome in CBT and psychological therapies.* Manuscript in preparation.

Sackett, D. L., Rosenberg, W. M. C., Gray, J. A. M., & Haynes, R. B. (1996). Evidence-based medicine: What is and what isn't. *British Medical Journal, 312,* 71–72.

Sheldon, T. A., Cullum, N., Dawson, D., Lankshear, A., Lowson, K., Watt, I., . . . Wright, J. (2004). What's the evidence that NICE guidance has been implemented? Results from a national evaluation using time series analysis, audit of patients' notes and interviews. *British Medical Journal, 329,* 999–1004.

Simon, J., Pilling, S., Burbeck, R., & Goldberg, D. (2006). Treating moderate and severe depression with anti-depressants, psychological therapy or their combination: A decision analytic model of effectiveness and costs developed to support a clinical guideline. *The British Journal of Psychiatry, 189,* 494–501.

Shooshtary, M. H., Panaghi, L., & Moghadam, J. A. (2008). Outcome of cognitive behavioral therapy in adolescents after natural disaster. *Journal of Adolescent Health, 42,* 466–472.

Starr, M., & Chalmers, I. (2003). *The evolution of the Cochrane Library, 1988–2003.* Oxford, England: Update Software. Retrieved from www.update software.com/history/clibhist.htm.

Steinbrook, R. (2008). Saying no isn't NICE—The travails of Britain's National Institute for Health and Clinical Excellence. *New England Journal of Medicine, 359,* 1997–1981.

Von Korff, M., & Goldberg, D. (2001) Improving outcomes in depression. *British Medical Journal, 323,* 948–949.

Wampold, B. E., Mondin, G. W., Moody, M., Stich, F., Benson, K., & Ahn, H. (1997). A meta-analysis of outcome studies comparing bona fide psychotherapies: Empirically, "all must have prizes." *Psychological Bulletin, 122,* 203–215.

Weisz, J. R., Jensen-Doss, A., & Hawley, K. M. (2006). Evidence-based youth psychotherapies versus usual clinical care: A meta-analysis of direct comparisons. *American Psychologist, 61,* 671–689.

Wensing, M., Wollersheim, H., & Grol, R. (2006). *Organizational interventions to implement improvements in patient care: A structured review of reviews.* Implementation Science. Retrieved from www.imple mentationscience.com/content/1/1/2

Westen, D., & Morrison, K. (2001). A multidimensional meta-analysis of treatments for depression, panic, and generalized anxiety disorder: An empirical examination of the status of empirically supported therapies. *Journal of Consulting and Clinical Psychology, 69,* 875–899.

Whitten, P. S., Mair, F. S., Haycox, A., May, C. R., Williams, T. L., & Hellmich, S. (2002). Systematic review of cost effectiveness studies of telemedicine interventions. *British Medical Journal, 324,* 1434–1437.

Whittington, C. J., Kendall, T., Fonagy, P., Cottrell, D., Cotgrove, A., & Boddington, E. (2004). Selective serotonin reuptake inhibitors in childhood depression: Systematic review of published versus unpublished data. *The Lancet, 363,* 1341–1345.

Wolpert, M., Fuggle, P., Cottrell, D., Fonagy, P., Philips, J., Pilling, S., . . . Target, M. (2006). *Drawing on the evidence: Advice for mental health professionals working with children and adolescents* (2nd ed.). London, England: CAMHS Publications.

Wood, A., Harrington, R., & Moore, A. (1996) Controlled trial of brief cognitive-behavioral intervention in adolescent patients with depressive disorders. *Journal of Child Psychology and Psychiatry, 37,* 737–746.

5

The Economics of Evidence-Based Practice in Disorders of Childhood and Adolescence

E. MICHAEL FOSTER AND KIMBERLY MCCOMBS-THORNTON

Economics has much to offer in understanding whether and how clients receive evidence-based treatment. Many steps are required between first determining efficacy, then effectiveness, then making a service or treatment widely available. At each step, economic incentives and effects likely inform decisions and/or can facilitate or block a policymaker's efforts to have those treatments delivered. Efficacy represents the first step and refers to the ability of the treatment to produce desired patient outcomes, generally under ideal circumstances. Multiple studies corroborating positive outcomes are necessary for establishing that a treatment is an evidence-based practice (EBP). This chapter starts at the point that an EBP has been established as efficacious.

The first half of the chapter provides an overview of the tools of economic analysis. These tools could be used to determine whether an efficacious intervention is cost-efficacious or, subsequently, that an effective one is cost-effective. We outline the forms of economic analysis and the principles that shape their conduct. Policymakers would use this information during the process to determine whether an efficacious intervention or treatment should be disseminated broadly.

In the second half of the chapter, we turn to the economics of dissemination. The contribution of economics at this stage reflects the broader field of health economics. That literature considers whether and how incentives can be used to induce economic agents to change their behavior. Little of the literature on incentives focuses on children's mental health or even mental health more generally. That literature, however, can inform thinking about EBP for children with emotional and behavioral problems because it is about effective implementation.

The chapter discusses the role of economics from the perspectives of three important stakeholders: the payers, the providers, and the consumers. We will illustrate our discussion by referring to our experience with the Incredible Years Series, an EBP targeting young children with emotional and behavioral problems.

BACKGROUND: THE INCREDIBLE YEARS SERIES

The Incredible Years Parents, Teachers, and Children Training Series (IYS)—developed by

Carolyn Webster-Stratton, PhD, and evaluated by colleagues at the University of Washington's Parenting Clinic—is a multicomponent program designed to treat young children with or at risk of early-onset conduct problems. The program has been adapted to serve as a cost-effective, community-based prevention program for children at risk for the development of CD (conduct disorder). Over the past 20 years, this intervention repeatedly has been implemented in both clinic and natural environment contexts such as mental health settings and schools.

Ultimately, the IYS strives to prevent delinquency, drug abuse, and violent acts among high-risk children. However, immediate goals of the program include the reduction of conduct problems in children; the enhancement of social, emotional, and academic capabilities of children; the promotion of parental competence and positive discipline strategies; the strengthening of families as well as the school-home connection; and the enhancement of teacher classroom management skills (Webster-Stratton, 2000).

The IYS comprises three components, each focusing on different contexts for and types of children's social interactions. The three treatment components include: (1) a child-based program (referred to as Child Training or CT), (2) a parent-based program (referred to as Parent Training or PT), and (3) a teacher-based program (referred to as Teacher Training or TT). (Since our focus is on the medical sector, this chapter does not discuss the last component in any detail.) The CT and PT leaders initially learn program curricula from certified IY trainers; following training, CT and PT leaders deliver program curricula to child and parent participants, respectively, during weekly small group sessions. For a detailed description of treatment component goals, curriculum, and implementation methods, please see Webster-Stratton (2000).

Webster-Stratton and colleagues have implemented the IYS using the three single treatment components either alone (i.e., CT program alone) or stacked in various combinations (i.e., CT plus TT and/or PT). Different combinations of the IY components are recommended depending on the targeted child population.

The IYS has been effective in reducing the frequency of children's conduct problems regardless of treatment locale. Service agencies (mental health agencies, child welfare systems, and schools) continue to implement the IYS; large-scale diffusion of the program has occurred across the United States, Canada, United Kingdom, and Norway. Agencies adopting the IYS are responsible for budgeting for initial training from certified IY trainers, program materials (videotapes, group leader manuals, parent and child materials, and handouts), program implementation, and ongoing consultation with IY trained staff. Following the initial materials and training fees, the IYS may be offered to participants from successive cohorts at minimal cost to the service agency.

Past literature has assessed the impact of participant characteristics, individual component intensity, and multicomponent delivery methods on the effectiveness of the IYS. Numerous randomized controlled group studies by the developer (e.g., Webster-Stratton, 1990; Webster-Stratton & Hammond, 1997; Webster-Stratton & Reid, 1999a, 1999b; Webster-Stratton, Reid, & Hammond, 2001) and by independent investigators (e.g., Barrera et al., 2002; Miller & Rojas-Flores, 1999; Scott, Spender, Doolan, Jacobs, & Aspland, 2001; Taylor, Schmidt, Pepler, & Hodgins, 1998) strongly support the assertion that the IYS consistently improves child behavior across a range of outcome indicators.

The IYS has been identified as an effective CD/oppositional defiant disorder (ODD) treatment and prevention program for young children by the Office of Juvenile Justice and Delinquency Prevention (Webster-Stratton, 2000). Additionally, when an independent review committee of the American Psychological Association reviewed findings from over 82 studies of CD interventions, the IYS was identified as only one of two behavioral intervention strategies that met the criteria for well-established efficacious CD treatments (Brestan & Eyberg, 1998).

With strong client outcomes, the IYS was a prime candidate for economic evaluation to determine the actual costs of the benefits. The first author led a team in conducting such an analysis. This chapter will discuss the process of conducting this economic evaluation and subsequent results.

Economic Evaluation: Is the EBP a Good Use of Society's Resources?

The formal tools of economic evaluation may take one of several forms: benefit-cost analysis, cost-effectiveness analysis, and cost-utility analysis. Perhaps best known is benefit-cost analysis. A benefit-cost analysis (BCA) provides a full accounting of the resource implications of an intervention, policy, or program. One measures both the costs and benefits of the intervention and then calculates net benefits—that is, the benefits of the intervention less its costs. If the net benefits are positive, then the intervention or treatment is desirable. A key feature of BCA is that the benefits should reflect societal willingness to pay for the resource or outcome involved. Economists use this societal perspective to gauge whether a program or service is a good investment. As discussed further on, however, one can assess net benefits from other perspectives, and these supplemental analyses can be informative. As we discuss, these additional perspectives can inform our efforts to understand provider and participant incentives.

A second form of economic evaluation is cost-effectiveness analysis (CEA). Although the term cost-effectiveness is often used as a synonym for economic evaluation, CEA actually refers to a specific form of such an evaluation. Unlike BCA, cost-effectiveness analysis does not require one to measure outcomes in dollar terms. Rather, the outcome measures remain in their natural metric (e.g., a 1-point difference on a symptom checklist or a percentage point reduction in the number of teenagers giving birth). The analyst then compares interventions or programs in terms of their added (or incremental) costs per added unit of the outcome measure (Zerbe & Dively, 1994). One could calculate such ratios for a variety of outcome measures.

A third form of economic evaluation, cost-utility analysis, is actually a specific form of CEA. The outcome or measure of effectiveness is a measure of overall well-being based on respondent ratings of several dimensions of well-being. The scores on the different dimensions are then combined using weights that reflect the relative desirability of different combinations of the attributes. Those weights capture caregiver or other stakeholder preferences for the attributes involved. A familiar measure of this sort is the quality-adjusted life year (QALY) (Drummond, O'Brien, Stoddart, & Torrance, 1997). The QALYs play an especially important role in the British National Health Service (NHS), as discussed later.

Finally, a related form of economic analysis involves costs of illness studies. Those studies involve estimating the broader societal costs of illness, such as alcoholism or cigarette smoking and many others (Rice, Hodgson, & Kopstein, 1985; Rice, Kelman, & Miller, 1991; Sobocki, Lekander, Borgstrom, Strom, & Runeson, 2007). A cost of illness study generally includes the costs of treatment as well as effects on employment (Gold, Russell, Siegel, & Weinstein, 1996). Because willingness to pay is difficult to measure, economists may use the reduction in costs of illness as the measure of the benefits of an intervention. This measure understates the full benefits of the intervention. Costs of illness, for example, generally do not capture pain and suffering (Kenkel, 1994).[1]

Regardless of the form of economic evaluation chosen, the foundation for each is a good estimate of a program's costs. The next subsection outlines economist's view of costs and their measurement.

Measuring the Costs of an EBP

In this subsection we begin by discussing the broad principles of cost estimation and then turn to the direct costs of the program. We then consider the morbidity-related costs and the impact of the intervention on those costs. Finally, we examine the direct costs of the IYS.

How Do Economists Think About Costs? Broad Principles

Economists' efforts to define and measure costs are guided by four principles. As mentioned before, the first is that the costs of a program or intervention vary depending on the perspective from which they are assessed. Economists emphasize the societal perspective, which encompasses impact of the program on all groups, such as intervention participants and taxpayers. By that standard, they assess whether a program is "efficient." By efficient, economists mean an allocation

---

[1] Indeed, the possibility that BCA may routinely understate the benefits of programs is one of the major criticisms of the method. It is worth noting that other areas of economic evaluation attempt to measure willingness to pay directly. These areas include environmental economics. In that field, the benefits of a program may be no less intangible than health; for example, environmental economists attempt to measure the value of a scenic lake (even to those who do not use the lake!). These methods include contingent valuation methodology. By comparison, health economists have made substantially less use of this method to measure the value of health improvements (Kenkel, Berger, & Blomquist, 1994).

of resources such that further reallocation could not improve societal well-being.

As noted, the societal perspective includes other relevant perspectives, such as those of patients, the insurer or other payer, the provider, and other citizens. As discussed in the following, all of these parties have to determine whether and how to do their part in delivering and receiving evidence-based care. Some costs may drive the decision making of one party but be completely irrelevant for another. For example, the travel or time costs for participants may be quite high. Unless an agency is reimbursing families, it may ignore those costs. The agency would consider them only indirectly and to the extent the costs manifest themselves on their budget sheet—for example, large travel costs might mean high rates of no-shows, which create costs for the agency.

In some instances, the effects of a program on different groups offset each other. In the case of reduced use of cash transfers (such as the Temporary Assistance to Needy Families program), the only (net) societal cost involves program administration: The gain to taxpayers offsets the losses born by the former recipients. There are other instances where the societal perspective diverges from that of other perspectives. For example, payments made for mental health service may not equal the costs of producing that service (Hargreaves, Shumway, Hu, & Cuffel, 1998). Those charges are the "costs" for the agency or program that pays for the services. These payments, however, may be a poor proxy for societal costs. This divergence exists for several reasons. As a result of market imperfections, payments made by some clients may implicitly subsidize other clients. The privately insured, for example, may subsidize the uninsured. As a result, payments made on behalf of the latter may understate the costs of society for the services involved. The societal perspective represents the bottom line for economists—it is used to gauge the "efficiency" or overall desirability of a societal allocation of resources.

The second through fourth principles involve this broader, societal perspective. A second principle is that economists measure costs in terms of opportunity costs, the value of a resource in its next best use (Gold et al., 1996). In many ways, this emphasis on foregone uses is what distinguishes an economist's approach from that of an accountant. This difference is most apparent in instances where a cost (or resource use) generates no bookkeeping entry. As an example, volunteer time requires no payment by the agency sponsoring an intervention. The time involved, however, has a value in alternative uses—the volunteer could spend that time at work or in leisure activities (or even volunteering at another program). These implicit time costs also might involve the time of program participants. Although economists may disagree somewhat as to how that time should be valued, they generally agree that such costs should be included.

A third principle shaping economists' reckoning of costs is that some costs are morbidity related. In a prevention program targeted to the mental health of children, these costs are particularly important. Children with emotional and behavioral problems are frequently involved in many child-serving sectors, and the costs of the services involved are potentially enormous. In many cases, these costs are actually reduced by a prevention program and so represent areas of so-called cost offset. For example, improvements in a child's mental health may reduce his or her use of health services or the use of mental health services by his or her parents (Foster & Bickman, 2000) or expenditures in the child-welfare sector (Foster & Connor, 2005). On the other hand, a preventive program may link families to these services and so increase their use (and related expenditures) as a result (e.g., the Starting Early, Starting Smart program; Karoly, Kilburn, Bigelow, Caulkins, & Cannon, 2001). In some cases, these indirect costs may not be immediately apparent. For example, an intervention may reduce school dropout. Although this effect has obvious

benefits, it also creates costs related to resources used while the individuals remain in school.

A fourth feature of an economist's view of costs is that marginal costs are the costs that matter (Warner & Luce, 1982). By "marginal" an economist means costs that change as a result of the activity involved. Consider, for example, an intervention that affects the use of special education. The relevant costs are those above and beyond the costs of education in a regular classroom—after all, the latter would be incurred even if the child were not in special education (unless the intervention affects the likelihood that a child leaves school altogether).

Costs seem rather concrete to the noneconomist, but the attentive reader will note the hypothetical nature of some of these costs—for example, the value of resources in alternative (i.e., hypothetical) uses. For that reason, even in estimating costs, economists often have to make assumptions about markets or the behavior of economic agents. It is important that the resulting estimates be subject to sensitivity analyses—that is, calculations based on alternative assumptions.

Before turning to the details of cost estimation, a key point about efficacy studies is worth making. In those studies, the delivery of services may differ from that anticipated in the real world. An interventionist, for example, may receive more supervision than is possible in an actual clinical setting. No doubt that researchers should consider this possibility in advance of the study (whether it involves a cost analysis or not), but the relevant point here is that the cost estimate must describe the use of resources used to generate the outcomes observed. High levels of supervision may be responsible for the improved outcomes; in that case, that supervision must be included in the corresponding cost estimates. Alternative costs estimates (such as those for lower levels of supervision) can be calculated when the corresponding outcomes become available through future studies.

In the next subsection, we consider how these principles would be applied to estimating the direct costs of EBP in an efficacy trial. We illustrate this discussion with our work evaluating the IYS in a clinical setting.

Measuring and Valuing the Direct Costs of EBP

With the broad principles outlined before, estimating costs involves a set of practical steps required to collect the necessary information and to perform the necessary calculations. Gold et al. (1996) identified three steps in measuring the costs of an intervention or service: identifying the resources involved, measuring their use, and valuing the resources used in dollar terms. We examine each of these for the direct costs of the CT and PT components of the IYS. Note that the following discussion presumes that evaluation and service delivery are conducted by the same unit. As a result, the two activities share space and administration; furthermore, some individuals work on both tasks. Although common, this sharing of tasks not only raises issues about blinding the individuals involved to the intervention status of participants but also complicates estimating the costs of the intervention. These personnel must track their allocation of time to intervention and research. This task might involve time sheets that relevant personnel complete weekly. Ideally, because retrospective reports may be unreliable, these sheets would be completed prospectively. For other shared resources, such as the costs of space, one can either track the use of space or divide the costs between the two activities based on other information (as discussed later).

Identifying resources involved. Consistent with the economic principles identified previously, we want to capture all of the resources involved in delivering an intervention. Such accounting includes implicit costs (those resources for which no explicit payments are made), such as parental time and donated space. Time contributed by volunteers also would be included.

Table 5.1 enumerates different resources used in delivering the IYS CT and PT Programs. Explicit costs of the intervention involve both fixed and variable costs. Fixed costs are those costs that do not change as the number of participants expands. In this case, fixed costs include the costs of facilities. Variable costs, on the other hand, depend on number of participants.

Some costs are quasi-fixed, such as staff training. For a given child, those costs are fixed—the training has occurred and will not increase as an additional child is treated. However, over time, one can anticipate that trained staff (e.g., a nurse) will turnover, and new training will be required. For that reason, to maintain the services over time, one would have to spread the costs of training over the

TABLE 5.1   Intervention Ingredients

Training Fees

CT Leader training by Cert. IYS Trainer (24 hrs total)

PT Leader training by Cert. IYS Trainer (24 hrs total)

CT Leader-in-training's time (24 hrs total)

PT Leader-in-training's time (24 hrs total)

Material Fees

CT Dina series session materials

CT Dina series lesson plans and handouts

PT training materials

PT session materials

PT Leader manual

CT and PT parent manuals (12)

Additional Fees—Staff Time

CT Leader's time in sessions

CT weekly supervision

PT Leader's time in sessions

PT Leader additional time

Additional Fees—IYS Implementation

PT small group session meals

PT small group session on-site babysitting fees

PT small group session cab vouchers

PT small group session off-site day care costs

anticipated tenure of the provider. In that case, the training is best viewed like a piece of equipment that will depreciate over time. From that perspective, a sensible practice would be to spread the costs of training over the expected number of children the provider could be expected to treat. An interventionist's tenure is not likely to be observed during the course of the study or in fact the study's funding may end, truncating tenure below that level that would be observed in the real world. For that reason, the analyst may perform calculations using a reasonable estimate.

Measuring resource use. Information on the resources involved could be determined from several sources. Principal among these are project budgets, which identify the resources used as well as costs to the project of those resources. In the case of some resources (particularly implicit costs), additional information would be needed from other sources, such as parental reports of time use.

Valuing the resources used in dollar terms. In the case of explicit costs, these costs are naturally expressed in dollar terms. The challenge here is to allocate these costs between intervention delivery and other activities, such as research. In the case of implicit costs, measuring the resources involved in dollar terms often requires additional information.

For many interventions, labor costs are a primary component of explicit costs. These costs can be calculated by using budget information on wages and salaries and on fringe benefits. Total labor costs would be allocated to the intervention based on the division of time use reported on the time sheets (discussed previously). Individuals devoting their time exclusively to research could be ignored or, if one were interested in the total costs of research, included in a separate tabulation. Note that administrative labor costs are included in the fixed costs allocated subsequently.

Next, one would estimate other variable costs, such as supplies and materials. To the extent these resources could be related directly to intervention delivery, expenditures would be included in the costs of the intervention. Expenditures on items that could not be linked to either the intervention or research (e.g., photocopying costs that were not tracked) could be included in (joint) fixed costs that are allocated as described later. Next, one would allocate fixed costs, including those costs that could not be divided between the intervention and research. Principal among these are space costs, including utilities and telecommunication costs. One could potentially include the costs of space used by specific personnel in the same proportion as they use their time. However, this would leave other space used by intervention and project personnel (such as conference rooms and meeting space) unallocated.

For that reason, following Hargreaves et al. (1998), we recommend that all space and similar shared costs be allocated based on the overall distribution of personnel time (and resulting costs) between the intervention and evaluation.[2] Note that some costs involve resources that are purchased in a given year but that are used by project staff over several years. These costs include equipment costs, such as computers. These costs can be amortized over time by using standard accounting principles. Also included in this category are training costs. Project staff may be trained in a given year but work with program participants over time. As a result, some portion of their training should be attributed to future years. Using an estimate of the average amount of time personnel remain with a project, one could amortize those costs as well.

As discussed previously, not all explicit costs can be tracked on project budgets. These costs include out-of-pocket costs of participation borne by families. Included here are transportation costs as well as babysitting costs

---

[2] These same principles could be used to allocate costs in situations where multiple interventions share resources. Such situations seem quite likely in real-world implementations.

for a participant's siblings. One could estimate those costs by having parents complete a short questionnaire at a few intervention sessions. These explicit costs represent the costs of the intervention to taxpayers (or other funding source) and participants. They also are part of the costs of the intervention to society.

Implicit costs are primarily of two types—time and space. The latter involves space used by an intervention for which no payments are made, such as classrooms used for evening parent training. One could argue that the opportunity cost for this space is often zero as well: These groups are conducted after the normal business day or at a time when the space would not otherwise be used. This point is debatable, however, and one might consider the sensitivity of one's conclusions to this assumption. Estimates of the opportunity cost include the costs of similar space one might rent in the community.

Time costs represent a second type of implicit costs. A treatment may require substantial amounts of a parent's time. Parents receive incentive payments in a research study, but those payments may not fully compensate them for their time.[3] Although family groups were scheduled at convenient times, parental participation reduces leisure time. Such time, however, is not without value. Because they conceivably could work during those hours, parents pay an implicit price for their leisure (in terms of reduced wages). This suggests that their leisure time is worth at least as much as their wage rate. For that reason, following Gorsky, Haddix, and Shaffer (1996), we recommend that one value parental time using parents' wage rate (Gorsky, Haddix, & Schaffer, 1996). One could calculate these costs using the results of a brief survey of

parents concerning time spent on intervention-related activities and their wage rate. (To avoid double-counting costs, one would only include the amount by which these costs exceed any incentive payments made.)

Measuring and Valuing Morbidity-Related Costs

As discussed previously, a second type of cost involves morbidity-related costs—namely, the costs of alternative services used. The first step in measuring these costs is identifying the resources (or services) involved. Having done that, we consider the means for measuring and valuing each service.

Identifying resources involved. The list of potential services and resources one might include is nearly endless. Children use many types of resources, and changes in their mental health likely will stimulate ripple effects through a range of child-serving sectors. Because research resources are not limitless, one has to prioritize based on what one knows about the prevention program and the population it targets. Possible criteria include the potential magnitude of costs involved as well as whether one would expect any relation between them and the intervention. In the case of the IYS, one system likely affected includes the educational system.

Measuring resource use. Increased use of school services likely include disciplinary referrals as well as special education. Potential sources of information include each parental report or, for older children, self-reports. Because of concerns about the accuracy of such reports, school records may prove more reliable if available. School records can report a level of detail of service use of which parents are unaware or unreliable, such as the percentage of time spent in a special classroom.

Valuing the resources used in dollar terms. For each type of service, one can convert measures of service use into dollar values using per-unit costs. A full discussion of the methods for valuing special education is

---

[3] One also could argue that those payments are for the research component (especially if the comparison or control group receives the same amount) and so should not offset any of the intervention time costs.

beyond the scope of this chapter. However, at least in the United States, schools do not determine special education costs at the child level. Rather, schools know what they spend on the "inputs"—teachers and other resources—but generally do not translate this figure into a per-child estimate. Even under the best of circumstances, therefore, obtaining per-unit costs for special education is challenging. As an alternative, one might turn to special studies of the costs of special education (Chambers, Parrish, & Harr, 2002; Chambers, Parrish, Lieberman, & Wolman, 1998). Those studies generally involve a district or a state, and whether and how well they would apply in another location is unknown.

Placing a dollar value on other uses of school services is difficult. For example, the marginal cost of one trip to the principal's office is likely small or zero for an individual child. The school will not have a principal devoted to just that child, no matter how poorly behaved. (Issues of additional costs arise if one were to think of large groups of children being treated or a universal program. In that situation, one might divert an assistant principal from disciplinary issues to other functions.)

The Costs of the Incredible Years Series

To estimate per-child costs of the IYS treatment combinations (excluding the control condition), total per-child costs were first estimated for the CT and PT components. Costs were derived using a series of detailed financial estimates provided by the developer of the IYS. The payer perspective was used to determine costs; that is, these financial estimates included all fees for which the agency implementing the IYS is responsible. Estimates included fees associated with training and ongoing supervision of CT and PT group leaders; group leader salary including time for peer review, self-study, and preparation; costs of providing materials for participants; and additional fees— both on- and off-site—necessary for actual program

implementation (i.e., on-site childcare, participant meals, cab vouchers, and off-site child-care compensation).

As reported in Foster, Olchowski, and Webster-Stratton (2007), the costs of CT in 2003 dollars was $1,164 per child; PT was $1,579. And when combined, the costs were $2,713, after discounting for duplicated resource materials.

The costs estimate depended on key assumptions. Total per-child cost estimates did not include costs associated with the space required for initial leader and teacher training and weekly small group sessions. It is assumed that agencies and schools implementing IY will provide on-site space in which group leader training and group sessions may be conducted. (If an agency does not have space available for training and small group sessions, the cost of space rental should be included when calculating total per-child cost estimates). It should also be noted that the combined condition required the purchase of only one set of parent manuals at the cost of $179.40 per 12 parents; therefore, this fee was not duplicated when summing total per-child costs for CT and PT to form the costs of the combined treatment combination.

Another assumption involved onetime program initiation costs. For example, estimates presented in the previous calculations assumed that each group leader, PT group leader, and trained teacher complete just one sequence of the IYS following certification. However, in real-world implementation, newly trained group and classroom facilitators who have completed training in CT, PT, and TT will likely lead more than one sequence of the IYS. Because group leaders and teachers complete training only prior to the first IYS sequence, training costs depreciate as the number of children participating in IYS increases. Similarly, after the first sequence of IYS, costs associated with onetime purchases of materials are not included in additional sequences of IYS. Therefore, with each additional cohort of participants treated, total per-child costs decrease for each treatment category. For these reasons, the total per-child estimates presented can be considered conservative.

Assessing Outcomes and Costs

A full economic assessment will incorporate outcomes in one of several forms. A cost of illness study would incorporate the direct costs of treatment as well as the broader societal costs (such as special education). One could consider whether evidence-based treatment reduces the broader costs of illness. Foster and colleagues, for example, consider whether spending on improved mental health services for adolescents reduces the costs of juvenile justice (Foster & Connor, 2005). Such studies are often labeled *BCA*s but technically are not and are best described as costs of illness (COI) impact study.[4] They do provide an estimate of the net benefits of the program by subtracting any cost savings from the direct costs of treatment.

A BCA would compare program costs with the benefits measured in terms of societal willingness to pay. The results would represent the net societal benefits of the program.[5] A comparison of program costs and the

willingness of society to pay for the program's benefits would definitely include the direct costs of the EBP. An issue of some fuzziness is whether to include reductions in the costs of other services, such as special education. Whether to do so would depend on how societal willingness to pay was assessed. Contingent valuation methodology would involve asking informants directly as to what they would be willing to pay to reduce mental disorder. In that case, whether and how the implications about schooling are included would determine whether the school costs were included in the costs calculation. Needless to say, obtaining such information is daunting, and it is not surprising that there are not many analyses of this type (Gunther et al., 2007; Healey & Chisholm, 1999; Konig, 2004; Konig, Bernert, & Angermeyer, 2005; O'Shea, Gannon, & Kennelly, 2008; Smith, 2007).

A third way of combining costs and benefits involves CEA. A CEA generates the "ICER," the incremental cost-effectiveness ratio. This ratio is the net costs of the program over its net benefits. The denominator (benefits) remains in its actual metric—problem cases of mental disorder avoided or improvement in a functioning scale.

One can see that the CEA takes considerably less effort than a BCA or even the COI assessment. Expressing program benefits in dollars or pounds is difficult and may require considerable effort. The CEA, therefore, require many fewer resources, and as a result, the vast majority of economic evaluations in health are CEA. The difficulty, however, is that one cannot easily compare interventions with disparate effects. For example, it is difficult to compare dollars spent per heart attack avoided with dollars spent per case of conduct disorder avoided. One would need a measure of the societal impact of the two disorders. The CEA, however, can be quite informative for comparing interventions with outcomes measured in the same way. In that case, the intervention with the lower ICER is clearly preferred. Even in those instances, however, problems arise

---

[4] Many prominent economic evaluations are mislabeled. The economic evaluation of the Perry Preschool, for example, is not a BCA but rather a "cost of illness impact" study (Barnett, 1985, 1996; Belfield, Nores, Barnett, & Schweinhart, 2006; Schweinhart, Barnes, & Weikart, 1993). The authors of the study mislabel their findings as well.

[5] Many noneconomists like to present the findings of such studies using benefit-cost ratios. Such ratios are misleading and considered "bad practice." The reason is that it is fairly easy to show that a program that produces net benefits of $1,000 (program costs = $2,000; program benefits = $3,000) is superior to one producing net benefits of $500 (program costs = $250; program benefits = $1,000), even though the latter might have a higher ratio of benefits to costs. (The benefit-cost ratios are 1.5 and 4.0, respectively.)

when there are multiple outcome measures. The ICERs for different measures may not be consistent with different measures identifying different treatments as cost-effective.

Policymakers constantly have to compare disparate uses of resources, and for that reason, they often want to compare programs that involve disparate outcomes. As noted, benefit-cost analysis represents one solution but a difficult one. As a result, health economists have created another outcome measure that they consider appropriate for disparate treatments and disorders—the QALY. The QALY is a measure of overall well-being ranging from 0 (death) to 1 (perfect health). By summing individual QALY scores over time, economists can capture the effect of a health intervention on longevity and quality of life. Scores are derived for various illnesses by asking consumers to rank alternative health states (as described in detail in terms of their level of impairment and discomfort). Economists believe that like willingness to pay estimates, QALY scores reflect patient preferences for alternative health states. The QALYs are surrounded by a range of controversies—for example, some would argue that consumers are unable to perform the cognitive tasks required to weight alternative health states. Other controversies include whether they measure disadvantages of the elderly relative to the young (Nord, 1999). Nonetheless, cost-utility analysis—cost-effectiveness with the QALY as the outcome—is the standard in health economics. The National Health Service makes key decisions about health-care delivery based on costs per QALY.

The Role of Morbidity-Related Costs

Morbidity-related costs (e.g., the use of special education) enter the analysis of costs and benefits in different ways depending on the type of analysis. For a true BCA, these costs would not enter at all—they would be reflected in the societal willingness to pay. In instances where we approximate willingness

to pay with impact on the costs of illness, any reductions in these costs would count as program benefits.

For CEAs, these morbidity-related costs would count in the numerator for the cost-effectiveness ratio depending on the perspective of the analysis. For example, if cost-effectiveness were assessed from the perspective of a health payer (e.g., a state Medicaid program), reductions in special education expenditures would be excluded. (Of course, this divergence in costs would influence payer behavior. The state education authority surely would have an incentive to shift costs onto the Medicaid program.) When calculated from a public taxpayer perspective, however, these costs would be included.

However, in the case of cost-effectiveness ratios where the denominator is a QALY, the morbidity-related costs would not be included. The effect on involvement in other public systems and other morbidity-related costs would be captured by quality of life. To count these costs both in the numerator and denominator would represent a form of double-counting (Gold et al., 1996).

The Cost-Effectiveness of the IYS

Using data from a series of clinical trials (described in more detail in Foster et al., 2007), we calculated the ICER for CT, PT, and CT+PT for a range of outcomes. The ICER combines the incremental cost of each treatment relevant to no treatment with the incremental benefits. The latter is scaled in terms of standard deviations of an observer rating of children's problem behavior. The CT and PT programs are indistinguishable—ICERs were $808 and $849, respectively. While the children who received both showed somewhat greater improvement, these gains were offset by higher costs—the ICER for the combined treatments was $1,028 (2007). A better investment of society's resources would be to treat more children with one of the less expensive, single treatments.

Note that we have not included morbidity-related costs here. As a result, the ICER should be interpreted here as the incremental costs and benefits from a health payer perspective. This role of morbidity-related costs related to the IYS is an area for future research.

ECONOMICS OF IMPLEMENTING EBP: PAYERS, PROVIDERS, AND CONSUMERS

Economic analysis is essential for determining the cost-effectiveness of an established EBP. Several steps, however, must be accomplished for the treatments to be actually delivered. The remainder of the chapter discusses how economic analyses may be applied to understanding the delivery and receipt of an EBP.

As noted, insurers or other possible payers must take the first step. After establishing effectiveness, the next step is to determine whether a treatment is likely cost-effective in real-world settings. In many instances, cost-effectiveness (or rather, cost efficacy) may be established based on efficacy studies alone. Researchers and policymakers may make the leap to assuming cost-effectiveness. The decision likely will reflect other considerations as well. The decision may be inherently emotional and political, reflecting how rational actors are influenced by their values and personal experiences. On a large scale, such a decision might take the form of social movements—for example, Ryan White's family championing government support for pediatric AIDS treatment and psychosocial support services.

Second, the payer must assess cost-effectiveness from its perspective. This decision involves a more objective BCA, comparing costs and outcomes of the newly established EBP to those of preexisting treatments. This situation might involve, for instance, a state Medicaid program or other insurer

determining whether or not to cover inpatient mental health services. When the payer is acting on behalf of taxpayers, this decision should be made with an eye toward societal well-being. Private insurers, of course, will consider their own bottom line. In the case of public systems (e.g., the National Health Service in the United Kingdom or the Medicaid program in the United States), the payer and societal perspective are identical. These programs are designed to accomplish social aims. Of course, public systems inevitably face budget limitations or at least budgetary implications, and so additional cost considerations enter as well.

When these two perspectives diverge, policymakers face a key challenge. A program may be advantageous for society yet not for the health-care payer. In that case, the policymaker must find a way to bring the payer's incentives into line with the social good. For example, better mental health services for troubled youth may increase spending on mental health services. However, those expenditures may reduce costs in the juvenile justice system. The key issue, therefore, for the policymaker is to find a way to transfer funds from the juvenile justice to the mental health system.

The contribution of economics is not limited to whether a payer should or will cover an EBP. That consumers have access to a service depends on several subsequent steps. Providers, for example, have to develop the capacity and be willing to deliver that service. Economic theory suggests that incentives can alter the provider's willingness to provide the EBP. The role of incentives and their potential to influence providers' behavior will be discussed throughout the chapter. For example, a community mental health center may be in the process of deciding whether or not to implement the IYS. Of course, this decision depends to a degree on the level at which reimbursement is set and/or other contractual arrangements, in addition to possible incentives. Driving this decision also will be an initial investment in the training required to provide the service and the potential return on that investment.

Finally, consumers have to be willing to engage in such treatment. Parents are a key player in compliance with prescribed treatment and EBP for children with mental health problems. Travel costs and costs of their time must be considered when encouraging their participation as active partners in their child's treatment. While physicians must prescribe the EBP, the patient will carry out part of the procedure. Incentives can also play a role with consumers and their families.

One can see that the delivery of evidence-based treatment involves several steps and players, and economic analyses improve our understanding of each.

Step 1: Payers Need to Pay

Economics plays a critical role in payers' decisions to include a given treatment in its benefits package. The nature of that decision, however, depends on the health-care system. The United States and the United Kingdom offer contrasts in how economic analysis might be used in coverage decisions about EBP. Before turning to a discussion of the basic tools of economic analysis, we discuss these two countries briefly.

Health Insurance in the United States

In the United States, decisions about what services to cover are made administratively by payers. Those decisions are made within a regulatory framework dictated by state or federal laws depending on the nature of the insurer and population covered. Private insurers are generally regulated by the laws of the states in which they practice. Those regulations are generally fairly broad in nature. For example, the state of New Jersey requires that insurers operating in that state cover all services for "biologically based mental illness" prescribed by physicians. This law is among broader laws addressing the coverage of

mental health services. A variety of other states have laws that require that copayments and deductibles for mental health be equal to those for services for physical disorders and illnesses.

Many private employers offer "self-funded" health insurance plans. These firms essentially fund their own insurance plan, spreading the risk across its employees. (Generally, they contract with a specialized firm to handle administrative details, such as enrollment.) Within the relevant laws, these plans have a wide flexibility in determining what services to offer.

These state laws generally do not apply to federally funded public programs such as Medicaid, Medicare, and the Veterans Administration. In the case of children, the Medicaid program is most relevant. Children become eligible through the program through a variety of means but most are poor or near-poor. The related State Children's Health Program (SCHIP) operates in a similar manner. Both states are funded with state funds and federal matching funds. The percentage mix varies from state to state depending on the state's level of poverty. States have considerable flexibility in determining what services they can or cannot cover but are required to offer services in several broad categories (e.g., inpatient hospitalization). Other categories of services are optional but are eligible for federal matching funds (e.g., rehabilitation and physical therapy services). States can obtain additional flexibility by applying for waivers from federal requirements. These can involve statewide demonstration projects or small experimental programs. Under these waivers, states maintain the federal matching funds to offer services that might otherwise not be eligible.

State Medicaid programs are only just beginning to explore linking service coverage to evidence. Currently, 12 states have pay for performance initiatives (Center for Medicare and Medicaid Services, 2008b). For example, the state of Washington has implemented what it calls Evidence-Based Medicaid. The heart of the program is the A-B-C-D Model (Center for Medicare and Medicaid Services, 2008a). That program assigns letter-grade values to services for which reimbursement is required. The state considers both the quality and strength of evidence in decision making. The grades range from A (indicating "proven benefit") through D ("investigational, experimental, ineffective, or unsafe"). At this time, cost or cost-effectiveness is not considered. Such programs as the Washington program are the exception rather than the rule, and most Medicaid programs make coverage decisions rather haphazardly.

The IYS illustrates the unmet potential of tapping health payer funding. The national IYS is housed at the University of Washington and used throughout the state. There is also a great deal of evidence corroborating its effectiveness, therefore likely classifying it as an EBP based on common criteria. Yet, despite the Evidence-Based Medicaid program in Washington, administrators of the IYS there are not aware if their program has a grade from Medicaid. Instead, the IYS is generally funded through grants from the Washington State Department of Health and Human Services. Tapping into Medicaid resources, allowing providers to bill on a fee for service basis, is unexplored territory for the IYS as well as other less traditional forms of children's mental health care.

Health Insurance in the United Kingdom

The National Health Service is the single-payer insurer for the United Kingdom. To some degree, the British system stands at the other end of the spectrum of decision making: Decisions about whether a service is funded by the National Health Service depend heavily on strictly regulated technological assessments. Those assessments are funded and regulated by the National Institute for Health and Clinical Excellence (NICE). The NICE produces appraisals (national guidance on individual technologies), clinical guidelines (the management of specific conditions), and clinical audits. The appraisals of new technologies are intended to encompass clinical effectiveness, cost-effectiveness, and wider implications of the technologies selected. The assessment guidelines recommend that a cost-effectiveness or cost-utility analysis be included (see the following) (Gafni & Birch, 2003). The NHS is legally obligated to fund medicines and treatments recommended by technology appraisals (National Institute for Health and Clinical Excellence, 2007). These appraisals have stimulated many of the advances in cost-effectiveness and economic evaluation developed by the researchers who prepare the appraisals.

Step 2: Providers Need to Deliver EBP

A budding literature examines incentives providers face when deciding whether to adopt and deliver EBP. A range of factors govern these processes, such as perceived professional standards and inertia in provider behavior. However, economists have explored whether and how financial and other incentives might shape providers' adoption of EBP. That literature grows out of the economists' approach to all human behavior—that people are rational actors. As such, economic agents make decisions that maximize their utility or well-being. Utility represents the goods, services, and state of being that an individual desires. These combine to make up one's "utility basket." The rational actor model posits that people respond to their environment in ways to increase items in their utility basket such as wealth, happiness, security, benefits for loved ones, and so on. They also act in ways to minimize negative consequences such as pay, pain, and extra workload—these outcomes decrease utility. For a health-care provider, utility is derived from patient outcomes, but not exclusively. (The issue of provider incentives and potential conflict with patient well-being is the focus of much research in health economics. The problem is known as the "principal agent problem.")

While economists are rarely mistaken for psychologists, the rational actor model describes human behavior. It also offers insight into how to influence that behavior. For instance, the rational actor model suggests that individuals are constantly performing rudimentary BCA. When perceived utility or benefits from an activity are thought to outweigh costs, a person decides to engage in the activity. This framework indicates that people can be influenced to change their decision based on altering the net benefits to them.

One common tool for changing the cost-effectiveness of a program or treatment is incentives. Incentives are designed to encourage behavior that achieves desired outcomes. To understand the potential case for incentives, it is important to first ask why people are not already acting in the ways that maximize these positive outcomes. From an economist's view, the short answer is that they perceive the costs to be greater than the benefits. Incentives seek to increase the benefit side of the equation so it outweighs the costs. Likewise, disincentives seek to influence behavior by increasing the costs of noncompliance.

EBPs are intended to maximize patient outcomes. Quality management literature also suggests that EBP can be cost-effective, minimizing unnecessary practices (Shortell et al., 2001). Incentives potentially increase the use of and adherence to evidence-based practices in children's mental health care. The following discusses the use of incentives for EBPs.

While little research is available on incentives in children's mental health care, the discussion highlights the small body of research in adolescent substance abuse. It also draws on literature from a wide range of other health conditions, pulling out lessons that could be applicable to children's mental health. The literature on other areas of health services can offer some guidance to research on EBP in mental health. That literature identifies key features of the link between incentives and provider behavior. These features involve the target of the incentives (either physicians or organizations) and the form (e.g., monetary or nonmonetary).

Target Audience: Physicians Versus Organizations

The rational actor model shows that to influence behavior, we must first determine whose behavior we want to shape. Using a simple economic framework, incentives could be used to influence those on the supply side (providers) or the demand side (users) of health services. The supply side includes physicians and the organizations for which they work. Health-care payers, such as the government and insurance companies, may offer incentives to providers for practicing evidence-based care. With EBP, the responsibility rests with the health-care provider to gain knowledge about these practices and prescribe them. As such, incentives for the supply side are central to our discussion.

Incentive programs have been targeted to both individual physicians and the health-care organizations for which they work. Some literature describes interventions at the individual physician level, offering direct payments to physicians for meeting criteria associated with EBP (Gilmore et al., 2007). Other research examines incentives at the organizational level, where the employers of the physicians actually receive the incentive (Grossbart, 2006; Roski et al., 2003; Shortell et al., 2001). For example, a community mental health center might receive additional payments by documenting that all of their psychologists have been trained to provide the IYS as an EBP.

Debate persists about whether to offer incentives to individual doctors or their employers. On the one hand, direct compensation to providers will have the most direct effect on their perceived benefits, and therefore, on their personal BCA. Managing this from the payer perspective, however, would be challenging. The data required for such monitoring is substantial. A payer would have to review cases for each doctor to determine compliance. Moreover, EBP focus on certain conditions. When a condition is relatively rare, a single physician may see few patients with those presenting symptoms. This will make it inefficient to measure improvement in care at the individual physician level (Christianson, Knutson, & Mazze, 2006).

Offering incentives to organizations that employ individual providers may be much more efficient for the payers. Patients across individual doctors in an organization can be pooled, providing many more patients with the targeted condition. However, providing incentives at the organizational level may not provide the same leverage for changing physician behavior. In some cases, the organization has discretion in deciding how to use the bonus or reward (Roski et al., 2003). It is possible that when the organization does not choose to pass it directly to the providers who use the EBP, the physicians are less motivated to change their behavior. Whether and how to pass long incentives to providers will reflect other economic considerations. Organizations may want to pass along the incentives in instances where monitoring specific providers is difficult. They may choose to keep the incentives in cases where they can guarantee provider compliance.

In extreme cases, it may also create a free-rider problem. Some physicians may ignore management's call for the use of EBP to save their time and resources needed for additional training or other costs. Yet they may benefit from increased remuneration or other perks if incentives are not shared exclusively with those who comply but rather spread across the organization. Another unintended consequence is that incentives to organizations could foster unhealthy competition among physicians (Ferguson & Lim, 2001). If the incentive is viewed as a finite sum that is divided among physicians based on performance, then perverse incentives could influence providers to forego collaboration and avoid peer consultation, a cornerstone of medical practice. In the end, hospitals and medical groups need participating physicians to share the same quality goals if the organization is to succeed in earning the financial incentive (Shaman, 2008).

Much of the current practice generally describes health payers giving incentives to organizations, with the assumption that the employers pass the money to individual physicians based on performance (Shaman, 2008). As such, the scenarios just described may be unfounded. However, this economic approach suggests that more research is needed on the potential latent effects of how the organization uses its incentives.

Type of Incentives

Incentives generally fall into two categories: monetary and nonmonetary, such as prestige. The type selected typically depends on the target group. For health-care providers, the literature largely focuses on monetary incentives. Pay for performance, often abbreviated as P4P, is an emerging tool in quality management practice. The Institute of Medicine's "Crossing the Quality Chasm" report of 2001 precipitated this movement (Christianson et al., 2006; Gilmore et al., 2007; Grossbart, 2006; Shaman, 2008; Shortell et al., 2001). The report stated that physician incentives needed to be more closely linked with their performance (Grossbart, 2006). Some even dub pay for performance as a "quality incentive program," actively linking the financial incentive to quality management practices (Gilmore et al., 2007). Financial disincentives for providers, such as docked pay for not meeting performance standards, are also described (Ferguson & Lim, 2001). However, the majority of the attention is on positive reinforcement or rewards rather than penalties (Shaman, 2008).

The Centers for Medicare and Medicaid Services (CMS) led the way with pay for performance. In the mid-2000s, CMS issued a new reimbursement policy for hospitals and physicians. Future increases in payment would depend on improvements in clinical care. Private sector health insurers followed suit. They have begun to implement pay for performance as well. Some even issue scorecards for hospitals and physicians that consumers may use in selecting a provider (Shaman, 2008). Now over half of the private-sector HMOs have a P4P program, covering over 80% of consumers enrolled in HMOs (Epstein, 2007).

To a lesser degree, health-care payers also use nonmonetary incentives for physicians and provider organizations. Those who meet quality targets may receive the designation as a preferred provider or other public recognition of their high-quality practices (Shaman, 2008). National accreditation and state licensure may also bestow prestige on an organization. Shortell invokes institutional theory, stating that providers will act in ways that either maintains or increases their credibility with key constituents (Shortell, 2004). Moreover, hospitals may also benefit from improved efficiencies. Use of the most appropriate care for patients would lead to saving money and time on unnecessary procedures. This would conceivably free up hospital beds earlier, allowing them to be filled by other patients (Shaman, 2008). Generally, however, financial incentives for health-care providers are most commonly described and studied in the research literature.

Evidence on Effectiveness of Incentives

While some studies find that physicians can be influenced by incentives (Gilmore et al., 2007; Shortell et al., 2001), research on the effectiveness of provider incentives is rather limited (Grossbart, 2006; Shortell, 2004; see also Epstein, 2007; Lindenauer et al., 2007). Little research is published on the use and effectiveness of financial incentives in mental health care, particularly for children. A few studies have considered incentives for other types of patient care. Although these studies vary in methodology, most find a surprising small effect size for incentives.

A number of studies has used observational data to assess the effectiveness of pay for performance. In an often-cited study, Lindenauer et al. assessed reported quality milestones of 613 hospitals over a 2-year period. A third of the sample participated in the CMS pay-for-performance program. The other two-thirds voluntarily reported their progress through a national initiative, but did not receive incentives. They found that the pay-for-performance hospitals improved across all areas of quality, significantly more so than the comparison hospitals. Hospitals that were performing the lowest at baseline made the greatest improvements. However, after controlling for baseline differences, the researchers found that pay for performance fostered more modest gains, ranging from 2.6% to 4.1% over the 2 years, compared to the hospitals with no incentives (Lindenauer et al., 2007).

Another large-scale observational study assessed change over time in mortality rates for patients diagnosed with key conditions. Werner and Barlow assessed results from 3,657 hospitals using data from the Center for Medicaid and Medicare Services Web site. They focused on myocardial infarction, pneumonia, heart failure, and pneumonia. For each of these conditions, there were only very small differences in risk-adjusted mortality rates between hospitals scoring in the top 25% in quality compared to those in the bottom quartile. Myocardial infarction had the largest, with only a 0.005 decrease in risk-adjusted mortality rates between the highest and the lowest performing hospitals. They suggest that quality performance measures should be reassessed to be more closely related to patient outcomes (Werner & Bradlow, 2006).

Smaller reviews also find preliminary evidence supporting the effectiveness of incentives. In a review of 10 hospitals located within one health system, Grossbart found that the hospitals that were provided incentives earned higher quality scores than those without incentives (Grossbart, 2006). However, hospitals chose whether or not to participate in the incentive process, suggesting the possibility of selection bias. Collier's study offered a financial incentive contract to a group representing 12 hospitalists working in a health system with two hospitals. The hospitalists improved in timely completion of medical records, maintaining 24-hour coverage and a lower target patient–physician ratio, as well as in many quality standards of the Joint Commission on Accreditation of Health Care Organizations (JCAHO) (Collier, 2007). This hospitalist group was favorably compared to another group that did not receive a contract for the incentive program. The comparison group, however, was not initially awarded a contract due to its insufficient number of physicians. Number of physicians is a key factor in being able to provide 24/7 coverage and a lower patient physician ratio. Comparing the unequal groups may confound the role of incentives in motivating physician behavior.

Most randomized studies have been small in scope. They do provide examples of a topic more closely related to mental health and psychosocial factors—smoking cessation. An et al. (2008) conducted a randomized experiment with clinics referring smokers to a hotline for tobacco cessation. These "quitlines" are considered to be a method to link smokers with evidence-based practices for quitting smoking. The study involved 49 clinics, half randomly assigned to receive incentives for making referrals to the quitline. Clinics receiving the incentive referred 11% of patients who smoked to the quitline, compared to 4% of the control clinics (An et al., 2008). While this difference is statistically significant, it still represents a small percentage of smokers referred for assistance.

Similarly, in a randomized study of smoking screening in adults, a medical group offered incentives to a portion of its clinics for identifying smokers and providing advice on quitting to a target number of patients. Clinics in the incentives group were significantly more likely to identify tobacco users than the control clinics. The researchers conclude, though, that

the incentives did not produce an effect that could significantly sustain the change in the physicians' behavior compared to the control group (Roski et al., 2003). This suggests that incentives may play a role in modifying physician and organizational behavior, but it should be viewed as one among several responses needed to change how clinical work is performed to better elicit quality results.

Challenges

As we discussed, evidence of effectiveness in the literature is mixed at best. Do these modest findings suggest that the rational actor model does not apply to health-care providers? On the contrary, the model would suggest that it is likely the physicians are responding quite appropriately to the incentive. Perhaps the incentives themselves are not large enough to alter the provider's internal BCA. In a review of 10 large pay-for-performance programs, Price Waterhouse found that incentives accounted for a range of 1% to 8% of physician pay. Health-care payers such as the participating insurance companies agreed that the amount should be at least 10% of salary to motivate physicians (Shaman, 2008). Other studies find that the current incentives are even lower, ranging from 1% to 2% of physician pay (Shortell, 2004).

Similarly, it may also be rational for providers to opt out of the financial incentive program. Each health payer determines its own set of quality criteria. One review of 10 major heath payers found that together they had 60 quality indicators. None of the measures, however, were shared by all 10 plans (Shaman, 2008). Participating physicians and organizations must track all of these indicators. Resources are needed to collect the data, enter it into a tracking system, and report the results. Some progressive institutions may already engage in data tracking for program monitoring and internal continuous quality improvement purposes. Many others, though, will note the burden required to meet the requirements of each payer. Finite resources may mean that the hospital takes money out of the direct care line item to cover increased administrative costs. Organizations as well as individuals must decide if the expected benefits outweigh the costs.

In addition to the provider's perspective, the payer must consider other challenges before embarking on a pay-for-performance program. Certain conditions must be evident before incentives are warranted, including:

Costs. Offering incentives could affect positive consumer outcomes. Managing the programs, however, can create significant costs. In most cases, payers must provide new funding to pay for the incentives themselves (Christianson et al., 2006). Additional costs include resources for monitoring quality compliance including data collection and even computerized tracking systems. Costs are to be expected, but so are increased benefits. Incentives make sense when expected benefits related to improved patient outcomes, productivity, cost savings, and so on outweigh the anticipated costs.

Ample resources. On both the supply side and the demand side, desired behaviors may involve referrals to resources. When the targeted service is scarce, it is not reasonable to offer incentives for using these resources. For instance, encouraging child protective services to place youth in therapeutic foster care would be misguided if the care was not widely available in the community. In this case, resources would be better spent trying to increase the availability of the service.

Ethical considerations. The use of incentives may be inappropriate for people in certain positions. This could be especially true of public officials. Incentives clearly should not be used if there is a possibility they could be construed as a bribe. In these cases, education-focused interventions that appeal to common interests may be more appropriate.

Latent consequences. Incentives inherently elevate the importance of the behaviors for which they are awarded. When people shift their priorities toward these activities, they may decrease the amount of time they spend doing other necessary practices that do not have an incentive (Christianson et al., 2006). Before instituting incentives, it is imperative to consider how they may affect people's other behaviors. Anticipated latent consequences may indicate that incentives may cause more harm than good.

Measurement error. Ultimately, the quality indicators linked to incentives must be measured. Sometimes the best measures of key behaviors are not necessarily the easiest to collect. Pay-for-performance indicators typically include those that are easiest and cheapest to monitor. As a result, behavior indicators related to incentives may not necessarily be closely related to the longer term patient outcomes of true importance (Christianson et al., 2006). Incentives would be appropriate when measures are most closely linked to the targeted health outcomes.

Applications to Mental Health EBP

At some point, the trend toward use of provider incentives, even with relatively little supporting evidence, will likely come to mental health. While there is little research on provider incentives in the mental health system, we can anticipate issues with incentives unique to mental health.

For instance, most EBPs are related to specific conditions. Mental health providers can spend much time determining a diagnosis. Conditions are often based on symptomology, which may vary naturally over time. For example, most depression scales have cutoff points representing clinical depression. At the same time, the latent condition of depression is continuous, ebbing and flowing. Time of measurement and assessment tools will become very important in determining whether or not the child meets the condition and therefore warrants an EBP. Moreover, incentives are only appropriate for conditions that have an established EBP. EBPs do not exist for some children's mental health issues. Acting rationally, it is possible that providers may (even subconsciously) give a diagnosis for borderline conditions that have an incentive tied to them. Clearly, much thought will need to be given to the range of conditions with EBPs before incentives are introduced to mental health.

Another issue to consider is the tracking of patient progress. Often the person who diagnoses the condition is the same one who implements the EBP and tracks changes over time in the client. Many organizations provide clinical supervision. The enhanced role of the supervisor, offering an objective view on the work done, will need to be explored within each agency. Review mechanisms will also need to be developed for solo practitioners if health payers decide to offer direct incentives to them as well.

Step 3: Consumers Need to Consume

Incentives for the demand side also have a place in the discussion of EBP. While physicians must prescribe the EBP, it is often up to the patient to carry out part of the procedure. This may involve making an appointment for ordered tests, purchasing and using medications as prescribed, following dietary and exercise regimens, and so on. The literature contains examples of programs that offer incentives for patients, typically related to treatment for specific conditions. These conditions often include traditional health problems such as diabetes (Taggart, Wan, Harris, & Powell Davies, 2008), but some are also related to mental health and substance use

issues like adolescent substance abuse (Godley, Godley, Wright, Funk, & Petry, 2008) and smoking during pregnancy (Heil et al., 2008), among others.

Types of Incentives

Improving consumer health behaviors and outcomes is the ultimate goal of EBP. Physicians and other health-care providers play an important role in educating patients and prescribing clinical recommendations. Incentives for providers, however, are not necessarily closely aligned with patient outcomes (Long, Helweg-Larsen, & Volpp, 2008; Werner & Bradlow, 2006). Patient adherence to their physician's recommendations is a central component of achieving optimal results. The consumer side of the supply-and-demand model also must be considered.

What motivates patients and consumers to comply with physician recommendations? Researchers have developed health and behavioral change theories to understand patient motivation. Interventions to improve patient adherence often involve education. More recently, tools such as motivational interviewing are receiving much attention. This approach involves exploring with the patient reasons for their resistance to compliance and facilitating their own discovery of mechanisms that can help them adhere to physician recommendations (Butterworth, 2008; Joy, 2008). Given the economic perspective that patients are rational actors, incentives may have a role in affecting patient adherence. Thus far, incentives are only a small piece of the patient motivation and compliance literature.

Incentives that have been described in the literature for patients and consumers include both monetary and nonmonetary rewards. Employers, insurance payers, and other health-supporting programs are beginning to use consumer incentives. Employers, for instance, are increasingly realizing the cost factors in having workers with a variety of taxing health conditions. Some have developed programs to encourage their employees to lose weight, exercise, and stop smoking, among other behaviors (Long et al., 2008). Others have offered payment to workers for completing programs in disease management (Wilhide, Hayes, & Farah, 2008). Disincentives also exist to encourage employee compliance with clinical recommendations, such as higher health-care premiums for persistent smokers or even the threat of termination (Long et al., 2008). National survey results indicate that 9 out of 10 employers with 50 or more workers offer some type of health promotion program. However, these tend to be small in scope, with only an estimated 7% offering comprehensive programs (Taitel, Haufle, Heck, Loeppke, & Fetterolf, 2008). Nonetheless, most organizations perceive that having a healthier workforce actually lowers their own costs of missed days of work and health-care premiums while ultimately increasing general productivity.

Some health payers are also beginning to explore patient incentives. One private company has implemented medical savings accounts for certain plan beneficiaries with chronic conditions. The payer deposits money into the client account for those who adhere to prescribed treatment. Disincentives are also being utilized. Most notable is the West Virginia Medicaid program's recent movement to reduce coverage for those who do not follow clinical recommendations (Long et al., 2008).

A small number of community-based health promotion programs has also begun to use incentives. For example, an adolescent substance abuse recovery program notes the use of drawings for prizes (ranging from candy to televisions) (Godley et al., 2008). Retail store vouchers also have been employed in a university hospital setting to encourage pregnant women to stop smoking (Heil et al., 2008).

Evidence

As use of incentives for consumers is evolving, so is the research on its effectiveness. Evidence generally falls into two groups. Employer-based incentives are relatively new and as such, limited evidence exists on their effectiveness. Much more research is available on contingency management, a common incentive-based system for treating substance abuse. Both will be discussed later.

Preliminary evidence suggests that work-based incentives have positive effects on patient/employer health outcomes. Wilhide and colleagues used data from 87 employers who each had at least 75 employees with a qualifying condition requiring disease management. Each employer decided whether or not to offer incentives to individuals for participating in a disease management program. Just over half provided incentives, most commonly gift cards and cash. The researchers found that incentives valued at least $50 at intake and again at completion of the disease management program were most effective in affecting employee participation (Wilhide et al., 2008). Taitel et al. (2008) studied the effect of incentives on employee participation on health risk assessments. Using data on 124 employers, they found that incentives did encourage participation. The necessary size of the incentive, however, depended on organizational characteristics. Those featuring high organizational support for employees could actually offer smaller incentives to inspire participation in the health assessment (Taitel et al., 2008). While preliminary studies such as these are promising, some in the field suggest that more evidence is needed before companies continue the move toward workplace incentives (Draper, Tynan, & Christianson, 2008).

Much more of the literature on demand-side incentives involves contingency management. This approach operationalizes the psychological theory of operant conditioning in which environmental factors can shape behavior through reinforcing rewards or negative consequences. Contingency management was developed specifically to address substance abuse. It uses incentives to induce behavior modification (Godley et al., 2008). The approach was first used with cocaine users. Using random assignment, Silverman et al. found that cocaine users were more likely to comply with treatment and submit clean urine tests when vouchers were offered as incentives (Silverman et al., 1998). While this study was small ($N = 59$), it inspired others to test contingency management for other substances including marijuana and alcohol dependence. Positive effects were found for these groups as well (Godley et al., 2008).

Since the earlier studies, contingency management has taken on the name voucher-based reinforcement therapy (Heil et al., 2008). Vouchers are offered to people for compliance with treatment, including maintaining sobriety. A meta-analysis of 30 studies using experimental designs found an average effect size of 0.32 when vouchers were used as incentives. Studies that offered incentives earlier on and that provided larger voucher amounts yielded the greatest results (Lussier, Heil, Mongeon, Badger, & Higgins, 2006). More recently, Heil and colleagues implemented a randomized controlled trial of 82 pregnant smokers. Both groups were encouraged to quit smoking. The treatment group was offered a voucher to use for retail items if they abstained from smoking. The comparison group was provided a voucher of similar amount for study participation. The study found that those in the treatment group were significantly more likely to have stopped smoking by the end of pregnancy (41% vs. 10%) and 12 weeks postpartum (24% vs. 3%) (Heil et al., 2008).

Evidence also suggests that contingency management can be effective for adolescent substance abusers. Most involve very small sample sizes. Corby and colleagues were among the first to assess the effects of contingency management for youth. They found that voucher interventions yielded positive results for young smokers. However, the study was framed as a feasibility study, likely due to the small sample size ($N = 8$) (Corby, Roll, Ledgerwood, & Schuster, 2000).

Kamon, Budney, and Stanger (2005) studied the use of vouchers in decreasing marijuana use among 19 adolescents. Teens with a history of marijuana use earned vouchers for clean drug tests. Vouchers were for socially acceptable services such as restaurants, clothing stores, and movie theaters. Values of the incentives increased with each clean screen and reverted to the initial amount when marijuana use was detected. Parents earned chances for prize drawings by supporting their children in the program as well. By the end of the 14-week intervention, 74% of youth tested free of marijuana, compared to only 37% at baseline. Just over half were clean 1 month following the program (Kamon et al., 2005).

More recently, Godley et al. (2008) conducted a descriptive contingency management study of 86 adolescents. They assessed the impact of prize drawing incentives on program compliance. Youth coming out of substance abuse residential treatment were encouraged to set goals related to developing socially acceptable activities. Participants set an average of 20 goals related to areas such as education, family, recreational activities, and so forth. The more steps a youth took to participate in activities that supported their chosen goals, the more opportunities they earned for participating in drawings. Youth completed 13 goals on average. Godley and colleagues suggest that prize drawing is a viable alternative to vouchers (S. H. Godley, Godley, Wright, Funk, & Petry, 2008).

Barriers

Most of the barriers related to measuring the effects of incentives in children's mental health involve observational data and small sample sizes. It is possible that additional research using larger scale randomized experiments will substantiate the current findings from smaller studies.

Most studies to date have not viewed incentives from the perspective of health behavior theory. This may elucidate additional approaches to incentives for consumers that have not been tested. Health behavior theory suggests that it is necessary to understand reasons why people have not already complied with the desired behavior before offering incentives. The PRECEDE–PROCEED model holds that interventions should address the target group's knowledge and attitudes, available resources for implementing the activity, and the opinions of others around them (Grol & Wensing, 2004). These can all serve as facilitators or barriers to implementing EBP. Incentives will be most effective when they help people overcome the barriers to participation. This may include being linked to activities that increase their knowledge (such as incentives for attending training), or perhaps provide increased resources that lower the costs of their participation (such as patient transportation assistance).

Applications to Mental Health EBP

The possibility of offering incentives to children with mental health conditions and/or their families requires significant discussion. One consideration is whether or not people will respond as predicted to incentives. Are children considered to be rational actors? Similarly, can we expect people with mental health conditions to respond rationally to an incentive? Depression itself can have great effects on a person's utility basket, perhaps driving it to zero. The answer to this may depend on the condition itself. Another possibility is to offer the incentive to the parents. Parents play a key role in assuring their children comply with provider recommendations. For instance, parents provide the transportation to appointments, administer medications, and so on. They essentially manage the illness on a daily basis.

CONCLUSION

Economics has an informative role to play in the field of children's mental health services. Cost-effectiveness techniques are necessary to fully understand the costs of the outcomes payers are "buying." This is an effective tool aiding in the selection among a variety of evidence-based programs. In addition to cost analysis, economics provides a framework for predicting human behavior. Incentives can play a role, albeit limited in some cases, in eliciting desired behavior among mental health providers and consumers including children and their parents or caregivers.

REFERENCES

An, L. C., Bluhm, J. H., Foldes, S. S., Alesci, N. L., Klatt, C. M., Center, B. A., . . . Manley, M. W. (2008). A randomized trial of a pay-for-performance program targeting clinician referral to a state tobacco quitline. *Archives of Internal Medicine, 168*, 1993–1999.

Barnett, W. S. (1985). *The Perry preschool program and its long-term effects : A benefit-cost analysis.* Ypsilanti, MI: High/Scope Educational Research Foundation.

Barnett, W. S. (1996). *Lives in the balance: Age-27 benefit-cost analysis of the High/Scope Perry Pre-school Program.* Ypsilanti, MI: High/Scope Educational Research Foundation.

Barrera, M., Jr., Biglan, A., Taylor, T. K., Gunn, B. K., Smolkowski, K., Black, C., . . . Fowler, R. C. (2002). Early elementary school intervention to reduce conduct problems: A randomized trial with Hispanic and non-Hispanic children. *Prevention Science, 3*, 83–94.

Belfield, C. R., Nores, M., Barnett, S., & Schweinhart, L. (2006). The High/Scope Perry Preschool Program: Costbenefit analysis using data from the age-40 followup. *Journal of Human Resources, 41*, 162–190.

Brestan, E. V., & Eyberg, S. M. (1998). Effective psychosocial treatments of conduct-disordered children and adolescents: 29 years, 82 studies, and 5,272 kids. *Journal of Clinical Child Psychology, 27*, 180–189.

Butterworth, S. W. (2008). Influencing patient adherence to treatment guidelines. *Journal of Managed Care Pharmacy, 14*(6 Suppl B), 21–24.

Center for Medicare and Medicaid Services. (2008a). Medicaid and SCHIP promising practices: Details for evidence-based practice. Retrieved from www.cms.hhs.gov/MedicaidSCHIPQualPrac/MSPPDL/ItemDetail.asp?ItemID=CMS1185908

Center for Medicare and Medicaid Services. (2008b). Pay for performance: Payment aligned with quality. Retrieved from www.cms.hhs.gov/MedicaidSCHIPQualPrac/04_P4P.asp#TopOfPage

Chambers, J., Parrish, T., & Harr, J. J. (2002). What are we spending on special education in the United States, 1999–2000? *Center for Special Education Finance Brief, 8*, 1–4.

Chambers, J., Parrish, T., Lieberman, J., & Wolman, J. (1998). What are we spending on special education in the U.S.? *Center for Special Education Finance Brief, 8*, 1–4.

Christianson, J. B., Knutson, D. J., & Mazze, R. S. (2006). Physician pay-for-performance. Implementation and research issues. *Journal of General Internal Medicine, 21* (Suppl 2), S9–S13.

Collier, V. U. (2007). Use of pay for performance in a community hospital private hospitalist group: A preliminary report. *Transactions of the American Clinical and Climatological Association, 118*, 263–272.

Corby, E. A., Roll, J. M., Ledgerwood, D. M., & Schuster, C. R. (2000). Contingency management interventions for treating the substance abuse of adolescents: A feasibility study. *Experimental and Clinical Psychopharmacology, 8*, 371–376.

Draper, D. A., Tynan, A., & Christianson, J. B. (2008). Health and wellness: The shift from managing illness to promoting health. *Issue Brief Center for Studying Health System Change, 121*, 1–4.

Drummond, M. F., O'Brien, B., Stoddart, G. L., & Torrance, G. W. (1997). Cost-utility analysis. In *Methods for the economic evaluation of health care programmes* (pp. 139–204). Oxford, England: Oxford University Press.

Epstein, A. M. (2007). Pay for performance at the tipping point. *New England Journal of Medicine, 356*, 515–517.

Ferguson, B., & Lim, J. N. (2001). Incentives and clinical governance: Money following quality? *Journal of Management in Medicine, 15*, 463–487.

Foster, E. M., & Bickman, L. (2000). Refining the costs analyses of the Fort Bragg Evaluation: The impact of cost offset and cost shifting. *Mental Health Services Research, 2*, 13–25.

Foster, E. M., & Connor, T. (2005). The public costs of better mental health services for children and adolescents. *Psychiatric Services, 56*, 50–55.

Foster, E. M., Olchowski, A. E., & Webster-Stratton, C. H. (2007). Is stacking intervention components cost-effective? An analysis of the Incredible Years program. *Journal of the American Academy of Child and Adolescent Psychiatry, 46*, 1414–1424.

Gafni, A., & Birch, S. (2003). NICE methodological guidelines and decision making in the National Health Service in England and Wales. *Pharmacoeconomics, 21*, 149–157.

Gilmore, A. S., Zhao, Y., Kang, N., Ryskina, K. L., Legorreta, A. P., Taira, D. A., & Chung, R. S. (2007). Patient outcomes and evidence-based medicine in a preferred provider organization setting: A six-year evaluation of a physician pay-for-performance program. *Health Services Research, 42*(6 Pt 1), 2140–2159; discussion 2294–2323.

Godley, S. H., Godley, M. D., Wright, K. L., Funk, R. R., & Petry, N. M. (2008). Contingent reinforcement of personal goal activities for adolescents with substance use disorders during post-residential continuing care. *American Journal of Addiction, 17*, 278–286.

Gold, M. R., Russell, L. B., Siegel, J. E., & Weinstein, M. C. (Eds.). (1996). *Cost-effectiveness in health and medicine*. New York, NY: Oxford University Press.

Gorsky, R. D., Haddix, A. C., & Schaffer, P. A. (1996). Cost of an intervention. In A. C. Haddix, S. M. Teutsch, P. A. Shaffer, & D. O. Dunet (Eds.), *Prevention effectivness: A guide to decision analysis and economic evaluation* (pp. 57–75). New York, NY: Oxford University Press.

Grol, R., & Wensing, M. (2004). What drives change? Barriers to and incentives for achieving evidence-based practice. *Medical Journal of Australia, 180* (6 Suppl), S57–S60.

Grossbart, S. R. (2006). What's the return? Assessing the effect of "pay-for-performance" initiatives on the quality of care delivery. *Medical Care Research and Review, 63*(1 Suppl), 29S–48S.

Gunther, O. H., Friemel, S., Bernert, S., Matschinger, H., Angermeyer, M. C., & Konig, H. H. (2007). The burden of depressive disorders in Germany—results from the European Study of the Epidemiology of Mental Disorders (ESEMeD). *Psychiatrische Praxis, 34*, 292–301.

Hargreaves, W. A., Shumway, M., Hu, T. W., & Cuffel, B. (1998). *Cost-outcome methods for mental health*. New York, NY: Academic Press.

Healey, A., & Chisholm, D. (1999). Willingness to pay as a measure of the benefits of mental health care. *Journal of Mental Health Policy and Economics, 2*, 55–58.

Heil, S. H., Higgins, S. T., Bernstein, I. M., Solomon, L. J., Rogers, R. E., Thomas, C. S., . . . Lynch, M. E. (2008). Effects of voucher-based incentives on abstinence from cigarette smoking and fetal growth among pregnant women. *Addiction, 103*, 1009–1018.

Joy, S. V. (2008). Clinical pearls and strategies to optimize patient outcomes. *Diabetes Education, 34*(Suppl 3), 54S–59S.

Kamon, J., Budney, A., & Stanger, C. (2005). A contingency management intervention for adolescent marijuana abuse and conduct problems. *Journal of the American Academy of Child and Adolescent Psychiatry, 44*, 513–521.

Karoly, L. A., Kilburn, M. R., Bigelow, J. H., Caulkins, J. P., & Cannon, J. S. (2001). *Assessing costs and benefits of early childhood intervention programs: Overview and application to the Starting Early Starting Smart Program*. Santa Monica, CA: Rand.

Kenkel, D. (1994). Cost of illness approach. In D. Kenkel & R. Fabian (Eds.), *Valuing health for policy: An economic approach* (pp. 42–71). Chicago, IL: University of Chicago Press.

Kenkel, D., Berger, M., & Blomquist, G. (1994). Contingent valuation of health. In D. Kenkel & R. Fabian (Eds.), *Valuing health for policy: An economic approach* (pp. 72–104). Chicago, IL: University of Chicago Press.

Konig, H. H. (2004). Measuring preferences of psychiatric patients. *Psychiatrische Praxis, 31*, 118–127.

Konig, H. H., Bernert, S., & Angermeyer, M. C. (2005). Measuring preferences for depressive health states. *Psychiatrische Praxis, 32*, 122–131.

Lindenauer, P. K., Remus, D., Roman, S., Rothberg, M. B., Benjamin, E. M., Ma, A., & Bratzler, D. W. (2007). Public reporting and pay for performance in hospital quality improvement. *New England Journal of Medcine, 356*, 486–496.

Long, J. A., Helweg-Larsen, M., & Volpp, K. G. (2008). Patient opinions regarding "pay for performance for patients." *Journal of General Internal Medicine, 23*, 1647–1652.

Lussier, J. P., Heil, S. H., Mongeon, J. A., Badger, G. J., & Higgins, S. T. (2006). A meta-analysis of voucher-based reinforcement therapy for substance use disorders. *Addiction, 101*, 192–203.

Miller, L. S., & Rojas-Flores, L. (1999). *Prevention study with parent program head start families*. New York: New York Child Study University Center.

National Institute for Health and Clinical Excellence. (2007). About NICE. Retrieved from www.nice.org.uk/aboutnice/about_nice.jsp.

Nord, E. (1999). *Cost-value analysis in health care: Making sense out of QALYs*. Cambridge, England, and New York, NY: Cambridge University Press.

O'Shea, E., Gannon, B., & Kennelly, B. (2008). Eliciting preferences for resource allocation in mental health care in Ireland. *Health Policy, 88*, 359–370.

Rice, D. P., Hodgson, T. A., & Kopstein, A. N. (1985). The economic costs of illness: A replication and update. *Health Care Financing Review, 7*, 61–80.

Rice, D. P., Kelman, S., & Miller, L. S. (1991). Estimates of economic costs of alcohol and drug abuse and mental illness, 1985 and 1988. *Public Health Reports, 106*, 280–292.

Roski, J., Jeddeloh, R., An, L., Lando, H., Hannan, P., Hall, C., & Zhu, S. H. (2003). The impact of financial incentives and a patient registry on preventive care quality: Increasing provider adherence to evidence-based smoking cessation practice guidelines. *Preventive Medicine, 36*, 291–299.

Schweinhart, L. J., Barnes, H. V., & Weikart, D. P. (1993). *Significant benefits: The High/Scope Perry Preschool Study through age 27*. Ypsilanti, MI: High/Scope Press.

Scott, S., Spender, Q., Doolan, M., Jacobs, M., & Aspland, H. (2001). Multicentre controlled trial of parenting groups for child antisocial behavior in clinical practice. *British Medical Journal, 323*, 1–5.

Shaman, H. (2008). What you need to know about pay for performance. *Healthcare Financing and Management, 62*, 92–96.

Shortell, S. M. (2004). Increasing value: A research agenda for addressing the managerial and organizational challenges facing health care delivery in the United States. *Medical Care Research Review, 61*(3 Suppl), 12S–30S.

Shortell, S. M., Zazzali, J. L., Burns, L. R., Alexander, J. A., Gillies, R. R., Budetti, P. P., . . . Zuckerman, H. S. (2001). Implementing evidence-based medicine: The role of market pressures, compensation incentives, and culture in physician organizations. *Medical Care, 39*(7 Suppl 1), I62–I78.

Silverman, K., Wong, C. J., Umbricht-Schneiter, A., Montoya, I. D., Schuster, C. R., & Preston, K. L. (1998). Broad beneficial effects of cocaine abstinence reinforcement among methadone patients. *Journal of Consulting and Clinical Psychology, 66*, 811–824.

Smith, R. D. (2007). Use, option and externality values: Are contingent valuation studies in health care misspecified? *Health Economics, 16*, 861–869.

Sobocki, P., Lekander, I., Borgstrom, F., Strom, O., & Runeson, B. (2007). The economic burden of depression in Sweden from 1997 to 2005. *European Psychiatry, 22*, 146–152.

Taggart, J., Wan, Q., Harris, M. F., & Powell Davies, G. (2008). Quality of diabetes care—a comparison of division diabetes registers. *Australian Family Physician, 37*, 490–492.

Taitel, M. S., Haufle, V., Heck, D., Loeppke, R., & Fetterolf, D. (2008). Incentives and other factors associated with employee participation in health risk assessments. *Journal of Occupational and Environmental Medicine, 50*, 863–872.

Taylor, T. K., Schmidt, F., Pepler, D., & Hodgkins, H. (1998). A comparison of eclectic treatment with Webster-Stratton's parent and children series in a children's mental health setting: A randomized controlled trial. *Behavior Therapy, 29*, 221–240.

Warner, K. E., & Luce, B. R. (1982). *Cost-benefit and cost-effectiveness analysis in health care*. Ann Arbor, MI: Health Administration Press.

Webster-Stratton, C. (1990). Enhancing the effectiveness of self-administered videotape for families and conduct-problem children. *Journal of Abnormal Psychology, 18*, 479–492.

Webster-Stratton, C., & Hammond, M. (1997). Treating children with early onset conduct problems: A comparison of child and parent training interventions. *Journal of Consulting and Clinical Psychology, 65*, 93–109.

Webster-Stratton, C. (2000). The Incredible Years training series. *Juvenile Justice Bulletin*, 1–23.

Webster-Stratton, C., Reid, M. J., & Hammond, M. (2001). Preventing conduct problems, promoting social competence: A parent teacher training partnership in headstart. *Journal of Clinical Child Psychology, 30*, 283–302.

Werner, R. M., & Bradlow, E. T. (2006). Relationship between Medicare's hospital compare performance measures and mortality rates. *Journal of the American Medical Association, 296*, 2694–2702.

Wilhide, C., Hayes, J. R., & Farah, J. R. (2008). The use and influence of employee incentives on participation and throughput in a telephonic disease management program. *Population Health Management, 11*, 197–202.

Zerbe, R. O., Jr., & Dively, D. D. (1994). *Benefit-cost analysis in theory and practice*. New York, NY: Harper Collins College.

PART II

Specific Disorders

6

Intellectual Disabilities

ROBERT DIDDEN, JEFF SIGAFOOS, RUSSELL LANG, MARK O'REILLY,
KLAUS DRIESCHNER, AND GIULIO E. LANCIONI

OVERVIEW OF DISORDER

Intellectual disability (ID) is diagnosed if an individual has a total IQ below 70, significant deficits in adaptive skills and onset before age of 18 years (American Psychiatric Association, 2000). Four levels of severity of ID are distinguished: (1) profound (IQ 0–20), (2) severe (IQ 20–35), (3) moderate (IQ 35–50), and (4) mild (IQ 50–70). Behavioral and/or psychiatric disorders are common among children and adults with ID. A growing number of studies have shown increased prevalence rates of a variety of behavioral and psychiatric disorders in ID as compared to nondisabled populations (Dekker & Koot, 2003; Emerson, 2003). A longitudinal study suggests that if untreated, such disorders are persistent (Einfeld et al., 2006). People with ID carry many risk factors for behavioral and psychiatric disorders such as communicative and social skills deficits and genetic abnormalities.

Interest in the causes and treatment of behavioral disorders in people with ID date back to the 1960s, especially in people with severe levels of ID (Lovaas & Simmons, 1969). Studies on behavioral and mental health problems in people with mild ID have been published since the 1980s. Substantial progress has been made on the understanding and hence treatment of behavior and/or psychiatric disorders in individuals with ID (Sigafoos,

Arthur, & O'Reilly, 2003; Sturmey, 2002). Recent years have shown an increased need for evidence-based practice in the analysis and treatment of psychopathology in people with ID (Matson, Terlonge, & Minshawi, 2008).

In this chapter, we will review the evidence base of psychosocial interventions for behavioral and psychiatric disorders in individuals with ID. The evidence base of treatment for these disorders will be evaluated according to criteria established by Chambless and Hollon (1998). An evidence-based and *effective treatment* for a given disorder requires: (a) at least two randomized controlled trials (RCTs) conducted by independent researchers, and/or (b) at least three small *N* experimental studies, each with at least nine participants in total with some studies conducted by at least two independent researchers. A treatment is *possibly effective* if there are fewer studies supporting a treatment's effectiveness and/or all of the research has been conducted by only one team of researchers. Treatments that do not attain these criteria are considered *not effective*.

AGGRESSIVE BEHAVIOR

The term *aggression* can be used to describe a wide variety of behavior. Aggression may be physical (e.g., hitting and kicking) or verbal (e.g., threatening statements and insults).

Aggression is a characteristic feature of many psychiatric disorders (e.g., conduct disorders, impulse control disorders, and some personality disorders), which may be comorbid with ID; however, individuals with ID who engage in aggression most likely do so, not because of a psychiatric disorder, but instead as a means of control or influence over their immediate environments (Antonacci, Manuel, & Davis, 2008).

In addition to the obvious risks to peers and caretakers, these behaviors also pose a substantial risk to the individual engaging in aggression. The aggressor is likely to be viewed negatively by the community and excluded from social activities. Additionally, the aggressor is at a high risk of being the victim of retaliatory aggression by peers or abuse by caretakers. Furthermore, many people with aggression are prescribed psychotropic medications intended to reduce aggression, but that may carry side effects or cause adverse drug interactions (Antonacci et al., 2008). Finally, aggression often results in higher service costs and staff turnover rates (Sigafoos, Elkins, Kerr, & Attwood, 1994).

Aggression is the most commonly cited reason for referral to behavior support teams and behavior specialists. Epidemiological studies of aggression report a wide range of prevalence from 9% to 42% of the ID population (Sigafoos et al., 2003). Higher rates of aggression are found in males and in institutional settings. Additionally, the prevalence, frequency, and intensity of aggression appear to increase with the severity of the disability (Antonacci et al., 2008).

Consensus Panel Recommendations

Rush and Frances (2000) surveyed 48 experts in the field of psychosocial treatment and 45 experts in the field of psychopharmacological treatment. Concerning the psychosocial treatment of aggression, both groups of experts were remarkably consistent regarding the recommendation to use applied behavior analysis (ABA). Regardless of the severity of disability or the intensity, frequency, and persistence of aggression, ABA was the most highly recommended approach. In addition to the use of ABA techniques, the consensus panel also made several general recommendations concerning the delivery of psychosocial services (e.g., use a multidisciplinary team approach, reduce stressors, enhance psychosocial supports).

Controlled Group Studies

The evaluation of psychosocial/ABA treatments with individuals with ID in controlled group designs is exceedingly rare. One such study (Matson, Fee, Coe, & Smith, 1991) evaluated the effects of a social skills training program on the aggressive behavior of 4- and 5-year-old girls with developmental disabilities in a school setting. Instruction in social skills was delivered twice a week for 6 weeks using puppets, peer modeling, role-playing, and reinforcement of target behaviors (i.e., polite verbal interaction, close proximity without aggression, and joint participation in an activity). A reduction in aggression for the experimental group compared to the control group was found.

Social skills training was less successful in reducing aggressive behaviors in preschoolers with developmental delays. Leblanc and Matson (1995) evaluated a 6-week treatment involving positive reinforcement, modeling, rehearsal, feedback, and time-out for appropriate and inappropriate (e.g., aggression) social skills. Compared to a control group, treatment resulted in a marked increase in appropriate social skills but not in a decrease in inappropriate behaviors. Outcomes of studies on social skills training are mixed. A critical review on the effectiveness of social skills training for aggression in individuals with ID is needed.

A number of group studies have examined the efficacy of cognitive behavioral interventions to manage anger in persons with mild ID (Lindsay et al., 2004; Rose, West, &

Clifford, 2000; Taylor, Novaco, Gillmer, Robertson, & Thorne, 2005; Taylor, Novaco, Gillmer, & Thorne, 2002; Taylor, Novaco, Guinan, & Street, 2004; Willner, Jones, Tams, & Green, 2002; Willner & Tomlinson, 2007) but only Willner et al. (2002) employed an RCT, and it will be described here. A total of 14 clients were randomly assigned (alternate referrals) to an immediate treatment group and a waiting list control group. Participants consisted of nine men and five women aged 19 to 58 years. The two groups were closely matched for age, IQ, and pretreatment anger ratings. Caretakers also rated the participants on anger rating scales prior to treatment. At 3 weeks and 3 months following treatment, all 14 participants and their caretakers were again asked to complete both anger scales. The intervention consisted of nine weekly 2-hour sessions of group therapy for the seven participants of the treatment group. The format of the intervention was similar to the anger management protocol described earlier. Participants in treatment improved on self and caretaker scores on the anger ratings relative to their own pretreatment scores and to control group scores. There was a high drop out of participants: Only two of the seven participants attended all treatment sessions. Two well-designed studies have demonstrated maintenance of CBT over time (6 to 30 months) and across settings (day service to residential facilities) (Lindsay, Allan, et al., 2004; Willner & Tomlinson, 2007); however, the overall amount of quality generalization data is sparse and future research is warranted (Sturmey, 2004, 2006).

Single-Subject Experimental Studies

Differential Reinforcement and Extinction

Matson, Dixon, and Matson (2005) reviewed 20 years of research regarding the treatment of aggression in individuals with ID. This review only included studies that had acceptable reliability and validity measures and demonstrated experimental control. The resulting review included 32 treatment studies, 29 of which were single-subject designs. ABA emerged as the treatment approach with the most single-subject empirical evidence. The ABA techniques with the most empirical support were differential reinforcement often combined with extinction, functional communication training (FCT), and noncontingent reinforcement.

Positive reinforcement is the most basic and significant of all ABA techniques. In the treatment of aggression, reinforcement can be used in four ways: differential reinforcement of alternative behavior (DRA), differential reinforcement of incompatible behavior (DRI), differential reinforcement of other behavior (DRO), and differential reinforcement of lower rates of behavior (DRL) (Sigafoos et al., 2003). One example comes from Zubicaray and Clair (1998), who treated a 46-year-old woman with a moderate ID who engaged in physical and verbal aggression in an institutional setting using a treatment package containing DRO, DRI, and restitution (i.e., apologizing to staff and patients). The DRI intervention component consisted of reinforcing prosocial interactions with staff members and patients and the DRO procedure reinforced behavior that did not involve interacting with others (e.g., looking at books, drawing). Aggression was reduced to zero. This effect maintained when the differential reinforcement components were removed; however, when restitution was no longer required, rates of aggression returned to near baseline levels. The findings of this study suggest that while differential reinforcement procedures may be effective, they are best used in conjunction with other intervention components. This assertion is supported by several other studies (Friman, Barnard, Altman, & Wolf, 1986; Luiselli, Suskin, & Slocum, 1984; Wacker et al., 1990).

The most common intervention component used in conjunction with reinforcement is extinction. Extinction involves withholding the reinforcement that maintained aggression following the occurrence of problem behavior.

Because the social environment surrounding an individual often responds to the occurrence of aggression, it is likely that the aggressor is in some way being inadvertently reinforced by environmental contingencies. This reinforcement may come in one or a combination of several forms; for example, reduction in task demands, provision of preferred stimuli (e.g., toys), and/or delivery of attention from peers or caretakers. Extinction consists of ensuring that these reinforcing consequences do not occur following aggression (Lerman & Iwata, 1996).

Functional Communication Training

One of the most substantial recent advances in the treatment of aggression and other forms of problem behavior is FCT (Carr & Durand, 1985). The FCT interventions have four components: (1) determination of the communicative intent of aggression (i.e., functional assessment); (2) selection and instruction of a behavior to replace aggression; (3) reinforcing the replacement behavior with the same reinforcer previously accessed by aggression (as determined during functional assessment); and (4) placing aggression on extinction (i.e., withholding reinforcement following aggression) (Durand & Merges, 2001). Over 100 single-subject research studies have been published evaluating the effects of FCT with almost entirely positive findings. Several literature reviews evaluating different cross-sections of this research base exist, each review reporting positive results following FCT (Durand & Merges, 2001; Mirenda, 1997). In Matson et al.'s 2005 review of aggression treatments, 32% of the studies analyzed implemented FCT interventions, all of which reported a substantial reduction in aggressive behavior.

Wacker et al. (2005) treated 25 children with moderate to profound ID engaged in some form of destructive behavior (including aggression) by training the children's parents to implement FCT within the home. Functional analysis identified target behavior functions for 84% (21 out of 25) of the children. Behaviors taught to replace aggression included vocal requests, manual signs, touching a picture card, or activating a micro-switch that produced synthesized speech. Once these new communication skills were acquired, they were reinforced with the stimuli identified by the functional analysis (e.g., break from work, attention from adults, or access to preferred items). Reinforcement was then withheld following the occurrence of destructive behavior (i.e., extinction). The mean pre-/post-decrease in destructive behavior across all children was 85%; one child did not respond to treatment. The results also showed substantial generalization to new settings and caretakers. Caretakers viewed the intervention to be both effective and social acceptable.

Noncontingent Reinforcement

The aforementioned treatments usually require some period of time to learn the replacement behavior in order to be effective. In some instances this time may not be available or the aggression is so severe instruction in replacement behavior is dangerous. Noncontingent reinforcement (NCR) is a form of antecedent control and works by reducing the reinforcing value of the consequence maintaining aggression. This is based on outcomes of a functional analysis and is done by providing unrestricted access to preferred stimuli, withdrawing all task demands, and removing all potential aversive stimuli from the individual's environment. If aggression is socially or environmentally maintained the individual's trigger or reason for aggressing should not be present (Tucker, Sigafoos, & Bushell, 1998). Compared to other interventions, the effects of NCR may be more immediate (O'Reilly, Lancioni, & Taylor, 1999). NCR is commonly used to reduce aggression to a level sufficient to make other interventions possible (Carr et al., 2000).

Several reviews that collectively evaluated over 40 single subject studies of NCR have concluded that NCR is often effective in the treatment of aberrant behavior (Carr et al., 2000; Tucker et al., 1998). For example, Vollmer, Ringdahl, Roane, and Marcus (1997) treated a 13-year-old with severe ID and high levels of aggression with NCR. Assessment revealed that aggression was most likely to occur when preferred items (e.g., magazines) were taken away. Aggression often resulted in having the items returned. The NCR consisted of providing free access to the preferred items and not attempting to remove them. Once such an environment in which aggression does not occur is created, additional instruction or fading can be accomplished.

Mindfulness Training

Single-case experimental designs are less frequently used in the published literature to evaluate the effectiveness of other therapies on aggression with individuals with ID. One noteworthy exception to this is the research program of Singh and colleagues, who have examined the effects of mindfulness procedures, a form of meditation, as a treatment for aggression (for a description of the mindfulness-based procedure, see Singh, Wahler, Adkins, & Myers, 2003). In one example, six adults with mild ID who were incarcerated in a forensic mental health facility due to a history of violence were taught these meditation techniques (Singh et al., 2008). Participants were taught to shift their attention from an anger-evoking stimulus (e.g., a negative interaction with a staff person) to a neutral stimulus (the soles of their feet). This meditation technique is designed to diffuse the anger and hence reduce aggression. Actual physical and verbal aggression was measured in this study. The intervention was staggered in a multiple baseline design fashion across the six participants in order to demonstrate experimental control. Incidents of physical and verbal aggression reduced substantially with the introduction of the intervention. Reductions in aggression continued for up to 2 years following the introduction of the treatment with all six participants. Data regarding

generalization of mindfulness training over time and setting is positive, particularly regarding generalization over time (i.e., up to 4 years; Singh, Lancioni, Winton, Adkins, Wahler, et al., 2007). The overall amount of across setting and therapist generalization data is sparse and future research is warranted, especially by researchers independent of Singh's group.

Conclusions

Effective treatments for aggression by individuals with ID are function-based ABA techniques such as differential reinforcement, NCR, extinction, and functional communication training. When the ID is borderline or mild, CBT techniques are effective. Some debate regarding the comparative research base of ABA and CBT exists (O'Reilly, Lancioni, Sigafoos, O'Donoghue, et al., 2004; Sturmey, 2004, 2006); however, it is important to note that most research examining the effects of CBT with individuals with mild ID has embedded ABA concepts into the procedures (e.g., functional analysis or differential reinforcement). Social skills training and mindfulness procedures are possibly effective in reducing aggressive behaviors in clients with mild (Singh et al., 2008) or moderate (Singh, Lancioni, Winton, Adkins, Singh, et al., 2007) ID, and through changing the behavior of parents (Singh, Lancioni, Winton, Singh, et al., 2007) and staff (Singh et al., 2006) toward their child and client with aggression, respectively. However, studies by Singh and colleagues await independent replication.

SELF-INJURIOUS BEHAVIOR

Common forms of self-injurious behavior (SIB) include head banging, face slapping, hitting other areas of the body with closed fists, and pinching, biting, or scratching and cutting oneself. (Chapter 13 provides a comprehensive review of treatment of self-injury.) Additional topographies of SIB are pulling out one's own hair, gouging self, skin picking, teeth grinding, self-induced vomiting, and pica (Sigafoos et al., 2003). (See the section later on pica and also Chapter 12 of this volume by McAdam, Breidbord, Levine, and Williams). Prevalence of SIB in children and adults with ID is relatively high and it often is a chronic condition that may persist for decades (Oliver, Murphy, & Corbett, 1987). Murphy, Hall, Oliver, and Kissi-Debra (1999) found that children with ID who eventually developed SIB often began with proto-injurious behavior before 2 years of age. Green, Sigafoos, O'Reilly, and Itchon (2005) studied 13 preschool children with intellectual and developmental disabilities and found that these children tended to develop aberrant behaviors as toddlers and showed little improvement in terms of the severity of their aberrant behavior over the 3-year preschool period.

Self-injurious behavior appears to be more prevalent among individuals with autism or autistic-like behaviors, severe ID, and with greater deficits in adaptive behavior functioning (Sigafoos et al., 2003). Deficits in the social skills and communication domains appear particularly important in terms of placing the individual at increased risk for the development of SIB (Matson, Anderson, & Bamburg, 2000). Self-injurious behavior has also been linked to certain genetic disorders, such as Lesch-Nyhan, Cornelia de Lange, and Prader-Willi syndromes, indicating that SIB is a behavioral phenotype of some genetic syndromes. Self-injurious behavior often causes serious health and medical problems, such as bruising, lacerations, bleeding, bone fractures and breakages, and other tissue damage and infections. In more extreme cases, SIB can lead to permanent disablement, such as loss of vision and brain damage. Frequent SIB may limit the person's community access and restrict participation in daily activities, such as participating in leisure activities with peers or gaining meaningful employment.

Consensus Panel Recommendations

In 1989, The National Institutes of Mental Health sponsored the Consensus Development Conference on the Treatment of Destructive Behaviors in Persons with Developmental Disabilities to evaluate the scientific evidence for the treatment of destructive behaviors, including SIB, in persons with developmental disabilities. Treatments were evaluated in terms of their magnitude, rapidity, and durability of effects. The general consensus was that while several behavioral treatments (e.g., differential reinforcement of other or incompatible behavior) had demonstrated effectiveness through replication via numerous single-case experiments, there was need for additional research to evaluate maintenance. Several contemporary approaches to the treatment of SIB (e.g., antecedent interventions, FCT) have received a considerable amount of empirical support since the 1989 conference.

Controlled Group Studies

In a nonrandomized controlled group study, Duker and Seys (2000) showed that contingent electric shock produced rapid suppression of life-threatening SIB in eight individuals, all of whom had severe to profound ID. No changes in SIB were noted in the control group ($N = 8$), who had received no treatment.

In an RCT, Mace, Blum, Sierp, Delaney, and Mauk (2001) investigated differential effectiveness of haloperidol and a function-based behavioral treatment on SIB in 15 individuals with ID. Individuals were allocated to either haloperidol or placebo and data were collected during sessions with a behavioral treatment and sessions without a behavioral treatment. Behavioral treatment was effective in decreasing SIB while haloperidol was not. More than 80% of participants responded to the behavioral treatment (in terms of a substantial reduction in SIB), whereas only 25% responded to haloperidol.

Single-Subject Experimental Studies

A range of psychological approaches has been developed for the treatment of SIB using single-case experimental designs including: (a) those based on the principles of ABA, (b) those based on notions of sensory integration, and (c) those aimed at enhancing interpersonal relationships. Several more specific procedures can often be identified within each of these three major classes.

Treatments Based on ABA

The ABA interventions have a long history of success in the treatment of SIB (Lovaas & Simmons, 1969; Matson et al., 2008). Within the class of ABA-based treatments, a number of more specific operant principles or procedures have been effectively applied. Operant techniques such as extinction, differential reinforcement, stimulus control, and punishment have been widely evaluated and validated for the treatment of SIB. In addition, considerable evidence has accumulated that shows ABA-based treatments are most effective when they are based on a prior functional assessment of the variables that maintain the person's SIB (Kahng, Iwata, & Lewin, 2002).

Since the early 1980s, considerable progress has been made in the behavioral treatment of SIB, based largely on consideration of operant functions of SIB. Numerous experiments on the effects of different reinforcement have shown that SIB often serves one or more operant functions for the individual (Iwata, Dorsey, Slifer, Bauman, & Richman, 1994). The main operant functions of SIB are: (a) positive social reinforcement (e.g., recruiting attention, gaining access to preferred objects or activities), (b) negative social reinforcement (e.g., escaping or avoiding nonpreferred objects or activities), and (c) automatic reinforcement; that is, in some cases, SIB might directly produce sensory reinforcement that maintains the behavior (Barrera, Violo, & Graver, 2007; Iwata et al., 1994).

Positive Reinforcement

Both differential reinforcement and noncontingent reinforcement have been shown to be effective. For example, Vollmer, Iwata, Zarcone, Smith, and Mazaleski (1993) have evaluated DRO and NCR in three persons with severe ID who showed high levels of SIB. Prior functional analysis revealed that SIB was maintained by social attention. During DRO the person received social attention provided she or he had refrained from SIB during the whole 15-second interval and SIB resulted in resetting the interval. In NCR the person received social attention at the end of each 15-second interval, irrespective whether she or he had exhibited SIB or not. Interval duration was based on the baseline mean interresponse time. Both procedures were effective in eliminating SIB in the three participants. The NCR may be more practical than differential reinforcement if it is implemented by staff members in daily situations.

Functional Communication Training

Building on the results of functional assessment, one of the more effective ABA-based packages for the treatment of SIB involves teaching efficient communication skills that serve the same operant function as the person's SIB. For example, Duker, Jol, and Palmen (1991) investigated the effect of teaching communicative manual gestures on SIB in 14 individuals with severe to profound ID and who lived in a residential facility. Results showed a decrease of about 40% in SIB as a collateral effect of an increased use of communicative gestures. Interestingly, there was a positive correlation between number of gestures learned and percentage of decrease in SIB. A limitation of this study was that the function of the SIB was not assessed prior to intervention.

In a more recent study, Wacker et al. (2005) provided training to parents of 25 children with developmental disabilities and various forms of aberrant behavior, including SIB. In this

4-year study, parents were taught to assess the operant function of the child's aberrant behavior and then implement teaching programs to replace aberrant behavior with alternative and more acceptable forms of communication (i.e., functional assessment followed by FCT). Wacker et al. reported that the program was associated with an 85% decrease in aberrant behavior on average. An important additional component of this type of treatment package is to ensure that SIB is placed on extinction (Hagopian, Fisher, Sullivan, Acquisto, & LeBlanc, 1998).

Aversive Stimulation

Severe SIB does not always respond to reinforcement-based interventions. Consequently, the addition of treatment packages that include punishment may be indicated. Punishment involves the application of some form of aversive stimulation contingent upon the occurrence of SIB. A variety of aversive stimuli have been evaluated, including overcorrection (Gibbs & Luyben, 1985), restraint (Gaylord-Ross, Weeks, Lipner, & Gaylord-Ross, 1983), water mist (Dorsey, Iwata, Ong, & McSween, 1980), facial screening (Lutzker, 1978), and electric shock (Duker & Seys, 1996). For example, Duker and Seys (1996) assessed the effectiveness of electric aversion therapy on SIB in 12 individuals with severe to profound ID who showed life-threatening SIB. With two individuals, treatment failed to suppress SIB. With seven individuals, however, suppression of SIB was nearly complete in that physical restraints were no longer necessary. With three individuals moderate effects were obtained in that, although a substantial decrease of imposed physical restraint had been achieved, they still needed daily administrations of electrical aversive stimuli. Long-term effectiveness was assessed for periods ranging from 2 to 47 months for the 12 individuals, respectively. Spontaneous generalization of treatment effects to other settings and therapists usually does not occur and has to be trained. Although potentially effective for

the treatment of severe SIB, electric shock is a controversial treatment.

Sensory Integration

Sensory integration is defined as "the neurological process that organizes sensations from one's own body and from the environment and makes it possible to use the body effectively within the environment" (Ayres, 1972, p. 11). It has been suggested that some of the learning difficulties and behavioral problems experienced by individuals with disabilities stem from sensory integration dysfunctions. In line with this reasoning, various sensory integration procedures—those that presumably address the underlying dysfunction—have been advocated in the treatment of individuals with developmental disabilities including swinging and rolling, brushing arms and thighs, and joint compression. These procedures are assumed to provide their therapeutic effect via stimulation of the vestibular, proprioceptive, and tactile systems.

With respect to potential specific effects on SIB, Mason and Iwata (1990) evaluated the effects of sensory integration procedures on SIB in three children with developmental disabilities. The evaluation was controlled through the use of multiple-baseline across subjects design. Self-injurious behavior increased for one child when sensory integration procedures were implemented. For the other two children SIB decreased, but data suggested that the increased attention from the therapist was the operative component of the intervention and not the actual sensory integration procedures. The variable results across children highlight the need for an individualized approach to treatment based in the operant function of SIB. When SIB is maintained by negative reinforcement in the form of escape from task demands, sensory integration sessions could represent a demand from which the child may seek to escape by engaging in SIB. This may account for the increase in SIB for one of the children in the Mason and Iwata study. In contrast, when SIB is maintained by positive reinforcement in the form of attention, then the increased attention associated with the application of sensory integration procedures may account for any reduction in SIB.

Baranek (2002) and Smith, Mruzek, and Mozingo (2005) provided comprehensive reviews of studies evaluating sensory integration therapy for individuals with developmental disabilities. These reviews included summaries of individual studies, systematic reviews, and one meta-analysis of 32 studies. Consistently, the studies reviewed by Baranek (2002) and Smith et al. (2005) failed to provide any convincing evidence for the therapeutic efficacy of sensory integration. While sensory integration is widely used in the treatment of individuals with developmental disabilities (Green et al., 2006), it lacks empirical support. Sensory integration therapy even may be harmful because it provides contingent reinforcement for the target behavior; for example, in case the person is taken to a sensory activity when the person is upset. This approach may thus strengthen the problem behavior if it is presented contingent on its occurrence.

Treatments Based on Building Interpersonal Relationships

There are several intervention programs that purport to achieve a therapeutic effect primarily through enhancing the interpersonal relationship between the individual with intellectual disabilities and his/her caregivers (Mudford, 1995). Perhaps the best known is Gentle Teaching, which is characterized by its emphasis on interpersonal bonding by engaging the person in positive social interactions (McGee & Menolascino, 1991). Gentle teaching also focuses on increasing participation in functional activities. Proponents of Gentle Teaching claim that as positive interpersonal bonds are established and participation increases, problem behavior will resolve without resort to any punishment-based procedures (McGee & Menolascino, 1991).

There are two major problems with Gentle Teaching. First, Gentle Teaching procedures are vague and ill-defined, making it impossible to replicate with any degree of treatment fidelity. Second, the claims related to the positive effects of Gentle Teaching have not withstood independent scrutiny (Mudford, 1995). While some evidences suggest the approach may reduce problem behavior in the short term, these results appear to be artifactual, and based on a poor understanding and contraindicated application of operant conditioning principles. For example, Gentle Teachers often seek to preempt problem behavior by reducing environmental demands. While this approach may temporarily stop escape-motivated problem behavior, it is also likely to inadvertently strengthen demand-related SIB over the long term if demands are reduced after problem behavior. Similarly, the continuous interaction used to enhance the bonding process may temporarily stop, but inadvertently strengthen, attention-maintained SIB. Overall, Gentle Teaching fails to meet the replication standard for an evidence-based treatment and may be contraindicated for individuals with escape- and attention-maintained SIB.

Meta-Analytic Studies

Harvey, Boer, Myer, and Evans (2009) analyzed 142 studies that provided intervention to 316 individuals with intellectual and developmental disabilities and various forms of aberrant behavior, including SIB. The treatment strategies evaluated in these 142 studies included a range of ABA-based techniques such as contingency management, modification of antecedents, and teaching replacement skills. These types of behavioral interventions—especially interventions that involved manipulation of antecedents, teaching of replacement skills, and use of reinforcement/ contingency management strategies—were most effective.

Systematic reviews confirm that specific ABA-based procedures have large effect sizes. For example, FCT consistently produces large effect sizes (Sigafoos, O'Reilly, & Lancioni, 2009). While the primary effects of punishment-based procedures have been demonstrated mainly in individual case or small-*N* studies, Didden, Duker, and Korzilius' (1997) meta-analytic review revealed that punishment-based procedures have relatively large effect sizes that are comparable to other ABA-based procedures.

Conclusions

Function-based ABA procedures are effective in the treatment of SIB in individuals with ID. More often than not, techniques are combined to create a multicomponent treatment package. At a minimum, ABA-based treatments typically include reinforcement of alternative behavior and extinction of SIB. The effect size of ABA treatments is enhanced when behavioral procedures are (a) combined into a more comprehensive treatment package (Harvey et al., 2009), and (b) based on outcomes of functional assessment (Didden et al., 1997). The most effective treatment procedures are those based on principles of applied behavior analysis, especially interventions that include replacing SIB by strengthening alternative behaviors. Also effective are punishment-based procedures for severe types of SIB; however, such procedures are controversial and should be used only if less intrusive procedures have remained ineffective.

Sensory integration therapy and gentle teaching are ineffective treatments for SIB. While sensory integration therapy is widely used, it lacks empirical support. Interventions that aim to reduce SIB by enhancing interpersonal relationships have often incorporated well-established behavioral principles, but in ways that may be contraindicated for escape- and attention-maintained SIB.

STEREOTYPIC BEHAVIOR

Stereotyped movement disorder is defined as "motor behavior that is repetitive, often seemingly driven, and non-functional" (American Psychiatric Association, 2000, p. 131). A significant percentage of individuals with ID engage in one or more forms of stereotyped motor behavior, such as body rocking, head weaving, hand flapping, finger flicking, and/or continually arranging and rearranging objects (Berkson, 2002). Stereotypic behavior is more common among individuals who function in the severe to profound range of ID. Frequent stereotyped movements interfere with learning and habilitation efforts, are socially stigmatizing, and in some cases can cause harm and lead to self-injury (Richman & Lindauer, 2005). Often, stereotypic behavior is a precursor to SIB from a developmental point of view. Chapter 19 of this volume by May, Kennedy, and Bruzek provides a comprehensive review of the treatment of stereotypy.

Consensus Panel Recommendations

There appear to be no formal consensus panel recommendations specific to the treatment of stereotyped movement disorders in persons with ID. There is general consensus that behavioral interventions are indicated in the treatment of this disorder (Kennedy, 2007; Rapp & Vollmer, 2005) including: (a) functional skill training, (b) environmental enrichment, (c) differential reinforcement of other behavior, (d) extinction, (e) response interruption, and (f) overcorrection.

Single-Subject Experimental Studies

Numerous single-case interventions studies have evaluated the effects of behavioral interventions for the treatment of stereotyped behaviors in individuals with ID. For example, Lancioni et al. (2008) demonstrated reductions in stereotyped hand mouthing by DRI in a girl with multiple disabilities. The child could gain automatic sensory reinforcement through object manipulation, but only when she was not engaged in hand mouthing. This procedure was evaluated in an ABAB design. Success with DRI has been replicated with other children (Lancioni, O'Reilly, Singh, Oliva, & Groeneweg, 2003).

Several procedures of antecedent control have been evaluated. For example, Sidener, Carr, and Firth (2005) and Rapp (2004) reduced stereotypy in two children with developmental disabilities by enriching the environment. Conroy, Asmus, Sellers, and Ladwig (2005) demonstrated the positive effects of bringing stereotypy under stimulus control via an antecedent intervention by using a visual cue to signal when stereotypy was acceptable versus when it was not acceptable.

Overcorrection has been found to be effective in reducing stereotypic behaviors in individuals with ID. For example, Cole, Montgomery, Wilson, and Milan (2000) showed that positive practice overcorrection eliminated stereotyped hand movements in adults with severe to profound ID. Longer durations (e.g., 8 minutes) were not more effective than shorter durations (30 seconds) of overcorrection.

A final treatment approach is sensory integration therapy. In one single-case study, sensory integrative therapy was compared to engagement in tabletop activities in seven children with ID (Smith, Press, Koenig, & Kinnealey, 2005). Each condition was implemented for a week, which alternated over 4 weeks, thus representing a type of ABAB design. The authors report that the sensory integration condition was associated with relatively less stereotypy compared to the tabletop activities condition; however, the tabletop condition was not a valid comparison. Instead, the effects of sensory integrative procedures would need to be compared to an established treatment, such as differential reinforcement procedures, to provide a meaningful evaluation of this procedure. Another type of sensory integration therapy procedure that has been evaluated using single-subject designs is wearing a weighted vest. Two studies have evaluated the use of weighted vests as a treatment for stereotyped behavior (Fertel-Daly, Bedell, & Hinojosa, 2001; Kane, Luiselli,

Dearborn, & Young, 2004). Both studies showed that weighted vests had no beneficial effect, but had a negative effect for some children.

Meta-Analytic and Narrative Reviews

Cannella, O'Reilly, and Lancioni (2006) systematically reviewed studies investigating the assessment and treatment of stereotyped behavior. Twenty-three studies met their criteria for review. Stereotyped behavior was most often maintained by automatic, sensory reinforcement. The most effective treatments combined differential reinforcement and antecedent intervention components. This review was limited to individuals with severe/profound ID and to a single topography of stereotypy (i.e., hand mouthing).

Rapp and Vollmer (2005) provided a narrative review of studies involving the behavioral assessment and treatment of stereotyped movements in persons with developmental disabilities. They concluded that these behaviors are most often maintained by automatic, sensory reinforcement. They identified two classes of effective behavioral treatments: (1) antecedent interventions, such as environmental enrichment; and (2) consequent strategies, such as the differential reinforcement of other behavior.

Didden et al.'s (1997) meta-analytic summary included 327 comparisons between the treatment and nontreatment phases of studies that focused on reducing stereotyped behavior in persons with ID. Stereotyped behaviors were classified along with SIB as a form of internal maladaptive behavior. The most effective treatments were behavioral procedures such as DRO and use of functional assessment procedures to identify the function of the behavior improved treatment outcomes, a finding confirmed by Harvey et al. (2009).

Conclusions

Behavioral treatment effectively reduces stereotyped movements in persons with ID.

The most effective behavioral interventions include antecedent and consequent components that address the automatic, sensory function of stereotyped behavior. Weighted vests are not effective and may be detrimental for some children. Sensory integrative therapy is not effective and should not be used.

PICA

Pica may be defined as the consumption of nonedible items. It is common in individuals with ID, especially in those with severe levels of ID. It may cause infestation, punctures, and blockage of the digestive tract and is potentially life-threatening (McAdam, Sherman, Sheldon, & Napolitano, 2008). Chapter 12 of this volume by McAdam, Breidbord, Levine, and Williams provides a comprehensive meta-analysis of treatment of pica.

Single-Subject Experimental Studies

Pica in individuals with ID has been treated using a combination of positive reinforcement and aversive stimulation. Differential reinforcement of alternative behavior was effective in reducing pica in 3 out of 4 adults with profound ID in a study by Goh, Iwata, and Kahng (1999). Observations in the participants' natural settings suggested that pica was automatically reinforced. An important part of the intervention was stimulus preference assessment that resulted in the identification of items that served as reinforcers during differential reinforcement. Noncontingent reinforcement was ineffective in the treatment of pica in these adults.

An effective intervention for pica is the presentation of an aversive stimulus contingent on pica. Physical restraint, response blocking, visual/facial screening, overcorrection, aversive stimuli (lemon juice), and negative practice have been used for the treatment of pica in ID (for an overview, see Chapter 12 by McAdam et al.). For example, Fisher et al. (1994) applied visual screening for pica

behavior in three young children with severe or profound ID. Pica consisted of ingestion of inedible objects such as grass, bugs, and strings. Prior to intervention, the aversiveness of the procedure was assessed through a stimulus avoidance assessment. During visual screening, the child received a verbal warning and his or her eyes were covered for 30 seconds following the occurrence of pica. Appropriate eating was positively reinforced. Screening was highly effective in reducing pica to near zero level and effects were maintained at a 9-month follow-up. Treatment effects were successfully generalized to other settings (e.g., home) and screening was gradually faded.

Recently, a study by Williams, Kirkpatrick-Sanchez, Enzinna, Dunn, and Borden-Karasack (2009) showed that a multicomponent treatment package consisting of environmental structuring and individualized behavior treatment programs was effective in establishing a marked reduction (75%–100%) of pica for 85% of the 41 participants. Other participants still had restrictive procedures (e.g., overcorrection); however, mechanical restraints were eliminated in all participants as well as pica surgeries. Treatment effects generalized to other settings (due to environmental structuring and antecedent procedures) and at a 9-year follow-up. Data were collected in individual AB designs.

Conclusions

Pica may be effectively treated using contingent aversive stimulation. Differential reinforcement of alternative behavior and environmental enrichment are possibly effective in reducing pica. The literature on pica in ID is restricted to small-N studies, people with profound ID, and institutional settings.

RUMINATION

Rumination is the chronic reurgitation and reswallowing of ingested food. As with severe feeding problems, rumination may have serious physical consequences such as malnutrition, weight loss, pneumonia, and teeth damage. It is sometimes managed with surgery, which may itself be life-threatening.

Single-Subject Experimental Studies

Food satiation has been most often used as treatment for rumination. Rast, Johnston, and Drum (1984) showed that satiation was effective in reducing rumination to near zero levels in three adults with profound ID who lived in a facility. The amount of extra food was related to the reduction in rumination: Small portions resulted in relatively small reductions in rumination while large portions resulted in a substantial decrease in rumination. These results have been replicated in other case studies (Johnston & Greene, 1992). Thibadeau, Blew, Reedy, and Luiselli (1999) evaluated the use of white bread as a satiation-based treatment of rumination displayed by an 18-year-old male with ID. White bread was made available during 1-hour periods following daily meals and this intervention produced a reduction in ruminating to near zero levels throughout the participant's waking hours. Long-term follow-up assessment revealed maintenance of low-frequency responding.

Foxx, Snyder, and Schroeder (1979) showed that adding an aversive procedure to satiation resulted in near zero levels or rumination in two clients with ID. The oral hygiene procedure consisted of cleansing the clients' teeth and gums with Listerine for 2 minutes following each instance of rumination. Treatment resulted in generalization across settings and effects were maintained at 16-month follow-up.

Lyons, Rue, Luiselli, and DiGennaro (2007) were the first to conduct a functional analysis of postmeal rumination in two youths with developmental disabilities who lived in a residential facility. Although rumination occurred in all conditions during analogue baselines its frequency was highest during the no interaction condition, suggesting that rumination was automatically reinforced.

Intervention consisted of noncontingent presentation of extra food on a fixed time 30 seconds schedule and was effective in reducing rumination to near zero levels. Data were collected in a multielement design for one participant and reversal design for the other participant. No data on generalization across settings or time was collected.

Conclusions

Despite a paucity of studies in this area, it may be concluded that food satiation is the most effective treatment for rumination in individuals with ID. An important side effect of satiation is overweight, so low-calorie foods should be used. Adding an aversive stimulus to satiation may result in lower levels of rumination.

FOOD REFUSAL

Feeding problems are identified if an individual refuses to eat or drink a sufficient quantity and variety of food items to maintain proper nutrition. Individuals with severe feeding problems are at risk for malnutrition and dehydration, which are serious adverse consequences (Kuhn & Matson, 2004). This broad category may consist of total food refusal and food selectivity, and disruptive mealtime behaviors. Prevalence rates of feeding problems among children and youngsters with developmental disabilities vary between 25% and 80%. Causes of severe feeding problems are medical and environmental. Medical conditions, such as reflux or oral-motor dysfunction, play an important role in the initiation of feeding problems. Environmental actors, such as caregiver behaviors that negatively reinforce escape and child avoidance behavior, maintain such problems. Functional analytic studies using analogue baseline methodology have shown that in most cases problematic feeding behaviors are often maintained by negative reinforcement (Kuhn & Matson, 2004; Piazza et al., 2002). Feeding problems tend to persist and do not resolve without intervention. Focus of treatment is on increasing caloric intake and improving health status and increasing appropriate mealtime behaviors. See Chapter 13 of this volume by Volkert and Piazza for a comprehensive review of feeding problems. Recently, Williams and Foxx (2007) have published a book that provides a overview on behavioral interventions for children with feeding problems.

Single-Subject Experimental Studies

Studies on the effectiveness of positive reinforcement on feeding problems show mixed results. In a study by Riordan, Iwata, Finney, Wohl, and Stanley (1984), differential positive reinforcement consisting of praise, access to preferred food, and toy play appeared effective in increasing food acceptance in four children with ID who had a history of food refusal. Amount of food consumed increased and improvements were maintained at 7 to 30 months follow-up. Positive reinforcement alone and noncontingent reinforcement were found ineffective in later studies. For example, Hoch, Babbitt, Coe, Krell, and Hackbert (1994) showed that escape extinction was necessary to increase food intake in two children. Escape extinction consisted of presenting food to the child and holding the food item at the child's lips until she or he accepted the food. Another type of escape extinction is physically guiding the child to open his or her mouth and deposit the food in the child's mouth. Escape extinction proved more effective in establishing food acceptance than positive reinforcement alone (Patel, Piazza, Martinez, Volkert, & Santana, 2002).

Simultaneous presentation of preferred and nonpreferred food has been shown to be effective in the treatment of food selectivity. Piazza et al. (2002) showed that simultaneous presentation increased food consumption in children with ID. In the simultaneous condition, preferred foods were presented at the same time as nonpreferred food (e.g., a piece of broccoli was presented on a chip). In the sequential condition, acceptance of the nonpreferred food resulted in presentation of the preferred food. Blending nonpreferred into preferred food is a form of simultaneous presentation that has been effective in treatment of food refusal of two children with ID (Mueller, Piazza, Patel, Kelley, & Pruett, 2004). Blending consisted of mixing nonpreferred foods into preferred foods in various ratios (e.g., 10% nonpreferred /90% preferred). Preferred food was then gradually faded in favor of nonpreferred food. Fading of food volume and/or texture is an important part of treatment packages for food refusal (Shore, Babbitt, Williams, Coe, & Snyder, 1998).

Conclusions

Behavioral treatment and blending are effective in the treatment of food refusal. Severe feeding difficulties require a multidisciplinary approach focusing on medical and psychological conditions (Kuhn & Matson, 2004). Severe food refusal has been treated in inpatient and/or outpatient settings and generalization of treatment procedure to other caregivers (e.g., parents, staff members) is important part of any treatment package. In case medical conditions can be ruled out, ABA procedures are the first choice of treatment of feeding problems in people with ID. Most often, treatment consists of a package of elements such as fading, reinforcement, and extinction techniques. Positive reinforcement alone is not sufficient to reduce feeding problems. Comparative research has shown that extinction is the most effective element in the treatment of feeding problems (Cooper et al., 1995).

SLEEP PROBLEMS

Children and adults have an increased risk for sleep problems (Didden & Sigafoos, 2001). Sleep problems frequently occur in genetic disorders, such as in Prader-Willi syndrome, Angelman syndrome, and Fragile-X syndrome, and in autism spectrum disorders. Three types of sleep problems are distinguished: (1) sleeplessness (insomnia), (2) excessive sleep (hypersomnia), and (3) unusual behaviors during sleep (parasomnias). Many factors may cause each of these three types of sleep problems, such as somatic (e.g., reflux disease), behavioral (parental reinforcement of disruptive behaviors), and/or other (e.g., circadian rhythm disorder). Chapter 27 (this volume) by Freeman, Palermo, and Scott and Chapter 19 (Volume 2) by Harvey and Dagys discuss evidence-based treatments of sleep disorders in children and adults, respectively.

Controlled Group Studies

Controlled group studies on the treatment of sleep problems are rare. In an RCT by Braam, Didden, Smits, and Curfs (2008) sleep problems were investigated in 51 individuals with severe to mild ID. Compared with placebo, melatonin significantly advanced mean sleep onset time by more than half an hour, increased mean total sleep time by almost 1 hour, and reduced frequency of night waking. Results of this study and measurement of melatonin levels during baseline and after treatment suggested that sleep problems were partly caused by delayed sleep phase disorder.

Meta-Analysis of Controlled Group Studies

Braam et al. (2009) conducted a meta-analysis of placebo-controlled randomized trials on melatonin in individuals with ID who have insomnia. Nine studies, including a total of 183 individuals, showed that melatonin treatment decreased sleep latency by about 34 minutes on average, increased total sleep time by mean of almost 1 hour, and decreased frequency of night waking.

Single-Subject Experimental Studies

There are several behavioral approaches available for the treatment of sleep problems.

Among these are several forms of extinction, stimulus control, differential reinforcement of appropriate sleep behavior, chronotherapy, desensitization, and sleep scheduling (Didden & Sigafoos, 2001; Lancioni, O'Reilly, & Basili, 1999; Richdale & Wiggs, 2005). In most cases, several techniques are applied simultaneously. For example, Bramble (1997), using AB designs, found extinction and stimulus control effective in the treatment of chronic sleep problems in 15 children with severe ID. Improvements in the children's night waking and settling problems occurred quickly; that is, within a few days. In most children, effects were maintained at 18-month follow-up.

Didden, Curfs, van Driel, and De Moor (2002) showed that crying in a 4-year-old child with mild disability was related to attention provided by her mother at bedtime. Anecdotal observations suggested that the child's crying and yelling were maintained by the mother's presence and attention. Data collected in a reversal design showed that the child's sleep disruption was indeed related to the presence/absence of mother's attention and extinction (mother ignored crying and yelling) was effective in eliminating the child's sleep problem. Using a nonconcurrent multiple baseline design, Didden et al. (2002) and Didden, Curfs, Sikkema, and de Moor (2004) showed that extinction and stimulus control were effective in other children with severe to mild ID who showed chronic sleep problems. Effects were maintained at 3- and 6-month follow up. In all cases, treatments were based on outcomes of functional assessment of stimuli that elicited and maintained the disruptive sleep behavior.

O'Reilly, Lancioni, and Sigafoos (2004) were the first to use functional analysis in assessing the variables maintaining the sleep problems in a young child with severe disabilities. Sleep problems consisted of frequently coming out of bed and leaving the bedroom. Using a paired-choice format, they found that parental reinforcement (cuddling) was a preferred stimulus that probably maintained the child's sleep onset problems. In the intervention condition, cuddling was used as a reinforcer for staying in bed. Data in a reversal design showed that the intervention, consisting of differential reinforcement of appropriate sleep behavior, was effective in eliminating the child's sleep problem.

Conclusions

Behavioral interventions and melatonin are effective in the treatment of sleep problems in individuals with ID. Behavioral interventions may consist of treatment packages including extinction and stimulus control. A functional assessment/analysis should precede a behavioral intervention (Didden & Sigafoos, 2001). Differential reinforcement and chronotherapy are possibly effective. Many disorders may cause a sleep problem in people with ID. To identify the sleep disorder(s) responsible for the sleep problem, a functional analysis of reinforcing event of sleep disruptive behavior, measurement of melatonin level (dim light melatonin onset), and assessment and treatment of any somatic factor (e.g., epilepsy, reflux, apnea) should be conducted.

ANXIETY DISORDERS

Several disorders, such as specific or social phobias, panic disorder, and obsessive-compulsive disorder, fall in the broad category of anxiety disorders. As with other psychiatric disorders, the diagnosis of anxiety disorders may be especially problematic in individuals with more severe levels of ID. At present, research in the etiology of anxiety disorders in ID is still sparse. Anxiety disorders may be related to certain genetic disorders, such as Fragile-X, Williams, and Prader-Willi and autism spectrum disorders. Other risk factors for anxiety disorders are traumatic events, childhood maltreatment, abuse and loss, client temperament, and stigmatization (Davis,

Saeed, & Antonacci, 2008). Several chapters in this and the accompanying volumes address various anxiety disorders in children and adults.

Consensus Panel Recommendations

There are no consensus panel statements on treatment of anxiety disorders in people with ID; however, treatment approaches developed for individuals without ID may be applicable to individuals with ID. These may consist of cognitive and behavioral therapies, change of environmental factors, and change of environmental and somatic factors (e.g., physical discomfort) (Deb, Matthews, Holt, & Bouras, 2001).

Randomized Controlled Trials

Lindsay, Baty, Michie, and Richardson (1989) evaluated two types of relaxation training on the level of anxiety in 50 clients with moderate to severe ID. They compared effectiveness of behavioral relaxation training and progressive relaxation training delivered in either an individual or a group format to a control group receiving no training. Progressive relaxation consisted of tension/release instructions for various body parts such as hands, arms, shoulders, and so forth. Behavioral relaxation taught clients to detect unrelaxed and relaxed states and reduce muscle activity when anxious. The same body parts were used as in the progressive relaxation training. Clients were randomly allocated to groups and assessments were taken during baseline, there were probes halfway through the intervention, and at the end of treatment. Relaxation training took place over twelve 30- to 45-minute individual sessions. Group progressive muscle relaxation training was delivered in 12 sessions that lasted 60–85 minutes. Assessments were conducted using 10 behavioral ratings (e.g., trunk, hands, feet) that were scored on a Likert-type 5-point scale, from completely relaxed to very anxious. At the end of treatment, both individual and group behavioral relaxation training was more effective in reducing clients' anxiety ratings than both types of progressive relaxation. Both treatments were more effective than the control group. There were no differences in heart rate between groups before and at the end of treatment.

Altabet (2002) examined the effect of a systematic desensitization procedure for dental phobia in individuals with severe and profound ID. Participation levels of 35 individuals receiving dental desensitization were compared to a group of 28 individuals that had not received an intervention. Those receiving desensitization showed greater improvement in toleration of dental procedures than did those in the comparison group.

Single-Subject Experimental Studies

Relatively many case studies have been published on the effectiveness of behavioral approaches to specific phobias (see Davis et al., 2008). In vivo desensitization has been shown to be effective in the treatment of a variety of specific fears, such as dog phobia, toilet phobia, fear of falling asleep alone, and phobia for physical examination. For example, Luiselli (1977) described an $N = 1$ experimental study of an institutionalised 15-year-old youth with ID, who displayed an intense fear of urinating in a toilet. As a result, he wet his pants at a frequent rate. Treatment consisted of token reinforcement and social reinforcement for appropriate toileting and time-out for urinary accidents. Treatment resulted in a substantial decrease in accidents. Frequency of accidents was reduced to zero at follow-up, during which all programmed consequences were discontinued. At the same time, he showed self-initiations to use the bathroom and toileting in an appropriate manner.

Contact desensitization was evaluated by Erfanian and Miltenberger (1990) as a treatment for two individuals with ID who showed an intense fear of dogs. During baseline, a behavioral avoidance test was used to measure approach/avoidance behaviors toward dogs. Contact desensitization resulted in successful approach to dogs in both individuals. These effects were maintained during a 2-month follow-up and the behaviors were successfully generalized to other settings.

The effects of a multicomponent treatment package on injection phobia in a 19-year-old adolescent with moderate ID was evaluated by Hagopian, Crockett, and Keeney (2001). Treatment consisted of differential reinforcement (tokens) for remaining still during drawing blood and restraint fading. Follow-up data show that level of restraint was markedly reduced while participant learned to accept increasing levels of medical examination and drawing blood.

Social anxiety in two adults with mild ID was treated by increasing positive verbal behavior in a study by Chiodo and Maddox (1985). Participants were taught to use positive self-statements (e.g., "I am doing a good job," "I do not care if you watch me") if they felt nervous in the presence of other people. There were four sessions that lasted 45 minutes each. Participants increased their helpful self-statements and anecdotal observations suggested that they used these statements in other settings (e.g., work setting).

Effectiveness of short-term cognitive behavioral treatment on symptoms of posttraumatic stress disorder was evaluated in an $N = 1$ study by Lemmon and Mizes (2002). The PTSD was caused by several sexual assaults in a woman with mild ID. Therapy consisted of imaginary exposure to a hierarchy of anxiety-arousing cues that were associated with sexual assaults. In a later phase of treatment, the woman was exposed in vivo to the environments in which the assaults took place. Exposure was highly effective in reducing PTSD symptoms, an effect that was maintained at follow-up.

Conclusions

Relaxation and desensitization are effective in the treatment of phobias and anxiety in individuals with ID. In most cases, multi-component treatment packages were used in which behavioral and cognitive techniques are combined. Though no formal component analysis has been conducted, it appears that behavioral procedures are effective. Data in a large proportion of studies have been collected in nonexperimental case studies (see Davis et al., 2008). Another notable problem with this literature is the absence of studies of complex phobias, such as panic and generalized anxiety disorder.

MOOD DISORDERS

Depressive behaviors are one of the most common mental health problems in individuals with ID. These individuals have an increased risk for developing depressive behaviors and mood disorders as compared to the general population. Important risk factors for depression in ID are social (e.g., lack of social support, life events, and social strain), behavioral (e.g., poor social competence and self-management skills), and/or cognitive (e.g., negative self-thoughts, low self-esteem) (McBrien, 2003). Diagnostic criteria usually are derived from the *DSM-IV* and *ICD-10* and several methods have been developed to screen for and diagnose depression in ID. Several chapters in this and the accompanying volume address depression and bipolar disorder.

Consensus Panel Recommendations

The diagnosis and treatment of several categories of mood disorders more or less follows the same guidelines as in individuals without ID. Prior to intervention, any causes of mood disorders should be examined and treated, such as somatic factors and diseases, medication, dementia, and environmental factors (e.g., social strain). Deb et al. (2001) provide guidelines for the examination and diagnosis of mood disorders. Intervention is based on

outcomes on diagnosis of mood disorder and may consist of a range of procedures varying from antidepressant medication, psychotherapy, and changes of environmental factors.

Controlled Group Studies

McCabe, McGillivray, and Newton (2006) have conducted a randomized controlled group study on the effectiveness of cognitive behavioral treatment on depression in adults with moderate to mild ID. Cognitive behavioral intervention was effective in decreasing levels of depressive symptoms, while increasing positive self-statements in 19 adults with moderate to mild ID working in supported employment. Changes were maintained at 3-month follow-up although more than half of clients' scores had deteriorated. Clients were randomly allocated to experimental conditions and data were collected within pretest/posttest control group design. The control group eventually received the treatment after completion of the therapy to the first group. Two hourly sessions were run over a period of 5 weeks. Therapy followed a precise protocol and was conducted on the premises of the workplace. Most clients showed improvement on measures of depression. In another study by this research team, McGillivray, McCabe, and Kershaw (2008) evaluated the effectiveness of a cognitive behavior therapy that was administered by 13 staff to 47 clients with mild ID and symptoms of depression. Therapy was implemented in a community-based setting. There was a waiting list control group ($N = 27$) who received no treatment. The therapy was effective in decreasing symptoms of depression and these effects were maintained at 3-month follow-up. Both studies are limited in that no data on generalization to home setting were collected, there was no potential response bias since raters were not blind to the experimental conditions, no social validity data were collected, and the influence of nonexperimental factors was probably large (absence of a true placebo-condition). The treatment component(s) responsible for treatment effectiveness are not clear.

Single-Subject Experimental Studies

One of the first controlled single-subject design studies on the treatment of depressive symptoms was conducted by Matson, Dettling, and Senatore (1979). They showed that a multi-component behavioral treatment package was effective in reducing depressive symptoms in a 32-year-old man with mild ID who lived in a residential facility. Depressive symptoms consisted of suicidal threats, depressed mood, sleep difficulties, and social withdrawal. The treatment package consisted of self-monitoring, modeling, and differential reinforcement aimed at increasing positive self-statements, decreasing negative self-statements, and increased social interactions. Treatment resulted in decrease of depressive symptoms and effects were maintained at follow-up.

In another study by Matson (1982), differential reinforcement within a token economy was shown to be highly effective in changing depressive behaviors in four adults who functioned in the moderate to mild range of ID. Individuals were treated in a mental health clinic and treatment consisted of psychoeducational interventions, feedback, and token economy. Tokens could be earned for appropriate emotional and negative verbal behaviors as well as adaptive behaviors (e.g., grooming). Effects were maintained at 6-month follow-up.

Environmental enrichment was used by Lindauer, DeLeon, and Fisher (1999) as an intervention for reducing signs of negative affect (e.g., crying, whining) and self-injury in a 23-year-old client with severe ID and major depression. Environmental enrichment was conducted in 10-minute sessions and consisted of providing her with 12 items that were highly preferred. Data on negative and positive affect were collected in a reversal design and a preference assessment of these items was conducted preceding data collection. Environmental enrichment resulted in a elimination of negative affect and an marked increase in positive affect. Unfortunately, data on generalization across settings and time were not collected.

A cognitive approach has been used by Lindsay, Howells, and Pitcaithly (1993) in two $N = 1$ studies involving two adults with mild ID. Dysfunctional thoughts were challenged and replaced. The intervention resulted in a marked decrease in suicidal thoughts and depressive feelings and effects were maintained at a 6-month follow-up.

Uncontrolled case studies have been published by Beail and Warden (1996) on effects of psychodynamic psychotherapy on severe mental health problems in 20 adults with ID and Tsiouris (2007) on the effects of light therapy for seasonal depression in four adults with ID.

Menolascino, Lazer, and Stark (1989) reported results of treatment of eight individuals with mild ID who were admitted to an inpatient mental health clinic. Treatment consisted of individual and group counseling, psychoactive medication and other approaches, and resulted in a marked decrease in depressive feelings. Long-term follow-up data collected between 2 and 5 years showed maintenance of effects. Clients were discharged into community settings and community support added to maintenance effects.

Conclusions

Cognitive behavior therapy is effective in the treatment of depression in individuals with ID. Cognitive therapy, psychodynamic therapy, and light therapy are possibly effective for depression and depressive symptoms. Studies in this area have included only clients who function in the mild range of ID.

OFFENDING

There is no conclusive evidence concerning the association between ID and offending (Holland, 2004). Sexual offending appears to be more prevalent among people with borderline intelligence than in the general population, and offending is rare among people with moderate, severe, or profound ID (Simpson & Hogg, 2001). Offenders with ID constitute a heterogeneous population. In treatment outcome research, a distinction is typically made between sexual offenders, violent offenders, and arsonists (Lindsay, Taylor, & Sturmey, 2004). Sometimes, individuals with offending-like behavior are included (Allan, Lindsay, MacLeod, & Smith, 2001; Murphy, Powell, Guzman, & Hays, 2007; Rose, Jenkins, O'Connor, Jones, & Felce, 2002), which is defendable because criminal behavior in institutions is often not reported to the police (Lyall, Holland, & Collins, 1995; Thompson, 1997). Cognitive behavioral approaches that aim at self-regulation are often used in the treatment of offenders with ID. Behavioral interventions, such as contingency management and environmental change, are less suitable to address offending behavior directly because offending is a low-frequency behavior and because control over contingencies is time-limited (Lindsay et al., 2004; Taylor, 2002). (See also Chapter 18, Volume 2, by Harkins and Beech on paraphilias and sexual offending).

Consensus Panel Recommendations

The widely accepted "what works" principles for offender treatment entail that treatments must target recognized risk behaviors for offending, such as substance abuse, offense-supportive attitudes, impulsivity, and must take into account the learning style and motivation of the offender. It has been argued that these principles also apply for offenders with ID (Harris & Tough, 2004), which is supported by the fact that treatments for offenders with ID are often derived from mainstream offender treatments.

Controlled Group Studies

No RCT (Ashman & Duggan, 2008) and only few controlled group studies on offending have been published. Taylor et al. (2005) evaluated the effect of an 18-session individual cognitive behavioral anger treatment containing cognitive restructuring, arousal reduction techniques, and skills training. In an inpatient sample of 36 people the effects of routine care in a waiting list control group was compared to routine care plus anger treatment. The results were in the expected direction but statistically significant for only one of the four anger measures. No reoffending data were reported. Lindsay and Smith (1998) evaluated the effect of 1 versus 2 years of cognitive group-therapy for offense-supportive attitudes of sex offenders. Both groups (each $N = 7$) were effective, but the 2-year treatment was more effective than the 1-year treatment.

In a sample of various types of offenders (72% sex offenders), Beail (2001) evaluated the effect of individual psychodynamic outpatient psychotherapy with an average duration of 16 months by comparing reoffending rates by individuals who accepted ($N = 13$) versus those who rejected ($N = 5$) treatment. Four years after treatment, reoffending rates were 15% and 100% for the treatment and control group, respectively. A limitation of this study was that the two groups were nonequivalent, resulting from selection bias.

Keeling, Rose, and Beech (2006) evaluated the effect of an intensive 12-month custody-based cognitive behavioral treatment program for sex offenders. Despite the small sample size ($N = 11$), significant changes between pre- and postmeasures were found for offence-supportive attitudes, self-control, and victim empathy. No follow-up data on reoffending were reported. Murphy et al. (2007) found significant changes in sexual knowledge and victim empathy but not in offense-supportive attitudes after a 12-month community-based cognitive behavioral treatment. Three of the eight participants engaged in sexually abusive behavior within 6 months after treatment. Craig, Stringer, and Moss (2006) found no changes in offense-supportive attitudes or coping skills in a small sample ($N = 6$) of sex offenders following a 7-month community-based cognitive behavioral group treatment. There were, however, no reconvictions within 12 months after treatment. Taylor, Thorne, Robertson, and Avery (2002) evaluated a cognitive behavioral group treatment for arsonists ($N = 14$). The 40-session treatment resulted in significant posttreatment improvements concerning fire attitudes, anger, and self-esteem. No follow-up or reconviction data were reported. Finally, Xenitidis, Henry, Russell, Ward, and Murphy (1999) evaluated the effectiveness of an inpatient facility that provides multicomponent treatment for people with ID and severe challenging behavior, most of whom committed offenses or engaged in offending-like behavior. Outcome indicators were type of living environment before and after the treatment, frequency of aggression, and use of seclusion in the first and last treatment phase. For patients who stayed in treatment for at least 12 months ($N = 57$), statistically significant effects were found on all outcome indicators. It is noteworthy that 80% of the patients who came from noncommunity settings (e.g., special hospitals, prisons) could be placed into community settings after the treatment. No reoffending or other follow-up data were reported.

Single-Subject Experimental Studies

There are no single-subject experiments on offending; however, several series of uncontrolled case studies were conducted to evaluate the effect of cognitive behavioral anger treatment. Lindsay, Allan, MacLeod, Smart, and Smith (2003) and Allan et al. (2001) evaluated a 40-session treatment with six male and five female violent offenders, respectively. A substantial reduction of experienced anger, which was maintained after 15 months, was found for almost all cases, and violent reoffending did not occur. Burns, Bird, Leach, and Higgins (2003) reported more mixed results for a similar 3-month anger treatment in a forensic inpatient facility. Taylor, Robertson, Thorne, Belshaw, and Watson (2006) evaluated effects of a 40-session inpatient treatment on six

female arsonists. They found an improvement with respect to anger, self-esteem, and depression but mixed results for fire-related attitudes. In several small case series, changes in offense-supportive attitudes after cognitive therapy were evaluated for exhibitionists (Lindsay, Neilson, Morrison, & Smith, 1998) and sexual offenders against children (Lindsay, Olley, Baillie, & Smith, 1999). All cases showed marked reductions of offence-supportive attitudes and absence of any reoffending during several years. Rose et al. (2002) evaluated changes in five sex offenders with respect to victim empathy, pro-offense attitudes, and sexual knowledge after 16 weeks of CBT. Most changes were in the intended direction but were less consistent and smaller than in the studies by Lindsay and colleagues.

Conclusions

The available evidence concerning reoffending and changes of more proximal outcome variables suggests that cognitive behavior therapies are effective and psychodynamic therapy and inpatient treatment are possibly effective for violent offenders, sex offenders, and arsonists with ID; however, the results are inconsistent, with a tendency for longer treatments to be more effective. This justifies the common practice of adapting mainstream offender treatments by increasing their length and providing more repetitions (Allam, Middleton, & Browne, 1997; Keeling & Rose, 2006). Research into effects of treatments for ID offenders has made considerable progress during the past decade, and this process should continue. Larger and well-designed outcome studies are on their way (see Craig & Hutchinson, 2005). A major challenge for future research results from the fact that offender treatment is typically delivered in the form of multimodal or multicomponent treatment packages, in which various elements interact during extensive periods of time in producing desirable outcomes. This complicates the attribution of observed changes during treatment and reoffending rates to specific interventions.

EVIDENCE-BASED PRACTICE

Since the 1960s, hundreds of small-N experimental studies have been published on the analysis and treatment of behavioral and psychiatric problems in individuals with ID (see, e.g., Didden et al., 1997; Didden, Korzilius, Van Oorsouw, & Sturmey, 2006). Most of these studies have included one or a relatively small number of participants, but have included proper experimental controls, through the use of multiple-baseline or reversal designs.

Table 6.1 provides a summary of the evidence base of treatments for various behavioral and psychiatric disorders. Evidence-based practice in individuals with ID is the use of function-based applied behavior analysis techniques. Outcomes of meta-analytic studies indicate that the effect size of ABA treatments is enhanced when behavioral procedures are based on outcomes of functional assessment (Didden, 2007). At present, there is no evidence that sensory integrative therapy and Gentle Teaching are effective. When the ID is borderline or mild, cognitive behavioral techniques are an evidence-based treatment for aggression and offending and some psychiatric conditions such as anxiety and mood disorder in ID. Mindfulness procedures are possibly effective but independent replication

TABLE 6.1   Evidence-Based Practice in Intellectual Disability

Behavior/ Disorder	Evidence Base of Treatment		
	Effective	Possibly Effective	Not Effective
Aggression	Cognitive behavior therapy	Mindfulness	
	Differential reinforcement	Social skills training	
	Noncontingent reinforcement		
	Extinction		
	Functional communication training		
Self-injury	Differential reinforcement		Sensory integration
	Functional communication training		Gentle Teaching
	Aversive stimulation		
Stereotypy	Differential reinforcement	Aversive stimulation	Sensory integration
	Stimulus control		
	Environmental enrichment		
Pica	Aversive stimulation	Stimulus control	Differential reinforcement
Rumination	Satiation		
Food refusal	Differential reinforcement		
	Extinction		
	Blending		
Sleep problem	Extinction	Chronotherapy	
	Stimulus control	Differential reinforcement	
	Melatonin		
Anxiety/phobia	Relaxation	Cognitive therapy	
	Desensitization		
Mood disorder	Cognitive behavior therapy	Cognitive therapy	
		Psychodynamic therapy	
		Light therapy	
Offending	Cognitive behavior therapy	Psychodynamic therapy	

is necessary. Other approaches such as cognitive therapies and psychodynamic therapy await further empirical validation.

REFERENCES

Allam, J., Middleton, D., & Browne, K. (1997). Different clients, different needs? Practice issues in community-based treatment for sex offenders. *Criminal Behaviour and Mental Health, 7*, 69–84.

Allan, R., Lindsay, W., MacLeod, F., & Smith, A. (2001). Treatment of women with intellectual disabilities who have been involved in the criminal justice system for reasons of aggression. *Journal of Applied Research in Intellectual Disabilities, 14*, 340–347.

Altabet, S. (2002). Decreasing dental resistance among individuals with severe and profound mental retardation. *Journal of Developmental and Physical Disabilities, 14*, 297–305.

American Psychiatric Association. (2000). *Diagnostic and statistical manual of mental disorders* (4th ed., text rev.). Washington, DC: Author.

Antonacci, D., Manuel, C., & Davis, E. (2008). Diagnosis and treatment of aggression in individuals with developmental disabilities. *Psychiatry Quarterly, 79*, 225–247.

Ashman, L., & Duggan, L. (2008). Interventions for learning disabled sex offenders. *Cochrane Database of Systematic Reviews, 1*, CD003682.

Ayres, A. (1972). *Sensory integration and learning disorders*. Los Angeles, CA: Western Psychological Services.

Baranek, G. (2002). Efficacy of sensory and motor interventions for children with autism. *Journal of Autism and Developmental Disorders, 32*, 397–422.

Barrera, F., Violo, R., & Graver, E. (2007). On the form and function of severe self-injurious behavior. *Behavioral Interventions, 22*, 5–33.

Beail, N. (2001). Recidivism following psychodynamic psychotherapy amongst offenders with intellectual disabilities. *The British Journal of Forensic Practice, 3*, 33–37.

Beail, N., & Warden, S. (1996). Evaluation of psychodynamic psychotherapy service for adults with intellectual disabilities: Rationale, design and preliminary outcome data. *Journal of Applied Research in Intellectual Disabilities, 9*, 223–228.

Berkson, G. (2002). Early development of stereotyped and self-injurious behaviors: II. Age trends. *American Journal on Mental Retardation, 104*, 107–116.

Braam, W., Didden, R., Smits, M., & Curfs, L. (2008). Melatonin treatment in individuals with intellectual disability and chronic insomnia: A randomised placebo-controlled study. *Journal of Intellectual Disability Research, 52*, 256–264.

Braam, W., Smits, M., Didden, R., Korzilius, H., van Geijlswijk, I., & Curfs, L. (2009). Exogenous melatonin for sleep problems in persons with intellectual disability: A meta-analysis. *Developmental Medicine and Child Neurology, 51*, 340–349.

Bramble, D. (1997). Rapid-acting treatment for a common sleep problem. *Developmental Medicine and Child Neurology, 39*, 543–547.

Burns, M., Bird, D., Leach, C., & Higgins, K. (2003). Anger management training: The effects of a structured programme on the self-reported anger experience of forensic inpatients with learning disability. *Journal of Psychiatric and Mental Health Nursing, 10*, 569–577.

Cannella, H., O'Reilly, M., & Lancioni, G. (2006). Treatment of hand mouthing in individuals with severe to profound developmental disabilities: A review of the literature. *Research in Developmental Disabilities, 27*, 529–544.

Carr, J., Coariaty, S., Wilder, D., Gaunt, B., Dozier, C., Britton, L., . . . Reed, C. (2000). A review of noncontingent reinforcement as a treatment for the aberrant behavior of individuals with developmental disabilities. *Research in Developmental Disabilities, 21*, 377–391.

Carr, E., & Durand, V. (1985). Reducing behavior problems through functional communication training. *Journal of Applied Behavior Analysis, 18*, 111–126.

Chambless, D., & Hollon, S. (1998). Defining empirically supported therapies. *Journal of Consulting and Clinical Psychology, 66*, 7–18.

Chiodo, J., & Maddox, J. (1985). A cognitive and behavioural approach to anxiety management of retarded individuals: Two case studies. *Journal of Child and Adolescent Psychotherapy, 2*, 16–20.

Cole, G., Montgomery, R., Wilson, K., & Milan, M. (2000). Parametric analysis of overcorrection duration effects: Is longer really better than shorter? *Behavior Modification, 24*, 359–378.

Conroy, M., Asmus, J., Sellers, J., & Ladwig, C. (2005). The use of an antecedent-based intervention to decrease stereotypic behavior in a general education classroom: A case study. *Focus on Autism and Other Developmental Disabilities, 20*, 223–230.

Cooper, L., Wacker, D., McComas, J., Brown, K., Peck, S., Richman, D., . . . Millard, T. (1995). Use of component analyses to identify active variables in treatment packages for children with feeding disorders. *Journal of Applied Behavior Analysis, 28*, 139–153.

Craig, L., & Hutchinson, R. (2005). Sexual offenders with learning disabilities: Risk, recidivism and treatment. *Journal of Sexual Aggression, 11*, 289–304.

Craig, E., Stringer, I., & Moss, T. (2006). Treating sex offenders with learning disabilities in the community: A critical review. *International Journal of Offender Therapy and Comparative Criminology, 50*, 369–390.

Davis, E., Saeed, S., & Antonacci, D. (2008). Anxiety disorders in persons with developmental disabilities: Empirically informed diagnosis and treatment. *Psychiatric Quarterly, 79*, 249–263.

Deb, S., Matthews, T., Holt, G., & Bouras, N. (2001). *Practice guidelines for the assessment and diagnosis of mental health problems in adults with intellectual disability.* Brighton, England: Pavilion.

Dekker, M., & Koot, H. (2003). DSM-IV disorders in children with borderline to moderate intellectual disability I: Prevalence and impact. *Journal of the American Academy of Child and Adolescent Psychiatry, 42*, 915–922.

Didden, R. (2007). Functional analysis methodology in developmental disabilities. In P. Sturmey (Ed.), *Functional analysis in clinical treatment* (pp. 65–86). New York, NY: Academic Press.

Didden, R., Curfs, L., Sikkema, S., & De Moor, J. (2004). Functional assessment and treatment of sleep problems with developmentally disabled children: Six case studies. *Journal of Behavior Therapy and Experimental Psychiatry, 29*, 85–97.

Didden, R., Curfs, L., van Driel, S., & de Moor, J. (2002). Sleep problems in children with developmental disabilities: Home-based functional assessment and treatment. *Journal of Behavior Therapy and Experimental Psychiatry, 33*, 49–58.

Didden, R., Duker, P., & Korzilius, H. (1997). Meta-analytic study on treatment effectiveness for problem behaviors with individuals who have mental retardation. *American Journal on Mental Retardation, 101*, 387–399.

Didden, R., Korzilius, H., Van Oorsouw, W., & Sturmey, P. (2006). Behavioral treatment of challenging behavior in individuals with mild mental retardation: A meta-analysis of single subject research. *American Journal on Mental Retardation, 111*, 290–298.

Didden, R., & Sigafoos, J. (2001). A review of the nature and treatment of sleep problems in individuals with developmental disabilities. *Research in Developmental Disabilities, 22*, 255–272.

Dorsey, M., Iwata, B., Ong, P., & McSween, T. (1980). Treatment of self-injurious behavior using a water mist: Initial response suppression and generalization. *Journal of Applied Behavior Analysis, 13*, 343–353.

Duker, P., Jol, K., & Palmen, A. (1991). The collateral decrease of self-injurious behavior with teaching communicative gestures to individuals who are mentally retarded. *Behavioral Residential Treatment, 6*, 183–196.

Duker, P., & Seys, D. (1996). Long-term use of electrical aversion treatment with self-injurious behavior. *Research in Developmental Disabilities, 17*, 293–301.

Duker, P., & Seys, D. (2000). A quasi-experimental study on the effect of electrical aversion treatment on imposed mechanical restraint for severe self-injurious behavior. *Research in Developmental Disabilities, 21*, 235–242.

Durand, M., & Merges, E. (2001). Functional communication training: A contemporary behavior analytic intervention for problem behaviors. *Focus on Autism and Other Developmental Disabilities, 16*, 110–119.

Einfeld, S., Piccinin, A., Mackinnon, A., Hofer, S., Taffe, J., Gray, K., . . . Tonge, B. (2006). Psychopathology in young people with intellectual disability. *Journal of the American Medical Association, 296*, 1981–1989.

Emerson, E. (2003). The prevalence of psychiatric disorders in children and adolescents with and without intellectual disabilities. *Journal of Intellectual Disability Research, 47*, 51–58.

Erfanian, N., & Miltenberger, R. (1990). Contact desensitization in the treatment of dog phobias in persons who have mental retardation. *Behavioral Residential Treatment, 5*, 55–60.

Fertel-Daly, D., Bedell, G., & Hinojosa, J. (2001). Effects of weighted vests on attention to task and self-stimulatory behaviors in preschoolers with pervasive developmental disorders. *American Journal of Occupational Therapy, 55*, 629–640.

Fisher, W., Piazza, C., Bowman, L., Kurtz, P., Sherer, M., & Lachman, S. (1994). A preliminary evaluation of empirically derived consequences for the treatment of pica. *Journal of Applied Behavior Analysis, 27*, 447–457.

Foxx, R., Snyder, M., & Schroeder, F. (1979). A food satiation and oral hygiene punishment program to suppress chronic rumination by retarded persons. *Journal of Autism and Developmental Disorders, 9*, 399–412.

Friman, P., Barnard, J., Altman, K., & Wolf, M. (1986). Parent and teacher use of DRO and DRI to reduce aggressive behavior. *Analysis and Intervention in Developmental Disabilities, 6*, 319–330.

Gaylord-Ross, R., Weeks, M., Lipner, C., & Gaylord-Ross, C. (1983). The differential effectiveness of four treatment procedures in suppressing self-injurious behavior among severely handicapped students. *Education & Training of the Mentally Retarded, 18*, 38–44.

Gibbs, J., & Luyben, P. (1985). Treatment of self-injurious behavior: Contingent versus noncontingent positive practice overcorrection. *Behavior Modification, 9*, 3–21.

Goh, H., Iwata, B., & Kahng, S. (1999). Multicomponent assessment and treatment of cigarette pica. *Journal of Applied Behavior Analysis, 32*, 297–316.

Green, V., Pituch, K., Itchon, J., Choi, A., O'Reilly, M., & Sigafoos, J. (2006). Internet survey of treatments used by parents of children with autism. *Research in Developmental Disabilities, 27*, 70–84.

Green, V., Sigafoos, J., O'Reilly, M., & Itchon, J. (2005). Persistence of early emerging aberrant behavior in children with developmental disabilities. *Research in Developmental Disabilities, 26,* 47–55.

Hagopian, L., Crockett, J., & Keeney, K. (2001). Multi-component treatment for blood-injury injection phobia in a young man with mental retardation. *Research in Developmental Disabilities, 21,* 141–149.

Hagopian, L., Fisher, W., Sullivan, M., Acquisto, J., & LeBlanc, L. (1998). Effectiveness of functional communication training with and without extinction and punishment: A summary of 21 inpatient cases. *Journal of Applied Behavior Analysis, 31,* 211–235.

Harris, A., & Tough, S. (2004). Should actuarial risk assessment be used with sex offenders who are intellectually disabled? *Journal of Applied Research in Intellectual Disabilities, 17,* 235–241.

Harvey, S., Boer, D., Meyer, L., & Evans, I. (2009). Updating a meta-analysis of intervention research with challenging behaviour: Treatment validity and standards of practice. *Journal of Intellectual and Developmental Disability, 34,* 67–80.

Hoch, T., Babbitt, R., Coe, D., Krell, D., & Hackbert, L. (1994). Contingency contacting: Combining positive reinforcement and escape extinction procedures to treat persistent food refusal. *Behavior Modification, 18,* 106–128.

Holland, A. (2004). Criminal behaviour and developmental disability: An epidemiological perspective. In W. Lindsay, J. Taylor, & P. Sturmey (Eds.), *Offenders with developmental disabilities* (pp. 23–34). Chichester, England: Wiley.

Iwata, B., Dorsey, M., Slifer, K., Bauman, K., & Richman, G. (1994). Toward a functional analysis of self-injury. *Journal of Applied Behavior Analysis, 27,* 197–209.

Iwata, B., Pace, G., Dorsey, M., Zarcone, J., Vollmer, T., Smith, R., . . . Willis, K. (1994). The functions of self-injurious behavior: An experimental-epidemiological analysis. *Journal of Applied Behavior Analysis, 27,* 215–240.

Johnston, J., & Greene, K. (1992). Relation between ruminating and quantity of food consumed. *Mental Retardation, 30,* 7–11.

Kahng, S., Iwata, B., & Lewin, A. (2002). The impact of functional assessment on the treatment of self-injurious behavior. In S. Schroeder, M. Oster-Granite, & T. Thompson (Eds.), *Self-injurious behavior. Gene-brain behavior relationships* (pp. 119–131). Washington, DC: American Psychological Association.

Kane, A., Luiselli, J., Dearborn, S., & Young, N. (2004). Wearing a weighted vest as intervention for children with autism/pervasive developmental disorder. *Scientific Review of Mental Health Practice, 3,* 19–24.

Keeling, J., & Rose, J. (2006). The adaptation of a cognitive behavioural treatment programme for special needs sexual offenders. *British Journal of Learning Disabilities, 34,* 110–116.

Keeling, J., Rose, J., & Beech, A. (2006). An investigation into the effectiveness of a custody-based cognitive-behavioural treatment for special needs sexual offenders. *The Journal of Forensic Psychiatry & Psychology, 17,* 372–392.

Kennedy, C. (2007). Stereotypic movement disorder. In P. Sturmey (Ed.), *Functional analysis in clinical treatment* (pp. 193–209). New York, NY: Academic Press.

Kuhn, D., & Matson, J. (2004). Assessment of feeding and mealtime behavior problems in persons with mental retardation. *Behavior Modification, 28,* 638–648.

Lancioni, G., O'Reilly, M., & Basili, G. (1999). Review of strategies for treating sleep problems in persons with severe to profound mental retardation or multiple handicaps. *American Journal on Mental Retardation, 104,* 170–186.

Lancioni, G., O'Reilly, M., Singh, N., Oliva, D., & Groeneweg, J. (2003). Using microswitches with persons who have profound multiple disabilities: Evaluation of three cases. *Perceptual and Motor Skills, 97,* 909–916.

Lancioni, G., Singh, N., O'Reilly, M., Sigafoos, J., Didden, R., Oliva, D., & Cingolani, E. (2008). A girl with multiple disabilities increases object manipulation and reduces hand mouthing through a switch-based program. *Clinical Case Studies, 7,* 238–249.

Leblanc, L., & Matson, J. (1995). A social skills training program for preschoolers with developmental delays: Generalization and social validity. *Behavior Modification, 19,* 234–246.

Lemmon, V., & Mizes, J. (2002). Effectiveness of exposure therapy: A case study of posttraumatic stress disorder and mental retardation. *Cognitive Behavioral Practice, 9,* 317–323.

Lerman, D., & Iwata, B. (1996). Developing a technology for the use of operant extinction in clinical settings: An examination of basic and applied research. *Journal of Applied Behavior Analysis, 29,* 345–382.

Lindauer, S., DeLeon, I., & Fisher, W. (1999). Decreasing signs of negative affect and correlated self-injury in an individual with mental retardation and mood disturbances. *Journal of Applied Behavior Analysis, 32,* 103–106.

Lindsay, W., Allan, R., Macleod, F., Smart, N., & Smith, A. (2003). Long-term treatment and management of violent tendencies of men with intellectual disabilities convicted of assault. *Mental Retardation, 41,* 47–56.

Lindsay, W., Allan, R., Parry, C., Macleod, F., Cottrell, J., Overend, H., & Smith, A. (2004). Anger and aggression in people with intellectual disabilities: Treatment and follow-up of consecutive referrals and a waiting list comparison. *Clinical Psychology and Psychotherapy, 11,* 255–264.

Lindsay, W., Baty, F., Michie, A., & Richardson, I. (1989). A comparison of anxiety treatments with adults who have moderate and severe mental retardation. *Research in Developmental Disabilities, 10*, 129–140.

Lindsay, W., Howells, L., & Pitcaithly, D. (1993). Cognitive therapy for depression with individuals with intellectual disabilities. *British Journal of Medical Psychology, 66*, 135–141.

Lindsay, W., Neilson, C., Morrison, F., & Smith, A. (1998). The treatment of six men with intellectual disabilities convicted of sexual offences with children. *British Journal of Clinical Psychology, 37*, 83–89.

Lindsay, W., Olley, S., Baillie, N., & Smith, A. (1999). Treatment of adolescent sex offenders with intellectual disabilities. *Mental Handicap, 37*, 201–211.

Lindsay, W., & Smith, A. (1998). Responses to treatment for sex offenders with intellectual disability: A comparison of men with 1- and 2-year probation sentences. *Journal of Intellectual Disability Research, 42*, 346–353.

Lindsay, W., Taylor, J., & Sturmey, P. (Eds.) (2004). *Offenders with developmental disabilities*. London, England: Wiley.

Lovaas, O., & Simmons, J. (1969). Manipulation of self-destruction in three retarded children. *Journal of Applied Behavior Analysis, 2*, 143–157.

Luiselli, J. (1977). An attendant-administered contingency management programme for the treatment of a toileting phobia. *Journal of Mental Deficiency Research, 21*, 283–288.

Luiselli, J., Suskin, L., & Slocum, P. (1984). Application of immobilization time-out in management programming with developmentally disabled children. *Child and Family Behaviour Therapy, 6*, 1–15.

Lutzker, J. (1978). Reducing self-injurious behavior by facial screening. *American Journal on Mental Deficiency, 82*, 510–513.

Lyall, I., Holland, A., & Collins, S. (1995). Offending by adults with learning disabilities and the attitude of staff to offending behaviour: Implications for service development. *Journal of Intellectual Disability Research, 39*, 501–508.

Lyons, E., Rue, H., Luiselli, J., & DiGennaro, F. (2007). Brief functional analysis and supplemental feeding for postmeal rumination in children with developmental disabilities. *Journal of Applied Behavior Analysis, 40*, 743–747.

Mace, F., Blum, N., Sierp, B., Delaney, B., & Mauk, J. (2001). Differential response of operant self-injury to pharmacologic versus behavioral treatment. *Journal of Developmental & Behavioral Pediatrics, 22*, 85–91.

Mason, S., & Iwata, B. (1990). Artifactual effects of sensory-integrative therapy on self-injurious behavior. *Journal of Applied Behavior Analysis, 23*, 361–370.

Matson, J. (1982). The treatment of behavioral characteristics of depression in the mentally retarded. *Behavior Therapy, 13*, 209–218.

Matson, J., Anderson, S., & Bamburg, J. (2000). The relationship of social skills to psychopathology for individuals with mild and moderate mental retardation. *British Journal of Developmental Disabilities, 46*, 15–22.

Matson, J., Dettling, J., & Senatore, V. (1979). Treating depression of a mentally retarded adult. *British Journal of Mental Subnormality, 26*, 86–88.

Matson, J., Dixon, D., & Matson, M. (2005). Assessing and treating aggression in children and adolescents with developmental disabilities: A 20-year review. *Educational Psychology, 25*, 151–181.

Matson, J., Fee, V., Coe, D., & Smith, D. (1991). A social skills program for developmentally delayed preschoolers. *Journal of Clinical Child Psychology, 20*, 428–434.

Matson, J., Terlonge, C., & Minshawi, N. (2008). Children with intellectual disabilities. In R. Morris & T. Kratochwill (Eds.), *The practice of child therapy* (4th ed.) (pp. 337–361). New York, NY: Erlbaum.

McAdam, D., Sherman, J., Sheldon, J., & Napolitano, D. (2008). Behavioral interventions to reduce pica of persons with developmental disabilities. *Behavior Modification, 28*, 45–72.

McBrien, J. (2003). Assessment and diagnosis of depression in people with intellectual disability. *Journal of Intellectual Disability Research, 47*, 1–13.

McCabe, M., McGillivray, J., & Newton, D. (2006). Effectiveness of treatment programmes for depression among adults with mild/moderate intellectual disability. *Journal of Intellectual Disability Research, 50*, 239–247.

McGee, J., & Menolascino, F. (1991). *Beyond Gentle Teaching: A nonaversive approach to helping those in need*. New York, NY: Plenum Press.

McGillivray, J., McCabe, M., & Kershaw, M. (2008). Depression in people with intellectual disability: An evaluation of a staff-administered treatment program. *Research in Developmental Disabilities, 29*, 524–536.

Menolascino, F., Lazer, J., & Stark, J. (1989). Diagnosis and management of depression and suicidal behavior in persons with severe mental retardation. *Journal of the Multihandicapped Person, 2*, 89–103.

Mirenda, P. (1997). Supporting individuals with challenging behavior through functional communication training and AAC: Research review. *Augmentative and Alternative Communication, 13*, 207–225.

Mudford, O. (1995). Review of the Gentle Teaching data. *American Journal on Mental Retardation, 99*, 345–355.

Mueller, M., Piazza, C., Patel, M., Kelley, M., & Pruett, A. (2004). Increasing variety of food consumed by blending nonpreferred foods into preferred foods. *Journal of Applied Behavior Analysis, 37*, 159–170.

Murphy, G., Hall, S., Oliver, C., & Kissi-Debra, R. (1999). Identification of early self-injurious behaviour in young children with intellectual disability. *Journal of Intellectual Disability Research, 43,* 149–163.

Murphy, G., Powell, S., Guzman, A., & Hays, S. (2007). Cognitive-behavioural treatment for men with intellectual disabilities and sexually abusive behaviour: A pilot study. *Journal of Intellectual Disability Research, 51,* 902–912.

National Institutes of Mental Health. (1989). *Consensus Development Conference statement: Consensus Development Conference on Treatment of Destructive Behaviors in Persons with Developmental Disabilities.* Washington, DC: Author.

Oliver, C., Murphy, G., & Corbett, J. (1987). Self-injurious behaviour in people with mental handicap: A total population study. *Journal of Mental Deficiency Research, 31,* 147–162.

O'Reilly, M., Lancioni, J., & Sigafoos, J. (2004). Using paired-choice assessment to identify variables maintaining sleep problems in a child with severe disabilities. *Journal of Applied Behavior Analysis, 37,* 209–212.

O'Reilly, M., Lancioni, G., Sigafoos, J., O'Donoghue, D., Lacey, C., & Edrisinha, C. (2004). Teaching social skills to adults with intellectual disabilities: A comparison of external control and problem-solving interventions. *Research in Developmental Disabilities, 25,* 399–412.

O'Reilly, M., Lancioni, G., & Taylor, I. (1999). An empirical analysis of two forms of extinction to treat aggression. *Research in Developmental Disabilities, 20,* 315–325.

Patel, M., Piazza, C., Martinez, C., Volkert, V., & Santana, C. (2002). An evaluation of two different reinforcement procedures with escape extinction to treat food refusal. *Journal of Applied Behavior Analysis, 35,* 363–374.

Piazza, C., Patel, M., Santana, C., Goh, H., Delia, M., & Lancaster, B. (2002). An evaluation of simultaneous and sequential presentation of preferred and non-preferred food to treat food selectivity. *Journal of Applied Behavior Analysis, 35,* 259–270.

Rapp, J. (2004). Effects of prior access and environmental enrichment on stereotypy. *Behavioral Interventions, 19,* 287–295.

Rapp, J., & Vollmer, T. (2005). Stereotypy I: A review of behavioral assessment and treatment. *Research in Developmental Disabilities, 26,* 527–547.

Rast, J., Johnston, J., & Drum, C. (1984). A parametric analysis of the relationship between food quantity and rumination. *Journal of Experimental Analysis of Behavior, 41,* 125–134.

Richdale, A., & Wiggs, L. (2005). Behavioral approaches to the treatment of sleep problems in children with developmental disabilities: What is the state of the art? *International Journal of Behavioral and Consultation Therapy, 1,* 165–189.

Richman, D., & Lindauer, S. (2005). Longitudinal assessment of stereotypic, proto-injurious, and self-injurious behavior exhibited by young children with developmental delays. *American Journal on Mental Retardation, 110,* 439–450.

Riordan, M., Iwata, B., Finney, J., Wohl, M., & Stanley, A. (1984). Behavioral assessment and treatment of chronic food refusal in handicapped children. *Journal of Applied Behavior Analysis, 17,* 327–341.

Rose, J., Jenkins, R., O'Connor, C., Jones, C., & Felce, D. (2002). A group treatment for men with intellectual disabilities who sexually offend or abuse. *Journal of Applied Research in Intellectual Disabilities, 15,* 138–150.

Rose, J., West, C., & Clifford, D. (2000). Group interventions for anger in people with intellectual disabilities. *Research in Developmental Disabilities, 21,* 171–181.

Rush, A., & Frances, A. (2000). Treatment of psychiatric and behavior problems in mental retardation. *American Journal of Mental Retardation, 105,* 161–228.

Shore, B., Babbitt, R., Williams, K., Coe, D., & Snyder, A. (1998). Use of texture fading in the treatment of food selectivity. *Journal of Applied Behavior Analysis, 31,* 621–633.

Sidener, T., Carr, J., & Firth, A. (2005). Superimposition and withholding of edible consequences as treatment for automatically reinforced stereotypy. *Journal of Applied Behavior Analysis, 38,* 121–124.

Sigafoos, J., Arthur, M., & O'Reilly, M. (2003). *Challenging behavior and developmental disability.* London, England: Whurr.

Sigafoos, J., Elkins, J., Kerr, M., & Attwood, T. (1994). A survey of aggressive behavior among a population of persons with intellectual disability in Queensland. *Journal of Intellectual Disability Research, 38,* 369–381.

Sigafoos, J., O'Reilly, M., & Lancioni, G. (2009). Functional communication training and choice-making interventions for the treatment of problem behavior in individuals with autism spectrum disorders. In P. Mirenda & T. Iacono (Eds.), *AAC interventions for individuals with autism spectrum disorders.* Baltimore, MD: Paul H. Brookes.

Simpson, M., & Hogg, J. (2001). Patterns of offending among people with intellectual disability: A systematic review. Part I: Methodology and prevalence data. *Journal of Intellectual Disability Research, 45,* 384–396.

Singh, N., Lancioni, G., Winton, A., Adkins, A., Singh, J., & Singh, A. (2007). Mindfulness training assists individuals with moderate mental retardation to maintain their community placements. *Behavior Modification, 31,* 800–814.

Singh, N., Lancioni, G., Winton, A., Adkins, A., Wahler, R., Sabaawi, M., & Singh, J. (2007). Individuals with mental illness can control their aggressive behaviour through mindfulness training. *Behavior Modification, 31*, 313–328.

Singh, N., Lancioni, G., Winton, A., Curtis, W., Wahler, R., Sabaawi, M., . . . McAleavy, K. (2006). Mindful staff increase learning and reduce aggression in adults with developmental disabilities. *Research in Developmental Disabilities, 27*, 545–558.

Singh, N., Lancioni, G., Winton, A., Singh, A., Adkins, A., & Singh, J. (2008). Clinical and benefit cost outcomes of teaching a mindfulness-based procedure to adult offenders with intellectual disabilities. *Behavior Modification, 32*, 622–637.

Singh, N., Lancioni, G., Winton, A., Singh, J., Curtis, W., Wahler, R., & McAleavy, K. (2007). Mindful parenting decreases aggression and increases social behavior in children with developmental disabilities. *Behavior Modification, 31*, 749–771.

Singh, N., Wahler, R., Adkins, A., & Myers, R. (2003). Soles of the feet: A mindfulness-based self-control intervention for aggression by an individual with mild mental retardation and mental illness. *Research in Developmental Disabilities, 24*, 158–169.

Smith, T., Mruzek, D., & Mozingo, D. (2005). Sensory integrative therapy. In J. Jacobson, R. Foxx, & J. Mulick (Eds.), *Controversial therapies for developmental disabilities: Fad, fashion and science in professional practice* (pp. 331–350). Mahwah, NJ: Erlbaum.

Smith, S., Press, B., Koenig, K., & Kinnealey, M. (2005). Effects of sensory integration intervention of self-stimulation and self-injurious behaviors. *American Journal of Occupational Therapy, 59*, 418–425.

Sturmey, P. (2002). Mental retardation and concurrent psychiatric disorder: Assessment and treatment. *Current Opinions in Psychiatry, 15*, 489–495.

Sturmey, P. (2004). Cognitive therapy with people with intellectual disabilities: A selective review and critique. *Clinical Psychology and Psychotherapy, 11*, 222–232.

Sturmey, P. (2006). On some recent claims for the efficacy of cognitive therapy for people with intellectual disabilities. *Journal of Applied Research in Intellectual Disabilities, 19*, 109–117.

Taylor, J. (2002). A review of the assessment and treatment of anger and aggression in offenders with intellectual disability. *Journal of Intellectual Disability Research, 46*, 57–73.

Taylor, J., Novaco, R., Gillmer, B., Robertson, A., & Thorne, I. (2005). Individual cognitive-behavioural anger treatment for people with mild-borderline intellectual disabilities and histories of aggression: A controlled trial. *British Journal of Clinical Psychology, 44*, 367–382.

Taylor, J., Novaco, R., Gillmer, B., & Thorne, J. (2002). Cognitive-behavioral treatment of anger intensity among offenders with intellectual disabilities. *Journal of Applied Research in Intellectual Disabilities, 15*, 151–165.

Taylor, J., Novaco, R., Guinan, C., & Street, N. (2004). Development of an imaginal provocation test to evaluate treatment for anger problems in people with intellectual disabilities. *Clinical Psychology and Psychotherapy, 11*, 233–246.

Taylor, J., Robertson, A., Thorne, I., Belshaw, T., & Watson, A. (2006). Responses of female fire-setters with mild and borderline intellectual disabilities to a group intervention. *Journal of Applied Research in Intellectual Disabilities, 19*, 179–190.

Taylor, J., Thorne, I., Robertson, A., & Avery, G. (2002). Evaluation of a group intervention for convicted arsonists with mild and borderline intellectual disabilities. *Criminal Behaviour and Mental Health, 12*, 282–293.

Thibadeau, S., Blew, P., Reedy, P., & Luiselli, J. (1999). Access to white bread as an intervention for chronic ruminative vomiting. *Journal of Behavior Therapy and Experimental Psychiatry, 30*, 137–144.

Thompson, D. (1997). Profiling the sexually abusive behaviour of men with intellectual disabilities. *Journal of Applied Research in Intellectual Disabilities, 10*, 125–139.

Tsiouris, J. (2007). Light therapy for seasonal depression in persons with intellectual disability: Literature review and four case series. *Mental Health Aspects in Developmental Disabilities, 10*, 137–144.

Tucker, M., Sigafoos, J., & Bushell, H. (1998). Use of noncontingent reinforcement in the treatment of challenging behavior: A review and clinical guide. *Behavior Modification, 22*, 529–547.

Vollmer, T., Iwata, B., Zarcone, J., Smith, R., & Mazaleski, J. (1993). The role of attention in the treatment of attention-maintained self-injurious behavior: Noncontingent reinforcement and differential reinforcement of other behavior. *Journal of Applied Behavior Analysis, 26*, 9–21.

Vollmer, T., Ringdahl, J., Roane, H., & Marcus, B. (1997). Negative side effects of noncontingent reinforcement. *Journal of Applied Behavior Analysis, 30*, 161–164.

Wacker, D., Berg, W., Harding, J., Barretto, A., Rankin, B., & Ganzer, J. (2005). Treatment effectiveness, stimulus generalization, and acceptability to parents of functional communication training. *Educational Psychology, 25*, 233–256.

Wacker, D., Steege, M., Northup, J., Sasso, G., Berg, W., Reimers, T., . . . Donn, L. (1990). A component analysis of functional communication training across three topographies of severe behavior problems. *Journal of Applied Behavior Analysis, 23*, 417–429.

Williams, K., & Foxx, R. (2007). *Treating eating problems of children with autism spectrum disorders and developmental disabilities: Interventions for professionals and parents.* Austin, TX: Pro-Ed.

Williams, D., Kirkpatrick-Sanchez, S., Enzinna, C., Dunn, J., & Borden-Karasack, D. (2009). The clinical management and prevention of pica: A retrospective follow-up of 41 individuals with intellectual disabilities and pica. *Journal of Applied Research in Intellectual Disabilities, 22,* 210–215.

Willner, P., Jones, J., Tams, R., & Green, G. (2002). A randomized controlled trial of the efficacy of a cognitive-behavioural anger management group for adults with learning disabilities. *Journal of Applied Research in Intellectual Disabilities, 15,* 224–235.

Willner, P., & Tomlinson, S. (2007). Generalization of anger-coping skills from day-service to residential settings. *Journal of Applied Research in Intellectual Disabilities, 20,* 553–562.

Xenitidis, K., Henry, J., Russell, A., Ward, A., & Murphy, D. (1999). An in-patient treatment model for adults with mild intellectual disability and challenging behaviour. *Journal of Intellectual Disability Research, 43,* 128–134.

Zubicaray, G., & Clair, A. (1998). An evaluation of differential reinforcement of other behavior, differential reinforcement of incompatible behavior, and restitution for the management of aggressive behaviors. *Behavioral Interventions, 13,* 157–168.

7

Learning Disabilities

T. STEUART WATSON, JANE E. COLE, SARAH GEBHARDT, AND TONYA S. WATSON

OVERVIEW OF THE DISORDER

A learning disability is defined in federal regulations as a severe discrepancy between a student's ability and their achievement in one or more of the following seven areas: (1) listening comprehension, (2) oral expression, (3) basic reading skills, (4) reading comprehension, (5) written expression, (6) mathematical calculation, and (7) mathematical reasoning (Individuals with Disabilities Education Improvement Act of 2004, PL 108-446). Because of the legal wording used to characterize a learning disability, there has been a great deal of focus on measuring this "discrepancy" between ability (usually measured by IQ tests) and achievement (usually measured by some form of standardized achievement test). Under this model of discrepancy identification, teachers or parents refer a child whom they believe is performing below their ability level to be tested by the school psychologist. If the results from intelligence and achievement testing demonstrate a "severe" discrepancy between the student's ability and his or her achievement, the student may be diagnosed as learning disabled. Although this has been a widespread practice in school districts throughout the United States for over 30 years, it unfortunately is not one based on empirical evidence and not one that is considered an evidence-based practice. There are a number

of reasons for the substantial shortcomings associated with the discrepancy model.

First, because the refer-test-diagnose system relies on subjective teacher and parent referrals, a student's problems have to become sufficiently severe to significantly impact his or her schoolwork before any intervention can begin, rather than being caught at the onset when the problem may be relatively minor. Waiting for a student to fall far behind his or her peers results in a phenomenon often referred to as the "wait-fail" effect, wherein a student first has to fail in order to receive any help. Second, the discrepancy model provides no direct link between learning disability classification and resulting treatment. In other words, diagnosing a student with a learning disability only applies a label to a problem, but does not prescribe an intervention. Furthermore, research suggests that neither IQ scores nor IQ-achievement discrepancies are relevant for treatment planning, nor do they predict or differentiate between children who are likely to respond well to treatment and those who will continue to struggle (Fletcher, Morris, & Lyon, 2003).

A third unfortunate outcome from the historical refer-test-diagnose model is the fact that the model attributes the failure to learn or the slow rate of learning to the child (Fletcher et al., 2003). Thus, the child himself is viewed as the source of the academic problem and the only factors truly considered in alleviating problem symptoms are in reference to the nature of the learning disability that exists *within* the child. These assumptions arise from the historical discrepancy-based model, which itself is based on a medical model of diagnosis. In the medical model, symptoms are assessed, a condition is diagnosed, and treatment is applied based on the diagnosis. While this model works remarkably well for the practice of medicine, it is woefully inadequate for helping students with learning problems to succeed in school (Steege & T. Steuart Watson, 2009). In addition, there is scant empirical evidence to support the idea that IQ-achievement discrepancy actually distinguishes different types of learning disorders or that children with learning disorders exhibit any qualitative differences from children with other forms of underachievement (Fletcher et al., 2003).

A fourth problem associated with the discrepancy model is psychometric in nature. That is, because the measurement of both ability and achievement are associated with error, the difference score is particularly prone to measurement error. In fact, difference scores reflect not only the error associated with measuring ability and achievement but also the error in computing a difference score. Thus, difference scores *maximize* measurement error rather than minimize it. Fifth, and on a related note, there is no agreement about the amount of difference that constitutes a severe discrepancy and how it is determined. As Kavale (2002) noted, the discrepancy model is most problematic when one uses a formula to determine the discrepancy. Unfortunately, Reschly and Hosp (2004) found that 29 states established a formula to use and 15 states quantified the discrepancy for it to be considered severe.

Finally, and most importantly for this chapter on evidence-based practices for students with learning problems, the scientific evidence that has accumulated since the 1970s consistently fails to support the discrepancy model for diagnosing learning disabilities. For further

reading on this topic, the interested reader is referred to Vellutino, Scanlon, and Lyon (2000). In fact, numerous professional organizations, special committees, and task forces have called for the elimination of the achievement-ability discrepancy model for identifying learning disabilities (Learning Disabilities Roundtable, 2002; National Association of School Psychologists [NASP], 2003).

THE RESPONSE TO INTERVENTION MODEL

The historical practice of using the IQ-achievement discrepancy model for identifying children with learning disabilities and assigning treatment based on their pattern of responding is rooted in the scientific medical model; however, it has not been shown effective. Therefore, there has been a movement away from this nonempirically supported model to an empirically based problem-solving model utilizing response to intervention for identifying children with significant learning problems and for treatment planning.

The problem-solving model is geared toward identifying interventions for student problems that are empirically linked to the problem itself and that evidence a high likelihood of improving the problem. Unlike the discrepancy model, the problem-solving model is oriented more toward the context in which the child is learning and socially interacting as a potential source of the problem, rather than viewing the problem as a reflection of an internal problem within the child. Instead of focusing on how to specifically classify learning disorders, the problem-solving model focuses on how to effectively treat academic deficits resulting from a variety of causes.

In order to link treatment, or intervention, directly to the problem, the variables producing the problem must first be operationalized by directly observing the child during academic engaged times and their resulting work products. Direct observations can include observing and recording specific behaviors of the student, the nature of the academic assignment, the teacher's instructional cues/direction, and other instructionally relevant stimuli in the classroom. A thorough observation will most likely include direct assessment of specific skills related to the academic problem area. For example, a young student who is struggling with reading would likely be assessed in phonemic and phonological awareness and oral reading fluency using curriculum-based measurements (CBM). CBM consist of probes that pinpoint specific skills necessary to achieve competency in areas such as reading. If a student shows a skill deficit in any particular area when his or her probe results are compared with results of other students that are the same age, these skill deficits can be targeted in intervention. Specific, measurable goals are set and interventions linked directly to the problem are then implemented. Student progress is monitored over the course of the intervention so the intervention may be modified during treatment if monitoring shows the student is not responding to the intervention.

In order to facilitate integration of the problem-solving model into the classroom setting, a new model of service delivery known as Response to Intervention (RTI) is now being adopted by many school districts (Gresham, 2008; Lichtenstein, 2008). This service delivery model takes a very different approach to identifying and dealing with learning disorders. Conceptualized as a way to provide problem-solving and intervention services to all students, not just those identified as requiring special education services, RTI is a prevention-focused model that provides specific and immediate intervention when a problem such as a deficit in reading skills or mathematics is first identified. The intensity of intervention is then increased if the problem persists.

In order to accomplish these goals, RTI is implemented within the structure of a three-tiered system. All students within a school are administered a brief curriculum-based measurement (i.e., test of reading fluency) to determine their skill level in a certain academic area. Those students who demonstrate adequate levels of performance according to predetermined benchmarks for their age fall within Tier 1 (80%–90% of students). It is expected that these students will respond to universal, school-wide interventions and continue to exhibit progress and growth. Tier 2 is comprised of the 5%–15% of students who are identified as being "at risk" for developing significant academic problems according to comparison with benchmark levels. These students should receive specialized small group interventions. Tier 3 (1%–7% of children) consists of children identified as having chronic and/or intense academic problems after failing to respond to Tier 2 interventions and who require specialized individual interventions.

All students are assessed with CBM periodically throughout the year to monitor progress and identify students who are having problems as soon as possible. Common research-based CBM systems include Dynamic Indicators of Basic Early Literacy Skills (DIBELS) and AIMSweb. Tier 1 screenings are generally conducted three times per year, once each in fall, winter, and spring. The results from screenings are compared with benchmark data and used to determine students who are not adequately responding to the general curriculum (i.e., universal intervention). Those students who are receiving Tier 2 and Tier 3 interventions are also monitored using CBMs, but much more frequently. Data from these assessments are used to determine whether or not students are responding to their Tier 2 and 3 interventions and make adjustments in instructional content or intensity accordingly.

EVIDENCE FOR RESPONSE TO INTERVENTION

Despite the wealth of articles now being published examining the effectiveness of different school-based academic interventions, it can be very challenging and confusing to determine what types of interventions should be used at which tier, and for which learning disorder. This chapter will attempt to provide clarity regarding the interventions that have been shown to be effective in the three most commonly diagnosed categories of learning disability: reading (fluency and comprehension), written expression, and math (calculation and reasoning). In addition, the vast majority of school-aged children diagnosed with a learning disability are comprised by these five areas (Bender, 2008; Lerner & Kline, 2006). Although some tiers and categories have a stronger empirical base than others, there is a degree of overlap between the interventions that are supported by empirical data, regardless of the content area to which they have been applied. Because RTI is still a fairly young movement, there is a limited amount of research available pertaining specifically to each of the seven learning disability categories. Although many schools now follow a fairly prescribed method of organizing interventions within the tiered system (Tilly, 2008), the bulk of RTI research focuses on developing strong interventions for Tier 2 students who require small group intervention. Nonetheless, we will present evidence-based practices for each tier of each disability category where it exists. If none exists, we will point that out as well. In some instances, we may surmise that strategies that have been shown effective across disability categories *may* be effective for those categories where there is little evidence-based practice.

READING SKILLS

In 2000, the National Reading Panel (NRP; National Institute of Child Health and Human Development) published a report that listed five critical skills considered most vital in developing reading proficiency: phonemic awareness, phonics, fluency, vocabulary, and text comprehension. Phonemic awareness involves teaching children to recognize the smallest units of language (phonemes) in spoken syllables and words. Phonics is instruction in letter-sound correspondence and their use in reading and spelling. Fluency refers to reading aloud with speed and accuracy. Vocabulary instruction involves teaching students the meaning of specific words, and text comprehension is the ability to derive meaning from text by using intentional, problem-solving cognitive processes. Due to the robust findings by the NRP, these five skills have become the gold standard in reading instruction content and will be the focus in this chapter's reading skill discussion.

Tier 1

Assessment. The most useful CBM assessments are designed to screen for progress and monitor student skills in the five specific areas listed by NRP (2000). A number of different tasks are used in such CBM assessments. For example, fluency tests in letter sounds, word identification, and passage reading fluency, also called oral reading fluency, are all common measures. Age-appropriate benchmarks for CBMs, such as oral reading fluency, can be found in various sources, including the DIBELS website (https://dibels.uoregon.edu/benchmark.php). Among older students, tasks such as maze probes, or reading passages where every seventh word has been deleted and the student chooses from among three words which is supposed to fill the blank, may also be used (L. S. Fuchs & Fuchs, 2007).

Curriculum/Strategies. Reading skill development typically receives the greatest emphasis during early education. Therefore, to ensure that every student has ample opportunity to learn basic reading skills and that instruction is delivered in an effective manner, it is critical that preschool, kindergarten, and early elementary general education classrooms use evidence-based reading curriculum. Justice (2006) offers a number of guidelines in her review of evidence-based practices to prevent reading disabilities. First, there must be protected time during the school day set aside exclusively for literacy instruction. Research suggests that at least 90 minutes of reading instruction is essential for beginning readers (Vaughn, Wanzek, Woodruff, & Linan-Thompson, 2007; Harn, Kame'enui, & Simmons, 2007). This instruction should be direct and explicit, specifically addressing the five critical elements of beginning reading such as phonics, phonemic awareness, and vocabulary. There are a number of empirically supported reading programs designed for general curriculum including Houghton Mifflin, Open Court, Reading Mastery, and Success for All (Vaughn et al., 2007). More information on reading programs and other interventions can be found at www.what works.ed.gov.

Second, care should be taken to create an organized environment in the classroom, including a daily instruction schedule that includes both physically structuring the classroom to encourage reading by providing resources such as a classroom library and using evidence-based curriculum (Justice, 2006). Research also suggests that teacher knowledge of instructional content and pedagogical constructs, or instructional strategies, is important to help ensure that scientifically based curriculum are implemented with integrity and that students are engaged during instruction (Foorman, Carlson, & Santi, 2007). Therefore, it is essential that teachers become involved in professional development related to both content (in phonics instruction, for example), and also in how to implement instruction within the problem-solving model, including how to assess and monitor student progress (Foorman et al., 2007; Vaughn et al., 2007).

Within the problem-solving model, Tier 1 instruction is viewed as a preventative measure aimed at decreasing the number of students who might later be classified as at risk or learning disabled. Growing evidence supports that the use of certain scientifically based early reading programs in Tier 1 can indeed reduce the number of students referred for Tiers 2 and 3 interventions for reading problems. For example, in their review of studies examining the use of ClassWide Peer Tutoring (CWPT) and Peer Assisted Learning Strategies (PALS), both of which can be implemented class-wide and involve teaching students how to teach basic reading skills to their fellow classmates, Greenwood, Kamps, Terry, and Linebarger (2007) found significant empirical support for both strategies, particularly when used in conjunction with teacher-assistive software, with effect sizes ranging from a modest 0.35 for language achievement to a robust 1.41 for academic engagement.

Tier 2

In many ways, the goals of Tier 2 instruction are the same as Tier 1, which is not surprising since Tier 2 instruction is intended as a supplement to Tier 1 general curriculum. Research suggests that Tier 2 instruction should still target phonemic awareness, phonics, fluency, vocabulary, and reading comprehension, and instruction should also still be systematic and explicit (Justice, 2006). However, the conceptual distinction between Tier 1 and Tier 2 instruction lies mostly in the difference in instructional intensity between the two levels. Research supports that increasing intensity of instruction by reducing group size, changing instructional delivery to prioritize content and include scaffolding (an instructional strategy whereby the teacher provides initial support and structure that are gradually removed as the student becomes more proficient in independently performing the task), and, most importantly, increasing instructional time, can significantly increase progress across measures of early literacy skills (Harn, Linan-Thompson, & Roberts, 2008). Research often recommends at least 20–30 minutes of Tier 2 instruction (in addition to the 90 minutes of general curriculum) be added to student schedules in order to impact progress (Vaughn et al., 2007).

In order to achieve this increased intensity, schools may elect to use research-based programs for their Tier 2 interventions. Programs similar to those found at Tier 1, including tutoring programs such as PALS, may also be used at the Tier 2 level. In the summary of a secondary intervention study funded by the National Research Center on Learning Disabilities, researchers chose to implement a small-group, adult-led tutoring intervention with groups of up to four first graders. Tutoring sessions met for 45 minutes, 4 times per week, and focused on building sight word recognition, letter sound recognition, and decoding. In comparison with a control group, the tutoring groups made significant, semester-long gains on CBMs measuring word identification fluency. Results obtained from multiple methods of analysis, including repeated measures ANOVA, chi-square analyses, linear modeling, and calculating effect sizes, indicated that students from the tutored groups showed greater gains at mid- and posttreatment on measures of word identification, word attack, sight word efficiency, and phonemic decoding efficiency than the untutored groups (L. S. Fuchs, Compton, Fuchs, Bryant, & Davis, 2008).

Peer tutoring, or teaching students to teach their classmates basic reading skills and progress monitoring techniques, has also been demonstrated to improve elementary students' reading fluency. One study examined the effects that peer tutors working with other students using techniques such as passage previewing, repeated readings, and contingent reward had on measures of reading fluency. The National Reading Panel report (2000) supports that passage previewing, or listening to a passage prior to reading the text, and repeated readings of a single passage can significantly improve word recognition, reading fluency, and comprehension. Other studies have found that the use of contingent reinforcement leads to a substantial increase in the performance of reading skills (Noell et al., 1998). Researchers conducting the peer

tutoring found that students responded positively to the peer tutoring lessons on measures of reading fluency (Dufrene, Henington, & Townsend, 2006).

Tier 3

Tier 3 intervention is usually synonymous with special education. As in Tier 2, Tier 3 instruction involves increasing the intensity of instruction, but there is a more dramatic difference between Tier 2 and Tier 3 instructional intensity and often the structure. In one study, researchers describe the most essential features of effective Tier 3 instruction: (a) protected time and grouping, whereby students receive at least 90 minutes of intensive small-group or individual instruction; (b) performance monitoring through at least monthly CBM administration; and (c) prioritized content and purposeful instructional design and delivery, or focusing on critical skills in sequence of area where the largest skill deficit is noted. For example, in their study examining Tier 3 interventions for kindergarteners, researchers used programs such as *Horizons*, *Reading Mastery*, and *Read Naturally* to help design targeted curriculums for Tier 3 students, most of which were implemented by specialized staff including special education and Title 1 teachers. The use of purposeful instructional design and prioritized content led to significant gains in phonemic segmentation fluency and nonsense word fluency skills over the course of a semester (Harn, Kame'enui, & Simmons, 2007). In fact, after treatment, student's achievement in these two skills closely approximated those of average achieving students. For instance, with regards to phonemic segmentation fluency, mean posttreatment scores of students in the treatment group were 47.84, compared to a mean of 49.62 for average achieving students. With regards to nonsense word fluency, mean posttreatment scores of the target students was 39.38, while the mean score of average achieving students on this skill was 39.68.

READING COMPREHENSION

Reading comprehension is a complex skill that is both challenging to assess and even more challenging to impact. Reading comprehension refers to a child understanding what he or she is reading (Justice, 2006). In a current overview of reading comprehension literature, Johnston, Barnes, and Desrochers (2008) explain that, in cognitive models of reading comprehension, fluent readers are able to identify the surface meaning of words, phrases, and sentences that they read and then use this meaningful interpretation of text to inform mental constructs of the text. Cognitive skills including working memory, the ability to identify text structure, and the ability to self-monitor support the process of comprehension. The authors also identify other skills such as vocabulary, grammar-related skills including syntax and morphology, making inferences about text, and using of context as critical to being good at decoding and comprehending text.

Because the processes of reading comprehension are so intricate, the measurement of comprehension is equally complex. Primary predictors of comprehension change as children age (Johnston et al., 2008). One study determined that the primary predictors among early elementary students were word reading skills, identified by measurements of letter knowledge and phonological awareness, while by third and fourth grade, oral language skills such as vocabulary, narrative recall, and syntactic performance were most predictive of successful comprehension, suggesting that reading comprehension becomes correlated with listening comprehension over time (Storch & Whitehurst, 2002). Although the processes underlying comprehension may change as students progress in school, the importance of being successful in reading comprehension never diminishes; if anything, individual capability in comprehension only becomes more imperative as children age. Therefore, while early intervention is of course

most desirable, this chapter will also address research on reading comprehension in secondary students.

Tier 1

Assessment. Assessment of reading comprehension often becomes assessment of fluency, particularly among older students. In general, students who can read fluently, or read with accuracy and speed, tend to be better readers and demonstrate better comprehension (Wexler, Vaughn, Edmonds, & Reutebuch, 2008). This may be because students who do not have to expend their focus solely on decoding tasks constructed meaning better from what they read (Wexler et al., 2008). Timed reading of passages assessed for accuracy and speed, such as the DIBELS oral reading fluency probe, are frequently used to assess fluency. Other reading comprehension skills such as vocabulary and syntax may be assessed using cloze passages (a reading passage where every seventh word has been deleted, allowing the student to predict the correct word) or maze passages (a reading passage where words have been deleted and students are given three words to choose from to fill in the blank), while making inferences may be assessed using questionnaires pertaining to passage content.

Curriculum/strategies. Concurrent with the dominance of fluency assessment, one of the most popular strategies to address reading comprehension is repeated reading, a task designed to increase reading fluency. Repeated reading is used with students of all ages and may be implemented in several ways. For example, students may engage in repeated reading after the reading passage has been read aloud, or previewed, by a model such as their teacher, after the passage has been previewed by a secondary model such as an audio tape, or with no passage preview of any kind. A recent synthesis of research on repeated reading studies with junior high and high school students found that repeated reading with modeling by an adult had the most significant impact on reading rate, with effect sizes ranging from 0.23 to 1.02. Despite these rather consistent effects for repeated reading, the authors caution that there is emerging evidence that suggests that there is not a significant difference in impact on reading comprehension between repeated readings and similar amounts of nonrepetitive readings (Wexler et al., 2008).

Other popular strategies focus on instruction in metacognition, or an awareness of one's own cognitive processes (Swanson, Hoskyn, & Lee, 1999). Students may be taught to monitor their own understanding of a text as they read it by stopping to ask themselves questions about the material or thinking about how the material connects to their previous knowledge. Before students can be cognitively aware of their own comprehension, they must also be sensitive to text structure; thus some successful instructional programs also teach students to identify different elements of story structure including characters, plot, and theme (Williams, 2003).

Tier 2

Students who exhibit continuing deficits in reading comprehension or related skills such as vocabulary or grammar may receive Tier 2 intervention. As in Tier 1 strategies, Tier 2 reading comprehension interventions focus on specific skills instruction and strategy instruction, only at a more intense level than Tier 1 curriculum (Johnston et al., 2008). For example, research suggests a number of small group programs such as Collaborative Strategic Reading (Vaughn, Klinger, & Bryant, 2001) and PALS (D. Fuchs, Fuchs, Mathes, & Simmons, 1997) have been particularly helpful in helping both learning disabled and average-achieving students improve their reading comprehension skills. More specifically, researchers who examined Collaborative Strategic Reading, a peer-mediated intervention that teaches students strategies to improve vocabulary, story structure identification, and

monitoring skills, found that students who participated made significant gains in both understanding text and learning content (Vaughn et al., 2001). The PALS is also peer-mediated and allows students to take turns being the "coach" or "reader" while working on three strategies: partner reading with retell, paragraph summary, and prediction relay. Researchers in one study found that participating students made significant gains on three measures of the Comprehensive Reading Assessment Battery as compared to control group students (D. Fuchs et al., 1997).

Tier 3

Tier 3 instruction for remediation of deficits in reading comprehension involves more intensive support using the same general strategies from Tier 2. Educators should not jump to the automatic conclusion that because a student can read, that same student can automatically comprehend text. Comprehension strategies and skills must be explicitly taught, especially for those students who struggle to understand what they have read. There is a paucity of research specific to tertiary interventions in reading comprehension; however, there are studies specific to reading comprehension instruction for students with mild/moderate disabilities.

Sencibaugh (2007) reviewed 15 studies of comprehension interventions and calculated effect sizes for each to determine which strategies were most effective. The studies were divided into two categories: visually dependent and auditory/language dependent. The effect sizes were categorized according to Cohen's (1988) guidelines: 0.20 or less is a small effect, ~0.50 is a moderate effect, and 0.80 or greater is a large effect. Sencibaugh found that an intervention involving a semantic feature analysis (Bos, Anders, Filip, & Jaffe, 1989, as cited in Sencibaugh, 2007) has the greatest effect size of the visually dependent studies. A semantic feature analysis is a graphic organizer that permits readers to visually organize and compare characteristics of concepts from the text.

Comprehension can be taught through auditory/language dependent strategies as well. Sencibaugh (2007) determined that interventions involving paragraph restatement and text-structure (Bakken, Mastropieri, & Scruggs, 1997, as cited in Sencibaugh, 2007) garnered the highest effect sizes in this category. The paragraph restatement intervention involved summarizing what was read from the text. This type of activity helps students learn to identify the main ideas of what they read. The text-structure–based intervention requires students to determine the type of text presented (narrative vs. expository) and approach the text with a framework geared toward understanding that particular type of text. For example, narrative text involves specific story grammar and readers can work through specific questions relating to parts of the story such as setting, plot, events, and so forth. Expository texts are more informational and readers must approach the text with the idea of making connections between concepts. The paragraph restatement intervention saw an effect size of 3.65 and the text-structure–based intervention had an effect size of 2.39. Both interventions were done at the middle school level with students identified as having a learning disability that affected reading performance.

However a teacher chooses to approach the various methods of teaching comprehension skills, there are a few things that have been determined to increase the effectiveness of instruction. First, the instruction must be explicit and systematic. Teachers should provide instruction in a sequential manner with frequent opportunities for practice and feedback. Varied types of text and genres should be used to teach the strategies in order to facilitate opportunities for generalization. Frequent assessment of student progress is necessary to determine the efficacy of instruction. The results of such assessment should be used to guide instruction as necessary.

WRITTEN EXPRESSION

Students with learning disabilities often find the writing process to be particularly challenging. Disabilities in written expression tend to surface beginning in fourth grade (Stotz, Itoi, Konrad, & Alber-Morgan, 2008), when it becomes clear that certain students are having problems with transcription skills and other related abilities. Specifically, students may exhibit difficulty with the physical process of handwriting or with more cognitively advanced skills such as spelling and composition. As writing develops with age, problems in these areas may be further compounded if students struggle with executive function in the areas of working memory, planning and revising, or self-regulation (V. W. Berninger & Amtmann, 2003). Because writing is such a vital process that can impact student performance in almost every area of study, it is imperative that measures be taken to both prevent and intervene as early and intensively as possible.

Tier 1

Assessment. Written expression probes are most often chosen as a CBM to assess writing skills. Students are given a lined paper with a "story starter" sentence and then allowed a set amount of time (i.e., 1 minute) to write as much as they can. The writing samples are then evaluated for Total Words Written (TWW) and Correct Word Sequences (CWS). Student performance is thus monitored and compared with age-appropriate benchmarks. Benchmarks may be developed locally or found in supporting literature (V. Berninger, 2001). These assessments are particularly useful because they can easily be implemented at any skill level, including with secondary school students.

Curriculum/strategies. Perhaps the most critical step in preventing written expression problems is helping students become proficient in handwriting and spelling. Handwriting fluency accounts for 66% and spelling for 41% of the variability in writing output for elementary and middle school students (Graham & Harris, 2003); therefore, a major focus of writing curriculum, particularly in elementary school, should be on developing automaticity in letter formation and spelling (V. W. Berninger & Amtmann, 2003). The development of automaticity helps circumvent problems that arise from both motor difficulties and problems with memory processes. If a child does not have to focus on the mechanics of how to write letters and correctly form words with those letters, he or she can focus on the processes of composition and developing content.

Handwriting training is an effective method of improving handwriting composition among early elementary students (V. W. Berninger & Amtmann, 2003). One study identified two particularly successful strategies: Having students study visual cues (numbered arrow cues) for a sequential plan for letter formation and writing letters from memory after increasing delays in how long the letter form had to be retained in memory. Compared with conventional techniques, such as repeated copying of letters, the combination of studying visual cues for a sequential plan for letter formation and long-term memory practice led to greater improvement in measures of automaticity and compositional fluency among first-graders (V. W. Berninger et al., 1997). Similarly, the same research suggests that spelling training, specifically training alphabetic principle both in isolation and in word context, can significantly improve spelling accuracy and length of composition.

Tier 2

If a student fails to respond to the strategies employed in general curriculum and performs below benchmark on written expression probes, they will likely be identified to receive Tier 2 intervention. A major focus in written expression research is implementing interventions that focus on self-regulation to help primary and intermediate students improve their writing skills and output. Graham and Harris (2003) conducted a meta-analysis of 26 studies that employed Self-Regulated Strategy Development (SRSD) interventions to improve writing skills. The SRSD instruction is characterized by teaching self-regulation procedures tailored to an individual child's needs in a series of six steps: (1) developing background knowledge needed to understand self-regulation processes, (2) discussing current performance and target strategies, (3) teacher modeling of target strategies, (4) memorization of strategies, (5) practicing, and (6) independent student use of target strategies in a new setting. Meta-analysis indicated that, overall, SRSD has the potential to produce a strong, positive effect on the quality, structure, and length of students writing with effect sizes ranging from 0.56 to 2.15.

Self-regulation interventions such as teaching error checking and self-correction have also been found effective in improving mechanical skills such as spelling with secondary students (Viel-Ruma, Houchins, & Fredrick, 2007). Direct instruction programs targeting the stages of the writing process, such as *Reasoning and Writing* and *Expressive Writing*, have also yielded promising results (Walker, Shippen, Alberto, Houchins, & Cihak, 2005). Direct instruction (DI) is a research-based instructional method that involves administering highly focused, fast-paced, and sequenced lessons to small groups of students. Students are given opportunities for immediate feedback and responses to instruction. One study that measured the effects of *Expressive Writing*, a DI program that teaches writing process skills such as sentence and paragraph construction, drafting, revising, and editing, found that three LD high school students who participated significantly improved their writing skills as measured by examining the number of correct word sequences during baseline and treatment and then analyzing the percentage of overlapping data points (POD). The POD for the three students was 7%, 5%, and 38%. Maintenance probes taken at 2-, 4-, and 6-week intervals indicated that all students maintained a stable level from treatment levels of correct word sequences at each of the intervals (Walker et al., 2005).

Tier 3

The SRSD techniques are often used at the Tier 3 intervention level as well, except that the intervention is then delivered in a one-to-one setting instead of in a small group (Graham & Harris, 2003). There is a paucity of extant research on tertiary writing interventions; however, there have been studies that explore effective writing interventions for students with mild/moderate disabilities. According to Graham and Perin's (2007) review of writing interventions, strategy instruction and summarization instruction had the largest effects on writing performance. Both interventions had an effect size of 0.82, indicating that they significantly impact performance. The strategy instruction explicitly taught students strategies for each step of the writing process (planning, revising, and editing) and included SRSD techniques as well as other strategies. Specific writing strategies permit students to easily recall steps in the writing process, leading to higher quality of writing. Summarization instruction explicitly taught students how to succinctly summarize information in writing, solidifying the students' ability to identify main ideas in both reading and writing. When implementing any type of writing intervention at the tertiary level, teachers must remember to teach the intervention explicitly in a sequential, systematic manner with frequent opportunities for practice, feedback, and progress monitoring.

Accommodations. Currently, computer technology offers a number of programs that may act as a support for students with transcription problems (V. W. Berninger & Amtmann, 2003). For example, keyboarding instead of writing may simplify the motor processes required for writing, making it easier for some students to express their thoughts on the page. Similarly, dictation using voice recognition software can wholly eliminate the motor component of writing for students with severe motor impairment. Students without severe impairment typically produce longer composition using dictation. Word prediction software, which generates a list of words based on what has already been written that the student then selects from, also reduces the number of keystrokes and improves spelling accuracy.

MATHEMATICAL SKILLS

Mathematics skills are fundamental to success in life. Without basic mathematic skills, one will struggle with finances, cooking, measuring, time management, transportation, or other major life skills. It is important that students are taught these skills to a proficient level prior to leaving a school setting in order to facilitate success in life. Unfortunately, helping students reach an appropriate level of proficiency has been a problem in the United States. According to Phillips (2007; as cited in *The Final Report of the National Mathematics Advisory Panel*, 2008), 78% of adults cannot detail how to compute interest paid on a loan, 71% of adults cannot calculate the number of miles per gallon of gas on a car trip, and 58% of adults cannot calculate a 10% tip due on a restaurant bill. The U.S. Department of Education (2004, as cited in *The Final Report of the National Mathematics Advisory Panel*, 2008) indicates that 27% of eighth graders could not correctly shade one third of a rectangle and 45% of eighth graders could not solve a problem requiring division of fractions on the National Assessment of Educational Progress. These statistics indicate there is a serious problem with the mathematics instruction provided in our schools.

Some students do not reach mathematics proficiency because they are affected by mathematical learning disabilities. According to L. S. Fuchs et al. (2005a), 5%–10% of school-aged children exhibit mathematics disabilities of varying degrees of severity. The Individuals with Disabilities Education Improvement Act (IDEIA, 2004) has even recognized mathematics disabilities (specifically in calculations and problem solving) as a type of learning disability. Bryant, Bryant, Gersten, Scammacca, and Chavez (2008) suggested that since early identification and intervention has assisted in the prevention of identified reading disabilities, the research efforts in that area should be replicated in mathematics in the hope that mathematics disabilities could also be prevented by early identification and intervention. Jordan, Kaplan, Locuniak, and Ramineni (2007) proposed early screening in kindergarten and first grade in order to facilitate intervention as early as possible and pointed out that, unlike early literacy screening instruments, early mathematics screening instruments are not as well-researched.

Multitiered instruction has been recommended as a method for identifying students with a learning disability (IDEIA, 2004). The premise of such instruction is that the first tier of instruction provides class-wide evidence-based core instruction; students who continue to struggle are provided with supplemental small-group instruction and ongoing progress monitoring in the second tier; and students who have not benefited sufficiently from the first two tiers are provided with intensive individualized interventions that may include additional instructional time beyond what is provided in Tier 2 instruction, adapted instructional content, different content materials, and/or special education services (Bryant, Bryant, Gersten, et al., 2008; Stecker, 2007; L. S. Fuchs et al., 2007). By ensuring that the entire class receives evidence-based practice in the first tier, educators can eliminate poor instruction as a potential cause for not achieving on target.

Mathematics skills can be divided into calculation skills and reasoning skills, both of which require diverse skill sets. Therefore, it is important that assessments and interventions

that are implemented as part of a multitiered instruction model reflect the appropriate skill set. If an inappropriate assessment or intervention is applied, the student will not progress and valuable instructional time will be lost.

MATHEMATICAL CALCULATION

Mathematical calculation can be defined as the foundational skills needed for applied mathematics (Codding, Eckert, Fanning, Shiyko, & Solomon, 2007). These basic skills must be learned fluently with the ability to be generalized in order to apply them to more complex mathematic skills that include money, time, measurement, algebra, and geometry. Due to the National Council of Teachers of Mathematics standards, much of today's mathematics instruction uses an inquiry-based pedagogy to increase student knowledge of conceptual mathematics (Bryant & Bryant, 2008). Current mathematics instruction typically limits the scope of calculation to focus on accuracy. While accuracy is important, it is also crucial for students to be able to recognize and solve computation problems across varied presentation formats. Therefore, assessments and interventions relating to mathematical calculation should consider both accuracy and format.

Tier 1

Interventions. Part of the Tier 1 instruction can include a universal screening instrument to determine which students are struggling with the content (Ardoin, Witt, Connell, & Koenig, 2005). This permits educators to administer necessary remedial instruction or Tier 2 interventions in a more timely fashion. Another Tier 1 intervention can include progress-monitoring measures that are administered periodically to the entire class. The purpose is the same as the universal screening instrument: to determine which students are struggling with content after receiving evidence-based instruction. L. S. Fuchs et al. (2007) identified CBM Computation probes as a valid indicator of the development of mathematical competence when administered over the first-grade year.

B. R. Bryant, Bryant, Kethley, et al. (2008) describe Tier 1, core instruction as meeting the needs of all students. Since Woodward (2006) contends that inquiry-based instructional practices may not be sufficient for students who struggle with mathematics due to a learning disability, educators may find it necessary to incorporate explicit, systematic instruction into the curriculum when focusing on math calculation. Swanson, Hoskyn, and Lee (1999) found high and significant effect sizes for studies implementing explicit instructional procedures compared to other instructional practices. Characteristics of explicit, systematic instruction include sequentially presented skill sets that build on previously learned skills, guided teaching questioning, teacher modeling/demonstration of new skills, guided practice with immediate feedback, and progress monitoring.

Another instructional intervention that benefits all students is the concrete-representational-abstract sequence (B. R. Bryant, Bryant, Kethley, et al., 2008). Educators begin teaching mathematical calculation facts using manipulatives to make the concept more concrete for students. The manipulatives are used until students can fluently demonstrate calculation skills, whereupon the educators can then move the students into the representational phase. Pictures, tally marks, and other non-manipulative representations are used to reinforce the skills learned during the concrete phase. Students remain in the representational phase until they fluently demonstrate the target skills. Finally, students move into the abstract phase. Here, the educator introduces numerical sentences using the digits, the most abstract form of mathematics calculation.

Tier 2

Interventions. When students are found to be unsuccessful in the core mathematics curriculum when evidence-based instructional practices are appropriately administered, educators need to implement Tier 2 interventions to supplement the Tier 1 instruction. Tier 2 interventions are considered to be slightly more individualized than Tier 1 interventions and are administered to small groups of students identified as struggling with the content (L. S. Fuchs et al., 2007). Students receiving Tier 2 interventions should receive more frequent and consistent progress monitoring measures to gauge the effectiveness of the interventions on their performance.

Vaughn, Moody, and Schumm (1998) recommended small-group instruction as an effective method to provide practice opportunities with immediate teacher feedback for reading. L. S. Fuchs et al. (2005b) used a combination of specific Tier 1 interventions in a small-group setting to determine the effects of the small-group instruction as a Tier 2 intervention for mathematics. They specifically focused on the concrete-representational-abstract sequence, emphasized problem solving and discussion of the solutions, and used technology to provide additional individualized practice for computation fluency. Children at risk for mathematical failure were identified from 41 first-grade classrooms and randomly assigned to either a control group or an intervention group. Small-group instruction was provided three times per week over the course of several months. Post-intervention measures to evaluate the impact on the dependent variable of mathematical achievement in computation indicated that the group receiving tutoring showed more growth than the students in the control group. Although the fluency measures were less strong than other computation measures, the technology has been redesigned to increase the focus in that area. The measures of computation and concepts had a moderate and significant effect size of 0.414, indicating that the tutoring had an impact on the performance of first-grade students who were not successful in the core mathematics curriculum.

D. P. Bryant, Bryant, Gersten, et al. (2008) also explored the use of small-group instruction as a Tier 2 intervention. The booster lessons in the small-group setting consisted of number, operation, and reasoning skills from the state achievement assessment. The lessons were provided three to four times per week over 18 weeks and lasted approximately 15 minutes per session. Teachers were provided with scripted lessons that incorporated modeling the skills, think-aloud procedures, guiding practice, pacing tips, and error correction suggestions. Performance measures and analysis of regression discontinuity (RD) did not indicate a significant effect for the first-graders who participated ($b = 0.04$), but were significant for the participating second-graders ($b = 0.19$, $p = 0.018$).

B. R. Bryant and Bryant (2008) consider the small-group instructional setting of Tier 2 interventions to be an appropriate placement to institute more intensive explicit, systematic instructions. As mentioned previously, explicit, systematic instruction involves modeling/demonstration, sequentially presented skill sets that build on previous knowledge, and guided practice opportunities with immediate feedback. B. R. Bryant and Bryant contend the small-group setting provides additional practice and feedback opportunities beyond what is offered during core instruction. In addition to explicit instruction, they also call for the use of strategic instruction in the small-group setting. Teaching small groups of struggling students to use specific strategies that can be immediately implemented into the core curriculum can positively impact those students to the point where they may become successful with the target skills.

Ardoin et al. (2005) implemented a Tier 2 intervention in a large-group setting because a class-wide screening instrument indicated that the majority of students were struggling with the target skill. The implemented intervention was a cover-copy-compare (CCC) strategy. Students were asked to cover the left column of a worksheet, complete the problems in the right column, and compare their completed problems to those on the left side. Any missed problems were reworked until the problems were correctly answered. No further instruction was provided. Performance was measured through the use of mathematics curriculum-based measurement probes consisting of 30 two-digit by two-digit subtraction problems with regrouping. These measures indicated that this intervention was successful for the majority of students who received it; those that were not successful received further interventions at the Tier 3 level.

Tier 3

Interventions. Tier 3 interventions differ among models of Response to Intervention. Some models consider Tier 3 interventions to be the equivalent of those seen in special education classes (D. P. Bryant, Bryant, Gersten, et al., 2008; L. S. Fuchs et al., 2007); others consider Tier 3 to be more intensive than Tier 2, but not quite on the level of special education (Ardoin et al., 2005). Stecker (2007) considers Tier 3 interventions to be part of special education and argues that individualized instruction has been the hallmark of special education. She contends that expecting general education teachers to provide the necessary intensive interventions that comprise Tier 3 is unreasonable and may overtax the general education resources. Regardless of the RTI model, Tier 3 interventions are generally reserved for those students who continue to struggle after receiving evidence-based core curriculum instruction with supplemental strategic, small-group instruction. As with students receiving Tier 2 interventions, students receiving Tier 3 interventions should receive regular progress monitoring measures that address the target skills. The data from these and previously administered measures should be used as part of the assessment process if and when the special education eligibility process is set into motion (Stecker, 2007).

D. P. Bryant, Bryant, Gersten, et al. (2008) and Stecker (2007) identified potential Tier 3 interventions as additional instructional time, (beyond what is provided during Tier 2 interventions), small instructional groups with no more than three students, adapting instructional content, or utilizing instructional material that differs from what is currently used in the class. Additional instructional time and smaller instructional groups allow teachers to further individualize the instruction for the students. Typically, Tier 3 interventions are provided by a special education teacher so the general education teacher will not have the pressure of attempting to find the time to plan and implement such individualized instruction on top of the regular classroom duties. Instructional content may be adapted to meet the students' needs in a number of ways. One adaptation might be to the presentation format of the content. The teacher may enlarge the print or darken the print to make it easier for the students to see. The teacher may decide to highlight or box certain parts of the problems to focus student attention. Another adaptation might be to the amount of content covered during the instructional period. The student may be required to complete a reduced number of problems in the lesson; if the student is able to demonstrate mastery within that reduced number of problems, the teacher moves on to the next skill. If the student is not able to demonstrate mastery, the teacher may provide remedial instruction and additional practice. Finally, the teacher may elect to use instructional material that is very different from what is currently used in the class. This may include material on a different ability level for the student, material that does not include distracting pictures or text, or material that is presented in a computer program.

Ardoin et al. (2005) administered a Tier 3 intervention that combined peer tutoring with the CCC Tier 2 intervention and instruction to the students that did not show improved performance after only the CCC intervention. The peer tutoring part of the intervention included practice of flashcards demonstrating the target skill. Students also completed the

CCC intervention and several performance probes of the target skill in each session. After completing the probes, the researcher provided corrective feedback and instruction on the missed problems in a one-on-one setting. Of the five students who received the Tier 3 intervention, one improved performance greatly, three improved moderately, and one did not improve. Ardoin and colleagues (2005) suggested that the student who did not improve would then be referred for special education services because she had "failed to improve" after three increasingly intensive levels of intervention to which her peers had adequately responded.

Mathematical calculation is an important foundation that must be solidified in order for the development of mathematical reasoning. Educators must provide solid, evidence-based core curriculum instruction that addresses the needs of all students to eliminate lack of appropriate instruction as a reason for below-average performance. For students failing to respond to such instruction, educators should implement Tier 2 interventions, which include small group supplemental instruction, strategy instruction, and additional progress monitoring measures. Finally, students that fail to respond to both Tier 1 and Tier 2 interventions should receive more intensive, individualized instruction. Such interventions may range from longer instructional periods to the use of adapted or different instructional materials.

MATHEMATICAL REASONING

Mathematical reasoning is the conceptual knowledge necessary for applying the appropriate set of skills to a problem or set of problems and demonstrates the interconnectedness of mathematical skills. Number sense, early numeracy skills, and problem-solving skills are all included under the umbrella of mathematical reasoning. L. S. Fuchs et al. (2007) found that the use of CBM Mathematical Concepts/Application probes provided valid identification of first-grade students at risk for poor overall mathematical development. Thus, mathematical reasoning should be a target of early intervention in order to facilitate performance and decrease the risk for poor mathematical development.

Tier 1

Interventions. Evidence-based core instruction makes up Tier 1. This instruction is provided for all students, including those receiving Tiers 2 and 3 interventions, and should address all of the needs exhibited by the students. B. R. Bryant and Bryant (2008) contended that the core instruction should include explicit and strategic instruction. Explicit instruction includes the use of modeling, practice, feedback, and progress monitoring on a specific skill, while strategic instruction focuses on the conceptual part of the mathematical knowledge base. B. R. Bryant and Bryant (2008) specify the combination of procedural rules, metacognitive cues, fact retention and retrieval techniques, and mnemonics as part of strategic instruction.

When addressing procedural rules in instruction, it is essential to provide students with both examples and nonexamples of the target concept. This permits the students to learn to generalize the concept across presentation formats as well as to learn when to apply and when not to apply the specific procedures; however, when presenting the examples and nonexamples, it is important to ensure the use of relevant, meaningful examples that do not address untaught concepts. Students will learn better if the examples employ concepts that have already been mastered.

Metacognitive instruction is also crucial to mathematical reasoning. Metacognition is the idea of self-understanding. For example, when reading an advanced text, a reader periodically will check his or her understanding. This may be done by asking oneself questions about the text, attempting to summarize what was read, or applying the knowledge gained from the text to an appropriate situation. Within

mathematical reasoning, metacognition is just as important. Students need to be explicitly taught to determine the level of their understanding of a concept through the use of metacognitive cues. These cues may include identifying key words or symbols in a problem to trigger specific procedural knowledge, using visual representation to map the necessary steps to the problem solution, or other activities that assist students in assessing their understanding of the conceptual task at hand.

Fact retention/retrieval and mnemonics are related. Fact retention/retrieval is a critical part of mathematical reasoning. Codding et al. (2007) contended that students lacking automaticity in fact retrieval are less able to comprehend underlying mathematical concepts and curricula that emphasizes problem solving. Mnemonics can be a solution to the issue of fact retention/retrieval. Keyword mnemonics involve the use of a similar sounding word to create a unique picture that triggers the idea to be retrieved. Wood and Frank (2000) developed a set of keyword mnemonics for multiplication fact families. An example from their set is for the multiplication fact of 2×2: an image of a skateboard with the focus on the two sets of wheels. Another type of mnemonics that can be used with mathematics is the pegword strategy. Pegwords involve the use of a consistent set of rhyming words that link to a visual image to help students retrieve a fact. Prior to the use of pegwords in retrieving facts, it is important that teachers ensure students have a solid understanding of the actual pegwords in order to associate them with specific numbers. Brigham and Brigham (2001) identified the list of pegwords and contended that the visual representations reduce the number of failures to recall links in chains of information. An example of this kind of mnemonic involves the multiplication fact of 6×6: the pegword for 6 is "sticks" and the pegword for 30 is "dirty," so the student would say "sticks times sticks equals dirty sticks" while visualizing the image. Another type of mnemonic is letter mnemonics, which involves acronyms and sentence mnemonics. An example of a problem-solving strategy acronym is STAR: Search the word problem, Turn the words into a picture equation, Answer the problem, and Review the solution. An example of a sentence mnemonic would be "Please Excuse My Dear Aunt Sally" to represent the order of operations (parentheses, exponents, multiplication, division, addition, and subtraction).

Chard et al. (2008) developed a curriculum specifically for kindergarten classes that focused on number sense. Number sense is an early component of mathematics reasoning in that it addresses the ability to use and manipulate numbers, the sense of the meaning of numbers, and the ability to make mental quantitative comparisons (Chard et al., 2008). The purpose of such a curriculum was to explicitly teach the skills necessary to develop number sense in young children, specifically those children who lack significant mathematical experiences in preschool or home settings. It is important to explicitly teach number sense skills because without intervention the gap between the students who have developed number sense and the students who have not developed number sense will continue to widen as mathematics instruction becomes more complex. The three main components of Chard and colleagues' curricula include: the use of mathematical models, mathematics vocabulary and discourse, and procedural fluency and automaticity. The mathematical models include tools such as a number line that permits the addition of numerals as they are learned, mathematical charts, and representations of numbers using traditional digits and symbols. Mathematical vocabulary is explicitly taught through scripted lessons and the inclusion of numerous practice opportunities. Procedural fluency and automaticity are taught through lessons that allow for systematic practice opportunities, frequent review of skills, progress monitoring, and feedback. Performance measures administered prior to and following the implementation of the curricula indicated a small but

significant effect size of 0.26, indicating that the curriculum is heading in the right direction. Due to several limitations of this study, further exploration of the effects of this curriculum on student performance is needed.

Miller and Hudson (2007) contended that the use of the concrete-representational-abstract (CRA) sequence is appropriate for development of conceptual knowledge. Use of the CRA sequence presents concepts in varied formats, allowing students opportunities to generalize their new conceptual knowledge to differing stimuli. Miller and Hudson (2007) also recommended that the instructional presentation of new skills be appropriate for the skills being taught. Three specific instructional formats are discussed, including compare/contrast, example/nonexample, and step-by-step structure. The compare/contrast instructional format is appropriate when teaching students to identify similarities and differences, such as equivalent fractions. Examples/nonexamples are used when illustrations are necessary to teach a concept such as geometric shapes. Finally, Miller and Hudson (2007) recommend using a step-by-step structure when concepts require the use of multiple, sequential steps, such as regrouping in the basic operations.

The *Reports of the Task Groups and Subcommittees of the National Mathematics Advisory Panel* (2008) identified several early numeracy programs appropriate for Tier 1, evidence-based whole class instruction. *Number Worlds* (Griffin, 2004) is a program that focuses on teaching children to form a mental "number line" to evaluate and perform arithmetic operations on sets of objects. The program also involves the use of mathematical language to familiarize children to the necessary vocabulary. The performance measure data from Griffin's research indicated that the program produced a large effect size of 1.79 for six of the measures at the posttest and 1.40 for 13 measures on a follow-up conducted at a later time. Student performance was measured using a researcher-designed instrument called the Number Knowledge Test. The test was subjected to evaluation for technical adequacy across age levels. It is administered several times as students work through the *Number Worlds* program (Griffin, 2007). The Berkley Math Readiness Project (Klein & Starkey, 2004, as cited in *Reports*, 2008) is a program that focuses on mathematics reasoning and number sense for preschoolers. Analysis of the data from this project indicated an effect size of 0.96 on nine measures of numerical understanding.

Tier 2

Interventions. D. P. Bryant, Bryant, Gersten, et al. (2008) recommend Tier 2 level interventions for students who do not demonstrate success when evidence-based core instruction is provided to the large group. Educators should use either a universal screening instrument or periodic progress monitoring measures to determine which students are struggling with the content.

Jordan, Kaplan, Oláh, and Locuniak (2006) measured the development of number sense in kindergartners over the period of a school year. The students' performance across the year was divided into groups; one particular group of students had consistently low and flat growth curves. Jordan and colleagues (2006) suggested that once that group entered the first grade interventions would be necessary to prevent further widening of the achievement gap between the low-performing and high-performing groups. One particular area of difficulty for the low-performing group related to place-value tasks. Jordan and colleagues recommended sustained, focused instructional time on place-value concepts for students identified as struggling with mathematics.

Ma (1999) asserted that mathematical interventions provided to struggling students should serve a corrective function by reteaching fundamental mathematical concepts. Ma was one of the creators of the Knowing Mathematics intervention designed for intermediate elementary

level students struggling with mathematics concepts necessary for more advanced mathematical topics. Students receiving the Knowing Mathematics intervention are generally at least 2 years below typical grade-level performance. The program begins with a warm-up exercise that engages the students in learning the new skill and/or reviewing previously learned material. The instructor then guides the students through a conversational overview of the target concepts for the current lesson. Opportunities for guided practice, immediate feedback, and independent practice are provided during the lesson. The final component includes an opportunity for student reflection and discussion.

Ketterlin-Geller, Chard, and Fien (2008) developed the Extended Core intervention in conjunction with classroom teachers. The intervention sessions for this program begins with an overview of content to be covered in the lesson, a review of content learned in the previous lessons, and a conversation about how the previous content would apply to the current lesson. The teacher demonstrates a strategy with explicit vocabulary instruction, concrete examples, step-by-step explanation of the concept, discussions, and practice opportunities that incorporate multiple representation formats. A guided practice activity with immediate corrective feedback is provided. Finally, students are encouraged to complete regularly assigned homework or reteaching pages as an independent practice opportunity. Ketterlin-Geller and colleagues' (2008) study that evaluated the Knowing Mathematics and Extended Core interventions led to evidence that supports both programs. First, student performance on both a district mathematics screener and a state mathematics achievement test were analyzed using a MANOVA procedure. The MANOVA did not find a statistically significant difference between groups ($p = 0.42$) on the two tests. Effect sizes between Knowing Math and Extended Core conditions were minimal ($ES = 0.03$), but stronger when each of those groups was compared to the control group ($ES = 0.65$ for Knowing Math; $ES = 0.62$ for Extended Core). When an ANOVA was conducted on student performance on the statewide achievement test, no significant differences were found ($p = 0.455$); however, the Extended Core had a greater effect size than the Knowing Math ($ES = 0.51$) and the control group ($ES = 0.35$). Finally, when the Knowing Math and Extended Core groups were compared on a publisher-created posttest, an ANOVA indicated that the Knowing Math score was significant, $F(1,49) = 6.18, p < 0.05$. On this measure, the Knowing Math group had an effect size of 1.16 over the Extended Core group. While the performances on the state assessment were not significant, the results are still important. The participants were selected because they performed below the fortieth percentile on the district screening instrument and by the end of the study, the average score of the students in the Extended Core group was above the state cut-score for meeting the mathematics benchmark.

Gersten, Jordan, and Flojo (2005) recommend explicit, systematic, and strategic instruction in mathematics vocabulary for students identified as struggling with the core curriculum. Mathematics vocabulary is important for students because it is the primary method of communicating an understanding of mathematical concepts as well as applying those concepts to mathematical tasks. The use of the different types of mnemonics (keyword, pegword, and letter/sentence) could prove to be effective in helping struggling students with the retention and retrieval of mathematics vocabulary.

Tier 3

Interventions. The Tier 3 interventions are targeted to students who have not responded to evidence-based whole class instruction (Tier 1) or to the strategic, small-group supplemental instruction (Tier 2). The interventions at this level are much more intensive and more likely to be implemented by a special education teacher. The interventions may include extended instructional time, beyond that which was provided in Tier 2, small instructional groups, adapted content, and different instructional materials (D. P. Bryant, Bryant, Gersten, et al., 2008).

The Final Report of the National Mathematics Advisory Panel (2008) identified explicit instruction to have consistently positive effects on problem-solving performance of students performing in the lowest third of a typical class. In Tier 3 level interventions, explicit instruction should feature prominently in each session. The instructional sessions should be very structured with specific opportunities for review of previously learned material, explicit instruction of necessary vocabulary, step-by-step explanation of target concepts with concrete links between previously learned and new content, teacher modeling/demonstration of target concepts, guided practice with immediate corrective feedback, independent practice, and frequent, regular formative assessment. Target concepts should be taught to mastery at this level. Examples used to illustrate the target concepts must be relevant, meaningful, and based on known skills.

D. P. Bryant, Bryant, Gersten, et al. (2008) contend that Tier 3 interventions may involve adapted content and/or varied instructional materials. Similar to Tier 3 mathematical computation interventions, teachers may decide to adapt the content for presentation format or number of problems required to demonstrate mastery to meet the needs of struggling students. In varying instructional materials, teachers may supplement a required textbook with additional practice pages, computer programs that encourage students to practice target skills or concepts, or use instructional materials on a level that is more appropriate to student knowledge. Teachers may also decide to include concrete manipulatives to assist struggling students in comprehending target concepts.

Mathematical reasoning is necessary for students to know when to apply specific computation skills and also make connections between related mathematical skills. Tier 1 instruction should be evidence-based instruction in the core curriculum that addresses the needs of all students, including those receiving supplemental Tier 2 and individualized Tier 3 instruction. It should also include a universal screening instrument or regular progress monitoring instruments. For students failing to respond to such instruction, educators should implement Tier 2 interventions, which include small group supplemental instruction, strategy instruction, and additional progress monitoring measures. Finally, Tier 3 interventions are applied to students who fail to respond to Tier 1 instruction and Tier 2 small-group supplemental instruction. These interventions are individualized specifically to the struggling students and may include working at a more appropriate level of instruction or adapting the current content to meet the needs of the students.

EVIDENCE-BASED TREATMENT OF LEARNING DISABILITIES

Historically, students have been identified as having specific learning disabilities through a severe discrepancy between ability to learn and achievement. Problems with this method of identification, including the "wait-fail" effect, lack of specified interventions, and inconsistent definitions of what constitutes a "severe" discrepancy have led to the development of an alternative method—a problem-solving model. The problem-solving model of identification incorporates RTI into the classroom for service delivery. The RTI is a prevention-focused model that implements tiered instruction, increasing in individualization and intensity as needed. Another characteristic of RTI is frequent progress monitoring at all levels of intervention, primarily through the use of CBM probes.

A number of empirically documented educational intervention strategies exist for the most common learning disabilities. The most critical skills for developing reading proficiency include phonemic awareness, fluency, phonics, vocabulary, and text comprehension. To achieve these skills, schools must engage in preventive efforts (e.g., setting aside 90 minutes each day for reading, direct and explicit instruction in beginning skills of phonics, phonemic awareness, and vocabulary) and use effective instructional practices (e.g., Class Wide Peer Tutoring, PALS). For students for whom the preventive efforts are insufficient, increasing instructional time, decreasing group size, prioritizing content, scaffolding, peer tutoring, and contingent positive reinforcement are strategies that have been shown to be effective.

Although there is a strong correlation between reading proficiency and reading comprehension, some students will find it difficult to comprehend what they are reading despite their level of fluency (or perhaps in conjunction with their diminished level of fluency). For students with reading comprehension difficulties, effective strategies include repeated reading and metacognitive strategies. Effective peer-mediated strategies include Collaborative Strategic Reading and PALS. Students who do not respond to these basic strategies may require more intensive intervention involving paragraph restatement and text structure, both of which generated high effect sizes.

The ability to express oneself in writing is becoming an increasingly important skill as rapidly developing technology requires proficiency in written expression. Two basic skills for fluency in written expression are handwriting (accounting for 66% of the variability in written output for elementary and middle school students) and spelling (accounting for 41% of the variability in written output). The most effective strategies for promoting automaticity of these basic skills include studying visual cues for letter formation and writing letters from memory (for handwriting) and alphabetic training and error-checking and self-correction (for spelling). When more intensive intervention is required, Direct Instruction and Self-Regulated Strategy Development have both been shown to be effective for improving length and quality of student's writing.

Roughly 5%–10% of school-aged children meet criteria for a mathematical disability. Difficulties in math are in either basic calculation or reasoning. Students who have difficulty with learning basic calculation skills are best taught with explicit instructional strategies that include sequentially presented skill sets that build on previously learned skills, guided questioning, teacher modeling/demonstration of new skills, guided practice with feedback, and progress monitoring. Explicit instructional strategies have been shown to produce larger effect sizes than other instructional strategies. An additional strategy with empirical support is use of the concrete-representational-abstract instructional sequence. Both of these strategies can be intensified by using them in small group settings with more frequent progress monitoring. Supplemental instructional strategies include peer tutoring and cover-copy-compare, both of which have been shown to promote moderate gains in math calculation skills.

Finally, mathematical reasoning requires a conceptual understanding of when and how to apply a particular mathematical operation. Some of the basic skills required for proficiency in this area include number sense, numeracy skills, and problem-solving skills. The core instruction in mathematical reasoning should include explicit strategies like those just mentioned for math calculation as well as strategic instruction (i.e., procedural rules, metacognitive cues, fact retention, and retrieval techniques) that focus on the conceptual aspect of mathematics. Two interventions/curricula that have shown to be effective and that utilize these strategies are the Knowing Mathematics and Extended Core programs.

It is unlikely that *all* students with learning difficulties in reading, writing, and math will respond to the evidence-based strategies that have been described in this chapter; however, it is likely that *most* students will at least respond positively to some degree using these interventions. For those students that do not, it is incumbent upon teachers, school psychologists, and parents to investigate the most effective instructional strategy or combination of strategies for that particular child. Doing so will add to the evidence base for those children for whom the extant strategies are insufficient for remediating their academic deficits.

REFERENCES

Ardoin, S. P., Witt, J. C., Connell, J. E., & Koenig, J. L. (2005). Application of a three-tiered response to intervention model for instructional planning, decision making, and the identification of children in need of services. *Journal of Psychoeducational Assessment, 23*, 362–380.

Bender, W. (2008). *Learning disabilities: Characteristics, identification, and teaching strategies* (6th ed.). Needham Heights, MA: Allyn & Bacon.

Berninger, V. (2001). *Process Assessment of the Learner (PAL) test battery for Reading and Writing (PAL-RW)*. San Antonio, TX: Psychological Corporation.

Berninger, V. W., & Amtmann, D. (2003). Preventing written expression disabilities through early and continuing assessment and intervention for handwriting and/or spelling problems: Research into practice. In H. L. Swanson, K. R. Harries, & S. Graham (Eds.), *Handbook of learning disabilities* (pp. 345–363). New York, NY: Guilford Press.

Berninger, V. W., Vaughn, K. B., Abbott, R. D., Abbott, S. P., Rogan, L. W., Brooks, A., . . . Graham, S. (1997). Treatment of handwriting problems in beginning writers: Transfer from handwriting to composition. *Journal of Educational Psychology, 89*, 652–666.

Brigham, F. J., & Brigham, M. (2001). *Current practice alerts: A focus on mnemonic instruction*. Retrieved from www.teachingld.org/pdf/Alert5.pdf

Bryant, B. R., & Bryant, D. P. (2008). Introduction to the special series: Mathematics and learning disabilities. *Learning Disability Quarterly, 31*, 3–8.

Bryant, B. R., Bryant, D. P., Kethley, C., Kim, S. A., Pool, C., & Seo, Y. (2008). Preventing mathematics difficulties in the primary grades: The critical features of instruction in textbooks as part of the equation. *Learning Disability Quarterly, 31*, 21–35.

Bryant, D. P., Bryant, B. R., Gersten, R., Scammacca, N., & Chavez, M. M. (2008). Mathematics intervention for first- and second-grade students with mathematics difficulties. *Remedial and Special Education, 29*, 20–32.

Chard, D. J., Baker, S. K., Clarke, B., Jungjohann, K., Davis, K., & Smolkowski, K. (2008). Preventing early mathematics difficulties: The feasibility of a rigorous kindergarten mathematics curriculum. *Learning Disability Quarterly, 31*, 11–20.

Codding, R. S., Eckert, T. L., Fanning, E., Shiyko, M., & Solomon, E. (2007). Comparing mathematics interventions: The effects of cover-copy-compare alone and combined with performance feedback on digits correct and incorrect. *Journal of Behavioral Education, 16*, 125–141.

Cohen, J. (1988). *Statistical power analysis for the behavioral sciences* (2nd ed.). New York, NY: Academic Press.

Dufrene, B. A., Henington, C., & Townsend, A. E. (2006). Peer tutoring for reading fluency: Student implementation and effects on reading fluency. *Journal of Evidence-Based Practices for Schools, 7*, 118–137.

Fletcher, J. M., Morris, R. D., & Lyon, G. R. (2003). Classification and definition of learning disabilities: An integrative perspective. In H. L. Swanson, K. R. Harries, & S. Graham (Eds.), *Handbook of learning disabilities* (pp. 30–55). New York, NY: Guilford Press.

Foorman, B. R., Carlson, C. D., & Santi, K. L. (2007). Classroom reading instruction and teacher knowledge in the primary grades. In D. H. Haager, J. K. Klingner, & S. Vaughn (Eds.), *Evidence-based reading practices for response to intervention* (pp. 45–71). Baltimore, MD: Paul H. Brookes.

Fuchs, D., Compton, D. L., Fuchs, L. S., Bryant, J., & Davis, G. N. (2008). Making "secondary intervention" work in a three-tier responsiveness-to-intervention model: Findings from the first-grade longitudinal reading study of the National Research Center on Learning Disabilities. *Reading and Writing, 21*, 413–436.

Fuchs, D., Fuchs, L. S., Mathes, P. G., & Simmons, D. C. (1997). Peer-assisted learning strategies: Making classrooms more responsive to diversity. *American Educational Research Journal, 34*, 174–206.

Fuchs, L. S., Compton, D. L., Fuchs, D., Paulsen, K., Bryant, J. D., & Hamlett, C. L. (2005a). The prevention, identification, and cognitive determinants of math difficulty. *Journal of Educational Psychology, 97*, 495–513.

Fuchs, L. S., Compton, D. L., Fuchs, D., Paulsen, K., Bryant, J. D., & Hamlett, C. L. (2005b). Responsiveness to intervention: Preventing and identifying mathematics disability. *Teaching Exceptional Children, 37*, 60–63.

Fuchs, L. S., Fuchs, D., Compton, D. L., Bryant, J. D., Hamlett, C. L., & Seethaler, P. M. (2007). Mathematics screening and progress monitoring at first grade: Implications for responsiveness to intervention. *Exceptional Children, 73*, 311–330.

Fuchs, L. S., & Fuchs, D. S. (2007). The role of assessment in the three-tier approach to reading instruction. In D. H. Haager, J. K. Klingner, & S. Vaughn (Eds.), *Evidence-based reading practices for response to intervention* (pp. 29–44). Baltimore, MD: Paul H. Brookes.

Gersten, R., Jordan, N. C., & Flojo, J. R. (2005). Early identification and interventions for students with mathematics difficulties. *Journal of Learning Disabilities, 38*, 293–304.

Graham, S., & Harris, K. R. (2003). Students with learning disabilities and the process of writing: A meta-analysis of SRSD studies. In H. L. Swanson, K. R. Harries, & S. Graham (Eds.), *Handbook of learning disabilities* (pp. 323–343). New York, NY: Guilford Press.

Graham, S., & Perin, D. (2007). What we know, what we still need to know: Teaching adolescents to write. *Scientific Studies of Reading, 11*, 313–355.

Greenwood, C. R., Kamps, D., Terry, B. J., & Linebarger, D. L. (2007). Primary intervention: A means of preventing special education? In D. H. Haager, J. K. Klingner, & S. Vaughn (Eds.), *Evidence-based reading practices for response to intervention* (pp. 73–103). Baltimore, MD: Paul H. Brookes.

Gresham, F. M. (2008). Best practices in diagnosis in a multitier problem-solving approach. In A. Thomas & J. Grimes (Eds.), *Best practices in school psychology-V* (pp. 281–294). Bethesda, MD: National Association of School Psychologists.

Griffin, S. (2004). Building number sense with Number Worlds: A mathematics program for young children. *Early Childhood Research Quarterly, 19*, 173–180.

Griffin, S. (2007). Early intervention for children at risk of developing mathematical learning difficulties. In D. B. B. Berch & M. M. M. Mazzocco (Eds.), *Why is math so hard for some children? The nature and origins of mathematical learning difficulties and disabilities* (pp. 373–395). Baltimore, MD: Paul H. Brookes.

Harn, B. A., Kame'enui, E. J., & Simmons, D. C. (2007). The nature and role of the third tier in a prevention model for kindergarten students. In D. H. Haager, J. K. Klingner, & S. Vaughn (Eds.), *Evidence-based reading practices for response to intervention* (pp. 161–184). Baltimore, MD: Paul H. Brookes.

Harn, B. A., Linan-Thompson, S., & Roberts, G. (2008). Intensifying instruction: Does additional instructional time make a difference for the most at-risk first graders? *Journal of Learning Disabilities, 41*, 115–125.

Individuals with Disabilities Education Improvement Act of 2004, P.L. 108-446, 20 U.S.C. § 1400 *et Seq* (2004).

Johnston, A. M., Barnes, M. A., & Desrochers, A. (2008). Reading comprehension: Developmental processes, individual differences, and interventions. *Canadian Psychology, 49*, 125–132.

Jordan, N. C., Kaplan, D., Locuniak, M. N., & Ramineni, C. (2007). Predicting first-grade math achievement from developmental number sense trajectories. *Learning Disabilities Research & Practice, 22*, 36–46.

Jordan, N. C., Kaplan, D., Oláh, L. N., & Locuniak, M. N. (2006). Number sense growth in kindergarten: A longitudinal investigation of children at risk for mathematics difficulties. *Child Development, 77*, 153–175.

Justice, L. M. (2006). Evidence-based practice, response to intervention, and the prevention of reading difficulties. *Language, Speech, and Hearing Services in Schools, 37*, 284–297.

Kavale, K. A. (2002). Discrepancy models in the identification of learning disability. In R. Bradley, L. Danielson, & D. P. Hallahan (Eds.), *Identification of learning disabilities: Research to practice* (pp. 369–426). Mahwah, NJ: Erlbaum.

Ketterlin-Geller, L. R., Chard, D. J., & Fien, H. (2008). Making connections in mathematics: Conceptual mathematics intervention for low-performing students. *Remedial and Special Education, 29*, 33–45.

Learning Disabilities Roundtable. (2002). *Specific learning disabilities: Finding common ground*. Washington, DC: U.S. Department of Education, Office of Special Education Programs.

Lerner, J., & Kline, F. (2006). *Learning disabilities and related disorders* (10th ed.). Boston, MA: Houghton Mifflin.

Lichtenstein, R. (2008). Best practices in identification of learning disabilities. In A. Thomas & J. Grimes (Eds.), *Best practices in school psychology-V* (pp. 295–318). Bethesda, MD: National Association of School Psychologists.

Ma, L. (1999). *Knowing and teaching elementary mathematics: Teachers' understanding of fundamental mathematics in China and the United States*. Mahwah, NJ: Erlbaum.

Miller, S. P., & Hudson, P. J. (2007). Using evidence-based practices to build mathematics competence related to conceptual, procedural, and declarative knowledge. *Learning Disabilities Research & Practice, 22*, 47–57.

National Association of School Psychologists. (2003). *NASP recommendations for IDEA reauthorization: Identification and eligibility determination for students with specific learning disabilities*. Retrieved from www.nasponline.org/advocacy/LDRecs_042803.pdf.

National Institute of Child Health and Human Development. (2000). *Report of the National Reading Panel. Teaching children to read: An evidence-based assessment of the scientific research literature on reading and its implications for reading instruction* (NIH Publication No. 00-4769). Washington, DC: U.S. Government Printing Office.

Noell, G. H., Gansle, K. A., Witt, J. C., Whitmarsh, E. L., Freeland, J. T., LaFleur, L. H., . . . Northup, J. (1998). Effects of contingent reward and instruction on oral reading performance at differing levels of passage difficulty. *Journal of Applied Behavior Analysis, 31*, 659–663.

Reschly, D. J., & Hosp, J. L. (2004). State SLD policies and practices. *Learning Disability Quarterly, 27*, 197–213.

Sencibaugh, J. M. (2007). Meta-analysis of reading comprehension interventions for students with learning disabilities: Strategies and implications. *Reading Improvement, 44*, 6–22.

Stecker, P. (2007). Tertiary intervention: Using progress monitoring with intensive services. *Teaching Exceptional Children, 39*, 50–57.

Steege, M. W., & Watson, T. Steuart (2009). *Conducting school-based functional behavioral assessments: A practitioner's guide* (2nd ed.). New York, NY: Guilford Press.

Storch, S. A., & Whitehurst, G. J. (2002). Oral language and code-related precursors to reading: Evidence from a longitudinal structural model. *Developmental Psychology, 38*, 934–947.

Stotz, K. E., Itoi, M., Konrad, M., & Alber-Morgan, S. R. (2008). Effects of self-graphing on written expression of fourth grade students with high-incidence disabilities. *Journal of Behavioral Education, 17*, 172–186.

Swanson, H. L., Hoskyn, M., & Lee, C. (1999). *Interventions for students with learning disabilities: A meta-analysis of treatment outcomes*. New York, NY: Guilford Press.

Tilly, W. D. (2008). The evolution of school psychology to science-based practice: Problem solving and the three-tiered model. In A. Thomas & J. Grimes (Eds.), *Best practices in school psychology-V* (pp. 17–36). Bethesda, MD: National Association of School Psychologists.

U.S. Department of Education. (2008). *The final report of the National Mathematics Advisory Panel*. Washington, DC: Author.

Vaughn, S., Klinger, J. K., & Bryant, D. P. (2001). Collaborative strategic reading as a means to enhance peer mediated instruction for reading comprehension and content-area learning. *Remedial and Special Education, 22*, 66–74.

Vaughn, S., Moody, S. W., & Schumm, J. S. (1998). Broken promises: Reading instruction in the resource room. *Exceptional Children, 64*, 211–225.

Vaughn, S., Wanzek, J., Woodruff, A. L., & Linan-Thompson, S. (2007). Prevention and early identification of students with reading disabilities. In D. H. Haager, J. K. Klingner, & S. Vaughn (Eds.), *Evidence-based reading practices for response to intervention* (pp. 11–27). Baltimore, MD: Paul H. Brookes.

Vellutino, F., Scanlon, D., & Lyon, G. R. (2000). Differentiating between difficult-to-remediate and readily remediated poor readers: More evidence against the IQ-achievement discrepancy definition of learning disability. *Journal of Learning Disabilities, 33*, 223–238.

Viel-Ruma, K., Houchins, D., & Fredrick, L. (2007). Error self-correction and spelling: Improving the spelling accuracy of secondary students with disabilities in written expression. *Journal of Behavioral Education, 16*, 291–301.

Walker, B., Shippen, M. E., Alberto, P., Houchins, D. E., & Cihak, D. F. (2005). Using the Expressive Writing program to improve the writing skills of high school students with learning disabilities. *Learning Disabilities Research & Practice, 20*, 175–183.

Wexler, J., Vaughn, S., Edmonds, M., & Reutebuch, C. K. (2008). A synthesis of fluency interventions for secondary struggling readers. *Reading and Writing, 21*, 317–347.

Williams, J. P. (2003). Teaching text structure to improve reading comprehension. In H. L. Swanson, K. R. Harries, & S. Graham (Eds.), *Handbook of learning disabilities* (pp. 293–205). New York, NY: Guilford.

Wood, D. K., & Frank, A. R. (2000). Using memory-enhancing strategies to learn multiplication facts. *Teaching Exceptional Children, 32*, 78–82.

Woodward, J. (2006). Developing automaticity in multiplication facts: Integrating strategy instruction with timed practice drills. *Learning Disability Quarterly, 29*, 269–289.

8

Stuttering

MARK ONSLOW, MARK JONES, SUSAN O'BRIAN, ANN PACKMAN, AND ROSS MENZIES

OVERVIEW OF DISORDER

Diagnostic Criteria

Stuttering is a speech disorder that begins during the first years of life and impairs verbal communication. The disorder is referred to as stammering in the United Kingdom. The diagnostic features of stuttering are disruptions to normal verbal behavior that can be referred to as *moments of stuttering* (Johnson, 1933), or more commonly, *stutters* or *stuttering*. These can be broadly categorized as (a) repeated movements, (b) fixed postures of the speech mechanism, and (c) superfluous behavior (Packman & Onslow, 1999; Teesson, Packman, & Onslow, 2003). These three behaviors are not mutually exclusive, with many or even all of them occurring during one moment of stuttering. Hence, the behaviors of stuttering can be complex. For example, a moment of stuttering may involve an incomplete syllable repetition, a fixed posture with audible airflow, a superfluous behavior that is verbal, and a superfluous behavior that is nonverbal. For the most part, clinical diagnosis is straightforward, with affected adults and parents of affected children coming to speech clinics correctly complaining of the disorder. When they occur at a clinically significant rate, the speech disruptions of stuttering are readily perceptible.

Demographic Variables

Stuttering has been recognized for thousands of years and occurs across cultures (Bloodstein & Bernstein Ratner, 2008). The generally accepted incidence of stuttering is 4%–5%; however, the first prospective, community ascertained cohort study of stuttering onset, with onset confirmed by expert diagnosis, reported a 3-year incidence of 8.6% (Reilly et al., 2009). Stuttering is unique among speech and language disorders because it appears without warning, typically after a period of apparently normal speech development. It has long been accepted that stuttering onset is variable in suddenness and severity (Yairi, Ambrose, & Niermann, 1993; Yairi & Lewis, 1984). Reilly et al. (2009) reported that, for the 96% of parents who could recall, stuttering began suddenly in many children, either over the course of a single day (37%) or 2 to 3 days (12%). For others, stuttering commenced a little more slowly, over 1 to 2 weeks (27%), 3 to 4 weeks (14%), and 5 weeks (6%).

Many children who begin to stutter recover naturally without the benefit of formal intervention; however, natural recovery from early stuttering has never been studied with ideal methods. The majority of studies commenced well after stuttering onset, were retrospective, and the participants were from clinics or were volunteers. With those caveats, spontaneous recovery rates are generally accepted to be between 70% and 80%. In one landmark United Kingdom study (Andrews & Harris, 1964), stuttering was reported to be transient and lasted shorter than 6 months in 37% of the children, with 42% recovering after an average of 2 years (range: 6 months to 6 years). Stuttering persisted until the conclusion of the study (16 years) in 21% of the participants. A Danish study (Mansson, 2000) found that 70.4% of the children stopped stuttering within 2 years of the study commencing.

The cause of stuttering is unknown (Buchel & Sommer, 2004) and at present there are many causal theories (Packman & Attanasio, 2004). Reilly et al. (2009) showed that early onset of stuttering in 137 children from a community ascertained cohort was "not associated with language delay, social and environmental factors, or preonset shyness/withdrawal" (p. 270). The current dominant causal theory of stuttering is that it results from a problem with neural processing underpinning speech, influenced by environmental and linguistic factors (Van Lieshout, Hulstijn, & Peters, 2004). Packman, Code, and Onslow (2007) argued that a deficit in neurological processing for spoken language, together with the triggering effects of certain aspects of spoken language, provide the best explanation for the onset and development of stuttering.

Stuttering as a problem of neural processing of speech is consistent with a meta-analysis of brain imaging studies (Brown, Ingham, Ingham, Laird, & Fox, 2005) showing unusual speech processing by those who stutter. In addition to functional anomalies, structural brain anomalies have been found in adults who stutter in speech-related areas (Foundas, Bollich, Corey, Hurley, & Heilman, 2001; Jäncke, Hanggi, & Steinmetz, 2004; Sommer, Koch, Paulus, Weiller, & Buchel, 2002). Increased size of right planum temporale has been shown to be associated with more severe stuttering (Foundas et al., 2004). Chang, Erickson, Ambrose, Hasegawa-Johnson and Ludlow (2008) reported anatomical differences in speech related areas for children who stutter, hence lending support to the idea that such anomalies are part of the cause, not the effects, of stuttering.

Impact of Disorder

Verbal communication is a distinguishing feature of humans and an essential component of adequate quality of life. Speech is the fundamental mechanism underpinning daily interactions with others, around which social and occupational networks are established, developed, and sustained. Consequently, failure to develop normal verbal communication because of stuttering can begin a destructive sequence in human development.

A fundamental impact of the disorder is that those who stutter do not say as much as their peers, or require longer to say as much. Depending on how it is measured, normal adult speech rate is in the range of 200–250 syllables per minute. Because stuttering moments consume time the disorder involves reduced speech output in comparison to others. In severe cases, fixed postures—speech "blockages"—can last for half a minute and render the speaker functionally mute. It appears that those who stutter speak at three quarters the rate of those who do not stutter (Johnson, 1961). With severe stuttering, at speech rate around 50 syllables per minute, verbal output would be less than a quarter of normal values.

Social anxiety is common with adults who stutter. Despite the fact that those who stutter are excluded from a *DSM-IV* diagnosis of social phobia (American Psychiatric Association, 1994), case reports in the psychiatric literature have affirmed the comorbidity of stuttering and social phobia in adults, and reported on pharmacological interventions (De Carle & Pato, 1996; Paprocki & Rocha, 1999). Stein, Baird, and Walker (1996) demonstrated that 44% of adults seeking treatment for stuttering warranted such a diagnosis because their anxiety and avoidance of social situations was not realistic considering the actual threat during everyday life because of stuttering. Subsequent reports indicated diagnosis rates of 40%

(Blumgart, Tran, & Craig, 2010) and 60% (Iverach et al., 2010) for clinical populations. Schneier, Wexler, and Liebowitz (1997) confirmed Stein et al.'s (1996) finding with a report that stuttering can be associated with similar levels of social anxiety that are experienced with socially phobic clients. Using a scale of social discomfort, Kraaimaat, Vanryckeghem, and Van Dam-Baggen (2002) reported that around half of a group of stuttering participants had scores that overlapped with "a group of highly socially anxious psychiatric patients" (p. 319). Mahr and Torosian (1999) reported that a group of stuttering participants scored higher on social anxiety than controls. Those who stutter are known also to be at risk for anxiety-related mood (Iverach, Jones, et al., 2010) and personality disorders (Iverach et al., 2009).

Messenger, Onslow, Packman, and Menzies (2004) showed that stuttering participants differ from controls with large effects sizes in the extent to which they expect negative social evaluation. Messenger et al. (2004) studied 34 stuttering and 34 nonstuttering participants with the Fear of Negative Evaluation (FNE) scale (Watson & Friend, 1969) and the Endler Multidimensional Anxiety Scales-Trait (EMAS-T; Endler, Edwards, Vitelli, & Parker, 1989). A large effect size was reported for the difference between stuttering and control participants for the FNE data. With the EMAS-T, significant group differences were reported for subtests concerning people and social interactions in which social evaluation would be possible (Social Evaluation and New/Strange Situations), but not for subtests with no reference to people and social interactions such as Physical Danger and Daily Routines. The thoughts and beliefs underlying these social anxiety problems with those who stutter are well known and measurable (Iverach, Menzies, et al., 2010; St. Clare et al., 2009).

The destructive developmental effects of stuttering can include failure to attain occupational potential. A negative linear relationship has been reported between stuttering severity and occupational attainment (O'Brian, Jones, Packman, Menzies, & Onslow, 2011). Hurst and Cooper (1983) reported employer beliefs that those who stutter are not as employable and promotable as others. Those who stutter believe this to be the case (Crichton-Smith, 2002; Hayhow, Cray, & Enderby, 2002), and there is evidence associating clinical control of stuttered speech with improved occupational outcomes (Craig & Calver, 1991).

EVIDENCE-BASED TREATMENT AND STUTTERING

Stuttering is treated by speech clinicians who are referred to variously in English-speaking countries as speech-language therapists (United Kingdom and New Zealand), speech-language pathologists (North America), and speech pathologists (Australia). A challenge in making recommendations based on stuttering treatment research is the diversity of methods applied over an extensive literature; Bloodstein and Bernstein Ratner (2008) identified around 300 published reports that describe the outcomes of various interventions for clients from preschool age to adulthood. Onslow, Jones, O'Brian, Menzies, and Packman (2008) have drawn on recommendations by authorities in the field (Bloodstein, 1995; Bothe, Davidow, Bramlett, & Ingham, 2006; Conture & Guitar, 1993; Curlee, 1993; Ingham, 1984; Ingham & Riley, 1998; Starkweather, 1993) to establish the following working definition of the methodological credentials of what might be considered a well-designed clinical trial of a stuttering treatment:

> A clinical trial of a stuttering treatment is a (a) prospective attempt to determine the outcome or outcomes of (b) at least one entire treatment with (c) at least one pretreatment and one follow-up outcome of at least 3 months in the case of a reported positive outcome, and (d) where outcomes involve speech observations that are independent of treatment and derived from recordings of conversational speech beyond the clinic. (Onslow et al., 2008, p. 404)

This definition of a clinical trial is used in this chapter. The prospective component of the definition excludes retrospective file audit reports (for example, Jones, Onslow, Harrison, & Packman, 2000; Starkweather & Gottwald, 1993; Yaruss, Coleman, & Hammer, 2006). The requirement for a clinical trial to evaluate an entire treatment excluded experiments where only a portion of a treatment was administered (for example, Franken, Kielstra-Van der Schalka, & Boelens, 2005; Lattermann, Euler, & Neumann, 2008). The criterion of measures based on recordings of conversational speech beyond the clinic is designed to reduce bias because of discriminated learning of stuttering reductions to a clinic setting, since there may be little correspondence between stuttering within and beyond the clinic (Ingham, 1980; Ingham & Packman, 1977).

Trials that met these criteria were identified from English language publications since 1965 in a generally accessible source. Papers were identified with online searches of the Web of Science, CINAHL, Journals@Ovid, Medline, Proquest, and PsycINFO databases, textbooks, and treatment manuals. Publications in non-peer-reviewed journals were eligible for review. Trials published in book chapters, published conference proceedings, and treatment manuals were eligible for review; however, conference abstracts, unpublished conference materials, and research dissertations were not eligible for review.

Around 50 reports were identified that met these criteria. All but one trial (Menzies et al., 2008) reported exclusively on speech outcomes using percent syllables stuttered (%SS) as an outcome measure. Recommendations are made only for treatments for which at least one randomized controlled trial (RCT) has been published. In such cases, supplementary evidence for treatment efficacy is also presented incorporating nonrandomized evidence within the phase-based taxonomy of clinical trials development as described in various sources (Herson, 1984; Piantadosi, 1997; Pocock, 1983).

VERBAL RESPONSE CONTINGENT STIMULATION

Verbal response contingent stimulation is a behavioral treatment where a verbal event occurs contingent on stuttering, stutter-free speech, and, less commonly, self-evaluation of whether stuttering has occurred. The essence of these treatments is the nature of the verbal contingencies, how often they occur, and by whom they are presented. These treatments are derived from an extensive body of laboratory research into the operant properties of stuttering in children and adults (Bloodstein & Bernstein Ratner, 2008).

The Lidcombe Program is a model of verbal response contingent stimulation designed for treatment of stuttering children less than 6 years old during the preschool years. The treatment guide for the Lidcombe Program is publicly available (Packman et al., 2011), details of the program and case studies are presented in a clinical text (Onslow, Packman, & Harrison, 2003), and an international continuing professional education network is available for Lidcombe Program training (Australian Stuttering Research Centre, 2007). The Lidcombe Program is administered by parents under the direction of a speech pathologist. During Stage 1, the child and parent visit the speech clinic each week, during which time the clinician teaches the parent how to control the child's stuttering with operant methods. Parents learn to present three verbal contingencies for the child's stutter-free speech and two verbal contingencies for stuttering. The verbal contingencies for stutter-free speech are acknowledgment, praise, and request for self-evaluation. The contingencies for stuttering are acknowledgment and request for self-correction. Parents then administer the contingencies for prescribed periods each day when conversing with the child in everyday situations. The clinician trains the parent to measure the child's stuttering severity each day on a 10-point scale. The clinician also measures the child's stuttering frequency in the clinic each week. Stage 1 of the treatment ends when stuttering is absent or at a very low criterion level beyond and within the clinic.

Time-out is a treatment for stuttering that has been used with children but is more commonly applied to adults in the form of self-managed time-out. The treatment involves the speaker ceasing speech contingent on a moment of stuttering. Hewat, Onslow, Packman, and O'Brian (2006) described one version of this treatment. During Stage 1 clients learn to self-impose time-out and then use this procedure in semi-natural speaking situations, incorporating self-evaluation. Subsequently, the procedure is used in the client's everyday speaking situations. During Stage 2 the clinician assists the client to maintain use of the time-out procedure in everyday situations.

A more complicated version of verbal response contingent stimulation treatment for stuttering is Gradual Increase in Length and Complexity of Utterance (GILCU) (Ryan, 2001). This treatment incorporates an establishment program with 18 steps across a progressive series of three speaking conditions: reading, monologue, and conversation. The duration and grammatical complexity of client utterances are systematically increased. The verbal contingency for stutter-free speech is praise, sometimes paired with redeemable tokens. The contingency for stuttering is verbal punishment using words such as "no," "stop," and "speak fluently." The treatment is more commonly used with children, and parents are trained to identify stuttering and to implement home practice. Score sheets are provided for the clinician to record the accuracy of the client's responses. Branching steps are included to provide additional, remedial training when a step is failed. Schedules for transfer and maintenance are provided, during which verbal contingencies are systematically withdrawn during transfer and maintenance.

Consensus Panel Recommendations

There have been two recent and comprehensive expert panel recommendations published for stuttering treatments. Both used different study selection criteria to the present ones. Bothe, Davidow, Bramlett, and Ingham (2006) used a more complicated set of criteria than those here, including a requisite treatment outcome for inclusion. Herder, Howard, Nye, and Vanryckeghem (2006) conducted a meta-analysis of treatment effects from randomized evidence for behavioral treatments, without regard for trial quality. Herder et al. (2006) concluded that stuttering interventions generally provided clinically beneficial effects and that there was no evidence of superior effects for any one treatment. Of available verbal response contingent treatments, Bothe et al. (2006) recommended the Lidcombe Program, time-out, and GILCU, and a variant of verbal response contingent stimulation for children (Reed & Godden, 1977). Additionally, Bothe et al. (2006) recommended a procedure for contingency management of generalization and maintenance of treatment effects (Ingham, 1980). Herder et al. (2006) included reports of the Lidcombe Program, time-out, GILCU, and a variant of that procedure in their meta-analysis.

Randomized Controlled Trials

There have been two Phase III RCTs of the Lidcombe Program (Jones et al., 2005; Lewis, Onslow, Packman, Jones, & Simpson, 2008). The Jones et al. (2005) Phase III trial was conducted at two clinical sites in Christchurch and Auckland, New Zealand. The design was an open plan, parallel group RCT. Blinded speech outcomes were measures of %SS collected from audiotape recordings made by parents beyond clinic speaking situations: speaking to a family member at home, a nonfamily member at home, and a nonfamily member away from home. Assessments occurred before randomization and 9 months postrandomization (not post the conclusion of treatment). Fifty-four children were randomized, 29 to the Lidcombe Program arm and 25 to a no-treatment control arm. Two children dropped out of the former group, and five dropped out of the latter group. Intention-to-treat analysis carried forward the last available data of participants for whom there were no follow-up data.

The control group showed some improvement; however, there was a large and statistically significant effect postrandomization. Mean prerandomization stuttering rate in the Lidcombe Program group was 6.4%SS, and 1.5%SS at postrandomization. It was the case that most children had not completed Stage 2 of the treatment at the 9-month follow-up assessment, because that maintenance phase of treatment requires a year or longer to complete. The mean prerandomization stuttering rate in the control condition was 6.8%SS and 3.9%SS at postrandomization. The odds ratio for this trial at 9 months postrandomization was 7.7%SS. Jones et al. (2008) followed up 19 children from the experimental arm of the trial at a mean of 5 years later (range 3.7–7.0 years). Only three children were stuttering appreciably above 1.0%SS, suggesting a long-term success rate of 84%.

Lewis et al. (2008) reported an open plan, parallel group RCT. A no-treatment control arm was compared with an arm that received a telehealth version of the treatment. Telehealth is the use of information technologies and telecommunications to support or deliver health services to remotely located sites (Project for Rural Health Communications and Information Technologies, 1996). These technologies include videoconferencing, standard telephone communication, Internet communication, and other data transfer methods. Telehealth treatment presentation is of value because of the large portions of populations of stuttering clients who are isolated from treatment services by distance and other factors. In Australia, where the Lewis et al. (2008) trial was conducted, one third of families live rurally. Adequate speech pathology services are simply unavailable and regular contact with a speech pathologist is difficult or impossible (Wilson, Lincoln, & Onslow, 2002). Twenty-two children were randomized: 13 to the control group and nine to the experimental group.

There were four dropouts. Mean %SS scores prerandomization for experimental and control groups were 6.7%SS and 4.5%SS, respectively. Mean %SS scores at 9 months postrandomization for experimental and control groups were 1.1%SS and 1.9%SS, respectively. After adjustment for baseline stuttering severity, ANCOVA showed a 69% decrease in the treatment group compared to the control group at 9 months postrandomization. Compared to the standard format, the treatment required 3 times the resources in telehealth format.

Meta-Analyses of Group Designs

The data from two RCTs for verbal response contingent stimulation treatments can be combined with data from two randomized controlled experiments (Harris, Onslow, Packman, Harrison, & Menzies, 2002; Lattermann, et al., 2008) for the purpose of meta-analysis of treatment effects for the treatment. The Harris et al. (2002) and Lattermann et al. (2008) studies randomized children to Lidcombe Program and control groups. These studies did not meet the present criteria for being considered a clinical trial because they only presented part of the Lidcombe Program treatment. Latterman et al. (2008) randomized 46 German preschool children who stuttered into either a no-treatment control group or to an experimental group who received the Lidcombe Program for 16 weeks. There was one dropout. Prerandomization %SS scores for the experimental and control groups were 9.5%SS and 8.9%SS, respectively, and postrandomization scores were 2.6%SS and 6.4%SS, respectively. Harris et al. (2002) randomly assigned 23 preschool children who stuttered to either a control group or a treatment group that received the Lidcombe Program for 12 weeks. There were six dropouts. Prerandomization %SS scores for the experimental and control groups were 8.6%SS and 8.3%SS, respectively, and postrandomization scores were 3.6%SS and 6.2%SS, respectively. Data from the four studies are summarized in Table 8.1.

TABLE 8.1 Mean Percent Syllables Stuttered Scores for Lidcombe Program and Control Groups in Four Randomized Studies of the Lidcombe Program

	Harris et al. (2002) (3 months)		Latterman et al. (2008) (4 months)		Lewis et al. (2008) (9 months)		Jones et al. (2005) (9 months)	
	Pre	Post	Pre	Post	Pre	Post	Pre	Post
Lidcombe	8.6% (5.2%)	3.6% (2.8%)	9.5% (4.8%)	2.6% (1.8%)	6.7% (4.5%)	1.1% (1.2%)	6.4% (4.3%)	1.5% (1.4%)
Control	8.3% (2.5%)	6.2% (3.6%)	8.9% (5.9%)	6.4% (4.0%)	4.5% (3.0%)	1.9% (1.4%)	6.8% (4.9%)	3.9% (3.5%)

Note: Standard deviations are presented in parentheses. Pre = Prerandomization; Post = Postrandomization.

The combination of these two studies with the Jones et al. (2005) and Lewis et al. (2008) studies would only be appropriate if the treatment effects for the shorter term studies are consistent with those for the longer term studies, which can be evaluated using a test for heterogeneity.

Analysis was performed using Stata, version for Windows 9.2. The average difference in %SS between the two treatment groups at final follow-up was estimated using a linear regression model with adjustment for baseline severity and treatment site. Similarly, the odds of attaining a minimal level of stuttering (less than 1.0%SS) at final follow-up were compared between the two treatment groups using logistic regression with adjustment for baseline severity and treatment site. For all trials the estimates of %SS for each participant were based on averages of all their beyond-clinic samples of speech at prerandomization and final follow-up. The four trials had 134 participants in total for whom follow-up data were available.

With adjustment for baseline severity and treatment site, the Lidcombe Program groups had lower stuttering by 2.9%SS (95% $CI =$ 1.90–3.8, $p < 0.001$) compared to control at final follow-up. Odds of success by treatment group, with adjustment for baseline severity and treatment site, showed that the Lidcombe Program group had higher odds of attaining minimal stuttering compared to controls ($OR = 7.5$, 95% $CI = 2.7$–20.9, $p < 0.001$). There was no evidence of heterogeneity for any of the analyses, therefore, it is reasonable to assume a fixed effect of treatment. Treatment with the Lidcombe Program over the short to medium term (3 to 9 months) was associated with a lower frequency of stuttering by an absolute difference of around 3.0%SS on average and a sevenfold increase in odds of attaining clinically minimal stuttering of less than 1.0%SS compared to no treatment. Lincoln, Onslow, and Reed (1997) showed that stuttering severity below that level is generally perceived as normal speech by unsophisticated listeners. The Jones et al. (2008) report of long-term follow-up of the Lidcombe Program showed that all 16 of the 19 children who completed the treatment and did not relapse were below this level of stuttering, with the exception of one child whose stuttering at follow-up was 1.1%SS.

Supplementary Data

The bulk of evidence for verbal response contingent stimulation treatment is at the level of nonrandomized Phase I or Phase II trials. Meta-analyses of nonrandomized data is hazardous at the best of times because results invariably inflate apparent effect sizes (Kunz & Oxman, 1998). Only RCTs, with intention-to-treat analyses, can offset this problem. Additionally, meta-analysis of pre- to posttreatment one-group data sets with standard methods is hazardous because of the marked positive skew of stuttering severity, resembling a gamma distribution (Jones, Onslow, Packman, & Gebski, 2006). Because of this, analysis of %SS data in stuttering trials using analysis of variance, *t*-test, or linear regression is dubious when sample sizes are less than 20 and variances are discrepant across pretreatment and posttreatment samples. These latter two scenarios apply to most Phase I and Phase II trials of stuttering treatment.

In addition to these considerations, an over-riding caveat to interpretation of nonrandomized clinical trials evidence is dropouts from trials. An estimate during the early 1980s was that this occurred for around a third of participants (R. Martin, 1981) and there may have been little improvement during subsequent decades (Bloodstein & Bernstein Ratner, 2008). With that in mind, in the following, instances are noted when a Phase II trial has recorded participant attrition and it is less than 20%. For those trials, an indication of stuttering reductions is given for the pre- to posttreatment period. For trials where greater than 20% participant attrition occurred, for trials where participant attrition was not addressed, and for Phase I trials ($N < 10$), the following indicates simply whether a treatment effect was reported or not.

For preschool children there have been three Phase I trials of the Lidcombe Program that reported an effect, with one using a telehealth adaptation of the treatment. There have been two successful Phase II trials of the Lidcombe Program. These trials are summarized in Table 8.2. The Rousseau, Packman, Onslow, Harrison, and Jones (2007) trial reported minimal drop out (5/34). Mean pretreatment stuttering rates were 3.0%SS and 0.8%SS during repeated assessments over 24 months post completion of Stage 1 of treatment. Long-term follow-up of participants in the Onslow, Costa, and Rue (1990) and Onslow, Andrews, and Lincoln (1994) trials was reported by Lincoln

and Onslow (1997) and showed similar, near-zero stuttering at 2 to 7 years follow-up (median 2 years) when the mean age of the children was 6 years 4 months (range 4 years 0 months to 9 years 8 months). For school-age children (7–12 years), Lincoln, Onslow, Lewis, and Wilson (1996) reported an effect for the Lidcombe Program with a Phase II study. Dropouts were minimal (2 of 13). Pretreatment mean stuttering severity was 6.3%SS and mean posttreatment stuttering severity was 0.3%SS during repeated assessments over a 12-month period. This trial is included in Table 8.2.

For adolescents (13–17 years) Hewat et al. (2006) reported, within the context of a larger trial mostly for adults, Phase I data showing that two participants responded to self-imposed time-out and two failed to show any treatment effect.

For adults (>17 years) Hewat, O'Brian, Onslow, and Packman (2001) reported Phase I data for self-imposed time-out, and subsequently a Phase II trial (Hewat et al., 2006). The latter trial showed the absence of an effect with many participants, with only half of them reducing their stuttering severity by more than 50%. This result may need to be interpreted with caution because of a high dropout rate for the trial (12 of 30 participants).

Single-Subject Experiments

There have been two successful single-subject experimental analyses of verbal response

TABLE 8.2 Nonrandomized Phase I and Phase II Trials of the Lidcombe Program With Preschool (< 6 Years) and School-Age (6–12 Years) Children

	Study Type	Treatment	Treatment Format	Age Group	N	Dropouts
Harrison, Wilson, and Onslow (1999)	Phase I trial	Lidcombe Program	Telehealth	Preschool	1	0
Onslow, Andrews, and Lincoln (1994)	Phase II trial	Lidcombe Program	Standard	Preschool	18	6[a]
Onslow, Costa, and Rue (1990)	Phase I trial	Lidcombe Program	Standard	Preschool	4	0
Rousseau et al. (2007)	Phase II trial	Lidcombe Program	Standard	Preschool	34	5
Wilson, Onslow, and Lincoln (2004)	Phase I trial	Lidcombe Program	Telehealth	Preschool	5	0
Lincoln et al. (1996)	Phase II	Lidcombe Program	Standard	School-age	13	2

[a] The initial design was a RCT; however, the control group was not retained because of a combination of participant drop out and drop in, and the trial is categorized here as Phase II. The drop-in children who were treated with the Lidcombe Program were not reported.

contingent stimulation with stuttering in pre-school children that meet the present criteria to be considered a clinical trial. R. R. Martin, Kuhl, and Haroldson (1972) applied time-out from speaking contingent on stuttering. This was achieved by having the two children converse with a puppet contained within a stage box, which was lit both while the puppet was talking and the children spoke without stuttering. When the children stuttered, the puppet ceased talking and the light was turned off for 10 seconds. The light switched back on and the conversation resumed at the end of this period. Using a different kind of verbal response contingent stimulation, Reed and Godden (1977) published a report using a verbal contingency for stuttering of "slow down," spoken by an experimenter contingent on stuttering. Both of these single-subject experimental analyses reported effects for all participants. No meta-analyses of single-subject experiments of verbal response contingent stimulation were located.

Gradual Increase in Length and Complexity of Utterance

For school-age children, Phase I and Phase II trials of two other types of verbal response contingent stimulation treatment have reported effects. Ryan and Van Kirk Ryan (1983, 1995) reported effects for GILCU. Treatments were provided in a U.S. school setting. The 1983 Phase I trial recruited four children, three of whom completed the treatment, and the 1995 Phase II trial recruited 12 children, six of whom completed the treatment. The Ryan and Van Kirk Ryan (1983) paper also contained a Phase I report of time-out with a school-age child. This trial recruited four children, also in a school setting, one of whom completed the treatment.

Self-Management

The only other single-subject experimental analyses of stuttering that could be considered a clinical trial was with a single adult (James,

1981) who was instructed to use self-imposed time-out. A clinically significant treatment effect was reported. James reported two experiments with an 18-year-old man who was trained to self-impose time-out for periods of at least 2 seconds. The first experiment was a multiple baseline across settings design, to determine the effects of self-administering time-out. The second experiment was designed to increase the reliability of self-administered time-out and therefore improve the treatment effect.

Conclusions

There is reasonable clinical trials evidence, with replication by independent researchers, that verbal response contingent stimulation treatment is particularly suitable for stuttering in children younger than 6 years. This may also be the case for school-age children. The best available evidence is for a version of this style of treatment known as the Lidcombe Program, for which there are RCTs. Those trials show clear benefits above the course of natural recovery of the disorder during the preschool years, with a favorable odds ratio. For children and families isolated from treatment services for various reasons, a telehealth version of the treatment is recommended. Although efficacious, treatment by telehealth consumes more clinical time than standard presentation of the treatment. Some evidence exists for the merit of verbal response contingent stimulation treatment with adolescents and adults; however, with those age groups, results appear to be inconsistent, although some clients appear to respond favorably.

SPEECH RESTRUCTURING

Speech restructuring is "use of a new speech pattern to reduce or eliminate stuttering while sounding as natural as possible" (Onslow & Menzies, 2010). The various aspects of speech production involved in the new speech pattern typically include several of the following: reduced speech rate, prolonged vowels, soft articulatory contacts, gentle vowel onsets, continuous airflow, and continuous vocalization. The technique was originally described by Goldiamond (1965). It was discovered during Goldiamond's use of delayed auditory feedback of the speech signal as an aversive contingency for stuttering. He observed that adults adopted a drawling speech pattern under such conditions, and demonstrated that they could remain stutter-free while shaping this slow, drawling speech pattern toward more natural sounding speech. Modern variants of this technique have replaced delayed auditory instruction with clinician instruction, aided by recorded speech models. Speech restructuring programs have proliferated around the world (Ingham, 1984) and are sometimes referred to as "prolonged speech" and "smooth speech."

Typical programs establish stutter-free speech with programmed instruction and then use procedures designed to generalize that treatment gain into everyday speaking situations. They are normally presented in a group intensive format with up to 15 clients in a group, often with a residential phase. For example, a well-known Canadian version of this treatment (Boberg & Kully, 1994) uses a programmed instruction sequence. Programmed instruction involves clinical targeting of a stepwise sequence toward the required goal. With speech restructuring treatments this is normally accomplished with programmed increases in speech rate. The Boberg and Kully treatment begins at a speech rate of 40 syllables per minute and moves progressively to a final rate of around 190 syllables per minute. At the conclusion of that sequence, clients undertake a series of beyond-clinic speaking assignments to facilitate generalization of stutter-free speech. The first 2 weeks of the treatment are intensive and residential, involving 7 hours per day of treatment, with the third week offering an option to remain in residence. Clients are typically followed up posttreatment to prevent relapse.

There is a version of this treatment—the Camperdown Program—that departs considerably from the multiday, intensive model just described that does not incorporate programmed instruction and formal generalization training (O'Brian, Onslow, Cream, & Packman, 2003). During weekly, individual teaching sessions clients learn the new speech pattern by watching and imitating a video of the speech pattern spoken at a speech rate of 70 syllables per minute. During these sessions clients learn to self-evaluate their stuttering severity. Subsequently, clients learn to control their stuttering while sounding as natural as possible. Clients attend in groups of three. In place of programmed instruction, during the day there is a series of 14 cycles, each involving three phases: (1) practicing the speech pattern displayed in the video exemplar, (2) speaking in monologue using the speech pattern with the aim of controlling stuttering while sounding as natural as possible, and (3) evaluating the speech produced during the previous phase. These cycles are 15 minutes in duration, each phase lasting 5 minutes. Subsequently, weekly, individual problem-solving sessions occur to assist clients to develop strategies for generalizing stutter-free speech. The treatment concludes with a generalization phase involving individual visits of 1 hour duration. During these visits the client engages in conversation with the clinician and presents tape recordings of everyday conversations during the previous week. These become less frequent as the client continues to meet the treatment criteria of near-zero stuttering and acceptable speech naturalness. The manual and video exemplar for the treatment are publicly available (O'Brian, Carey, Onslow, Packman, & Cream, 2010). The Camperdown Program may be adapted for use without an intensive day, as occurs with the telehealth versions of the treatment.

Table 8.3 presents nonrandomized Phase I and Phase II trials of speech restructuring treatment for school-age children, adolescents and adults.

Consensus Panel Recommendations

Consensus panel recommendations indicate that speech restructuring treatments are the

TABLE 8.3   Nonrandomized Phase I and Phase II Trials of Speech Restructuring Treatment and School-Age (6–12 Years) Children, Adolescents (13–17 Years), and Adults (17 years plus)

	Study Type	Age Group	N	Dropouts
Boberg & Kully (1994)	Phase II	School-age	5	[a]
Craig et al. (1996)	Phase II[b]	School-age	52	9
Kully & Boberg (1991)	Phase I	School-age	10	Not reported
Ryan & Van Kirk Ryan (1995)	Phase I	School-age	12	7
Block et al. (2005)	Phase II	Adult	80	2
Boberg & Kully (1994)	Phase II	Adult	17	[a]
Boberg (1981)	Phase II[b]	Adult	24	4
Harrison, Onslow, Andrews, Packman, & Webber (1998)	Phase I	Adult	3	6
Howie, Tanner, & Andrews (1981)	Phase II	Adult	36	Not reported
Ingham & Andrews (1973)	Phase II	Adult	23	0
James et al. (1989)	Phase II	Adult	24	4
Langevin & Boberg (1993)	Phase I	Adult	10	0
Langevin et al. (2006)	Phase II	Adult	39	Not reported
O'Brian et al. (2003)	Phase II	Adult	30	14
O'Brian et al. (2008)[c]	Phase II	Adult	10	0
Onslow et al. (1996)	Phase II	Adult	32	20
Perkins, Rudas, Johnson, Michael, & Curlee (1974)	Phase II	Adult	44	Not reported
Boberg & Kully (1994)	Phase II	Adolescent	20	[a]
Harrison et al. (1998)	Phase I	Adolescent	3	0
Hearne, Packman, Onslow, & O'Brian (2008)	Phase I	Adolescent	3	1
Langevin & Boberg (1993)	Phase I	Adolescent	1	0

[a] This trial included school age, adolescent and adults participants, with a total $N = 49$ and seven dropouts in total.
[b] These trials contained a control arm and an experimental arm comparing variants of the treatment. However, allocation was not randomized and hence they were classified as Phase II trials.
[c] This trial was for a telehealth format.

most efficacious for stuttering in adults and adolescents. This consensus was established in an early meta-analysis (Andrews, Guitar, & Howie, 1980) and the view has not changed with recent recommendations. Bothe, Davidow, Bramlett, and Ingham (2006) recommend 14 clinical reports of speech restructuring treatment. Because of the limited randomized clinical evidence for speech restructuring, Herder et al. (2006) included only one report of a speech restructuring treatment in their meta-analysis. This was a small trial ($N = 11$) that did not meet the present trial standards, comparing speech restructuring to GILCU.

Randomized Controlled Trials

There have been two RCTs of a speech restructuring that meet the present criteria for a clinical trial. Carey, O'Brian, Onslow, Block, and Jones (2010) reported a parallel group, noninferiority randomized controlled trial to compare the standard version of this treatment (O'Brian et al., 2003) with a telehealth adaptation. A noninferiority trial tests the hypothesis that one treatment is not worse than another. Speech outcomes involved multiple blinded assessments of %SS based on recordings of unscheduled telephone calls to clients during everyday situations. Assessments were made prerandomization and at 9 months

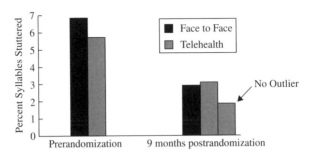

Figure 8.1   Summary of the Results of the Carey et al. (2010) RCT of the Camperdown Program, With and Without the Outlier Data for One Participant Whose Scores Exerted Undue Influence on Analyses

postrandomization, when treatment was completed. Twenty participants were randomized to each group. Two dropped out from the standard group and two dropped out from the telehealth group. Intention-to-treat analysis carried forward the last available data of participants for whom there were no follow-up data. The telehealth and standard group mean %SS scores prerandomization were, respectively, 6.7%SS ($SD = 4.8\%SS$) and 5.4%SS ($SD = 3.8\%SS$). At 9 months postrandomization the telehealth and standard group mean %SS scores were, respectively, 3.0%SS ($SD = 5.1\%SS$) and 2.7%SS ($SD = 2.8\%SS$). There was no statistically or clinically significant difference between the two groups at 9 months postrandomization. Analysis of covariance adjusting for prerandomization severity showed that the telehealth group had 0.8%SS lower stuttering rates at 9 months postrandomization than the standard group. This effect is enhanced with the removal of one participant's data, which exerted undue influence on analyses. This participant was unique in being completely unresponsive to the treatment and retaining stuttering rates greater than 20.0%SS throughout all assessments. Figure 8.1 presents results with and without this participant. Analyses showed no significant difference in the speech naturalness scores between the telehealth and face-to-face groups; however, the control group of normal speakers produced a mean naturalness score that was 1 scale value lower (more natural) than that of

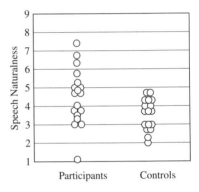

Figure 8.2   Speech Naturalness Scores of Participants in the O'Brian et al. (2003) Clinical Trial and Control Speakers

both treatment groups combined ($p = .003$). This is a common outcome with speech restructuring treatment (see Figure 8.2). A secondary outcome was clinician contact time. The telehealth group consumed statistically less than the standard group. The telehealth group required a mean of 10 hours, 17 minutes contact time and the standard group required a mean of 12 hours, 54 minutes.

Saint-Laurent and Ladouceur (1987) reported an open plan, parallel group RCT of a variant of speech restructuring known as regulated breathing (Azrin & Nunn, 1974). It is clear that this method involves a hybrid of various behavioral techniques for the control of stuttering, including relaxation, emphasizing the start of utterances, speaking for short periods, using deep and regular breathing during speech, and ceasing stuttering contingent on stuttering and taking a deep breath. Regardless, the procedure warrants classification as a variant of speech restructuring (Ingham, 1984).

In a rather ambitious project, Saint-Laurent and Ladouceur (1987) randomized 40 adult participants to five treatment arms. Four were variants of Azrin and Nunn's (1974) procedure and the fifth was an alternative treatment involving self-monitoring. Dropouts were not mentioned in the report. Any form of regulated breathing was statistically significantly superior to the self-monitoring procedure. Reductions in stuttering severity were smaller than reported, with more traditional speech restructuring programs being approximately 50%, with stuttering severity around 5.0%SS at follow-up. Speech rate increased for all groups, significantly so for the groups that received regulated breathing training.

Meta-Analyses of Group Designs

Although reasonably comprehensive, and containing many independent replications of findings, the remainder of clinical trials evidence for the efficacy of speech restructuring treatments is at the level of Phase I and Phase II trials. The caveats described earlier about dropouts from these clinical trials are applied here also. There has been no meta-analysis of these designs.

There has been no clinical trial of a speech restructuring treatment reported for preschool (<6 years) children that meets the present definition criteria. For school-age children (7–12 years) there have been three successful Phase I trials reported. There has been one Phase II trial of speech restructuring for school-age children (Craig et al., 1996), which reported less than 20% dropout (9/52). Pretreatment mean %SS was 10.9%SS and at 12 months posttreatment was 3.0 %SS. Long-term follow-up outcomes at 2–6 years posttreatment were reported by Hancock et al. (1998), showing retention of those treatment effects. For adolescents (13–17 years), there have been four successful Phase I trials of speech restructuring. For adults (>17 years) there have been two successful Phase I trials of a

speech restructuring treatment and 10 successful Phase II trials. One of these has been a trial of a telehealth format (O'Brian, Packman, & Onslow, 2008). Onslow, O'Brian, Packman, and Rousseau (2004) followed up the participants in the Onslow, Costa, Andrews, Harrison, and Packman (1996) trial and reported that treatment effects were sustained 7–12 years posttreatment.

Of particular note is the Block, Onslow, Packman, Gray, and Dacakis (2005) trial with 78 participants, not only because this is the largest trial reported for speech restructuring treatment, but because only two of the 80 participants recruited to the trial dropped out. Pretreatment mean stuttering rates were 5.4%SS and at 3.5 years posttreatment mean stuttering rates were 1.6%SS during an unexpected phone call during everyday life. The Boberg and Kully (1994) Phase II trial reported data for 17 adults at 12 months posttreatment, with no dropouts, and showed a reduction from a mean of around 25.0%SS pretreatment to around 6.0%SS posttreatment. There were three extreme outlying scores above 20.0%SS at 12 months posttreatment, and with these removed the mean score posttreatment was close to that reported by Block et al. (2005) at around 2.0%SS. Boberg and Kully (1994) reported similar results for their 20 adolescent participants. James, Ricciardelli, Hunter, and Rogers (1989) also reported few dropouts. It is difficult to interpret stuttering reductions in this report because data were presented graphically; however, it appears that pretreatment scores were all in the range of 4–10%SS, and the scores at a 6-month follow-up period were mostly in the range of 1–4%SS, with scores during a phone call in the range of 4%–6%SS. The O'Brian, Onslow, et al. (2008b) report of a telehealth adaptation reported no participant attrition, which the authors attributed to the flexibility of the treatment format. Mean pretreatment %SS for the group, based on an unscheduled phone call from a stranger during daily life, was 7.2%SS and at 6 months posttreatment was 1.9%SS.

Single-Subject Experimental Analyses

There has been one single-subject experimental analysis of speech restructuring treatment involving the regulated breathing technique. De Klinder and Boelens (1998) conducted a multiple baseline across subjects experiment with one school-age and one adolescent participant. For the school-age participant, pretreatment stuttering rates were in the range of around 5%–12%SS, and for the adolescent participant, pretreatment stuttering rates were in the range of around 10%–20%SS. For both participants, the last two data points at follow-up around a year later showed %SS scores to be consistently below 5.0%SS in the clinic, at home, and school. We identified no meta-analyses of single-subject experiments of speech restructuring.

Conclusions

There have been more clinical trials reported for speech restructuring than for any other speech pathology technique for the control of stuttering. Only two of these have been RCTs. The majority of clinical trials reported have been at the Phase I and Phase II, with 21 such reports. Despite that methodological limitation of this body of research, there is reasonably compelling evidence of the medium and long-term benefits of this treatment for the control of stuttering. With the caveats in mind about bias in estimating effect sizes from nonrandomized data (see earlier), it seems reasonable to conclude that adults and adolescents are able to achieve and maintain posttreatment stuttering rates at or below 2.0%SS.

There is no clinical trials evidence available to address whether speech restructuring treatments have any benefit for preschool children. For school-age children there is independently replicated Phase I and Phase II clinical trials evidence that treatment effects will occur with that age group. However, it is hazardous to assess the effect size that might occur with school-age children because there is no randomized Phase III evidence available and only

one substantive Phase II trial has been reported. Considering the complexity of speech restructuring treatment, which in essence teaches the client a new way of speaking, and considering the possibility of unnatural sounding speech as an outcome, verbal response contingent stimulation treatments would be considered a first treatment choice for school-age children.

There is independently replicated Phase I and Phase II evidence of the efficacy of this treatment style with adolescents, with a Phase II trial showing reasonably convincing stuttering reductions without substantial dropouts. There is reasonably compelling evidence, including an RCT, that speech restructuring is efficacious for the control of stuttering in adults and that stuttering reductions to 2.0%SS can be obtained and sustained for clinically significant periods. There is reasonably compelling evidence that a telehealth adaptation of speech restructuring treatment is suitable for clients isolated from treatment services.

One striking limitation of speech restructuring treatments is that they may produce speech that sounds unnatural as a trade-off for control of stuttering. From research into this issue, it appears that around half of clients achieve control of stuttering and sound within the range of control speakers in terms of speech naturalness, and around half score beyond the range of control speakers. This is illustrated in Figure 8.2 with results of O'Brian et al. (2003) using a 9-point speech naturalness scale where 1 = highly natural and 9 = highly unnatural.

COGNITIVE BEHAVIOR THERAPY

Consensus Panel Recommendations

Because the application of contemporary anxiolytic cognitive behavior therapy (CBT) techniques to stuttering treatment is a recent development, there have been no published consensus panel recommendations for the method.

Randomized Controlled Trials

CBT is the most efficacious intervention available for treating social anxiety (Andrews, Crino, Hunt, Lampe, & Page, 2003) and has been evaluated extensively in the nonstuttering population (Heimberg, 2002). In response to the prevalence of social anxiety in stuttering, McColl, Onslow, Packman, and Menzies (2001) designed a CBT package specifically for the speech-related anxiety of clients who stutter. The design of the treatment was driven by the common thoughts and beliefs of stuttering clients reported by St. Clare et al. (2009). The treatment involves 10 weekly sessions of individual, 1-hour treatment and three extended sessions of treatment, totaling 15 hours of treatment time. The cognitive restructuring and graded exposure components were as described by Mattick, Peters, and Clarke (1989), and the behavioral experiments component was as described by Butler (1996).

Menzies et al. (2008) reported an open plan, parallel group RCT of this treatment. Thirty-two participants were allocated to either a speech restructuring treatment alone or a speech restructuring treatment followed by the McColl et al. (2001) treatment package. Follow up measures of psychological function and stuttering severity were made 12 months postrandomization. Sixty percent of participants were diagnosed with social phobia: 10 of the 15 participants in the experimental group and 8 of the 15 participants in the control group. At blinded follow-up assessment none of the experimental group were diagnosed with social phobia and the eight participants in the control group retained their diagnoses of social phobia. In relation to control participants, experimental participants showed statistically and clinically significant improvements on a range of psychological assessments. These included the Global Assessment of Functioning scale (*DSM-IV*, APA, 1994), and the percentage of situations on a fear hierarchy that participants were able to enter. Measures of *%SS* made before and after the speech restructuring treatments and at follow-up showed clearly that CBT promoted no further stuttering reductions than did the speech restructuring treatment.

Conclusions

Here is only one published RCT of CBT for speech-related social anxiety in those who stutter.[1] That trial showed positive results for social anxiety. However, until there are replications of the efficacy of CBT, adaptation of that technique into a specific treatment for stuttering clients needs to be guarded.

RHYTHMIC STIMULATION

It is known that rhythmic speech—saying each word or syllable in time to a regular beat—has powerful controlling effects on stuttering (Packman, Onslow, & Menzies, 2000). Based on this information, Trajkovski, Andrews, O'Brian, Onslow, and Packman (2006) reported a case study, and Trajkovski, Andrews, Onslow, Packman, and O'Brian (2009) reported a multiple baseline across subjects experiment showing some promise for rhythmic stimulation as an early stuttering

---

[1] Conference abstracts were not eligible to be included in the present review; however, it is of note that an abstract of an unpublished conference presentation (Ezrati-Vinacour, Gilboa-Schechtman, Anholt, Weizman, & Hermesh, 2007) reported on a group CBT package for 13 adults who stuttered and who also had a diagnosis of social phobia. Participants received 18 weekly group sessions of 1.5 hours. Posttreatment scores were significantly lower on the Liebowitz Social Anxiety Scale (Liebowitz, 1987) for social phobia. Additionally, participants showed improvement on a checklist about anxiety of speaking situations (Hanson, Gronhovd, & Rice, 1981). As was the case for the Menzies et al. (2008) trial, CBT did not improve stuttering.

intervention. The children were provided a parental model of rhythmic speech several times each day and were encouraged to follow the model. Both Phase I reports showed promising results. A subsequent Phase II trial (Trajkovski et al., 2011) reported that eight of 17 recruited children completed the treatment and showed a mean posttreatment stuttering reduction of 96%.

MACHINE-DRIVEN THERAPIES

The discipline of speech pathology has long searched for machine-driven therapies for stuttering. The benefits of such devices would be to move much of the responsibility for the treatment process from the clinician to the client. Recent times have seen some preliminary clinical trials of such devices. Craig et al. (1996) reported initially promising results in a Phase II trial of an electromyographic feedback device. However, two subsequent studies failed to find a clinically meaningful treatment effect with an identical treatment (Block, Onslow, Roberts, & White, 2004; Huber, O'Brian, Onslow, & Packman, 2003). A recent Phase I trial of a device similar to a hearing aid, which changes aspects of auditory feedback of the speech signal, showed no effect (Pollard, Ellis, Finan, & Ramig, 2009). The one promising machine-driven therapy that has been reported in a Phase I trial is the modification of phonation intervals technique (Ingham et al., 2001). This procedure uses computer software and hardware to provide biofeedback on a computer screen to the speaker. The treatment is mostly client-directed and is designed to remove vocalizations shorter than a set duration from the speech signal. Ingham et al. (2001) showed, with single-subject experiments on five adults, that stuttering appeared to be eliminated in daily speaking situations after treatment. Further clinical trials evidence for the efficacy of this procedure would be welcomed.

FAMILY-BASED EARLY INTERVENTION

A popular, but arguably dubious (Packman & Attanasio, 2004), causal theory of stuttering contends that the origins and perpetuation of the disorder can be found in the environments in which children live. This theory suggests that a clinical approach to early stuttering lies in identifying stressors in the child's daily environment and alleviating them. The majority of stressors thought to be responsible for stuttering reside in the language habits of parents. The parental changes that would normally occur with this style of treatment include reduced speech rate, use of simple sentences, numerous pauses, and reduced demands for nonspontaneous speech (Starkweather & Gottwald, 1993).

S. K. Millard, Nicholas, and Cook (2008) presented a Phase I trial of a treatment based on such premises. Results were not particularly promising, with the six children showing a mean stuttering reduction of only 64%. A second similar trial of six children (S. Millard, Edwards, & Cook, 2009) produced an equivalent result of a 66% reduction in stuttering severity. A second similar trial of six children (S. Millard, Edwards, & Cook, 2009) produced an equivalent result of a 66% reduction in stuttering severity. Stuttering reductions of greater than 90% have been reported for Phase I and Phase II trials of other treatments (see above).

EVIDENCE-BASED PRACTICES

Chambless and Hollon (1998) proposed a set of often-cited criteria for use in determining the extent to which psychological treatments have adequate empirical support. Chambless and Hollon make the incontrovertible statement that the best demonstration of treatment efficacy is the RCT. The evidence-based speech pathology practitioner has access to only five RCTs that meet the liberal standards of trial quality outlined in the current chapter: two for verbal response contingent stimulation, two for speech restructuring, and one for CBT. Chambless and Hollon argued that the most compelling clinical trials evidence is that determining the relative efficacy of one treatment compared to another. No such trials have been reported for stuttering; however, the Carey et al. (2010) trial established the non-inferiority of telehealth compared to standard presentation of speech restructuring. This trial met Chambless and Hollon's (1998) criteria for demonstrating treatment equivalence, with the exception that 20 subjects were recruited to each trial arm rather than their suggestion of 25–30. However, the participant numbers in the Carey et al. (2010) trial were based on power analysis.

Chambless and Hollon (1998) also drew attention to the need for independent replication of clinical trials evidence for it to be believable. Verbal response contingent stimulation treatments meet this requirement, with replication of treatment effects reported by five independent research teams over more than three decades. That body of research has shown treatment effects to occur for preschool children, school-age children, and adults. The most developed of verbal response contingent stimulation treatments, the Lidcombe Program, has not been replicated with a clinical trial that conforms to the present trial standards. However, the randomized experiment with German children by Lattermann et al. (2008) provided 16 weeks of treatment rather than a complete treatment. As such, that report might be admissible as an independent replication of a treatment effect with the Lidcombe Program. Speech restructuring treatments have also been well replicated, with successful clinical trials being reported by 10 independent research teams over more than three decades, with trials including school-age, adolescent, and adult participants. The application of CBT to stuttering treatment is a recent development and there has only been one clinical trial of the procedure. Only these three treatments meet Chambless and Hollon's (1998) criterion of adequate manualization.

Chambless and Hollon (1998) draw attention to the need for diagnostic rigor. In the case of stuttering, diagnosis of the disorder in any age group is straightforward (Onslow, Packman, & Payne, 2007). The Menzies et al. (2008) trial of CBT incorporated a multiaxial psychiatric interview (American Psychiatric Association, 1994). Chambless and Hollon point out that evidence for long-term treatment effects is particularly important for disorders that are notoriously unstable. That is certainly the case for stuttering, where posttreatment relapse is a recurring problem (Craig & Hancock, 1995; R. Martin, 1981). Hence, it is noteworthy that evidence exists that both treatments are capable of providing treatment effects for many years posttreatment. There is no doubt that the reductions of stuttering severity reported in this body of literature are clinically significant. Preschoolers are capable of attaining, and sustaining in the long term, reductions of stuttering severity to 1.0%SS and below. In the case of adults who stutter, efficacious control of the disorder in the long term appears to be a realistic goal, with reductions to around 2.0%SS attainable.

Chambless and Hollon (1998) raised the important issue of treatment effectiveness in contrast to efficacy: the extent to which a treatment is shown to work in general clinical practice. It appears that evidence of treatment effectiveness is a shortcoming of the body of research described in this chapter. The majority of clinical trials have been conducted under conditions that invoke many of the issues identified by Chambless and Hollon (1998) concerning generalizing results of clinical trials to standard clinical practice. The majority of trials have been conducted in university or university-affiliated clinics and the clinicians have been either specialist clinicians for stuttering or have been trained specifically for the purposes of the trials. In fact, the development of new models of speech restructuring treatment (O'Brian et al., 2003) and evaluation of them in telehealth format (Carey et al., 2010; O'Brian et al., 2008a), was driven by the demonstrable incapacity of Australian speech pathology services to provide these treatments in the multiday, intensive format in which they were originally developed. In the case of the Lidcombe Program, despite the existence of an international continuing professional education network for this treatment (Australian Stuttering Research Centre, 2007), the effectiveness of the treatment at the level of the clinical community is currently unknown and awaiting research.

Chambless and Hollon (1998) were also mindful of the costs of treatment. The median time for attainment of adequate stuttering reductions during treatment is 12 clinical hours in the Lidcombe Program for preschool children (Jones et al., 2000), and around 23 hours mean total treatment time, including maintenance services (Webber & Onslow, 2003). Treatment of adults who stutter appears to require at least 20 hours (O'Brian et al., 2003), supplemented with subsequent maintenance services to prevent relapse, and intensive residential programs typically require more than 100 hours of treatment (Andrews et al., 1980). On balance, considering the deleterious effects of stuttering on development, evidence of superior outcomes and shorter treatment times for preschool children, and the simplicity of verbal response contingent stimulation as a treatment, a recommendation for early intervention is compelling in terms of outcomes and cost-effectiveness.

It is tempting to relate the apparent deterioration of outcomes across the life span to the dominant causal theory of the disorder as a problem with neural processing of speech. Wohlert and Smith (2002) suggested that there is some loss of flexibility of speech motor activity from the preschool years onward. Perhaps, as suggested by Packman et al. (2007), verbal response contingent stimulation for early stuttering is efficacious "because it prompts children to learn to adjust for the underlying neural processing deficit at a critical time of speech development, before neural networks for speech become established" (p. 360). In light of such speculation, it is surprising that only one treatment for early stuttering has been developed to the Phase III clinical trial stage. It might be anticipated that a variety of treatments would be shown to be efficacious in assisting preschoolers to make such adjustments, and that outcome is anticipated in the future.

Another potentially profitable line of research for the future would be the combination of pharmacological interventions with speech restructuring treatments for adults. There have been numerous drug trials for adults who stutter; however, there is a consensus recommendation (Bothe, Davidow, Bramlett, Franic, et al., 2006) from a review of 31 reports, that there is insufficient evidence of treatment effects for any drug to be recommended for the treatment of stuttering. Considering the prevalence of speech-related social anxiety in stuttering that has become apparent during recent years, it is now timely to begin Phase I trials of combined pharmacological and speech restructuring approaches.

REFERENCES

American Psychiatric Association. (1994). *Diagnostic and statistical manual of mental disorders* (4th ed.). Washington, DC: Author.

Andrews, G., Crino, R., Hunt, C., Lampe, L., & Page, A. (2003*). The treatment of anxiety disorders: Clinician guides and patient manuals* (2nd ed.). Cambridge, England: Cambridge University Press.

Andrews, G., Guitar, B., & Howie, P. (1980). Meta-analysis of the effects of stuttering treatment. *Journal of Speech and Hearing Disorders, 45,* 287–307.

Andrews, G., & Harris, M. (1964) *The syndrome of stuttering*. London, England: Heinemann.

Australian Stuttering Research Centre. (2007). Lidcombe Program Trainers Consortium. Retrieved from http://sydney.edu.au/health_sciences/asrc/health_professionals/lptc.shtml

Azrin, N., & Nunn, R. C. (1974). A rapid method of eliminating stuttering by a regulated-breathing method. *Behaviour Research and Therapy, 12,* 279–286.

Block, S., Onslow, M., Packman, A., Gray, B., & Dacakis, G. (2005). Treatment of chronic stuttering: Outcomes from a student training clinic. *International Journal of Language and Communication Disorders, 40,* 455–466.

Block, S., Onslow, M., Roberts, R., & White, S. (2004). Control of stuttering with EMG feedback. *Advances in Speech Language Pathology, 6*, 100–106.

Bloodstein, O. (1995). *A handbook on stuttering* (5th ed.). San Diego, CA: Singular Publishing Group.

Bloodstein, O., & Bernstein Ratner, N. (2008). *A handbook on stuttering* (6th ed.). Clifton Park, NY: Delmar.

Blumgart, E., Tran, Y., & Craig, A. (2010). Social anxiety disorder in adults who stutter. *Depression and Anxiety, 27*, 687–692.

Boberg, E. (1981). Maintenance of fluency: An experimental program. In E. Boberg (Ed.), *Maintenance of fluency* (pp. 71–111). New York, NY: Elsevier.

Boberg, E., & Kully, D. (1994). Long-term results of an intensive treatment program for adults and adolescents who stutter. *Journal of Speech and Hearing Research, 37*, 1050–1059.

Bothe, A. K., Davidow, J. H., Bramlett, R. E., Franic, D. M., & Ingham, R. J. (2006). Stuttering treatment research 1970–2005: II. Systematic review incorporating trial quality assessment of pharmacological approaches. *American Journal of Speech-Language Pathology, 15*, 342–352.

Bothe, A. K., Davidow, J. H., Bramlett, R. E., & Ingham, R. J. (2006). Stuttering treatment research 1970–2005: I. Systematic review incorporating trial quality assessment of behavioral, cognitive, and related approaches. *American Journal of Speech-Language Pathology, 15*, 321–341.

Brown, S., Ingham, R. J., Ingham, J. C., Laird, A. R., & Fox, P. T. (2005). Stuttered and fluent speech production: An ALE meta-analysis of functional neuroimaging studies. *Human Brain Mapping, 25*, 105–117.

Buchel, C., & Sommer, M. (2004). What causes stuttering? *Plos Biology, 2*, 159–163.

Butler, G. (1996). Research and practice in the treatment of complex anxiety disorders: Developing more effective treatments. In W. Dryden (Ed.), *Research in counselling and psychotherapy: Practical applications* (pp. 79–100). Thousand Oaks, CA: Sage Publications.

Carey, B., O'Brian, S., Onslow, M., Block, S., & Jones, M. (2010). Randomised controlled non-inferiority trial of a telehealth treatment for chronic stuttering: The Camperdown Program. *International Journal of Language and Communication Disorders, 45*, 108–120.

Chambless, D., & Hollon, S. (1998). Defining empirically supported therapies. *Journal of Consulting and Clinical Psychology, 66*, 7–18.

Chang, S. E., Erickson, K. I., Ambrose, N. G., Hasegawa-Johnson, M. A., & Ludlow, C. L. (2008). Brain anatomy differences in childhood stuttering. *Neuro-Image, 39*, 1333–1344.

Conture, E. G., & Guitar, B. E. (1993). Evaluating efficacy of treatment of stuttering—School-age-children. *Journal of Fluency Disorders, 18*, 253–287.

Craig, A. R., & Calver, P. (1991). Following up on treated stutterers: Studies of perceptions of job status. *Journal of Speech and Hearing Research, 34*, 279–284.

Craig, A. R., & Hancock, K. (1995). Self-reported factors related to relapse following treatment for stuttering. *Australian Journal of Human Communication Disorders, 23*, 48–60.

Craig, A., Hancock, K., Chang, E., McCready, C., Shepley, A., McCaul, A., & Reilly, K. (1996). A controlled clinical trial for stuttering in persons aged 9 to 14 years. *Journal of Speech and Hearing Research, 39*, 808–826.

Crichton-Smith, I. (2002). Communicating in the real world: Accounts from people who stammer. *Journal of Fluency Disorders, 27*, 333–352.

Curlee, R. F. (1993). Evaluating treatment efficacy for adults: Assessment of stuttering disability. *Journal of Fluency Disorders, 18*, 319–331.

De Carle, A. J., & Pato, M. T. (1996). Social phobia and stuttering [Letter]. *American Journal of Psychiatry, 153*(10), 1367–1368.

De Klinder, M., & Boelens, H. (1998). Habit-reversal treatment for children's stuttering—Assessment in three settings. *Journal of Behavior Therapy and Experimental Psychiatry, 29*, 261–265.

Endler, N. S., Edwards, J. M., Vitelli, R., & Parker, J. D. A. (1989). Assessment of state and trait anxiety: Endler Multidimensional Anxiety Scales. *Anxiety Research: An International Journal, 2*, 1–14.

Ezrati-Vinacour, R., Gilboa-Schechtman, E., Anholt, G., Weizman, A., & Hermesh, H. (2007, July). *Effectiveness of cognitive behaviour group therapy (CBGT) for social phobia (SP) in people who stutter (PWS) with social phobia (SP)*. Paper presented at the 5th World Congress of Behavioural and Cognitive Therapies, Barcelona.

Foundas, A. L., Bollich, A. M., Corey, D. M., Hurley, M., & Heilman, K. M. (2001). Anomalous anatomy of speech-language areas in adults with persistent developmental stuttering. *Neurology, 57*, 207–215.

Foundas, A. L., Bollich, A. M., Feldman, J., Corey, D. M., Hurley, M., Lemen, L. C., & Heilman, K. M. (2004). Aberrant auditory processing and atypical planum temporale in developmental stuttering. *Neurology, 63*, 1640–1646

Franken, M. C. J., Kielstra-Van der Schalka, C. J., & Boelens, H. (2005). Experimental treatment of early stuttering: A preliminary study. *Journal of Fluency Disorders, 30*, 189–199.

Goldiamond, I. (1965). Stuttering and fluency as manipulatable operant response classes. In L. Krasner & L. Ullmann (Eds.), *Research in behavior modification* (pp. 106–156). New York, NY: Holt, Rinehart, and Winston.

Hancock, K., Craig, A., McCready, C., McCaul, A., Costello, D., Campbell, K., & Gilmore, G. (1998).

Two- to six-year controlled-trial stuttering outcomes for children and adolescents. *Journal of Speech, Language, and Hearing Research, 41*, 1242–1252.

Hanson, B. R., Gronhovd, K. D., & Rice, P. L. (1981). A shortened version of the Southern Illinois University speech situation checklist for the identification of speech-related anxiety. *Journal of Fluency Disorders, 6*, 351–360.

Harris, V., Onslow, M., Packman, A., Harrison, E., & Menzies, R. (2002). An experimental investigation of the impact of the Lidcombe Program on early stuttering. *Journal of Fluency Disorders, 27*, 203–214.

Harrison, E., Onslow, M., Andrews, C., Packman, A., & Webber, M. (1998). Control of stuttering with prolonged speech: Development of a one-day instatement program. In A. K. Cordes & R. J. E. Ingham (Eds.), *Treatment efficacy in stuttering* (pp. 191–212). San Diego, CA: Singular Publishing.

Harrison, E., Wilson, L., & Onslow, M. (1999). Distance intervention for early stuttering with the Lidcombe Programme. *Advances in Speech Language Pathology, 1*, 31–36.

Hayhow, R., Cray, A. M., & Enderby, P. (2002). Stammering and therapy views of people who stammer. *Journal of Fluency Disorders, 27*, 1–16.

Hearne, A., Packman, A., Onslow, M., & O'Brian, S. (2008). Developing treatments for adolescents who stutter: A Phase I trial of the Camperdown Program. *Language, Speech, and Hearing Services in Schools, 39*, 487–497.

Heimberg, R. G. (2002). Cognitive Behavioral Therapy for social anxiety disorder: Current status and future directions. *Biological Psychiatry, 51*, 101–108.

Herder, C., Howard, C., Nye, C., & Vanryckeghem, M. (2006). Effectiveness of behavioral stuttering treatment: A systematic review and meta-analysis. *Contemporary Issues in Communication Science and Disorders, 33*, 61–73.

Herson, J. (1984). Monitoring data logistics with a PC. *Controlled Clinical Trials, 5*, 308–308.

Hewat, S., O'Brian, S., Onslow, M., & Packman, A. (2001). Control of chronic stuttering with self-imposed time-out: Preliminary outcome data. *Asia Pacific Journal of Speech, Language, and Hearing, 6*, 97–102.

Hewat, S., Onslow, M., Packman, A., & O'Brian, S. (2006). A Phase II clinical trial of self-imposed time-out treatment for stuttering in adults and adolescents. *Disability and Rehabilitation, 28*, 33–42.

Howie, P. M., Tanner, S., & Andrews, G. (1981). Short-term and long-term outcome in an intensive treatment program for adult stutterers. *Journal of Speech and Hearing Disorders, 46*, 104–109.

Huber, A., O'Brian, S., Onslow, M., & Packman, A. (2003). Results of a pilot study of EMG biofeedback for the control of stuttering in adolescents. *Proceedings of the Speech Pathology Australia National Conference*, 177–182.

Hurst, M. I., & Cooper, E. B. (1983). Employer attitudes toward stuttering. *Journal of Fluency Disorders, 8*, 1–12.

Ingham, J. C., & Riley, G. (1998). Guidelines for documentation of treatment efficacy for young children who stutter. *Journal of Speech, Language, and Hearing Research, 41*, 753–770.

Ingham, R., & Andrews, G. (1973). An analysis of a token economy in stuttering therapy. *Journal of Applied Behavior Analysis, 6*, 219–229.

Ingham, R. J. (1980). Modification of maintenance and generalization during stuttering treatment. *Journal of Speech and Hearing Research, 23*, 732–745.

Ingham, R. J. (1984). *Stuttering and behavior therapy: Current status and experimental foundations.* San Diego, CA: College-Hill Press.

Ingham, R. J., Kilgo, M., Ingham, J. C., Moglia, R., Belknap, H., & Sanchez, T. (2001). Evaluation of a stuttering treatment based on reduction of short phonation intervals. *Journal of Speech Language and Hearing Research, 44*, 1229–1244.

Ingham, R. J., & Packman, A. (1977). Treatment and generalization effects in an experimental treatment for a stutterer using contingency management and speech rate control. *Journal of Speech & Hearing Disorders, 42*, 394–407.

Iverach, L., Jones, M., O'Brian, S., Block, S., Lincoln, M., Harrison, E., . . . Onslow, M. (2009). Screening for personality disorders among adults seeking speech treatment for stuttering. *Journal of Fluency Disorders, 34*, 173–186.

Iverach, L., Jones, M., O'Brian, S., Block, S., Lincoln, M., Harrison, E., . . . Onslow, M. (2010). Mood and substance use disorders among adults seeking speech treatment for stuttering. *Journal of Speech, Language, and Hearing Research, 53*, 1178–1190.

Iverach, L., Menzies, R., Jones, M., O'Brian, S., Packman, A., & Onslow, M. (2010). Further development and validation of the Unhelpful Thoughts and Beliefs About Stuttering (UTBAS) scales: relationship to anxiety and social phobia among adults who stutter. *International Journal of Language and Communication Disorders.* doi:10.3109/13682822.2010.495369

James, J. E. (1981). Behavioral self-control of stuttering using time-out from speaking. *Journal of Applied Behavior Analysis, 14*, 25–37.

James, J. E., Ricciardelli, L. A., Hunter, C. E., & Rogers, P. (1989). Relative efficacy of intensive and spaced behavioral treatment of stuttering. *Behavior Modification, 13*, 376–395.

Jäncke, L., Hanggi, J., & Steinmetz, H. (2004). Morphological brain differences between stutterers and non-stutterers. *BMC Neurology, 4*, 1–8.

Johnson, W. (1933). An interpretation of stuttering. *Quarterly Journal of Speech, 19*, 70–77.

Johnson, W. (1961). Measurements of oral reading and speaking rate and disfluency of adult male and female stutterers and nonstutterers. *Journal of Speech and Hearing Disorders Monograph Supplement, 7*, 1–20.

Jones, M., Onslow, M., Packman, A., O'Brian, S., Hearne, A., Williams, S., . . . Schwarz, I. (2008). Extended follow-up of a randomized controlled trial of the Lidcombe Program of Early Stuttering Intervention. *International Journal of Language and Communication Disorders, 7*, 1–13.

Jones, M., Onslow, M., Harrison, E., & Packman, A. (2000). Treating stuttering in young children: Predicting treatment time in the Lidcombe Program. *Journal of Speech, Language, and Hearing Research, 43*, 1440–1450.

Jones, M., Onslow, M., Packman, A., & Gebski, V. (2006). Guidelines for statistical analysis of percentage of syllables stuttered data. *Journal of Speech, Language, and Hearing Research, 49*, 867–878.

Jones, M., Onslow, M., Packman, A., Williams, S., Ormond, T., Schwarz, I., & Gebski, V. (2005). Randomised controlled trial of the Lidcombe programme of early stuttering intervention. *British Medical Journal, 331*, 659–661.

Kraaimaat, F. W., Vanryckeghem, M., & Van Dam-Baggen, R. (2002). Stuttering and social anxiety. *Journal of Fluency Disorders, 27*, 319–331.

Kully, D., & Boberg, E. (1991). Therapy for school-age children. *Seminars in Speech and Language, 12*, 291–300.

Kunz, R., & Oxman, A. (1998). The unpredictability paradox: Review of empirical comparisons of randomised and non-randomised clinical trials. *British Medical Journal, 317*, 1185–1190.

Langevin, M., & Boberg, E. (1993). Results of an intensive stuttering therapy program. *Journal of Speech-Language Pathology and Audiology, 17*, 158–166.

Langevin, M., Huinck, W. J., Kully, D., Peters, H. F., Lomheim, H., & Tellers, M. (2006). A cross-cultural, long-term outcome evaluation of the ISTAR Comprehensive Stuttering Program across Dutch and Canadian adults who stutter. *Journal of Fluency Disorders, 31*, 229–256.

Lattermann, C., Euler, H. A., & Neumann, K. A. (2008). Randomized control trial to investigate the impact of the Lidcombe Program on early stuttering in German-speaking preschoolers. *Journal of Fluency Disorders, 33*, 52–65.

Lewis, C., Onslow, M., Packman, A., Jones, M., & Simpson, J. A. (2008). Phase II trial of telehealth delivery of the Lidcombe Program of Early Stuttering Intervention. *American Journal of Speech-Language Pathology, 17*, 139–149.

Liebowitz, M. (1987). Social phobia. *Modern Problems of Pharmacopsychiatry, 22*, 141–173.

Lincoln, M., & Onslow, M. (1997). Long-term outcome of an early intervention for stuttering. *American Journal of Speech-Language Pathology, 6*, 51–58.

Lincoln, M., Onslow, M., Lewis, C., & Wilson, L. (1996). A clinical trial of an operant treatment for school-age children who stutter. *American Journal of Speech-Language Pathology, 5*, 73–85.

Lincoln, M., Onslow, M., & Reed, V. (1997). Social validity of the treatment outcomes of an early intervention program for stuttering. *American Journal of Speech-Language Pathology, 6*, 77–84.

Mahr, G. C., & Torosian, T. (1999). Anxiety and social phobia in stuttering. *Journal of Fluency Disorders, 24*, 119–126.

Mansson, H. (2000). Childhood stuttering: Incidence and development. *Journal of Fluency Disorders, 25*, 47–57.

Martin, R. (1981). Introduction and perspective: Review of published research. In E. Boberg (Ed.), *Maintenance of fluency* (pp. 1–30). New York, NY: Elsevier.

Martin, R. R., Kuhl, P., & Haroldson, S. (1972). An experimental treatment with two preschool stuttering children. *Journal of Speech and Hearing Research, 15*, 743–752.

Mattick, R. P., Peters, I., & Clarke, J. C. (1989). Exposure and cognitive restructuring for social phobia: A controlled study. *Behavior Therapy, 20*, 3–23.

McColl, T., Onslow, M., Packman, A., & Menzies, R. G. (2001). A cognitive behavioral intervention for social anxiety in adults who stutter. *Proceedings of the Speech Pathology Australia National Conference*, 93–98.

Menzies, R., O'Brian, S., Onslow, M., Packman, A., St. Clare, T., & Block, S. (2008). An experimental clinical trial of a cognitive behavior therapy package for chronic stuttering. *Journal of Speech, Language and Hearing Research, 51*, 1451–1464.

Messenger, M., Onslow, M., Packman, A., & Menzies, R. (2004). Social anxiety in stuttering: Measuring negative social expectancies. *Journal of Fluency Disorders, 29*, 201–212.

Millard, S., Edwards, S. I., & Cook, F. M. (2009). Parent-child interaction therapy: Adding to the evidence. *International Journal of Speech Language Pathology, 11*, 61–67.

Millard, S. K., Nicholas, A., & Cook, F. M. (2008). Is Parent-Child Interaction Therapy effective in reducing stuttering? *Journal of Speech, Language, and Hearing Research, 51*, 636–650.

O'Brian, S., Carey, B., Onslow, M., Packman, A., & Cream, A. (2010). The Camperdown Program for Stuttering: Treatment Manual. Retrieved from http://sydney.edu.au/health_sciences/asrc/docs/camperdown_manual.pdf

O'Brian, S., Jones, M., Packman, A., Menzies, R., & Onslow, M. (2011). Stuttering severity and educational attainment. *Journal of Fluency Disorders, 36*, 86–92.

O'Brian, S., Onslow, M., Cream, A., & Packman, A. (2003). The Camperdown Program: Outcomes of a new prolonged-speech treatment model. *Journal of Speech Language and Hearing Research, 46,* 933–946.

O'Brian, S., Packman, A., & Onslow, M. (2008a). Tele-health delivery of the Camperdown Program for adults who stutter. *Journal of Speech, Language and Hearing Research, 51,* 1–12.

O'Brian, S., Packman, A., & Onslow, M. (2008b). Tele-health delivery of the Camperdown Program for adults who stutter: A phase I trial [Clinical Trial, Phase I Research Support, Non-U.S. Gov't]. *Journal of Speech Language & Hearing Research, 51,* 184–195.

Onslow, M., Andrews, C., & Lincoln, M. (1994). A control-experimental trial of an operant treatment for early stuttering. *Journal of Speech & Hearing Research, 37,* 1244–1259.

Onslow, M., Costa, L., Andrews, C., Harrison, E., & Packman, A. (1996). Speech outcomes of a prolonged-speech treatment for stuttering. *Journal of Speech and Hearing Research, 39,* 734–749.

Onslow, M., Costa, L., & Rue, S. (1990). Direct early intervention with stuttering: Some preliminary data. *Journal of Speech & Hearing Disorders, 55,* 405–416.

Onslow, M., Jones, M., O'Brian, S., Menzies, R., & Packman, A. (2008). Defining, identifying, and evaluating clinical trials of stuttering treatments: A tutorial. *American Journal of Speech Language Pathology, 17,* 401–415.

Onslow, M., & Menzies, R. (2010) *Speech restructuring.* Accepted entry in www.commonlanguagepsychotherapy.org/fileadmin/user_upload/Accepted_procedures/speechrestr.pdf.

Onslow, M., O'Brian, S., Packman, A., & Rousseau, I. (2004). Long term follow up of speech outcomes for a prolonged-speech treatment for stuttering: The effects of paradox on stuttering treatment research. In A. K. Bothe (Ed.), *Evidence-based treatment of stuttering: Empirical issues and clinical implications* (pp. 231–244). Mahwah, NJ: Erlbaum.

Onslow, M., Packman, A., & Harrison, E. (2003). *The Lidcombe Program of early stuttering intervention: A clinician's guide.* Austin, TX: Pro-Ed.

Onslow, M., Packman, A., & Payne, P. (2007). Clinical identification of early stuttering: Methods, issues, and future directions. *Asia Pacific Journal of Speech Language and Hearing, 10,* 15–31.

Packman, A., & Attanasio, J. S. (2004). *Theoretical issues in stuttering.* London, England: Taylor & Francis.

Packman, A., Code, C., & Onslow, M. (2007). On the cause of stuttering: Integrating theory with brain and behavioral research. *Journal of Neurolinguistics, 20,* 353–362.

Packman, A., & Onslow, M. (1999). Fluency disruption in speech and in wind instrument playing. *Journal of Fluency Disorders, 24,* 293–298.

Packman, A., Onslow, M., & Menzies, R. (2000). Novel speech patterns and the treatment of stuttering. *Disability and Rehabilitation, 22,* 65–79.

Packman, A., Onslow, M., Webber, M., Harrison, E., Lees, S., Bridgman, K., & Carey, B. (2011). The Lidcombe Program of earling stuttering intervention treatment guide. Retrieved from http://sydney.edu.au/health_sciences/asrc/docs/lp_manual_2011.pdf

Paprocki, J., & Rocha, F. L. (1999). Stuttering associated with social phobia. Results with pharmacological treatment. *Jornal Brasileiro de Psiquiatria, 48,* 263–273.

Perkins, W. H., Rudas, J., Johnson, L., Michael, W. B., & Curlee, R. F. (1974). Replacement of Stuttering with Normal Speech. 3. Clinical Effectiveness. *Journal of Speech and Hearing Disorders, 39,* 416–428.

Piantadosi, S. (1997). *Clinical trials: A methodological perspective.* New York, NY: Wiley.

Pocock, S. J. (1983). *Clinical trials.* Chichester, England: Wiley.

Pollard, R., Ellis, J. B., Finan, D., & Ramig, P. R. (2009). Effects of the SpeechEasy on objective and perceived aspects of stuttering: A six-month, Phase I clinical trial in naturalistic environments. *Journal of Speech Language and Hearing Research, 52,* 516–533.

Project for Rural Health Communications and Information Technologies. (1996). *Telehealth in rural and remote Australia.* Moe, Victoria, Australia: Monash University, Australian Rural Health Research Institute.

Reed, C., & Godden, A. (1977). An experimental treatment using verbal punishment with two preschool stutterers. *Journal of Fluency Disorders, 2,* 225–233.

Reilly, S., Onslow, M., Packman, A., Wake, M., Bavin, E., Prior, M., . . . Ukoumunne, O. C. (2009). Predicting stuttering onset by age 3 years: A prospective, community cohort study. *Pediatrics, 123,* 270–277.

Rousseau, I., Packman, A., Onslow, M., Harrison, L., & Jones, M. (2007). Language, phonology, and treatment time in the Lidcombe Program: A prospective study in a Phase II trial. *Journal of Communication Disorders, 40,* 382–397.

Ryan, B. P. (2001). *Programmed therapy for stuttering in children and adults* (2nd ed.). Springfield, IL: Charles C Thomas.

Ryan, B. P., & Van Kirk Ryan, B. (1983). Programmed stuttering therapy for children: Comparison of four establishment programs. *Journal of Fluency Disorders, 8,* 291–322.

Ryan, B. P., & Van Kirk Ryan, B. (1995). Programmed stuttering treatment for children: Comparison of two establishment programs through transfer, maintenance, and follow-up. *Journal of Speech and Hearing Research, 38,* 61–75.

Saint-Laurent, L., & Ladouceur, R. (1987). Massed versus distributed application of the regulated-breathing method for stutterers and its long-term effect. *Behavior Therapy, 18,* 38–50.

Schneier, F. R., Wexler, K. B., & Liebowitz, M. R. (1997). Social phobia and stuttering. *American Journal of Psychiatry, 154,* 131.

Sommer, M., Koch, M. A., Paulus, W., Weiller, C., & Buchel, C. (2002). Disconnection of speech-relevant brain areas in persistent developmental stuttering. *Lancet, 360*, 380–383.

Starkweather, C. W. (1993). Issues in the efficacy of treatment for fluency disorders. *Journal of Fluency Disorders, 18*, 151–168.

Starkweather, C. W., & Gottwald, S. R. (1993). A pilot study of relations among measures obtained at intake and discharge in a program of prevention and early intervention for stuttering. *American Journal of Speech-Language Pathology, 2*, 51–58.

St Clare, T., Menzies, R. G., Onslow, M., Packman, A., Thompson, R., & Block, S. (2009). Unhelpful thoughts and beliefs linked to social anxiety in stuttering: Development of a measure. *International Journal of Language and Communication Disorders, 44*(3), 338–351.

Stein, M. B., Baird, A., & Walker, J. R. (1996). Social phobia in adults with stuttering. *American Journal of Psychiatry, 153*, 278–280.

Teesson, K., Packman, A., & Onslow, M. (2003). The Lidcombe behavioral data language of stuttering. *Journal of Speech Language and Hearing Research, 46*, 1009–1015.

Trajkovski, N., Andrews, C., O'Brian, S., Onslow, M., & Packman, A. (2006). Treating stuttering in a preschool child with syllable timed speech: A case report. *Behaviour Change, 23*, 270–277.

Trajkovski, N., Andrews, C., Onslow, M., O'Brian, S., Packman, A., & Menzies, R. (2011). A Phase II trial of the Westmead Program: Syllable-timed speech treatment for preschool children who stutter. *International Journal of Speech-Language Pathology, 13*, 500–509.

Trajkovski, N., Andrews, C., Onslow, M., Packman, A., & O'Brian, S., & Menzies, R. (2009). Using syllable-timed speech for treat preschool children who stutter: A multiple baseline experiment. *Journal of Fluency Disorders, 34*, 1–10.

Van Lieshout, P. H. H. M., Hulstijn, W., & Peters, H. F. M. (2004). Searching for the weak link in the speech production chain of people who stutter: A motor skill approach. In B. Maassen, R. Kent, H. F. M. Peters, P. H. H. M. Van Lieshout, & W. Hulstijn (Eds.), *Speech motor control in normal and disordered speech* (pp. 313–355). Oxford, England: Oxford University Press.

Watson, D., & Friend, R. (1969). Measurement of social-evaluative anxiety. *Journal of Consulting and Clinical Psychology, 33*, 448–457.

Webber, M., & Onslow, M. (2003). Maintenance of treatment effects. In M. Onslow, A. Packman, & E. Harrison (Eds.), *The Lidcombe Program of early stuttering intervention: A clinician's guide* (pp. 81–90). Austin, TX: Pro-Ed.

Wilson, L., Lincoln, M., & Onslow, M. (2002). Availability, access, and quality of care: Inequities in rural speech pathology services and a model for redress. *Advances in Speech Language Pathology, 4*, 9–22.

Wilson, L., Onslow, M., & Lincoln, M. (2004). Telehealth adaptation of the Lidcombe Program of early stuttering intervention: Preliminary data. *American Journal of Speech Language Pathology, 13*, 81–93.

Wohlert, A. B., & Smith, A. (2002). Developmental change in variability of lip muscle activity during speech. *Journal of Speech Language and Hearing Research, 45*, 1077–1087.

Yairi, E., Ambrose, N. G., & Nierman, R. (1993). The early months of stuttering: A developmental study. *Journal of Speech and Hearing Research, 36*, 521–528.

Yairi, E., & Lewis, B. (1984). Disfluencies at the onset of stuttering. *Journal of Speech and Hearing Research, 27*, 154–159.

Yaruss, I. S., Coleman, C., & Hammer, D. (2006). Treating preschool children who stutter: Description and preliminary evaluation of a family-focused treatment approach. *Language Speech and Hearing Services in Schools, 37*, 118–132.

9

Autism Spectrum Disorders

GLEN O. SALLOWS AND TAMLYNN D. GRAUPNER

OVERVIEW OF DISORDER

Autism is a neurodevelopmental disorder characterized by problems and delays in social interaction, social use of language, and the presence of atypical behaviors, including motor stereotypies and intense but unusual interests or preferences (American Psychiatric Association, 2000). Regression during the second year of life has been noted in 25% to 35% or more of children (Volkmar, Chawarska, & Klin, 2008). The mean age at which parents first report concerns is around 18 months (Landa, 2008), but subtle symptoms are typically present during the first year of life (Zwaigenbaum et al., 2005). Geneticists report heritability as high as 70% to 90% (Abrahams & Geschwind, 2008). There is strong evidence of abnormalities during fetal brain development, which continues postpartum. Autopsy and neuroimaging studies of children at risk for autism have shown several anatomical abnormalities, such as rapid brain growth reflected in large head circumference during the first year followed by slower growth (Dawson et al., 2007), developmental abnormalities in the fusiform face area, involved with gaining social information from faces; the cerebellum, involved in intellectual and affective functions (Courchesne, Piven, Saliba, Bailey, & Arndt, 1999); and the amygdala, involved in recognition of emotional stimuli (Dawson, 2008). These abnormalities are likely the result of

malfunctioning genes. Several genes have been identified that are expressed in the brain and are regulated by neuronal activity, the result of which is synaptogenesis and neuroplasticity (Morrow et al., 2008). This is one avenue through which early intervention may cause improvements in the cognitive and social skills of children with autism (Thompson, 2007) and is most easily accomplished during early childhood when there is an overabundance of synapses.

Diagnosis

The *DSM-IV* (American Psychiatric Association, APA, 2000) lists 12 autism symptoms and requires that a child meet a total of six to qualify for a diagnosis of autism. There are three categories of symptoms: (1) impairments in social interaction, (2) impairments in communication, and (3) restrictive and repetitive behavior, interests, and activities. Deficits in one of the three areas must occur prior to age three. Children with later onset can be diagnosed with atypical autism. Asperger's disorder (AD) is a disorder with delays in social skills and restricted interests, but without significant language delays. Language content is somewhat odd, including prolonged speech about favorite topics, and there are problems with social understanding, often leading to increasing difficulties in adolescence. Whether Asperger's is fundamentally different from high-functioning autism (HFA) is unclear (R. L. Koegel & Koegel, 2006). Pervasive developmental disorders not otherwise specified (PDD-NOS) is a diagnosis for children who do not quite meet criteria for any of the other pervasive developmental disorders because they do not meet criteria in all three areas or because symptoms are mild. Children with Rett's disorder and childhood disintegrative disorder (CDD) undergo regressions that include loss of motor and physical skills such as use of the hands in Rett's disorder and bowel and bladder control in CDD (Bishop, Luyster, Richler, & Lord, 2008; Fombonne, 2002). In both conditions, there is a pre-regression period of apparent normalcy: 6 to 18 months for Rett's disorder and 2 to 3 years in CDD. Both conditions are rare—less than 2 per 100,000 for CDD and 1 in 10,000 to 15,000 for Rett's disorder. Rett's disorder can be caused by a mutation in the sequence of a single gene (National Institute of Mental Health [NIMH], 2008).

Epidemiology

In the *DSM-IV-TR* (APA, 2000), the median prevalence of autism is listed as 5 per 10,000 people (range 2 to 20 per 10,000). During the past 10 years, there have been reports of even higher prevalence, up to 1 in 110 children (Centers for Disease Control and Prevention, 2009). This apparent increase is probably not due to the MMR vaccine (Volkmar, Westphal, Gupta, & Weisner, 2008) or thimerosal (NIMH, 2008; Smith & Wick, 2008), but some have suggested that it may be due to broadening of diagnostic criteria (Chakrabarti & Fombonne, 2005; Fombonne, 2005) and diagnostic substitution (Shattuck, 2006).

COMPREHENSIVE TREATMENT PROGRAMS

Applied Behavior Analysis

Applied Behavior Analysis (ABA) is based on over 50 years of research with persons with autism focusing on understanding how behavior is learned, maintained, and generalized, how problems develop, and how individuals can learn to succeed in everyday life. Intervention begins with an assessment of relevant medical conditions, environmental antecedents, child skills, and consequences for both appropriate and inappropriate behaviors. An intervention is then designed to modify environmental events such as antecedents and consequences, as well as building new skills, which are broken down into small steps so that they can be easily learned. In comprehensive treatment, a team of trained and supervised staff work 1:1 with the child daily, optimally for 30–35 hours per week, to provide sufficient repetition so skills are learned quickly. A curriculum is used to guide the intervention based on standard developmental progression, modified to utilize the strengths of autistic children, including visual learning. As skills are learned, interventionists plan the generalization of these new skills to new materials, partners, and settings to ensure that the child can use them in daily life.

Consensus Panel Recommendations

The New York State Department of Health (NYSDOH, 1999) identified five studies examining the effects of intensive behavioral treatment using control group designs that met the criteria for adequate evidence about efficacy (Birnbrauer & Leach, 1993; Lovaas, 1987; McEachin, Smith, & Lovaas, 1993; Sheinkopf & Siegel, 1998; Smith, Eikeseth, Klevstrand, & Lovaas, 1997). All used independent diagnosticians and evaluators, compared effects of treatment to control groups, and used group assignment strategies designed to avoid bias. All found that children receiving intensive ABA showed greater improvement than control group children. Several studies showed that intensive behavioral treatment was successful without the use of aversives in settings outside a university and that treatment could be successfully implemented by trained paraprofessionals and parents. Recommendations supported by "strong evidence" were: (a) Principles of ABA should be included as an important element of any intervention program for young children with autism; (b) intensive behavioral programs should include a minimum of 20 hours per week of individualized behavioral intervention, not including time spent by parents; (c) hours of behavioral intervention should be based on child and family characteristics such as age, severity of autistic symptoms, rate of progress, tolerance of the child for the intervention, and family participation; (d) parents should be included as active participants in the intervention team; (e) parents should be trained in behavioral techniques and encouraged to provide additional hours of intervention, including regular consultation with a qualified professional; and (f) physical aversives are not recommended and are not necessary for successful outcome.

The National Research Council (NRC, 2001) chapter on "Comprehensive Programs," the primary responsibility of Gail McGee, included reviews of ten programs representing ABA, Positive Behavioral Support, Pivotal Response Training (PRT), Incidental Teaching, and TEACCH (Treatment and Education of Autistic and Communication related handicapped Children). McGee recommended beginning intervention before 4 or 5 years of age, providing at least 25 hours per week for 12 months per year, training staff using standard protocols, the active involvement of parents, and ongoing assessment to guide treatment plans based on a curriculum addressing communication, social, cognitive, academic, self-help, and motor skills as well as behavioral challenges using research-based procedures with planning for maintenance, generalization, and transition to school.

The National Professional Development Center on autism spectrum disorder, funded by the U.S. Department of Education, performed an extensive literature review using criteria similar to those of Chambless and Hollon (1998) to identify evidence-based practices

(EBPs) and strategies, rather than comprehensive programs, as well as identifying the target behaviors each practice successfully changed (Odom, Collet-Klingenberg, Rogers, & Hatton, 2010). Most of the 24 EBPs were behavioral: prompting, reinforcement, task analysis and chaining, time delay, discrete trial, naturalistic interventions and Pivotal Response Training (use of behavioral strategies in natural settings), peer-mediated interventions, functional behavioral assessment, stimulus control, response interruption/redirection, Functional Communication Training, extinction, differential reinforcement, self-management, social skills training, video modeling, and visual schedules/supports. The group also identified five other EBPs: Picture Exchange Communication System (PECS), social narratives, parent training/involvement, voice output devices, and computer aided instructions. The group has posted step-by-step instructions for how to implement each of the strategies online.

Review of Comprehensive ABA Programs

Smith (1999) reviewed the literature regarding comprehensive early intervention for children with autism who were 5 years old or younger published in peer-reviewed journals from 1980 to early 1998. Twelve studies met these criteria: nine behavioral, one from TEACCH, and two from Colorado Health Sciences. Smith (1999) noted that in all programs some children made large gains while others showed little change, regardless of intervention approach. He concluded that ABA, also referred to as Early Intensive Behavioral Intervention (EIBI), was supported by research as an effective approach, but that neither the TEACCH nor Colorado Health Science programs had adequate research support.

Eikeseth (2009) reviewed 26 comprehensive treatment studies, including those reviewed by Smith (1999), rating each by scientific merit. Twenty-one were based on principles of ABA. Level 1 scientific merit denoted the most scientifically sound studies, required blind diagnosis, random assignment, assessment of cognitive and adaptive skills using normed and standardized measures, and evidence of treatment fidelity. Only one study met Level 1 standards (Smith, Groen, & Wynn, 2000). Children with a mean age of 36 months and matched on pretreatment IQ (51) were randomly assigned to an ABA ($N = 15$, mean 24.5 hours per week for 33 months) or a parent training group ($N = 13$, twice weekly 2–3 hour sessions for 3–9 months). After a mean of 33 months of treatment, the ABA group showed significantly better outcome than the parent-training group on IQ, nonverbal IQ, total language, school placement, and academic skills, but not on Vineland subscales (changes for both groups were small) or the Child Behavior Checklist. The ABA group showed a mean increase in IQ of 16 points versus a loss of 1 point for the parent-training group. Twenty-seven percent of the ABA group (4 out of 15) versus none of the parent training group achieved average post-treatment scores and were in regular classrooms without support (Cohen's $d = 1.43$, large). These improvements were not as large as those found by other comprehensive ABA studies and the authors commented that their sample might have been atypical in that 23 of 28 children were mute compared to approximately 50% in the general population of children with autism.

Level 2 studies met all of the requirements of Level 1 except that group assignment was not random—instead being based on geographical location, parental choice, or staff availability—which has been described as not resulting in noticeable bias (Baer, 1993; NYSDOH, 1999). Five group studies met Level 2 criteria and all compared outcome of children receiving ABA with that of children receiving eclectic approaches in preschool classrooms (Cohen, Amerine-Dickens, & Smith, 2006; Eikeseth, Smith, Jahr, and Eldevik, 2002, 2007; Howard, Sparkman, Cohen, Green, & Stanislaw, 2005; Remington et al., 2007). Altogether, there were 63 children in intensive ABA and 49 in eclectic classrooms. The IQ averaged 60.9 for ABA children and 60.5 for controls. There were no significant differences in pretreatment child variables. Hours per week for ABA groups were 35 to 40 for studies treating younger children, 28 hours for the older group (Eikeseth et al., 2002, 2007), and 25 to 30 for eclectic classrooms. The ABA intervention included discrete trial targeting language, social and cognitive skills, generalization strategies including Incidental Teaching and practicing skills in community and school settings, and social skills training, including supervised and prompted interactions with typical peers several times per week. Eclectic classrooms offered discrete trial, TEACCH, sensory integration, and group activities common in preschool settings. After a mean of 2.3 years of treatment (14 months to 3 years), all ABA groups scored significantly higher than eclectic classrooms on IQ (mean increase of 27 points vs. 10 points), and adaptive functioning (mean increase of 10.5 points vs. loss of 4.9 points). Remington et al. (2007) showed that ABA programs using lower hours (20–30) and team meeting every 2–12 weeks, with consultant visits every 2–6 months, showed lower gains (12 IQ points), but were still superior to eclectic classrooms (loss of 2.2 IQ points). Two other studies compared ABA with eclectic classrooms (Eldevik, Eikeseth, Jahr, & Smith, 2006; Magiati, Charman, & Howlin, 2007), bringing the total to seven studies; only Magiati et al. (2007) found that the classroom approach was equally effective. The ABA program in their study showed a decrease in IQ, not typical of well-run programs (Peyton, Mruzek, & Smith, 2008), and the "autism-specific" classroom showed no change in IQ. Overall, where EIBI was implemented correctly, all studies found that EIBI was more effective than eclectic approaches on most if not all measures.

Sallows and Graupner (2005) used random assignment to compare two versions of EIBI over 4 years: A clinic-directed group (UCLA model, $N = 13$, age $= 35$ months, IQ $= 50.9$) and a parent-directed EIBI group, where parents could select the number of hours and supervision was biweekly rather than weekly ($N = 10$, age $= 37.1$ months, IQ $= 52.1$). It was initially anticipated that this would be a low-hour EIBI control group; however, parents selected an average of 32 hours per week (range 25–40 hours), versus the 39 hours that was provided to the clinic-directed group, changing the parent-directed condition from a control group to a second treatment group with slightly fewer (but still intensive) hours, and less intensive supervision. After 4 years there were no significant differences between clinic- and parent-directed groups, indicating that twice-monthly supervision and slightly lower hours were as effective as treatment following the UCLA model. Combining data from both treatment groups, children showed a mean improvement in IQ from 51 to 76 ($d = 2.56$, large) as well as significant improvements in Vineland Adaptive Behavior Scales (VABS) communication and socialization, language comprehension (Clinical Evaluation of Language Fundamentals, [CELF-III]), and Autism Diagnostic Interview-Revised (ADI-R) reciprocal social interaction and communication scales. Eleven of 23 children (48%) learned new skills quickly, their IQ scores reached the average range, increasing from 55 (range 44–73) to 104 (range 85–126), achieved post-treatment scores in the average range on language, socialization, adaptive, and academic skills tests, and succeeded in regular first-grade classrooms.

Howlin, Magiati, and Charman (2009) reviewed 13 EIBI studies and concluded that these studies produced large increases in IQ, especially during the first year, and language scores. They questioned the superiority of EIBI, hypothesizing that less well-trained staff in other types of interventions may have led to poorer results, and that intensity rather than the intervention itself may have been responsible for the differences. The authors interpreted the observation that the largest gains occurred during the first year as evidence that the effects

of ABA were brief and then deteriorated. We noted that this was an artifact of increasing age. In our study (Sallows & Graupner, 2005), IQ of rapid learners increased 18 months per year throughout treatment. Using a ratio estimate of IQ for illustrative purposes, we can see that from an IQ of 50, a gain of 18 months during the 1 year from age 3 to 4 yields an increase in IQ from 50 (18/36) to 75 (36/48), a 25-point increase; however, a gain of 18 months from an IQ of 100 during the 1 year from age 6 to 7 yields an increase in IQ from 100 (72/72) to 107 (90/84), a 7-point increase. Graphing these data points yields a decreasing slope in spite of a constant rate of gain.

Meta-Analyses of Comprehensive ABA Programs

Eldevik (2007) performed a meta-analysis of 255 children in 14 ABA programs. Age at start of treatment was strongly related to outcome ($r = 0.926, p < 0.000$), but treatment duration was not, perhaps reflecting a nonlinear response to duration. Eldevik (2007) found that children increased about 18 IQ points from baseline during the first year, then lost about 3 points during the second year and increased about 8 more points to end at about 22 points above baseline after the third year. Weekly hours were strongly related to outcome, with 0–14 hours resulting in less than a 5-point IQ gain, 15–24 hours resulting in a 5-point increase, 25–34 hours resulting in a 15-point increase, and 35+ hours resulting in a mean increase of 21 points.

Makrygianni and Reed (2008) presented a meta-analysis of 22 studies. Mean age at start of treatment was 39 months and mean pre-treatment IQ was 50. Mean number of hours per week was 27 and the mean duration of treatment was 28 months. Mean pre-/post-Cohen's d was 0.967 for IQ (large), 0.877 for language (large), and 0.669 for adaptive behavior (moderate). Mean d's comparing behavioral treatment with control groups were 0.924 for IQ (large), 0.781 for language (moderate to large), and 0.504 for adaptive behavior (moderate). Higher treatment intensity, longer treatment duration, younger age, presence of speech, and higher preintervention adaptive skills were associated with more positive outcome.

Ospina et al. (2008) published a meta-analysis of studies using the UCLA model, which showed that it was significantly more effective than special education on measures of intellectual functioning, language, socialization, and adaptive behaviors. Rogers and Vismara (2008) reached similar conclusions and using Chambless et al. criteria (1998) for evaluating treatment effectiveness, determined that the UCLA model of EIBI met the criteria for a "well-established" treatment.

THE TEACCH PROGRAM

The TEACCH program is primarily classroom-based and consists of a range of approaches to minimize stress during learning, such as use of visual schedules and instructions to compensate for poor language skills, keeping task difficulty low, and allowing children time to engage in self-stimulatory behavior (Schopler, Reichler, & Lansing, 1980). This program accepts rather than remediates the deficits common in autism (Mesibov & Shea, 2005; Smith, 1996), which follows from the program philosophy that these deficits are for the most part irreversible (Erba, 2001; Schopler et al., 1980). The curriculum focuses on basic cognitive, language, and functional skills, such as sorting and assembly tasks, that will be helpful when the children are old enough to work in sheltered workshop settings.

The TEACCH program began in the late 1970s and parent satisfaction surveys have been generally positive (Marcus, Schopler, & Lord, 2001). Two studies evaluated TEACCH. Lord and Schopler (1989) evaluated 213 children aged 2 to 7 prior to beginning TEACCH services and again 2–5 years later. Three-year-olds gained 7 IQ points, 4-year-olds gained

3 points, and 6-year-olds lost 1 point. Three-year-olds whose pretreatment IQ was below 50 showed a gain from 38 to 57 using the Bayley Scales of Infant Development at baseline, whereas post-testing used the Merrill-Palmer Scale of Mental Tests. Children who had been tested with the Merrill-Palmer at both pre- and post-testing scored only 2.5 points higher. Lord and Schopler noted that the Merrill-Palmer scored spuriously high compared to the Bayley and concluded that "IQ is a relatively stable characteristic, even of young autistic children" (p. 495). Proponents of TEACCH, however, have subsequently omitted Lord and Schopler's disclaimer when referring to this study (Smith, 1999), stating instead that "substantial increases in IQ are quite common in children first assessed at age 3 or 4" (Marcus et al., 2001, p. 228).

Ozonoff and Cathcart (1998) compared a behaviorally-based classroom with a home-based version of TEACCH utilizing weekly parent training sessions and focusing on teaching imitation, communication, preacademics, and prevocational skills, similar to an ABA curriculum. Pre-post testing was done by each child's own treatment staff, rather than by blind evaluators. Results after 10 weeks of treatment (the pre- to posttest interval was 16.5 weeks) found that the mean Psycho-Educational Profile (PEP-R) total scores were higher for the treatment group, but this was due to increases in motor skills, imitation, and nonverbal performance items, not verbal reasoning or language items. There have been no other outcome studies using standardized measures.

DEVELOPMENTAL INTERVENTIONS

In Greenspan and Wieder's (1997) theory, children with autism are seen as having biological deficiencies in sensory processing and modulation. Autism is understood as the result of the mother-child relationships breaking down due to parents' inability to maintain a bond with the infant because of these deficiencies. Treatment is intended to help parents work around their child's processing difficulties so as to reestablish affective contact, posited as necessary for the normal developmental process to resume. To accomplish this, Greenspan teaches parents to implement several strategies in "floor time": for example, following the child's lead, offering help, prompting interaction by asking permission to join, interfering with the child's activities ("playful obstruction"), and playing "dumb" while requesting the child's help.

Consensus Panel Recommendations

The NRC (2001) chapter by Amy Wetherby stated "the empirical support for developmental approaches is more limited than for behavioral approaches" (p. 54). The NYSDOH (1999) concluded that some aspects of Greenspan's Developmental, Individual Difference, Relationship (DIR) model may be consistent with elements of effective interventions—for example, "playful obstruction," which is similar to the Incidental Teaching strategy of withholding a desired toy until the child requests it (Smith & Wick, 2008). However, due to the lack of validating research, the NYSDOH recommended that approaches based on DIR theory and practices not be used as primary intervention methods.

Studies reviewed for this chapter included DIR/Floortime (Greenspan & Wieder, 1997), the Denver Model (Rogers & DiLalla, 1991; Rogers & Lewis, 1989), the PLAY Project (Solomon, Necheles, Ferch, & Bruckman, 2007), Relationship Development Intervention (RDI, Gutstein, unpublished, 2003; Gutstein, Burgess, & Montfort, 2007), and Responsive Teaching (Mahoney & Perales, 2005). All of these studies had serious methodological problems, including retrospective selection of subjects, lack of matched controls, non-standard tests and measures, unblinded diagnoses, and data consisting of ratings by parents or treatment staff. We conclude that, based on the above shortcomings, comprehensive

developmental interventions do not meet the requirements for evidence-based treatments.

Combining Developmental and Behavioral Approaches

The SCERTS model (Social Communication, Emotional Regulation, and Transactional Support) is intended to be a comprehensive intervention bridging the gap between developmental and behavioral approaches (Prizant, Wetherby, Rubin, & Laurent, 2003). The authors base the legitimacy of SCERTS on shared philosophies with other well-known approaches including Floor Time, Responsive Teaching, RDI, Hanen, PRT, and results of other studies, for example, Aldred et al. (2004), Kasari, Freeman, and Paparella (2006), and Drew et al. (2002). Except for PRT, none of these programs or studies meet criteria for evidence-based comprehensive interventions. SCERTS includes a few other evidence-based behavioral interventions, such as Functional Communication Training (FCT), Positive Behavioral Supports (PBS), and visual supports, but no outcome research exists on the effectiveness of SCERTS as a whole, so that it cannot be considered evidence-based.

Dawson et al. (2010) described an RCT with 48 young autistic children (mean age 24 months at start of treatment), randomly assigned to treatment (Early Start Denver Model) or available community services. The ESDM intervention is manualized in Rogers and Dawson (2010), and is based on Pivotal Response Training combined with a developmental focus on increasing parental sensitivity and responsiveness to child cues, joint attention and shared engagement. The therapist sets out toys, and when the child shows interest in a toy or activity, the therapist implements specific interactions designed to address several of the child's goals during each play episode. This pattern is repeated every few minutes in order to address each of the 20 or so goals five times per hour. Mean pre-treatment IQ was 60 (Mullen) and Vineland ABC was 70 for both groups. Treatment was provided by trained staff, scheduled for 20 hours per week (mean 15), supervised weekly by an experienced clinician. Parents were trained to provide treatment and reported doing so 16 hours per week. Results after 2 years, 4 months showed an increase in IQ for the ESDM group of 17.6 points versus 6.9 points for the control group. On the Vineland ABC, the ESDM group showed no change (–0.8 points), whereas the control group lost 10.8 points. The ESDM group gained 13.7 points on the Communication subscale and lost points on all other scales, as did the control group. Based on ADOS scores, there were no changes in autism symptoms and no difference between groups in autism severity (ESDM 7.0; control 7.3). To put these results in context, less able children (IQ 51, Vineland ABC 60) who received the UCLA version of ABA for 2 years (from Sallows & Graupner, 2005) showed similar gains in IQ (20.7 points) and Vineland Communication (16.6 points), but also showed larger gains in Vineland ABC (8.3, 9.1 points higher), socialization (10.39, 15.0 points higher), and significant improvements in autism symptoms (ADI-R).

SOCIAL SKILLS INTERVENTIONS

Social skill delays of children with ASD do not improve with age (White, Koenig, & Scahill, 2007). Although many parents send their preschool-age children with ASD to school to foster social skills, the results are often disappointing. Acquisition of social skills does not occur without training and preparation of teachers (Wetherby & Woods, 2006), classmates (Kamps et al., 2002; Terpstra, Higgins, & Pierce, 2002), or the children with autism (Anderson, Moore, Godfrey, & Fletcher-Flinn, 2004; R. L. Koegel & Koegel, 2006; Olley, 2005; Owen-DeSchryver, Carr, Cale, & Blakley-Smith, 2008). Without a specific intervention, neurotypical children tend to play with each other or to victimize children with autism (R. L. Koegel & Koegel, 2006), while

children with autism tend to isolate (DiSalvo & Oswald, 2002; Pierce & Schreibman, 1997; Terpstra et al., 2002), even when typical classmates are nearby (Anderson et al., 2004; R. L. Koegel & Koegel, 2006). Children with Asperger's Disorder and high-functioning autism become aware of their differences and view themselves as greater than one *SD* lower than their typical peers in social skills, with 30% to 40% showing symptoms of anxiety and depression as they enter adolescence and adulthood (Rao, Bidel, & Murray, 2008; Solomon, Goodlin-Jones, & Anders, 2004; White et al., 2007). Preschool children with ASD who avoid peers tend to continue this pattern and use less language as they age (Ingersoll, Schreibman, & Stahmer, 2001).

Consensus Panel Recommendations

The NRC chapter on interventions to build social skills was the primary responsibility of Sally Rogers. She noted that "more empirical data are available to support the efficacy of behavioral interventions than developmental interventions," and that there is "very little data on the effectiveness of developmental approaches for social development in early autism" (p. 81). She concluded that for children with little appropriate spontaneous behavior, adult-directed approaches were more effective for building new skills, but child-directed interventions such as Incidental Teaching, PRT, or peer mediated approaches, should be used to build fluency, generalization, and maintenance. For more able children, Rogers postulated that child-directed "naturalistic" approaches may be as effective as adult-directed interventions.

The NYSDOH concluded that effective approaches included peer mediation, although generalization to untrained peers was weak; direct teaching of specific social skills including initiating play, cooperative play, and giving compliments, behavioral momentum, and training parents and peers to implement Incidental Teaching.

Precursors to Social and Communication Skills

Several skills that normally appear in infancy or early childhood are correlated with later language, social skills, and cognitive functioning (Kasari, Freeman, & Paparella, 2006). Pointing and showing appears at 9 months (Jones & Carr, 2004), joint attention (JA) is typically present by 1 to 1.5 years (Bono, Daley, & Sigman, 2004; Whalen & Schreibman, 2003), pretend or symbolic play is present in the second year of life (Jones & Carr, 2004; Stahmer, 1999), and theory of mind skills (ToM) appear at about age 4 (Charlop-Christy & Daneshvar, 2003).

Joint Attention

There are two aspects of JA: Responding to others' bids for attention and initiating JA. Whalen and Schreibman (2003) observed six typical preschoolers (mean age 2 years, 4 months, MA 2 years, 5 months) in an unstructured JA assessment, during which an adult played with the child and initiated JA every 30 seconds by showing objects, pointing, or shifting gaze toward an object or picture on the wall. Typical children responded to 82% of their partner's JA initiations and initiated during 23% of intervals throughout the 30-minute session. When involved with an object, typical children initiated JA about every 10 seconds or roughly six times per minute. Bono et al. (2004) noted that 49% of children with autism respond to bids for JA prior to treatment. Joint attention can be increased (Hwang & Hughes, 2000; Ingersoll & Schreibman, 2006; Whalen & Schreibman, 2003; Yoder & Stone, 2006), with response to JA showing more improvement than initiation (Jones & Carr, 2004; Whalen & Schreibman, 2003).

Joint attention may underlie more complex social-communicative skills and several writers have stated that it should therefore be directly addressed (Baron-Cohen, 1995; Kasari, Paparella, Freeman, & Jahromi, 2008; Wetherby & Woods, 2006); however, several studies in which JA has been targeted have found contradictory results. For example, when JA has increased, predicted improvements in speech and play skills have not occurred (Ingersoll & Schreibman, 2006; Tsao & Odom, 2006) and increasing maternal responsiveness resulted in increases in child social-communicative skills, but not JA (Aldred, Green, & Adams, 2004). When treatment ends, JA has often dropped to baseline levels (Ingersoll & Schreibman, 2006; Whalen & Schreibman, 2003) or failed to generalize to other adults (Hwang & Hughes, 2000; Ingersoll & Schreibman, 2006; Whalen & Schreibman, 2003), whereas child social-communication skills were maintained (Hwang & Hughes, 2000; Ingersoll & Schreibman, 2006).

Kasari et al. (2008) published the largest JA study in which 65 children with autism were randomly assigned to three groups: One targeted JA directly, one targeted symbolic play, and one was a no-treatment control group. Treatment was 30 minutes per day for 5 to 6 weeks. Follow-up 12 months later found that both treatment groups increased expressive language by 15 months compared to 10 months for the control group, showing that JA training was not necessary to improve social-communicative behaviors. Bono et al. (2004) noted that interventions of all kinds include episodes of JA because treatment staff have to get the child to attend to the same object or activity in order to impart or request information about it. The best predictor of increases in expressive language was pretreatment expressive language rather than pretreatment JA; however, among children who had poor pretreatment expressive language, those in the JA group showed the largest improvement in expressive language, from a language age of about 15 months to about 28–29 months at follow-up 15 months later when the children were 58 months old. Analyzing more data from their earlier study, Whalen and Schreibman (2006) found that JA training did not affect level of play, but did improve initiation of social behaviors;

however, these returned to near baseline at 3-month follow-up.

Yoder and Stone (2006) randomly assigned 36 children with autism, ages 2 to 9 years old, to a PECS, or a naturalistic strategy to teach JA. Results showed the naturalistic procedure was more effective in increasing JA initiations for children who already had some JA prior to treatment, whereas PECS was more effective for children with only minimal pretreatment JA.

While JA training resulted in some improvements, abilities of treated children remained far below those of typical children, raising questions about clinical significance. R. L. Koegel and Koegel (2006) commented that it is not yet clear whether directly targeting JA will produce lasting collateral changes in other behaviors.

Theory of Mind

A lack of the ability to understand another person's point of view, termed *ToM*, is thought by some to underlie the difficulties that children with ASD have in interpreting social gestures, facial expressions, other's intentions, or in general how to act so as to have friends (Baron-Cohen, 1995). Although children with ASD do poorly on ToM tasks, they can learn to do better (Charlop-Christy & Daneshvar, 2003). However, Olley (2005) concluded that attempts to teach ToM have been largely unsuccessful and that there have been no reports of generalization to other cognitive or social behaviors.

Yoder and Stone (2006) hypothesized that true JA and its consequences are internal events. Charlop-Christy and Daneshvar (2003) pointed out that the usual behaviors by which the presence of JA or ToM are inferred may not be valid indicators of these internal events. Jones and Carr (2004) hypothesized that pointing, showing, and giving may in young children be reinforced by getting attention, rather than by shared focus, and that response to JA bids may be reinforced by seeing an interesting object.

INCREASING SOCIAL INTERACTION SKILLS

Peer Mediation

There are a number of approaches to peer mediation, including integrated groups, peer tutoring, peer buddies, and extensively trained peers. Roeyers (1996) reported the largest study of integrated groups ($N = 85$) with one peer assigned to each child. Training consisted of informing peers about the problems of children with autism, but not what the peers should do. Results showed that the children with ASD increased interaction by 20%, but their interactions remained idiosyncratic (i.e., still unusual).

Two studies used peer tutoring. In one (Kamps, Barbetta, Leonard, & Delquadri, 1994), classroom peers were assigned as tutors for children with autism and in the other (Kamps, Dugan, Potucek, & Collins, 1999), 9-year-old children with ASD tutored typical first graders. In both studies interaction increased but data on generalization was contradictory.

Using peer buddies, Laushey and Heflin (2000) instructed each peer to play and talk with their assigned child with high-functioning autism on the playground ($N = 2$, reversal design). Compared to baseline, when there was no peer buddy, children with HFA increased initiation by about 37%. Using a similar strategy, Goldstein, Schneider, and Thiemann (2007) reported generalization to different trained peers ($N = 8$).

Several studies have extensively trained groups of peers of various sizes (from two to the entire class) to initiate and maintain conversation, respond to conversation, give compliments, share, and give instructions to the child with autism. Two studies by Kamps and colleagues (Garrison-Harrell, Kamps, & Kravits, 1997; Kamps, Potucek, Lopez, Kravitz, & Kemmerer, 1997) found that children with autism increased their interactions, and two of three children showed generalization to nontreatment settings with trained peers present. Two studies by Strain and colleagues (Kohler et al., 1995; Lefebvre & Strain, 1989) added group reinforcement contingencies and found that interaction increased over that achieved through social skills training alone, but children showed high variability in the amount of interaction during treatment and maintenance was poor.

Pivotal Response Training

Robert Koegel developed PRT (Koegel et al., 1989) as a way to shorten the treatment process and increase generalization by imbedding discrete trials in real-life settings and activities that the child is interested in at the moment. The PRT procedures also include varying activities, rewarding attempts, using reinforcers that are powerful at the moment, taking turns, and narrating thought processes or actions (Harper, Symon, & Frea, 2008). Three studies taught peers to use PRT strategies when interacting with children with autism (Harper et al., 2008; Pierce & Schreibman, 1995, 1997). All six children ($N = 2$ per study) began to take turns, initiate play, and interact, but only one child generalized these skills to an untrained peer. Stahmer (1995) found that PRT was effective in increasing pretend play in seven children. They also observed some generalization to other adults but much less so to peers, and generalization mostly involved JA responses rather than JA initiations. Studies using methods other than PRT also found increases in social interactions and results were better with more peers, with girls tending to be better (Owen-DeSchryver et al., 2008). One of three children increased initiations almost to the range of typical peers during the intervention, but there were no data on maintenance.

Social Scripts

Krantz and McClannahan (1993) taught four children with autism to initiate interactions with peers by using a script containing 10 written statements that were gradually faded. Results showed increases in scripted and unscripted initiations, with generalization and maintenance in three of four children. Goldstein et al. (2007) described several of their own studies, one of which involved three children with ASD who learned sociodramatic play scripts (e.g., customer, salesperson, and animal handler in a pet shop). Children learned the roles, each of which contained 10 statements and demonstrated generalization to a new trained peer.

Modeling

Video Self-Modeling

Bellini and Akullian (2007) reviewed 29 studies published between 1987 and 2005 using video modeling in single-subject designs, 15 of which addressed social-communication skills. For example, Wert and Neisworth (2003) used video self-modeling (VSM) in which the target child was the model, to increase requesting. During videotaped structured peer play sessions, verbal children were prompted to request play items. Afterward, the prompts were edited out. The edited tapes, which depicted the child seeming to independently request a toy, were then shown to the children. All four children showed substantial increases in spontaneous verbal requests (Percent of Nonoverlapping Data [PND] = 96%). A PND over 90% indicates a "highly effective" treatment, and these increases were maintained at follow-up (PND = 100%). Buggey, Toombs, Gardner, and Cervetti (1999) used VSM with three children to increase answering questions during play (PND = 75%; a PND of 70% to 90% indicates an "effective" treatment), but once the video modeling sessions were stopped, maintenance was poor (PND = 44%; a PND under 50% indicates an ineffective intervention). Buggey (2005) used VSM to address several social behaviors with five children, ages 5 to 11 years, including social initiations, responding to questions, pushing others, and tantrums. All children showed immediate acquisition of the targeted behaviors (PND = 87%) and maintenance was high

(PND = 100%). Unfortunately, studies with small numbers of participants do not allow interpretation of disparate results, and outcomes may not be representative of those found in other small groups. Further, increases in PND scores compare improvements with baseline, not with scores of typical peers, leaving unanswered the question of whether participants behave like typical peers. This is relevant at least in young children with ASD, because improvements to the typical range are possible for many children with effective treatments.

Video Modeling

Simpson, Langone, and Ayres (2004) used a computer-based program showing a picture card with the definition of the target behavior, after which the four children, ages 5 to 6 years, observed a video of peers demonstrating examples and nonexamples of the targeted behavior, such as sharing, complying with teacher directions, and social greetings. All children acquired the skills rapidly (PND = 97%). Apple, Billingsley, and Schwartz (2005) found that video modeling alone led to increases in responding to compliments, but not giving compliments until tangible reinforcers were introduced. Maintenance of giving complements was poor.

Sherer et al. (2001) compared video modeling with VSM in teaching conversation skills with five children, ages 4 to 11 years. Three of the five children reached 100% mastery, whereas the other two did not reach mastery with either method (PND = 78% for all five children). There were no overall differences between video modeling and video self-modeling.

In Vivo Modeling

Jahr, Eldevik, and Eikeseth (2000) used an intensive in vivo modeling approach to teach cooperative play and conversation to six children with autism. Children were verbal 4- to 12-year-olds. During training, children observed familiar adults demonstrate a scripted episode of cooperative play, with each adult demonstrating one action. For example, one adult says "Let's play," and builds a fence, followed by the other putting a cow inside the fence. After the demonstration, children were asked to describe in order what both models had done and to take the place of one of the models as the episode was repeated. All six children met mastery criteria that included generalization and use of novel responses. Follow-up after 10 months showed maintenance of gains.

Charlop-Christy, Le, and Freeman (2000) compared the effectiveness of video modeling versus in vivo modeling for teaching conversational speech, spontaneous greetings, and play behavior to five children, ages 7 to 11. Children learned the tasks (PND = 73%) faster using video modeling than in vivo modeling.

Meta-Analysis of Video Modeling

Bellini and Akullian (2007) completed a meta-analysis of 23 studies using video modeling published between 1987 and 2005 with children and adolescents diagnosed with autism, PDD-NOS, or Asperger's disorder. The studies included 73 subjects (ages 3 to 20 years) and 20 primary researchers across 13 states and 4 countries. Fourteen of the 23 studies were done in schools. The mean PND was 80% for treatment, 83% for maintenance, and 74% for generalization, all in the "effective" range. Age of participants was not a significant factor in outcome.

Self-Management

Self-management programs begin with teaching children to observe and count their own behavior accurately, with the teacher reinforcing accurate self-observation. Next, children learn to reinforce their own behavior only when it meets criterion. Finally, the teacher withdraws, leaving children observing, counting, and reinforcing their own behavior independently (L. K. Koegel, Koegel, & Parks, 1992). Apple et al. (2005) found that, after gains returned to baseline following an earlier intervention, self-management was effective for rebuilding compliment giving (PND = 98%), and maintenance was high (PND = 100%). Stahmer and Schreibman (1992) described a self-management program used to teach appropriate play to three children, ages 7–13 years, with mild to moderate delays. Appropriate play increased from 10%–15% at baseline to 80%–96% during self-management, and remained high as the three children took over the procedure. Concurrently, self-stimulation decreased from 13% for two children and 66% for the third at baseline to 2%–3% for all three during self-management.

Newman, Tuntigian, Ryan, and Reinecke (1997) described a self-management procedure to reduce problem behaviors in a classroom, including being out-of-seat and self-stimulating with three children ages 4, 6, and 12 with mild to moderate intellectual disability and autism. Following treatment, results showed reduction in out-of-seat to zero and self-stimulation to 10% of intervals. These gains were maintained during the shift to independent self-reinforcement. Interestingly, none of the children were accurate in terms of reinforcing their own behavior, but their inappropriate behaviors nevertheless remained near zero.

Meta-Analysis of Self-Management Procedures

Lee, Simpson, and Shogren (2007) found 11 articles between 1992 and 2004 where self-management was used to increase positive behaviors. The meta-analysis included data from 34 children, aged 3 to 17 years. Twenty-nine percent were preschool age (3–5 years), 71% were school-age (6–17 years), and 53% of the studies were done in school settings. The overall PND for all subjects was 81.9% (effective).

Social Skills Groups

While social skills groups are a common strategy for addressing social interaction deficits, no studies have used randomized controlled designs with blind evaluators and standardized tests. Solomon, Goodlin-Jones, and Anders (2004) described a study conducted at the UC Davis MIND Institute in which children were randomly assigned to a social skills group ($N = 10$) or to a waiting list control group ($N = 9$). Children were 8- to 12-years-old, high-functioning (had IQs over 75), and could pass a first-order ToM task. The group met weekly for 1.5 hours for 20 weeks and addressed emotional face recognition, body language, perspective-taking and interpersonal problem solving, conversation skills such as staying on topic, and handling teasing. Concurrently, parents attended a group where they learned to understand their children's behavior within the context of the social deficits of autism, and helped each other develop strategies for addressing their child's day-to-day problems. Results showed that a subgroup of the highest functioning children learned to identify facial emotions. Other than this, there were no effects for face recognition, ToM, social problem solving, child depression, maternal depression, or maternal satisfaction and confidence in dealing with their child's behavior.

Several other studies of social skills groups used role-playing and practice to address specific skills, including: giving compliments, helping, sharing ideas, and self-control, plus teacher and parent training (Kroeger, Schultz, & Newsom, 2007; Webb, Miller, Pierce, Strawser, & Jones, 2004); eye contact, introductions, awareness of and expression of feelings, reading nonverbal communication, conversational skills, negotiation, dealing with teasing and bullying, hygiene, and dining etiquette at a restaurant (Tse, Strulovitck, Tagalaskis, Meng, & Fombonne, 2007), with time to practice with trained peers (Barry et al., 2003; Bauminger, 2002). These studies all found significant results using observational data, written tests or parent rating of skills, but not using normed tests completed by persons uninvolved in treatment.

White et al. (2007) reviewed 14 studies from 1985 to 2006 using social skills groups. Their findings were similar to those found here; that is, positive findings based on observational data and qualitative measures, such as parent questionnaires, but little improvement based on standardized tests. They also found poor generalization to other skills and to peer interaction outside the group. In a review of meta-analyses of social skills, Gresham, Sugai, and Horner (2001) reported poor generalization and maintenance, and suggested that 30 hours of intervention over 10–12 weeks was not enough. DiSalvo and Oswald (2002) hypothesized that poor generalization may result from only teaching a few skills and not building those to the level of neurotypical children, leaving children without enough skills to interact with untrained peers.

Brinton, Robinson, and Fujiki (2004) described a program for a 14-year-old child with HFA, who experienced anxiety over his social isolation and inability to converse satisfactorily with peers. The 2-year treatment (two 1-hour sessions per week) began with identifying others' feelings, emotions, and intentions by watching movie clips, followed by training in maintaining conversational topic, drawing others into the conversation, introducing new topics, and responding to others' statements. Although it always required conscious thought, the boy learned to converse and interact normally enough that peers began to invite him to participate in their social activities.

Meta-Analysis of Social Skills Treatments

Matson, Matson, and Rivet (2007) reviewed 79 studies, over 90% of which were single-subject designs, most of which were school-based, and included studies using modeling, peer mediation, reinforcement and activity schedules, scripts, and social stories. No summary data were reported. The authors recommended using a pretreatment assessment to identify deficits and to be sure that

there was actually a deficit rather than another explanation for poor interaction—such as lack of reinforcement for existing skills, beginning treatment of social skill before age 5 years, and continuing treatment for an extended period—targeting social communication for lower-functioning children and social interaction skills for higher-functioning children.

Bellini, Peters, Benner, and Hopf (2007) reviewed 55 single-subject design school-based studies. The overall PND was 70%, at the bottom of the "effective" range (70%–90%). The PND was 80% for maintenance and 53% during generalization ("ineffective"). There were no significant differences between group versus individual treatment, intensity, or age of participants; however, treatment within the classroom or on the playground was more effective than treatment done in pullout sessions (PND for treatment 76% vs. 62%, maintenance 88% vs. 67%, generalization 67% vs. 29%), consistent with earlier suggestions that decontextualized interventions resulted in poorer outcomes. The authors noted that none of the reviewed studies provided more than 30 hours of intervention, as had been recommended in earlier reviews.

Social Skills in Comprehensive ABA Programs

Combining data from four recent studies (Cohen et al., 2006; Eikeseth et al., 2007; Howard et al., 2005; Sallows & Graupner, 2005), Vineland socialization scores for all children (total $N = 86$) increased from 69 (range 60–73) prior to treatment, to 79 (range 72–86) after 1 to 4 years of treatment. By comparison, children in eclectic special education classes showed no change in socialization standard scores ($N = 40$), with 72 (range 62–76) prior to treatment and 72 (range 58–78) 1 to 3 years later. In our study (Sallows & Graupner, 2005), rapid learners ($N = 11$ of 23) increased socialization standard scores from 62 prior to treatment to 88 4 years later, and the mean posttreatment standard scores based on teacher ratings was 90.

COMMUNICATION INTERVENTIONS

Without treatment, only about 50% of children with autism develop functional speech (NRC, 2001) and many children with minimal communication skills use inappropriate behavior to communicate. The FCT and alternative communication strategies, such as sign language, PECS, and voice output devices are helpful in providing a way for children with poor spoken language skills to express their needs and to communicate with others. Bondy and Frost (1994) reported that after 2 years of using PECS, 39 of 66 children (59%) developed independent speech, although it remained quite limited for many. Howlin, Kate-Gordon, Pasco, Wade, and Charman (2007) found that PECS did not lead to increases in level of speech or general communication development. Sign plus speech has been shown to be more effective than speech alone in helping children learn words; however, none of these strategies is likely to result in acquisition of fluent and flexible typical speech (NRC, 2001, p. 58). In this section, we address strategies for developing spoken language, since difficulty in this area is a major impediment to being able to succeed in mainstream social situations.

Consensus Panel Recommendations

The NRC chapter on communication was the primary responsibility of Amy Wetherby. She stated that the core communication deficits in autism are social communication and pragmatics, reflecting poor joint attention and symbol use as in pretend play. She organized language-building strategies into (a) those modeled after Lovaas and colleagues; (b) "more contemporary behavioral approaches," such as PRT, Incidental Teaching, Time Delay, and Milieu Treatment; and (c) "developmentally oriented approaches," such as Greenspan's DIR and Rogers' Colorado Health Sciences program. She recommended direct intervention to build joint attention and symbolic play as a way to build speech. The NYDOH found support for sign plus speech, Time Delay, peer modeling, and Pivotal Response Training.

ABA Approaches

Following relationship building through positive interaction and increased responsiveness to child cues, the earliest programs in an ABA curriculum for a nonverbal child build attention and generalized imitation. Concurrently, receptive language is targeted using visual cues; for example, "give" accompanied by holding the hand out palm-up near an object. The child experiences success 80%–90% of the time by breaking tasks down to small steps, initially prompting success (errorless prompting) and using powerful reinforcers. Expressive speech begins with increasing rates of vocalization and imitation of simple sounds. Visual cues may be used, including pictures, objects, signs, or a mirror. Once a child can imitate about 10 single sounds, most can combine them without confusion. A typical standard speech therapy curriculum proceeds as follows: (a) consonant-vowel (cv), such as "ma," "bee"; (b) cvc, such as "mom," "dad"; (c) cvcv, such as "papa," "mama"; (d) cv(1) cv(2), such as "puppy," "baby," "cookie"; and finally (e) c(1)vc(2), such as "cat," "juice." Lovaas (1981) recommended that once children could say a few words or stable approximations, they should be taught to use the words as requests for desired items, since making words functional is a powerful way to increase their use. Vocabulary is built by first using receptive strategies; for example, the adult requests an object by labeling it, followed by an errorless prompt to give the correct object (Lovaas, 1981). Generalization is accomplished by having many adults present many examples of the object in different settings, although in practice, problems with generalizing labels are uncommon (see Sallows, 2005, for a more detailed description).

Brief Review of ABA Comprehensive Studies

Several comprehensive ABA intervention programs have found large increases in language skills using standardized tests (Cohen et al., 2006; Eikeseth et al., 2002, 2007; Eldevik et al., 2006; Howard et al., 2005; Sallows & Graupner, 2005; Smith, Groen, & Wynn, 2000). Eikeseth et al. (2002) found an increase in expressive language of 22.6 points on the Reynell Developmental Language Scale (RDLS) following 1 year of treatment versus a loss of 2.2 points for an eclectic group. Howard et al. (2005) reported an increase of 17.2 months in expressive language over 14 months of treatment on the RDLS, compared to 7.5 months for an autism-specific classroom and 4.5 months for generic special education. In our study, scores for receptive language of rapid learners (48% of treated children) increased from below the bottom of the scale (12 months, RDLS) to a standard score of 93.6 (CELF-III) after 3 to 4 years of treatment. Expressive language increased from below the bottom of the scale (15 months, RDLS) to a standard score of 85.7 (CELF-III). These children spoke fluently in social situations as reported by parents and teachers using the classroom version of the Vineland.

Naturalistic Approaches

Incidental Teaching (Hart & Risley, 1968) involves waiting for the child to approach a toy (child choice), and reach for it (showing it was a reinforcer at that moment), then intervening by holding the toy while looking expectantly to cue the child to request it. In Time Delay, the therapist waits for a predetermined interval before modeling the correct response. Naturalistic strategies were developed as a way to improve generalization after it was observed that some children treated with the UCLA approach had trouble using mastered language outside the therapy setting (Lovaas, Koegel, Simmons, & Long, 1973). Robert Koegel further developed this approach as the Natural Language Paradigm (R. L. Koegel, O'Dell, & Koegel, 1987) and in 1989 as PRT (R. L. Koegel et al., 1989). He and his colleagues had the child select from an array of preferred items (*environmental arrangement*), demonstrated and described appropriate play with the object (*linguistic mapping*), labeling it as the child reached for it, intermixing mastered items to increase response motivation, and reinforcing all vocalizations and attempts by the child to communicate, rather than waiting for closer approximations. Milieu Teaching (Hancock & Kaiser, 2002) is a similar approach.

Brief Review of Naturalistic Studies

McGee, Morrier, and Daly (1999) used Incidental Teaching to increase speech with 28 children ages 2 to 5 years. The number of children who spoke words increased from 36% to 82% 1 year later; however, no data were presented on the number of words spoken, the number of children who could speak in phrases, or whether the words spoken were used in social contexts. Several single-subject design studies have shown that naturalistic procedures have been effective in increasing number of utterances and verbal imitation (McGee et al., 1999); spontaneous object labels (McGee, Krantz, Mason, & McClannahan, 1983); short phrases (Charlop-Christy & Carpenter, 2000); articulation (R. L. Koegel, O'Dell, & Dunlap, 1988), which generalized to home and school (R. L. Koegel, Camarata, Koegel, Ben-Tall, & Smith, 1998); "Yes" and "No" in response to questions (Neef, Walters, & Egel, 1984); expressive prepositions (McGee, Krantz, & McClannahan, 1985); and asking questions (L. K. Koegel, Koegel, Shoshan, & McNerney, 1999). Parents have learned to implement naturalistic procedures (Laski, Charlop, & Schreibman, 1988;

Stahmer & Gist, 2001), and both parents and children have shown positive affect during intervention (Schreibman, Kaneko, & Koegel, 1991).

While naturalistic approaches are effective in building new skills, there have been few comparisons to skills of typical children and improvements have not always been very large. R. L. Koegel et al. (1988) reported that three out of four children showed improved articulation of sounds, but it was unclear whether any learned to say words correctly. Laski et al. (1988) found that seven out of eight children improved verbal imitation, but only half showed improvement in use of spontaneous words. Stahmer and Gist (2001) found increases in number of words used, but there was disagreement between a parent measure and direct observation regarding whether this was due to PRT. R. L. Koegel et al. (1987) and Neef et al. (1984) found that learning to label an object to request it did not generalize to labeling it when asked "What is it?" or "Is this a ball?" when shown a ball. McGee et al. (1985) found that children learned expressive prepositions in treatment (e.g., "The bear is under the box"), but did not respond correctly with untrained items. Other studies have found that "linguistic mapping" may not add much to PRT treatment effects (Ingersoll & Schreibman, 2006) and that imbedding intervention into a daily activity may result in only limited improvement in dissimilar settings where the intervention was not used (Woods, Kashinath, & Goldstein, 2004). Hancock and Kaiser (2002) implemented Milieu Teaching for 5 months with four preschool-age children who could already speak 10 words, and reported that language-age increased 6 months over 12 months time, representing a low rate of gain.

Comparison of ABA and Naturalistic Studies

Several of the aforementioned studies have compared naturalistic and ABA approaches,

concluding that naturalistic interventions were superior (Delprato, 2001; R. L. Koegel & Koegel, 2006); however, there were problems with the comparisons, rendering many of the results uninterpretable. The most common problem was providing an inaccurate representation of ABA intervention; for example, repeatedly instructing a child who had no speech to say "ball" (R. L. Koegel et al., 1987), and 45-minute sessions focusing only on verbal imitation (R. L. Koegel, Koegel, & Surratt, 1992). Also, not allowing standard ABA generalization strategies, such as having the child identify and label items around the house once having learned them both receptively and expressively in a less distracting setting (McGee et al., 1985), not allowing therapists to demonstrate correct practices, or parents to observe therapists working (Schreibman et al., 1991), only reinforcing children for equaling or surpassing earlier performance (R. L. Koegel et al., 1988), and learning to say "yes" or "no" with regard to desires in the naturalistic condition versus "yes" or "no" for facts in the ABA condition, which is a later developing skill (Rossetti, 2006).

In summary, naturalistic approaches have resulted in improved language skills and have shown some evidence of generalizing to new settings, but less so to untrained items, indicating that using naturalistic approaches does not remove the need to program for generalization. Given the shortcomings in the comparison studies, Goldstein (2002) concluded in a review of treatment efficacy of interventions for communication deficits in autism that "there is no compelling evidence that milieu teaching procedures [referring to naturalistic procedures] are clearly more effective than the procedures that have been developed out of discrete trial procedures. . . . Many interventions using discrete trial training have produced impressive generalization" (p. 388). Proponents of naturalistic approaches have yet to publish comprehensive or group studies of effectiveness and Schreibman and Ingersoll (2005) commented that it is unclear whether naturalistic approaches can provide the magnitude of gains shown by comprehensive ABA approaches.

Developmental Approaches

Developmental approaches described here aimed to increase parental sensitivity and responsiveness to the child's rudimentary attempts to communicate and interact, thereby providing an intensified version of the normal pathway by which children acquire language. The Hanen program is one example. It is a manualized 11-week parent training program. McConachie, Randle, Hammal, and Le Couteur (2005) compared 17 children receiving treatment with 12 children on a wait-list. Results after 7 months showed no change in the Autism Diagnostic Observation Schedule (ADOS) communication, social interaction scales, or in behavior problems. Vocabulary based on parent report increased for the treatment group, but these figures may reflect different expectations on the part of parents in treatment versus those waiting for treatment. Girolametto, Sussman, and Weitzman (2007) implemented Hanen with three children and measured effects using coded videotapes. Results when the children were about 39 months old showed that they all increased the number of spoken words, while the number of new words increased from a mean of 13 to 32, which is a fairly small improvement compared to the typical 3-year-old, who uses hundreds of words. The authors noted that the child's rate of speech was highly dependent on the mother's rate of initiations, raising concerns regarding maintenance and generalization.

Aldred et al. (2004) reported results of an RCT with random assignment of 14 children to treatment and 14 to a no-treatment control group matched on total ADOS scores. In this manualized treatment, parents were trained to increase coordinated attention and decrease intrusive demands, while increasing synchronous communications, such as ongoing verbal commentary on the child's actions, interpreting the child's vocalizations as words, establishing predictable play routines (e.g., peek-a-boo), and promoting intentionality using teasing and pauses to create opportunities for the child to initiate communicative acts. After 1 year of intervention, ADOS scores in social interaction were better for children in treatment, but there were no differences for ADOS communication or stereotypic behavior. Increases in parent-reported vocabulary were higher for children in treatment. Vineland Communication raw scores favored the treatment group, but increases in age equivalents were quite similar and standard scores (correcting for maturation) showed no gains for either group. By comparison, after 1 year of treatment, children in our study ($N = 23$) showed increases in Vineland Communication of 14 points ($p < .002$).

INAPPROPRIATE BEHAVIOR

Aggression, self-injurious behavior, property destruction, pica, self-stimulation, noncompliance, and disruptive behavior are major barriers to educational and social development (Horner, Carr, Strain, Todd, & Reed, 2002) and are the behaviors most likely to prevent school inclusion (Olley, 2005). Children displaying such problem behavior are also at risk for exclusion from social relationships, typical home environments, and community activities (Horner et al., 2002). Once problem behaviors are established as part of a child's repertoire, they are unlikely to change and are instead more likely to get worse without treatment (Bregman, Zager, & Gerdtz, 2005; Horner et al., 2002).

Consensus Panel Recommendations

The NRC chapter on interventions to reduce behavior problems was prepared primarily by Marie Bristol-Powers and Sam Odom, who noted that long-term reduction of behavior problems requires that intervention programs build positive and prosocial alternative behaviors to take their place. The authors stated "Forty years of single-subject-design research testifies to the efficacy of time-limited, focused ABA methods in reducing or eliminating specific problem behaviors and in teaching new skills to children and adults with autism or other developmental disorders" (NRC, 2001, p. 120). Specific effective interventions include use of visual cues and schedules, modifying curricula and reducing demands, differential reinforcement and extinction, PRT, self-management, and using functional analysis to develop interventions. The authors noted that punishment often results in faster reduction of severe problem behaviors compared to reinforcement-based procedures, and may be necessary to suppress competing problem behaviors before reinforcement of functional appropriate alternative behaviors can be effective; however, strategies to prevent problem behaviors should be the primary approach.

The NYSDOH reached similar conclusions. The studies reviewed showed that using a functional analysis and reinforcement assessment prior to intervention resulted in more successful outcomes.

Visual Strategies

Many writers have noted the effectiveness of a variety of visual strategies for reducing problem behaviors. MacDuff, Krantz, and McClannahan (1993) taught four 9- to 14-year-old children to use photo schedules and physical prompts to complete leisure tasks. Following training, children were on-task for roughly 90% of observation intervals, showed generalization to new schedules without additional training, and no longer required an adult to prompt them to follow schedules. Pierce and Schreibman (1994) combined self-management training and use of picture schedules to help three children become independent in daily living tasks. Results showed increases in task completion and

decreases in inappropriate behavior for all children. Improvements were maintained at 2-month follow-up and generalized to new settings, but all children had trouble when picture schedules were removed. Coyle and Cole (2004) used videotaped self modeling to reduce off-task behavior in the classroom for four children, ages 9 to 11 years. The children were also trained to use a self-monitoring procedure to increase awareness of on-task behavior. Results showed large decreases in off-task behavior (PND = 95%) and the gains were maintained.

Schreibman, Whalen, and Stahmer (2000) described "priming," a procedure used to prepare a child for entering a new situation by first describing what will happen. Videos were made of walking through a typical shopping trip, ending at the child's favorite store. Results showed a rapid drop in tantrums from about 60% prior to intervention to 20%, reaching 0 after 25–30 sessions for all three children. Maintenance data were available for two children and both showed good maintenance. Generalization to another setting occurred immediately for one of the two, and the other generalized after one priming video.

Functional Communication Training

FCT, first described in 1985 by Carr and Durand, is an example of teaching a replacement behavior to reduce an inappropriate behavior that is maintained by the same consequences (*functional equivalence*). Individuals who lacked communication skills learned to use a few basic verbalizations, pictures, or signs to communicate desires, such as "want," "no," and "help." This has been shown effective in decreasing a variety of problem behaviors used to get attention, request desired materials, or to remove demands (Durand & Carr, 1987, 1991). For example, Reeve and Carr (2000) described a study in which eight children with autism, who displayed a variety of problem behaviors maintained by attention, were randomly assigned to FCT or control groups. During times when the teacher was busy, the treatment group used FCT and disruptions decreased; however, the control group showed escalation of intensity and frequency of problem behaviors. When the control group children were switched to the FCT treatment, their problem behaviors also decreased.

Building Alternative Prosocial Behaviors

Teaching appropriate toy play to reduce inappropriate behavior is another example of building replacement behaviors. Eason, White, and Newsom (1982) taught three children a series of play steps with each of several toys. Appropriate play increased from a mean of 11% to 92% of intervals and was maintained and generalized to the classroom 3 months after treatment was discontinued. Concurrently, self-stimulation decreased from 45% to 2% of intervals and remained low at 4% 3 months later in the classroom. Stahmer and Schreibman (1992) found that building appropriate toy play resulted in decreased self-stimulation and that gains were maintained and generalized to new settings and new toys. Turner (1999) described a study in which six autistic children were taught appropriate play skills as a way to decrease self-stimulation. Self-stimulation decreased and the play skills generalized across settings and were maintained at 3-month follow-up.

Behavioral Momentum

Behavioral momentum is based on the observation that if a person is successful with a series of easy tasks, he is more likely to give extra effort when the next task is somewhat more difficult, than he would be if he had not just experienced several preceding successes. Several studies with one or two participants have addressed problem behaviors such as self-stimulation, refusal to take medications, and noncompliance by first getting compliance with several easy instructions (e.g., identifying body parts). Davis, Brady, Hamilton, McEvoy, and Williams (1994) used this strategy to increase compliance with one-step instructions to initiate social interaction in play contexts by three children with autism; for example, "Give the marble to Dave." The rate of initiation increased from near zero at baseline to 0.76 per minute (0.8 is average for typical peers), and time spent interacting increased from 0% to 35% (89% is average for typical peers, according to Jahr, Eikeseth, Eldevik, & Aase, 2007). At follow-up several weeks later, the rate of initiations had decreased to 0.48, but percent of time interacting was maintained. These results generalized to trained and familiar peers in other settings.

Social Stories

Social stores are brief descriptions of problem situations with solutions that are intended to increase a child's understanding of why it is important to respond in a new way. Sansosti, Powell-Smith, and Kincaid (2004) reviewed the literature and found eight empirical studies published since 1995. All were single-subject designs showing that social stories were effective for a variety of behaviors, including reducing an 8-year-old girl's talking to herself at lunchtime, increasing quiet waiting and getting attention politely to reduce tantrums in a 12-year-old boy with moderate intellectual disabilities and autism, and tantrums in a high-functioning boy where tantrums were reinforced by tangibles. Sansosti and Powell-Smith (2006) used social stories successfully with three 9- to 11-year-old children to build initiating conversation and social interaction as a way of decreasing yelling, leaving in the middle of a conversation, and blurting out inappropriate comments. Scattone, Wilczynski, Edwards, and Rabian (2002) used social stories successfully to reduce inappropriate behavior in three children with autism in a special education classroom.

Meta-Analysis of Social Stories

Reynhout and Carter (2006) found 11 peer-reviewed studies and five dissertations on social stories. These represented 60 boys and 17 girls, ages 3 to 15 years. One group study (Feinberg, 2002) included 25 boys and 9 girls, ages 8 to 13 years divided into a treatment and control group. Mean IQ was 71.3 and all could speak in two- to three-word phrases. Target behaviors included staying on-task, asking to play, asking others what they wanted to play, and accepting the peer's choice. Social skills increased only in the experimental group ($d = 0.99$, highly effective).

For the 13 single-subject design studies, the overall PND was 51% (low end of "questionably effective" range 50%–70%) and there was large variability in children's responses. Within studies, some children showed clear improvement, whereas for others the intervention seemed ineffective. Studies using social stories that adhered to Gray's 2003 guidelines regarding story construction were no more effective than stories that did not. Those studies that included more than the recommended proportion of directive and consequence sentences were more effective, with a mean PND of 79% for stories with more directive sentences versus 56% for stories following the guidelines, and 70% for stories with more consequence sentences versus 47% for stories following the guidelines. Due to the low overall PND and the fact that social stories were rarely used alone, the authors concluded that effectiveness of social stories was "not determined."

Differential Reinforcement

There are several types of differential reinforcement, but differential reinforcement of other behavior (DRO) has been used most frequently. In practice, DRO often means reinforcing nonoccurrence of the undesirable target behavior. Bregman et al. (2005) described a study of 5-year-old quadruplets with intellectual disabilities (mental retardation) and pervasive developmental disorder, who displayed aggression and self-injury maintained by attention. The intervention consisted of providing reinforcement every 10 seconds of no problem behavior, and gradually increasing the interval to every 5 minutes. Problem behaviors decreased significantly and were maintained at 1- and 2-month follow-up.

Charlop-Christy and Haymes (1996) compared the effectiveness of DRO using the child's obsessional object versus food as a reinforcer, as well as the effectiveness of reductive procedures such as time-out versus only positive reinforcers. Four children with autism, 4 to 5 years old, including one with an IQ of 129 and one who was nonverbal, engaged in tantrumming, aggression, property destruction, and self-stimulation. The DRO using food was ineffective, but using obsessive objects as reinforcers with or without reductive procedures was the most effective for all children. Problem behaviors decreased from 40%–50% of intervals at baseline to zero for two children, to about 8% for another, and about 20% for the nonverbal child. These improvements generalized to play sessions for three of the four children and on-task performance increased during all of the experimental conditions.

Punishment

Bregman et al. (2005) described 13 articles using punishment to reduce problem behavior. Matson and LoVullo (2008) reported that for lower-functioning persons with self-injurious behavior, positive reinforcement strategies, including differential reinforcement, were less effective than punishment. Punishers, individualized to each person, were almost always used in conjunction with reinforcement to strengthen the alternative behavior. Effective punishers included verbal reprimand, overcorrection, and time-out for aggression in children with intellectual disabilities and ASDs. Varied punishers were more effective than one punisher. Movement suppression time-out, requiring the child to stand facing a wall and not move or make noises, was effective for decreasing biting in preschoolers, including a 1- to 4-month follow-up. Turner (1999) noted that sensory extinction procedures that remove the sensory consequences of behavior; for example, masking the auditory stimulation from repetitive vocalizations with earphones, have also been shown to be successful in several studies.

Positive Behavioral Support

Positive behavioral support (PBS) involves training parents and staff to use visual schedules, responding to nonverbal cues, building routines out of day-to-day activities, and promoting play and interaction with peers (Dunlap & Fox, 1999). Antecedent strategies include increasing child choices, using transition warnings, increasing social attention to the child, and interspersing preferred activities between difficult activities. Replacement skills, such as PECS or FCT, are taught to replace problem behavior. Continued problem behavior typically results in redirecting the child away from the problem behavior toward the replacement skill. Escape extinction and differential reinforcement of alternate behavior is used with some children. The child is prompted to request a break and this response, rather than escape, is reinforced with a break. Dunlap and Fox (1999) described three cases using these approaches. One nonverbal 2½-year-old girl with moderate intellectual disabilities had few skills and spent her time self-stimulating. Prevention strategies included increasing toy play, choices, and social interaction opportunities. She was also taught to use nonverbal signals to request social interaction, including "more," "want," and "no." Continued self-stimulation was redirected to this replacement skill. Self-stimulation decreased immediately, from 50% to just over 20% and to 0% of intervals after 5 months of treatment. Two 3-year-old children

with moderate intellectual disabilities, one of whom was nonverbal, had frequent serious tantrums, and were successfully treated using similar procedures. Problem behavior decreased immediately, from 50% of intervals at baseline to 5%–10% and finally to near 0% of intervals. Unfortunately, the data represented therapist-child rather than parent-child interactions, leaving it unclear whether gains had or would generalize to parents once therapists left.

Meta-Analysis of Positive Behavior Support

Carr et al. (1999) published a meta-analysis of 366 cases (all ages) involving PBS interventions. Ten percent of participants were autistic and 40% were diagnosed with autism and intellectual disabilities plus other problems such as brain damage and seizures. Half of all clients showed decreases in problem behaviors of 90% from baseline and maintenance at 1–2 years was 71%. Behaviors that were maintained by attention, escape, or tangible rewards showed a mean decrease from baseline of 60%, whereas behaviors maintained by sensory reinforcers showed a mean decrease of 23.5%.

Meta-Analyses of Treatments for Inappropriate Behavior

Campbell (2003) reviewed 117 articles using single-subject designs to treat persons with autism published between 1966 and 1998. The studies described behavioral treatment for 181 individuals, age 2 to 31 years (mean = 10.1 years), with an IQ from 6 to 129 (mean = 42.2). One third were mute, another third had minimal to some functional language, and only about 2% were in the average range for language. Participant IQs were predominantly in the moderate (40–54, 23.2%) and severe (39 and below, 35.9%) range of intellectual disability, with 8.8% in the mild range (55 to 70) and 4.4% greater than 70. Behavior problems addressed in the studies included self-injury (17.9%), self-stimulation (29%), aggression (5.1%), and property destruction (0.9%). Combining all studies, problem behaviors decreased 76% from baseline. The PND was 84% ("effective") and PZD (percent of zero data) was 43%, all effect size measures significant at $p = .001$. Comparisons of effectiveness of aversive, positive, combination, and extinction interventions and target behavior category were not significant. All treatments were equally effective regardless of targeted behavior and treatment used.

Regression analysis was used to determine which participant variables contributed to treatment effects. The IQ, age, gender, diagnosis, and verbal ability added little. As in previous studies, Campbell found that studies using functional analysis had higher PZD scores than studies without functional analysis (58.4% vs. 37.0%, $p = .012$). Type of functional analysis, experimental versus descriptive (e.g., ABC charts, staff interviews, or rating scales) was related to outcome, with experimental FA resulting in PZD scores 30 points higher (mean = 66.84% vs. 36.71%, $p = .009$).

Turner (1999) described a meta-analysis of treatments for self-stimulatory behavior, showing that the most effective procedures for reducing self-stimulation were response contingent procedures, such as overcorrection or aversive conditioning. The next most effective procedures were those that used DRO or DRI. Medication was the least effective.

CONCLUSIONS

In defining empirically supported treatments, Chambless and Hollon (1998) stated that for a treatment to be defined as efficacious, it must be supported by two group design RCTs, each by a different research group, or at least two single-subject design studies with three or more participants by separate research groups, without conflicting data. If the study compares the treatment with that of another standard treatment, rather than with a nontreated control group, the treatment has additional merit and is defined as *efficacious and specific*, the most rigorous indication of effectiveness. The research must also have been conducted using adequate methods, including clear definition of the population, outcome measures with known reliability and construct validity, and blind evaluators. Evidence of clinical significance—for example, comparison to normative standards or to some other meaningful outcome—is also important, as is maintenance of gains at follow-up.

Comprehensive ABA treatments using random assignment and normed, standardized tests have been shown to be superior to no-treatment groups in two studies by the UCLA group (Lovaas, 1987; Smith, Groen, & Wynn, 2000). In studies conducted by four groups using quasi-random assignment, based on parental choice or staff availability, EIBI was more effective than special education, including classrooms specifically designed for children with autism (Cohen et al., 2006; Eikeseth et al., 2002, 2007; Howard et al., 2005; Remington et al., 2007). Therefore, EIBI meets the Chambless and Hollon (1998) criteria for efficacious and specific. Similarly, Rogers and Vismara (2008), using a related set of criteria (Chambless et al., 1998), determined that ABA met the highest standard, "well established." The ABA interventions have resulted in some children with pretreatment standard scores in the 40s and 50s improving at an accelerated rate and catching up to peers, testing in the average range in cognitive, language, academic, and social areas following treatment. No other intervention has shown this large an effect.

For naturalistic interventions, small group or single-subject design studies by five different groups have demonstrated improvements in various aspects of language using observational, but not standardized, measures. While some generalization has been observed, it has not been more pronounced than that in other approaches, and comparisons with other interventions, primarily discrete-trial, have been flawed and uninterpretable. Rogers and Vismara (2008) concluded that naturalistic procedures could not be rated using the Chambless and Hollon (1998) criteria because of the lack of standardized measures; however, we found three studies from two research groups using single-subject multiple baseline designs and observational data that could be rated (Laski et al., 1988; Neef et al., 1984; Stahmer, 1995). These studies included reliable data showing improvements to the level of typical children and evidence of generalization. We therefore conclude that naturalistic interventions meet the standards for a rating of efficacious, but there is as yet no data that would support naturalistic approaches as a comprehensive intervention.

No outcome studies of developmental interventions have used RCTs or small N experiments, or compared treatment outcomes with skills of typically developing children using reliable and valid measures so that readers could interpret the clinical significance of reported gains. In a less theoretically based intervention targeting increased parental responsiveness, studies have produced some increases in child interaction, but no unequivocal increases in language. Maintenance and generalization have not been assessed. Currently, developmental approaches do not meet Chambless and Hollon (1998) criteria for effectiveness, nor is there research support for these approaches as comprehensive interventions.

Although TEACCH has published studies documenting the effectiveness of structural and visual strategies in decreasing disruptive and noncompliant behavior, as well as positive parent satisfaction, few studies have addressed increases in skills. The largest study (Lord and Schopler, 1989) found that increases in IQ were negligible following 2 to 5 years of intervention. In an in-home version of TEACCH using much more one-to-one intervention than is provided in TEACCH classrooms, Ozonoff and Cathcart (1998) found

increases in nonverbal, motor, and imitation skills, but not in verbal skills. In the absence of additional outcome studies during the subsequent 12 years, the TEACCH approach, especially in its classroom form, does not meet Chambless and Hollon (1998) criteria for effectiveness, and cannot be considered an effective comprehensive intervention.

We found six studies of peer-mediated interventions by four research groups with three or more participants that showed that peer mediation increased interaction between children with autism and trained peers, but generalization was less impressive (Garrison-Harrel et al., 1997; Goldstein et al., 2007; Owen-DeSchryver et al., 2008). While peer mediation is an efficacious procedure for building social interaction, it is less clear that new skills are built, possibly accounting for the lesser findings in areas of maintenance and generalization to untrained peers. Therefore, we conclude that it is possibly efficacious.

Video modeling has been an effective strategy for building new skills, such as initiating and responding to peers, sharing, answering questions, conversation skills, and complying with teacher directions. These skills have also been successfully used as replacements for reducing inappropriate behaviors. Six different groups reported effectiveness and high maintenance in six studies with three or more participants (Buggey, 2005; Charlop-Christy et al., 2000; Coyle & Cole, 2004; Sherer et al., 2001; Simpson et al., 2004; Wert & Neisworth, 2003). A meta-analysis (Bellini & Akullian, 2007) found an overall PND of 80% for treatment, 83% for maintenance, and 74% for generalization. Video modeling meets criteria as an efficacious intervention.

Visual schedules were found to be effective by three different groups, each treating three or more children (MacDuff et al., 1993; Pierce & Schreibman, 1994; Turner, 1999). Maintenance and generalization were strong. Visual schedules therefore meet criteria as an efficacious intervention.

Self-management training was found to be effective by three groups, each publishing studies with three or more participants (Apple et al., 2005; Newman et al., 1997; and three studies by Schreibman and colleagues, e.g., Stahmer & Schreibman, 1992). Target behaviors included increasing appropriate behaviors and decreasing maladaptive behaviors. A meta-analysis (Lee et al., 2007) found that treatment effects (PND = 81.9%) and maintenance were high. Self-management meets criteria as an efficacious intervention.

Priming, in which the child is provided a preview of what will happen, has been shown to be effective in reducing problem behavior on community trips for three children (Schreibman et al., 2000). Maintenance was good and generalization to new settings occurred for some children. For others, generalization required repeating the intervention. Because we found only one study with three or more participants, priming meets the criteria for possibly efficacious.

Social skills groups have targeted skills including awareness of one's own feelings, reading nonverbal behavior of others, conversation skills, and dealing with teasing, as well as practicing new skills with each other and typical peers. Results have shown skill gains within the group based on observational or parent rating data, but not standardized measures, and generalization to peers outside the group has been weak. Social skills groups do not meet criteria for effectiveness, perhaps because they do not teach enough skills to mastery (DiSalvo & Oswald, 2002) or because the group represents a decontextualized setting, where poor generalization is a common problem.

Training children in conversation skills using scripts has been more effective. Goldstein et al. (2007) reviewed several studies in which learning several sociodramatic scripts resulted in improved interaction in other settings. Krantz & McClannahan (1993) also used scripts to teach children with ASD to converse and found increases in scripted and unscripted initiations to peers, which generalized to others. Jahr et al. (2000) similarly provided detailed instruction in social interaction scenarios with scripted language and found maintenance and generalization to untrained peers in different settings. Each study included three or more participants, indicating that learning scripts is an efficacious intervention for building interaction.

Social stories were found to be effective in one RCT (N = 34, Feinberg, 2002) and in at least three smaller studies with three or more participants (Sansosti & Powell-Smith, 2006; Scattone et al., 2002; Turner, 1999). Reviews of social stories report variability in Response to Intervention, with some children showing clear improvement and others showing none. Stories containing more directive and consequence statements than are recommended were more effective. A recent meta-analysis (Reynhout & Carter, 2006) concluded that the effectiveness of social stories was "not determined"; however, the aforementioned studies found successful outcome for most participants, resulting in a rating of possibly efficacious due to conflicting data from other studies. Larger studies are required to determine which combination of sentence types are most effective and which child characteristics are associated with larger responses.

The FCT has been shown to be effective in one small RCT (Reeve & Carr, 2000) and three single-subject design studies with three or more participants (Carr & Durand, 1985; Carr & Kemp, 1989; Durand & Carr, 1991), with Carr being a coauthor on each of these studies. Other authors have used FCT as part of a more comprehensive intervention (Dunlap & Fox, 1999). While FCT may not be effective for reducing more complex behaviors of lower-functioning participants (Matson & LoVullo, 2008), it seems to us that an intervention need not be effective with all populations to be considered effective. Because we did not find studies using FCT alone by more than one group of researchers, we conclude that FCT meets criteria for possibly efficacious.

Increasing appropriate toy play was shown to be an effective strategy for reducing self-stimulatory behavior with maintenance and generalization of gains several months later in three studies with three or more children, each by a different research group (Eason et al., 1982; Stahmer & Schreibman, 1992; Turner, 1999). This meets the criteria of an efficacious approach. Similarly, behavior momentum has been shown to be effective in increasing compliance to instructions previously met with refusal, applying this approach to following prompts to initiate play (Davis et al., 1994), resulting in a rating of possibly efficacious.

The DRO was effective for reducing problem behaviors such as out-of-seat, aggression, disruption, self-stimulation, tantrums, and property destruction in three single-subject design studies, each with three or more participants, by three different research teams (Charlop-Christy & Haymes, 1996; Kennedy & Haring, 1993; Newman et al., 1997). The DRO, therefore, meets criteria as an efficacious intervention.

Punishment procedures (e.g., verbal reprimand, time-out, movement suppression time-out, and overcorrection) were shown to be effective in two studies with three or more participants by separate research teams, making punishment an efficacious intervention (see Bregman et al., 2005). In several other studies, punishment was used as part of a broader intervention in which positive reinforcement strategies were used to increase desirable behavior while problem behaviors were reduced. Both consensus panels recommended this combination when using punishment.

Positive behavioral support was found in a large meta-analysis (Carr et al., 1999) to be quite effective for half of those treated with good maintenance, and all persons treated for problems maintained by attention, escape, or reward demonstrated a mean decrease from baseline of 60%. This intervention can be considered to be efficacious.

REFERENCES

Abrahams, B. S., & Geschwind, D. H. (2008, May). Advances in autism genetics: On the threshold of a new neurobiology. *Nature Reviews/Genetics, 9*, 341–355. Retrieved from www.nature.com/reviews/genetics

Aldred, C., Green, J., & Adams, C. (2004). A new social communication intervention for children with autism: Pilot randomized controlled study suggesting effectiveness. *Journal of Child Psychology and Psychiatry, 45*, 1420–1430.

Anderson, A., Moore, D. W., Godfrey, R., & Fletcher-Flinn, C. M. (2004). Social skills assessment of children with autism in free-play situations. *Autism, 8*, 369–385.

American Psychiatric Association. (2000). *Diagnostic and statistical manual of mental disorders* (4th ed., text rev.). Washington, DC: Author.

Apple, A. L., Billingsley, F., & Schwartz, J. S. (2005). Effects of video modeling alone and with self-management on compliment-giving behaviors of children with high functioning ASD. *Journal of Positive Behavior Interventions, 7*, 33–46.

Baer, D. M. (1993). Quasi-random assignment can be as convincing as random assignment. *American Journal on Mental Retardation, 97*, 373–375.

Baron-Cohen, S. (1995). *Mindblindness*. Cambridge, MA: MIT Press.

Barry, T. D., Klinger, L. G., Lee, J. M., Palardy, N., Gilmore, T., & Bodin, S. D. (2003). Examining the effectiveness of an outpatient clinic-based social skills group for high-functioning children with autism. *Journal of Autism and Developmental Disorders, 33*, 685–701.

Bauminger, N. (2002). The facilitation of social-emotional understanding and social interaction in high-functioning children with autism: Intervention outcomes. *Journal of Autism and Developmental Disorders, 32*, 283–298.

Bellini, S., & Akullian, J. (2007). A meta-analysis of video modeling and video self-modeling interventions for children and adolescents with autism spectrum disorders. *Exceptional Children, 73*, 264–287.

Bellini, S., Peters, J. K., Benner, L., & Hopf, A. (2007). A meta-analysis of school-based social skills interventions for children with autism spectrum disorders. *Remedial and Special Education, 28*, 153–162.

Birnbrauer, J. S., & Leach, D. J. (1993). The Murdoch early intervention program after 2 years. *Behavior Change, 10*, 63–74.

Bishop, S. L., Luyster, R., Richler, J., & Lord, C. (2008). Diagnostic assessment. In K. Chawarska, A. Klin, and F. R. Volkmar (Eds.), *Autism spectrum disorders in infants and toddlers* (pp. 23–49). New York, NY: Guilford Press.

Bondy, A., & Frost, L. (1994). The Picture Exchange Communication System. *Focus on Autistic Behavior, 9*, 1–19.

Bono, M. A., Daley, T., & Sigman, M. (2004). Relations among joint attention, amount of intervention and language gain in autism. *Journal of Autism and Developmental Disorders, 34*, 495–505.

Bregman, J. D., Zager, D., & Gerdtz, J. (2005). Behavioral interventions. In F. R. Volkmar, R. Paul, S. Klin, & D. Cohen (Eds.), *Handbook of autism and pervasive disorders: Vol. 2. Assessment, interventions, and policy* (3rd ed., pp. 897–924). Hoboken, NJ: Wiley.

Brinton, B., Robinson, L. A., & Fujiki, M. (2004). Description of a program for social language intervention: "If you can have a conversation, you can have a relationship." *Language, Speech, and Hearing Services in the Schools, 35*, 283–290.

Buggey, T. (2005). Video self-modeling applications with children with autism spectrum disorder in a small private school. *Focus on Autism and Other Developmental Disabilities, 20*, 52–63.

Buggey, T., Toombs, K., Gardner, P., & Cervetti, M. (1999). Training responding behaviors in students with autism: Using videotaped self-modeling. *Journal of Positive Behavior and Intervention, 1*, 205–214.

Campbell, J. M. (2003). Efficacy of behavioral interventions for reducing problem behavior in persons with autism: A quantitative synthesis of single-subject research. *Research in Developmental Disabilities, 24*, 120–138.

Carr, E. G., & Durand, V. M. (1985). Reducing behavior problems through functional communication training. *Journal of Applied Behavior Analysis, 18*, 111–126.

Carr, E. G., Horner, R. H., Turnbull, A. P., Marquis, J. G., Magito-McLaughlin, D., McAtee, M. L., . . . Doolabh, A. (1999). *Positive behavior support for people with developmental disabilities.* Washington, DC: American Association on Mental Retardation Monograph Series.

Carr, E. G., & Kemp, D. C. (1989). Functional equivalence of autistic leading and communicative pointing: Analysis and treatment. *Journal of Autism and Developmental Disorders, 19*, 561–578.

Centers for Disease Control and Prevention. (2009). Prevalence of autism spectrum disorders—Autism and developmental disabilities monitoring network, United States, 2006. Surveillance Summaries. *Morbidity and Mortality Weekly Report, 58*(SS–10), 1–20.

Chakrabarti, S., & Fombonne, E. (2005). Pervasive developmental disorders in preschool children: Confirmation of high prevalence. *American Journal of Psychiatry, 126*, 1133–1141.

Chambless, D. L., Baker, M. J., Baucom, D. H., Beutler, L. E., Calhoun, K. S., Crits-Christoph, P., . . . Woody, S. R. (1998). Update on empirically validated therapies, II. *The Clinical Psychologist, 51*, 3–16.

Chambless, D. L., & Hollon, S. D. (1998). Defining empirically supported therapies. *Journal of Consulting and Clinical Psychology, 66*, 7–18.

Charlop-Christy, M. H., & Carpenter, M. H. (2000). Modified incidental teaching sessions: A procedure for parents to increase spontaneous speech in their children with autism. *Journal of Positive Behavior Interventions, 2*, 98–112.

Charlop-Christy, M. H., & Daneshvar, S. (2003). Using video modeling to teach perspective taking to children with autism. *Journal of Positive Behavior Interventions, 5*, 12–21.

Charlop-Christy, M. H., & Haymes, L. K. (1996). Using obsessions as reinforcers with and without mild reductive procedures to decrease inappropriate behaviors of children with autism. *Journal of Autism and Developmental Disorders, 26*, 527–546.

Charlop-Christy, M. H., Le, L., & Freeman, K. A. (2000). A comparison of video modeling with in-vivo modeling for teaching children with autism. *Journal of Autism and Developmental Disorders, 30*, 537–552.

Cohen, H., Amerine-Dickens, M., & Smith, T. (2006). Early intensive behavioral treatment: Replication of the UCLA model in a community setting. *Developmental and Behavioral Pediatrics, 27*, 145–155.

Courchesne, E., Piven, J., Saliba, K., Bailey, J., & Arndt, S. (1999). An MRI study of autism: The cerebellum revisited. *Neurology, 52*, 1106–1111.

Coyle, C., & Cole, P. (2004). A videotaped self-modeling and self-monitoring treatment program to decrease off-task behaviour in children with autism. *Journal of Intellectual and Developmental Disabilities, 29*, 3–15.

Davis, C. A., Brady, M. P., Hamilton, R., McEvoy, M. A., & Williams, R. E. (1994). Effects of high-probability requests on the social interactions of young children with severe disabilities. *Journal of Applied Behavior Analysis, 27*, 619–637.

Dawson, G. (2008). Early behavioral intervention, brain plasticity, and the prevention of autism spectrum disorder. *Development and Psychopathology, 20*, 775–803.

Dawson, G., Munson, J., Webb, S. J., Nalty, T., Abbott, T. R., & Toth, K. (2007). Rate of head growth decelerates and symptoms worsen in the second year of life in autism. *Biological Psychiatry, 61*, 458–464.

Dawson, G., Rogers, S. J., Smith, M., Munson, J., Winter, J, Greenson, J., . . . Varley, J. (2010). Randomized controlled trial of the Early Start Denver Model: A relationship-based developmental and behavioral intervention for toddlers with autism spectrum disorders: Effects on IQ, adaptive behavior and autism diagnosis. *Pediatrics, 125*, 1–7.

Delprato, D. J. (2001). Comparison of discrete-trial and normalized behavioral language interventions for young children with autism. *Journal of Autism and Developmental Disorders, 31*, 315–325.

DiSalvo, C.A., & Oswald, D. P. (2002). Peer-mediated interventions to increase the social interaction of children with autism: Considerations of peer expectancies. *Focus on Autism and Other Disabilities, 17*, 198–207.

Drew, A., Baird, G., Baron-Cohen, S., Cox, A., Slonims, V., Wheelwright, S., . . . Charman, T. (2002). A pilot randonised control trial of a parent training intervention for pre-school children with autism: Preliminary fimndings and methodological challenges. *European Child & Adolescent Psychiatry, 11*, 266–272.

Dunlap, G., & Fox, L. (1999). A demonstration of behavioral support for young children with autism. *Journal of Positive Behavior Interventions, 1*, 77–87.

Durand, V. M., & Carr, E. G. (1987). Social Influences on "self-stimulatory" behavior: Analysis and treatment application. *Journal of Applied Behavior Analysis, 20*, 119–132.

Durand, V. M., & Carr, E. G. (1991). Functional communication training to reduce challenging behavior: Maintenance and application in new settings. *Journal of Applied Behavior Analysis, 24*, 251–264.

Eason, L. J., White, M. J., & Newsom, C. (1982). Generalized reduction of self-stimulatory behavior: An effect of teaching appropriate play to autistic children. *Analysis and Intervention in Developmental Disabilities, 2*, 157–169.

Eikeseth, S. (2009). Outcome of comprehensive psychoeducational interventions for young children with autism. *Research in Developmental Disabilities, 30*, 158–178.

Eikeseth, S., Smith, T., Jahr, E., & Eldevik, S. (2002). Intensive behavioral treatment at school for 4- to 7-year-old children with autism: A 1-year comparison controlled study. *Behavior Modification, 26*, 49–68.

Eikeseth, S., Smith, T., Jahr, E., & Eldevik, S. (2007). Outcome for children with autism who began intensive behavioral treatment between ages 4 and 7: A comparison controlled study. *Behavior Modification, 31*, 264–278.

Eldevik, S. (2007). *Prediction of outcomes of early behavioral treatment for children with autism: A meta-analysis.* Paper presented at the annual meeting of the Association for Behavior Analysis, San Diego, CA.

Eldevik, S., Eikeseth, S., Jahr, E., & Smith, T. (2006). Effects of low-intensity behavioral treatment for children with autism and mental retardation. *Journal of Autism and Developmental Disorders, 36*, 211–224.

Erba, H. W. (2001). Early intervention programs for children with autism: Conceptual frameworks for implementation. *American Journal of Orthopsychiatry, 70*, 82–94.

Feinberg, M. J. (2002). *Using social stories to teach specific social skills to individuals with autism* (Unpublished doctoral dissertation). California School of Professional Psychology, San Diego, California.

Fombonne, E. (2002). Prevalence of childhood disintegrative disorder. *Autism, 6*, 149–157.

Fombonne, E. (2005). Epidemiology of autistic disorder and other pervasive developmental disorders. *Journal of Clinical Psychiatry, 66*(suppl 10), 3–8.

Garrison-Harrell, L., Kamps, D., & Kravitz, T. (1997). The effects of peer networks on social-communicative behaviors for students with autism. *Focus on Autism and Other Developmental Disabilities, 12*, 241–254.

Girolametto, L., Sussman, F., & Weitzman, E. (2007). Using case study methods to investigate the effects of interactive intervention for children with autism spectrum disorders. *Journal of Communication Disorders, 40*, 470–492.

Goldstein, H. (2002). Communication intervention for children with autism: A review of treatment efficacy. *Journal of Autism and Developmental Disorders, 32*, 373–396.

Goldstein, H., Schneider, N., & Thiemann, K. (2007). Peer-mediated social communication intervention. *Topics in Language Disorders, 27*, 182–199.

Gray, C. (2003). *Social stories.* Retrieved from www.thegraycenter.org

Greenspan, S. I., & Wieder, S. (1997). Developmental patterns and outcomes in infants and children with disorders in relating and communicating: A chart review of 200 cases of children with autism spectrum diagnoses. *Journal of Developmental and Learning Disorders, 1*, 87–141.

Gresham, F. M., Sugai, G., & Horner, R. H. (2001). Interpreting outcomes of social skills training for students with high-incidence disabilities. *Teaching Exceptional Children, 67*, 331–344.

Gutstein, S. E., Burgess, A. F., & Montfort, K. (2007). Evaluation of the Relationship Development Intervention program. *Autism, 11*, 397–411.

Hancock, T. B., & Kaiser, A. P. (2002). The effects of trainer-implemented enhanced milieu teaching on the social communication of children with autism. *Topics in Early Childhood Special Education, 22*, 39–54.

Harper, C. B., Symon, J. B. G., & Frea, W. D. (2008). Recess time is time-in: Using peers to improve social skills of children with autism. *Journal of Autism and Developmental Disorders, 38*, 815–826.

Hart, B. M., & Risley, T. R. (1968). Establishing use of descriptive adjectives in the spontaneous speech of disadvantaged preschool children. *Journal of Applied Behavior Analysis, 1*, 109–120.

Horner, R. H., Carr, E. G., Strain, P. S., Todd, A. W., & Reed, H. K. (2002). Problem behavior interventions for young children with autism: A research synthesis. *Journal of Autism and Developmental Disorders, 32*, 423–446.

Howard, J. S., Sparkman, C. R., Cohen, H. G., Green, G., & Stanislaw, H. (2005). A comparison of intensive behavior analytic and eclectic treatments for young children with autism. *Research in Developmental Disabilities, 26*, 359–383.

Howlin, P., Kate-Gordon, R., Pasco, G., Wade, A., & Charman, T. (2007). The effectiveness of Picture Exchange Communication System (PECS) training for teachers of children with autism: A pragmatic, group randomized controlled trial. *Journal of Child Psychology and Psychiatry, 48*, 473–481.

Howlin, P., Magiati, I., & Charman, T. (2009). Systematic review of early intensive behavioral interventions for children with autism. *American Journal on Intellectual and Developmental Disabilities, 114*, 23–41.

Hwang, B., & Hughes, C. (2000). Increasing early social-communicative skills of preverbal preschool children with autism through social interactive training. *Journal of the Association for Persons with Severe Handicaps, 25*, 18–28.

Ingersoll, B., & Schreibman, L. (2006). Teaching reciprocal imitation skills to young children with autism using a naturalistic behavioral approach: Effects on language, pretend play, and joint attention. *Journal of Autism and Developmental Disorders, 36*, 487–505.

Ingersoll, B., Schreibman, L., & Stahmer, A. C. (2001). Brief report: Differential treatment outcomes for children with autistic spectrum disorder on level of peer social avoidance. *Journal of Autism and Developmental Disorders, 31*, 343–349.

Jahr, E., Eikeseth, S., Eldevik, S., & Aase, H. (2007). Frequency and latency of social interaction in an inclusive kindergarten setting: A comparison between typical children and children with autism. *Autism, 11*, 349–363.

Jahr, E., Eldevik, S., & Eikeseth, S. (2000). Teaching children with autism to initiate and sustain cooperative play. *Research in Developmental Disabilities, 21*, 151–169.

Jones, E. A., & Carr, E. G. (2004). Joint attention in children with autism: Theory and intervention. *Focus on Autism and Other Developmental Disabilities, 19*, 13–26.

Kamps, D. M., Barbetta, P. M., Leonard, B. R., & Delquadri, J. (1994). Classwide peer tutoring: An integration strategy to improve reading skills and promote peer interactions among students with autism and general education peers. *Journal of Applied Behavior Analysis, 27*, 49–61.

Kamps, D. M., Dugan, E., Potucek, J., & Collins, A. (1999). Effects of cross-age peer tutoring networks among students with autism and general education students. *Journal of Behavioral Education, 9*, 97–115.

Kamps, D. M., Potucek, J., Lopez, A. G., Kravitz, T., & Kemmerer, K. (1997). The use of peer networks across multiple settings to improve social interaction for students with autism. *Journal of Behavioral Education, 7*, 335–357.

Kamps, D. M., Royer, J., Dugan, E., Kravits, T., Gonzalez-Lopez, A., Garcia, J., . . . Kane, L. G. (2002). Peer training to facilitate social interaction for elementary students with autism and their peers. *Exceptional Children, 68*, 173–187.

Kasari, C., Freeman, S., & Paparella, T. (2006). Joint attention and symbolic play in young children with autism: A randomized controlled intervention study. *Journal of Child Psychology and Psychiatry, 47*, 611–620.

Kasari, C., Paparella, T., Freeman, S., & Jahromi, L. B. (2008). Language outcome in autism: Randomized comparison of joint attention and play interventions. *Journal of Consulting and Clinical Psychology, 76*, 125–137.

Kennedy, C. H., & Haring, T. G. (1993). Combining reward and escape DRO to reduce the problem behavior of students with severe disabilities. *Journal of the Association of Persons with Severe Disabilities, 18*, 85–92.

Koegel, L. K., Koegel, R. L., & Parks, D. R. (1992). *How to teach self-management to people with severe disabilities: A training manual*. University of California, Santa Barbara: Author.

Koegel, L. K., Koegel, R. L., Shoshan, Y., & McNerney, E. (1999). Pivotal response intervention II: Preliminary long-term outcome data. *Journal of the Association for Persons with Severe Handicaps, 24*, 186–198.

Koegel, R. L., Camarata, S., Koegel, L. K., Ben-Tall, A., & Smith, A. E. (1998). Increasing speech intelligibility in children with autism. *Journal of Autism and Developmental Disorders, 28*, 241–251.

Koegel, R. L., & Koegel, L. K. (2006). *Pivotal response treatments for autism: Communication, social and academic development*. Baltimore, MD: Paul H. Brookes.

Koegel, R. L., Koegel, L. K., & Surratt, H. A. (1992). Language intervention and disruptive behavior in preschool children with autism. *Journal of Autism and Developmental Disorders, 22*, 141–153.

Koegel, R. L., O'Dell, M., & Dunlap, G. (1988). Producing speech use in nonverbal autistic children by reinforcing attempts. *Journal of Autism and Developmental Disorders, 18*, 525–538.

Koegel, R. L., O'Dell, M. C., & Koegel, L. K. (1987). A natural language paradigm for nonverbal autistic children: Attempts to improve verbal language acquisition. *Journal of Autism and Developmental Disorders, 17*, 187–200.

Koegel, R. L., Schreibman, L., Good, A., Cerniglia, L., Murphy, C., & Koegel, L. K. (1989). *How to teach pivotal behaviors to children with autism: A training manual*. University of California, Santa Barbara: Author.

Kohler, F. W., Strain, P. S., Hoyson, M., Davis, L., Donna, W. M., & Rapp, N. (1995). Using group-oriented contingency to increase social interactions between children with autism and their peers: A preliminary analysis of corollary supportive behaviors. *Behavior Modification, 19*, 10–32.

Krantz, P. J., & McClannahan, L. E. (1993). Teaching children with autism to initiate to peers: Effects of a script-fading procedure. *Journal of Applied Behavior Analysis, 26*, 121–132.

Kroeger, K. A., Schultz, F. R., & Newsom, C. (2007). A comparison of two group-delivered social skills programs for young children with autism. *Journal of Autism and Developmental Disorders, 37*, 808–817.

Landa, R. J. (2008). Diagnosis of autism spectrum disorders in the first 3 years of life. *Nature Clinical Practice Neurology, 4*, 138–146.

Laski, K. E., Charlop, M. H., & Schreibman, L. (1988). Training parents to use the natural language paradigm to increase their autistic children's speech. *Journal of Applied Behavior Analysis, 21*, 391–400.

Laushey, K. M., & Heflin, L. J. (2000). Enhancing social skills of kindergarten children with autism through the training of multiple peers as tutors. *Journal of Autism and Developmental Disorders, 30*, 183–193.

Lee, S. H., Simpson, R. L., & Shogren, K. A. (2007). Effects and implications of self-management for students with autism: A meta-analysis. *Focus on Autism and Other Developmental Disabilities, 22*, 2–13.

Lefebvre, D., & Strain, P. S. (1989). Effects of a group contingency on the frequency of social interactions among autistic and non-handicapped preschool children: Making LRE efficacious. *Journal of Early Intervention, 13*, 329–341.

Lord, C., & Schopler, E. (1989). The role of age at assessment, developmental level, and test in the stability of intelligence scores in young autistic children. *Journal of Autism and Developmental Disorders, 19*, 483–499.

Lovaas, O. I. (1981). *Teaching developmentally disabled children: The me book.* Austin, TX: Pro-Ed.

Lovaas, O. I. (1987). Behavioral treatment and normal educational and intellectual functioning in young autistic children. *Journal of Consulting and Clinical Psychology, 55*, 3–9.

Lovaas, O. I., Koegel, R. L., Simmons, J. Q., & Long, J. S. (1973). Some generalization and follow-up measures on autistic children in behavior therapy. *Journal of Applied Behavior Analysis, 6*, 131–166.

MacDuff, G. S., Krantz, P. J., & McClannahan, L. E. (1993). Teaching children with autism to use photographic activity schedules: Maintenance and generalization. *Journal of Applied Behavior Analysis, 26*, 89–97.

Magiati, I., Charman, T., & Howlin, P. (2007). A two-year prospective follow-up study of community-based early intensive behavioural intervention and specialist nursery provision for children with autism spectrum disorders. *Journal of Child Psychology and Psychiatry, 48*, 803–812.

Mahoney, G., & Perales, F. (2005). Relationship-focused early intervention with children with pervasive developmental disorders and other disabilities: A comparative study. *Developmental and Behavioral Pediatrics, 26*, 77–85.

Makrygianni, M., & Reed, P. (2008). *The effectiveness of behavioral early intervention for children with autism: A meta-analysis* [Power point]. Presented at the Division of Educational and Child Psychology Annual Professional Development Event, Bournemouth, Australia. Retrieved from www.wsanswa.ac.uk.

Marcus, L., Schopler, E., & Lord, C. (2001). TEACCH services for preschool children. In J. S. Handleman & S. I. Harris (Eds.), *Preschool education programs for children with autism* (2nd ed., pp. 215–232). Austin, TX: Pro-Ed.

Matson, J. L., & LoVullo, S. V. (2008). A review of behavioral treatments for self-injurious behaviors of persons with autism spectrum disorders. *Behavior Modification, 32*, 61–76.

Matson, J. L., Matson, M. L., & Rivet, T. T. (2007). Social-skills treatments for children with autism spectrum disorders: An overview. *Behavior Modification, 31*, 682–707.

McConachie, H., Randle, V., Hammal, D., & Le Couteur, A. (2005). A controlled trial of a training course for parents of children with suspected autism disorder. *Journal of Pediatrics, 147*, 335–340.

McEachin, J. J., Smith, T., & Lovaas, O. I. (1993). Long-term outcome for children with autism who received early intensive behavioral treatment. *American Journal on Mental Retardation, 97*, 359–372.

McGee, G. G., Krantz, P. J., Mason, D., & McClannahan, L. E. (1983). A modified incidental-teaching procedure for autistic youth: Acquisition and generalization of receptive object labels. *Journal of Applied Behavior Analysis, 16*, 329–338.

McGee, G. G., Krantz, P. J., & McClannahan, L. E. (1985). The facilitative effects of incidental teaching on preposition use by autistic children. *Journal of Applied Behavioral Analysis, 18*, 17–31.

McGee, G. G., Morrier, M. J., & Daly, T. (1999). An incidental teaching approach to early intervention for toddlers with autism. *Journal of the Association for Persons with Severe Handicaps, 24*, 133–146.

Mesibov, G. B., & Shea, V. (2005). The TEACCH method: Structured teaching. In L. S. Wankoff (Ed.), *Innovative methods in language intervention, treatment outcome measures: Can the data support the claims* (pp. 85–109). Austin, TX: Pro-Ed.

Morrow, E. M., Seung-Yun, Y., Flavell, S. W., Tae-Kyung, K., Lin, Y., Hill, R. S., . . . Walsh, C. A. (2008). Identifying autism loci and genes by tracing recent shared ancestry. *Science, 321*, 218–223.

National Institute of Mental Health (NIMH). (2008). *Autism spectrum disorders (pervasive developmental disorders)*. Washington, DC: Author. Retrieved from www.nih.gov/health/publications/autism/complete-publication.shtml

National Research Council (NRC). (2001). *Educating children with autism*. Washington, DC: National Academies Press.

Neef, N. A., Walters, J., & Egel, A. L. (1984). Establishing generic yes/no responses in developmentally disabled children. *Journal of Applied Behavior Analysis, 17*, 453–460.

Newman, B., Tuntigian, L., Ryan, C. S., & Reinecke, D. R. (1997). Self-management of a DRO procedure by three students with autism. *Behavioral Interventions, 12*, 149–156.

New York State Department of Health (NYSDOH), Early Intervention Program. (1999, May). *Clinical practice guideline: The guideline technical report. Autism/pervasive developmental disorders, assessment and intervention for young children (ages 0–3 years)*. 1999 Publication No. 4217. Albany, NY: Author.

Odom, S. L., Collet-Klingenberg, L., Rogers, S. L., & Hatton, D. O. (2010). Evidence-based practices in intervention for children and youth with autism spectrum disorders. *Preventing School Failure, 54*, 275–282.

Olley, J. G. (2005). Curriculum and classroom structure. In F. R. Volkmar, R. Paul, A. Klin, & D. Cohen (Eds.), *Handbook of autism and pervasive developmental disorders*: Vol. 2. *Assessment, interventions, and policy* (3rd ed., pp. 863–881). Hoboken, NJ: Wiley.

Ospina, M. B., Seida, J. K., Clark, B., Karkhaneh, M., Hartling, L., Tjosvold, L., . . . Smith, V. (2008). Behavioral and developmental interventions for autism spectrum disorder: A clinical systematic review. *PLoS ONE, 3*(11). Retrieved from www.plosone.org

Owen-DeSchryver, J. S., Carr, E. G., Cale, S. I., & Blakley-Smith, A. (2008). Promoting social interactions between students with autism spectrum disorders and their peers in inclusive school settings. *Focus on Autism and Other Developmental Disabilities, 23*, 15–28.

Ozonoff, S., & Cathcart, K. (1998). Effectiveness of a home program intervention for young children with autism. *Journal of Autism and Developmental Disorders, 28*, 25–32.

Peyton, R. T., Mruzek, D. W., & Smith, T. (2008). What do we know about early intensive behavioral intervention? In E. Cipani (Ed.), *Triumphs in early autism treatment*. New York, NY: Springer.

Pierce, K. L., & Schreibman, L. (1994). Teaching daily living skills to children with autism in unsupervised settings through pictorial self-management. *Journal of Applied Behavior Analysis, 27*, 471–481.

Pierce, K., & Schreibman, L. (1995). Increasing complex social behaviors in children with autism: Effects of peer-implemented pivotal response training. *Journal of Applied Behavior Analysis, 28*, 285–295.

Pierce, K., & Schreibman, L. (1997). Multiple peer use of pivotal response training social behaviors of classmates with autism: Results from trained and untrained peers. *Journal of Applied Behavior Analysis, 30*, 157–160.

Prizant, B. M., Wetherby, A. M., Rubin, E., & Laurent, A. C. (2003). The SCERTS Model: A transactional, family-centered approach to enhancing communication and socioemotional abilities of children with autism spectrum disorders. *Infants and Young Children, 16*, 296–316.

Rao, P. A., Bidel, D. C., & Murray, M. J. (2008). Social skills interventions for children with Asperger's syndrome or high-functioning autism: A review and recommendations. *Journal of Autism and Developmental Disorders, 38*, 353–361.

Reeve, C. E., & Carr, E. G. (2000). Prevention of severe behavior problems in children with developmental disorders. *Journal of Positive Behavior Interventions, 2*, 144–160.

Remington, B., Hastings, R. P., Kovshoff, H., degli Espinosa, F., Jahr, E., Brown, T., . . . Ward, N. (2007). Early intensive intervention: Outcomes for children with autism and their parents after two years. *American Journal on Mental Retardation, 112*, 418–438.

Reynhout, G., & Carter, M. (2006). Social Stories™ for children with disabilities. *Journal of Autism and Developmental Disorders, 36*, 445–469.

Roeyers, H. (1996). The influence of non-handicapped peers on the social interactions of children with a pervasive developmental disorder. *Journal of Autism and Developmental Disorders, 26*, 303–320.

Rogers, S. J., & Dawson, G. (2010). *Early Start Denver Model for Young Children with Autism: Promoting language, learning, and engagement*. New York, NY: Guilford Press.

Rogers, S. J., & DiLalla, D. L. (1991). A comparative study of the effects of a developmentally based instructional model on young children with autism and young children with other disorders of behavior and development. *Topics in Early Childhood Special Education, 11*, 29–47.

Rogers, S. J., & Lewis, H. (1989). An effective day treatment model for young children with pervasive developmental disorders. *Journal of the American Academy of Child and Adolescent Psychiatry, 28*, 207–214.

Rogers, S. J., & Vismara, L. A. (2008). Evidence-based comprehensive treatments for early autism. *Journal of Clinical Child and Adolescent Psychology, 37*, 8–38.

Rossetti, L. (2006). *The Rossetti Infant-Toddler Language Scale*. East Moline, IL: LinguiSystems.

Sallows, G. O. (2005). Applied behavior analysis and the acquisition of social language in autistic children. In L. S. Wankoff (Ed.), *Innovative methods in language intervention: Can the data support the claims.* (pp. 55–83) Austin, TX: Pro-Ed.

Sallows, G. O., & Graupner, T. D. (2005). Intensive behavioral treatment for children with autism: Four-year outcome and predictors. *American Journal on Mental Retardation, 110,* 417–438.

Sansosti, F. J., & Powell-Smith, K. A. (2006). Using social stories to improve the social behavior of children with Asperger syndrome. *Journal of Positive Behavior Interventions, 8,* 43–57.

Sansosti, F. J., Powell-Smith, K. A., & Kincaid, D. (2004). A research synthesis of social story interventions for children with autism spectrum disorders. *Focus on Autism and Other Developmental Disorders, 19,* 194–204.

Scattone, D., Wilczynski, S. M., Edwards, R. P., & Rabian, B. (2002). Decreasing disruptive behaviors of children with autism using social stories. *Journal of Autism and Developmental Disorders, 32,* 535–543.

Schopler, E., Reichler, R. J., & Lansing, M. (1980). *Individualized assessment and treatment for autistic and developmentally disabled children: Vol. 2. Teaching strategies for parents and professionals.* Baltimore, MD: University Park Press.

Schreibman, L., & Ingersoll, B. (2005). Behavioral interventions to promote learning in individuals with autism. In F. R. Volkmar, R. Paul, A. Klin, & D. Cohen (Eds.), *Handbook of autism and pervasive disorders: Vol. 2. Assessment, interventions, and policy* (3rd ed., pp. 882–896). Hoboken, NJ: Wiley.

Schreibman, L., Kaneko, W. M., & Koegel, R. L. (1991). Positive affect of parents of autistic children: A comparison across two teaching techniques. *Behavior Therapy, 22,* 479–490.

Schreibman, L., Whalen, C., & Stahmer, A. C. (2000). The use of video priming to reduce disruptive transition behavior in children with autism. *Journal of Positive Behavior Interventions, 2,* 3–11.

Shattuck, P. T. (2006). The contribution of diagnostic substitution to the growing administrative prevalence of autism in U.S. special education. *Pediatrics, 117,* 1028–1037.

Sheinkopf, S. J., & Siegel, B. (1998). Home-based behavioral treatment of young children with autism. *Journal of Autism and Developmental Disorders, 28,* 15–23.

Sherer, M., Pierce, K. L., Paredes, S., Kisacky, K. L., Ingersoll, B., & Schreibmen, L. (2001). Enhancing conversation skills in children with autism via video technology: Which is better, "self" or "other" as a model? *Behavioral Modifications, 25,* 140–158.

Simpson, A., Langone, J., & Ayres, K. M. (2004). Embedded video and computer based instruction to improve social skills for students with autism. *Education and Training in Developmental Disabilities, 39,* 240–252.

Smith, T. (1996). Are other interventions effective? In C. Maurice (Ed.), *Behavioral intervention for young children with autism* (pp. 45–59). Austin, TX: Pro-Ed.

Smith, T. (1999). Outcome of early intervention for children with autism. *Clinical Psychology: Science & Practice, 6,* 33–49.

Smith, T., Eikeseth, S., Klevstrand, M., & Lovaas, O. I. (1997). Intensive behavioral treatment for preschoolers with severe mental retardation and pervasive developmental disorder. *American Journal on Mental Retardation, 102,* 238–249.

Smith, T., Groen, A. D., & Wynn, J. W. (2000). Randomized trial of intensive early intervention for children with pervasive developmental disorder. *American Journal on Mental Retardation, 105,* 269–285.

Smith, T., & Wick, J. (2008). Controversial treatments. In K. Chawarska, A. Klin, & F. R. Volkmar (Eds.), *Autism spectrum disorders in infants and toddlers: Diagnosis, assessment, and treatment* (pp. 243–273). New York, NY: Guilford Press.

Solomon, M., Goodlin-Jones, B. L., & Anders, T. F. (2004). A social adjustment intervention for high functioning autism, asperger's syndrome, and pervasive developmental disorder NOS. *Journal of Autism and Developmental Disorders, 34,* 649–668.

Solomon, R., Necheles, J., Ferch, C., & Bruckman, D. (2007). Pilot study of a parent training program for young children with autism: The PLAY project home consultation program. *Autism, 11,* 205–224.

Stahmer, A. C. (1995). Teaching symbolic play skills to children with autism using pivotal response training. *Journal of Autism and Developmental Disorders, 25,* 123–141.

Stahmer, A. C. (1999). Using pivotal response training to facilitate appropriate play in children with autistic spectrum disorders. *Child Language Teaching and Therapy, 15,* 29–40.

Stahmer, A. C., & Gist, K. (2001). The effects of an accelerated parent education program on technique mastery and child outcome. *Journal of Positive Behavior Interventions, 3,* 75–82.

Stahmer, A. C., & Schreibman, L. (1992). Teaching children with autism appropriate play in unsupervised environments using a self-management treatment package. *Journal of Applied Behavior Analysis, 25,* 447–459.

Terpstra, J. E., Higgins, K., & Pierce, T. (2002). Can I play? Classroom-based interventions for teaching play skills to children with autism. *Focus on Autism and Other Developmental Disabilities, 17,* 119–127.

Thompson, T. (2007). Relations among functional systems in behavior analysis. *Journal of the Experimental Analysis of Behavior, 87,* 423–440.

Tsao, L., & Odom, S. L. (2006). Sibling-mediated social interaction intervention for young children with autism. *Topics in Early Childhood Special Education, 26,* 106–123.

Tse, T., Strulovitck, J., Tagalaskis, V., Meng, L., & Fombonne, E. (2007). Social skills training for adolescents with Asperger syndrome and high-functioning autism. *Journal of Autism and Developmental Disorders, 37*, 1960–1968.

Turner, M. (1999). Annotation: Repetitive behaviour in autism: A review of psychological research. *Journal of Child Psychology & Psychiatry, 40*, 838–849.

Volkmar, F. R., Chawarska, K., & Klin, A. (2008). Autism spectrum disorders in infants and toddlers: An introduction. In K. Chawarska, A. Klin, & F. R. Volkmar (Eds.), *Autism spectrum disorders in infants and toddlers: Diagnosis, assessment, and treatment* (pp. 1–22). New York, NY: Guilford Press.

Volkmar, F. R., Westphal, A., Gupta, A. R., & Wiesner, L. (2008). Medical issues. In K. Chawarska, A. Klin, & F. R. Volkmar (Eds.), *Autism spectrum disorders in infants and toddlers: Diagnosis, assessment, and treatment* (pp. 274–299). New York, NY: Guilford Press.

Webb, B. J., Miller, S. P., Pierce, T. B., Strawser, S., & Jones, P. (2004). Effects of social skill instruction for high-functioning adolescents with autism spectrum disorders. *Focus on Autism and Other Developmental Disabilities, 19*, 52–62.

Wert, B. Y., & Neisworth, J. T. (2003). Effects of video self-modeling on spontaneous requesting in children with autism. *Journal of Positive Behavior Interventions, 5*, 30–34.

Wetherby, A. M., & Woods, J. J. (2006). Early social interaction project for children with autism spectrum disorders beginning in the second year of life: A preliminary study. *Topics in Early Childhood Special Education, 26*, 67–82.

Whalen, C., & Schreibman, L. (2003). Joint attention training for children with autism using behavior modification procedures. *Journal of Child Psychology and Psychiatry, 44*, 456–468.

Whalen, C., & Schreibman, L. (2006). The collateral effects of joint attention training on social initiations, positive affect, imitation, and spontaneous speech for young children with autism. *Journal of Autism and Developmental Disorders, 36*, 655–664.

White, S. W., Koenig, K., & Scahill, L. (2007). Social skills development in children with autism spectrum disorders: A review of the intervention research. *Journal of Autism and Developmental Disorders, 37*, 1858–1868.

Woods, J., Kashinath, S., & Goldstein, H. (2004). Effects of embedding caregiver-implemented teaching strategies in daily routines on children's communication outcomes. *Journal of Early Intervention, 26*, 175–193.

Yoder, P., & Stone, W. L. (2006). Randomized comparison of two communication interventions for preschoolers with autism spectrum disorders. *Journal of Consulting and Clinical Psychology, 74*, 426–435.

Zwaigenbaum, L., Bryson, S., Rogers, T., Roberts, W., Brian, J., & Szatmari, P. (2005). Behavioral manifestations of autism in the first year of life. *International Journal of Developmental Neuroscience, 23*, 143–152.

10

Attention-Deficit/ Hyperactivity Disorders

REBECCA J. HAMBLIN AND ALAN M. GROSS

OVERVIEW

Attention-deficit/hyperactivity disorder (ADHD) is one of the most well-studied child psychopathologies, and a tremendous amount of research has been published related to its etiology, primary problems and impact, demographic and contextual variability, and treatment methods. The label has also received heavy criticism as being an artificial U.S. construct for labeling normally exuberant children; however, early clinical descriptions of attention impairments date to 1798 (Barkley, 2006; Palmer & Finger, 2001). Attention-deficit/hyperactivity disorder symptoms are reported to occur in all countries in which ADHD has been studied (Polanczyk, de Lima, Horta, Biederman, & Rohde, 2007). Despite early conceptualization of the disorder as resulting from poor character or wayward parenting, ADHD is now seen as a neurologically based disorder (Barkley, 2006).

ADHD is one of the most common disorders of childhood, affecting an estimated 3% to 5% of children in the United States, and is the most common reason for clinical referral of children to psychiatric clinics (American Psychiatric Association, 2000). Children with ADHD display symptoms of inattention, impulsivity, and hyperactivity across multiple situations beginning at an early age. The frequency of these behaviors is out of bounds with respect to normal development, and symptoms cause significant impairments in family and peer relationships, academic functioning, and emotional well-being (Barkley, 2006).

This chapter will provide an overview of the core symptoms and current diagnostic features of the disorder, describe its prevalence and epidemiology, impairments to daily life, comorbid disorders, and long-term outcomes. The next sections will describe various psychosocial treatments that have been empirically explored, and will review the most current research on treatment efficacy. The chapter concludes with a summary and list of evidence-based treatments for ADHD.

CORE SYMPTOMS

Inattention

Relative to children without ADHD, those with the disorder have difficulty maintaining attention or vigilance in responding to environmental demands. That is, they have trouble sustaining effort in tasks, particularly for activities that are tedious, difficult, or with little intrinsic appeal (Barkley, 2006). In the classroom setting, impairment in attention and task vigilance may be evident in inability to complete independent assignments or listen to class instruction. In unstructured settings, inattention may be apparent in frequent shifts between play activities. Parents and teachers report that these children have difficulty focusing, are often forgetful, lose things, frequently daydream, fail to complete chores and schoolwork, and require more redirection and supervision than others the same age. Children with high levels of inattentive symptoms in the absence of hyperactive or impulsive symptoms may also have a different kind of attention problem marked by sluggish cognitive processing and deficiency in selective attention (Barkley, 2003).

Hyperactivity and Impulsivity

Hyperactivity and impulsivity almost always co-occur and are therefore considered a single dimension of ADHD. The hyperactive-impulsive dimension of the disorder is often conceptualized as behavioral disinhibition. Hyperactivity is displayed in fidgeting, restlessness, loud and excessive talking, and excessive levels of motor activity. Impulsive behaviors include interrupting or intruding on others, difficulty waiting and taking turns, and blurting out without thinking. Children and adolescents with hyperactive-impulsive features are described by caregivers as reckless, irresponsible, rude, immature, squirmy, and on the go (APA, 2000; Barkley, 2006).

Diagnostic Criteria and Subtypes

Diagnostic criteria for ADHD are defined by the *Diagnostic and Statistical Manual of Mental Disorders, Fourth Edition, Text Revision* (*DSM-IV-TR*) as presence of several symptoms in inattention, hyperactivity-impulsivity, or both, as seen in Table 10.1 (APA, 2000). Individuals with symptoms in both domains are classified as having ADHD, combined type (ADHD-C). Those who manifest multiple symptoms of inattention but no or few hyperactive-impulsive characteristics are diagnosed with ADHD,

predominately inattentive type (ADHD-PI). The ADHD, predominately hyperactive-impulsive type (ADHD-PHI) describes individuals with behavioral disinhibition without significant symptoms of inattention. Table 10.1 contains the complete diagnostic contained in the *DSM-IV-TR*.

PREVALENCE AND DEMOGRAPHIC VARIABLES

Nearly 5 million children in the United States are diagnosed with ADHD (Centers for Disease Control and Prevention [CDC], 2005). Prevalence rates of ADHD translate, on average, to one to two children in every classroom in America (APA, 2000). The most commonly diagnosed subtype is ADHD-C, representing about 50% to 75% of children diagnosed. Another 20% to 30% are classified with ADHD-PI, while fewer than 15% are diagnosed with ADHD-PHI. It is thought that ADHD-PHI may be a developmental precursor to the combined type, seen in preschool-age children who have not yet manifested symptoms of inattention.

Boys are 2 to 9 times more likely than girls to be diagnosed with ADHD (APA, 2000). The gender discrepancy is more pronounced in clinic referred than in community samples. Higher rates among males may be at least partially attributable to a stronger tendency for males to present ADHD-C and comorbid disruptive behavior disorders, which are more likely to rise to the level of clinical attention. Girls are more likely to have ADHD-PI and comorbid disorders are more likely to be internalizing disorders. Because symptoms of ADHD-PI and emotional disorders are more likely to go unnoticed, girls with ADHD may be underidentified and undertreated (Biederman, 2005).

ADHD is present among all socioeconomic levels and ethnic groups within the United States, though prevalence and symptoms vary by gender, age, and ethnicity (Barkley, 2003;

TABLE 10.1 *DSM-IV-TR* Criteria for Attention-Deficit/Hyperactivity Disorder

I. Either A or B:

A. Six or more of the following symptoms of inattention have been present for at least 6 months to a point that is inappropriate for developmental level:

Inattention

1. Often does not give close attention to details or makes careless mistakes in schoolwork, work, or other activities.

2. Often has trouble keeping attention on tasks or play activities.

3. Often does not seem to listen when spoken to directly.

4. Often does not follow through on instructions and fails to finish schoolwork, chores, or duties in the workplace (not due to oppositional behavior or failure to understand instructions).

5. Often has trouble organizing activities.

6. Often avoids, dislikes, or doesn't want to do things that take a lot of mental effort for a long period of time (such as schoolwork or homework).

7. Often loses things needed for tasks and activities (e.g., toys, school assignments, pencils, books, or tools).

8. Is often easily distracted.

9. Is often forgetful in daily activities.

B. Six or more of the following symptoms of hyperactivity-impulsivity have been present for at least 6 months to an extent that is disruptive and inappropriate for developmental level:

Hyperactivity

1. Often fidgets with hands or feet or squirms in seat when sitting still is expected.

2. Often gets up from seat when remaining in seat is expected.

3. Often excessively runs about or climbs when and where it is not appropriate (adolescents or adults may feel very restless).

4. Often has trouble playing or doing leisure activities quietly.

5. Is often "on the go" or often acts as if "driven by a motor."

6. Often talks excessively.

Impulsivity

7. Often blurts out answers before questions have been finished.

8. Often has trouble waiting one's turn.

9. Often interrupts or intrudes on others (e.g., butts into conversations or games).

II. Some symptoms that cause impairment were present before age 7 years.

III. Some impairment from the symptoms is present in two or more settings (e.g., at school/work and at home).

IV. There must be clear evidence of clinically significant impairment in social, school, or work functioning.

V. The symptoms do not happen only during the course of a Pervasive Developmental Disorder, Schizophrenia, or other Psychotic Disorder. The symptoms are not better accounted for by another mental disorder (e.g., Mood Disorder, Anxiety Disorder, Dissociative Disorder, or a Personality Disorder).

Based on these criteria, three types of ADHD are identified:

IA. ADHD, *Combined Type*: If both criteria IA and IB are met for the past 6 months.

IB. ADHD, *Predominantly Inattentive Type*: If criterion IA is met but criterion IB is not met for the past six months.

IC. ADHD, *Predominantly Hyperactive-Impulsive Type*: If criterion IB is met but criterion IA is not met for the past 6 months.

Source: Reprinted with permission from the *Diagnostic and Statistical Manual of Mental Disorders, Fourth Edition, Text Revision* (Copyright © 2000). American Psychiatric Association.

Cuffe, Moore, & McKeown, 2005). World-wide prevalence estimates typically range from 3% to 8% of the world population. Estimates vary by geographic region, but this is thought to be primarily due to differences in diagnostic criteria and study methodologies (Biederman, 2005; Polanczyk et al., 2007).

Studies of current and lifetime prevalence rates in the United States indicate that Hispanics and Latinos have lower risk for ADHD than either African Americans or Caucasians. Some studies show a higher rate of ADHD diagnosed among African Americans than in Caucasians, but these differences are not always statistically significant (Breslau et al., 2006; Cuffe et al., 2005). Lower socioeconomic status is related to higher incidence of ADHD. This difference may be attributable to lower socioeconomic status being a risk factor for development of the disorder; additionally, parents of children with ADHD are likely to also have ADHD, and therefore may have low educational obtainment and occupational difficulties (Barkley, 2003; Cuffe et al., 2005). Results of the 2003 National Survey of Children's Health (CDC, 2005) showed that ADHD was more commonly diagnosed among children whose parents had obtained a high school education than those whose parents had achieved more or less education. Children in ethnic minority populations and uninsured children were less likely than others to receive medication treatment. Finally, prevalence of reported ADHD increased with age and was greater for children 9 years and up than for younger children (CDC, 2005; Visser, Lesesne, & Perou, 2007).

IMPACT OF ADHD

Social

Children with ADHD experience a great deal of difficulty in their family and peer relationships. They tend have more conflict with their parents over issues like chores and homework. Parents are more likely to be harsh and inconsistent in their discipline, and children respond with greater hostility and avoidance of their parents than their non-ADHD peers. This pattern of negative interaction results in strained and distant parent-child relationships (Anastopolous, Sommer, & Schatz, 2009; Wehmeier, Schacht, & Barkley, 2010).

Children and teens with ADHD also engage in more conflict with their siblings than do other children of the same age. Externalizing behavior problems seem to be one of the major sources of this conflict; when comorbid disruptive behavior disorders are present, conflict increases substantially. While children with ADHD generally do not rate their sibling relationships as less close than do other children, the presence of comorbid internalizing or externalizing disorders has been shown to relate to less warmth and closeness in these interactions (Mikami & Pfiffner, 2008).

Social skills deficits and conflictual interactions extend to peer relations as well. A majority (70%) of these children have been found to have serious problems in peer and friend relationships. Younger children with ADHD can be difficult playmates as they have a harder time waiting and taking turns, and paying attention to and following rules of games. Those with ADHD-C in particular tend to interact in an impulsive, intrusive manner, and are disruptive (Wehmeier et al., 2010). In contrast, children with ADHD-PI are often characterized as being socially passive, shy, and withdrawn (Barkley, 2006). As a result of these skill deficits, they tend to be less well-liked, experience more frequent rejection, and have fewer reciprocal friendships than their peers. Those with oppositional defiant disorder (ODD) or conduct disorder (CD) display the most serious social problems; for these youth, most do not develop any close friendships by the third grade, and in adolescence are more likely to become bullies or victims of bullies (Wehmeier et al., 2010). Treatment with psychostimulant medication frequently does not improve social problems even when it decreases aggression and other negative behaviors (Pelham & Fabiano, 2008).

Academic

The academic environment may be the most challenging context that students with ADHD have to navigate. Symptoms appear dramatically in the school setting, where children are required to remain vigilant to instruction and tasks at longer intervals than at home or in social settings (Barkley, 2003). Nearly all children with ADHD experience significant impairment in academic achievement throughout their school years, and on average score a full standard deviation below classmates on achievement tests (G. J. DuPaul & Stoner, 2003; Loe & Feldman, 2007). Problems with inattention manifest in increased off-task behavior, and increased time to return to an activity after being distracted, resulting in decreased productivity. Children with ADHD have difficulty completing homework and assignments, organizing materials and tasks, and planning completion for long-term projects. Hyperactivity and impulsivity appear in such behaviors as getting up without permission, disturbing others, talking noisily, and rule-breaking, which lead to punishments and negative interactions with teachers. They may spend less time in the classroom as a result of frequent disciplinary action, and thus miss out on instruction. It is not surprising that children with ADHD are at higher risk than their peers for grade retention, suspension, expulsion, and school drop out (Barkley, 2006; G. J. DuPaul et al., 2006).

Emotional

Adolescents and children with ADHD experience rejection, failure, frustration, and conflict on a day-to-day basis. The ADHD-related impairments often take an emotional toll on these children as they navigate a variety of social and performance situations, often facing criticism from all sides. They may learn to anticipate failure instead of success, developing a sense of learned helplessness and dejection (Wehmeier et al., 2010). They also tend to have poorer self-perception than their peers and rate themselves more negatively on social and communication skills (Klimkeit et al., 2006). Related to the impairment in behavioral inhibition, children with ADHD are less able to moderate or regulate their emotions and to suppress their external emotional reactions. Consequently, they may experience extreme emotional reactions to stressful situations (Barkley, 2006).

COMORBID DISORDERS

Children with ADHD frequently have one or more comorbid psychiatric disorders. Recent studies suggest that around 80% of children and adolescents with ADHD have at least one comorbid disorder, and over half have two or more (Biederman, Petty, Evans, Small, & Faracone, 2010; Cuffe et al., 2005). The most common pattern of comorbidity seen in children with ADHD is that of ADHD-C with other externalizing behavior disorders. About half of youth diagnosed with ADHD also meet diagnostic criteria for ODD or CD. ODD is characterized by a pattern of defiant behavior and rule-breaking, including noncompliance with direct commands, denying responsibility for actions, and arguing. CD is more severe, defined by a pattern of aggression, destruction, lying, stealing, or truancy (APA, 2000).

Internalizing disorders also commonly co-occur with ADHD. About 30% of youth with ADHD have a comorbid anxiety disorder, and about 25% have a mood disorder (Biederman, 2005). Rates of anxiety disorders may be slightly higher in individuals with ADHD-PI. Anxiety disorders are found to reduce the risk of impulsiveness compared to ADHD without anxiety. As noted before, children with ADHD experience considerable rejection and failure;

it may be that high rates of comorbidity are related to such a negative learning history (Barkley, 2003; Wehmeier et al., 2010). ADHD and mood disorders may share a common genetic factor predisposing an individual to both disorders, but no genetic link or familial pattern has been found for comorbidity of anxiety disorders (Barkley, 2003; Biederman, 2005). Learning disabilities, tic disorders, and sleep disorders and disturbances are other problems frequently seen in children with ADHD (Barkley, 2003).

DEVELOPMENTAL COURSE

Although usually diagnosed in childhood, ADHD is increasingly conceptualized as a chronic disorder, often persisting through adulthood. Hyperactivity and impulsivity tend to present in the preschool years, at around age 3 to 4 years, and symptoms of inattention typically appear slightly later at 5 or 6 years. Some evidence suggests that ADHD-PI has a slightly later onset than ADHD-C, and symptoms may not occur until age 8 or later. Almost all cases of ADHD have an onset prior to age 16 years (Barkley, 2003, 2006).

Hyperactivity symptoms begin to decline in adolescence, and at this time take on a more internalized subjective sense of restlessness rather than external motor activity. For this reason, ADHD was previously thought to be a remitting disorder in which most children outgrew their symptoms; however, while hyperactivity tends to decline, symptoms of inattention typically do not, and most children with ADHD continue to have impairments as adolescents and as adults. Symptoms of ADHD decline in a similar manner for males and females (Monuteaux, Mick, Faraone, & Biederman, 2010). A longitudinal study that followed boys with ADHD showed that 78% of participants continued to experience clinically significant symptoms as young adults (Beiderman et al., 2010). Adults with ADHD also continue to display high rates of psychiatric comorbidity relative to comparisons, with higher lifetime prevalence for mood and anxiety disorders, substance use disorders, externalizing disorders, bulimia nervosa, Tourette's, and language disorders (Beiderman et al., 2010; Kessler et al., 2006). For adults, anxiety disorders are the most common comorbid diagnoses; estimates suggest that around 50% of adults with ADHD also have an anxiety disorder (Biederman, 2005).

TREATMENT APPROACHES

Treatments for ADHD proliferate and include such various approaches as behavioral parent training, academic interventions, classroom management, summer treatment programs, neurofeedback, psychostimulant medication, and cognitive behavior therapy, among others. The two most empirically tested interventions for ADHD are psychostimulants and behavior contingency management, which is usually delivered as parent or teacher training.

Administration of psychotropic medication, generally in the form of central nervous system stimulants, is the most commonly employed treatment method for ADHD. Evidence for the effectiveness of psychostimulant medication for ADHD is extensive; it is considered the gold standard of treatment as it results in large improvements in the short term for ADHD symptoms of inattention, hyperactivity, and impulsivity and in some related impairments, such as aggression, compliance, and productivity at school. About 80% of individuals treated with psychostimulants show some improvement in symptoms, but the remaining portion are considered nonresponders to medication. Among those who show a positive response, most do not achieve normalized functioning with medication alone. Still others experience significant adverse effects, such as dry mouth, loss of appetite, nausea, and insomnia and prefer not to take medications for those reasons. Parents commonly prefer alternative treatment options. Additionally, psychostimulants may not be adequate in addressing all significant life impairments, such as parent–child relationships, social skills and peer relations, long-term academic achievement, and comorbid disorders. Because of these limitations, a number of psychosocial interventions for ADHD have been developed and investigated both as stand-alone therapies and as adjunctive treatments to psychostimulant medication (Biederman, 2005; Pelham & Fabiano, 2008).

The second most commonly implemented treatment is behavior modification, also known as contingency management, usually delivered as training in behavior techniques to parents and teachers. For this treatment, parents and teachers are instructed by a professional in methods to systematically administer consequences to reduce unwanted behavior and increase desired behavior. By contrast, direct contingency management is delivered directly to children by clinicians, and also involves shaping consequences to promote desired behavior. For children with ADHD, direct contingency management is delivered in summer treatment programs. A combination of these behavioral strategies is frequently used to maximize effectiveness and generalize gains.

BEHAVIOR MODIFICATION

Behavior contingency management/behavior modification was initially used for children with hyperactive and inattentive symptoms because they had successfully been implemented with children with intellectual disabilities. Their use was originally driven by the idea that faulty learning or social contingencies were the cause of the disorder, and that correcting the contingencies by training the parents would produce lasting changes. Although social learning is not to blame for the symptoms and impairments that arise from ADHD, training parents and teachers to manipulate antecedents and consequences is a technique that may serve to cue and motivate appropriate behavior (Antshel & Barkley, 2008). Antecedent modification involves using cues to prompt desired behavior (e.g., effective commands, visual reminders). Reinforcement contingencies are created to increase desired behaviors, such as compliance with commands, completion of schoolwork, and so forth, and are often implemented in the form of point systems or token economies. Punishments are applied to reduce inappropriate behaviors such as arguing and aggression; a common punishment for young children is time-out. Parents and teachers are trained in the use of operant conditioning techniques in the child's natural environment. Behavior management strategies are not likely to completely eliminate symptoms and impairments of such a strongly neurologically based disorder; however, if delivered consistently and appropriately, behavior management strategies that are focused on immediate and significant relationships and environmental settings often reduce some of the more devastating psychosocial consequences of ADHD through improving parent-child relationships, social functioning, academic achievement, and reducing or eliminating comorbid psychiatric problems. No one treatment approach is likely to be adequate in addressing every area of difficulty for a child with ADHD.

Behavioral parent training (BPT) is the most frequently implemented behavioral intervention for ADHD. Several manualized BPT programs have been effective in the treatment of ODD and have been used in children with ADHD and with comorbid ADHD and ODD. Barkley's (1987) Defiant Children program has been adapted for use with ADHD and is described here as a representation of a typical program; similar programs include Community Parent Education Program, and the Incredible Years Series (IYS) (Cunningham, Bremner, & Secord, 1997; Webster-Stratton, 1992).

Barkley's (1987) BPT program consists of 8–12 weekly training sessions taught by a mental health professional either to groups or individual parents. Each session focuses on a different behavioral technique that parents then apply at home. Treatment begins with psychoeducation on ADHD, behavior problems, and basic learning/behavior principles. Parents are taught to increase positive attention by spending daily one-on-one special time with the child. Attention is used to reinforce compliance and independent play. Increasing compliance is one of the more important targets for children with ADHD (even those without ODD) because parents so often have to cue appropriate behavior (e.g., "stop at the curb," "look at your homework"). The program incorporates the use of a token economy for increasing individualized target behaviors and teaches use of appropriate time-out as a mild punisher for misbehavior. A daily report card system between parents and teachers is implemented to generalize behavioral gains to the school environment. Table 10.2 provides an example sequence of steps in a BPT program.

Consensus Panel Recommendations

Expert panels created among medical and psychiatric associations and government health organizations periodically review existing empirical research and develop guidelines to aid practitioners in choosing the most well-established, scientifically supported treatments for ADHD. Published guidelines include recommendations of best practice for assessment, treatment, and treatment maintenance of ADHD. The American Academy of Child and Adolescent Psychiatry (2007) practice parameters for the assessment and treatment of ADHD recommend psychopharmalogical treatment with an FDA-approved psychostimulant as the first line of treatment for most individuals with ADHD. Behavior therapy, including BPT and behavioral classroom management, is suggested as the first-line treatment option for cases in which ADHD symptoms are mild or in which parents reject treatment with psychostimulants. Behavior therapy is recommended as the second intervention alternative when an individual does not respond to an FDA-approved drug. A combination of treatment with medication and behavioral intervention is recommended for children with less than optimal response to medication and for those with comorbid psychiatric disorders or significant impairments in daily functioning. These recommendations include behavior therapy as treatment consideration for a considerable portion of children and adolescents with ADHD.

The National Institute for Health and Clinical Excellence (NICE) of the United Kingdom guidelines for assessment and treatment of ADHD (NICE, 2009) endorse behavioral treatments for all children and adolescents diagnosed with ADHD. Group parent training

---

TABLE 10.2   Sequence of Sessions for Behavioral Parent Training

1. Overview of ADHD and ODD and behavior management principles
2. Establishing special time, increasing positive attention
3. Attending to appropriate behavior (e.g., compliance) and ignoring minor, inappropriate behaviors (e.g., whining)
4. Giving effective commands and reprimands
5. Establishing and enforcing rules and contingencies
6. Teaching effective time-out procedures
7. Home token economy system for rewards and sometimes response costs
8. Enforcing contingencies in public places; planning ahead for misbehavior outside the home
9. Implementing a daily school behavior report card
10. Troubleshooting techniques, managing future misconduct
11. One month booster session

programs are recommended as the first-line treatment for all preschool-age children. For school-age children and adolescents with moderate levels of symptoms and psychosocial impairments, the NICE guidelines recommend a combination of a parent training program and behavioral interventions implemented in the classroom. Medication is recommended as an adjunctive therapy when school-age children and adolescents do not show adequate response to behavioral and psychological interventions. In instances in which symptoms and impairments are severe, the guidelines recommend a combination of psychostimulant medication, parent training, and classroom behavior management. The NICE guidelines state that pharmacological ADHD treatments should always be accompanied by a comprehensive treatment plan that includes behavioral, psychological, educational, and interventions.

Randomized Controlled Trials

Development of clinical practice guidelines is based upon a review of empirical studies of various treatment methods and comparison of cumulative support of each therapy. Particular weight is given to randomized controlled trials (RCTs), which compare a particular treatment method with control groups and alternative treatments. A number of early RCTs that compared BPT to wait-list controls established a base of empirical support for BPT in the treatment of children with ADHD (Gittelman-Klein et al., 1980; Horn, Ialongo, Greenberg, Packard, & Smith-Winberry, 1990; Horn et al., 1991; Pisterman et al., 1989). These studies generally showed BPT to reduce problem behaviors in children as rated by parents, improve parent-child interactions, and decrease parental stress (Chronis, Chacko, Fabiano, Wymbs, & Pelham, 2004).

For example, one early study examined the effectiveness of BPT for ADHD symptoms and parental stress among families of school-aged children randomly assigned to either a BPT group or wait-list control. The BPT group received nine sessions of BPT training. Pre- and postmeasures of parent and child functioning were taken. The BPT participants showed significant gains in comparison to the control group on measures of parent-reported child ADHD symptoms, parenting stress, and parenting self-esteem. These gains were shown to be maintained in a 2-month follow-up measure (Anastopoulos, Shelton, DuPaul, & Guevremont, 1993).

A more recent study compared the effectiveness of BPT as adjunct to routine care with routine care alone (treatment as usual). Children ages 4 through 12 years receiving care in an outpatient clinic for treatment of ADHD were randomly assigned to either 5 months of BPT in conjunction with routine clinical care ($N = 47$) or to routine care alone, which consisted of family support and medication treatment as indicated (BPT consisted of 12 group training sessions). Parent-reported ADHD symptoms, conduct problems, internalizing symptoms, and parenting stress were assessed for both groups pre- and posttreatment, and a follow-up assessment of the BPT group was conducted 25 weeks after treatment. Both treatment groups improved on all measures. The BPT group showed larger improvements for conduct problems and internalizing symptoms than the routine care group, but no group differences were found for either parenting stress or ADHD symptoms. Results were equivalent for children receiving medication and not receiving medication, although those in the BPT treatment received less medication treatment. The researchers suggested that BPT enhances the effectiveness of routine clinical treatment for children with ADHD for behavioral and internalizing problems, but not for ADHD symptoms or parenting stress. They also suggest that BPT may limit the need for medication treatment (Van den Hoofdakker et al., 2007).

As a result of consistent positive findings regarding the effectiveness of BPT for enhancing parent behavior management skills and reducing child externalizing behavior, attention has increasingly focused on enhancing BPT programs to increase effectiveness for core ADHD symptoms and to address correlates associated with poor treatment response, such as low socioeconomic status, parental psychopathology, and single-parenting. For example, single mothers of children with ADHD face special challenges and barriers to receiving treatment, and tend to show decreased treatment response to BPT. In response to this special need, an enhanced version of BPT was created, including additional treatment components addressing treatment influences identified in this population (e.g., low-intensity, didactic format). In order to evaluate the efficacy of the program, 120 single mothers of 5- to 12-year-old children with ADHD were randomly assigned to a wait-list control group, a traditional behavioral parent training program, or an enhanced behavioral parent training program—the Strategies to Enhance Positive Parenting (STEPP) program. Both traditional BPT and STEPP resulted in significant improvements in several areas of functioning, including oppositional behavior, and parent-child relations. While both treatments were superior to the control group, the STEPP group demonstrated superior outcomes to the standard BPT group for these domains (overall mean effect sizes were 0.36 and 0.44 across all outcomes). Participants in the STEPP program attended more frequently, were more engaged, and were more satisfied with treatment compared to single mothers in the traditional BPT program. Similar to other studies of BPT, the BPT and STEPP programs in this study did not significantly improve core ADHD symptoms and improvements were not maintained at 3-month follow-up (Chacko et al., 2009).

A similar BPT program was designed to increase fathers' engagement in BPT. Fathers of 6- to 12-year-old children with *DSM* diagnoses of ADHD were randomly assigned to attend either a standard BPT program or the Coaching Our Acting-Out Children: Heightening Essential Skills (COACHES) program. The COACHES program included BPT plus sports skills training for the children and parent-child interactions in which the fathers practiced parenting techniques in the context of a soccer game. Children's ADHD and ODD symptoms were similarly improved across groups, but fathers who participated in the COACHES program were significantly more engaged in the treatment process, as demonstrated by more frequent punctuality and attendance of sessions, increased compliance with homework assignments, and greater consumer satisfaction on posttreatment measures (Fabiano et al., 2009). The studies demonstrating benefits of enhanced BPT programs indicates the possibility that tailoring psychosocial treatments to meet individual client needs may be an effective means of increasing treatment compliance and may result in larger treatment gains for children targeted in the interventions.

A number of studies have shown BPT to result in greater improvement for conduct problems and internalizing problems than for core ADHD symptoms (inattention, hyperactivity) among school-aged children (Barkley et al., 2000; Chacko et al., 2009; Corcoran and Dattalo, 2006; MTA, 1999; Van den Hoofdakker et al., 2007). A handful of enhanced BPT programs have shown more favorable results on both ADHD symptoms and related impairments for preschool-aged children. The New Forest Parenting Package (NFPP) (Weeks, Thompson, & Laver-Bradbury, 1999) is a BPT intervention that was evaluated in a community sample of 78 three-year-olds diagnosed with ADHD. Participants were randomized to NFPP, parent counseling and support, or a waiting-list control group. The NFPP group received directive coaching in child management techniques while the counseling group received only nondirective support and counseling. The management techniques were not geared only toward oppositional behavior, but also trained parents to help children self-regulate through a variety of activities. Pre-, post-, and follow-up measures of child ADHD symptoms and mother's sense of well-being were obtained. The BPT group proved superior to the counseling and wait-list groups for both ADHD symptom reduction and increased maternal well-being. The ADHD symptom improvement was clinically significant for 53% of children in the BPT group, and treatment effects were maintained at the 15-week posttreatment follow-up. Authors concluded that BPT is a valuable treatment option for preschoolers with ADHD, and that constructive training in parenting strategies is an essential component of BPT over and above therapist contact and support (Sonuga-Barke, Daley, Thompson, Laver-Bradbury, & Weeks, 2001).

A more recent study of the NFPP program showed similarly positive outcomes. Forty-one preschoolers were randomly assigned to either NFPP or treatment as usual conditions. Measures of ADHD and ODD symptoms, mothers' mental health, and the quality of mother–child interactions were taken pre- and posttreatment, and at a 9-week follow-up. The ADHD symptoms were significantly lower for the treatment groups versus control group (effect size > 1) and were maintained at a 9-week follow-up measure. Improvement in ODD symptoms was more moderate but favored the treatment group. No improvements were seen in maternal mental health or parenting behavior during mother–child interactions, although mothers spoke more positively of their children in a speech sample following treatment. The authors concluded that results support efficacy of the NFPP program, though replication with a larger sample size is needed (Thompson et al., 2009).

Similar evaluations of the IYS and the Triple P Positive Parenting Program with preschool children have shown reductions in ADHD and disruptive behavior problems for families randomized to BPT compared to wait-list conditions (Jones, Daley, Hutchings, Bywater, & Eames, 2007; Bor, Sanders, & Markie-Dadds, 2002). The IYS participants showed maintenance in treatment gains at 18-month follow-up (Jones, Daley, Hutchings, Bywater, & Eames, 2008). Other RCTs evaluating the Triple P program have shown clinically significant reductions in conduct problems in preschoolers, though these studies were not specific to children with ADHD (Sanders, Markie-Dadds, Tully, & Bor, 2000). Such positive findings from BPT with preschoolers are especially encouraging considering the potential long-term outcomes associated with the disorder.

Parent training for adolescents with ADHD has been studied far less than for younger children. The BPT programs that were developed for younger children are modified for use with a teenage population. Behavior targets for adolescents are decided on by child and parent, and privilege loss (grounding) is used in place of time-out. Positive reinforcement and token economies are adjusted to be appropriate with teenagers (Antshel & Barkley, 2008; Young & Myanthi Amarasinghe, 2010). A few uncontrolled studies have shown BPT to be modestly beneficial for this age group, but no controlled studies have been conducted to date demonstrating superiority of BPT to other treatment options (Young & Myanthi Amarasinghe, 2010).

Barkley, Edwards, Laneri, Fletcher, and Metevia (2001) compared two family-based psychosocial therapies for adolescents with ADHD. Families ($N = 97$) were assigned to either 18 sessions of problem-solving communication training or behavior management training for nine sessions followed by PSCT for nine sessions. Posttreatment, both groups were equally improved on ratings and observations of parent–teen conflicts, although significantly more families dropped out of PSCT alone than out of BMT/PSCT. For both treatment groups, only about one fourth demonstrated reliable, clinically significant improvement, and some families worsened in their degree of conflict. Thus the verdict is out regarding parent training with adolescent ADHD.

Improvements at home resulting from BPT are not likely to generalize to the school environment because the structure and contingencies created by the parent are not immediately present for the child at school. In order to improve behavior and performance at school, antecedent modification and contingency management need to be implemented there as well (Abramowitz & O'Leary, 1991). Some school-based behavioral programs have focused on school-wide training of teachers and programs that are inclusive of many children in the school with ADHD (e.g., Pfiffner et al., 2007). More commonly, mental health professionals are contacted as consultants for individual children when ADHD symptoms create behavioral disruptions in the classroom and interfere with academic progress (Abramowitz & O'Leary, 1991; G. J. DuPaul et al., 2006; Fabiano & Pelham, 2003). Behavioral training procedures used with parents are generally very similar to those used to help teachers manage ADHD in the classroom. Behavioral classroom management is a parallel form of behavior modification treatment in which the child's classroom teacher is trained in the use of effective commands, time-out, token systems, immediate feedback, and increased positive reinforcement (Antshel & Barkley, 2008).

As with BPT, a frequent behavioral target in classroom management is increasing compliance with commands. A recent study focused on the effectiveness of Barkley's method of reducing repetition of commands to increase compliance within the school setting. Elementary school teachers were randomly assigned to either a treatment group (which received instruction on reducing repetition and increasing effectiveness of commands) or to a nontreatment control group. Students whose teachers received the training significantly reduced noncompliance while students in the control group did not. The author concluded that this method is effective in the classroom setting and should be implemented for students with ADHD (Kapalka, 2005).

One study examined the effects of an intensive classroom treatment in 158 kindergartners identified as having high levels of hyperactive, inattentive, impulsive, and aggressive behaviors. Participants were randomly assigned to one of four treatment groups: no treatment, parent training, classroom behavioral treatment, or a combination of classroom and parent training treatments. Unfortunately, parents assigned to the BPT-only group showed very poor attendance and this group did not demonstrate treatment gains; however, the classroom management treatment condition resulted in improvements in objective observations of externalizing behavior in the classroom, teacher ratings of attention, social skills, self-control, and aggression, as well as parent ratings of adaptive behavior. Behavior improvements in the classroom did not generalize to the home environment per parent ratings. Additionally, while externalizing behaviors improved, no gains were seen in academic achievement or laboratory-based measures of attention (i.e., Continuous Performance Test). The intervention was conducted for one school year only (Barkley et al., 2000). A 2-year follow-up of the intervention indicated no difference between those treated in the classroom condition and those not treated, and the children continued to display high levels of ADHD and ODD symptoms compared to peers (Shelton et al., 2000). These results again demonstrate that behavioral gains resulting from contingency management in one setting are not likely to generalize to other settings or to persist once the contingencies have been removed; therefore, it is important that contingency management be implemented across settings.

Several other investigation teams have found beneficial results in both home and school settings, as indicated by parent and teacher ratings when incorporating parent training and classroom management into the same treatment package. Corkum, McKinnon, and Mullane (2005) demonstrated superior results when adding a behavioral training intervention with children's teachers to the behavior training provided to parents alone. Similarly, Owens et al. (2005) reported treatment gains across contexts from a small-scale RCT of a behavioral package that included parent and teacher behavior contingency management strategies. A study that compared a behavioral package to medication found superior results for the medication group, although the behavioral group showed gains at home and at school (Van der Oord, Prins, Oosterlaan, & Emmelkamp, 2008).

Meta-Analyses of Group Designs

Corcoran and Dattalo (2006) examined a small set of studies examining BPT published between 1980 and 2003. Studies that compared BPT to control or comparison groups were included. The overall effect size (Cohen's d) of BPT on ADHD symptoms was relatively low (0.40), as was the effect size (0.36) on externalizing symptoms. A moderate effect was observed for family functioning (0.67) and internalizing symptoms (0.64). This finding is also consistent with those of individual RCTs; however, an effect size of 8.2 was reported for academic performance. This finding is not consistent with data from RCTs, which failed to show generalization of treatment gains to the school environment. This discrepancy may be at least partially attributable to inclusion of only two studies that reported this outcome. Consistent with a number of studies the effects of BPT on social functioning were near zero. Similar to individual RCTs described earlier, the findings indicate that BPT produces some change in ADHD symptoms of inattention and hyperactivity, and results in more substantial improvements in family relationships and internalizing symptoms.

A meta-analytic review of BPT studies to identify effective components of BPT programs examined 77 published evaluations of BPT outcomes for children up to age 7 years. Component analysis was conducted by using content and delivery methods of training programs to predict effect sizes on measures of children's externalizing behavior and parenting behaviors, controlling for differences among research designs. Components of BPT programs consistently associated with larger effect sizes were teaching parents the use of time-out and the value of consistency, increasing positive parent–child interactions, enhancing emotional communication skills, and incorporating practice of new skills with their children during training sessions. Program components consistently associated with smaller effects included teaching parents problem solving; teaching parents to promote children's cognitive, academic, or social skills; and providing various additional services (Kaminski, Valle, Filenne, & Boyle, 2008).

G. DuPaul and Eckert (1997) conducted a meta-analysis examining the effects of school-based interventions for children and teenagers with ADHD. Studies included were those based on either contingency management, academic interventions that use antecedent modification (such as adding structure to a task), or cognitive behavior therapy (which includes teaching of strategies such as reflective problem solving). Behavior effect sizes (weighted least squares) for within-subject and between-subject designs were computed for all three types of interventions. For within-subjects design studies, behavior effect sizes were greater for contingency management (0.94) and academic interventions (0.69) than for cognitive behavioral interventions (0.19). Behavior effect sizes for between-subjects designs were not different among the three types of interventions. Academic outcome effect sizes for within-subjects designs were small among all three interventions types; the effect size for contingency management was 0.11. Academic effect sizes were not available for between-subjects designs. The authors concluded that behavior modification techniques are more effective than cognitive techniques in improving behavioral outcomes for children with ADHD.

Single-Subject Experimental Analyses

Between-group design studies evaluating behavior modification techniques are based on positive findings from earlier work using single-case designs. Results of single-subject studies demonstrate effectiveness of behavioral principles in managing ADHD. For example, in a study of a 6-year-old girl with ADHD, a system of positive reinforcement and response costs was implemented in the classroom. The teacher was trained to implement the class-wide management system. An ABA reversal design was used in order to determine effectiveness of the behavioral interventions used in combination. Direct behavioral observations were made to determine baseline levels of appropriate versus oppositional and on-task versus off-task behaviors. Preintervention, the child displayed appropriate behavior for 61% of observed intervals. During the intervention phase, her appropriate behavior increased to 79%, and when the treatment was withdrawn, appropriate behavior decreased, though not to baseline level (71%). On-task behavior increased from 76% at baseline to 88% during the treatment interval, and dropped to 82% when the treatment was withdrawn (Anhalt, McNeil, & Bahl, 1998).

Similarly, McGoey and DuPaul (2000) used a single-subject withdrawal design to compare the effects of a token reinforcement and a response cost intervention in improving classroom behavior for four preschool-age children with ADHD. A reversal design was used to compare behavior at baseline (A), with implementation of a token economy system (B), and with a response cost intervention (C). Two participants received the ABACABAC intervention, and the other two received treatments in the opposite order. The results of behavior observations and teacher rating scales showed that both interventions were effective in improving behavior for all four children. Three of the children improved to levels equal to their peers. The teachers found the response cost procedures to be easier to administer in a large group setting.

An 8-year-old boy attending the third grade was the subject of a consultant directed behavior modification program. John was in a general education classroom and received remediation in math and reading in a small group special education setting. John received special education services because ADHD significantly impaired his academic progress. His disruptive behaviors at the start of treatment included interrupting others, poor academic work, being out of his seat without permission, talking back when corrected, teasing peers, and noncompliance. John's teachers expressed frustration with his behavior and his peers did not want to be seated next to him. In addition to small group instruction, John also received a behavioral intervention that involved a behavior tracking sheet through which John could earn biweekly rewards. Five behavior goals were identified for John, and he met with his teacher at the end of each academic period to determine whether he had achieved his goals. With this intervention in place for several weeks, John had not earned a reinforcer. The behavioral consultant observed John and his classmates in the morning and afternoon for a few weeks in order to gather baseline data on the frequency of John's disruptive and off-task behavior in relation to that of his classmates. In order to make his behavioral targets more objective and clear for John, and to provide him with immediate feedback when he was violating a rule, John's teacher was instructed to issue a reprimand when he was violating a rule (i.e., off-task or disruptive). In order to receive reinforcement, John had to have fewer than three violations of each objective. Instead of receiving a delayed reinforcer, John earned the opportunity to play a video game for a few minutes after each academic period in which he met his behavioral targets (fewer than three violations). John's off-task behavior declined immediately with the implementation of the new plan. Over a few weeks, both off-task behavior and classroom disruptions were brought to the level of the average for his class. Unfortunately, the authors did not report on academic achievement or work productivity gains as a result of the intervention. It was not possible to follow-up with John's progress because the school year ended (Fabiano & Pelham, 2003).

Meta-Analyses of Single-Subject Experiments

Although behavioral interventions were developed based on findings and methods of small N experiment, few meta-analytic reviews have been devoted to single-subject designs. Thirty-eight single-case designs were included within a larger meta-analysis (G. DuPaul & Eckert, 1997) of school-based interventions for ADHD. Both published and unpublished studies that used behavioral (contingency management or antecedent modification) or cognitive behavioral interventions were included. The overall weighted least squares effect size for behavioral outcomes was 1.16 with a median of 0.80. Interventions using contingency management (ES = 1.44) and antecedent modification (academic intervention) (ES = 1.61) were significantly more effective than cognitive behavioral treatments (ES = 0.80). Interestingly, interventions based in public school settings were significantly more effective than those implemented in private schools. Effect sizes from cases in special education settings (ES = 1.52) were significantly greater than those obtained in general education or combined general education/ special education programs (0.96; 1.30). The mean effect size for academic outcomes was 0.82 with a median of 0.30 for all treatment interventions. No differences were found among types of treatment on academic outcomes. For both behavioral and academic outcomes, effect sizes from published studies were significantly greater than those from unpublished studies.

Conclusions

Results of RCTs, single-subject studies, and meta-analyses show that stand-alone behavior modification interventions are effective treatments for ADHD. They are not as effective as psychostimulant medication for core symptoms of ADHD (inattention and hyperactivity), but are especially helpful in targeting specific impairments including oppositional behavior, parent–child relationships, externalizing behavior, and internalizing disorders. Many programs are based on treatments originally developed for ODD and tend to focus on conduct or externalizing problems more so than attention impairments; this is a major limitation on the part of behavior management. Many studies do not address academic performance, inattention symptoms, or organization and time management, but more recently developed programs are beginning to include strategies targeting these areas (Pfiffner et al., 2007). Parents tend to prefer behavioral interventions over stimulant medication as a first line of treatment, which is important to consider when deciding how beneficial contingency management strategies are in comparison to medication. These treatments tend to be time consuming in comparison to stimulant medication, but if offered in community mental health settings or in public schools, they may be provided in a more cost-effective manner. A major limitation of behavioral modification strategies is that treatment gains are usually not maintained postintervention and do not generalize across settings in which contingencies are not implemented (Antshel & Barkley, 2008; Barkley et al., 2000; Kaiser, Hoza, & Hurt, 2008; MTA, 1999). Psychostimulants also do not result in lasting gains and are not effective on days when the child does not take them (Biederman, 2005). Common impediments to both treatments include single-parent household, low socioeconomic status, and ethnic minority status (Chronis et al., 2004). While behavior modification improves areas of functioning not affected by medication, neither intervention has consistently shown enhancement of academic achievement, although some of the more recent school-based treatments have begun to focus more intensely on this area (Evans, Serpell, Schultz, & Pastor, 2007). Overall, behavior contingency management would likely be beneficial for nearly all children who have ADHD, as they result in some gains in ADHD symptoms and larger gains in family functioning, academic productivity, and symptom improvement for internalizing and externalizing disorders. In order for lasting effects to occur, treatment boosters should be delivered and contingencies maintained across settings.

SUMMER TREATMENT PROGRAM

Summer treatment programs (STPs) were developed in order to provide a comprehensive treatment model for children and teenagers with ADHD in a camp-like recreational setting. The STPs do not focus directly on ADHD symptoms as listed in the *DSM-IV-TR*, but instead focuses on social, academic, and parenting functional impairments that are theorized to moderate long-term outcomes for children with ADHD. Goals of treatment are to improve peer relationships, interactions with adults, academic performance, and self-efficacy, each of which is related to long-term functioning (Pelham et al., 2010).

The STPs are held in the summer months during school breaks. Programs generally are conducted for 7 to 8 weeks, 5 days per week, 8 or 9 hours per day. The STPs are designed for children between the ages of 5 and 15 years. Small groups of 12 to 16 youth matched by age are created at the beginning of the program and are led by trained interns. Treatment components include social reinforcement for appropriate behavior, teaching the use of effective commands, a reward/response cost point system, social skills training, daily report cards to parents, sports training, time-out, and academic instruction. Camp participants spend 3 hours per day in a classroom setting that employs a point system for managing behavior and encouraging work completion. Much of the remainder of each day is devoted to recreational activities (Pelham et al., 2010; Pelham, Greiner, & Gnagy, 1997).

Social skills training is delivered in 10-minute group sessions, and appropriate social behavior is prompted and reinforced throughout the day. While clinic-based social skills training has not been shown to be effective, developers of the STP system argue that social skills can be targeted more directly in STP. Sports skills training is also included in order to promote social interaction and to enhance motor skills, which are typically poor in children with ADHD. Parents attend weekly BPT sessions in order to acquire management skills for facilitating generalization and maintenance of treatment gains. Many children involved in STPs also take stimulant medication; optional placebo-controlled evaluations are provided in order to find the most effective dose or to determine whether medication provides benefits beyond those produced by the program (Pelham et al., 2010; Pelham, Greiner, & Gnagy, 1997).

This intensive, multicomponent treatment is based on conceptualization of ADHD as a chronic disorder with long-lasting psychosocial consequences. Developers argue that in order to be effective in improving quality of life and produce meaningful changes, intensive long-term psychosocial interventions need to be implemented across settings. The STP also includes intensive monitoring through the daily point system, academic work, and daily ratings by adults (Pelham et al., 2010).

Consensus Panel Recommendations

The APA Task Force (Brown et al., 2007) review of behavioral, pharmacological, and combined treatments recommended behavioral treatments as the first-line intervention and medication as an adjunct treatment for those who need it. The panel concluded that behavioral, pharmacological, and combined treatments are each effective interventions. Considering side effects of medication and consumer preference for psychosocial treatment, a cost-benefit analysis favored behavioral treatment.

The American Academy of Pediatrics (AAP) guidelines are less clear concerning which treatments to try first but recommend stimulant medication and/or behavior therapy as appropriate treatments. Further, the guidelines suggest establishing a treatment program that recognizes ADHD as a chronic condition, collaboration among the clinician, parents, child, and school to specify target outcomes, and continued monitoring of progress with information from parents, teachers, and the child. Evaluation of the treatment plan, original diagnosis, and possibility of comorbid disorders is recommended when target outcomes are not reached (American Academy of Pediatrics [AAP], 2001).

Although not specifically endorsed, STPs are consistent with AAP practice guidelines. The STP allows for easy identification of target outcomes, collaboration with parents, clinician, school, and child, and systematic monitoring of treatment outcomes. Maintenance of parent and school contingency strategies through the school year addresses the chronic nature of the disorder. In the clinical setting, such intensive management is impractical if not impossible. Inclusion of the placebo-controlled medication trials and communication with parents and teachers helps to meet individual treatment needs and maximize positive outcomes.

Randomized Controlled Trials

No between-group RCTs have been published for STPs as a stand-alone treatment; however, RCTs have been published that demonstrate the efficacy of individual components of STPs. Additionally, the Multimodal Treatment Study of Children with ADHD (MTA) included STP as part of a multicomponent behavioral treatment package along with BPT and classroom contingency management. While the MTA did not evaluate the effectiveness of STP as a stand-alone treatment, examining the results of

the study is beneficial in determining the potential for STPs.

The MTA is the largest, multisite RCT to date. Based on research supporting psychostimulants and behavior therapy as efficacious treatments, the MTA study compared the two treatments, their combination, and treatment as usual regarding efficacy, generalizeability, and sustained improvement. Participants were 579 children ages 7–9.9 years in grades one to four who met *DSM-IV* criteria for ADHD-C. Children with comorbid disorders were included in the study. All were randomly assigned to one of four treatment strategies: (1) medication management carefully monitored and titrated by the research group; (2) behavioral treatment package including behavioral parent training based on Barkley's and Forehand and McMahon's procedures, the summer treatment program developed by Pelham, and school-based contingency management; (3) combined medication and behavioral interventions; or (4) treatment as usual (community care). Most of the participants (67.4%) in the treatment as usual group were on medication but did not receive treatment from the study group. Participants were assessed and monitored before, during, and after 14 months of treatment on outcomes including core ADHD symptoms and impairment domains related to ADHD. All treatment groups showed clinically meaningful symptom reduction. Medication management and combined treatment were superior to community care and behavioral treatments for core ADHD symptom reduction and did not differ from one another. Those in the combined group required significantly lower doses of medication than those in the medication management group. Combined treatment was superior to treatment as usual and behavioral treatments for internalizing symptoms, opposition/aggression, teacher-rated social skills, parent–child relations, and reading achievement score, while medication management was not. Behavior treatment outperformed treatment as usual in improving parent–child relations. Parents of children in the behavioral and combined treatment groups rated treatments with greater satisfaction than the medication management group; the study group suggested that behavioral treatment components likely benefitted family functioning. Using success rates, a significantly higher success rate is reported for the combined treatment condition (67%) compared to the methylphenidate treatment condition (55%) (Swanson et al., 2001).

Overall, results suggest that medication management and combination treatment are efficacious treatments for reducing ADHD symptoms, and that a combination of intensive behavioral treatments and medication are most effective in improving secondary impairments. Thus for pure ADHD-C, medication alone may be adequate to treat symptoms, but for those with comorbid disorders or significant family disruption, combination treatment provides incremental improvement in functioning. The authors note that these findings cannot be generalized to other subtypes (ADHD-PI) or age groups. Additionally, the authors caution that results do not suggest that behavioral treatment was ineffective, as those in the treatment condition showed significant improvements in the course of treatment (MTA Cooperative Group, 1999).

The lack of greater impact of the intensive behavioral intervention in the absence of medication and on ADHD/ODD symptoms generally was unexpected. A limitation of the study is that posttreatment measures were gathered after the behavioral interventions were discontinued and were no longer implemented at their highest intensity, while medication was still being used at its most effective dose. The absence of maintenance of treatment gains following the cessation of behavioral interventions has been a significant problem. As noted before, return to baseline levels of problem behavior is also reported when individuals with ADHD discontinue taking medication.

Secondary analyses for the MTA study derived a composite score of treatment outcome across measures and showed that the combination treatment was significantly better than the other treatments on the composite. For children with a comorbid anxiety disorder, behavioral treatment was as effective as the medication management, and the combination condition proved superior to other conditions, particularly when a disruptive behavior disorder was also present. This finding is particularly noteworthy when considering that nearly 40% of the sample had a comorbid anxiety disorder, and nearly one fourth had both an anxiety and disruptive behavior disorder (Jensen et al., 2001). Also noteworthy is the finding that 8 years after completion of the study, the MTA treatment groups did not differ significantly from one another on repeated measures or newly analyzed variables including hospitalizations and academic achievement. Despite having received intensive intervention, the adolescents fared more poorly than their non-ADHD peers on 91% of measures. Neither the type nor intensity of treatment delivered in the 14-month trial predicted functioning for the teenagers (Molina et al., 2009).

Meta-Analyses of Group Designs

In order to provide an updated quantitative account of the magnitude of the effectiveness of behavioral interventions for ADHD, a comprehensive meta-analysis of behavioral treatment reports was conducted using 174 studies indentified in the literature (Fabiano et al., 2009). Authors aimed to incorporate all behavioral treatment studies conducted to date, across type of intervention (BPT, Summer Treatment Program, Classroom Contingency Management) and study design. Effect sizes varied by study design. Effect sizes in pre-post studies (0.70), between-group studies (0.83), and within-group studies (2.64) demonstrate effectiveness. Authors concluded that results add to an existing body of strong evidence that behavioral treatments are effective for treating ADHD.

Van der Oord et al. (2008) conducted a meta-analysis of group design studies comparing medication, behavioral, and combination medication and behavioral interventions for ADHD in order to evaluate the relative effectiveness of each. Analyses were conducted using RCTs published from 1985–2006 with children ages 6–12 years. Medication and combined treatments yielded large effect sizes for ADHD symptoms, ODD, and conduct problems. By contrast, behavioral treatments had moderate effect sizes for these outcomes. All treatment modalities had a moderate effect size for social behavior and small effect size for academic functioning. Efficacy rates of combined conditions were larger than medication on all outcome domains, but these differences were not statistically significant. Based on these results, researchers concluded that behavioral treatments are less effective than medication and do not appear to have additive treatment effects when used in combination with medication. The researchers also noted that children who are nonresponders to medication or who take low doses would likely benefit from behavioral interventions.

Single-Subject Experimental Analyses

In order to evaluate individual response to behavior modification within the STP, four children aged 11–12 years participated in a treatment withdrawal study. The comprehensive behavioral treatment package was delivered and withdrawn in a BABAB reversal design over the course of the 8-week program. Measures were frequency of negative behaviors, counts of rule violations in recreational and classroom settings, and accuracy and completion in academic work. Behavioral intervention was effective for each of the children, as demonstrated by rapid increase in rule violations and negative behavior, and decrease in accuracy and completion of academic work when the treatment was withdrawn. Behavior worsened increasingly over the course of the withdrawal weeks.

Following the second withdrawal, behaviors took longer to return to levels seen in the initial treatment condition. In general, behavior worsened progressively during the withdrawal period (Coles et al., 2005).

Meta-Analyses of Single-Subject Experiments

Fabiano et. al (2009) recently reported on single-case experiments within a larger meta-analysis of behavioral interventions of ADHD that included group designs (described earlier). A total of 100 single-case studies for ADHD published from 1968–2006 were included in the analysis. Outcomes were based on parent observations of ADHD symptoms, direct observations of child behavior, and academic productivity. Effect sizes were large across these domains. The unweighted effect size for behavioral treatments averaged 3.78.

Conclusions

STPs offer numerous advantages compared to other behavioral interventions, including the direct administration of intensive behavior therapy, combination of multiple well-established treatment components, and collaboration among treatment providers, teachers, and parents. STPs also demonstrate high attendance and low dropout rate compared to other psychosocial interventions. Parents and children rate STPs very favorably. The recreational setting seems to make STPs a particularly palatable treatment option. Additionally, children who attend STPs have shown decreased need for stimulants, an important outcome considering incremental adverse effects with increased doses of psychostimulants (Pelham et al., 2010).

Research support for the efficacy of STP comes primarily from the laboratory of the original developers. Chambless and Hollon (1998) require independent replication of treatment effects in a randomized controlled design by more than one investigation team in order for a treatment to be considered efficacious and specific. No published studies have yet compared STP as a stand-alone treatment with a nontreatment control group in a randomized trial, although several crossover designs have shown efficacy. Existing research including multiple single-case studies and within-group designs have shown promising results. Additionally, while the MTA study incorporated multiple behavior treatments into the behavior treatment condition, two out of those three treatments are delivered in STPs: STP and BPT.

As with other treatment for ADHD, much of the treatment gains made during the STP disappear almost immediately upon removal of treatment (Coles et al., 2005). While direct contingency management demonstrates results, it is not feasible for clinicians and STP staff to follow children through their daily routines year-round. Therefore, following direct contingency management as delivered in STP with parent and teacher training in contingency management is critical to maintain improvements gained during the summer weeks.

EVIDENCE-BASED PRACTICES

BPT is the most widely implemented and thoroughly researched behavioral treatment for ADHD. BPT, classroom management, and STPs have strong support. None of these psychosocial treatments is as effective as psychostimulant medication for ADHD symptoms (inattention, hyperactivity), but each is more efficacious in reducing secondary functional impairments, though only while treatment is in place (MTA, 1999; Molina et al., 2009). Multimodal treatment includes a combination of behavior contingency modification at home and at school, STP, and psychostimulant medication, and is the most effective mode of addressing ADHD and its secondary impairments.

BPT and classroom management are relatively costly and time-consuming compared to stimulant medication, and STP is the most expensive and time-intensive intervention available. Evaluation of the long-term cost-effectiveness of STPs when delivered across multiple consecutive summers could provide crucial information in selecting the best treatments; if STPs result in long-term benefits to psychosocial functioning, it may be that they serve as an investment preventing significant future costs. Some evidence supports the notion that BPT programs developed specifically for preschoolers with ADHD may be effective in curtailing ADHD symptoms and result in lasting gains, though longitudinal analyses of such programs are needed. More research is needed in areas of dissemination and implementation of evidence-based practices in general and specifically in ADHD. Also of concern is how to tailor treatments to meet the individual needs of the child and family, and how to gain generalization and maintenance of treatment effects.

REFERENCES

Abramowitz, A. J., & O'Leary, S. G. (1991). Behavioral interventions for the classroom: Implications for children with ADHD. *School Psychology Review, 20,* 220–233.

American Psychiatric Association. (2000). *Diagnostic and statistical manual of mental disorders* (4th ed., text rev.). Washington, DC: Author.

American Academy of Child and Adolescent Psychiatry. (2007). Practice parameters for the assessment and treatment of children and adolescents with attention-deficit/hyperactivity disorder. *Journal of the American Academy of Child and Adolescent Psychiatry, 46,* 894–921.

American Academy of Pediatrics (AAP). (2001). Clinical practice guideline: Treatment of the school-aged child with attention-deficit/hyperactivity disorder. *Pediatrics, 108,* 1033–1044.

Anastopoulos, A. D., Shelton, T. L., DuPaul, G., & Guevremont, D. C. (1993). Parent training for attention-deficit hyperactivity disorder: Its impact on parent functioning. *Journal of Abnormal Child Psychology, 21,* 581–596.

Anastopoulos, A. D., Sommer, J. L., & Schatz, N. K. (2009). ADHD and family functioning. *Current Attention Disorders Report, 1*, 167–170.

Anhalt, K., McNeil, C. B., & Bahl, A. B. (1998). The ADHD classroom kit: A whole classroom approach for managing disruptive behavior. *Psychology in the Schools, 35*, 67–79.

Antshel, K. M., & Barkley, R. A. (2008). Psychosocial interventions in attention deficit hyperactivity disorder. *Child and Adolescent Psychiatric Clinics of North America, 17*, 421–437.

Barkley, R. A. (1987). *Defiant children: A clinician's manual for assessment and parent training.* New York, NY: Guilford Press.

Barkley, R. A. (2003). Attention-deficit/hyperactivity disorder. In E. J. Mash & R. A. Barkley (Eds.), Child psychopathology (2nd ed.) (pp. 75–143). New York, NY: Guilford Press.

Barkley, R. A. (2006). *Attention-deficit/hyperactivity disorder: A handbook for diagnosis and treatment* (3rd ed.). New York, NY: Guilford Press.

Barkley, R. A., Edwards, G., Laneri, M., Fletcher, K., & Metevia, L. (2001). The efficacy of problem-solving communication training alone, behavior management training alone, and their combination for parent–adolescent conflict in teenagers with ADHD and ODD. *Journal of Consulting and Clinical Psychology, 69*, 926–941.

Barkley, R. A., Shelton, T. L., Crosswait, C., Moorehouse, M., Fletcher, K., Barrett, S., . . . Metevia, L. (2000). Multi-method psychoeducational intervention for preschool children with disruptive behavior: Preliminary results at post-treatment. *Journal of Child Psychology and Psychiatry and Allied Disciplines, 41*, 319–332.

Biederman, J. (2005). Attention-deficit/hyperactivity disorder: A selective overview. *Biological Psychiatry, 57*, 1215–1220.

Biederman, J., Petty, C. R., Evans, M., Small, J., & Faracone, S. V. (2010). How persistent is ADHD? A controlled 10-year follow-up study of boys with ADHD. *Psychiatry Research, 177*, 299–304.

Bor, W., Sanders, M., & Markie-Dadds, C. (2002). The effects of the Triple P-Positive Parenting Program on preschool children with co-occurring disruptive behavior and attentional/hyperactive difficulties. *Journal of Abnormal Child Psychology, 30*, 571–587.

Breslau, J., Aguilar-Gaxiola, S., Kendler, K. S., Su, M., Williams, D. R., & Kessler, R. C. (2006). Specifying race-ethnic differences in risk for psychiatric disorder in a U.S. national sample. *Psychological Medicine, 36*, 57–68.

Brown, R. T., Anonuccio, D. O., DuPaul, G. J., Fristad, M. A., King, C. A., Leslie, L. K., . . . Vilello, B. (2007). *Childhood mental health disorders: Evidence base and contextual factors for psychosocial, psychopharmacological, and combined interventions.* Washington, DC: American Psychological Association.

Centers for Disease Control and Prevention (2005). Mental health in the United States: Prevalence of diagnosis and medication treatment for attention-deficit/hyperactivity disorder. *Morbidity and Mortality Weekly Report, 54*, 842–847.

Chacko, A., Wymbs, B., Wymbs, F., Pelham, W., Swanger-Gagne, M., Girio, E., . . . O'Connor, B. (2009). Enhancing traditional behavioral parent training for single mothers of children with ADHD. *Journal of Clinical Child & Adolescent Psychology, 38*, 206–218.

Chambless, D. L., & Hollon, S. D. (1998). Defining empirically supported therapies. *Journal of Consulting and Clinical Psychology, 66*, 7–18.

Chronis, A. M., Chacko, A., Fabiano, G. A., Wymbs, B. T., & Pelham, W. E. (2004). Enhancements to the behavioral parent training paradigm for families of children with ADHD: Review and future directions. *Clinical Child and Family Psychology Review, 7*, 1–27.

Coles, E. K., Pelham, W. E., Gnagy, E. M., Burrows-MacLean, L., Fabiano, G. A., Chacko, A., . . . Robb, J. A. (2005). A controlled evaluation of behavioral treatment with children with ADHD attending a summer treatment program. *Journal of Emotional and Behavioral Disorders, 13*, 99–112.

Corcoran, J., & Dattalo, P. (2006). Parent involvement in treatment for ADHD: A meta-analysis of the published studies. *Research on Social Work Practice, 16*, 561–570.

Corkum, P. V., McKinnon, M., & Mullane, J. C. (2005). The effect of involving classroom teachers in a parent training program for families of children with ADHD. *Child & Family Behavior Therapy, 27*, 29–49.

Cuffe, S. P., Moore, C. G., & McKeowen, R. E. (2005). Prevalence and correlates of ADHD symptoms in the national health interview survey. *Journal of Attention Disorders, 9*, 392–402.

Cunningham, C. E., Bremner, R., & Secord, M. (1997). *COPE: The Community Parent Education Program: A school-based family systems oriented workshop for parents of children with disruptive behavior disorders.* Hamilton, Ontario: COPE Works.

DuPaul, G., & Eckert, T. (1997). The effects of school-based interventions for attention deficit hyperactivity disorder: A meta-analysis. *School Psychology Review, 26*, 5–27.

DuPaul, G. J., Jitendra, A. K., Volpe, R. J., Tresco, K. E., Lutz, G., Vile Junod, R. E., . . . Mannella, M. C. (2006). Consultation-based academic interventions for children with ADHD: Effects on reading and mathematics achievement. *Journal of Abnormal Child Psychology, 34*, 633–646.

DuPaul, G. J., & Stoner, G. (2003). *ADHD in the schools: Assessment and intervention strategies* (2nd ed.). New York, NY: Guilford Press.

Evans, S. W., Serpell, Z. N., Schultz, B. K., & Pastor, D. A. (2007). Cumulative benefits of secondary school-based treatment of students with Attention-Deficit Hyperactivity Disorder. *School Psychology Review, 26,* 256–272.

Fabiano, G. A., Chacko, A., Pelham, W. E., Robb, J. A., Walker, K. S., Wienke, A. L., . . . Pirvics, L. (2009). A comparison of behavioral parent training programs for fathers of children with attention deficit/hyperactivity disorder. *Behavior Therapy, 40,* 190–204.

Fabiano, G. A., & Pelham, W. E. (2003). Improving the effectiveness of behavioral classroom interventions for attention-deficit/hyperactivity disorder: A case study. *Journal of Emotional and Behavioral Disorders, 11,* 122–128.

Gittelman-Klein, R., Abikoff, H., Pollack, E., Klein, D., Katz, S., & Mattes, J. (1980). A controlled trial of behavior modification and methylphenidate in hyperactive children. In C. Whalen & B. Henker (Eds.), *Hyperactive children: The social ecology of identification and treatment* (pp. 221–246). New York, NY: Academic Press.

Horn, W. F., Ialongo, N., Greenberg, G., Packard, T., & Smith-Winberry, C. (1990). Additive effects of behavioral parent training and self-control therapy with attention deficit hyperactivity disordered children. *Journal of Clinical Child Psychology, 19,* 98–110.

Horn, W. F., Ialongo, N. S., Pascoe, J. M., Greenberg, G., Packard, T., Lopez, M., . . . Puttler, L. (1991). Additive effects of psychostimulants, parent training, and self-control therapy with ADHD children. *Journal of the American Academy of Child and Adolescent Psychiatry, 30,* 233–240.

Jensen, P. S., Hinshaw, S. P., Kraemer, H. C., Lenora, N., Newcorn, J. H., & Abikoff, H. B. (2001). ADHD comorbidity findings from the MTA study: Comparing comorbid subgroups. *Journal of the American Academy of Child and Adolescent Psychiatry, 40,* 147–158.

Jones, K., Daley, D., Hutchings, J., Bywater, T., & Eames, C. (2007). Efficacy of the Incredible Years Basic Parent Training programme as an early intervention for children with conduct problems and ADHD. *Child Care, Health and Development, 33,* 740–756.

Jones, K., Daley, D., Hutchings, J., Bywater, T., & Eames, C. (2008). Efficacy of the Incredible Years Basic Parent Training program as an early intervention for children with conduct problems and ADHD: Long-term follow-up. *Child Care, Health and Development, 34,* 380–390.

Kaiser, N. M., Hoza, B., & Hurt, E. A. (2008). Multimodal treatment for childhood attention-deficit/hyperactivity disorder. *Expert Review of Neurotherapeutics, 8,* 1573–1583.

Kaminski, J. W., Valle, L. A., Filenne, J. H., & Boyle, C. L. (2008). A meta-analytic review of components associated with parent training program effectiveness. *Journal of Abnormal Child Psychology, 36,* 567–589.

Kapalka, G. M. (2005). Avoiding repetitions reduces ADHD children's management problems in the classroom. *Emotional and Behavioural Difficulties, 10,* 269–279.

Kessler, R. C., Adler, L., Barkley, R., Biederman, J., Conners, C. K., Demler, O., . . . Zaslavsky, A. M. (2006). The prevalence and correlates of adult ADHD in the United States: Results from the National Comorbidity Survey Replication. *American Journal of Psychiatry, 163,* 716–723.

Klimkeit, E., Graham, C., Lee, P., Morling, M., Russo, D., & Tonge, B. (2006). Children should be seen and heard: Self-report of feelings and behaviors in primary-school-age children with ADHD. *Journal of Attention Disorders, 10,* 181–191.

Loe, I. M., & Feldman, H. M. (2007). Academic and educational outcomes of children with ADHD. *Journal of Pediatric Psychology, 32,* 643–654.

McGoey, K. E., & DuPaul, G. J. (2000). Token reinforcement and response cost procedures: Reducing the disruptive behavior of preschool children with ADHD. *School Psychology Quarterly, 15,* 330–343.

Mikami, A. Y., & Pfiffner, L. J. (2008). Sibling relationships among children with ADHD. *Journal of Attention Disorders, 11,* 482–492.

Multi-Modal Treatment (MTA) Cooperative Group: Moderators and mediators of treatment response for children with attention-deficit/hyperactivity disorder (ADHD). (1999). *Archives of General Psychiatry, 56,* 1088–1096.

Multi-Modal Treatment (MTA) Study of Children with Attention-Deficit/Hyperactivity Disorder Cooperative Group. (1999). A 14-month randomized clinical trial of treatment strategies for attention-deficit/hyperactivity disorder. *Archives of General Psychiatry, 56,* 1073–1086.

Molina, B. S. G., Hinshaw, S. P., Swanson, J. M., Arnold, L. E., Vitiello, B., Jensen, P. S., & the MTA Cooperative Group. (2009). The MTA at 8 years: prospective follow-up of children treated for combined type ADHD in a multisite study. *Journal of the American Academy of Child Adolescent Psychiatry, 48,* 484–500.

Monuteaux, M. C., Mick, E., Faraone, S. V., & Biederman, J. (2010). The influence of sex on the course and psychiatric correlates of ADHD from childhood to adolescence: A longitudinal study. *Journal of Child Psychology and Psychiatry, 51,* 233–241.

National Institute for Health and Clinical Excellence (NICE). (2009, March). *Attention deficit hyperactivity disorder: Diagnosis and management of ADHD in children, young people and adults. NICE Clinical Guideline 72.* London, England: Author.

Owens, J. S., Richerson, L., Beilstein, E. A., Crane, A., Murphy, C. E., & Vancouver, J. B. (2005). School-based mental health programming for children with inattentive and disruptive behavior problems: First-year treatment outcomes. *Journal of Attention Disorders, 9,* 261–274.

Palmer, E. D., & Finger, S. (2001). An early description of ADHD (Inattentive Subtype): Dr. Alexander Crichton and "mental restlessness" (1798). *Child Psychology and Psychiatry Review, 6*, 66–73.

Pelham, W. E., & Fabiano, G. A. (2008). Evidence-Based psychosocial treatments for attention-deficit/hyperactivity disorder. *Journal of Clinical Child & Adolescent Psychology, 37*, 184–214.

Pelham, W. E., Gnagy, E. M., Greiner, A. R., Waschbusch, D. A., Fabiano, G. A., & Burrows-MacLean, L. (2010). Summer treatment programs for attention-deficit/hyperactivity disorder. In A. E. Kazdin & J. R. Weisz (Eds.), *Evidence-based psychotherapies for children and adolescents* (2nd ed.). New York, NY: Guilford Press.

Pelham, W. E., Greiner, A. R., & Gnagy, E. M. (1997). *Summer treatment program manual.* Buffalo, NY: Comprehensive Treatment for Attention Deficit Disorders, Inc.

Pfiffner, L. J., Mikami, A. Y., Huang-Pollock, C., Zalecki, C., Easterlin, B., & McBurnett, K. (2007). A randomized controlled trial of integrated home-school behavioral treatment for ADHD, predominantly inattentive type. *Journal of the American Academy of Child and Adolescent Psychiatry, 46*, 1041–1050.

Pisterman, S., McGrath, P., Firestone, P., Goodman, J. T., Webster, I., & Mallory, R. (1989). Outcome of parent-mediated treatment with preschoolers with attention deficit disorder with hyperactivity. *Journal of Consulting and Clinical Psychology, 57*, 628–635.

Polanczyk, G., de Lima, M. S., Horta, B. L., Biederman, J., & Rohde, L. A. (2007). The worldwide prevalence of ADHD: A systematic review and meta-regression analysis. *American Journal of Psychiatry, 164*, 942–948.

Sanders, M., Markie-Dadds, C., Tully, L., & Bor, W. (2000). The Triple P-Positive Parenting Program: A comparison of enhanced, standard, and self-directed behavioral family intervention for parents of children with early onset conduct problems. *Journal of Consulting and Clinical Psychology, 68*, 624–640.

Shelton, T. L., Barkley, R. A., Crosswait, C., Moorehouse, M., Fletcher, K., Barrett, S., . . . Metevia, L. (2000). Multimethod psychoeducational intervention for preschool children with disruptive behavior: Two-year post-treatment follow-up. *Journal of Abnormal Child Psychology, 28*, 253–266.

Sonuga-Barke, E., Daley, D., Thompson, M., Laver-Bradbury, C., & Weeks, A. (2001). Parent-based

therapies for preschool attention-deficit/hyperactivity disorder: A randomized, controlled trial with a community sample. *Journal of the American Academy of Child & Adolescent Psychiatry, 40*, 402–408.

Swanson, J. M., Kraemer, H. C., Hinshaw, S. P., Arnold, L. E., Conners, K. C., Abikoff, H. B., . . . Wu, M. (2001). Clinical relevance of the primary findings of the MTA: Success rates based on severity of ADHD and ODD symptoms at the end of treatment. *Journal of the American Academy of Child and Adolescent Psychiatry, 40*, 168–179.

Thompson, M. J., Laver-Bradbury, C., Ayres, M., Le Poidevin, E., Mead, S., Dodds, C., . . . Sonuga-Barke, E. J. (2009). A small-scale randomized controlled trial of the revised new forest parenting programme for preschoolers with attention deficit hyperactivity disorder. *European Child & Adolescent Psychiatry, 18*, 605–616.

Van den Hoofdakker, B. J., van der Veen-Mulders, L., Sytema, S., Emmelkamp, P. M., Minderaa, R. B., & Nauta, M. H. (2007). Effectiveness of behavioral parent training for children with ADHD in routine clinical practice: A randomized controlled study. *Journal of American Academy of Child and Adolescent Psychiatry, 46*, 1263–1271.

Van der Oord, S., Prins, P. J. M., Oosterlaan, J., & Emmelkamp, P. M. G. (2008). Efficacy of methylphenidate, psychosocial treatments, and their combination in school-aged children with ADHD: A meta-analysis. *Clinical Psychology Review, 28*, 783–800.

Visser, S. N., Lesesne, C. A., & Perou, R. (2007). National estimates and factors associated with medication treatment for childhood attention-deficit/hyperactivity disorder. *Pediatrics, 119*, 99–106.

Weeks, A., Thompson, M., & Laver-Bradbury, C. (1999). *Information manual for professionals working with families with hyperactive children aged 2–9 years.* Ashurst, England: Ashurst Child & Family Evidence Centre.

Wehmeier, P. M., Schacht, A., & Barkley, R. A. (2010). Social and emotional impairment in children and adolescents with ADHD and the impact on quality of life. *Journal of Adolescent Health, 46*, 209–217.

Webster-Stratton, C. (1992). Individually administered videotape parent training: "Who benefits?" *Cognitive Therapy and Research, 16*, 31–35.

Young, S., & Myanthi Amarasinghe, J. (2010). Practitioner review: Non-pharmacological treatments for ADHD: A lifespan approach. *Journal of Child Psychology and Psychiatry, 51*, 116–133.

11

Conduct, Oppositional Defiant, and Disruptive Behavior Disorders

MICHAEL HANDWERK, CLINT FIELD, ANGIE DAHL, AND JESSICA MALMBERG

OVERVIEW OF THE DISORDERS

Childhood disruptive behavior disorders (DBD) are some of the most frequent childhood problems. DBD represent the majority of referrals to child mental health practitioners, accounting for almost half of all outpatient referrals and the majority of admissions for psychiatric inpatient hospitalizations (Kazdin, 1995; Lock & Strauss, 1994). Behavioral problems associated with DBD are also the most common problems mentioned to pediatricians by parents during pediatric exams (Arndorfer, Allen, & Aljazireh, 1999). Long-term outcomes for youth with DBD are poor, and the cost of treating these disorders is high (Foster & Jones, 2005). There have been numerous published empirical evaluations of interventions for childhood and adolescent DBD, perhaps more than any other child disorder. Despite this, many clinicians report utilizing interventions with little or no evidence base (Kazdin, 2000), and many graduate training programs do not consistently train students in evidence-based practices for children with DBD (Crits-Christoph, Frank, Chambless, Brody, & Karp, 1995; Woody, Weisz, & McLean, 2005). As evidence-based treatments for childhood problems generally outperform typical community-delivered treatment (Weisz, Jensen-Doss, & Hawley, 2006), it is imperative to evaluate and disseminate effective interventions for DBD.

Diagnostic Criteria

Childhood DBD are differentiated from developmentally typical antisocial activity by frequency, intensity, chronicity, and impairment. Isolated problem behaviors, such as lying, noncompliance, temper tantrums, and sibling aggression are developmentally typical. For example, parents reported that 53% of 6-year-old children tell lies, and 20% of 5-year-old children destroy other's things (Achenbach, 1991). Similarly, approximately 33% of high-school students reported being in a physical fight at least once during the past year and 17% reported carrying a weapon within the past 30 days (Grunbaum et al., 2004).

The Diagnostic and Statistical Manual of Mental Disorders, 4th edition, text revision (*DSM-IV-TR*; American Psychiatric Association, 2000) sets forth diagnostic criteria that capture the features of childhood disruptive, noncompliant, oppositional, and antisocial behaviors in the diagnoses oppositional defiant disorder (ODD) and conduct disorder (CD).[1] ODD is defined by a persistent and recurrent pattern of defiant, oppositional, and hostile behavior toward adult authority. Children with ODD frequently are disobedient, defiant, and argumentative. They have difficulty compromising or negotiating, may deliberately try to annoy others (adults and peers), and often blame others for their mistakes. Diagnostic criteria state that at least four of the following eight criteria must be present for at least a period of 6 months: often loses temper, often argues with adults, often actively defies or refuses to comply with adults' requests or rules, often deliberately annoys people, often blames others for his or her mistakes or misbehavior, "touchy" or easily annoyed by others, often angry and resentful, and often spiteful or vindictive.

CD is defined by chronic, serious violations of societal norms and rules that cause significant problems in social relationships or academic/occupational functioning. Considerable data suggests that CD reflects the developmental progression of ODD (Lahey, Loeber, Burke, & Rathouz, 2002; Quay, 1999). Children and adolescents with CD often engage in aggression to people or animals, destruction of property, theft or deceitfulness, and major rule violations (e.g., staying out all night, skipping school, running away).

The *DSM-IV-TR* criteria for aggression include: often bullying, threatening, or intimidating others; frequently initiating physical fights; using a dangerous weapon in a fight; being physically cruel to people; being physically cruel to animals; stealing while confronting a victim; and forcing someone into sexual activity. Destruction of property is

---

[1] Attention-deficit/hyperactivity disorder is sometimes considered a DBD along with ODD and CD. However, ADHD does not involve direct, intentional defiance of societal norms, though it does potentially entail inability to comply with environmental demands (see Chapter 10 for a thorough discussion of interventions for ADHD).

defined by two criteria: fire-setting with the intent to cause damage and deliberately destroying others' property. Theft and deceitfulness is captured in three criteria: breaking into a house, building, or car; often lying to obtain favors or goods or to avoid obligations; and stealing something of nontrivial value without confronting a victim (e.g., shoplifting). Three criteria capture serious rule violations, including staying out late at night despite parental prohibitions (beginning before age 13), running away from home overnight at least twice (or once without returning for a lengthy period), and frequently being truant from school (beginning before age 13 years). Diagnostic criteria state that at least three of these 15 criteria must be present within the last year, with at least one symptom occurring within the past 6 months. All criteria are weighted equally (e.g., staying out late and forcing someone into sex).

The *DSM-IV-TR* defines two subtypes of the disorder based on age of onset. Childhood onset, as opposed to adolescent onset, is defined by presence of at least one criterion being present before the age of 10. Approximately 75%–95% of children with CD also demonstrate behaviors consistent with ODD (Hinshaw & Anderson, 1996), though a diagnosis of ODD is not given if criteria for CD are met. Children and adolescents with CD often demonstrate associated concerns such as early onset of persistent drug and alcohol use, low self-esteem, school problems, low academic achievement, early sexual activity or persistent promiscuity, and legal problems (APA, 2000; Bloomquist & Schnell, 2002; Connor, 2002).

Demographic Variables

Prevalence of DBD is high. Conservative estimates of the rate of ODD in the general population range from 6% to 10%, while rates of CD range from 2% to 10% (Costello, 1990; Lahey, Miller, Gordon, & Riley, 1999). Boys tend to be clearly more aggressive than girls in childhood (Bierman et al., 2004), though rates of ODD are relatively equal between boys and girls across development (Lahey et al., 1999; Webster-Stratton, 1996). However, 3 to 5 times more males than females are diagnosed with CD, though in later adolescence this ratio tends to be more equal due to an increase in girls' nonaggressive antisocial activity (Bierman et al., 2004; Hinshaw & Anderson, 1996; Zoccolillo, 1993). ODD symptoms tend to peak around the age of 8 and remain fairly constant throughout childhood (Loeber, Lahey, & Thomas, 1991). In contrast, rates of CD increase dramatically in older children, with peak rates around the ages of 10 to 13 (Lahey et al., 1999). Earlier onset of DBD is associated with more severe symptomotology and poorer outcomes (Quay, 1999). Rates of DBD appear to be influenced by context, as prevalence of CD tends to be somewhat higher in urban and lower SES groups (Bloomquist & Schnell, 2002; Lahey et al., 1999).

Most children don't "grow out of it": Both ODD and CD tend to be stable over time. Over a period of several years, only 25% of children diagnosed with ODD exhibit spontaneous symptom reduction (Lahey, Loeber, Quay, Frick, & Grimm, 1992). Of the other 75%, about half continued to show behavior characteristic of ODD, while another 25% progressed to more serious antisocial behavior associated with CD. Approximately 25%–33% of children diagnosed with CD show persistent and severe antisocial behavior into adulthood (Robbins, 1978; Zoccolillo, Pickles, Quinton, & Rutter, 1992).

DBDs occur comorbidly with a number of other *DSM-IV-TR* disorders (Loeber & Keenan, 1994). Attention-deficit/hyperactivity disorder (ADHD) frequently co-occurs with ODD and CD, with comorbidity rates around 40%–75%. Children exhibiting the combination of comorbid DBD and ADHD seem to have particularly dire outcomes, as they demonstrate a greater range and more severe forms of antisocial behavior, higher rates of peer rejection, higher rates of academic learning problems, and increased drug use. These deficits seem to be specific to comorbid DBD and ADHD and do not appear when

ODD or CD co-occur with other conditions (Lynam, 1996; Waschbush, 2002). CD also has a high comorbidity rate with substance use disorders (SUD) and rates of substance use are dramatically increased for youth with CD (Molina, Smith, & Pelham, 1999). DBD also co-occurs with internalizing disorders. More than 25% of youth with DBD also exhibit an internalizing disorder (i.e., major depression, dysthymia, phobias, generalized anxiety, separation anxiety; Frick, 1998; Loeber & Keenan, 1994; Zoccolillo, 1992).

Impact of the Disorder

DBDs are among the most costly of mental health problems encountered in our society, both in terms of human suffering and economic expenditures (Connor, 2002). Children are at high risk for an overabundance of negative short-term and long-term outcomes including engagement in violent behaviors, significant mental health problems, school failure and drop out, chemical dependency, occupational difficulties, marital and family dysfunction, and criminal offending (Bloomquist & Schnell, 2002). Early-onset CD is associated with more violent and aggressive behavior, lower academic achievement, solitary (as opposed to group) aggressive and antisocial activity, comorbid attention and neurological impairments, and a significantly poorer prognosis and outcome. Adults diagnosed with CD as children are more likely to engage in criminal behavior, become alcoholics, struggle occupationally, and display comorbid psychiatric diagnoses (Connor, 2002). Interventions for DBD are extremely costly, as per capita expenditures for youth with CD far exceeded youth with other mental health problems (Foster & Jones, 2005).

INTERVENTIONS FOR DBD

There are thousands of published studies of interventions for DBD (Weisz, Chu, & Polo, 2004). However, most are bridled by methodological shortcomings that fall short of evidence-based research standards (i.e., random assignment, clear inclusion/exclusion criteria, an appropriate control group or clearly established experimental control, reliable and valid outcome measures, cf. Behan & Carr, 2000; Eyberg, Nelson, & Boggs, 2008; Farmer, Compton, Burns, & Robertson, 2002). Further, within this literature there are investigations of specific treatment techniques (e.g., time-out) and investigations of combinations of techniques (e.g., time-out, rule-setting, and token economy combined) that approximate a comprehensive approach to treatment such as is typical of most manualized treatments. Due to pragmatic limitations, and in an effort to align with social and professional efforts to specify evidence-based practices within the profession of clinical psychology, we have confined our review to studies that: (a) possess significant methodological rigor and (b) examine well-defined "treatment packages" (e.g., Incredible Years, Multisystemic Therapy) rather than individual procedures (e.g., time-out). The majority of evidence-based interventions for DBD derive from a research history rich in the use of single-case and small sample methods. Nonetheless, we have limited this review to well-defined treatment packages that tend to utilize group-based research designs, often leaving a significant void of rigorous single-subject experimental design studies. For example, in a meta-analyses of behavioral parent training, Maughan, Christiansen, Jenson, Olympia, and Clark (2005) identified 79 group and single-case design studies that met minimal criteria for including in a meta-analysis evaluating the effectiveness of parent training for DBD. Only 15 of the 79 studies were single-case design studies; several of these came from unpublished sources (i.e., dissertations), and several were "precursor" studies in the development of treatment packages.

At a broad level, interventions for DBD can be classified into one of a few categories: behavioral parent training (BPT), cognitive behavioral interventions (CBI) for children, and other interventions. As the body of literature supporting each category is large enough to consider as a whole, and several meta-analytic studies have done just that, we will present evidence as to the entirety of each approach, followed by descriptions of specific programs within each category. A description of each category will be provided, followed by a review of consensus panel recommendations (where applicable), and general meta-analytic conclusions. Then RCTs, treatment-specific meta-analysis data, and single-subject studies evaluating specific treatments will be reviewed, after which summary conclusions are drawn.

BEHAVIORAL PARENT TRAINING

Considered as a whole, behavioral parent training (BPT) for DBD probably has as much evidence for its effectiveness as any other treatment for any childhood problem. BPT has its roots in the pioneering work of Gerald Patterson, Rex Forehand, and Constance Hanf, among others, who developed early models that utilized principles of operant conditioning and social learning theory to teach parents to more effectively interact with and manage their disruptive children. Although there are many different models and versions of BPT, almost all share common characteristics, including parents being the primary target of intervention, and the content of the training being the effective application of operant-based behavior modification strategies (e.g., issuing commands, contingent delivery of praise and attention, administering time-out, etc.) delivered via instruction, modeling, and role-playing. Early versions of BPT were primarily administered to mothers, individually. However, innovation over the past few decades has led to the development of group parent training, videotape modeling, and mass media models of dissemination. Modern day BPT models utilize multiple modes of intervention that target parents, children, and teachers. Presented next are several lines of support for BPT as a whole, followed by specific BPT programs.

Consensus recommendations. Kutcher et al. (2004) described an international consensus meeting on ADHD and DBD that was convened due to the concern that youth with ADHD and DBD were not accessing appropriate treatment. Eleven experts on ADHD and DBD were invited to participate in the meeting with the specific goal of highlighting existing empirical support for the etiology, assessment, diagnosis, and treatment of ADHD and DBD. The participants concluded that for oppositional behaviors, parent training is a first-line, primary intervention. In another international consensus statement commissioned by the European Union (Jané-Llopis & Braddick, 2008), a panel of international experts from many different European countries recommended group-based parent training for children to reduce problems associated with conduct problems.

Parent training, as a general approach, has also been recommended as an evidence-based intervention by the American Psychological Association (APA) Division 12 (Clinical Psychology; Chambless et al., 1996) and Division 53 (Society of Clinical Child and Adolescent Psychology; Brestan & Eyberg, 1998). The evidence-based status of specific treatment programs are reviewed in respective sections throughout this chapter.

Meta-analysis of group design. Shadish et al. (1993) conducted a meta-analysis of family and marital psychotherapies on various outcomes, which included BPT. Based on the literature review, 163 studies were found to meet their inclusion criteria that subjects were randomly assigned to treatment conditions, subjects were in some way distressed, and studies examined a marital or family therapy. As it relates to the current chapter, Shadish et al. (1993) computed effect size estimates (ES) for various theoretical orientations in family therapy for different types of problems,

including childhood conduct problems. They report an average ES of 0.55 ($N = 13$) for behavioral family therapy interventions, ES $= 0.26$ ($N = 8$) for systemic family interventions, and ES $= 0.57$ ($N = 7$) for eclectic family therapies in treating CD. Most of the studies in the behavioral family therapy interventions analyses were BPT programs.

In one of the earliest meta-analysis specific to BPT, Serketich and Dumas (1996) conducted a comprehensive search of electronic databases to identified studies using BPT to treat DBD. Only 26 studies met inclusionary criteria, which included having a comparison or control group, at least five subjects per group, and at least one outcome measure relating to the child's behavior (observed or reported). On average, across all studies, the age of participants was 6 years, and parents participated in nine-and-a-half BPT sessions. The overall effect size on child behavioral adjustment was 0.86 and was relatively consistent across parent, teacher, and independent observer reports of child behavior. The effect size for parental adjustment was also significant, ES $= 0.44$, indicating parents benefited from the intervention as well. Only one demographic factor, age of the child, was related to outcomes. The ES was larger for older children relative to younger children, though the oldest mean age of any study was 10.1, suggesting that elementary-aged children benefited the most from BPT.

Maughan et al. (2005) conducted a meta-analysis examining the effectiveness of BPT for children and adolescents with externalizing behaviors and DBD. Seventy-nine studies met the inclusion criteria, including that the treatment had to involve training of parents in the use of reinforcement and/or time-out and one additional behavioral procedure (e.g., differential attention, precision requests, or contracts). Children were between the ages of 3 and 16 years. Mean weighted ES were calculated for each of the three design categories (between-subjects, within-subjects, and single-subjects). For between-subjects designs, the mean weighted ES was 0.30. For within-subjects design, the mean weighted ES was 0.68. For single-subject design studies, the mean weighted ES was calculated using two different statistical methods, with one yielding a modest weighted ES of 0.54, and alternate method yielding a very large weighted ES of 1.56. Mean age of the targeted child was found to be a significant moderating variable for between-subjects design studies and single-subject design studies. Among the between-subjects studies, the ES values for studies of children with a mean age of 9 to 11 years was significantly greater than those of children with a mean age of 3 to 5 years or 6 to 8 years. Among the single-subject studies, studies that used children with a mean age of 9 to 11 years again yielded the highest ES, and the 12 to 16 year group yielded the lowest ES value. Finally, in general, ES were larger for parent reports of child behavior than for direct observations of child behavior, possibly indicating an expectation bias on the part of participating parents.

A meta-analysis by Lundahl, Risser, and Lovejoy (2006) analyzed 63 studies of parent training to evaluate the effectiveness of both behavioral and nonbehavioral programs at posttreatment and follow-up. Parent training studies targeting disruptive behaviors were included in the meta-analysis if they had at least one treatment and control group drawn from the same population of at least five participants each. Dependent measures included child behaviors (e.g., compliance and amount of disruptive behaviors), parent behaviors (e.g., changes made in parenting practices), and self-perception of parenting (e.g., stress, effectiveness).

BPT produced moderate ES immediately following treatment, ES = 0.42 (child behavior), ES = 0.47 (parent behavior), and ES = 0.53 (parental perception). No differences were found between the behavioral and nonbehavioral programs, though the quality of the research methodology greatly favored studies of behavioral programs. Moderators were analyzed only

for the behavioral programs due to the homogenous nature of the nonbehavioral programs. Families with more economic disadvantage were found to benefit less from BPT. However, families with low SES had better outcomes when treatment was delivered individually as opposed to a group modality. Additionally, no increased benefit was found for the inclusion of child-only therapy along with parent training. At follow-up, there was a reduction in treatment gain from posttreatment as ES for the behavioral programs were in the small to moderate range: ES = 0.21 (child behavior), ES = 0.25 (parent behavior), and ES = 0.45 (parent perceptions). Only four studies provided follow-up data for the nonbehavioral programs and were not interpreted.

Parent Management Training Oregon Model

Parent Management Training Oregon Model (PMTO) is a type of behavioral parent training that focuses on teaching parents basic behavioral principles for modifying child behavior (Patterson, Reid, Jones, & Conger, 1975). The PMTO model is an extension of Patterson's theory of coercive family interactions where the focus of treatment is on teaching parents strategies that effectively allow them to break out of coercive cycles of escalating aversive interactions with their child through the application of operant condition principles. PMTO is generally used with children between ages 3 and 12 years. Unlike some other models of parent training, length of treatment varies based on the individual needs of the family rather than utilizing a predetermined number of sessions. Therapy includes weekly treatment sessions and telephone contact with parents. Parents are taught how to monitor and modify their child's behavior. Over time, parents become increasingly responsible for designing and implementing various behavioral management strategies. Progression through treatment is data-driven and based on parental skill display and behavioral improvements in the child. Treatment manuals, *Living with Children* (Patterson & Guillion, 1968) and *Families* (Patterson, 1975), are often utilized to supplement therapist coaching, and have been utilized as treatment manuals in several studies.

Consensus recommendations. PMTO has been recommended by APA Division 53 as an evidence-based treatment for children with ODD. Further, it is the only treatment for ODD and CD to gain a designation of "well-established" in a review published in a Division 53 journal, *Journal of Clinical Child and Adolescent Psychology*, special issue on devoted evidence-based treatments (Eyberg et al., 2008).

Randomized controlled trials. There have been numerous studies of PTMO. Bernal, Klinnert, and Schultz (1980) randomly assigned 36 families of children with disruptive behaviors to a PMTO condition, a client-centered parent counseling condition, or a wait-list control condition. Children were 5 to 12 years of age ($M = 8.44$), primarily male (86%), referred for disruptive behaviors, and had at least two of three indices of disruptive or aggressive behavior including scoring substantially above the mean on a measure of observed disruptive behavior and/or two behavior checklists. Treatment groups met for 8 weeks that included 10 one-hour individual therapy sessions. Follow-up occurred at 6 months and 2 years for only the two treatment groups. Outcome measures included parent-report behavioral checklists and a measure of direct observation of disruptive behavior during home observations. On checklists, PMTO was significantly better than either client-centered parent counseling or the control condition. However, on measures of direct observation, there were no differences between groups. At 6-month follow-up, one measure showed no differential treatment outcomes, while another indicated treatment gains were not maintained for the PMTO group relative to the client-centered group. At 2 years, there were no differences between groups. Of note, this

study was conducted by independent researchers, though PMTO was not delivered in its usual time-unlimited fashion.

Patterson, Chamberlain, and Reid (1982) randomly assigned 19 families to PMTO or a treatment as usual (TAU) condition. Participants were youth (68% male) between the ages of 3 to 12 years old ($M = 6.8$) referred for disruptive behavior, and who scored above the 90th percentile on a measure of observed in-home disruptive behavior. PMTO was individually administered to families by a trained therapist. Average treatment consisted of 17 hours of PMTO but ranged from 4 to 48 hours across participants. In the TAU condition, eight of nine children were treated by a variety of providers using an assortment of treatment modalities for 1 to 32 sessions ($M = 12$ sessions). Outcome measures included direct observation of disruptive behaviors at home and daily parental reports of problem behavior. Results indicated that the PMTO sample evidenced greater reduction in the rates of child disruptive behaviors relative to the comparison condition on measures of direct observations. However, on the parent-report measure, no differences were observed.

Christensen, Johnson, Phillips, and Glasgow (1980) randomly assigned 36 families of disruptive children ages 4 to 12 ($M = 7.0$) to individually administered PMTO, group-administered PMTO, or a minimal contact, self-administered, bibliotherapy the PMTO condition (MCB). *Living with Children* (Patterson & Gullion, 1968) was utilized as the treatment manual for all conditions. In the MCB condition, parents met with a therapist once, where they received a copy of the manual, an outline of treatment, and a weekly log to keep track of completed activities. In both individual and group conditions, PMTO was time-limited, lasting 10 weeks. In the group condition, six families participated in parent training at a time. Parent observations of disruptive behavior and three measures of disruptive behavior coded from home audio recordings of parent–child interactions were the primary outcome measures. In addition to posttreatment, outcome measures were collected in a follow-up period that ranged from 2 to 10 weeks after treatment ($M = 5$ weeks). On the parent observational data, at both posttreatment and follow-up, results indicated that individual and group treatments showed larger reductions in parent-observed disruptive behavior than the MCB group but did not differ from each other. On the three home audio recordings variables, there were no significant reductions from pre- to posttreatment. However, only 13 families had complete pre- and post data.

Hughes and Wilson (1988) compared a time-limited version of PMTO to a communication skills/problem-solving condition (CSPS) and a wait-list control. Participants were 42 children between the ages of 6 and 15 and their families. All children had been referred for serious disruptive behavior problems. Of the participating children, 81% were male, all had at least four disruptive behaviors reported by parents on a standardized measure, half were being considered for out-of-home placement, and a third had court involvement due to disruptive behavior. Treatment conditions met weekly for 1½ hours for 7 weeks. In addition to treatment, another independent variable was assessed: child present or child not present in the therapy. In the "child present" conditions, the children participated fully in the therapy. The CSPS group received training in effective communication, problem-solving, and conflict resolution. There were nine outcome variables that included a number of parent completed problem behavior checklists, parent-reported observations of disruptive behavior, subscales from a family functioning scale, and a child-reported measure of self-concept. Results indicated that participants in the two treatment groups showed greater improvement than those in the wait-list control group on two measures: the overall score on a standardized problem behavior checklist, and a subscale measuring "family understanding" on the family functioning measure. There was a higher proportion of children in the PMTO group that met criterion for significant reductions (greater than 30%) in parent-observed problem behavior than either the CSPS or control groups. The CSPS group showed more improvement than the PMTO group on a subscale of family functioning measuring "acceptance." No other differences between groups were found.

In one of the few studies of BPT applied to adolescents with DBD, Bank, Marlowe, Reid, Patterson, and Weinrott (1991) examined a variant of PMTO in a group of 55 chronically offending adolescent boys (average age of 14). The boys were assigned to PMTO or "treatment as usual" conditions. PMTO was modified to stress parental monitoring and supervision, grounding and restrictions as primary punishments rather than time-out, and involvement of the adolescent in setting up behavioral contracts. Outcomes were court-documented offenses. Average treatment duration for the PMTO group was 45 hours (half of which was telephone consultation) and for the treatment control group was 50 hours. About half of the families in the PMTO group received booster sessions. After a year of treatment, the ES for recidivism rate (i.e., re-arrest) was 0.7 for PMTO relative to the control group. However, at a 3-year follow-up, the advantage for the PMTO had dissipated, with the ES for recidivism dropping to 0.1. The ES for incarceration, or time in jail/detention, was 0.5 at both posttreatment and 3-year follow-up.

Dishion and Andrews (1995) assigned 158 "at-risk families" to a modified PMTO group, a child training group (CT), a combined group (PMTO + CT), a self-directed change group (SDC), or a no-control control group (CON). Youth were 10 to 14 years of age ($M = 12.4$), 95% Caucasian, and 52% male. Inclusionary criteria for disruptive behavior were not clear, though average parent ratings of externalizing problems on a standardized behavior checklist fell at the clinical cut-off for the sample. Treatment occurred during 12 weekly 90-minute sessions completed over 3 to 4 months.

The PMTO group consisted of eight families, and curriculum and training methods were similar to those described earlier. The CT training emphasized skills of self-regulation, self-monitoring, prosocial goal setting, developing positive peer networks, problem solving, and communications. SDC participants were mailed materials (written and video) that were utilized in parent and group training. Engagement in the two active treatment groups was high, with approximately 70% attendance in each. In contrast, nearly half of families in the CON group reported not watching the videotapes as scheduled. Outcome measures included direct observation of family interaction, a measure of parent-reported family conflict, parent (mother) and teacher ratings of youth behavior, and a self-reported measure of smoking. All active treatments resulted in improvement on observed interaction variables, with the exception of a marginally significant result for observed teen negativity for the CT group. There were no improvements for the SDC group. Mother reports on the measure of family conflict showed improvement from pre- to posttreatment for only the PMTO + CT group. There were no intervention effects for any group on mothers' ratings of externalizing behavior on a standardized behavior checklist. In general, there was a reduction in reported problem behaviors for teenagers in all groups at posttreatment and follow-up, including the SDC and CON groups. For teacher reports, there was a marginally statistically significant effect ($p > 0.06$) for the parent groups (PMTO and PMTO + CT) relative to controls at posttreatment. At 1-year follow-up, teens participating in CT (CT or PMTO + CT) demonstrated higher rates of teacher-rated externalizing problems (i.e., an iatrogenic effect). A similar result was reported for self-reported rates of smoking, where teens in the CT groups reported higher rates of smoking at posttreatment and 1-year follow-up.

Conclusions. PMTO is the only intervention for DBD that has obtained the status of a "well-established" treatment, as it is one of the few treatments tested in several independent studies (Eyberg et al., 2008). However, although results have been generally positive, several studies have found mixed outcomes. For example, in Bernal et al. (1980), there were no differences between treatment groups at posttreatment on observations of child behavior, at 6-month follow-up PMTO was no longer superior to client-centered counseling, and at 2 years neither treatment group differed from the wait-list control group on any measure. In contrast, Patterson et al. (1982) found significant posttreatment differences between PMTO and treatment as usual controls on observed child behaviors, but no differences on a parent-reported outcome measure. In Christensen et al. (1980), differences between the PMTO groups and a self-administered bibliotherapy group indicated reductions in parent-recorded frequency of child problem behaviors but not on three measures of parent and child behavior derived from coding of audiotapes. Similarly, Hughes and Wilson (1988) found few differences between PMTO-treated families and control on several outcome measures. Part of the reason for this might be the small sample sizes in many studies of PMTO. In the four studies reviewed here, a total of 47 parents of children with younger oppositional behavior underwent PMTO treatment. Also, as Patterson et al. (1982) have noted, PMTO was designed to be flexible and individually tailored to meet the needs of families. Many studies of PMTO did not did not utilize it in this manner, perhaps not providing an adequate "dose" of PMTO. Finally, attempts to modify PMTO to address adolescent disruptive behavior have been only modestly successful. It appears that to achieve modest success with this population, a large dosage of treatment is required over a substantial period of time.

Parent–Child Interaction Therapy

Parent–child interaction therapy (PCIT) is one of many models of BPT that has derived from the early work of Hanf (as cited in McMahon,

Wells, & Kotler, 2006). In developing the PCIT model, Brinkmeyer and Eyberg (2003) drew heavily from developmental, attachment, and social learning theories to mold an approach to working with parents and children that emphasized relationship to a greater degree than many parent training programs. Generally speaking, treatment in the context of PCIT unfolds across two areas of emphasis: child-directed interactions (CDI)—a type of play therapy designed to promote relationship development—and parent-directed interactions (PDI), which reflect traditional behavior management strategies (e.g., issuing commands, using time-out) as conceptualized within a social learning framework. The general format of treatment involves teaching, modeling, and practicing of specific skills with feedback provided by the therapist designed to shape parental behavior. As mastery of a skill is attained, additional skills are targeted. PCIT has yielded positive treatment effects with children of various ages, although it is most often used with children 3 to 6 years of age. On average, families participate in 13 therapy sessions, although length of treatment varies widely as termination decisions are predicated on parent performance and degree of parental confidence.

Consensus recommendations. PCIT has been recommended by Division 53 of the APA as an evidence-based practice in the treatment of ODD and CD. More specifically, based on a review of methodologically sound studies, Eyberg et al. (2008) concluded that PCIT is a "probably efficacious" treatment for DBD.

Randomized controlled trials. A number of RCTs have been conducted documenting the merits of PCIT as a treatment for conduct problems. Schuhmann, Foote, Eyberg, Boggs, and Algina (1998) conducted a study in which 22 families that completed treatment were compared to a similar number of wait-list control families. Children in the study were between 3 and 6 years of age and each had been diagnosed with ODD. PCIT was delivered using a manualized format, although the number of treatment sessions varied across families with treatment families participating in an average of 13 therapy sessions. Dependent measures included a variety of observed parent and child behaviors, child behavior questionnaires, parent questionnaires, and measures of satisfaction. Follow-up data extending to approximately 4 months posttreatment was also collected. The investigators stated specific interest in a group of heterogeneous dependent variables that included child behavior problems as well as a number of family functioning variables such as marital satisfaction and parental experience of depression. Pre- and post-scores were collected for most variables and subsequently subjected to a series of ANCOVA analyses. Overall, results were supportive of PCIT and significant shifts in the direction of improved child and parenting behaviors were observed along with reported decreases in levels of parental stress. For example, parents in the PCIT condition exhibited greater rates of praising and lower rates of criticism following intervention. Rate of compliance increased significantly among PCIT children, and scores on a parent report behavior checklist fell from the clinical into the nonclinical range of functioning, but only for those receiving PCIT. PCIT parents reported decreased levels of stress following treatment, but experience of depression remained unchanged. Finally, all observed gains at the conclusion of therapy appeared to maintain for at least 4 months posttreatment.

Nixon, Sweeney, Erickson, and Touyz (2003) also conducted a study examining the effects of PCIT. They compared a standard 12-session version of PCIT to an abbreviated PCIT and a wait-list condition. The abbreviated condition differed from the standard condition primarily in that parenting skills were trained via the use of videotapes observed in the home setting. Fifty-four children that had been previously diagnosed with ODD and ranged in age from 3 to 5 years were participants in this study. Dependent variables included observed and parent-reported rates of child problem behavior, observed rates of parenting strategies, and self-report measures of parenting stress and confidence. Data was analyzed using ANCOVA analyses and results uniformly indicated that the standard and abbreviated PCIT conditions yielded improved child behavior, increased use of effective parenting strategies, and improvement in parent-specific variables such as satisfaction and reactivity to child behavior. The investigators generally concluded that the effectiveness of PCIT had been replicated with an independent sample and that such gains may also be attained with an abbreviated approach to intervention, although further replication of that finding would be needed to draw firm conclusions.

Meta-analysis of group studies. PCIT has been evaluated via meta-analytic technique by Thomas and Zimmer-Gembeck (2007). This study evaluated 13 investigations completed between the years of 1980 and 2004. Across studies, most children fell in the range of 4 to 5 years of age and combined sample size exceeded 500 children. The authors noted that child behavior, measured in a number of ways (e.g., observational methods, parent report) changed positively immediately following treatment with ES ranging from 0.54 to 1.31 depending on the informant and type of outcome measure. However, gains appeared to diminish at follow-up, with the exception of maternal endorsement of change, which remained high. Further, relative to all wait-list comparison groups, medium and large treatment effects were observed, suggesting that PCIT effectively altered the problem behaviors of children and parents alike.

Conclusions. Generally speaking, PCIT results have been supportive and participants have exhibited greater improvement with fewer drop-outs than typically evidenced in psychotherapy with children. Brinkmeyer and Eyberg (2003) have provided a fairly detailed overview of a number of studies of PCIT, most of which have utilized a wait-list comparison group. However, most of these studies suffer from methodological shortcomings, causing PCIT to be acknowledged by a task force of the APA as having only "probably-efficacious" status as an evidence-based practice for DBD (Eyberg et al., 2008).

Helping the Noncompliant Child (HNC)

The HNC program (McMahon & Forehand, 2003) is closely related to the original Hanf parent training model and therefore overlaps significantly with many other behavioral parent training programs such as PCIT. The HNC program targets children between the ages of 3 and 8, and is typically utilized in traditional clinical settings as the therapist works with individual families. The general approach to skills training involves providing parents instructions and rationales, modeling skills, and completing role-plays and actual practice with children in the clinic setting. Parents are expected to implement skills learned within therapy sessions independently in the home setting. The HNC program is comprised of two phases of skill training. The first phase is designed to promote alterations in parent–child interactions as parents employ differential attention skills, engage in appropriate responding and ignoring to children's behavior, and create individual playtime with children each day. Phase 2 training is focused on techniques for managing conduct problems and is generally referred to as "compliance training." This phase reflects the overarching philosophy of the HNC program, which is that noncompliance is a keystone behavior that occurs early in the developmental progression of DBD. The instruction–time-out sequence is a critical component of Phase 2 training, which also includes training in specific techniques such as establishing home rules and, if warranted, managing problem behavior in community settings.

Consensus recommendations. HNC has been recommended by Division 53 of the APA as an evidence-based practice in the treatment of ODD and CD. More specifically, based on a review of methodologically sound studies, Eyberg et al. (2008) concluded that HNC is a "probably efficacious" treatment for DBD.

Randomized controlled trials. Although there has been a series of uncontrolled and minimally controlled studies demonstrating the effectiveness of the HNC program (e.g., Baum & Forehand, 1981; Forehand & Long, 1988; Peed, Roberts, & Forehand, 1977), there has only been a single RCT study of HNC with DBD that possessed requisite methodological rigor. Wells and Egan (1988) conducted this study in which families of 18 children, aged 3 to 8 years old, who had been diagnosed with ODD and exhibited high rates of noncompliance to commands were randomly assigned to either parent training using the HNC model or systems family therapy. Dependent variables included rates of parent and child observed behavior, maternal experience of anxiety and depression, and marital adjustment. Results indicated that each treatment program had similar effects on parental adjustment (e.g., mood concerns, anxiety, and marital adjustment). However, HNC significantly outperformed family therapy on observational measures of parent–child interactions associated with ODD. Specifically, parents assigned to the HNC condition engaged in affection (e.g., praise statements) and effective discipline behaviors (e.g., use of time-out) significantly more frequently. Also, rates of child compliance were significantly higher in the HNC condition than in the family therapy group following treatment.

Conclusions. HNC has been studied extensively, as evidenced by the thorough review of the empirical bases of the program provided by McMahon and Forehand (2003). Unfortunately, much of this work has not occurred in the context of well-controlled RCT. Thus, while the treatment is deemed effective in treating and preventing DBD, consensus agreement limits HNC to probably efficacious status as an evidence-based practice.

The Incredible Years Training Series

The Incredible Years Training Series (IYTS) is a comprehensive program that includes a parent management training component, a teacher training component, and a child training component (Webster-Stratton, 1992; Webster-Stratton & Reid, 2003). The program targets children between the ages of 2 to 8 years of age. IYTS uses video presentations embedded in training modules that are run by therapists and trainers.

The parent management program has three modules spanning basic parent management skills (e.g., praise, prompts, ignoring, time-out), advanced management skills (e.g., conflict management, communication, anger management, social support), and school functioning (e.g., parent–teacher collaboration, homework). The basic module consists of 26 hours of tapes (utilizing over 250 vignettes) and is typically completed in 13 or 14 two-hour weekly sessions. The advanced module consists of 14 hours of tapes (with 60 vignettes). Typically, parent training occurs in groups of 8 to 12 parents. Parent training components are also enhanced by a printed manual that accompanies the video presentations. The child module is a social skills training component for children covering conflict resolution, negative attributions, perspective-taking, cooperation, communications, and problem solving. Children meet weekly in groups of six or seven for 2 hours for 18 weeks. Groups are typically led by two therapists.

Consensus recommendations. IYTS has been recommended by Division 53 of the APA as an evidence-based practice in the treatment of ODD and CD. More specifically, based on a review of methodologically sound studies, Eyberg et al. (2008) concluded that IYTS is a probably efficacious treatment for DBD. The IYTS has also been recommended as a consensus model program in the Blueprints for Violence Prevention by the Center for the Study and Prevention of Violence at the University of Colorado (2006).

Randomized controlled trials. IYTS has been evaluated in several RCTs, all but one of which were conducted by the lead developer and associates. Webster-Stratton (1984) compared individually administered parent training, group parent training with trainer facilitated videotape-modeling, and wait-list control groups. Participants were 35 families with children (ages 3 to 8 years) diagnosed with ODD. Treatment conditions were approximately nine sessions and covered the same content across formats. Outcome measures included attitudinal measures (six measures encompassing two standardized behavior rating scales, and three subscales from a formal measure of parent-reported frequency of problem behavior) and structured observations that included eight categories of behavior. Additionally, standardized teacher ratings were collected at 1-year follow-up only.

At the end of treatment, there were no differences between the two treatment groups on any attitudinal measure and only one significant difference on observational measures (higher ratio of direct commands relative to all commands in group treatment compared to individual treatment). For attitudinal measures, each treatment group demonstrated significant improvement over the control group on most outcome measures, with the group condition outperforming controls on five of the six measures, and the individual group being significantly better on four of the six measures. Among observational variables, the group condition improved on five of the eight measures, and the individual condition on three of eight measures relative to the control condition. Consumer satisfaction ratings were similar between the two treatment conditions. At 1-year follow-up, there were no differences between treatment groups on any attitudinal measure, and measure-based treatment gains were maintained. Observation-based gains were also maintained; and for child noncompliance and deviancy, there was significant improvement beyond posttreatment measures. There were no differences between treatment conditions on behavioral observation measures at 1 year.

Webster-Stratton, Reid, and Hammond (2004) compared parent training (PT) only, child training (CT) only, PT + teacher training (PT + TT), CT + TT, and all three programs combined (PT + CT + TT) against a waist-list control. One hundred and fifty-nine children (143 boys, 16 girls) between the ages of 4 and 8 with a diagnosis of ODD and their families were randomly assigned to groups. Outcome measures included nine composite variables composed of ratings of observations of interactions between children and caretakers at home, school, and in the clinic; questionnaires; and standardized rating scales. The composite measures were mother and father positive parenting, mother and father negative parenting, mother and father child conduct problems at home, child conduct problems at school, child social competence with peers, and negative teacher classroom management. In addition, there was a measure of parent and teacher satisfaction, and a 1-year follow-up with the treatment conditions only (no control group). Conditions that included PT tended to produce the most robust change. PT demonstrated significant changes on seven of the nine outcome measures, PT + TT on seven of nine measures, and PT + CT + TT on eight of nine measures. The child conditions brought about significant change on about half the outcome measures (CT on five of nine, CT + TT on four of nine). Treatments generally had the most impact on treatment-related measurements (i.e., PT had larger effect sizes for parent behavior, teacher training for teacher-rated child behavior, child training for child-rated peer competence), though, somewhat surprisingly, both PT and CT generalized across settings (e.g., children in the PT group had significantly improved ratings of behavior at school; CT led to reductions in parents' use of harsh punishment). Treatment gains were maintained at 1-year follow-up for seven of the eight composite scores (child negative behavior at school deteriorated; teacher-negative behavior was not assessed as the children had different teachers).

Webster-Stratton and Hammond (1997) evaluated efficacy of PT, CT, and PT + CT treatment compared to a wait-list control in a group of 97 families with children (72 boys, 25 girls) between 2 and 7 years of age diagnosed with ODD. Children were randomly assigned to one of the four conditions. Twenty-nine outcome variables included multiple standardized behavior checklists completed by parents (mothers and fathers) and one by teachers, a measure of parental problem solving, parental reports of observed behaviors, independent observations of parent–child and child–peer interactions, and child-reported social problem solving. Of 29 outcome measures, 19 demonstrated significant between-groups differences. All three treatment groups demonstrated more improvement on standardized behavior ratings as well as on observation of conflict management compared to the control group. The PT condition tended to be superior to the CT condition on parent ratings of problem behavior at home as well as observed parenting behavior, while the CT conditions produced more significant positive changes on ratings and observations of child social problem solving. The combined group (PT + CT) showed improvements over the broadest array of outcome measures. However, neither PT, CT, nor PT + CT significantly affected teacher ratings of problem behavior. Conditions that included parent training were rated significantly more positive on a consumer satisfaction measure. At 1-year follow-up, treatment gains on all measures assessed were maintained.

Webster-Stratton, Reid, and Hammond (2001) examined the CT against a wait-list control (CONT). Participants were 99 children between the ages of 4 and 8 with early-onset CD. The CT condition lasted 18 to 22 sessions and consisted of groups of five to six children who watched videotapes of models performing skills (i.e., videotaped modeling), participated in group discussion utilizing unique props

(i.e., the use of puppets), and were exposed to a motivation system. Outcome measures included a composite measure of child behavior problems derived from standardized behavior ratings from parents and teachers, structured home observations, and a child self-report measure of social competence and problem solving. Results indicated that the CT group performed better on parent ratings of externalizing problem behaviors, teacher ratings of aggression, observational measures of child deviance, and two scales of child-reported social problem solving. Within-group analyses indicated that there were significant reductions in conduct problems in the treatment group, and significant increases in conduct problems in the control group. Treatment gains were maintained at 1-year follow-up.

Lavigne et al. (2008) reported outcomes for 117 children with ODD, aged 3 to 6, assigned to either 12-session PT or a minimal contact, bibliotherapy condition. Trainer degree was also examined, resulting in two PT groups (PT-psychologist led or PT-nurse led). The study consisted of randomly assigning 24 pediatric clinics to one of the three conditions. Families in the PT condition watched the IYTS videos and participated in related discussion. Webster-Stratton's book, *The Incredible Years* (1992), was utilized as a treatment manual and guide. Participants assigned to the minimal contact, bibliotherapy condition did not meet with a therapist and only received a copy of *The Incredible Years*. Results indicated that all three treatment conditions showed significant improvement over a 12-month follow-up—there was no difference between either of the PT groups and the bibliotherapy group. However, there was a dose effect where children of parents who attended seven or more treatment sessions demonstrated greater gains on one outcome measure than the bibliotherapy group, and children of parents who attended nine or more sessions exhibited greater gains on two outcome measures.

Conclusions. Webster-Stratton's IYTP has been extensively studied and has solid support for both the parent training and child training components. Studies of IYTP have benefited from large sample sizes, utilization of multiple outcome measures, and consistent inclusion of control conditions. Treatment gains have been maintained for up to a year after treatment. The teacher component has not been sufficiently evaluated at this point. IYTP has been revolutionary in its use of videotaped modeling to facilitate parent and child training while reducing the staff time necessary to direct training. Evaluation of IYTP has been hampered by a lack of replication by independent research teams, leaving open the possibility that transportability of the intervention may be problematic due to the comprehensive nature of the programs. For example, in Lavigne et al. (2008), the treatment effects of IYTP appeared to be dose dependent, and in real-world settings a full treatment dose may be less likely to occur.

Positive Parenting Program (Triple P)

Triple P is another approach to BPT that shares many similarities with previously reviewed BPT models (Sanders, 1999). Unique to Triple P is an approach to treatment that targets children from birth to 16 years of age across five levels of formal intervention. Level 1, or Universal Triple P, is intended to be a universal prevention program able to provide all parents with easy access to parenting information and multimedia support (e.g., tip sheets, videotaped guidance). Level 2, or Selected Triple P, is a brief intervention program usually limited to only a few sessions and often implemented by primary health-care staff to address a specific behavioral concern. Level 3, or Primary Care Triple P, is also often provided by a primary health-care provider but is greater in duration and is designed to teach parents basic skills in managing a variety of mild conduct problems. Level 4, or Standard Triple P, is a more traditional BPT program typically implemented by mental health

providers, often in a 12-session format. Standard Triple P is considered a primary treatment for DBD. Level 5, or Enhanced Triple P, is a more general, broader approach to intervention that targets child behavior concerns and family concerns such as parental psychopathology and relational problems. As is typical of all BPT approaches, across Triple P interventions (albeit at varying degrees of intensity), parents are taught critical parenting skills such as ignoring misbehavior and implementing consequences for inappropriate behavior, while emphasizing increased display of positive behaviors and improvements in the parent–child relationship.

Consensus recommendations. Triple P has been recommended by Division 53 of the APA as an evidence-based practice in the treatment of ODD and CD. More specifically, based on a review of methodologically sound studies, Eyberg et al. (2008) concluded that Triple P is a probably efficacious treatment for DBD.

Randomized controlled trials. Sanders (1999) has provided a detailed description of each level of Triple P and a brief review of RCTs describing the effectiveness of the program. However, two studies in particular, both completed by the same team of investigators, possess high standards of methodological rigor and will be reviewed in some detail. Based on these studies, two levels of Triple P (Level 4 and Level 5) have been assigned probably efficacious status in the treatment of disruptive behavior disorders.

Sanders, Markie-Dadds, Tully, and Bor (2000) conducted a large study that targeted 3- and 4-year-old children who were exhibiting high rates of conduct problems as reported by their mothers. Children were assigned to one of four conditions: Level 5 Triple P, Level 4 Triple P, Triple P (Self-Help), and a wait-list control group. Mothers and children were observed in order to identify rates of negative child behavior (e.g., noncompliance) and parent behavior. Additionally, a number of parent self-report measures were completed to further assess child and parent functioning. Across all conditions, parents participated in 10 to 12 therapy sessions and were trained to implement 17 specific intervention strategies. The format of delivery differed across groups, and Level 5 participants were also provided treatment designed to target family functioning. Participants in the Level 4 and 5 conditions exhibited significant improvements in displaying fewer negative behaviors than their wait-list counterparts on both observational and self-report measures. Parents in these conditions also reported greater confidence and satisfaction as a result of treatment. Further, treatment gains were maintained for approximately 1 year following treatment.

In a subsequent study, Bor, Sanders, and Markie-Dadds (2002) replicated these outcomes in a study that targeted 3- and 4-year-old children exhibiting significant conduct problems and comorbid attentional/hyperactive concerns. Participants in this study were randomly assigned to one of three groups including Level 4 Triple P, Level 5 Triple P, and a wait-list control group. Families participating in this study were assessed via direct observational strategies and through a variety of parent report measures that assessed child behavior concerns as well as a number of parent variables (e.g., depression, anxiety, degree of overreactivity, etc.). Outcomes of this study indicated that children assigned to one of the treatment conditions exhibited improved behavior relative to wait-list control children immediately following intervention and at 1-year postintervention. Additionally, parents reported decreased rates of stress, enhanced competence, and satisfaction with each of the Triple P interventions. Interestingly, Level 5 Triple P was not observed to produce significantly greater treatment gains than Level 4 Triple P.

Meta-analysis. Two meta-analyses have been conducted in an attempt to evaluate Triple P by pooling evidence across studies. One group of investigators (De Graaf, Speetjens, Smit, de Wolff, & Tavecchio, 2008)

studied the specific effects of level 4 Triple P across multiple studies. The investigators were particularly interested in assessing the impact of this program on parenting style or competency at the conclusion of treatment and maintenance of such effects over time. Nineteen studies ($N = 19$) were included in the analyses, and sample characteristics were observed to vary widely in terms of service modality (e.g., group vs. individual intervention), type of sample recruited (e.g., typically developing vs. developmentally disabled), sex and age of children, dependent measures employed, and sample size (e.g., ranging from 9 to 691). The results of this meta-analysis indicated that parenting style did reliably improve as a result of Level 4 intervention (mean ES = 0.51, moderate) and that parental competency similarly improved (mean ES = 0.57, moderate) regardless of intervention modality or age of children. Overall, the intervention appeared to be more effective for parents of boys than girls and effects were maintained over time, across studies.

A second meta-analysis conducted by Thomas and Zimmer-Gembeck (2007) examined the effectiveness of Level 4 and 5 Triple P across 11 studies. Participants were children between the ages of 3 and 12 and their parents. Significant variability was observed across variables such as sex and age of child and degree of disruptive behavior present, although most children were at or within clinical cutoff ranges at treatment onset. Most studies included parent report of child behavior using behavioral checklists and many included behavioral observations of parent and child behavior. Medium and large effects were observed for Level 4 Triple P, relative to wait-list control groups, for both child and parent behaviors as reported by parents. Significant effects were not observed for observational data. In contrast, Level 5 Triple P yielded medium to large effects for improvements across parent-reported and observed rates of child and parenting behavior. Finally, the authors considered the efficacy of Triple P and PCIT relative to one another and concluded that each produced positive effect sizes, although variability in efficacy appeared to be related to outcome measure utilized. Overall, the authors argued that PCIT exhibited larger effects than Triple P despite each being recognized as efficacious.

Conclusions. Triple P represents a unique approach to BPT in that it is closely aligned with primary care health settings and covers a significant age range with multiple levels of intensity. Thus far, only Level 4 and 5 Triple P have been extensively evaluated, and the advantage of adding more intense services in Level 5 is unclear.

BPT With Supportive Enhancements

Similar to Enhanced Triple P, several different programs have been designed to enhance the effectiveness of BPT by adding adjunctive treatment for parents and caretakers. Specifically, these programs aim to decrease parental stress, provide social support for parents, and address nonparenting concerns of care providers.

Randomized controlled trials. Griest et al. (1982) offered enhancement therapy as an adjunctive treatment in addition to BPT. Seventeen mothers of young oppositional children were assigned to a traditional BPT group, or BPT + Enhancement. BPT covered standard topics and was delivered individually. The enhancement condition included addressing mother's perception of their child's behavior, parents' personal adjustment, parents' marital adjustment, and parents' extrafamilial relationships. Outcomes were home observations of child behavior conducted by independent observers. Results indicated that BPT + Enhancement resulted in increased compliance and less child disruption at posttreatment and 2-month follow-up.

Dadds, Schwartz, and Sanders (1987) assigned 24 single parents who had children with ODD to a BPT-only or a BPT + partner support training (PST) condition. In addition, parents were assigned to groups based on their level of marital discord (i.e., high or low). The BPT training occurred individually at a clinic for 1 hour over no more than six sessions. Children were approximately 4 years of age. The PST component provided brief marital therapy that focused on parents' immediate responses to challenges by utilizing problem-solving skills. Outcome measures included a behavior checklist completed by parents, and three scales derived from observations of mother-child interactions. At posttreatment, there were no group differences; however, at 6-month follow-up, treatment effects were maintained for all groups except the BPT-only with marital discord. Both treatment groups without marital discord maintained treatment effects at follow-up, as did the group of mothers reporting high marital discord and receiving BPT with enhanced PST.

Wahler, Cartor, Fleischman, and Lambert (1993) compared a typical BPT program with an enhancement called synthesis training. Synthesis training was designed to help parents discriminate the stresses from nonchild sources (e.g., lack of monetary resources, social isolation, coercive adult relationships) from parenting stresses, thus allowing more effective attending and responding, and less indiscriminate responding to child behavior (i.e., "taking it out on the children"). Mothers were assigned to a BPT-only group ($N = 10$), or a BPT + synthesis training (ST) group, or a BPT + ST + friendship liaison group (where a chosen friend accompanied the mother to the synthesis training session). Because there were no differences between the ST and friendship liaison groups, these were combined for analyses ($N = 19$). Outcome measures were observations of parent–child interactions coded along a number of dimensions. At posttreatment, there was no improvement in child behavior in either group. However, mothers in BPT + ST reduced their indiscriminate reactions. At 12-month follow-up, mothers in the BPT + ST group were more consistent in responding to their children, and the children displayed less aversive behavior.

Conclusions. It appears as if BPT with supportive interventions can enhance the effects of BPT for some parents. This may be particularly true of highly stressed, lower socioeconomic status (SES) families. As SES has been found to be a significant moderator of treatment gains, these studies are important in demonstrating that barriers to effective treatment can be addressed. Nevertheless, optimism should be tempered based on the relatively small number of studies, the small number of participants, the relatively weak treatment effects, and the methodological variability that was present across studies. Additionally, there have been several attempts to enhance BPT that did not prove successful and are not reviewed here (Dadds & McHugh, 1992).

Conclusions for BPT as an Intervention for DBD

There is overwhelming support for BPT as a general class of interventions for childhood noncompliance and disruptive behaviors. There are a plethora of well-designed studies that have consistently demonstrated the superiority of BPT over no-treatment or minimal-treatment conditions, regardless of the specific BPT program or delivery systems (e.g., group, individual, child-present/not-present, etc.). In general, effects have been maintained up to 1 year, though in several studies, and in at least one meta-analysis, significant decrements in treatment effects are evident at 1-year follow-up.

However, there are many gaps in the effective delivery of these programs. Relatively few studies have specifically studied BPT for the treatment of ODD and CD. Instead, many BPT programs are utilized with "children referred for disruptive behaviors" but who do not necessarily qualify for a DBD diagnoses. This is probably not a critical flaw in evaluating this body of interventions, as Lundahl et al. (2006) found that severity of

child behavior at pretreatment was unrelated to treatment outcome except for child behaviors. For child behavior, contrary to expectations, more severe disruptive behavior resulted in more improvement on measures of child behavior, though this might be accounted for by the statistical phenomenon of regression to the mean.

Also, there is limited evidence that BPT is effective for older children and adolescents with DBD. Finally, it is clear that as a group, BPT programs overlap considerably. However, pertinent differences do exist across programs. Further work in evaluating specific components of each approach to treatment may be valuable.

COGNITIVE BEHAVIORAL INTERVENTIONS (CBI)

Cognitive behavioral interventions have also been utilized in the treatment of DBD. CBI are generally rooted in social-cognitive processing theories. Children with DBD demonstrate distortions and deficits in social-cognitive processing such as generating alternative solutions to interpersonal problems, identifying consequences for their actions, identifying accurate attributions to others' actions, and perceiving how others feel (Lochman, Whidby, & Fitzgerald, 2000). The overarching goal of CBI as applied to DBD is to train aggressive children to utilize effective skills and strategies to alter dysfunctional cognitive processes, better manage their emotional responding, and develop more functional repertoires. We will present several meta-analyses of CBI before describing and presenting specific CBI.

Meta-analyses of group design. Sukhodolsky, Kassinove, and Gorman (2004) conducted a meta-analysis of studies that utilized CBI for the treatment of anger in children and adolescents ages 6 to 18 years. The specific goals of this meta-analysis included evaluating the overall effect of CBI for anger-related problems, comparing effect sizes for specific types of CBI (i.e., skills development, affective education, problem solving, and eclectic treatment), and evaluating the effects of CBI across different outcome measures and informants. A comprehensive search yielded 21 published and 19 unpublished studies from 1974 to 1997. To be included in the meta-analysis, studies were required to have a control group (either no treatment or attention control) and treatment needed to be explicitly aimed at anger or aggression reduction or improvement of anger control skills. Additionally, at least one aggression-related outcome measure needed to be included. Three sets of effect sizes were calculated for each study: overall effect size, outcome measure effect size, and informant effect size.

Overall, CBI for children and adolescents for anger problems produced a mean ES of 0.67. Within specific CBI, skills training (ES = 0.79) and eclectic/multimodal treatment (ES = 0.74) were significantly more effective than affective education and most effective in reducing aggressive behavior and improving social skills. Problem-solving training (ES = 0.67) was not significantly different than any of the other intervention types but was most effective in reducing subjective anger experiences. There were no differences in ES caused by duration of treatment, informant (teacher, parent, observation, or self-report), or treatment format (group or individual).

McCart, Priester, Davies, and Azen (2006) conducted a meta-analytic study comparing the effectiveness of BPT and CBI for the treatment of youth with antisocial behavior problems. In addition, youth demographic variables were examined as potential moderators of the effectiveness of these two types of interventions. Thirty BPT studies and 41 CBI studies met the inclusion criteria for this meta-analysis. BPT was defined as any treatment involving the training of parents in the use of behavior management principles. CBI was coded when treatment involved anger management, conflict resolution, social skills training, or cognitive restructuring.

The weighted mean ES for the 71 studies at posttreatment was 0.40. The mean ES of BPT was 0.47 and the mean ES of CBI was 0.35, placing each in the small to medium range. There were an insufficient number of BPT studies that reported follow-up data to calculate an ES for long-term outcomes. For CBI, weighted mean effect size at follow-up, which on average was 8 months, was 0.22. Results suggested that youth age may moderate outcome of the two interventions, with BPT having a stronger effect for preschool and school-aged youth and CBI having a stronger effect for adolescents. Session length, outcome source, and degree of disturbance failed to account for significant differences between BPT and CBI. Inconsistent reporting of demographic variables in many of the studies prevented analysis of gender and ethnicity as potential moderator variables.

Problem-Solving Skills Training (PSST)

PSST was developed as an intervention to ameliorate deficits in the interpersonal cognitive problem-solving skills often seen in children with DBD. The goal of PSST is to foster cognitive changes in the way the child approaches interpersonal problems and the process of generating potential behavioral solutions to these problems.

PSST was developed as both an alternative and adjunctive treatment to BPT for youth with DBD. As Kazdin (2003) notes, in both inpatient and outpatient work, sometimes there is not an available parent with which to conduct BPT. In such cases, working directly with the child may be a viable alternative. In other cases where there is an available parent, PSST complements and supplements BPT. Thus, the focus of BPT is on changing the way the parent interacts with their child while the focus of PSST is on changing the way the child interacts with significant others in their environment.

PSST is delivered in an individual format. Typically a therapist meets with a child weekly for 30 to 50 minutes across 12 to 20 therapy sessions. Initially, sessions focus on teaching and understanding the steps in problem solving (problem identification, generating alternative solutions, evaluating alternatives, choosing a plan, and evaluating the outcome), and subsequently, sessions emphasize skills generalization outside of therapy by utilizing role-playing and promoting application in the context of real-life situations. Consideration of interpersonal problems and conflicts dominate therapist-led discussions.

Consensus recommendations. PSST has been recommended by Division 53 of the APA as an evidence-based practice in the treatment of ODD and CD, and by Eyberg et al. (2008) as a "probably efficacious" treatment for DBD.

Randomized controlled trials. Kazdin, Esveldt-Dawson, French, and Unis (1987a) evaluated the efficacy of PSST by comparing it to relationship therapy and a therapist-contact control group in a group of 56 children 7 to 13 years of age who resided in a medium-stay (2 to 3 months) inpatient psychiatric facility. Among other criteria, children were included if they had exhibited antisocial behavior, scored at or above the 98th percentile on parent-report measures of aggression, and were not taking psychotropic medication. Seventy percent of children had a principal diagnosis of CD. Participating youth were primarily white males with a mean age of 10.9. Twenty children were randomly assigned to PSST, which included 20 sessions. Nineteen children were assigned to relationship therapy (RT), which consisted of 20 individualized nondirective therapy sessions lasting about 45 minutes each. Within this condition, therapists were instructed to develop a strong relationship with the child as well as provide empathy, warmth, and unconditional positive regard. Seventeen youth were assigned to a treatment-contact control group (TC) in order to control for contact effects. These youth met with therapists for 20 sessions lasting 20 minutes during which the child was engaged in discussions of routine unit activities. Outcome measures included standardized parent and teacher ratings. Posttreatment data was collected for 47 children and longitudinal data (1 year) was collected for 42 children.

Between-group comparisons of posttreatment means indicated that the PSST group improved significantly better (less pathology and/or better adjustment) across five parent-report scales and three teacher-report scales relative to RT or TC groups, which did not differ from each other on any measures. Within-group comparisons indicated significant improvement for the PSST group on the majority of outcome measures at both posttreatment and 1-year follow-up. The RT group demonstrated significant improvement on two of eight measures at posttreatment, and on no scales at 1-year follow-up. The TC group demonstrated significant improvements on two of eight measures at posttreatment, and on a single measure at follow-up.

In a very similar study, Kazdin, Esveldt-Dawson, French, and Unis (1987b) evaluated combined PSST and BPT (PSST/BPT) relative to a contact-control condition (CC). Participants were 40 children 7 to 12 years of age who resided in a medium-stay (2 to 3 months) inpatient psychiatric facility. Inclusionary criteria were identical in this study. Conduct disorder was the principal diagnosis for 78% of the children. The majority was Caucasian and male with a mean age of 10.1. Twenty-four children were randomly assigned to PSST/BPT group. PSST consisted of 20 sessions lasting about 50 minutes and BPT consisted of 13 sessions lasting about 2 hours each. Sixteen children participated in the CC group consisting of individual sessions with a therapist whose task was to engage the child in conversations related to routine activities. Parents in the CC group met with inpatient staff biweekly to discuss the progress of their child. Attrition was equal between the groups. Several parent-report outcome measures were used in this study as well.

Between-group comparisons of posttreatment means indicated that children in PSST/

BPT group demonstrated significantly less deviance than those in the CC condition across all measures. Within-group comparisons indicated significant improvement for the PSST/ BPT group on all measures at both posttreatment and 1-year follow-up. The control group demonstrated significant improvements on two measures at posttreatment and at 1-year follow-up.

Kazdin, Siegel, and Bass (1992) evaluated PSST, BPT, and a combined PSST/BPT condition in 97 children (7 to 13 years old; $M = 10.3$) referred to an outpatient clinic for antisocial behavior. Among other inclusionary criteria, children had to be rated at or above the 90th percentile on a parent-report measure of disruptive behavior and not be taking psychotropic medication. Sixty-nine percent of the children were Caucasian, and 78% were male. Almost all (91%) of the children had a primary diagnosis of CD or ODD. Twenty-nine children were assigned to PSST, which consisted of 25 individual weekly sessions lasting about 50 minutes. Thirty-one parents participated in the BPT condition, which consisted of 16 individual sessions with parents lasting approximately 1½ to 2 hours. Sessions were weekly over the first two-thirds of the program, then faded to biweekly for the final three or four sessions. Participants in the combined PSST/BPT condition ($N = 37$) received each treatment as described previously. Of the 97 initial participants, 22% did not complete treatment, though attrition rates did not vary between groups. Outcomes included a parent-report measure, a parent-informant semistructured interview, parent reports of observed child behavior, two teacher-report behavioral rating scales, two child-report measures of problem behavior, two measures of parent-report of family environment/stress, and two measures of parental psychopathology. In sum, a total of 19 outcome measures were utilized.

Within-group repeated measures analyses indicated that all three treatment conditions resulted in improved functioning. At posttreatment, of the 19 outcome measures, the PSST group showed significant improvement from pretreatment on 13, BPT on 10, and PSST/BPT on all 19. Nonsignificant results for PSST and BPT primarily occurred on measures of family functioning and parental psychopathology, but not indices of child behavior. At 1-year follow-up, the PSST and PSST/BPT groups continued to demonstrate improvement from pretreatment on most measures (13 and 17 of 19, respectively), though treatment gains in BPT condition were largely attenuated (4 of 19). Between-group comparisons at posttreatment indicated that the PSST/BPT group displayed significantly fewer antisocial and conduct problems, better family functioning, and less parental psychopathology relative to comparison conditions. At 1-year follow-up, the advantage for the combined treatment was maintained, with between-group differences favoring the PSST/ BPT group on child conduct problem, family functioning, and parental psychopathology measures. At 1-year follow-up, the PSST groups (PSST/BPT and PSST) were superior to the BPT group on teacher-rated behaviors, self-reported aggression, parent-observed conduct problems at home, and parental psychopathology.

Conclusions. Problem-solving skills training is a CBI that has been documented as effective in the treatment of DBD. Unique to the research base that supports PSST is its use in combination with BPT that appears to add incrementally to its efficacy. Rigorous studies of PSST have been conducted but are limited in number—a factor that relegates PSST to the status of a "probably efficacious" evidence-based practice. Unfortunately, a limited amount of well-controlled research on PSST appears to have been conducted over the past 5 to 7 years.

Anger Control Training

Anger control training (ACT), also referred to as Anger Coping Program, is a cognitive-behavioral intervention aimed at helping angry, aggressive, and peer-rejected children (Larson & Lochman, 2002; Lochman, Barry, &

Pardini, 2003). The goal of ACT is to help youth develop cognitive and behavioral skills through increased awareness of feelings and emotions, enhance anger management techniques, develop problem-solving skills, learn coping strategies, and integrate this knowledge into a child's behavioral repertoire. Anger control training has been implemented in both school and clinic settings. Participants typically meet in groups, once a week, for 60 to 90 minutes over 18 sessions. Groups are typically run by coleaders with a master's degree. Throughout each session, participants are taught, modeled, and given the opportunity to practice new skills including: positive self-statements, coping strategies (e.g., relaxation skills training), and social communication techniques. Additionally, youth participate in hypothetical social vignettes to develop problem-solving skills and practice appropriate responses to emotionally charged situations. Throughout the intervention, group members work together to provide feedback and support each other in the proper demonstration and implementation of anger management strategies. A recent version of ACT, called the Coping Power Program, is a more intensive curriculum (33 sessions over 15 months) and also includes a parent component targeting effective discipline, monitoring and supervision, and family communication.

Consensus recommendations. ACT has been recommended by Division 53 of the APA as an evidence-based practice in the treatment of ODD and CD. More specifically, based on a review of methodologically sound studies, Eyberg et al. (2008) concluded that ACC is a "probably efficacious" treatment for DBD.

Randomized controlled trials. Several studies have evaluated ACT with children and adolescents. Lochman, Burch, Curry, and Lampron (1984) evaluated an early version of the Anger Control Program. Participants were 76 aggressive boys, 4th through 6th grade, randomly assigned to an anger coping group (AC, 12 sessions), goal-setting intervention (GS, eight sessions), a combined anger coping and goal-setting condition (AC/GS), or an untreated control (C). Participants were 53% African American. The boys in the AC conditions (AC and AC/GS) were rated as having less parent-reported aggression and lower rates of observed disruptive behavior in the classroom than either the GS or C groups. A study of the long-term effects demonstrated continued treatment effects at 3 years for the boys receiving AC on measures of drug use, alcohol use, self-esteem, and problem solving, but not for aggressive behavior (Lochman, 1992).

Lochman, Coie, Underwood, and Terry (1993) compared two groups of youth (aggressive rejected and nonaggressive rejected youth) treated in ACT groups to a control condition. Participants were 52 African American fourth-grade children. In this study, the two treatment groups participated in 26 individual and 8 group sessions twice weekly over a 6-month period. The intervention included problem-solving practice, social skills training (e.g., appropriate play and engagement in social relationships), group-entry skills instruction, and feelings identification. As areas of skills weaknesses were recognized, students were taught and modeled new skills, and given the opportunity for practice and feedback. To encourage skill implementation, behavioral contracts and social reinforcement were utilized.

While the intervention was not effective for nonaggressive rejected children, the intervention was effective with the aggressive rejected children. On both teacher and peer report, the aggressive rejected intervention group had significantly fewer problems than the aggressive rejected control group at both posttreatment and follow-up. Additionally, the aggressive rejected intervention group showed gains in prosocial behavior.

Robinson, Smith, and Miller (2002) independently examined ACT in a study of 41 sixth-, seventh-, and eighth-grade male students exhibiting conduct problems. Four classrooms were randomly assigned to either ACT or a control condition. The intervention group participated in 10 weeks of treatment, biweekly sessions for the first 5 weeks and weekly sessions for the remaining 5 weeks. Sessions included teaching, modeling, role-play, discussion, and feedback for the specific skills targeted: anger identification and coping skills (e.g., relaxation techniques), social communication, problem solving, modeling, and practice of anger control skills. Youth in the ACT group were rated as being less aggressive at posttreatment and at follow-up on several standardized measures of aggression as rated by teachers and the youth.

Conclusions. ACT is a cognitive behavioral intervention that has been evaluated in several RCTs. ACT has been found to be more effective than wait-list control conditions in several studies, and in one study, more effective than a modest, but legitimate, treatment comparison condition. In general, ACT has targeted grade school children. Long-term effects have been mixed, with one study demonstrating maintenance of effects at 6 months, while another study did not find maintenance of effects on measures of aggression at 3 years.

Conclusion about CBI as an intervention for DBD. The two programs reviewed here have solid support for older, school-aged children. There are several other CBI approaches, including anger management interventions (e.g., Feindler & Ecton, 1986), rational-emotive interventions (Block, 1978), and assertiveness training (Huey & Rank, 1984), that have promising, but insufficient, support to recommend as evidence-based practice. Meta-analyses have indicated that CBI produce small to medium effects, and relative to behavioral parent training, produce slightly smaller treatment effects, though some studies have indicated equal if not superior effects for CBI over BPT. Importantly, as many BPT target younger children, CBI tend to be effective for older school-age children and fill an important gap in service delivery for children with DBD.

OTHER INTERVENTIONS

Multisystemic Therapy (MST)

Multisystemic therapy is a comprehensive intervention approach for treating adolescents with serious disruptive, delinquent, and anti-social behavior. The approach is a philosophy of intensive intervention that is individually administered, combining treatments and approaches as needed for individual families and adolescents. An overarching philosophy of MST is that youth are embedded in multiple interconnected systems (e.g., family, neighborhood, school, peer culture, community, etc.). The role of the MST therapist is to identify the bidirectional influences and risk factors within and across these systems relative to the adolescents' problematic behaviors. Families are considered the primary agents of change. Nine treatment principles guide the actions of MST therapists, which include: (1) how problems "make sense" in the context of the youth's social ecology, (2) focusing on strengths, (3) increasing responsibility with family members, (4) being present and action-focused, (5) targeting specific and sequenced behavior, (6) implementing developmentally appropriate strategies, (7) establishing intensive and continuous requirements of the family, (8) constantly evaluating the intervention and accountability of the MST therapist, and (9) programming for generalization. There is no one specific treatment that is espoused other than utilization of the treatment that is most appropriate for a particular problem in a specific context. Typical treatments include cognitive behavioral approaches, behavior therapy, BPT, pragmatic family therapies, and pharmacological interventions that have an evidence-base (Henggeler & Lee, 2003).

MST is delivered in the natural environment of the youth, including home, school, and neighborhood. MST therapists have a small caseload (four to five families), are the primary point-of-contact between the family and other systems, and are available for families 24 hours a day, 7 days a week. Treatment is time-limited, typically 3 to 5 months.

Consensus

MST has been recommended by Division 53 of the APA as an evidence-based practice for the treatment of CD. MST was one of several National Institute of Health (NIH) recommended programs to reduce violence and juvenile offending (2004), and has been recommended a model program in the Blueprints for Violence Prevention by the Center for the Study and Prevention of Violence at the University of Colorado (2006).

Randomized controlled trials. MST has been evaluated in a number of studies using random assignment that have directly targeted delinquent adolescents. Several published MST evaluations have utilized sample data from previously published accounts, and because of space limitations, will not be covered in this review (Henggeler et al., 1991; Scherer, Brondino, Henggeler, Melton, & Hanley, 1994).

Henggeler, Melton, and Smith (1992) evaluated youth referred by a social service agency who were judged to be at imminent risk for out-of-home placement. Ninety-six youth were referred. Pre- and postintervention arrest data was obtained for 84 youth, but only 56 youth and their families participated to the extent that complete pre- and postassessment data were collected. Youth were randomly assigned to receive MST services or "services as usual." MST families remained in treatment on average 13.4 weeks, encompassing an average of 33 hours of direct contact, with sessions usually lasting less than 90 minutes and held as frequently as every day or as infrequently as once a week. "Services as usual" consisted of terms of probation (e.g., seeking therapeutic services, attending school, curfews). Probation officers met with the youth at least once a month where officers stressed the importance of compliance with

the probation terms and consequences for not doing so. Youth not in compliance with probation were ordered back to court where judges could send them to a youth detention facility or place them back on probation.

Youth in the final intervention sample (MST; $n = 33$; control $n = 23$) averaged 3.4 previous arrests, 8.1 weeks of prior incarceration, and 59% of them had at least one arrest for a violent crime. Mean age was 15.0 years ($SD = 1.4$), 75% were male, 66% were African American, and 34% were Caucasian. Treatment groups did not differ on any demographic or criminal history variables. Outcome variables collected posttreatment, which averaged 59 weeks postreferral, included arrest and incarceration records, self-reported delinquency, standardized checklists measuring family functioning, peer relationships, adolescent social competence, adolescent symptomatology, and parental symptomatology. Results indicated that adolescents in the MST group had significantly fewer arrests, shorter incarcerations, and less self-reported delinquency. Only two of the eight psychosocial measures were significantly different between treatment groups, with the MST group showing improved family cohesion and decreased peer aggression.

Borduin et al. (1995) evaluated the effectiveness of MST with 176 delinquent youth between 12 to 17 years of age ($M = 14.8$). All youth had been referred from a juvenile court, had been arrested multiple times, and had been detained for at least 4 weeks. Youth and their families were randomly assigned to MST or individual therapy (IT). IT was described as "treatment as usual" for juvenile offenders in this district and consisted of an eclectic blend of psychodynamic, client-centered, and positive behaviors approaches. Outcomes included measures of individual adjustment (mother, father, and child mental health; parent-rated disruptive behavior), standardized measures of family functioning and relationships, direct observation of parent–child interactions, standardized measures of peer relationships, and court-reported criminal activity (i.e., rearrests). There were no differences between MST drop-outs, IT drop-outs, and treatment refusers on any preintervention measure.

The MST group improved significantly more than the IT group on the maternal and paternal mental health as well as mother-reported adolescent disruptive behavior. However, adolescents in the MST group did not report greater improvement than the IT group on a measure of general mental health. On 8 of 11 measures of family functioning, the MST had treatment gains that were superior to the IT condition, including on standardized parent-reported measures as well as formal observations of family interactions. There were no treatment effects for combined mother/teacher ratings of peer interactions on three composite scales. Survival analyses of the arrest data indicated that MST completers were less likely to be rearrested after a 4-year follow-up compared to IT completers (22.1% vs. 71.4%, respectively), and less likely to be arrested for violent crimes as well.

Henggeler, Melton, Brondino, Scherer, and Hanley (1997) evaluated MST in a study of "violent or chronic juvenile offenders" designed to test the effectiveness of the intervention in a realistic setting and assess the role of treatment fidelity in outcomes. Absent in the MST condition was the usual weekly supervision and feedback from an expert MST trainer. The study took place in two public mental health facilities that each housed two full-time therapists and a supervisor. Participants were 155 violent or chronic juvenile offenders between the ages of 11 and 17 who had committed a serious crime or had at least three nonstatus criminal offenses (40% had been arrested for a violent crime; mean arrests = 3.07), and were at imminent risk of being placed out-of-home. Average age of the participants was 15.2, 82% were male, and 81% were African American. Participants were randomly assigned to the MST condition or treatment as usual. Treatment as usual

consisted of probation for a minimum of 6 months, and potential further restitution. Probation officers saw youth at least once per month. School attendance was monitored, and youth were often referred to other social services agencies for treatment (e.g., therapy). Youth not making progress could be placed in an alternative school or in out-of-home treatment. Outcome measures of parent and adolescent psychological distress, adolescent disruptive behavior problems, adolescent self-report on a measure of delinquency, official court records of arrests and incarcerations, family functioning as defined by several scales from standardized measures of family functioning, parent and adolescent reports of parental monitoring, and peer relationships and peer conformity were utilized. Although the treatment groups tended to improve over time on most measures, the MST group demonstrated statistically significantly better outcomes than the comparison group on only 2 of 22 outcome comparisons. Specifically, the youth in the MST condition rated their emotional functioning as more improved than treatment as usual youth, and MST youth were incarcerated fewer days (33.2 vs. 70.4, respectively). There was no other group difference on any other outcome measures. In a subsequent analysis, various aspects of therapist fidelity to MST principles were found to be positively associated with positive changes in several measures over the course of treatment in the MST group.

Meta-analysis of group design. A recent meta-analysis (Curtis, Ronan, & Borduin, 2004) evaluated 11 published studies between 1987 and 2002 that utilized MST as an intervention in randomized group design studies targeting a total of 798 children and adolescents, many of whom demonstrated behaviors consistent with ODD and CD diagnoses. Study sample sizes ranged from 16 to 176 ($Mdn = 116$). Youth ranged in age from 8.3 to 17.6 years ($Mdn = 14.8$), 70% were male, and 81% lived with at least one biological parent.

About 45% of participants were African American and another 45% were Caucasian. Most of the youth (55%) were classified as chronic, at-risk, and/or violent juvenile offenders; 17% ($N = 118$) were classified as substance abusers; 16% ($N = 116$) required emergency psychiatric hospitalization (presenting problems included suicidal ideation, homicidal ideation, and psychosis); 6% ($N = 43$) were classified as abused and/or neglected; 2% were classified as sexual offenders. Eighty-four percent ($N = 593$) of the youths had been arrested previously.

The comparison group in four of the studies was "usual services," which included services provided through juvenile justice agencies, community mental health center, an outpatient substance abuse treatment program, and an inpatient psychiatric hospital. In the three other studies, one utilized a comparison parent training condition and two utilized individual therapy. Parent training consisted of weekly group sessions in which caregivers received instruction on human development, behavioral management techniques, and positive parent–child interactions. Individual therapy for the youths included an eclectic blend of psychodynamic, client-centered, and behavioral approaches in which therapists focused on personal, family, and academic issues and provided encouragement for behavior change (Curtis et al., 2004).

Results indicated that the average ES for MST was 0.55. The ES was higher for measures assessing critical domains (arrests, self-reported delinquency; ES = 0.50), family functioning variables (e.g., observation of family interactions, self-reported measures of functioning; ES = 0.57), and school attendance (ES = 0.54), while effect sizes for peer relationships (ES = 0.11) and individual adjustment (ES = 0.28) were generally lower. Studies ($N = 3$) utilizing closely supervised graduate students as therapists yielded larger effect sizes than those studies ($N = 4$) using therapist in community-based facilities, ES = 0.81 and ES = 0.26, respectively. Some

methodological limitations of the study were the small number of studies included, the presence of possible allegiance effects (as all studies were conducted by the primary investigators), and the pooling of studies with overlapping samples (Curtis et al., 2004).

Conclusions. MST is one of the more promising approaches for serious delinquency in adolescents. Unlike many of the other interventions where the intended target is younger children, MST has targeted difficult adolescents with serious delinquency and antisocial behavior. As such, MST represents a legitimate community-based treatment option for youth who would otherwise be incarcerated or placed in a long-term residential care setting.

Family Therapy

Family therapy is a philosophy of treatment that assumes that problems are not unique to individuals, but rather are inherent within the systems in which the target individual resides. Thus, interventions target the entire family system. The emphasis of family therapy is placed on the interactive dynamics between individuals in the family, family communication patterns, and roles, allegiances, and alliances within families. Family therapies tend to incorporate skills and strategies from an eclectic and broad array of interventions. There are many different schools of family therapy, each of which has a different emphasis resulting in some differences in practice. Two versions of family therapy are particularly promising interventions for DBD.

Brief strategic family therapy (BSFT) was developed primarily to treat Hispanic adolescents who were demonstrating antisocial behavior (Robbins et al., 2003), a population that has been grossly overlooked in evidence-based treatments (Eyberg et al., 2008). BSFT is a blend of the structural family and strategic family interventions. BSFT targets family interactional patterns that are most directly relevant to the problematic behavior. BSFT is problem-focused and follows a prescribed sequence of steps, including joining, diagnoses and assessment of the family, developing an individualized treatment plan to address youth problem behaviors, and restructuring. Restructuring is the implementation of therapeutic strategies through typical family therapy interventions, including reframing, shifting family alliances, redirecting family communications, bolstering the strength of the parental subsystem, developing and promoting family conflict skills, and teaching parents effective behavior management skills (Robbins et al., 2003).

Functional family therapy (FFT) is a multisystemic prevention and intervention for high-risk adolescents and families (Parsons & Alexander, 1973). Across an average of 12 sessions, adolescents and their families participate in both individual and family therapy. There are three phases of treatment in FFT that include: engagement and motivation, behavior change, and generalization. In the first phase, therapists work to develop rapport with the individual and their family, develop a family-focused understanding of the presenting problem, and increase hope in order to decrease resistance, encouraging treatment "buy in." During the second phase of treatment, immediate and long-term behavioral goals and commitments are established that target interactional patterns, parenting practices, communication skills, existing personal pathologies, cognitive processes, and coping strategies. The goal of the second phase is to extinguish existing maladaptive relational patterns and provide reinforcement for the positive utilization of coping skills and effective communication patterns (Parsons & Alexander, 1973). Finally, during the third phase, clients and their families are connected to resources in the community and continue treatment in order to maintain treatment progress and prevent relapse.

Consensus Statements

FFT was recommended by a National Institute of Health (NIH) consensus panel as an effective program to reduce violence and juvenile offending (2004). This recommendation was largely based on the status of FFT as a model program in the Blueprints for Violence Prevention by the Center for the Study and Prevention of Violence at the University of Colorado. BSFT is cited as a "promising program" by Blueprints for Violence Prevention (2006).

Randomized controlled trials. Santisteban et al. (2003) assigned 126 disruptive (delinquent, behavior-problem, substance using) Hispanic adolescents, aged 12 to 18 ($M = 15.6$) and their families to either a BSFT intervention or a group-intervention control (GC). Youth participants were 75% male. BSFT was conducted weekly with all family members, and families participated in an average of 11 sessions. The GC condition was described as "group therapy as usual," and consisted of four to eight adolescents who were encouraged to discuss and solve problems by the group facilitator who emphasized group cohesion, disseminated information regarding criminality and drug use, and strove to maintain a problem-solving atmosphere. The average number of group sessions attended by youth was nine and each lasted about 90 minutes. Outcome measures included a parent-report measure of disruptive behavior, parent- and child-report measures of family-functioning, and observations of family-interactions. Attrition rates were high (30% to 37%), but did not differ between groups. Adolescents in the BSFT condition demonstrated significant improvements relative to the GC condition on parent-report measures of behavior problems and adolescent-report measures of family cohesion. However, no other differences were significant.

FFT has been evaluated in a number of studies. The first published outcome study utilized a twice-weekly FFT intervention with 40 families of male juvenile delinquents previously arrested for a behavioral offense (Parsons & Alexander, 1973). The adolescents and their families were assigned to one of four treatment conditions (no treatment control, placebo control, a pre-post test treatment group, and posttest-only treatment group). The treatment included training in differentiating rules from requests in order to add structure to the family system, the implementation of a family-wide token economy, communication training, and training in reinforcing the display of positive, solution-focused communication patterns. Results supported the utilization of FFT with juvenile delinquents and their families as the treatment groups were significantly different than the control groups on positive family interaction. Specifically, there was decreased silence, increased equality of speech, and increased frequency and duration of simultaneous speech on taped 20-minute family interactions in the treatment groups as compared to the control groups. However, no differences were found in agreement to social vignettes and/or degree of noticed behavioral change between groups.

In a series of reports of FFT with delinquent adolescents and their families (Alexander & Parsons, 1982; Klein, Alexander, & Parsons, 1977), families of 86 adolescents (38 male and 48 female) were randomly assigned to one of four groups: no-treatment control, FFT group, an eclectic-dynamic approach, and a client-centered family group. Outcome measures indicated a significant reduction in 6- to 18-month recidivism rates for the FFT program as compared to the other groups. Additionally, rates of sibling court referrals over a 2½ to 3½ year period were 20% for the FFT intervention group and 40 to 60% court contacts for the siblings of families in the control or alternative treatment conditions, further offering support for FFT with adolescents exhibiting conduct problems.

Finally, an independent team has applied FFT to adolescent offenders in rural areas. In a series of reports, Gordon, Arbuthnot, Gustafson, and McGreen (1988) and Gordon, Graves, and Arbuthnot (1995) compared FFT ($N = 27$) and a probation-only control group ($N = 27$) for delinquent adolescents. The FFT was delivered in-home by experienced therapists for 16 sessions. Follow-up recidivism rates were collected at 2½ years posttreatment. Results strongly favored FFT. The recidivism rate for the FFT group was 11%, compared to 67% for the probation control group. Followed several years into adulthood, the advantage for FFT continued, where recidivism rates were 9% for the FFT group and 41% in the comparison group.

Meta-analysis of group design studies. As mentioned previously, Shadish et al. (1993) conducted a meta-analysis that yielded support for the effectiveness of family therapy in general. However, the ES for systemic family therapy (0.28) in particular was not significantly different from zero, and comparisons of family therapy to individual therapy for child and adolescent conduct problems yielded a higher ES for individual therapy, raising some questions regarding the relative value of systemic family therapy in the treatment of DBD.

Conclusions. There is accumulating evidence regarding the efficacy of family therapy for adolescent disruptive behavior. Several models of family therapy have been tested in rigorous designs. Relative to other treatments for adolescent DBD (e.g., MST, residential placement), family therapy offers a relatively low-intensity intervention that can be delivered in the clinic or home, and appears effective for at least mild to moderate cases of adolescent DBD. However, some caution is warranted in that meta-analytic reviews have not indicated that family therapy, broadly defined, is more effective than other types of interventions for youth with DBD. Further, not all trials of BSFT have provided such positive results (Szapocznik et al., 1989). Nevertheless, FFT and, to a lesser extent, BSFT clearly have a place in the arsenal of evidence-based practices for adolescents with DBD.

CONCLUSIONS REGARDING EVIDENCE-BASED PRACTICES FOR DBD

There are significant developmental considerations when evaluating evidence-based practices for DBD. For prepubescent children with DBD, BPT is the clear treatment of choice. The evidence-base for BPT is impressive and unequivocal. In general, BPT has overwhelming empirical support suggesting substantive treatment gains relative to no treatment or minimal treatment controls. Further, there is persuasive, though not irrefutable, evidence for its superiority relative to other legitimate treatments. The choice of individually administered versus group-administered parent training is a matter of preference and economics, not efficacy, as there is sufficient evidence that either individual- or group-administered BPT is effective in reducing the disruptive behavior of younger children with DBD. Finally, for some families, it appears as if adding a support component addressing familial problems (e.g., parental psychopathology) can be very helpful for some, but not necessarily all, parents (Dadds et al., 1987; Sanders et al., 2000).

CBI has also demonstrated promising results, though its evidence base is not as impressive as BPT. Although several CBI programs have been demonstrated to be efficacious (e.g., PSST, Anger Coping), many are supported by only a single, well-conducted study. Examination of effect sizes of treatment from several meta-analyses indicates that overall CBI produce small to moderate effects. In one meta-analysis directly comparing BPT and CBI, BPT produced a larger treatment effect than CBI for children aged 6 to 12 (McCart et al., 2006). In sum, CBI appears to be more effective for older children and adolescents than with prepubescent children (McCart et al., 2006; Sukhodolsky et al., 2004).

The available evidence has also indicated that treatment outcomes may be maximized when BPT is augmented with an evidence-based CBI targeting the child directly. Unfortunately, only a few studies have directly compared BPT, CBI, and a combined condition. In these well-conducted studies, Kazdin et al. (1992), Webster-Stratton and Hammond

(1997), and Webster-Stratton et al. (2004) found that when CBI was added to BPT, the results were superior to the BPT-only group. Somewhat surprisingly, in two of these studies, CBI alone was as effective as BPT in ameliorating the conduct problems of children with DBD. However, at least one meta-analysis of BPT concluded that there was no significant benefit to BPT programs when adjunctive CBI programs for children were added to them (Lundahl et al., 2006). Given the equivocal results and the relatively small number of studies that have evaluated combined programs, it is premature to recommend combined BPT and CBI as an evidence-based practice, though the potential seems promising. Given the rich tradition and empirical support for both BPT and CBI, it is truly surprising that there have been so few studies that have examined this possibility.

Unlike the abundance of evidence-based studies for children with DBD, fewer treatments have demonstrated strong empirical support for their effectiveness as an intervention for adolescents with DBD. The few extensions of BPT to adolescents with DBD have resulted in mixed findings, suggesting that the intensity of BPT has to be significantly enhanced to achieve even modest effects (Bank, Marlowe, Reid, Patterson, & Weinrott, 1991; Dishion & Andrews, 1995) for older youth.

Taken as a whole, several forms of family therapy have a solid evidence base for adolescent DBD, including BSFT and FFT. The most comprehensive intervention for adolescents, MST, probably has the most promising and consistently positive body of evidence with highly disruptive and antisocial adolescents.

Perhaps not surprisingly, interventions for adolescents with DBD tend to be much more intensive when compared to BPT and CBI for children. For example, modified PMTO for adolescents averaged 45 hours of treatment over a year, while average MST treatment requires around 30 hours of therapist contact over 3 to 4 months, and FFT requires between 12 to 30 hours of treatment. Although the required intensity of these interventions may seem daunting, they are nonetheless effective, which is not true of a myriad of alternative treatments that have historically been implemented for adolescents with DBD. Treating adolescents with DBD is difficult, and many reasonable approaches have not produced substantially positive outcomes (Dishion & Andrews, 1995; Lipsey & Wilson, 1998; Szapocznik et al., 1989), often resulting in the placement of adolescents in juvenile detention or out-of-home treatment facilities (Farmer, Mustillo, Burns, & Holden, 2008).

Despite there being greater empirical evidence for effective treatments for DBD than perhaps any other childhood disorder, there are many unresolved issues and lingering questions. First, the long-term effectiveness of treatments has not been demonstrated beyond a few years. In fact, in several studies, treatment effects have not maintained at long-term follow-up (greater than 1 to 2 years). Whether long-term effects could be enhanced through additional sessions, combined treatments, and/ or enhanced versions of treatments remains largely unknown.

Second, with a few exceptions, mediators and moderators of treatment outcome have not been addressed in treatment programs. Simply stated, there are likely limits to the benefits of these treatments that are largely unknown (Weisz & Kazdin, 2003). For example, data have indicated that SES is significantly related to BPT treatment outcomes (Dumas, 1984; Lundhal et al., 2006), which has led to modifications in treatment delivery to low SES families (Brestan & Eyberg, 2008; Dadds et al., 1987). There are many other factors that could similarly alter treatment efficacy and remain in need of systematic evaluation, such as ethnicity, cultural factors, and comorbidity.

Third, issues related to the transportability of interventions are concerning. Most of the treatments reviewed here have been evaluated in controlled environments, often by the developers of the intervention. Further, studies have utilized strict manualized training protocols, and clinically atypical supervision (Eyberg et al., 2008). Whether these treatments can be transported to environments where there is less control is largely unknown, though some evidence indicates there are significant decrements in outcomes for youth with DBD during this transportation process (Henggeler et al., 1997; Lavigne et al., 2008).

Fourth, mechanisms of action remain largely unknown for most effective treatments of DBD. An emphasis on how evidence-based treatments effect change would yield critical feedback regarding the functional components of treatment. "Dismantling" studies conducted with a variety of treatments for other disorders have demonstrated surprising and controversial results that have significantly altered the practice of evidence-based therapies (Feske & Goldstein, 1997; Jacobson et al., 1996).

Despite these gaps, evidence-based practice for childhood DBD remains on solid footing. There are numerous effective interventions for children and adolescents with DBD that span a range of theoretical orientations and delivery systems.

REFERENCES

Achenbach, T. M. (1991). *Manual for the child behavior checklist/4-18 and 1991 profile*. Burlington: University of Vermont, Department of Psychiatry.

Alexander, J., & Parsons, B. V. (1982). *Functional family therapy*. Monterey, CA: Brooks/Cole.

Arndorfer, R. E., Allen, K. D., & Aljazireh, L. (1999). Behavioral health needs in pediatric medicine and the acceptability of behavioral solutions: Implications for behavioral psychologists. *Behavior Therapy, 30*, 137–148.

American Psychiatric Association. (2000). *Diagnostic and statistical manual of mental disorders* (4th ed., text rev.). Washington, DC: Author.

Bank, L., Marlowe, J. H., Reid, J. B., Patterson, G. R., & Weinrott, M. R. (1991). A comparative evaluation of parent-training interventions for families of chronic delinquents. *Journal of Abnormal Child Psychology, 19*, 15–33.

Baum, C. G., & Forehand, R. (1981). Long term follow-up assessment of parent training by use of multiple outcome measures. *Behavior Therapy, 12*, 643–652.

Behan, J., & Carr, A. (2000). Oppositional defiant disorder. In A. Carr (Ed.), *What works with children and adolescents?: A critical review of psychological interventions with children, adolescents and their families* (pp. 102–130). Florence, KY: Taylor & Frances/Routledge.

Bernal, M. E., Klinnert, M. D., & Schultz, L. A. (1980). Outcome evaluation of behavioral parent training and client-centered parent counseling for children with conduct problems. *Journal of Applied Behavior Analysis, 13*, 677–691.

Bierman, K. L., Bruschi, C., Domitrovich, C., Fang, G. Y., Miller-Johnson, S., & Conduct Problems Prevention Research Group. (2004). Early disruptive behaviors associated with emerging antisocial behavior among girls. In M. Putallaz & K. L. Bierman (Eds.), *Aggression, antisocial behavior, and violence among girls: A developmental perspective. Duke series in child development and public policy* (pp. 137–161). New York, NY: Guilford Press.

Block, J. (1978). Effects of a rational-emotive mental health program on poorly achieving, disruptive high school students. *Journal of Counseling Psychology, 25*, 61–65.

Bloomquist, M. L., & Schnell, S. V. (2002). *Helping children with aggression and conduct problems: Best practices for intervention*. New York, NY: Guilford Press.

Bor, W., Sanders, M. R., & Markie-Dadds, C. (2002). The effects of the Triple P-Positive Parenting Program on preschool children with co-occurring disruptive behavior and attentional/hyperactive difficulties. *Journal of Abnormal Child Psychology, 30*, 571–587.

Borduin, C. M., Mann, B. J., Cone, L. T., Henggeler, S. W., Fucci, B. R, Blaske, D. M., & Willaims, R. A. (1995). Multisystemic treatment of serious juvenile offenders: Long-term prevention of criminality and violence. *Journal of Consulting and Clinical Psychology, 63*, 569–578.

Brestan, E. V., & Eyberg, S. M. (1998). Effective psychosocial treatments of conduct-disordered children and adolescents: 29 years, 82 studies, and 5,272 kids. *Journal of Clinical Child Psychology, 27*, 180–189.

Brinkmeyer, M. Y., & Eyberg, S. M. (2003). Parent–child interaction therapy for oppositional children. In A. E. Kazdin & J. R. Weisz (Eds.), *Evidence-based psychotherapies for children and adolescents* (pp. 204–223). New York, NY: Guilford Press.

Chambless, D. L., Sanderson, W. C., Shoham, V., Bennett Johnson, S., Pope, K. S., Crits-Christoph, P., . . . McCurry, S. (1996). An update on empirically validated therapies. *The Clinical Psychologist, 49*, 5–18.

Christensen, A., Johnson, S. M., Phillips, S., & Glasgow, R. E. (1980). Cost effectiveness in behavioral family therapy. *Behavior Therapy, 11*, 208–226.

Connor, D. F. (2002). *Aggression and antisocial behavior in children and adolescents: Research and treatment.* New York, NY: Guilford Press.

Costello, E. J. (1990). Child psychiatric epidemiology: Implications for clinical research and practice. In B. B. Lahey & A. E. Kazdin (Eds.), *Advances in clinical child psychology* (Vol. 13, pp. 53–90). New York, NY: Plenum Press.

Crits-Christoph, P., Frank, E., Chambless, D. L., Brody, C., & Karp, J. F. (1995). Training in empirically validated treatments: What are clinical psychology students learning? *Professional Psychology: Research and Practice, 26*, 514–522.

Curtis, N. M., Ronan, K. R., & Borduin, C. M. (2004). Multisystemic treatment: A meta-analysis of outcome studies. *Journal of Family Psychology, 3*, 411–419.

Dadds, M. R., & McHugh, T. A. (1992). Social support and treatment outcome in behavioral family therapy for child conduct problems. *Journal of Consulting and Clinical Psychology, 60*, 252–259.

Dadds, M. R., Schwartz, S., & Sanders, M. R. (1987). Marital discord and treatment outcome in behavioral treatment of child conduct disorders. *Journal of Consulting and Clinical Psychology, 55*, 396–403.

De Graaf, I., Speetjens, P., Smit, F., de Wolff, M., & Tavecchio, L. (2008). Effectiveness of the Triple P Positive Parenting Program on behavioral problems in children: A meta-analysis. *Behavior Modification, 32*, 714–735.

Dishion, T. J., & Andrews, D. W. (1995). Preventing escalation in problem behaviors with high-risk young adolescents: Immediate and 1-year outcomes. *Journal of Consulting and Clinical Psychology, 63*, 538–548.

Dumas, J. E. (1984). Interactional correlates of treatment outcome in behavioral parent training. *Journal of Consulting and Clinical Psychology, 52*, 946–954.

Eyberg, S. M., Nelson, M. M., & Boggs, S. R. (2008). Evidence-based psychosocial treatments for children and adolescents with disruptive behavior. *Journal of Clinical Child & Adolescent Psychology, 37*, 215–237.

Farmer, E. M. Z., Compton, S. N., Burns, J. B., & Robertson, E. (2002). Review of the evidence base for treatment of childhood psychopathology: Externalizing disorders. *Journal of Consulting and Clinical Psychology, 70*, 1267–1302.

Farmer, E. M. Z., Mustillo, S., Burns, B. J., & Holden, E. W. (2008). Use and predictors of out-of-home placements within systems of care. *Journal of Emotional and Behavioral Disorders, 16*, 5–14.

Feindler, E. L., & Ecton, R. B. (1986). *Adolescent anger control: Cognitive-behavioral techniques*. New York: Pergamon.

Feske, U., & Goldstein, A. J. (1997). Eye movement desensitization and reprocessing treatment for panic disorder: A controlled outcome and partial dismantling study. *Journal of Consulting and Clinical Psychology, 65*, 1026–1035.

Forehand, R., & Long, N. (1988). Outpatient treatment of the acting out child: Procedures, long term follow-up data, and clinical problems. *Advances in Behaviour Research & Therapy, 10*, 129–177.

Foster, E. M., & Jones, D. E. (2005). The high costs of aggression: Public expenditures resulting from conduct disorder. *American Journal of Public Health, 95*, 1767–1772.

Frick, P. J. (1998). *Conduct disorders and severe antisocial behavior.* New York, NY: Plenum Press.

Gordon, D. A., Arbuthnot, J., Gustafson, K. E., & McGreen, P. (1988). Home-based behavioral-systems family therapy with disadvantaged juvenile delinquents. *American Journal of Family Therapy, 16*, 243–255.

Gordon, D. A., Graves, K., & Arbuthnot, J. (1995). The effect of functional family therapy for delinquents on adult criminal behavior. *Criminal Justice and Behavior, 22*, 60–73.

Griest, D. L., Forehand, R., Rogers, T., Breiner, J. L., Furey, W., & Williams C. A. (1982). Effects of parent enhancement therapy on the treatment outcome and generalization of a parent training program. *Behaviour Research and Therapy, 20*, 429–436.

Grunbaum, J. A., Kann, L., Kinchen, S., Ross, J., Hawkins, J., & Lowry, R. (2004). Youth Risk Behavior Surveillance—United States, 2003. *Morbidity and Mortality Weekly Report, 53*(SS-2).

Henggeler, S. W., Borduin, C. M., Melton, G. B., Mann, B. J., Smith, L., Hall, J. A., . . . Fucci, B. R. (1991). Effects of Multisystemic therapy on drug use and abuse in serious juvenile offenders: A progress report from two outcome studies. *Family Dynamics of Addiction Quarterly, 1*, 40–51.

Henggeler, S. W., & Lee, T. (2003). Multisystemic treatment of serious clinical problems. In A. E. Kazdin & J. R. Weisz (Eds.), *Evidence-based psychotherapies for children and adolescents* (pp. 301–322). New York, NY: Guilford Press.

Henggeler, S. W., Melton, G. B., Brondino, M. J., Scherer, D. G., & Hanley, J. H. (1997). Multisystemic therapy with violent and chronic juvenile offenders and their families: The role of treatment fidelity in successful dissemination. *Journal of Consulting and Clinical Psychology, 65*, 821–833.

Henggeler, S. W., Melton, G. B., & Smith, L. A. (1992). Family preservation using multisystemic therapy: An effective alternative to incarcerating serious juvenile offenders. *Journal of Consulting and Clinical Psychology, 60*, 953–961.

Hinshaw, S. P., & Anderson, C. A. (1996). Conduct and oppositional defiant disorders. In E. J. Mash & R. A. Barkley (Eds.), *Child psychopathology* (pp. 113–149). New York, NY: Guilford Press.

Huey, W. C., & Rank, R. C. (1984). Effects of counselor and peer-led group assertive training on black adolescent aggression. *Journal of Counseling Psychology, 31*, 95–98.

Hughes, R. C., & Wilson, P. H. (1988). Behavioral parent training: Contingency management versus communication skills training with or without the participation of the child. *Child & Family Behavior Therapy, 10*, 11–23.

Jacobson, N. S., Dobson, K. S., Truax, P. A., Addis, M. E., Koerner, K., Gollan, J. K., . . . Prince, S. E. (1996). A component analysis of cognitive-behavioral treatment for depression. *Journal of Consulting and Clinical Psychology, 64*, 295–304.

Jané-Llopis, E., & Braddick, F. (Eds). (2008). *Mental health in youth and education.* Consensus paper. Luxembourg: European Communities.

Kazdin, A. E. (1995). *Conduct disorders in childhood and adolescence* (2nd ed.). Thousand Oaks, CA: Sage Publications.

Kazdin, A. E. (2000). *Psychotherapy for children and adolescents: Directions for research and practice.* New York, NY: Oxford University Press.

Kazdin, A. E. (2003). Problem-solving skills training and parent management training for conduct disorder. In A. E. Kazdin & J. R. Weisz (Eds.), *Evidence-based psychotherapies for children and adolescents* (pp. 241–262). New York, NY: Guilford Press.

Kazdin, A. E., Esveldt-Dawson, K., French, N. H, & Unis, A. S. (1987a). Effects of parent management training and problem-solving skills training combined in the treatment of antisocial child behavior. *Journal of the American Academy of Child & Adolescent Psychiatry, 26*, 416–424.

Kazdin, A. E., Esveldt-Dawson, K., French, N. H., & Unis, A. S. (1987b). Problem-solving skills training and relationship therapy in the treatment of antisocial child behavior. *Journal of Consulting and Clinical Psychology, 55*, 76–85.

Kazdin, A. E., Siegel, T. C., & Bass, D. (1992). Cognitive problem-solving skills training and parent management training in the treatment of antisocial behavior in children. *Journal of Consulting and Clinical Psychology, 60*, 733–747.

Knaus, W. (1974). *Rational-emotive education.* New York, NY: Albert Ellis Institute.

Kutcher, S., Aman, M., Brooks, S. J., Buitelaar, J., van Daalen, E., Fegert, J., . . . Tyano, S. (2004). International consensus statement on attention-deficit/hyperactivity disorder (ADHD) and disruptive behaviour disorders (DBDs): Clinical implications and treatment practice suggestions. *European Neuropsychopharmacology, 14*, 11–28.

Lahey, B. B., Loeber, R., Burke, J., & Rathouz P. J. (2002). Adolescent outcomes of childhood conduct disorder among clinical-referred boys: Predictors of improvement. *Journal of Abnormal Child Psychology, 30*, 333–348.

Lahey, B. B., Loeber, R., Quay, H. C., Frick, P. J., & Grimm, J. (1992). Oppositional defiant and conduct disorders: Issues to be resolved for *DSM-IV*. *Journal of the American Academy of Child & Adolescent Psychiatry, 31*, 539–546.

Lahey, B. B., Miller, T. L., Gordon, R. A., & Riley, A. W. (1999). Developmental epidemiology of the disruptive behavior disorders. In H. C. Quay & A. E. Hogan (Eds.), *Handbook of disruptive behavior disorders* (pp. 23–48). Dordrecht, Netherlands: Kluwer Academic.

Larson, J., & Lochman, J. E. (2002). *Helping school-children cope with anger*. New York, NY: Guilford Press.

Lavigne, J. V., LeBailly, S. A., Gouze, K. R., Cicchetti, C., Pochyly, J., Arend, R., . . . Binns, H. J. (2008). Treating oppositional defiant disorder in primary care: A comparison of three models. *Journal of Pediatric Psychology, 33*, 449–461.

Lipsey, M. W., & Wilson, D. B. (1998). Effective intervention for serious juvenile offenders: A synthesis of research. In R. Loeber & D. P. Farrington (Eds.), *Serious & violent juvenile offenders: Risk factors and successful interventions* (pp. 313–345). Thousand Oaks, CA: Sage Publications.

Lochman, J. E. (1992). Cognitive-behavioral intervention with aggressive boys: Three-year follow-up and preventive effects. *Journal of Consulting and Clinical Psychology, 60*, 426–432.

Lochman, J. E., Barry, T. D., & Pardini, D. A. (2003). Anger control training for aggressive youth. In A. E. Kazdin & J. R. Weisz (Eds.), *Evidence-based psychotherapies for children and adolescents* (pp. 263–281). New York, NY: Guilford Press.

Lochman, J. E., Burch, P. R., Curry, J. F., & Lampron, L. B. (1984). Treatment and generalization effects of cognitive-behavioral and goal-setting interventions with aggressive boys. *Journal of Consulting and Clinical Psychology, 52*, 915–916.

Lochman, J. E., Coie, J. D., Underwood, M. K., & Terry, R. (1993). Effectiveness of a social relations intervention program for aggressive and nonaggressive, rejected children. *Journal of Consulting and Clinical Psychology, 61*, 1053–1058.

Lochman, J. E., Whidby, J. M., & Fitzgerald, D. P. (2000). Cognitive-behavioral assessment and treatment with aggressive children. In P. C. Kendall (Ed.), *Child & Adolescent Therapy: Cognitive-Behavioral Procedures* (2nd ed., pp. 31–87). New York, NY: Guilford Press.

Lock, J., & Strauss, G. D. (1994). Psychiatric hospitalization of adolescents for conduct disorder. *Hospital & Community Psychiatry, 45*, 925–928.

Loeber, R., & Keenan, K. (1994). Interaction between conduct disorder and its comorbid conditions: Effects of age and gender. *Clinical Psychology Review, 14*, 497–523.

Loeber, R., Lahey, B. B., & Thomas, C. (1991). Oppositional defiant disorder and conduct disorder in boys: Patterns of behavioral covariation. *Journal of Clinical Child Psychology, 20*, 202–208.

Lundahl, B., Risser, H. J., & Lovejoy, M. C. (2006). A meta-analysis of parent training: Moderators and follow-up effects. *Clinical Psychology Review, 26*, 86–104.

Lynam, D. (1996). Early identification of chronic offenders: Who is the fledgling psychopath? *Psychological Bulleting, 120*, 209–234.

Maughan, D. R., Christiansen, E., Jenson, W. R., Olympia, D., & Clark, E. (2005). Behavioral parent training as a treatment for externalizing behaviors and disruptive behavior disorders: A meta-analysis. *School Psychology Review, 34*, 267–286.

McCart, M. R., Priester, P. E., Davies, W. H., & Azen, R. (2006). Differential effectiveness of behavioral parent-training and cognitive-behavioral therapy for antisocial youth: A meta-analysis. *Journal of Abnormal Child Psychology, 34*, 527–543.

McMahon, R. J., & Forehand, R. L. (2003). *Helping the noncompliant child: Family-based treatment for oppositional behavior* (2nd ed.). New York, NY: Guilford Press.

McMahon, R. J., Wells, K. C., & Kotler, J. S. (2006). Conduct Problems. In E. J. Mash & R. A. Barkley (Eds.), *Treatment of childhood disorders* (3rd ed.) (pp. 137–268). New York, NY: Guilford Press.

Molina, B. S. G., Smith, B. H., & Pelham, W. E. (1999). Interactive effects of attention deficit hyperactivity disorder and conduct disorder on early adolescent substance use. *Psychology of Addictive Behaviors, 13*, 348–358.

Nixon, R. D. V., Sweeney, L., Erickson, D. B., & Touyz, S. W. (2003). Parent–child interaction therapy: A comparison of standard and abbreviated treatments for oppositional defiant preschoolers. *Journal of Consulting and Clinical Psychology, 71*, 251–260.

Parsons, B. V., & Alexander, J. F. (1973). Short-term behavioral intervention with delinquent families: Impact on family process and recidivism. *Journal of Abnormal Psychology, 81*, 219–225.

Patterson, G. R. (1975). *Families: Applications of social learning to family life*. Champaign, IL: Research Press.

Patterson, G. R., Chamberlain, P., & Reid, J. B. (1982). A comparative evaluation of a parent-training program. *Behavior Therapy, 13*, 638–650.

Patterson, G. R., & Guillion, M. E. (1968). *Living with children: New methods for parents and teachers*. Champaign, IL: Research Press.

Patterson, G. R., Reid, J. B., Jones, R. R., & Conger, R. E. (1975). *A social learning approach to family intervention: Families with aggressive children* (vol. 1). Eugene, OR: Castalia.

Peed, S., Roberts, M., & Forehand, R. (1977). Evaluation of the effectiveness of a standardized parent training program in altering the interaction of mothers and their noncompliant children. *Behavior Modification, 1,* 323–350.

Quay, H. C. (1999). Classification of disruptive behavior disorders. In H. C. Quay & A. E. Hogan (Eds.), *Handbook of disruptive behavior disorders* (pp. 3–21). Dordrecht, Netherlands: Kluwer Academic.

Robbins, L. N. (1978). Sturdy childhood predictors of adult antisocial behavior: Replications from longitudinal studies. *Psychological Medicine, 8,* 611–622.

Robbins, M. S., Szapocznik, J., Santisteban, D. A., Hervis, O. E., Mitrani, V. B., & Schwartz, S. J. (2003). Brief strategic family therapy for Hispanic youth. In A. E. Kazdin & J. R. Weisz (Eds.), *Evidence-based psychotherapies for children and adolescents* (pp. 407–424). New York, NY: Guilford Press.

Robinson, T. R., Smith, S. W., & Miller, M. D. (2002). Effect of a cognitive-behavioral intervention on responses to anger by middle school students with chronic behavior problems. *Behavioral Disorders, 27,* 256–271.

Sanders, M. R. (1999). Triple P-Positive Parenting Program: Towards an empirically validated multilevel parenting and family support strategy for the prevention of behavior and emotional problems in children. *Clinical Child and Family Psychology Review, 2,* 71–90.

Sanders, M. R., Markie-Dadds, C., Tully, L. A., & Bor, W. (2000). The Triple P-Positive Parenting Program: A comparison of enhanced, standard, and self-directed behavioral family intervention for parents of children with early onset conduct problems. *Journal of Consulting and Clinical Psychology, 68,* 624–640.

Santisteban, D. A., Coatsworth, J. D., Perez-Vidal, A., Kurtines, W. M., Schwartz, S. J., LaPerriere, A., & Szapocznik, J. (2003). Efficacy of brief strategic family therapy in modifying Hispanic adolescent behavior problems and substance use. *Journal of Family Psychology, 17,* 121–133.

Scherer, D. G., Brondino, M. J., Henggeler, S. W., Melton, G. B., & Hanley, J. H. (1994). Multisystemic Family Preservation Therapy: Preliminary findings from a study of rural and minority serious adolescent offenders. *Journal of Emotional and Behavioral Disorders, 2,* 198–206.

Schuhmann, E. M., Foote, R. C., Eyberg, S. M., Boggs, S. R., & Algina, J. (1998). Efficacy of parent–child interaction therapy: Interim report of a randomized trial with short-term maintenance. *Journal of Clinical Child Psychology, 27,* 34–45.

Serketich, W. J., & Dumas, J. E. (1996). The effectiveness of behavioral parent training to modify antisocial behavior in children: A meta-analysis. *Behavior Therapy, 27,* 171–186.

Shadish, W. R., Montgomery, L. M., Wilson, P., Wilson, M. R., Bright, I., & Okwumabua, T. (1993). Effects of family and marital psychotherapies: A meta-analysis.

Journal of Consulting and Clinical Psychology, 61, 992–1002.

Sukhodolsky, D. G., Kassinove, H., & Gorman, B. S. (2004). Cognitive-behavioral therapy for anger in children and adolescents: A meta-analysis. *Aggression and Violent Behavior, 9,* 247–269.

Szapocznik, J. R. A., Murray, E., Cohen, R., Scopetta, M., Rivas-Vazquez, A., Hervis, O., . . . Kurtines, W. (1989). Structural family versus psychodynamic child therapy for problematic Hispanic boys. *Journal of Consulting and Clinical Psychology, 57,* 571–578.

Thomas, R., & Zimmer-Gembeck, M. J. (2007). Behavioral outcomes of Parent–Child Interaction Therapy and Triple P-Positive Parenting Program: A review and meta-analysis. *Journal of Abnormal Child Psychology, 35,* 475–495.

Wahler, R. G., Cartor, P. G., Fleischman, J., & Lambert, W. (1993). The impact of synthesis teaching and parent training with mothers of conduct-disordered children. *Journal of Abnormal Child Psychology, 21,* 425–440.

Waschbush, D. A. (2002). A meta-analytic examination of comorbid hyperactive-impulsive-attention problems and conduct problems. *Psychological Bulletin, 128,* 118–150.

Webster-Stratton, C. (1984). Randomized trial of two parent-training programs for families with conduct-disordered children. *Journal of Consulting and Clinical Psychology, 52,* 666–678.

Webster-Stratton, C. (1992). *The incredible years: A trouble-shooting guide for parents of children aged 3–8.* Toronto, Ontario, Canada: Umbrella Press.

Webster-Stratton, C. (1996). Early onset conduct problems: Does gender make a difference? *Journal of Consulting and Clinical Psychology, 64,* 540–551.

Webster-Stratton, C., & Hammond, M. (1997). Treating children with early-onset conduct problems: A comparison of child and parent training interventions. *Journal of Consulting and Clinical Psychology, 65,* 93–109.

Webster-Stratton, C., & Reid, M. J. (2003). The Incredible Years parents, teachers and children training series: A multifaceted treatment approach for young children with conduct problems. In A. E. Kazdin & J. R. Weisz (Eds.), *Evidence-based psychotherapies for children and adolescents* (pp. 224–240). New York, NY: Guilford Press.

Webster-Stratton, C., Reid, M. J., & Hammond, M. (2004). Treating children with early-onset conduct problems: Intervention outcomes for parent, child, and teacher training. *Journal of Clinical Child and Adolescent Psychology, 33,* 105–124.

Weisz, J. R., Chu, B. C., & Polo, A. J. (2004). Treatment dissemination and evidence-based practice: Strengthening intervention through clinician-researcher collaboration. *Clinical Psychology: Science and Practice, 11,* 300–307.

Weisz, J. R., Jensen-Doss, A., & Hawley, K. M. (2006). Evidence-based youth psychotherapies versus usual clinical care: A meta-analysis of direct comparisons. *American Psychologist, 61*, 671–689.

Weisz, J. R., & Kazdin, A. E. (2003). Concluding thoughts: Present and future of evidence-based psychotherapies for children and adolescents. In A. E. Kazdin & J. R. Weisz (Eds.), *Evidence-based psychotherapies for children and adolescents* (pp. 439–451). New York, NY: Guilford Press.

Wells, K. C., & Egan, J. (1988). Social learning and systems family therapy for childhood oppositional disorder: Comparative treatment outcome. *Comprehensive Psychiatry, 29*, 138–146.

Woody, S. R., Weisz, J., & McLean, C. (2005). Empirically supported treatments: 10 years later. *The Clinical Psychologist, 58*, 5–11.

Zoccolillo, M. (1993). Gender and the development of conduct disorder. *Development and Psychopathology, 5*, 65–78.

Zoccolillo, M., Pickles, A., Quinton, D., & Rutter, M. (1992). The outcome of childhood conduct disorder: Implications for defining adult personality disorder and conduct disorder. *Psychological Medicine, 22*, 971–986.

12

Pica

DAVID B. MCADAM, JONATHAN BREIDBORD, MICHELLE LEVINE, AND DON E. WILLIAMS

OVERVIEW OF DISORDER

Impact

Pica is an eating disorder characterized by consumption of nonfood items or compulsive eating of edible and nonedible items (Albin, 1977; Bell & Stein, 1992; Kalfus, Fisher-Gross, Marvullo, & Nau, 1987; McAdam, Sherman, Sheldon, & Napolitano, 2004; Myles, Simpson, & Hirsch, 1997). Individuals who display pica have been found to eat glass, cigarettes, pebbles, metal screws, excessive amounts of food items such as ice or baking soda, and nonedible plants (Choure, Quinn, & Franco, 2006; Mihailidou, Galanakis, Paspalaki, Borgia, & Mantzouranis, 2002; Starn & Udall, 2008). Pica often occurs in persons with intellectual disabilities (i.e., mental retardation; McAlpine & Singh, 1986), specific genetic mental retardation syndromes (e.g., Prader-Willi syndrome; Duker & Nielen, 1993), and biochemical abnormalities (e.g., iron anemia), and some physical illnesses (e.g., sickle-cell disease; Allen & O'Donovan, 2007; Lemanek et al., 2002). Pica is associated with a variety of negative side effects including puncture or blockage of the digestive tract, infestation by gastrointestinal parasites (Foxx & Martin, 1975), and poisoning, such as lead toxicity (Singh & Bakker, 1984). In severe cases, pica results in death; McLoughlin (1988), for example, described the case of a 22-year-old man with an intellectual disability who died from a chest infection related to a 20-year history of pica. The number of deaths resulting from pica is unknown, although follow-up data suggests that some people with pica may die prematurely (Foxx & Livesay, 1984).

Diagnosis and Prevalence

A pica diagnosis is typically made using the criteria described in the *Diagnostic and Statistical Manual of Mental Disorders* (4th ed., rev.) (*DSM-IV-R*; American Psychological Association, 2000) and the *International Classification of Diseases* (10th ed.) (World Health Organization, 1994). The essential feature within these diagnostic systems is eating one or more nonnutritive substances on a persistent basis for a period of at least 1 month. This behavior must be developmentally inappropriate and not part of a culturally sanctioned practice. If it occurs exclusively during the course of another mental disorder,

Address correspondence to David McAdam, Division of Neurodevelopmental and Behavioral Pediatrics, 601 Elmwood Avenue, Box 671, Rochester, New York, 14642. We thank Deborah Napolitano for useful comments on an earlier version of this chapter. Specific procedures of the meta-analytic review are available from the authors upon request.

pica may only be diagnosed if it is sufficiently severe to warrant independent clinical attention. Generally, it is not diagnosed in children younger than 18 months because the mouthing of objects is considered developmentally appropriate behavior (Barltrop, 1966).

Clinical and research reports confirm the incidence of pica in children (Stawar, 1978) and adults (McAdam et al., 2004) with typical or above-range of intellectual functioning and children (Kern, Starosta, & Adelman, 2006) and adults (Duker & Nielen, 1993) with intellectual disabilities. Limited prevalence data have been published. Studies of adults with intellectual disabilities living in an institutional setting have estimated the prevalence between 6% (Matson & Bamburg, 1999) and 25% (Danford & Huber, 1982). In a statewide survey of adults with intellectual disabilities living in Texas, Griffin, Williams, Stark, Altmeyer, and Mason (1986) found approximately 17% of males and 8% of females engaged in pica. The wide range of these statistics may reflect several factors such as failure to use a standard operational definition of this severe eating disorder (McAdam et al., 2004) and underreporting in medical records (Danford & Huber, 1982). Thus, researchers and clinicians could both benefit from additional documentation of the clinical incidence of pica and the systematic study of its prevalence.

Conceptualization

Derived from the Latin *picus* for magpie, a bird with indiscriminate appetite (Ali, 2001), pica describes consumption of a wide variety of nonfood items in various combinations. Table 12.1 summarizes various cases from clinical reports and research literature.

TABLE 12.1   Physical Classes of Nonedible Materials Associated With Pica

Biological secretions		Organic material	
Feces	Coprophagia	Laundry starch	Amylophagia
Vomit	Emetophagia	Book pages	Bibliophagia
Blood	Hematophagia	Dust	Coniophagia
Mucous	Mucophagia	Acorns, grass,	Foliophagia
Urine	Urophagia	pinecones, leaves	
Biological solids		Dirt, sand, clay	Geophagia
Skin	Dermaphagia	Ice, freezer frost	Pagophagia
Fingernails	Onycophagia	Cigarette ashes	Stachtophagia
Bone	Osteophagia		
Hair	Trichophagia		
Chemicals		**Physically damaging material**	
Copper	Cuprophagia	Sharp items	Acuphagia
Pharmaceuticals	Pharmacophagia	Burnt matches	Cautopyreiophagia
Lead chips	Plumbophagia	Glass	Hyalophagia
Foodstuffs		Bark, twigs	Lignophagia
Raw potatoes	Geomelophagia	Stones	Lithophagia
Peanuts	Gooberphagia	Cigarette butts	Tobaccophagia
Lettuce	Lectophagia	Wood	Xylophagia
Eggs	Oophagia		

Cultural Practices

The diversity of people who engage in pica suggests that it is not a disease entity but, rather, a behavior that results from the interaction of biological, environmental, and psychological factors (Ali, 2001). Published literature rooted in psychology, cultural anthropology, and medicine emphasizes each of these aspects. Although clinical reports focus on undesirable behavior in Western settings, pica occurs in commercial, medical, and cultural contexts across the world (Stiegler, 2005). Consumption of clay (geophagia) often augments procedures used for folk-style management of various medical conditions. For example, blends of soil sold by street vendors in Uganda are described as having unique curative powers (Geissler et al., 1999). Clay may be consumed to treat diarrhea and intestinal discomfort and, due to its ability to absorb dietary toxins and reduce hunger, may be added to specific meals (e.g., fish) and to a pregnancy diet. More common in females than males (Stiegler, 2005), geophagia is part of cultural practices related to pregnancy, childbearing, and breastfeeding (McKenna, 2006). Geissler et al. (1999) interviewed 52 pregnant women in Kenya and found 73% explained their consumption of clay in terms of cultural beliefs about blood, fertility, and femininity. In India, pregnant women reported eating ash, brick, clay, lime, and mud to reduce pregnancy cravings (Bhatia et al., 1988). Mainly seen in southern areas of the United States, geophagia appears to have originated through transfer of cultural practices during the slave trade (Vermeer & Frate, 1979).

Neurological Model

Studies of brain structure and function demonstrate an association between damage to specific brain areas and pica in animals. For example, pica has been observed in domesticated cats and rats with experimental amygdala lesions (Ali, 2001; Uno et al., 1997). In support of a dopaminergic theory ascribing pica to dopamine deficiency, Singh, Ellis, Crews, and Singh (1994) found that three persons with intellectual disabilities displayed more pica when taking thioridazine (an antidopaminergic medication) than when taking methylphenidate (a dopamine agonist). Studies of the elderly population describing occurrence of pica at the onset of dementia lend further support to a neuropathological basis of this behavior (Dumaguing, Singh, Sethi, & Devanand, 2003).

Nutritional Hypothesis

Theories based on malnutrition implicate specific mineral deficiencies in consumption of nonnutritive substances (Hoyt, 1997). Medical literature contains numerous references suggesting an association between pica and an individual's nutritional status, particularly iron deficiency, that date as far back as 1,000 A.D. (Parry-Jones & Parry-Jones, 1992). Other minerals of interest, which are interdependent in human biology, include calcium, zinc, and copper. The nutritional model has preliminary—albeit long-standing—support from some data-based studies that show a relationship between specific mineral status and occurrence of pica with some discrepant results likely due to differences between research participants.

Behavior-Analytic Hypothesis

According to the behavior-analytic model, pica is a learned behavior, which can be explained in terms of reinforcement, stimulus control, punishment, and learning history (Mace & Wacker, 1994; Progar et al., 2001; Wacker, 2000). It is specifically conceptualized as a stimulus-control problem. That is, persons with intellectual disabilities engage in pica because they do not discriminate edible from nonedible items. This discrimination hypothesis is supported by studies that evidence that teaching persons to discriminate edible from nonedible items reduces their pica (Finney, Russo, & Cataldo, 1982). Behavior analysts also have demonstrated that pica is maintained by nonsocial factors and thus is described as being "automatically" reinforced (Hagopian & Adelinis, 2001; Piazza, Hanley, & Fisher, 1996).

DATA-BASED TREATMENT STUDIES

Overview

Conceptual models have guided development of various interventions for pica; however, the extent of their effects and empirical support remain unclear. Based on quantitative meta-analysis and specific criteria for evaluation (i.e., 3+ participants per study) and independent replication (i.e., 3+ experimental studies) of treatment effects (Chambless & Hollon, 1998), this review aims to summarize current intervention methods and to identify evidence-based practice for clinical treatment of pica.

Published reviews or reports of original research related to nonpsychopharmacological interventions were found by initially searching Medical Literature Analysis and Retrieval System Online (MEDLINE) and PsycINFO databases using pearl-growing procedures (Schlosser, Wendt, Bhavnani, & Nail-Chiwetalu, 2006). Studies of nutritional interventions were identified by searching for terms used to index early investigations (Gutelius, Millican, Layman, Cohen, & Dublin, 1962; Lanzkowsky, 1959) and terms used to index subsequently identified experimental studies. Recent studies of interventions based on behavior-analytic principles and procedures were found by searching for terms used to index experimental studies included in earlier reviews (Ali, 2001; Bell & Stein, 1982; Carter, Wheeler, & Mayton, 2004; Lacey, 1990; McAdam et al., 2004; Stiegler, 2005) and for terms used to index subsequently identified experimental studies. Other studies were found

by searching Google Scholar for publications containing *pica* or any of its common descriptors with -agia (Table 12.1) and -agy suffixes and by reviewing literature ancestry.

Most empirical studies used a single-case experimental design to evaluate the effects of nutritional ($N = 3$) or behavioral ($N = 39$) interventions on pica displayed by 31 females (age 2–57 years) and 38 males (age 2–48 years). Participants were frequently ($N = 60$, 87%) described as having profound ($N = 42$), severe ($N = 13$), moderate ($N = 3$), or unspecified ($N = 2$) intellectual disability with ($N = 32$, 53%) or without ($N = 28$, 47%) another diagnosis. Comorbid conditions included physical disabilities (e.g., blindness), genetic conditions (e. g., autism-spectrum disorders, Prader-Willi syndrome, Cornelia de Lange syndrome), and neurological symptoms (e.g., seizures, lead poisoning). Participants without an intellectual disability were described as having a clinical autism diagnosis ($N = 5$), lead poisoning ($N = 3$), or typical development ($N = 1$). Although the report of nonspecific history was common, direct-observation data reflected participants' attempted or successful oral insertion of physically damaging materials ($N = 17$), organic items ($N = 5$), food scraps ($N = 3$), chemicals ($N = 1$), biological solids ($N = 2$), biological secretions ($N = 2$), multiple items ($N = 20$), and unspecified material ($N = 19$). Other studies comprise three randomized controlled trials (RCTs) of nutritional interventions for pica displayed by children (age 1–4 years) with intellectual disabilities.

Nutritional Interventions

Based on evidence of a baseline chemical deficit in people with pica as compared to typical controls (Edwards et al., 1959) and as compared to blood levels following iron supplementation (Lanzkowsky, 1959), early group-design studies and RCTs investigated effects of nutritional interventions on chemical measures and behavior ratings. Gutelius, Millican, Layman, Cohen, and Dublin (1962) and McDonald and Marshall (1964) gave intramuscular injections of iron and saline, respectively, to age-matched samples of 12–13 children with pica. Participants who received treatment showed significantly increased blood-level hemoglobin and significantly improved pica scores. A similar change in behavior seen in control samples from iron (Gutelius et al., 1962) and multivitamin (Gutelius et al., 1963) studies may reflect their high level of hemoglobin, which was associated with maintenance of pica ratings for other children who had received iron therapy (McDonald & Marshall, 1964).

Recent investigations with a single-case experimental design have evaluated intervention effects on objectively measured pica. Lofts, Schroeder, and Maier (1990) gave chelated zinc to a woman with intellectual disabilities and low serum zinc. Pica frequency decreased upon 100-mg supplementation, increased upon withdrawal of the intervention, and was fully suppressed at a larger dosage (150 mg). Lofts et al. (1990) reported a significant reduction of serum zinc for this participant during baseline conditions and for three other adults who participated in a baseline-treatment pilot study. Using similar single-case experimental methods, Pace and Toyer (2000) achieved higher latency to pica by administering iron to a 9-year-old girl with intellectual disabilities and a history of iron anemia; further pica reduction was observed following combined administration of iron and a multivitamin. Bugle and Rubin (1993) also observed reduction of coprophagy upon addition of a powdered supplement containing numerous readily absorbable nutrients to the institutional diets of a 13-year-old girl and two men with profound intellectual disabilities.

The nutritional-deficiency approach involves laboratory measurement and clinical review of an individual's biochemical profile and identification of any compound(s) in clinically significant proportion. Investigations to date describe various methods of supplement administration (e.g., oral, intramuscular) and collaboration among health-care providers. Clinical gains following multivitamin therapy suggest possible benefit of nonspecific supplementation, though well-controlled investigations are needed to replicate this effect—and its key multivitamin components—on levels of specific chemicals and pica engagement measured by direct observation of behavior.

BEHAVIORAL INTERVENTIONS

Overview

Interventions based on behavior-analytic principles include one or more specific procedures either involving punishment (e.g., overcorrection) or not (e.g., environmental enrichment). Procedures may be ranked by restrictiveness (Table 12.2) and have been used by clinicians in various combinations. Pretreatment assessments have been used fairly commonly to develop interventions that are minimally restrictive and most likely to be effective for a specific, individual case of pica. Methods have been established for evaluation of a person's preferences (i.e., preference assessment; W. Fisher et al., 1992) and the antecedents (i.e., stimulus-control assessment; Gardner, 1986) and consequences thought to maintain engagement in pica. Emphasis on pretreatment assessment is a recent development in the pica literature (Hanley, Iwata, & McCord, 2003), and may result in the development of the minimally restrictive most effective intervention for an individual (McAdam et al., 2004).

Among empirical investigations, 13 studies identified potentially effective positive or negative consequences and 10 studies conducted a functional behavior assessment or analog functional analysis using established protocols or manuals (Cipani, 2008; O'Neil et al., 1997; Watson & Steege, 2003); others used common assessment tools to identify variables thought to maintain pica (e.g., antecedent-behavior-consequence charts).

TABLE 12.2　Summary of Behavioral Interventions and Common Supplementary Assessments

Intervention	Description/Example	Data-based assessments in research					
		AF	FB	Pr	Pu	Re	SC
Not restrictive							
Environmental enrichment	Add a variety of high-preference items to a setting	✓		✓	✓	✓	✓
Reinforcement	Providing attention according to a fixed time schedule	✓	✓	✓			
Discrimination training	Teaching a person to only eat food off of a plate	✓		✓	✓	✓	
Habit reversal	Improve identification of pica and performance of alternative, behavior using aversive and nonaversive techniques						
Restrictive							
Negative practice	Initiate unpleasant simulation of pica following pica						
Response blocking	Physically preventing pica	✓		✓	✓		✓
Highly restrictive							
Aversive stimuli	Play unpleasant tone following pica	✓		✓			✓
Overcorrection	Assign a nonpreferred task requiring extra effort following pica						
Physical restraint	Restrict hand movement following pica						

Note: AF, analog functional analysis; *FB*, functional behavior assessment; *Pr*, preference assessment; *Pu*, punisher assessment; *Re*, reinforcer assessment; *SC*, stimulus-control assessment

These studies were commonly conducted in a residential facility or other well-controlled, analog environment, with most interventions implemented by research staff. Treatment evaluations in a participant's naturalistic setting (i.e., home, classroom, or worksite) often involved informal social validation post-hoc by indirect (i.e., parents, support staff) or immediate-community (i.e., teachers, employers) intervention stakeholders (Schlosser, 1999).

Environmental Enrichment

In a frequently cited study, Favell, McGimsey, and Schell (1982) enriched the living environment of three men aged 22 years or less and with profound intellectual disabilities, with a variety of toys and food (e.g., popcorn). Environmental enrichment demonstrated a clinically significant reduction in pica displayed by each participant. In a systematic examination of procedures for presenting of pica and alternative items, Piazza, Roane, Keeney, Boney, and Abt (2002) reported several findings, including reduction of pica when alternative items were present. They also reported a relative increase in pica when the effort necessary for a participant to obtain alternative items was increased. In the low-effort condition alternate items were continuously present and in the high-effort condition participants had to press a microswitch to obtain alternate items. Follow-up data collected quarterly demonstrated limited evidence of behavior-change maintenance (W. W. Fisher, Piazza, Bowman, Kurtz, & Lachman, 1994).

Studies comparing noncontingent presentation of toys in the absence or presence of either response interruption (Piazza et al., 1996) or verbal reprimand (W. W. Fisher et al., 1994; Rapp, Dozier, & Carr, 2001) demonstrated better performance of intervention packages that included the use of punishment. Similar results were observed in intervention analyses comparing environmental enrichment with or without either response blocking (Carr, Dozier, Patel, Adams, & Martin, 2002; Piazza et al., 1998) or time-out (Falcomata, Roane, & Pabico, 2007). Piazza et al. (1998) also examined environmental enrichment with stimuli identified by preference assessment. It substantially improved combination with noncontingent attention for reduction of pica displayed by a 17-year-old female with autism and profound intellectual disability.

Differential and Noncontingent Reinforcement

Differential reinforcement has been examined in naturalistic (Kalfus et al., 1987; Kern et al., 2006) and analog settings (Bogart, Piersel, & Gross, 1995; Donnelly & Olczak, 1990; Favell et al., 1982; Goh, Iwata, & Kahng, 1999; Kern et al., 2006; Paniagua, Braverman, & Capriotti, 1986). Smith (1987) described reduction of pica displayed by a 23-year-old man with autism and a profound intellectual disability via differential reinforcement of incompatible behaviors using verbal praise provided for on-task behavior such as keeping hands busy. The intervention was conducted in a vocational setting and was implemented by the participant's one-on-one vocational counselor. Similarly, Donnelly and Olczak (1990) used small volumes of coffee, contingent on independent gum chewing, to reduce pica displayed by two men with intellectual disabilities; investigators gradually increased the time-based criteria for reinforcement, leading to longer periods of gum chewing without pica. Paniagua et al. (1986) effectively used a combination of overcorrection, physical restraint, and differential reinforcement of other behavior (i.e., verbal praise provided contingent on absence of pica for 1 minute) with a 4-year-old girl with a profound intellectual disability. In an analog setting, Mace and Knight (1986) implemented a functional

analysis-derived intervention package to reduce pica displayed by a 19-year-old man with spastic quadriplegia and a profound intellectual disability. Pretreatment analyses suggested that pica was maintained by social attention and that a protective helmet worn by the participant did not prevent pica. As part of treatment, the participant's helmet was removed and experimenters made eye contact with the participant, on average, every minute and talked to the participant, on average, every 5 minutes.

These studies include observational data collected at 1-year follow-up (Smith, 1987) or continuously for a period of 7 months (Favell et al., 1982) or 57 months (Bogart et al., 1995) after intervention, thus demonstrating maintenance of behavior change. Differential reinforcement used in conjunction with response interruption (Goh et al., 1999), response blocking (Kern et al., 2006), or physical restraint (Bogart et al., 1995) showed a more clinically significant reduction of pica when differential reinforcement is augmented punishment.

Discrimination Training

Discrimination training has been examined in analog settings. Johnson, Hunt, and Siebert (1994) reduced pica displayed by two teenage boys with profound intellectual disabilities and taught them to eat food from a specific placemat using differential reinforcement. Contingent on pica, the participants' eyes were covered briefly and they were instructed to only eat food on their place mat. Piazza, Hanley, Blakeley-Smith, and Kinsman (2000) also used discrimination training to reduce pica displayed by a 9-year-old boy with profound intellectual disability who was being treated for severe problem behavior at an inpatient facility.

Other investigations have evaluated a combination of discrimination training and either verbal reprimands with empirically derived consequences (W. W. Fisher et al., 1994), physical restraint (Bogart et al., 1995; Stawar, 1978), and overcorrection (Madden,

Russo, & Cataldo, 1980) to reduce pica displayed by participants with intellectual disabilities. No data are available for maintenance of behavior change following discrimination training.

Habit Reversal

Habit reversal has been examined in a naturalistic setting. Woods, Miltenberger, and Lumley (1996) used a simplified habit-reversal procedure to reduce the pica-related chewing of a typically developing 6-year-old boy. Simplified habit reversal consisted of awareness training, competing response training, and increased social support. During awareness training, the participant learned to identify and label the occurrence of pica-related chewing during live sessions and during review of videos. Social support consisted of his mother and sister providing verbal praise contingent on correctly using the competing response and verbally prompting him to use the competing response (i.e., removing the object from his mouth and pursing his lips for a minute) when he did not do so. Authors noted the necessity of a booster session in which the participant and his mother received follow-up training to support maintenance of behavior change 30 weeks postintervention.

Negative Practice

Negative practice has been evaluated in an analog setting. Duker and Nielen (1993) reduced the pica of a woman with Prader-Willi syndrome and intellectual disability by holding a desired item to her lips—but not allowing her to bite it—for 2 minutes following each pica attempt. Data collected at 7 months follow-up suggest long-term maintenance of behavior change.

Response Blocking

Response blocking has been examined in analog settings. Hagopian and Adelinis (2001) demonstrate an assessment-based approach to intervention for pica displayed by a 26-year-old man with moderate intellectual disability and bipolar disorder. Based on results of an analog functional analysis suggesting an automatic function, investigators first blocked every attempt to eat nonedible items. Since such response blocking resulted in increased aggression and limited pica reduction, it was subsequently paired with redirection—delivered contingently—to eat popcorn instead of engaging in pica. Popcorn was identified as a highly preferred item via paired-choice preference assessment (W. Fisher et al., 1992) and its use as part of a multicomponent intervention package was associated with reduced pica without the negative side effect of aggression. McCord, Grosser, Iwata, and Powers (2005) compared effects of different response-blocking techniques and found that using a sweeping motion to move the participant's hand away from his mouth, which terminated pica earlier in the response chain, was more effective for pica reduction than placing a hand between the hand and mouth of three men with profound intellectual disabilities. The authors suggest that blocking by sweeping worked better because it reduced the likelihood of ingesting an item, thus preventing the unintentional, intermittent reinforcement of pica. Furthermore, LeBlanc, Piazza, and Krug (1997) evaluated the effects of response blocking with or without protective equipment (i.e., arm restraint, helmet) on pica displayed by a 4-year-old girl with a severe intellectual disability. Less therapist effort was associated with response blocking used in isolation because the participant would resist wearing the protective equipment.

No data are available for maintenance of behavior change following interventions based on response blocking. Response blocking has also been evaluated both as an alternative to and part of reinforcement-based interventions (Carr et al., 2002; Kern et al., 2006; Piazza et al., 1998).

Aversive Stimuli

Ferreri, Tamm, and Wier (2006) used a food aversion to reduce the pica of a 4-year-old boy with autism. As part of early intensive behavioral intervention for consumption of plastic toys and food refusal, experimenters lightly coated toys with tapioca pudding, which was selected based on the participant's history of food-refusal behaviors (e.g., gagging, spitting, crying) when prompted to eat it. Results showed a reductive effect on pica and no adverse effect on engagement in appropriate toy play. Other data suggested maintenance of behavior after intervention fading, intervention withdrawal, and at 1-year follow-up.

Contingent aversive presentation has been examined in analog settings. Paisey and Whitney (1989) sprayed a small amount of lemon juice into the mouth of a 16-year-old adolescent with profound intellectual disability following each pica attempt. Similarly, Rojahn, McGonigle, Curcio, and Dixon (1987) found better results for contingent presentation of water mist than aromatic ammonia and used the former to reduce pica displayed by a 16-year-old girl with severe intellectual disability, autism, and other medical conditions. Singh and Winton (1984) used a blindfold to cover the eyes of a 24-year-old female with right hemipalegia and profound intellectual disability for 1 minute. This visual screen procedure successfully reduced pica and collateral behaviors, such as stereotypy in three different settings within the participant's residential facility. Based on pretreatment analyses suggesting that pica displayed by a 6-year-old girl with autism was not maintained by social factors and after various less-restrictive interventions (e.g., noncontingent access to food, verbal reprimand contingent on pica) were ineffective, Rapp et al. (2001) used contingent auditory stimulation (i.e., presentation of a loud tone) for pica reduction.

These studies included maintenance data collected over 2 weeks following transfer of the intervention to support staff (Singh & Winton, 1984) and follow-up data collected continuously for 90 days (Rojahn et al., 1987) or over the course of 6 months after intervention had been withdrawn (Paisey & Whitney, 1989; Singh &

Winton, 1984), thus demonstrating maintenance of behavior change. Contingent aversive presentation has also been included in intervention packages based on overcorrection (Matson, Stephens, & Smith, 1978) and discrimination training (W. W. Fisher et al., 1994).

Overcorrection

Overcorrection (Foxx & Bechtel, 1983) has been evaluated in naturalistic (Ricciardi, Luiselli, Terrill, & Reardon, 2003) and analog settings (Foxx & Martin, 1975; Matson et al., 1978; Mulick, Barbour, Schroeder, & Rojahn, 1980; Singh & Winton, 1985). Foxx and Martin (1975) used overcorrection contingent on pica to reduce pica of two men with profound intellectual disabilities. Participants were required to spit out the nonedible item, brush their teeth with a mouthwash-soaked toothbrush, and perform other corrective acts (e.g., floor-mopping). Similarly, Matson et al. (1978) included tooth brushing and various corrective cleaning tasks as part of a contingent-aversive procedure (i.e., oral administration of diluted hot sauce). This multicomponent intervention achieved reduction of pica and collateral behavior (i.e., hair-pulling) displayed by a woman with profound intellectual disability. Mulick et al. (1980) compared overcorrection of either pica or behavior that preceded pica (i.e., picking up and handling of nonedible items) displayed by a man and woman, both age 23 years, with profound intellectual disabilities, and found greater reduction of pica when overcorrection was implemented earlier contingent of antecedent behavior. Ricciardi et al. (2003) used contingent practice—oral expulsion of a nonedible item and repeated practice of its appropriate disposal—to reduce pica displayed by a 7-year-old boy with autism.

Follow-up data collected at 3 months post-treatment (Matson et al., 1978) or daily over the course of 4 months while treatment was still in effect (Ricciardi et al., 2003) demonstrated maintenance of behavior change.

Overcorrection also has been compared to physical restraint (Singh & Bakker, 1984) and has been used to augment reinforcement-based intervention strategies (Madden et al., 1980; Paniagua et al., 1986).

Physical Restraint

Physical restraint has been examined in analog settings. Bucher, Reykdal, and Albin (1976) described reduction of pica displayed by a boy and a girl, both with profound intellectual disabilities, via contingent delivery of a verbal reprimand ("No!") and removal of the nonedible material followed by holding both arms at the child's sides for 30 seconds. Following treatment analysis (i.e., comparison of physical-restraint duration: 10 seconds vs. 30 seconds for one participant, 3 seconds vs. 10 seconds for another participant), Winton and Singh (1983) achieved reduction of pica displayed by two teenage boys, both age 19 years or less with profound intellectual disabilities, in various settings within a residential facility. Singh and Bakker (1984) used brief-duration physical restraint to reduce pica, antecedent behavior, and collateral behavior (e.g., stereotypy, toy play) of two males, ages 20 and 21, with profound intellectual disabilities.

No data are available for maintenance of behavior change following interventions based on physical restraint. Physical restraint also has been used as a component of reinforcement-based interventions packages that successfully produced a reduction in pica (Bogart et al., 1995; Paniagua et al., 1986).

META-ANALYSIS OF BEHAVIORAL STUDIES

Intervention efficacy was evaluated via meta-analysis of all studies with direct-observation data. The 35 eligible studies with a single-case design comprised 59 participants (1–4 participants per study) and 172 baseline-treatment comparisons. Exclusion criteria identified studies with unclear data due to graph degradation (Rojahn, McGonigle, Curcio, & Dixon, 1987), summary statistics of unreported raw data (Hirsch & Myles, 1996; Rojahn, Schroeder, & Mulick, 1980; Stawar, 1978), treatment-only data (Ausman, Ball, & Alexander, 1974), and use of an alternating-treatments design (Barlow & Hayes, 1979) to simultaneously compare the effects of two interventions (LeBlanc et al., 1997; Piazza et al., 2002). Although articles discuss therapeutic effects of specific interventions, 18 studies also implemented other interventions unsuccessfully; these data, comprising 37.2% of all baseline-treatment comparisons, were also included in the meta-analysis.

Data extraction involved estimation of rectangular coordinates for all graphical observations, based on manually input minima and maxima of each graph, using GraphClick v3.0 computer software (www.arizona-software.ch /graphclick/). Separate effect sizes were calculated for pica reduction and pica suppression. Pica reduction was measured as the percentage of nonoverlapping data (PND) between each intervention phase and a baseline condition. Interventions with mean effect size between 51 PND and 70 PND were considered questionably effective, those with mean effect size between 71 PND and 90 PND were considered moderately effective, and those with mean effect size exceeding 90 PND were considered highly effective (Scruggs, Mastropieri, Cook, & Escobar, 1986). Percentage of zero data (PZD), a stringent index of behavior suppression (Campbell, 2004), was calculated as the proportion of intervention-phase observations with frequency of pica at zero or its latency exceeding a session's length (Didden, Korzilius, van Oorsouw, & Sturmey, 2006). Interventions with mean effect size between 18 PZD and 54 PZD were considered questionably effective, those with mean effect size between 55 PZD and 80 PZD were considered moderately effective, and those with mean effect size exceeding 80 PZD were considered highly effective (Scotti, Evans, Meyer, & Walker, 1991).

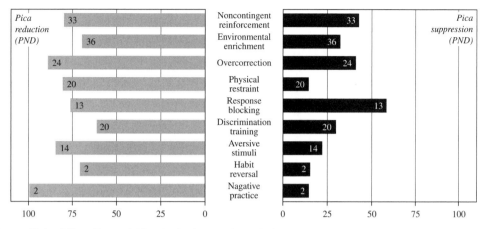

Figure 12.1   Effect Sizes of Pica Reduction (Left) and Pica Suppression (Right) for Various Behavioral Interventions
Note: Numbers with the bars represent the number of comparisons used to calculate effect sizes.

Behavioral interventions demonstrated moderate efficacy for pica reduction (mean PND = 77) and some efficacy for pica suppression (mean PZD = 33). Most interventions spanned the relatively narrow range above 70 PND. Largest effect sizes were associated with negative practice (100 PND), overcorrection (89 PND), and aversive presentation (85 PND). In contrast, efficacy of pica suppression varied between none and moderate with response blocking (58 PZD) and reinforcement procedures (43 PZD) performing best and some punishment-based strategies (i.e., aversive presentation, 22 PZD, and physical restraint, 15 PZD) being questionbly efficious. Comparison of effect sizes shows a discrepancy for habit reversal and negative practice—interventions each subject to a single study (see Figure 12.1). Based on independently replicated research, discrimination training and aversive presentation performed inconsistently. Overcorrection, response blocking, and reinforcement procedures demonstrated efficacy for both the reduction and suppression of pica.

Shown in Figure 12.2, this trend favoring aversive procedures continued in comparison of interventions with no punishment component (e.g., noncontingent social attention) and those with punishment as either a primary procedure (e.g., brief physical restraint contingent on pica)

or as part of a reinforcement-based package (e.g., noncontingent social attention with brief physical restraint contingent on pica). In terms of pica suppression, performance was comparable for interventions with (34 PZD) or without (33 PZD) aversive components; however, those that combined reinforcement and punishment (i.e., differential reinforcement, noncontingent presentation) notably performed best.

Contrary to expectation, effect size for pica reduction was comparable between interventions that included (79 PND) a pretreatment assessment (e.g., analog functional analysis, functional behavior assessment, preference assessment) and those that did not (75 PND). Interventions associated with relatively less pica reduction performed better when developed after consideration of pretreatment information (discrimination training, 75 PND; response blocking, 78 PND) than when implemented in isolation (discrimination training, 54 PND; response blocking, 67 PND). Collection of pretreatment data was associated with increased mean pica suppression (38 PZD vs. 31 PZD) seen in discrimination training (52 PZD vs. 18 PZD) and response blocking (62 PZD vs. 35 PZD).

Effect sizes were used along with specific criteria (Chambless & Hollon, 1998) of treatment evaluation (i.e., 3+ participants per

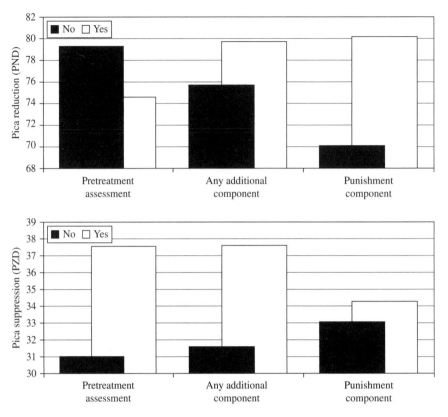

Figure 12.2 Reduction (Top) and Suppression (Bottom) Effect Sizes for Modified Behavioral Interventions

study) and independent replication (i.e., 3+ investigations) to summarize the empirical basis of each intervention (see Table 12.3). Synthesis of single-case research demonstrates *well-established clinical efficacy* of reinforcement procedures, environmental enrichment, and overcorrection. These interventions were evaluated in five or more independent studies with 10 or more participants. Two behavioral procedures (i.e., physical restraint, response blocking) and mineral supplementation show *limited clinical efficacy* characterized by substantial effects on pica displayed by five or more participants from three or more independent studies. Remaining interventions with modest effect sizes (i.e., discrimination training) or insufficient independent evaluations (i.e., contingent aversive presentation, habit reversal, negative practice) do not yet meet criteria for evidence-based practice.

EVIDENCE-BASED TREATMENT OF PICA

Highly varied research and other case reports with positive results confirm the relevance of mineral deficiency to the clinical treatment of pica; however, the paucity of data-based investigations and limited collection of direct-observation data suggest the need for additional, well-controlled investigations of specific nutritional interventions. In contrast, evaluation based on criteria of research evaluation and independent replication (Chambless & Hollon, 1998) finds substantial support for some behavioral interventions developed by applied behavior analysts or behavioral therapists. Thus, in the absence of a specific chemical abnormality, evidence-based practice for the treatment of pica should include implementation of behavior-analytic

TABLE 12.3 Summary of Empirical Support for Interventions to Reduce (percentage of nonoverlapping data, PND) or Suppress (percentage of zero-value data, PZD) Pica Displayed by Research Participants With or Without an Intellectual Disability (ID).

Intervention	Studies	Participants	PND	PZD	Appraisal
Noncontingent reinforcement	10	16 ID	80	43	A nonrestrictive procedure with well-established evidence of clinical efficacy for short-term pica reduction.
Environmental enrichment	8	13 ID 3 no ID	70	32	A nonrestrictive procedure with well-established evidence of clinical efficacy for short-term pica reduction.
Overcorrection	5	9 ID 1 no ID	89	41	A highly restrictive procedure with well-established evidence of clinical efficacy for short-term pica reduction.
Physical restraint	4	8 ID	80	15	A highly restrictive procedure with limited evidence of clinical efficacy for short-term pica reduction.
Nutritional treatment	3	5 ID	89	56	A nonrestrictive procedure with limited evidence of clinical efficacy for short-term pica reduction.
Response blocking	3	4 ID 1 no ID	76	58	A highly restrictive procedure with limited evidence of clinical efficacy for short-term pica reduction.
Discrimination training	5	10 ID	62	30	A nonrestrictive procedure with insufficient experimental evidence of clinical efficacy for short-term pica reduction.
Aversive stimuli	4	2 ID 2 no ID	85	22	A highly restrictive procedure with insufficient experimental evidence of clinical efficacy for short-term pica reduction.
Habit reversal	1	1 ID 1 no ID	71	15	A nonrestrictive procedure with insufficient experimental evidence of clinical efficacy for short-term pica reduction.
Negative practice	1	1 ID	100	15	A restrictive procedure with insufficient experimental evidence of clinical efficacy for short-term pica reduction.

interventions developed by an applied behavior analyst or behavioral psychologist.

Hierarchical Approach to Clinical Interventions

Staff at common settings for people with severe and profound intellectual disabilities— schools, facilities, state agencies—should track local trends of pica prevalence. Individualized treatment plans should establish standards for clinical efficacy based on fundamental objectives of health promotion and risk management. Behavior psychologists and Board-Certified Behavior Analysts with training and extensive experience in the

treatment of pica should participate in intervention development.

When implementing behavioral interventions clinicians generally follow the least-restrictive approach (Bailey & Burch, 2005), which mandates that less-restrictive, potentially effective procedures be evaluated before consideration of aversive, punishment-based interventions (Green, 1990). This approach, nicely demonstrated by Rapp et al. (2001), is recommended when pica is not life-threatening. The most effective intervention approach (Van Houten et al., 1988) may be justified when a person is at immediate risk of harm or death. In this case, a clinical treatment team should identify the intervention package they believe is most likely to produce an immediate reduction in pica. Consent should be obtained prior to implementation and, subsequently, the outcome should undergo peer review. Clinicians are strongly encouraged to conduct analyses of intervention packages using appropriate single-case experimental designs (Kazdin, 1982).

Assessment as Part of Clinical Interventions

Clinicians should conduct a functional-behavioral assessment or analog functional analysis in order to better identify the factors maintaining a person's pica (Hanley et al., 2003). Training in these contemporary functional assessment methods (Iwata et al., 2000; Moore & Fisher, 2007) is appropriate for all members of clinical treatment teams, especially those who work in more restrictive settings such as institutions and segregated schools likely to include people with serious pica. Training and experience in these assessment procedures may facilitate individualized planning of minimally restrictive, maximally effective intervention packages.

According to Baer, Wolf, and Risley (1968) behavior change has generalized if it is durable over time, if it occurs in a number of different environments, and if it is observed across behaviors. Although often emphasized in the literature, generalization is rarely assessed in studies of interventions designed to reduce severe problem behaviors (Foxx, 1990; Foxx & Meindl, 2007). McAdam et al. (2004) found that most controlled evaluations of treatment of pica before 2004 did not specifically program for generalization; among 11 studies describing generalization, two articles described intervention effects across settings or behaviors and a single article reported generalization across any combination of settings, staff, and behaviors. This review and the current research summary confirm the need for active programming of generalization (Stokes & Baer, 1977) when developing

interventions for pica, and precise assessment of generalization across settings and care providers when evaluating interventions for pica.

Since evidence-based clinical practice comprises empirical support and consumer satisfaction, interventions for pica—especially those with well-established clinical efficacy or probable clinical efficacy—should be further analyzed according to standards of conceptually distinct stakeholders (i.e., social validation). In addition to assessment of social validity as perceived by members of a person's family and community, information about treatment acceptability should also be collected to aide in the selection between alternate interventions (Hanley, Piazza, Fisher, Contrucci, & Maglieri, 1997). Selection of multiple agents, measures, and dimensions of social validity is feasible in most experimental settings and is potentially useful for increasing the implementation and acceptability of empirically supported intervention for pica.

Systems of Clinical Interventions

This chapter summarizes interventions for pica often used with people with intellectual and other developmental disabilities (e.g., autism with or without an intellectual disability). Future work should extend research findings to other populations. For example, studies of habit reversal used with typical participants (see Tucker et al., Chapter 14, this volume) have demonstrated the efficacy of this treatment for habit disorders. Similarly, the analog functional analysis protocol may be useful for developing behavioral interventions for elderly people who display pica related to dementia (Dwyer-Moore & Dixon, 2007).

Although basic constitutional rights (*Youngberg v. Romeo*, 1982) ensure protection from serious harm and risk, interventions for pica are often administered only in response to a major medical incident (McAlpine & Singh, 1986); this delay may reflect its misinterpretation as merely object mouthing instead of a serious problem behavior akin to aggression. Since pica remains a leading cause of federal involvement in state programs (Department of Justice, 2007), there should be a requirement that its adverse outcomes (i.e., emergency surgery, death) be reported in similar fashion as injury or death following restraint. Development of a valid severity measure is warranted. The development of such a measure would improve differentiation between mild and life-threatening forms of pica, potentially leading to less self-injury in severe cases. A dimensional scale would advance studies of correlation between pica and other behaviors of interest, physiological measures, susceptibility loci, and neural substrates. This tool would also be useful for subtle assessment of behavior maintenance; despite some evidence of reduction in emergency surgery throughout 9-year follow-up (Williams, Kirkpatrick-Sanchez, Enzinna, Dunn, & Borden-Karasack, 2009), current research falls short of sensitive measurement and systematic scope.

REFERENCES

References marked with an asterisk indicate studies included in the meta-analysis.

Albin, J. B. (1977). The treatment of pica (scavenging) behavior in the retarded: A critical analysis and implications for research. *Mental Retardation, 15,* 14–17.

Ali, Z. (2001). Pica in people with intellectual disability: A literature review of aetiology, epidemiology and complications. *Journal of Intellectual & Developmental Disability, 26,* 205–215.

Allen, N. M., & O'Donovan, D. J. (2007). Foam eater. *The Journal of Pediatrics, 151,* 710–710.

American Psychiatric Association. (2000). *Diagnostic and statistical manual of mental disorders* (4th ed., text rev.). Washington, DC: Author.

Ausman, J., Ball, T. S., & Alexander, D. (1974). Behavior therapy of pica with a profoundly retarded adolescent. *Mental Retardation, 12,* 16–18.

Baer, D. M., Wolf, M. M., & Risley, T. R. (1968). Some current dimensions of applied behavior analysis. *Journal of Applied Behavior Analysis, 1,* 91–97.

Bailey, J. S., & Burch, M. R. (2005). *Ethics for behavior analysts: A practical guide to the Behavior Analyst Certification. Board guidelines for responsible conduct.* New York, NY: Erlbaum.

Barlow, D. H., & Hayes, S. C. (1979). Alternating treatments design: One strategy for comparing the effects of two treatments in a single subject. *Journal of Applied Behavior Analysis, 12,* 199–210.

Barltop, D. (1966). The prevalence of pica. *American Journal of Diseases in Children, 112,* 116–123.

Bell, K. E., & Stein, B. M. (1992). Behavioral treatments for pica: A review of empirical studies. *International Journal of Eating Disorders, 11,* 377–389.

Bhatia, M. S., Rai, S., Singhbal, P. K., Nigam, V. R., Bohra, N., & Malik, S. C. (1988). Pica: Prevalence and etiology. *Indian Pediatrics, 25,* 1165–1170.

*Bogart, L. C., Piersel, W. C., & Gross, E. J. (1995). The long-term treatment of life-threatening pica: A case study of a woman with profound mental retardation living in an applied setting. *Journal of Developmental and Physical Disabilities, 7,* 39–50.

*Bucher, B., Reykdal, B., & Albin, J. (1976). Brief physical restraint to control pica in retarded children. *Journal of Behavior Therapy and Experimental Psychiatry, 7,* 137–140.

*Bugle, C., & Rubin, H. B. (1993). Effects of a nutritional supplement on coprophagia: A study of three cases. *Research in Developmental Disabilities, 14,* 445–456.

Campbell, J. M. (2004). Statistical comparison of four effect sizes for single-subject designs. *Behavior Modification, 28,* 234–246.

*Carr, J. E., Dozier, C. L., Patel, M. R., Adams, A. N., & Martin, N. (2002). Treatment of automatically reinforced object mouthing with noncontingent reinforcement and response blocking: Experimental analysis and social validation. *Research in Developmental Disabilities, 23,* 37–44.

Carter, S. L., Wheeler, J. J., & Mayton, M. R. (2004). Pica: A review of recent assessment and treatment procedures. *Education and Training in Developmental Disabilities, 39,* 346–358.

Chambless, D. L., & Hollon, S. D. (1998). Defining empirically supported therapies. *Journal of Consulting and Clinical Psychology, 66,* 7–18.

Choure, J., Quinn, K., & Franco, K. (2006). Baking-soda pica in an adolescent patient. *Psychosomatics, 47,* 531–532.

Cipani, E. (2008). *Classroom management for all teachers: Plans for evidence-based practice.* Upper Saddle River, NJ: Pearson Merrill Prentice-Hall.

Danford, D. E., & Huber, A. E. (1982). Pica among mentally retarded adults. *American Journal of Mental Deficiency, 87,* 141–146.

Department of Justice. (2007). *Department of Justice Activities Under the Civil Rights of Institutionalized Persons Act Fiscal Year 2007.* Washington, DC: U.S. Government Printing Office.

Didden, R., Korzilius, H., van Oorsouw, W., & Sturmey, P. (2006). Behavioral treatment of challenging behavior in individuals with mild mental retardation:

Meta-analysis of single-subject research. *American Journal on Mental Retardation, 111,* 290–298.

*Donnelly, D. R., & Olczak, P. V. (1990). The effects of differential reinforcement of incompatible behaviors (DRI) on pica for cigarettes in persons with intellectual disability. *Behavior Modification, 14,* 81–96.

*Duker, P. C., & Nielen, M. (1993). The use of negative practice for the control of pica behavior. *Journal of Behavior Therapy and Experimental Psychiatry, 24,* 249–253.

Dumaguing, N. I., Singh, I., Sethi, M., & Devanand, D. P. (2003). Pica in the geriatric mentally ill: Unrelenting and potentially fatal. *Journal of Geriatric Psychiatry and Neurology, 16,* 189–191.

Dwyer-Moore, K. J., & Dixon, M. R. (2007). Functional analysis and treatment of problem behavior of elderly adults in long-term care. *Journal of Applied Behavior Analysis, 40,* 679–683.

Edwards, C. H., McDonald, S., Mitchell, J. R., Jones, L., Mason, L., Kemp, A. M., . . . Trigg, L. (1959). Clay and cornstarch-eating women. *Journal of the American Dietetic Association, 35,* 810–815.

Falcomata, T. S., Roane, H. S., & Pabico, R. R. (2007). Unintentional stimulus control during the treatment of pica displayed by a young man with autism. *Research in Autism Spectrum Disorders, 1,* 350–359.

*Favell, J. E., McGimsey, J. F., & Schell, R. M. (1982). Treatment of self-injury by providing alternative sensory activities. *Analysis and Intervention in Developmental Disabilities, 2,* 83–104.

*Ferreri, S. J., Tamm, L., & Wier, K. G. (2006). Using food aversion to decrease severe pica by a child with autism. *Behavior Modification, 30,* 456–471.

Finney, J., Russo, D., & Cataldo, M. (1982). Reduction of pica in young children with lead poisoning. *Journal of Pediatric Psychology, 7,* 197–207.

Fisher, W., Piazza, C. C., Bowman, L. G., Hagopian, L. P., Owens, J. C., & Slevin, I. (1992). A comparison of two approaches for identifying reinforcers for persons with severe and profound disabilities. *Journal of Applied Behavior Analysis, 25,* 491–498.

*Fisher, W. W., Piazza, C., Bowman, L. G., Kurtz, P. F., & Lachman, S. R. (1994). A preliminary evaluation of empirically derived consequences for the treatment of pica. *Journal of Applied Behavior Analysis, 26,* 23–36.

Foxx, R. M. (1990). "Harry": A ten year follow-up of the successful treatment of a self-injurious man. *Research in Developmental Disabilities, 11,* 67–76.

Foxx, R. M., & Bechtel, D. R. (1983). Overcorrection: A review and analysis. In S. Axelrod & J. Apsche (Eds.). *The effects of punishment on human behavior.* New York, NY: Academic Press.

Foxx, R. M., & Livesay, J. (1984). Maintenance of response suppression following overcorrection: A 10-year retrospective examination of eight cases.

Analysis and Intervention in Developmental Disabilities, 4, 65–79.

Foxx, R. M., & Martin, E. D. (1975). Treatment of scavenging behavior (coprophagy and pica) by overcorrection. *Behaviour Research and Therapy, 13,* 153–162.

Foxx, R. M., & Meindl, J. (2007). The long term successful treatment of aggressive/destructive behavior of a preadolescent with autism. *Behavioral Interventions, 22,* 83–97.

Gardner, W. I. (1986). Reducing aggression in individuals with developmental disabilities: An expanded stimulus control, assessment, and intervention model. *Education and Training of the Mentally Retarded, 21,* 3–12.

Geissler, P. W., Prince, R. J., Levene, M., Poda, C., Beckerleg, S. E., Mutemi, W., & Shulman, C. E. (1999). Perceptions of soil-eating and anaemia among pregnant women on the Kenyan coast. *Social Science & Medicine, 48,* 1069–1079.

Goh, H. L., Iwata, B. A., & Kahng, S. W. (1999). Multicomponent assessment and treatment of cigarette pica. *Journal of Applied Behavior Analysis, 32,* 297–315.

Green, G. (1990). Least restrictive use of reductive procedures: guidelines and competences. In A. C. Repp & N. N. Singh (Eds.), *Perspectives on the use of non-aversive and aversive interventions for persons with developmental disabilities.* Sycamore, IL: Sycamore.

Griffin, J. C., Williams, D. E., Stark, M. T., Altmeyer, B. K., & Mason, M. (1986). Self-injurious behavior: A statewide prevalence survey of the extent and circumstances. *Applied Research in Mental Retardation, 7,* 105–116.

*Gutelius, M. F., Millican, F. K., Layman, E. M., Cohen, G. J., & Dublin, C. C. (1962). Nutritional studies of children with pica: I. Controlled study evaluating nutritional status, II. Treatment of pica with iron given intramuscularly. *Pediatrics, 29,* 1012–1023.

*Gutelius, M. F., Millican, F. K., Layman, E. M., Cohen, G. J., & Dublin, C. C. (1963). Treatment of pica with a vitamin and mineral supplement. *American Journal of Clinical Nutrition, 12,* 388–393.

*Hagopian, L. P., & Adelinis, J. D. (2001). Response blocking with and without redirection for the treatment of pica. *Journal of Applied Behavior Analysis, 34,* 527–530.

Hanley, G. P., Iwata, B. A., & McCord, B. E. (2003). Functional analysis of problem behavior: A review. *Journal of Applied Behavior Analysis, 36,* 147–185.

Hanley, G. P., Piazza, C. C., Fisher, W. W., Contrucci, S. A., & Maglieri, K. A. (1997). Evaluation of client preference for function-based treatment packages. *Journal of Applied Behavior Analysis, 30,* 459–473.

Hirsch, N., & Myles, B. S. (1996). The use of a pica box in reducing pica behavior in a student with autism. *Focus on Autism and Other Developmental Disabilities, 11*, 222–225.

Hoyt, R. E. (1997). Popcorn, pica, and impaction. *The American Journal of Medicine, 103*, 70.

Iwata, B. A., Wallace, M. D., Kahng, S., Lindberg, J. S., Roscoe, E. M., Conners, J., . . . Wordsell, A. S. (2000). Skill acquisition in the implementation of functional analysis methodology. *Journal of Applied Behavior Analysis, 33*, 181–194.

Johnson, C. R., Hunt, F. M., & Siebert, M. J. (1994). Discrimination training in the treatment of pica in a developmentally delayed child. *Behavior Modification, 18*, 214–229.

*Kalfus, G. R., Fisher-Gross, S., Marvullo, M. A., & Nau, P. A. (1987). Outpatient treatment of pica in a developmentally delayed child. *Child and Family Behavior Therapy, 9*, 49–63.

Kazdin, A. E. (1982). *Single case research design: Methods for clinical and applied settings.* New York, NY: Oxford University Press.

*Kern, L., Starosta, K., & Adelman, B. E. (2006). Reducing pica by teaching children to exchange inedible items for edibles. *Behavior Modification, 30*, 135–158.

Lanzkowsky, P. (1959). Investigation into the aetiology and treatment of pica. *Archives of Disease in Childhood, 34*, 140–148.

Lacey, E. P. (1990). Broadening the perspective of pica: Literature review. *Public Health Reports, 105*, 29–35.

LeBlanc, L. A., Piazza, C. C., & Krug, M. A. (1997). Comparing methods for maintaining the safety of a child with pica. *Research in Developmental Disabilities, 18*, 215–220.

Lemanek, K. L., Brown, R. T., Armstrong, F. D., Hood, C. H., Pegelow, C., & Woods, G. (2002). Dysfunctional eating patterns and symptoms of pica in children and adolescents with sickle cell disease. *Clinical Pediatrics, 41*, 493–500.

*Lofts, R. H., Schroeder, S. R., & Maier, R. H. (1990). Effects of serum zinc supplementation on pica behavior of persons with mental retardation. *American Journal on Mental Retardation, 95*, 103–109.

*Mace, F. C., & Knight, D. K. (1986). Functional analysis and treatment of severe pica. *Journal of Applied Behavior Analysis, 19*, 411–416.

Mace, F. C., & Wacker, D. P. (1994). Toward greater integration of basic and applied behavioral research: An introduction. *Journal of Applied Behavior Analysis, 27*, 569–574.

*Madden, N. A., Russo, D. C., & Cataldo, M. F. (1980). Behavioral treatment of pica in children with lead poisoning. *Child Behavior Therapy, 2*, 67–81.

Matson, J. L., & Bamburg, J. W. (1999). A descriptive study of pica behavior in persons with mental retardation. *Journal of Developmental and Physical Disabilities, 11*, 353–361.

*Matson, J. L., Stephens, R. M., & Smith, C. (1978). Treatment of self-injurious behavior with overcorrection. *Journal of Mental Deficiency Research, 22*, 175–178.

McAdam, D. B., Sherman, J. A., Sheldon, J. B., & Napolitano, D. A. (2004). Behavioral interventions to reduce the pica of persons with developmental disabilities. *Behavior Modification, 28*, 45–72.

McAlpine, C., & Singh, N. N. (1986). Pica in institutionalized mentally retarded persons. *Journal of Mental Deficiency Research, 30*, 171–178.

*McCord, B. E., Grosser, J. W., Iwata, B. A., & Powers, L. A. (2005). An analysis of response-blocking parameters in the prevention of pica. *Journal of Applied Behavior Analysis, 38*, 391–394.

McDonald, R., & Marshall, S. R. (1964). The value of iron therapy in pica. *Pediatrics, 34*, 558–562.

McKenna, D. (2006). Myopathy, hypokalaemia, and pica (geophagia) in pregnancy. *The Ulster Medical Journal, 75*, 159–159.

McLoughlin, J. (1988). Pica as a cause of death in three mentally handicapped men. *British Journal of Psychiatry, 152*, 842–845.

Mihailidou, H., Galanakis, E., Paspalaki, P., Borgia, P., & Mantzouranis, E. (2002). Pica and the elephant's ear. *Journal of Child Neurology, 17*, 855–856.

Moore, J. W., & Fisher, W. W. (2007). The effects of videotape modeling on staff acquisition of functional analysis methodology. *Journal of Applied Behavior Analysis, 40*, 197–202.

*Mulick, J. A., Barbour, R., Schroeder, S. R., & Rojahn, J. (1980). Overcorrection of pica in two profoundly retarded adults: Analysis of setting events, stimulus, and response generalization. *Applied Research in Mental Retardation, 1*, 241–252.

Myles, B. S., Simpson, R. L., & Hirsch, N. C. (1997). A review of literature on interventions to reduce pica in individuals with developmental disabilities. *Autism, 1*, 77–95.

O'Neil, R. E., Horner, R. H., Albin, R. W., Sprague, J. R., Storey, K., & Newton, J. S. (1997). *Functional assessment and program development for problem behavior.* Florence, KY: Brooks/Cole Publishing Company.

*Pace, G. M., & Toyer, E. A. (2000). The effect of a vitamin supplement on the pica of a child with severe mental retardation. *Journal of Applied Behavior Analysis, 33*, 619–622.

*Paisey, T. J., & Whitney, R. B. (1989). A long-term case study of analysis, response suppression, and treatment maintenance involving life-threatening pica. *Behavioral Residential Treatment, 4*, 191–211.

*Paniagua, F., Braverman, C., & Capriotti, R. M. (1986). Use of a treatment package in management of a profoundly mentally retarded girl's pica and self-stimulation. *American Journal of Mental Deficiency, 90*, 550–557.

Parry-Jones, B., & Parry-Jones, W. L. (1992). Pica: Symptom or eating disorder? A historical assessment. *British Journal of Psychiatry, 160*, 341–354.

*Piazza, C. C., Fisher, W. W., Hanley, G. P., LeBlanc, L. A., Worsdell, A., Lindauer, S., . . . Keeneey, K. M. (1998). Treatment of pica through multiple analyses of its reinforcing functions. *Journal of Applied Behavior Analysis, 35*, 165–189.

*Piazza, C. C., Hanley, G. P., Blakeley-Smith, A. B., & Kinsman, A. M. (2000). Effects of search skills training on the pica of a blind boy. *Journal of Developmental and Physical Disabilities, 12*, 35–41.

*Piazza, C. C., Hanley, G. P., & Fisher, W. W. (1996). Functional analysis and treatment of cigarette pica. *Journal of Applied Behavior Analysis, 29*, 437–450.

Piazza, C. C., Roane, H. S., Keeney, K. M., Boney, B. R., & Abt, K. A. (2002). Varying response effort in the treatment of pica maintained by automatic reinforcement. *Journal of Applied Behavior Analysis, 35*, 233–246.

Progar, P. R., North, S. T., Bruce, S. S., DiNovi, B. J., Nau, P. A., Eberman, E. M., . . . Nussbaum, C. N. (2001). Putative behavioral history effects and aggression maintained by escape from therapists. *Journal of Applied Behavior Analysis, 34*, 69–72.

*Rapp, J. T., Dozier, C. L., & Carr, J. E. (2001). Functional assessment and treatment of pica: A single-case experiment. *Behavioral Interventions, 16*, 111–125.

*Ricciardi, J. N., Luiselli, J. K., Terrill, S., & Reardon, K. (2003). Alternative response training with contingent practice as intervention for pica in a school setting. *Behavioral Interventions, 18*, 219–226.

Rojahn, J., McGonigle, C., Curcio, C., & Dixon, M. J. (1987). Suppression of pica by water mist and aromatic ammonia. *Behavior Modification, 11*, 65–74.

Rojahn, J., Schroeder, S., & Mulick, J. A. (1980). Ecological assessment of self-protective devices in three profoundly retarded adults. *Journal of Autism and Developmental Disorders, 10*, 59–66.

Schlosser, R. W. (1999). Social validation of interventions in augmentative and alternative communication. *Augmentative and Alternative Communication, 15*, 234–247.

Schlosser, R. W., Wendt, O., Bhavnani, S., & Nail-Chiwetalu, B. (2006). Use of information-seeking strategies for developing systematic reviews and engaging in evidence-based practice: The application of traditional and comprehensive pearl growing. A review. *International Journal of Language & Communication Disorders, 41*, 567–582.

Scotti, J. R., Evans, I. M., Meyer, L. H., & Walker, P. (1991). A meta-analysis of intervention research with problem behavior: Treatment validity and standards of practice. *American Journal on Mental Retardation, 96*, 233–256.

Scruggs, T. E., Mastropieri, M. A., Cook, S. B., & Escobar, C. (1986). Early interventions for children with conduct disorders: A quantitative synthesis of single-subject research. *Behavioral Disorders, 11*, 260–271.

*Singh, N. N., & Bakker, L. W. (1984). Suppression of pica by overcorrection and physical restraint: A comparative analysis. *Journal of Autism and Developmental Disorders, 14*, 40–45.

*Singh, N. N., Ellis, C. R., Crews, W. D., & Singh, Y. N. (1994). Does diminished dopaminergic neurotransmission increase pica? *Journal of Child and Adolescent Psychopharmacology, 4*, 93–99.

*Singh, N. N., & Winton, A. S. (1984). Effects of screening procedures on pica and collateral behaviors. *Journal of Behavior Therapy and Experimental Psychiatry, 15*, 59–65.

*Singh, N. N., & Winton, A. S. (1985). Controlling pica by components of an overcorrection procedure. *American Journal of Mental Deficiency, 90*, 40–45.

*Smith, M. D. (1987). Treatment of pica in an adult disabled by autism by differential reinforcement of incompatible behavior. *Journal of Behavior Therapy and Experimental Psychiatry, 18*, 285–288.

Starn, A. L., & Udall, J. N. (2008). Iron deficiency anemia, pica, and restless legs syndrome in a teenage girl. *Clinical Pediatrics, 47*, 83–85.

Stawar, T. L. (1978). The modification of coprophagic behavior in a 1-month-old boy using errorless discrimination learning. *Journal of Behavior Therapy and Experimental Psychiatry, 9*, 373–376.

Stiegler, L. N. (2005). Understanding pica behavior: A review for clinical and education professionals. *Focus on Autism and Other Developmental Disabilities, 20*, 27–38.

Stokes, T. F., & Baer, D. M. (1977). An implicit technology of generalization. *Journal of Applied Behavior Analysis, 10*, 349–367.

Uno, A., Takeda, N., Horii, A., Morita, M., Yamamota, Y., Yamatodani, A., & Kubo, T. (1997). Histamine release from the hypothalamus induced by gravity change in rats and space motion sickness. *Physiology & Behavior, 61*, 883–887.

Van Houten, R., Axelrod, S., Bailey, J. S., Favell, J. E., Foxx, R. M., Iwata, B. A., & Lovass, O. I. (1988). The right to effective behavioral treatment. *Journal of Applied Behavior Analysis, 21*, 381–384.

Vermeer, D. E., & Frate, D. A. (1979). Geophagia in rural Mississippi: Environmental and cultural contexts and nutritional implications. *The American Journal of Clinical Nutrition, 32*, 2129–2135.

Wacker, D. P. (2000). Building a bridge between research in experimental and applied behavior analysis.

In J. C. Leslie, & D. Blackman (Eds.), *Experimental and applied analysis of human behavior* (pp. 205–212). Reno, NV: Context.

Watson, T. S., & Steege, M. W. (2003). *Conducting school-based functional behavior assessments: A practitioner's guide*. New York, NY: Guilford Press.

Williams, D. E., Kirkpatrick-Sanchez, S., Enzinna, C., Dunn, J., & Borden-Karasack, D. (2009). The clinical management and prevention of pica: A retrospective follow-up of 41 individuals with intellectual disabilities and pica. *Journal of Applied Research in Intellectual Disabilities, 22,* 210–215.

*Winton, A. S., & Singh, N. N. (1983). Suppression of pica using brief duration physical restraint. *Journal of Mental Deficiency Research, 27,* 93–103.

World Health Organization. (1994). *The international statistical classification of diseases and related health problems* (10th ed.). Geneva, Switzerland: Author.

*Woods, D. W., Miltenberger, R. G., & Lumley, V. A. (1996). A simplified habit reversal treatment for pica-related chewing. *Journal of Behavior Therapy and Experimental Psychiatry, 27,* 257–262.

Youngberg v. Romeo, 457 U.S. 307 (1982).

13

Pediatric Feeding Disorders

VALERIE M. VOLKERT AND CATHLEEN C. PIAZZA

OVERVIEW OF DISORDER

A child's growth in height, weight, and head circumference is dependent on the complex and dynamic process of eating (Kerwin, 1999). Feeding is typically thought of as an instinctual process related to survival. However, some children fail to eat or fail to advance to age-appropriate eating. Feeding difficulties may lead to poor weight gain; weight loss; malnutrition; dehydration; imbalances in electrolytes; impairments related to cognitive, emotional, or academic functioning; hospitalization; recurrent infections; a compromised immune system; dependency on tube feedings (e.g., nasogastric or gastrostomy); high medical costs; and in severe cases if left untreated, death (Cohen, Piazza, & Navathe, 2006; Schwartz, 2000). Feeding difficulties may also greatly increase parental stress or anxiety due to frequent contact with medical personnel, and unconventional feeding routines often are required to manage the child's medical and nutritional needs (Franklin & Rodger, 2003; Winters, 2003). In addition, the relationship between the parent and child may suffer (Schwartz, 2000).

Identification and Diagnosis of Pediatric Feeding Disorders

A number of terms have been developed to describe infants and children with feeding difficulties, the earliest dating as far back as 1897, and no standard system of classification is currently used by mental health professionals (Chatoor, 2002; Schwartz, 2000). The tenth edition of *The Diseases of Infancy and Childhood* (Holt & Howland, 1933) first contained the term *failure to thrive* (Schwartz, 2000). Although there is not a consensus as to the definition of failure to thrive, this term generally encompasses impaired growth, a decrease in growth to below the 3rd or 5th percentile in weight-for-height or height-for-age, or a decrease in weight of two major percentiles over a month in infants or young children (Chatoor, 2002; Kerwin, 1999; Schwartz, 2000). Failure to thrive has been further classified into three categories: organic, nonorganic, and mixed. Organic failure to thrive is related to "a major disease process or a single or multiple organ dysfunction" or medical cause, and nonorganic failure to thrive is related to "insufficient emotional or physical nurturing without distinct pathophysiologic abnormality" (Schwartz, 2000, p. 59). Mixed failure to thrive would then relate to a combination of organic and nonorganic factors. Other terms, such as infantile anorexia nervosa, maternal/paternal deprivation syndrome (Schwartz, 2000), reactive attachment disorder (*Diagnostic and Statistical Manual, DSM-III*, American Psychiatric Association [APA], 1980), posttraumatic feeding disorder, and food phobia (Chatoor, 2002), have also been used to describe children with feeding problems.

The *DSM-IV* (APA, 1994) included the diagnostic category "Feeding Disorder of Infancy and Early Childhood" (307.59; Chatoor, 2002). Four criteria must be met for this diagnosis to be applied: (1) a feeding disturbance displayed by persistent failure to eat adequately with significant failure to gain weight or significant loss of weight over at least 1 month; (2) disturbance is not due to an associated gastrointestinal or other general medical condition; (3) disturbance is not better accounted for by another mental disorder or by lack of available food; and (4) onset is before age 6 years (APA, 1994). This diagnostic code has helped mental health professionals to become more aware of pediatric feeding disorders; however, it has not been widely used because the term is too broad (Chatoor, 2002; Piazza, 2008). That is, feeding disorders are specific and may be manifested as: (a) total food refusal; (b) food selectivity by type and/or texture or failure to advance to table texture; (c) oral motor difficulties or delays (e.g., tongue thrust or chewing deficits); (d) dysphasia, aspiration, or difficulty with coordination of swallowing; (e) oppositional, objectionable, or inappropriate mealtime behavior (e.g., child will not remain seated at the table, head turning, disruptions, tantrums, crying); (f) expulsion; (g) gagging and/or vomiting; and (h) delays in or lack of self-feeding skills (Chatoor, 2002; Field, Garland, & Williams, 2003; Kerwin, 1999; Munk & Repp, 1994; Winters, 2003).

Some diagnoses of feeding disorders state that insufficient growth must not be attributed to a medical cause (e.g., feeding disorder of infancy or early childhood, *DSM-IV*, 307.59). Others require that deficits in social or developmental achievement are present for the diagnosis to be given (Schwartz, 2000). Differences such as these may arise due to the various etiologies of feeding disorders. Although many diagnostic systems rely on the etiology of the feeding disorder, Babbitt, Hoch, and Coe (1994) state that a feeding disorder can be identified regardless of etiology (Piazza, Fisher, et al., 2003). The etiologies of feeding disorders are multifaceted and likely involve the interaction of medical factors (e.g., anatomical abnormalities; cardiac, respiratory, and gastrointestinal problems; food allergies), behavioral/environmental factors, psychosocial factors (e.g., parental anxiety, the parent–child relationship), skill deficits, and sensory processing difficulties (Field et al., 2003; Franklin & Rodger, 2003; Kerwin, 1999; Winters, 2003). Differences in the description and diagnoses of feeding disorders also may exist as the result of the diverse range of professionals who are involved in the assessment and treatment of feeding difficulties (Chung & Kahng, 2006; Cohen et al., 2006). Psychologists, pediatricians, gastroenterologists, nutritionists/dieticians, speech pathologists, and occupational therapists all may be involved in the treatment of a feeding disorder. On the other hand, given that multiple factors are involved in the development of a feeding disorder, a team approach is warranted to treat the feeding problem (Schwartz, 2000).

Prevalence of Pediatric Feeding Disorders

Between 6% and 45% of typically developing infants, toddlers, and early elementary-age children experience transient feeding difficulties (Archer, Rosenbaum, & Streiner, 1991; Franklin & Rodger, 2003; Kerwin, 1999; O'Brien, Repp, Williams, & Christophersen, 1991). Parents have reported that their typically developing children do not experience hunger at mealtime, attempt to stop a meal after taking a couple of bites, or are food selective (Kerwin, 1999; Reau, Senturia, Iebailly, & Christoffel, 1996). The feeding difficulties displayed by typical children are often mild and relatively easy to treat by pediatricians, and many times are resolved with no intervention (Kerwin, 1999).

Children with medical problems or developmental disabilities experience more severe and persistent feeding difficulties not as easily addressed by pediatricians. Up to 80% of children with developmental disabilities display feeding problems (Field et al., 2003; Kerwin, 1999; Manikam & Perman, 2000; Perske, Clifton, McClean, & Stein, 1977; Rommel, DeMeyer, Feenstra, & Veereman-Wauters, 2003; Stein, 2000; Williams, Witherspoon, Kavsak, Patterson, & McBlain, 2006). Between 26% and 90% of children with physical disabilities and 8% to 49% of children with prematurity or low birth weight exhibit feeding problems (Drewett, Corbett, & Wright, 1999; Field et al., 2003; Kerwin, 1999).

Field et al. (2003) explored the prevalence of feeding disorders in children with autism spectrum disorders (ASD), Down syndrome, and cerebral palsy. The most common feeding problem displayed by children with ASD was food selectivity by type and/or texture (62%). These children were less likely to experience food refusal or oral motor deficits such as dysphasia. Oral motor delays were present in 80% of the children with Down syndrome and 68% of the children with cerebral palsy. In children with Down syndrome, food selectivity by texture was the most common feeding concern (45%). Children with Down syndrome often present with a tongue thrust or chewing deficits; thus, issues with texture selectivity are not unexpected. Although food refusal was not the most prevalent feeding disorder among any of the three groups, a high correlation was found between gastroesophageal reflux disease and food refusal, regardless of the child's diagnosis. Several additional studies have also documented oral motor delays as a common feeding difficulty in children diagnosed with Down syndrome and cerebral palsy (e.g., Frazer & Friedman, 1996; Gisel, Applegate-Ferrante, Benson, & Bosma, 1996; Gisel, Lange, & Niman, 1984a, 1984b; Reilly, Skuse, & Poblete, 1996; Spender et al., 1996).

Assessment of Pediatric Feeding Disorders

Clinical assessment of pediatric feeding disorders should involve the input of pediatricians, gastroenterologists, psychologists, occupational therapists, speech pathologists, nutritionists or dieticians, and social workers (Cohen et al., 2006; Piazza, 2008). During assessment, these specialists gather information regarding the history of the presenting problem; antecedents and consequences surrounding the feeding problem, which includes caregiver behavior; the child's feeding skills; and previous attempts to resolve the feeding difficulty (Cohen et al., 2006). Primary caregivers are typically interviewed and medical records are reviewed to collect information regarding the child's health, growth, nutrition, feeding, developmental, medical, and motor history (Cohen et al., 2006). In addition, a meal is typically observed during the assessment process. Informant-based measures such as the Childhood Eating Behavior Inventory (Archer et al., 1991) and the Behavioral Pediatrics Feeding Assessment Scale (Crist, McDonnell, & Beck, 1994) may be used during the assessment process. Assessment tools such as the Global Scale for Feeding Situations (Stark, Bowen, Tyc, Evans, & Passero, 1990) and the Mealtime Observation Schedule (Sanders, Patel, Le Grice, & Shepherd, 1993) may be used during the mealtime observation.

Feeding difficulties are likely maintained partially by environmental variables or are learned behaviors (Ahearn, Kerwin, Eicher, Shantz, & Swearingin, 1996; Cooper et al., 1999; Hoch, Babbitt, Coe, Krell, & Hackbert, 1994; Piazza, Fisher, et al., 2003). That is, a functional relation may exist between the child's inappropriate mealtime behavior (e.g., head turning and pushing the feeder's hand) and the environment. Regardless of the etiology of the feeding disorder, caregivers attempt to motivate their children to eat by providing various consequences following refusal behavior (Piazza, Fisher, et al., 2003). For example, the caregiver may provide brief breaks from eating (e.g., 1 minute) from eating or meal termination, following instances of inappropriate mealtime behavior. Caregivers may also try to coax or reprimand the child (e.g., "Yum. Peas are good," or "You like this") following inappropriate mealtime behavior. Finally, after the child displays inappropriate mealtime behavior, the caregiver may provide preferred foods or toys (Piazza, Fisher, et al., 2003). Assessment to determine the variables influencing inappropriate mealtime behavior is important in developing prescriptive treatment for pediatric feeding disorders. Once these variables are identified, a specific treatment can be tailored to reduce inappropriate mealtime behavior.

Piazza, Fisher, et al. (2003) observed parents and children with feeding problems during meals. The authors instructed the parents "to feed the child as you would at mealtime." Data collected on parent and child behavior indicated that parents implemented a variety of consequences following child inappropriate mealtime behavior including: (a) providing escape from presentations of liquids or solids, (b) providing attention, and (c) giving the child a preferred toy or preferred food following refusal of a nonpreferred food. The authors conducted analog assessments to test the effects of the consequences used by parents, using a modification of the functional analysis procedures described by Iwata, Dorsey, Slifer, Bauman, and Richman (1982/1994). The authors assessed child inappropriate behavior during two or three test conditions (escape, attention, tangible) and a control condition.

In the escape condition, no toys or attention were available. If the child engaged in inappropriate mealtime behavior, the therapist removed the spoon for a brief period (5–30 seconds). The purpose of this condition was to test whether inappropriate mealtime behavior was maintained by negative reinforcement in the form of escape from eating. In the attention condition, no toys or escape were available. If the child exhibited inappropriate mealtime behavior, the spoon remained at midline, but

the feeder provided attention (e.g., "You like this") for 5–10 seconds. The purpose of this condition was to determine whether inappropriate mealtime behavior was maintained by positive reinforcement in the form of adult attention. In the tangible condition, no attention or escape was available. If the child displayed inappropriate mealtime behavior, the spoon remained at midline, but the feeder gave a preferred toy or food to the child for a brief period (5–30 seconds). The purpose of this condition was to test whether inappropriate mealtime behavior was maintained by positive reinforcement in the form of access to preferred items. The final condition was a control condition. During this condition, the spoon remained at midline, toys were available, and the feeder interacted with the child throughout the meal and did not provide differential consequences for child inappropriate mealtime behavior. A clear function of inappropriate mealtime behavior was identified for 10 of the 15 participants, and negative reinforcement by escape and avoidance of feeding was the predominant function identified.

EMPIRICALLY SUPPORTED TREATMENT OF PEDIATRIC FEEDING DISORDERS

Given the complex etiology of pediatric feeding disorders, the importance of a multidisciplinary approach cannot be overemphasized; however, in the majority of studies, interventions based on the principles of applied behavior analysis have been found effective in the treatment of feeding disorders (Kerwin, 1999; Piazza, 2008; Piazza & Carroll-Hernandez, 2004). To determine whether the interventions were *well-established* or *probably efficacious*, the guidelines described by the Task Force on Promotion and Dissemination of Psychological Procedure and the Society for Pediatric Psychology described in Kerwin were used, and the following treatment discussion is intended to be an extension of Kerwin (1999).

Well-established interventions have at least two good between-group design experiments or at least nine single-subject experiments demonstrating (a) the superiority of an intervention to pill, psychological placebo, or alternative treatment or (b) equivalence to an already established treatment. Experiments are conducted with treatment manuals or with specified treatment protocol; characteristics of the client samples are clearly specified; and effects are demonstrated by at least two different investigative groups. *Probably efficacious* treatments have two experiments showing the treatment is more effective than a waiting-list control, or one or more experiments meeting the criteria for a well-established treatment conducted by the same investigative group. *Promising* interventions have at least one well-controlled study and a less rigorously controlled study by a separate investigator, or two or more well-controlled studies with either small sample size or conducted by the same investigative group. (Kerwin, 1999, p. 196)

In most of the studies reviewed in this chapter, single-subject designs were employed, and the baseline condition served as the no-treatment control.

Differential Reinforcement of Alternative Behavior (DRA)—Well-Established

Differential reinforcement of alternative behavior (DRA) procedures involve the delivery of positive or negative reinforcement following appropriate behavior, which in the case of feeding is often acceptance of solids or liquids, while no differential consequences are typically provided for any other behavior. In most DRA interventions, attention/praise, preferred edibles, preferred toys/activities, and tokens were delivered following appropriate feeding behavior (positive reinforcement). Kahng, Boscoe, and Byrne (2003) demonstrated the effectiveness of differential negative reinforcement of alternative behavior (DNRA). They used tokens, which could be

exchanged to discontinue the meal, which they delivered following acceptance.

Nineteen studies demonstrated the effectiveness of DRA in increasing acceptance and consumption of nonpreferred foods (see Table 13.1 for a complete list). Increases in overall caloric intake, appropriate behavior, and weight were also noted when DRA treatments were implemented (Kerwin, 1999; Stark et al., 1990, 1993, 1996; Turner, Sanders, & Wall, 1994). Follow-up data were reported in 12 of the 19 DRA studies. Treatment gains maintained from 1 month to 2 years (Kerwin, 1999).

In 9 of the 19 investigations referred to earlier, other components such as time-out (e.g., Linscheid, Oliver, Blyler, & Palmer, 1978; Werle, Murphy, & Budd, 1993), response cost (e.g., Kahng, Tarbox, & Wilke, 2001), relaxation procedures (e.g., Stark et al., 1993, 1996), behavior management training (e.g., Stark et al., 1993, 1996; Turner et al., 1994), and stimulus fading (Kahng, Boscoe, & Byrne, 2003; Siegel, 1982) were used in conjunction with DRA. Thus, the independent contributions of these components require further evaluation.

Escape Extinction (EE)—Well-Established

Piazza, Fisher, et al. (2003) found negative reinforcement in the form of escape from eating to be the most predominant function of inappropriate mealtime behavior. Thus, the importance of escape extinction (EE) in the treatment of feeding disorders is not surprising. Two EE procedures have been described in the literature: nonremoval of the spoon (NRS) and physical guidance (PG) (Ahearn et al., 1996). Both procedures involve the elimination of the escape contingency following instances of inappropriate mealtime behavior. With NRS, the spoon or cup is held at the child's lips even if the child turns his head or bats at the spoon. The feeder maintains the spoon or cup at the child's lips until the presentation of solid or liquid can be deposited into the child's mouth. With PG, after a brief

TABLE 13.1   Well-Established Interventions

Intervention	Article
Differential Reinforcement of Alternative Behavior	Madsen, Madsen, and Thompson (1974) Thompson, Palmer, and Linscheid (1977) Linscheid, Oliver, Blyler, and Palmer (1978) Riordan, Iwata, Wohl, and Finney (1980) *Siegel, 1982* Riordan, Iwata, Finney, Wohl, and Stanley (1984) Luiselli, Evans, & Boyle (1985) Linscheid, Tarnowski, Rasnake, and Brams (1987) Stark, Bowen, Tyc, Evans, and Passero (1990) *Johnson & Babbitt (1993)* Stark et al. (1993) Werle, Murphy, and Budd (1993) Luiselli (1994) Stark, Powers, Jelalian, Rape, and Miller (1994) Turner, Sanders, and Wall (1994) Stark et al. (1996) *Kahng, Tarbox, and Wilke (2001)* *Kahng, Boscoe, and Bryne (2003)* *Casey, Cooper-Brown, Wacker, and Rankin (2006)*
Escape Extinction (Nonremoval of the Spoon or Physical Guidance)	*O'Brien, Bugle, and Azrin (1972)* *Riordan et al. (1984)* Hoch et al. (1994) Kerwin, Ahearn, Eicher, and Burd (1995) Ahearn et al. (1996) *Kern and Marder (1996)* *Coe et al. (1997)* *Freeman and Piazza (1998)* *Shore et al. (1998)* *Benoit, Wang, and Zlotkin (2000)* *Babbitt et al. (2001)* *Patel et al. (2001)* *Patel, Piazza, Martinez, et al. (2002)* *Piazza et al. (2002)* *Sevin et al. (2002)* *Dawson et al. (2003)* *Najdowski et al. (2003)* *Piazza et al. (2003)* *Mueller et al. (2004)* *Reed et al. (2004)* *Gulotta et al. (2005)* *Patel, Piazza, et al. (2005)* *Patel, Reed, et al. (2005)*
Physical Guidance of Self-Feeding Behavior	O'Brien et al. (1972) Nelson et al. (1975) Stimbert et al. (1977) Reidy (1979) Sisson and Dixon (1986a) Sisson and Dixon (1986b) Luiselli (1988a) Luiselli (1988b) Piazza et al. (1993) Luiselli (1993)

Note: The italicized studies have either been classified differently than in Kerwin (1999) or have been published since that article.

period of time (e.g., 5 seconds), if the child has not accepted the bite, slight pressure is applied to the mandibular joint to guide the child's mouth open, at which time the feeder deposits the bite into the child's mouth. Generally, if the child expels the bite, NRS or PG is used to re-present the bite. Across most of the studies using EE, a reinforcement component (e.g., praise, toys, continuous access to attention) typically was incorporated for acceptance or swallowing (see the following discussion).

Since the publication of Kerwin (1999), escape extinction (EE) has been shown to be a *well-established* treatment. Twenty-three studies have demonstrated the effectiveness of EE in increasing acceptance or consumption (see Table 13.1 for complete list of articles).

Kerwin (1999) reported parental dissatisfaction as a concern when using EE interventions. Two investigations actually found that when given a choice, parents chose the seemingly more intrusive EE treatment. In Ahearn et al. (1996), NRS and PG were equally effective in increasing acceptance; however, parents rated PG as more preferred, and behaviors such as disruption or self-injury were lower under this treatment. In Piazza, Patel, Gulotta, Sevin, and Layer (2003) parents were given the choice between NRS and PG. Half of the parents chose NRS and half chose PG. When these same parents were asked to choose between the EE procedures alone or in combination with reinforcement, all parents chose to implement the EE intervention alone.

A series of studies have examined using EE alone or in conjunction with DRA, non-contingent reinforcement (NCR), and behavioral momentum procedures (e.g., Dawson et al., 2003; Patel, Reed, et al., 2005; Patel, Piazza, Martinez, Volkert, & Santana, 2002; Reed et al., 2004; Piazza, Patel, et al., 2003). These adjunctive procedures (DRA, NCR, momentum) were ineffective in increasing acceptance alone and were ineffective unless used in conjunction with EE. In most cases, acceptance increased under EE regardless of whether reinforcement or behavioral momentum procedures were present. However, in some cases, when DRA or NCR was combined with EE, levels of inappropriate mealtime behavior and negative vocalizations were lower than when EE was used alone (Piazza, Patel, et al., 2003; Reed et al., 2004).

EE was part of a treatment package that included components other than reinforcement in several studies. In six studies, EE was combined with stimulus fading (see further discussion later). Other studies combined EE with simultaneous presentation (Kern & Marder, 1996; Piazza et al., 2002), establishing operation manipulations (Patel, Piazza, Layer, Coleman, & Swartzwelder, 2005; Patel, Piazza, Santana, & Volkert, 2002), and redistribution (Gulotta, Piazza, Patel, & Layer, 2005; Sevin, Gulotta, Sierp, Rosica, & Miller, 2002). In Piazza et al. (2002) and Kern and Marder (1996), bite presentations consisted of the simultaneous presentation of nonpreferred and preferred foods. In Patel, Piazza, Santana, et al. (2002) and Patel, Piazza, et al. (2005), the texture of one or all foods was lowered to decrease expulsion or packing. In addition, for some particpants, in both of these studies a Nuk brush was used to replace bites that were expelled or to redistribute packed bites by moving the food that the child was holding in his or her mouth onto the tongue. In Gulotta et al. (2005) and Sevin et al. (2002), EE was effective in increasing acceptance; however, redistribution was necessary to increase swallowing (see swallow redistribution treatments for further discussion). The contribution of each component of these treatments has not been completely established; thus, further research is warranted.

Generalization or follow-up data were reported in 10 of the 23 EE studies. Results were maintained from 2 months up to 1 year, parents were taught to implement the treatments (e.g., Mueller, Piazza, Patel, Kelley, & Pruett, 2004; Patel, Piazza, et al., 2005; Patel, Reed, et al., 2005), and sessions were conducted in home or restaurant settings (e.g., Najdowski, Wallace, Doney, & Ghezzi, 2003).

Physical Guidance of Self-Feeding Behavior—Well-Established

As noted by Kerwin (1999), 10 studies have shown physical guidance to be effective in increasing appropriate utensil use or self-feeding skills (see Table 13.1 for complete list of articles). All studies also combined physical prompting with a reinforcement procedure (e.g., praise, toy, or preferred food provided for appropriate feeding behavior). Physical guidance involves using hand-over-hand prompting to help the child complete a behavior. For example, to increase self-feeding, the feeder would place his hand over the child's hand, and together they would pick up the spoon and lift it to the child's mouth. In three studies, a physical prompt was part of a more elaborate procedure such as backward chaining (Luiselli, 1993) or three-step guided compliance (Piazza, Andersen, & Fisher, 1993; Sisson & Dixon, 1986a). In five investigations, other components such as interruption of stereotypic behavior or using hands to pick up food (Reidy, 1979), positive practice (Stimbert, Minor, & McCoy, 1977), and time-out were used in conjunction with physical guidance (Kerwin, 1999; Sisson & Dixon, 1986b). Generalization or follow-up data were reported in 7 of the 10 studies. Treatment effects generalized to a cafeteria or dining room (Nelson, Cone, & Hanson, 1975; Sisson & Dixon, 1986a), and treatment effects were maintained from 1 week up to 1 year (Kerwin, 1999).

Kerwin (1999) classified two additional studies under physical guidance; however, when further examined, these studies seemed to be a more appropriate fit for the EE intervention as NRS or PG (applying pressure to the jaw) were described. In the majority of the studies in which physical prompting was used, the spoon was guided to the child's mouth but not actually placed in the mouth as described with the EE treatments (e.g., Nelson et al., 1975; Luiselli, 1988a, 1993). This was probably the case because food refusal was not listed as a participant characteristic in these studies. Several participants ate fairly well (i.e., consumed solids and liquids), but did not exhibit appropriate self-feeding skills.

Nonnutritive Sucking—Probably Efficacious

Children who are born less than 32 weeks from gestation typically are not able to efficiently feed from the bottle or breast because of a lack of coordination between sucking, swallowing, and breathing (Pinelli & Symington, 2008). Nonnutritive Sucking (NNS) involves allowing premature infants to suck on a pacifier either during nasogastric tube feedings (Field et al., 1982; Sehgal, Prakash, Gupta, Mohan, & Anand, 1990) or prior to bottle feedings (Pickler & Reyna, 2004; Yu & Chen, 1999).

Five studies using group designs have established NNS as an effective intervention in increasing oral intake and decreasing the transition time between tube feedings to bottle feedings in preterm infants (Pinelli & Symington, 2008; see Table 13.2 for complete list of articles). In Rocha, Moreira, Pimenta, Ramos, and Lucena (2007), NNS was used in conjunction with oral stimulation, so the separate effects of NNS were unclear. Currently, the long-term effectiveness of NNS is unknown, because data are not yet available (Pinnelli & Symington, 2008).

TABLE 13.2   Probably Efficacious Interventions

Intervention	Article
Nonnutritive Sucking	*Field et al. (1982)*
	Sehgal et al. (1990)
	Yu and Chen (1999)
	Pickler and Reyna (2004)
	Rocha et al. (2007)
Oral Stimulation	*Fucile et al. (2002)*
	Fucile et al. (2005)
	Rocha et al. (2007)

Note: The italicized studies have either been classified differently than in Kerwin (1999) or have been published since that article.

Oral Stimulation—Probably Efficacious

Three group studies (Fucile, Gisel, & Lau, 2002, 2005; Rocha et al., 2007) have demonstrated the efficacy of oral stimulation in increasing oral intake and facilitating and reducing the time required to transition from tube feedings to full oral feedings in preterm infants. Oral stimulation consists of rubbing or compressing the perioral (e.g., cheeks and lips) and intraoral (e.g., tongue, palate, and gums) structures for 15 to 30 minutes prior to a tube feeding for a period of at least 10 days before oral feedings are initiated (Fucile et al., 2005). The long-term effects of oral stimulation have not been evaluated.

Oral Support—Promising

To administer oral support, the feeder uses one or both hands to support and compress the cheeks toward the lips and uses one finger to support the chin and stabilize the jaw while holding the bottle in the infant's mouth. The feeder also attempts to create a seal of the infant's lips around the nipple. Two group studies have shown oral support to be effective in increasing oral intake in premature infants (Boiron, Nobrega, Roux, Henrot, & Saliba, 2007; Einarsson-Backes, Deitz, Price, Glass, & Hays, 1994). Additional research is needed to further establish the effectiveness of oral support.

Stimulus Fading—Promising

Stimulus fading involves the gradual changing of antecedent stimuli so that stimulus control is transferred from one stimulus to another (Shore, Babbitt, Williams, Coe, & Snyder, 1998). Eight studies have demonstrated the effectiveness of stimulus fading in increasing acceptance and consumption (see Table 13.3 for complete list of articles). Najdowski et al. (2003) incorporated fading of bite number; Freeman and Piazza (1998) faded food amount and variety; Hagopian, Farrell, and Amari (1996) gradually increased liquid amount;

Tiger and Hanley (2006) faded from chocolate milk to plain milk; Shore et al. gradually increased texture from pureed to chopped; and Babbitt, Shore, Smith, Williams, and Coe (2001) faded from presenting liquid on a spoon to a cup. In the six aforementioned studies, four used stimulus fading in conjunction with EE (Babbitt, Shore, Smith, Williams, & Coe, 2001; Freeman & Piazza, 1998; Najdowski et al., 2003; Shore et al., 1998).

In two studies, after EE was ineffective on its own in increasing acceptance, stimulus fading procedures were also implemented. When consumption of Carnation Instant Breakfast (CIB) and milk did not increase under EE with one participant, Patel, Piazza, Kelly, Ochsner, and Santana (2001) gradually added CIB and milk to water (a fluid the child would drink readily). For two children in Mueller et al. (2004), acceptance of nonpreferred foods increased when the foods were blended gradually with a preferred food and not when EE was implemented alone. Reinforcement (e.g.,

TABLE 13.3   Promising Interventions

Intervention	Article
Oral Support	*Einarsson-Backes et al. (1994)*
	Boiron et al. (2007)
Stimulus Fading	*Hagopian et al. (1996)*
	Freeman and Piazza (1998)
	Shore et al. (1998)
	Babbitt et al. (2001)
	Patel et al. (2001)
	Najdowski et al. (2003)
	Mueller et al. (2004)
	Tiger and Hanley (2006)
Simultaneous Presentation	*Riordan et al. (1984)*
	Piazza et al. (2002)
	Ahearn (2003)
	Buckley and Newchok (2005)
Swallow Facilitation and Redistribution	*Lamm and Greer (1988)*
	Sevin et al. (2002)
	Gulotta et al. (2005)

Note: The italicized studies have either been classified differently than in Kerwin (1999) or have been published since that article.

praise or preferred toys) was a common element across all studies using stimulus fading and a backward chaining procedure was combined with stimulus fading in Hagopian et al.

Generalization or follow-up data were collected in three of the seven studies that evaluated stimulus fading. Parents were taught to implement the treatment, and treatment effects were demonstrated at home, a restaurant, or the living unit of an inpatient hospital. In addition, treatment effects maintained up to 7 months (Hagopian et al., 1996; Mueller et al., 2004; Najdowski et al., 2003). We categorized stimulus fading as promising because in most of the studies cited earlier, investigators used stimulus fading in conjunction with other procedures; therefore, the effects of stimulus fading alone have been tested less frequently.

Simultaneous Presentation Without EE—Promising

Most interventions that address feeding disorders have involved consequence-based procedures. Simultaneous presentation is really the only antecedent-based intervention found to be effective without using EE. Simultaneous presentation involves presenting a bite of nonpreferred food and a bite of preferred food together. The nonpreferred food may be embedded in the preferred food (Piazza et al., 2002), placed on top of the nonpreferred food (Ahearn, 2003), or placed behind the nonpreferred food (Buckley & Newchok, 2005). This procedure is often contrasted with sequential presentation in which the preferred bite is presented following the nonpreferred bite (Piazza et al., 2002).

Four studies have demonstrated the effectiveness of simultaneous presentation in increasing acceptance of nonpreferred foods in children with food selectivity independent of an EE procedure (see Table 13.3 for complete list of articles). In Riordan, Iwata, Finney, Wohl, and Stanley (1984) simultaneous and sequential procedures were equally effective in increasing acceptance for three participants; however, the simultaneous presentation was only in place briefly before the presentation could be described as sequential (a 2- to 3-second delay was introduced between the presentation of foods). Piazza et al. (2002) also compared the effectiveness of the simultaneous versus sequential presentation procedures in increasing consumption of nonpreferred foods. Simultaneous presentation was most effective for all participants; however, EE was necessary for one of three participants.

A common component of all of the studies except Ahearn (2003) was reinforcement (e.g., praise, preferred items) for acceptance or consumption, and a response cost for packing was used in Buckley and Newchok (2005). Follow-up was conducted in two of the four studies, and consumption of nonpreferred foods maintained for up to 2 years. Research is still necessary to support the efficacy of this intervention.

Swallow Facilitation and Redistribution—Promising

Swallow facilitation consists of eliciting a swallow by means of touching the posterior area of the tongue with a finger (Lamm & Greer, 1988) or applying slight pressure to the posterior area of the tongue with a utensil when depositing the bite. Redistribution consists of using a utensil (e.g., Nuk) to first collect pocketed food and then deposit the food on the middle rather than the posterior of tongue (Gulotta et al., 2005; Sevin et al., 2002). Although redistribution may facilitate a swallow, it is unclear whether the swallow is elicited. The effect of bite placement on swallow facilitation is unclear at this point. Three studies have demonstrated the efficacy of swallow facilitation and redistribution in increasing swallowing of food or liquids (Gulotta et al., 2005; Lamm & Greer, 1988; Sevin et al., 2002). Only one of the three studies reported follow-up data. Lamm and Greer found the functional swallow response maintained up to 2 years. Additional research will be necessary to further support the effectiveness of this treatment.

EVIDENCE-BASED PRACTICES

Pediatric feeding disorders can pose serious risks to a child's growth and development (Cohen et al., 2006; Kerwin, 1999). Feeding disorders are more common in children with physical disabilities and developmental disabilities and children who are born premature. Although the etiology of feeding problems is often unknown, several treatments have been shown to be effective. The majority of these studies used behavior-analytic practices and employed single-subject designs. Three treatments are well-established: Differential reinforcement of alternative behavior and escape extinction are well-established treatments for increasing acceptance and consumption of food and liquids, and physical guidance is a well-established intervention found to increase self-feeding skills. Several interventions have been identified as promising but require more research: stimulus fading is a promising intervention shown to increase acceptance and consumption of solids and liquids; simultaneous presentation without escape extinction is a promising treatment found to increase acceptance in children diagnosed with food selectivity; and swallow facilitation and/or redistribution is a promising treatment shown to increase swallowing.

Three interventions did not incorporate behavior analytic procedures and were aimed to increase oral intake in premature infants. The studies examining these treatments employed group designs and used procedures common to pediatric medicine and occupational therapy. In preterm infants, nonnutritive sucking and oral stimulation are probably efficacious interventions, and oral support is a promising intervention for decreasing transition time between tube feedings and bottle feedings and in increasing oral consumption. All these interventions require more research.

Several treatments have been found to be effective in treating pediatric feeding disorders. However, since Kerwin (1999), behavioral treatments continue to be the primary interventions that meet the criteria to be considered empirically supported. Evidence is now available to support procedures used by pediatric medicine and occupational therapists, but further research is warranted to establish the effectiveness of these practices. The effects of most of the behavioral treatments were maintained over time. However, the long-term effects (10 or more years) of these interventions are still unclear. Future research is needed to determine whether these children are eating well in adolescence or early adulthood. Given that the nature of pediatric feeding disorders requires a multidisciplinary approach, more research is warranted to provide evidence to support treatments implemented by other disciplines. This will only strengthen the current approaches to treat pediatric feeding disorders.

REFERENCES

Ahearn, W. H. (2003). Using simultaneous presentation to increase vegetable consumption in a mildly selective child with autism. *Journal of Applied Behavior Analysis, 36,* 247–250.

Ahearn, W. H., Kerwin, M. E., Eicher, P. S., Shantz, J., & Swearingin, W. (1996). An alternating treatments comparison of two intensive interventions for food refusal. *Journal of Applied Behavior Analysis, 29,* 321–332.

American Psychiatric Association. (1980). *Diagnostic and statistical manual of mental disorders* (3rd ed.). Washington, DC: Author.

American Psychiatric Association. (1994). *Diagnostic and statistical manual of mental disorders* (4th ed.). Washington, DC: Author.

Archer, I. A., Rosenbaum, P. L., & Streiner, D. L. (1991). The children's eating behavior inventory: Reliability and validity results. *Journal of Pediatric Psychology, 16,* 629–642.

Babbitt, R. L., Hoch, T. A., & Coe, D. A. (1994). Behavioral feeding disorders. In D. N. Tuchman & R. S. Walter (Eds.), *Disorders of feeding and swallowing in infants in children* (pp. 77–95). San Diego, CA: Singular Publishing Group.

Babbitt, R. L., Shore, B. A., Smith, M., Williams, K. E., & Coe, D. A. (2001). Stimulus fading in the treatment of adipsia. *Behavioral Interventions, 16*, 197–207.

Benoit, D., Wang, E. E., & Zlotkin, S. H. (2000). Discontinuation of enterostomy tube feeding by behavioral treatment in early childhood: A randomized controlled trial. *Journal of Pediatrics, 137*, 498–503.

Boiron, M., Nobrega, L. D., Roux, S., Henrot, A., & Saliba, E. (2007). Effects of oral stimulation and oral support on non-nutritive sucking and feeding performance in preterm infants. *Developmental Medicine & Child Neurology, 49*, 439–444.

Buckley, S. D., & Newchok, D. K. (2005). An evaluation of simultaneous presentation and differential reinforcement with response cost to reduce packing. *Journal of Applied Behavior Analysis, 38*, 405–409.

Casey, S. D., Cooper-Brown, L. J., Wacker, D. P., & Rankin, B. E. (2006). The use of descriptive analyses to identify and manipulate schedules of reinforcement in the treatment of food refusal. *Journal of Behavioral Education, 15*, 41–52.

Chatoor, I. (2002). Feeding disorders in infants and toddlers: Diagnosis and treatment. *Child and Adolescent Psychiatric Clinics, 11*, 163–183.

Chung, K.-M., & Kahng, S. W. (2006) Pediatric feeding disorders. In J. E. Fisher & W. T. O'Donohue (Eds.), *Practitioner's guide to evidence-based psychotherapy.* New York, NY: Springer.

Coe, D. A., Babbitt, R. L., Williams, K. E., Hajimihalis, C., Snyder, A. M., Ballard, C., & Efron, L. A. (1997). Use of extinction and reinforcement to increase food consumption and reduce expulsion. *Journal of Applied Behavior Analysis, 30*, 581–583.

Cohen, S. A., Piazza, C. C., & Navathe, A. (2006). Feeding and nutrition. In I. L. Rubin & A. C. Crocker (Eds.), *Medical care for children and adults with developmental disabilities* (pp. 295–307). Baltimore, MD: Paul Brook.

Cooper, L. J., Wacker, D. P., Brown, K., McComas, J. J., Peck, S. M., Drew, J., . . . Kayser, K. (1999). Use of a concurrent operants paradigm to evaluate positive reinforcers during treatment of food refusal. *Behavior Modification, 23*, 3–40.

Crist, W., McDonnell, P., & Beck, M. (1994). Behavior at mealtimes and the young child with cystic fibrosis. *Journal of Developmental & Behavioral Pediatrics, 15*, 157–161.

Dawson, J. E., Piazza, C. C., Sevin, B. M., Gulotta, C. S., Lerman, D., & Kelley, M. L. (2003). Use of the high-probability instructional sequence and escape extinction in a child with food refusal. *Journal of Applied Behavior Analysis, 36*, 105–108.

Drewett, R. F., Corbett, S. S., & Wright, C. M. (1999). Cognitive and educational attainments of school-aged children who failed to thrive in infancy: A population-based study. *Journal of Child Psychology and Psychiatry, 40*, 551–561.

Einarsson-Backes, L. M., Deitz, J., Price, R., Glass, R., & Hays, R. (1994). The effect of oral support on sucking efficiency in preterm infants. *American Journal of Occupational Therapy, 48*, 490–498.

Field, D., Garland, M., & Williams, K. (2003). Correlates of specific childhood feeding problems. *Journal of Pediatric Child Health, 39*, 299–304.

Field, T., Ignatoff, E., Stringer, S., Brennan, J., Greenberg, R., Widmayer, S., & Andersen, G. C. (1982). Nonnutritive sucking during tube feedings: Effects on preterm neonates in an intensive care unit. *Pediatrics, 70*, 381–384.

Franklin, L., & Rodger, S. (2003). Parents' perspectives on feeding medically compromised children: Implications for occupational therapy. *Australian Occupational Therapy Journal, 50*, 137–147.

Frazer, J. B., & Friedman, B. (1996). Swallow function in children with Down syndrome: A retrospective study. *Developmental Medicine and Child Neurology, 38*, 695–703.

Freeman, K. A., & Piazza, C. C. (1998). Combining stimulus fading, reinforcement, and extinction to treat food refusal. *Journal of Applied Behavior Analysis, 31*, 691–694.

Fucile, S., Gisel, E. G., & Lau, C. (2002). Oral stimulation accelerates the transition from tube to oral feeding in preterm infants. *Journal of Pediatrics, 141*, 230–236.

Fucile, S., Gisel, E. G., & Lau, C. (2005). Effect of an oral stimulation program on sucking skill maturation of preterm infants. *Developmental Medicine and Child Neurology, 47*, 158–162.

Gisel, E. G., Applegate-Ferrante, T., Benson, J., & Bosma, J. F. (1996). Oral-motor skills following sensorimotor therapy in two groups of moderately dysphagic children with cerebral palsy: Aspiration vs. nonaspiration. *Dysphasia, 11*, 59–71.

Gisel, E. G., Lange, L. J., & Ninman, C. W. (1984a). Chewing cycles in 4- and 5-year-old Down syndrome children: A comparison of eating efficacy with normals. *American Journal of Occupational Therapy, 38*, 666–671.

Gisel, E. G., Lange, L. J., & Niman, C. W. (1984b). Tongue movements in 4- and 5-year-old Down syndrome children during eating: A comparison with normal children. *American Journal of Occupational Therapy, 38*, 660–665.

Gulotta, C. S., Piazza, C. C., Patel, M. R., & Layer, S. A. (2005). Using food redistribution to reduce packing in children with severe food refusal. *Journal of Applied Behavior Analysis, 38*, 39–50.

Hagopian, L. P., Farrell, D. A., & Amari, A. (1996). Treating total liquid refusal with backward chaining and fading. *Journal of Applied Behavior Analysis, 29*, 573–575.

Hoch, T. A., Babbitt, R. L., Coe, D. A., Krell, D. M., & Hackbert, L. (1994). Contingency contacting:

Combining positive reinforcement and escape extinction procedures to treat persistent food refusal. *Behavior Modification, 18*, 106–128.

Holt, L. E., & Howland, J. (1933). *Holt's diseases of infancy and childhood* (10th ed.). New York, NY: Appleton-Century.

Iwata, B. A., Dorsey, M. F., Slifer, K. J., Bauman, K. E., & Richman, G. S. (1994). Toward a functional analysis of self-injury. *Journal of Applied Behavior Analysis, 27*, 197–209. (Reprinted from *Analysis and Intervention in Developmental Disabilities, 2*, 3–20, 1982.)

Johnson, C. R., & Babbitt, R. L. (1993). Antecedent manipulation in the treatment of primary solid food refusal. *Behavior Modification, 17*, 510–521.

Kahng, S., Boscoe, J. H., & Byrne, S. (2003). The use of an escape contingency and a token economy to increase food acceptance. *Journal of Applied Behavior Analysis, 36*, 349–353.

Kahng, S., Tarbox, J., & Wilke, A. E. (2001). Use of a multicomponent treatment for food refusal. *Journal of Applied Behavior Analysis, 34*, 93–96.

Kern, L., & Marder, T. J. (1996). A comparison of simultaneous and delayed reinforcement as treatments for food selectivity. *Journal of Applied Behavior Analysis, 29*, 243–246.

Kerwin, M. E. (1999). Empirically supported treatments in pediatric psychology: Severe feeding problems. *Journal of Pediatric Psychology, 24*, 193–214.

Kerwin, M. E., Ahearn, W. H., Eicher, P. S., & Burd, D. M. (1995). The costs of eating: A behavioral economic analysis of food refusal. *Journal of Applied Behavior Analysis, 28*, 245–260.

Lamm, N., & Greer, R. D. (1988). Induction and maintenance of swallowing responses in infants with dysphagia. *Journal of Applied Behavior Analysis, 21*, 143–156.

Linscheid, T. R., Oliver, J., Blyler, E., & Palmer, S. (1978). Brief hospitalization for the behavioral treatment of feeding problems in the developmentally disabled. *Journal of Pediatric Psychology, 3*, 72–76.

Linscheid, T. R., Tarnowski, L., Rasnake, K., & Brams, J. S. (1987). Behavioral treatment of food refusal in a child with short-gut syndrome. *Journal of Pediatric Psychology, 12*, 451–459.

Luiselli, J. K. (1988a). Behavioral feeding intervention with deaf-blind, multihandicapped children. *Child and Family Behavior Therapy, 10*, 49–72.

Luiselli, J. K. (1988b). Improvement of feeding skills in multihandicapped students through paced-prompting interventions. *Journal of the Multihandicapped Person, 1*, 17–30.

Luiselli, J. K. (1993). Training self-feeding skills in children who are deaf and blind. *Behavior Modification, 17*, 457–473.

Luiselli, J. K. (1994). Oral feeding treatment of children with chronic food refusal and multiple developmental disabilities. *American Journal on Mental Retardation, 98*, 646–655.

Luiselli, J. K., Evans, T. P., & Boyle, D. A. (1985). Contingency management of food selectivity and oppositional eating in a multiply handicapped child. *Journal of Clinical Child Psychology, 14*, 153–156.

Madsen, C. H., Madsen, C. K., & Thompson, F. (1974). Increasing rural Head Start children's consumption of middle-class meals. *Journal of Applied Behavior Analysis, 7*, 257–262.

Manikam, R., & Perman, J. A. (2000). Pediatric Feeding Disorders. *Journal of Gastroenterology, 30*, 34–46.

Mueller, M. M., Piazza, C. C., Patel, M. R., Kelley, M. E., & Pruett, A. (2004). Increasing variety of foods consumed by blending nonpreferred foods into preferred foods. *Journal of Applied Behavior Analysis, 37*, 159–170.

Munk, D. D., & Repp, A. C. (1994). Behavioural assessment of feeding problems of individuals with severe disabilities. *Journal of Applied Behavior Analysis, 27*, 241–250.

Najdowski, A. C., Wallace, M. D., Doney, J. K., & Ghezzi, P. M. (2003). Parental assessment and treatment of food selectivity in natural settings. *Journal of Applied Behavior Analysis, 36*, 383–386.

Nelson, G. L., Cone, J. D., & Hanson, C. R. (1975). Training correct utensil use in retarded children: Modeling vs. physical guidance. *American Journal of Deficiency, 80*, 114–122.

O'Brien, F., Bugle, C., & Azrin, N. H. (1972). Training and maintaining a retarded child's proper eating. *Journal of Applied Behavior Analysis, 5*, 67–72.

O'Brien, S., Repp, A. C., Williams, G. E., & Christophersen, E. R. (1991). Pediatric feeding disorders. *Behaviour Modification, 15*, 394–418.

Patel, M. R., Piazza, C. C., Kelly, M. L., Ochsner, C. A., & Santana, C. M. (2001). Using a fading procedure to increase fluid consumption in a child with feeding problems. *Journal of Applied Behavior Analysis, 34*, 357–360.

Patel, M. R., Piazza, C. C., Layer, S., Coleman, R., & Swartzwelder, D. (2005). A systematic evaluation of food textures to decrease packing and increase oral intake in children with pediatric feeding disorders. *Journal of Applied Behavior Analysis, 38*, 89–100.

Patel, M. R., Piazza, C. C., Martinez, C. J., Volkert, V. M., & Santana, C. M. (2002). An evaluation of two differential reinforcement procedures with escape extinction to treat food refusal. *Journal of Applied Behavior Analysis, 35*, 363–374.

Patel, M. R., Piazza, C. C., Santana, C. M., & Volkert, V. M. (2002). An evaluation of food type and texture in the treatment of a feeding problem. *Journal of Applied Behavior Analysis, 35*, 183–186.

Patel, M. R., Reed, G. K., Piazza, C. C., Bachmeyer, M. H., Layer, S. A., & Pabico, R. S. (2005). An evaluation of a high-probability instructional sequence to increase acceptance of food and decrease inappropriate behavior in children with pediatric feeding disorders. *Research in Developmental Disabilities, 27*, 430–442.

Perske, R., Clifton, A., McClean, B. M., & Stein, J. I. (1977). *Mealtimes for severely and profoundly handicapped persons: New concepts and attitudes.* Baltimore, MD: University Park Press.

Piazza, C. C. (2008). Feeding disorders and behavior: What have we learned? *Developmental Disabilities Research Reviews, 14*, 174–181.

Piazza, C. C., Anderson, C., & Fisher, W. (1993). Teaching self-feeding skills to patients with Rett syndrome. *Developmental Medicine and Child Neurology, 35*, 991–996.

Piazza, C. C., & Carroll-Hernandez, T. A. (2004). Assessment and treatment of pediatric feeding disorders. In R. E. Trembly, R. G. Barr, & R. DeV. Peters (Eds.), *Centre of Excellence for Early Childhood Development.* Retrieved from www.child encyclopedia.com/pages/PDF/Piazza-Carroll-Hernan dezANGxp.pdf

Piazza, C. C., Fisher, W. F., Brown, K. A., Shore, B. A., Patel, M. R., Katz, R. M., . . . Blakeley-Smith, A. (2003). Functional analysis of inappropriate mealtime behaviors. *Journal of Applied Behavior Analysis, 36*, 187–204.

Piazza, C. C., Patel, M. R., Gulotta, C. S., Sevin, B. M., & Layer, S. A. (2003). On the relative contributions of positive reinforcement and escape extinction in the treatment of food refusal. *Journal of Applied Behavior Analysis, 36*, 309–324.

Piazza, C. C., Patel, M. R., Santana, C. M., Goh, H. L., Delia, M. D., & Lancaster, B. M. (2002). An evaluation of simultaneous and sequential presentation of preferred and nonpreferred food to treat selectivity. *Journal of Applied Behavior Analysis, 35*, 259–270.

Pickler, R. H., & Reyna, B. A. (2004). Effects of nonnutritive sucking on nutritive sucking, breathing, and behavior during bottle feedings of preterm infants. *Advances in Neonatal Care, 4*, 226–234.

Pinelli, J., & Symington, A. (2008). Non-nutritive sucking for promoting physiologic stability and nutrition in preterm infants (Review). *The Cochran Library, 3*, 1–22.

Reau, N. R., Senturia, Y. D., Lebailly, S. A., & Christoffel, K. K. (1996). Infant and toddler feeding patterns and problems: Normative data and a new direction. *Journal of Developmental and Behavioral Pediatrics, 17*, 140–153.

Reed, G. K., Piazza, C. C., Patel, M. R., Layer, S. A., Bachmeyer, M. H., Bethke, S. D., & Gutshall, K. A. (2004). On the relative contributions of noncontingent reinforcement and escape extinction in the treatment of food refusal. *Journal of Applied Behavior Analysis, 37*, 27–41.

Reidy, T. J. (1979). Training appropriate eating behavior in a pediatric rehabilitation setting: Case study. *Archives of Physical Medicine and Rehabilitation, 60*, 226–230.

Reilly, S., Skuse, D., & Poblete, X. (1996). Prevalence of feeding problems and oral motor dysfunction in children with cerebral palsy: A community survey. *Journal of Pediatrics, 129*, 877–882.

Riordan, M. M., Iwata, B. A., Finney, J. W., Wohl, M. K., & Stanley, A. E. (1984). Behavioral assessment and treatment of chronic food refusal in handicapped children. *Journal of Applied Behavior Analysis, 17*, 327–341.

Riordan, M. M., Iwata, B. A., Wohl, M. K., & Finney, J. W. (1980). Behavioral treatment of food refusal and selectivity in developmentally disabled children. *Applied Research in Mental Retardation, 1*, 95–112.

Rocha, A. D., Moreira, M. E., Pimenta, H. P., Ramos, J. R., & Lucena, S. L. (2007). A randomized study of the efficacy of sensory-motor-oral stimulation and non-nutritive sucking in very low birth weight infants. *Early Human Development, 83*, 385–388.

Rommel, N., DeMeyer, A. M., Feenstra, L., & Veereman-Wauters, G. (2003). The complexity of feeding problems in 700 infants and young children presenting to a tertiary care institution. *Journal of Pediatric Gastroenterology and Nutrition, 37*, 75–84.

Sanders, M. R., Patel, R. K., Le Grice, B., & Shepherd, R. W. (1993). Children with persistent feeding difficulties: An observational analysis of feeding interactions of problem and non-problem eaters. *Health Psychology, 12*, 64–73.

Schwartz, D. (2000). Failure to thrive: An old nemesis in the new millennium. *Pediatrics in Review, 21*, 257–264.

Sehgal, S. K., Prakash, O., Gupta, A., Mohan, M., & Anand, N. K. (1990). Evaluation of beneficial effects of nonnutritive sucking in preterm infants. *Indian Pediatrics, 27*, 263–266.

Sevin, B. M., Gulotta, C. S., Sierp, B. J., Rosica, L. A., & Miller, L. J. (2002). Analysis of response covariation among multiple topographies of food refusal. *Journal of Applied Behavior Analysis, 35*, 65–68.

Shore, B. A., Babbitt, R. L., Williams, K. E., Coe, D. A., & Synder, A. (1998). Use of texture fading in the treatment of food selectivity. *Journal of Applied Behavior Analysis, 31*, 621–633.

Siegel, L. J. (1982). Classical and operant procedures in the treatment of a case of food aversion in a young child. *Journal of Clinical Child Psychology, 27*, 105–110.

Sisson, L. A., & Dixon, M. J. (1986a). A behavioral approach to the training and assessment of feeding skills in multihandicapped children. *Applied Research in Mental Retardation, 7*, 149–163.

Sisson, L. A., & Dixon, M. J. (1986b). Improving mealtime behaviors through token reinforcement. *Behavior Modification, 10*, 333–354.

Spender, Q., Stein, A., Dennis, J., Reilly, S., Percy, E., & Cave, D. (1996). An explanation of feeding difficulties in children with Down syndrome. *Developmental Medicine and Child Neurology, 38*, 681–694.

Stark, L. J., Bowen, A. M., Tyc, V. I., Evans, S., & Passero, M. A. (1990). A behavioral approach to increasing calorie consumption in children with cystic fibrosis. *Journal of Pediatric Psychology, 15*, 309–326.

Stark, L. J., Knapp, L. G., Bowen, A. M., Powers, S. W., Jelalian, E., Evans, S., . . . Hovell, M. (1993). Increasing calorie consumption of children with cystic fibrosis: Replication with 2-year follow-up. *Journal of Applied Behavior Analysis, 26*, 435–450.

Stark, L. J., Mulvihill, M. M., Powers, S. W., Jelalian, E., Keating, K., Creveling, S., . . . Hovell, M. F. (1996). Behavioral intervention to improve calorie intake of children with cystic fibrosis: Treatment vs. wait-list controls. *Journal of Pediatric Gastroenterology and Nutrition, 23*, 240–253.

Stark, L. J., Powers, S. W., Jelalian, E., Rape, R. N., & Miller, D. L. (1994). Modifying problematic mealtime interactions of children with cystic fibrosis and their parents via behavioral parent training. *Journal of Pediatric Psychology, 19*, 751–768.

Stein, K. (2000). Children with feeding disorders: An emerging issue. *Journal of the American Dietetic Association, 100*, 1000–1001.

Stimbert, V. E., Minor, J. W., & McCoy, J. F. (1977). Intensive feeding training with retarded children. *Behavior Modification, 1*, 517–530.

Thompson, R. J., Palmer, S., & Linscheid, T. R. (1977). Single-subject design and interaction analysis in the behavioral treatment of a child with a feeding problem. *Child Psychiatry and Human Development, 8*, 43–53.

Tiger, J. H., & Hanley, G. P. (2006) Using reinforcer pairing and fading to increase the milk consumption of a preschool child. *Journal of Applied Behavior Analysis, 39*, 399–403.

Turner, K. M., Sanders, M. R., & Wall, C. R. (1994). Behavioural parent training versus dietary education in the treatment of children with persistent feeding difficulties. *Behavior Change, 11*, 242–258.

Werle, M. A., Murphy, T. B., & Budd, K. S. (1993). Treating chronic food refusal in young children: Home-based parent training. *Journal of Applied Behavior Analysis, 26*, 421–433.

Williams, S., Witherspoon, K., Kavsak, P., Patterson, C., & McBlain, J. (2006). Pediatric feeding and swallowing problems: An interdisciplinary team approach. *Canadian Journal of Dietetic Practice and Research, 67*, 185–190.

Winters, N. C. (2003). Feeding problems in infancy and early childhood. *Primary Psychiatry, 10*, 30–34.

Yu, M., & Chen, Y. (1999). The effects of nonnutritive sucking on behavioral state and feeding in premature infants before feeding. *Nursing Research (China), 7*, 468–478.

14

Tics and Tourette Disorders

BENJAMIN T. P. TUCKER, CHRISTINE A. CONELEA, AND DOUGLAS W. WOODS

OVERVIEW OF TIC DISORDERS

Diagnostic Criteria

Tics are sudden, repetitive, recurrent motor movements or vocalizations that are typically experienced as uncontrollable but that can be suppressed to varying degrees (American Psychiatric Association [APA], 2000). The *DSM-IV-TR* includes four diagnostic categories of tic disorders (TD). Chronic motor or vocal tic disorders (CTD) are characterized by the presence of single or multiple motor or vocal tics, but not both, while Tourette's syndrome (TS) is characterized by the presence of both multiple motor tics and one or more vocal tics. Diagnostic criteria for TS and CTD also stipulate that tics must occur multiple times per day or intermittently for a period of at least 1 year, without a tic-free period of 3 consecutive months. The diagnosis of transient tic disorder (TTD) is conferred when motor and/or vocal tics are present for at least 1 month but less than 1 year. All tic disorder diagnoses require an onset of tics before age 18 years, and tics must not be better accounted for by the effects of a substance or by another medical condition (APA, 2000). If an individual has tics but does not meet criteria for any of the aforementioned TD, a diagnosis of tic disorder not otherwise specified (TD-NOS) is given. Due to the more chronic nature of TS and CTD, these disorders tend to be more frequently studied and treated than TTD or TD-NOS.

Demographic Variables

The prevalence of tics among children and adolescents ranges from 6.6% to 18.5%, suggesting that tics are not as rare as previously believed (Khalifa & von Knorring, 2003; Kurlan et al., 2001; Mason, Banerjee, Eapen, Zeitlin, & Robertson, 1998). The prevalence of TS is thought to range from 0.04% to 3.8% (APA, 2000; Kurlan et al., 2001), while CTD are thought to affect 0.5% to 0.8% of the population (APA, 2000; Khalifa & von Knorring, 2003). Tourette's syndrome is more common in males than females by a ratio of between 2 and 9:1 (Apter, Pauls, Bleich, & Zohar, 1993; Burd, Kerbeshian, Wikenheiser, & Fisher, 1986).

The severity of tics typically changes across the life span. Onset generally occurs between the ages of 5 and 7 years. Motor tics of the face and head develop first, followed the emergence of other motor tics in the torso and extremities (Leckman, King, & Cohen, 1999). Phonic tics usually develop after motor tics, and simple tics (e.g., movements involving single muscle groups or brief vocalizations) typically precede complex tics (e.g., sequences of movements or whole words or phrases). The severity, frequency, and intensity of tics often fluctuate in a waxing and waning pattern, and an overall diminution of symptoms often occurs between childhood and adolescents in many cases (Coffey et al., 2000).

An important phenomenological feature of TD is the "premonitory urge," an aversive somatic sensation experienced as an itch, tingle, or tension that precedes tic occurrence (Leckman et al., 1999). Tics are associated with temporary alleviation or reduction of the urge, leading some to hypothesize that tics may in part be maintained by negative reinforcement associated with urge removal (Himle, Woods, Conelea, Bauer, & Rice, 2007). Up to 93% of those diagnosed with TS report the experience of a premonitory urge (Leckman, Walker, & Cohen, 1993). Young children may experience the urge; however, the ability to reliably report urge awareness is thought to emerge around the age of 10 years (Woods, Piacentini, Himle, & Chang, 2005).

It has been suggested that up to 90% of individuals diagnosed with a TD also meet criteria for another psychiatric disorder (Robertson, 2000). The most common co-occuring conditions are attention-deficit/hyperactivity disorder (ADHD), which has been shown to occur in 50% to 90% of those with TS, and obsessive-compulsive disorder (OCD), which co-occurs with TS at a rate of 25% to 80% (Walkup et al., 1999). In addition, research has suggested elevated rates of other anxiety, mood, and disruptive behavior disorders in children with tics (Kurlan et al., 2002). It is unclear whether the elevated rates of these conditions reflect a shared genetic association with TD or the psychosocial difficulties secondary to having a TD (Gaze, Kepley, & Walkup, 2006).

Impact of Tic Disorders

Many children and adults with TD experience functional impairment and a diminished quality of life due to the presence of tics (Elstner, Selai, Trimble, & Robertson, 2001; Storch et al., 2007). Those with TS may experience decreased social acceptability, peer relationship problems, poor self-concept, and increased difficulty with academic and occupational functioning (Woods, Marcks, & Flessner, 2007). Families are also impacted, as parents of children with TD experience increased parenting frustration, family conflict, marital difficulties, and decreased quality of parent–child interactions (Cohen, Ort, Leckman, Riddle, & Harding, 1988). Finally, tics can produce physical injury, such as pain in tic-related muscles, oral inflammation or infection, skin abrasions, bone fractures, or ocular injury (Woods, Friman, & Teng, 2001).

An Evaluation of Evidence-Based Practice for Tic Disorders

The following review of behavioral treatments for TD utilizes the evidence-based treatment criteria described by the American Psychological Association Task Force for Promotion and Dissemination of Psychological Procedures (Task Force, 1995) and by Chambless et al. (1998). The Task Force (1995) identified two different types of empirically supported treatments. *Well-established* treatments are those that meet the highest standard of scientific support. The efficacy of well-established treatments must be demonstrated in at least two rigorous randomized controlled trials comparing the treatment to a placebo condition or to another established treatment. Efficacy may also be demonstrated in a large series of rigorous single-subject experimental design studies. Finally, the treatment must be clearly described and effects must be demonstrated by at least two different research teams. *Probably efficacious* treatments are those supported by at least one randomized controlled trial comparing the treatment to a wait-list control. Treatments classified as *probably efficacious* are also those that are promising but do not yet have enough research support to be classified as *well-established* (e.g., need independent replication, larger sample size, descriptive manual, more single-subject analyses).

In a recent review of the literature on behavioral treatments for TD, Cook and Blacher (2007) noted that methodologically rigorous studies have been conducted for seven different psychosocial treatments for tics: habit reversal training (HRT), exposure and response prevention (ERP), cognitive-behavioral therapy (CBT), self-monitoring, massed negative practice (MNP), contingency management, and psychotherapy. In addition to these seven treatments, the current chapter also reviews the efficacy of relaxation as a monotherapy for TD. To our knowledge, there have not yet been any meta-analyses examining any of these treatments, nor have there been any consensus panel recommendations regarding their use. Therefore, only results from randomized controlled trials and single-subject experimental studies are discussed in the following sections.

HABIT REVERSAL TRAINING

Despite TD's neurobiological etiology (Leary, Reimschisel, & Singer, 2007; Pauls & Leckman, 1986), environmental factors play a large role in the disorder's maintenance and symptom fluctuations (Conelea & Woods, in press). Antecedent variables such as the presence of others (Watson & Sterling, 1998), tic-related talk (Woods, Watson, Wolfe, Two-hig, & Friman, 2001), boredom, stress, and anxiety (K. O'Connor, Brisebois, Brault, Robillard, & Loiselle, 2003; Silva, Munoz, Barickman, Friedhoff, 1995) have all been implicated as factors that can increase tic frequency. Environmental consequences including social attention (Watson & Sterling, 1998), tangible reinforcers (Himle & Woods, 2005; Woods & Himle, 2004), and the reduction of premonitory sensations contingent on tic occurrence (Himle et al., 2007; Verdellen et al., 2008) also appear to have tic-controlling properties. Such evidence suggests that behavioral interventions designed to alter such environmental factors and interrupt stimulus-response chains may be effective means of reducing tic frequency and facilitating symptom management.

Habit reversal training (HRT) is a multi-component behavioral treatment package, designed to treat TD by targeting such factors. Azrin and Nunn (1973) first introduced HRT

and it has since undergone slight revisions and become the subject of much research. HRT treats TD through (a) training awareness of tics and their warning signs, (b) instituting behaviors incompatible with tics (i.e., competing responses), (c) recruiting social support to facilitate compliance, (d) promoting generalization of treatment gains, (e) psychoeducation, and (f) function-based interventions (Azrin & Nunn, 1973; Woods et al., 2008). In awareness training, the client is trained to recognize his or her tics and their warning signs (e.g., premonitory urge sensations and/or the beginning stages of the movement or vocalization) as they occur in session and is instructed to monitor tics as they occur in the everyday environment. The purpose is to increase awareness of the tics themselves and the stimulus-response chains leading to their occurrence. Competing response training involves teaching the client to perform tic-incompatible behaviors (e.g., slow controlled blinking for an eye-blinking tic or diaphragmatic breathing for a vocal tic) for several minutes following a tic or its warning sign. Competing responses are introduced for tics sequentially, beginning with the most distressing tic and moving to the less troublesome tics. Social support involves recruiting significant individuals in the child's life (e.g., parents or teachers) to provide support, reminders, and praise for performing competing responses. This is done to increase treatment compliance and facilitate the generalization of competing responses to the everyday environment. Psychoeducation involves teaching children about the brain regions involved in TD, the high prevalence of tics in children, and other important information in order to normalize the child's experience and remove any self-stigmatization. HRT also emphasizes altering environmental factors identified in a functional analysis of tics. This may include removing tic-contingent reinforcers (e.g., parental attention or sympathy), introducing techniques to alter affective states associated with increases in tics (e.g., relaxation training for anxiety-provoking situations), or altering the environment so the client is less likely to come into contact with tic-exacerbating settings or events.

HRT usually requires 8 to 16 sessions. The first session includes gathering detailed background information, psychoeducation, introducing the rationale for HRT and its structure, and creating a tic hierarchy based on level of distress accompanying individual tics. In the second session, the therapist targets the highest tic on the hierarchy using the techniques just described. During the following session, the therapist treats the next tic on the hierarchy.

This process continues until all tics have been treated.

Randomized Controlled Trials

The first RCT of HRT was published in 1980 and showed superiority of HRT to massed negative practice (MNP) in 22 individuals (Azrin, Nunn, & Frantz, 1980). Since then, six additional well-designed RCTs have been conducted (Table 14.1). Of note, we were able to locate one additional RCT (Deckersbach, Rauch, Buhlmann, & Wilhelm, 2006) not

TABLE 14.1 Randomized Controlled Trials of Habit Reversal

Reference	Sample Characteristics	Comparison (N per condition)	Outcome Variable(s)	Findings
Azrin, Nunn, and Frantz (1980)	Adults and children (aged 11–16) with tics	HRT (10) vs. MNP (12)	SN	Significantly greater reduction in tics in HRT (92% reduction) than NP (33% reduction). Gains maintained for HRT group at 18-month follow-up.
Azrin and Peterson (1990)	Adults and children (aged 6–36) with TS	HRT (5) vs. WL (5)	DO (clinic and home)	Significantly greater percent reduction in tic frequency in HRT than WL.
K. P. O'Connor, Gareau, and Borgeat (1997)	Adults (aged 23–49) with chronic motor tics	HRT (7) vs. HRT + CT (6)	SM	Reductions at posttreatment and 3-month follow-up in HRT (54%, 77%) and HRT + CT group (57%, 86%).
K. P. O'Connor et al. (2001)	Adults with chronic tics	HRT + CT (47) vs. WL (22)	SM	Significant reductions in tic frequency (pre- to posttreatment) in HRT + CT, but not WL. Gains maintained in HRT + CT group at 12-month follow-up.
Wilhelm et al. (2003)	Participants with TS	HRT (16) vs. SP (13)	YGTSS	Greater reductions in tic severity scores in HRT than in SP at posttreatment. Gains maintained in HRT group at 10-month follow-up.
Verdellen, Keijsers, Cath, and Hoogduin (2004)	Adults and children (aged 7–55) with TS	HRT (22) vs. ERP (21)	YGTSS DO (clinic and home)	Statistically equivalent reductions post-treatment on all outcome measures in both conditions. Gains maintained in both groups at 3-month follow-up.
Deckersbach, Rauch, Buhlmann, and Wilhelm (2006)	Participants with TS	HRT (14) vs. SP (16)	YGTSS	Greater reductions in tic severity scores in HRT than in SP at posttreatment. Gains maintained in HRT group at 6-month follow-up.

Note: CT = cognitive therapy; ERP = exposure and response prevention; DO = direct observation; HRT = habit reversal training; MNP = massed negative practice; SM = self-monitoring; SP = supportive psychotherapy; TS = Tourette syndrome; WL = wait-list; YGTSS = Yale global tic severity scale included in Cook and Blacher's (2007) review. Over 200 participants (children and adults) with TS or another CTD have been included in these studies. Investigators have used a variety of control conditions (e.g., wait-list and alternative treatments) and outcome measures (e.g., self-monitored tic frequency, direct observation of tics, and clinician-rated symptom severity scales) to test its efficacy. All of these approaches have yielded favorable results for HRT.

Overall research design. In evaluating an RCT's research design, there are several important considerations essential to drawing sound causal inferences. Beyond design features common to all RCTs (i.e., random assignment of participants to either the treatment under investigation or one or more control conditions), one must also consider the characteristics of the study sample, the validity and reliability of the main outcome measures, the integrity of the treatment delivery, and the appropriateness of the data analytic approach. Examination of these features is essential for determining the extent to which a group of studies supports a specific treatment for a specific population.

In terms of characteristics, all studies have included either mixed child and adult samples (e.g., Azrin et al., 1980; Azrin & Peterson, 1990; Verdellen, Keijers, Cath, & Hoogduin, 2004) or adult-only samples (e.g., K. P. O'Connor et al., 2001; K. P. O'Connor, Gareau, & Borgeat, 1997). In all studies, participants met existing criteria for TS or another CTD, with the exception of Azrin and colleagues (1980), who included participants who would almost certainly have been diagnosed with TS or a CTD by today's standards (i.e., daily occurrence of tics, present for at least a year, and with childhood onset).

Habit reversal researchers have measured outcome in several ways. Direct methods have included acquiring data on tic frequency from self-monitoring or direct observation. Researchers using direct observation have quantified tics in several ways (e.g., raw frequency, tics per minute, or the percent of discrete time intervals in which a tic occurs). A 5-minute observation period yields a valid and reliable measure of tics regardless of the scoring method used (Himle et al., 2006). Additionally, researchers have used global symptom severity measures to assess primary outcome. The most common is the clinician-rated Yale Global Tic Severity Scale (YGTSS; Leckman et al., 1989), which has demonstrated excellent psychometric properties and yields overall severity ratings for motor, vocal, and total tics as well as a rating for tic-related functional impairment.

In all RCTs, the researchers delivered HRT in a manualized format or according to the guidelines of the treatment creators (e.g., Azrin & Nunn, 1973; Azrin & Peterson, 1988, 1990). The majority of the studies included only HRT-specific elements in the active treatment condition. However, two studies (K. P. O'Connor et al., 2001; K. P. O'Connor et al., 1997) included additional training in muscle control in tic-affected areas using biofeedback and cognitive restructuring along with HRT. Like Cook and Blacher (2007), we decided to include any well-designed RCT that used competing response training in the active treatment condition, since this element is arguably the central component to HRT (Woods, Miltenberger, & Lumley, 1996).

Outcome on symptom-specific measures. In all seven studies, there was a significant mean pre- to posttreatment improvement in the HRT group (see Table 14.1). The percentage of participants in the HRT condition experiencing substantial improvement at posttreatment tended to be quite high in these studies. For instance, Deckersbach, Rauch, Buhlmann, and Wilhelm (2006) found that 67% of HRT participants were "much improved" or "very much improved" at posttreatment. Other studies have found that over 80% of participants receiving HRT were virtually tic-free posttreatment (Azrin et al., 1980) and 90% showed at least an 88% reduction in tic frequency (Azrin & Peterson, 1990). The values of Cohen's *d* for HRT treatment on YGTSS tic severity scores tend to be large in these studies and have ranged from 1.06–1.50 (Verdellen, Keijers, Cath, & Hoogduin, 2004; Wilhelm et al., 2003).

In the five studies in which a between-group comparison (HRT vs. control) on main outcome measures was conducted, HRT outperformed the control group in four. HRT has demonstrated superiority to wait-list (Azrin & Peterson, 1990), negative practice (Azrin et al., 1980), and supportive psychotherapy (Deckersbach et al., 2006; Willhelm et al., 2003). In a direct comparison, exposure and response prevention (ERP) was equivalent to HRT (Verdellen et al., 2004). The remaining two investigations (K. P. O'Connor et al., 2001; K. P. O'Connor et al., 1997) do not allow one to determine whether HRT was superior to control. O'Connor and colleagues (2001) showed that the active treatment condition was statistically superior to wait-list. However, because individuals with both tic and habit disorders were included in the analyses comparing outcome between treatment groups, one cannot draw conclusions about its effect for the TD sample specifically. K. P. O'Connor and colleagues' (1997) study found statistically equivalent outcomes in the group treated with HRT alone compared to the group treated with HRT plus cognitive therapy, thus preventing any conclusions regarding the basic efficacy of HRT in this sample; however, large reductions in tic frequency from pretreatment to posttreatment were observed in both groups.

Follow-up. Establishing the durability of therapeutic gains is difficult due to problems maintaining contact with participants, the possibility that participants have sought additional treatment during the maintenance period, and the ubiquity of study dropouts (Chambless & Hollon, 1998). These difficulties notwithstanding, RCTs suggest that symptomatic improvements stemming from HRT are maintained after treatment has ended. The RCTs included in this review have examined follow-up data ranging from 2 to 18 months and

have found that participants tend to maintain treatment gains (Azrin et al., 1980; Deckersbach et al., 2006; K. P. O'Connor et al., 2001; K. P. O'Connor et al., 1997; Willhelm et al., 2003).

Clinical significance. Although HRT has a clear effect on tics, less is known about the treatment's effect on general functioning and quality of life. In general, RCTs have confined outcome measurement to symptom-specific indices; however, more recent studies have assessed impact on broad areas of functioning. For instance, the YGTSS includes a subscale score for overall impairment (range = 0–50) resulting from tics and HRT has been shown to produce substantially greater improvement on this scale compared to supportive psychotherapy (Wilhelm et al., 2003). In a later RCT, Deckersbach et al. (2006) tested the effect of HRT on self-report measures of general psychosocial functioning and quality of life. Although the HRT group improved in both domains, the improvement was no greater than that found in the supportive psychotherapy group.

Another dimension of clinical significance is the magnitude of symptomatic improvement. A magnitude of change placing participants either outside the distribution of the dysfunctional population or within the distribution of the functional population is a generally accepted definition of clinical significance (Jacobson & Truax, 1991). Although no RCTs have examined clinical significance using these criteria, some researchers (Azrin et al., 1980; Azrin & Peterson, 1990) have shown a near-100% reduction in tics posttreatment for some participants, potentially indicating clinical significance (Kazdin, 2003), although others (e.g., Verdellen et al., 2004) have not shown as dramatic an effect on tic frequency. Thus, the complete disappearance of tics following HRT can occur, but such a result is unlikely to occur in the majority of cases. Rather, the findings of Deckersbach et al. (2006) may offer a more reasonable estimate of HRT's clinical significance. In this study, approximately 67% of HRT participants were significantly improved at posttreatment.

Single-Subject Experimental Analyses

Because HRT was created within the field of applied behavior analysis, the majority of treatment studies have employed single-subject experimental designs. Cook and Blacher (2007) identified 14 studies (see Table 14.2). As is the case in RCTs, single-subject studies consistently support the effectiveness of HRT.

Overall research design. Single-subject studies of HRT for TD are designed to test the effect of the intervention or its individual components within subjects, not groups of subjects. Such designs rely on multiple repeated observations of the target behavior to account for general variance in the subject's behavior. As a result, the outcome measures often involve such strategies as direct observation or self-monitoring because they are more easily administered than clinician-rated instruments, which capture behavior over longer time frames (e.g., the YGTSS measures tics over the past week). Investigators use various designs to

TABLE 14.2   Single-Subject Experimental Analyses of Habit Reversal

Reference	Sample Characteristics	Design	Outcome Variable	Findings
Ollendick (1981)	2 participants (males, age 9–11) with tics	Multiple baselines across settings with FU	DO	Both children showed clear reductions in tics.
Finney, Rapoff, Hall, and Christopherson (1983)	2 participants (males, ages 11 & 12) with chronic motor tics	Multiple baselines across subjects and behaviors with FU	DO	Both participants' tics dropped to near zero levels following treatment. Gains maintained at 12-month FU.
Miltenberger and Fuqua (1985)	1 participant (female, age 67) with a squinting tic	Multiple baselines across subjects with FU	SM	Participant showed a decrease in mean tic frequency. At 1-month FU, tic returned to baseline levels.
Miltenberger, Fuqua, and McKinley (1985)	9 participants (3 males, 6 females, age 12–60) with chronic motor tics	Multiple baselines across subjects with FU	DO	8 subjects showed clear reductions in tics, maintained at FU.
Azrin and Peterson (1989)	1 participant (female, age 9) with an eye-blinking tic	Withdrawal design for first 2 experiments; AB with FU for 3rd experiment	DO	Participant's tic dropped to near- zero levels following treatment and remained at this level at 2-year FU.
Sharenow, Fuqua, and Miltenberger (1989)	3 participants (2 males, 1 female, age 24, 32, 66) with chronic motor tics	Multiple baselines across subjects and behaviors with FU	DO	All participants showed marked decline in tics. 2 participants were available at FU and maintained gains.
Peterson and Azrin (1992)	6 participants (males, 2 children, 4 adults) with TS	Alternating treatments design	DO	Significant reductions in tics during treatment conditions across participants.
Carr and Bailey (1996)	1 participant (male, age 9) with TS	Alternating treatments with withdrawal and FU	DO	Participant's tics were reduced and maintained at 1-month FU.
Carr, Bailey, Carr, and Coggin (1996)	2 participants (males, age 12) with TS	Alternating treatments design	DO	No significant reductions in tics for either participant. Authors noted that treatment was not implemented as planned.
Woods, Miltenberger, and Lumley (1996)	4 participants (3 males, 1 female, ages 8–12) with chronic tics	Multiple baselines across motor behaviors and subjects with FU	DO	Marked reductions in tics in all participants. For the 3 participants available at FU, gains were maintained in 2.

(Continued)

TABLE 14.2 Single-Subject Experimental Analyses of Habit Reversal *(Continued)*

Reference	Sample Characteristics	Design	Outcome Variable	Findings
Clarke, Bray, Kehle, and Truscott (2001)	4 participants (males, ages 11–16) with TS	Multiple baselines across subjects with FU	DO	3 of 4 showed reductions. Gains maintained at FU.
Woods and Twohig (2002)	3 participants (males, age 7, 9, 16) with chronic vocal tics	Multiple baselines across subjects with FU	DO	2 participants showed reductions in tics and 1 maintained gains at FU.
Woods, Twohig, Flesssner, and Roloff (2003)	5 participants (5 males, ages 10–13) with TS	Multiple baselines across subjects with FU.	DO	The treatment targeted vocal tics and was effective for 4 participants. 3 maintained gains at FU.
Carr, Sidener, Sidener, and Cummings (2005)	2 participants (males, age 8 & 12) with TS	Multiple baselines across subjects	DO	Both participants showed significant reductions in tics.

Note: DO = direct observation; FU = follow-up; SM = self-monitoring; TS = Tourette syndrome

address possible alternative explanations for observed reductions in tic frequency following implementation of treatment (e.g., the natural waxing and waning course of TD; Leckman et al., 1999). For instance, withdrawal designs (e.g., Azrin & Peterson, 1989), alternating treatment designs (e.g., Carr & Bailey, 1996), and multiple baselines across settings (e.g., Ollendick, 1981), subjects (e.g., Finney, Rapoff, Hall, & Christophersen, 1983), and behaviors (e.g., Miltenberger & Fuqua, 1985) have all been employed to address threats to internal validity in single-subject studies of HRT for TD. The reader is directed to Barlow and Hersen (1984) for a review of appropriate strategies for establishing experimental control in single-subject designs.

A total of 45 participants with TS or another CTD have been included in these studies. Of these, 30 (68%) were children and 35 (80%) were male. The treatment has been delivered and investigated in a variety of ways. Some investigators have examined the effect of HRT as a complete package (e.g., Finney et al., 1983; Woods & Twohig, 2002; Woods, Twohig, Flessner, & Roloff, 2003), while others have focused on the effect of individual treatment components. For example, researchers have investigated the effects of competing

response training, relaxation, awareness training, self-monitoring, and social support, alone or in various combinations with each other (e.g., Azrin & Peterson, 1989; Miltenberger, Fuqua, & McKinley, 1985; Peterson & Azrin, 1992; Woods et al., 1996).

Outcome. The majority of participants in these studies have shown a clear reduction in tics during treatment. Of the 45 participants included in these studies, only six have failed to respond to the intervention. Two of these nonresponders were identified in a study in which the authors noted that the treatment was not implemented as planned (Carr, Bailey, Carr, & Coggin, 1996). The overall response in individual subjects varies, with some subjects showing a clear but partial reduction in tics during treatment (e.g., Carr, Sidener, Sidener, & Cummings, 2005; Clarke, Bray, Kehle, & Truscott, 2001; Woods et al., 2003) and others reaching zero or near-zero levels in their target tic(s) (e.g., Azrin & Peterson, 1989; Miltenberger et al., 1985; Woods et al., 1996).

The efficacy of individual components of HRT. Habit reversal includes several components and there have been some attempts to identify those that are most active in producing tic reduction. For instance, Miltenberger and colleagues (1985) compared the effects of a complete HRT package (consisting of awareness training, a tic inconvenience review, relaxation, competing response practice, social support, and self-monitoring) to simplified HRT (awareness and competing response training alone). Five of 5 subjects receiving simplified HRT showed clinically significant reductions in their tics, and 3 out of 4 responded to the complete package. These nearly equivalent results suggest that awareness and competing response training were the essential ingredients in the treatment. A follow-up study of simplified HRT (Woods et al., 1996) supported the efficacy of a simplified treatment. The investigators examined the individual effects of four major treatment components: awareness training, self-monitoring, social support, and competing response training, when delivered in sequence to four children. These results provided the greatest support for the combination of awareness training, competing response training, and social support. Others have examined the effect of different delivery schedules of the competing response. Competing responses are more effective when delivered contingent upon the tics than when practiced in a noncontingent fashion (Miltenberger & Fuqua, 1985). Competing responses that were dissimilar in topography from the tic itself (e.g., tightening the bicep for a mouth twitching tic) were as effective as those that were physically incompatible with the tics (Sharenow, Fuqua, & Miltenberger, 1989).

Follow-up. Like RCTs, single-subject studies suggest that the effects of HRT are generally maintained after treatment has ended. Of the 14 studies, 11 reported follow-up data for periods ranging from 1 week to 24 months. In general, the reduction in tics at posttreatment remained at follow-up. For example, Azrin and Peterson (1989) observed a 100% reduction posttreatment in a participant's eye blinking tic, which remained absent at 2-year follow-up. In another study, of the three subjects responding to treatment and available at follow-up (8–17 weeks), two maintained near-zero levels of tics and one showed a partial return to his baseline level (Woods et al., 1996). Also, in a large single-

subject study including nine participants, eight responded to treatment and maintained gains at 1 to 15 week follow-up (Miltenberger et al., 1985). For the over 20 participants in these studies who showed a clear response to treatment and for which follow-up data were reported, treatment gains were maintained in all but four.

Clinical significance. Single-subject studies have rarely investigated changes in psychosocial functioning and general well-being in HRT. Two studies (Carr & Bailey, 1996; Miltenberger et al., 1985) delivered consumer satisfaction surveys to participants and showed some evidence that participants saw their tics as less distressing to themselves and others and were less uncomfortable around others as a result of treatment; however, these conclusions were made from responses to single items and not tested for statistical significance, making it difficult to draw strong conclusions. In another study, Woods and colleagues (1996) had observers rate participants' tics according to how problematic they appeared before and after treatment and found that observers rated each participants' tics as significantly less problematic after treatment. Also, the parents of the children participating in this study completed self-report measures and rated their children's tics as less distressing after treatment.

As has been observed in RCTs, the magnitude of symptom reduction is often substantially large to suggest clinical significance. For instance, in some studies, some participants have completely or nearly completely eliminated the target tic following treatment and at follow-up (e.g., Azrin & Peterson, 1989; Finney et al., 1983; Woods et al., 1996). Again, while the majority of participants have not demonstrated such a remarkable improvement, a minority appears to have experienced a near-100% improvement in the targeted tic.

Conclusions

Habit reversal is a psychosocial treatment for TD with a fairly large empirical basis. Twenty-one well-designed trials (7 RCTs, 14 single-subject studies) have been conducted and all but one (Carr et al., 1996) have shown evidence of effectiveness. In RCTs, significant improvements in the immediate symptoms of TD are statistically more pronounced than comparison treatments (e.g., negative practice and supportive psychotherapy), suggesting that outcome is treatment specific. Additionally, 13 well-designed single-subject studies have supported the treatment. Positive results are consistent regardless of the outcome measure used, sample characteristics (e.g., adults, children, or both), or the investigative team conducting the study. The magnitude of improvement is usually quite pronounced, with values of Cohen's *d* generally above 1 and a substantial minority of participants approaching a nearly complete elimination of their tic(s). Treatment gains are, in general, well-maintained at follow-up. Based on these data, HRT meets the criteria set forth by Chambless et al. (1998) for a *well-established* treatment. However, there is a need for further investigations on the efficacy of HRT, specifically in child and adolescent populations. Although three RCTs on HRT (Azrin et al., 1980; Azrin & Peterson, 1990; Verdellen et al., 2004) included children or adolescents in their study sample, no RCT has examined the effect of HRT in a child and adolescent only sample and only five large *N* (≥ 3) single-subject studies have shown HRT to be effective in child and adolescent participants.

EXPOSURE AND RESPONSE PREVENTION

Exposure and response prevention (ERP) is a *well-established* treatment for OCD (Chambless & Ollendick, 2001) that has also been investigated as a potentially effective treatment for TD. In the context of OCD, ERP involves directly exposing the client to his or her feared obsessions while preventing the performance of behaviors (i.e., compulsions) designed to reduce distress caused by these obsessions. Over repeated exposures, anxiety gradually decreases, leading to improvements in the symptoms of

OCD (Grayson, Foa, & Steketee, 1982). Given the frequent comorbidity of OCD and TD and the similar functional relationship premonitory urges and tics share with obsessions and compulsions, some have proposed that ERP can be adapted and used as an effective treatment for TD (Verdellen et al., 2004). Exposure and response prevention for TD involves exposing the client to premonitory sensations usually relieved by tics, while suppressing the tics themselves. The goal of treatment is to decrease the intensity of premonitory urges and their control over tic occurrence (Verdellen et al., 2004).

Randomized Controlled Trials

This treatment was first tested in an RCT by Verdellen and colleagues (2004). Forty-three participants (ages 7–55 years) with TS were randomized to HRT or ERP. Exposure and response prevention consisted of two training sessions in which participants were taught to suppress their tics for increasingly longer periods of time, followed by ten 2-hour sessions of ERP. Exposure involved focusing attention on the urge and the bodily areas in which they were located and/or exposure to tic-eliciting objects, along with instructions and encouragement to suppress tics. Following treatment, the two groups showed statistically equivalent changes in clinician-rated tic severity measures and in direct observation measures. The ERP group showed a large effect size on the YGTSS ($d = 1.42$) and moderate effect sizes on direct observation at home and in the clinic (d's = 0.90, 0.88, respectively). Following crossover, the group initially receiving HRT showed substantial incremental improvements in tic severity scores after completing ERP. The group initially receiving ERP showed no further improvement after HRT. Both groups maintained gains at 3-month follow-up.

Single-Subject Experimental Analyses

There has been only one small single-subject study of ERP for TD. Wetterneck and Woods (2006) examined the effect of an ERP protocol on three repetitive behaviors in a boy with TS.

Using multiple baselines across behaviors design and direct observation as an outcome measure, they observed a clear decline in the frequency of two of these behaviors. However, at 3-month follow-up, these behaviors had returned to baseline levels.

Conclusions

Exposure and response prevention is a new and promising treatment for TD. The treatment is thought to work through repeated exposures to urges in the context of tic suppression, which results in decreases in urge intensity and their control over tics (Verdellen et al., 2008). Exposure and response prevention has been shown to produce at least equivalent outcomes as HRT in a sample of participants with TS (Verdellen et al., 2004). Given these findings, the treatment may be considered *probably efficacious* according to the criteria set forth by Chambless et al. (1998). Nevertheless, there is a need to test the efficacy of ERP for TD in child and adolescent populations specifically, rather than in mixed adult and child samples.

COGNITIVE BEHAVIOR THERAPY

Cognitive approaches to the treatment of TD incorporate cognitive restructuring procedures aimed at challenging and modifying the client's thoughts related to tics. For example, treatment could target thoughts related to anticipation of high-risk tic situations and the appearance of tics to oneself and to others. When cognitive therapy is included in the treatment of a TD, it is typically used in conjunction with other behavioral treatments, such as HRT and ERP, rather than as a stand-alone approach. In HRT, cognitive techniques may be used as part of a function-based intervention to target thoughts that precede high-risk tic situations.

Randomized Controlled Trials

Two studies have examined the use of cognitive therapy in TD. K. P. O'Connor et al.

(1997) randomly assigned medication naive participants to either standard HRT ($N = 7$) or to CBT ($N = 7$), which included cognitive restructuring for thoughts related to tic anticipation. Outcome did not differ between the two groups. Both groups showed reductions in tic frequency and EMG levels and an increased perceived control over the tic. However, the study is limited by its small sample size. Studies with small samples are unlikely to detect differences between two treatments unless those differences are very large. Therefore, it is possible differences between the treatments would have been found if the sample had been larger. In addition to the low sample size, the study is limited because the HRT and CBT treatments shared awareness training as a treatment component, which alone can result in changes in tic frequency (Woods et al., 1996).

K. P. O'Connor et al. (2001) also examined the use of HRT plus cognitive restructuring in adults with TD and other habit disorders, such as nail biting, hair pulling, face scratching, and teeth grinding. Participants were randomly assigned to a 4-month treatment program consisting of HRT plus cognitive restructuring (TD: $N = 47$), or to a wait-list control (TD: $N = 22$). Tic frequency, tic intensity, and degree of tic control were assessed using daily self-report diaries completed by participants. Only participants in the treatment group showed a significant decrease in tic/habit frequency, decrease in tic/habit intensity, and increase in degree of control; however, participants with TD were not separated from those with habit disorders in analyses, limiting the conclusions that can be drawn about the efficacy of the treatment on TD alone. Another limitation concerned the authors' decision to examine the combined effect of HRT plus cognitive restructuring. Although this study lends some support to the CBT approach, it is unclear if the cognitive restructuring provides any incremental benefit beyond the effects of HRT alone.

Conclusions

Although CBT appears to be a promising treatment worthy of further investigation, the existing data do not support its classification as a probably efficacious or well-established treatment at this time (Cook & Blacher, 2007). To date, only one well-designed study has examined the efficacy of CBT alone as a treatment for TD (K. P. O'Connor et al., 1997). Although the O'Connor et al. study was limited by a small sample, results indicated that the treatment is not more efficacious than HRT. Several limitations in the existing research on CBT should be addressed in the future. First, research should be conducted to examine whether tic expression changes following cognitive restructuring alone. Second, future examinations comparing CBT and HRT should do their best to avoid overlapping treatment components that alone can produce changes in tic expression, such as awareness training. Third, given that all of the research on the efficacy of CBT has been conducted with adults, it would be helpful to examine the efficacy of this treatment in a sample of children and adolescents.

MASSED NEGATIVE PRACTICE

Massed negative practice is a behavioral procedure in which the client overrehearses a tic by purposefully performing it quickly and repeatedly. The tic is repeated for a specified duration of time, and practice trials are interspersed with periods of rest. MNP is based on the idea that tics are simple learned habits that can be reduced through a process called *reactive inhibition* (Yates, 1958). Reactive inhibition refers to a reduction in a behavior due to a high frequency of the behavior in the past. According to Yates, MNP causes the individual to become "tired" of performing the movement, resulting in a decreased tic frequency.

Randomized Controlled Trials

In the only controlled trial of MNP (Azrin, et al., 1980), participants were randomly assigned to either MNP ($N = 12$) or HRT ($N = 10$). Although results showed a 33% tic reduction following the first day of MNP, the average tic reduction was only 25% at 4-week follow-up. In comparison, HRT was associated with an 84% tic reduction following the first day of treatment, and gains appeared to be maintained through an 18-month follow-up. Because the study did not include an inactive control group, nothing specific can be said about the effects of MNP. The study does suggest that MNP may be a minimally effective treatment for tics, albeit much less effective than HRT.

Single-Subject Experimental Analyses

Although 18 single-subject designed studies have utilized MNP as a major or solitary treatment component, most of these are uncontrolled case studies (see Peterson & Azrin, 1993, for a review). Three single-subject experimental analyses found tic reductions following MNP (Knepler & Sewall, 1974; St. James-Roberts & Powell, 1979; Turpin & Powell, 1984), while one study found no lasting therapeutic change after the treatment (Canavan & Powell, 1981). Therefore, the support of MNP from single-subject research is limited and inconsistent.

Conclusions

The paucity of evidence supporting the efficacy of MNP and its inferiority to HRT have led to the conclusion that MNP is not a well-established or probably efficacious treatment (Cook & Blacher, 2007).

SELF-MONITORING

Self-monitoring involves training the individual with a TD to systematically observe and record tic occurrences for specific amounts of time on an ongoing basis. Although self-monitoring is frequently used as a method of data collection or as a component of awareness training in HRT, some research has examined its use as a monotherapy.

Single-Subject Experimental Analyses

Four studies using a multiple baseline across behaviors design examined the effect of self-monitoring as a sole treatment procedure for TD. Thomas, Abrams, and Johnson (1971) treated an 18-year-old male with multiple motor and vocal tics. One vocal tic decreased immediately and significantly on the first day of self-monitoring, but the other tics did not improve until other treatment procedures, such as reciprocal inhibition, were implemented. Billings (1978) instructed a 17-year-old female in self-monitoring and observed reductions in tic frequency and intensity. Hutzell, Platzek, and Logue (1974) used self-monitoring to treat an 11-year-old male with TS. Posttreatment and 1.5- and 12-month follow-up assessments indicated that tic frequencies remained low in the therapeutic setting and decreased to zero in other settings, such as home and school. Finally, Wright and Miltenberger (1987) found that self-monitoring was effective in reducing head and facial tics in a 19-year-old male. Wright and Miltenberger observed generalization effects in nonclinic situations.

Peterson and Azrin (1992) used an alternating treatments design to compare the impact of a single session of training in self-monitoring, relaxation, and HRT in six adult males with TS. Tic frequencies were assessed in the clinic using direct observation procedures. Tic frequencies were reduced by an average of 44% following self-monitoring, which was lower than the reductions observed following HRT (55%) and higher than those observed following relaxation training (32%).

Conclusions

To date, self-monitoring has not been examined in an RCT, which would be needed to determine whether the treatment is impacted by demand or placebo effects. Although three single-subject analyses demonstrate the efficacy of self-monitoring, one study found that it was only effective for one of the individual's tics (Thomas et al., 1971), and another study found that it was less efficacious than HRT (Peterson & Azrin, 1992). In addition, the majority of these studies were conducted with adults, limiting the conclusions that can be drawn about the efficacy of self-monitoring as a monotherapy for children with tics. Based on the limited support for self-monitoring as a monotherapy, Cook and Blacher (2007) concluded that it does not meet criteria for an empirically supported treatment.

CONTINGENCY MANAGEMENT

Contingency management is a behavioral treatment approach based on operant learning theory. From this perspective, tics are thought to be maintained, at least temporarily, by consequences that follow them. Contingency management can include reinforcement procedures, such as rewarding a child for tic-free periods, or punishment procedures, such as presenting an aversive stimulus contingent on tic occurrence.

Single-Subject Experimental Analyses

Although many studies have examined the use of contingency management, the majority of these studies employed an AB design or used contingency management as one of several behavioral procedures (see Peterson & Azrin, 1993, for a review). Three single-case experimental analyses have used strict operant contingency management procedures to treat TD.

Wagaman, Miltenberger, and Williams (1995) examined the efficacy of a differential reinforcement (DRO) procedure using an ABAB design. The participating child was a 9-year-old male with chronic vocal tics. The authors reinforced the absence of tics with money for each specified tic-free period. Tic frequencies decreased to near-zero levels when the DRO contingency was in place and returned to baseline levels when the contingency was removed, demonstrating the efficacy of the DRO contingency in controlling tic frequencies. For treatment purposes, the reinforcement contingency was faded out after 3 weeks. Treatment effects were maintained through a 50-week follow-up.

Watson and Sterling (1998) conducted a functional analysis to identify possible reinforcement contingencies maintaining a vocal tic in a 4-year-old female. Parental reports suggested that the tic only occurred during meals. The impact of social attention and tangible reinforcers on tic frequencies were assessed using a functional analysis during mealtimes. The tic was maintained by parental attention. The parents were instructed to withhold attention following tic occurrences and instead provide attention contingent upon tic-free periods. Following this intervention, the tic rate decreased to zero.

Roane, Piazza, Cercone, and Grados (2002) conducted a functional analysis in a 22-year-old male with vocal tics and autism. A preference assessment was then conducted to identify items that would compete with the occurrence of tics. Finally, the participant was seated at a table and given continuous access to preferred items as well as attention on a fixed interval schedule of reinforcement. Competing stimuli produced brief decreases in tics but did not reduce tic frequencies over longer periods of time. The noncontingent presentation of competing stimuli may have limited their ability to produce tic decreases. Instead, it may have been more effective for the participant to be given access to these preferred items contingent upon tic-free periods. It is also unclear whether the comorbid diagnosis of autism may have impacted the efficacy of contingency management.

Conclusions

Although the Wagaman et al. (1995) study provides support for the use of contingency management, this treatment alone may not be effective in all cases (Roane et al., 2002). In order to better understand the efficacy of contingency management as a treatment for TD, more research examining the impact of contingency management alone must be conducted using single-subject experimental designs and RCTs. At this time, contingency management does not meet criteria for an empirically validated treatment.

RELAXATION

Relaxation training is most often included as a component of a larger treatment package for TD. When relaxation is used as a monotherapy for TD, the individual is typically taught to engage in targeted relaxation of tic-related muscles contingent upon sensation of the urge, to regularly practice progressive muscle relaxation, and/or to use diaphragmatic breathing regularly or in high-risk tic situations.

Randomized Controlled Trials

One study has examined the efficacy of relaxation therapy as a stand-alone treatment. Bergin, Waranch, Brown, Carson, and Singer (1998) compared relaxation therapy ($N = 7$) to a "minimal therapy" condition ($N = 9$) for children and adults with TD (age: $M = 11.8$ years, $SD = 2.8$). The relaxation therapy condition consisted of instruction in multiple relaxation techniques, including awareness training, diaphragmatic breathing, behavioral relaxation, applied relaxation, and biofeedback. Participants in each condition received six weekly hour-long individual sessions. The groups did not differ in terms of tic severity at posttreatment and 3-month follow-up, suggesting that relaxation training alone is an ineffective treatment for tics; however, the study had a very small sample size and thus was unlikely to detect any differences between the two groups.

Single-Subject Experimental Analyses

As described in the previous section on self-monitoring, Peterson and Azrin (1992) examined the impact of relaxation training using a counterbalanced design. Videotapes were used to assess changes in tic frequency across conditions. As compared to baseline, tics were reduced by an average of 32% following relaxation training, suggesting that relaxation was less effective than self-monitoring and HRT in reducing tics. These results reflect immediate changes in tic frequency following a single session of relaxation training, which may obscure the benefit of long-term, repeated relaxation practice.

Conclusions

The majority of research examining relaxation training for TD has included it as a component in a larger treatment package, limiting the conclusions that can be drawn about the efficacy of relaxation training alone. Only one RCT has evaluated relaxation training as a monotherapy for TD and found that it is not superior to a placebo condition (Bergin et al., 1998). The only single-subject analysis of relaxation training indicated that relaxation training is less effective than other treatment strategies (Peterson & Azrin, 1992). Due to the lack of research supporting its efficacy, relaxation training does not meet empirically supported treatment criteria.

SUPPORTIVE PSYCHOTHERAPY

Supportive psychotherapy for tics aims to reduce distress and to improve self-esteem, global psychosocial functioning, life-satisfaction, and coping abilities. Treatment typically consists of psychoeducation about TS and discussion about the client's functioning, both related and unrelated to TS. As the client expresses feelings about current life issues, therapists provide encouragement, clarification, and reassurance.

Therapists also normalize the client's experience, model appropriate behavior, and reframe issues in an attempt to alter the client's perspective.

Randomized Controlled Trials

In the research literature, supportive psychotherapy has primarily been used as a control condition to examine the efficacy of HRT. As such, supportive psychotherapy in these studies was specifically designed to utilize a nondirective approach and did not include specific instruction in tic reduction strategies.

Wilhelm et al. (2003) examined the efficacy of supportive psychotherapy ($N = 13$) and HRT ($N = 16$) in a sample of adults with TS. Following 14 sessions of therapy, tic severity and functional impairment were unchanged from pretreatment in the supportive psychotherapy group, whereas tic severity and impairment significantly decreased in the HRT group. Deckersbach et al. (2006) conducted a similar RCT, assigning participants to either supportive psychotherapy ($N = 15$) or HRT ($N = 15$) for 14 sessions of treatment. As in the Wilhelm et al. study, only HRT was found to significantly reduce tic severity. However, results indicated that both groups significantly improved on measures of life satisfaction and psychosocial functioning at posttreatment, leading the authors to conclude that supportive psychotherapy may be beneficial as an adjunct to HRT or as an alternative for individuals who do not respond to HRT.

Conclusions

Although the Deckersbach et al. (2006) study shows that supportive psychotherapy may improve the lives of those with TS more globally, there is currently no evidence to suggest that the treatment reduces tic symptoms. Furthermore, HRT was demonstrated to be a more efficacious treatment for TS than supportive psychotherapy alone in two RCTs (Deckersbach et al., 2006; Wilhelm et al.,

2003). Given the lack of data supporting the efficacy of supportive psychotherapy, the treatment does not meet empirically supported treatment criteria. However, there may be promise for the treatment as an adjunct, as mentioned by Deckersbach and colleagues (2006). Future research will need to examine whether supportive psychotherapy procedures enhance the efficacy of other empirically supported treatments for TS.

EVIDENCE-BASED PRACTICES

Tic disorders are common conditions among children and adolescents that are associated with psychiatric comorbidity and impairments in general functioning and quality of life. The past three decades have seen the introduction and rigorous testing of several psychosocial treatments. Although TDs are commonly seen in clinical practice, many treatment providers know very little about appropriate psychological treatments and how they are to be implemented (Marcks, Woods, Teng, & Twohig, 2004). As such, there is a pressing need to disseminate accurate knowledge of evidence-based psychotherapy approaches for TD (Woods, Conelea, & Walther, 2007). The purpose of this review was to describe the most common psychosocial approaches to treating TD and to evaluate their empirical support.

Habit reversal and ERP were found to meet criteria for an evidence-based practice, with the labels of *well-established* and *probably efficacious*, respectively. Other interventions (e.g., MNP, CBT, self-monitoring, relaxation, contingency management, and supportive psychotherapy) have been tested and sometimes shown positive results; however, because of inferiority to a *well-established* treatment (e.g., MNP and supportive psychotherapy), research designs that do not allow for adequate testing of the intervention (e.g., CBT), and a limited number of well-conducted studies (e.g., self-monitoring, contingency management, and relaxation), designation of

these treatments as *probably efficacious* or *well-established* is premature.

For HRT, we evaluated the findings of 7 RCTs and 14 single-subject studies that tested HRT as either a complete treatment package or its major components. Single-subject analyses have shown clear reductions in tics as a result of treatment for the large majority of participants. Between-group experimental studies show HRT to be superior to no treatment (Azrin & Peterson, 1990), MNP (Azrin et al., 1980), and supportive psychotherapy (Deckersbach et al., 2006; Wilhelm et al., 2003). Evidence that HRT produces greater gains than alternative treatments suggests that the treatment is also *efficacious and specific* (Chambless & Hollon, 1998), meaning the effect appears to be a result of techniques specific to HRT and not simply caused by factors common to all forms of psychotherapy (e.g., regular contact with a professional, support, and a treatment rationale). The most active components appear to be competing response training, awareness training, and self-monitoring, with the addition of social support possibly serving an additionally important role in the treatment of children (Woods et al., 1996).

Although ERP is a *well-established* treatment for OCD, it has only recently been tested in the context of TD. The findings of a single RCT showed that the treatment was at least equivalent to HRT and one small single-subject study showed a reduction in repetitive behaviors associated with TS following treatment. Based on the results of the RCT, we can reasonably conclude that ERP is an evidence-based treatment for TD, but in need of further investigation by other researchers and replication in child and adolescent populations.

Despite the evidence supporting the use of HRT and ERP for TD, there are several important issues pertaining to HRT and ERP that have yet to be adequately investigated. First, while these treatments have an established effect on the tics themselves, improvements in general functioning and quality of life have rarely been examined. For instance, given that many children with TD experience problems in peer, family, and school functioning (Boudjouk, Woods, Miltenberger, & Long, 2000; Packer, 2005; Stokes, Bawden, Camfield, Backman, & Dooley, 1991; Wilkinson et al., 2002; Woods, 2002), it would be valuable to examine whether improvements in tic symptoms are accompanied by improvements in other domains of functioning. Second, there is a need to examine whether HRT and ERP can be disseminated to community settings and whether positive results are also seen in these settings. Third, little has been done to examine factors that may moderate the treatment's effects. Since children with TD often have co-occurring psychiatric disorders (e.g., ADHD and OCD; Kadesjö & Gillberg, 2000; Kurlan et al., 2002) and receive medication treatment for these other psychiatric disorders, it makes sense to examine whether these factors attenuate response to treatment. Finally, relatively little is known about processes through which these treatments exert their effect. Several hypotheses have been proposed. For instance, the creators of HRT (Azrin & Nunn, 1973) propose that the overcorrection procedure involved in competing response training may positively punish tics, thereby reducing their frequency. They also suggest that a growing awareness of tics during the course of treatment may mediate the effect of HRT on tics. Although these processes are likely to account for a proportion of the gains seen in HRT, the introduction of ERP as an efficacious treatment and recent research on the functional role of premonitory urges in tics suggest that changes in urge characteristics may mediate treatment effects. Self-reported urge severity increases during short periods of suppression (Himle et al., 2007) and gradually declines both within and across ERP sessions (Verdellen et al., 2008). Insofar as tic symptoms are maintained by negative reinforcement through reductions of premonitory

sensations and HRT and ERP involve suppression of tics in response to these sensations, successful treatment may depend on decreasing premonitory urges' intensity and control over tics. Future studies of mechanisms of change in HRT and ERP will be valuable to understanding treatment effects and modifying approaches to target mediating factors more directly.

It is also important to note that several medications have shown benefit for treating TD and constitute the mainstay of treatment for the disorder. The majority of these medications are dopamine antagonists (e.g., haloperidol, pimozide, and risperidone) that have shown evidence of greater effect than pill placebo (e.g., Ross & Moldofsky, 1978; Scahill, Leckman, Schultz, Katsovich, & Peterson, 2003; A. K. Shapiro & Shapiro, 1984; E. Shapiro, Shapiro, Fulop, & Hubbard, 1989). However, various aversive side effects may result in poor medication adherence (Jagger et al., 1982). To date, there have been no head-to-head trials comparing the effectiveness of medications to psychosocial treatments for TD. Future studies would do well to examine the relative efficacy of medication compared to psychosocial treatments and whether there are advantages to one treatment over the other in terms of cost-effectiveness in both the short and long term.

In conclusion, psychologists have at their disposal two evidence-based treatments for TD in children: HRT and ERP. Given HRT's more extensive research base, especially when used in treating children, it should be used as the first-line treatment. Exposure and response prevention, despite being an efficacious treatment, has not been rigorously tested as a treatment for children, and should therefore be used with more caution and an understanding of the limitations in its empirical basis. As scientists continue to examine these treatments, we are likely to gain further information on the boundaries of their effect and how to maximize overall effectiveness. We also hope to see their greater use in routine clinical practice.

REFERENCES

American Psychiatric Association. (2000). *Diagnostic and statistical manual of mental disorders* (4th ed., text rev.). Washington, DC: Author.

Apter, A., Pauls, D. L., Bleich, A., & Zohar, A. H. (1993). An epidemiologic study of Gilles de la Tourette's syndrome in Israel. *Archives of General Psychiatry, 50*, 734–738.

Azrin, N. H., & Nunn, R. G. (1973). Habit-reversal: A method of eliminating nervous habits and tics. *Behaviour Research and Therapy, 11*, 619–628.

Azrin, N. H., Nunn, R. G., & Frantz, S. E. (1980). Habit reversal vs. negative practice treatment of nervous tics. *Behavior Therapy, 11*, 169–178.

Azrin, N. H., & Peterson, A. L. (1988). Habit reversal for the treatment of Tourette syndrome. *Behaviour Research and Therapy, 26*, 347–351.

Azrin, N. H., & Peterson, A. L. (1989). Reduction of an eye tic by controlled blinking. *Behavior Therapy, 20*, 467–473.

Azrin, N. H., & Peterson, A. L. (1990). Treatment of Tourette syndrome by habit reversal: A wait-list control group comparison. *Behavior Therapy, 21*, 305–318.

Barlow, D. H., & Hersen, M. (1984). *Single case experimental designs: Strategies for studying behavior change* (2nd ed.). Needham Heights, MA: Allyn & Bacon.

Bergin, A., Waranch, H. R., Brown, J., Carson, K., & Singer, H. S. (1998). Relaxation therapy in Tourette syndrome: A pilot study. *Pediatric Neurology, 18*, 136–142.

Billings, A. (1978). Self-monitoring in the treatment of tics: A single-subject analysis. *Journal of Behavior Therapy and Experimental Psychiatry, 9*, 339–342.

Boudjouk, P. J., Woods, D. W., Miltenberger, R. G., & Long, E. S. (2000). Negative peer evaluation in adolescents: Effects of tic disorders and trichotillomania. *Child and Family Behavior Therapy, 22*, 17–28.

Burd, L., Kerbeshian, J., Wikenheiser, M., & Fisher, W. (1986). A prevalence study of Gilles de al Tourette syndrome in North Dakota school-age children. *Journal of the American Academy of Child Psychiatry, 25*, 552–553.

Canavan, A. G. M., & Powell, G. E. (1981). The efficacy of several treatments of Gilles de la Tourette's syndrome as assessed in a single case. *Behaviour Research and Therapy, 19*, 549–556.

Carr, J. E., & Bailey, J. S. (1996). A brief behavior therapy protocol for Tourette syndrome. *Journal of Behavior Therapy and Experimental Psychiatry, 27*, 33–40.

Carr, J. E., Bailey, J. S., Carr, C. A., & Coggin, A. M. (1996). The role of independent variable integrity in the behavioral management of Tourette syndrome. *Behavioral Interventions, 11*, 35–45.

Carr, J. E., Sidener, T. M., Sidener, D. W., & Cummings, A. R. (2005). Functional analysis and habit-reversal treatment of tics. *Behavioral Interventions, 20*, 185–202.

Chambless, D. L., Baker, M. J., Baucom, D. H., Beutler, L. E., Calhoun, K. S., Crits-Christoph, P., . . . Woody, S. R. (1998). Update on empirically validated therapies, II. *The Clinical Psychologist, 51*, 3–16.

Chambless, D. L., & Hollon, S. D. (1998). Defining empirically supported therapies. *Journal of Consulting and Clinical Psychology, 66*, 7–18.

Chambless, D. L., & Ollendick, T. H. (2001). Empirically supported psychological interventions: Controversies and evidence. *Annual Review of Psychology, 52*, 685–716.

Clarke, M. A., Bray, M. A., Kehle, T. J., & Truscott, S. D. (2001). A school-based intervention designed to reduce the frequency of tics in children with Tourette's syndrome. *School Psychology Review, 30*, 11–22.

Coffey, B. J., Biederman, J., Geller, D. A., Spencer, T., Park, K. S., Shapiro, S. J., & Garfield, S. B. (2000). The course of Tourette's disorder: A literature review. *Harvard Review of Psychiatry, 8*, 192–198.

Cohen, D. J., Ort, S. I., Leckman, J. F., Riddle, M. A., & Harding, M. T. (1988). Family functioning and Tourette's syndrome. In D. J Cohen, R. D. Brunn, & J. F. Leckman (Eds.), *Tourette's syndrome and tic disorders: Clinical understanding and treatment* (pp. 179–196). Oxford, England: Wiley.

Conelea, C. A., & Woods, D. W. (2008). The influence of contextual factors on tic expression in Tourette's syndrome: A review. *Journal of Psychosomatic Research, 65*, 487–496.

Cook, C. R., & Blacher, J. (2007). Evidence-based psychosocial treatments for tic disorders. *Clinical Psychology: Science and Practice, 14*, 252–267.

Deckersbach, T., Rauch, S., Buhlmann, U., & Wilhelm, S. (2006). Habit reversal versus supportive psychotherapy in Tourette's disorder: A randomized controlled trial and predictors of treatment response. *Behaviour Research and Therapy, 44*, 1079–1090.

Elstner, K., Selai, C. E., Trimble, M. R., & Robertson, M. M. (2001). Quality of life (OQL) of patients with Gilles de la Tourette's syndrome. *Acta Psychiatrica Scandinavica, 103*, 52–59.

Finney, J. W., Rapoff, M. A., Hall, C. L., & Christophersen, E. R. (1983). Replication and social validation of habit reversal treatment for tics. *Behavior Therapy, 14*, 116–126.

Gaze, C., Kepley, H. O., & Walkup, J. T. (2006). Co-occurring psychiatric disorders in children and adolescents with Tourette syndrome. *Journal of Child Neurology, 21*, 657–664.

Grayson, J. B., Foa, E. B., & Steketee, G. (1982). Habituation during exposure treatment: Distraction vs. attention focusing. *Behaviour Research and Therapy, 20*, 323–328.

Himle, M. B., Chang, S., Woods, D. W., Pearlman, A., Buzzella, B., Liviu, B., & Picentini, J. C. (2006). Establishing the feasibility of direct observation in the assessment of tics in children with chronic tic disorders. *Journal of Applied Behavior Analysis, 39*, 429–440.

Himle, M. B., & Woods, D. W. (2005). An experimental evaluation of tic suppression and the tic rebound effect. *Behaviour Research and Therapy, 43*, 1443–1451.

Himle, M. B., Woods, D. W., Conelea, C. A., Bauer, C. C., & Rice, K. A. (2007). Investigating the effects of tic suppression on premonitory urge ratings in children and adolescents with Tourette's syndrome. *Behaviour Research and Therapy, 45*, 2964–2976.

Hutzell, R. R., Platzek, D., & Logue, P. E. (1974). Control of symptoms of Gilles de la Tourette's syndrome by self-monitoring. *Journal of Behavior Therapy and Experimental Psychiatry, 5*, 71–76.

Jacobson, N. S., & Truax, P. (1991). Clinical significance: A statistical approach to defining meaningful change in psychotherapy research. *Journal of Consulting and Clinical Psychology, 59*, 12–19.

Jagger, J., Prusoff, B. A., Cohen, D. J., Kidd, K. K., Carbonari, C. M., & John, K. (1982). The epidemiology of Tourette's syndrome: A pilot study. *Schizophrenia Bulletin, 8*, 267–278.

Kadesjö, B., & Gillberg, C. (2000). Tourette's disorder: Epidemiology and comorbidity in primary school children. *Journal of the American Academy of Child and Adolescent Psychiatry, 39*, 548–555.

Kazdin, A. E. (2003). *Research design in clinical psychology* (4th ed.). Boston, MA: Allyn & Bacon.

Khalifa, N., & von Knorring, A. (2003). Prevalence of tic disorders and Tourette syndrome in a Swedish school population. *Developmental Medicine & Child Neurology, 45*, 315–319.

Knepler, K. N., & Sewall, S. (1974). Negative practice paired with smelling salts in the treatment of a tic. *Journal of Behavior Therapy and Experimental Psychiatry, 5*, 189–192.

Kurlan, R., Como, P. G., Miller, B., Palumbo, D., Deeley, C., Andresen, E. M., . . . McDermott, M. P.. (2002). The behavioral spectrum of tic disorders. *Neurology, 59*, 414–420.

Kurlan, R., McDermott, M. P., Deeley, C., Como, P. G., Brower, C., Eapen, S., et al. (2001). Prevalence of tics in schoolchildren and association with placement in special education. *Neurology, 57*, 1035–1048.

Leary, J., Reimschisel, T., & Singer, H. S. (2007). Genetic and neurobiological bases of Tourette syndrome. In D. W. Woods, J. C. Piacentini, & J. T. Walkup (Eds.), *Treating Tourette syndrome and tic disorders: A guide for practitioners* (pp. 58–84). New York, NY: Guilford Press.

Leckman, J. F., King, R. A., & Cohen, D. J. (1999). Tic and tic disorders. In J. F. Leckman & D. J. Cohen (Eds.), *Tourette's Syndrome: Tics, obsessions, compulsions*. New York, NY: Wiley.

Leckman, J. F., Riddle M. A., Hardin M., Ort S. I., Swartz K. L., Stevenson J., & Cohen, D. J. (1989). The Yale global tic severity scale: Initial testing of a clinician-rated scale of tic severity. *Journal of the American Academy of Child and Adolescent Psychiatry, 28*, 566–573.

Leckman, J. F., Walker, D. E., & Cohen, D. J. (1993). Premonitory urges in Tourette's syndrome. *American Journal of Psychiatry, 151*, 98–102.

Marcks, B. A., Woods, D. W., Teng, E. J., & Twohig, M. P. (2004). What do those who know, know? Investigating providers' knowledge about Tourette's syndrome and its treatment (2004). *Cognitive and Behavioral Practice, 11*, 298–305.

Mason, A., Banerjee, S., Eapen, V., Zeitlin, H., & Robertson, M. M. (1998). The prevalence of Tourette syndrome in a mainstream school population. *Developmental Medicine and Child Neurology, 40*, 292–296.

Miltenberger, R. G., & Fuqua, R. W. (1985). A comparison of contingent vs. non-contingent competing response practice in the treatment of nervous habits. *Journal of Behavior Therapy and Experimental Psychiatry, 16*, 195–200.

Miltenberger, R. G., Fuqua, R. W., & McKinley, T. (1985). Habit reversal with muscle tics: Replication and component analysis. *Behavior Therapy, 16*, 39–50.

O'Connor, K. P., Brault, M., Robillard, S., Loiselle, J., Borgeat, F., & Stip, E. (2001). Evaluation of a cognitive behavioral program for the management of chronic tic and habit disorders. *Behaviour Research and Therapy, 39*, 667–681.

O'Connor, K., Brisebois, H., Brault, M., Robillard, S., & Loiselle, J. (2003). Behavior activity associated with onset in chronic tic and habit disorder. *Behaviour Research and Therapy, 41*, 241–249.

O'Connor, K. P., Gareau, D., & Borgeat, F. (1997). A comparison of a behavioural and cognitive-behavioural approach to the management of chronic tic disorders. *Clinical Psychology and Psychotherapy, 4*, 105–117.

Ollendick, T. H. (1981). Self-monitoring and self-administered overcorrection: The modification of nervous tics in children. *Behavior Modification, 5*, 75–84.

Packer, L. E. (2005). Tic-related school problems: Impact on functioning, accommodations, and interventions. *Behavior Modification, 29*, 876–899.

Pauls, D. L., & Leckman, J. F. (1986). The inheritance of Gilles de la Tourette's syndrome and associated behaviors: Evidence for autosomal dominant transmission. *New England Journal of Medicine, 315*, 993–996.

Peterson, A. L., & Azrin, N. H. (1992). An evaluation of behavioral treatments for Tourette syndrome. *Behaviour Research and Therapy, 30*, 167–174.

Peterson, A. L., & Azrin, N. (1993). Behavioral and pharmacological treatments for Tourette Syndrome: A review. *Applied and Preventive Psychology, 2*, 231–242.

Roane, H. S., Piazza, C. C., Cercone, J. J., & Grados, M. (2002). Assessment and treatment of vocal tics associated with Tourette's syndrome. *Behavior Modification, 26*, 482–498.

Robertson, M. M. (2000). Tourette syndrome, associated conditions and the complexities of treatment. *Brain, 123*, 425–462.

Ross, M. S., & Moldofsky, H. (1978). A comparison of primozide and haloperidol in the treatment of Gilles de la Tourette's syndrome. *American Journal of Psychiatry, 135*, 585–587.

Scahill, L., Leckman, J. F., Schultz, R. T., Katsovich, L., & Peterson, B. S. (2003). A placebo-controlled trial of risperidone in Tourette syndrome. *Neurology, 60*, 1130–1135.

Shapiro, A. K., & Shapiro, E. (1984). Controlled study of primozide vs. placebo in Tourette's syndrome. *Journal of the American Academy of Child Psychiatry, 23*, 161–173.

Shapiro, E., Shapiro, A. K., Fulop, G., & Hubbard, M. (1989). Controlled study of haloperidol, primozide, and placebo for the treatment of Gilles de la Tourette syndrome. *Archives of General Psychiatry, 46*, 722–730.

Sharenow, E. L., Fuqua, R. W., & Miltenberger, R. G. (1989). The treatment of muscle tics with dissimilar competing response practice. *Journal of Applied Behavior Analysis, 22*, 35–42.

Silva, R. R., Munoz, D. M., Barickman, J., & Friedhoff, A. J. (1995). Environmental factors and related fluctuations of symptoms in children and adolescents with Tourette's disorder. *Journal of Child Psychology & Psychiatry, 36*, 305–312.

St. James-Roberts, N., & Powell, G. E. (1979). A case-study comparing the effects of relaxation and massed practice upon tic frequency. *Behaviour Research and Therapy, 17*, 401–403.

Stokes, A., Bawden, H. N., Camfield, P. R., Backman, J. E., & Dooley, J. M. (1991). Peer problems in Tourette's disorder. *Pediatrics, 87*, 936–942.

Storch, E. A., Lack, C. W., Simons, L. E., Goodman, W. K., Murphy, T. K., & Geffken, G. R. (2007). A measure of functional impairment in youth with Tourette's syndrome. *Journal of Pediatric Psychology, 32*, 950–959.

Task Force on Promotion and Dissemination of Psychological Procedures. (1995). Training in and dissemination of empirically validated psychosocial treatments: Report and recommendations. *The Clinical Psychologist, 48*, 3–23.

Thomas, E. J., Abrams, K. S., & Johnson, J. B. (1971). Self-monitoring and reciprocal inhibition in the modification of multiple tics of Gilles de la Tourette's syndrome. *Journal of Behavior Therapy and Experimental Psychiatry, 2*, 159–171.

Turpin, G., & Powell, G. E. (1984). Effects of massed practice and cue-controlled relaxation on tic frequency in Gilles de la Tourette's syndrome. *Behaviour Research and Therapy, 22*, 165–178.

Verdellen, C. W. J., Hoogduin, C. A. L., Kato, B. S., Keijers, G. P. J., Cath, D. C., & Hoijtink, H. B. (2008). Habituation of premonitory sensations during exposure and response prevention treatment of Tourette's syndrome. *Behavior Modification, 32*, 215–227.

Verdellen, C. W. J., Keijers, G. P. J., Cath, D. C., & Hoogduin, C. A. L. (2004). Exposure with response prevention versus habit reversal in Tourettes's syndrome: A controlled study. *Behaviour Research and Therapy, 42*, 501–511.

Wagaman, J. R., Miltenberger, R. G., & Williams, D. E. (1995). Treatment of a vocal tic by differential reinforcement. *Journal of Behavior Therapy and Experimental Psychiatry, 26*, 35–39.

Walkup., J. T., Khan, S., Schuerholz, L., Paik, Y.-S., Leckman, J. F., & Schultz, R. T. (1999). Phenomenology and natural history of tic-related ADHD and learning disabilities. In J. F. Leckman & D. J. Cohen (Eds.), *Tourette's syndrome: Developmental psychopathology and clinical care* (pp. 63–79). New York, NY: Wiley.

Watson, T. S., & Sterling, H. E. (1998). Brief functional analysis and treatment of a vocal tic. *Journal of Applied Behavior Analysis, 31*, 471–474.

Wetterneck, C. T., & Woods, D. W. (2006). An evaluation of the effectiveness of exposure and response prevention on repetitive behaviors associated with Tourette's syndrome. *Journal of Applied Behavior Analysis, 39*, 441–444.

Wilhelm, S., Deckerbach, T., Coffey, B. J., Bohne, A., Peterson, A. L., & Baer, L. (2003). Habit reversal versus supportive psychotherapy: A randomized controlled trial. *American Journal of Psychiatry, 160*, 1175–1177.

Wilkinson, B. J., Newman, M. B., Shytle, R. D., Silver, A. A., Sanberg, P. R., & Sheehan, D. (2002). Family impact of Tourette's syndrome. *Journal of Child and Family Studies, 10*, 477–483.

Woods, D. W. (2002). The effect of video based peer education on the social acceptability of adults with Tourette's syndrome. *Journal of Developmental and Physical Disabilities, 14*, 51–62.

Woods, D. W., Conelea, C. A., & Walther, M. R. (2007). Barriers to dissemination: Exploring the criticisms of behavior therapy for tics. *Clinical Psychology: Science and Practice, 14,* 279–282.

Woods, D. W., Friman, P. C., & Teng, E. J. (2001). Physical and social impairments in persons with repetitive behavior disorders. In D. W. Woods and R. G. Miltenberger (Eds.), *Tic disorders, trichotillomania, and other repetitive behavior disorders: Behavioral approaches to analysis and treatment* (pp. 33–51). Boston, MA: Kluwer Academic.

Woods, D. W., & Himle, M. B. (2004). Creating tic suppression: Comparing the effects of verbal instruction to differential reinforcement. *Journal of Applied Behavior Analysis, 37,* 417–420.

Woods, D. W., Marcks, B. A., & Flessner, C. A. (2007). Management of social and occupational difficulties in persons with Tourette syndrome. In D. W. Woods, J. C. Piacentini, & J. T. Walkup (Eds.), *Treating Tourette syndrome and tic disorders* (pp. 265–278). New York, NY: Guilford Press.

Woods, D. W., Miltenberger, R. G., & Lumley, V. A. (1996). Sequential application of major habit-reversal components to treat motor tics in children. *Journal of Applied Behavior Analysis, 29,* 483–493.

Woods, D. W., Piacentini, J., Himle, M. B., & Chang, S. (2005). Premonitory urge for tics scale (PUTS): Initial psychometric results and examination of the premonitory urge phenomenon in youths with tic disorders. *Journal of Developmental & Behavioral Pediatrics, 26,* 397–403.

Woods, D. W., Piacentini, J. C., Chang, S., Deckersbach, T., Ginsberg, G., Peterson, A. L., . . . Wilhelm, S. (2008). *Managing Tourette's syndrome: A behavioral intervention for children and adults (therapist guide).* New York, NY: Oxford University Press.

Woods, D. W., & Twohig, M. P. (2002). Using habit reversal to treat chronic vocal tic disorder in children. *Behavioral Interventions, 17,* 159–168.

Woods, D. W., Twohig, M. P., Flessner, C. A., & Roloff, T. J. (2003). Treatment of vocal tics in children with Tourette syndrome: Investigating the efficacy of habit reversal. *Journal of Applied Behavior Analysis, 36,* 109–112.

Woods, D. W., Watson, T. S., Wolfe, E., Twohig, M. P., & Friman, P. C. (2001). Analyzing the influence of tic-related talk on vocal and motor tics in children with Tourette's syndrome. *Journal of Applied Behavior Analysis, 34,* 353–356.

Wright, K. M., & Miltenberger, R. G. (1987). Awareness training in the treatment of head and facial tics. *Journal of Behavior Therapy and Experimental Psychiatry, 18,* 269–274.

Yates, A. J. (1958). The application of learning theory to the treatment of tics. *Journal of Abnormal and Social Psychology, 56,* 175–182.

15

Encopresis

MICHAEL W. MELLON

OVERVIEW OF ENCOPRESIS

In the last decade, the field of clinical psychology has endeavored to explore the concept of *evidence-based psychosocial treatments* in an effort to summarize and better disseminate knowledge about which psychological treatments appear to provide the greatest to human maladaptive behavior. Given that epidemiology studies (Bellman, 1966; Van der Wal, Benninga, & Hirasing, 2005) would estimate in the United States between 604,000 and 3 million children would meet the diagnostic criteria for encopresis, the need for evidence-based knowledge for treating this elimination disorder is even more relevant.

Although there seems to be a lack of interest in childhood encopresis, this author believes this *biobehavioral* disorder may provide some of the best examples in which evidence-based psychosocial treatments, or those combined with medical interventions, have been established. Further, the research literature provides an interesting body of evidence as to the possible mechanisms of action that not only account for the etiology of the disorders but also the mediating and moderating variables through which and for whom particular treatments work. This chapter reviews the literature regarding psychosocial treatments of functional fecal soiling or encopresis primarily since the 1990s and focuses discussion on the effectiveness of biofeedback and combined

medical and behavioral interventions. Conclusions regarding the treatment of encopresis are less confident than the most common elimination disorder, nocturnal enuresis, although certain methods seem to be more effective than others. The author emphasizes a biobehavioral conceptualization of encopresis, as this perspective is related to greater efficacy in treatment.

Diagnostic Criteria

The passage of feces into one's clothing after the age of 4 years, occurring with a frequency of at least one soiling accident per month and lasting at least 6 months, with the soiling not due to organic disease, is referred to as encopresis (American Psychiatric Association, 1994). Currently, there is discussion regarding the definition of encopresis with some researchers distinguishing between fecal soiling with or without constipation and stool withholding, or age of onset for constipation and soiling (Benninga, Voskuijl, & Taminiau, 2004; Loening-Baucke, 2004). This discussion is quite necessary to better define research populations and treatment relevant characteristics of children who present with encopresis.

For example, a European pediatric gastroenterology research group (Rasquin-Weber et al., 1999) developed a new set of diagnostic criteria known as the "Rome II Criteria in Childhood Defecation Disorders" in order to standardize definitions so that different researchers would better coordinate their work. The Rome II criteria was compared to more traditional definitions for constipation and fecal soiling with evidence that neither approach fully captures all the various presentations of defecation disorders (Voskuijl et al., 2004). The Rome II criteria failed to recognize 16% of children with pediatric constipation, and the standard criteria failed to recognize 11% of children with functional constipation and functional fecal retention in a cohort of 198 consecutive clinic patients. Eighty-four percent of the cohort met the criteria for encopresis, and of these patients, 79% exhibited functional constipation and functional fecal retention. This study continues to tell the same story of encopresis: Soiling is often and primarily associated with symptoms of constipation and a history of painful defecation.

For the purpose of this book chapter, the classic criteria encopresis (Loening-Baucke, 2002) will be used and is described as follows: defecation frequency less than three times per week, two or more episodes of encopresis per week, periodic passage of very large amounts of stool every 7 to 30 days (often so large they clog the toilet), and a palpable abdominal or rectal mass at physical examination. Although not part of this definition, descriptions of the child engaging in retentive posturing, actively avoiding defecation by purposefully contracting the pelvic floor muscles and gluteus muscles, are often reported by parents or caregivers.

Demographic Variables

Among school-age children, as many as 1.5% to 7.5% will meet the diagnostic criteria, with boys at least 2 times more likely to evidence constipation and soiling (Bellman, 1966; Van der Wal et al., 2005). The symptom evolution of constipation that frequently leads to overflow soiling can span more than 5 years until the child presents for treatment (Partin,

Hamill, Fischel, & Partin, 1992). Complaints of constipation in infants and children account for approximately 3% of pediatric visits and as many as 25% of pediatric gastroenterology visits each year (Lewis & Rudolph, 1997), with as many as 68% to 86% experiencing pain with defecation (Loening-Baucke, 1993). Even after standard medical treatment for the encopresis, as many as 36% to 42% of children will persist with constipation and soiling, attesting to the difficulty in effectively treating this common childhood disorder (Procter & Loader, 2003; Rockney, McQuade, Days, Linn, & Alario, 1996).

The behavioral and emotional characteristics of children with encopresis described in the literature are meager and somewhat inconsistent. However, several trends bear mentioning in respect to effective management of the encopretic child. Psychological and behavioral factors are thought to have an effect not only on the evolution of fecal incontinence (e.g., coercive toilet training, birth of a sibling, start of school) but also on the maintenance of the problem (e.g., externalizing behavior and nonadherence, low self-esteem and hopelessness, family conflict, psychiatric problems in parents) (Cox et al., 2003). For example, children with soiling demonstrate significantly more symptoms of anxiety or depression, less expressiveness and organization in the family environment, greater attention and social problems, more disruptive behaviors, and poorer school performance than nonsymptomatic children (Cox, Morris, Borowitz, & Sutphen, 2002). Furthermore, 20% more of the encopretic sample exceeded clinical thresholds in their behavioral symptoms compared with nonencopretic children. Additional evidence suggests lower levels of social competency in encopretic children versus nonclinical children (Young et al., 1995). Thus, encopretic children appear to have demonstrable behavioral dysregulation. Finally, in a population-based study of 8,242 children between the ages of 7 and 8 years old in the United Kingdom, Joinson, Heron, Butler, and Von Gontard

(2006) reported that children who soil have significantly more emotional and behavioral problems than those who do not soil, including more problems with attention, hyperactivity, obsessions and compulsions, oppositional behavior, and higher rates of being involved in overt bullying (both as victim and perpetrator). Whether these differences precede or are the result of the stress incurred by having encopresis has yet to be disentangled. However, the behavioral–emotional difficulties observed in encopretic children attest to the differences in the complexity of this problem compared to children with mono-symptomatic nocturnal enuresis. This emotional–behavioral complexity, combined with the greater physiological complexity in the mastery of bowel continence, will likely have to be addressed in the design of effective treatments for childhood encopresis.

Summary of Evidence-Based Bio-Psychosocial Intervention Studies

The history of treating encopresis has included singular medical attempts to reduce the obvious problems of constipation using bowel cathartics and stool softeners, singular psychological attempts to reduce the obvious stool withholding and avoidance of stooling using reinforcement procedures for appropriate toileting and clean underwear, invasive biofeedback to eradicate the paradoxical contraction of the external anal sphincter, or combinations of all of the above. Many of the investigations have included single case (primarily for psychologically-oriented treatments) or small group intervention designs, which preclude drawing reliable conclusions about what works versus natural spontaneous recovery. The conservative conclusions drawn from the review by McGrath, Mellon, and Murphy (2000) were that no empirically established treatments have emerged from the literature. However, treatments that combine medical interventions for constipation with behavioral procedures to increase appropriate toileting

have an average cure rate of 55%–63%. Combining biofeedback and medical management to treat abnormal defecation dynamics and constipation have an average cure rate of 67%. Both types of interventions were considered to meet the criteria for "probably efficacious" treatments. These reviewers also indicated that reliable conclusions about the literature could not be made due to inconsistent definitions of outcome, few randomized controlled studies, and a general lack of manualized treatments. Similar conclusions were drawn by Brazzelli and Griffiths (2008), who completed a comprehensive review of behavioral and cognitive interventions for defecation disorders in children. They reported no significant benefit from biofeedback therapy compared to conventional medical management plus behavior therapy and measured in terms of long-term recovery from soiling. Combined medical management and behavior therapy is significantly better than either treatment component alone. These authors also report the lack of well-controlled studies of adequate sample sizes.

This chapter reviews studies that report the most informative findings regarding the treatment of encopresis. These areas include studies for the use of new types of laxatives for constipation, biofeedback, and those treatments that combine medical and behavioral interventions to address the fecal soiling (detailed in summary tables). When available, information regarding mediators and moderators of treatment are discussed. Further review of the psychosocial burden of encopresis is also presented. Finally, a biobehavioral model conceptualizing the emergence and maintenance of encopresis in the context of learning processes is presented in an effort to suggest future research directions.

The reader will appreciate that the eventual mastery of fecal continence is more complicated than that of nocturnal urinary continence for several reasons. Urination happens more frequently than defecation, and thus, there are more opportunities for practice and eventual mastery. Because the problem of fecal incontinence is essentially a daytime phenomenon, there are significantly more environmental distractions that compete with appropriate toileting compared to nocturnal enuresis, which occurs during a state of sleep. Finally, the effect of constipation and fecal retention is thought to significantly reduce the internal sensations that signal the need to use the toilet, further making the mastery of fecal continence more difficult for the encopretic child. Encopresis is likely governed primarily by operant and social-learning influences in its treatment as compared to those less behaviorally complex responses (i.e., pelvic floor contraction and possible arousal from sleep to visit toilet) necessary to maintain urinary continence during sleep.

TREATMENTS FOR CONSTIPATION: LAXATIVES

Given that the vast majority of children with encopresis have struggled with chronic constipation, nearly all of these children will be treated for this problem. Research on effective treatments for constipation has a long history with significant confusion over definitions. As indicated early, the Rome II criteria has been described as too restrictive and misses a substantial portion of children who are described with traditional definitions. The Paris Consensus on Childhood Constipation Terminology (Benninga et al., 2005) recommends defining constipation in a child if over the past 8 weeks there have been fewer than three bowel movements per week, more than one soiling accident per week, large amounts of stool in the rectum or palpable stool in an abdominal examination, large diameter stool that when passed obstructs the toilet, retentive posturing and withholding behavior, and painful defecation. Thus, constipation is the first target of most encopresis treatments for more than 85% of these children. Although considered an essential part of treatment, used

as a unitary intervention for constipation and soiling it is considered to lack efficacy (McGrath et al., 2000).

Consensus Panel Recommendations

The North American Society for Pediatric Gastroenterology and Nutrition (NASPGN) published evidence-based guidelines for assessing and treating pediatric constipation that includes four steps (Baker et al., 1999). Step one includes education to demystify the problem for the patient and caregiver regarding the development of constipation, painful defecation, and withholding behavior that leads to soiling. Step two involves disimpaction of the hard and large amount of stool in the rectum through the use of oral or rectal laxatives, and for long-term maintenance. The third step is the prevention of reaccumulation of stool in the rectum with dietary interventions or long-term use of laxatives. Finally, the last step requires long-term follow-up with the child to manage any relapses that might occur, as these are common. The types of stimulant laxatives to achieve successful treatment and management of constipation are numerous.

Randomized Controlled Trials

Given that as many as 70% to 90% of children who present with encopresis struggle with constipation, the initial treatment includes laxatives and stool softeners (Benninga et al., 2004). There are many choices available for stool softeners with newer preparations coming on the market. The literature lists constipation treatments that lubricate the bowel such as mineral oil, products that stimulate bowel movements such as senna extract or bisacodyl, and osmotic laxatives such as phosphate enemas or magnesium citrate. The osmotic laxative called polyethylene glycol is now considered a mainstay for constipation treatment and has undergone considerable scrutiny for efficacy. Its safety record is good and is now available over the counter. Table 15.1

TABLE 15.1 Summary of Recent Medical Interventions for Constipation and Encopresis

Study	Pashankar and Bishop (2001)	Pashankar, Bishop, and Loening-Baucke (2003)	Loening-Baucke et al. (2004)	Voskuijl et al. (2004)
Sample Size	N = 24 (4 dropped out)	N = 74; (Grp1: constipation only = 43 Grp2: constipation + Encopresis = 31)	Grp1 (placebo): n = 11 Grp2 (Glucomannan fiber): n = 20	Grp1: (PEG 3350) N = 50. 4 withdrew Grp2: (Lactulose) N = 50. 5 withdrew
Ethnicity	American	American	American, Italian	Dutch
Mean Age	6.09 years, range 1.5 to 11 years	Grp1: 6.6 years Grp2: 8.4 years	Grp1: 6.6 years Grp2: 7.4 years	Grp1: 6.5 years Grp2: 6.5 years
Gender (male)	9 males	Grp1: 23 male Grp2: 17 male	Grp1: 5 male Grp2: 11 male	Grp1: 27 males Grp2: 28 males
Outcome Measures	Stools/week, stool consistency, soiling/week, frequency of reported fear of, pain with or blood in stooling.	Stools/week, stool consistency, soiling/week, frequency of reported fear of, pain with or blood in stooling. Successful Tx = >/= 3 BMs/week and no soiling in last month of Tx.	Stools/week, stool consistency, soiling/week, frequency of reported fear of, pain with or blood in stooling. Successful Tx = >/= 3 BMs/week and < 1 soiling in last 3 weeks of Tx. Frequency of abdominal discomfort during Tx.	Stools/week, stool consistency, soiling/week. Successful Tx = >/= 3 BMs/week and < 1 soiling in last 2 weeks of Tx. Frequency of abdominal discomfort during Tx and follow period.
Therapists	Physicians	Physicians	Physicians	Not reported
Setting	University Hospital	University Hospital	Pediatric clinics in Iowa and Italy	4 Pediatric Hospitals
Treatments	Polyethylene glycol 3350 (Miralax) for 8 weeks	Polyethylene glycol 3350 (Miralax). Grp1: 8.3 months; Grp2: 10 months	Grp1: placebo = maltodextrins; Grp2: glucomannan— a polysaccharide. 4 weeks of initial treatment and then crossed over to other treatment for 4 weeks.	Grp1: PEG 3350 (Miralax®) Grp2: Lactulose Children in both groups on toileting schedule and given rewards for adhering to schedule.
Results	Weekly stooling increased from 2.3 to 16.9; softened significantly; soiling declined from 10 to 1.3 per week. Mean effective dose 0.84 g/kg/d.	Grp1: stools/week 2.2 to 9.9; significant reduction in all measures of constipation. Grp2: stools/week 3.0 to 12.5; soiling/week 11.0 to 1.8: significant reduction in all measures of constipation. Mean effective dose 0.7 g/kg/d for both groups.	Grp1: (placebo) stools significantly softer and less soiling; Grp2: significantly more BMs/week vs. baseline and placebo, and significantly softer stools and less soiling vs. baseline, significantly less abdominal pain vs. placebo, significantly more patients successfully treated and improved compared to placebo.	Significant increase in stools, decrease in soiling for both groups throughout 8 weeks of Tx. No differences between groups at end of 8-week trial. Significantly more subjects in Grp1 successfully treated than Grp2. When Grp2 switched to PEG 3350, significantly more successes compared to lactulose trial. Significantly more side effects with lactulose vs. PEG 3350. PEG 3350 tasted significantly worse than lactulose.

(Continued)

TABLE 15.1 Summary of Recent Medical Interventions for Constipation and Encopresis (*Continued*)

Study	Pashankar and Bishop (2001)	Pashankar, Bishop, and Loening-Baucke (2003)	Loening-Baucke et al. (2004)	Voskuijl et al. (2004)
Follow-Up	None	None	None	18 weeks after treatment with open label of PEG 3350 for all subjects.
Main Findings	Miralax very effective in short-term relief of constipation and soiling with no significant side effects.	Miralax very effective in short-term relief of constipation and soiling with no significant side effects.	Glucomannan more effective than placebo in increasing frequency of BMs/ week and general improvement of soiling.	PEG 3350 had significantly more successes than lactulose, had significantly less side effects, but tasted worse than lactulose.
Type of Study	Single group, open-label, pretest-posttest.	Two group, open-label, pretest-posttest.	Double blind, placebo-controlled crossover study with 4 weeks of each phase of study.	Double blind, parallel groups, randomized, prospective and multicenter study. 8 weeks of treatment, then all subjects in 18-week follow-up treated with PEG 3350.
Significance to Literature	Effective osmotic laxative for constipation with minimal side effects.	Effective osmotic laxative for constipation with minimal side effects.	New stool softener with minimal side effects to deal with constipation.	Miralax significantly more effective for constipation and soiling than lactulose.

reviews several studies that utilize polyethylene glycol, or PEG 3350 (Miralax), in effectiveness studies (Pashankar & Bishop, 2001) and compared to other laxatives such as lactulose (Voskuijl et al., 2004) or glucomannan fiber (Loening-Baucke, Miele, & Staiano, 2004). These studies certainly argue for the superiority of PEG 3350 in managing constipation as a first step in treating the majority of children who present with encopresis. Voskuijl et al. (2004) are the only researchers who completed a true RCT with PEG 3350, although the findings for all studies listed in Table 15.1 are consistent with the conclusion that this treatment is effective for its stated purpose and with minimal side effects. A recent randomized trial of liquid paraffin compared to lactulose demonstrated greater efficacy for the former (Farahmand, 2007). The robustness of the research findings is diminished, as the study was not blinded.

Meta-Analyses of Group Designs

A systematic review of stimulant laxatives use for constipation was undertaken through the Cochrane Collaboration (Price & Elliott, 2008). The purpose of this meta-analysis of the literature was to determine the effect of stimulant laxative treatment in children with constipation and soiling, including randomized controlled trials that compared stimulant laxatives to placebo or alternative treatments. However, the authors concluded that there were no studies that met the stringent inclusion criteria for review. There continues to be a significant need for additional research in studies of adequate size and appropriate controls to allow consensus statements regarding evidence-based practice for stimulant laxative therapy in the treatment of constipation and soiling.

Single-Subject Experimental Analyses

Use of single-subject research designs are essentially nonexistent in the medical literature,

as this methodology is typically associated with behavioral psychology research.

Meta-Analyses of Single-Subject Experiments

Use of meta-analysis methodology to summarize treatment effects over large populations of subjects has been available for more than two decades. However, the use of metaanalysis for single-case experimental designs is just now being promulgated with ongoing discussion of how to actually do this research (Schlosser, 2005; Schlosser & Sigafoos, 2008). At this time, there have been no published studies using this methodology to summarize any types of treatments for children with constipation and encopresis.

Conclusions

In spite of the fact that few, if any, systematic and well-controlled investigations of the use of laxatives have been completed, their use is common and considered an essential first step in the treatment of children with chronic constipation and encopresis. This is clearly the conclusion of Price and Elliot (2008): "The need clearly exists to establish a more secure footing for treatment decisions and adequately sized trials are required to provide comparative data on commonly used drugs." Others (van Dijk, Benninga, Grootenhuis, Onland-van Nieuwenhuizen, & Last, 2007) indicate it is difficult to judge the effectiveness of laxatives separately from behavioral interventions as studies commonly include both. Nonetheless, the constipation subcommittee of the North American Society for Pediatric Gastroenterology and Nutrition strongly indicates that disimpaction and long-term prevention of reaccumulation of stool is achieved with the use of laxatives. The initial clean-out can be accomplished by either oral or rectal treatment using hypertonic phosphate enemas, hyperosmolar milk of molasses enema, polyethylene glycol oral lavage solution, and high dosages of laxatives (Loening-Baucke, 2002).

TREATMENT: MEDICAL-BEHAVIORAL INTERVENTIONS

The use of singular behavioral interventions in the treatment of encopresis has been explored and found to have some level of efficacy. However, the trend in the research literature is to combine the medical components that address chronic constipation with the behavioral interventions that are needed to make necessary behavioral and lifestyle changes in the encopretic child in order to overcome the fecal soiling. This next section will review what kinds of combined treatments have the best evidence for recovery from encopresis. Further, the reader will recognize that the role of biofeedback in the treatment of retentive encopresis is considered largely ineffective (and perhaps unnecessary) compared to standard treatment methods that combine laxatives and traditional behavioral interventions that utilize contingency management strategies.

Consensus Panel Recommendations

Partly informed by the recommendations of the North American Society for Pediatric Gastroenterology and Nutrition (NASPGN), a European clinical research group has recently published guidelines for a protocolized behavioral approach for chronic constipation and fecal incontinence (van Dijk et al., 2007). The authors' goals were to thoroughly review the treatment literature with regard to behavioral interventions to determine effectiveness and then develop a protocolized intervention for children 4–8 years old and children 9–18 years old. The behavioral interventions consist of five steps labeled with the keywords describing the components of treatment: "Know" involves the psychoeducational effort to understand the etiology of the disorder, "Dare" to deal with the anxiety and avoidance behavior associated with defecation, "Can" is

when the child learns to do the medical aspects of treatment and master efficient defecation technique, "Will" is when the parents are taught how to reinforce the child for adherence to treatment, and "Do" is when the necessary long-term toileting routines are established. The program is modified for older children and reflects their capacity for a greater sophistication and understanding of the problem and their ability to participate in record keeping. The authors hope that the operationally defined protocol will contribute to improved quality of research by standardizing the intervention.

In the United States, a recent guideline was published by clinical experts at the University of Michigan and disseminated through the federally funded National Guidelines Clearinghouse (University of Michigan, 2008). The guideline team reviewed the existing literature regarding diagnosis and treatment to provide clearly defined algorithms to manage constipation and soiling in children. The algorithms differentiate between children less than 1 year and older than 1 year and provide guidance for accurate diagnosis, thorough assessment of the disorder, and broad spectrum treatment including education, specific cleanout procedures, diet modification, behavioral training, and steps for long-term management and fading of treatment. These guidelines are a valuable contribution to the proper management of chronic constipation and encopresis.

Randomized Controlled Trials

The types of treatments for encopresis that have been examined in the context of randomized controlled trials have included biofeedback alone, or combined with standard medical interventions that utilized laxatives, scheduled toilet visits, and simple reinforcement procedures to promote adherence to the medical regimen and BMs in the toilet. This section will highlight the most important findings. Specific details of each cited study are listed in Table 15.2.

TABLE 15.2 Summary of Recent Medical and Behavioral Treatments for Encopresis

Study	Cox et al. (1998)	Van Ginkel et al. (2000)	Borowitz et al. (2002)	Van Ginkel et al. (2003)	Hibi et al. (2003)	Ritterband et al. (2003)	Croffie et al. (2005)	Unal and Pehlivanturk (2005)
Sample Size	Grp1: N = 29 Grp2: N = 27 Grp3: N = 31 All patients with constipation/ Encopresis	Grp1: N = 25 Grp2: N = 23 All patients with constipation/ Encopresis	Reanalysis of the same subjects in the Cox et al. (1998) study with 6- and 12-month follow-up.	N = 418 primarily constipated children. 90% were soiling (84% soiling > 2 times/ week; 60% having < 3 BMs in toilet per week).	N = 19 children with Encopresis (13 had received conventional medical treatment of enemas, suppositories, or laxatives).	Grp1: N = 12 Grp2: N = 12 All patients with constipation/ Encopresis.	Grp1: N = 24 Grp2: N = 12 All patients with dyssynergic defecation and constipation/ encopresis who failed conventional medical treatment (laxative + behavior toilet training for at least 6 months).	N = 86. 67 (78%) children were re-evaluated after 6 years of follow-up.
Ethnicity	American	Dutch	American	Dutch	Japanese	Grp1: 11 White, 1 Black Grp2: 10 White, 2 Black	American	Turkish
Mean Age	Grp1: 8.5 years Grp2: 8.7 years Grp3: 8.4 years	Grp1: 8.0 years Grp2: 8.0 years	Grp1: 8.5 years Grp2: 8.7 years Grp3: 8.4 years	Median age = 8.0 (6 to 10 years)	8.1 years (range 5–13 years)	Grp1: 8.57 years Grp2: 8.34 years	For total sample N = 36: 9.2 years (range 6–14 years)	Baseline: 8 years (range 4.1 to 13.7 years). At follow-up: 14.1 years. (range 9.7 to 20.0 years)
Gender (male)	Grp1: 22 male Grp2: 25 male Grp3: 25 male	Grp1: 21 male Grp2: 20 male	Grp1: 22 male Grp2: 25 male Grp3: 25 male	279 male (67%)	14 males	Grp1: 10 male Grp2: 9 male	For total sample N = 36: 30 males	At follow-up: 52 males (77.6%)
Outcome Measures	No. of soiling/day for 14 days before and after 3 months Tx; Successful vs. Unsuccessful; cost of Tx; BMs in toilet/day, self-initiated BMs, parental prompts to	No. of soiling/ week; No. of BMs in toilet/week; colonic transit time; anorectal manometry (anal rest pressure, max. squeeze pressure,	No. of soiling/day for 14 days before and after 3 months Tx: Successful vs. Unsuccessful; cost of Tx; BMs in toilet/ day, self-initiated BMs, parental	No. of soiling/ week, No. of BMs in toilet/ week, defecation details and abdominal discomfort, use of laxatives.	Kelly scores reflect presence of soiling, fecal straining, and pelvic floor function on a 3 point scale of frequency of	No. soiling/ week, No. BMs in toilet/week, bathroom use with/without parent prompt, Encopresis knowledge	No. of soiling/week; No. BMs in toilet/week; days of laxative use/week. Recovered = >3 BMs in toilet/week with no discomfort + <2 soiling episodes/months with no or rare use of laxatives.	No. soiling/ months, demographic questionnaire of school progress, parental education, Encopresis type, presence of

(Continued)

TABLE 15.2 Summary of Recent Medical and Behavioral Treatments for Encopresis (*Continued*)

Study	Cox et al. (1998)	Van Ginkel et al. (2000)	Borowitz et al. (2002)	Van Ginkel et al. (2003)	Hibi et al. (2003)	Ritterband et al. (2003)	Croffie et al. (2005)	Unal and Pehlivanturk (2005)
	toilet, painful defecation.	sensory threshold, critical volume, normal defecation dynamics. Success = < 1 soiling episode per 2 weeks; relapses at follow-up (not defined).	prompts to toilet, painful defecation.	Success = >/= 3 BMs/week, < 2 soiling/month, while not on any laxatives. Lesser outcomes determined by use of laxatives and less frequency of BMs in toilet or increased frequency of soiling.	occurrence and strength of pelvic floor squeeze.	Questionnaire (EKQ) and the Virginia Encopresis/ Constipation Apperception Test (VECAT).		constipation, other psychiatric comorbidities.
Therapists	Physicians, psychologists	Physicians	Physicians, psychologists	Physicians	Physicians	Psychologists	Physician and nurse. Parent support in BF	Child Psychiatrists
Setting	Medical Center	Medical Center	Medical Center	Medical Center	Children's Research Hospital	Subject's primary care MD, Web group used service over Internet in home	Children's Hospital	University Hospital, Department of Child Psychiatry
Treatments	Grp1: Intensive Medical Care—IMC (enemas, stool softeners, dietary changes). Grp2: Enhanced Toilet Training—ETT (IMC +, defecation instruction, incentives for independent toileting).	Grp1: Biofeedback alone (sensory training, expelling saline filled balloon). Grp2: Biofeedback + oral lactulose (5 g/10 kg of body weight / day divided into 2 doses).	Grp1: Intensive Medical Care— IMC (enemas, stool softeners, dietary changes). Grp2: Enhanced Toilet Training— ETT (IMC +, defecation instruction, incentives for	All children got standard conventional treatment (enemas, lactulose of 5 g/10 kg of body wt/day, high-fiber diet, constipation education, praise and small gifts for compliance. 297 of	If subject had constipation they were cleaned out prior to biofeedback (BF). BF completed 2 sessions/day for 7 days while in hospital.	All subjects were under the care of primary MD (67% taking laxatives at start of study). Grp1: Web (Enhanced Toilet Training delivered over Internet with 27	All subjects got cleansing enemas prior to BF training. Grp1: Anorectal manometry + biofeedback to change dyssynergic defecation response. Subjects had 5, 30 minute sessions at 2-week intervals in an outpatient clinic. Grp2: same clinic training as for Grp1 + home-based	Verbal therapy for child and parent to address causes of and stress of soiling, behavior therapy for bowel habits, psychoactive meds when needed for psychiatric problem, dietary

	Study 1	Study 2	Study 3	Study 4	Study 5	Study 6	Study 7	Study 8
	Grp3: Biofeedback-BF (IMC + ETT + anal EMG recording to relax sphincter while doing valsalva).	Subjects randomly assigned to groups, but nonblinded to laxatives.	independent toileting). Grp3: Biofeedback-BF (IMC + ETT + anal EMG recording to relax sphincter while doing valsalva).	children also got 5 biofeedback sessions or 2 anorectal manometry sessions. Laxatives continued until successful. Relapsed retreated with same protocol.	Subjects were taught to relax external anal sphincter while defecating saline filled balloon.	training modules about constipation, soiling, and its management). Home visit to set up computer and complete pretest questionnaires and follow-up phone calls for 3 weeks. Grp2: No-Web. Home visit to set up computer and complete pretest questionnaires and follow-up phone calls for 3 weeks.	EMG external anal sphincter feedback for 2, 5-minute sessions each day. The home-based training lasted until last day of clinic-based training.	modification and stool softeners when needed.
Results	Groups equivalent on all baseline measures. ETT and BF significantly less soiling than IMC; ETT significantly more successes than IMC and BF; ETT sign. Less costly than IMC only; for all groups significant reduction in BM's in toilet, self-toileting,	Group were equivalent in all baseline measures, colonic transit times, and % of children with abnormal defecation dynamics. Both groups showed equal and significant reduction in	Groups equivalent on all baseline measures. No sign. Differences between groups in soiling/day at 3 months, 6 months, and 12 months after initiation of treatment. Grp 2 showed significantly more children improving, but no	At baseline, significantly more boys were encopretic (68% vs. 52%) and soiling more often than girls. At 1-year follow-up 59% successful, 83% successful but still on laxatives. After 5 years, 70% successful.	Significant improvement in Kelly scores at end of treatment, and 3, 6, and 12 months after treatment. 65% of patients showed clinical improvement with no soiling after 1 week of BF treatment.	Groups equivalent on all pretest measures. Web group showed significant reduction in soiling/week, increase in BMs in toilet/week, increase use of bathroom with and without	Pretreatment group differences on outcome variables were not reported. All subjects learned appropriate defecation dynamics after 5 BF sessions. No significant differences between groups at posttreatment, 2 months, 4 months, or long-term follow-up on any outcome measure. 71%, 92%, and 61% of Grp1 and 83%, 83%,	First analysis compared the baseline variables of 67 children to the 19 lost to follow-up, and there were no differences in demographic or clinical variables. The total sample of 67 children at follow-up showed

(Continued)

TABLE 15.2 Summary of Recent Medical and Behavioral Treatments for Encopresis *(Continued)*

Study	Cox et al. (1998)	Van Ginkel et al. (2000)	Borowitz et al. (2002)	Van Ginkel et al. (2003)	Hibi et al. (2003)	Ritterband et al. (2003)	Croffie et al. (2005)	Unal and Pehlivanturk (2005)
	reduced parent prompting.	soiling/week (7 to 2 episodes). BF only showed significantly more successes than BF + laxatives with 100% of later grp relapsing between 12 and 26 weeks after treatment.	group differences in number of children cured. No differences between groups in self-initiated BMs in toilet at 6 and 12 months.	Successful Tx associated with less severe soiling at baseline and if constipation emerged after 4 years-old. Seventeen percent of girls and 41.8% of boys relapsed within 1 year. Boys relative risk of relapse 1.73 vs. girls.	60% of successful treated children had soiling at 6 months follow-up.	parent prompts. No differences on EKQ or VECAT between groups.	and 58% of Grp2 recovered at 2 months, 4 months, and long-term follow-up, respectively. For total sample ($N = 36$), significant increase in BMs in toilet/week, reduction in soiling/week, and reduction in laxative use/week at all time points.	that 41.8%, 70.1%, and 83.6% recovered completely in an average time of 21.2 months when assessed by 1, 3, and 6 years after treatment. Only 36% of subjects were constipated. Second analysis compared those recovered vs. not-recovered. Recovery significantly related to child having better school performance, greater parent education, having secondary Encopresis, and shorter period of constipation.
Follow-Up	None	12 weeks, 26 weeks, 12 months	6 and 12 months after treatment	Median of 5 years (range 1–8 years)	3, 6, and 12 months after treatment	None	2 months, 4 months, and long-term follow-up (mean = 44 months)	1, 3, and 6 years

Main Findings	Combined medical and behavioral intervention superior to medical alone. Behavior therapy with direct instruction of toileting superior to biofeedback on multiple measures.	Children without constipation do not benefit from laxative treatment when combined with BF. BF helpful with nonconstipated children. Normalization of defecation dynamics unrelated to success.	Combined medical and behavioral intervention lead to more children succeeding in treatment with less visits. Significant findings from 1998 did not hold up at 6 and 12 months.	Recovery is steady and slow over 5 years. Early symptoms of constipation and Encopresis related to poor outcome. Relapse more likely with males than females.	One intense week of BF shows significant improvement in soiling. Relapse of 60% at 6 months after treatment suggests additional training is needed.	Internet treatment program for Encopresis that is paired with regular care from primary MD is more effective at reducing soiling and increasing BMs in toilet than non-Internet contact.	BF training in the clinic produced a significant improvement in Encopresis. Home BF practice did not enhance treatment outcome.	Complete recovery from Encopresis associated with absence of constipation, more educated children and parents, and when symptom duration was shorter.
Type of Study	Randomized trial of 3 treatments with pretest-posttest measures.	Randomized trial of 2 treatments with pretest-posttest measures.	Randomized trial of 3 treatments with pretest-posttest measures.	Single group, multiple measures, and followed up to 8 years.	Single group, pre-test, posttest study with up to 12 months of follow-up.	Randomized trial of treatment vs. no-treatment, pretest-posttest.	Randomized trial of two treatments, with posttest and extended follow-up comparisons.	Single group, pretest, follow-up at 1, 3, and 6 years.
Significance to Literature	Combined medical/ behavior Txs with specific instruction for toileting and incentives for independent use of toilet is probably effective. The "additive strategy" of treatments likely diminished unique treatment effects.	Success rates with BF only poor at 12 weeks (44%), 26 weeks (32%), 12 months (36%). Using laxatives with nonconstipated children may lead to more soiling.	Significant improvement and cure at 12 months predicted by success in first 2 weeks of treatment for all groups. The "additive strategy" of treatments likely diminished unique treatment effects.	Conventional treatment with minimal behavioral treatment is helpful over extended follow-up period. Not a controlled study.	Poorly defined outcome measures allows for authors to suggest some benefit to BF.	First Internet treatment site for Encopresis that shows significant improvement in soiling and BMs in toilet. Families highly satisfied with Internet program.	Positive outcome of BF for Encopresis at long-term follow-up. Pretest measures not reported and equivalent groups not demonstrated. Unequal and small sample sizes. Study may have lacked statistical power.	Even with poorly defined treatment, many children with Encopresis recover in a 6-year period. Shorter duration of symptoms associated with greater recovery.

Biofeedback (i.e., bringing into a person's awareness subtle bodily functions through visual or auditory projection) interventions have been applied to the problem of chronic constipation and the retention of feces, which are characteristics of encopretic children. Biofeedback appeared promising in treating the assumed conditioned paradoxical contraction of the external anal sphincter (EAS) during defecation attempts, which is thought to be the primary mechanism leading to constipation and eventual overflow soiling in as many as 50% of encopretic children (Benninga et al., 2004).

Several research teams since the late 1990s have conducted randomized controlled studies looking at the singular effects of biofeedback (BF) or effects of BF combined with either standard medical care for constipation or behavioral interventions for appropriate toileting (Borowitz, Cox, Sutphen, & Kovatchev, 2002; Cox, Sutphen, Borowitz, Kovatchev, & Ling, 1998; Croffie et al., 2005; Hibi, Iwai, Kimura, Sasaki, & Tsuda, 2003; Ritterband et al., 2003; Van Ginkel et al., 2000; Van Ginkel et al., 2003). Important characteristics of these studies are detailed in Table 15.2. The purpose of using biofeedback to treat the children evidencing the paradoxical contraction of the EAS was to make defecation more efficient and regular by bringing into the child's awareness the maladaptively learned contraction of the EAS as an avoidance response to painful defecation. Other reviewers have concluded that normalizing the dyssyrnergic anorectal response does not lead to recovery and is no better than standard medical care combined with behavioral interventions at the time of follow-up (Brazzelli & Griffiths, 2003; Brooks et al., 2000). The only finding as yet that deserves further investigation regarding BF is whether this intervention significantly reduces the length of treatment, and thus, the psychosocial burden of fecal soiling.

Researchers from the University of Virginia Health Sciences Center have recently made significant contributions to the treatment outcome literature for encopresis due primarily to their understanding of the disorder as a *biobehavioral* problem (also see Table 15.2). The breadth of their work is exemplified in the undertaking of randomized controlled studies, the development of combined medical treatment with a unique method of teaching and reinforcing the necessary behaviors for appropriate toileting, an automated voicemail data collection system over the telephone, and the application of this combined treatment over the Internet. Their unique biobehavioral treatment is called "enhanced toilet training," which employs the typical and intensive medical management of enemas and stool softeners with behavioral training for appropriate toileting. Patients are instructed about the pathophysiology of retentive encopresis and the reduced rectal sensitivity and paradoxical contraction of the EAS resulting from chronic constipation. As such, an incentive plan is developed to target independent toileting and clean underwear. This basic intervention is enhanced by the therapist instructing the patient about proper sitting technique and using one's hands placed on one's abdomen to recognize the muscles involved in enacting a Valsalva contraction with prompting to simultaneously relax the EAS. Once the sequence is understood by the encopretic child and parent, the parents were instructed to prompt this practice at home while the patient was sitting on the toilet after two meals during the day. The sitting practice lasted 12 minutes, with the first 4 minutes having the child contracting/relaxing the EAS to localize control and to fatigue the sphincter. The second 4 minutes emphasized nothing more than a fun activity, such as reading, to desensitize the child to toileting. The last 4 minutes involved the child actually trying to have a bowel movement while relaxing his/her feet, legs, and EAS. This procedure was faded out 2 weeks after the last treatment session.

Cox, Sutphen, Ling, Quillian, and Borowitz (1996) conducted a randomized controlled experiment comparing standard intensive medical intervention (Group 1); brief medical intervention combined with a behavioral intervention for appropriate toileting (Group 2, enhanced toilet training, or ETT); and a bio-feedback intervention (Group 3). Groups 2 and 3 contributed to significantly less soiling than Group 1, but no differences between Groups 2 and 3. Children classified as significantly improved were 19%, 71%, and 69% for Groups 1, 2, and 3, respectively.

Cox et al. (1998) replicated the previous study with an additive strategy utilizing intensive medical management (IMM), enhanced toilet training (ETT), and biofeedback (BF) to reflect clinical practice. The authors demonstrated that ETT significantly benefited more children, used less laxatives and fewer treatment sessions, and at a lower cost than either the intensive medical care group or the biofeedback group. The researchers also reported that a child's success during the first 2 weeks of treatment, regardless of the intervention, was strongly related to success at 3 months. Borowitz et al. (2002) reanalyzed the data from the Cox et al. (1998) study and reported multiple outcomes for the end of treatment, and at 3, 6, and 12 months post-treatment (see details in Table 15.2). At the 12-month follow-up, there were no differences in the number of children cured, or in the frequency of self-initiated visits to the toilet. However, all treatments resulted in significant reduction in soiling accidents and increases in bowel movements in the toilet. The most significant advantages of the ETT were that fewer children remained on laxative therapy, a trend toward fewer office visits, and lower cost of treatment. These results are less impressive than other reported combined medical and extensive behavioral interventions. It is suspected that the study samples were possibly more difficult to treat, as they had all previously failed conventional treatment. Further, the "additive strategy" used in these studies likely masked true effects of each treatment.

Finally, Ritterband et al. (2003) evaluated the ETT intervention delivered via the Internet and at multiple study sites. Subjects were randomly assigned to Web-ETT or no Web-ETT. The Web-ETT group (referred to as the U-CAN-POOP-TOO Internet program) had significantly more cured, significantly increased self-initiated toileting, and increased number of bowel movements in the toilet. The most impressive finding of this study is that the treatment was essentially delivered in the patient's home as an additive component to standard medical care delivered in their home community. The interactive and educational website included 27 modules regarding the pathophysiology of encopresis and medical/behavioral intervention with illustrations and tutorials, and with previously demonstrated high levels of user satisfaction (Borowitz & Ritterband, 2001).

These studies conducted by the University of Virginia research group have contributed to conclusions that the use of biofeedback is not associated with greater effectiveness than combined medical and behavioral treatments. They have also demonstrated that a complex medical/behavioral treatment can be delivered in a cost-effective way over the Internet and with outcomes consistent with those reported using face-to-face procedures. Yet the researchers still conclude that their interventions are in need of improvement. The self-assessment of their work has prompted the University of Virginia researchers to develop psychosocial measures of child and parent characteristics that might reveal process variables related to treatment outcome. The influence of psychosocial variables on treatment outcome is reviewed in the section regarding mediators and moderators of treatment.

Meta-Analyses of Group Designs

Two contemporary systematic reviews have contributed to a better understanding of what types of interventions have the best evidence for the treatment of encopresis. McGrath et al. (2000) reviewed 65 treatment studies and employed the "Chambless Criteria"

(Chambless et al., 1996) to determine which studies met the rigorous criteria for an empirically supported treatment. They concluded that no well-established treatments have yet to emerge. However, treatments that combine medical interventions plus positive reinforcement, medical interventions plus biofeedback for abnormal defecation dynamics, and medical interventions plus positive reinforcement of skills to relax the external anal sphincter were considered "probably efficacious" treatments.

Brooks et al. (2000) reviewed only studies utilizing a randomized controlled design and identified only nine reports for school-aged children that compared medical, behavioral, psychological, and biofeedback treatments. The authors summarized that the literature is devoid of standardized and operationally defined treatments that are necessary in order to draw firm conclusion of each intervention. They reported that biofeedback was not more effective than medical–behavioral treatment at the time of follow-up comparisons, and that the problem of abnormal defecation dynamics was not related to outcome.

The only meta-analysis of encopresis treatments is that by Brazzelli and Griffiths (2008). As part of the Cochrane Database of Systematic Reviews, these authors applied only the most rigorous standards for inclusion and exclusion for analysis for those studies that employed randomized and quasirandomized trials of behavioral and/or cognitive interventions to treat defecation disorders in children. This resulted in the identification of 18 randomized controlled trials and involved 1,168 children. The authors concluded that fecal soiling was more likely to persist at 12-month follow-up with treatments that included biofeedback. There is some evidence that laxative therapy plus behavioral interventions (i.e., toilet training, positive reinforcement, and dietary advice) is better than either treatment delivered individually for either primary or secondary encopresis. The authors concluded that the existing studies need to be replicated and evaluated with standardized treatments compared to other singular treatments or no-treatment control groups.

Single-Subject Experimental Analyses

Single-case experimental designs (Barlow & Hersen, 1984) are primarily associated with "psychological or behavioral" treatments and are rarely found in the professional literature of other disciplines, especially the medical literature. However, the literature regarding psychological treatments for encopresis using single-case methodology is informative. Perhaps one of the best examples is that provided by Doleys, McWhorter, Williams, and Gentry (1977). They employed a standard, multiple baseline across three boys who were 4, 8, and 9 years old. After the completion of a medical exam to rule out an organic cause for soiling, the treatment was considered uniquely behavioral with periodic pant checks, scheduled toileting, overcorrection for accidents, and positive reinforcement for appropriate toileting behaviors. All three subjects met the success criteria of at least 4 consecutive accident-free weeks. Forty-eight weeks after treatment, subject 1 had only two accidents and subjects 2 and 3 were completely accident-free 12 and 36 weeks after ending treatment.

In a similar single-case design using a multiple baseline across subjects, Houts, Mellon, and Whelan (1988) employed a combination treatment of stimulus control of the gastroileal reflex to produce a bowel movement, combined with an incentive to increase dietary fiber. All subjects successful reached 4 consecutive accident-free weeks and these gains were maintained at 1-year follow-up. This study was important in demonstrating the effectiveness of increasing dietary fiber in the treatment of constipation and soiling, in addition to reestablishing a regular habit of defecation.

Finally, Boles, Roberts, and Vernberg (2008) utilized a single-case method in treating a nonretentive encopretic child by rewarding scheduled toilet visits. The study focused on a 10-year-old boy in an elementary school for children with serious emotional disturbances and employed a multiple baseline across settings (home and school). The target behaviors were frequency of soiling accidents and sitting on the toilet without opposition. The treatment used a simple positive reinforcement system of giving tokens for cooperating with a toileting schedule of up to 11 two-minute periods of sitting. After 7 weeks of treatment, the tokens were given for bowel movements in the toilet. The experiment began in the classroom and then was initiated at home after 5 weeks of baseline recording of accidents and sits on the toilet. The treatment had a significant influence on accidents as they dropped from and average of seven per week to only three when the toilet visits were reinforced. When the contingency changed to rewarding BMs in the toilet at the seventh week, the average accidents per week then fell to zero at school and home. Frequency of toilet sits increased to an average of 15 times per week during treatment compared to only four times during baseline. The authors demonstrated how the reinforcement procedure shaped the appropriate toileting behaviors of first sitting on the toilet without opposition and then specifically reinforcing BMs in the toilet as they anticipated resistance from the child from the start.

These three examples of single-subject designs clearly demonstrate the utility and efficiency of this methodology to understanding what types of treatments might ultimately prove to be a promising and perhaps an empirically supported intervention.

Meta-Analyses of Single-Subject Experiments

As mentioned in the review of laxatives for encopresis, the use of meta-analysis methodology to summarize treatment effects in the context of group studies is common. However, the use of meta-analysis to summarize single-case experimental designs is considered new.

At this time, there have been no published studies using this methodology to summarize any types of treatments for children with constipation and encopresis.

Conclusions

The conclusions regarding which treatments meet the criteria as an effective intervention for encopresis are still incomplete. Others (McGrath et al., 2000; Brazzelli & Griffiths, 2008) explain that the current literature is limited by inconsistently defined outcome measures (i.e., cure vs. improved), heterogeneous study samples, and prominent variability in the treatments utilized. Further, there are a limited number of randomized controlled trials that have compared different treatment types, and rarely do the treatments include standardized manuals. Nonetheless, at the time of follow-up, there appears to be ample evidence that the use of biofeedback has no added benefit over standard medical treatment alone or combined with complex behavioral interventions. The extensive work by the University of Virginia research group, which has astutely included many previously helpful components of treatment, has made significant strides in further demonstrating that biobehavioral treatments utilizing intensive medical care, combined with complex behavioral interventions designed to promote independent toileting, appear to demonstrate the greatest efficacy for managing the complex disorder of encopresis.

As certain treatments are established as being evidence-based, research then turns to the question of what mechanisms seem to best account for specific outcomes. These mechanisms include social-behavioral and physiological influences that are involved in the emergence of a problem and its ultimate resolution. The following section explores, in a preliminary way, mediators and moderators of treatment outcome. It is also suggested that these mechanisms of action call for different areas of research that may well push the current treatment literature closer to clearly identifying evidence-based interventions for encopresis.

PROPOSED MECHANISMS OF ACTION

Mediators of Encopresis Treatment

Researchers in quantitative psychology (Kraemer, Wilson, Fairburn, & Agras, 2002; Rose, Holmbeck, Coakley, & Franks, 2004) describe the phenomena through which psychosocial treatments work as "mediating variables." These would include both physiological and psychological processes that influence encopresis treatment outcome. This section describes the physiological processes involved in the normal development of fecal continence and points out where this process breaks down and ultimately manifests itself in encopresis. Emphasized are those influences leading to the state of chronic constipation and overflow incontinence, as this accounts for up to 90% of children presenting with encopresis (Benninga et al., 2004). Further, a description of those psychosocial variables that appear to affect treatment outcome and the long-term recovery from this complex biobehavioral problem of childhood is explored. With this discussion, the reader should also appreciate the complexity of this problem in the encopretic child's efforts to overcome and maintain recovery from constipation and soiling.

Most children undergo a developmental process that culminates in completed bowel training approximately 98% of the time by the age of 4 years (Benninga et al., 2004). Fecal continence is maintained as a dynamic balance between the influences of a functional anal sphincter, anorectal sensitivity, "the anal sampling reflex," rectal compliance, and the consistency of fecal material. The sensory nerve cells of the anal canal allow a person to differentially recognize and respond to various qualities of stool and are reported to evidence tactile sensitivity equal to that of the index finger (Bartolo & Macdonald, 2002). This sensitivity allows for the discrimination of the state of rectal contents as solid, liquid, or gas and enables the child to make socially appropriate decisions about how to respond in order to maintain continence. As stool enters the distal portions of the rectum from the sigmoid colon, it activates stretch receptors in the wall of the rectum. This in turn produces contraction of the rectal wall and causes the internal anal sphincter, through spinal nuclei, to reflexively relax and allow the contents (solid, liquid, or gas) to move into the anal canal. The physical state of the rectal contents, perceived by the sensitive tissue of the anus, allows for the child to determine the most socially appropriate response at the time.

This process of selectively allowing the rectal contents into the anus is referred to as the "anal sampling reflex" and can occur up to seven times in an hour until the call to stool becomes undeniable. If it is determined that passage of the rectal contents is inappropriate, then the person voluntarily contracts the external anal sphincter, which pushes the contents back into the upper rectal area and reestablishes resting tone in the internal anal sphincter. When defecation is deemed appropriate, assuming a squatting position on the toilet allows for more efficient passage of stool. Simultaneously executing a Valsalva contraction and relaxing the external anal sphincter allows for formed and soft stool to pass without discomfort. As the stool leaves the anus, the external anal sphincter reflexively contracts with the puborectalis muscle to once again reestablish the normal resting tone or contraction of the internal anal sphincter. Fecal continence is maintained by greater muscle tone in the external anal sphincter and puborectalis muscle compared to pressures in the sigmoid rectum, with the anus acting essentially as the valve that selectively allows feces or flatus to pass.

Appropriate defecation and fecal continence is unique from urinary continence in that it is primarily a daytime phenomenon. During sleep, bowel motility is slowed with fecal accidents happening rarely during that time. Fecal continence is also different in terms of the frequency in which a person must deal with this function, as normal regularity is considered to range from a bowel movement occurring daily to once every third day. Peristalsis is stimulated by meal ingestion or vigorous physical activity, and this moves the contents of the bowel forward with a wave-like contraction (Quigley, 2002). The normal defecatory response appears to be a state of inhibition, which is described as a "guarding reflex." However, a state of chronic constipation or severe fecal impaction in which the rectal area is stretched full will produce inhibition or deactivation of the tone of the internal anal sphincter and also relaxation of the external anal sphincter, which can lead to fecal incontinence.

Constipation is considered the precursor to fecal soiling or encopresis in the majority cases, as it is associated with decreased rectal sensitivity (Loening-Baucke, 2002). The loss of sensation to rectal filling will lead to soiling when rectal pressures rise and exceed the weakened anal pressure prior to the person even being aware of the need to defecate (Bartolo & Macdonald, 2002). The rectal sensitivity can be further compromised by the stool consistency with high volumes of liquid stool or small, hard pellets being difficult to discriminate (i.e., flatus or liquid feces) and effectively passed (i.e., small and hard stool). In most circumstances, fecal incontinence results from the loss of the signal indicating the need to defecate, due to the chronic constipation that causes reduced rectal and anal sensitivity. The signal of rectal distention and a disrupted anal sampling reflex is lost in the background noise of chronic fecal impaction.

Further, intensely painful defecation resulting from the passage of large diameter stool is thought to precipitate avoidance of defecation by prompting the contraction of the gluteal muscles and the pelvic floor while standing in a rigid posture until the urge to defecate subsides. Unfortunately, this further contributes to worsening constipation. Accidents occur as a result of small amounts of stool in the distal end of the fecal mass breaking away or with liquid stool bypassing the hardened impaction. It is suspected that the defecation "avoidance" response becomes overgeneralized to more complex aspects of toileting, including visiting the bathroom to attempt defecation, compliance with treatment, and the social consequences of soiling by ignoring accidents or hiding soiled underwear. In essence, all aspects of bowel functioning become associated with aversive experiences that are to be avoided due to the anticipation of pain and frustration in losing control of toileting skills. It is at this point that a feeling of "learned helplessness" and indifference to toileting begins. Also often mentioned in the mental health literature is the alleged involvement of sexual abuse as a precursor to encopresis. This proposed relationship is based more on single-case reports and lore as opposed to objective evidence. Mellon, Whiteside, and Friedrich (2006) have demonstrated that encopresis is no more effective at identifying children with known sexual abuse than general behavior problems. They also found that "sexually acting-out" behaviors were much more powerful predictors of sexual abuse than ecopresis and behavior problems.

Cox et al. (2003) developed a complex measure of behavioral and emotional problems regarding fecal soiling, completed by both child and parent, and called the VECAT (Virginia Encopresis-Constipation Apperception Test), with demonstrated acceptable levels of reliability and validity. This measure is important because it has clearly demonstrated differences between children with encopresis and controls in bowel-specific versus general problems. Themes covered by the VECAT relate to the sensation or experience of defecation, parent–child relationship, and social consequences of soiling, which are likely useful in identifying bowel-specific psychological variables involved in mediating treatment outcome. It is proposed as a research tool that may well be useful in predicting which children recover from the soiling and those mechanisms that maintain the soiling and those that change as a result of treatment. Given that biofeedback (which specifically treats the physiological aspects of disrupted defecation) is not helpful to the long-term recovery of encopretic children, much work is yet to be done in identifying psychosocial mechanisms of action involved in overcoming encopresis.

Cox et al. (1998) proposed a linear model that describes the development of encopresis through experiences that commence and shape the paradoxical contraction of the external anal sphincter while attempting defecation. This in turn leads to later disruptions to appropriate toileting, and the psychosocial factors influencing the soiling problem. There is a suggestion of both respondent and operant conditioning processes combined with a physiological predisposition involved in the evolution of the problem, but not clearly articulated as such. This author suggests that Cox et al.'s (1998) model does not capture the complexity of the biobehavioral problems involved in encopresis. It fails to explain the disorder as a reciprocally interacting pattern of behavior by the encopretic child within his or her environment. It is suggested that the delicate balancing act of fecal continence, as well as its loss when encopresis occurs, is better conceptualized using the "four term contingency" of operant behaviorism (Bijou, 1995). This is described in the following section.

Moderators of Encopresis Treatment

Moderators of treatment include those variables that affect the strength and/or direction of treatment (Kraemer et al., 2002; Rose et al., 2004). This author proposes that psychosocial influences on the delivery of treatment should be pursued as an "adherence" issue similar to other chronic disorders (i.e., asthma, diabetes, etc.). Rapoff (1999) has clearly articulated the problem of nonadherence to medical regimens

and noted the patient/family, disease, and treatment regimen correlates that affect adherence. Patient and family factors include the following: demographics such as age, gender, and socioeconomic status; child and parent knowledge of the disease; adjustment and coping problems in the parent and child; and how much parental monitoring occurs. Disease factors include the duration, symptom type, and severity, and the child and parent perceived severity of the illness have been related to adherence. Finally, treatment regimen factors such as the type and complexity of the intervention, costs, side effects, and the perceived efficacy of the treatment affect adherence.

Adherence issues involved in encopresis treatment have yet to be adequately explored and may be due to more significant problems related to poorly defined treatment outcome measures, poorly delineated treatment samples, and the need for more scientific rigor in this area. This author proposes that psychosocial moderators play an even greater role in the delivery of treatment for encopresis compared to enuresis, and what influences the delivery of treatment is the relevant question to ask.

Several studies have explored psychological and behavioral characteristics of the child and parents related to encopresis. Cox et al. (2003) explored the concept of bowel-specific and general emotional and behavioral problems that were related to encopresis. These psychological and behavioral factors are thought to have an impact not only on the evolution of fecal incontinence (coercive toilet training, birth of sibling, start of school), but also on the maintenance of the problem (externalizing behavior and nonadherence, low self-esteem and hopelessness, family conflict, psychiatric problems in parents), and deserve further systematic study.

With regard to psychological and behavioral characteristics of encopretic children that might impact treatment outcome, few evidence-based conclusions can be made, but several studies bear mentioning. Most of these studies have found a variety of emotional and behavioral problems in encopretic children that differentiate them from control samples, although most of these problems are at subclinical levels. For example, Levine, Mazonson, and Bakow (1980) indicated that unsuccessfully treated encopretic children demonstrated higher antisocial-aggressive behaviors at pretreatment. Gabel, Hegedus, Wald, Chandra, and Chiponis (1986) reported children with encopresis showed poorer social competency and more behavioral problems compared to a nonreferred sample. In contrast, Friman, Mathews, Finney, Christophersen, and Leibowitz (1988) reported no behavioral differences between children with soiling and a matched comparison sample. More recently, Young et al. (1995) reported lower levels of social competency and greater behavioral problems for encopretic children versus a matched, nonclinical sample on a standardized behavior rating scale (Child Behavior Checklist), although the differences were at subclinical levels. Contemporary researchers are beginning to identify important patient characteristics of encopretic children that predict recovery of constipation and soiling. Van Ginkel et al. (2003) reported that successful treatment was more likely in children whose constipation emerged after 4 years of age versus prior to 4, and a greater level of soiling at the start of treatment was associated with a negative outcome. In a 6-year study of 67 cases of encopresis, Unal and Pehlivanturk (2005) report that good school performance in the child, higher levels of parental education, and absence of constipation were associated with recovery of encopresis. They further reported that secondary onset of soiling, if symptoms were present for less than a year, were associated with successful treatment. These studies suggest that less severe symptoms of constipation and greater emotional resources are associated with successful treatment.

Cox et al. (2002), in a large sample of encopretic children ($N = 86$), indicated that children with soiling demonstrated significantly more anxiety/depression symptoms, less expressiveness and organization in the family environment, greater attention and social problems, more disruptive behaviors, and poorer school performance compared to 62 nonsymptomatic children. Further, the authors reported that 20% more of the encopretic sample exceeded clinical thresholds compared to nonsymptomatic children, and this suggests that a small portion of encopretic children should also have their behavioral/emotional difficulties addressed in their treatment. Collectively, these studies suggest that there is demonstrable behavioral dysregulation involved with encopretic children. The question of whether these differences precede or are the result of the stress incurred by having encopresis is yet to be answered. This emotional/behavioral complexity, combined with the greater physiological complexity in the mastery of bowel continence, will likely have to be addressed in the design of more effective treatments for childhood encopresis.

Rapoff's (1999) conceptualization of factors affecting adherence to pediatric regimens identifies those areas that should be addressed in future investigation. This author suggests this model should guide all future research efforts to target adherence to a fairly simple, but behaviorally challenging treatment. The treatment is simple (i.e., bowel clean-out, stool softeners and dietary fiber intake, scheduled toileting to reestablish bowel regularity), but the emotional and behavioral characteristics of the child and family system make the need for a biobehavioral treatment even more necessary. Rappoff (1999) recommends that treatments must be successful in motivating the patient and family to follow the regimen, must provide effective role modeling, must help the families set specific goals in treatment and monitor patient progress, must teach the child and parent the necessary skills to follow in the treatment, and must help the child and family arrange more reinforcing consequences for following treatment versus the status quo of soiling.

This author offers the following model of normal development of fecal continence and explanation of influences that ultimately lead to encopresis (Figure 15.1). This model utilizes the four-term conceptualization of operant behavior that includes antecedent cues (i.e., discriminative stimuli or S^D), behavioral responses (R), and those consequences (i.e., positive and negative reinforcement, or S^{R+}/S^{R-}) that shape the responses. The fourth term is often referred to as setting events that affect the strength of the relationship between the discriminative stimuli and the response. The dynamic interaction between the child and both the internal and external environments are highlighted in the developmental history leading to fecal soiling. The complexity of defecation and learning processes of fecal continence are emphasized.

Section I of Figure 15.1 describes the complex behavioral chain involved in actual defecation that is elicited by the introduction of stool into the rectum as an S^D. This chain includes both reflexes and learned responses. It is assumed that this response is naturally reinforced by the experience of relief from bowel pressure. Also emphasized is the normal state of inhibition of defecation with resting tone in the internal anal sphincter (IAS), referred to as the "guarding reflex," and is thought to have been shaped both through praise for clean pants and reprimand for accidents. This guarding reflex or generalized inhibition of defecation is overcome by the initiation of defecation via a Valsalva maneuver, or bearing down to produce a bowel movement. Socially appropriate defecation is the result of this complex behavioral chain and the interacting physiological and social influences that shape the where and when of this process.

Section II explains the complex process of the child learning to discriminate between the three states of matter present in the rectum via the "anal sampling reflex." The ability to discriminate the physical properties of the rectal

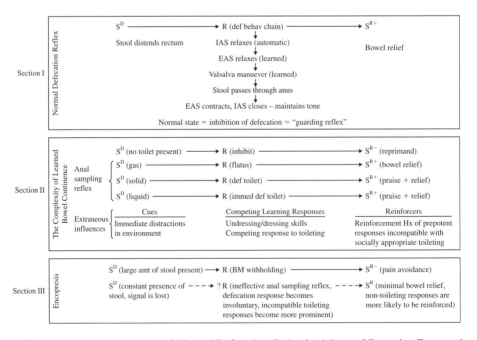

Figure 15.1   A Biobehavioral Model of Normal Defecation, Pathophysiology of Retentive Encopresis, and Is Remediation Through Combined Medical/Psychological Treatment

Source: © 2011 Mayo Foundation for Medical Education and Research

contents allows the child to appropriately respond to the need to toilet or the socially appropriate passage of flatus. Making the correct stimulus prompted response is likely shaped through relief of bowel pressure, social praise, and reprimand. Even more amazing is that this process occurs in the context of competing distractions in the environment for incompatible toileting behaviors (i.e., playing) and in coordination with other complex motor responses necessary to appropriately produce a bowel movement in the toilet (i.e., dressing/undressing skills, proper sitting on toilet, personal hygiene responses, etc.). Even more challenging is that this process occurs less frequently than urination and during the daytime under circumstances that make the learning process less efficient.

The process leading to fecal incontinence or encopresis is depicted in Section III of the model. This author believes that the state of chronic constipation and passage of painful, large diameter stool contributes to an exaggerated guarding reflex and stool withholding in order to avoid pain. Small, hard, and pebble-like stool is especially difficult to pass and leads to accumulation of feces. Excessive amounts of stool in the rectum lead to stretching of the bowel tissue, which reduces anorectal sensitivity and defecation efficiency. It is proposed that the presence of large amounts of stool in the rectum may also disinhibit the IAS, which allows stool to come into constant contact with the anus and thus disrupts the discriminative sensitivity of the anal sampling reflex. Because stool is always impinging upon the anus, the anal sampling reflex would periodically milk fecal matter through the anal opening, which results in small soiling accidents. Decreased anorectal sensitivity likely allows for the accidental passage of small amounts of stool, which is below the awareness of the child. It is assumed that years of soiling, and the resulting odor, also contributes to the habituation to the aversive smell of feces. In essence, the encopretic child has an enhanced guarding reflex to

avoid the passage of painfully large stool that only contributes to a worsening of the constipation. With the disruption of an efficient anal sampling reflex, and small accidents that occur outside of the awareness of the child, the child is generally incapable of preventing soiling. This process is even further compromised as the avoidance of defecation is generalized to the avoidance of toileting via ignoring the need to visit the toilet (if perceived at all), denying or lying about accidents, and attempting to hide soiled underwear. It is also believed that the child develops a state of learned helplessness or indifference to soiling accidents, as he truly is unable to control the function of his bowel.

With this model the reader will appreciate the true complexity of not only fecal continence, but also the difficulty in effectively treating encopresis. This complexity may explain the less than satisfying success rates ranging from 47% to 64% cured for combined medical/behavioral treatments (McGrath et al., 2000) versus the consistently reported cure rates of 70% to 80% for complex behavioral treatments utilizing the urine alarm for nocturnal enuresis (Mellon & McGrath, 2000). The model also indicates that treatments should address the physiological aspects of chronic constipation and the social-behavioral aspects of avoidance of appropriate toileting in the context of biobehavioral treatments. Clearly, much more research is needed to understand those factors affecting adherence to necessary medical regimens in order to reverse chronic constipation and those social influences needed to reestablish appropriate toileting behaviors.

EVIDENCE-BASED PRACTICES

Most children who present for treatment of fecal soiling will have been symptomatic for up to five years (Fishman, Rappaport, Schonwald, & Nurko, 2003; Partin et al., 1992). Further, Rockney et al. (1996) have reported that children who have failed previous treatment for constipation are less likely to recover from encopresis. This author suggests the best interventions should be ones designed to intervene early and with enough intensity to properly manage the predisposing constipation and eventual frustrating parent–child interactions. Early screening and monitoring of constipation and toileting refusal has been recommended by the American Academy of Pediatrics in published guidelines (1999). A conventional treatment approach that consists of child/parent education and demystification, medical intervention to treat impaction and constipation, prevention of recurrence of constipation, behavioral intervention to reinforce compliance with medical treatment and improve bowel habits, and fading out treatment (except for dietary changes) is recommended (Loening-Baucke, 2002). It is encouraging that trends in referral to an encopresis clinic over a 20-year period suggest that encopretic children are tending to be younger, have been symptomatic for less time, and are receiving more appropriate treatments for the chronic constipation by primary care physicians prior to referral to the encopresis clinic (Fishman et al., 2003). Finally, there appears to be less difficulty in obtaining adequate insurance coverage for effective encopresis treatment. Perhaps this is due to the nature of the biobehavioral etiology of the disorder and its multidisciplinary treatment.

Future Directions in Encopresis Treatment

This author hopes that the model (see Figure 15.1) of normal development of socially appropriate defecation, and disruption of this process that leads to encopresis, will lead to more organized and focused research efforts to better understand the encopretic child. Given that the spontaneous remission rate for encopresis is not clearly defined, a watchful waiting approach to managing constipation and infrequent soiling is not the best recommendation to give to patients and parents, as

these symptoms appear to get worse over time and can persist for years prior to the child's eventual referral for treatment.

Investigators of children with encopresis would also make significant contributions to the literature if they conducted descriptive studies with adequate sample sizes to further understand the characteristics that might predict which children are more likely to be successfully treated with standard interventions. The use of standardized measures of a child's emotional and behavioral functioning, family interaction patterns and demographics, toilet training history, and measures of treatment satisfaction would serve the purpose of obtaining reliable information that could be compared across studies. One such disorder-specific measure previously described was the VECAT (Cox et al., 2003). Clearly, all investigations of treatments should be conducted as randomized controlled studies of adequate sample sizes or well-controlled studies utilizing single-case experimental designs. Less rigorous methodology will only further delay obtaining reliable knowledge regarding effective treatment of encopresis.

Specific research regarding components of effective treatment should reflect the biobehavioral nature of the problem. Much is already known about effectively relieving constipation and preventing its return (see Table 15.1). The long-term role of dietary fiber to prevent the return of constipation and as a necessary component of effective treatment has yet to be fully investigated. The research literature describes two perspectives on constipation treatment: one that promotes the use of medicinal stool softeners and cathartics and another that advocates for the use of natural fiber found in foods such as grains, fruits, and vegetables as a means of preventing the recurrence of constipation and to promote bowel regularity.

Factors related to behavioral adherence to the medical regimens must be better understood. Reestablishing in the child the ability to detect the presence of fecal material in the rectum and then appropriately enact socially learned toileting behaviors is necessary for recovery from encopresis. This concept is easy to understand but difficult to implement, as evidenced by the less than pleasing reported outcomes for treatment. Much has been discovered about efficiently teaching toileting skills to not only developmentally delayed children, but also typical children. Azrin and Foxx (1974) and Christophersen (1991) have described highly structured and operant-based methods of assessing readiness for toileting and then teaching the chain of behaviors necessary to master socially appropriate toileting. Discovering the necessary components of this structured approach is worth the research effort. What is not known is how rule-governed or verbal behavior not only maintains the problem but might also be important in the recovery from encopresis. Rule-governed behaviors are those verbal antecedents that control human behavior and can take different forms such as instructions, advice, and laws. These rules imply contingencies related to one's own behavior. How these rules relate to adherence to effective encopresis treatment certainly warrants further investigation, as they may explain how a child eventually gains complete independence in socially appropriate toileting.

The common childhood problem of encopresis is an important example of a biobehavioral problem that is influenced by physiological and psychological processes that contribute to their pathophysiology and effective treatment. The systematic study of encopresis may contribute important lessons to the research psychologist in an effort to more fully understand even more complex psychosocial disorders.

REFERENCES

American Academy of Pediatrics. (1999). Physiological and clinical considerations regarding toilet training: An updated review. *Pediatrics, 103*(Suppl 6), Pt 2 of 3.

American Psychiatric Association. (1994). *Diagnostic and statistical manual of mental disorders* (4th ed.). Washington, DC: Author.

Azrin, N., & Foxx, R. (1974). *Toilet training in less than a day.* New York, NY: Simon & Schuster.

Baker, S., Liptak, G., Colleti, R., Croffie, J., Di Lorenzo, C. Ector, W., & Nurko, S. (1999). Constipation in infants and children: Evaluation and treatment. A medical position statement of the North American Society for Pediatric Gastroenterology and Nutrition. *Journal of Pediatric Gastroenterology and Nutrition, 29,* 612–626.

Barlow, D., & Hersen, M. (1984). *Single case experimental designs: Strategies for studying behavior change.* New York, NY: Pergamon.

Bartolo, D., & Macdonald, A. (2002). Fecal continence and defecation. In J. Pemberton, M. Swash, & M. Henry (Eds.), *The pelvic floor—Its function and disorders* (pp. 77–93). New York, NY: W. B. Saunders.

Bellman, M. (1966). Studies on encopresis. *Acta Paediatrica Scandinavica, 1*(Suppl 170), 7–132.

Benninga, M., Candy, D., Catto-Smith, A., Clayden, G., Loening-Baucke, V., Lorenzo., . . . Staiano, A. (2005). The Paris Consensus on Childhood Constipation Terminology (PACCT) group. *Journal of Pediatric Gastroenerology and Nutrician, 40,* 272–275.

Benninga, M., Voskuijl, W., & Taminiau, J. (2004). Childhood constipation: Is there new light in the tunnel? *Journal of Pediatric Gastroenterology and Nutrition, 39,* 448–464.

Bijou, S. (1995). *Behavior analysis of child development.* Reno, NV: Context Press.

Boles, R., Roberts, M., & Vernberg, E. (2008). Treating non-retentive encopresis with rewarded scheduled toilet visits. *Behavior Analysis in Practice, 1,* 68–72.

Borowitz, S., Cox, D., Sutphen, J., & Kovatchev, B. (2002). Treatment of childhood encopresis: A randomized trial comparing three treatment protocols. *Journal of Pediatric Gastroenterology & Nutrition, 34,* 378–384.

Borowitz, S., & Ritterband, L. (2001). Using the Internet to teach parents and children about constipation and encopresis. *Medical Informatics & the Internet in Medicine, 26,* 283–295.

Brazzelli, M., & Griffiths, P. (2008). Behavioural and cognitive interventions with or without other treatments for defaecation disorders in children. *Cochrane Database of Systematic Reviews, 4,* CD002240.

Brooks, R., Copen, R., Cox, D., Morris, J., Borowitz, S., & Sutphen, J. (2000). Review of the treatment literature for encopresis, functional constipation, and stool-toileting refusal. *Annals of Behavioral Medicine, 22,* 260–267.

Chambless, D., Sanderson, W. C., Shoham, V., Johnson, S. B., Pope, K. S., Crits-Christoph., . . . McCurry, S.

(1996). An update on empirically validated therapies. *Clinical Psychologist, 49*, 5–18.

Christophersen, E. (1991). Toileting problems in children. *Pediatric Annals, 20*, 240–244.

Cox, D., Morris, J., Borowitz, S., & Sutphen, J. (2002). Psychological differences between children with and without chronic encopresis. *Journal of Pediatric Psychology, 27*, 585–591.

Cox, D., Ritterband, L., Quillian, W., Kovatchev, B., Morris, J., Sutphen, J., & Borowitz, S. (2003). Assessment of behavioral mechanisms maintaining encopresis: Virginia Encopresis-Constipation Apperception Test. *Journal of Pediatric Psychology, 28*, 375–382.

Cox, D., Sutphen, J., Borowitz, S., Kovatchev, B., & Ling, W. (1998). Contribution of behavior therapy and biofeedback to laxative therapy in the treatment of pediatric encopresis. *Annals of Behavioral Medicine, 20*, 70–76.

Cox, D., Sutphen, J., Ling, W., Quillian, W., & Borowitz, S. (1996). Additive benefits of laxative, toilet training, and biofeedback therapies in the treatment of pediatric encopresis. *Journal of Pediatric Psychology, 21*, 659–670.

Croffie, J., Fitzgerald, J., Ammar, M., Gupta, S., Pfefferkorn, M., Molleston, J., . . . Klipsch, A. (2005). Assessment of the effectiveness of biofeedback in children with dyssynergic and recalcitrant constipation/encopresis: Does home biofeedback improve long-term outcomes? *Clinical Pediatrics, 44*, 63–71.

Doleys, D., McWhorter, A., Williams, S., & Gentry, W. (1977). Encopresis: Its treatment and relation to nocturnal enuresis. *Behavior Therapy, 8*, 77–82.

Farahmand, F. (2007). A randomized trial of liquid paraffin versus lactulose in the treatment of chronic functional constipation in children. *Acta Medica Iranica, 45*, 183–188.

Fishman, L., Rappaport, L., Schonwald, A., & Nurko, S. (2003). Trends in referral to a single encopresis clinic over 20 years. *Pediatrics, 111*, e604–e607.

Friman, P., Mathews, J., Finney, J., Christophersen, E., & Leibowitz, J. (1988). Do encopretic children have clinically significant behavior problems? *Pediatrics, 82*(3 Pt 2), 407–409.

Gabel, S., Hegedus, A., Wald, A., Chandra, R., & Chiponis, D. (1986). Prevalence of behavior problems and mental health utilization among encopretic children: Implications for behavioral pediatrics. *Journal of Developmental & Behavioral Pediatrics, 7*, 293–297.

Hibi, M., Iwai, N., Kimura, O., Sasaki, Y., & Tsuda, T. (2003). Results of biofeedback therapy for fecal incontinence in children with encopresis and following surgery for anorectal malformations. *Disorders of the Colon and Rectum, 46*(Suppl), 854–858.

Houts, A., Mellon, M., & Whelan, J. (1988). Use of dietary fiber and stimulus control to treat retentive encopresis: A multiple baseline investigation. *Journal of Pediatric Psychology, 13*, 435–445.

Joinson, C., Heron, J., Butler, U., & Von Gontard, A. (2006). Psychological differences between children with and without soiling problems. *Pediatrics, 117*, 1575–1584.

Kraemer, H., Wilson, T., Fairburn, C., & Agras, S. (2002). Mediators and moderators of treatment effects in randomized clinical trials. *Archives of General Psychiatry, 59*, 877–883.

Levine, M., Mazonson, P., & Bakow, H. (1980). Behavioral symptom substitution in children cured of encopresis. *American Journal of Diseases of Children, 134*, 663–667.

Lewis, L., & Rudolph, C. (1997). Practical approach to defecation disorders in children. *Pediatric Annals, 26*, 260–268.

Loening-Baucke, V. (1993). Constipation in early childhood: Patient characteristics, treatment, and long-term follow up. *Gut, 34*, 1400–1404.

Loening-Baucke, V. (2002). Encopresis. *Current Opinion in Pediatrics, 14*, 570–575.

Loening-Baucke, V. (2004). Functional fecal retention with encopresis in childhood. *Journal of Pediatric Gastroenterology and Nutrition, 38*, 79–84.

Loening-Baucke, V., Miele, E., & Staiano, A. (2004). Fiber (glucomannan) is beneficial in the treatment of childhood constipation. *Pediatrics, 113*, 259–264.

McGrath, M., Mellon, M., & Murphy, L. (2000). Empirically supported treatments in pediatric psychology: Constipation and encopresis. *Journal of Pediatric Psychology, 25*, 225–254.

Mellon, M. W., & McGrath, M. (2000). Empirically supported treatments in pediatric psychology: Nocturnal enuresis. *Journal of Pediatric Psychology, 25*, 193–214.

Mellon, M., Whiteside, S., & Friedrich, W. (2006). The relevance of fecal soiling as an indicator of sexual abuse: A preliminary analysis. *Journal of Developmental and Behavioral Pediatrics, 27*, 25–32.

Partin, J., Hamill, S., Fischel, J., & Partin, J. (1992). Painful defecation and fecal soiling in children. *Pediatrics, 89*, 1007–1009.

Pashankar, D., & Bishop, W. (2001). Efficacy and optimal dose of daily polyethylene glycol 3350 for treatment of constipation and encopresis in children. *Journal of Pediatrics, 139*, 428–432.

Pashankar, D., Bishop, W., & Loening-Baucke, V. (2003). Long-term efficacy of polyethylene glycol 3350 for the treatment of chronic constipation in children with and without encopresis. *Clinical Pediatrics, 42*, 815–819.

Price, K., & Elliott, T. (2008). Stimulant laxatives for constipation and soiling in children (Review). *Cochrane Database of Systematic Reviews, 3*, Art. No. CD002040.

Procter, E., & Loader, P. (2003). A 6-year follow-up study of chronic constipation and soiling in a specialist paediatric service. *Child: Care, Health & Development, 29,* 103–109.

Quigley, E. (2002). Colonic motility and colonic function. In J. Pemberton, M. Swash, & M. Henry (Eds.), *The pelvic floor. Its function and disorders* (pp. 84–93). New York, NY: W. B. Saunders.

Rapoff, M. (1999). *Adherence to pediatric medical regimens.* New York, NY: Kluwer Academic/Plenum Publishers.

Rasquin-Weber, A., Hyman, P., Cucchiara, S., Fleisher, D., Hyams, J., Milla, P., . . . Staiano, A. (1999). Childhood functional gastrointestinal disorders. *Gut, 45,* 60–68.

Ritterband, L., Cox, D., Walker, L., Kovatchev, B., McKnight, L., Patel, K., . . . Sutphen, J. (2003). An Internet intervention as adjunctive therapy for pediatric encopresis. *Journal of Consulting & Clinical Psychology, 71,* 910–917.

Rockney, R., McQuade, W., Days, A., Linn, H., & Alario, A. (1996). Encopresis treatment outcome: Long-term follow-up of 45 cases. *Journal of Developmental & Behavioral Pediatrics, 17,* 380–385.

Rose, B., Holmbeck, G., Coakley, R., & Franks, E. (2004). Mediator and moderator effects in developmental and behavioral pediatric research. *Journal of Developmental & Behavioral Pediatrics, 25,* 58–67.

Schlosser, R. (2005). Reply to Pennington: Meta-analysis of single-subject research: How should it be done? *International Journal of Language and Communication Disorders, 40,* 375–378.

Schlosser, R. W., & Sigafoos, J. (2008). Meta-analysis of single-subject experimental designs: Why now? *Evidence-based Communication Assessment and Intervention, 2,* 117–119.

Unal, F., & Pehlivanturk, G. (2005). Encopresis: Long-term clinical outcome of 67 cases. *The Turkish Journal of Pediatrics, 47,* 53–57.

University of Michigan Health System. (2008). *Functional constipation and soiling in children.* Ann Arbor:Author. Retrieved from http://cme.med.umich.edu/pdf/guideline/peds08.pdf.

Van der Wal, M., Benninga, M., & Hirasing, R. (2005). The prevalence of encopresis in a multicultural population. *Journal of Pediatric Gastroenterology and Nutrition, 40,* 345–348.

van Dijk, M., Benninga, M., Grootenhuis, M., Onland-van Nieuwenhuizen, A., & Last, B. (2007). Chronic childhood constipation: A review of the literature and the introduction of a protocolized behavioral intervention program. *Patient Education and Counseling, 67,* 63–77.

Van Ginkel, R., Benninga, M., Blommaart, P., Van der Plas, R., Boeckxstaens, G., Buller, H., & Taminiau, J. (2000). Lack of benefit of laxatives as adjunctive therapy for functional nonretentive fecal soiling in children. *The Journal of Pediatrics, 137,* 808–813.

Van Ginkel, R., Reitsma, J., Buller, H., Van Wijk, M., Taminiau, J., & Benninga, M. (2003). Childhood constipation: Longitudinal follow-up beyond puberty. *Gastroenterology, 125,* 357–363.

Voskuijl, W., de Lorijn, F., Verwijs, W., Hogeman, P., Heijmans, Taminiau, J., & Benninga, M. (2004). PEG 3350 versus lactulose in the treatment of childhood functional constipation: A double blind, randomized controlled, multicenter trail. *Gut, 53,* 1590–1594.

Voskuijl, W., Heijmans, J., Heijmans, H., Makel, W., Taminiau, J., & Benninga, M. (2004). Use of Rome II criteria in childhood defecation disorders: Applicability in clinical research practice. *Journal of Pediatrics, 45,* 213–217.

Young, M., Brennen, L., Baker, R., & Baker, S. (1995). Functional encopresis: Symptom reduction and behavioral improvement. *Developmental and Behavioral Pediatrics, 16,* 226–232.

16

Enuresis

W. LARRY WILLIAMS AND MARIANNE JACKSON

OVERVIEW OF DISORDER

Diagnostic Criteria

Enuresis is the medical term that refers to the involuntary discharge of urine. Although this is the literal meaning of the word, many clinicians erroneously use the term to refer to urinary incontinence that occurs during sleep (nocturnal enuresis). Primary enuresis refers to urinary incontinence from birth and secondary enuresis refers to urinary incontinence that develops after the child has been dry for at least 6 months. Diurnal enuresis refers to urinary incontinence that occurs during the day and mixed enuresis refers to urinary incontinence that occurs day and night. Monosymptomatic enuresis refers to nocturnal enuresis that occurs without any other symptoms. Polysymptomatic nocturnal enuresis refers to nocturnal incontinence that occurs in association with urinary urgency, the sensation that one must urinate immediately, urge incontinence, voiding due to the presence of an urge to void, or staccato voiding and bursts of voiding.

The process by which our bodies' physiological maturation interacts with daily psychological events as exemplified in our learning to gain control over urinating is complex and rife with opportunity for learning to go wrong. It involves the establishment of a complex communication between our voluntary and involuntary nervous systems and our bladder and its surrounding pelvic floor muscles. The bladder is very elastic and is comprised of smooth muscle fibers that permit its expansion. Silverstein (2004) noted that:

> Filling of the bladder is achieved by a complex interaction between the sympathetic and parasympathetic nervous systems and the bladder musculature. Briefly, sympathetic (originating from T11 to L2 of the spinal cord) stimulation of beta adrenergic receptors in the bladder body, or the detrusor muscle induces bladder relaxation, allowing for filling. Filling is also achieved by contraction of the bladder neck (internal sphincter) smooth muscle fibers, under sympathetic control, and the striated muscle fibers of the external sphincter, the latter under voluntary control. In contrast, bladder emptying is controlled by parasympathetic, or somatic control, from S2 to S4. Parasympathetic receptor sites are located throughout the detrusor muscle and the proximal urethra. When these receptors are activated, the detrusor muscle contracts, increasing intravesical pressure. (p. 218)

In newborns urination is a spinal cord reflex. During the first or second year of life, bladder capacity increases as well as simultaneous maturation of the central nervous system, resulting in a greater awareness of bladder filling but still an inability to voluntarily control voiding. Voluntary control of voiding is eventually achieved by the coordinated development of: (a) increased bladder capacity, (b) voluntary control over the external sphincter, and (c) central nervous system control over voiding or inhibition of micturition independent of bladder capacity. (MacKeith, 1972).

As we have observed elsewhere,

> Acquisition of urinary continence is a complex physiological process (Muellner, 1951; Vincent, 1974). Normal continence is attained through appropriate voluntary elimination via sphincter release upon the lowering of the bladder neck when it is full and preventing micturation by contraction of pelvic floor muscles which raises the top of the bladder.
>
> Continence involves an appropriate bladder capacity, and the development of stimulus control of a full bladder over prevention of micturation until an appropriate situation for urination is present. This involves becoming aware of the need to urinate to avoid the emergency condition of "urgency" when urination is eminent, as well as the inhibition of urination while awake or sleeping. Incontinence can result from physical anomalies, neurological anomalies, and the lack of training oneself to recognize full bladder stimulation and act upon it. (Williams, Jackson, & Friman, 2007, p. 178)

Considered for some time to be primarily a sleep disorder (Wolfish, Pivik, & Busby, 1997), recent research (Nevéus, 2003) indicates that the sleep of enuretic children is quite normal polysomnographically, but it is also very "deep": Children with enuresis have high arousal thresholds.

Clinical treatment and research into childhood enuresis has revealed a variety of possible contributors, including: faulty suppression of urine production by the kidneys to the bladder during sleep (Muellner, 1951); malfunction or lack of maturation of the bladder, detrusor, and pelvic floor muscles responsible for adjusting the bladder position as it fills and empties (Muellner, 1960); neurological signaling between the cortex and the musculature controlling the bladder, especially during sleep (Yeung, Diao, & Sreedhar, 2008); anatomical irregularity or immature growth of the bladder resulting in small bladder capacity (Kawauchi et al., 2003); an unsuccessful development of operant or classical conditioning control over awakening in time to void appropriately or to not void until awakening (Gaber El-Anany, Maghraby, El-Din Shaker, & Abdel-Moneim,1999); and either infections anywhere in the urinary tract or a significant number of rare anatomical and physiological anomalies that result in the label of mixed enuresis and that require specific medical interventions. Treatments for nocturnal enuresis have closely followed these general known causes for primary and secondary nocturnal and diurnal enuresis and can be categorized generally as pharmacological, behavioral, and other. Interventions specific to the variety of medical conditions that are associated with mixed enuresis will not be discussed.

Demographic Variables

If one parent is enuretic, then enuresis occurs in children with a 40% increase from the general population and with a 70% increase if both parents are enuretic (Bakwin, 1993). By 5 years of age, 85% of children have complete diurnal and nocturnal control of urination. The remaining 15% of children gain urinary continence at a rate of approximately 15% per year. By 12 to 13 years of age, between 2% and 5% of children will continue to have urinary incontinence or primarily nocturnal enuresis. The incidence of primary nocturnal enuresis in adults has been reported to range between approximately 1.5% and 3%. Secondary enuresis occurs in approximately 3% to 8% of children between the ages of 5 and 13 years, and spontaneously resolves at approximately the same rate as primary enuresis (Husmann, 1996).

Impact of the Disorder

Estimated to affect 5 to 7 million children in North America, primary nocturnal enuresis is 3 times more prevalent than daytime wetting and occurs 3 times more often in boys. Secondary causes account for less than 25% of cases (Ramakrishnan, 2008); however, treatment efficacy is greatly dependent on proper ruling out of multiple symptoms (R. Butler & Heron, 2006). Indeed, Van de Walle and Van Laecke (2008) noted the inconsistent reporting of actual participant admission symptoms due to differences in symptoms reported in the *Diagnostic and Statistical Manual of the American Psychiatric Association* (APA, 1994) and the terminology outlined in the International Children's Continence Society (Nevéus et al., 2006). This has resulted in a general lack of clarity as to the relative effects of different treatments on different subpopulations of persons with enuresis. This observation limits all past and current research findings and conclusions and can only be addressed in future research with standardized reporting of a variety of participant symptoms or lack thereof in all research. It is increasingly being shown that different subgroups of mono-symptomatic enuresis may benefit more from different treatments that have been developed for specific patient characteristics and studies should describe those characteristics to arrive at meaningful conclusions regarding the different forms and treatments of enuresis. This review will also suffer from these limitations.

PHARMACOLOGICAL INTERVENTIONS

Imipramine

Imipramine is a tricyclic antidepressant with anticholinergic effects that can affect nocturnal enuresis by reducing muscle tone of the bladder and by lowering arousal levels of deep sleep, especially in the latter third of nighttime sleeping. Functionally, imipramine increases bladder capacity and assists in arousing the patient. Unfortunately, the effects of imipramine are closely tied to serum levels and the effective dosage to achieve an effective serum level has been shown to vary as much as 700% from one person to another (Fritz, Rockney, & Yeung, 1994). Additionally, some have reported negative side effects, such as upset stomach, and potentially fatal cardiac arrhythmias can be produced by higher dosages of imipramine (Husmann, 1996).

Less than two wet nights per month have been reported with imipramine for 20%–36% of patients, but cure rate is the same as for no treatment when medication is stopped (Kardash, Hillman, & Werry, 1968; Kunin, Limbert, Platzker, & McGinley, 1970; Martin, 1971; Monda & Husmann, 1995). Most recently Nevéus & Tullus (2008) reported on a trial of imipramine compared to placebo and tolterodine. Although better than placebo, tolterodine was not as effective as imipramine, which resulted in a mean of only 7.8 +/− 5.1 wet nights in a 2-week period with 25 children.

Imipramine is not reliably effective at eliminating monosymptomatic nocturnal enuresis and is the same as placebo for curing enuresis once medication is stopped. Reports of some side effects and the danger of over-consumption causing heart disrythmia reduce its attractiveness as a treatment.

Desmopressin

Desmopressin is an analog of the natural pituitary hormone vasopressin acetate, which is responsible for reducing urinary production while we sleep and is believed to be at fault in many monosyptomatic noctural enuresis cases (Rittig, Knudsen, Norgaard, Pedersen, & Djurhuus, 1989). Desmopressin produces an antidiuretic effect resulting in more reabsorption of water by the kidney, more concentrated volume of urine entering the bladder, and overall lower urine production. Its effects are only observed as long as the medication is taken.

Snajderova et al. (2001) reported on the use of desmopressin as a long-term treatment for 55 children with primary nocturnal enuresis. Intranasal desmopressin was administered in progressively higher doses (7–21 μg) until bed-wetting stopped in 89.1% of participants. Every 3 months, the drug was weaned and, if relapse occurred, the previous successful dose was reinstated. At the end of each of the 3 months, the number of responders remained higher (72.7%, 70.9%, 61.6%) than the spontaneous cure rate of 15%. Tullus, Bergström, Fosdal, Winnergård, and Hjälmås (1999) found similar results in an open study of 300 children in Sweden. Wolfish, Barkin, Gorodzinsky, and Schwarz (2002) reported on the 12-month effects of oral desmopressin on a group of 256 children from Canada. They found that 49% showed an effect of greater than 50% reduction in wet nights from baseline.

Meta-Analysis of Group Designs

Glazener and Evans (2002) reported a meta-analysis of 16 randomized controlled trials and found that nasal desmopressin was better than placebo in reducing the number of wet nights per week (mean 1.34 fewer wet nights/week; 95% confidence interval, 1.11–1.57). Desmopressin at doses of 20 μg, 40 μg, and 60 μg similarly increased the likelihood of a cure defined as 14 consecutive dry nights during treatment in three trials reporting this outcome (relative risk for failure to achieve 14 dry nights with 20 μg = 0.84; NNT for cure = 5.6). Unfortunately, no difference was found in cure rates after treatment was stopped.

The benefits of desmopressin are temporary, with a high relapse rate once treatment is discontinued (Diehr, 2003). Desmopressin is most effective in children with nocturnal polyuria and normal bladder capacity. Desmopressin may be functional for temporary reduction in symptoms for purposes of sleepovers or camping, and so forth.

Oxybutinin

Anticholinergics such as oxybutynin decrease detrusor muscle tone, frequency, and urgency of urination and increase bladder capacity. Oxybutinin has been used in children with primary nocturnal enuresis and daytime wetting showing restricted bladder capacity caused by an overactive detrusor muscle. It is also used in patients who have not responded to desmopressin.

Lovering, Tallett, and McKendry (1988) and Marconi, Felici, Roggia, and Torelli (1985) are two poorly designed random control trials of oxybutinin with large dropout rates such that no sound conclusions could be reached regarding effective treatment. Adverse side effects included dry mouth, blurred vision, headache, nausea, dizziness, gastrointestinal upset, and tachycardia (Glazener & Evans, 2002).

Summary of Pharmacological Treatments

The research evidence for the effects of Imipramine and Desmopressin meets acceptable criteria for evidence-based practice and provides support for these treatments as short-term control over enuresis; however, this same literature provides evidence that these interventions are not at all effective once medication is stopped, and therefore evidence for their nonuse in the long-term treatment of enuresis. There is also no support for the effectiveness of anticholinergics such as Oxubutinin in the long-term treatment of enuresis as appropriately controlled randomized controlled studies have yet to be conducted.

BEHAVIORAL INTERVENTIONS

Behavioral treatments teach the skills necessary for continence and attempt to reduce or stop incidents of wetting. In contrast to drugs and other treatments, the effects of behavioral treatments often continue long after treatment has been terminated, although rates of relapse will be discussed later. Behavioral approaches to diurnal and nocturnal enuresis often involve many of the same treatment components or variations of these. Evidence for one approach is often evaluated as a component of treatment. So for this reason, each of these treatments and components will be described more generally before the evidence for the effectiveness is examined and discussed with respect to diurnal or nocturnal enuresis. Variations of each treatment or component and the effectiveness of such variations will also be addressed.

Common Behavioral Interventions

Urine Alarm

The urine alarm (bell and pad apparatus) is probably the most well-known and most researched treatment for enuresis. Mowrer first examined it in 1938, and since then studies of its effectiveness have led to the identification of strengths and weaknesses of this technique in the treatment of enuresis. Variations in implementation have been developed to allow it to be used in a variety of different settings, with a variety of different individuals, and to enhance its effectiveness. In general, the urine alarm consists of a moisture-sensitive switch that closes, setting off the alarm, in the presence of moisture (i.e., urine). For nocturnal enuresis, the moisture sensor is often placed inside the child's pajamas or under the bed sheets and is activated when the child urinates. In cases of diurnal enuresis the child usually wears the device inside of his or her underwear. The development of a silent but vibrating alarm has also allowed it to be utilized for cases of diurnal enuresis without the public embarrassment of an audible alarm (Ruckstuhl, 2003).

Retention Control Training

Many studies have shown a correlation between enuresis and a reduced functional bladder capacity (De Wachter, Vermandel, De Moerloose, & Wyndaele, 2002). For example, Hallman (1950) assessed the bladder capacity of 192 children by giving them a large amount of water and then instructing them to refrain from voiding for as long as possible.

Their urine outputs were then measured over the next 4–6 hours and the largest void was used as a measure of functional bladder capacity. This original finding was then confirmed by subsequent studies (Esperanca & Gerrard, 1969; Starfield, 1967), and has been shown to be true both diurnally and nocturnally (Troup & Hodgson, 1971).

These findings have led to a treatment approach that involves requiring individuals to drink more fluids and then delay urination for an increasingly longer time to remediate the disparate functional bladder capacities of enuretic individuals, but does not directly train skills that may be associated with nocturnal continence. This approach assumes that the correlation between enuresis and functional bladder capacity is causal, meaning that continence problems are seen as a direct result of a smaller functional bladder capacity.

Positive Practice

Positive practice has been a common element of treatment in both diurnal and nocturnal enuresis. It involves the repeated practice of going to the bathroom and sitting on the toilet numerous times, in the absence of the urge to urinate. In the case of diurnal enuresis this is often conducted many times throughout the day and the child is required to interrupt ongoing activities to go to the bathroom a specified number of times. In the case of nocturnal enuresis, the child is required to lie in bed for a specified period of time and then get up out of bed, go to the bathroom, and sit on the toilet. This is often done during waking hours before going to bed and is practiced repeatedly in a given time period. Such practices may also be implemented contingent on an incident of wetting behavior. When the child has an accident they are required to repeat the practice of going to the bathroom and sitting on the toilet.

When an accident has occurred, positive practice is often combined with procedures that involve the restitution of the surrounding environment. This means that the child is required to change clothes or pajamas, clean themselves, clean up the area where urination occurred (for example, remove bedding and replace with clean bedding, and perhaps even do laundry that includes bedding or clothing that contacted urine). These procedures have also been referred to as "Responsibility Training" (Friman & Jones, 1998) and "Cleanliness Training" (Azrin, Sneed, & Foxx, 1974).

Stream Interruption Exercises

Stream interruption exercises consist of practice in the initiation and then termination of urine flow during a urinary episode. This approach is derived from the treatment of incontinence in women where they are required to contract and relax Kegel muscles in the pelvic floor. As these are the same muscles utilized to stop the flow of urine, this approach seems to be relevant to the treatment of enuresis and is often included as part of a treatment package for enuresis (Friman & Jones, 1998).

Waking Schedule

Waking schedules are only applicable to the treatment of nocturnal enuresis and typically involve waking the child at some predetermined interval and guiding them to the bathroom (Azrin et al., 1974). The initial interval until waking may be based on the typical period from the onset of sleep until an incident of wetting occurs. Waking may occur throughout the night, for example, every hour, or may just occur at the critical time before wetting. These awakenings are then systematically faded out by awakening the child progressively less or earlier in the evening until they can go to the bathroom before bed and stay dry until morning. This fading is typically based on a criterion of dry nights.

Positive Reinforcement

A number of procedures based on the principle of reinforcement have been utilized in the treatment of enuresis, often used in conjunction with other approaches. Positive reinforcement is often viewed not as a method by which to cure enuresis, but as a way to increase or maintain participation. Children are often allowed to select items that they would like to earn. Then conditioned reinforcers, such as tokens, points, stars, and so forth, are delivered for appropriate continence-related behaviors and later exchanged for the larger, significant preferred item or activity selected by the child (Friman & Jones, 1998; Harris & Purohit, 1977; Lassen & Fluet, 1979; Paschalis, Kimmel, & Kimmel, 1972; Popler, 1976). Other reinforcement-based procedures have delivered preferred items such as food, toys, or activities directly following appropriate voiding or other continence-related behaviors (LeBlanc, Carr, Crossett, Bennett, & Detweiler, 2005; Samaan, 1972). Reinforcement procedures have been utilized in the treatment of both diurnal and nocturnal enuresis.

Dry Bed Training

A combination of many of the aforementioned treatments was first utilized by Azrin et al. (1974). Their treatment package, dry bed training (DBT), included increased fluid intake, scheduled awakenings and reduced intensity of prompts to waken, positive practice, reinforcement of appropriate voiding, use of the urine alarm, wetness awareness (some children need training in discriminating that they have wet underwear or wet bed sheets), and cleanliness or responsibility training.

Evidence for Effectiveness of the Urine Alarm

Mowrer (1938) first reported the use of the urine alarm for the treatment of enuresis and since then, many other studies have examined the effectives and the underlying mechanisms responsible. Although the alarm has primarily been used for the treatment of nocturnal enuresis, there is also evidence for its effectiveness in treating diurnal enuresis and these will be discussed separately. There is a literature on the potential learning processes that may underlie the effectiveness of the urine alarm. Early work emphasized possible classical conditioning (Lovibond, 1963, 1964), whereas later work emphasized operant mechanisms (Azrin et al., 1974; Hansen, 1979; Mace & Parrish, 1984; Turner, Young, & Rachman, 1970). The reader is referred to these sources for a more detailed discussion of this question.

Single-Subject Experiments

Friman and Vollmer (1995) used a urine alarm to treat the diurnal enuresis of a 15-year-old female. Treatment resulted in arrest of accidents almost immediately and the authors suggested that the underlying mechanism was negative reinforcement, specifically avoidance of the embarrassment of the alarm signal in public. This treatment was examined using a reversal design and, although accidents increased again with the withdrawal of the treatment, they did not return to baseline levels. Reduction of accidents to near-zero levels was achieved after only two learning trials and the effects were maintained at a 3- and 6-month follow-up. Caution should be used in considering the use of such a treatment for diurnal enuresis, as the child may suffer further negative effects of the embarrassment of the alarm such as social withdrawal, anxiety, and so forth, and may attempt to remove the alarm and interfere with treatment. One way to avoid this issue is to use a silent vibrating version of the alarm, which was evaluated for effectiveness in treating nocturnal enuresis and found to be effective in arresting accidents in almost half of the participants (Ruckstuhl, 2003); however, if avoiding embarrassment was the key consequence in this intervention, then this may result in ineffective treatment.

Randomized Controlled Trials

Fielding (1980) examined the effects of urine alarms on 45 children with nocturnal enuresis and 30 children with both diurnal and nocturnal enuresis. In this section attention will be drawn to the effects of alarm treatment on the daytime wetting of the day and night participants. Individuals from both categories were divided into two treatment groups, with one group being exposed to the urine alarm immediately after baseline and the other group being exposed to retention control training for the first 4 weeks and then, if continence was not achieved, they were exposed to the alarm treatment. Although the alarm was only used at night, effects on both day and night wetting were measured. The criterion for success was 14 consecutive dry days or nights and failure to attain this criterion was decided after 14 weeks of treatment.

Despite some slight reductions in the day wetting frequencies under both treatment regimes, neither treatment showed a significant effect during the first 4 weeks of treatment. A comparison of baseline daytime wetting frequencies with frequencies of wetting in the first 4 weeks of treatment failed to reach statistical significance for either groups (retention control training: $t = 0.973$, $df = 6$; alarm: $t = 0.17$, $df = 6$). Over subsequent months of alarm-only treatment for both groups, there was a gradual reduction in the frequency of day wetting under both treatment regimes; however, comparisons of the frequencies of day wetting in baseline to those of the first, second, and third month of alarm treatment failed to reach statistical significance. Of the 17 children in the day and night wetting group who completed the study with a full data set, eight achieved the success criterion during the day, with four of these eight also achieving dryness at night. Four of these eight participants were in the retention control training then the alarm group, and four were in the alarm-only group. In general the response of day wetting to the alarm treatment was varied, with success being achieved for some participants and not for others. The source of this variation was unknown. In addition, of the eight participants who met the success criterion, 66% had relapsed at 3- and 6-month follow-up, with relapse defined as two instances of wetting. Moreover, children with both day and night wetting relapsed earlier than the children who only experienced night wetting, and there were a greater number of dropouts from day and night wetting participants.

Noctural Enuresis: Single-Subject Experiments

Hansen (1979) provided a variation on the standard urine alarm by using a twin-signal device that allowed escape and avoidance conditioning. This procedure involved one alarm that went off after urination on the pad, and then stopped. If the child did not awaken, get up, and turn off the alarm system, the second alarm would sound and did not stop until turned off. This procedure was explained to the child before the treatment began. When awakened by the first alarm they were required not only to get up to turn it off but also go to the bathroom and finish urinating and change pajamas, while the parents changed bedding and pad and reset the alarm. This device was utilized with two children aged 8 and 9 years and was successful in arresting the nocturnal enuresis of both participants over a treatment period of 200 days. Furthermore, these effects were shown to have been maintained at a 1-year follow-up.

Samaan (1972) reported the failure of urine alarm procedures to treat the nocturnal enuresis of one individual. A 7-year-old child described as a "slow learner" (p. 103) with primary enuresis participated. His parents were trained to use the traditional pad and bell alarm treatment and to report their results daily. After 2 weeks of intermittent success, a waking schedule and a reinforcement-based procedure were introduced as treatment, and then gradually faded. This led to zero levels of bed-wetting and maintenance of these effects at a 2-year follow-up. Although the author reported the failure of alarm procedures for this case of nocturnal enuresis, it should be noted that this treatment was only in effect for 2 weeks and that many other studies have assessed the effectiveness of treatment procedures over much longer periods of time (DeLeon & Mandell, 1966; Young & Turner, 1965).

Single-Subject Experiments: Treatment Packages

LeBlanc et al. (2005) demonstrated effective treatment for two of the three participants diagnosed with autism who had not yet been effectively toilet trained despite numerous attempts by parents. Treatment involved many components in addition to the urine alarm, including a sitting schedule, reinforcement contingencies for successful voids and self-initiations, increased fluid intake, communication training, and positive practice for accidents. The criteria for success in this study was no accidents for 2 consecutive days with at least one self-initiated void in the toilet, or 80% success for 2 consecutive days with at least 40% of successful voids being self-initiated. For the two participants who met this criteria they remained continent at a 4-week follow-up.

Mace and Parrish (1984), in a staggered multiple case study intervention, demonstrated the complete elimination of nocturnal enuresis in two brothers, by treating one sibling who was deaf and explaining to the other sibling that they could avoid treatment with the urine alarm if they had 14 consecutive dry nights. Given that one child was unable to hear the alarm, the parents awoke to the sound of the alarm and then woke the child. The child was then required to go to the bathroom, complete the void, change clothes, linens, and complete a datasheet. Here the procedures of cleanliness training were also utilized. The second child shared a bedroom with the first child and so observed treatment; some reduction in the frequency of bed-wetting was observed from this. Use of the alarm and cleanliness procedures were then introduced for the second child and both children achieved the success criterion of 14 dry nights. Treatment gains were maintained at a 10-month follow-up.

Nocturnal Enuresis: Randomized Controlled Trials

Mowrer (1938) and Mowrer and Mowrer (1938) first introduced the urine alarm as a treatment for nocturnal enuresis and reported a 100% success rate for 30 participants. They did not report any follow-up data. Since then a number of random controlled trials have been conducted to assess the effectiveness of this treatment and the results for the alarm treated groups are described following. The control groups received a variety of treatments including drug treatments, psychotherapy, and wakening, whereas others were simply kept on a wait-list. All of these studies showed that treatment with the urine alarm was better than treatment by the control condition, and this finding was shown to be statistically significant.

Young and Turner (1965) treated 105 patients with the urine alarm and reported that 65% of these participants showed an initial arrest of nocturnal enuresis, with 13% of these relapsing at 6- and 12-month follow-up. Their criterion for success was 14 consecutive dry nights and treatment took an average of 2.2 months. Similarly, DeLeon and Mandell (1966) reported successful treatment of 79% of their 56 participants with nocturnal enuresis, with a similar criterion of 14 dry nights. These authors report that 79% of those individuals had relapsed at a 6-month follow-up. Novick (1966) treated 36 individuals with the urine alarm and reported 89% success with a criterion of 14 nights of no wetting, and a relapse rate of 50%. Baker (1969) successfully treated 27 individuals using the standard urine alarm, using a success criterion of 28 consecutive dry nights, and reported relapse in 20% of these individuals. Forsythe and Redmond (1970) successfully treated 66% of the 200 individuals in their study; 23% of this 66% having relapsed at the 12- and 36-month follow-up.

R. J. Butler and Robinson (2002) reported on an interesting application of the alarm to 66 children with nocturnal enuresis. They achieved a 54.5% successful elimination of wet beds (14 consecutive nights dry), but also noted that 80% of these successful children slept through the entire night, reporting a result that is not commonly found and that draws into question the underlying effective ingredient of the alarm method. These studies are summarized in Table 16.1.

Ikeda, Koga, and Minami (2006) conducted an analysis of the treatment outcomes for 38 successfully treated enuretics (achieving 3 weeks of no wet nights) and 19 unsuccessful cases. Although the purpose of their study was isolation of variables in successful versus unsuccessful cases to support an active avoidance mechanism for the dry alarm method, their 66% success rate was accompanied by no significant differences in their participants in wet nights at baseline, age, and length of participation.

TABLE 16.1   Example Outcomes of Group Studies Using the Wet Bed Alarm for Nocturnal Enuresis

Author(s)	Participants	Initial Success Rate	Rate at Follow-Up
Mowrer and Mowrer, 1938	30	100%*	100%
Young and Turner, 1965	105	65%*	55% at 12 months
DeLeon and Mandell, 1966	56	79%*	16% at 6 months
Novick, 1966	36	89%*	50% at 8–12 months
Baker, 1969	27	100%+	80% at 6 months
Forsythe and Redmond, 1970	200	66%*	43% at 36 months
R. J. Butler and Robinson, 2002	66	54.5%*	Not reported
Cutting et al., 2007	522	79%*	64% at 24 months

Note: * = 14 consecutive nights dry; + = 28 consecutive dry nights

More recently, Cutting, Pallant, and Cutting (2007) reported on one of the largest ($N = 522$) groups of children treated with alarms alone for monosymptomatic enuresis. Their report was based on 505 of 849 enuretic children seen over a 5-year period and included a 6-month and 24-month follow-up with 99% response rates. A total of 79.0% achieved initial dryness within a median of 10 weeks. Of those achieving initial dryness, 73.0% remained dry at 6-month follow-up and 64% had remained dry at 24 months with no gender differences. Nineteen percent of children required more than 16 weeks' management with 56% achieving dryness. More girls achieved dryness than boys and more quickly. No difference in initial success was found with respect to severity of wetting or age. Additionally, relapse rates were unrelated to gender, age, or initial severity.

Nocturnal Enuresis: Meta-Analyses and Systematic Reviews

Kristensen and Jensen (2003) reported on a meta-analysis of 35 random control studies from Mowrer and Mowrer (1938) to 1996. This capitalized on a previous review of 34 of those studies by Forsyth and Butler (1989) and 237 patients treated by Jensen and Kristensen (1999, 2001a, 2001b). This meta-analysis indicated an approximately 38% success rate over four studies conducted between 1989 and 1996, as opposed to a 98% success rate for four studies from 1938–1958, supporting a steady decline in the effectiveness of the urine alarm for nocturnal enuresis. The authors attributed this to the systematic changes in reporting practice and underestimation of the problem of relapse. The probability of the success of alarm treatment for nocturnal enuresis increased with the frequency of wet nights, confirming previous findings.

R. J. Butler and Gasson (2005) reported a systematic review of 38 articles from 1980–2002 involving at least 10 children and a stand-alone alarm treatment. Success rates ranged from 30% to 87% (mean 64%) and were influenced by the type of enuresis, the treatment duration, and the success criteria adopted. In a subset of 20 studies involving 721 children who were treated for at least 6 weeks, 467 (65%) achieved 14 consecutive dry nights with only the alarm treatment. Again, a lack of standard inclusion criteria and definitions of success and relapse made conclusions on treatment effectiveness hard to make.

Relapse: Urine Alarm

Issues of relapse have been extremely prevalent in the literature on treatments for enuresis, especially in group studies. One study by Sacks and DeLeon (1983) illustrates this problem well. Fifty-two participants with nocturnal Enuresis were treated with the standard urine alarm and of the 44 (84.6% of the total) successful treatments, only 16 (30.8% of the total) remained continually dry throughout a 1-year follow-up. Positive outcomes increased to 24 (46.2% of the total), with the addition of successful retrainings (for those with at least 1 wet night per week for 4 consecutive weeks) who were followed for an additional year. In other words, although most of the individuals in this study were initially successful in meeting the dryness criterion, less than one-third remained dry.

As mentioned previously, Turner et al. (1970) demonstrated that relapse rates using the urine alarm were reduced when it was applied intermittently; however, treatment to criterion took many more sessions. Other studies have replicated this finding. For example, Finley, Besserman, Bennett, Clapp, and Finley (1973) reported the treatment of nocturnal enuresis with the urine alarm, on a continuous and intermittent schedule of application, with 90% and 80% initial success rates, and 44% and 12% relapse rates, respectively. Finley, Wansley, and Blenkarn (1977) treated 80 children using the urine alarm on a 70% schedule of application and reported a 94% success rate, with treatment taking longer than the average reported in the literature for 100% schedules, but relapse rates lower than typically reported for 100% schedules, a statistically significant difference. Taylor and Turner (1975) reported similar findings treating 61 children, divided into three groups: continuous application of the urine alarm, intermittent application of the urine alarm, and overlearning with the urine alarm. These authors reported 69% relapse on a continuous schedule of application, and a 44% relapse rate on an intermittent schedule of application. Furthermore, Taylor and Turner examined the effects of overlearning on relapse and found that this reduced relapse further to only 23%. Overlearning involves increasing fluid intake before bedtime and continuing treatment until a given criterion is achieved with a given fluid intake. Overlearning appears to be more effective in reducing relapse rates, with intermittent application being the next most effective compared to continuous application. It should also be noted that mean treatment was longest (114 days) with intermittent application, followed by overlearning (87 days), and shortest for continuous application (69 days) of the urine alarm.

Morgan (1978) reviewed the literature reporting the effects of intermittent application and overlearning on the relapse rates of alarm treatment. Although both have consistently been shown to reduce relapse, overlearning was reliably found to be the most effective method of countering relapse using urine alarm treatment; however, studies have varied widely on their definition of relapse with some describing significant relapse as a return to pretreatment levels of wetting, and others describing it as one incidence of wetting. This makes such reviews and analyses of the effects of treatment variations on relapse difficult.

Summary of Urine Alarm Treatment

Many research studies have examined the effectiveness of the urine alarm since it was first used in 1938. Although a few of these have examined the use of the urine alarm for diurnal enuresis, the majority of these studies have examined its utility in treating nocturnal enuresis. The reasons for this may be that many more approaches are available for use in diurnal enuresis where the individual is awake, but also that the use of an alarm in daily social situations could be particularly aversive for the individual, and may even result in a number of additional problems and side effects resulting from the treatment itself. There is support for the position that the effective process in treating enuresis is active avoidance of the general nuisance associated with it. That is, the alarm may function simply as the occasion for operant learning involving positive practice, response cost, social disapproval, and so forth. This position is also supported by evidence that any awakening system using these additional procedures is associated with success.

In 1977, Doleys provided a review of the literature to that point and concluded that, using each researcher's criterion for successful treatment, bed-wetting was arrested in 75% of individuals. The duration of treatment ranged from 5 weeks to 12 weeks with a relapse rate of 41%, most of these occurring within 6 months of treatment. From those studies presenting data on retreatment, approximately 68% were successfully retreated. Although other meta-analyses of urine alarm treatments around the same time reported higher success rates of 80%–90% (Lovibond, 1964), all data support the overall conclusion that initial success rates using the urine alarm are high, the relapse rates continue to be high, and variations such as overlearning and intermittent application should be incorporated into treatment to reduce these. In addition, the frequent reporting of ulcers associated with use of the alarm (Doleys, 1977) suggest that procedures requiring as few exposures as possible may be desirable.

More recently, Glazener and Evans (2002) reported that children given alarms as part of a treatment package were 13 times more likely to become dry as children treated without alarms and that somewhere between 29% and 69% of children relapse after initially successful treatment. Moreover, attrition rates may be as high as 26% using alarm treatments, although Glazener and Evans stated that this is not significantly different to attrition rates for other treatments of nocturnal enuresis. Nevertheless, we would argue that such attrition rates are problematic and should be addressed in future research. Ruckstuhl (2003) attempted to address this by examining the social validity of alarm treatments for 32 participants and their parents. Results suggested that the treatment was socially acceptable to the individuals surveyed; however, it should be noted that only 19 of the 32 participants initially involved actually completed the study.

Despite the high attrition and relapse rates, R. J. Butler, Golding, and Heron (2005) reported that enuresis alarms were used by 19.2% of parents surveyed on treatments used to treat their enuretic children. This was less common than restricting fluid intake in the evening and waking schedules, but more common than medications.

Collectively, these data make it clear that the urine alarm is an evidence-based practice for the treatment of nocturnal enuresis; however, it is not successful for everyone, and relapse rates are high. Further, the use of intermittent schedules and overlearning are also evidence-based practices that enhance the efficacy of the alarm; however, there is much less evidence for use of the alarm for treatment of diurnal enuresis. Given these general findings and issues in the use of the urine alarm, procedures such as retention control training, waking schedules, positive practice, responsibility or cleanliness training, and stream interruption exercises, continue to be investigated as stand-alone treatments or components of a treatment package, and are discussed in the following.

EVIDENCE FOR RETENTION CONTROL TRAINING

Retention Control Training for Diurnal Enuresis

Although many treatments using retention control training (RCT) for nocturnal enuresis

have conducted retention control training during the day, few have examined its effectiveness with diurnal enuresis. Fielding (1980) examined the RCT in a group of 45 nocturnal enuretic children, and a group of 30 nocturnal and diurnal enuretic children exposed to either urine alarm procedures or RCT. As discussed previously, results suggest that alarm procedures were far superior to RCT and the RCT groups were subsequently exposed to alarm treatment; however, although there were some slight reductions in the frequency of day wetting under both treatments, this failed to reach statistically significant levels. Mean bladder capacities increased significantly for day and night wetters who became dry by the end of treatment (both alarm-only and RCT plus alarm), but not for those who did not become dry by the end of treatment. This study showed that RCT did not produce significant improvement for nocturnal enuresis, or diurnal and nocturnal enuresis.

Single-Subject Research on Retention Control Training

Kimmel and Kimmel (1970) applied RCT to three individuals with nocturnal enuresis, increasing fluid intake and increasing the retention interval gradually until it reached 30 minutes. Reinforcement was provided at the end of the required retention interval. All three participants became dry by the end of treatment, which lasted just 7 days for two of the participants, and 14 days for the other. All were still dry at a 12-month follow-up. Stedman (1972) conducted a variation on RCT by teaching one individual to discriminate bladder distention and to chart their own data on the number of nighttime wets. This treatment took 14 weeks; however, some relapse had occurred at the 3-month follow-up. Miller (1973) examined the utility of RCT for two individuals with nocturnal enuresis. The study involved two children with nocturnal enuresis, and the numbers of wet nights, as well as the frequency of diurnal voiding, were taken as dependent measures. No tangible reinforcers were provided and RCT was examined using a standard ABAB reversal design. The children charted their own data and were treated for 14–16 weeks, when both participants met the success criterion for dryness. At 4- and 7-month follow-up, neither had relapsed. Doleys and Wells (1975) treated one individual using RCT as part of a package involving forced increase in fluid intake, a waking schedule, and reinforcement for voiding appropriately. Again, the mean amount voided at each occurrence during the day was taken as a dependent measure, in addition to the number of dry nights. The individual was dry after 50 days of treatment and remained dry at a 14-week follow-up.

In general, single-subject analyses of the effects of RCT typically take a long time and often involve additional procedures such as reinforcement. Although the reinforcement is programmed to follow the retention interval it also directly correlates with appropriate voiding, and so it is possible that many successful applications could be due to the reinforcement of appropriate voiding and not the RCT itself.

Group Research on Retention Control Training

Starfield and Mellits (1968) investigated the effects of RCT with 83 individuals with nocturnal enuresis. Parents were instructed to allow free access to fluids throughout the day and to ask the children to withhold urination until it caused minimal discomfort. Pre- and posttreatment measures of bladder capacity and bed-wetting were taken, and the change in bladder capacity for successfully treated and unsuccessfully treated individuals was significantly different.

Paschalis et al. (1972) trained diurnal retention of urine for 31 individuals diagnosed with nocturnal enuresis. This training continued until the individuals could retain urine for 45 minutes before voiding, and took an average of 20 days. Enuretic participants were divided into two treatment groups: one group receiving treatment immediately after the collection of baseline data and the second receiving treatment after a period of no treatment. There was also a third group of nonenuretic participants whose data were also analyzed for differences in mean number of voids per day. Fifteen of the treated individuals were nocturnally dry, another eight showed significant improvements, and the remainder showed no effect, suggesting that RCT conducted during the day may have some inconsistent effect on nocturnal enuresis but the results are inconclusive.

Harris and Purohit (1977) compared the effects of RCT with a no-treatment control group with 18 enuretic children. Results showed a significant increase in bladder capacity for the treatment group over the control group but that the frequency of bed-wetting did not change significantly for the treatment group, suggesting that while RCT may increase functional bladder capacity, this increase may not necessarily change the incidents of bed-wetting for individuals with nocturnal enuresis.

Summary

In general, the use of RCT as a stand-alone treatment has been inconsistent in its effectiveness. Although evidence-based criteria for number of studies and participants have been met, variations in procedures, the absence of substantial follow-up data, and the lack of evidence for a causal relation between functional bladder capacity and enuresis, make evaluation difficult; however, RCT has frequently been included as a component of larger treatment packages discussed later.

EVIDENCE FOR REINFORCEMENT-BASED PROCEDURES

Few studies have examined the effectiveness of reinforcement-based procedures alone. Historically, these have utilized both positive and aversive contingencies, although the most recent applications emphasize the use of positive reinforcement. Although reinforcement procedures have been used in conjunction with a variety of other procedures, only those primarily focused on the isolated use of reinforcement procedures will be described here. These studies have typically been conducted using a single-subject design and have targeted cases of nocturnal enuresis.

Several independent studies have shown that reinforcement of appropriate behavior can result in acquisition of continence. For example, Nordquist (1971) used time out from positive reinforcement and differential reinforcement of appropriate behavior to reduce tantruming and other noncompliant behaviors. The hypothesis was that the child's wetting was part of the same response class as the other targeted behaviors. This involved one child, and was conducted using a reversal design where the treatment was implemented, removed, and then reimplemented. Procedures reduced both the targeted responses and incidents of wetting, with treatment taking 20 weeks to reach complete elimination of enuresis. The child was still free from wetting accidents at the 16-month follow-up.

Samaan (1972) examined the effects of reinforcement for urination in the toilet for a child with nocturnal enuresis. The child was also exposed to a waking schedule where she was wakened every 2–3 hours and guided to the bathroom to sit on the toilet. If she urinated while on the toilet she was given a piece of chocolate and a hug. After only 10 days of treatment, the child began to waken independently to urinate. Throughout treatment the schedule of reinforcement and the waking schedule were gradually faded. The participant remained dry at the 2-year follow-up. Popler (1976) investigated the use of a token economy for nonenuretic behaviors with one individual diagnosed with nocturnal enuresis. The individual was instructed to record whether he was wet or dry each night, and during treatment he had a weekly meeting where records were discussed and verified, and one token was given for each dry night. The individual kept a graph of data posted on the meeting room wall, and was given $5 for every 15 tokens collected. The frequency of bed-wetting reduced to zero after 28 weeks of treatment and this had been maintained by the 6-month follow-up. Allgeier (1976) investigated the effects of modeling and reinforcement on the enuretic behaviors of two sisters, both diagnosed with nocturnal enuresis. Both individuals were required to fill out a chart in the kitchen of their home indicating whether or not they had remained dry the night before, and they lost some of their allowance for not reporting their data and for reporting inaccurately. During baseline, no additional contingencies were programmed for bed-wetting. When accurate reporting had been established, treatment began by consequating bed-wetting with a restriction on nighttime fluid intake. They were not allowed any liquid intake after 6:00 P.M. until they had been continent for 21 days. Some reduction in the frequency of bed-wetting was observed after the implementation of the self-monitoring system, and both individuals became dry and remained dry for 44 and 65 days by the end of the study. No follow-up data was reported. More recently, Hagopian, Fisher, Piazza, and Wierzbicki (1993) examined the effectiveness of a continuous schedule of reinforcement for continent urinations of one individual with diurnal enuresis. In addition, minimal attention was given following accidents, the child was taken to the bathroom every 30 minutes, and directed to sit on the toilet while lukewarm water was poured over the genital area to increase the likelihood of urination. Accidents were reduced and continent urination increase from 17% to 84%. The treatment was implemented in an additive manner and these results were obtained using all elements just described. No follow-up data were available.

Only one study used a punishment approach. Tough, Hawkins, MacArthur, and Ravensway (1971) provided contingent punishment in the form of a cool bath for incidents of bed-wetting. Two individuals were involved in this study that lasted for 22 and 28 days until both became dry at night; however, one had relapsed at the 18-month follow-up.

Reinforcement-based procedures alone can be effective in eliminating enuresis but may require extended periods of treatment in order to have such an effect. The available data suggest that relapse rates may be fairly low. Many studies utilizing reinforcement procedure have also used other components of treatment. Currently, it appears that neither the volume of studies nor participants meet the requirements for evidence-based practice, and the limited numbers of studies on the effectiveness of these procedures alone make further conclusions difficult and tentative. This also makes this area of research important and necessary.

EVIDENCE OF EFFECTIVENESS OF DRY BED TRAINING

Many of the treatments described so far have been utilized as part of a treatment package referred to as DBT. This was first examined by Azrin et al. (1974) and has since been investigated and utilized by many researchers, exclusively in the area of nocturnal enuresis. A few of the individual treatment approaches described at the beginning of this section have not been discussed with respect to their effectiveness, primarily because they are not typically used, or at least not reported, as stand-alone treatments and so will be discussed and evaluated in terms of their role in DBT. Treatments involving many of the components involved in DBT will also be discussed here.

Single-Subject Research Dry Bed Training

Browning (1967) implemented a treatment package similar to DBT. Browning treated one individual with nocturnal enuresis using the urine alarm, a wakening schedule, reinforcement for wakening and going to the bathroom, and required the individual to change bedding.

The participant was dry by week 7 of treatment. Follow-up data was not reported.

Singh, Phillips, and Fischer (1976) used a procedure similar to DBT with the exception that positive practice and the urine alarm were excluded. Instead of the urine alarm, these authors used an alarm clock that woke the individual 2 hours after falling asleep and then progressively earlier. Upon waking to the alarm the individual had to go to the bathroom and sit on the toilet. If accidents occurred she was required to change bedding, and praise was provided for dry nights. Although the nocturnal enuresis was eliminated using these operant procedures without the use of the urine alarm, it took 15 months for treatment to be effective; however, treatment effects had maintained at an 8-month follow-up.

Lassen and Fluet (1979) used DBT to treat the nocturnal enuresis of a 10-year-old child, including use of a urine alarm, a requirement to get up and wash face, void in toilet, wake parents, change bed, and reset alarm. An overlearning procedure was also added, possibly to reduce relapse, and involved an increased fluid intake before bed. Parents were trained to implement this procedure and conducted the treatment. Nocturnal enuresis was eliminated after 13 weeks, and treatment was terminated after 30 consecutive dry nights. Parents reported that effects were maintained at follow-up, although the time to follow-up was not reported by the authors.

Papworth (1989) used DBT to treat a 42-year-old male with nocturnal enuresis. The treatment involved RCT, scheduled awakenings, a urine alarm, cleanliness training, positive practice, and reinforcement for dry nights. Enuresis was successfully treated after only 4 weeks of treatment and the individual had remained dry by a 6-month follow-up.

More recently, LeBlanc et al. (2005) used a DBT-type package to treat diurnal and nocturnal incontinence in three individuals using a nonconcurrent multiple baseline intervention strategy. This consisted of a treatment package including a urine alarm, schedule for sitting on the toilet, reinforcement of successful voids and self-initiations, increased fluid intake, communication training, and positive practice. Incontinence was eliminated for two of the three individuals and accidents were reduced for the third.

Group Design Research on Dry Bed Training

Azrin et al. (1974) were the first to describe and investigate DBT. They examined the treatment of 24 individuals who were randomly assigned to four groups. One group received standard urine alarm procedures, another group received DBT where only the child heard the urine alarm, a third group received DBT where only the parents heard the alarm, and the last group received DBT where both parent and child heard the alarm. The DBT consisted of increased fluid intake, hourly awakenings, teaching child to awaken to a signal by sitting the child up or gently shaking them, positive practice of waking and going to the toilet, reinforcement for urinating in the toilet at night, a urine alarm, training in awareness of the dry versus wet condition of the bed, and cleanliness training. Successful treatment was reported for all 24 participants and was fairly rapid, with the average participant having only 2 wet nights before the success criterion of 2 consecutive dry weeks was achieved. No major relapses were reported and no intensive retraining was required by the 6-month follow-up.

Bollard and Woodroffe (1977) examined the effectiveness of parent-administered DBT on the nocturnal enuresis of 34 children. One group of participants used parent-administered DBT and the other had parent-administered DBT without the use of the alarm. Enuresis was eliminated for all children exposed to parent-administered DBT using the alarm and took only 12 days, with only two relapses. Although reductions were achieved, in the group exposed to DBT without the alarm, enuresis was not completely eliminated for any

of the children. The authors suggest that the use of the alarm with other procedures allows for the more immediate and effective application of relevant consequences.

Keating, Butz, Burke, and Heimberg (1983) further investigated the necessity of an alarm in DBT, and the effects of training parents to implement treatment. Twenty-three individuals were divided into three treatment groups that varied on the training setting (home or office) and whether training was conducted with the parent and child or just the parent. Seven individuals on a wait-list were monitored. Although the treatment groups did improve compared to the wait-list group, enuresis was not successfully eliminated for any of the participants. Furthermore, 6 of the 23 participants in the treatment groups dropped out of the study.

Bollard and Nettelbeck (1981) also investigated the level of supervision necessary for parents to effectively implement DBT and compared the effects of DBT to a standard alarm procedure. In the first experiment they compared the application of standard urine alarm procedures implemented by parents who were closely supervised and parents who received no supervision after initial instructions. Parental supervision while implementing treatment with a urine alarm resulted in greater decreases in enuretic incidents. The second experiment compared DBT under four conditions: (1) by the child's parents at home, (2) by a professional trainer at home, (3) by a professional trainer in the hospital, and (4) by the child's parents without use of an alarm. The DBT was successful under all conditions except where no buzzer was used, in which case it was only marginally more effective than no treatment at all. Furthermore, DBT was superior to standard urine alarm treatment.

Van Londen, Van Londen-Barentsen, Van Son, and Mulder (1995) investigated the effectiveness of bibliotherapy by parents, allowing them to act as therapists for their child's nocturnal enuresis. Parents were given a set of instructions and a urine alarm. One group was instructed to give or remove stickers immediately after the child's alarm goes off, they wake to urinate, or their bed is dry in the morning. A second group was given instructions to apply consequences only the next morning. A third group used only the alarm and were not given instructions to provide specific programmed consequences. Ninety-seven percent of group 1 was successfully treated to eliminate nocturnal enuresis, with only 84% for group 2, and 72% of group 3. At a 2½-year follow-up, maintenance of results were reduced to 92% for group 1, reduced to 77% for group 2, and stayed the same at 72% for group 3. Again, the authors suggested that the increased success using the urine alarm is simply that it allows for more immediate application of consequences for wetting.

Summary of Dry Bed Training

Dry bed training was originally shown by Azrin et al. (1974) to be very effective and efficient in arresting nocturnal enuresis. Since then other studies have not had quite the same degree of success but have demonstrated that it is an effective and rapid method for treating, and often eliminating, enuresis. The literature indicates that DBT meets the requirements for evidence-based treatment with the alarm, and may be effective alone as long as the enuretic is awakened. Studies investigating the use of parents as therapists not only increase the accessibility to treatment but make it more cost-effective, as it is often difficult to find a professional willing to conduct all-night intensive treatment and the cost of that can be high. Given this, it is important to simplify procedures as much as possible without losing the effectiveness of the treatment.

The literature on DBT suggests that some components may be necessary while others may be less critical to the success of treatment. The use of a urine alarm in DBT has been repeatedly shown to be critical. The role of the alarm in DBT seems to be to provide the opportunity to implement other contingencies and elements of the treatment package. Consistent with studies on the use of the urine alarm, overlearning has been shown to be a useful addition to treatment packages as it reduces the likelihood of future relapse. Further, a waking schedule, or reinforcement for waking to minimal prompts, has been shown to be relevant to treatment success, as well as some procedure by which to ensure that the child is fully awake. This could be served by washing their face, showering, or by completing a task that is effortful and requires wakening, such as changing bedding.

Alternatively, the literature suggests that some elements are not necessary for treatment success. Retention control training appears to be less relevant to success and does not consistently show increased continence either alone or as part of a treatment package such as DBT. Other elements, such as positive practice, require further research to determine the role they play. Other treatments such as Kegel exercises have often been added to treatment packages (Friman & Jones, 1998) but have not been evaluated and thus remain non-evidence-based practice. Tarbox, Williams, and Friman (2004) also suggest that the wearing of diapers should be considered as an important variable when considering treatment for continence issues, although further research is also required on this issue.

OVERVIEW OF RESEARCH ON BEHAVIORAL TREATMENTS

Urine alarms, although often effective, are also associated with frequent relapse. Relapse can be reduced by the addition of procedures such as overlearning and intermittent schedules. The addition of reinforcement for appropriate behaviors and other contingencies such as those described in DBT provide a treatment that is consistently effective in a short period of time with few relapses. Parents, given some minimal level of instruction and supervision, can effectively implement DBT.

Evaluation and comparison of treatment approaches and success rates in the treatment of enuresis is made difficult by variability surrounding treatment success criteria. Research has varied widely on definitions of successful treatment of enuresis, with some only requiring an improvement from baseline and others requiring 14 consecutive days of dryness. Given this, success in one study may not be considered a success in another study. Furthermore, relapse has suffered the same fate. Some studies have considered relapse to be one incidence of wetting, with others not considering relapse to occur unless wetting has returned to baseline levels. This also raises the variability of follow-up periods, as follow-up data cannot be collected until a minimal period of dryness, considered as successful treatment in the original criterion, has passed. If a follow-up period is extremely short, then relapse by any criteria is less likely and an extremely long follow-up period may be considered somewhat unethical given that there is often a social stigma associated with problems of continence. Moreover, a reasonable treatment time should elapse before a treatment is considered as a failure and other methods are considered. A resolution of these issues may make conclusions regarding effective treatment stronger than the current analysis.

OTHER TREATMENT APPROACHES

A recent Cochrane Review provides a summary of several alternative approaches and the state of our knowledge regarding their effectiveness. Glazener, Evans, and Cheuk (2008) conducted this meta-analysis. They reviewed 15 randomized trials describing a variety of treatment approaches and concluded that the studies provided weak evidence to support the use of hypnosis, psychotherapy, acupuncture,

and chiropractic; however, the studies in general were small, and of weak methodological caliber.

EVIDENCE-BASED PRACTICES FOR ENURESIS

Evidence-based practices as reported in the Cochrane database for enuresis suffer from a general lack of specific comparisons of treatments for differing types and classifications of enuresis as outlined at the beginning of this chapter. The most recent available papers published as 2008 updates of earlier studies (Glazener & Evans, 2002, 2004; Glazener, Evans, & Peto, 2004) reported that meta-analyses are not available for complex treatments of enuresis that include alarms and other further interventions such as medications or DBT, and conclusions that can only be drawn from small single-subject trials indicate that alarm and other interventions such as DBT are more effective than alarm alone but that any treatment with alarms appears better than any treatment without alarms. For simple enuresis, outside of the known effect of desmopressin (while the drug is being taken), simple behavioral interventions may be effective for some children, but further comparison trials of components are needed. Simple methods could be tried as first-line therapy before considering alarms and DBT types of procedures, because these later treatments may be more demanding and may provide increased opportunity for stress and inconsistency.

The large-scale study by Cutting et al. (2007) provides strong support for alarm treatment of monosymptomatic nocturnal enuresis, albeit not shown in a randomized study. Indeed, 70 years after Mowrer first reported on the original alarm treatment, randomized controlled studies of combination treatments are still needed.

See Table 16.2, which summarizes the evidence for the effectiveness of various treatments for enuresis.

TABLE 16.2   A Summary of the Evidence for Effectiveness of the Different Enuresis Treatments

Category	Treatment	Strong Evidence	Weak Evidence	Needs More Study
Pharmacological	Imipramine		Y*	Y
	Desmopressin	Y*		
	Oxybutinin		Y*	Y
Behavioral	Alarm	Y		Relapse
	Dry bed training	Y		
	Reinforcement		Y	
	Retention training		Y	Y
	Kegel exercises		Y	Y
	Waking schedule		Y	Y
	Positive practice		Y	Y
Other	Acupuncture			Y
	Psychotherapy			Y
	Hypnosis			Y
	Chiropractic			Y

Note: * = Only effective while the medication is being taken

REFERENCES

Allgeier, A. R. (1976). Minimizing therapist supervision in the treatment of enuresis. *Journal of Behavior Therapy & Experimental Psychiatry, 7*, 371–372.

American Psychiatric Association. (1994). *Diagnostic and statistical manual of mental disorders* (3rd ed.). Washington, DC: Author.

Azrin, N. H., Sneed, T. J., & Foxx, R. M. (1974). Dry-bed: Rapid elimination of childhood enuresis. *Behavior Therapy, 12*, 147–156.

Baker, B. L. (1969). Symptom treatment and symptom substitution in Enuresis. *Journal of Abnormal Psychology, 74*, 42–49.

Bakwin, H. (1993). The genetics of enuresis. In I. Koluk, R. C. MacKeith, & S. R. Medow (Eds.), *Bladder control and enuresis* (pp. 73–77). London, England: W. Heinemann Medical Book.

Bollard, J., & Nettelbeck, T. (1981). A comparison of dry-bed training and standard urine-alarm conditioning treatment of childhood bedwetting. *Behaviour Research and Therapy, 19*, 215–226.

Bollard, J., & Woodroffe, O. (1977). The effect of parent-administered dry-bed training on nocturnal enuresis. *Behaviour Research and Therapy, 15*, 159–165.

Browning, R. M. (1967). Operant strengthening UCR (awakening) as a prerequisite to treatment of persistent enuresis. *Behaviour Research and Therapy, 5*, 371–372.

Butler, R. J., & Gasson, S A. (2005). Enuresis alarm treatment. *Scandinavian Journal of Urology and Nephrology, 39*, 349–357.

Butler, R., & Heron, J. (2006). Exploring the differences between mono- and polysymptomatic nocturnal enuresis. *Scandinavian Journal of Urology and Nephrology, 40*, 313–319.

Butler, R. J., Golding, J., & Heron, J. (2005). Nocturnal enuresis: A survey of parental coping strategies at 7 1/2 years. *Child: Care, Health, and Development, 31*, 659–667.

Butler, R. J., & Robinson, J. C. (2002). Alarm treatment for childhood nocturnal enuresis: An investigation of within-treatment variables. *Scandinavian Journal of Urology and Nephrology, 36*, 268–272.

Cutting, D. A., Pallant, J. F., & Cutting, F. M. (2007). Nocturnal enuresis: Application of evidence-based medicine in community practice. *Journal of Paediatrics and Child Health, 43*, 167–172.

DeLeon, G., & Mandell, W. (1966). A comparison of conditioning and psychotherapy in the treatment of functional enuresis. *Journal of Clinical Psychology, 22*, 326–330.

De Wachter, S., Vermandel, A., De Moerloose, K., & Wyndaele, J. J. (2002). Value of increase in bladder capacity in treatment of refractory monosymptomatic nocturnal enuresis in children. *Urology, 60*, 1090–1094.

Diehr, S. (2003). How effective is desmopressin for primary nocturnal enuresis? *The Journal of Family Practice, 30*, 568–569.

Doleys, D. M. (1977). Behavioral treatments for nocturnal enuresis in children: A review of the recent literature. *Psychological Bulletin, 84*, 30–54.

Doleys, D. M., & Wells, K. C. (1975). Changes in functional bladder capacity and bed-wetting during and after retention control training: A case study. *Behavior Therapy, 6*, 685–688.

Esperanca, M. D., & Gerrard, J. W. (1969). Nocturnal enuresis: Studies in bladder function in normal children and enuretics. *Canadian Medical Assessment Journal, 101*, 324–327.

Fielding, D. (1980). The response of day and night wetting children and children who wet only at night to retention control training and the enuresis alarm. *Behaviour Research and Therapy, 18*, 305–317.

Finley, W. W., Besserman, R. L., Bennett, L. F., Clapp, R. K., & Finley, P. M. (1973). The effect of continuous, intermittent, and "placebo" reinforcement on the effectiveness of the conditioning treatment for enuresis nocturna. *Behaviour Research and Therapy, 11*, 289–297.

Finley, W. W., Wansley, R. A., & Blenkarn, M. M. (1977). Conditioning treatment of enuresis using a 70% intermittent reinforcement schedule. *Behaviour Research and Therapy, 15*, 419–427.

Forsythe, W. I., & Butler, R. J. (1989). Fifty years of enuretic alarms. *Archives of the Disabled Child, 64*, 879–885.

Forsythe, W. I., & Redmond, A. (1970). Enuresis and the electric alarm: Study of 200 cases. *British Medical Journal, 1*, 211–213.

Friman, P. C., & Jones, K. M. (1998). Elimination disorders in children. In S. Watson & F. Gresham (Eds.), *Handbook of child behavior therapy* (pp. 239–260). New York, NY: Plenum Press.

Friman, P. C., & Vollmer, D. (1995). Successful use of the nocturnal urine alarm for diurnal enuresis. *Journal of Applied Behavior Analysis, 28*, 89.

Fritz, G. K., Rockney, R. M., & Yeung, A. S. (1994). Plasma levels and efficacy of imipramine treatment for enuresis. *Journal of the American Academy of Child and Adolescent Psychiatry, 33*, 60–64.

Gaber El-Anany, F., Maghraby, H., El-Din Shaker, S., & Abdel-Moneim, A. (1999). Primary nocturnal enuresis: A new approach to conditioning treatment. *Urology, 53*, 405–409.

Glazener, C. M. A., & Evans, J. H. (2002). Desmopressin for nocturnal enuresis in children. *Cochrane Database of Systematic Reviews, 3*, Art. No. CD002112.

Glazener, C. M. A., & Evans, J. H. C. (2004). Simple behavioural and physical interventions for nocturnal enuresis in children. *Cochrane Database of Systematic Reviews, 2*, Art. No. CD003637.

Glazener, C. M. A., Evans, J. H. C., & Cheuk, D. K. L. (2008). Complementary and miscellaneous interventions for nocturnal enuresis in children. *Cochrane Database of Systematic Reviews, 2*, Art. No. CD005230.

Glazener, C. M. A., Evans, J. H. C., & Peto, R. E. (2004). Complex behavioural and educational interventions for nocturnal enuresis in children. *Cochrane Database of Systematic Reviews, 1*, Art. No. CD004668.

Hagopian, L. P., Fisher, W., Piazza, C. C., & Wierzbicki, J. J. (1993). A water-prompting procedure for the treatment of urinary incontinence. *Journal of Applied Behavior Analysis, 26*, 473–474.

Hallman, N. (1950). On the ability of enuretic children to hold urine. *Acta Paediatrica, 39*, 87–93.

Hansen, G. D. (1979). Enuresis control through fading, escape, and avoidance training. *Journal of Applied Behavior Analysis, 12*, 303–307.

Harris, L. S., & Purohit, A. P. (1977). Bladder training and enuresis: A controlled trial. *Behaviour Research and Therapy, 15*, 485–490.

Husmann, D. (1996). Enuresis. *Urology, 48*(2), 184–193.

Ikeda, A., Koga, A., & Minami, S. (2006). Evaluation of a cure process during alarm treatment for nocturnal enuresis. *Journal of Clinical Psychology, 62*, 1245–1257.

Jensen, I. N., & Kristensen, G. (1999). Alarm treatment: Analyses of response and relapse. *Scandinavian Journal of Urology and Nephrology, 202*, 73–75.

Jensen, I. N., & Kristensen, G. (2001a). Frequency of nightly wetting and the efficiency of alarm treatment of nocturnal enuresis. *Scandinavian Journal of Urology and Nephrology, 35*, 357–363.

Jensen, I. N., & Kristensen, G. (2001b). *Nightly voiding habits of enuretic patients: The first 40 days with the alarm treatment for nocturnal enuresis* (Research Report 32). Odense, Denmark: Department of Statistics and Demography, University of Southern Denmark.

Kardash, S., Hillman, E. S., & Werry, J. (1968). Efficacy of imipramine in childhood enuresis: A double-blind control study with placebo. *Canadian Medical Association Journal, 99*, 263–266.

Kawauchi, A., Tanaka, Y., Naito, Y., Yamao, Y., Ukimura, O., Yoneda, K., . . . Miki, T. (2003). Bladder capacity at the time of enuresis. *Urology, 61*, 1016–1018.

Keating, J. C., Butz, R. A., Burke, E., & Heimberg, R. G. (1983). Dry bed training without a urine alarm: Lack of effect of setting and therapist contact with child. *Journal of Behaviour Therapy & Experimental Psychiatry, 14*, 109–115.

Kimmel, H. D., & Kimmel, E. C. (1970). An instrumental conditioning method for the treatment of enuresis. *Journal of Behaviour Therapy & Experimental Psychiatry, 1*, 121–123.

Kristensen, G., & Jensen, I. N. (2003). Meta-analyses of results of alarm treatment for nocturnal enuresis. *Scandinavian Journal of Urology and Nephrology, 37*, 232–238.

Kunin, S. A., Limbert, D. J., Platzker, A. C. G., & McGinley, J. (1970). The efficacy of imipramine in the management of enuresis. *Urology, 104*, 612–615.

Lassen, M. K., & Fluet, N. R. (1979). Multifaceted behavioral intervention for nocturnal enuresis. *Journal of Behavior Therapy & Experimental Psychiatry, 10*, 155–156.

LeBlanc, L. A., Carr, J. E., Crossett, S. E., Bennett, C. A., & Detweiler, D. D. (2005). Intensive outpatient behavioral treatment of primary urinary incontinence of children with autism. *Focus on Autism and Other Developmental Disabilities, 20*, 98–105.

Lovibond, S. H. (1963). The mechanism of conditioning treatment of enuresis. *Behaviour Research and Therapy, 1*, 17–24.

Lovibond, S. H. (1964). *Conditioning and enuresis.* Oxford, England: Pergamon Press.

Lovering, J. S., Tallett, S. E., & McKendry, J. B. (1988). Oxybutinin efficacy in the treatment of primary enuresis. *Pediatrics, 82*, 104–106.

Mace, F. C., & Parrish, J. M. (1984). A preliminary investigation of three issues pertaining to a common behavioral treatment for nocturnal enuresis. *Journal of Behavior Therapy & Experimental Psychiatry, 15*, 265–269.

MacKeith, R. C. (1972). Is maturation delay a frequent factor in the origins of primary nocturnal enuresis? *Developmental Medical Child Neurology, 14*, 217.

Marconi, A. M., Felici, E., Roggia, A., & Torelli, F. (1985). Anticholinergic treatment in the therapy of primary enuresis. Effectiveness of oxybutinin hydrochloride in a controlled trial of 58 patients (in Italian). *Pediatria Medica E Chirurgica, 7*, 573–576.

Miller, P. M. (1973). An experimental analysis of retention control training in the treatment of nocturnal enuresis in two institutionalized adolescents. *Behavior Therapy, 4*, 288–294.

Morgan, R. T. (1978). Relapse and therapeutic response in the conditioning treatment of enuresis: A review of recent findings on intermittent reinforcement, overlearning, and stimulus intensity. *Behaviour Research and Therapy, 16*, 273–279.

Mowrer, O. H. (1938). Apparatuses for the study and treatment of enuresis. *Journal of Psychology, 51*, 163–165.

Mowrer, O. H., & Mowrer, W. M. (1938). Enuresis: A method for its study and treatment. *American Journal of Orthopsychiatry, 18*, 436–459.

Muellner, S. R. (1951). The physiology of micturition. *The Journal of Urology, 65*, 805–813.

Muellner, S. R. (1960). Development of urinary control in children. *Journal of the American Medical Association, 172*, 1256–1261.

Nevéus, T. (2003). The role of sleep and arousal in nocturnal enuresis. *Acta Pædiatrica, 92*, 1118–1123.

Nevéus, T., & Tullus, K. (2008). Tolterodine and imipramine in refractory enuresis; a placebo-controlled crossover study. *Pediatric Nephrology, 23*, 263–267.

Nevéus, T., von Gontard, A., Hoebeke, P., Hjalmas, K., Bauer, S., Bower, W., . . . Djurhuus, J. C. (2006). The standardization of terminology of lower urinary tract function in children and adolescents: Report from the Standardisation Committee of the International Children's Continence Society. *Journal of Urology, 176*, 314–324.

Nordquist, V. M. (1971). The modification of a child's enuresis: Some response-response relationships. *Journal of Applied Behavior Analysis, 4*, 241–247.

Novick, J. (1966). Symptomatic treatment of acquired and persistent enuresis. *Journal of Abnormal Psychology, 71*, 363–368.

Papworth, M. A. (1989). The behavioral treatment of nocturnal enuresis in a severely brain-damaged client. *Behavior Therapy & Experimental Psychiatry, 30*, 365–368.

Paschalis, A. P., Kimmel, H. D., & Kimmel, E. (1972). Further study of diurnal instrumental conditioning in the treatment of enuresis nocturna. *Journal of Behavior Therapy & Experimental Psychiatry, 3*, 253–256.

Popler, K. (1976). Token reinforcement in the treatment of nocturnal enuresis: A case study and six month follow up. *Behavior Therapy & Experimental Psychiatry, 7*, 83–84.

Ramakrishnan, K. (2008). Evaluation and treatment of enuresis. *American Family Physician, 78*, 489–496.

Rittig, S., Knudsen, U. B., Norgaard, J. P., Pedersen, E. B., & Djurhuus, J. C. (1989). Abnormal diurnal rhythm of plasma vasopressin and urinary output in patients with enuresis. *American Journal of Physiology, 256*, 664–671.

Ruckstuhl, L. E. (2003). Evaluation of the vibrating urine alarm: A study of effectiveness, social validity, and path to continence for enuretic children. *Dissertation Abstracts International: Section B: The Sciences and Engineering, 64*, 2376.

Sacks, S., & DeLeon, G. (1983). Conditioning functional enuresis: Follow-up after retraining. *Behaviour Research and Therapy, 21*, 693–694.

Samaan, M. (1972). The control of nocturnal enuresis by operant conditioning. *Journal of Behavior Therapy & Experimental Psychiatry, 3*, 103–105.

Silverstein, D. M. (2004). Enuresis in children: Diagnosis and management. *Clinical Pediatrics, 43*, 217–221.

Singh, R., Phillips, D., & Fischer, S. C. (1976). The treatment of enuresis by progressively earlier wakening. *Behavior Therapy & Experimental Psychiatry, 7*, 277–278.

Snajderova, M., Lehotska, V., Kemova, T., Kocnarova, N., Archmanova, E., Jandam, P., & Lanska, V. (2001). Desmopressin in a long-term treatment of children with primary nocturnal enuresis: A symptomatic therapy? *European Family Pediatrician, 160*, 197–198.

Starfield, B. (1967). Functional bladder capacity in enuretic and nonenuretic children. *Journal of Pediatrics, 70*, 777–781.

Starfield, B., & Mellits, E. D. (1968). Increase in functional bladder capacity and improvements in enuresis. *Journal of Pediatrics, 72*, 483–487.

Stedman, J. M. (1972). An extension of the Kimmel treatment method for enuresis to an adolescent: A case report. *Journal of Behavior Therapy & Experimental Psychiatry, 3*, 307–309.

Tarbox, R., Williams, W. L., & Friman, P. C. (2004). Extended diaper wearing: Effects on continence in and out of the diaper. *Journal of Applied Behavior Analysis, 37*, 97–100.

Taylor, P. D., & Turner, R. K. (1975). A clinical trial of continuous, intermittent, and overlearning "bell and pad" treatments for nocturnal enuresis. *Behaviour Research and Therapy, 13*, 281–293.

Tough, J. H., Hawkins, R. P., MacArthur, M. M., & Ravensway, S. V. (1971). Modification of enuretic behavior by punishment: A new use for an old device. *Behavior Therapy, 2*, 567–574.

Troup, C. W., & Hodgson, N. B. (1971). Nocturnal functional bladder capacity in enuretic children. *Urology, 105*, 129–132.

Tullus, K., Bergström, R., Fosdal, I., Winnergård, I., Hjälmås, K., for the Swedish Enuresis Trial Group (1999). Efficacy and safety during long-term treatment of primary monosymptomatic nocturnal enuresis with desmopressin. *Acta Pediatrica, 88*, 1271–1278.

Turner, R. K., Young, G. C., & Rachman, S. (1970). Treatment of nocturnal enuresis by conditioning techniques. *Behaviour Research and Therapy, 8*, 367–381.

Van de Walle, J., & Van Laecke, E. (2008). Pitfalls in studies of children with monosymptomatic nocturnal enuresis. *Pediatric Nephrology, 23*, 173–178.

Van Londen, A., Van Londen-Barentsen, M. L., Van Son, M. J., & Mulder, G. (1995). Relapse rate and subsequent parental reaction after successful treatment of children suffering from nocturnal enuresis: A 2 1/2 year follow-up of bibliotherapy. *Behaviour Research and Therapy, 33*, 309–311.

Vincent, S. A. (1974). Mechanical, electrical and other aspects of enuresis. In J. H. Johnston & W. Goodwin (Eds.), *Reviews in pediatric urology* (pp. 280–313). New York, NY: Elsevier.

Williams, W. L., Jackson, M., & Friman, P. (2007). Encopresis and enuresis. In P. Sturmey (Ed.), *Handbook of clinical psychology and functional analysis* (pp. 171–192). New York, NY: Elsevier.

Wolfish, N. M., Barkin, J., Gorodzinsky, F., & Schwarz, R. (2002). The Canadian Enuresis study and evaluation: Short and long-term safety and efficacy of an oral desmopressin preparation. *Scandinavian Journal of Urology and Nephrology, 37*, 22–27.

Wolfish, N. M., Pivik, R. T., & Busby, K. A. (1997). Elevated sleep arousal thresholds in enuretic boys: Clinical implications. *Acta Paediatrica, 86*, 381–384.

Yeung, C. K., Diao, M., & Sreedhar, B. (2008). Cortical arousal in children with severe enuresis. *New England Journal of Medicine, 358*, 2414–2415.

Young, G. C., & Turner, R. K. (1965). CNS stimulant drugs and conditioning of nocturnal enuresis. *Behaviour Research and Therapy, 3*, 93–101.

17

Separation Anxiety Disorder

MAAIKE H. NAUTA AND PAUL M. G. EMMELKAMP

OVERVIEW OF DISORDER

Diagnostic Criteria and Clinical Picture

Separation anxiety disorder (SAD) is characterized by developmentally inappropriate and excessive anxiety concerning separation from home or from those to whom the child is attached. Children can either be afraid that something bad might happen to them, such as being kidnapped or getting lost, or that something bad might happen to their parents, such as getting in an accident or falling ill. The anxiety causes significant distress or impairment in social, academic, or other important areas of functioning for at least 4 weeks and the onset must be before the age of 18 (American Psychiatric Association [APA], 1994). Children with SAD may avoid staying home alone, playing in the house of a friend, staying with a babysitter, or sleeping over at a friend's or relatives' house. Homesickness is extremely common. In addition, children with SAD may call their parents frequently when away from them and ask repeatedly for reassurance. Children may report physical symptoms, such as stomachaches and headaches, and may have nightmares about being separated from their parents.

Using the *Diagnostic and Statistical Manual* (4th ed.) (*DSM-IV*) criteria for SAD (APA, 1994), children must exhibit at least three of the following eight symptoms: (1) recurrent

excessive distress when separation from home or major attachment figures occurs or is anticipated; (2) persistent and excessive worry about losing, or about possible harm befalling major attachment figures; (3) persistent and excessive worry that an untoward event will lead to separation from a major attachment figure (e.g., getting lost or being kidnapped); (4) persistent reluctance or refusal to go to school or elsewhere because of fear of separation; (5) persistently and excessively fearful or reluctant to be alone or without major attachment figures at home or without significant adults in other settings; (6) persistent reluctance or refusal to go to sleep without being near a major attachment figure or to sleep away from home; (7) repeated nightmares involving the theme of separation; (8) repeated complaints of physical symptoms, such as headaches, stomachaches, nausea, or vomiting, when separation from major attachment figures occurs or is anticipated. Additionally, the problem must last at least 4 weeks, begin before age 18 years, must cause clinically significant distress or impairment, and must not be due to other mental health problems, such as a pervasive developmental disorder or panic disorder with agoraphobia. A classification for SAD gives little information about the exact clinical manifestation or the intensity of the disorder, since two children with the disorder may not share any symptoms, and may vary a great deal with regard to interference in daily functioning; however, the core of the disorder is the "developmentally inappropriate and excessive anxiety concerning separation from home or from those to whom the individual is attached" (APA, 1994, p. 113).

Worry is common in children with SAD. Worries specifically related to separation are more prevalent in children with SAD than in children with other anxiety disorders, children with attention-deficit/hyperactivity disorder (ADHD), or control children (Perrin & Last, 1997). In addition, children with ADHD and control children report separation-related worries among their most prevalent intense worries.

Separation anxiety often occurs with somatic complaints, such as headaches and tension, stomachaches, rapid heartbeats, sweating, and trembling (Livingston, Taylor, & Crawford, 1988). Egger, Costello, Erkanli, and Angold (1999) reported that higher levels of stomachaches and musculoskeletal pains, but not headaches, were typical for girls (but not boys) with SAD; however, these somatic complaints may not be specific to SAD and may occur equally in other childhood anxiety disorders, and even more so in children with comorbid mood disorders (Hofflich, Hughes, & Kendall, 2006). The level of somatic complaints is associated with poor academic performance in children with anxiety disorders (Hughes, Lourea-Waddell, & Kendall, 2008), and may therefore be an important focus for clinical practice.

Relatively few studies have addressed SAD in childhood. In a recent review of publication trends on childhood anxiety disorders over the past 25 years nearly 1,400 papers were found: 367 were on obsessive-compulsive disorder, 377 on posttraumatic stress disorder, 206 on multiple anxiety disorders, 177 on social phobia, 99 on panic disorder/agoraphobia, 83 on specific phobia, and only 51 papers addressed SAD (Muris & Broeren, 2009). The authors concluded that research on childhood anxiety disorders has been dominated by posttraumatic stress disorder and obsessive-compulsive disorder, and multiple anxiety disorders. Thus, we still have little empirical data on SAD, which is odd given that it is the only anxiety disorder specific to children.

Separation Anxiety in Typical Development

Most children experience distress at separation and stranger anxiety in certain developmental phases. Toward the end of the first year most infants go through a phase of separation distress or anxiety (Gullone, 2000) that is mostly minor and transient (Menzies & Harris, 2001). Weems and Costa (2005) investigated developmental differences in the expression of childhood anxiety symptoms. The results revealed systematic age differences. Separation anxiety symptoms were predominant in 6- to 9-year-olds, but steadily decreased as children grew into adolescence. In contrast, generalized anxiety and social anxiety symptoms were relatively infrequent among the 6- to 9-year olds, but were found much more frequently during adolescence. Analyses of developmental trajectories in community samples also showed that SAD symptoms typically decreased in adolescence (Hale, Raaijmakers, Muris, van Hoof, & Meeus, 2008). This was in contrast to the severity of other anxiety disorders, such as social phobia, that tended to increase during adolescence (Cohen, Cohen, Kasen, & Velez, 1993; R. M. Rapee, 2001). The level of self-reported SAD symptoms is generally higher for girls than for boys, in both children and adolescents (Hale et al., 2008).

Prevalence of Separation Anxiety Disorder and Comorbidity

In a recent epidemiological study (Costello, Mustillo, Erklani, Keeler, & Angold, 2003; Costello, Egger, & Angold, 2004), specific phobia, social phobia, generalized anxiety disorder (GAD), and SAD were the most common childhood anxiety disorders. Prevalence rates of SAD were estimated to be around 4% in community samples—3.6% in Emmelkamp and Scholing (1997) and 4.1% in Shear, Jin, Ruscio, Walters, and Kessler (2006). Prevalence rates are typically higher for girls than for boys in community samples, for instance, 6.8% and 3.2% for boys and girls, respectively (Foley et al., 2008), whereas clinical samples usually have equal numbers of boys and girls (Last, Strauss, & Francis, 1987).

SAD tends to co-occur with a range of other disorders. In a large clinical sample, Verduin and Kendall (2003) found that as many as 78% of children with SAD had comorbid GAD, 20% also had social phobia, 58% had a specific phobia, and 34% also met criteria for externalizing disorders such as ADHD and/or oppositional defiant disorder. In addition, children with SAD were more likely to suffer from enuresis (8%) and less likely to suffer from mood disorders (2%) relative to children with primary GAD (1% and 17%, respectively) or social phobia (2% and 15%, respectively). Nighttime fears and nightmares are extremely common in children with SAD. Childhood anxiety disorders, including SAD, also show considerable comorbidity with depression (Costello et al., 2004).

In addition, anxiety disorders are a quite common comorbid condition in a variety of common childhood mental problems. Anxiety disorders frequently co-occur with ADHD, with prevalence rates of SAD much higher for girls (14%) than for boys (5%) (Levy, Hay, Bennett, & McStephen, 2005). In children with pervasive developmental disorder (PDD), as many as 13.6% had clinically significant internalizing problems, causing clear interference with functioning. Additionally, 8.5% of parents of children with PPD reported that their children also met criteria for SAD (Kim, Szatmari, Bryson, Streiner, & Wilson, 2000).

In OCD, the theme of separation is sometimes quite prevalent in obsessions, and OCD and SAD often co-occur (Geller, Biederman, Griffin, Jones, & Lefkowitz, 1996). In children

with Tourette's disorder, comorbid SAD was also found in one third of all cases and was more strongly associated with tic severity than other anxiety disorders (Coffey et al., 2000). Children with depression often have a comorbid anxiety disorder, with rates up to 41% (Kovacs, Gatsonis, Paulauskas, & Richards, 1989), and SAD being the most prevalent anxiety disorder.

Due to the high comorbidity rates and overlap in symptoms between the childhood anxiety disorders, some authors have raised the question whether SAD is indeed a separate construct. It is noteworthy that four out of five children with SAD also fulfill the diagnostic criteria for GAD. This may be because children with SAD are typically characterized by separation-related worries. On the other hand, Ferdinand et al. (2006) suggested that a distinction between anxiety disorders may be useful. The results indicated that separation anxiety represents a different construct than social anxiety in referred children. This did not hold, however, for children in the general population. Also, psychometric studies on various self-report measures suggest that separation anxiety is a separate construct (Birmaher, Khetarpal, Brent, & Cully, 1997; Chorpita, Yim, Moffitt, Umemoto, & Francis, 2000; Spence, 1997) and can be distinguished from the other clusters of anxiety symptoms. Factor analyses showed that separation anxiety can be regarded as a separate factor loading on a general factor of overall anxiety in both child and parent reports of child anxiety symptoms (Nauta et al., 2004; Spence, 1997). Also, in preschoolers aged 2 to 5 years, symptoms of anxiety and depression cluster into different categories along the lines of the diagnostic classifications of *DSM-IV*, rather than being essentially undifferentiated as one construct of internalizing symptoms (Sterba, Egger, & Angold, 2007).

Informant agreement between parent(s) and child tends to be poor for childhood anxiety in general, especially when the symptoms are formulated in terms of feelings and thoughts rather than observable behavior. Of all clusters of anxiety symptoms, SAD symptoms typically show the highest informant agreement between child and parents in paper and pencil reports, with correlations in the moderate to high range, $r = 0.66$ in anxious children and 0.60 in a control sample (Nauta et al., 2004); $r = 0.47$ and 0.39 in two studies with anxious children (Birmaher et al., 1997, 1999); $r = 0.62$ in anxious children, $r = 0.50$ in children with other mental health problems (Muris, Dreessen, Bögels, Weckx, & van Melick, 2004); and $r = 0.71$ (child–mother) and 0.63 (child–father) in a community sample (March, Parker, Sullivan, Stallings, & Conners, 1997). Informant agreement between parents was also the highest for separation anxiety ($r = 61$; March et al., 1997); however, parent–child agreement decreases with the age of the child: Birmaher et al. (1999) found a correlation of 0.39 between parent and child report, and a correlation of only 0.08 between parent and adolescent self-report. In a large, retrospective study, parent-child agreement was poor for SAD lifetime diagnosis (Foley et al., 2004).

Impact of Disorder

In childhood, anxiety disorders in general are associated with low levels of adaptive functioning, including difficulties in peer relations, school performance, and self-esteem (Chansky & Kendall, 1997; Essau, Conradt, & Petermann, 2000; Strauss, Frame, & Forehand, 1987); however, relatively little research has focused specifically on SAD. In a large community twin sample, children and adolescents with three or more SAD symptoms reported relatively little impairment: Only 19% of them had functional impairment in important life domains such as family, school, and peers (Foley et al., 2008). This percentage of impairment was equal across age and gender. The more symptoms the youth reported, the higher the impairment rates were.

Separation anxiety is not only of influence on the child's and family's current functioning.

Children with an anxiety disorder were still likely to fulfill diagnostic criteria up to 8 years after the onset of the disorder (Kovacs & Devlin, 1998); however, the content of anxiety symptoms may differ over time. Comorbid depression in childhood in addition to anxiety disorder may be of particular influence on poorer functioning in young adulthood (Last, Hansen, & Franco, 1997). There is evidence that children with a history of SAD are at risk of developing psychopathology in later childhood and adulthood. In a large, longitudinal study on children and adolescents who were followed from age 11 to 19 years, separation anxiety at a younger age was specifically predictive of separation anxiety later in adolescence, rather than being a nonspecific factor predicting various kinds of psychopathology (Bittner et al., 2007). In a large sample of adults, retrospectively reported childhood SAD was a precursor of adult mental health diagnoses in 36.1% of cases (Shear et al., 2006). In another retrospective study, SAD was a risk factor in the development of mental problems in 78.6% of adults, specifically, panic disorder and depression (Lewinsohn, Holm-Denoma, Small, Seeley, & Joiner, 2008). Other studies also found evidence for early and severe SAD as a main and specific risk factor for developing adult panic disorder with agoraphobia (Manicavasagar, Silove, & Hadzi-Pavlovic, 1998; Silove, Manicavasagar, Curtis, & Blaszczynski, 1996), even though the specificity of this relationship has been questioned. For instance, two recent prospective studies concluded that SAD is a precursor of many types of psychopathology, such as other anxiety disorders (Aschenbrand, Kendall, Webb, Safford, & Flannery-Schroeder, 2003), bipolar disorder, alcohol dependence, and pain disorder (Brückl et al., 2006).

In all, SAD symptoms may not directly lead to significant impairment in the majority of children (Foley et al., 2008); however, these children are at risk for the development of other psychopathology later in life. Therefore, treatment may be considered, even for the children who do not fulfill the *DSM* criterion for functional impairment (Foley et al., 2008).

TREATMENT OF SEPARATION ANXIETY DISORDER

In the past 15 years, many randomized controlled trials (RCTs) on the treatment of anxiety disorders in children have been published, and meta-analyses and systematic reviews have weighed the evidence for the efficacy and effectiveness of the different treatments (Cartwright-Hatton et al., 2004; In-Albon & Schneider, 2006; Silverman, Pina, & Viswesvaran, 2008). In these RCTs, children with various anxiety disorders are included and treated within the same treatment protocol. Most treatment manuals have been developed for the range of anxiety disorders in childhood, and do not provide specific techniques or working models for each individual anxiety disorder. Virtually all treatment programs have adapted this universal approach. Therapists are encouraged to flexibly adapt the treatment manual to the specific child and disorder is one characteristic of this approach (Kendall, Chu, Gifford, Hayes, & Nauta, 1998). The body of literature with regard to treatment outcome in anxious children in general contrasts with the scarcity of outcome studies on SAD in particular. In all, only three noncontrolled studies provided data on pure SAD samples.

In the next section, we will describe several psychological interventions, including cognitive behavior therapy (CBT); both individual and group CBT interventions, and child-, parent-, and family-focused CBT interventions; and psychodynamic psychotherapy (PP). For each, we will first describe available evidence in specific SAD samples, and we will then proceed to describe the available guidelines and panel consensus statements with regard to the treatment of anxiety disorders in children in general, including children with SAD, the available RCTs, meta-analyses, and systematic reviews. At the end of each section, we will

draw conclusions with regard to the effectiveness of the interventions mentioned in the context of the Chambless and Hollon (1998) criteria, along with other considerations for clinical practice.

Cognitive Behavior Therapy

Typically, CBT includes techniques based on principles of classical and operant conditioning. Interventions based on classical conditioning typically involve respondent extinction of learned maladaptive conditioned responses. The best-known and most commonly applied strategy is exposure in vivo (Kendall et al., 2005). During this procedure, children are exposed to their feared stimuli in a stepwise fashion. Feared situations are commonly rated by the child by means of a fear thermometer and ranked in a fear hierarchy. The child is exposed to the feared situations starting at the least anxiety-provoking situation. Exposure in vivo is thought to be the key ingredient to change in CBT for anxiety-disordered children (Kendall et al., 2005). Techniques based on the principles of operant conditioning consist of reinforcing brave behavior and operant extinction of maladaptive fearful behavior (Sturmey, 2007, 2008). Positive reinforcement can be performed by the parents or the therapist, and the child can learn to reinforce his or her own brave behavior. Other available CBT techniques include modeling, social skills training, learning of coping behavior such as relaxation skills, and emotive imagery. Cognitive techniques, such as challenging maladaptive thoughts, are primarily based on more cognitive-oriented theories.

CBT in Children With SAD Only: Single-Subject Experiments

To date, only one CBT-based program has been developed especially for children with SAD (A. E. Eisen & Schaefer, 2005). The intervention was a parent training program and contained three components: (1) child coping skills (progressive relaxation and cognitive restructuring), (2) parent coping skills (education on the nature of SAD and associated parental behavior, child-anxiety management skills such as reinforcing courageous behavior and parental communication), and (3) developing a fear hierarchy and conducting exposure exercises. Even though these components seem universal for all anxiety disorders, every aspect has been elaborated for SAD, giving particular attention to the interaction between parents and children. The treatment takes 10 parent sessions of 1.5 hours each. This treatment was evaluated in six families with children with SAD aged 7–9 years, in a multiple baseline design. Treatment started after a 3- to 6-week baseline phase. After treatment, five out of six children no longer met criteria for SAD. In addition, parents reported improvement in self-efficacy and parenting stress. This study provides preliminary evidence for the efficacy of a CBT-based parent training program that specifically targets SAD. Thus, in terms of the Chambless and Hollon (1998) criteria, CBT parent training for SAD qualifies as *possibly efficacious*, pending replication in larger samples, embedded in at least one other research group. We found no studies on the evaluation of individual or group CBT for children with SAD only.

CBT in Children With All Anxiety Disorders, Including SAD

Consensus panel recommendations. To the best of our knowledge, there are no consensus panel recommendations available for the treatment of anxiety disorders that include SAD. Neither Britain's National Institute for Clinical Excellent (NICE) nor the National Institute for Mental Health (NIMH) provide such guidelines, since children and adolescents are beyond the scope of their guidelines on anxiety disorders. There has been a recent publication on practice parameters for child and adolescent anxiety disorders that may be regarded closest to panel consensus available at this point (Connolly & Bernstein, 2007). The authors performed searches on relevant

databases with the keywords *child, adolescent,* and *anxiety disorders*. They examined all of these papers and only included the most relevant references. It is unclear from the publication exactly how this decision was made. Included papers were described with the headings of screening, evaluation, treatment, comorbidity, and prevention. Recommendations were formulated following each description of available literature. The authors then categorized the recommendations into four categories of endorsement: minimal standard (based on rigorous empirical evidence and/or overwhelming clinical consensus), clinical guidelines (based on empirical evidence and/or strong clinical consensus), options (acceptable practices with insufficient empirical evidence and/or consensus), and not endorsed (ineffective or contra-indicated practices). The authors did not further define the operationalization of *rigorous empirical evidence* versus *empirical evidence*, and did not clarify criteria or a transparent procedure for clinical consensus. In these practice parameters, a multimodal treatment approach for anxiety disorders in children and adolescents was recommended, where a clinician should consider multiple options. Exposure-based CBT is described as the psychotherapy with the most empirical support (i.e., clinical guidelines, based on numerous RCTs with positive outcome with regard to the reduction of anxiety symptoms). The authors concluded that most evidence of CBT is related to its superiority above a wait-list control and (to a lesser extent) to its superiority above attention placebo or other treatments. The practice parameters do not provide specific recommendations with regard to SAD.

Randomized controlled trials. Treatment outcome for children and adolescents with anxiety disorders has been thoroughly studied during the past 15 years. We found 6 non-controlled and 25 controlled clinical trials that included children with SAD. (See Tables 17.1 and 17.2, respectively.) The noncontrolled trials included a total of 79 children, of whom

TABLE 17.1 Uncontrolled Studies of CBT for Separation Anxiety Disorder

Study	Included Primary Disorders	N	N Primary SAD (%)	Research Setting or Clinical Setting	Age (years)	Conditions	Conclusions (effect on anxiety symptoms)	% Recovery (no more principal diagnosis of an anxiety disorder at posttreatment and follow-up)	Specific Conclusions With Regard to SAD
Bögels and Siqueland 2006	GAD, SAD, SoPh, SP, ANOS	17	5 (29%)	Clinical setting	8–18	Family-based CBT following wait-list	Intervention superior to baseline wait-list	41% (57% / 71%) (3 / 12-month follow-up)	No information
Howard and Kendall, 1996	Anxiety disorders	6	3 (50%)	Research	9–13	Family-based CBT intervention program	Program superior to baseline	83% (83%) (4-month follow-up)	No information
Eisen, Raleigh, and Neuhoff, 2008	SAD	6	6(100%)	Clinical setting	7–10	CBT-based parent training	Positive outcome, maintained at 6-month follow-up	83% (83%) (6-month follow-up)	Only children with SAD
Ollendick, Hagopian, and Huntzinger, 1991	SAD + night fears	2	2(100%)	Not clear	8–10	CBT: self-control training + contingent reinforcement	CBT superior to baseline, reinforcement phase seemed especially beneficial in reducing anxiety and avoidance	100% (100%) (2-year follow-up)	Only children with SAD
Thienemann, Moore, Tompkins, 2006	SoPh, GAD, SP, SAD, PD	24	2 (8%)	Research	7–16	Parent group training	Positive effects on anxiety severity and impairment. Less improvement for children with anxious parents.	25%	Authors conclude that PT was most efficacious for SAD and SP, and less so for GAD and SoPh. They argue that parents may have most influence on anxiety within the parent-child interaction or at home, as well as anxiety for specific stimuli.
Toren et al., 2000	SAD, GAD	24	23(96%)	Clinical setting	6–13	1. CBT + parents 2. Wait-list	1 > 2	1. 70% (91%) 2. no symptomatic change (3-year follow-up)	No information

Note: SAD = separation anxiety disorder; GAD = generalized anxiety disorder; CBT = cognitive behavior therapy; SoPh = social phobia

TABLE 17.2 Controlled Treatment Outcome Studies on CBT for Anxiety Disordered Children and Adolescents

Study	Included Primary Disorders	N	N Primary SAD (N, %)	Research Setting or Clinical Setting	Age (years)	Conditions	Conclusions (effect on anxiety symptoms with regard to treatment condition)	Conclusions on Recovery Rates (% of children no longer meeting their principle anxiety diagnosis at posttreatment follow-up)	Specific Conclusions With Regard to SAD
	SAD, OAD, SoPh	79	30(38%)	Research, specialized anxiety clinic	7–14	1. FAMCBT 2. ICBT 3. WL	1 > 2 >> 3	1. 84% (96%) 2. 57% (70%) 3. 26% (12-month follow-up)	Results were equal for all primary anxiety diagnoses
Barrett, 1998	SAD, OAD, SoPh	60	26(43%)	Research, specialized anxiety clinic	7–14	1. GCBT 2. group FAMCBT 3. WL	1 = 2 >> 3 (at post) 1 > 2 on family measures and at 12-month follow-up	1. 71% (85%) 2. 56% (65%) 3. 25% (12-month follow-up)	No information
Bodden, Bögels, et al., 2008	SAD, GAD, SoPh, PDAG, SP	128	34(27%)	Clinical settings for mental health	8–17	1. ICBT 2. FAMCBT 3. WL	1 > 2 >> 3 Less improvement for children with anxious parents in both active treatment conditions 1 = 2 at follow-up	1. 53%* (56%*) 2. 28%* (47%*) 3. 0%* (3-month follow-up)	No information
Cartwright-Hatton et al., 2011	DSM-IV anxiety disorders	74	5 (7%)	Research	2–9	1. GPT 2. TAU/WL	1 > 2	1. 57% (54%) 2. 15% (24%) (12-month follow-up)	No information
Cobham, Dadds, and Spence, 1998	SAD, SoPh, GAD, OAD, SP, AG	67	8 (12%)	Research	7–14	1. ICBT 2. ICBT + PAM	1 = 2 1 < 2 if parental anxiety	1. 82% (67%) 2. 80% (75%) (12-month follow-up)	No information
De Groot, Cobham, Leong, and McDermott, 2007	GAD, SoPh, SAD, SP	29	3 (10%)	Research	7–12	1. Individual FAMCBT 2. Group FAMCBT	1 = 2	1. 57% (50%) 2. 47% (53%) (6-month follow-up)	All 3 SAD children, all randomized to individual FAMCBT, only one recovered, only at 6-month follow-up.

Study	Diagnoses	N		Setting	Age	Conditions	Comparison	Outcome	Notes
Flannery-Schroeder and Kendall, 2000	GAD, SAD, SoPh	37	11 (30%)	Research setting	8–14	1. ICBT 2. GCBT 3. WL	1 = 2 > 3 on most measures 1 > 2 >> 3 on child reports	1. 73% (79%) 2. 50% (53%) 3. 8% (3-month follow-up)	No information
Heyne et al., 2002	School refusal	61	6 (10%)	Research	7–14	1. ICBT 2. PT/TT 3. Combination of 1+2	1 = 2 = 3	Not reported, 69% overall	No information
Kendall, 1994	SAD, SoPh, GAD	47	8 (17%)	Research	9–13	1. ICBT 2. WL	1 >> 2	1. 66% 2. 5% Treatment gains were maintained at 12-month follow-up	No information
Kendall, Flannery-Schroeder, Panichelli-Mindel, Southam-Gerow, Henin, and Warman, 1997	SAD, SoPh, GAD	94	22(23%)	Research	9–13	1. ICBT 2. WL	1 >> 2	1. 71% 2. 6% Treatment gains were maintained at 12-month follow-up	Results equal for all principal diagnoses
Kendall et al., 2008	SAD, GAD, SoPh, SP	161	47(29%)	Research	7–14	1. ICBT 2. FAMCBT 3. FESA	1 = 2 > 3, all effective 1 > 2 and 3 on teacher ratings	1. 64% (67%) 2. 64% (64%) 3. 42% (46%) (12-month follow-up)	No differential effect with regard to principal diagnosis
King et al., 1998	School refusers	34	8 (24%)	Research	5–15	1. ICBT + PT + TT 2. WL	1 > 2	Not reported	No information
Last et al., 1998	School phobia	56	18(32%)	Research	6–17	1. ICBT 2. ES	1 = 2	1. 65% 2. 50%	No significant differential effect
Liber et al., 2008	SAD, GAD, SoPh, SP	127	52(41%)	Clinical settings	8–12	1. GCBT 2. ICBT	1 = 2	1. 54% 2. 62%	No information

(Continued)

419

TABLE 17.2 Controlled Treatment Outcome Studies on CBT for Anxiety Disordered Children and Adolescents *(Continued)*

Study	Included Primary Disorders	N	N Primary SAD (N, %)	Research Setting or Clinical Setting	Age (years)	Conditions	Conclusions (effect on anxiety symptoms with regard to treatment condition)	Conclusions on Recovery Rates (% of children no longer meeting their principle anxiety diagnosis at posttreatment follow-up)	Specific Conclusions With Regard to SAD
Lyneham and Rapee, 2006	GAD, SAD, SoPh, OCD, SP, PD	100	22 (22%)	Research setting (rural sample)	6–12	1. telephone 2. e-mail 3. client-initiate 4. WL	1 >> 2 = 3 > 4	1. 79% (88%) 2. 33% (92%) 3. 31% (67%) 4. 0% (12-month follow-up; NB follow-up data of 52% of original subjects, mostly treatment responders)	No information
Manassis et al., 2002	GAD, SAD, SoPh, SP, PD	78	20(26%)	Clinical setting	8–12	1. GCBT 2. ICBT	1 = 2 on most measures, 1 < 2 for high socially anxious children	No data on diagnostic status	Results better for GAD than for SAD and SP (on maternal reports only)
Mendlowitz et al., 1999	*DSM-IV* Anxiety disorders	62	No info	Clinical setting	7–12	1. GCBT 2. GCBT + PT 3. PT 4. WL	1 = 2 = 3 >> 4 GCBT + PT superior on active coping, but not on anxiety	No information on diagnostic status	No information
Muris, Meesters, and van Melick, 2002	SAD, GAD, SoPh	30	10(33%)	School/research	9–12	1. GCBT 2. ED (placebo) 3. No intervention	1 > 2 = 3	Based on a normative cut-off for self-report: 1. 80% 2. 40% 3. 30%	No difference in effectiveness between CBT and ED with regard to principal diagnosis
Nauta et al., 2001	SAD, GAD, SoPh	18	8(44%)	Clinical setting	8–15	1. ICBT 2. ICBT + CPT	1 = 2	1. 44% (78%) 2.11% (63%) (15-month follow-up)	No information
Nauta et al., 2003	SAD, GAD, SoPh, SP	79	26(33%)	Clinical settings (N = 51) and	8–17	1. ICBT 2. ICBT + CPT 3. WL	1 = 2 >> 3	1. 54%* (68%*) 2. 59%* (69*) 3. 10%* (3-month follow-up)	No differential effect with regard to primary diagnosis

				research (N=28)					
R. Rapee et al., 2006	GAD, SAD, SoPh, OCD	267	51(19%)	Research setting	6–12	1. GCBT 2. parent bibliotherapy 3. WL	1 > 2 > 3	1. 49%* (61%*) 2. 18%* (19%*) 3. 6%* (3-month follow-up)	No information
Shortt, Barrett, & Fox, 2001	GAD, SoPh, SAD	71	19(27%)	Research	6–10	1. group FAMCBT 2. WL	1 > 2	1. 69% (68%) 2. 6%	No significant difference between the diagnostic groups.
Siqueland et al., 2005	GAD, SAD	11	1 (9%)	Research	12–17	1. ICBT + ABFT 2. ICBT	1 = 2	1. 40% (80%) 2. 67% (100%) (9-month follow-up)	Only one adolescent with SAD
Spence et al., 2006	GAD, SoPh, SAD	72	15(21%)	Research	7–14	1. GCBT 2. Internet + half GCBT 3. WL	1 = 2 >> 3	1. 65% (90%) 2. 56% (74%) 3. Waitlist (12-month follow-up)	No information
J. Wood et al., 2006	GAD, SoPh, SAD	40	27 current SAD (68%)	Research	6–13	1. ICBT 2. FAMCBT	1 < 2	1. 53%* 2. 79%*	No information

* These figures describe the percentage free of any anxiety disorder (not just the principal diagnosis).

Note: SAD = separation anxiety disorder; GAD = generalized anxiety disorder; SoPh = social phobia; SP = specific phobia; AG = agoraphobia; ABFT = attachment-based family therapy; ICBT = individual cognitive behavior therapy; GCBT = group cognitive behavior therapy; CPT = cognitive parent training; FAMCBT = family-based cognitive behavior therapy; FESA = family-based education/support/attention; WL = wait-list; ES = educational support; PT = parent training; TT = teacher training; ED = emotional disclosure

41 (52%) had a primary diagnosis of SAD. In the 25 RCTs, a total of 1,855 anxious children have been studied, including 462 children (25%) with SAD as their primary diagnosis, with no study specifically consisting only of SAD children.

Several delivery formats for CBT have been developed, including individual, family-based, and group CBT. There has been considerable effort to set up effective family-based treatment programs. Family-based treatments build upon the evidence that anxiety disorders tend to run in families, that parenting of anxious children is often characterized by less autonomy granting and more conflict, and that parents often play a role in the maintenance of anxious behavior. The different family-based programs have put their own emphasis on different interventions within the CBT framework. "Building confidence" (J. Wood, Piacentini, Southam-Gerow, Chu, & Sigman, 2006) emphasizes exposure exercises, and also communication related specifically to intrusiveness and autonomy granting. In the attachment-based family CBT (Siqueland, Rynn, & Diamond, 2005) the main focus is on autonomy for the adolescent by open communication and negotiation. Bodden, Bögels, et al. (2008) describe a family-based CBT program that has sessions for the parents, the child, and the family, including the siblings. In this program, parents are in charge of guiding and reinforcing child exposure. In addition, parents are encouraged to model courageous behavior and to challenge and change their maladaptive thoughts about anxiety or their anxious child. In the family sessions, family communication is addressed with all family members, and problem solving is introduced. Granting autonomy is an important theme throughout the treatment. Another family-based CBT program was developed as an addition to an individual CBT program ("Coping Cat"; Kendall, Kane, Howard, & Siqueland, 1990; Kendall, 1994) and consists of in vivo exercises and anxiety management skills (Kendall, Hudson, Gosch, Flannery-Schroeder, & Suveg, 2008). The family component addresses parental beliefs and expectations, parental reactions to the child's distress, parental support, and communication. A last parent-based addition to CBT has been described in Nauta, Scholing, Emmelkamp, and Minderaa (2003), where parents followed a seven-session cognitive training addressing their own (dysfunctional) cognitions and behaviors with regard to the anxious behavior of their child. This parent training took place in addition to an individual CBT program for the child. Group training programs have been developed, from the perspective of sharing with peers and modeling, as well as issues of cost-effectiveness. Family interventions can also be provided in group format.

As Table 17.2 shows, individual CBT has been studied most frequently in RCTs, with recovery rates of the principal diagnosis as high as 53%–82%, which was superior to wait-list control in all studies. Effects do not seem to be limited to anxiety symptoms only: Evidence suggests that associated problems such as depressive symptomatology also ameliorates, and that CBT has a positive influence on general functioning, including school performance and social functioning (Suveg et al., 2009; J. J. Wood, 2006). In addition, group and family CBT have both been found effective. In general, little support was found for one active CBT treatment over another. Most studies found no difference in effectiveness between family- and child-based programs (P. Barrett, 1998; Heyne et al., 2002; Kendall et al., 2008; Nauta, Scholing, Emmelkamp, & Minderaa, 2001, 2003). Three studies found a superior effect of family-based relative to child-based treatment (P. M. Barrett, Dadds, & Rapee, 1996; Cobham, Dadds, & Spence, 1998; J. Wood et al., 2006); however, two studies reported favorable outcome for child-based relative to family-based CBT (Bodden, Bögels, et al., 2008; Kendall et al., 2008, on teacher ratings). Both the individual and group treatment modalities seem equally effective in reducing anxiety disorders in children over a waiting list (De Groot, Cobham, Leong, & McDermott, 2007; Flannery-Schroeder & Kendall, 2000; Liber et al., 2008).

With regard to the specific benefits of CBT versus other active treatments, four RCTs included an attention placebo condition, two of which found superiority for CBT. The most recent study showed that CBT was more effective than an attention placebo condition controlling for general factors related to therapeutic outcome, such as the therapeutic relationship, attention, and expectancy for change (Kendall et al., 2008). However, Last, Hansen, and Franco (1998) found no difference between CBT-based psychoeducation compared to a CBT treatment, but the power of that study may have been insufficient to detect a difference between active treatments ($N = 56$). Evidence of the effectiveness of CBT for children with anxiety disorders has been further established by studies demonstrating that treatment gains were maintained up to 6 or 7 years after individual or family CBT (P. M. Barrett, Duffy, Dadds, & Rapee, 2001; Kendall & Southam-Gerow, 1996).

Recently, some other formats of CBT have found to be efficacious relative to a waiting list control. These include (a) group parent training for younger children (Cartwright-Hatton et al., 2011); (b) parent–teacher training (Heyne et al., 2002); (c) CBT using telephone, e-mail, or client-initiated contact with therapist, with telephone contact providing the best results (Lyneham & Rapee, 2006); (d) parent bibliotherapy (R. Rapee, Abbott, & Lyneham, 2006); and (e) a minimal group CBT combined with Internet interventions (Spence, Holmes, March, & Lipp, 2006).

All of these trials included a heterogeneous set of anxious children but none exclusively focused on SAD. Only 9 of these 25 studies evaluated whether treatment effects were different for the various anxiety disorders. In all studies but one, the conclusion was drawn that the treatment effectiveness was equal across diagnoses. In the Mendlowitz et al. study

(1999), mothers, but not children or clinicians, reported better outcome for children with GAD than for children with either SAD or simple phobia, regardless of individual or group treatment modality (20 of 78 children had primary SAD in this study). It is not clear why the intervention was more successful for children with GAD in the eyes of the mothers, since the interventions offered were very similar to the interventions in the other RCTs, where no such differences in effectiveness were found between children with different anxiety disorders. In practically all of these studies, the same CBT program was applied in all children, without any tailoring to the specific disorders. In contrast, highly specialized interventions have been developed for each anxiety disorder. Perhaps more specific interventions may enhance treatment gains in children with anxiety disorders.

Meta-analyses and systematic reviews. We will describe one systematic review and two meta-analyses that have been conducted on the effectiveness of CBT for children with anxiety disorders. We will also describe possible differential effectiveness of the different formats of CBT delivery (Cartwright-Hatton, Roberts, Chitsabesan, Fothergill, & Harrington, 2004; In-Albon & Schneider, 2006; Silverman et al., 2008).

In the systematic review by Cartwright-Hatton et al. (2004), 10 CBT studies were reviewed. After CBT, 56.6% of children no longer met criteria for their principal anxiety disorder versus 34.8% after no treatment. The general conclusion was that CBT is effective in treating anxiety disordered children. Silverman et al. (2008) conducted a systematic review and a series of meta-analyses on evidence-based practice in anxiety disordered children. Thirty-two studies were evaluated along a continuum of methodological rigor, the majority of the studies being either methodologically robust or fairly rigorous. Further, each treatment was classified according to Chambless and Hollon's (1998) criteria for *well-established, probably efficacious, possibly efficacious*, and *experimental* treatments. None of the studied treatments fulfilled the criteria for well-established. Individual and group CBT and group CBT with parents each met criteria for probably efficacious. Cohen's *d* relative to control conditions for overall CBT was 0.44 for child ratings and 0.63 for parent ratings, which are both in the moderate range. No significant differences were found between individual and group treatments on diagnostic recovery rates and anxiety symptom reductions. Similarly, there was no evidence that parental involvement in CBT was more effective than parental noninvolvement.

In-Albon and Schneider's (2006) meta-analysis contained 24 RCTs, all on CBT. These studies were selected through the databases of PsychInfo and Medline, and included only published and peer-reviewed papers. All studies had random assignment to active treatment and a control condition, used a standard treatment protocol, and included at least 10 subjects per treatment group. The mean effect size for CBT was 0.86 (large) versus 0.13 for waiting list and 0.58 for attention placebo control. This does not contradict the smaller effect sizes reported by Silverman et al. (2008), since In-Albon and Schneider (2006) reported the within-group effect sizes and Silverman et al. reported the more conservative between-group effect sizes, where the effects of the control groups have been subtracted from the effects of the active treatment. Overall, 68.9% of the children treated with CBT no longer met criteria for their principal diagnosis at posttreatment, versus 12.9% of children in waiting-list control groups. There was no differential outcome with regard to individual and group treatments or child- and family-focused treatments. None of these publications could draw separate conclusions for SAD.

Conclusions With Regard to CBT for SAD

Strictly speaking, only the CBT parent training qualifies for a probably efficacious treatment for SAD; however, the evidence for the effectiveness of CBT can be indirectly derived from the RCTs and meta-analyses on heterogeneous samples with all anxiety disorders. Summarizing the research evidence discussed before, overall individual CBT for childhood anxiety disorders including SAD seem to be efficacious; however, a recent RCT by Kendall et al. (2008) changes the status for individual CBT in a positive way. If we add this study to the other studies discussed in the meta-analyses, individual CBT would fulfill the criteria for a well-established treatment since it is supported by several good group-design experiments, by at least two independent research groups, and was found statistically significantly superior over a placebo treatment. The other CBT-based interventions, including CBT with family involvement, group CBT, and family-based group CBT can be rated as probably efficacious, since their efficacy was supported by at least two studies by independent research teams. There is still insufficient evidence for the effectiveness of other psychological treatments, with some qualifying for possibly efficacious, such as parent bibliotherapy, Internet-based treatment, parent or parent-teacher training for school refusal, as well as CBT-based parent training for young children. If we assume that there is no reason to assume that the treatments were less effective for SAD than for the total sample, the conclusion that CBT is a well-established treatment is probably equally true for children with SAD.

Parent–Child Interaction Therapy (PCIT)

Parent–child interaction therapy is a treatment for parents of 2- to 6-year-old children and is based upon attachment and social learning theories. The PCIT focuses on building a warm and responsive relationship between the child and the parent(s) in the first phase of treatment, as a starting point for managing child behavior in the second phase in a more directive fashion (Hembree-Kigin & McNeil, 1995). PCIT is considered an efficacious treatment for young children with disruptive problems and their families. Different outcome studies showed a significant improvement in disruptive behavior, as well as on parent–child interaction and parental distress (Herschell & McNeil, 2005); these results were maintained at longer term follow-up (Hood & Eyberg, 2003). PCIT usually consists of 10–16 sessions and typically has two phases: Child-Directed Interaction (CDI), and Parent-Directed Interaction (PDI). In CDI, parents learn skills to ameliorate parent–child interaction in terms of warmth and supportiveness. In PDI, parents are taught the use of positive and negative reinforcement, including the time-out procedure. The main focus of these operant conditioning principles is noncompliance in children. PCIT for SAD is described by Pincus, Eyberg, and Choate (2005) and contains one extra phase that the authors have scheduled in between the two regular phases: Bravery-Directed Interaction (BDI). In BDI, parents get psychoeducation on anxiety and anxiety management. A "bravery ladder" is construed to work on exposure exercises with homework assignments. Parents are encouraged to reward steps on the bravery ladder as well as any behavior toward new or scary situations. For brave behavior, such as exposure during homework assignments, children's brave behavior is reinforced with spending special time with their parents. Note that there is a considerable overlap with traditional CBT interventions.

Small-N Experimental Designs on PCIT

PCIT was not mentioned in the American Academy of Child and Adolescent Psychiatry practice parameter, or in any of the meta-analyses or systematic reviews. One multiple baseline experiment has been conducted including three children with SAD aged 5, 7, and 8 years (Choate, Pincus, Eyberg, & Barlow, 2005). All three children significantly improved on both separation anxiety symptoms as well as disruptive behavior, and treatment gains were maintained at 3-month follow-up. In terms of the classification system

by Chambless and Hollon (1998), PCIT qualifies for a possibly efficacious treatment for young children with SAD, based on one well-conducted small-N experiment, waiting for replication in other small-N experimental studies and larger samples by at least two different research groups.

Psychodynamic Psychotherapy

Psychodynamic psychotherapy has been used and is continuously being used in treatment of SAD, although there is hardly any evidence and no controlled studies supporting its effectiveness. Nevertheless, in the American Association of Child and Adolescent Psychiatry Practice Parameters (Connolly & Bernstein, 2007), PP is mentioned as one of the psychotherapeutic options to be considered for the treatment of anxiety disorders in children in general.

Noncontrolled Study on Psychodynamic Psychotherapy

There are no meta-analyses or RCTs available evaluating treatment outcome of PP with SAD. One nonexperimental study has specifically addressed the treatment of children with SAD. Muratori et al. (2005) evaluated PP with a quasi-experimental design, in which 24 children with SAD received either PP or treatment as usual. There was no random assignment; children were assigned to either treatment condition based on therapist availability. No statistical test analyses of baseline equivalence were reported. The main emphasis was on the core conflictual theme and attempts were made to elucidate its relationship with the child's anxiety and mood symptoms. After PP, children improved significantly in clinician ratings of global functioning and on parent reports of internalizing problems. Children continued to improve between the end of treatment and 2-year follow-up. Based on this one experimental study on PP for children with SAD, PP qualifies as a "possibly efficacious" intervention.

The same group of researchers published another study on PP (Muratori, Picchi, Bruni, Patarnello, & Romagnoli, 2003). Fifty-eight children, 6–10 years of age, meeting *DSM-IV* criteria for anxiety or depressive disorder, were assigned nonrandomly to either active psychodynamic treatment or treatment as usual; 31% of these children fulfilled the criteria of SAD. At baseline, there were no significant differences between the two groups in demographical or clinical measures. The PP contained 11 weekly sessions, including 5 parent sessions, 5 child sessions, and 1 parent–child session. Substantial improvements occurred on the Children's-Global Assessment Scale at 6 months, and on the Child Behavior Checklist at 2-year follow-up. It is not clear whether this study includes the same SAD subjects as the Muratori et al. (2005) study participants; however, the design of the study and conclusions are similar (Muratori et al., 2005).

In all, since there are two quasi-experimental studies by one research group, PP qualifies for a possibly efficacious treatment for emotional disorders in general and SAD in particular (Chambless & Hollon, 1998). More methodologically sound research is required to further test the merits of PP.

Evidence-Based Practices and SAD

Only about 20% of adults that retrospectively report childhood SAD reported to have received professional help for emotional problems as a child, most often at a mental health center (Shear et al., 2006). Only in 25% of these cases was SAD indeed the focus of the treatment. In line with these findings, in current primary care for children, anxiety disorders are highly prevalent, yet relatively few parents and children receive treatment (Chavira, Stein, Bailey, & Stein, 2004). Child SAD may not be treated if comorbid with another principal diagnosis, such as ADHD, autism spectrum, disruptive behavior, or depression. Some early evidence is emerging

that a CBT intervention on anxiety as a secondary disorder may be effective (e.g., Chalfant, Rapee, & Carroll, 2007, for high-functioning autism). This type of intervention may have an important clinical utility, since recovery from SAD or other comorbid anxiety disorders may improve the level of functioning of these children and their parents.

From a societal point of view, it is important to also consider the costs of anxiety disordered children, and the cost-effectiveness of treatment. Bodden, Dirksen, and Bögels (2008) computed that the costs for a family with an anxiety disordered child are 21 times higher than for a family with no such child. The same group also investigated the cost-effectiveness of individual and family CBT (Bodden, Dirksen, et al., 2008). They calculated the costs (e.g., health care and additional costs such as extra babysitters) and benefits (in terms of symptom reduction and quality of life). They concluded that family CBT was not cost-effective as compared to individual CBT: Family CBT was more expensive and led to less symptom reduction. It should be noted that effective treatment for SAD is not limited to anxiety reduction in the child. As shown by J. Wood et al. (2006), reduction of anxiety is also associated with better social functioning and school performance. These additional benefits should be taken into account when considering the cost-effectiveness of CBT for children with SAD.

EASE OF DISSEMINATION

Even though most treatment programs were developed in research settings, they have also been conducted in real life clinical settings. As reported in Table 17.2, 6 of 25 studies (24%) were carried out in clinical settings. Results from these clinical settings, working with referred rather than recruited children, seem similar to those from research settings. More specifically, Nauta et al. (2003) included children from two mental health clinics as well as one research department, and found no differences between the groups in sample characteristics or treatment outcome. Taken together, the results just discussed suggest that CBT can be implemented in clinical practice, provided that adequate training and supervision is provided.

So, why do very few practitioners use evidence-based protocols in clinical practice (Powers & Emmelkamp, 2009)? Even with probably efficacious CBT treatments available for SAD, poor dissemination of treatments to the clinicians is a serious problem. One reason might be the costs involved in the training and supervision of efficacious treatments for each childhood anxiety disorder. There is now a growing trend in the field of anxiety disorders in adults to develop trans-diagnostic treatment protocols (Norton & Philipp, 2008). So, in the field of childhood anxiety disorders, the disadvantage of having few specific treatment protocols for each separate anxiety disorder may turn out to be a blessing in disguise. Trans-diagnostic approaches to treating childhood anxiety disorders may be an advantage for the dissemination of efficacious CBT treatments in clinical practice.

In contrast to anxiety disorders in adults, where a number of studies have compared the relative effectiveness of psychological treatment versus pharmacotherapy, there has only been one such recent study (Walkup et al., 2008). The research on the effectiveness of medication for anxiety disordered children, and SAD in particular, is relatively scarce. In several studies, the results were inconclusive with regard to the relative effectiveness for active medication versus placebo. The two studies that specifically addressed SAD found no superiority of medication above placebo on the primary outcome, namely for imipramine (Klein, Koplewicz, & Kanner, 1992 [$N = 21$, all SAD]) and clonazepam (Graae, Milner, Rizzotto, & Klein, 1994 [$N = 15$, 73% primary SAD]). In school refusal, children with medication (imipramine or alprazolam) reported somewhat more improvement at posttreatment, but the effect disappeared when controlling for pretreatment differences (G. A. Bernstein, Garfinkel, & Borchardt, 1990 [$N = 24$, % SAD not reported]), However, the number of children treated in these studies was small, and there were often baseline differences between the various conditions. Therefore, the studies may have been underpowered to detect a difference. In a later study on the treatment of school refusal, the combination of imipramine and CBT proved more effective than placebo in school attendance, but not in anxiety levels (G. Bernstein et al., 2000; $N = 63$, % SAD not reported). There is one positive trial on fluoxetine in children with anxiety disorders; however, the results did not hold for children with SAD (Birmaher et al., 2003; $N = 74$, 47% with current SAD). In a multicenter trial the SSRI fluvoxamine was more effective than placebo (Pine et al., 2001; $N = 128$, 75% current SAD). No separate conclusions were drawn with regard to SAD. Finally, one large and recent study directly compared the SSRI sertraline and CBT as monotherapies, versus their combination (Walkup et al., 2008; $N = 488$, 54% current SAD). The conclusion was that both monotherapies were effective in reducing the severity of anxiety relative to placebo, while the combination treatment had superior response rates. No conclusions were drawn with respect to SAD in particular. In terms of Chambless and Hollon (1998), treatments with fluvoxamine and sertraline are probably efficacious, which is a lower rating than the well-established rating of CBT for childhood anxiety disorders.

Overall, there are good possibilities of treating SAD effectively in children and adolescents. Even though the studies on SAD specifically are scarce, there are multiple studies on childhood anxiety disorders. Post hoc comparisons between the different anxiety disorders within these studies revealed no reason to assume differential effectiveness for SAD. Individual CBT has the highest level of evidence available, and qualifies as well-established for anxiety disorders in children.

Other formats of CBT delivery, such as group CBT or family-based CBT, are other good options. Future research may shine more light on the effectiveness of these programs in clinical practice, the ease of dissemination, and the generalizability of the positive findings to children who have SAD as a comorbid disorder.

REFERENCES

American Psychiatric Association. (1994). *Diagnostic and statistical manual of mental disorders* (4th ed.). Washington, DC: Author.

Aschenbrand, S., Kendall, P., Webb, A., Safford, S., & Flannery-Schroeder, E. (2003). Is childhood Separation Anxiety Disorder a predictor of adult Panic Disorder and Agoraphobia? A seven-year longitudinal study. *Journal of the American Academy of Child & Adolescent Psychiatry, 42*, 1478–1485.

Barrett, P. (1998). Evaluation of cognitive-behavioral group treatments for childhood anxiety disorders. *Journal of Clinical Child Psychology, 27*, 459–468.

Barrett, P. M., Dadds, M. R., & Rapee, R. M. (1996). Family treatment of childhood anxiety: A controlled trial. *Journal of Consulting and Clinical Psychology, 64*, 333–342.

Barrett, P. M., Duffy, A. L., Dadds, M. R., & Rapee, R. M. (2001). Cognitive-behavioral treatment of anxiety disorders in children: Long-term (6-year) follow-up. *Journal of Consulting and Clinical Psychology, 69*, 135–141.

Bernstein, G., Borchardt, C., Perwien, A., Crosby, R., Kushner, M., Thuras, P., & Last, C. G. (2000). Imipramine plus cognitive-behavioral therapy in the treatment of school refusal. *Journal of the American Academy of Child & Adolescent Psychiatry, 39*, 276–283.

Bernstein, G. A., Garfinkel, B. D., & Borchardt, C. M. (1990). Comparative studies of pharmacotherapy for school refusal. *Journal of the American Academy of Child & Adolescent Psychiatry, 29*, 773–781.

Birmaher, B., Axelson, D. A., Monk, K., Kalas, C., Clark, D. B., Ehmann, M., . . . Brent, D. A. (2003). Fluoxetine for the treatment of childhood anxiety disorders. *Journal of the American Academy of Child & Adolescent Psychiatry, 42*, 415–423.

Birmaher, B., Brent, D. A., Chiappetta, L., Bridge, J., Monga, S., & Baugher, M. (1999). Psychometric properties of the Screen for Child Anxiety Related Emotional Disorders (SCARED): A replication study. *Journal of the American Academy of Child & Adolescent Psychiatry, 38*, 1230–1236.

Birmaher, B., Khetarpal, S., Brent, D., & Cully, M. (1997). The Screen for Child Anxiety Related Emotional Disorders (SCARED): Scale construction and psychometric characteristics. *Journal of the American Academy of Child & Adolescent Psychiatry, 36*, 545–553.

Bittner, A., Egger, H., Erkanli, A., Costello, E., Foley, D., & Angold, A. (2007). What do childhood anxiety disorders predict? *Journal of Child Psychology and Psychiatry, 48*, 1174–1183.

Bodden, D. M., Bögels, S. M., Nauta, M. H., De Haan, E., Ringrose, J., Appelboom, C., . . . Appelboom-Geerts, K. J. (2008). Child versus family cognitive-behavioral therapy in clinically anxious youth: An efficacy and partial effectiveness study. *Journal of the American Academy of Child & Adolescent Psychiatry, 47*, 1384–1394.

Bodden, D. M., Dirksen, C. D., Bögels, S. M., Nauta, M. H., De Haan, E., Ringrose, J., . . . Appelboom-Geerts, K. J. (2008). Costs and cost-effectiveness of family CBT versus individual CBT in clinically anxious children. *Clinical Child Psychology and Psychiatry, 13*, 543–564.

Bögels, S., & Siqueland, L. (2006). Family cognitive behavioral therapy for children and adolescents with clinical anxiety disorders. *Journal of the American Academy of Child & Adolescent Psychiatry, 45*, 134–141.

Brückl, T., Wittchen, H., Höfler, M., Pfister, H., Schneider, S., & Lieb, R. (2006). Childhood separation anxiety and the risk of subsequent psychopathology: Results from a community study. *Psychotherapy and Psychosomatics, 76*, 47–56.

Cartwright-Hatton, S., McNally, D., Field, A. P., Rust, S., Laskey, B., Dixon, C., . . . Woodham, A. (2011). A new parenting-based group intervention for young anxious children: Results of a randomized controlled trial. *Journal of the American Academy of Child & Adolescent Psychiatry, 50*, 242–251.

Cartwright-Hatton, S., Roberts, C., Chitsabesan, P., Fothergill, C., & Harrington, R. (2004). Systematic review of the efficacy of cognitive behaviour therapies for childhood and adolescent anxiety disorders. *British Journal of Clinical Psychology, 43*, 421–436.

Chalfant, A., Rapee, R., & Carroll, L. (2007). Treating anxiety disorders in children with high functioning autism spectrum disorders: A controlled trial. *Journal of Autism and Developmental Disorders, 37*, 1842–1857.

Chambless, D., & Hollon, S. (1998). Defining empirically supported therapies. *Journal of Consulting and Clinical Psychology, 66*, 7–18.

Chansky, T. E., & Kendall, P. C. (1997). Social expectancies and self-perceptions in anxiety-disordered children. *Journal of Anxiety Disorders, 11*, 347–363.

Chavira, D., Stein, M., Bailey, K., & Stein, M. (2004). Child anxiety in primary care: Prevalent but untreated. *Depression and Anxiety, 20*, 155–164.

Choate, M., Pincus, D., Eyberg, S., & Barlow, D. (2005). Parent-Child Interaction Therapy for treatment of

Separation Anxiety Disorder in young children: A pilot study. *Cognitive and Behavioral Practice, 12*, 126–135.

Chorpita, B. F., Yim, L., Moffitt, C., Umemoto, L. A., & Francis, S. E. (2000). Assessment of symptoms of *DSM-IV* anxiety and depression in children: A revised child anxiety and depression scale. *Behaviour Research and Therapy, 38*, 855.

Cobham, V. E., Dadds, M. R., & Spence, S. H. (1998). The role of parental anxiety in the treatment of childhood anxiety. *Journal of Consulting and Clinical Psychology, 66*, 893–905.

Coffey, B. J., Biederman, J., Smoller, J. W., Geller, D. A., Sarin, P., Schwartz, S., & Kim, G. S. (2000). Anxiety disorders and tic severity in juveniles with Tourette's disorder. *Journal of the American Academy of Child & Adolescent Psychiatry, 39*, 562–568.

Cohen, P., Cohen, J., Kasen, S., & Velez, C. N. (1993). An epidemiological study of disorders in late childhood and adolescence: I. Age- and gender-specific prevalence. *Journal of Child Psychology and Psychiatry, 34*, 851–867.

Connolly, S., & Bernstein, G. (2007). Practice Parameter for the assessment and treatment of children and adolescents with anxiety disorders. *Journal of the American Academy of Child & Adolescent Psychiatry, 46*, 267–283.

Costello, E. J., Egger, H. L., & Angold, A. (2004). Developmental epidemiology of anxiety disorders. In T. H. Ollendick & J. S. March (Eds.), *Phobic and anxiety disorders in children and adolescents. A clinician's guide to effective psychosocial and pharmacological interventions* (pp. 61–91). New York, NY: Oxford University Press.

Costello, E. J., Mustillo, S., Erkanli, A., Keeler, G., & Angold, A. (2003). Prevalence and development of psychiatric disorders in childhood and adolescence. *Archives of General Psychiatry, 60*, 837–844.

De Groot, J., Cobham, V., Leong, J., & McDermott, B. (2007). Individual versus group family-focused cognitive-behaviour therapy for childhood anxiety: Pilot randomized controlled trial. *The Australian and New Zealand Journal of Psychiatry, 41*, 990–997.

Egger, H. L., Costello, E. J., Erkanli, A., & Angold, A. (1999). Somatic complaints and psychopathology in children and adolescents: Stomach aches, musculoskeletal pains, and headaches. *Journal of the American Academy of Child and Adolescent Psychiatry, 38*, 852–860.

Eisen, A., Raleigh, H., & Neuhoff, C. (2008). The unique impact of parent training for separation anxiety disorder in children. *Behavior Therapy, 39*, 195–206.

Eisen, A. E., & Schaefer, C. E. (2005). *Separation anxiety in children and adolescents.* New York, NY: Guilford Press.

Emmelkamp, P. M. G., & Scholing, A. (1997). Anxiety disorders in childhood and adolescence. In F. Petermann & C. A. Essau (Eds.), *Developmental psychopathology: Epidemiology, diagnostics and treatment* (pp. 219–264). Amsterdam, Netherlands: Harwood Academic Publishers.

Essau, C. A., Conradt, J., & Petermann, F. (2000). Frequency, comorbidity, and psychosocial impairment of anxiety disorders in German adolescents. *Journal of Anxiety Disorders, 14*, 263–279.

Ferdinand, R. F., Bongers, I. L., van der Ende, J., van Gastel, W., Tick, N., Utens, E., & Verhulst, F. C. (2006). Distinctions between separation anxiety and social anxiety in children and adolescents. *Behaviour Research and Therapy, 44*, 1523–1535.

Flannery-Schroeder, E. C., & Kendall, P. C. (2000). Group and individual cognitive-behavioral treatments for youth with anxiety disorders: A randomized clinical trial. *Cognitive Therapy and Research, 24*, 251–278.

Foley, D., Rowe, R., Maes, H., Silberg, J., Eaves, L., & Pickles, A. (2008). The relationship between separation anxiety and impairment. *Journal of Anxiety Disorders, 22*, 635–641.

Foley, D., Rutter, M., Pickles, A., Angold, A., Maes, H., Silberg, J., & Eaves, L. (2004). Informant disagreement for separation anxiety disorder. *Journal of the American Academy of Child & Adolescent Psychiatry, 43*, 452–460.

Geller, D., Biederman, J., Griffin, S., Jones, J., & Lefkowitz, T. (1996). Comorbidity of juvenile obsessive-compulsive disorder with disruptive behavior disorders. *Journal of the American Academy of Child and Adolescent Psychiatry, 35*, 1637–1646.

Graae, F., Milner, J., Rizzotto, L., & Klein, R. (1994). Clonazepam in childhood anxiety disorders. *Journal of the American Academy of Child and Adolescent Psychiatry, 33*, 372–376.

Gullone, E. (2000). The development of normal fear: A century of research. *Clinical Psychology Review, 20*, 429–451.

Hale, W., Raaijmakers, Q., Muris, P., van Hoof, A., & Meeus, W. (2008). Developmental trajectories of adolescent anxiety disorder symptoms: A 5-year prospective community study. *Journal of the American Academy of Child and Adolescent Psychiatry, 47*, 556–564.

Hembree-Kigin, T., & McNeil, C. (1995). *Parent-child interaction therapy.* New York, NY: Plenum Press.

Herschell, A., & McNeil, C. (2005). Parent-Child Interaction therapy for children experiencing externalizing behavior problems. In L. A. Reddy, T. M. Files-Hall, & C. E. Schaefer (Eds.), *Empirically based play interventions for children* (pp. 169–190). Washington, DC: American Psychological Association.

Heyne, D., King, N. J., Tonge, B. J., Rollings, S., Young, D., Pritchard, M., & Ollendick, T. H. (2002). Evaluation of child therapy and caregiver training in the treatment of school refusal. *Journal of the American Academy of Child & Adolescent Psychiatry, 41*, 687–695.

Hofflich, S., Hughes, A., & Kendall, P. (2006). Somatic complaints and childhood anxiety disorders. *International Journal of Clinical and Health Psychology, 6,* 229–242.

Hood, K., & Eyberg, S. (2003). Outcomes of Parent-Child Interaction Therapy: Mothers' reports of maintenance three to six years after treatment. *Journal of Clinical Child and Adolescent Psychology, 32,* 419–429.

Howard, B., & Kendall, P. (1996). Cognitive-behavioral family therapy for anxiety-disordered children: A multiple-baseline evaluation. *Cognitive Therapy and Research, 20,* 423–443.

Hughes, A., Lourea-Waddell, B., & Kendall, P. (2008). Somatic complaints in children with anxiety disorders and their unique prediction of poorer academic performance. *Child Psychiatry & Human Development, 39,* 211–220.

In-Albon, T., & Schneider, S. (2006). Psychotherapy of Childhood Anxiety Disorders: A meta-analysis. *Psychotherapy and Psychosomatics, 76,* 15–24.

Kendall, P. C. (1994). Treating anxiety disorders in children: Results of a randomized clinical trial. *Journal of Consulting and Clinical Psychology, 62,* 100–110.

Kendall, P. C., Chu, B., Gifford, A., Hayes, C., & Nauta, M. (1998). Breathing life into a manual: Flexibility and creativity with manual-based treatments. *Cognitive and Behavioral Practice, 5,* 177–198.

Kendall, P. C., Flannery-Schroeder, E., Panichelli-Mindel, S. M., Southam-Gerow, M., Henin, A., & Warman, M. (1997). Therapy for youths with anxiety disorders: A second randomized clinical trial. *Journal of Consulting and Clinical Psychology, 65,* 366–380.

Kendall, P. C., Hudson, J., Gosch, E., Flannery-Schroeder, E., & Suveg, C. (2008). Cognitive-behavioral therapy for anxiety disordered youth: A randomized clinical trial evaluating child and family modalities. *Journal of Consulting and Clinical Psychology, 76,* 282–297.

Kendall, P. C., Kane, M., Howard, B., & Siqueland, L. (1990). *Cognitive-behavioral therapy for anxious children: Treatment manual.* Philadelphia, PA: Department of Psychology, Temple University.

Kendall, P. C., Robin, J., Hedtke, K., Suveg, C., Flannery-Schroeder, E., & Gosch, E. (2005). Considering CBT with anxious youth? Think exposures. *Cognitive and Behavioral Practice, 12,* 136–150.

Kendall, P. C., & Southam-Gerow, M. (1996). Long-term follow-up of a cognitive-behavioral therapy for anxiety-disordered youth. *Journal of Consulting and Clinical Psychology, 64,* 724–730.

Kim, J., Szatmari, P., Bryson, S., Streiner, D., & Wilson, F. (2000). The prevalence of anxiety and mood problems among children with Autism and Asperger syndrome. *Autism, 4,* 117–132.

King, N. J., Tonge, B. J., Heyne, D., Pritchard, M., Rollings, S., Young, D., . . . Ollendick, T. H. (1998). Cognitive-behavioral treatment of school-refusing children: A controlled evaluation. *Journal of the American Academy of Child & Adolescent Psychiatry, 37,* 395–403.

Klein, R., Koplewicz, H., & Kanner, A. (1992). Imipramine treatment of children with separation anxiety disorder. *Journal of the American Academy of Child and Adolescent Psychiatry, 31,* 21–28.

Kovacs, M., & Devlin, B. (1998). Internalizing disorders in childhood. *Journal of Child Psychology and Psychiatry, 39,* 47–63.

Kovacs, M., Gatsonis, C., Paulauskas, S., & Richards, C. (1989). Depressive disorders in childhood. IV. A longitudinal study of comorbidity with and risk for anxiety disorders. *Archives of General Psychiatry, 46,* 776–782.

Last, C. G., Hansen, C., & Franco, N. (1997). Anxious children in adulthood: A prospective study of adjustment. *Journal of the American Academy of Child and Adolescent Psychiatry, 36,* 645–652.

Last, C. G., Hansen, C., & Franco, N. (1998). Cognitive-behavioral treatment of school phobia. *Journal of the American Academy of Child and Adolescent Psychiatry, 37,* 404–411.

Last, C. G., Strauss, C., & Francis, G. (1987). Comorbidity among childhood anxiety disorders. *The Journal of Nervous and Mental Disease, 175,* 726–730.

Levy, F., Hay, D., Bennett, K., & McStephen, M. (2005). Gender differences in ADHD subtype comorbidity. *Journal of the American Academy of Child & Adolescent Psychiatry, 44,* 368–376.

Lewinsohn, P., Holm-Denoma, J., Small, J., Seeley, J., & Joiner, T. (2008). Separation anxiety disorder in childhood as a risk factor for future mental illness. *Journal of the American Academy of Child & Adolescent Psychiatry, 47,* 548–555.

Liber, J. M., Van Widenfelt, B. M., Utens, E. J., Ferdinand, R. F., Van der Leeden, A. M., Van Gastel, W., & Treffers, P. A. (2008). No differences between group versus individual treatment of childhood anxiety disorders in a randomised clinical trial. *Journal of Child Psychology and Psychiatry, 49,* 886–893.

Livingston, R., Taylor, J., & Crawford, S. (1988). A study of somatic complaints and psychiatric diagnosis in children. *Journal of the American Academy of Child and Adolescent Psychiatry, 27,* 185–187.

Lyneham, H., & Rapee, R. (2006). Evaluation of therapist-supported parent-implemented CBT for anxiety disorders in rural children. *Behaviour Research and Therapy, 44,* 1287–1300.

Manassis, K., Mendlowitz, S. L., Scapillato, D., Avery, D., Fiksenbaum, L., Freire, M., . . . Owens, M. (2002). Group and individual cognitive-behavioral therapy for childhood anxiety disorders. A randomized trial. *Journal of the American Academy of Child & Adolescent Psychiatry, 41,* 1423–1430.

Manicavasagar, V., Silove, D., & Hadzi-Pavlovic, D. (1998). Subpopulations of early separation anxiety: Relevance to risk of adult anxiety disorders. *Journal of Affective Disorders, 48*, 181–190.

March, J., Parker, J., Sullivan, K., Stallings, P., & Conners, C. (1997). The Multidimensional Anxiety Scale for Children (MASC): Factor structure, reliability, and validity. *Journal of the American Academy of Child and Adolescent Psychiatry, 36*, 554–565.

Mendlowitz, S. L., Manassis, K., Bradley, S., Scapillato, D., Miezitis, S., & Shaw, B. F. (1999). Cognitive-behavioral group treatments in childhood anxiety disorders: The role of parental involvement. *Journal of the American Academy of Child and Adolescent Psychiatry, 38*, 1223–1229.

Menzies, R., & Harris, L. (2001). Nonassociative factors in the development of phobias. In M. W. Vasey and M. R. Dadds (Eds.), *The developmental psychopathology of anxiety* (pp. 183–204). New York, NY: Oxford University Press.

Muratori, F., Picchi, L., Apicella, F., Salvadori, F., Espasa, F., Ferretti, D., & Bruni, G. (2005). Psychodynamic psychotherapy for separation anxiety disorders in children. *Depression and Anxiety, 21*, 45–46.

Muratori, F., Picchi, L., Bruni, G., Patarnello, M., & Romagnoli, G. (2003). A two-year follow-up of psychodynamic psychotherapy for internalizing disorders in children. *Journal of the American Academy of Child and Adolescent Psychiatry, 42*, 331–339.

Muris, P., & Broeren, S. (2009). Twenty-five years of research on childhood anxiety disorders: Publication trends between 1982 and 2006 and a selective review of the literature. *Journal of Child and Family Studies, 18*, 388–395.

Muris, P., Dreessen, L., Bögels, S., Weckx, M., & van Melick, M. (2004). A questionnaire for screening a broad range of *DSM*-defined anxiety disorder symptoms in clinically referred children and adolescents. *Journal of Child Psychology and Psychiatry, and Allied Disciplines, 45*, 813–820.

Muris, P., Meesters, C., & van Melick, M. (2002). Treatment of childhood anxiety disorders; A preliminary comparison between cognitive-behavioral group therapy and a psychological placebo intervention. *Journal of Behavior Therapy and Experimental Psychiatry, 33*, 143–158.

Nauta, M. H., Scholing, A., Emmelkamp, P. M. G., & Minderaa, R. B. (2001). Cognitive-behavioural therapy for anxiety disordered children in a clinical setting: Does additional cognitive parent training enhance treatment effectiveness? *Clinical Psychology and Psychotherapy, 8*, 330–340.

Nauta, M. H., Scholing, A., Emmelkamp, P. M. G., & Minderaa, R. B. (2003). Cognitive-behavioural therapy for anxiety disordered children in a clinical setting: No additional effect of a cognitive parent

training. *Journal of the American Academy of Child and Adolescent Psychiatry, 42*, 1270–1278.

Nauta, M. H., Scholing, A., Rapee, R. M., Abbott, M., Spence, S. H., & Waters, A. (2004). A parent-report measure of children's anxiety: Psychometric properties and comparison with child-report in a clinic and normal sample. *Behaviour Research and Therapy, 42*, 813–839.

Norton, P., & Philipp, L. (2008). Transdiagnostic approaches to the treatment of anxiety disorders: A quantitative review. *Psychotherapy: Theory, Research, Practice, Training, 45*, 214–226.

Ollendick, T., Hagopian, L., & Huntzinger, R. (1991). Cognitive-behavior therapy with nighttime fearful children. *Journal of Behavior Therapy and Experimental Psychiatry, 22*, 113–121.

Perrin, S., & Last, C. (1997). Worrisome thoughts in children clinically referred for anxiety disorder. *Journal of Clinical Child Psychology, 26*, 181–189.

Pincus, D., Eyberg, S., & Choate, M. (2005). Adapting parent-child interaction therapy for young children with separation anxiety disorder. *Education & Treatment of Children, 28*, 163–181.

Pine, D. S., Walkup, J. T., Labellarte, M. J., Riddle, M. A., Greenhill, L., Klein, R., . . . Roper, M. (2001). Fluvoxamine for the treatment of anxiety disorders in children and adolescents. *The New England Journal of Medicine, 344*, 1279–1285.

Powers, M. B., & Emmelkamp, P. M. G. (2009). Dissemination of research findings. In D. Richard & S. Huprich (Eds.), *Clinical psychology: Assessment, treatment, and research* (pp. 495–524). Burlington, MA: Elsevier Academic Press.

Rapee, R. M. (2001). The development of generalized anxiety. In M. W. Vasey & M. R. Dadds. (Eds.), *The developmental psychopathology of anxiety* (pp. 481–503). London, England: Oxford University Press.

Rapee, R., Abbott, M., & Lyneham, H. (2006). Bibliotherapy for children with anxiety disorders using written materials for parents: A randomized controlled trial. *Journal of Consulting and Clinical Psychology, 74*, 436–444.

Shear, K., Jin, R., Ruscio, A., Walters, E., & Kessler, R. (2006). Prevalence and correlates of estimated *DSM-IV* child and adult separation anxiety disorder in the National Comorbidity Survey Replication. *The American Journal of Psychiatry, 163*, 1074–1083.

Shortt, A., Barrett, P., & Fox, T. (2001). Evaluating the FRIENDS program: A cognitive-behavioral group treatment for anxious children and their parents. *Journal of Clinical Child Psychology, 30*, 525–535.

Silove, D., Manicavasagar, V., Curtis, J., & Blaszczynski, A. (1996). Is early separation anxiety a risk factor for adult panic disorder? A critical review. *Comprehensive Psychiatry, 37*, 167–179.

Silverman, W., Pina, A., & Viswesvaran, C. (2008). Evidence-based psychosocial treatments for phobic and anxiety disorders in children and adolescents. *Journal of Clinical Child and Adolescent Psychology, 37*, 105–130.

Siqueland, L., Rynn, M., & Diamond, G. (2005). Cognitive behavioral and attachment based family therapy for anxious adolescents: Phase I and II studies. *Journal of Anxiety Disorders, 19*, 361–381.

Spence, S. H. (1997). Structure of anxiety symptoms among children: A confirmatory factor-analytic study. *Journal of Abnormal Psychology, 106*, 280–297.

Spence, S., Holmes, J., March, S., & Lipp, O. (2006). The feasibility and outcome of clinic plus Internet delivery of cognitive-behavior therapy for childhood anxiety. *Journal of Consulting and Clinical Psychology, 74*, 614–621.

Sterba, S., Egger, H., & Angold, A. (2007). Diagnostic specificity and nonspecificity in the dimensions of preschool psychopathology. *Journal of Child Psychology and Psychiatry, and Allied Disciplines, 48*, 1005–1013.

Strauss, C. C., Frame, C. L., & Forehand, R. (1987). Psychosocial impairment associated with anxiety in children. *Journal of Clinical Child Psychology, 16*, 235–239.

Sturmey, P. (2007). *Functional analysis in clinical treatment*. New York, NY: Academic Press.

Sturmey, P. (2008). *Behavioral case formulation and intervention: A behavioral approach*. Hoboken, NJ: Wiley.

Suveg, C., Hudson, J. L., Brewer, G., Flannery-Schroeder, E., Gosch, E., & Kendall, P. C. (2009). Cognitive-behavioral therapy for anxiety-disordered youth: Secondary outcomes from a randomized clinical trial

evaluating child and family modalities. *Journal of Anxiety Disorders, 23*, 341–349.

Thienemann, M., Moore, P., & Tompkins, K. (2006). A parent-only group intervention for children with anxiety disorders: Pilot study. *Journal of the American Academy of Child & Adolescent Psychiatry, 45*, 37–46.

Toren, P., Wolmer, L., Rosental, B., Eldar, S., Koren, S., Lask, M., . . . Laor, N. (2000). Case series: Brief parent–child group therapy for childhood anxiety disorders using a manual-based cognitive–behavioral technique. *Journal of the American Academy of Child & Adolescent Psychiatry, 39*, 1309–1312.

Verduin, T. L., & Kendall, P. C. (2003). Differential occurrence of comorbidity within childhood anxiety disorders. *Journal of Clinical Child & Adolescent Psychology, 32*, 290–295.

Walkup, J. T., Albano, A., Piacentini, J., Birmaher, B., Compton, S. N., Sherrill, J. T., . . . Kendall, P. C. (2008). Cognitive behavioral therapy, sertraline, or a combination in childhood anxiety. *The New England Journal of Medicine, 359*, 2753–2766.

Weems, C., & Costa, N. (2005). Developmental differences in the expression of childhood anxiety symptoms and fears. *Journal of the American Academy of Child & Adolescent Psychiatry, 44*, 656–663.

Wood, J. J. (2006). Effect of anxiety reduction on children's school performance and social adjustment. *Developmental Psychology, 42*, 345–349.

Wood, J., Piacentini, J., Southam-Gerow, M., Chu, B., & Sigman, M. (2006). Family Cognitive Behavioral Therapy for child anxiety disorders. *Journal of the American Academy of Child & Adolescent Psychiatry, 45*, 314–321.

18

Reactive Attachment Disorder and Severe Attachment Disturbances

THOMAS G. O'CONNOR, MARY SPAGNOLA, AND J. GERARD BYRNE

OVERVIEW OF DISORDER

Reactive attachment disorder (RAD) has been in the psychiatric nomenclature for more than a quarter of a century, appearing in the *Diagnostic and Statistical Manual* (*DSM*) (3rd ed.) in 1980. Its formulation in *DSM-IV-TR* (American Psychiatric Association, 2000) differs in some notable ways from the earlier diagnostic definition, but most of the central features remain. RAD is now a focus of considerable debate; there is a wide range of opinions about the disorder and its treatment among clinicians and scientists, social care professionals, and parents. Significantly, this debate has occurred and, by and large, continues to occur in the absence of very substantial progress in understanding the disorder or how it is best managed in clinical practice. Indeed, RAD has a dubious distinction of being a disorder about which there are probably more review papers than there are solid empirically based clinical studies. In short, the evidence base is quite limited and much of the existing clinical research assesses a phenotype that is far broader than the *DSM-IV* or *International Classification of Diseases* (*ICD*) (10th ed.) (World Health Organization, 1992) definition. Nevertheless, a chapter on evidence-based treatments for RAD is appropriate in this volume because there is substantial clinical scientific interest in RAD and there is an abiding need to differentiate which of the various treatments so far proposed have merit or promise.

Preliminary Points and Clarifications

Given the definitional confusion and lack of an established clinical protocol, it is important to provide some preliminary comments about how we define RAD. In that regard, we considered for analysis those studies that include *DSM-* or *ICD*-based diagnoses, but also extended our reach to those papers that did not explicitly assess *DSM/ICD* criteria. The need to extend beyond conventional diagnostic boundaries is inevitable because the application of diagnostic criteria in clinical assessment is typically difficult to decipher and most studies avoided formal diagnostic assessments altogether. We pick up on this issue in a subsequent section.

A major source of confusion about the disorder is its link with the concepts, methods, findings, and interventions based on the attachment theory developed by Bowlby (1982), Ainsworth (1967), Ainsworth, Blehar, Waters, and Wall (1978), and others. As we discuss later, it is not yet clear how or if RAD and attachment theory are linked (O'Connor, 2002). This has proved to be a controversial matter, especially regarding intervention, with some writers claiming that certain interventions, such as holding therapies, are based on attachment theory, whereas others suggest that those same interventions are antithetical to attachment theory. Perhaps the only point that can be agreed upon is that RAD is "attachment"-related insofar as it is invariably associated with severe early caregiving deprivation or the absence of a consistently available attachment figure.

A final preliminary comment is that the literature on interventions for RAD per se is limited. That is a consequence of the confusion about the diagnosis, its very low prevalence, and tendency for those working in this area to resist empirical scrutiny, at least until recently. Therefore, we are well short of being able to compare evidence of alternative treatments in a systematic way. In response to that, we have structured our review of the intervention data in the following manner. First, and most centrally, we address the available evidence base for RAD intervention research, but we add two subsequent sections. One concerns interventions for children at risk for RAD, namely those with a history of severe caregiving (de) privation, such as children in foster care. This is an important additional set of studies, although the overlap with RAD as such is unclear. Also, we include a brief intervention section dealing with more conventional attachment-based interventions for the more conventional kinds of disturbances, namely, insecure attachment. Although probably none of the children in these interventions would meet criteria for RAD, a brief discussion of these interventions is instructive to make clear what conventional attachment interventions look like and how effective they are in addressing more common problems in child–parent attachment. Whether these interventions will have carry-over benefits for treating children with RAD is, at present, unknown. On the other hand, considering these studies and their effects may help to reduce the confusion that now exists about what constitutes an attachment therapy.

Historical Overview

The concept of RAD has a particularly rich history that predates its appearance in the *DSM-III* in 1980. Indeed, the core behavioral symptoms of what is now referred to as the "Disinhibited" form of RAD were evident in reports on institutionalized children from the first half of the 20th century. An interesting observation from these early reports is that there is consistency in these descriptions despite substantial differences in the backgrounds and biases of the authors. "Superficially affectionate" was a term used in an early paper by Levy (1937), and Goldfarb (1943) commented on indiscriminate behavior toward unfamiliar persons and an "excessive need for adult attention" that persisted after children were placed from the institution into families. Anna Freud and Dorothy Burlingham (1973) studied children's behavior in a residential nursery who likely did not have a history of consistent care, and perhaps even had poor care. They used the phrase "indiscriminate exhibition" to describe how particular children engaged and approached strange adults in order to show off clothes or belongings. In their classic study of infants who experienced institutional care, Provence and Lipton (1962) used the term "indiscriminately friendly" to describe the approach of children to virtual strangers. And Wolkind (1974) provided suggestive evidence that what he referred to as "affectionless psychopathy" was particularly linked with *early* institutional care.

The last decades of the 20th century witnessed several additional reports. These are notable because the children being studied were not necessarily experiencing profound deprivation secondary to being made orphans because of World War II, for example. Thus, the studies reported by Tizard and colleagues (Tizard & Hodges, 1978; Tizard & Rees, 1975) were based on children in residential placements in which there was adequate nutritional, social, and cognitive stimulation, although there was not individual care of the child— what we would now refer to as a lack of opportunity to form a selective or discriminating attachment relationship. Despite what was thought to be adequate care by social care organizations, a sizable minority of those children followed by Tizard and colleagues exhibited what they described as "indiscriminately friendly" behavior toward strangers— an apparent synonym for the core feature of disinhibited RAD in *DSM-IV-TR*. Other studies identifying this behavioral pattern in children in foster or residential settings include the work of Roy (Roy, Rutter, & Pickles, 2000), which was on a similar cohort to Tizard but published much later and, more recently, the work of Rushton (Rushton, Treseder, & Quinton, 1995), Vorria (Vorria et al., 2006), Zeanah and Boris (Boris et al., 2004; Zeanah et al., 2004), and Minnis (Minnis, Green, O'Connor, Liew, & the RADAR team, 2009). The work of Zeanah, Rushton, and Minnis may prove especially valuable because they assessed the RAD phenotype in children in foster care, a more common population than children with an institutional care history.

Perhaps the most important spur for the increased attention to attachment disorder derives from the flurry of studies of children who experienced early institutional care in Romania and eastern Europe, Russia, China, and elsewhere, and were adopted into families in Australia, Europe, and North America (Chisholm, 1998; Gunnar, Morison, Chisholm, Shuder, 2001; O'Connor, Rutter, Beckett, et al., 2000).

There is also the Bucharest Early Intervention Project, which assessed children in Romanian institutions as well as those who

were placed in foster families and a comparison group of nondeprived children (Nelson et al., 2007). These studies reflected the increased awareness of international adoption and the fact that, in many circumstances, children's experiences prior to adoption included profound deprivation. Significantly, none of these studies used accepted *DSM* or *ICD* definitions of RAD. Nevertheless, it is ironic but not a contradiction that the findings from these studies provide probably the most important set of results that inform our understanding of the causes and course of RAD.

A fundamental issue in contemporary research is how well the findings from samples of institutional children, by far the most common source of data on RAD and RAD-related behaviors, extends to children in the adoption and foster care system, which is now the most common source of clinical concern. At this point in the clinical science, it is not clear that findings from one population will extend to the other; that remains an open question that requires concentrated clinical study.

A proposed second form of attachment disorder, referred to as the "inhibited" variety in the *DSM-IV*, has a much less clear historical and clinical basis. Children with a history of severe maltreatment have been described as showing extreme fear and even terror of strangers (Albus & Dozier, 1999; Gaensbauer & Harmon, 1982; Goldfarb, 1943; Zeanah, 1996)—a marked contrast to what is seen in children with the disinhibited form. Descriptions by the Robertsons (Robertson & Robertson, 1989), Bowlby (1982), and Spitz (1946) are significant here insofar as they describe a tendency to withdraw substantially from the social and caregiving environment. Children with a history of severe caregiving deprivation have been reported to show lack of seeking care when it would be expected, such as following an injury or illness; however, these reports are mostly of a clinical and anecdotal manner; systematic study into this form of disturbance is very limited.

Summary of Main Research Findings

Several decades of research into RAD and RAD-related behaviors suggest the following (Boris et al., 2004; Chisholm, 1998; Goldfarb, 1943; Minnis et al., 2009; O'Connor, Rutter, & the English and Romanian Adoptees Study Team, 2000; O'Connor et al., 2003; Provence & Lipton, 1962; Rushton et al., 1995; Rutter et al., 2007; Smyke, Dumitrescu, & Zeanah, 2002; Tizard & Rees, 1975; Zeanah, Smyke, & Dumitrescu, 2002; Zeanah et al., 2004). First, children who experience early caregiving deprivation show severe disturbances with caregivers and other social partners. It is especially important to note that disturbances are found even when children receive adequate nutrition, cognitive stimulation, and opportunities for social interaction—as in the case of the Tizard studies, for example. This implies that RAD and particularly the disinhibited behavioral disturbance is not an "institutional syndrome," but rather a "caregiver deprivation" syndrome that is associated with the lack of opportunity to form a stable consistent relationship with a particular caregiver. Second, the disturbance is persistent; that is, it continues to be observed long after the termination of the depriving environment and despite the presence of a consistent caring environment in which there is ready availability of a stable attachment figure. Indeed, RAD, and particularly the disinhibited pattern of behavioral disturbance, is one of the more impressive examples of a persisting effect of early adversity. Third, caregiving deprivation is associated with RAD-related behaviors, but not, apparently, with insecure attachment, the form of attachment problem found in children who had the opportunity to form selective attachments but had caregivers who were significantly insensitive and unresponsive. This provides one of several pieces of evidence that RAD is qualitatively different from insecure attachment. Fourth, RAD and related disturbances can be distinguished from frequently comorbid conditions, such as attentional

problems and cognitive delay and other forms of social impairments. On the other hand, although systematic study is still absent, there is general clinical agreement that children with RAD do show elevated rates of comorbid attention and other behavioral problems, as well as fundamental problems in detecting, interpreting, and responding to emotions and social clues. This is important because it implies that the disturbance can be explained by fundamental problems in using and detecting interpersonal information, which is more basic than attachment. Fifth, there is a widespread presumption that the children with RAD and RAD-related behaviors will show substantial disturbances in one of several biological systems, from those involved in stress physiology (Gunnar et al., 2001) to neuropeptides associated with social relationships (Fleming, O'Day, & Kraemer, 1999), and structural changes in the brain (Eluvathingal et al., 2006). This work remains somewhat exploratory, but holds considerable promise as a way of offering additional evidence for disturbance and possibly as a means of evaluating treatment success (Dozier, Peloso, Lewis, Laurenceau, & Levine, 2008). Sixth, there is now substantial evidence that children who are reported to show disinhibited behavior may nevertheless show apparently normal and even secure-looking behavior toward their caregivers. That presents an important conceptual puzzle (e.g., is it possible that a child with disinhibited behavior could nevertheless have a genuinely secure attachment relationship with a caregiver?). It also raises the additional clinical question about whether or not "success" in treating RAD should require a reduction in disinhibited behavior. Finally, perhaps the most impressive finding on RAD-related behaviors is how much variability there is, even following severe deprivation lasting several years. So, for example, in the study of children adopted into the United Kingdom following institutional rearing in institutions in Romania (O'Connor, Rutter, & the English and Romanian Adoptees Study Team, 2000), only a sizable minority of children who experienced 2 or more years of institutional rearing showed severe disturbance; a sizable minority showed no obvious impairments in this area, as far as could be determined.

Diagnostic Criteria

According to *DSM-IV-TR*, RAD of childhood exists in two forms, disinhibited and inhibited. The disinhibited form is defined as "diffuse attachments as manifest by indiscriminate sociability with marked inability to exhibit appropriate selective attachments (e.g., excessive familiarity with relative strangers or lack of selectivity in choice of attachment figures)" (APA, 2000, p. 118). The inhibited form is defined as

> persistent failure to initiate or respond in a developmentally appropriate fashion to most social interactions, as manifest by excessively inhibited, hypervigilant, or highly ambivalent and contradictory responses (e.g., the child may respond to caregivers with a mixture of approach, avoidance, and resistance to comforting, or may exhibit 'frozen watchfulness,' hypervigilance while keeping an impassive and still demeanor. (p. 118)

These definitions are familiar to those who have read the clinical and more recent empirical studies of children who experienced severe deprivation, and seem generally to capture the major behavioral manifestation in clinical practice. As noted, however, these definitions have not proved to be influential in research and there is not yet an established clinical protocol, although efforts are underway" (Minnis et al., 2009; O'Connor & Zeanah, 2003).

In addition to specifying which of the two forms is more prevalent, there is also a diagnostic requirement to confirm that there is "markedly disturbed and developmentally inappropriate social relatedness" in most contexts; that is, the problem is not relationship-specific, the disinhibited or inhibited disturbance is not accounted for by developmental

delay and the child does not also meet diagnostic criteria for pervasive developmental disorder (PDD), there is an onset before 5 years of age, and there is a documented history of significant neglect.

There are a number of concerns that have been expressed about the diagnostic approach in *DSM-IV-TR* (O'Connor & Zeanah, 2003; Zeanah, 1996). One of the most significant is that the behavioral features are focused on preschool to early school-aged children. Given that this is presumed to be a stable disorder, with problems persisting well past early childhood, there is a need to consider formally if the behavioral features now in *DSM* and *ICD* are relevant beyond the preschool period. Very little work of this kind has been reported. A second concern is to do with terminology. Specifically, the notion, from *DSM-IV-TR*, that a child has "diffuse attachments" is an oxymoron: Attachments are not, by their nature, diffuse. Thus, the term may contribute to ongoing uncertainty about the disinhibited pattern. Also, there is no consensus on what would constitute "sufficient" neglect, a precondition for the diagnosis. So, for example, in the many studies of attachment in maltreated children, there is virtually no mention of RAD but considerable mention of insecure attachment, particularly of the disorganized form. The absence of RAD in these studies could be because the investigators were not looking for these features or used insensitive assessment procedures; on the other hand, it seems more likely that maltreatment is not adequate to lead to RAD. Indeed, it has been appreciated for some time that children who were maltreated nevertheless develop *selective but insecure* attachment relationships toward their abusive/neglectful parent (Cicchetti, Rogosch, & Toth, 2006). This presents one further piece of evidence that RAD and insecure attachment are etiologically distinct. The former seems more closely associated with a lack of available attachment relationship, whereas the latter is associated with a history of insensitive, unresponsive, or abusive care.

The *ICD-10* has a somewhat different approach to the disorder, at least in terms of organizing the symptoms. For example, there is a formal disjunction between RAD, which is essentially equivalent to the inhibited form of RAD according to *DSM-IV-TR*, and Disinhibited Attachment Disorder of Childhood, a separate disorder, which is essentially equivalent to the disinhibited form from *DSM-IV-TR*. Also, unlike the *DSM-IV-TR*, the *ICD-10* refers to poor social interaction with peers and self- and other-directed aggression. It is not clear that the mild differences in how *DSM-IV-TR* and *ICD-10* handle attachment disorder have any practical clinical consequence; what is clear is that the research base is inadequate to make preferential decisions about one or other nosology.

Interestingly, both *DSM-IV-TR* and *ICD-10* note that disinhibited problems may be quite persistent, an impression strongly supported by a long history of social care reports and the more recent empirical data. Thus, *ICD-10* notes that "indiscriminate sociability may persist even after the child has developed selective attachments" and *DSM-IV-TR* states that disinhibited problems tend "to persist despite marked changes in environmental circumstances." As we discussed earlier, this raises very substantial questions about whether or not disinhibited behaviors would be a reliable clinical outcome. These recent updates to the diagnostic systems imply that clinical improvement may occur without major reductions in disinhibited behavior; if that is so, it could have a major impact on how disinhibited behavior is conceptualized in clinical practice and what it means for understanding the link between attachment patterns and RAD.

Although the specific diagnostic criteria have not had a major influence on clinical research as of yet, they do provide a solid beginning and, in any event, provide a solid starting point. Other approaches to assess RAD-related behaviors have been proposed. Probably the best known is that put forth by

Zeanah and colleagues (Zeanah, Boris, & Lieberman, 2000). That approach also requires systematic clinical study. There are approaches to defining RAD that can and should be dismissed outright, including a wide array of questionnaires that are promoted on the Internet and not yet rigorously evaluated as a possible clinical-scientific tool (e.g., Randolph, 2000). Such measures should be discarded because they serve only to maintain confusion about what RAD is, what the diagnostic boundaries may be, and what treatments—if effective—are changing. The absence of an established evidence-based assessment protocol is maintaining the confusion about RAD in clinical practice; establishing an evidence-based model for assessment that is clinically feasible is a major challenge for clinical research.

Demographic Variables

Demographic data on RAD are essentially nonexistent, apart from the dramatic circumstance of caregiving deprivation that is found in institutional rearing and, in an unknown subset of children, foster care. However, samples from these studies are too small to make firm conclusions. Thus, nothing is known about the epidemiology of the disorder. By way of example, data from the English and Romanian Adoptees study (O'Connor, Rutter, & the English and Romanian Adoptees Study Team, 2000) of children adopted into the United Kingdom following severe deprivation in Romania indicated that over 30% of children who experienced between 24 and 42 months of institutional care exhibited severe disinhibited disturbance when they were assessed at age 6 years; the rate was less than 10% in those for whom institutional care was limited to the first 6 months or less following birth. Rates of RAD in foster care samples are unreliable as yet. A recent study of a large sample of children in foster care in Utah (Steele & Buchi, 2008) reported a rate of 17%

with reactive attachment and adjustment disorders, although inexplicably, the two diagnoses were combined in the reporting. How these diagnoses were made was also not clear from the report, making the estimates unreliable. In their assessment of 94 maltreated toddlers in foster care, Zeanah et al. (2004) found that the rate of *DSM-IV* and *ICD-10* RAD was 38%–40%. There is also the report from Minnis and colleagues (2007), who reported rates of RAD-related behaviors in a normative sample of young children. Although the rates of more severe problems were predictably low in this nonmaltreated community sample, it was notable that disinhibited and inhibited items were endorsed by parents of children who had not experienced caregiving deprivation, although the meaning of these behaviors in a nondeprived sample may differ from that in a deprived sample. Significantly, there is no good evidence that any of the other well-known sources of psychosocial risk for more typical behavioral/emotional problems— such as social economic status, poverty, or parental mental illness—have anything to do with RAD.

Impact of Disorder

Comparatively few studies assessed impact of RAD as such or the costs associated with it. Regarding the individual child, there is little question that the impact and cost would be substantial because of the frequent involvement of residential placement. Clinical and anecdotal experience also shows that the cost and impact on the lives of families is unquestionably severe, albeit difficult to quantify with available data. At the public health level, the impact of RAD is completely unknown because the epidemiological findings are so uncertain. It may be safer, at this early stage, to presume that the impact of disorder is comparable to what it is for children in foster care (Becker, Jordan, & Larsen, 2006; Minnis, Everittt, Pelosi, Dunn, & Knapp, 2006).

OVERVIEW OF TREATMENT MODELS

As noted, the evidence base of effective treatments for RAD is limited. There are, for example, no randomized controlled trials (RCTs) for RAD, although there are some uncontrolled trials, described following; a few case studies have been reported. And, although some treatment guidelines have been discussed by professional bodies, they function primarily to warn against certain dangerous and unsupported treatments (e.g., Boris, Zeanah, and the Work Group on Quality Issues, 2005). This is perhaps all that treatment guidelines could be expected to do, given the poor evidence base now available. Some attention is paid in our discussion to treatment conceptualization models because there remains considerable need to elucidate how— as well as if—treatment works.

Behavioral and Psychoeducational Approaches

Uncontrolled Trials

Data from uncontrolled trials that use behaviorally based approaches have been reported for RAD. Mukkades and colleagues (Mukaddes, Bilge, Alyanak, & Kora, 2000; Mukaddes, Kaynack, Kinali, Besikci, & Issever, 2004) reasoned that PDD, autism, and RAD share similar symptoms. They applied an intervention that had been successful with treatment of children with PDD and autism to children with RAD. These psychoeducational interventions were derived from Treatment and Education of Autistic and Related Communication Handicapped Children (TEACCH; Schopler, 1987; Schopler et al., 1984), a program that teaches parents strategies to help their children to address problematic behavior by using behavioral techniques. The first study (Mukaddes et al., 2000) included 15 children (nine boys, six girls) diagnosed with RAD who had initially been misdiagnosed with PDD. These children had a history of pathogenic care and showed impairments in social interaction, communication, and language development. They participated with their current primary caregivers in the 3-month TEACCH outpatient program. Following treatment, children showed improvements in social behavior (increased eye contact, reciprocal play, and social imitation) and ability to form sentences, and decreased stereotyped behavior. The second study (Mukaddes et al., 2004) used a home-based version of TEACCH and compared the progress of ten boys with diagnoses of autism to eleven boys and girls with diagnoses of RAD, all of preschool age. Children in both the autism and the RAD group showed overall improvements following the intervention, measured by parents' reports on the *Ankara Developmental Screening Inventory* (Savasir, Sezgin, & Erol, 1998); children with RAD showed greater improvement than children with autism on the total development score. Specifically, they showed greater improvement on the subscales of language-cognition, social and self-care, and fine and gross motor skills.

Both studies showed evidence of positive change in the social behavior of children with RAD; however, the particular social behavior that was targeted is not the most clinically relevant to RAD. That is, the intervention improved eye contact and turn-taking behavior, but did not address the problematic social behavior associated with RAD, such as indiscriminate social relating and/or failure to seek a caregiver in times of distress. In addition, impaired social functioning in disorders such as PDD and autism may be more indicative of cognitive deficits, whereas those consistent with RAD may derive from a history of pathogenic care and may be more indicative of impairments in social and emotional functioning related to this type of care; whether this potential difference in etiology translates to differential capacity to change is unclear. It is also significant that the studies did not use random assignment, but rather capitalized on the existence of children with RAD who had

been—perhaps mistakenly—referred to an autism service.

Single-Case Studies

Behavioral modification approaches, of the sort in such evidence-based programs such as Incredible Years (Reid, Webster-Stratton, & Baydar, 2004; Scott, Spender, Doolan, Jacobs, & Aspland, 2001) and the Oregon Social Learning Center (Forgatch & DeGarmo, 1999) have a prominent role in treating a range of behavioral/emotional problems in children. A single-case report (Buckner, Lopez, Dunkel, & Joiner, 2008) used a behavioral modification approach to treat RAD. The authors described a 12-session treatment of a 7-year-old Caucasian girl who was recently adopted by her grandparents following many years of presumed severe neglect and likely maltreatment from her biological father, who had retained custody of the child when the parents separated before the child's first birthday. At presentation, the child showed the predictable pattern of wide-ranging disruptive and "socially annoying" behaviors alongside poor self-care and some sexualized behavior; notably, the child also engaged in painful hugging with peers and adults across multiple settings. A diagnosis of RAD was suggested. Using Barkley's *Defiant Children* model, the authors report substantial success in reducing disruptive behavioral problems and, perhaps more significantly, disturbed social relations with caregivers and peers. At the conclusion of treatment, the authors report that the child no longer met diagnostic criteria for RAD and was mildly ill, down from markedly ill at intake.

Single-case reports are obviously of limited value, but this one may have more impact than most because it challenges the presumption—which had been built on no empirical data—that a behaviorally based intervention would not yield sizable clinical improvements in attachment disturbances. The origins of this notion are not quite clear, but the argument most often heard from parents and clinicians is that a problem as severe as RAD requires a more intensive or extreme treatment. As we note elsewhere, there is no connection between how extreme or intensive an intervention is and its likelihood of success, and there are disastrous results for certain invasive interventions, as we discuss later. Rather than immediately assuming that an intensive intervention is needed, it seems a safer position to try noninvasive approaches that are evidence-based. More broadly, there is a growing literature that shows attachment-based interventions may have the strongest effects on child attachment security and parental sensitivity if they incorporate behavioral strategies and principles (Bakermans-Kranenburg, van Ijzendoorn, & Juffer, 2003). This work helps to break down the artificial divide that has been built up between attachment and behavioral approaches. Of course, the Bakermans-Kranenburg et al. meta-analysis is of attachment-based interventions for insecure attachment; none of the children had RAD. It does not follow that these same interventions would have any clinical benefit for RAD—a possibility that we consider in a subsequent section.

"Holding" and Related Therapies

The most controversial treatment by far is a form of treatment that we label "holding" therapy, a general term to represent a range of treatment approaches that are difficult to categorize precisely. The reason for this is that the descriptions of the treatments have changed somewhat, partly reflecting the rising resistance to the more coercive techniques that have been/are used in some approaches. So, for instance, in the case of the intervention described by Hughes (1997, 2004) generally labeled "Dyadic Developmental Psychotherapy" (DDP), there is some inconsistency about the usefulness and meaning of the therapist's uninvited holding of the child in the course of treatment. In any event, there is little doubt that an aversion to coercive holding has now taken hold. Therapies that encouraged the use of

coercive holding had been promoted by several authors (Keck & Kupecky, 1995; Levy, 2000; Welch, 1989) on the presumption that, for example, the intense physical contact was needed to "break through" the child's defenses. That approach is no longer reputable and the conceptualization was, in any event, severely flawed. A number of professional organizations have explicitly rejected coercive holding as harmful (Boris et al., 2005). Indeed, deaths of several children resulted from coercive therapies such as "rebirthing therapy," perhaps the most infamous form.

On the other hand, the use of *noncoercive* holding—which may be difficult to distinguish from coercive holding in many instances—has not been completely rejected and continues to be one of the most distinguishing characteristics of treatments promoted for RAD. We use the term "holding therapy" to describe the treatments in this section, but recognize that the treatment procedures are often not well-specified, vary among adherents, and may have altered over time. It is significant that most of the literature on holding and related therapies is in the form of books, pamphlets, and Internet material. Those sources provide no attempt to assess the value of this kind of treatment, and so are not included here. We similarly do not include descriptive accounts of interventions that do not allow for any formal evaluation; that is, clinical descriptions without a formal case study, for example.

Uncontrolled Trials

To date, only uncontrolled trials have been reported in this area. Becker-Weidman (2006, 2008) examined the effectiveness of DDP, an intervention developed by Hughes (1997, 2004). Sixty-four maltreated children (aged 5–16) and their primary caregivers participated in the study: 34 children in the treatment group were seen regularly for DDP with their foster-parent caregivers on an outpatient basis and 30 children in the control group received care as usual on an outpatient basis. DDP emphasized the development and maintenance of an attachment relationship between the child and caregiver by aiming to alter negative internal working models by increasing use of the caregiver as a secure base. The intervention also targeted grief associated with loss due to abuse, neglect, or foster placement; also addressed were formation of social relationships, aggression, and socially acceptable behavior. Caregivers and children participated in this treatment with the therapist. Methods included modeling healthy attachment, reducing shame, and providing "safe and nurturing physical contact" that is containing so that the child can "re-experience the affect associated with the trauma" and "integrate the experience."

Following treatment, caregivers of children in the DDP group reported significant decreases in problem behavior and symptoms of attachment disorder. They also reported significant decreases in withdrawal, anxiety, and depression. In a follow-up study (Becker-Weidman, 2008), the long-term effects of DDP were examined by comparing the initial post-treatment scores on the *Child Behavioral Checklist* (Achenbach, 1991) and the *Randolph Attachment Disorder Questionnaire* (Randolph, 2000) with those acquired 1 year and approximately 4 years later. Children in the DDP group maintained their gains from the intervention, with scores on the two measures remaining in the normal range and behavior improvements that continued to be clinically significant 4 years later.

The studies of DDP provide an interesting start to developing an evidence base, but there are limitations to the studies. Specifically, these studies did not provide evidence for a specific manualized treatment that could be easily replicated, an important issue because the intervention description was somewhat vague regarding specific therapeutic techniques. Moreover, it is unclear if the children included in the studies actually had a diagnosis of RAD and too few details on the assessment of RAD symptoms were provided. Aside from the problem of uncertain measurement of

RAD, there are other more conventional and serious limitations, including the lack of randomization, independence of assessment, and fidelity of treatment administration. In other words, the studies fall short of providing a solid level of evidence.

Another published report indicated that a "2-week intensive" inpatient treatment regiment for children with suspected RAD reduced aggression according to parent report (Myeroff, Mertlich, & Gross, 1999). This study of about a dozen cases offered the first evidence that a holding treatment-based approach was better than a nontreated group, but this study also had serious flaws, including small and very selective samples without randomization, and, as in the case of the DDP studies, the concerns about the potential independence of the evaluation (i.e., avoiding potential conflicts of interest) were not considered. In addition, a core aim of the holding therapy, an improvement in the relationship between parent and child, was not part of the assessment. This is a particularly important oversight because many methods for reducing aggressive behavior are available that are far less costly and invasive than an inpatient treatment, and do not have the adverse effects that are associated with holding therapy.

Consensus panel recommendations from numerous professional bodies explicitly reject the use of coercive holding as a treatment technique for children with RAD (Boris et al., 2005). One reason for that view is the simple case that there is nothing to recommend it; that is, no empirical evidence. Based on our review of the available data, this continues to be the case, with a possible footnote about weak studies of uncertain value. More significant is the fact that coercive holding treatments have caused injury and death, and there is a general suspicion, based on clinical-anecdotal evidence, that the coercive holding may retraumatize children. Aside from these substantial rationales is the further concern that the conceptualizations often used to justify holding—and certainly coercive holding—are theoretically bereft and, in some cases, frankly bizarre. All responsible clinicians now reject coercive holding therapy, but it is noteworthy that there has not been a robust consideration of the possible ill effects of noncoercive holding. Accordingly, that remains highly controversial, with some suggesting that even noncoercive holding may be traumatizing to the child and others suggesting that it may be clinically helpful. It is unfortunate that such a discrepancy of opinion exists; that is an indictment of the quality of the clinical literature in this area.

Altering the Caregiving Context

Uncontrolled Trials

One of the more novel treatments for RAD-related problems was carried out in an institutional setting in Romania. Smyke and colleagues (Smyke et al., 2002) assessed three groups of children. One group consisted of 32 children, aged 4–68 months, who were living in a conventional institutional setting with approximately 30–35 children looked after by two or three caregivers. A second group of children ($N = 29$; aged 18–70 months) were living in an experimental institutionalized pilot program that reduced substantially the child:caregiver ratio and reduced the number of caregivers with whom the children had regular contact. The third group ($N = 33$) of children included never-institutionalized children, although some of these children ($N = 17$) attended "weekly nursery" that lasted from Monday morning through Friday afternoon. Interviews were conducted with caregivers regarding children who had achieved a developmental level of 10 months; questions about RAD-related behaviors were asked using the *Disturbances of Attachment Interview* developed by the authors. In the case of institutionalized children, those who were familiar with the child acted as informants. Results indicated that children in the conventional institutional setting exhibited substantially more inhibited and indiscriminate behavior

than children in the pilot institutional setting and those in the noninstitutionalized group. Effect sizes were clearly clinically meaningful, and varied a bit according to which measure of RAD symptoms was used.

These results are consistent with many previous studies of children in institutional settings, but provide additional, suggestive evidence that altering the caregiving context, even modestly, may substantially reduce RAD-like behaviors. Indeed, this is the study showing the strongest effect on reducing RAD-like behaviors so far reported. It does have important methodological limitations, including lack of randomization and a complicated and diverse comparison group. Importantly, the implications may extend beyond the particular case of Romania. That is because institutional care for children is, in some settings, a necessity because of the loss of parents from AIDS, for example. Thus, institutional care in parts of Africa and China is inevitable, and findings from Smyke et al. could go some way to help optimize the institutional setting. Furthermore, institutional care of infants in the United States, referred to as "congregate care," is still practiced, despite its well-documented drawbacks when compared to foster care (Jones Harden, 2002). Moreover, the findings from altering the caregiving context are compatible with a long history of largely anecdotal data on the increased rates and severity of disturbance associated with multiple placements (e.g., Penzerro & Lein, 1995). Smyke et al. demonstrated that increasing consistency and availability of the caregiver reduces RAD-related behavior. It has long been suspected, but not yet clearly shown, that reducing the number of placements in foster care might have comparable effects.

Although not focused on RAD-like behavior, the Bucharest Early Intervention Project is an institution-based intervention that did set out to alter institutional caregiving conditions using an RCT design (Nelson et al., 2007). Findings revealed that children who were placed in a foster care setting showed considerably better cognitive recovery than those children who stayed in an institutional setting. Whether or not comparable gains are noted in RAD would be notable.

What does come through in the institution- or systems-based (e.g., social services) studies is how difficult it is to conduct an RCT in these settings. That same message is evident in studies of children in foster care, which are reviewed next. An important methodological point here is that the gold standard RCT model may be too rigid and impractical for some settings, particularly to the extent that the study relies on the cooperation of other systems without an RCT gold standard and a primary statutory obligation to intervene rather than to evaluate (e.g., legal system, social services). This does not allay concerns about the interpretability of the findings from these complex interventions using less than ideal designs, but it does mean that it may not be feasible to count only those studies that use the RCT standard—they may not soon be reported.

ALTERNATIVE TREATMENT STUDIES THAT MAY BE RELEVANT

Children in Foster Care

Foster care is an index of the kind of severe or "pathogenic care" that would constitute a risk for RAD. Accordingly, interventions for children in foster care may prove useful for evaluating interventions for children with RAD. It is significant that the foster care setting is the most common source of reports of children with RAD after institutional care. Although still uncommon, RCTs for children in the foster care setting are more numerous than are RCTs for RAD per se.

A recent Cochrane Review (Turner, MacDonald, & Dennis, 2007) examined cognitive behavioral-based interventions for foster caregivers to improve child behavior. That is, the focus here was on altering parenting in children with, in most cases, clinically elevated rates of general behavioral and emotional disturbance. The design mimics a standard parenting intervention approach with biological parents in which the children are not the focus of the intervention; rather, the study design evaluates if the alteration of parenting induced by the intervention trickles down to alter child behavior.

Overall, there is little evidence for clinically or statistically significant improvements in child behavior. Specifically, Turner et al. noted that there is "no evidence that training foster carers in cognitive-behavioural methods has a significant impact on psychological functioning in looked after children" (p. 15). The review also noted little evidence for a change in placement breakdown, a particularly important outcome for RAD-behavior—which would be expected to increase with increasing placements.

Whether or not these findings provide a directly contrary outcome to the case report using CBT for RAD as described earlier is unclear because, for example, RAD behaviors were not targeted or even assessed in these foster care studies. In that context, the intervention trial for foster parents conducted by Minnis et al. (Minnis, Pelosi, Knapp, & Dunn, 2001) is noteworthy because it is one of few to assess RAD-related behaviors alongside more typical behavioral/emotional problems in the child; RAD-related behaviors were assessed using a questionnaire developed by the authors. Importantly, children were selected into the study through foster care involvement and not because of presenting symptoms of RAD. In the Minnis et al. study, the 3-day training program, which was focused on communication and attachment, did not significantly improve child behavioral/emotional problems, including RAD-related behavioral problems.

A separate Cochrane Review of children in Treatment Foster Care (TFC; Macdonald & Turner, 2008), for more severely disturbed and older children in restrictive settings, reported more positive findings from trials assessing behavioral/emotional problems. TFC interventions are typically longer in duration (9–12 months) and intensive, with extensive coordination among care providers in the residential and home settings and the case supervisor. Features of the program are familiar to cognitive behavioral and parent training models, and include close supervision, limit-setting, consequences for rule-breaking, and a supportive therapeutic relationship with the case supervisor, and social skills training.

TFC has been evaluated using standard RCT designs; the Cochrane Review includes many of the key studies. It could be safely inferred that children in this set of studies were at even higher risk for RAD than the children in studies reviewed by Turner et al., 2007. Here again, any relevance to RAD can only be indirect, as the studies neither targeted nor assessed RAD-related behaviors. An implication here is that there may be very relevant interventions in the foster care system that could provide very valuable information to clinicians working with children with RAD—but room needs to be made in the assessment and protocol to consider possible RAD behaviors. It is not clear if the positive gains in delinquent, suicide, and other psychiatric problems would also been seen for RAD behaviors, and that is an obvious and important next step for research.

Other intervention studies of children in foster care that might be relevant to treating RAD were not covered in the Cochrane Review and warrant mention. Chief among these is the work of Dozier and colleagues, who have designed an intervention for infants and toddlers in foster care titled "Attachment and Biobehavioral Catch-up," or ABC. Dozier (2003); Dozier, Higley, Albus, and Nutter (2002); Dozier et al. (2006); and Dozier et al. (2008) adopted a more explicit attachment orientation to their intervention. Specifically, they argued that foster care children are at heightened risk because they may signal adult caregivers to provide non-nurturing care; an additional problem may be that some caregivers are uncomfortable with providing this type of care. They developed an intervention for children and their foster caregivers to address the following concerns: (a) the failure of foster children to properly signal need for care to the caregiver, and a related difficulty in care-providers' skills at reading their signals for care; (b) caregivers' discomfort with providing nurturing care to their foster children; and (c) foster children may frequently show difficulties with emotional, behavioral, and neuroendocrine regulation. The ABC targets these three areas in its intervention designed for infants and toddlers entering long-term foster or adoptive care. The attachment-based intervention consists of ten 60-minute sessions in caregivers' homes. The therapist/trainer meets with both the caregiver and the foster child as well as with the caregiver alone.

Dozier and colleagues examined the effectiveness of the ABC intervention in an RCT of infants and toddlers in the foster care system who were assigned either to ABC or to a control intervention. The sample consisted of 60 children and their foster caregivers who completed either the treatment or control intervention based on an educational model. Results indicated that children in the ABC group showed lower levels of cortisol, an index of stress, than those in the control intervention. Work using this intervention is still somewhat preliminary, but it seems to be the leading intervention model for infants in the foster care system. It is likely that further reports will contain data directly relevant to RAD.

An additional set of studies for somewhat older children in foster care was reported by Fisher and colleagues (Fisher, Gunnar, Chamberlain, & Reid, 2000). They, too, use an RCT design, but the intervention focused on cognitive behavior and social learning models rather than attachment or RAD-related outcomes. Findings so far suggest that there may be beneficial effects on the stress response system of the intervention, as in Dozier's work; here, too, it is in the somewhat early stages of the results, but the promise for providing data that may be at least indirectly relevant to RAD is considerable.

Adoption as Treatment

Adoption is rarely seen as a "treatment," but no intervention is more substantial and pervasive. And, if we view adoption as an extreme form of intervention, then we may be able to draw some inferences from the many naturalistic studies of children who were adopted following severe early caregiving deprivation that would be expected to increase the likelihood of RAD.

Studies of children adopted following early institutional rearing provide the most relevant information; results from these studies were mentioned earlier, but several lessons are worth reiterating in the context of intervention. The first is that adoptive families are, in general, quite resourceful and, through screening, have demonstrated a basic competence to look after the adopted child. The second lesson is, as noted, that there is a sizable minority of children who show persisting RAD-related behaviors several years after adoption (Chisholm, 1998; O'Connor, Rutter, & the English and Romanian Adoptees Study Team, 2000; Rutter et al., 2007). It is obviously not possible to conclude from these naturalistic studies anything about interventions that might be used in clinical practice, and these adoption studies are not controlled in any way. Nonetheless, the persistence of RAD-like behavior in children who experienced many years of a supportive parenting environment might be interpreted as a caution against the potential intervention effectiveness of a brief treatment trial. Indeed, an important clinical question to address is why, despite auspicious circumstances, a minority of adopted children show persisting problems in attachment and social relationships, even after living in the adoptive home for many years. That finding may be just as important as any RCT-derived finding for treatment planning and developing reasonable treatment goals with the child and family.

Attachment Theory-Based Treatments for Insecure Attachment

We include in a final section a brief review of some attachment-based interventions. Attachment-based treatments now have a substantial evidence base (Bakermans-Kranenburg et al., 2003); however, as we also noted, there is wide variation in the understanding of attachment-based interventions. Accordingly, some mention of well-documented attachment-based interventions seems warranted. The aim here is not to identify the best examples, but to provide some concrete examples of evidence-based programs. It is not at all clear that these programs will benefit children with RAD.

With the notable exception of the behavioral management approach described before, most proposed treatments for RAD have claimed to incorporate attachment theory, at least to a significant extent. Whether or not that is actually true is a matter of intense disagreement. For example, as we described, advocates of the holding therapy-based models have argued that their approach is based on attachment, but most clinical scientists in the attachment field would claim that there is much about these programs that is antithetical to attachment theory and research. On the other hand, there are a number of interventions that are firmly grounded in attachment theory that have been developed and meet conventional RCT criteria for evidence-based. Unfortunately, we were unable to locate systemic research using these interventions for RAD and related developmental and relationship problems. That gap is a striking indictment about how slow clinical attachment research has addressed the clinical matter of RAD (O'Connor & Zeanah, 2003).

In this section, we review several evidence-based interventions that are rooted in attachment theory and that have been shown to be successful with caregiver–child dyads with an insecure attachment relationship. Before doing that, however, we need to consider how treatment conceptualization may differ qualitatively between RAD and insecure attachment. For example, a central feature of the attachment treatment model is that, to some substantial degree, it is the caregiver's insensitivity that is a major contributor to the child's difficulties. That is not to say that there are not important child-based factors, but the focus is on improving the caregiver's ability to sensitively and consistently respond to the child's need for safety, security, and comfort, and to promote the child's exploration. If parental sensitivity is improved, it is expected that the child's attachment to the parent will become more secure. This situation is very different from most instances of reported RAD. In a typical RAD case, the child is placed with adoptive/foster caregivers who may be at least typically sensitive, or using Winnicott's term, "good enough" (e.g., as perhaps demonstrated with older biological children who have normative, if not ideally secure attachments to them). In other words, the parenting quality of the foster/adoptive parent was not the cause of the RAD behavior and, just as importantly, we do not yet know if improving foster/adoptive caregiver sensitivity could be expected to reduce RAD-related behaviors. Anecdotal clinical data suggest that may be, but then there are other clinical data and findings from naturalistic follow-up studies implying that RAD behaviors may persist despite sensitive caregiving—what this means in the case of children with RAD who are still living with their biological parents is even less clear. There is then the issue that attachment-based interventions are designed to shift a child from an insecure to a more secure relationship; these interventions are not designed to create or help from a *new* attachment. Yet, that is presumably what is needed for children with RAD who, by definition, fail to show a selective attachment to their caregiver. Notwithstanding these important caveats, a brief review of attachment interventions is provided here to distinguish them from the kinds of "attachment therapy" interventions sometimes used for children with RAD.

One attachment-based model is Child–Parent Psychotherapy (CPP), developed by Alicia Lieberman and colleagues for parent–infant and parent–toddler dyads (Lieberman, Ippen, & Van Horn, 2006) to increase attachment security in children at high levels of parenting and social risk. The model has several key features, including the presumption that parenting ability is shaped by the quality of the individual's own experience of being parented and that the infant develops a representation of the self and other based on the quality of his/her interactions with the caregiver. The CPP is attachment-based because it emphasizes how the attachment system organizes the young child's response to perceived threat and safety.

Cicchetti, Toth, and colleagues (Cicchetti, Toth, & Rogosch, 1999; Toth, Rogosch, Manly, & Cicchetti, 2006) examined the efficacy of CPP in the context of maternal depression. When children were approximately 20 months of age, they were seen with their mothers in joint therapy sessions. The treatment continued until the children were 3 years old. A community sample of mothers who had experienced depression within the first 18 months of their children's lives participated in the study along with their toddlers. Depressed and nondepressed women were recruited for the study. Depressed participants were randomly assigned to the group receiving TPP ($N = 67$) or to the depressed control group ($N = 64$). A third group of mothers who had not been depressed nor had experienced any other psychopathology was recruited as well ($N = 70$).

Mothers and their toddlers were seen in joint therapy sessions. Therapists helped mothers to recognize and change how their behavior and representations may have a negative influence on their relationship with their children. This took place through play, observation, sensitivity training, and corrective guidance, changing how they see their children and themselves. Mothers also attended individual therapy designed to provide a corrective emotional experience with the therapist to improve representations of self and other, which would then influence their representation and interactions with their own children. Results of the intervention were that mother–child dyads that received TPP showed higher rates of secure attachment among children. These rates were comparable to children of mothers without a history of depression. Children in the depressed control group continued to show rates of attachment insecurity that were greater than those in the nondepressed control group.

Cichetti and colleagues (2006) compared child–parent psychotherapy to Psychoeducational Parenting Intervention (PPI), based on the work of Olds and colleagues (e.g., Olds & Kitzman, 1990) that targeted parenting attitudes, child-rearing stress, and social support. Infants in maltreating families, along with their mothers, were assessed on the quality of their relationship and parenting. The maltreated sample consisted of 137 infants (60 boys, 77 girls) and their mothers. A nonmaltreated comparison group consisted of 52 infants (28 boys, 24 girls) and their mothers. Prior to intervention, infants in the maltreatment group showed higher rates of insecure attachment compared to those in the nonmaltreating group. Of the insecure children in the maltreatment group, nearly 90% were classified as having a disorganized (Type D) style of attachment, compared to about 42% of children in the nonmaltreating group (infants in the nonmaltreated group also experienced high risk due to factors such as poverty). Following the intervention, when infants were approximately two years old, the rate of secure attachment had increased in the child–parent psychotherapy and PPI groups to over 50%; there was no evidence of significant change in attachment security among those in the maltreated control group. The results imply that training in sensitive parenting, evident in both types of therapy, was the common therapeutic factor. That would comport with the meta-analyses of sensitivity and attachment interventions in early childhood (Bakermans-Krananburg et al., 2003). Seventy studies of treatment interventions for increasing sensitivity and security of attachment, 29 of which were focused specifically on attachment security, were included. Findings were that the most effective interventions included a moderate number of sessions, and a behavioral focus. They also found that interventions focused on improving parental sensitivity to their children's cues were more effective in improving attachment security. Perhaps PPI, with its focus on lowering parenting stress and increasing social support, also increased parenting sensitivity and thus the attachment relationship.

GENERAL CONCLUSIONS

The most obvious conclusion to draw is that the existing clinical intervention data are too weak to endorse any particular intervention. That this has been the case for so many years, and despite the existence of RAD as a psychiatric disorder for more than a quarter of a century, requires interpretation. That is, why does a disorder that presents such a fascinating developmental puzzle that may hold important lessons for understanding the behavioral and neuroscientific basis of attachment and early experience been virtually ignored in the clinical treatment literature? Moreover, why is it that strikingly diverse views continue to be expressed about treatment conceptualization—in the absence of adequate clinical findings to justify any particular view? Answers to these questions will involve more than an analysis of research findings, and will instead rely on analyzing the process of clinical research: How are clinical questions identified? How is the notion of "evidence" understood differently among parents, clinicians, and those in academic settings? How are ideas about clinical treatment proliferated? There is surely something to be learned about how to improve evidence-based practice in psychology from an analysis of the particular failures in the area of RAD.

What, then, can be concluded about evidence-based treatment for RAD if the evidence base is inadequate? One is that there are some interventions with more promise than others. Behaviorally based interventions have a decidedly mixed report, but some positive signs mean that they warrant further systematic attention. Children with RAD often present with an unusual admixture of additional symptoms and problems, including hoarding, smearing, and deficits in social skills. These kinds of difficulties would normally attract behavioral approaches, and so it is natural to consider if parallel behavioral approaches might also be applied to manage symptoms more central to RAD.

The status of holding therapies is less salutary. On one hand, there is absolutely no reason to endorse the more coercive forms of holding therapy; avoiding such interventions is probably the only strong consensus among professional organizations. On the other hand, there remain advocates of less coercive holding therapy models. Available evidence does not support the use of this approach, and the only evidence so far offered is based on poorly designed evaluations. And, there continues to be an unfortunate level of ambiguity about what these interventions actually entail, even to the point of how coercive or unwelcome any contact between the child and therapists may be. In the absence of sound clinical evidence that physical contact is therapeutic, and given reasonable concerns that physical contact may be countertherapeutic, the safest clinical approach is to avoid physical contact altogether and focus first on the nonphysical features in these interventions. That is, there may be some positive aspects of these interventions, but the rationale for any form of physical contact with the child in these treatments is weak, absent, or dubious.

The third form of intervention, altering the caregiving environment to improve caregiver consistency and availability, has received little formal evaluation, but nevertheless stands as the strongest form of intervention. The implications likely extend beyond the residential setting but, because of the obvious ethical and practical reasons of conducting a study that manipulates the number of placements for a child in foster care, practitioners should not wait to act on this evidence until "gold standard" evidence is delivered.

Other kinds of intervention, often implicit or subsidiary in existing intervention studies, require formal analysis in their own right. Probably the most obvious of these is interventions to improve social skills and peer relationships. Available data do suggest—and ICD-10 makes this explicit—that problems in peer relationships are common in children with RAD. The implication is that it may be misguided to focus only on the child–parent or family relationships, which is the format of as many interventions. There are encouraging data on improving social and peer skills through child training (Webster-Stratton, Reid, & Hammond, 2001), and this would constitute a safe and important intervention. Both positive and negative findings from these trials would provide valuable information for further devising clinical management models.

Treatment guidelines that have been offered (Boris et al., 2005; Chaffin et al., 2006; Hanson & Spratt, 2008; Haugaard & Hazan, 2004; O'Connor & Zeanah, 2003) tend to suggest fairly general, common sense approaches that emphasize, for example, support to caregivers, availability to the child of a warm and consistent caregiver, and promotion of social skills; however sensible these clinical recommendations may be, they too are without evidence base. Indeed, knowing how much clinical improvement can be expected is unclear from existing studies. It is in this context that clinicians and parents should attend to the adoption study findings, which imply that substantial improvement may be unlikely.

The fact that the clinical research literature is as undeveloped as it is also requires action in the form of further clinical investigation. As we suggested, one rate-limiting factor in the clinical literature is uncertainty about how to define RAD and assess it in routine clinical practice. Applied studies that contrast alternative methods of defining the RAD phenotype are needed before any real progress on treatment can be expected. Some work in that area was noted, but assessment uncertainties remain strong and will undermine progress in treatment. There is also a note of caution about how interventions should be disseminated; namely, the promotion of any intervention should be driven by the quality of the evidence rather than by the ambition or optimism of the framer of the intervention. Finally, progress in understanding and managing RAD in clinical practice will require greater coordination among academic psychology and psychiatry, pediatrics, social care services, and sharing concepts and methods in assessment and treatment.

REFERENCES

Achenbach, T. M. (1991). *Manual for the Child Behavior Checklist/4-18 and 1991 profile*. Burlington: University of Vermont Department of Psychiatry.

Ainsworth, M. D. S. (1967). *Infancy in Uganda: Infant care and the growth of attachment*. Baltimore, MD: Johns Hopkins University Press.

Ainsworth, M. D. S., Blehar, M. C., Waters, E., & Wall, S. (1978). *Patterns of attachment: A psychological study of the strange situation*. Hillsdale, NJ: Erlbaum.

Albus, K., & Dozier, M. (1999). Indiscriminate friendliness and terror of strangers in infancy: Contributions from the study of infants in foster care. *Infant Mental Health Journal, 20*, 30–41.

American Psychiatric Association (APA). (2000). Diagnostic and statistical manual of mental disorders (4th ed., text rev.). Washington, DC: Author.

Bakermans-Kranenburg, M., van Ijzendoorn, M., & Juffer, F. (2003). Less is more: Meta-analyses of sensitivity and attachment interventions in early childhood. *Psychological Bulletin, 129*, 195–215.

Becker, M., Jordan, N., & Larsen, R. (2006). Behavioral health service use and costs among children in foster care. *Child Welfare, 85*, 633–647.

Becker-Weidman, A. (2006). Treatment for children with trauma-attachment disorders: Dyadic developmental psychotherapy. *Child and Adolescent Social Work Journal, 23*, 147–171.

Becker-Weidman, A. (2008). Treatment for children with reactive attachment disorder: Dyadic developmental psychotherapy. *Child and Adolescent Mental Health, 13*, 52–59.

Boris, N. W., Hinshaw-Fuselier, S. S., Smyke, A. T., Scheeringa, M. S., Heller, S. S., & Zeanah, C. H. (2004). Comparing criteria for attachment disorders: Establishing reliability and validity in high-risk samples. *Journal of the American Academy of Child and Adolescent Psychiatry, 43*, 568–577.

Boris, N. W., Zeanah, C. H., and the Work Group on Quality Issues. (2005). Practice parameter for the assessment and treatment of children and adolescents with reactive attachment disorder of infancy and early childhood. *Journal of the American Academy of Child and Adolescent Psychiatry, 44*, 1206–1219.

Bowlby, J. (1982). *Attachment and loss: Attachment* (2nd ed.). New York, NY: Basic Books.

Buckner, J. D., Lopez, C., Dunkel, S., & Joiner, T. E. (2008). Behavior management training for the treatment of reactive attachment disorder. *Child Maltreatment, 13*, 289–297.

Chaffin, M., Hanson, R., Saunders, B. E., Nicols, T., Barnett, D., Zeanah, C., . . . Miller-Perrin, C. (2006). Report to the APSAS Task Force on attachment therapy, reactive attachment disorder, and attachment problems. *Child Maltreatment, 11*, 76–89.

Chisholm, K. (1998). A three year follow-up of attachment and indiscriminate friendliness in children adopted from Romanian orphanages. *Child Development, 69*, 1092–1106.

Cicchetti, D., Rogosch, F. A., & Toth, S. L. (2006). Fostering secure attachment in infants in maltreating families through preventive interventions. *Development and Psychopathology, 18*, 623–649.

Cicchetti, D., Toth, S. L., & Rogosch, F. A. (1999). The efficacy of toddler-parent psychotherapy to increase attachment security in offspring of depressed mothers. *Attachment and Human Development, 1*, 34–66.

Dozier, M. (2003). Attachment-based treatment for vulnerable children. *Attachment and Human Development, 5*, 253–257.

Dozier, M., Higley, E., Albus, K. E., & Nutter, A. (2002). Intervening with foster infants' caregivers: targeting three critical needs. *Infant Mental Health Journal, 23*, 541–554.

Dozier, M., Peloso, E., Lewis, E., Laurenceau, J., & Levine, S. (2008). Effects of an attachment-based intervention on the cortisol production of infants and toddlers in foster care. *Development and Psychopathology, 20*, 845–859.

Dozier, M., Peloso, E., Lindhiem, O., Gordon, K., Manni, M., Sepúlveda, S., & Ackerman, J. (2006). Developing evidence-based interventions for foster children: An example of a randomized clinical trial with infants and toddlers. *Journal of Social Issues, 62*, 767–785.

Eluvathingal, T. J., Chugani, H. T., Behen, M. E., Juhász, C., Muzik, O., Maqbool, M., . . . Makki, M. (2006). Abnormal brain connectivity in children after early severe socioemotional deprivation: A diffusion tensor imaging study. *Pediatrics, 117*, 2093–2100.

Fisher, P. A., Gunnar, M. R., Chamberlain, P., & Reid, J. B. (2000). Preventive intervention for maltreated preschool children: Impact on children's behavior, neuroendocrine activity, and foster parent functioning. *Journal of the American Academy of Child and Adolescent Psychiatry, 39*, 1356–1364.

Fleming, A. S., O'Day, D. H., & Kraemer, G. W. (1999). Neurobiology of mother-infant interactions: Experience and central nervous system plasticity across development and generations. *Neuroscience and Biobehavioral Reviews, 23*, 673–685.

Forgatch, M., & DeGarmo, D. S. (1999). Parenting through change: An effective prevention program for single mothers. *Journal of Consulting and Clinical Psychology, 67*, 711–724.

Freud, A., & Burlingham, D. (1973). *The writings of Anna Freud: Volume III. Infants without families 1939–1945*. New York, NY: International Universities Press.

Gaensbauer, T. J., & Harmon, R. J. (1982). Attachment in abused/neglected and premature infants. In R. N. Emde & R. J. Harmon (Eds.), *The development of attachment and affiliative systems* (pp. 263–280). New York, NY: Plenum Press.

Goldfarb, W. (1943). The effects of early institutional care on adolescent personality. *Journal of Experimental Education, 12*, 106–129.

Gunnar, M. R., Morison, S. J., Chisholm, K., & Schuder, M. (2001). Salivary cortisol levels in children from Romanian orphanages. *Development and Psychopathology, 13*, 611–628.

Haugaard, J. J., & Hazan, C. (2004). Recognizing and treating uncommon behavioral and emotional disorders in children and adolescents who have been severely maltreated: Reactive attachment disorder. *Child Maltreatment, 9*, 154–160.

Hanson, R. F., & Spratt, E. G. (2008). Reactive attachment disorder: What we know about the disorder and implications for treatment. *Child Maltreatment, 5*, 137–145.

Jones Harden, B. (Ed.). (2002). Congregate care for infants and toddlers: Shedding new light on an old question. *Infant Mental Health Journal, 23*, 476–495.

Hughes, D. A. (1997). *Facilitating developmental attachment: The road to emotional recovery and behavioral change in foster and adopted children*. New York, NY: Jason Aronson.

Hughes, D. (2004). An attachment-based treatment for maltreated children and young people. *Attachment & Human Development, 6*, 263–278.

Keck, G. C., & Kupecky, R. (1995). *Adopting the hurt child*. Colorado Springs, CO: Pinon Press.

Levy, D. (1937). Primary affect hunger. *American Journal of Psychiatry, 94*, 643–652.

Levy, T. (Ed.). (2000). *Handbook of attachment interventions*. New York, NY: Academic Press.

Lieberman, A. F., Ippen, S. G., & Van Horn, P. (2006). Child-parent psychotherapy: 6-month follow-up of a randomized controlled trial. *Journal of the Academy of Child and Adolescent Psychiatry, 45*, 913–918.

Macdonald, G., & Turner, W. (2008). Treatment Foster Care for improving outcomes in children and young people. *Cochrane Database of Systematic Reviews, 1*, Art. No. CD005649. doi:10.1002/14651858.CD005649.pub2

Minnis, H., Everittt, K., Pelosi, A. J., Dunn, J., & Knapp, M. (2006). Children in foster care: Mental health, service use and costs. *European Journal of Child and Adolescent Psychiatry, 15*, 63–70.

Minnis, H., Green, J., O'Connor, T. G., Liew, A., & the RADAR team. (2009). An exploratory study of the association between reactive attachment disorder and attachment narratives in early school-age children. *Journal of Child Psychology and Psychiatry, 50*, 931–942.

Minnis, H., Pelosi, A., Knapp, M., & Dunn, J. (2001). Mental health and foster carer training. *Archives of Disease in Childhood, 84*, 302–306.

Minnis, H., Reekie, J., Young, D., O'Connor, T. G., Ronald, A., Gray, A., & Plomin, R. (2007). Genetic, environmental and gender influences on attachment disorder behaviours. *British Journal of Psychiatry, 190*, 490–495.

Mukkades, N. M., Bilge, S., Alyanak, B., & Kora, M. E. (2000). Clinical characteristics and treatment responses in cases diagnosed as reactive attachment disorder. *Child Psychiatry and Human Development, 30*, 273–287.

Mukaddes, N. M., Kaynak, F. N., Kinali, G., Besikci, H., & Issever, H. (2004). Psychoeducational treatment of children with autism and reactive attachment disorder. *Autism, 8*, 101–109.

Myeroff, R., Mertlich, G., & Gross, J. (1999). Comparative effectiveness of holding therapy with aggressive children. *Child Psychiatry and Human Development, 29*, 303–331.

Nelson, C. A., Zeanah, C. H., Fox, N., Marshall, P. J., Smyke, A. T., & Guthrie, D. (2007). Cognitive recovery in socially deprived young children: The Bucharest Early Intervention Project. *Science, 318*(5858), 1937–1940.

O'Connor, T. G. (2002). Attachment disorders in infancy and childhood. In M. Rutter & E. Taylor (Eds.), *Child and adolescent psychiatry: Modern approaches* (4th ed., pp. 776–792). Oxford, England: Blackwell Scientific Publications.

O'Connor, T. G., Marvin, R. S., Rutter, M., Olrick, J., Britner, P. A., & the English and Romanian Adoptees Study Team. (2003). Child-parent attachment following early institutional deprivation. *Development and Psychopathology, 15*, 19–38.

O'Connor, T. G., Rutter, M., Beckett, C., Kreaveny, L., Kreppner, J. M., & Romanian Adoptees Study Team. (2000). The effects of global severe privation on cognitive competence: Extension and longitudinal follow-up. *Child Development, 71*, 376–390.

O'Connor, T. G., Rutter, M., & the English and Romanian Adoptees Study Team. (2000). Attachment disorder behavior following early severe deprivation: Extension and longitudinal follow-up. *Journal of the American Academy of Child and Adolescent Psychiatry, 39*, 703–712.

O'Connor, T. G., & Zeanah, C. H. (2003). Attachment disorders: Assessment strategies and treatment approaches. *Attachment and Human Development, 5*, 233–244.

Olds, D. L., & Kitzman, H. (1990). Can home visitation improve the health of women and children at environmental risk? *Pediatrics, 86*, 108–116.

Penzerro, R. M., & Lein, L. (1995). Burning their bridges: Disordered attachment and foster care discharge. *Child Welfare, 74*, 351–366.

Provence, S., & Lipton, R. C. (1962). *Infants reared in institutions*. New York, NY: International Universities Press.

Randolph, E. (2000). *The manual for the Randolph Attachment Disorder Questionnaire* (3rd ed.). Evergreen, CO: The Attachment Center Press.

Reid, M. J., Webster-Stratton, C., & Baydar, N. (2004). Halting the development of conduct problems in head start children: The effects of parent training. *Journal of Clinical Child and Adolescent Psychology, 33*, 279–291.

Robertson, J., & Robertson, J. (1989). *Separation and the very young*. London, England: Free Association Books.

Roy, P., Rutter, M., & Pickles, A. (2000). Institutional care: Risk from family background or pattern of rearing? *Journal of Child Psychology and Psychiatry, 41*, 139–149.

Rushton, A., Treseder, J., & Quinton, D. (1995). An eight-year prospective study of older boys placed in permanent substitute families: A research note. *Journal of Child Psychology and Psychiatry, 36*, 687–696.

Rutter, M., Colvert, E., Kreppner, J., Beckett, C., Castle, J., Groothues, C., . . . Sonuga-Barke, E. (2007). Early adolescent outcomes for institutionally-deprived and non-deprived adoptees. I: Disinhibited attachment. *Journal of Child Psychology and Psychiatry, 48*, 17–30.

Savasir, I., Sezgin, N., & Erol, N. (1998). *Ankara Gelisim Envanteri El Kitabi. Turk Psikologlar Dernegi, 2*. Ankara: Basim.

Scott, S. B., Spender, Q., Doolan, M., Jacobs, B., & Aspland, H. (2001). Multicentre controlled trial of parenting groups for childhood antisocial behaviour in clinical practice. *British Medical Journal, 323*, 194–198.

Sheperis, C. J., Doggett, R. A., Hoda, N. E., Blanchard, T., Renfro-Michel, E. L., Holdiness, S. H., & Schlagheck, R. (2003). The development of an assessment protocol for reactive attachment disorder. *Journal of Mental Health Counseling, 25*, 291–310.

Schopler, E. (1987). Specific and nonspecific factors in the effectiveness of a treatment system. *American Psychologist, 42*, 376–383.

Schopler, E., Mesibov, G. B., Shigly, R. H., & Bashfend, A. (1984). Helping autistic children through their parents: The TEACCH model. In E. Schopler & G. B. Mesibov (Eds.), *The effects of autism on the family* (pp. 65–81). New York, NY: Plenum Press.

Smyke, A. T., Dumitrescu, A., & Zeanah, C. H. (2002). Attachment disturbances in young children. I: The continuum of caretaking casualty. *Journal of the American Academy of Child and Adolescent Psychiatry, 41*, 972–982.

Spitz, R. (1946). Anaclitic depression: An inquiry into the genesis of psychiatric conditions in early childhood. *Psychoanalytic Study of the Child, 1*, 53–74.

Stafford, B., Zeanah, C. H., & Scheeringa, M. (2003). Exploring psychopathology in early childhood: PTSD and attachment disorders in DC: 0-3 and *DSM-IV*. *Infant Mental Health Journal, 24*, 398–409.

Steele, J. S., & Buchi, K. F. (2008). Medical and mental health of children entering the Utah foster care system. *Pediatrics, 122*, e703–e709.

Tizard, B., & Hodges, J. (1978). The effect of early institutional rearing on the development of eight-year-old children. *Journal of Child Psychology and Psychiatry, 19*, 99–118.

Tizard, B., & Rees, J. (1975). The effect of early institutional rearing on the behavioral problems and affectional relationships of four-year-old children. *Journal of Child Psychology and Psychiatry, 16*, 61–73.

Toth, S. L., Rogosch, F. A., Manly, J. T., & Cicchetti, D. (2006). The efficacy of toddler-parent psychotherapy to reorganize attachment in the offspring of mothers with major depressive disorder: A randomized preventive trial. *Journal of Consulting and Clinical Psychology, 74*, 1006–1016.

Turner, W., Macdonald, G. M., & Dennis, J. A. (2007). Behavioural and cognitive behavioural training interventions for assisting foster carers in the management of difficult behaviour. *Cochrane Database of Systematic Reviews, 1*, Art. No. CD003760. doi:10.1002/14651858.CD003760.pub3

Vorria, P., Papaligoura, Z., Sarafidou, J., Kopakaki, M., Dunn, J., Van Ijzendoorn, M. H., & Kontopoulou, A. (2006). The development of adopted children after institutional care: A follow-up study. *Journal of Child Psychology and Psychiatry, 47*, 1246–1253.

Welch, M. G. (1989). *Holding time*. New York, NY: Fireside.

Webster-Stratton, C., Reid, J., & Hammond, M. (2001). Social skills and problem-solving training for children with early-onset conduct problems: Who benefits? *Journal of Child Psychology and Psychiatry, 42*, 943–952.

Wolkind, S. N. (1974). The components of "affectionless psychopathology" in institutionalized children. *Journal of Child Psychology and Psychiatry, 15*, 215–220.

World Health Organization (WHO). (1992). *The ICD-10 classification of mental and behavioral disorders: Clinical descriptions and diagnostic guidelines.* Geneva, Switzerland: Author.

Zeanah, C. H. (1996). Beyond insecurity: A reconceptualization of attachment disorders of infancy. *Journal of Consulting and Clinical Psychology, 64*, 42–52.

Zeanah, C. H., Boris, N. W., & Lieberman, A. F. (2000). Attachment disorders of infancy. In A. J. Sameroff, M. Lewis, & S. M. Miller (Eds.), *Handbook of developmental psychopathology* (2nd ed., pp. 293–307). New York, NY: Plenum Press.

Zeanah, C. H., Scheeringa, M., Boris, N. W., Heller, S. S., Smyke, A. T., & Trapani, J. (2004). Reactive attachment disorder in maltreated toddlers. *Child Abuse and Neglect, 28*, 877–888.

Zeanah, C. H., Smyke, A. T., & Dumitrescu, A. (2002). Attachment disturbances in young children. II: Indiscriminate behavior and institutional care. *Journal of the American Academy of Child and Adolescent Psychiatry, 41*, 983–989.

19

Stereotypic Behavior Disorder

MICHAEL E. MAY, CRAIG H. KENNEDY, AND JENNIFER L. BRUZEK

OVERVIEW OF STEREOTYPIC BEHAVIOR DISORDER

Stereotypic behavior disorder (SBD) encompasses a broad range of response topographies that are emitted for a variety of reasons. The psychological study of human SBD began in the 1960s by Gershon Berkson, who previously studied nonhuman primate models of stereotypical response patterns with Harry Harlow at the University of Wisconsin at Madison (Harlow, 1965). Berkson's early work was descriptive and cataloged environmental and demographic variables associated with SBD, primarily in institutionalized individuals with intellectual/developmental disabilities (I/DDs). The research of Berkson and colleagues has established an increased prevalence in stereotypic behaviors associated with lower intellectual functioning (Berkson & Davenport, 1962; Berkson, Tupa, & Sherman, 2001). Indeed, the pervasiveness of stereotypic behaviors in some diagnostic categories associated with I/DD are part of the diagnostic criteria (e.g., autism spectrum disorders). Overall, 34% to 82% of people with I/DDs engage in stereotypic behaviors. Typically, the earlier these behaviors are observed in a person with I/DDs, the more likely they will persist throughout the person's life span (Ballaban-Gil, Rapin, Tuchman, & Shinnar, 1996). Since stereotypic behaviors can interfere with learning and persist across a variety of contexts, several treatment approaches have been developed to reduce stereotypic responding. The purpose of this chapter, therefore, is to review diagnostic features and evidence-based treatments for SBD in people with I/DDs.

Identification and Diagnosis of SBD

Stereotypic behaviors are part of normal development, emerging around 6 months of age. Most forms of repetitive behaviors decrease in frequency after 18 months of age, although there is evidence some forms persist into adulthood (Berkson, Rafaeli-Mor, & Tarnovskys, 1999). Early repetitive behaviors in typical development include body rocking, body arching, head banging, hand waving, and tooth grinding (Thelen, 1996). Although these behaviors typically subside after 18 months of age, they can become a predominant aspect of an individual's behavioral repertoire. It is in these individuals that repetitive behaviors are symptomatic of SBD.

Most investigators consider stereotypic behaviors to be voluntary actions that are repeated over long periods of time, remain impervious to environmental changes, and are developmentally inappropriate (Berkson & Davenport, 1962; Thelen, 1996; Lewis &

Bodfish, 1998). Examples of stereotypic behaviors range from repetitive motor movements to preoccupation with objects to ritualistic routines (South, Ozonoff, & McMahon, 2005). Repetitive motor movements may include hand waving, head banging, or other behaviors seen in early typical development. Object preoccupations can include focused attention on particular objects, people, or activities extending beyond a normal level of interest (e.g., obsessively engaging in conversations about dinosaurs). Finally, ritualistic routines can include insistence on maintaining sameness in the environment (e.g., room furniture remaining in the same location) to elaborate rituals (e.g., always engaging in certain hand movements before walking through a doorway).

Categorical definitions are constructs and general topographical descriptions of stereotypic behaviors have defied a more precise operationalization, even in very specific subpopulations (Bodfish, Parker, Lewis, Sprague, & Newell, 2001). A major limitation in accurately defining stereotypic behaviors is that they often resemble other repetitive behaviors. Compulsions, for example, are repetitive behaviors such as excessive hand washing, ordering objects, counting, or hoarding with the goal of avoiding perceived noxious stimulation (Lewis & Bodfish, 1998). Conversely, tics are abrupt involuntary acts involving simple or complex muscle movements (Cummings, 1985).

Stereotypic behaviors are often considered to serve little instrumental purpose. Developmentally, repetitive behaviors are part of a typical process of motor refinement in infants but are later replaced by more consequence-directed behaviors. Therefore, some researchers view chronic and persistent stereotypic behaviors as fixations on early developmental actions (Berkson & Davenport, 1962; Evans et al., 1997). Other researchers suggest the difference between repetitive behaviors defining SBD from those waning over the first few years of life is most likely a result of central nervous system impairment (Lewis, Baumeister, & Mailman, 1987); however, developmental and neurobiological constructs may evade functional aspects of stereotypic behaviors. For example, some researchers describe stereotypic behaviors based on the reinforcing events maintaining them in a variety of environmental contexts (Kennedy, 2002; Kennedy, Meyer, Knowles, & Shukla, 2000; Lovaas, Newsom, & Hickman, 1987). Defining stereotypic behaviors by their environmental functions may be a more pragmatic approach to determining appropriate and effective treatments for SBD.

From a behavior-analytic perspective, stereotypic behaviors are currently classified into five functional categories: negative reinforcement, positive reinforcement, nonsocial reinforcement, multiply determined, or undifferentiated (Asmus et al., 2004; Hanley, Iwata, & McCord, 2003). *Negative reinforcement* is a process by which stereotypic behaviors are emitted to avoid or escape people, places, or things. An example would be an adolescent who engages in hand waving to avoid academic instruction or the people and places associated with academic instruction. *Positive reinforcement* is a process by which stereotypic behaviors are reliably followed by stimuli such as people, places, or things. For example, an adolescent's hand waving could gain attention from parents, particularly in settings where the behaviors cannot be ignored (e.g., a shopping mall or grocery store). This attention can be affirming social interactions or critical social comments. *Nonsocial reinforcement* is a process by which stereotypic behaviors produce perceptual consequences. Positive nonsocial reinforcement occurs when the behavior itself produces a rewarding consequence. For example, hand waving may produce visual stimulation, increasing the probability of hand waving. Negative nonsocial reinforcement occurs when the behavior removes or attenuates aversive internal stimulation, such as discomfort. For example, a child may engage in stereotypical ear stimulation to reduce pain from an ear infection. *Multiply determined functions* involve any combination of the three previous reinforcement types. For example, the hand waving may be negatively reinforced by avoiding instruction and positively reinforced by adult attention. Finally, an *undifferentiated function* is noted if no clear behavioral outcome is identified.

Although no epidemiological data are available regarding the prevalence of functions relating to SBD, most experimental analyses have identified nonsocial reinforcement as the sole or most prevalent function (cf. Guess & Carr, 1991; Richman & Lindauer, 2005). When a behavior is maintained by nonsocial reinforcement, isolating the specific type of reinforcement (e.g., positive or negative) is more complicated. Often, stereotypic behaviors are maintained by putative reinforcers that are more than likely interoceptive, making it impractical for investigators to manipulate them directly. Thus, research techniques have overcome these boundaries by manipulating stimuli other than the specific reinforcers themselves (e.g., from the same hypothesized sensory modality).

Although it is often assumed that stereotypic behaviors are maintained by nonsocial reinforcement, there is growing evidence that social positive and/or negative reinforcement can maintain them (Kennedy et al., 2000; Rapp & Vollmer, 2005a). In such instances, stereotypic behaviors become forms of communication because the behaviors function to alter the behavior of others. Therefore, appropriate behavior, possibly a communicative response, must be shaped and reinforced in the person's repertoire to contact reinforcement in socially meaningful ways.

Functional Behavior Assessment of SBD

Assessing the functions of stereotypic behaviors involves a process referred to as functional behavior assessment (FBA). FBA is a problem-solving strategy for identifying the variables associated with stereotypic behaviors, and includes a series of increasingly complex assessment techniques. The first step in conducting a FBA is to operationally define stereotypic behaviors. Operationalizing stereotypic behaviors requires defining the response in terms of observable physical characteristics (see Sulzer-Azaroff & Mayer, 1990).

The next step in completing an FBA is to identify the specific contextual factors increasing the likelihood of the stereotypic behaviors by collecting information on the conditions when a person is most and least likely to engage in the behaviors. Information about the contextual factors allows a trained observer to make predictions about when stereotypic behaviors will occur, and how to prevent the opportunity for inappropriate behavior to emerge. The most commonly used sequence of assessments consists of record reviews/interviews, descriptive assessments, and experimental analyses. Once the behavioral function has been identified, treatment is based on these findings.

Record reviews include health records, educational documents, psychological assessments, and any other information contributing to an understanding of environmental influences on stereotypic behaviors. Interviews require respondents to answer open-ended questions and/or to complete questionnaires (Miltenberger, 2003; O'Neill, Horner, Albin, Storey, & Sprague, 1996). Interviews should be structured so that information is obtained about the settings the behaviors do and do not occur in, who and how many people are present when the behaviors occur, the activities or interactions that take place just *before* the behaviors occur, and what happens *after* the behaviors occur. It is important to obtain information about setting events that can lead to stereotypic behaviors, such as task difficulty (or lack thereof), problems with transitions or interruptions in preferred activities, and predictability of routines. Multiple informants may be necessary to gather information about contextual factors, especially if stereo-typic behaviors are situation-specific. If a clear hypothesis regarding behavioral function is identified at this point (e.g., attention from adults as positive reinforcement) qualified professionals proceed with developing a treatment plan; however, if hypotheses are questionable, or multiple functions seem likely, trained professionals conduct descriptive assessments.

Descriptive assessment involves directly observing and recording situational factors surrounding stereotypic behaviors. A range of data collection protocols have been developed to conduct descriptive assessments, but all share a common focus on collecting direct observation data on the antecedents and consequences relating to stereotypic behaviors (O'Neill et al., 1996; Thompson, Felce, Symons, & Symons, 1999; Touchette, Macdonald, & Langer, 1985; Vollmer, Borrero, Wright, Van Camp, & Lalli, 2001). The events that occur just before the stereotypic behaviors are noted, followed by the behaviors and what occurred directly after the behaviors. This approach identifies the behavioral dimensions (e.g., rate, duration, or percentage of intervals of occurrence), possible environmental variables, and/or temporal factors influencing the behaviors; however, there is no systematic testing of hypotheses to ensure a direct relation exists between stereotypic behaviors and the environment. For instance, when descriptive assessments in conjunction with record reviews/interviews do not yield clear hypotheses regarding function, experimental analysis are used.

Experimental analyses are small-scale experiments using some type of single-case methodology (Kennedy, 2005). Conditions are explicitly arranged to test specific reinforcement contingencies in relation to problem behaviors (Iwata, Dorsey, Slifer, Bauman, & Richman, 1982; Wacker, Berg, Harding, & Cooper-Brown, 2004). The goal of such an analysis is to present and/or remove the suspected environmental consequences contingent on the occurrence or nonoccurrence of stereotypic behaviors. If the behaviors reliably occur when the consequences are presented and/or removed, the functional relation between the behaviors and the environment has been empirically validated.

In general, treatment for problem behaviors is most effective when based on the functions of the behaviors (Rapp & Vollmer, 2005a); however, it was not common for functional analyses to be conducted when assessing stereotypic behaviors prior to the mid-1990s. Many behavioral treatments presupposed a nonsocial or self-stimulatory function for stereotypic behaviors, and were sometimes punitive and/or aversive. Nonetheless, non-function-based treatments have effectively reduced stereotypic behaviors. Because of ethical concerns surrounding the aversive nature of some non-function-based treatments, they should only be used after exhausting less aversive alternatives (Lerman & Vorndan, 2002).

EMPIRICALLY SUPPORTED TREATMENT OF SBD

The Task Force on Promotion and Dissemination of Psychological Procedure (1995) and Chambless and Hollon (1998) established guidelines for defining empirically supported treatments for behavioral problems. First, a treatment is considered "well-established" if two or more independent research teams obtain therapeutic effects using randomized controlled trials in group designs, or at least two independent teams use well-designed single-case experiments with at least nine participants combined. Second, empirical investigations explicitly describe treatment procedures and the participants who benefit from treatment. If less than three studies demonstrate therapeutic effects with at least three participants, or if the same investigators directly replicate their own research, then a treatment is deemed "possibly efficacious." Finally, the efficacy of a treatment is demonstrated by comparing it to drug therapies, a placebo treatment or control condition, an alternative treatment, or a treatment already established as effective. A preponderance of treatments for SBD over the past 30 years use single-subject methodology.

WELL-ESTABLISHED FUNCTION-BASED TREATMENTS

Enriched Environment

A total of 30 studies were found that used enriched environment (EE) as a treatment for SBD. The EE generally consists of providing items for a person to engage with that compete with nonsocial stereotypic behaviors. The focus is on providing alternative forms of stimulation functioning as positive reinforcement and decreasing the probability of stereotypic behaviors (Horner, 1980). The primary approach to EE, *noncontingent reinforcement* (NCR), is supported by numerous experiments conducted over the past three decades (Table 19.1). Currently, evidence-based practice suggests trained professionals begin with a preference assessment to establish what stimuli function as positive reinforcers for an individual (Piazza, Adelinis, Hanley, Goh, & Delia, 2000; Roscoe, Iwata, & Goh, 1998). Once these stimuli have been identified, they can be provided to the individual in settings where stereotypic behaviors are identified as problematic. By having care providers present the stimuli frequently and noncontingently, the density of reinforcement available to the individual is increased, resulting in a substantial decrease in the probability of stereotypic behaviors (Rapp, 2004).

For example, Piazza et al. (2000) conducted a functional analysis of stereotypic behaviors for three children with I/DDs and found the behaviors to be maintained by nonsocial reinforcement. A preference assessment was conducted to identify stimuli that matched the sensory consequences of the behaviors, as well as stimuli that produced consequences dissimilar to those maintaining the behaviors. Sensory items were made continuously available to participants during treatment. Results suggested stimuli matching the specific sensory modality of reinforcement were effective at reducing stereotypic behaviors than arbitrarily chosen sensory stimuli.

In a similar study, Ringdahl, Vollmer, Marcus, and Roane (1997) evaluated the role of stimulus preference in EE conditions on the reduction of nonsocial stereotypic behaviors. The matched sensory stimuli most preferred during a preference assessment were more effective at reducing stereotypic behaviors and increasing object manipulation. Ringdahl et al. (1997) also compared EE to alternative treatment approaches. Differential reinforcement and a response restriction procedure during EE sessions were shown to be effective when the preferred stimuli were made contingent on either asking for the stimuli, or on the absence of stereotypic behavior. What this data suggests is that preferred sensory stimuli can be used both contingently and noncontingently to reduce stereotypic behaviors.

Roscoe and colleagues (1998) also compared NCR procedures with sensory extinction for stereotypic behaviors maintained by nonsocial consequences. Preference assessments revealed specific stimuli to use in the NCR condition for each participant. During the sensory extinction condition, participants wore protective equipment selected to prevent sensory reinforcement when engaging in targeted behaviors. Both procedures were effective at reducing stereotypic behaviors; however, stereotypic behaviors under the NCR condition reduced more rapidly than the sensory extinction condition.

Several interventions focusing on arbitrary reinforcement or matching stimulation to sensory modalities have been developed and shown to be effective. EE sessions have been used over the past 30 years with and without

TABLE 19.1 Function- and Non-Function-Based Treatments

Treatment	Reference

Enriched Environment
Noncontingent Reinforcement:
  Well-Established
  (Function Based)
	Britton, Carr, Kellum, Dozier, and Well, 2000; Britton, Carr, Landaburu, and Romick, 2002; J. E. Carr, Dozier, Patel, Adams, and Martin, 2002; Cuvo et al., 2001; Fisher, Lindauer, Alterson, and Thompson, 1998; Fisher et al., 1992; Goh et al., 1995; Horner, 1980; Lindberg, Iwata, and Kahng, 1999; Lindberg, Iwata, Roscoe, Worsdell, and Hanley, 2003; Mace and Lalli, 1991; Muller and Kafka, 2006; Piazza et al., 2000; Rapp, 2006, 2007; Rapp, Miltenberger, Galensky, Ellingson, and Long, 1999; Rapp, Vollmer, St. Peter, Dozier, and Cotnoir, 2004; Realon, Favell, and Cacace, 1995; Ringdahl et al., 1997; Roane, Kelly, and Fisher, 2003; Roscoe, Iwata, and Goh, 1998; Sidener, Carr, and Firth, 2005; Shore, Iwata, DeLeon, Kahng, and Smith, 1997; Simmons, Smith, and Kliethermes, 2003; Sprague, Holland, and Thomas, 1997; Tierny, McGuire, and Walton, 1979; Vollmer, Marcus, and LeBlanc, 1994; Wilder, Draper, Williams, and Higbee, 1997; Wilder, Kellum, and Carr, 2000; Yang and Bruner, 1996

Differential Reinforcement:
  Well-Established
  (Function Based)
	Aurand et al., 1989; Azrin and Wesolowski, 1980; Barmann, 1980; Barton, Brulle, and Repp, 1986; Barton, Repp, and Brulle, 1985; Beare et al., 2004; Cavalier and Ferretti, 1980; Charlop, Kurtz, and Casey, 1990; Charlop-Christy and Haymes, 1996; Derwas and Jones, 1993; Durand and Carr, 1987; Dyer, 1987; Fellner, Laroche, and Sulzer-Azaroff, 1984; Foxx, McMorrow, Fenlon, and Bittle, 1986; Handen et al., 1984; Hanley, Iwata, Thompson, and Lindberg, 2000; Haring, Breen, Pitts-Conway, and Gaylord-Ross, 1986; Hung, 1978; Jones and Baker, 1988, 1989; Jones, Baker, and Murphy, 1988; Kennedy, Meyer, Knowles, and Shukla, 2000; Lancioni et al., 2004; Lancioni et al., 2006; Lancioni et al., 2007a; Lancioni et al., 2007b; Lockwood and Williams, 1994; Loftin, Odom, and Lantz, 2008; Luiselli, Colozzi, Helfen, and Follow, 1980; Mason and Newsom, 1990; McClure, Moss, McPeters, and Kirkpatrick, 1986; McEntee, Parker, Brown, and Poulson, 1996; McGonigle and Rojahn, 1989; Miller and Jones, 1997; Patel, Carr, Kim, Robles, and Eastridge, 2000; Pierce and Schreibman, 1994; Rehfeldt and Chambers, 2003; Repp, Barton, and Brulle, 1983; Saunders and Saunders, 1997; Saunders, Saunders, and Marquis, 1998; Shabani, Wilder, and Flood, 2001; Singh et al., 1981; Tang, Patterson, and Kennedy, 2003; Wacker et al., 1990; Wolery et al., 1985

Sensory Extinction:
  Well-Established
  (Function Based)
	Aiken and Salzberg, 1984; Deaver et al., 2001; Jordan, Singh, and Repp, 1989; Maag, Wolchik, Rutherford, and Parks, 1986; McGonigle, Duncan, Cordisco, and Barrett, 1982; Rapp, Dozier, Carr, Patel, and Enloe, 2000; Rapp et al., 1999; Rapp et al., 2000; Rincover, 1978; Rincover, Cook, Peoples, and Packard, 1979; Singh et al., 1993; Tang, Kennedy, Koppekin, and Caruso, 2002

Antecedent Exercise:
  Well-Established
  (Non-Function Based)
	Allison, Faith, and Franklin, 1995; Bachman and Fuqua, 1983; Bachman and Sluyter, 1988; Celiberti, Bobo, Kelly, Harris, and Handleman, 1997; Elliott et al., 1994; Ellis, MacLean, and Gazdag, 1989; Jansma and Combs, 1987; Kern, Koegel, and Dunlap, 1984; Kern, Koegel, Dyer, Blew, and Fenton, 1982; Lancioni, Olivia, Coppa, and Boelens, 1991; Levinson and Reid, 1993; McGimsey and Favell, 1988; Morrissey et al., 1992; Powers et al., 1992; Prupas and Reid, 2001; Reid, Factor, Freeman, and Sherman, 1988; Rosenthal-Malek and Mitchell, 1997; Watters and Watters, 1980

Self-Monitoring:
  Well-Established
  (Non-Function Based)
	R. L. Koegel and Koegel, 1990; Pope and Jones, 1996; Stahmer and Schreibman, 1992

Response Restriction:
  Well-Established
  (Non-Function Based)
	Ahearn et al., 2007; Duker and Schaapveld, 1996; Irvin, Thompson, Turner, and Williams, 1998; Lerman, Kelley, Vorndran, and Van Camp, 2003; McEntee and Saunders, 1997; Reid, Tombaugh, and Vanden Heuvel,

Treatment	Reference
	1981; Richmond, 1983; Rolider, Williams, Cummings, and van Houten, 1991; Tarbox, Tarbox, Ghezzi, Wallace, and Yoo, 2007; Turner, Realon, Irvin, and Robinson, 1996; Zhou and Goff, 2000
Overcorrection: Well-Established (Non-Function Based)	Barrett and Linn, 1981; Barrett and Shapiro, 1980; Carey and Bucher, 1983; Cole, Montgomery, Wilson, and Milan, 2000; Coleman, Whitman, and Johnson, 1979; Czyzewski, Barrera, and Sulzer-Azaroff, 1982; Denny, 1980; Harris and Wolchik, 1979; Higgs, Burns, and Meunier, 1980; Luiselli, Pemberton, and Helfen, 1978; Marholin and Townsend, 1978; Matson, Ollendick, and Martin, 1979; Matson and Stephens, 1981; Ollendick, Matson, and Martin, 1978; Ollendick, Shapiro, and Barrett, 1981; Roberts, Iwata, McSween, and Desmond, 1979; Rollings and Baumeister, 1981; Shapiro, Barett, and Ollendick, 1980
Inhibitory Stimulus Control: Possibly Efficacious (Non-Function Based)	Brusa and Richman, 2007; Conroy, Asmus, Sellers, and Ladwig, 2005; Doughty, Anderson, Doughty, Williams, and Saunders, 2007; Rollings and Baumeister, 1981; Woods, 1983

identifying the specific sensory modality of reinforcement (e.g., Cuvo, May, & Post, 2001; Vollmer, Marcus, & LeBlanc, 1994). However, the hallmark of treatments for behaviors producing their own reinforcement is the identification of effective forms of alternative stimulation that effectively compete with the response-produced stimulation. Therefore, the use of preference assessments has become an integral component in the effective treatment of nonsocially reinforced stereotypic behaviors.

Differential Reinforcement

Forty-five studies have implemented treatment protocols based on differential reinforcement for treatment of stereotypic behaviors (Table 19.1). The use of differential reinforcement builds on EE by making the delivery of alternative stimuli contingent on the absence of stereotypic behaviors or the presence of an alternative response (Repp, Felce, & Barton, 1988). A preference assessment should be conducted prior to the development of the treatment. Once stimuli are identified, baseline rates of the stereotypic behaviors are established and a reinforcement interval shorter than the median interresponse time (IRT) is used as the initial reinforcement interval. The interval

size is increased systematically over time as stereotypic behaviors are reduced.

There is a variety of differential reinforcement procedures used to decrease stereotypic behaviors. The most common include differential reinforcement of other behaviors (DRO), alternative behaviors (DRA), and low-rate behaviors (DRL). The DRO contingencies specify that reinforcement be delivered for the nonoccurrence of stereotypic behaviors (Charlop-Christy & Haymes, 1996). The DRA schedules specify an alternative topography or topographies of behaviors that are reinforced (Roane, Fisher, Sgro, Falcomata, & Pabico, 2004). Because of its social-communicative bases, socially mediated stereotypic behaviors typically require some form of communication-focused treatment, such as functional communication training (FCT). FCT focuses on reinforcing alternative forms of behavior (E. G. Carr & Durand, 1985). Thus, functionally equivalent behaviors in the same response class as stereotypic behaviors are selected for shaping to occasion similar positive or negative social reinforcement (Sprague & Horner, 1992). For example, if stereotypic behaviors are positively reinforced in the form of adult attention, then alternative, socially appropriate responses (e.g., signing, verbalization, or gesture) could be taught and reinforced with adult attention. Finally, research has also supported the use of DRL reinforcement contingencies with the goal of reinforcing longer IRTs (Singh, Dawson, & Manning, 1981). For example, a trained care provider might begin by targeting a frequency lower than the existing baseline and then gradually reducing that number over time.

Patel, Carr, Kim, Robles, and Eastridge (2000) used a DRO procedure to reduce non-social stereotypic behaviors. The investigators subsequently identified auditory stimulation as a source of reinforcement for one participant's behavior and tactile stimulation for another. A list of most-to-least preferred stimuli were identified for each participant during a preference assessment of stimuli providing similar sensory reinforcement as the behaviors. The DRO procedure was implemented so that reinforcement would be provided in the absence of stereotypic behaviors.

DRO procedures have been compared with other treatment strategies. For example, Charlop-Christy and Haymes (1996) used object preoccupations to reinforce periods of time with no stereotypic behaviors. An initial assessment of DRO using food reinforcement for the absence of stereotypic behavior showed the procedure to be ineffective. This was most likely because food reinforcement may not compete with the sensory reinforcement provided by the stereotypic behaviors. The food reinforcement was replaced with object preoccupation and effectively reduced stereotypic behaviors. The addition of a mild punitive procedure (i.e., time-out from positive reinforcement) was more effective than the preoccupation DRO alone. A final condition compared the food DRO with the food DRO plus mild reductive procedure and found that the latter procedure was also more effective. Thus, although DRO is an effective procedure when the appropriate reinforcers are identified through preference assessments, the rate of stereotypic behaviors may decrease to lower rates quicker with a mild punitive procedure.

There are two possible disadvantages that can conceivably make a DRO procedure less effective for some people. First, DRO procedures require a behavior to be absent for a specified period of time. Without a punitive procedure to decrease responding, the person may never contact the scheduled reinforcement because the behavior would occur during the period it is supposed to be absent. Second, DRO procedures often do not specify that collateral behaviors must be absent. Thus, the procedure could adventitiously reinforce other inappropriate behaviors that occur contiguously with reinforcement delivery; however, punitive procedures are not absolutely necessary when implementing a DRO procedure. For example, Beare, Severson, and Brandt (2004) combined DRO with a DRA procedure to reduce escape-maintained stereotypic behaviors and increase work productivity. Clothes manipulation was interfering with task engagement at work, making it difficult for the participant to reintegrate into community employment. The participant received food reinforcement for completing the work task (DRA) as long as he refrained from stereotypic behavior (DRO).

DRA has been successful at reducing stereotypic behaviors as a stand-alone procedure and in combination with other procedures. Wolery, Kirk, and Gast (1985) used stereotypic behaviors emitted by children with autism to reinforce correct responses during academic skills training. When stereotypic behaviors were allowed contingent on correct responding, task performance increased and stereotypic behaviors during instruction time decreased; however, restricting the stereotypic response may be necessary before task engagement will occur (Hanley, Iwata, Thompson, Lindberg, 2000). In the Hanley et al. (2000) study, participants were exposed to four conditions: continuous access to leisure materials, prompted use of the leisure materials, restricted access to stereotypic behaviors through response blocking, and access to stereotypic behaviors contingent on using leisure materials. NCR was ineffective for reducing stereotypic behaviors, even when participants were prompted to use the materials. Task engagement only increased after restricting the stereotypic response.

Stereotypic behaviors as reinforcers for alternative behavior are not essential for DRA to be effective. The effects are largely due to the stimuli used as reinforcement for alternative behavior. For example, Rehfeldt and Chambers (2003) conducted a functional analysis and determined verbal perseverations of a man with autism were maintained by social attention. The treatment required the man to engage in appropriate conversation to receive adult attention, and verbal perseverations were extinguished. Dyer (1987) found that preferred items delivered contingent on task completion reduced stereotypic behaviors for three students; however, another three students required response blocking to increase task completion.

As mentioned previously, FCT can be used to reinforce alternative communication that competes with stereotypic behaviors. Durand and Carr (1987) analyzed socially maintained stereotypic behaviors of four children with I/DDs. Initial assessments indicated all participants used behaviors to escape academic demands. Participants were taught to request assistance on difficult tasks, resulting in a reduction in stereotypic behaviors. Kennedy et al. (2000) analyzed the multiple functions of stereotypic behaviors for a child with autism. Alternative responses were taught for each identified function. The results showed stereotypic behaviors reduced when differential reinforcement for communication was implemented. What the Durand and Carr (1987) and Kennedy et al. (2000) studies demonstrate is that appropriate behavior can be reinforced with DRA procedures without the use of external suppression techniques.

The final differential reinforcement treatment is the DRL procedure. Singh et al. (1981) analyzed the stereotypic behaviors of three children with I/DDs before using the DRL procedure to determine the average IRT for the behaviors. Descriptive praise was delivered following a stereotypic behavior if that behavior was separated from a previous occurrence by 12 seconds. Stereotypic behaviors decreased and social behaviors increased by using the DRL procedure. Handen, Apolito, and Seltzer (1984) used a DRL procedure to reduce stereotypic behaviors of a child with autism. Tokens were provided contingent on the child withholding verbal perseverations according to a specified criterion level. Stereotypic behaviors reduced substantially over the course of the study and maintained at low rates for over a year.

Sensory Extinction

A total of 12 studies used sensory extinction as a treatment for stereotypic behaviors (Table 19.1). This intervention approach focuses on identifying the sensory system(s) associated with the stereotyped response and then intervening to eliminate the sensory consequences maintaining the behavior. One requirement for this type of intervention is that a sensory modality assessment be completed and then some means of altering the response to eliminate the sensory stimulation be used (see Sidener, Carr, & Firth 2005; Tang, Patterson, & Kennedy, 2003). The approach was initially demonstrated by Rincover, Cook, Peoples, and Packard (1979). A female engaging in repetitive plate spinning underwent a sensory assessment indicating that sound produced by plate spinning was the sensory modality maintaining the response. The investigators blocked the sensory consequence, reducing the behavior to near-zero levels. Deaver, Miltenberger, and Stricker (2001) analyzed nonsocial hair twirling in a young girl with I/DDs. Noncontingent application of mittens was used to block tactile stimulation. Results of the study showed hair twirling dramatically decreased as a result of sensory extinction. Tang and colleagues (2003) analyzed specific sensory modalities maintaining nonsocial stereotypic behaviors of students with multiple profound disabilities. The investigators used sensory extinction to block visual or tactile stimulation. Alternative stimulation was provided that competed with the sensory consequences of stereotypic behaviors.

Sensory extinction has been compared to other treatments. For example, Singh, Landrum, Ellis, and Donatelli (1993) evaluated the effects of thioridazine and visual screening on stereotypic and social behaviors. Conditions included a double-blind, placebo-controlled condition in which two doses of thioridazine (1.25 and 2.5 mg/kg/day) were administered alone, or in combination with, visual screening. Initial functional analyses revealed a nonsocial function for stereotypic behaviors. The higher dose of thioridazine produced a modest decrease in stereotypic behaviors and minimal increase in social behaviors, compared to the smaller dose. The combination of thioridazine and visual screening produced a larger reduction of stereotypic behaviors. Visual screening alone produced the best results in terms of increases in social behaviors and decreases in stereotypic behaviors. It is important for more comparative studies to examine the beneficial treatment of medication and behavioral treatments on stereotypic behaviors.

WELL-ESTABLISHED NON-FUNCTION-BASED TREATMENTS

Antecedent Exercise

Antecedent manipulations are sometimes used to treat stereotypic behaviors when the consequences cannot be controlled. Sometimes these manipulations are function based, as in NCR procedures just described. However, for NCR to be a function-based treatment, the maintaining variables must be known. When the consequent events are not known, the environment is altered in an attempt to prevent the stereotypic behaviors from occurring. The aim of antecedent exercise is to provide people

with I/DDs opportunity to engage in stimulating activities that produce kinesthetic, vestibular, and tactile stimulation that competes with stereotypic behaviors (Bachman & Fuqua, 1983). There are 18 studies of the effects of antecedent exercise on stereotypic behaviors (Table 19.1). Exercise can include vigorous exercise—including jogging, dancing, or calisthenics—or mild exercise—such aswalking or tossing a ball. Various combinations of exercise have been evaluated based on their type, duration, and frequency.

Powers, Thibadeau, and Rose (1992) evaluated the effects of vigorous exercise on the stereotypic behaviors of a child with I/DDs. The child roller-skated for 10 minutes before being observed. Vigorous exercise increased on-task behavior for the child and decreased stereotypic behaviors 30 minutes after the exercise. Elliott, Dobbin, Rose, and Soper (1994) found similar results when comparing vigorous aerobic exercise with general motor training. General motor training consisted of increasing the heart rate to between 90 and 120 beats per minute after 20 minutes of riding a bike, using a stair-stepper, lifting weights, or walking on a treadmill. Aerobic exercise consisted of elevating the heart rate above 130 beats per minute after 20 minutes. Stereotypic behaviors were reduced substantially for over 30 minutes after vigorous aerobic exercise.

Kern, Koegel, and Dunlap (1984) compared vigorous and mild exercise programs on three people with I/DDs. Participants were exposed to 15 minutes of tossing a ball in one condition, and then exposed to 15 minutes of continuous vigorous jogging. Results suggested stereotypic behaviors decreased after vigorous exercise. Vigorous exercise has also been demonstrated to decrease stereotypic behaviors and increase on-task behavior when compared to behavioral relaxation training (Morrissey, Franzini, & Karen, 1992).

The duration of exercise has been evaluated for its effects on stereotypic behaviors. For example, Levinson and Reid (1993) examined the effects of a 15-minute walk (mild intensity) or 90 minutes of jogging (vigorous intensity). The investigators specifically noted only motor stereotypic behaviors were reduced with 90 minutes of jogging for all three participants. This may suggest the possibility of a matched consequence for stereotypic behaviors (e.g., proprioceptive stimulation produced by motor stereotypic behaviors may be attenuated by providing the same stimulation through functional activities).

The frequency of exercise has also been examined for its effects on stereotypic behaviors. For example, Prupas and Reid (2001) evaluated one daily 10-minute walk or jog compared to three 10-minute walks or jogs for four children with I/DDs. Stereotypic behaviors were observed immediately before and after exercise. Both exercise frequencies reduced stereotypic behaviors by half; however, multiple exercise opportunities reduced stereotypic behaviors for longer periods of time throughout the day.

Self-Monitoring

Self-monitoring is a well-established non-function-based treatment. Three studies, including 12 participants with I/DDs, have demonstrated its effects on stereotypic behaviors and improvement in social skills in a variety of settings (Table 19.1). People with I/DDs are taught to discriminate and self-record the occurrence or nonoccurrence of stereotypic and prosocial behaviors. Self-monitoring encourages self-control by allowing the person to observe their own behavior and to regulate when the behaviors occur. The procedure can also be used in the absence of care providers. R. L. Koegel and Koegel (1990) taught students to discriminate stereotypic behaviors from others by watching a model demonstrate the behaviors. The students were then taught to record when their stereotypic behaviors occurred. Prompts to self-record were slowly faded until the students were recording the stereotypic behaviors on their own. After a recording period ended, a therapist provided reinforcement if the students recorded without prompts. Stereotypic behaviors were attenuated using self-monitoring, and the procedure was generalized to community settings.

Although prompts were faded during discrimination training in the study just mentioned, external reinforcement was necessary to maintain self-recording of stereotypic behaviors. Pope and Jones (1996) demonstrated that external reinforcement is not necessary to maintain the effects of self-monitoring. Participants in the study were taught to monitor and record the frequency of their stereotypic behaviors. Stereotypic behaviors were substantially attenuated for all participants. The successful use of self-monitoring without external reinforcement for continued performance may be due, in part, to the level of disability of the participants. People with mild to moderate I/DDs may contact natural reinforcers more quickly than people with more severe I/DDs. For example, people with mild to moderate I/DDs may have contacted social reinforcement more frequently. Thus, the increase in social reinforcement strengthened the probability of further reduction in inappropriate behavior with concomitant increases in prosocial behaviors.

Response Restriction

Response restriction is sometimes used in conjunction with differential reinforcement treatments to reduce stereotypic behaviors (Aurand, Sisson, Aach, & Van Hasselt, 1989; R. L. Koegel, Firestone, Kramme, and Dunlap, 1974; Roscoe et al., 1998; Vollmer et al., 1994). Response restriction can be in the form of an interruption or blocking of the response (Ahearn, Clark, MacDonald, & Chung, 2007; Duker & Schaapveld, 1996), increased response effort (Zhou & Goff, 2000), or brief mechanical or physical restraint (Irvin, Thompson, Turner, & Williams, 1998). The purpose of response restriction is to temporarily suppress stereotypic behaviors so that other prosocial behaviors emerge. Eleven studies have demonstrated the effects of response restriction alone or in comparison to other treatments (Table 19.1).

Ahearn and colleagues (2007) conducted a functional analysis on vocal stereotypies of children with I/DDs and found the behaviors were maintained by nonsocial consequences. Response interruption with redirection was implemented, requiring a teacher issue vocal demands to gain compliance contingent upon vocal stereotypies. The continuous demands to comply with other academic behaviors successfully reduced stereotypic vocal behaviors and increased appropriate verbal communication. Duker and Schaapveld (1996) evaluated the effects of interruption of stereotypic behavior on on-task behavior in five people with severe I/DDs. Investigators briefly interrupted the stereotypic responses while prompting appropriate on-task behaviors. Results indicated substantial increases in on-task behaviors. These studies demonstrated that both verbal and motor stereotypic behaviors can be interrupted long enough to reinforce appropriate communicative and academic skills.

Zhou and Goff (2000) evaluated the effects of increased response effort on stereotypic behaviors. Soft flexion sleeves were used to increase the physical effort required to bend the arms. Results showed decreased stereotypic behaviors and increased object manipulation. Irvin et al. (1998) also used increased response effort to reduce stereotypic behaviors in people with I/DDs. Arm restraints were used to alter the amount of effort necessary to engage in hand mouthing. Hand mouthing decreased substantially with little effect on activity engagement. Follow-up sessions revealed that the treatment effects were maintained.

There can be some deleterious effects of using response restriction as sole treatment for reducing stereotypic behaviors. Lerman, Kelley, Vorndran, and Van Camp (2003) examined the effects of response blocking on stereotypic behaviors in a woman with I/DDs.

Blocking stereotypic behaviors was associated with decreases in leisure-item interaction and increases in other forms of stereotypic behaviors. By blocking inappropriate use of leisure items, appropriate use of the same items was also punished. An attempt to reinforce appropriate use of sensory items attenuated the new stereotypic behaviors.

Overcorrection

Another treatment considered by many investigators to be punitive is overcorrection. Overcorrection is often still used for rapid reduction of stereotypic behaviors and functional analysis results are inconclusive; however, many early studies of overcorrection focused almost exclusively on the time-out and response cost components of the procedure (Azrin & Welsolowski, 1980; Foxx & Azrin, 1973; Foxx, McMorrow, Fenlon, & Bittle, 1986). The focus of overcorrection tends to be on removing the person from the reinforcing consequences of the stereotypic behavior by requiring practice of responses that are incompatible with the stereotypic responses. A total of 18 studies demonstrated the effects of overcorrection on stereotypic behaviors (Table 19.1).

Carey and Bucher (1983) examined the effects of long (3 minutes) and short (30 seconds) durations of overcorrection for stereotypic behaviors interfering with performance of an object placement task. Stereotypic behaviors resulted in positive practice of the object placement task. Appropriate task performance occurred at a greater rate, with decreased stereotypic behaviors during the 30-second positive practice technique. Cole, Montgomery, Wilson, and Milan (2000) expanded on the Carey and Bucher analysis by examining three different positive practice durations. The different durations were equally effective in reducing the stereotypic behaviors. These studies demonstrate that the effective duration of positive practice ranges between 30 seconds and 8 minutes.

Overcorrection can be effective at eliminating stereotypic behaviors. Some suggest it is more effective than differential reinforcement procedures (Harris & Wolchik, 1979). Overcorrection can be used in brief bouts to eliminate inappropriate behavior while strengthening alternative behaviors. Future research should focus on positive practice of functionally equivalent responses to obtain reinforcement similar to that produced by stereotypic behaviors.

POSSIBLY EFFICACIOUS NON-FUNCTION-BASED TREATMENTS

Inhibitory Stimulus Control

Another antecedent treatment used since the 1980s is inhibitory stimulus control. One difficulty experienced while using differential reinforcement procedures is that behaviors maintained by nonsocial consequences are resistant to extinction procedures inherent to those procedures. Thus, response restriction is often part of the treatment package for reduction of stereotypic behaviors. Inhibitory stimulus control procedures follow a similar concept (i.e., reinforcement and punishment procedures combined) by providing cues signaling when reinforcement or punishment consequences are in effect. Five studies have been conducted on its effectiveness with people with I/DDs (Table 19.1).

Inhibitory stimulus control uses discrimination training with some cue signaling when engagement in stereotypic behaviors is acceptable. Engagement in stereotypic behaviors when the cue for a nonresponse is present results in some sort of punishment, such as overcorrection or response blocking (Brusa & Richman, 2008; Rollings & Baumeister, 1981). Stereotypic behaviors occurring in the presence of the appropriate cue allow the person time to engage in the behaviors without punishment. For example, Rollings and Baumeister (1981) used discrimination training to reduce stereotypic behaviors in two adults

with I/DDs. Discrimination training used an overcorrection technique to punish stereotypic behaviors in the presence of a red light. Another light signaled to the participants that stereotypic behaviors would go unpunished. Stereotypic behaviors decreased significantly in the punishment contingency (i.e., when the red light was on), and increased significantly when the light signaling reinforcement was on.

EVIDENCE-BASED PRACTICES

Function-based treatments are tailored to the specific needs of individuals with I/DDs. The treatment literature shows a trend toward appropriate functional behavior assessment of problem behaviors and basing the treatment decisions on those results; however, stereotypic behaviors are complex, persistent, and often resistant to treatment. This observation was made early in the study of SBD and continues to be accurate today, even though our assessment and treatment techniques have continued to increase in terms of accuracy and sophistication. Such an observation suggests stereotypic behaviors may be different from other forms of problem behavior, at least in part, because of the type of reinforcement that is associated with their occurrence. Unlike socially mediated reinforcement, nonsocial reinforcement does not lend itself to environmental analyses because, by their nature, they are internal events (Kennedy, 1994; Moore, 1984). This suggests that behavioral treatments may have an inherent limitation in their ability to affect behavior that is response-produced and reinforced by the sensory consequences of the region.

On the other hand, there are many effective behavioral interventions for reducing levels of stereotypic behaviors. The interventions are effective as long as they are delivered with fidelity and are sustained over time; however, when they are removed, the stereotypic behaviors typically resume at levels consistent with the original baseline levels. This suggests that current interventions for stereotypic behaviors are not curative in their nature, but instead are palliative. Such an observation should not be interpreted as being overly pessimistic. Science often advances by noting current limitations in evidence-based practices. Such an observation should be interpreted, however, as a prediction that stereotypic behaviors will continue to be complex, persistent, and often resistant to treatment. At the moment, we know a great deal about why stereotypic behaviors occur and posses a reasonable armamentarium of treatments to suppress their occurrence; but more work remains to be done.

A treatment protocol is emerging in the literature. First, an FBA must be conducted on the maintaining consequences of behavior. Second, nonsocially maintained behavior must be examined further to determine specific sensory modalities of reinforcement. Third, an appropriate preference assessment must be conducted to find competing stimuli for nonsocially maintained stereotypic behaviors. For socially maintained behaviors, reinforcers must be withheld to increase the probability that a more adaptable response can be taught to acquire those reinforcers. Finally, treatments must be function based if the behavioral function can be determined. If the function cannot be determined, antecedent or more restrictive treatments are often used. Thus, all of the treatments mentioned before are acceptable treatments for SBD.

Enriched environments provide noncontingent access to stimuli that provide the same consequences as stereotypic behaviors. Differential reinforcement can be used to reduce stereotypic behaviors while reinforcing alternative behavior with similar consequences. Sensory extinction can be used to mask the sensory consequences of stereotypic behaviors while determining alternative stimulation, including when and where stereotypic behaviors are acceptable. Antecedent exercise is effective at producing sensory consequences similar to some forms of stereotypic behaviors (e.g., vestibular stimulation). Teaching students with mild to moderate I/DDs to self-monitor when stereotypic behaviors occur can decrease the behaviors without the presence of care providers. Response restriction is useful for immediate suppression of stereotypic behaviors when teaching new skills, but has little long-term effects on stereotypic behaviors. Overcorrection results in immediate suppression of stereotypic behaviors while attempting to teach new skills; however, overcorrection is most often focused on removing the person from the source of stimulation. Future research will focus on using this treatment to positively practice alternative behaviors that provide similar sensory stimulation as the stereotypic behaviors. Finally, inhibitory stimulus control is possibly efficacious as a treatment for stereotypic behaviors. More research is needed for this treatment alone, in comparison with other treatments for superior effects, or in combination with other treatments for an enhanced effect on stereotypic behaviors.

REFERENCES

Ahearn, W. H., Clark, K. M., MacDonald, R. P., & Chung, B. I. (2007). Assessing and treating vocal stereotypy in children with autism. *Journal of Applied Behavior Analysis, 40,* 263–275.

Aiken, J. M., & Salzberg, C. L. (1984). The effects of a sensory extinction procedure on stereotypic sounds of two autistic children. *Journal of Autism and Developmental Disorders, 14,* 291–299.

Allison, D. B., Faith, M. S., & Franklin, R. D. (1995). Antecedent exercise in the treatment of disruptive behavior: A meta-analytic review. *Clinical Psychology: Science and Practice, 2,* 279–303.

Asmus, J. M., Ringdahl, J. E., Sellers, J. A., Call, N. A., Andelman, M. S., & Wacker, D. P. (2004). Use of a short-term inpatient model to evaluate aberrant behavior: Outcome data summaries from 1996 to 2001. *Journal of Applied Behavior Analysis, 37,* 283–304.

Aurand, J. C., Sisson, L. A., Aach, S. R., & Van Hasselt, V. B. (1989). Use of reinforcement plus interruption to reduce self-stimulation in a child with multiple handicaps. *Journal of Developmental and Physical Disabilities, 2,* 51–61.

Azrin, N. H., & Wesolowski, M. D. (1980). A reinforcement plus interruption method of eliminating behavioral stereotypy of profoundly retarded persons. *Behaviour Research and Therapy, 18*, 113–119.

Bachman, J. E., & Fuqua, R. W. (1983). Management of inappropriate behaviors of trainable mentally impaired students using antecedent exercise. *Journal of Applied Behavior Analysis, 16*, 477–484.

Bachman, J. E., & Sluyter, D. (1988). Reducing inappropriate behaviors of developmentally disabled adults using antecedent aerobic dance exercises. *Research in Developmental Disabilities, 9*, 73–83.

Ballaban-Gil, K., Rapin, I., Tuchman, R., & Shinnar, S. (1996). Longitudinal examination of the behavioral, language, and social changes in a population of adolescents and young adults with autistic disorder. *Pediatric Neurology, 15*, 217–223.

Barmann, B. C. (1980). Use of contingent vibration in the treatment of self-stimulatory hand-mouthing and ruminative vomiting behavior. *Journal of Behavior Therapy and Experimental Psychiatry, 11*, 307–311.

Barrett, R. P., & Linn, D. M. (1981). Treatment of stereotyped toe-walking with overcorrection and physical therapy. *Applied Research in Mental Retardation, 2*, 13–21.

Barrett, R. P., & Shapiro, E. S. (1980). Treatment of stereotyped hair-pulling with overcorrection: A case study with long-term follow-up. *Journal of Behavior Therapy and Experimental Psychiatry, 11*, 317–320.

Barton, L. E., Brulle, A. R., & Repp, A. C. (1986). Maintenance of therapeutic change by momentary DRO. *Journal of Applied Behavior Analysis, 19*, 277–282.

Barton, L. E., Repp, A. C., & Brulle, A. R. (1985). Reduction of stereotypic behaviours using differential reinforcement procedures and momentary restraint. *Journal of Mental Deficiency Research, 29*, 71–79.

Beare, P. L., Severson, S., & Brandt, P. (2004). The use of a positive procedure to increase engagement on-task and decrease challenging behavior. *Behavior Modification, 28*, 28–44.

Berkson, G., & Davenport, R. K. (1962). Stereotyped movements of mental defectives. I. Initial survey. *American Journal on Mental Deficiency, 66*, 849–852.

Berkson, G., Rafaeli-Mor, N., & Tarnovskys, S. (1999). Body-rocking and other habits of college students and persons with mental retardation. *American Journal of Mental Retardation, 104*, 107–116.

Berkson, G., Tupa, M., & Sherman, L. (2001). Early development of stereotyped and self-injurious behaviors: I. Incidence. *American Journal on Mental Retardation, 106*, 539–547.

Bodfish, J. W., Parker, D. E., Lewis, M. H., Sprague, R. L., & Newell, K. M. (2001). Stereotypy and motor control: Differences in the postural stability dynamics of persons with stereotyped and dyskinetic movement disorders. *American Journal on Mental Retardation, 106*, 123–134.

Britton, L. N., Carr, J. E., Kellum, K. K., Dozier, C. L., & Well, T. M. (2000). A variation of noncontingent reinforcement in the treatment of aberrant behavior. *Research in Developmental Disabilities, 21*, 425–435.

Britton, L. N., Carr, J. E., Landaburu, H. J., & Romick, K. S. (2002). The efficacy of noncontingent reinforcement as treatment for automatically reinforced stereotypy. *Behavioral Interventions, 17*, 93–103.

Brusa, E., & Richman, D. (2008). Developing stimulus control for occurrences of stereotypy exhibited by a child with autism. *International Journal of Behavioral Consultation and Therapy, 4*, 264–269.

Carey, R. G., & Bucher, B. (1983). Positive practice overcorrection: The effects of duration of positive practice on acquisition and response reduction. *Journal of Applied Behavior Analysis, 16*, 101–109.

Carr, E. G., & Durand, V. M. (1985). Reducing behavior problems through functional communication training. *Journal of Applied Behavior Analysis, 18*, 111–126.

Carr, J. E., Dozier, C. L., Patel, M. R., Adams, A. N., & Martin, N. (2002). Treatment of automatically reinforced object mouthing with noncontingent reinforcement and response blocking: Experimental analysis and social validation. *Research in Developmental Disabilities, 23*, 37–44.

Cavalier, A. R., & Ferretti, R. P. (1980). Stereotyped behaviour, alternative behavior and collateral effects: A comparison of four intervention procedures. *Journal of Mental Deficiency, 24*, 219–230.

Celiberti, D. A., Bobo, H. E., Kelly, K. S., Harris, S. L., & Handleman, J. S. (1997). The differential and temporal effects of antecedent exercise on the self-stimulatory behavior of a child with autism. *Research in Developmental Disabilities, 18*, 139–150.

Chambless, D. L., & Hollon, S. D. (1998). Defining empirically supported treatments. *Journal of Consulting and Clinical Psychology, 66*, 7–18.

Charlop, M. H., Kurtz, P. F., & Casey, F. G. (1990). Using aberrant behaviors as reinforcers for autistic children. *Journal of Applied Behavior Analysis, 23*, 163–181.

Charlop-Christy, M. H., & Haymes, L. K. (1996). Using obsessions as reinforcers with and without mild reductive procedures to decrease inappropriate behaviors of children with autism. *Journal of Autism and Developmental Disorders, 26*, 527–546.

Cole, G. A., Montgomery, R. W., Wilson, K. M., & Milan, M. A. (2000). Parametric analysis of overcorrection duration effects. *Behavior Modification, 24*, 359–378.

Coleman, R. S., Whitman, T. L., & Johnson, M. R. (1979). Suppression of self-stimulatory behavior in a profoundly retarded boy across staff and settings: An assessment of situational generalization. *Behavior Therapy, 10*, 266–280.

Conroy, M., Asmus, L., Sellers, L., & Ladwig, C. (2005). The use of an antecedent-based intervention to decrease stereotypic behavior in a general education classroom: A case study. *Focus on Autism and Other Developmental Disabilities, 20*, 223–230.

Cummings, J. L. (1985). Psychosomatic aspects of movement disorders. *Advances in Psychosomatic Medicine, 13*, 111–132.

Cuvo, A. J., May, M. E., & Post, T. M. (2001). Effects of living room, Snoezelen room, and outdoor activities on stereotypic behavior and engagement by adults with profound mental retardation. *Research in Developmental Disabilities, 22*, 183–204.

Czyzewski, M. J., Barrera, R. D., & Sulzer-Azaroff, B. (1982). An abbreviated overcorrection program to reduce self-stimulatory behaviors. *Journal of Behavior Therapy & Experimental Psychiatry, 13*, 55–62.

Deaver, C. M., Miltenberger, R. G., & Stricker, J. M. (2001). Functional analysis and treatment of hair twirling in a young child. *Journal of Applied Behavior Analysis, 34*, 535–538.

Denny, M. (1980). Reducing self-stimulatory behavior of mentally retarded persons by alternative positive practice. *American Journal of Mental Deficiency, 84*, 610–615.

Derwas, H., & Jones, R. S. P. (1993). Reducing stereotyped behavior using momentary DRO: An experimental analysis. *Behavioural Residential Treatment, 8*, 45–53.

Doughty, S. S., Anderson, C. M., Doughty, A. H., Williams, D. C., & Saunders, K. J. (2007). Discriminative control of punished stereotyped behavior in humans. *Journal of the Experimental Analysis of Behavior, 87*, 325–336.

Duker, P. C., & Schaapveld, M. (1996). Increasing on-task behaviour through interruption-prompting. *Journal of Intellectual Disabilities Research, 40*, 291–297.

Durand, V. M., & Carr, E. G. (1987). Social influences on "self-stimulatory" behavior: Analysis and treatment application. *Journal of Applied Behavior Analysis, 20*, 119–132.

Dyer, K. (1987). The competition of autistic stereotyped behavior with usual and specially assessed reinforcers. *Research in Developmental Disabilities, 8*, 607–626.

Elliott, R. O., Dobbin, A. R., Rose, G. D., & Soper, H. V. (1994). Vigorous, aerobic exercise versus general motor training activities: Effects on maladaptive and stereotypic behaviors of adults with both autism and mental retardation. *Journal of Autism and Developmental Disorders, 24*, 565–576.

Ellis, D. N., MacLean, W. E., & Gazdag, G. (1989). The effects of exercise and cardiovascular fitness on stereotyped bodyrocking. *Journal of Behavior Therapy and Experimental Psychiatry, 20*, 251–256.

Evans, D. W., Leckman, A. C., Reznick, J. S., Henshaw, D., King, R. A., & Pauls, D. (1997). Ritual, habit, and perfectionism: The prevalence and development of compulsive-like behavior in normal young children. *Child Development, 68*, 58–68.

Fellner, D. J., Laroche, M., & Sulzer-Azaroff, B. (1984). The effects of adding interruption to differential reinforcement on targeted and novel self-stimulatory behaviors. *Journal of Behavior Therapy & Experimental Psychiatry, 15*, 315–321.

Fisher, W. W., Lindauer, S. E., Alterson, C. J., & Thompson, R. H. (1998). Assessment and treatment of destructive behavior maintained by stereotypic object manipulation. *Journal of Applied Behavior Analysis, 31*, 513–527.

Fisher, W. W., Piazza, C. C., Bowman, L. G., Hagopian, L. P., Owens, J. C., & Slevin, I. (1992). A comparison of two approaches for identifying reinforcers for persons with severe and profound disabilities. *Journal of Applied Behavior Analysis, 25*, 491–498.

Foxx, R. M., & Azrin, N. H. (1973). The elimination of autistic self-stimulatory behavior by overcorrection. *Journal of Applied Behavior Analysis, 6*, 1–14.

Foxx, R. M., McMorrow, M. J., Fenlon, S., & Bittle, R. G. (1986). The reductive effects of reinforcement on the genital stimulation and stereotypy of a mentally retarded adolescent male. *Analysis and Intervention in Developmental Disabilities, 6*, 239–248.

Goh, H. L., Iwata, B. A., Shore, B. A., DeLeon, I. G., Lerman, D. C., Ulrich, S. M., & Smith, R. G. (1995). An analysis of the reinforcing properties of hand mouthing. *Journal of Applied Behavior Analysis, 28*, 269–283.

Guess, D., & Carr, E. G. (1991). Emergence and maintenance of stereotypy and self-injury. *American Journal on Mental Retardation, 96*, 299–319.

Handen, B. L., Apolito, P. M., & Seltzer, G. B. (1984). Use of differential reinforcement of low rates of behavior to decrease repetitive speech in an autistic adolescent. *Journal of Behavior Therapy & Experimental Psychiatry, 15*, 359–364.

Hanley, G. P., Iwata, B. A., & McCord, B. E. (2003). Functional analysis of problem behavior: A review. *Journal of Applied Behavior Analysis, 36*, 147–185.

Hanley, G. P., Iwata, B. A., Thompson, R. H., & Lindberg, J. S. (2000). A component analysis of "stereotypy as reinforcement" for alternative behavior. *Journal of Applied Behavior Analysis, 33*, 285–297.

Haring, T. G., Breen, C. G., Pitts-Conway, V., & Gaylord-Ross, R. (1986). Use of differential reinforcement of other behavior during dyadic instruction to reduce stereotyped behavior of autistic students. *American Journal of Mental Deficiency, 90*, 694–702.

Harris, S. L., & Wolchik, S. A. (1979). Suppression of self-stimulation: Three alternative strategies. *Journal of Applied Behavior Analysis, 12*, 185–198.

Harlow, H. F. (1965), Total social isolation: Effects on Macaque monkey behavior. *Science, 148*, 666.

Higgs, R., Burns, G., & Meunier, G. (1980). Eliminating self-stimulation vocalizations of a profoundly retarded girl through overcorrection. *The Journal of the Association for the Severely Handicapped, 5,* 264–269.

Horner, R. D. (1980). The effects of an environmental enrichment program on the behavior of institutionalized profoundly retarded children. *Journal of Applied Behavior Analysis, 13,* 473–491.

Hung, D. (1978). Using self-stimulation as reinforcement for autistic children. *Journal of Autism and Developmental Disorders, 8,* 355–366.

Irvin, D. S., Thompson, T. J., Turner, W. D., & Williams, D. E. (1998). Utilizing increased response effort to reduce chronic hand mouthing. *Journal of Applied Behavior Analysis, 31,* 375–385.

Iwata, B. A., Dorsey, M. F., Slifer, K. J., Bauman, K. E., & Richman, G. S. (1982). Toward a functional analysis of self-injury. *Analysis and Intervention in Developmental Disabilities, 2,* 3–20. (Reprinted in the *Journal of Applied Behavior Analysis, 27* [1994], 197–209)

Jansma, P., & Combs, C. S. (1987). The effects of fitness training and reinforcement on maladaptive behaviors of institutionalized adults classified as mentally retarded/emotionally disturbed. *Education and Training of the Mentally Retarded, 22,* 268–279.

Jones, R. S. P., & Baker, L. J. V. (1988). Reducing stereotyped behaviour using differential reinforcement: A comparison of DRO and DRI schedules. *Mental Handicap, 16,* 171–174.

Jones, R. S. P., & Baker, L. J. V. (1989). Reducing stereotyped behaviour: A component analysis of the DRI schedule. *British Journal of Clinical Psychology, 28,* 255–266.

Jones, R. S. P., Baker, L. J. V., & Murphy, M. J. (1988). Reducing stereotyped behaviour: The maintenance effects of a DRO reinforcement procedure. *Journal of Practical Approaches to Developmental Handicap, 12,* 24–30.

Jordan, J., Singh, N. N., & Repp, A. C. (1989). An evaluation of gentle teaching and visual screening in the reduction of stereotypy. *Journal of Applied Behavior Analysis, 22,* 9–22.

Kennedy, C. H. (1994). Automatic reinforcement: Oxymoron or hypothetical construct? *Journal of Behavioral Education, 4,* 387–396.

Kennedy, C. H. (2002). The evolution of stereotypy into self-injury. In S. Schroeder, M. L. Oster-Granite, & T. Thompson (Eds.), *Self-injurious behavior: Gene-brain-behavior relationships* (pp. 133–143). Washington, DC: American Psychological Association.

Kennedy, C. H. (2005). *Single-case designs for educational research.* Boston, MA: Allyn & Bacon.

Kennedy, C. H., Meyer, K. A., Knowles, T., & Shukla, S. (2000). Analyzing the multiple functions of stereotypical behavior for students with autism: Implications for assessment and treatment. *Journal of Applied Behavior Analysis, 33,* 559–571.

Kern, L., Koegel, R. L., & Dunlap, G. (1984). The influence of vigorous versus mild exercise on autistic stereotyped behaviors. *Journal of Autism and Developmental Disorders, 14,* 57–67.

Kern, L., Koegel, R. L., Dyer, K., Blew, P. A., & Fenton, L. R. (1982). The effects of physical exercise on self-stimulation and appropriate responding in autistic children. *Journal of Autism and Developmental Disorders, 12,* 399–419.

Koegel, R. L., Firestone, P. B., Kramme, K. W., & Dunlap, G. (1974). Increasing spontaneous play by suppressing self-stimulation in autistic children. *Journal of Applied Behavior Analysis, 7,* 521–528.

Koegel, R. L., & Koegel, L. K. (1990). Extended reductions in stereotypic behavior of students with autism through a self-management treatment package. *Journal of Applied Behavior Analysis, 23,* 119–127.

Lancioni, G. E., Olivia, D., Coppa, M. M., & Boelens, H. (1991). Self-stimulation and occupational responding in low-functioning persons. *International Journal of Rehabilitation Research, 14,* 235–238.

Lancioni, G. E., O'Reilly, M. F., Singh, N. N., Sigafoos, J., Oliva, D., Baccani, S., & Groeneweg, J. (2006). Microswitch clusters promote adaptive responses and reduce finger mouthing in a boy with multiple disabilities. *Behavior Modification, 30,* 892–900.

Lancioni, G. E., Singh, N. N., O'Reilly, M. F., Oliva, D., Campodonico, F., & Groeneweg, J. (2004). Impact of favorite stimuli on the behavior of persons with multiple disabilities while using a treadmill. *Journal of Visual Impairment and Blindness, 98,* 304–309.

Lancioni, G. E., Singh, N. N., O'Reilly, M. F., Sigafoos, J., Oliva, D., Pidala, S., . . . Bosco, A. (2007a). Promoting adaptive foot movement and reducing hand mouthing and eye poking in a boy with multiple disabilities through microswitch technology. *Cognitive Behaviour Therapy, 36,* 85–90.

Lancioni, G. E., Singh, N. N., O'Reilly, M. F., Sigafoos, J., Oliva, D., Severini, L., . . . Tamma, M. (2007b). Microswitch technology to promote adaptive responses and reduce mouthing in two children with multiple disabilities. *Journal of Visual Impairment and Blindness, 101,* 628–636.

Lerman, D. C., Kelley, M. E., Vorndan, C. M., & Van Camp, C. M. (2003). Collateral effects of response blocking during the treatment of stereotypic behavior. *Journal of Applied Behavior Analysis, 36,* 119–123.

Lerman, D. C., & Vorndan, C. M. (2002). On the status of knowledge for using punishment: Implications for treating behavior disorders. *Journal of Applied Behavior Analysis, 35,* 431–464.

Levinson, L. J., & Reid, G. (1993). The effects of exercise intensity on the stereotypic behaviors of individuals with autism. *Adapted Physical Activity Quarterly, 10,* 255–268.

Lewis, M. H., Baumeister, A. A., & Mailman, R. B. (1987). A neurobiological alternative to the perceptual reinforcement hypothesis of stereotyped behavior: A commentary on "Self-stimulatory behavior and perceptual reinforcement." *Journal of Applied Behavior Analysis, 20,* 253–258.

Lewis, M. H., & Bodfish, J. W. (1998). Repetitive behavior disorders in autism. *Mental Retardation and Developmental Disabilities Research Reviews, 4,* 80–89.

Lindberg, J. S., Iwata, B. A., & Kahng, S. W. (1999). On the relation between object manipulation and stereotypic self-injurious behavior. *Journal of Applied Behavior Analysis, 32,* 51–62.

Lindberg, J. S., Iwata, B. A., Roscoe, E. M.,Worsdell, A. S., & Hanley, G. P. (2003). Treatment efficacy of noncontingent reinforcement during brief and extended application. *Journal of Applied Behavior Analysis, 36,* 1–19.

Lockwood, K., & Williams, D. E. (1994). Treatment and extended follow-up of chronic hand mouthing. *Journal of Behavior Therapy & Experimental Psychiatry, 25,* 161–169.

Loftin, R. L., Odom, S. L., & Lantz, J. F. (2008). Social interaction and repetitive motor behaviors. *Journal Autism and Developmental Disorders, 38,* 1124–1135.

Lovaas, I., Newsom, C., & Hickman, C. (1987). Self-stimulatory behavior and perceptual reinforcement. *Journal of Applied Behavior Analysis, 20,* 45–68.

Luiselli, J. K., Colozzi, G. A., Helfen, C. S., & Follow, R. S. (1980). Differential reinforcement in treating classroom management problems of developmentally disabled children. *Psychological Record, 30,* 261–270.

Luiselli, J. K., Pemberton, B. W., & Helfen, C. S. (1978). Effects and side-effects of a brief overcorrection procedure in reducing multiple self-stimulatory behaviour: A single case analysis. *Journal of Mental Deficiency Research, 22,* 287–293.

Maag, J. W., Wolchik, S. A., Rutherford, R. B., & Parks, B. T. (1986). Response covariation on self-stimulatory behaviors during sensory extinction procedures. *Journal of Autism and Developmental Disorders, 16,* 119–132.

Mace, F. C., & Lalli, J. S. (1991). Linking descriptive and experimental analysis in the treatment of bizarre speech. *Journal of Applied Behavior Analysis, 24,* 553–562.

Marholin, D., & Townsend, N. M. (1978). An experimental analysis of side effects and response maintenance of a modified overcorrection procedure. *Behavior Therapy, 9,* 383–390.

Mason, S. A., & Newsom, C. D. (1990). The application of sensory change to reduce stereotyped behavior. *Research in Developmental Disabilities, 11,* 257–271.

Matson, J. L., Ollendick, T. H., & Martin, J. E. (1979). Overcorrection revisited: A long-term follow-up. *Journal of Behavior Therapy and Experimental Psychiatry, 10,* 11–14.

Matson, J. L., & Stephens, R. M. (1981). Overcorrection treatment of stereotyped behaviors. *Behavior Modification, 5,* 491–502.

McClure, J. T., Moss, R. A., McPeters, J., & Kirkpatrick, M. A. (1986). Reduction of handmouthing by a boy with profound mental retardation. *Mental Retardation, 24,* 219–222.

McEntee, J. E., Parker, E. H., Brown, M. B., & Poulson, R. L. (1996). The effects of response interruption DRO and positive reinforcement on the reduction of hand-mouthing behavior. *Behavioral Interventions, 11,* 163–170.

McEntee, J. E., & Saunders, R. R. (1997). A response-restriction analysis of stereotypy in adolescents with mental retardation: Implications for applied behavior analysis. *Journal of Applied Behavior Analysis, 30,* 485–506.

McGimsey, J. E., & Favell, J. E. (1988). The effects of increased physical exercise on disruptive behavior in retarded persons. *Journal of Autism and Developmental Disorders, 18,* 167–179.

McGonigle, J. J., Duncan, D., Cordisco, L., & Barrett, R. P. (1982). Visual screening: An alternative method for reducing stereotypic behaviors. *Journal of Applied Behavior Analysis, 15,* 461–467.

McGonigle, J. J., & Rojahn, J. (1989). An experimental analysis of visual screening and DRO for stereotyped behavior in young children with developmental disabilities. *Journal of the Multihandicapped Person, 2,* 251–270.

Miller, B. Y., & Jones, R. S. P. (1997). Reducing stereotyped behavior: A comparison of two methods of programming differential reinforcement. *British Journal of Clinical Psychology, 36,* 297–302.

Miltenberger, R. G. (2003). *Behavior modification: Principles and procedures.* Independence, KY: Wadsworth Publishing.

Moore, J. (1984). On privacy, causes, and contingencies. *Behavior Analyst, 7,* 3–16.

Morrissey, E. A., Franzini, L. R., & Karen, R. L. (1992). The salutary effects of light calisthenics and relaxation training on self-stimulation in the developmentally disabled. *Behavioral Residential Treatment, 7,* 373–389.

Muller, M. M., & Kafka, C. (2006). Assessment and treatment of object mouthing in a public school classroom. *Behavioral Interventions, 21,* 137–154.

Ollendick, T. H., Matson, J. L., & Martin, J. E. (1978). Effectiveness of hand overcorrection for topographically similar and dissimilar self-stimulatory behavior. *Journal of Experimental Child Psychology, 25,* 396–403.

Ollendick, T. H., Shapiro, E. S., & Barrett, R. P. (1981). Reducing stereotypic behaviors: Analysis of treatment procedures using an alternating treatment design. *Behavior Therapy, 12,* 570–577.

O'Neill, R. E., Horner, R. H., Albin, R. W., Storey, K., & Sprague, J. R. (1996). *Functional assessment and program development for problem behavior: A practical handbook*. Independence, KY: Wadsworth Publishing.

Patel, M. R., Carr, J. E., Kim, C., Robles, A., & Eastridge, D. (2000). Functional analysis of aberrant behavior maintained by automatic reinforcement: Assessments of specific sensory reinforcers. *Research in Developmental Disabilities, 21*, 393–407.

Piazza, C. C., Adelinis, J. D., Hanley, G. P., Goh, H. L., & Delia, M. D. (2000). An evaluation of the effects of matched stimuli on behaviors maintained by automatic reinforcement. *Journal of Applied Behavior Analysis, 33*, 13–27.

Pierce, K. L., & Schreibman, L. (1994). Teaching daily living skills to children with autism in unsupervised settings through pictorial self-management. *Journal of Applied Behavior Analysis, 27*, 471–481.

Pope, S. T., & Jones, R. S. (1996). The therapeutic effect of reactive self-monitoring on the reduction of inappropriate social and stereotypic behaviours. *British Journal of Clinical Psychology, 35*, 585–594.

Powers, S., Thibadeau, S., & Rose, K. (1992). Antecedent exercise and its effects on self-stimulation. *Behavioral Residential Treatment, 7*, 15–22.

Prupas, A., & Reid, G. (2001). Effects of exercise frequency on stereotypic behaviors of children with developmental disabilities. *Education and Training in Mental Retardation and Developmental Disabilities, 36*, 196–206.

Rapp, J. T. (2004). Effects of prior access and environmental enrichment on stereotypy. *Behavioral Interventions, 19*, 287–295.

Rapp, J. T. (2006). Toward an empirical method for identifying matched stimulation: A preliminary investigation. *Journal of Applied Behavior Analysis, 39*, 137–140.

Rapp, J. T. (2007). Further evaluation of methods to identify matched stimulation. *Journal of Applied Behavior Analysis, 40*, 73–88.

Rapp, J. T., Dozier, C. L., Carr, J. E., Patel, M. R., & Enloe, K. A. (2000). Functional analysis of hair manipulation: A replication and extension. *Behavioral Interventions, 15*, 121–133.

Rapp, J. T., Miltenberger, R. G., Galensky, T. L., Ellingson, S. A., & Long, E. S. (1999). A functional analysis of hair pulling. *Journal of Applied Behavior Analysis, 32*, 329–337.

Rapp, J. T., Miltenberger, R. G., Galensky, T. L., Ellingson, S. A., Stricker, J., Garlinghouse, M., & Long, E. S. (2000). Treatment of hair pulling maintained by digital-tactile stimulation. *Behavior Therapy, 31*, 381–393.

Rapp, J. T., & Vollmer, T. (2005a). Stereotypy I: A review of behavioral assessment and treatment. *Research in Developmental Disabilities, 26*, 527–547.

Rapp, J. T., Vollmer, T. R., St. Peter, C., Dozier, C. L., & Cotnoir, N. M. (2004). Analysis of response allocation in individuals with multiple forms of stereotyped behavior. *Journal of Applied Behavior Analysis, 37*, 481–501.

Rehfeldt, R. A., & Chambers, M. R. (2003). Functional analysis and treatment of verbal perseverations displayed by an adult with autism. *Journal of Applied Behavior Analysis, 36*, 259–261.

Reid, J. G., Tombaugh, T. N., & Vanden Heuvel, K. (1981). Application of contingent physical restraint to suppress stereotyped body rocking of profoundly mentally retarded persons. *American Journal of Mental Deficiency, 86*, 78–85.

Reid, P. D., Factor, D. C., Freeman, N. L., & Sherman, J. (1988). The effects of physical exercise on three autistic and developmentally disordered adolescents. *Therapeutic Recreation Journal, 22*, 42–55.

Realon, R. E., Favell, J. E., & Cacace, S. (1995). An economical, humane, and effective method for short-term suppression of hand mouthing. *Behavioral Interventions, 10*, 141–147.

Repp, A. C., Barton, L. E., & Brulle, A. R. (1983). A comparison of two procedures for programming the differential reinforcement of other behaviors. *Journal of Applied Behavior Analysis, 16*, 435–445.

Repp, A. C., Felce, D., & Barton, L. E. (1988). Basing the treatment of stereotypic and self-injurious behaviors on hypotheses of their causes. *Journal of Applied Behavior Analysis, 21*, 281–289.

Richman, D. M., & Lindauer, S. E. (2005). Longitudinal assessment of stereotypic, proto-injurious, and self-injurious behavior exhibited by young children with developmental delays. *American Journal on Mental Retardation, 110*, 439–450.

Richmond, G. (1983). Evaluation of a treatment for a hand-mouthing stereotypy. *American Journal of Mental Deficiency, 87*, 667–669.

Rincover, A. (1978). Sensory extinction: A procedure form eliminating self-stimulatory behavior in developmentally disabled children. *Journal of Abnormal Child Psychology, 6*, 299–310.

Rincover, A., Cook, R., Peoples, A., & Packard, D. (1979). Sensory extinction and sensory reinforcement principles for programming multiple adaptive behavior change. *Journal of Applied Behavior Analysis, 12*, 221–233.

Ringdahl, J. E., Vollmer, T. R., Marcus, B. E., & Roane, H. S. (1997). An analogue evaluation of environmental enrichment: The role of stimulus preference. *Journal of Applied Behavior Analysis, 30*, 203–216.

Roane, H. S., Fisher, W. W., Sgro, G. M., Falcomata, T. S., & Pabico, R. R. (2004). An alternative method of thinning reinforcer delivery during differential reinforcement. *Journal of Applied Behavior Analysis, 37*, 213–218.

Roane, H. S., Kelly, M. L., & Fisher, W. W. (2003). The effects of noncontingent access to food on the rate of object mouthing across three settings. *Journal of Applied Behavior Analysis, 36*, 579–582.

Roberts, P., Iwata, B. A., McSween, T. E., & Desmond, E. F. (1979). An analysis of overcorrection movements. *American Journal of Mental Deficiency, 83*, 588–594.

Rolider, A., Williams, L., Cummings, A., & van Houten, R. (1991). The use of a brief movement restriction procedure to eliminate severe inappropriate behavior. *Journal of Behavior Therapy & Experimental Psychiatry, 22*, 23–30.

Rollings, J. P., & Baumeister, A. A. (1981). Stimulus control of stereotypic responding: Effects on target and collateral behavior. *American Journal of Mental Deficiency, 86*, 67–77.

Roscoe, E. M., Iwata, B. A., & Goh, H. (1998). A comparison of noncontingent reinforcement and sensory extinction as treatment for self-injurious behavior. *Journal of Applied Behavior Analysis, 31*, 635–646.

Rosenthal-Malek, A., & Mitchell, S. (1997). The effects of exercise on the self-stimulatory behaviors and positive responding of adolescents with autism. *Journal of Autism and Developmental Disorders, 27*, 193–202.

Saunders, M. D., & Saunders, R. R. (1997). An analysis of stereotypy during prevocational instruction of an adolescent with severe mental retardation. *Behavioral Interventions, 12*, 1–26.

Saunders, M. D., Saunders, R. R., & Marquis, J. G. (1998). Comparison of reinforcement schedules in the reduction of stereotypy with supported routines. *Research in Developmental Disabilities, 19*, 99–122.

Shabani, D. B., Wilder, D. A., & Flood, W. A. (2001). Reducing stereotypic behavior through discrimination training, differential reinforcement of other behavior, and self-monitoring. *Behavioral Interventions, 16*, 279–286.

Shapiro, E. S., Barett, R. P., & Ollendick, T. H. (1980). A comparison of physical restraint and positive practice overcorrection in treating stereotypic behavior. *Behavior Therapy, 11*, 227–233.

Shore, B. A., Iwata, B. A., DeLeon, I. G., Kahng, S., & Smith, R. G. (1997). An analysis of reinforcer substitutability using object manipulation and self-injury as competing responses. *Journal of Applied Behavior Analysis, 30*, 21–41.

Sidener, T. M., Carr, J. E., & Firth, A. M. (2005). Superimposition and withholding of edible consequences as treatment for automatically reinforced stereotypy. *Journal of Applied Behavior Analysis, 38*, 121–124.

Simmons, J. N., Smith, R. G., & Kliethermes, L. (2003). A multiple-schedule evaluation of immediate and subsequent effects of fixed-time food presentation on automatically maintained mouthing. *Journal of Applied Behavior Analysis, 36*, 541–544.

Singh, N. N., Dawson, M. J., & Manning, P. (1981). Effects of spaced responding DRL on the stereotyped

behavior of profoundly retarded persons. *Journal of Applied Behavior Analysis, 14*, 521–526.

Singh, N. N., Landrum, T. J., Ellis, C. R., & Donatelli, L. S. (1993). Effects of thioridazine and visual screening on stereotypy and social behavior in individuals with mental retardation. *Research in Developmental Disabilities, 14*, 163–177.

South, M., Ozonoff, S., & McMahon, W. M. (2005). Repetitive behavior profiles in Asperger syndrome and high-functioning autism. *Journal of Autism and Developmental Disorders, 35*, 145–158.

Sprague, J., Holland, K., & Thomas, K. (1997). The effect of noncontingent sensory reinforcement, contingent sensory reinforcement, and response interruption on stereotypical and self-injurious behavior. *Research in Developmental Disabilities, 18*, 61–77.

Sprague, J. R., & Horner, R. H. (1992). Covariation within functional response classes: Implications for treatment of severe problem behavior. *Journal of Applied Behavior Analysis, 25*, 735–745.

Stahmer, A. C., & Schreibman, L. (1992). Teaching children with autism appropriate play in unsupervised environments using a self-management treatment package. *Journal of Applied Behavior Analysis, 25*, 447–459.

Sulzer-Azaroff, B., & Mayer, R. (1990). *Applying behavior analysis procedures with children and youth.* New York, NY: Holt, Rinehardt, & Winston.

Tang, J. C., Kennedy, C. H., Koppekin, A., & Caruso, M. (2002). Functional analysis of stereotypical ear covering in a child with autism. *Journal of Applied Behavior Analysis, 35*, 95–98.

Tang, J. C., Patterson, T. G., & Kennedy, C. H. (2003). Identifying specific sensory modalities maintaining the stereotypy of students with multiple profound disabilities. *Research in Developmental Disabilities, 24*, 433–451.

Tarbox, R. S., Tarbox, J., Ghezzi, P. M., Wallace, M. D., & Yoo, J. H. (2007). The effects of blocking mouthing of leisure items on their effectiveness as reinforcers. *Journal of Applied Behavior Analysis, 40*, 761–765.

Task Force on Promotion and Dissemination of Psychological Procedures (1995). Training in and dissemination of empirically validated treatments: Report and recommendations. *The Clinical Psychologist, 48*, 3–23.

Thelen, E. (1996). Normal infant stereotypes: A dynamic systems approach. In R. L. Sprague & K. M. Newell (Eds.), *Stereotyped movements: Brain and behavior relationships* (pp. 139–165). Washington, DC: American Psychological Association.

Thompson, T., Felce, D., Symons, F., & Symons, F. J. (1999). *Behavioral observation: Technology and applications in developmental disabilities.* Baltimore, MD: Paul H. Brookes.

Tierny, I. R., McGuire, R. J., & Walton, H. J. (1979). Reduction of stereotyped body-rocking using variable time reinforcement: Practical and theoretical implications. *Journal of Mental Deficiency Research, 23*, 175–185.

Touchette, P. E., MacDonald, R. F., & Langer, S. N. (1985). A scatter plot for identifying stimulus control of problem behavior. *Journal of Applied Behavior Analysis, 18*, 343–351.

Turner, W. D., Realon, R. E., Irvin, D., & Robinson, E. (1996). The effects of implementing program consequences with a group of individuals who engaged in sensory maintained hand mouthing. *Research in Developmental Disabilities, 17*, 311–330.

Vollmer, T. R., Borrero, J. C., Wright, C. S., Van Camp, C., & Lalli, J. S. (2001). Identifying possible contingencies during descriptive analyses of severe behavior disorders. *Journal of Applied Behavior Analysis, 34*, 269–287.

Vollmer, T. R., Marcus, B. A., & LeBlanc, L. (1994). Treatment of self-injury and hand mouthing following inconclusive functional analyses. *Journal of Applied Behavior Analysis, 27*, 331–344.

Wacker, D. P., Berg, W., Harding, J., & Cooper-Brown, L. (2004). Use of brief experimental analyses in outpatient clinic and home settings. *Journal of Behavioral Education, 13*, 213–226.

Wacker, D. P., Steege, M. W., Northup, J., Sasso, G., Berg, W., Reimers, T., . . . Donn, L. (1990). A component analysis of functional communication training across three topographies of severe behavior problems. *Journal of Applied Behavior Analysis, 23*, 417–429.

Watters, R. G., & Watters, W. E. (1980). Decreasing self-stimulatory behavior with physical exercise in a group of autistic boys. *Journal of Autism and Developmental Disorders, 4*, 379–387.

Wilder, D. A., Draper, R., Williams, W. L., & Higbee, T. S. (1997). A comparison of noncontingent reinforcement, other competing stimulation, and liquid rescheduling for the treatment of rumination. *Behavioral Interventions, 12*, 55–64.

Wilder, D. A., Kellum, K. K., & Carr, J. E. (2000). Evaluation of satiation resistant head rocking. *Behavioral Interventions, 15*, 71–78.

Wolery, M., Kirk, K., & Gast, D. L. (1985). Stereotypic behavior as a reinforcer: Effects and side effects. *Journal of Autism and Developmental Disorders, 15*, 149–161.

Woods, T. S. (1983). The selective suppression of stereotypy in an autistic child: A stimulus control approach. *Behavioural Psychotherapy, 11*, 235–248.

Yang, L. J., & Bruner, J. D. (1996). Effects of providing sensory stimulation to decrease self-stimulatory behavior: Using additional food to suppress hand-mouthing behavior. *Behavioral Interventions, 11*, 119–130.

Zhou, L., & Goff, G. A. (2000). Effects of increased response effort on self-injury and object manipulation as competing responses. *Journal of Applied Behavior Analysis, 33*, 29–40.

20

Self-Injurious Behavior

PETER STURMEY, LINDSAY MAFFEI-ALMODOVAR, MAYA S. MADZHAROVA, AND JOSHUA COOPER

OVERVIEW

Diagnostic Criteria

The *Diagnostic and Statistical Manual* (4th ed., text rev. [*DSM-IV-TR*]) of the American Psychiatric Association (American Psychiatric Association [APA], 2000) defined self-injurious behavior (SIB) as a subtype of stereotypic movement disorder. A stereotypic movement disorder was defined by six criteria:

> A. Repetitive, seemingly driven, and non-functional motor behavior . . . . B. [which], markedly interferes with normal activities or results in self-inflicted bodily injuries that requires medical treatment . . . C. If mental retardation is present, the stereotypic or self-injurious behavior is of sufficient severity to become a focus of treatment. D. . . . [and] is not better accounted for by a compulsion . . . a tic . . . a stereotypy that is part of a Pervasive Developmental Disorder, or hair pulling . . . E. . . . not due to the direct physiological effects of a substance or a general medical condition. F. The behavior persists for 4 weeks or longer. (p. 121)

The *DSM-IV-TR* then adds a specifier that stated, "With self-injurious behavior: if the behavior results in bodily damage that requires specific treatment (or that would result in bodily damage if protective measures were not used)" (p. 121). The *International Classification of Diseases*, 10th edition (*ICD-10*;

World Health Organization, 1993), used the same approach and essentially the same criteria. The *ICD-10*'s guide for intellectual disabilities (mental retardation) (World Health Organization, 1996) also included *repetitive self-injury*, defined as "repeated self-injury among adults sufficient to cause tissue damage. It includes self-injury which would cause tissue damage if protection or restraint were not used. Repeated self-injurious behavior includes head banging, face slapping, eye poking and biting of hands, lips or other body parts. *Excludes* Stereotyped movement disorders of childhood F98.4, nailbiting and thumbsucking F98.8" (p. 5).

Similar definitions of SIB can also be found in modified diagnostic criteria designed specifically for use with people with developmental disabilities. These modified diagnostic criteria generally have made few substantive modifications to standard criteria. For example, the *Diagnostic Manual—Intellectual Disability* (*DM-ID*) (Fletcher, Loschen, Stravrakaki, & First, 2007) made no modification to the *DSM-IV-TR* criteria other than to add "without obsessions and cognitive symptoms" (p. 198) to criterion A. Thus, there is a general agreement among different diagnostic systems about the inclusion criteria, namely that SIB is a subtype of stereotyped movement disorder because of its repetitive and apparently nonfunctional nature and must present a significant problem above and beyond that accounted for by intellectual disabilities alone if present. There is also agreement concerning the exclusion criteria, namely exclusion of other disorders, such as trichotillomania, obsessive-compulsive disorder (OCD), Tourette's syndrome, and so forth.

The most common forms of SIB include head banging, self-biting, picking at skin or body orifices. SIB may also include hitting body parts, which sometimes involving use of objects (American Psychiatric Association, 2000, p. 119). As noted by Christiansen (2009, p. 9), although these are the most common topographies of SIB, there are many other less common forms (Furniss & Biswas, 2009; Griffin, Williams, Stark, Altmeyer, & Mason, 1984; Iwata et al., 1994; Matson & LoVullo, 2008; Maurice & Trudel, 1982) including "hair pulling, eye pressing or gouging, hitting one's knuckles together, finger or arm biting, chin hitting, self-pinching, self-hitting or slapping, hand mouthing, and skin abrasions caused by rubbing one's skin against objects" (Christiansen, 2009, p. 9).

Despite this convergence of opinion, clinical experience indicates that things are not so simple. For example, although many forms of SIB are indeed repetitive and sometimes topographically very similar to stereotypic movement disorder, some are not. For example, a person may smash their arm through a window resulting in lacerations, or a person may throw themselves on the floor one time in response to some social interaction resulting in head injuries. These examples are not repetitive behavior, but rather a single occurrence of SIB. A second consideration is that, although diagnostic criteria exclude other disorders, such as various anxiety disorders, some research has explicitly linked stereotypy and SIB as forms of anxiety disorders such as OCD (Hellings & Warnock, 1994). Finally, the notion that stereotypic movement disorders and SIB are "seemingly driven and nonfunctional" is directly challenged by the extensive empirical behavioral literature showing that both are operant

behavior maintained by social and nonsocial consequences (Iwata et al., 1994; Newell, Sprague, Pain, Deutsch, & Meinhold, 1999; Oliver, Hall, & Murphy, 2005; Richman & Lindauer, 2005).

SIB is often distinguished from self-harm, such as that found in people with borderline personality disorder, major depressive disorder, bulimic and anorexic disorders, and some forms of adolescent acting out. Self-harm can be distinguished from SIB both topographically and functionally. Self-harm often involves cutting or burning one's body or ingesting dangerous objects or substances and is related to para-suicidal behavior and suicide in some people. Self-harm appears to function to regulate mood in persons who do not have other forms of effective self-regulation to do so (Gratz & Chapman, 2007; Jeglic, 2005), whereas mood regulation is generally not imputed as a function of SIB.

Demographic Variables

Some forms of repetitive behavior and even SIB are commonly observed in typically developing infants (Thelen, 1979), but they typically wax and wane during development and never come to dominate the child's behavioral repertoire. In contrast, intellectual disability (ID) is a specific risk factor for SIB. The degree of intellectual disability is positively correlated with risk of SIB. For example, Rojahn, Borthwick-Duffy, and Jacobson (1993) found that the prevalence of SIB was 4%, 7%, 16%, and 25% in people with mild, moderate, severe, and profound ID. Certain genetic syndromes associated with ID are also associated with increased risk of SIB and also with specific topographies of SIB. For example, Lesch-Nyhan syndrome is often associated with finger- and lip-biting as well as other forms of SIB, whereas Prader-Willi syndrome is often associated with secretive skin picking.

Impact of Disorder

The impact of the disorder varies widely. Some forms of SIB may be mild, relatively transient, and easily managed. Other forms result in significant medical concerns ranging from mild abrasions to chronic skin infections, such as those associated with chronic hand mouthing, fractures, blindness, and probable increased brain damage, and require lifelong, intrusive, and expensive treatments. Indeed, in some rare cases SIB may directly or indirectly result in death, although data on this question are contradictory (Nissen & Haverman, 1997; Wieseler, Hanson, & Nord, 1995). SIB also places people at risk for restrictive and/or dangerous behavior management practices. For example, SIB may commonly be managed in both institutional and community settings by physical, personal, or chemical restraint, PRN ("as-needed") medication, time-out, and seclusion. Some forms of SIB, such as chronic regurgitation, are sometimes treated by risky medical procedures, such as gastric surgery, which itself caries risk of death. Sometimes SIB is managed by medical interventions such as removal of teeth for self-biting or teeth guards, for example, in Lesch Nyhan Syndromes (Hall, Oliver, & Murphy, 2001). SIB often places the person at risk of restrictive residential programming, one-on-one staffing, and social rejection and ostracism from family members, staff, professionals, and peers. Thus, although the impact of the disorder is quite varied, in some cases the impact is lifelong and very negative.

APPLIED BEHAVIOR ANALYSIS

Consensus Panel Recommendations

We reviewed two expert panels for possible recommendations relating to SIB. One made no specific recommendations related to SIB (National Autism Center [NAC], 2009); however, Rush and Frances (2000) recommended specific treatments to reduce SIB in individuals with developmental disabilities.

These authors reported the opinions of a large number of leading experts regarding treatment decisions for multiple problem behaviors present among individuals with intellectual disabilities. They reported that applied behavioral analysis, client and/or family education, and managing the environment were the treatment of choice for a wide range of problem behaviors including SIB. Specifically regarding SIB, their expert panel recommended (from most to least preferred): (a) behavioral parent and teacher/staff training, (b) accelerating differential reinforcement procedures, (c) social skills and communication training, (d) decelerating differential reinforcement procedures, (e) response interruption and prevention, and (f) response cost. Thus, this expert panel recommended behavioral treatments of SIB as the preferred method of psychosocial treatment and did not recommend other psychosocial interventions, such as cognitive therapy, sensory treatments, or psychotherapy for SIB.

Randomized Controlled Trials

Although literature searches conducted for this chapter identified no randomized controlled trials (RCTs) specifically for SIB, some RCTs evaluated behavioral treatment for some broadly defined category of behavior problems that included SIB (e.g., Aman et al., 2009); however, one group design study was already known to the first author.

Noting that both pharmacological and behavioral treatments of SIB had support in the literature, Mace, Blum, Sierp, Delaney, and Mauk (2001) conducted a group experiment with compared placebo, haloperidol, and applied behavior analytic interventions based on functional analyses. The authors selected 15 participants from a larger group of 30 children and adults with intellectual disabilities and SIB who were admitted to an inpatient unit specializing in treatment of SIB. After a thorough medical evaluation, the authors selected 15 participants who were diagnosed with operant SIB. These 15 participants were aged approximately between 4 and 32 years. Eleven were male and four were female. Eleven had diagnoses related to intellectual and other developmental disabilities, of whom seven had a diagnosis of autism and one had a diagnosis of attention-deficit/hyperactivity disorder. All participants took part in functional analyses to identify the function of their SIB. Prior to the functional analyses all psychotropic medication was stopped for 11 participants. The remaining two participants continued to take their psychotropic medications because of the severity of their SIB and because it would have taken too long to taper the high doses of their medication; thus, these participants remained on constant doses of medication during this experiment. The dependent variables were the change in the rate of SIB over the highest functional analysis condition, differences between rate of SIB between haloperidol and placebo and scores on the *Aberrant Behavior Checklist* (Aman, Singh, Stewart, & Field, 1985). The authors defined treatment responders as those participants who had a 75% or greater reduction in SIB over baseline.

Ten of 12 participants who received ABA were responders and only two of eight who received haloperidol were responders (Fisher exact test, $p = 0.054$.) ABA also resulted in a significant reduction in SIB compared to baseline ($p = 0.015$) and placebo ($p = 0.021$.) Haloperidol plus ABA was also more effective than baseline ($p = 0.038$) and haloperidol alone ($p = 0.012$), but haloperidol alone did not differ from baseline. There were no differences detected on the *Aberrant Behavior Checklist*, perhaps due to the small samples or other factors related to lack of experimental power. A review of the data in Aman et al.'s (1985) Table 2 indicated that all but one participant receiving ABA had large reductions in SIB and none had increases, whereas the response of participants receiving haloperidol varied, ranging from 100% reduction to 217% increase. The authors concluded that individuals with operant SIB were more likely to respond to ABA than haloperidol. Although

promising, this study had one very significant limitation, which was that it did not report treatment integrity, generalization, and maintenance data. Thus, this study did not meet Chambless and Hollon's (1998) criteria for a well-designed study. Further, there are not yet any independent replications. Thus, there is no acceptable evidence from RCTs that identifies evidence-based practices for SIB.

Meta-Analyses of Single-Subject Experiments

We searched PsychINFO, ERIC, PubMed, and MEDLINE® using the following terms: "(Self injury or self-injury OR SIB OR head banging OR skin picking OR hair pulling OR trichotillomania OR self-biting OR scratch OR eye poking OR rectal digging) AND (meta-analysis OR randomized control trial OR RCT OR systematic review OR literature review or review of research)." Articles were retained only if they were meta-analyses or systematic reviews examining treatment of SIB among individuals with intellectual or other developmental disabilities. Studies examining SIB among typically developing individuals, or examining treatments of behavior problems other than SIB were excluded. This search identified 136 abstracts from PsychINFO, 19 from ERIC, and 3,362 from PubMed and MEDLINE. Four systematic reviews and meta-analyses were identified from this group of articles and a hand search of Christiansen (2009) also identified one additional systematic review (Christiansen, 2005).

The earliest systematic review of treatment of SIB came from Sternberg, Taylor, and Babkie (1994), who reviewed intervention research on SIB in individuals with severe and profound intellectual disabilities conducted between 1980 and 1990. They identified 143 studies that contained 195 participants. They calculated Chi-square statistics with Yates correction through cross tabulations for type of SIB and type of intervention. They defined efficacy of intervention as the mean percentage decrease in SIB from baseline level to treatment. The authors also coded 39 study variables, such as demographic variables, SIB characteristics, and treatment variables, and calculated the percentage reduction over baseline for each paper and then ranked the effectiveness of five treatment types and the relationship between the 39 study variables and treatment effectiveness.

The five treatments ranked from most to least effective and mean percentage reduction in SIB over baseline were: (1) differential reinforcement with another simultaneously administered approach, such as Differential Reinforcement of Other Behavior (DRO) and response interruption ("over 95% decrease"); (2) other combined approaches using more than one intervention in different phases of the treatment (the authors did not state an average percentage reduction); (3) overcorrection or only differential reinforcement used alone ("approximately 80% reduction"); (4) aversives ("approximately 75% reduction"); and (5) use of instructional/environmental approaches ("only 50% reduction"). Sternberg et al. (1994) also reported that drug interventions were ineffective for more than 50% of participants.

Kahng, Iwata, and Lewin (2002) conducted the second systematic review, which focused on behavioral treatment of SIB. These authors generated a database of articles on the assessment and treatment of SIB through searches of *Current Contents*, PsychINFO, and ERIC published between 1964 and 2000. Their inclusion criteria were: (a) the study presented data on the behavioral intervention used for treatment of SIB, either alone or in conjunction with other problem behaviors; (b) the participants were diagnosed with developmental disability; (c) if the study used multiple participants, only those who engaged in SIB were included in the analysis; (d) the study used a single-subject experimental design. The exclusion criteria were: (a) the study assessed SIB but there was no treatment implemented; (b) there was no individual data reported;

(c) the study involved only pharmacological interventions or combination with behavioral interventions. There were 296 studies with 706 participants.

Kahng et al. (2002) divided the treatments reviewed into seven categories: (1) antecedent manipulation; (2) extinction; (3) reinforcement; (4) punishment; (5) restraint; (6) response blocking; (7) several subcategories, such types of reinforcement (e.g., DRO and Differential Reinforcement of Alternate Behavior [DRA]) and punishment (e.g., timeout and overcorrection). The authors calculated the effect size by determining the value of the last five data points from the baseline and treatment phases. If there were fewer than five data points, they used the maximum and equal number of data points available in baseline and treatment. They measured the distance between a data point and the x-axis and y-axis using an Alvin divider to calculate the approximate value of these points. They used these approximate values to then obtain condition means for baseline and treatment. Finally, they calculated the treatment effect size by subtracting the mean treatment value from the mean baseline value, dividing by the mean baseline value, and multiplying by 100%. The results indicated a percentage of change.

The overall mean effect size was an 83.7% reduction in SIB. When they analyzed each treatment type individually they found that the mean effect sizes (and number of studies) ranked from largest to smallest effect sizes were: (a) mechanical restraint (91.4%, $N = 33$); (b) response blocking (90.6%, $N = 4$); (c) antecedent manipulation (87.2%, $N = 39$); (d) punishment (83.2%, $N = 194$); (e) extinction (82.6%, $N = 26$); and (f) reinforcement (73.2%, $N = 195$). The results for combination of interventions from most to least effective were: (a) antecedent manipulation and reinforcement (100%, $N = 4$), (b) antecedent manipulation and mechanical restraint (99.5%, $N = 2$) and extinction and mechanical restraint (99.5%, $N = 1$), (c) extinction and punishment

(97.8%, $N = 4$), (d) extinction and response blocking (97.2%, $N = 2$), (e) antecedent manipulation and response block (95.8%, $N = 6$), (f) punishment and mechanical restraint (94.7%, $N = 2$), (g) antecedent manipulation and extinction (94.3%, $N = 15$), (h) punishment and mechanical restraint (87.7%, $N = 4$), (i) reinforcement and punishment (83.7%, $N = 92$), (j) extinction and reinforcement (77.4%, $N = 36$), and (k) reinforcement and response block (72.6%, $N = 8$). In addition, the authors indicated that the mean effectiveness increased from 1964 to 1995 (mean = 82.4%, range = 32.1% to 100%) and from 1996 to 2000 (mean = 98.8%, range = 85.6% to 93.7%.) Thus, Kahng et al. (2002) concluded that behavioral treatments for SIB are effective. Despite the relatively large differences between effect sizes for different types of treatment, Kahng et al. (2002) were reluctant to conclude which treatments were most effective due to two main reasons. First, the authors stated there was a possibility that studies may have been reluctant to report treatment failures. Second, since not all studies based their intervention on functional assessment, this may have also affected the treatment efficacy. For example, interventions such as extinction and differential reinforcement have been shown to be largely affected by the results of functional assessment, whereas interventions such as nonreinforcement procedures and mechanical restraints may not be affected by behavioral function (Kahng et al., 2002).

A third systematic review of treatment of SIB comes from Lang et al. (2010), who systematically reviewed behavioral interventions for chronic skin-picking in individuals with developmental disabilities. They searched only English-language-peer-reviewed studies in ERIC, MEDLINE, Psychology and Behavioral Sciences Collection, and PsychINFO with no restriction on the year of publication. Articles retained had to meet two inclusion criteria: (1) the definition of skin-picking had to include the use of fingers or a handheld object to self-inflict tissue damage by pulling, scratching, lancing, digging, or gouging anywhere on the body, including eye socket, mouth, nose, and rectum; and (2) a behavioral intervention had to be used as treatment for at least one person with a developmental disability. The authors excluded articles that focused only on assessment, description, or prevalence and those focused on medication treatments without behavioral interventions. They identified 16 studies with 19 participants that met inclusion criteria, which included treatments such as the use of protective clothing, DRO, Differential Reinforcement of Incompatible Behavior (DRI), DRA, antecedent manipulation, and punishment. The authors described each study in terms of five predetermined categories to provide and compare behavioral interventions used. The five categories were: participant characteristics, assessment procedures and results, intervention procedures, results of the intervention, and certainty of evidence.

Behavioral treatment had large effect sizes across all 16 studies: The mean Proportion of Nonoverlapping Data (PND) was 97% (range 75%–100%). They found large effect sizes for different types of dependent variables, such as frequency of skin picking and number of open sores. Additionally, nine studies reported that treatment persisted from 2 to 35 months posttreatment. Aversive or restrictive interventions, and antecedent- and reinforcement-based interventions were all effective; however, due to the small number of studies and participants and because most studies implemented multiple treatment components simultaneously, Lang et al. (2010) were unable to compare the effectiveness of different treatments. Thus, they concluded that there was preliminary evidence that behavioral treatments were effective for skin-picking, but also noted that the number of participants ($N = 19$) and use of treatment packages limited the confidence in these conclusions. Although these authors were correctly cautious about the limits to this research literature, we note that this literature does meet Chambless and

Hollon's criteria for an effective treatment since there were more than three small-N experiments with more than nine participants, all with very large reductions in SIB.

Christiansen (2005) conducted the third meta-analysis of behavioral treatment of SIB among individuals with autism in her Master's thesis. She searched PsychINFO, ERIC, PubMed, and Digital Dissertations databases in addition to individualized hand searches of 13 relevant journals. Her inclusion criteria were: (a) published in English; (b) had graphic display of the treatment data; (c) each participant had a diagnosis of autism, Asperger's disorder, or pervasive developmental disorder; (d) the age of participants ranged from 18 months to 21 years 11 months; (e) the target behavior included at least one form of SIB; (f) the studies were published in peer-reviewed journals between 1965 and 2003; (g) there was enough information reported to allow calculation or estimation of an ES statistic; (h) each single-subject design study included at least 5 data points in each phase; (i) each study used an AB, ABA, ABAB, multiple baseline design, multiple probe design, or alternating treatment design. Twenty studies with a total of 21 participants met inclusion criterion. She compared the results for overall ES of behavioral interventions obtained through two different statistical measures: interpreted-time-series analysis for autocorrelated data (ITSACORR) and hierarchical linear model (HLM).

The results from both ITSACORR and HLM calculations indicated an ES of –2.32 and an ES of –1.45, respectively. (Negative ES indicated reductions in SIB.) According to the ITSACORR results, the most effective treatment for SIB was the use of aversive interventions yielding an ES of –2.83. Interventions employing positive and combined techniques were found to have much smaller effect, yielding an ES of –0.52 and –0.67, respectively. Interestingly, however, results obtained using the HLM measure yielded almost equal ES for effectiveness of positive (–2.34), aversive (–2.24), and combined (–2.43)

interventions. Therefore, Christiansen (2005) concluded that behavioral treatments for SIB were effective in children with autism spectrum disorders. She also noted several significant limitations to this literature, including that there were no studies involving parents as change agents and no participants with Asperger's syndrome. The reader should note that this study only included papers published up to 2003 and thus may not include many more recent studies on treatment of SIB in people with autism spectrum disorders.

Christiansen (2009) went on to expand her earlier study to conduct the most comprehensive meta-analysis of treatment of SIB among children and adolescents with all developmental disabilities for her doctoral dissertation. She used three search methods: electronic databases; search of reference lists of relevant studies, review articles, chapters, and books; and computer and hand searches of available volumes of relevant journals. The inclusion criteria were: (a) published in English; (b) participants were diagnosed with developmental disability; (c) participants were between the age of 11 months and 21 years 11 months; (d) target behavior included at least one form of self-injury; (e) studies were dissertations or published articles; (f) studies were published between 1964 and 2008; (g) there was sufficient quantitative information to permit calculation or estimation of effect size statistic; (h) studies used single-subject designs; (i) there was a graph display of raw data demonstrating changes in behavior; and (j) each study used AB, ABA, ABAB, multiple baseline designs or multiple-probe designs, or alternating treatment designs. The total number of studies included in the review was 224, which included 343 participants. Christiansen (2009) used only the HLM to calculate the average effect sizes across all studies and estimate the reliable variance of each individual study.

The overall ES was –3.35, which was large and significantly different from 0. This indicated that behavioral treatments are very effective for the reduction of SIB. Christiansen (2009) also compared the effectiveness of different behavioral interventions and rank ordered them from most to least effective. The combination of aversive and nonaversive methods was the most effective intervention (ES = –4.19), followed by aversive methods alone (ES = –3.67), communication-based interventions (ES = –3.32), combination of aversive and communication-based interventions (ES = –2.91), and last nonaversive interventions yielded the smallest ES (–2.33). Sensory interventions had no significant effect, as the ES did not differ from 0 (ES = –0.89). (See the following section on sensory treatments, which also indicates that sensory treatments for SIB are ineffective.) Christiansen (2009) concluded that behavioral interventions for SIB were very effective and resulted in very large effect sizes that were robust.

Summary and Comment

These five meta-analyses converge on an overall conclusion, namely, that behavior analytic treatment of SIB is highly effective. We can be confident in these conclusions because they result from hundreds of experimental studies conducted by many independent researchers over a 50-year period. Further, all five meta-analyses reported large effect sizes. Thus, this literature far surpasses Chambless and Hollon's (1998) modest criteria for evidence-based practice.

These five meta-analyses diverge on several points, such as the precise ranking of the effectiveness of behavioral treatments. It is difficult to interpret Sternberg et al.'s (1994) study since it did not report complete and precise data and it is difficult to be confident in Christiansen's (2005) conclusions because of the relatively small sample size (N = 20 studies). Lang et al. (2010) only focused on skin picking and refrained from rank ordering treatments by effectiveness. This leaves two

systematic reviews with very large samples of studies (Christiansen, 2009; Kahng et al., 2002). These two studies concurred on certain general points. For example, both ranked combined punishment and reinforcement procedures as more effective than other procedures. Similarly, both ranked punishment alone as more effective than reinforcement alone or antecedent interventions alone. (Kahng et al., 2002 themselves refrained from making conclusions about the relative ranking of the effectiveness of different forms of behavioral treatment.) Thus, although reinforcement procedures alone and antecedent interventions alone may sometimes result in large effect sizes, they are less effective than combined punishment plus other procedures or combined punishment plus reinforcement procedures. This finding may be controversial to some and echoes the controversy over the use of punishment (Cipani, 2004; Favell et al., 1982). It is likely that these two papers both review overlapping sets of papers; nevertheless, the additional research since 2002 appears not to have materially changed the conclusions of Kahng et al. (2002).

These five meta-analyses demonstrated that behavioral treatments meet and, indeed, greatly exceed Chambless and Hollon's (1998) criteria for evidence-based practice. They also did not identify any alternate psychosocial treatments that might be evidence-based practices. Nevertheless, these studies have significant limitations. First, none reported ES for replacement behaviors. Second, although ES might be related to speed or response to treatment—a very clinically significant consideration in selecting treatment for SIB—none explicitly measured this outcome. Third, like many meta-analyses, all were considerably out of date at the time of this review and thus were incomplete since they excluded many recent studies. Finally, none reported measures of the quality of the studies and thus the question as to whether ES were smaller when studies were conducted in a more rigorous fashion remains unanswered.

Training Caregivers

Training routine caregivers, such as family members and staff, to implement effective interventions is an important component for the treatment of developmental disabilities. Thus, we conducted a literature search using MEDLINE, PsychINFO, and ERIC. The search strings utilized were: "(self injury OR self-injury OR SIB OR head banging OR skin picking OR hair pulling OR self-biting OR scratch* OR eye poking OR rectal digging) AND (parent training OR staff training OR caregiver training OR parent-training OR staff-training OR caregiver-training OR train parents OR train caregivers OR staff training OR train staff)." Inclusion criteria were: (a) the study must have had a parent or staff training component; (b) treatment integrity data must have been collected for the caregiver training component; (c) each subject must have exhibited SIB and had a developmental disability; (d) the study must have been an experiment such as an RCT, multiple-baseline, or reversal design or other small N experimental design; (e) the study must have measured SIB; and (f) the study must have been published in a peer-reviewed journal. The database searches returned a total of 446 abstracts, of which 26 were potentially relevant studies; only one study met all inclusion criteria (Northup, Wacker, Berg, Kelly, Sasso et al., 1994).

Northup et al. investigated whether school staff could learn to conduct a functional analysis and implement an intervention to decrease the occurrence of SIB. Five children with a developmental disability aged 5 to 11 years participated, of whom four displayed SIB; two, Mike and Rebecca, wore restraint devices in school. The other two children displaying self-injury, Kit and Jane, were not fitted with any restraint devices. SIB included head banging, self-hitting, and hand mouthing. All teachers who volunteered to participate were certified special education teachers with 1 to 10 years' experience, but none had any experience conducting functional analysis or Functional Communication Training (FCT). The three target child behaviors were appropriate classroom behavior, inappropriate behavior (such as aggression and SIB), and manding. The authors reported SIB data separately from other inappropriate behavior. The authors collected data weekly during both active treatment times and during 2 years of treatment during nontreatment times using 10-second partial interval sampling. A second observer scored 36% of the functional analysis sessions and 26% of the treatment sessions. Mean interobserver agreement was 93% for functional analysis and 85% for treatment.

Treatments were individualized for each subject based on their functional analysis and typically used FCT, except for Kit, whose intervention used noncontingent music and time-out from music for SIB. All the other subjects learned to mand for either breaks or attention via sign or recorded message on a cassette.

Following a 2-day workshop to train staff to implement and maintain interventions, Northup et al. evaluated treatment using brief treatment withdrawal reversal designs. Northup et al. trained staff using instruction, rehearsal, and feedback; they systematically faded feedback as staff achieved proficiency. Northup et al. also used modeling during on-site technical assistance, which continued throughout the study on a weekly or biweekly basis. The study took place over a 2-year period for each participant.

Following treatment there was a dramatic decrease in SIB to low and often near-zero levels for all four children. The PNDs were 95%, 98%, 100%, and 100% (mean PND = 98%). Additionally, for some children appropriate behavior approached 100% of intervals. The authors also collected data on treatment integrity, which included observations of teachers correctly delivering consequences for mands and for SIB. Treatment integrity data were 100%, 100%, 27%, and 52% for Jane, Kit, Rebecca, and Mike, respectively; treatment integrity was generally markedly higher for mands than for SIB. Despite the low treatment integrity for Rebecca and Mike, SIB for both subjects were reduced to near-zero levels by the end of the treatment.

This search revealed only one small *N* experimental study with four participants that met inclusion criteria; thus, caregiver training meets Chambless and Hollon's (1998) criteria for a promising rather than evidence-based treatment. Note that, although Rush and Francis' (2000) consensus panel recommended both staff training and parent training as the highest ranked intervention for psychosocial treatment of problem behavior, the evidence to support this opinion in the specific case for treatment of SIB is very limited. One limitation to this study is the data on treatment integrity. On the one hand, it might be tempting to dismiss the study on the basis of low treatment integrity data, especially for staff response to SIB. Alternatively, one might argue that it was sufficient to thin but not eliminate reinforcement schedule for SIB and increase the reinforcement density for the alternate response to reduce SIB (Piazza et al., 1997; Worsdell, Iwata, Hanley, Thompson, & Khang, 2000). Since the authors did not experimentally evaluate the relative contributions of different components of the treatment package, however, this point remains moot.

SNOEZELEN

Snoezelen includes two treatment components: an environment that includes visual, auditory, tactile, and olfactory stimulation such as a variety of lights, gently stimulating music, aromas, and tactile objects; and an interaction component in which staff encourage patients to select desired activities and assist patients with the equipment when necessary (Chan, Thompson, Chau, Tam, & Chiu, 2009). Research on the use of the Snoezelen rooms

for clients with developmental and intellectual disabilities has increased in recent years (Hogg, Cavet, Lambe, & Smeddle, 2001) and a number of studies have attempted to establish the efficacy of Snoezelen to decrease SIB (Carson, Clare, & Murphy, 1998; Fagny, 2000; Fava & Strauss, 2009; Kwok, To, & Sung, 2003; Martin, Gaffan, & Williams, 1998; McKee, Harris, Rice, & Silk, 2007; Savarimuthu, 2005; Shapiro, Parush, Green, & Roth, 1997; Singh et al., 2004; Stadele & Melaney, 2001; Withers and Ensum, 1995). There have also been a few systematic reviews of Snoezelen (Chan et al., 2009; Hogg et al., 2001; Lancioni, Cuvo, & O'Reilly, 2002). These reviews have noted significant limitations in the literature, such as identifying only one experiment in the literature (Chan et al., 2009) and poor quality of the studies (Lancioni et al., 2002), leading Hogg et al. (2001) to conclude that the use of Snoezelen to treat SIB was highly questionable.

We searched PsycArticles, PsycInfo, PubMed, ERIC, and Education and Research Complete using the following combination of terms: "Self injury or self-injury OR SIB OR head banging OR skin picking OR hair pulling OR trichotillomania OR self-biting OR scratch OR eye poking OR rectal digging AND Snoezelen OR multi sensory OR multisensory OR multi-sensory OR multi sensory environment OR multi-sensory environment OR multisensory environment OR MSE." This search yielded only three potentially relevant articles. Therefore, we extended the search to Google Scholar using the same search terms. This search yielded an additional nine articles. A hand search of each article's reference section identified four more articles. The inclusion criteria were: (a) published in a peer-reviewed journal either in English or translated to English, (b) included participants with developmental or intellectual disabilities exhibiting SIB, (c) included SIB as a behavior targeted for decrease and measured self-injury separately from other behaviors, (d) employed RCTs (or small *N* experimental designs) to measure the effects of a Snoezelen room on SIB for included participants, (e) reported using treatment manuals, and (f) used outcome measure tools that have demonstrated reliability and validity in previous research.

Three articles were systematic reviews (Chan et al., 2009; Hogg et al., 2001; Lancioni et al., 2002), seven did not collect data on SIB separately from other behaviors (De Bunsen, 1994; Fagny, 2000; Fava & Strauss, 2009; Kenyon & Hong, 1998; Kwok et al., 2003; McKee et al., 2007; Shapiro et al., 1997), and six were case studies (Carson et al., 1998; Savarimuthu, 2005; Stadele & Melaney, 2001; Withers & Ensum, 1995) or quasi-experimental designs (Fava & Strauss, 2009; Kwok et al., 2003). Martin et al. (1998) was excluded as it did not randomly assign subjects to conditions and Singh et al. (2004) did not measure treatment integrity or use a treatment manual. Thus, no studies met all inclusion criteria. Therefore, there is no evidence that Snoezelen is an evidence-based practice for SIB.

SENSORY INTEGRATION THERAPY

We reviewed one meta-analysis (Vargas & Camilli, 1999) and several recent systematic reviews of sensory integration therapy (SIT) (Baranek, 2002; Case-Smith & Jane-Arbesman, 2008; Hyatt, Stevenson, & Carter, 2009; May-Benson & Koomar, 2010; Stephenson & Carter, 2009). None of these systematic reviews specifically assessed the effects of SIT in reducing SIB in individuals with developmental disabilities. (Recall also that Christensen's [2009] meta-analysis of treatment of SIB also concluded that the effect size for sensory treatments did not differ significantly from zero and hence was an ineffective treatment for SIB.) However, two experiments compared SIT with behavioral interventions.

Mason and Iwata (1990) assessed the effects of SIT and behavioral interventions in reducing SIB in three individuals with severe to profound intellectual disabilities. The experiment had three phases. In Phase 1, experimenters conducted functional analyses to assess the functions of participants' SIB. In Phase 2, they exposed participants to 15-minute SIT sessions during which participants had noncontingent access to apparatus delivering auditory, kinesthetic, tactile, vestibular, and visual stimulation. During Phase 3, experimenters treated participants' SIB using behavioral interventions including extinction for attention- and escape-maintained SIB and DRO, response interruption, and noncontingent access to toys for stereotyped SIB. Experimenters employed reversal designs during the second and third phases of the experiment.

The experimenters found that attention-maintained SIB varied as a function of withheld or noncontingent attention during SIT sessions and decreased during behavioral intervention when attention was withdrawn contingent on SIB occurrence. Similarly, escape-maintained SIB varied with the presentation of demands during SIT and decreased as a function of escape extinction during behavioral intervention. Stereotypic SIB increased during SIT and decreased in response to a combination of DRO, response interruption, and noncontingent access to toys during behavioral intervention. Thus, SIB was a direct function of the manipulation of its controlling variables and the effects that occurred during SIT seemed to be artifactual and not due to SIT itself.

Devlin, Leader, and Healy (2009) also conducted a direct comparison of SIT and ABA to treat SIB in 9-year-old boy with autism. A functional analysis indicated that the function of his SIB was to escape demands. Using an alternating treatment design, Devlin et al. (2009) compared an ABA, function-based intervention with SIT. They found that during the alternating treatment design the behavioral intervention was consistently superior to SIT. Further, continued implementation of behavioral treatment resulted in yet further reductions in SIB. They concluded that the behavioral intervention was more effective than SIT for this child's SIB.

These systematic searches and two experimental studies lead to the conclusion that SIT has indeed been evaluated for its effects on SIB, but it is not an evidence-based treatment for SIB. These conclusions are also supported by Christiansen's (2009) meta-analysis, which found that the ES for SIT were not significantly different from zero. Further, in two comparisons of SIT with ABA, ABA was consistently superior to SIT for both experiments, providing limited evidence, since they only involved two experiments with a total of four participants, indicating that ABA is a more effective treatment than SIT for SIB.

SOCIAL STORIES

A literature search for "(self injur* OR self-injur* OR SIB OR head banging OR skin picking OR hair pulling OR self-biting OR scratch*) AND (social stories)" on MEDLINE, PsycInfo, and ERIC returned five abstracts. None of those results were relevant to social stories or self-injury. These findings are congruent with the NAC's (2009) systematic review of social stories and autism, which also found some evidence that social stories may be effective in improving interpersonal and self-regulatory skills, but found no evidence that social stories were an effective treatment for any type of problem behavior.

OTHER PSYCHOSOCIAL TREATMENTS

We searched PsychINFO, ERIC, PubMed, and MEDLINE using the following combination of terms: "self injury or self-injury or SIB or head banging or skin picking or hair pulling or trichotillomania or self-biting or scratch or eye poking or rectal digging and meta-analysis OR randomized control trial OR RCT OR

systematic review OR literature review OR review of research and meta-analysis or randomized control trial or RCT or systematic review or literature review or review of research." The inclusion criteria were: (a) studies were meta-analyses or systematic reviews, (b) examining treatment of SIB, and (c) among individuals with intellectual or other developmental disabilities. No abstracts met these criteria. Again, these results are in agreement with the Rush and Frances (2000) expert panel and the NAC report, both of which found no or little evidence to support other psychosocial treatments for SIB at this time. For example, the NAC only found three studies of cognitive behavior therapy and did not include a review of psychotherapy, presumably because of the absence of outcome research.

EVIDENCE-BASED PRACTICES

This chapter conducted multiple literature searches to identify evidence-based practices for treatment of SIB: Five systematic reviews only found evidence to support ABA as an evidence-based practice, often with large effect sizes (Christiansen, 2009; Kahng et al., 2002). These two largest systematic reviews provided evidence that punishment and combined treatments that included punishment and other interventions were associated with the largest effects sizes. There was also evidence that reinforcement alone and antecedent interventions alone could also be effective, although these interventions were associated with smaller effect sizes. We also identified two experiments showing that ABA was superior to SIT. These empirical results concur with Rush and Frances (2000) expert panel and the NAC's (2009) recent review of treatment for autism spectrum disorders. Thus, we conclude that: (a) ABA is an evidence-based practice in the treatment of SIB; (b) ABA often has large effect sizes, especially for combined packages of punishment and other interventions; (c) other behavioral interventions, such as reinforcement alone and antecedent interventions alone are also evidence-based practices, but have smaller effect sizes than combined packages; (d) there is limited evidence that ABA may be superior to SIT; therefore (d) ABA is the preferred psychosocial treatment for SIB.

There were many important limitations to this literature. For example, there was very limited evidence—only one experimental study with four children—to support caregiver-mediated interventions for SIB. Although Lang et al. (2010) found strong evidence of maintenance over many months for behavioral treatment of skin picking, other systematic reviews did not report data on this important issue. Similarly, none of these systematic reviews reported data on generalization. Although some systematic reviews included studies with adults, Christiansen (2005, 2009) excluded studies with adults. Although there are studies of behavioral treatment of SIB with adults, there are far fewer studies with adults than with children and adolescents. Thus, although behavioral interventions meet Chambless and Hollon's criteria for evidence-based practice, much is left unanswered by these systematic reviews. Nevertheless, ABA remains the psychosocial treatment of choice. Rush and Frances' (2000) expert panel also reached this conclusion. Thus, both systematic reviews and the only expert panel on this question have reached the same conclusion.

We found no evidence to support the effectiveness of any other psychosocial treatment. This included treatments such as SIT, Snoezelen, and social stories, which have extensive empirical literatures, but were of poor quality, largely failed to address SIB specifically, and sometimes contained well-designed experiments with negative results. It is possible that some sensory treatments, such as Snoezelen and SIT, might be effective when these methods are combined with the results of functional assessments and analyses. For example, Snoezelen might be an effective treatment for SIB maintained by automatic positive reinforcement if it provided that reinforcement noncontingently. Similarly, if Snoezelen incorporated the results of preference assessments for sensory items and the availability of those items was associated with low rates of SIB then Snoezelen might be an effective treatment for SIB. On the other hand, if a particular Snoezelen environment provided aversive sensory stimulation and the function of a person's SIB was to escape that aversive stimulation, or if Snoezelen failed to deliver the sensory reinforcer maintaining a person's SIB noncontingently, then Snoezelen might be a harmful treatment. Future research should evaluate whether combining the results of functional analyses can enhance the effectiveness of sensory treatments and eliminate harmful sensory interventions.

We also found no evidence to support the effectiveness of other types of psychosocial treatments such as cognitive behavior therapy, counseling psychoanalytic, and psychodynamic therapies, where we were unable to find any empirical literature evaluating their efficacy in treating SIB. This chapter did not review the evidence for pharmacological and other biological treatments or the potential interactions between these and psychosocial treatments. This area remains controversial and future systematic reviews should address this issue.

This chapter was based upon searches of databases such as PubMed, and so forth. These searches have significant limitations. For example, there are numerous synonyms for terms related to SIB and developmental disabilities and it is likely that it is impossible to detect all relevant articles using any systematic searches. For example, Duggan, Morris, and Adams (1997) identified all 56 RCTs published in the *Journal of Intellectual Disabilities Research* between 1974 and 1994. They then searched PsychLit and MEDLINE and only found 36 and 37 of these RCTs abstracted in these databases, respectively. Further, electronic searches in a variety of databases using a variety of search terms never identified all these RCTs using any search strategies. They observed that many titles and abstracts of these articles omitted relevant words and terms, such as "randomized," which would have facilitated accurate and complete searches. Further, the databases we searched may be limited, both in terms of which journals they include and how far back their databases go and thus, may not include some relevant articles.

REFERENCES

Aman, M. G., McDougle, C. J., Scahill, L., Handen, B., Arnold, L. E., Johnson, C., . . . Wagner, A. (2009). Medication and parent training in children with pervasive developmental disorders and serious behavior problems: Results from a randomized clinical trial. *Journal of the American Academy of Child and Adolescent Psychiatry, 48*, 1143–1154.

Aman, M. G., Singh, N. N., Stewart, A. W., & Field, C. J. (1985). The Aberrant Behavior Checklist: A behavior rating scale for the assessment of treatment effects. *American Journal of Mental Deficiency, 89*, 485–491.

American Psychiatric Association (APA). (2000). *Diagnostic and statistical manual of mental disorders* (4th ed., text rev.). Washington, DC: Author.

Baranek, G. T. (2002). Efficacy of sensory and motor interventions for children with autism. *Journal of Autism and Developmental Disorders, 32*, 397–422.

Carson, G., Clare, I., & Murphy, G. (1998). Assessment and treatment of self-injury with a man with a profound learning disability. *British Journal of Learning Disabilities, 26*, 51–57.

Case-Smith, J., & Jane-Arbesman, M. (2008). Evidence based review of interventions for autism used in or of relevance to occupational therapy. *The American Journal of Occupational Therapy, 62*, 416–429.

Chambless, D. L., & Hollon, S. D. (1998). Defining empirically supported therapies. *Journal of Consulting and Clinical Psychology, 66*, 7–18.

Chan, S., Thompson, D., Chau, P., Tam, W., & Chiu, I., (2009). Effects of multisensory therapy on behaviour of adult clients with developmental disabilities. *JBI Library of Systematic Reviews, 7*, 309–353.

Christiansen, E. (2005). Effectiveness of behavioral treatments for the reduction of self-injury in Autism: A meta-analysis (Unpublished master's thesis, University of Utah, Salt Lake City, Utah). *Abstracts International: Section B. Sciences and Engineering, 71*(1-B), 647.

Christiansen, E. (2009). Effectiveness of interventions targeting self-injury in children and adolescents with developmental disabilities: A meta-analysis. *Dissertation Abstracts International: Section B. Sciences and Engineering, 71*(1-B), 647.

Cipani, E. (2004). *Punishment on trial*. Reno, NV: Context Press.

De Bunsen, A. (1994). A study in the use and implications of the Snoezelen resource at the Limington House School. In R. Hutchinson & J. Kewin (Eds.), *Sensations and disability: Sensory environments for leisure, Snoezelen, education and therapy*, (pp. 138–162). Chesterfield, England: Rompa.

Devlin, S., Leader, G., & Healy, O. (2009). Comparison of behavioral intervention and sensory-integration therapy in the treatment of self-injurious behavior. *Research in Autism Spectrum Disorders, 3*, 223–231.

Duggan, L. M., Morris, M., & Adams, C. E. (1997). Prevalence study of the randomized controlled trials in the *Journal of Intellectual Disability Research*: 1957–1994. *Journal of Intellectual Disability Research, 41*, 232–237.

Fagny, M. (2000). L'impact de la technique du Snoezelen sur les comportements indiquant l'apaisement chez les adultes autistes [Impact of Snoezelen technique on the calming behaviors of autistic adults]. *Revue Francophone de la Defiance Intellectuelle, 11*, 105–115.

Fava, L., & Strauss, K. (2009). Multi-sensory rooms: Comparing effects of the Snoezelen and the stimulus preference environment on the behavior of adults with profound mental retardation. *Research in Developmental Disabilities, 31*, 160–171.

Favell, J. E., Azrin, N. H., Baumeister, A. A., Carr, E. G., Dorsey, M. F., Forehand, R., . . . Solnick, J. V. (1982). The treatment of self-injurious behavior. *Behavior Therapy, 13*, 529–554.

Fletcher, R., Loschen, E., Stavrakaki, C., & First, M. (Eds.). (2007). *Diagnostic Manual-Intellectual Disability (DM-ID): A textbook of diagnosis of mental disorders in persons with intellectual disability*. Washington, DC: National Association for the Dually Diagnosed Press and American Psychiatric Association.

Furniss, F., & Biswas, A. (2009). Treatment of self-injurious behaviour in children with intellectual disabilities. In J. L. Matson, F. Andrasik, & M. L. Matson (Eds.), *Treating childhood psychopathology and developmental disabilities* (pp. 333–372). New York, NY: Springer Science+Business Media.

Gratz, K. L., & Chapman, A. L. (2007). The role of emotional responding and childhood maltreatment in the development and maintenance of deliberate self-harm among male undergraduates. *Psychology of Men and Masculinity, 8*, 1–14.

Griffin, J. C., Williams, D. E., Stark, M. T., Altmeyer, B. K., & Mason, M. (1984). Self injurious behavior: A statewide prevalence survey, assessment of severe cases, and follow-up of aversive programs. In J. C. Griffin, M. T. Stark, D. E. Williams, B. K. Altmeyer, & H. K. Griffin (Eds.), *Advances in the treatment of self injurious behavior* (pp. 1–25). Austin, TX: Department of Health and Human Services.

Hall, S., Oliver, C., & Murphy, G. (2001). Self-injurious behaviour in young children with Lesch-Nyhan syndrome. *Developmental Medicine and Childhood Neurology, 43*, 745–749.

Hellings, J. A., & Warnock, J. K. (1994). Self-injurious behavior and serotonin in Prader-Willi Syndrome. *Psychopharmacology Bulletin, 30*, 245–250.

Hogg, J., Cavet, J., Lambe, L., & Smeddle, M. (2001). The use of "Snoezelen" as multisensory stimulation with people with intellectual disabilities: A review of research. *Research in Developmental Disabilities, 22*, 353–372.

Hyatt, K., Stephenson, J., & Carter, M. (2009). A review of three controversial educational practices: Perceptual motor programs, sensory integration and tinted lenses. *Education and Treatment of Children, 32*, 313–342.

Iwata, B. A., Pace, G. M., Dorsey, M. F., Zarcone, J. R., Vollmer, T. R., Smith, R. G., . . . Willis, K. D. (1994). The functions of self-injurious behavior: An experimental- epidemiological analysis. *Journal of Applied Behavior Analysis, 27*, 215–240.

Jeglic, E. (2005). The function of self-harm behavior in a forensic population. *International Journal of Offender Therapy and Comparative Criminology, 49*, 131–142.

Kahng, S. W., Iwata, B. A., & Lewin, A. B. (2002). Behavioral treatment of self-injury, 1964 to 2000. *American Journal of Mental Retardation, 107*, 212–221.

Kenyon, J., & Hong, C. S. (1998). An explorative study of the function of a multisensory environment. *British Journal of Therapy and Rehabilitation, 5*, 619–623.

Kwok, H. W. M., To, Y. F., & Sung, H. F. (2003). The application of a multisensory Snoezelen room for people with learning disabilities—Hong Kong experience. *Hong Kong Medical Journal, 9*, 122–126.

Lancioni, G. E., Cuvo, A. J., & O'Reilly, M. F. (2002). Snoezelen: An overview of research with people with developmental disabilities and dementia. *Disability and Rehabilitation, 24*, 175–184.

Lang, R., Didden, R., Machalicek, W., Rispoli, M., Sigafoos, J., Lancioni, G., . . . Soyean, K. (2010). Behavioral treatment of chronic skin-picking in individuals with developmental disabilities: A systematic review. *Research in Developmental Disabilities, 31*, 304–315.

Mace, F. C., Blum, N. A. J., Sierp, B. J., Delaney, B. A., & Mauk, J. E. (2001). Differential response of operant self-injury to pharmacologic versus behavioral treatment. *Journal of Developmental & Behavioral Pediatrics, 22*, 85–91.

Martin, N. T., Gaffan, E. A., & Williams, T. (1998). Behavioral effects of long-term multisensory

stimulation. *British Journal of Clinical Psychology, 37*, 69–82.

Mason, S. A., & Iwata, B. A. (1990). Artifactual effects of sensory-integrative therapy on self-injurious behavior. *Journal of Applied Behavior Analysis, 23*, 361–370.

Matson, J. L., & LoVullo, S. V. (2008). A review of behavioral treatments for self injurious behaviors of persons with autism spectrum disorders. *Behavior Modification, 32*, 61–76.

Maurice, P., & Trudel, G. (1982). Self-injurious behavior: Prevalence and relationships to environmental events. In J. H. Hollis & C. E. Meyers (Eds.), *Life-threatening behavior: Analysis and intervention* (pp. 81–103). Washington, DC: American Association on Mental Deficiency.

May-Benson, T. A., & Koomar, J. A. (2010). Systematic review of the research evidence examining the effectiveness of interventions using a sensory integrative approach for children. *American Journal of Occupational Therapy, 64*, 403–414.

McKee, S. A., Harris, G. T., Rice, M. E., & Silk, L. (2007). Effects of a Snoezelen room on the behavior of three autistic clients. *Research in Developmental Disabilities, 28*, 304–316.

National Autism Center (NAC). (2009). *National standards report*. Retrieved from www.nationalautism center.org/pdf/NAC%20Standards%20Report.pdf

Newell, K. M., Sprague, R. L., Pain, M. T., Deutsch, K. M., & Meinhold, P. (1999). Dynamics of self-injurious behaviors. *American Journal on Mental Retardation, 104*, 11–21.

Nissen, J. M., & Haverman, M. J. (1997). Mortality and avoidable death in people with severe self-injurious behaviour: Results of a Dutch study. *Journal of Intellectual Disabilities Research, 41*, 252–257.

Northup, J., Wacker, D. P., Berg, W. K., Kelly, L., Sasso, G., & DeRaad, A. (1994). The treatment of severe behavior problems in school settings using a technical assistance model. *Journal of Applied Behavior Analysis, 27*, 33–47.

Oliver, C., Hall, S., & Murphy, G. (2005). The early development of self-injurious behavior: Evaluating the role of social reinforcement. *Journal of Intellectual Disability Research, 48*, 591–599.

Piazza, C. C., Fisher, W. W., Hanley, G. P., Remick, M. L., Contrucci, S. A., & Aitken, T. L. (1997). The use of positive and negative reinforcement in the treatment of escaper maintained destructive behavior. *Journal of Applied Behavior Analysis, 30*, 279–298.

Richman, D. M., & Lindauer, S. E. (2005). Longitudinal assessment of stereotypical, proto injurious, and self-injurious behavior exhibited by young children with developmental delays. *American Journal on Mental Retardation, 110*, 439–450.

Rojahn, J., Borthwick-Duffy, S. A., & Jacobson, J. W. (1993). The association between psychiatric diagnoses and severe behavior problems in mental retardation. *Annals of Clinical Psychiatry, 5*, 163–170.

Rush, J. A., & Frances, A. (Eds.). (2000). Treatment of psychiatric and behavioral problems in mental retardation. *American Journal on Mental Retardation, 105*, 159–228.

Savarimuthu, D. (2005). Can the "Snoezelen" affect self-injurious behaviour? A case study. In J. P. Morgan (Ed.), *Psychology of aggression* (pp. 161–172). Hauppauge, NY: Nova Science Publishers.

Shapiro, M., Parush, S., Green, M., & Roth, D. (1997). The efficacy of the "Snoezelen" in the management of children with mental retardation who exhibit maladaptive behaviors. *The British Journal of Developmental Disabilities, 43*, 140–155.

Singh, N. N., Lancioni, G. E., Winton, A. S. W., Molina, E. J., Sage, M., Brown, S., & Groeneweg, J. (2004) Effects of Snoezelen room, activities of daily living skills training, and vocational skills training on aggression and self-injury by adults with mental retardation and mental illness. *Research in Developmental Disabilities, 25*, 285–293.

Stadele, N. D., & Melaney, N. A. (2001). The effects of a multisensory environment on negative behavior and functional performance on individuals with autism. *University of Wisconsin-La Crosse: Journal of Undergraduate Research, 4*, 211–218.

Stephenson, J., & Carter, M. (2009). The use of weighted vests with children with autism spectrum disorders and other disabilities. *Journal of Autism and Developmental Disorders, 39*, 105–114.

Sternberg, L., Taylor, R. L., & Babkie, A. (1994). Correlates of interventions with self-injurious behavior. *Journal of Intellectual Disabilities Research, 38*, 475–485.

Thelen, E. (1979). Rhythmical stereotypies in normal human infants. *Animal Behaviour, 27*, 699–715.

Vargas, S., & Camilli, G. (1999). A meta-analysis of research on sensory integration treatment. *American Journal of Occupational Therapy, 53*, 189–198.

Wieseler, N. A., Hanson, R. H., & Nord, G. (1995). Investigation of mortality and morbidity associated with severe self-injurious behavior. *American Journal on Mental Retardation, 100*, 1–5.

Withers, P. S., & Ensum, I. (1995). Successful treatment of self-injury incorporating the use of DRO, a Snoezelen room, and orientation cues. *British Journal of Learning Disabilities, 23*, 164–167.

Worsdell, A. S., Iwata, B. A., Hanley, G. P., Thompson, R. T., & Khang, S. W. (2000). Effect of continuous and intermittent reinforcement for problem behavior during functional communication training. *Journal of Applied Behavior Analysis, 33*, 167–179.

World Health Organization (WHO). (1993). *The ICD-10 classification of mental and behavioural disorders: Diagnostic criteria for research.* Geneva, Switzerland: Author. Retrieved from www.who.int/classifications/icd/en/GRNBOOK.pdf

World Health Organization (WHO). (1996). *ICD-10 guide for mental retardation.* Geneva, Switzerland: Author. Retrieved from www.who.int/mental_health/media/en/69.pdf

21

Smoking in Children and Adolescents

ROGER E. THOMAS

OVERVIEW OF DISORDER

Diagnostic Criteria

There are three nicotine-related disorders: nicotine dependence, nicotine withdrawal, and nicotine-related disorder not otherwise specified (NOS) (American Psychiatric Association, 2000). Substance-related disorders are characterized by tolerance, withdrawal, increased consumption, persistent desire or unsuccessful attempts to reduce consumption, spending a great deal of time related to the substance, reduction or discontinuation in important activities, and continued use despite knowledge of harm. Substance withdrawal disorders are characterized by a substance-specific syndrome due to cessation of heavy and prolonged use that causes clinically significant distress or impairment on functioning not due to a general medical disorder. Nicotine-related disorders (NOS) are other disorders that do not meet the criteria for these disorders. There are a number of measures of smoking and nicotine-related disorders (Piper, McCarthy, & Baker, 2006; Richardson et al., 2007).

Demographic Variables

A search in MEDLINE and EMBASE was conducted on December 20, 2008, using the terms *smoking* or *tobacco* or *cigarette* and

adolescent or *child* and *prevalence*. The Global Youth Tobacco Surveillance organization surveys students 13–15 years old at 4–5-year intervals in 140 World Health Organization member states, and 11 other areas (Warren et al., 2008). The sampling frame is all public and private schools in a geographic area, the probability of school selection is proportional to the number of students in the specified grades, and classes in the schools are selected randomly. Students participate voluntarily and anonymously (Warren et al., 2008). The average prevalence of cigarette smoking in surveys between 2000 and 2007 was 9.5% and ranged from 19.2% in Europe to 4.9% in the Eastern Mediterranean. Boys were significantly more likely than girls to smoke cigarettes in all regions except Europe and the Americas. Tobacco other than cigarettes in the form of bidis, pipes, smokeless tobacco, or water pipes were used by 10% of students, with the highest rate in Europe (12.0%) and the lowest in Western Pacific (6.6%).

Impact of Disorder

Tobacco smoke is a complex mixture of thousands of different molecules including aldehydes, carbon monoxide, hydrogen cyanide, ketones, nicotine and other alkaloids, nitrogen oxides, *N*-nitrosamines, polyaromatic hydrocarbons, and quinine, many of which have been demonstrated to independently contribute to the adverse cardiovascular and carcinogenic effects of tobacco smoke (Frobisher et al., 2008). A search in MEDLINE and EMBASE was conducted on December 22, 2008, using the terms *smoking* or *tobacco* or *cigarette* and *morbidity* or *mortality* or *adverse effects*. In national data in 22 European countries for ages 30–69 years, the key factor accounting for differences in mortality rates was educational status: Males with less education had mortality rates 2 to 5 times greater than those with more education and females 2 to 3 times more. Smoking accounted for 22% of mortality differences for males and 6% for females, compared to 11% for alcohol for males and 6% for females. Smoking rates were strongly correlated with educational status (Mackenbach et al., 2008; Ozasa et al., 2008; Woloshin, Schwartz, & Welch, 2008).

Smoking is related to early aging, organ dysfunction, morbidity, and mortality. It causes a wide range of cancers, including cancers of the esophagus, stomach, pancreas, liver, pharynx, larynx, lung, bladder, kidney, cervix, and myeloid leukemia (Frobisher et al., 2008). It affects male sterility (Said, Ranga, & Agarwal, 2005); causes adverse effects during pregnancy, such as abruption, preterm delivery, smaller fetuses, altered placental development (Zdravkovic, Genbacev, McMaster, & Fisher, 2005), stillbirths, and perinatal deaths (Lavezzi, Ottaviani, & Matturi, 2005). It also causes vascular problems, such as early vascular aging (Nilsson, 2008), decreases blood vessel dilatation, increases prothrombotic and proinflammatory blood vessel processes (Adamopoulos, van de Borne, & Argacha, 2008), and intermittent claudication (Kollerits et al., 2008) and lung problems, such as chronic obstructive lung disease, chronic bronchitis, asthma (Pelkonen, 2008), and worsening of asthma (Thomson, Chaudhuri, & Livingston, 2004). It is estimated that smoking causes 7% of all deaths annually, and costs more than $200 billion annually, with half the costs in the developing countries. Expenditures on tobacco are greater than health expenditures in all developing countries (Centers for Disease Control, 2008).

EVIDENCE-BASED PREVENTION AND TREATMENT OF SMOKING IN CHILDREN AND ADOLESCENTS

Systematic Reviews and Meta-Analyses

The Cochrane Collaboration Tobacco Review Group has systematically reviewed a wide range of preventive and treatment interventions. Their reviews constitute the main body of this chapter. Before the authors of a Cochrane Collaboration Systematic Review conduct a review, they specify in a protocol their review of the literature to derive an answerable, focused question, the literature search, how they will review abstracts and full-text articles for relevance, and their data entry, risk of bias, and statistical analysis methods. The protocol is then critiqued by international experts, and after the reviewers have satisfactorily responded to the experts' and group editor's suggestions, they conduct a thorough literature search with the help of a librarian expert in the area, including Central, a database of over 525,000 randomized controlled trials (RCTs) in medicine and related areas, the Cochrane Tobacco Review Group database, and the Grey literature. Two reviewers independently screen abstracts and full-text articles and enter study data onto prespecified data collection forms. The reviewers write to authors of potentially includable articles to ask for details of methods or results not presented in the original articles.

In October 2008 the Cochrane Collaboration introduced a uniform method of assessing bias across all reviews, by asking for every RCT the answers to six questions: (1) Is there adequate sequence generation (i.e., allocation of individuals or groups to intervention or control)?; (2) Is there allocation concealment?; (3) Is there blinding?; (4) Are incomplete outcome data addressed?; (5) Are the articles reporting the study free of selective reporting?; and (6) Is the study free of other bias? The answers are either Yes, Unclear, or No. Higgins and Green (2008) provide a detailed table of ways of assessing the answers. A method of integrating evidence from different types of study designs is now coded using GRADE-PRO software.

The reviews described in the following were all conducted before these new uniform methods were introduced. Future versions of this chapter will report systematic reviews updated with these new methods. We report the methods of assessing risk of bias used by the reviewers, and the methods the reviewers used to evaluate evidence from different types of study when they included nonrandomized studies. For each systematic review the primary article that states the main data is cited by author and date. The study design and additional data for many studies are often presented in several additional publications, and readers of this chapter can access them in the original reviews. Some studies tested several interventions that were appropriately assessed by different reviews; thus, some studies form the database for more than one review. Where it was appropriate to pool data, pooled odds ratios are reported. Where it was not possible, individual trial results are reported. There is a problem in this "head counting" approach, because this ignores the different strength of results in different studies. The Cochrane Collaboration Systematic Review by Sowden and Arblaster (1998) on mass media interventions to prevent smoking in young people will not be presented because it has not been updated since 1998.

PREVENTION

School-Based Interventions

Systematic Review and Meta-Analyses

R. Thomas and Perera (2006) performed a Cochrane Collaboration Systematic Review of

school-based interventions to prevent never-smokers from starting smoking, with the most recent substantive amendment on April 20, 2006. Researchers have tested five types of interventions: (1) information-giving (Bangert-Drowns, 1988); (2) social competence (Bandura, 1977), which teaches self-management, social, cognitive, and stress management skills; (3) social influence, based on persuasive communications theory (McGuire, 1968) and Evans' (1976) theory of psychological inoculation, which teaches students about current adolescent and societal norms about smoking, skills to resist offers of tobacco, how to assess influences to smoke from the media, peers, and family, and encourages a public commitment not to smoke; (4) combined social competence and social influence; and (5) multimodal, which combines school and community interventions to prevent child and adolescent tobacco use, including involving parents, stop-smoking programs for parents and teachers, and initiatives to change school, community, and state policies about tobacco use. One problem in assessing the independent effectiveness of interventions in schools is that there is a background of uneven activity involving many different tobacco education curricula, but few of these often state-mandated curricula have been rigorously evaluated (U.S. 2000 National Youth Tobacco Survey, 2001; Wenter, Blackwell, Davis, & Farrelly, 2002) or have been shown to be ineffective (Wiehe, Garrison, Christakis, Ebel, & Rivara, 2005). Studies often use different measures of tobacco use, either recording frequency (monthly, weekly, daily), or the number of cigarettes smoked, or they construct an index from multiple measures. This variety of measures is often intended to record the fact that young children begin smoking on a monthly basis, and as they get older proceed to weekly and daily smoking. We included all measures of smoking behavior.

We assessed the likelihood of four forms of bias and the extent to which RCTs minimized them. We first assessed selection bias, the systematic differences in comparison groups, due to imperfect randomization. Second, we assessed performance bias, such as problems with the implementation of the intervention, often due to incomplete intervention or contamination of the control group. Third, we assessed attrition bias, such as losses to follow-up or systematic differences in the rate of loss to follow-up among different groups. We considered studies with an overall attrition rate of greater than 20% to be at significant risk from attrition bias and where there was differential attrition between groups. We also considered bias more likely if there was no sensitivity analysis of the effect of this attrition on outcomes. Finally, we considered detection bias such as significant differences in outcome assessment. Additionally, we applied two statistical criteria: (1) whether there was a power calculation with attainment of the desired sample size, and (2) whether the statistical analysis was appropriate to the unit of randomization. Intraclass correlations (ICCs) in smoking behavior vary by school grade, frequency of smoking, gender, ethnicity, and time of school year. The ICCs typically inflate the needed sample size, and failure to take account of ICCs may lead to inadequate sample size and, thus, the risk of drawing false negative conclusions (Dielman, 1994; Murray & Hannan, 1990; Murray & Short, 1997; Palmer, Graham, White, & Hansen, 1998). We considered statistical analysis to be appropriate if: (a) the analysis used the same unit as randomization (e.g., if the intervention was delivered at the level of the school then the school was the unit of analysis), or (b) if ICCs were computed to adjust the analysis, or (c) if methods such as multilevel modeling accounted for cluster effects. We assigned studies to three quality categories: Category One, minimal risk of bias in all six areas previously noted; Category Two, a risk of bias in one or more areas; and Category Three, risks of bias in design and execution such that no conclusions can be drawn from the study. Odds ratios were obtained from individual

randomized trials with the control group as comparator, and using intention-to-treat analyses whenever possible (i.e., including in the denominator all participants originally randomized). Adjusted odds ratios from cluster RCTs were obtained either directly from those trials that reported them or by adjusting the original, nonadjusted odds ratios using an intraclass correlation coefficient of 0.097 for current smoking status averaged among all ethnicities (Siddiqui, Hedeker, Flay, & Hu, 1996). This allowed the pooling of both cluster and individually randomized trials. A pooled estimate of the effect was obtained using the generalized inverse variance method and a fixed-effect model. The adjusted odds ratio (logarithms) and the standard errors were calculated in Excel before entering them into RevMan 4.3. The χ^2 and I^2 statistics (Higgins, Thompson, Deeks, & Altman, 2003) were used to test the adequacy of the assumption of homogeneity for each set of comparisons. None of the 94 RCTs stated that they concealed the allocation of individuals or clusters to intervention or control.

We identified 23 Category One RCTs that met the criteria, 31 Category Two RCTs that contained one or more problems in design or conduct that could threaten the validity of their conclusions, and 40 Category Three RCTs with serious problems. Data to support these judgments are presented in the Notes column of the Included Studies Table in the Cochrane Review in the RevMan software. We focus on the 23 Category One and 31 Category Two studies, which tested the five psychological theories (Table 21.1).

Information-Giving Curricula Versus Control

There were 10 RCTs of information-giving, but only one Category One (Crone et al., 2003) and one Category Two (Ausems, Mesters, Van Breukelen, & De Vries, 2004) studies. Two trials (Ausems et al., 2004; Crone et al., 2003) provided information for statistical analysis of short-term prevention. Ausems et al. (2004)

TABLE 21.1 Evidence-Based Interventions in Schools to Prevent Children Starting Smoking

Intervention	Evidence-Based Effect
Information	1 Category One and 1 Category Two RCTs; both found positive significant effects; inappropriate to pool results
Social competence	2 Category One RCTS; no significant pooled effect
Social influences	13 Category One, 20 Category Two RCTS; no significant pooled effect
Social competence and influences	3 Category One, 7 Category Two RCTS: no significant pooled effect
Multimodal programs	4 Category One, 3 Category Two RCTS: 3 Category One RCTs found significant positive effects

reported that the in-school group was less likely to continue smoking compared to the control at 12 months (OR = 0.49; 95% CI = 0.29 to 0.84); and at 18 months the out-of-school group was less likely to start smoking compared to the Control (OR = 0.42; 95% CI = 0.18 to 0.96). Crone et al. (2003) reported a significant effect of the intervention (OR = 0.61; 95% CI = 0.41 to 0.91). Randomization in Ausems et al. (2004) occurred within two different groups. Nineteen schools already in the in-school intervention were randomly assigned to either receive or not receive the out-of-school intervention, and the other 17 schools were randomly assigned to receive or not receive the out-of-school intervention. This could be thought of as two separate RCTs, with out-of-school status being the intervention studied. The results presented do not make this separation, and pool the results from both RCTs, which breaks the randomization process and compares nonrandomized groups for the in-school intervention. Bias in the results, therefore, cannot be ruled out.

Social Competence Interventions Versus Control

There were three RCTs with two Category One trials, no Category Two trials, and one Category Three trial (Furr-Holden, Ialongo, Anthony, Petras, & Kellam, 2004; Kellam & Anthony, 1998; Storr, Ialongo, Kellam, & Anthony, 2002), which provided information for statistical analysis of long-term prevention. A nonsignificant positive effect was obtained from the pooled estimate (OR = 0.77; 95% CI = 0.48 to 1.22). The χ^2 (0.10, $p = 0.76$) and I^2 (0%) statistics were consistent with the assumption of homogeneity.

Social Influences Interventions Versus Control

There were 56 RCTs that met the inclusion criteria, with 13 Category One RCTs (Aveyard et al., 1999; Botvin, Griffin, Diaz, & Ifill-Williams, 2001; Brown et al., 2002; Cameron et al., 1999; Dijkstra, Mesters, De Vries, van Breukelen, & Parcel, 1999; Elder, Sallis, Woodruff, & Wildey, 1993; Ellickson & Bell, 1990; Ellickson, McCaffrey, Ghosh Dastidar, & Longshore, 2003; Hansen & Graham, 1991; Murray et al., 1992; Noland et al., 1998; Peterson, Kealey, Mann, Marek, & Sarason, 2000; Walsh et al., 2003), 20 Category Two RCTs (Abernathy & Bertrand, 1992; Armstrong, De Klerk, Shean, Dunn, & Dolin, 1990; Ary et al., 1990; Biglan, Glasgow, et al., 1987; Biglan, Severson, et al., 1987; Bush et al., 1989; Clarke, MacPherson, Holmes, & Jones, 1986; Clayton, Cattarello, & Johnstone, 1996; De Vries et al., 1994; Flay et al., 1995; Murray, Luepker, Johnson, & Mittelmark, 1984; Nutbeam, Macaskill, Smith, Simpson, & Catford, 1993; Schinke, Gilchrist, Schilling, & Senchal, 1986; Severson et al., 1991; Unger et al, 2004; Vartiainen, Paavola, McAlister, & Puska, 1998; Walter, Hofman, Connelly, Barrett, & Kost, 1985; Walter et al., 1986) and 23 Category Three trials. Thirteen trials (Abernathy & Bertrand, 1992; Armstrong et al., 1990; Ary et al., 1990; Aveyard et al., 1999; De Vries et al., 1994; De Vries et al., 2003; Ellickson & Bell, 1990; Ellickson et al., 2003; Flay et al., 1985; Hansen, Johnson, Flay, Graham, & Sobel, 1988; Lloyd et al., 1983; Telch, Miller, Killen, Cooke, & Maccoby, 1990; Unger et al., 2004) provided information for statistical analysis on short-term prevention and seven (Abernathy & Bertrand, 1992; Armstrong et al., 1990; Brown et al., 2002; Flay et al., 1985; Focarile & Scaffino, 1994; Hansen et al., 1988; Vartiainen et al., 1998) on long-term prevention. A nonsignificant positive effect on short-term prevention was obtained from the pooled estimate (OR = 0.93; 95% CI = 0.84 to 1.03); and a nonsignificant negative effect on long-term prevention (OR = 1.19; 95% CI = 0.99 to 1.42). For short-term prevention, the χ^2 (6.59, $p = 0.88$) and I^2 (0%) statistics are consistent with the assumption of homogeneity; while for long-term prevention the χ^2 (11.72, $p = 0.07$) and I^2 (48.8%) statistics are slightly above the numbers that provide complete reassurance about the homogeneity of the data. To test for possible bias in terms of trial quality, sensitivity analyses were done, including only high-quality trials. In the short-term outcome, seven studies provided information for the pooled effect estimate (Aveyard et al., 1999; De Vries et al., 1994; De Vries et al., 2003; Ellickson & Bell, 1990; Ellickson et al., 2003; Flay et al., 1985; Lloyd et al., 1983). The pooled effect estimate from these high-quality trials was OR = 0.97 (95% CI = 0.86 to 1.09). A similar analysis was performed for the long-term effect with only one trial (Brown et al., 2002) providing information of a beneficial but not statistically significant effect (OR = 0.86; 95% CI = 0.44 to 1.71).

Combined Social Competence and Social Influences Versus Control

There were 16 trials with three Category One RCTs (Spoth, Redmond, & Shin, 2001; Spoth, Redmond, Trudeau, & Shin, 2002; Sussman et al., 1995) and seven Category Two RCTs (Botvin, Baker, Dusenbury, Tortu, & Botvin, 1990; Botvin, Baker, Filazzola, & Botvin, 1990; Botvin, Griffin, Diaz, Miller, & Ifill-Williams, 1999; Gersick, Grady, & Snow, 1988; Jøsendal, Aarø, Torsheim, & Rasbash, 2005; Jøsendal, Aarø, & Bergh, 1998; Scheier, Botvin, & Griffin, 2001; Sussman et al., 1993). Six trials (Botvin & Eng, 1980, 1982; Botvin, Renick, & Baker, 1983; Botvin et al., 1999;

Scheier et al., 2001; Spoth et al., 2002) provided information for statistical analysis on short-term prevention and one trial reported on long-term prevention (Spoth et al., 2001). A nonsignificant positive effect on short-term prevention was obtained from the pooled estimate (OR = 0.72; 95% CI = 0.45 to 1.16), while the only trial on long-term prevention reported a nonsignificant positive effect (Spoth et al., 2001, OR = 0.55; 95% CI = 0.30 to 1.01). For short-term prevention, the χ^2 (0.39, $p = 1$) and I^2 (0%) statistics are consistent with the assumption of homogeneity. We carried out sensitivity analyses including only high-quality trials. In the short-term outcome only one study (Spoth et al., 2002) provided information showing a nonsignificant positive effect (OR = 0.75; 95% CI = 0.12 to 4.60), while for long-term prevention only Spoth et al. (2001) provided information.

Multimodal Compared to Single-Component Interventions

There were nine RCTs, with four Category One (Biglan, Ary, Smolkowski, Duncan, & Black, 2000; Elder et al., 1996; Perry et al., 1996; Perry et al., 2003) and three Category Two RCTs (De Vries et al., 2003; Piper, Moberg, & King, 2000; Schofield, Lynagh, & Mishra, 2003). Three of the Category One studies found positive significant results. Biglan et al. (2000) found after 3 years that the communities that received the community-plus-school program had net 4.0% less smoking ($p < 0.038$) and smokeless tobacco ($p < 0.04$) than communities that received the school-only program. Perry et al. (1996) found less smoking in the intervention group compared to control after 3 years for baseline nonusers of alcohol ($p < 0.05$). Perry et al. (2003) found that growth rates in tobacco use were lower in the DARE group compared to control ($p < 0.04$); and lower for DARE Plus compared to DARE ($p < 0.04$) for males, but found no significant differences for females. Elder et al. (1996) found there were no significant differences in the percentages in the experimental (4.7%) and control groups (5%) stating that they had ever smoked (OR = 1.01; 95% CI = 0.79 to 1.30) at 36 months; however, there was an increase from 55% to 75% among control schools in smoke-free policies, and from 45% to 78% among experimental schools (no statistical analysis reported). The authors stated that differences in the rate of policy adoption could not necessarily be attributed to the CATCH intervention, and that Minnesota schools already had a policy of 100% smoke-free schools.

Conclusions

Three of the four high-quality multimodal interventions showed a positive and significant effect. It is possible that combining social influences models with other components, such as community interventions and generic social competence training, may improve effectiveness; however, these interventions have not been subject to rigorous evaluation. In addition, there are few data from direct comparisons to suggest how large an increment might be achieved.

There are three problems in deciding whether the theories have been fully tested. Many studies set out to test a theoretical orientation, yet there are differences in components between studies testing the same theory, eclectic mixes of interventions, and, hence, disagreement about which are the effective intervention elements. A second problem is the relative lack of long-term studies testing interventions. Recognizing that the culture and social structure of adolescent populations varies widely both between and within societies, there are studies that have introduced ethnic-, age-, and gender-specific interventions; yet there are few studies that draw on the key elements of modern adolescent culture and no interventions designed by adolescents. Finally, program costs have not yet been evaluated.

Family Interventions

Systematic Review

R. E. Thomas, Baker, and Lorenzetti (2007) performed a Cochrane Collaboration Systematic

Review of interventions in families to prevent smoking, with the most recent substantive amendment on November 27, 2006. We identified 22 RCTs of family interventions to prevent smoking and, based on the four key Cochrane assessments for bias, rated six trials as Category One (Bauman et al., 2001; Curry et al., 2003; Schinke, Schwinn, Di Noia, & Cole, 2004; Spoth et al., 2001; Spoth et al., 2002; Storr et al., 2002, and follow-up report in Furr-Holden et al., 2004), 10 trials as Category Two (Ary et al., 1990; Biglan, Glasgow, et al., 1987; Cullen & Cullen, 1996; Elder et al., 1996; Forman, Linney, & Brondino, 1990; Jackson & Dickinson, 2003, 2006; Jøsendal et al., 1998; Jøsendal et al., 2005; Nutbeam et al., 1993; Stevens et al., 2002, and follow-up study Jones et al., 2005; Wu et al., 2003, and follow-up study Stanton et al., 2004), and six RCTs were placed in Category Three. The interventions were varied: Six focused exclusively on preventing smoking; five on preventing smoking and other addictions; one on alcohol and tobacco with a control intervention about gun safety and the use of bicycle helmets and car seatbelts; one on safe sex to reduce HIV risk, drugs, alcohol, drug selling, and monitoring and communicating techniques by parents; four to reduce cardiovascular risks and tobacco use or increase exercise; one counseled high-risk fathers about risk factors for coronary heart disease, smoking, and exercise; three improved parenting skills without a specific focus on tobacco control, although tobacco use was measured after the intervention; and one compared improvement in classroom management techniques compared to a family–school partnership to reduce children's risk behaviors. Follow-up varied from 1 year (eight trials), to 20 months (one trial), 2 years (two trials), 3 years (six trials), and one trial each at 6, 7, 15, and 27 to 29 years.

When the 16 Category One and Two studies were analyzed together it was found that: (a) When a family intervention was tested against a control group, four of the nine RCTs had significant positive effects, one showed significant negative effects, and four found no effect; (b) when a family intervention was tested against a school intervention, only one of the five RCTs had a significant positive effect and four showed no difference; (c) when a family program was added to a school program, none of seven RCTs found an incremental effect to a school program, which by itself had significant positive effects; (d) one RCT tested a family tobacco intervention against a family nontobacco safety intervention and showed no effects; and (e) two RCTs used family-based risk reduction programs, which did not include a specific tobacco intervention but measured tobacco outcomes, and both showed a decrease in tobacco use (see Table 21.2). The RCT that used general risk reduction interventions found the group that received the parent and teen interventions had less smoking than the one that received only the teen intervention. In the RCT that used CD-ROMs to reduce alcohol use, both groups receiving the alcohol reduction intervention had less smoking than the control. Heterogeneity did not permit pooling of data within interventions or overall.

TABLE 21.2 Evidence-Based Interventions in Families to Prevent Children Starting Smoking

Intervention	Evidence-Based Effect
Family intervention vs. control	4 of the 9 RCTs significant positive effects, 1 significant negative effects
Family intervention vs. school intervention	1 of the 5 RCTs significant positive effect
Family intervention added to school program	0 of 7 RCTs found an incremental significant positive effect
Family tobacco intervention vs. family nontobacco safety intervention	1 RCT no effects
Family risk reduction intervention	2 RCTs significant decrease

Conclusions

We did not find any explanation for these findings in differences in the number of sessions between studies. Intensity of training and/or fidelity of implementation by those who presented the interventions, however, appeared to be related to positive outcomes (see Table 21.3).

School Competitions

A search in MEDLINE and EMBASE was conducted on December 29, 2008, using the terms "smoking OR tobacco OR cigarette AND contest OR competition." By 2006 over 600,000 students in 16 European countries had participated in a European Community-sponsored competition "Be Smart—Don't Start," which asked classes to stay smoke-free for a 6-month period, defined as less than 10% of class members smoking, but the intervention has only been tested by two RCTs (Etter & Bouvier, 2006). No meta-analyses of RCTs were found.

Schulze, Mons, Edler, and Pötschke-Langer (2006) (cf. Schulze, Ehrmann, Schunk, & Pötschke-Langer, 2005) randomized 172 classes in 68 schools to either the "Be Smart—Don't Start" contest plus three weekly lessons ($N = 59$ classes; 2,163 students) or the control group ($N = 83$ classes; 1,880 students). At baseline there were significant differences between groups in percentages of never smokers (intervention: 61.7%; control: 52.1%) and current smokers (7.7% vs. 12.2%; $p < 0.05$). Smoking rates were measured 18 months later in the intervention group ($N = 980$) and control ($N = 872$) for a follow-up rate of 46%. No differences were found in percentages never smoking in the intervention (62.1%) or control groups (61.5%) (OR = 1.02; 95% CI = 0.83 to 1.24), or in the percentage of ex-smokers who had not relapsed in the intervention (45.1%) or control (41.4%) groups (OR = 1.07; 95% CI = 0.77 to 1.49); however, Hanewinkel, Wiborg, Isensee, Nebot, and Vartiainen's (2006) re-analysis noted that at 18 months 32 of 980 students in the intervention group and 116 of 872 in the control

TABLE 21.3 Effect of Intensity of Training and Fidelity of Implementation in Family Interventions

Category One and Two trials with positive outcomes

- Forman et al. (1990): Average completion rate of intervention activities in all coping skills sessions was 74%, with two-thirds of the students completing 9 or 10 of the 10 planned intervention sessions, although only 44% had a parent participate in the parent training intervention.
- Jackson and Dickinson (2006): Interviewers had 2 years of experience working with children and received an additional 30 hours of training.
- Jøsendal et al. (1998); Jøsendal et al. (2005): Two days of training were provided, plus a manual and evaluation questionnaire.
- Spoth et al. (2001): High levels of coverage of key concepts in both interventions.
- Storr et al. (2002): Sixty hours of training, with feedback on compliance and coverage from teachers and parents.
- Schinke et al. (2004): Did not describe any training for the research staff, and Wu et al. (2003) provided no process analysis.

Trials with negative or no effects

- Ary et al. (1990): Provided only 2 to 3 hours training to implementers.
- Curry et al. (2003): Found low levels (3%–22%) of discussion of tobacco use.
- Elder et al. (1996): Variable levels of program fidelity.
- Nutbeam et al. (1993): One day of training to implementers.
- Stevens et al. (2002): Only 47%–51% fidelity to program delivery.
- Biglan, Glasgow, et al. (1987) and Cullen and Cullen (1996) did not report on training or program fidelity.
- Spoth et al. (2002) reported relatively high levels of program compliance.

group did not provide information on their current smoking behavior.

Crone et al. (2003) invited all 54 community health services, except three participating in another study, to participate in the RCT by providing the names of schools "probably prepared to participate"; 14 community health services did participate and provided the names of 48 schools. A power computation showed that 1,400 students were needed in both the intervention and control groups to find a difference of a 5% increase in smoking rates with power of 80%, $\alpha = 0.05$, and an intraclass correlation of smoking by class $= 0.075$. Schools were ranked by size and whether they used a national drug education program. Some intervention and control schools continued to use this program during the intervention. The intervention was three classroom lessons on knowledge and attitudes about smoking and social influences to smoke, followed by a class agreement not to smoke or to quit for the next 5 months, with the possibility of winning six class prizes of €220 to 450. Twenty-six schools were randomized,

with 1,444 students in the intervention and 1,118 in the control group (average age 13 years). The control group had significantly more boys than the intervention. The final questionnaire 20 months later was completed by 537 in the intervention and 404 in the control for a follow-up rate of 37%, with higher nonresponse rates among smokers, especially in the control group. After 8 months there was a lower initiation rate in the intervention group (OR $= 0.61$; 95% CI $= 0.41$ to 0.90), but no difference after 20 months. The control group at baseline was not as large as the power computation required, and there was a high attrition rate.

The study in Germany (Hanewinkel & Wiborg, 2002, 2003; Wiborg & Hanewinkel, 2002; Wiborg, Hanewinkel, & Kliche, 2002) was not an RCT, and two other evaluations did not have a control group (Hanewinkel & Wiborg, 2006; Hrubá, Zachovalová, Matějová, & Daňková, 2007). The cost-effectiveness analysis by Hoeflmayr and Hanewinkel (2008) is moot because of the uncertainty about evaluation of the program.

Conclusion

There were no methodologically sound studies of smoking competitions.

Community Interventions

Systematic Reviews and Meta-Analyses

Sowden and Stead (2003) performed a Cochrane Collaboration Systematic Review with the last recent substantive amendment on 24 September 2002, and identified 17 studies. In two studies allocation of communities was random (Kaufman, Jason, Sawlski, & Halpert, 1994; Schinke, Tepavac, & Cole, 2000) and in four allocation was random after communities or areas had been matched on a number of different factors (Biglan et al., 2000; Hancock et al., 2001; Piper et al., 2000; Sussman, Dent, Stacy, & Craig, 1998). We will limit the data presented here to these six RCTs.

Biglan et al. (2000) randomly allocated eight communities in Oregon to a school-based program to prevent drug and tobacco use, and eight to a school-based program plus community intervention. The school-based intervention consisted of five sessions over a 1-week period in grades 6 (11 years of age) through 12 (17 years of age) with health facts, refusal skills, modeling refusal skills, public commitment, and peer-led discussion components. The community program included media advocacy, youth antitobacco activities, family communications about tobacco through parent–child activities arranged by the school or civic organizations, and activities to reduce illegal sales of tobacco to young people. Biglan et al. (2000) found no significant effects on the prevalence of cigarette smoking in the prior month using a random coefficients analysis for nested cross-sectional designs; however, when pairwise analysis comparing time points over the 3-year follow-up period was used, there was a decrease in smoking in communities that received the school plus community intervention that was 4.8% greater

($p = 0.022$) compared to the school-only communities, and 3.8% less after 3 years ($p = 0.038$). The prevalence of smoking in communities that received the schools-only intervention increased significantly from the first follow-up to the 3-year follow-up, with no significant change in the communities that received the schools plus community intervention; however, when biochemically verified measures were used (expired CO) there were no differences at any time point between the communities that received the schools intervention and those which received the schools plus community intervention.

Hancock et al. (2001) tested the Cancer Action in Rural Towns intervention in rural Australian towns with community facilitators, and accessed students through health-care providers, community organizations, media, retailers, schools, and workplaces. The interventions varied across towns and included media coverage, letters to schools in eight towns, letters to parents in five towns, surveys about smoking policies, and encouragement of smoke-free venues. The duration of the study varied from 2 to 3 years because the interventions were introduced at different rates in different towns. There was a problem with attrition, with 3,973 students in 20 towns at baseline and 3,230 in 19 towns providing 81% follow-up at evaluation 2 to 3 years later. Moreover, about 10% of the surveys contained some responses evaluated by the researchers as "nonsensical" and these students were not included. Smoking prevalence measured over the previous 4-week period increased over time in all towns, with intervention towns showing a greater increase, but in view of the methodological problems encountered, the interpretation of the results must be cautious.

Kaufman et al. (1994) evaluated a "culturally relevant" program to increase knowledge about the harmful effects of smoking and decrease cigarette use among 11- to 12-year-old inner city African American adolescents in Chicago. Two schools (131 students) were randomized to the seven-session school plus media intervention. This treatment consisted of homework with parents; children were prompted to read, watch, and participate in media interventions; a newspaper curriculum; eight radio announcements; a call-in talk show; a rap contest; and a billboard contest. One school was allocated to the media-only intervention with no prompts to participate (76 students). There were several methodological concerns: The intervention students at pretest smoked significantly more cigarettes than the media-only group ($p < 0.02$), the 11-year-olds in the media-only group had been exposed to the DARE antismoking program in the year prior to the intervention, and no adjustment was made for clustering. Smoking rates for both intervention and control schools decreased significantly from pretest to follow-up (3.20 vs. 4.04, $p < 0.0011$), but were not significantly different from each other at posttest or follow-up.

Piper et al. (2000) matched 21 schools in suburbs, small cities, and towns in Wisconsin on baseline risk of smoking, allowed them to choose between an intensive or age-appropriate intervention, then randomly assigned them to one of two Healthy for Life Project (HFL) intervention groups or a control group. Six schools were randomized to the age-appropriate intervention: The school-based components were inoculation, use of peer leaders, family values, health advocacy, short-term health effects, advertising and media influences, public commitment, peer norms, incentives to attend classes and complete assignments, and a parent orientation session prior to the program; the community-based intervention was a community organizer for 6 months in each of the 3 years. Seven schools were randomized to the intensive intervention: The school component was the same as for the age-appropriate intervention but the 54-lesson curriculum was delivered in one sequential 12-week block to the seventh-grade students, and the community component involved a community organizer for 15 months. Eight schools were randomized to

the control group, which received the standard health education curriculum. The study involved 2,483 students aged 11–15 years.

Past month cigarette use for the HFL group was 5% at pretest in the sixth grade, 22% in the ninth grade, and 28% in the tenth grade; for the age-appropriate HFL curriculum 4%, 24%, and 36%; and for the control group 5%, 24%, and 30%. For the HFL group compared to the control group the likelihood of smoking was significantly reduced ($p < 0.05$), but for the age-appropriate condition the likelihood of smoking was nonsignificantly increased compared to control.

Schinke et al. (2000) randomized by school 1,396 Native American youth in the third to fifth grades in 27 tribal or public schools on 10 reservations in five states to a school-based, a school-based plus community intervention, or a control group. The school-based intervention involved fifteen 50-minute sessions during one school term and two session boosters semiannually, with culturally tailored instruction with skills modeling by older peers, rehearsal, problem solving, personal coping and interpersonal communication, and an emphasis on local cultural traditions counter to substance abuse. The school plus community intervention used the same school intervention plus mobilization of Native American constituents including families, teachers, school guidance counselors, neighborhood residents, law enforcement, and commercial establishments, with activities to raise awareness of substance abuse prevention such as media releases, flyers and posters, meetings for parents and others, poster-making, mural painting, and skits. The control communities received no intervention. Smoking rates more than trebled to 35%–40% over the 3½ year period, but there were no significant differences in weekly smoking rates between the intervention and control groups.

Sussman et al. (1998), in Project Towards No Drug Abuse, randomized by school 1,074 high-risk youths aged 14–19 years in 21 Continuation high schools from a five-county region in southern California either to the classroom program (seven schools), the classroom program plus school-as-community intervention (seven schools), or to a control group with standard care (seven schools). The classroom program included a nine-lesson drug abuse prevention curriculum and a community newsletter to the schools. The classroom plus school-as-community used the same school component, and the community intervention consisted of weekly Associated Student Body Core group meetings for 6 months with six events per school, with drug-free parties, a drug awareness week, job training, and sports participation. No significant effects on cigarette use in the past 30 days were found.

Additional methodological concerns are that none of these six studies concealed allocation. Four verified nonsmoking biochemically: Three used expired air carbon monoxide (Biglan et al., 2000; Piper et al., 2000; Sussman et al., 1998), and Schinke et al. (2000) collected saliva samples but only analyzed a small percentage. The sample size in Biglan et al. (2000) increased from 1,303 at baseline to 1,430 after 3 years due to additions to the study. Of the 1,396 students at pretest in Schinke et al. (2000), 1,199 provided data after 3½ years (14% attrition). Two studies showed considerable attrition: Of the 1,981 sixth graders in Piper et al. (2000), 80% provided data in the ninth grade and 68% in the tenth; and of the 2,001 students at pretest in Sussman et al. (1998), 33% provided follow-up data after 1 year.

Conclusions

Three of six RCTs found no effects, one found lower smoking rates in the community intervention, one found higher rates in the community intervention, and one found lower smoking rates in one intervention arm (intensive community intervention) and nonsignificantly higher rates in another intervention arm (the age-appropriate community intervention) (Piper et al., 2000). The results are very mixed and no overall conclusions can be drawn.

Prevention of Tobacco Sales to Minors

Systematic Reviews and Meta-Analyses of Group Designs

Stead and Lancaster (2005) conducted a Cochrane Collaboration Systematic Review, last assessed as up-to-date on April 30, 2008. They identified 35 studies, of which 9 were RCTs, and we will focus on those. Additional data on design and outcomes has been added for this chapter from a reading of the primary studies. The store was the unit of randomization in six studies (Altman, Foster, Rasenick-Douss, & Tye, 1989; Altman, Rasenick-Douss, Foster, & Tye, 1991; Chapman et al., 1994; Gemson et al., 1998; Jason, Billows, Schnopp Wyatt, & King, 1996; Schofield, Sanson-Fisher, & Gulliver, 1997; Skretny, Cummings, Sciandra, & Marshall, 1990) and the community in three studies (Altman, Wheelis, McFarlane, Lee, & Fortmann, 1999; Cummings et al., 1998, and follow-up Cummings, Hyland, Perla, & Giovino, 2003; Forster, Wolfson, Murray, Wagenaar, & Claxton, 1997, and follow-up articles Blaine et al., 1997, Forster et al., 1998, and Chen & Forster, 2006). An additional five studies are not discussed here further: Four used a control group without randomization (Baggot, Jordan, Wright, & Jarvis, 1998; Keay, Woodruff, Wildey, & Kenney, 1993; Rigotti et al., 1997; Staff et al., 1998), and Tutt, Bauer, Edwards, and Cook (2000) compared local smoking prevalence rates with state rates. The six RCTs with the school as the unit of randomization will be presented first.

Altman et al. (1989, 1991) provided community education in Santa Clara County, California, about underage smoking through the mass media and presentations to community groups. They also randomly allocated 412 stores that sold cigarettes over the counter and 30 with vending machines to one of two retailer education interventions, which consisted either of mailed information, visits from the project staff, and an education kit; or contact with the chief executives of the companies that owned major chains and franchises; or a no personal contact control condition. Fourteen- to 16-year-olds visited all 412 stores that sold over the counter and all 30 that sold through vending machines, and attempted to purchase tobacco before the intervention and 6 months after. At 6 months after the intervention, 408 stores were assessed; and at 1 year, a 25% stratified random sample of 97 were assessed. The rate of illegal purchases in all 412 stores at baseline was 74%. This decreased to 39% at 6 months and increased to 59% at 1 year ($p = 0.01$), and there was no effect on illegal sales by the type of contact project staff had with storekeepers and no effect on sales from vending machines.

Chapman et al. (1994) in Sydney, Australia, sent pairs of children aged 12 to 13 years, who told their correct age if asked, to a sample of 255 retail outlets to purchase cigarettes. Retailers who had sold cigarettes to minors were then randomized to receive either a warning letter and threat of subsequent prosecution ($N = 50$) or to control ($N = 49$). After 2 months, the same pairs of children attempted to buy cigarettes at 244 stores and their undercover buying operation was reported by the media. In the group that received publicity about undercover buying plus warning letters that threatened prosecution, illegal sales of cigarettes to minors declined by 29%, and only 31% of these shopkeepers continued to sell to minors, compared to 60% of those who did not receive a letter. Regrettably, 24% of those who had not sold to minors at baseline started to sell to minors at the follow-up date.

Gemson et al. (1998) in Harlem, New York City, randomly assigned 181 stores licensed to sell tobacco to one of two interventions or a control group. Twenty-nine stopped selling tobacco by the end of the study and the final sample size was 152 stores. The intervention groups were the enforcement group ($N = 49$), which were fined if they violated regulations at the baseline or at 6 months, and the education group ($N = 48$), which received a visit within 3 months of the baseline to explain the law and

provide leaflets. The control group ($N = 55$) received no intervention. The baseline enforcement survey was reported in the media. African American students aged 12 to 14 years attempted to purchase a single, "loosie" cigarette, and if unsuccessful another student attempted to purchase a pack of cigarettes. A researcher or faculty member accompanied the student to the store, stayed out of sight, and recorded the attempted purchase. Illegal sales of single cigarettes or packs at baseline were uniformly high (average 98%), with a decline after 6 months in the enforcement group from 100% to 55% ($p < 0.05$), in the education group from 100% to 89.6% (NS), and in the control group from 94.5% to 87.3% (NS). After 1 year there was a further decline to 46.9% in the enforcement compared to baseline ($p < 0.05$), and to 77.1% in the education (NS), and a slight increase in the control group to 89.1% (NS).

Jason et al. (1996), using 1990 U.S. census data for Chicago, identified wards with the highest proportions of African Americans, Caucasians, and Latinos, and identified 40 stores in each ethnic neighborhood. These 120 stores were then randomized to one of three interventions or the control group. Seven went out of business, yielding a final sample size of 113. A different youth each month, who appeared to be aged 16–17 years and who told his or her correct age if asked, attempted to purchase cigarettes. A research assistant drove them to the store, waited outside, and recorded the attempted purchase. After 4 months shopkeepers who had illegally sold cigarettes were informed, warned that inspectors would check their sales, were provided with educational materials, and randomized to four schedules of enforcement (every 2, 4, or 6 months, or never). Monthly compliance checks continued and $200 fines for infractions were issued. Shopkeepers who did not sell to minors were given a congratulatory letter and educational materials. Illegal sales rates at baseline were high (87%–89%) and similar for all types of store. For the period from 4 to 10 months after the warnings to shopkeepers, average illegal sales of cigarettes declined to 19% in stores receiving checks every 2 months, 34% in those checked every 4 months, 42% in those checked every 6 months, and 84% in the control group. No statistical analysis was provided. At baseline merchants who asked for age identification sold to minors 33% of the time, and those did not ask for age identification 89% of the time ($p < 0.001$), and during the last month of the intervention the percentages were 0% and 100% ($p < 0.001$). At baseline there were significant differences in the percentage of illegal sales by type of store: 100% of gas stations, 94% of convenience stores, 78% of grocery stores, 72% of "mom and pop" stores, and 61% of pharmacies ($p < 0.01$). During the last month of the intervention there were sharp declines in all categories of stores to 20% of gas stations, 14% of convenience stores, 27% of grocery stores, 8% of "mom and pop" stores, and 27% of pharmacies (NS).

Schofield et al. (1997) in New South Wales, Australia, identified supermarkets, corner stores, takeaway food stores, newsagents, service stations, and tobacconists in a telephone area and randomly assigned 300 (90%) by computer-generated random numbers to one of two intervention groups or control. In the education intervention ($N = 100$) the Public Health Unit sent a letter about the new law and the need to check ages and put up signs, and in the education and threat of enforcement intervention ($N = 100$) the same intervention was used plus a letter warning about enforcement, and a public health officer visited the shop. The control group ($N = 100$) received only the survey. Eighteen-year-olds who looked younger than their age and wore school uniforms attempted to purchase cigarettes. Twenty-eight shops had either closed down or were not open at the compliance check times, so 272 (91%) were checked for compliance and 217 completed both the pre- and posttest telephone surveys. The number of retailers requiring proof of age increased from 8% at pretest to 35% at posttest in the education

group, from 11.7% to 33% in the education plus threat of enforcement group, and from 1% to 32% in the control (NS). There was an increase in the number of stores who displayed signs from 49% to 61%, but no significant differences between groups. Retailers' knowledge about the legal age for buying tobacco was very high and there was little scope for change; knowledge about fines increased but nonsignificantly, and the percentages in the intervention groups stating it was "okay" to sell to minors who appeared nearly 18 remained very low in both intervention groups (1%), but rose from 0% to 12% in the control group.

Skretny et al. (1990) in Buffalo, New York, randomly allocated convenience stores, pharmacies, and supermarkets to the intervention ($N = 60$) or control ($N = 58$) group. Intervention stores received an educational package and a letter stating New York state law about tobacco sales to minors, were asked for assistance in observing this law about sales to minors, and were provided with signs and a tip sheet to educate employees. There was no baseline assessment of sales. Students who appeared to be 14–16 years of age attempted to buy cigarettes 2 weeks later. There were no significant differences in illegal sales between intervention (77%) and control groups (86%); warning signs about illegal sales were put up in only 40% of the intervention stores and none of the control stores. The three RCTs with the community as the unit of randomization will be presented next.

Altman et al. (1999) studied two community pairs (Gonzales/Soledad and Greenfield/King City) in Monterey County, California, because students from each community pair attended the same high school, the communities were relatively isolated so that purchasing cigarettes from another community involved a 15-minute drive, and there was no public transport. The communities varied from 67% to 90% Hispanic. The pairs were assigned by coin toss to intervention or control. In the intervention group, all the managers and staff of each retail outlet were contacted directly with "numerous personal visits, mailings, and phone calls" to raise awareness about illegal sales to minors, provided with training for employees, signs, and education about community norms and ways of reducing sales. There were mass mailings to all postal patrons, messages at point of purchase, presentations at community group, fairs, and at council meetings by the youth coalition, and the media reported the campaign. Stores that sold to minors received additional education for their staff, and stores not selling to minors received favorable publicity. During the 34-month study period, 13- to 17-year-olds purchased candy, and another student, who would provide his correct age if asked, then attempted to purchase cigarettes, and also attempted to buy cigarettes several additional times throughout the study. Minors were driven to stores by adult escorts. The percentage of minors able to buy cigarettes declined from 75% to 0% in the intervention and from 64% to 39% in the control communities ($p < 0.0001$), with the final drop in the control group attributed to a "massive statewide campaign on minor's access to tobacco." The percentage of salespersons asking for proof of age increased from 5% to 71% in the intervention and from 6% to 26% in the control communities ($p < 0.0001$). After a year of discussion the police chiefs of Soledad and Gonzales agreed to cite merchants if the District Attorney would prosecute, but the District Attorney declined to prosecute any shopkeepers making illegal sales. Generalized estimating equations of the results of the Stanford Tobacco Survey of tobacco use found that "The seventh grade analysis revealed significant effects for treatment condition, time, and sex. The ninth grade analysis revealed significant effects for sex. The eleventh grade analysis revealed significant effects for time and sex" (Altman et al., 1999, p. 767). The levels of significance were not stated and the authors concluded that there were "significant effects" in reducing smoking in the intervention communities only for the seventh graders and females.

In Minnesota, in the Tobacco Policy Options for Prevention study (TPOP), Forster et al. (1998; cf. also Blaine et al., 1997; Chen & Forster, 2006; Forster et al., 1997) studied 14 communities that had neither received the ASSIST antismoking intervention nor had made recent ordinance changes controlling tobacco use. Communities were randomized either to the intervention group, which introduced eight new ordinances, compliance checks, community awareness, and media campaigns, or to the control group, which introduced weaker, less thorough ordinances. Surveys were completed by 91.8% of eligible students ($N = 6,014$) in 1993 and 92.9% ($N = 6,269$) in 1996. Fifteen-year-old females attempted illegal purchases on two successive days. Clustering of data was adjusted for in mixed-model regression. Illegal sales to minors decreased sharply, from 36.7% to 3.1% in intervention communities and from 41% to 8.8% in control communities. Although the differences between communities were not statistically significant, nor were there significant differences in requests for proof of age or display of signs, there was a significant increase in the number of stores keeping cigarettes behind counters. Intervention communities had 4.9% less daily smoking (95% CI = −9.0 to −0.7), 5.6% less weekly smoking (95% CI = −11.7 to 0.5), and 6.7% less monthly smoking (95% CI = −14.9 to 1.5). The difference in smoking rates was maintained through the 5-year assessment but not by the 7-year assessment, which was attributed to the control communities enacting similar ordinances to the intervention communities.

Cummings et al. (1998) and Cummings et al. (2003) in Erie County, New York, matched six pairs of communities on socioeconomic characteristics and the number of retail outlets selling tobacco and then randomized them to either enforcement or control conditions. Stores in the enforcement arm were randomly assigned to either receive 1, 2, or 3 enforcement checks over an 8-month period, with fines for violators and congratulatory letters for compliers. All retail stores selling tobacco over the counter in each community also received a reminder about the law not to sell tobacco to minors. The control group only received warnings. Adolescents aged 15–17 years, who told their age if asked, made compliance checks in 366 stores in the 12 communities by asking to purchase cigarettes, then said they did not have the money for the purchase. The police hired minors aged 14–16 years old to perform enforcement checks, but the number of checks (385) was fewer than planned. Compliance rates were similar at baseline in enforcement (36%) and nonenforcement (35%) communities and increased markedly at follow-up in both to 74% and 72%, but with no significant differences. There were no significant differences in sales between stores that had received fines (70%) or had not (73%), but clerks in stores that were checked twice were 1.8 (95% CI = 1.0 to 3.3) times more likely to ask for age identification compared to stores that had been checked once, and 2.1 times (95% CI = 1.1 to 4.0) more likely in stores checked three times. Rates of adolescent smoking within a 30-day period increased from 26.2% to 30.8% in communities that achieved less than 80% compliance, and from 25.6% to 25.5% in communities that achieved more than 80% ($p = 0.06$), and in frequent smoking from 9.9% to 12.7%, with a decrease from 9.2 % to 7.7% in communities that achieved more than 80% compliance ($p = 0.04$).

Conclusions

Four of six RCTs in which stores were randomized and three of three RCTs where communities were randomized found significant decreases in illegal sales to minors over the study period. The interpretation of these findings may be affected by the fact that interventions consisted of both community education campaigns of varying intensity, which all storekeepers could have heard, and direct educational and enforcement strategies at the store levels. Stead and Lancaster (2005)

commented that in studies where adolescents are sent in to attempt illegal purchases, sales may be underestimated if a single purchase is made per store, or if attempted purchasers are older youths or experienced smokers. Moreover, adolescents may obtain cigarettes by using invalid IDs, shoplifting, stealing from parents, and by asking older adults to purchase for them, and sales clerks may recognize known adolescent customers and sell to them. If legal sources of purchase are restricted, some minors may resort to more illegal forms of access.

Impact of Tobacco Advertising

Systematic Reviews and Meta-Analyses of Group Designs

Lovato, Linn, Stead, and Best (2003) performed a Cochrane Systematic Review of the effect of tobacco advertising, most recently amended on May 13, 2003. They identified nine longitudinal studies with over 12,000 baseline nonsmokers. All used self-report of smoking behavior, widely differing definitions of smoking, and different follow-up periods. Only two studies assessed reliability: Pucci and Siegel (1999) read the magazines the students reported they had read and counted the number of cigarette advertisements, and Sargent et al. (2000) tested the reliability of the receptivity and smoking items in his questionnaire with a separate sample and obtained kappas > 0.7. Most studies measured and adjusted for age, socioeconomic status, and the smoking behavior of friends, siblings, and parents. Alexander et al. (1983) retained 87% (5,616/6,455) at follow-up; Armstrong et al. (1990) 64% (1,514/2,366); Biener and Siegel (2000) 57.8% (618/1069); Diaz, Villalbi, Nebot, Auba, and Sanz (1998) 89% (1,003/1,126); Pierce, Choi, Gilpin, Farkas, & Berry (1998) 61.5% (3,376/5,531); Pucci and Siegel (1999) 59% (627/1,069); Sargent et al. (2000) 74% (537/727); and While, Kelly, Huang, and Charlton (1996) had questionnaires for 1,490 at baseline and completion and discarded 2.7% as incomplete.

Three studies assessed whether being receptive to tobacco advertising and promotions was related to beginning smoking. Biener and Siegel (2000) defined receptivity as being able to name a brand and found that 14% of the nonsmokers who neither owned an item that promoted smoking nor named a brand became established smokers 4 years later, 18% who either owned an item or could name a brand (defined as moderate receptivity), and 46% of those who owned a tobacco promotional item and named a brand advertisement that attracted their attention (defined as high receptivity) ($p < 0.001$). For those who were highly receptive at baseline, when family and peer smoking and rebelliousness were controlled, the OR (odds ratio) of them becoming established smokers was 2.70 (95% CI = 1.24 to 5.85).

Pierce et al. (1998) defined having a favorite advertisement as moderate receptivity and owning or being willing to use a promotional item as high receptivity. Pierce found that, with demographic factors and school performance controlled, those with a favorite advertisement were more likely to become smokers than those without one (OR = 1.82; 95% CI = 1.04 to 3.20), and those who owned or were willing to use a promotional item were more likely to become smokers than those who were not (OR = 2.89; 95% CI = 1.47 to 5.68). Sargent et al. (2000) defined owning or being willing to use a personal item bearing a cigarette brand logo as being receptive, and for those who were receptive the OR of becoming smokers was 1.9 (95% CI = 1.3 to 2.9).

Three studies assessed the effect of advertising by cigarette brands. Charlton and Blair (1989) found for boys that having a favorite advertisement or being able to name a brand did not predict smoking uptake, and for girls naming a brand—but not having a favorite advertisement—was related to starting smoking. Pucci and Siegel (1999) found that exposure to advertising by specific brands was related to starting smoking. While et al. (1996) found for boys that those who named the largest number of advertised brands were not more

likely to start smoking, but girls who named the most brands were more likely to start smoking.

Three studies assessed the relationship between approving advertising, perceiving it as influential, and starting smoking. Alexander et al. (1983) found that those who approved of cigarette advertising had a 27% rate of beginning to smoke, those who were ambivalent 19.3%, and those who were opposed 12% ($p < 0.001$). Armstrong et al. (1990) found at the 1-year follow-up for those who perceived smoking advertisements as having some influence, for females the smoking prevalence rate was 8.4% higher (95% CI = −1.2 to 18.1) than those who did not perceive smoking as influencing them, and for males was 5.3% higher (95% CI = −5.2 to 15.8). At the 30-month follow-up for females, the difference in prevalence rates was 15% (95% CI = 2.1 to 27.9), and for males was 15.3% (95% CI = 4.0 to 26.6). Diaz et al. (1998) found that for those who accepted cigarette advertising the RR of smoking was 2.1 (95% CI = 1.5 to 3.0). Armstrong et al. (1990) found that those who owned a personal item with a cigarette brand logo on it had an OR = 1.9 of smoking (95% CI = 1.3 to 2.9).

Conclusions

No RCTs were identified and, therefore, the results of the non-RCT designs are reported. Interventions to oppose the effects of advertising were often used as part of school interventions, and are described in the tables of the Cochrane Schools Review by R. Thomas and Perera (2006), but the individual effects of the interventions to oppose advertising cannot be disentangled from the larger interventions.

Four of six RCTs in which stores were randomized and three of three RCTs where communities were randomized found significant decreases in illegal sales to minors over the study period. Thus, advertising to promote cigarette sales to adolescents is effective, and although the Schools Review by R. Thomas and Perera (2006) listed many antiadvertising interventions within larger school interventions, the results of the antismoking interventions cannot be seprarately assessed. There is a key role for new studies in this area to measure the effects of interventions opposing advertising.

Family and Caregiver Interventions

Systematic Reviews and Meta-Analyses of Group Designs

Priest et al. (2008) conducted a Cochrane Systematic Review of interventions to prevent exposure of children to environmental tobacco smoke, and the most recent substantive amendment was August 7, 2008. They identified 36 studies, and in 30 of which there was random allocation of the control group (of which 10 had adequate concealment of allocation), 10 of the RCTs found a significant effect in reducing children's exposure to environmental tobacco smoke, but because of heterogeneity of designs there was no pooling of data.

Although Zhang and Qiu (1993) was not an RCT, we report it here because of the unique intervention involving children asking fathers to quit smoking. In 44 primary schools in China with 20,382 children, Zhang used a tobacco prevention curriculum including the social and health consequences of tobacco use, refusal skills, and antismoking policies in schools, and the intervention group children wrote letters to their fathers asking them to quit smoking and watched their father's smoking behavior. Control schools received the usual curriculum. At baseline more intervention group fathers were smokers (6,843 of 9,953 = 68.8%) than control group fathers (6,274 of 9,580 = 65.5%), but after 8 months there was a large decline in the proportion of fathers who stopped smoking for at least 180 days in the intervention group (800 of 9,953 = 11.7%) compared to the control (14 of 6,274 = 0.2%).

Conclusion

Of 30 RCTs, 10 found a significant decrease in children's exposure to environmental tobacco smoke.

TREATMENT

Tobacco Cessation Interventions

Systematic Reviews and Meta-Analyses of Group Designs

A Cochrane Collaboration Systematic Review by Grimshaw and Stanton (2006) received its last substantive amendment on August 15, 2006 and identified seven cluster RCTs, six RCTs, and two controlled trials with a total of 3,605 young people. There was a wide range of definitions of the smoking outcome, mostly point prevalence, ranging from 1–30 days. Eight verified smoking abstinence by carbon monoxide and salivary cotinine levels, and three by salivary cotinine levels. The reviewers rated nine RCTs as "A" for allocation concealment, losses to follow-up ranged from 10% to 50%, and seven trials used intention-to-treat analyses.

Nine RCTs tested motivational enhancement or behavioral management techniques. Five used cognitive behavioral techniques, three motivational interviewing, and one compared fact and attitude interventions (see Table 21.4). Of the five cognitive behavioral interventions, three RCTs tested the "Not on Tobacco" intervention with smokers recruited from 84 schools in three different states. Dino, Goldcamp, Fernandes, Kalsekar, and Massey (2001) ($N = 402$) found an OR = 1.63 (95% CI = 0.82 to 3.24); Horn, Dino, Kalsekar, and Mody (2005) ($N = 122$) found an OR = 2.03 (95% CI = 0.18 to 23.04); and Horn, Fernandes, Dino, Massey, and Kalsekar (2003) and Horn, Dino, Kalsekar, and Fernandes (2004) ($N = 128$) found an OR = 5.65 (95% CI = 0.61 to 52.02), none of which showed a statistically significant effect at 6-month follow-up with intention-to-treat data, but pooled data did show a statistically significant effect (OR = 1.87; 95% CI = 1.00 to 3.50). Lipkus et al. (2004) ($N = 402$) contacted individuals in shopping malls and an amusement arcade and offered them telephone counseling, self-help materials, and a video, and after 6 months found an OR = 1.12 (95% CI = 0.69 to

TABLE 21.4   Interventions to Help Adolescents Stop Smoking

Intervention	Evidence-Based Effect
Cognitive behavior therapy	The 5 individual RCTs did not achieve statistically significant results, but pooled data for 3 "Not on Tobacco" trials had an OR with a lower 95% CI limit, which just included unity.
Stages of change theory	3 RCTs pooled at 1 year had an OR = 1.70 (95% CI = 1.25 to 2.33) and at 2 years an OR = 1.38 (95% CI = 0.99 to 1.92).
Motivational interviewing	3 RCTs had a pooled OR = 2.05 (95% CI = 1.10 to 3.80), but the reviewers could not separately identify the effect of the motivational interviewing component.
Medication	Neither small RCT achieved significance.
All 15 RCTs	Pooled OR = 2.39 (95% CI = 0.98 to 5.84).

1.83). Myers and Brown (2005) ($N = 54$) contacted individuals in an outpatient substance abuse program and offered them six 1-hour group sessions of motivational enhancement, and after 12 months found an OR = 4.91 (95% CI = 0.51 to 47.16).

Three RCTs used motivational interviewing and for all three the 95% confidence interval included unity. Brown et al. (2003) ($N = 181$), for inpatients at a psychiatric hospital at 6 month follow-up, found an OR = 1.71 (95% CI = 0.63 to 4.62). Colby et al. (2005) ($N = 85$), for individuals in a hospital outpatient department or the emergency room at 6 months, found an OR = 3.08 (95% CI = 0.31 to 30.82). Sussman, Dent, and Litchman (2001) ($N = 335$, with 259 in the intervention and 76 in the control group) found an OR = 2.39 (95% CI = 0.98 to 5.84). One RCT (Greenberg & Deputat, 1978) compared fact, scare, and attitudinal interventions and found an OR = 5.65 (95% CI = 0.61 to 52.22). Seven of the RCTs using motivational techniques were pooled and at 6 months the OR = 2.39 (95% CI = 0.98 to 5.84).

Three RCTs tested Prochaska's stages of change model. Aveyard et al. (1999) and follow-up (2001) ($N = 1,089$) arranged for students to work with computer messages oriented to their smoking situation and found an OR = 1.52 (95% CI = 1.02 to 2.26) at 12 months, and OR = 1.16 (0.76 to 1.75) at 24 months. Hollis et al. (2005) ($N = 448$) used a computer expert system with clinical messages, motivational counseling, and booster sessions and found an OR = 2.04 (95% CI = 1.24 to 3.35) at 12 months and an OR = 1.86 (95% CI = 1.07 to 3.23) at 24 months. The pooled result for both RCTs at 12 months is OR = 1.70 (95% CI = 1.25 to 2.33) and at 24 months OR = 1.38 (95% CI = 0.99 to 1.92). Lipkus et al. (2004) ($N = 402$) used telephone motivational enhancement and cognitive behavior therapy and after 8 months found an OR = 1.12 (95% CI = 0.69 to 1.83), and because of the combined intervention, his results were not pooled with the other two RCTs.

Two RCTs tested medications, for both of which the confidence intervals included unity. Moolchan et al. (2005) ($N = 86$) compared nicotine patches to placebo and after 6 months found an OR = 4.93 (95% CI = 0.95 to 25.6), and when nicotine gum was compared to placebo OR = 1.81 (95% CI = 0.31 to 10.4). Killen et al. (2004) ($N = 213$) compared nicotine patches and bupropion to nicotine patches and placebo and found an OR = 1.05 (95% CI = 0.38 to 2.92).

Conclusions

Three interventions using cognitive behavior therapy interventions were tested in five trials and individual RCTs did not achieve statistically significant results, but pooled data for three Not on Tobacco trials had an OR with a lower 95% CI limit, which just included unity. The interventions testing Prochaska's stages of change theory, when pooled at 1 year had an OR = 1.70 (95% CI = 1.25 to 2.33) and at 2 years an OR = 1.38 (95% CI = 0.99 to 1.92). The three RCTs using motivational interviewing had a pooled OR = 2.05 (95% CI = 1.10 to 3.80), but the reviewers could not separately identify the effect of the motivational interviewing component. Neither of the small RCTs of medication achieved significance. When all 15 RCTs were pooled the OR = 2.39 (95% CI = 0.98 to 5.84).

Interventions for Smokeless Tobacco

Systematic Reviews and Meta-Analyses of Group Designs

The Cochrane Collaboration Systematic Review by Ebbert et al. (2007), with the most recent substantive amendment on July 20, 2007, includes three studies of adolescents (Severson, Andrews, Lichtenstein, Danaher, & Akers, 2007; Stotts, Roberson, Hanna, Jones, & Smith, 2003; Walsh et al., 2003), but Severson et al. (2007) included individuals older than 15 years and the results for those of adolescent age cannot be separated.

Stotts et al. (2003) randomized by computer-generated code 303 male 14- to 19-year-old smokeless tobacco users in 41 U.S. high schools to one of three intervention groups: nicotine patch plus behavioral therapy, placebo patch plus behavioral therapy, or minimal intervention control. All participants were offered screening by a dentist to detect any oral problems including cancers, and were offered incentives to attend and to complete assessments. The nicotine patch plus behavioral therapy group received patches whose initial strength was tailored to their baseline cotinine level, and the six sessions of proactive counseling were according to Prochaska's Stages of Change Theory. The nicotine patch and placebo groups participated in the same behavioral therapy sessions, and the educators and participants were both blinded to their group assignment. The minimal intervention group served as a control, as participants received only 5–10 minutes of counseling and a phone call. Most participants (80%–90%) used snuff and 66%–81% also used cigarettes. Tobacco use at baseline was lower for the group that received the placebo patch. The dropout rate was higher in the minimal intervention group, perhaps because they guessed they would not receive free patches, and the intention-to-treat analysis may underestimate the quit rates for the control group. Abstinence was higher in the intervention (42 of 198) groups than control (12 of 105): OR = 2.09 (95% CI = 1.05 to 4.16).

Walsh et al. (2003) randomly selected 44 rural U.S. high schools then stratified them on the number and size of their baseball teams and smokeless tobacco prevalence, and from the 1,084 students who played baseball selected 307 who used smokeless tobacco. They were randomized to either a behavioral therapy group or no-intervention control group. The behavioral therapy group received education within their teams by peers using videotape and then a discussion, slides that the peers chose, and discussions about how the tobacco industry uses advertising. Then a dentist or dental hygienist conducted an oral cancer screening exam, gave advice to quit, provided counseling in small groups how to quit, and telephoned each participant on the date they had agreed to quit. Abstinence at 12 months was higher in the intervention (38 of 141) than control group (23 of 166): OR = 2.29 (95% CI = 1.29 to 4.08). Smoking status was not biochemically verified.

Conclusions

There were two RCTs of behavioral and nicotine replacement therapies for smokeless tobacco and both were effective, thus behavioral and nicotine replacement therapies are evidence-based practice for smokeless tobacco cessation.

EVIDENCE-BASED PRACTICES

Prevention

With respect to school-based interventions, the evidence summarized in Table 21.1 shows that it is possible that combining social influences models with other components, such as community interventions and generic social competence training, may improve effectiveness; however, these interventions have not been subject to the same rigorous evaluation as the social influences approach. In addition, there are few data from direct comparisons to suggest how large an increment might be achieved. Although half of the highest quality social influences RCTs had significant positive results, the pooled group results were not significant. Future interventions need to reflect contemporary adolescent culture, which is heavily oriented to music, iPods, cartoons, games, and dancing. Table 21.2 shows that there is only modest evidence that family programs are effective, and no evidence that they are strong enough to provide additive effects in conjunction with school programs. The interventions to date may not be strong enough when used in an additive role.

For competitions in schools there is no systematic review, and a literature search identified no methodologically sound evidence for the effectiveness of competitions.

For community interventions the results are limited to the six RCTs in Sowden and Arblaster's (2002) systematic review: Three of six RCTs found no effects; one found lower smoking rates in the community intervention; one found higher rates in the community intervention; and one found lower smoking rates in one intervention arm (intensive community intervention) and nonsignificantly higher rates in another intervention arm (the age-appropriate community intervention) (Piper et al., 2000). The results are very mixed and no overall conclusions can be drawn.

For interventions to prevent sales of tobacco, the results are limited to the nine RCTs in Stead and Lancaster's (2005) systematic review. Four of six RCTs in which stores were randomized and three of three RCTs where communities were randomized found significant decreases in illegal sales to minors over the study period. Interpretation is complicated

by the dual educational interventions in the community and to storekeepers, and storekeepers in control groups possibly learning about the direct storekeeper enforcement components. Adolescents can also obtain cigarettes by many illegal routes other than stores. Nevertheless, the effects on reducing sales to minors make these interventions among the most effective in preventing adolescent tobacco use.

Advertising is strongly correlated with smoking by adolescents. All nine nonrandomized studies on the impact of tobacco advertising found a significant relationship between cigarette advertising and smoking. Although causality cannot be proven by nonrandomized designs, all of these nine studies found a relationship between receptivity to tobacco advertising, approval of advertising, perceiving advertising as influential, owning a personal item with a tobacco logo on it, and knowledge of specific brands and smoking. Interventions to oppose advertising are part of many of the school interventions reviewed in the Schools Review by R. Thomas and Perera (2006) but, unfortunately, cannot be disentangled from the other interventions. Undertaking RCTs to oppose the effects of advertising is, thus, a wide-open field for research.

For family and caregiver interventions to prevent smoking, the Cochrane Systematic Review by Priest et al. (2008) identified 36 studies, of which 30 had random allocation of the control group. Ten of the RCTs found a significant reduction in children's exposure to environmental tobacco smoke.

Treatment

For interventions to help adolescents stop smoking, Table 21.4 summarizes the evidence. The stages of change, "Not on Tobacco," and motivational RCTs were all effective, although the motivational component could not be separately analyzed in the motivational studies. This is a very promising area for future research, and more, larger trials with medication, motivational, stages of change, CBT, and combined arms are needed. Combined behavior and nicotine replacement therapies are also a very promising area.

For preventing smokeless tobacco use, two RCTs found significant decreases in smokeless tobacco usage: Stotts et al. (2003) (OR = 2.09, 95% CI = 1.05 to 4.16) and Walsh et al. (2003) (OR = 2.29, 95% CI = 1.29 to 4.08). Future research with more, larger trials of medication, motivational stages of change, CBT, and combined arms are needed.

REFERENCES

Abernathy, T. J., & Bertrand, L. D. (1992). Preventing cigarette smoking among children: Results of a four-year evaluation of the PAL program. *Canadian Journal of Public Health, 83*, 226–229.

Adamopoulos, D., van de Borne, P., & Argacha, J. F. (2008). New insights into the sympathetic, endothelial and coronary effects of nicotine. *Clinical and Experimental Pharmacology & Physiology, 35*, 458–463.

Alexander, H. M., Callcott, R., Dobson, A. J., Hardes, G. R., Lloyd, D. M., O'Connell, D. L., & Leeder S. R. (1983). Cigarette smoking and drug use in schoolchildren: IV—factors associated with changes in smoking behaviour. *International Journal of Epidemiology, 12*, 59–66.

Altman, D. G., Foster, V., Rasenick-Douss, L., & Tye, J. B. (1989). Reducing the illegal sale of cigarettes to minors. *Journal of the American Medical Association, 261*, 80–83.

Altman, D. G., Rasenick-Douss, L., Foster, V., & Tye, J. B. (1991). Sustained effects of an educational program to reduce sales of cigarettes to minors. *American Journal of Public Health, 81*, 891–893.

Altman, D. G., Wheelis, A. Y., McFarlane, M., Lee, H., & Fortmann, S. P. (1999). The relationship between tobacco access and use among adolescents: A four community study. *Social Science & Medicine, 48*, 759–775.

American Psychiatric Association. (2000). *Diagnostic and statistical manual of mental disorders* (4th ed., text rev.). Washington, DC: Author.

Armstrong, B. K., De Klerk, N. H., Shean, R. E., Dunn, D. A., & Dolin, P. J. (1990). Influence of education and advertising on the uptake of smoking by children. *Medical Journal of Australia, 152*, 117–124.

Ary, D. V., Biglan, A., Glasgow, R., Zoref, L., Black, C., Ochs, L., . . . Brozovsky, P. (1990). The efficacy of social-influence prevention programs versus "standard

care": Are new initiatives needed? *Journal of Behavioral Medicine, 13*, 281–296.

Ausems, M., Mesters, I., Van Breukelen, G., & de Vries, H. (2004). Effects of in-school and tailored out-of-school smoking prevention among Dutch vocational school students. *Health Education Research, 19*, 51–63.

Aveyard, P., Cheng, K. K., Almond, J., Sherratt, E., Lancashire, R., Lawrence, T., . . . Aveyard, P. (1999). Cluster randomised controlled trial of expert system based on the transtheoretical ("stages of change") model for smoking prevention and cessation in schools. *British Medical Journal, 319*, 948–953.

Aveyard, P., Sherratt, E., Almond, J., Lawrence, T., Lancashire, R., Griffin, C., & Cheng, K. K. (2001). The change-in-stage and updated smoking status results from a cluster-randomized trial of smoking prevention and cessation using the transtheoretical model among British adolescents. *Preventive Medicine, 33*, 313–324.

Bagott, M., Jordan, C., Wright, C., & Jarvis, S. (1998). How easy is it for young people to obtain cigarettes, and do test sales by trading standards have any effect? A survey of two schools in Gateshead. *Child Care, Health and Development, 24*, 207–216.

Bandura, A. (1977). *Social learning theory*. Englewood Cliffs, NJ: Prentice-Hall.

Bangert-Drowns, R. L. (1988). The effects of school-based substance abuse education. A meta-analysis. *Journal of Drug Education, 18*, 243–264.

Bauman, K. E., Foshee, V. A., Ennetts, S. T., Pemberton, M., Hicks, K. A., King, T. S., & Koch, G. G. (2001). The influence of a family program on adolescent tobacco and alcohol use. *American Journal of Public Health, 91*, 604–610.

Biener, L., & Siegel, M. (2000). Tobacco marketing and adolescent smoking: More support for a causal inference. *American Journal of Public Health, 90*, 407–411.

Biglan, A., Ary, D. V., Smolkowski, K., Duncan, T., & Black, C. (2000). A randomized controlled trial of a community intervention to prevent adolescent tobacco use. *Tobacco Control, 9*, 24–32.

Biglan, A., Glasgow, R. E., Ary, D. V., Thompson, R., Severson, H., Lichtenstein, E., . . . Gallison, C. (1987). How generalizable are the effects of smoking prevention programs? Refusal skills training and parent messages in a teacher-administered program. *Journal of Behavioral Medicine, 10*, 613–628.

Biglan, A., Severson, H., Ary, D., Faller, C., Gallison, C., Thompson, R., . . . Lichtenstein, E. (1987). Do smoking prevention programs really work? Attrition and the internal and external validity of an evaluation of a refusal skills training program. *Journal of Behavioral Medicine, 10*, 159–171.

Blaine, T. M., Forster, J. L., Hennrikus, D., O'Neil, S., Wolfson, M., & Pham, H. (1997). Creating tobacco control policy at the local level: Implementation of a direct action organizing approach. *Health Education and Behavior, 24*, 640–651.

Botvin, G. J., Baker, E., Dusenbury, L., Tortu, S., & Botvin, E. M. (1990). Preventing adolescent drug abuse through a multimodal cognitive-behavioral approach: Results of a 3-year study. *Journal of Consulting and Clinical Psychology, 58*, 437–446.

Botvin, G. J., Baker, E., Filazzola, A. D., & Botvin, E. M. (1990). A cognitive-behavioral approach to substance abuse prevention: One-year follow-up. *Addictive Behaviors, 15*, 47–63.

Botvin, G. J., & Eng, A. (1980). A comprehensive school-based smoking prevention program. *Journal of School Health, 50*, 209–213.

Botvin, G. J., & Eng, A. (1982). The efficacy of a multicomponent approach to the prevention of cigarette smoking. *Preventive Medicine, 11*, 199–211.

Botvin, G. J., Griffin, K. W., Diaz, T., & Ifill-Wiliams, M. (2001). Drug abuse prevention among minority adolescents: Posttest and one-year follow-up of a school-based preventive intervention. *Prevention Science, 2*, 1–13.

Botvin, G. J., Griffin, K. W., Diaz, T., Miller, N., & Ifill-Williams, M. (1999). Smoking initiation and escalation in early adolescent girls: One-year follow-up of a school-based prevention intervention for minority youth. *Journal of the American Medical Women's Association, 54*, 139–143, 152.

Botvin, G. J., Renick, N. L., & Baker, E. (1983). The effects of scheduling format and booster sessions on a broad-spectrum psychosocial approach to smoking prevention. *Journal of Behavioral Medicine, 6*, 359–379.

Brown, K. S., Cameron, R., Madill, C., Payne, M. E., Filsinger, S., Manske, S. R., & Best, J. A. (2002). Outcome evaluation of a high school smoking reduction intervention based on extracurricular activities. *Preventive Medicine, 35*, 506–510.

Brown, R. A., Ramsey, S. E., Strong, D. R., Myers, M. G., Kahler, C. W., Lejuez, C. W., . . . Abrams, D. B. (2003). Effects of motivational interviewing on smoking cessation in adolescents with psychiatric disorders. *Tobacco Control, 12*(Suppl 4), iv3–iv10.

Bush, P. J., Zuckerman, A. E., Theiss, P. K., Taggart, V. S., Horowitz, C., Sheridan, M. J., & Walter, H. J. (1989). Cardiovascular risk factor prevention in black schoolchildren: Two-year results of the "Know Your Body" Program. *American Journal of Epidemiology, 129*, 466–482.

Cameron, R., Brown, K. S., Best, J. A., Pelkman, C. L., Madill, C. L., Manske, S. R., & Payne, M. E. (1999). Effectiveness of a social influences smoking prevention program as a function of provider type, training method, and school risk. *American Journal of Public Health, 89*, 1827–1831.

Centers for Disease Control and Prevention. (2008). *Smoking & tobacco use.* Retrieved from www.cdc.gov/tobacco

Chapman, S., King, M., Andrews, B., McKay, E., Markham, P., & Woodward, S. (1994). Effects of publicity and a warning letter on illegal cigarette sales to minors. *Australian Journal of Public Health, 18*, 39–42.

Charlton, A., & Blair, V. (1989). Predicting the onset of smoking in boys and girls. *Social Science and Medicine, 29*, 813–818.

Chen, V., & Forster, J. L. (2006). The long-term effect of local policies to restrict retail sale of tobacco to youth. *Nicotine & Tobacco Research, 8*, 371–377.

Clarke, J. H., MacPherson, B., Holmes, D. R., & Jones, R. (1986). Reducing adolescent smoking: A comparison of peer-led, teacher-led, and expert interventions. *Journal of School Health, 56*, 102–106.

Clayton, R. R., Cattarello, A. M., & Johnstone, B. M. (1996). The effectiveness of Drug Abuse Resistance Education (Project DARE): 5-year follow-up results. *Preventive Medicine, 25*, 307–318.

Colby, S. M., Monti, P. M., O'Leary Tevyaw, T., Barnett, N. P., Spirito, A., Rohsenow, D. J., . . . Lewander, W. (2005). Brief motivational intervention for adolescent smokers in medical settings. *Addictive Behaviors, 30*, 865–874.

Crone, M. R., Reijneveld, S. A., Willemsen, M. C., van Leerdam, F. J., Spruijt, R. D., & Sing, R. A. (2003). Prevention of smoking in adolescents with lower education: A school based intervention study. *Journal of Epidemiology and Community Health, 57*, 675–680.

Cullen, K. J., & Cullen, A. M. (1996). Long-term follow-up of the Busselton six-year controlled trial of prevention of children's behavior disorders. *Journal of Pediatrics, 129*, 136–139.

Cummings, K. M., Hyland, A., Perla, J., & Giovino, G. A. (2003). Is the prevalence of youth smoking affected by efforts to increase retailer compliance with a minors' access law? *Nicotine & Tobacco Research, 5*, 465–471.

Cummings, K. M., Hyland, A., Saunders-Martin, T., Perla, J., Coppola, P. R., & Pechacek, T. F. (1998). Evaluation of an enforcement program to reduce tobacco sales to minors. *American Journal of Public Health, 88*, 932–936.

Curry, S. J., Hollis, J., Bush, T., Polen, M., Ludman, E. J., Grothaus, L., & McAfee, T. (2003). A randomized trial of a family-based smoking prevention intervention in managed care. *Preventive Medicine, 37*, 617–626.

De Vries, H., Backbier, E., Dijkstra, M., Van Breukelen, G., Parcel, G., & Kok, G. (1994). A Dutch socal influence smoking prevention approach for vocational school students. *Health Education Research, 9*, 365–374.

De Vries, H., Mudde, A., Leijs, I., Charlton, A., Vartiainen, E., Buijs, G., . . . Kremers, S. (2003). The European Smoking Prevention Framework Approach (EFSA): An example of integral prevention. *Health Education Research, 18*, 611–626.

Diaz, E., Villalbi, J. R., Nebot, M., Auba, J., & Sanz, F. (1998). Smoking initiation in students: Cross-sectional and longitudinal study of predictive factors. *Medical Clinics (Barcelona), 110*, 334–339.

Dielman, T. E. (1994). *Correction for the design effect in school-based substance use and abuse prevention research: Sample size requirements and analysis considerations.* NIDA Research Monographs. Vol. 139, 115–126. Washington, DC: National Institute of Drug Addiction.

Dijkstra, M., Mesters, I., Devries, H., van Breukelen, G., & Parcel, G. S. (1999). Effectiveness of a social influence approach and boosters to smoking prevention. *Health Education Research, 14,* 791–802.

Dino, G., Goldcamp, J., Fernandes, A., Kalsekar, I., & Massey, C. (2001). A 2-year efficacy study of Not On Tobacco in Florida: An overview of program successes in changing teen smoking behavior. *Preventive Medicine, 33,* 600–605.

Ebbert, J. O., Montori, V., Vickers, K. S., Erwin, P. C., Dale, L. C., & Stead, L. F. (2007). Interventions for smokeless tobacco use cessation. *Cochrane Database of Systematic Reviews, 4,* Art. No. CD004306. doi:10.1002/14651858.CD004306.pub3

Elder, J. P., Perry, C. L., Stone, E. J., Johnson, C. C., Yang, M., Edmundson, E. W., . . . Parcel, G. S. (1996). Tobacco use measurement, prediction, and intervention in elementary schools in four states: The CATCH study. *Preventive Medicine, 25,* 486–494.

Elder, J. P., Sallis, J. F., Woodruff, S. I., & Wildey, M. R. (1993). Tobacco-refusal skills and tobacco use among high-risk adolescents. *Journal of Behavioral Medicine, 16,* 629–641.

Ellickson, P. L., & Bell, R. M. (1990). Drug prevention in junior high: A multi-site longitudinal test. *Science, 247,* 1299–1305.

Ellickson, P. L., McCaffrey, D. F., Ghosh Dastidar, B., & Longshore, D. L. (2003). New inroads in preventing adolescent drug use: Results from a large-scale trial of Project ALERT in middle schools. *American Journal of Public Health, 93,* 1830–1836.

Etter, J. F., & Bouvier, P. (2006). Some doubts about one of the largest smoking prevention programmes in Europe, the smokefree class competition. *Journal of Epidemiology & Community Health, 60,* 757–759.

Evans, R. I. (1976). Smoking in children: Developing a social psychological strategy of deterrence. *Preventive Medicine, 5,* 122–127.

Flay, B. R., Miller, T. Q., Hedeker, D., Siddiqui, O., Britton, C. F., Brannon, B. R., . . . Dent, C. (1995). The Television, School, and Family Smoking Prevention and Cessation Project. VIII student outcomes and mediating variables. *Preventive Medicine, 24,* 29–40.

Flay, B. R., Ryan, C. B., Best, J. A., Brown, K. S., Kersell, M. W., d'Avernas, J. R., & Zanna, M. P. (1985). Are social-psychological smoking programs effective? The Waterloo study. *Journal of Behavioral Medicine, 8,* 37–59.

Focarile, F., & Scaffino, L. (1994). Risultati di uno studio controllato randomizzato sulla prevenzione dell'abitudine al fumo degli adolescenti. [Results of a randomized controlled trial on preventing the smoking habit in adolescents]. *Epidemiologia e Prevenzione, 18,* 157–163.

Forman, S. G., Linney, J. A., & Brondino, M. J. (1990). Effects of coping skills training on adolescents at risk for substance use. *Psychology of Addictive Behavior, 4,* 67–76.

Forster, J. L., Murray, D. M., Wolfson, M., Blaine, T. M., Wagenaar, A. C., & Hennrikus, D. J. (1998). The effects of community policies to reduce youth access to tobacco. *American Journal of Public Health, 88,* 1193–1198.

Forster, J. L., Wolfson, M., Murray, D. M., Wagenaar, A. C., & Claxton, A. J. (1997). Perceived and measured availability of tobacco to youth in 14 Minnesota communities: The TPOP study. *American Journal of Preventive Medicine, 13,* 167–174.

Frobisher, C., Winter, D. L., Lancashire, E. R., Reulen, R. C., Taylor, A. J., Eiser, C., . . . British Childhood Cancer Survivor Study. (2008). Extent of smoking and age at initiation of smoking among adult survivors of childhood cancer in Britain. *Journal of the National Cancer Institute, 100,* 1068–1081.

Furr-Holden, C. D. M., Ialongo, N. S., Anthony, J. C., Petras, H., & Kellam, S. G. (2004). Developmentally inspired drug prevention: Middle school outcomes in a school-based randomized prevention trial. *Drug and Alcohol Dependence, 73,* 149–158.

Gemson, D. H., Moats, H. L., Watkins, B. X., Ganz, M. L., Robinson, S., & Healton, E. (1998). Laying down the law: Reducing illegal tobacco sales to minors in central Harlem. *American Journal of Preventive Medicine, 88,* 936–939.

Gersick, K. E., Grady, K., & Snow, D. L. (1988). Social-cognitive skill development with sixth graders and its initial impact on substance use. *Journal of Drug Education, 18,* 55–70.

Greenberg, J. S., & Deputat, Z. (1978). Smoking intervention: Comparing three methods in a high school setting. *Journal of School Health, 48,* 489–502.

Grimshaw, G. M., & Stanton, A. (2006). Tobacco cessation interventions for young people. *Cochrane Database of Systematic Reviews, 4,* Art. No. CD003289. doi:10.1002/14651858.CD003289.pub4

Hancock, L., Sanson-Fisher, R., Perkins, J., Girgis, A., Howley, P., & Schofield, M. (2001). The effect of a community action intervention on adolescent smoking rates in rural Australian towns: The CART project. Cancer Action in Rural Towns. *Preventive Medicine, 32,* 332–340.

Hanewinkel, R., & Wiborg, G. (2002). Primär- und Sekundärprevention des Rauchens im Jugendalter: Effekte der Kampagne "Be Smart—Don't Start." [Primary and secondary prevention of smoking in adolescents: Results of the campaign "Be Smart—Don't Start"]. *Gesundheitswesen, 64*(8–9), 492–498.

Hanewinkel, R., & Wiborg, G. (2003). Förderung des Nichtrauchens in der Schule: Ergebnisse einer prospektiven kontrollierten Interventionsstudie. *Sucht, 49*, 333–341.

Hanewinkel, R., & Wiborg, G. (2006). Initial evaluation of a real-world self-help smoking cessation programme for adolescents and young adults. *Addictive Behaviors, 31*, 1939–1945.

Hanewinkel, R., Wiborg, G., Isensee, B., Nebot, M., & Vartiainen, E. (2006). "Smoke-free Class Competition": Far-reaching conclusions based on weak data. *Preventive Medicine, 43*, 150–151.

Hansen, W. B., & Graham, J. W. (1991). Preventing alcohol, marijuana and cigarette use among adolescents: Peer pressure resistance training versus establishing conservative norms. *Preventive Medicine, 20*, 414–430.

Hansen, W. B., Johnson, C. A., Flay, B. R., Graham, J. W., & Sobel, J. (1988). Affective and social influences approaches to the prevention of multiple substance abuse among seventh grade students: Results from Project SMART. *Preventive Medicine, 17*, 135–154.

Higgins, J. P., Thompson, S. G., Deeks, J. J., & Altman, D. G. (2003). Measuring inconsistency in meta-analyses. *British Medical Journal, 327*(7414), 557–560.

Hoeflmayr, D., & Hanewinkel, R. (2008). Do school-based tobacco prevention programmes pay off? The cost-effectiveness of the "Smoke-free Class Competition." *Public Health, 122*, 34–41.

Hollis, J. F., Polen, M. R., Whitlock, E. P., Lichtenstein, E., Mullooly, J. P., Velicer W. F., & Redding, C. A. (2005). Teen Reach: Outcomes from a randomized, controlled trial of a tobacco reduction program for teens seen in primary medical care. *Pediatrics, 115*, 981–989.

Horn, K. A., Dino, G. A., Kalsekar, I. D., & Fernandes, A. W. (2004). Appalachian teen smokers: Not On Tobacco 15 months later. *American Journal of Public Health, 94*, 181–184.

Horn, K., Dino, G., Kalsekar, I., & Mody, R. (2005). The impact of Not On Tobacco on teen smoking cessation. *Journal of Adolescent Research, 20*, 640–661.

Horn, K., Fernandes, A., Dino, G., Massey, C. J., & Kalsekar, I. (2003). Adolescent nicotine dependence and smoking cessation outcomes. *Addictive Behaviours, 28*, 769–776.

Hrubá, D., Zachovalová, V., Matějová, H., & Daňková, I. (2007). "Our class does not smoke"; the Czech version of the "smoke-free class competition" programme. *Central European Journal of Public Health, 15*, 163–166.

Jackson, C., & Dickinson, D. (2003). Can parents who smoke socialise their children against smoking? Results from the Smoke-free Kids intervention trial. *Tobacco Control, 12*, 52–59.

Jackson, C., & Dickinson, D. (2006). Enabling parents who smoke to prevent their children from initiating smoking. Results from a 3-year intervention evaluation. *Archives of Pediatric and Adolescent Medicine, 160*, 56–62.

Jason, L., Billows, W., Schnopp Wyatt, D., & King, C. (1996). Reducing the illegal sales of cigarettes to minors: Analysis of alternative enforcement schedules. *Journal of Applied Behavioral Analysis, 29*, 333–344.

Jones, D. J., Olson, A. L., Forehand, R., Gaffney, C. A., Zens, M. S., & Bau, J. J. (2005). A family-focused randomized controlled trial to prevent adolescent alcohol and tobacco use: The moderating roles of positive parenting and adolescent gender. *Behavior Therapy, 36*, 347–355.

Jøsendal, O., Aarø, L. E., & Bergh, I. (1998). Effects of a school-based smoking prevention program among subgroups of adolescents. *Health Education Research, 13*, 215–224.

Jøsendal, O., Aarø, L. E., Torsheim, T., & Rasbash, J. (2005). Evaluation of the school-based smoking-prevention program "BE smokeFREE." *Scandinavian Journal of Psychology, 46*, 189–199.

Kaufman, J. S., Jason, L. A., Sawlski, L. M., & Halpert, J. A. (1994). A comprehensive multi-media program to prevent smoking among black students. *Journal of Drug Education, 24*, 95–108.

Keay, K. D., Woodruff, S. I., Wildey, M. B., & Kenney, E. M. (1993). Effect of a retailer intervention on cigarette sales to minors in San Diego County, California. *Tobacco Control, 2*, 145–151.

Kellam, S. G., & Anthony, J. C. (1998). Targeting early antecedents to prevent tobacco smoking: Findings from an epidemiologically based randomized field trial. *American Journal of Public Health, 88*, 1490–1495.

Killen, J. D., Robinson, T. N., Ammerman, S., Hayward, C., Rogers, J., Stone, C., . . . Schatzberg, A. F. (2004). Randomized clinical trial of the efficacy of bupropion combined with nicotine patch in the treatment of adolescent smokers. *Journal of Consulting and Clinical Psychology, 72*, 729–735.

Kollerits, B., Heinrich, J., Pichler, M., Rantner, B., Klein-Weigel, P., Wolke, G., . . . Erfurt Male Cohort. (2008). Intermittent claudication in the Erfurt Male Cohort (ERFORT) Study: Its determinants and the impact on mortality. A population-based prospective cohort study with 30 years of follow-up. *Atherosclerosis, 198*, 214–222.

Lavezzi, A. M., Ottaviani, G., & Matturri, L. (2005). Adverse effects of prenatal tobacco smoke exposure on biological parameters of the developing brainstem. *Neurobiology of Disease, 20*, 601–607.

Lipkus, I. M., McBride, C. M., Pollak, K. I., Schwartz-Bloom, R. D., Bloom, P. N., & Tilson, E. (2004). A randomized trial comparing the effects of self-help materials and proactive telephone counseling on teen smoking cessation. *Health Psychology, 23*, 397–406.

Lovato, C., Linn, G., Stead, L. F., & Best, A. (2003). Impact of tobacco advertising and promotion on increasing adolescent smoking behaviours. *Cochrane*

Database of Systematic Reviews, 3, Art. No. CD003439. doi:10.1002/14651858.CD003439

Lloyd, D. M., Alexander, H. M., Callcott, R., Dobson, A. J., Hardes, G. R., O'Connell, D. L., & Leeder, S. R. (1983). Cigarette smoking and drug use in school-children: III—Evaluation of a smoking prevention education programme. *International Journal of Epidemiology, 12*, 51–58.

Mackenbach, J. P., Stirbu, I., Roskam, A. J., Schaap, M. M., Menvielle, G., Leinsalu, M., . . . European Union Working Group on Socioeconomic Inequalities in Health. (2008). Socioeconomic inequalities in health in 22 European countries. *New England Journal of Medicine, 358*, 2468–2481.

McGuire, W. J. (1968). The nature of attitudes and attitude change. In G. Lindzey & E. Aronson (Eds.), *Handbook of social psychology* (pp. 136–314). Reading, MA: Addison-Wesley.

Moolchan, E. T., Robinson, M. L., Ernst, M., Cadet, J. L., Pickworth, W. B., Heishman, S. J., & Schroeder, J. R. (2005). Safety and efficacy of the nicotine patch and gum for treatment of adolescent tobacco addiction. *Pediatrics, 115*, 407–414.

Murray, D. M., & Hannan, P. J. (1990). Planning for the appropriate analysis in school-based drug-use prevention studies. *Journal of Consulting and Clinical Psychology, 58*, 458–468.

Murray, D. M., Luepker, R. V., Johnson, C. A., & Mittelmark, M. B. (1984). The prevention of cigarette smoking in children: A comparison of four strategies. *Journal of Applied Social Psychology, 14*, 274–288.

Murray, D. M., Perry, C. L., Griffin, G., Harty, K. C., Jacobs, D. R., Jr., Schmid, L., . . . Pallonen, U. (1992). Results from a statewide approach to adolescent tobacco use prevention. *Preventive Medicine, 21*, 449–472.

Murray, D. M., & Short, B. J. (1997). Intraclass correlation among measures related to tobacco use by adolescents: Estimates, correlates, and applications in intervention studies. *Addictive Behaviors, 22*, 1–12.

Myers, M. G., & Brown, S. A. (2005). A controlled study of a cigarette smoking cessation intervention for adolescents in substance abuse treatment. *Psychology of Addictive Behaviors, 19*, 230–233.

Nilsson, P. M. (2008). Early vascular aging (EVA): Consequences and prevention. *Vascular Health Risk Management, 4*, 547–552.

Noland, M. P., Kryscio, R. J., Riggs, R. S., Linville, L. H., Ford, V. Y., & Tucker, T. C. (1998). The effectiveness of a tobacco prevention program with adolescents living in a tobacco-producing region. *American Journal of Public Health, 88*, 1862–1865.

Nutbeam, D., Macaskill, P., Smith, C., Simpson, J. M., & Catford, J. (1993). Evaluation of two school smoking education programmes under normal classroom conditions. *British Medical Journal, 306*(6870), 102–107.

Ozasa, K., Katanoda, K., Tamakoshi, A., Sato, H., Tajima, K., Suzuki, T., & Sobue, T. (2008). Reduced life expectancy due to smoking in large-scale cohort studies in Japan. *Journal of Epidemiology, 18*, 111–118.

Palmer, R. F., Graham, J. W., White, E. L., & Hansen, W. B. (1998). Applying multilevel analytic strategies in adolescent substance use prevention research. *Preventive Medicine, 27*, 328–336.

Pelkonen, M. (2008). Smoking: Relationship to chronic bronchitis, chronic obstructive pulmonary disease and mortality. *Current Opinion in Pulmonary Medicine, 14*, 105–109.

Perry, C. L., Komro, K. A., Veblen-Mortenson, S., Bosma, L. M., Farbakhsh, K., Munson, K. A., & Lytle, L. A. (2003). A randomized controlled trial of the middle and junior high school D.A.R.E. and D.A.R.E. Plus programs. *Archives of Pediatric and Adolescent Medicine, 157*, 178–184.

Perry, C. L., Williams, C. L., Veblen-Mortenson, S., Toomey, T. L., Komro, K. A., Anstine, P. S., & Wolfson, M. (1996). Project Northland: Outcomes of a communitywide alcohol use prevention program during early adolescence. *American Journal of Public Health, 86*, 956–965.

Peterson, A.V., Jr., Kealey, K. A., Mann, S. L., Marek, P. M., & Sarason, I. G. (2000). Hutchinson Smoking Prevention Project: Long-term randomized trial in school-based tobacco use prevention-results on smoking. *Journal of the National Cancer Institute, 92*, 1979–1991.

Pierce, J. P., Choi, W. S., Gilpin, E. A., Farkas, A. J., & Berry, C. C. (1998). Tobacco industry promotion of cigarettes and adolescent smoking. *Journal of the American Medical Association, 279*, 511–515.

Piper, M. E., McCarthy, D. E., & Baker, T. B. (2006). Assessing tobacco dependence: A guide to measure evaluation and selection. *Nicotine & Tobacco Research, 8*, 339–351.

Piper, D. L., Moberg, D. P., & King, M. J. (2000). The healthy for life project: Behavioral outcomes. *Journal of Primary Prevention, 21*, 47–73.

Priest, N., Roseby R., Waters, E., Polnay, A., Campbell, R., Spencer, N., . . . Ferguson-Thorne, G. (2008). Family and carer smoking control programmes for reducing children's exposure to environmental tobacco smoke. *Cochrane Database of Systematic Reviews, 4*, Art. No. CD001746. doi:10.1002/14651858.CD001746.pub2

Pucci, L. G., & Siegel, M. (1999). Exposure to brand-specific cigarette advertising in magazines and its impact on youth smoking. *Preventive Medicine, 29*, 313–320.

Richardson, C. G., Johnson. J. L., Ratner, P. A., Zumbo, B. D., Bottorff, J. L., Shoveller, J. A., & Prkachin, K. M. (2007). Validation of the Dimensions of Tobacco Dependence Scale for adolescents. *Addictive Behaviors, 32*, 1498–1504.

Rigotti, N. A., DiFranza, J. R., Chang, Y., Tisdale, T., Kemp, B., & Singer, D. E. (1997). The effect of enforcing tobacco-sales laws on adolescents' access to tobacco and smoking behavior. *New England Journal of Medicine, 337*, 1044–1051.

Said, T. M., Ranga, G., & Agarwal, A. (2005). Relationship between semen quality and tobacco chewing in men undergoing infertility evaluation. *Fertility & Sterility, 84*, 649–653.

Sargent, J. D., Dalton, M., Beach, M., Bernhardt, A., Heatherton, T., & Stevens, M. (2000). Effect of cigarette promotions on smoking uptake among adolescents. *Preventive Medicine, 30*, 320–327.

Scheier, L. M., Botvin, G. J., & Griffin, K. W. (2001). Preventive intervention effects on developmental progression in drug use: Structural equation modeling analyses using longitudinal data. *Prevention Science, 2*, 91–112.

Schinke, S. P., Gilchrist, L. D., Schilling, R. F., II, & Senechal, V. A. (1986). Smoking and smokeless tobacco use among adolescents: Trends and intervention results. *Public Health Reports, 101*, 373–378.

Schinke, S. P., Schwinn, T. M., Di Noia, J., & Cole, K. C. (2004). Reducing the risks of alcohol use among urban youth: Three-year effects of a computer-based intervention with and without parent involvement. *Journal of Studies in Alcohol, 65*, 443–449.

Schinke, S. P., Tepavac, L., & Cole, K. C. (2000). Preventing substance use among Native American youth: Three-year results. *Addictive Behavior, 25*, 387–397.

Schofield, M. J., Lynagh, M., & Mishra, G. (2003). Evaluation of a Health Promoting Schools program to reduce smoking in Australian secondary schools. *Health Education Research, 18*, 678–692.

Schofield, M. J., Sanson-Fisher, R. W., & Gulliver, S. B. (1997). Interventions with retailers to reduce cigarette sales to minors: A randomised controlled trial. *Australian and New Zealand Journal of Public Health, 21*, 590–596.

Schulze, A., Ehrmann, K., Schunk, S., & Pötschke-Langer, M. (2005). Ergebnisse aus zwei bundesweiten "Rauchfrei"-Kampagnen. [Results of two nationwide "smokefree" campaigns]. *Gesundheitswesen, 67*, 872–878.

Schulze, A., Mons, U., Edler, L., & Pötschke-Langer, M. (2006). Lack of sustainable prevention effect of the "Smoke-Free Class Competition" on German pupils. *Preventive Medicine, 42*, 33–39.

Severson, H. H., Andrews, J. A., Lichtenstein, E., Danaher, B. G., & Akers, L. (2007). Self-help cessation programs for smokeless tobacco users: Long-term follow-up of a randomized trial. *Nicotine & Tobacco Research, 9*, 281–289.

Severson, H. H., Glasgow, R., Wirt, R., Brozovsky, P., Zoref, L., Biglan, A., . . . Weissman, W. (1991). Preventing the use of smokeless tobacco and cigarettes by teens: Results of a classroom intervention. *Health Education Research, 6*, 109–120.

Siddiqui, O., Hedeker, D., Flay, B., & Hu, F. (1996). Intraclass correlation estimates in a school-based

smoking prevention study. *American Journal of Epidemiology, 144*, 425–433.

Skretny, M. T., Cummings, K. M., Sciandra, E., & Marshall, J. (1990). An intervention to reduce the sale of cigarettes to minors in New York State. *New York State Journal of Medicine, 92*, 521–525.

Sowden, A. J., & Arblaster, L. (1998). Mass media interventions for preventing smoking in young people. *Cochrane Database of Systematic Reviews, 4*, Art. No. CD001006. doi:10.1002/14651858.CD001006

Sowden, A., & Stead, L. (2003). Community interventions for preventing smoking in young people. *Cochrane Database of Systematic Reviews, 1*, Art. No. CD001291. doi:10.1002/14651858.CD001291

Spoth, R. L., Redmond, C., & Shin, C. (2001). Randomized trial of brief family interventions for general populations: Adolescent substance use outcomes 4 years following baseline. *Journal of Consulting and Clinical Psychology, 69*, 627–642.

Spoth, R. L., Redmond, C., Trudeau, L., & Shin, C. (2002). Longitudinal substance initiation outcomes for a universal preventive intervention combining family and school programs. *Psychology of Addictive Behaviors, 16*, 129–134.

Staff, M., March, L., Brnabic, A., Hort, K., Alcock, J., Coles, S., & Baxter, R. (1998). Can non-prosecutory enforcement of public health legislation reduce smoking among high school students? *Australian and New Zealand Journal of Public Health, 22*, 332–335.

Stanton, B., Cole, M., Galbraith, J., Li, X., Pendleton, S., Cottrel, L., . . . Kaljee, L. (2004). Randomized trial of a parent intervention: Parents can make a difference in long-term adolescent risk behaviors, perceptions, and knowledge. *Archives of Pediatrics and Adolescent Medicine, 158*, 947–955.

Stead, L. F., & Lancaster, T. (2005). Interventions for preventing tobacco sales to minors. *Cochrane Database of Systematic Reviews, 1*, Art. No. CD001497. doi:10.1002/14651858.CD001497.pub2

Stevens, M. M., Olson, A. L., Gaffney, C. A., Tosteson, T. D., Mott, L. A., & Starr, P. (2002). A pediatric, practice-based, randomized trial of drinking and smoking prevention and bicycle helmet, gun, and seatbelt safety promotion. *Pediatrics, 109*, 490–497.

Storr, C. L., Ialongo, N. S., Kellam, S. G., & Anthony, J. C. (2002). A randomized controlled trial of two primary school intervention strategies to prevent early onset tobacco smoking. *Drug and Alcohol Dependence, 66*, 51–60.

Stotts, R. C., Roberson, P. K., Hanna, E. Y., Jones, S. K., & Smith, C. K. (2003). A randomized clinical trial of nicotine patches for treatment of spit tobacco addiction among adolescents. *Tobacco Control, 12*(Suppl 4), iv11–iv15.

Sussman, S., Dent, C. W., & Litchman, K. L. (2001). Project EX: Outcomes of teen smoking cessation program. *Addictive Behaviors, 26*, 425–438.

Sussman, S., Dent, C. W., Simon, T. R., Stacy, A. W., Galaif, E. R., Moss, A. M., . . . Johnson, C. A. (1995). Immediate impact of social influence-oriented substance abuse prevention curricula in traditional and continuation high schools. *Drugs & Society, 8*(3/4), 65–81.

Sussman, S., Dent, C. W., Stacy, A. W., & Craig, S. (1998). One-year outcomes of Project Towards No Drug Abuse. *Preventive Medicine, 27,* 632–642.

Sussman, S., Dent, C. W., Stacy, A. W., Hodgson, C. S., Burton, D., & Flay, B. R. (1993). Project Towards No Tobacco Use: Implementation, process and post-test knowledge evaluation. *Health Education Research, 8,* 109–123.

Telch, M. J., Miller, L. M., Killen, J. D., Cooke, S., & Maccoby, N. (1990). Social influences approach to smoking prevention: The effects of videotape delivery with and without same-age peer leader participation. *Addictive Behaviors, 15,* 21–28.

Thomas, R. E., Baker, P., & Lorenzetti, D. (2007). Family-based programmes for preventing smoking by children and adolescents. *Cochrane Database of Systematic Reviews, 1,* Art. No. CD004493. doi:10.1002/14651858.CD004493.pub2

Thomas, R., & Perera, R. (2006). School-based programmes for preventing smoking. *Cochrane Database of Systematic Reviews, 3,* Art. No. CD001293. doi:10.1002/14651858.CD001293.pub2

Thomson, N. C., Chaudhuri, R., & Livingston, E. (2004). Asthma and cigarette smoking. *European Respiratory Journal, 24,* 822–833.

Tutt, D., Bauer, L., Edwards, C., & Cook, D. (2000). Reducing adolescent smoking rates. Maintaining high retail compliance results in substantial improvements. *Health Promotion Journal of Australia, 10,* 20–24.

Unger, J. B., Chou, C. P., Palmer, P. H., Ritt-Olson, A., Gallaher, P., Cen, S., . . . Johnson, C. A. (2004). Project FLAVOR: 1-year outcomes of a multicultural, school-based smoking prevention curriculum for adolescents. *American Journal of Public Health, 9,* 263–265.

U.S. 2000 National Youth Tobacco Survey. (2001). Youth tobacco surveillance—United States, 2000. *Morbidity & Mortality Weekly Report. CDC Surveillance Summaries, 50*(4), 1–84 [erratum in *MMWR CDC Surveillance Summaries, 2001 Nov 23, 50*(46), 1036].

Vartiainen, E., Paavola, M., McAlister, A., & Puska, P. (1998). Fifteen-year follow-up of smoking prevention effects in the North Karelia Youth Project. *American Journal of Public Health, 88,* 81–85.

Walsh, M. M., Hilton, J. F., Ellison, J. A., Gee, L., Chesney, M. A., Tomar, S. L., & Ernster, V. L. (2003). Spit (smokeless) tobacco intervention for high school athletes. Results after 1 year. *Addictive Behaviors, 28,* 1095–1113.

Walter, H. J., Hofman, A., Connelly, P. A., Barrett, L. T., & Kost, K. L. (1985). Primary prevention of chronic disease in childhood: Changes in risk factors after one year of intervention. *American Journal of Epidemiology, 122,* 772–781.

Walter, H. J., Hofman, A., Connelly, P. A., Barrett, L. T., & Kost, K. L. (1986). Coronary heart disease prevention in childhood: One-year results of a randomized intervention study. *American Journal of Preventive Medicine, 2,* 239–249.

Warren, C. W., Jones, N. R., Peruga, A., Chauvin, J., Baptiste, J. P., Costa de Silva, V., . . . Centers for Disease Control and Prevention (CDC). (2008). Global youth tobacco surveillance, 2000–2007. *Morbidity & Mortality Weekly Report. Surveillance Summaries, 57,* 1–28.

Wenter, D. L., Blackwell, S., Davis, K. S., & Farrelly, M. C. (2002). *Using multiple strategies in tobacco use prevention. Legacy first look report 8.* Washington, DC: American Legacy Foundation. Retrieved from http://www.americanlegacy.org/content/PDF/FLR8.pdf.

While, D., Kelly, S., Huang, W., & Charlton, A. (1996). Cigarette advertising and onset of smoking in children: Questionnaire survey. *British Medical Journal, 313*(7054), 398–399.

Wiborg, G., & Hanewinkel, R. (2002). Effectiveness of the "Smoke-Free Class Competition" in delaying the onset of smoking in adolescence. *Preventive Medicine, 35,* 241–249.

Wiborg, G., Hanewinkel, R., & Kliche, K.-O. (2002). Verhütung des Einstiegs in das Rauchen durch die Kampagne "Be Smart—Don't Start": eine Analyse nach Schularten. ["Be smart—don't start" campaign to prevent children from starting to smoke: An analysis according to type of school attended]. *Deutsche Medizinische Wochenschrift, 127,* 430–436.

Wiehe, S. E., Garrison, M. M., Christakis, D. A., Ebel, B. E., & Rivara, F. P. (2005). A systematic review of school-based prevention trials with long-term follow-up. *Adolescent Health, 36,* 162–169.

Woloshin, S., Schwartz, L. M., & Welch, H. G. (2008). The risk of death by age, sex, and smoking status in the United States: Putting health risks in context. *Journal of the National Cancer Institute, 100,* 845–853.

Wu, Y., Stanton, B. F., Galbraith, J., Kaljee, L., Cottrell, L., & Li, X. (2003). Sustaining and broadening intervention impact: A longitudinal randomized trial of 3 adolescent risk reduction approaches. *Pediatrics, 111,* e32–e36.

Zdravkovic, T., Genbacev, O., McMaster, M. T., & Fisher, S. J. (2005). The adverse effects of maternal smoking on the human placenta: A review. *Placenta, 26*(Suppl. A), S81–S86.

Zhang, D., & Qiu, X. (1993). School-based tobacco-use prevention—People's Republic of China, May 1989–January 1990. *Morbidity & Mortality Weekly Report, 42,* 370–371, 377.

22

Depressive Disorders in
Children and Adolescents

WILLIAM MARTINEZ, KRISTEN ZYCHINSKI, AND ANTONIO J. POLO

OVERVIEW OF DEPRESSIVE DISORDERS

Depression is a widespread and pervasive condition, affecting functioning in a multitude of areas; however, it was only recently that depression was recognized as a disorder impacting children and adolescents. A line of research from the 1970s provided evidence that depression significantly impacts youth, and the research base has been growing since that point (Lewinsohn, Rohde, & Seeley, 1998). Despite this increasing body of literature, less is known about the existence and presentation of depression in youth relative to its presence in and impact on adults. Although depressive symptoms may manifest differently among youth, general consensus identifies two main forms of depression for both adults and youth: major depressive disorder (MDD) and dysthymic disorder (DD).

Diagnostic Criteria

According to the *Diagnostic and Statistical Manual of Mental Disorders* (4th ed., text revision) (*DSM-IV-TR*), MDD is defined as the presence over time of one or more major depressive episodes without a history of manic, mixed, or hypomanic episodes (American Psychiatric Association [APA], 2000). A major depressive episode involves five criteria (A–E). The first criterion (A) requires the presence of at least five symptoms, including one or more of the following primary symptoms: depressed mood or a decreased interest or sense of pleasure in activities. Additional symptoms include changes in weight or appetite, sleep disturbances, psychomotor agitation or retardation, diminished energy, feelings of worthlessness or guilt, difficulty concentrating or making decisions, and thoughts of death or suicide. Beyond the presence of these symptoms, criteria B through D stipulate that an individual with MDD must not meet criteria for a mixed episode (B); must experience impairment in social, occupational, or other areas of functioning (C); and must not have developed symptoms as a result of a medical condition or substance (D). Additionally, the experience of the episode should not be the result of bereavement, or the death of a loved one, within the previous 2 months (criterion E). MDDs can be further described by severity descriptors, such as mild, moderate, or severe (with and without psychotic features). Additional diagnostic specifiers include: chronic, with catatonic features (e.g., motor disturbance, echolalia); with melancholic features (e.g., loss of pleasure or interest, depression worse in the morning); with atypical features (e.g., mood reactivity, hypersomnia); and with postpartum onset (i.e., episode onsets within 4 weeks postpartum; APA, 2000).

In addition to MDD, the experience of depressive symptoms may result in a diagnosis of DD, described as less severe but with a more chronic course than MDD (APA, 2000). Criterion A in DD involves the presence of depressed mood for more days than not over the course of 2 years. In addition to depressed mood, individuals with DD must experience at least two of the following symptoms: disturbances in weight, appetite, or sleep; fatigue; low self-esteem; difficulty concentrating or making decisions; and feeling hopeless (criterion B). Over the course of 2 years, these symptoms must never be absent for longer than 2 months (criterion C), and an individual must not meet criteria for a major depressive episode (criterion D). Further, there must not be a history of manic, mixed, or hypomanic episodes (criterion E), and the symptoms must not occur during a psychotic disorder (criterion F) or as a result of substance use or a general medical condition (criterion G). Individuals with DD must also experience some level of impairment in at least one area of functioning (criterion H). The *DSM-IV-TR* includes several considerations when applying diagnoses of MDD and DD to children and adolescents. First, youth may experience the primary symptom of depressed mood as irritability. Additionally, symptoms need only be experienced over the course of 1 year when considering a diagnosis of DD for youth.

Demographic Variables

According to a review of epidemiological literature on child and adolescent mood disorders, prevalence estimates vary by study. Across studies, point prevalence of MDD ranges from 1% to 6%, and lifetime prevalence falls between 4% and 25% (Kessler, Avenevoli, & Merikangas, 2001). Based on findings from the National Comorbidity Survey, the lifetime prevalence of MDD for 15- to 18-year-olds is estimated to be about 14% (Kessler et al., 1994); however, this statistic is slightly lower than the lifetime prevalence rate of 20.4% found in a large study of 14- to 18-year-old high school students (Lewinsohn et al., 1998). The point prevalence for this same sample of adolescents was estimated to be 2.9%, and the incidence of MDD during the 12-month study period was found to be 7.8%.

The majority of epidemiological research has focused on adolescents, as this is typically the time during which MDD rates increase; however, the Great Smoky Mountains Study of Youth estimates a 3-month MDD prevalence rate of 0.03%, with a rate of 0.13% for DD and 1.45% for depressive disorder not otherwise specified in preadolescent children (Costello et al., 1996). Rates of depression in preschool-age children are generally thought to be much lower, and a recent study of racially and socioeconomically diverse 4-year-olds found prevalence rates of 0.3% for MDD and DD (Lavigne, LeBailly, Hopkins, Gouze, & Binns, 2009). A meta-analysis of epidemiological studies with youth samples confirmed the pattern seen earlier: prevalence rates of depressive disorders in adolescents are about twice as large as those found in children under the age of 13 (5.6% vs. 2.8%; Costello, Erkanli, & Angold, 2006). Notably, Kessler et al. (2001) found that, across epidemiological studies, 20%–50% of child and adolescent respondents exceeded cut-off scores for clinically significant depression on self-report measures. This may indicate that a substantial segment of the youth population experiences moderate to severe levels of depressive symptoms without meeting full criteria for a depressive disorder.

Based on a sample of high-school students, onset of MDD occurs at a mean age of 14.9 years. Further, incidence rates increase from 1% to 2% among 13-year-olds to 3%–7% among 15-year-olds (Lewinsohn et al., 1998). Retrospective reports from the National Comorbidity Survey indicate that about 50% of adults with a history of MDD experienced their first episode prior to the age of 18 (Kessler et al., 2003). Evidence suggests that, among individuals from an adolescent community sample, the mean duration of major depressive episodes was 26 weeks, with a median of 8 weeks (Lewinsohn et al., 1994). Across studies, depression was found to be generally consistent over time, with high rates of recurrence (Kessler et al., 2001). In a community sample, 5% of adolescents experienced a depressive disorder within 6 months of the previous episode, whereas 12% went on to report an episode within 1 year and about 33% within 4 years (Lewinsohn et al., 1994). In contrast to the mean duration and time to recurrence found in a community sample, children and adolescents from clinical samples are more likely to experience longer depressive episodes and report less time between episodes. In a review of research on clinical samples, the mean duration was found to be 7 to 9 months, and 70% of youth experienced a recurrent episode within 5 years (Kovacs, 1996).

Across childhood and adolescence, symptom presentation appears to be relatively consistent. Based on retrospective reports, symptoms experienced during depressive episodes before the age of 14 have not been found to be significantly different from symptoms occurring after the age of 14 (Lewinsohn et al., 1998). Similarly, longitudinal data suggests that symptoms do not change significantly from adolescence to young adulthood (Lewinsohn, Pettit, Joiner, & Seeley, 2003). A comparison of symptom prevalence rates in adolescence to those found among adults in the Epidemiologic Catchment Area Study reveals that the course of depression remains generally similar over time; however, adolescents were more likely to report symptoms related to worthlessness and guilt, whereas adults reported higher rates of weight/appetite disturbances and suicidal ideation (Lewinsohn et al., 1998). Additionally, in adolescence, the most frequently reported symptoms were depressed mood, difficulties concentrating and making decisions, and changes in sleeping and/or eating habits (R. E. Roberts, Lewinsohn, & Seeley, 1995). Moreover, symptom prevalence has been found to be generally similar in groups of male and female adolescents (Lewinsohn et al., 2003).

Prevalence rates of depression overall, however, are significantly different for males and females. A review of studies involving children and adolescents reports slightly higher levels of depressed mood in males prior to adolescence; however, females' reports of depressive symptoms rise significantly during the period of early adolescence (Kessler et al., 2001). In a community sample of 14- to 18-year-olds, for example, the lifetime prevalence of MDD was estimated at 24.8% for females and 11.6% for males (Lewinsohn et al., 1998). In a meta-analysis of studies involving the Children's Depression Inventory (CDI), girls' scores remained stable from the ages of 8 to 11 and then increased significantly between 12 and 16. In contrast, boys' CDI scores were reported to be similar across age groups (Twenge & Nolen-Hoeksema, 2002). Higher rates of depression across female samples are found across studies (Allgood-Merten, Lewinsohn, & Hops, 1990; R. Roberts & Sobhan, 1992; Siegel, Yancey, Aneshensel, & Schuler, 1999), and a recent meta-analysis of epidemiological studies confirms that rates of depression in female adolescents are higher than those found for males (Costello et al., 2006).

Although less work has been done to study the differences in depression rates across racial and ethnic groups, results are consistent across studies in this area. In a diverse community sample of middle school students, Mexican American youth had higher prevalence rates of MDD than all other racial and ethnic groups, including European, African, and Asian Americans (R. Roberts, Roberts, & Chen, 1997). Similarly, in a national survey of 12- to 17-year-olds, Mexican American males and females reported higher levels of depressive symptoms on a self-report symptom scale (R. Roberts & Sobhan, 1992). In studies involving the CDI, Latino youth have scored significantly higher on this scale than children and adolescents from all other racial and ethnic groups sampled (Siegel et al., 1999; Twenge & Nolen-Hoeksema, 2002).

With regard to socioeconomic status (SES), results are mixed across studies. One meta-analysis involving the CDI found no differences across SES groups with respect to depressive symptoms (Twenge & Nolen-Hoeksema, 2002). In another study, however, children and adolescents who reported having fewer financial resources also reported higher levels of depression (R. Roberts et al., 1997).

Etiological Factors

A review of twin, family, and adoption studies involving depression in children and adolescents concluded that biology and genetics are important factors in influencing the development of depression in youth (Kessler et al., 2001). Additionally, this same review found that parental psychopathology was the most important factor in predicting the occurrence of depression in youth, pointing to the influence of both genetics and environment (Kessler et al., 2001). Other research has focused on the impact of psychosocial risk factors in predicting the onset of depressive disorders. Lewinsohn et al. (1994), for example, found that the most significant risk factors preceding the development of depression included internalizing problems, a suicide attempt, and the presence of a non-affective disorder. Physical impairments due to medical conditions also significantly predicted the onset of depression in adolescents (Lewinsohn, Seeley, Hibbard, Rohde, & Sack, 1996). It is hypothesized that, given the strong evidence for the influence of genetic, biological, and psychosocial factors in impacting the development of depression, it is the complex interplay of these factors that ultimately determines the onset and course of depressive disorders (Lewinsohn et al., 1998). As the literature suggests, depression is a complicated and multiply determined condition, and a full discussion of its etiology is beyond the scope of this chapter. For more detailed information, the reader is directed to Abela and Hankin (2007).

Impact of Depression

Depression is regarded as a disorder with a wide-ranging, debilitating impact on a variety of domains in children and adolescents. In adolescents, depression has been associated with difficulties in adaptive functioning, higher levels of negative cognitions and stress, lower self-esteem, interpersonal conflict, and smaller social support networks (Lewinsohn et al., 1998). Literature also suggests that depression in youth is negatively correlated with measures of academic achievement, including standardized test scores and grades (Accordino, Accordino, & Slaney, 2000; Ialongo, Edelsohn, & Kellam, 2001). Depressive symptoms may also be linked to lower self-efficacy in youth (Muris, 2002). Further, experiencing MDD as an adolescent serves as a risk factor for impairment and disease as an adult (Lewinsohn et al., 1998; Rice, Lifford, Thomas, & Thapar, 2007). Areas of functioning that may be impacted into adulthood include occupational performance, physical health, substance use, smoking, quality of life, and continuing psychopathology (Lewinsohn et al., 2003; Rice et al., 2007). Notably, suicidal ideation and attempts are significantly associated with depression in children and adolescents, and the majority of children and adolescents with depression also suffer from a comorbid psychiatric disorder (Kessler et al., 2001). In light of the substantial impact that youth depression has on current and future outcomes, it is increasingly necessary to develop and investigate interventions aimed at treating this pervasive disorder.

EVIDENCE-BASED TREATMENT CRITERIA

The American Psychological Association Task Force for Promotion and Dissemination of Psychological Procedures, along with subsequent modifications, established criteria for determining the efficacy of psychosocial treatments for both group and single-subject designs (Chambless et al., 1998; Chambless & Hollon, 1998; Chambless & Ollendick, 2001). Based largely on these classifications, Silverman and Hinshaw (2008) proposed that treatments and protocols be classified into three categories: *well-established*, *probably efficacious*, and *experimental*. This chapter will outline treatments designed to treat depression in children and adolescents based on the aforementioned standards and categories; however, due to the dearth of studies focusing on youth depression treatments employing single-subject designs, this chapter will only review between-group designs.

Two major reviews of the literature on psychosocial treatments for depression employing the Chambless and Hollon (1998) criteria have been completed. In the first, Kaslow and Thompson (1998) found that two cognitive behavior therapy (CBT) protocols, *Self-Control Therapy* (Stark, Reynolds, & Kaslow, 1987; Stark, Rouse, & Livingston, 1991) and *Adolescents Coping with Depression* (Lewinsohn, Clarke, Hops, & Andrews, 1990; Lewinsohn, Clarke, Rohde, Hops, & Seeley, 1996), were found to be probably efficacious and no protocols were found to be well-established. Ten years later, David-Ferdon and Kaslow (2008) updated the original review and found that, in contrast to earlier findings, both CBT and interpersonal psychotherapy (IPT) treatment orientations had earned the well-established classification. Classifications were additionally presented separately for specific intervention modalities within these treatments (e.g., individual, individual with parent, group only) and, responding to developmental considerations, separately for children and adolescents.

The present review of psychosocial treatments for youth depression employs a structure similar to the aforementioned published reviews of the literature. Information is first organized by treatment orientation (e.g., CBT, IPT), followed by a review of different modalities within each orientation (e.g., group

treatment, individual treatment) and specific protocols within each modality (e.g., *Adolescents Coping with Depression*, *Self-Control Therapy*, *Penn Prevention Program*). Additionally, the discussion will be organized to include evidence for the efficacy of treatment orientations, modalities, and protocols for children (12 years and younger) and for adolescents (13 years and older) as outlined by David-Ferdon and Kaslow (2008). Treatment orientations and modalities with *experimental* classification, according to Silverman and Hinshaw's (2008) criteria, will not be reviewed. These include nondirected support/psychoeducational and family systems theoretical orientations.

The information in the 2008 review is supplemented by studies published since 2007. A literature search was completed using the PsycINFO and PubMed databases and utilized the same search terms as those described by David-Ferdon and Kaslow. In addition, the same inclusion and exclusion criteria were used. The literature search of studies published since 2007 yielded 25 treatment outcome studies; however, only eight met inclusion criteria. Studies were excluded because they (a) did not employ a control group (e.g., Richardson, McCauley, & Katon, 2009), (b) were part of an experimental treatment orientation such as family systems or psychoeducation (e.g., Hoek, Schuurmans, Koot, & Cuijpers, 2009), or (c) were not a randomized controlled trial (RCT) (e.g., Jungbluth & Shirk, 2009).

The classification system to determine empirically validated treatments, as they were originally called, has not gone without criticism and controversy. One concern is that treatments may earn a well-established classification despite evidence that they are not always efficacious. Therefore, a broader discussion of the overall efficacy and potency of CBT and IPT will also be included. Specifically, clinical significance, or the degree to which an intervention improves a person's functioning, will be discussed as it relates to the current evidence base for each modality. In addition, studies examining the comparative effects of CBT and IPT versus active treatments will be reviewed. Finally, meta-analytic reviews of treatment outcome studies (e.g., J. R. Weisz, Weiss, Han, Granger, & Morton, 1995) will be compared as these reviews include all treatment outcome studies regardless of whether or not they found statistically significant effects in favor of these treatment orientations. The chapter will conclude with recommendations for moving beyond the use of efficacy as a marker for treatment excellence and the provision of evidence-based practice guidelines according to the most recent research findings.

COGNITIVE BEHAVIOR THERAPY

The most widely used and researched psychosocial treatment orientation for depression in children and adolescents is cognitive behavior therapy (Harrington, Whittaker, Shoebridge, & Campbell, 1998). Most intervention models of CBT for depression are based on Beck, Rush, Shaw, and Emery's (1979) cognitive theory of depression, which posits that depressed individuals engage in thinking that is characterized as being overly negative and pessimistic regarding themselves, the world, and their futures. An underlying assumption of CBT is that disturbances in cognitive processes are directly connected to emotional distress. Thus, the goal of CBT is to address these maladaptive cognitions and behavioral patterns to combat depressed mood through psychoeducation and the promotion of adaptive coping skills. Mood-enhancing techniques employed in CBT include relaxation, activity selection, cognitive restructuring, problem solving, and social skills training.

CBT for Depression in Children

In David-Ferdon and Kaslow's (2008) review, CBT was found to be a well-established treatment for depression in children 12 years or younger who have been diagnosed with a depressive disorder. Based on a total of 10 distinct studies (Asarnow, Scott, & Mintz, 2002; Gillham, Reivich, Jaycox, & Seligman, 1995; Jaycox, Reivich, Gillham, & Seligman, 1994; Kahn, Kehle, Jenson, & Clark, 1990; Nelson, Barnard, & Cain, 2003; C. Roberts, Kane, Thomson, Bishop, & Hart, 2003; Stark, Rouse, & Livingston, 1991; Stark et al., 1987; J. R. Weisz, Thurber, Sweeney, Proffitt, & LeGagnoux, 1997; Yu & Seligman, 2002), CBT demonstrated superior effects when compared to both active treatments and no-treatment control groups. One additional study focusing on individual CBT for depression among children was published after 2007 (J. Weisz et al., 2009); however, it did not meet the methodological criteria outlined in the David-Ferdon and Kaslow (2008) review because CBT was not found to be superior to the comparison intervention (usual care). Therefore, the evidence-based efficacy classification of individual CBT for children remains unchanged. A summary of the evidence base for the well-established CBT modalities for children and adolescents as well as information on the specific CBT treatment protocols will be presented next.

CBT Group Treatments for Children

Seven well-designed studies provided evidence for the efficacy of the CBT group modality (David-Ferdon & Kaslow, 2008). Child-only group treatments and child-plus-parent group interventions are the two well-established CBT modalities with children 12 years of age and under. Two specific treatment protocols were found to be probably efficacious: *Self-Control Therapy* and the *Penn Prevention Program.*

The *Self-Control Therapy* program developed by Stark, Reynolds, and Kaslow (1987) is a school-based group intervention approach whose goal is to teach children self-management skills. A version of *Self-Control Therapy* with a parent component is also available (Stark et al., 1991). Whereas two well-designed RCTs demonstrated that Self-Control Therapy performed better than a psychological placebo and included a treatment manual, the same research group performed both studies. In addition, the Stark et al. (1991) study employed a parent component version of Self-Control Therapy, making the intervention slightly different than the one delivered in the Stark et al. (1987) study. Thus, criteria were not met for a well-established treatment.

Similarly, the *Penn Prevention Program* (Gillham, Hamilton, et al., 2006; Gillham et al., 1995; Jaycox et al., 1994; C. Roberts et al., 2003; Yu & Seligman, 2002) is a group-based intervention delivered in school settings. Its CBT approach focuses on both identifying negative thoughts and improving social problem-solving skills. It is also known as the *Penn Resiliency Program*, and the evidence base includes a modification for Chinese children in mainland China named the *Penn Optimism Program* (Yu & Seligman, 2002). The Penn Prevention Program studies include a treatment manual and have been carried out by independent research groups. In addition, at least two RCTs have demonstrated that the Penn Prevention Program is better than a no-treatment control group; however, the intervention falls short of meeting the criteria for a well-established treatment because only one study has found that the Penn Prevention Program is superior to a psychological placebo.

CBT for Depression in Adolescents

David-Ferdon and Kaslow's (2008) review also classified CBT as a well-established theoretical orientation for adolescents ages 13 through 18 years. Up to that point, a total of 15 studies had found that a CBT program for adolescent depression was better than a no-treatment control group or a psychological placebo (Ackerson, Scogin, McKendree-Smith, & Lyman, 1998; Asarnow et al., 2005; Brent et al., 1997; G. N. Clarke et al., 1995; G. N. Clarke et al., 2001; G. N. Clarke, Rohde,

Lewinsohn, Hops, & Seeley, 1999; Kowalenko et al., 2005; Lewinsohn et al., 1990; Lewinsohn et al., 1996; Melvin et al., 2006; Reynolds & Coats, 1986; Rohde, Clarke, Mace, Jorgensen, & Seeley, 2004; Rosselló & Bernal, 1999; Treatment for Adolescents with Depression Study (TADS) Team, 2004; Wood, Harrington, & Moore, 1996). Several modalities have been tested for adolescents within the CBT theoretical orientation, including adolescent-only group, group with parent component, individual treatment, and individual treatment with parent component. No group treatment protocols were found to be well-established, and one, *Adolescents Coping with Depression* (CWD-A), was found to be probably efficacious.

In addition to the 15 studies identified in the David-Kerdon and Kaslow (2008) review, five RCTs have been published since 2007 involving CBT treatments for adolescent depression (Brent et al., 2008; Garber et al., 2009; Rosselló, Bernal, & Rivera-Medina, 2008; Stice, Burton, Bearman, & Rohde, 2007; Stice, Rohde, Seeley, & Gau, 2008). All five studies included a group CBT condition. In one of these studies (Rosselló et al., 2008), both group and individual CBT modalities were included and compared to group and individual IPT modalities. Overall, CBT was significantly more effective at reducing depressive symptoms than IPT; however, information was not provided comparing treatment modalities within each orientation (e.g., group CBT vs. individual IPT, individual CBT vs. individual IPT). Therefore, the results do not represent evidence for either individual or group CBT treatments. Cognitive behavior therapy with adolescents was already found to be a well-established treatment orientation for depression. Therefore, these studies further support the efficacy of this modality but do not change the classification given in David-Ferdon and Kaslow's (2008) review.

CBT Group Treatments for Adolescents

Adolescent-only group treatment is the only CBT modality that was supported by enough research to be classified by David-Ferdon and Kaslow (2008) as well-established. The support included six clinical trials (G. N. Clarke et al., 1995; G. N. Clarke et al., 1999; Kowalenko et al., 2005; Lewinsohn et al., 1990; Lewinsohn et al., 1996; Reynolds & Coats, 1986) completed by at least two independent research groups, and in which at least two studies found the adolescent-only group modality to be superior to a psychological placebo. As noted earlier, two more studies (Stice et al., 2007; Stice et al., 2008) have been published since 2007. In the first study, the adolescent-only brief CBT delivered in groups was superior to a wait-list control group. In their most recent trial, the adolescent-only brief CBT intervention was superior to both supportive-expressive therapy and bibliotherapy conditions at posttreatment. Adolescent-only CBT group modalities were already well-established by the David-Ferdon and Kaslow (2008) review, and the addition of these two studies does not change the classification but provides further support for the efficacy of this treatment modality.

The adolescent group with parent component CBT modality was classified by David-Ferdon and Kaslow (2008) as probably efficacious, supported by five RCTs (G. N. Clarke et al., 2001; G. N. Clarke et al., 1999; Lewinsohn et al., 1990; Lewinsohn et al., 1996; Rohde et al., 2004). None of these studies were completed by an independent research group, thus failing to meet criteria for a well-established treatment. Since 2007, two additional RCTs employing a group with parent component modality have been published (Brent et al., 2008; Garber et al., 2009). Both provide evidence supporting the efficacy of adolescent CBT group with parent component; however, this treatment modality falls short of being eligible for a well-established treatment classification because neither study was conducted by an independent group. The group CBT with parent component modality therefore continues to be classified as probably efficacious.

As previously mentioned, no specific group treatment protocols have been found to be well-established, but one, *Adolescents Coping with Depression* (CWD-A), was found to have enough support to merit the classification of probably efficacious (David-Ferdon & Kaslow, 2008). The CWD-A treatment protocol is a modified version of an adult group treatment protocol for depression comprised of various CBT modules, including relaxation training, cognitive restructuring, and problem-solving skills among other CBT techniques (G. N. Clarke et al., 1995; G. N. Clarke et al., 2001; G. N. Clarke et al., 1999; Lewinsohn et al., 1990; Lewinsohn et al., 1996; Rohde et al., 2004). Two versions of CWD-A are available. The first is an adolescent-only version and the second adds a parent component. In David-Ferdon and Kaslow's (2008) review, both of these modalities were classified as probably efficacious and failed to meet criteria for well-established classification because evidence of efficacy had not been established by an independent research team.

Since 2007, four clinical trials including modified versions of CWD-A were published (Brent et al., 2008; Garber et al., 2009; Stice et al., 2007; Stice et al., 2008). In the Stice et al. (2007) and Stice et al. (2008) studies, evidence is found for the efficacy of a brief six-session version of CWD-A without a parent component. The study published by Brent et al. (2008) used a protocol that was based on the CWD-A along with other CBT protocols. Finally, Garber et al. (2009) tested the effects of a modified CWD-A protocol with a parent component (eight sessions plus six monthly continuation visits). Although these studies provide additional support for the general efficacy of CBT for depressed adolescents, they do not change the evidence-based classification of CWD-A for two reasons. First, all were modified versions of CWD-A and none used the original CWD-A manual. Second, none of the studies were carried out by independent research groups. Therefore, both CWD-A and CWD-A with a parent component retain their probably efficacious classification.

CBT Individual Treatments for Adolescents

David-Ferdon and Kaslow (2008) classified adolescent-only CBT and adolescent-plus-parent CBT modalities as probably efficacious. Two RCTs (Rosselló & Bernal, 1999; Wood et al., 1996) evaluated the efficacy of adolescent-only CBT, whereas three RCTs (Brent et al., 1997; Melvin et al., 2006; TADS Team, 2004) evaluated the adolescent-plus-parent CBT modality. At least two RCTs were completed by independent research groups for each modality; however, none of the protocols for individual CBT have been classified as at least probably efficacious. Therefore, the individual CBT category could not be classified as well-established (David-Ferdon & Kaslow, 2008). No adolescent-only CBT or adolescent-plus-parent CBT studies for adolescent depression were published since 2007. Therefore, individual CBT remains classified as probably efficacious.

Clinical Significance in CBT

Clinical significance is defined as either the degree to which an intervention improves a person's functioning relative to a population affected by the same disorder or improvement to a point equivalent to a normal functioning population (Jacobson & Truax, 1991). Functioning can include social, work, and home dimensions. Among youth, functioning is often also evaluated in terms of academic achievement and relationships with teachers and parents. Clinical significance allows reviewers of studies to ascertain whether a treatment has demonstrated the ability to not only statistically significantly reduce symptoms associated with a disorder but to assess whether that change in symptoms has also positively and meaningfully impacted a participant's life. A treatment may cause a significant decrease in depressive symptoms, but if that decrease does not allow the person to function at a nonclinical level, the efficacy is less clinically significant. Even if the magnitude of effects is strong, the results may not have real-world impact.

An example of a RCT in which clinical significance was evaluated in a study conducted by Rohde et al. (2004). In this study, the efficacy of a group-based CBT intervention aimed at preventing depressive symptoms in adolescents with comorbid conduct disorder was evaluated. The intervention used was a slightly modified version of the group CWD-A protocol with a parent component. The study included 93 (48% female; 19.4% ethnic minorities) participants who were randomized into either the CWD-A group or a life skills group. The participants were referred by the Department of Youth Services of the state where the clinical trials were undertaken.

Assessment of depressive symptoms included the use of a semi-structured interview protocol, the Schedule for Affective Disorders and Schizophrenia for School-Age Children, Epidemiological Version (K-SADS-E); the Hamilton Depression Rating Scale (HAM-D); and the Beck Depression Inventory (BDI). The K-SADS-E was completed with the adolescents, the HAM-D was completed by the interviewer, and the BDI was completed by the adolescents. Parents completed the Achenbach Child Behavior Checklist (CBCL), which contains questions about children's internalizing and externalizing behavior, as well as social functioning items. In addition, the Children's Global Adjustment Scale (CGAS) was utilized to assess the impact of CWD-A on global. Finally, adolescents completed the Social Adjustment Scale–Self Report for Youth (SAS-SR), a scale measuring interpersonal adjustment over the previous 2 weeks. All measures were administered by an interviewer who was not aware of the child's conditional status within the experiment nor had participated in administering the experimental intervention or usual care interventions.

The results indicated that youth in the CWD-A treatment group were more likely to recover from a depressive disorder following treatment when compared to the control group (39% vs. 19%). In addition, significant effects were found in favor of the CWD-A group in the reporting of depressive symptoms as evidenced by the HAM-D ($d = 0.39$) and the BDI ($d = 0.17$). Youth also reported small to moderate increases in social functioning on the SAS-SR when compared to the active treatment control ($d = 0.30$). No significant increases were detected in global functioning as measured by the CGAS.

Comparative Effects of CBT

Although a large number of studies have compared CBT to a wait-list or other placebo control, there is evidence of its efficacy when compared to other active treatments. Nelson et al. (2003) compared the efficacy of a face-to-face individual version of CBT for children that included a parent component to a similar CBT protocol that delivered the treatment through videoconferencing. Both groups showed significant decreases in depressive symptoms. The videoconferencing group, however, showed a significantly greater reduction in depressive symptoms as measured by the CDI when compared to the face-to-face group ($d = 0.56$).

Two studies have also compared the efficacy of adding a parent component to group CBT (Lewinsohn et al., 1990; Lewinsohn et al., 1996). Both studies provided evidence that CBT, with or without the parent condition, is more efficacious than a wait-list control group at reducing depressive symptomatology; however, the CBT with parent component did not significantly further reduce symptoms when compared to the CBT group without the parent component.

A number of studies have compared the efficacy of CBT psychotherapy interventions in children and adolescents with psychopharmacological interventions. The TADS RCT (2004) is the largest study to date to compare CBT to both psychopharmacological treatments and pharmacological placebo, involving 439 participants and 13 academic and community clinics across the United States. The TADS trial indicated increased efficacy when CBT was combined with fluoxetine, a selective serotonin reuptake inhibitor (SSRI), than when either treatment was administered alone, as compared to a pharmacological placebo group receiving the same doses as the fluoxetine-only group.

Other smaller trials found results that diverged from those of the TADS study. Goodyer and colleagues (2007) examined the efficacy of CBT in combination with an SSRI versus SSRI and usual care alone. Although both the CBT with SSRI and SSRI alone groups significantly improved depressive symptoms in adolescents, the CBT with SSRI group did not demonstrate significantly improved reduction in symptoms over the SSRI only group. Another study examined the effect of treatments on adolescents who met *DSM-IV* criteria for a depressive disorder and included three treatment conditions: a group receiving CBT only, a sertraline-only group, and a group receiving both CBT and sertraline (Melvin et al., 2006). Sertraline is a psychopharmacological treatment classified in the SSRI group. All three treatment groups resulted in significantly lower rates of depressive symptoms; however, no significant differences were found between the groups on any measures of depression. G. Clarke et al. (2005) similarly found that adolescents receiving CBT plus an SSRI responded equally as well as their counterparts receiving SSRI without CBT. Although these studies suggest that the addition of CBT to SSRIs does not provide additional benefits, the evidence is not conclusive. Meta-analytic studies are needed to interpret these findings with more confidence.

INTERPERSONAL PSYCHOTHERAPY

Interpersonal psychotherapy (IPT) is a brief intervention originally designed to treat depression in adult outpatients, and strong support in the literature exists for its efficacy with this population (Weissman, Markowitz, &

Klerman, 2000). The main assumption underlying IPT is that irrespective of what caused an individual's depressive condition, interpersonal relationships are involved. Interpersonal psychotherapy's assumptions are based on the interpersonal theories of depression of Sullivan (1953) and Meyer (1957), as well as Bowlby's (1978) attachment theory. The goal of treatment is to improve the interpersonal functioning of individuals in their significant relationships and its focus is on current conflicts in this domain. Techniques employed during the course of IPT include communication analysis, problem-solving skills related to interpersonal relationships, and role-playing (Mufson & Dorta, 2003). Other techniques are employed based on the specific problem-area affecting the individual (e.g., grief).

IPT has been categorized as a well-established treatment for depression in adolescents according to David-Ferdon and Kaslow's (2008) guidelines. Four RCTs conducted by at least two independent research groups found IPT to be more effective than a psychological placebo and, with the inclusion of a treatment manual, formed the basis for the highest efficacy classification (Mufson, Weisman, Moreau, & Garfinkel, 1999; Mufson et al., 2004; Rosselló & Bernal, 1999; Young, Mufson, & Davies, 2006a). Similar evidence, however, was not found for IPT's efficacy in children 12 years and under, as no RCT employing IPT as a theoretical orientation had been, at the time of the review, completed with children.

Since 2007, two RCTs have been published in which IPT was employed as a treatment orientation (Gunlicks-Stoessel, Mufson, Jekal, & Turner, 2010; Rosselló et al., 2008). Gunlicks-Stoessel et al. (2010) most recently provided evidence of individual IPT's efficacy relative to treatment-as-usual delivered by school clinicians. Rosselló et al. (2008) included IPT-A in both group and individual modalities; however, the results were not reported separately for each modality. Therefore, the present review will only focus on individual-only IPT for adolescents. IPT's classification as a treatment orientation, therefore, continues to be well-established for adolescents.

Individual IPT With Depressed Adolescents

Three RCTs provide the research base in David-Ferdon and Kaslow's (2008) review for classifying individual-only IPT as a well-established treatment for depression in adolescents. Of the three RCTs, two employed the treatment protocol *Interpersonal Psychotherapy for Depressed Adolescents* (IPT-A). The IPT-A protocol is similar to the IPT protocol for adults with depression but focuses on interpersonal issues that are unique to adolescence (Mufson et al., 2004; Mufson et al., 1999). The two studies examining the effectiveness of the IPT-A protocol were not conducted by independent research groups; thus, IPT-A was classified as probably efficacious. The third study employing IPT in an individual modality utilized a different adaptation of the adult IPT protocol for Puerto Rican adolescents (Rosselló & Bernal, 1999).

One RCT (Gunlicks-Stoessel et al., 2010) employing an individual IPT modality was located by the authors in their review of the treatment literature since 2007. The study demonstrated the effectiveness of IPT-A versus treatment as usual; however, the study was not completed by an independent research group. In addition, the literature already had established individual IPT as a well-established treatment. Therefore, the IPT-A protocol's classification remains as probably efficacious and individual-only IPT, as a modality, continues to be well-established.

Clinical Significance in IPT

Young, Mufson, and Davies's (2006a) IPT-AST study provides an example of the clinical significance of IPT-AST with a school-based population of adolescents at risk for depressive disorders. At posttreatment, none of the 27 participants in the IPT-AST condition met criteria for a depressive disorder on the K-SADS-PL. In contrast, 3 of the 14 the usual care group participants met criteria for a depressive disorder at posttreatment. Scores on the CGAS, a measure of global functioning completed by clinicians, were significantly higher for the IPT-AST group than the usual care group at posttreatment $(d = -0.96)$, at 3-month follow-up $(d = -0.82)$, and at 6-month follow-up $(d = -1.21)$. The results indicate that IPT-AST not only was able to significantly improve depressive symptoms when compared to usual care in a school setting, but it was also able to significantly increase the child's overall functioning.

Comparative Effects of IPT

There are fewer studies on the effects of IPT than CBT. Furthermore, no RCT has examined the comparative efficacy of IPT to psychopharmacological treatment. Two studies have compared IPT to CBT for youth depression and both were carried out in Puerto Rico (Rosselló & Bernal, 1999; Rosselló et al., 2008). In the first study, 71 adolescents meeting *DSM-III-R* criteria were evaluated (Rosselló & Bernal, 1999). Both CBT and IPT significantly improved symptoms compared to a wait-list control group. No significant differences were found between IPT and CBT in regards to depressive symptom improvement; however, when examining effect sizes on the CDI scores, the CBT treatment displayed a smaller effect $(d = 0.35)$ than the IPT treatment group $(d = 0.76)$ when each was compared to a wait-list control group. In the second study, Rosselló, Bernal, and Rivera-Medina (2008) examined both individual and group modalities when comparing CBT and IPT. A total of 112 adolescents were randomly assigned to either a CBT-individual, CBT-group, IPT-individual, or IPT-group condition. Again, both CBT and IPT significantly decreased symptoms of depression. No differences were found between the individual and group treatment conditions; however, the

CBT conditions produced significantly greater reductions in depressive symptoms than the IPT conditions $(d = 0.43)$.

IPT and CBT are the two treatment orientations that have generated the largest number of RCTs and are the only two with a well-established classification status. There are several modalities and protocols within these orientations that are currently designated as probably efficacious or experimental, which were not systematically reviewed here. Other treatment orientations that have attracted substantial attention in the adult literature are not represented in the child and adolescent field. Notably, RCTs for depression among youth have yet to be published for treatments such as behavioral activation (BA) and mindfulness-based cognitive therapy (MB-CT), which have growing support among adult populations (see Cuijpers, Van Straten, & Warmerdan, 2007; Dimidjian & Davis, 2009; Mazzucchelli, Kane, & Rees, 2009).

REVIEW OF META-ANALYSES

Three meta-analyses were completed between 1998 and 2002 examining the effects of psychotherapy treatments of depression in children and adolescents (Lewinsohn & Clarke, 1999; Michael & Crowley, 2002; Reinecke, Ryan, & DuBois, 1998). The effects in these studies ranged from mean effect sizes of 0.72 to 1.02, suggesting that the effects of treatments for youth depression were as strong or stronger than those found for psychosocial interventions for youth with other mental health problems (J. R. Weisz et al., 1995). Since those early meta-analytic studies were published, two comprehensive meta-analyses on psychosocial treatments for depression in children and adolescents have been published that revealed much smaller effects of psychosocial treatments for depression in youth (Watanabe, Hunot, Omori, Churchhill, & Furukawa, 2007; J. R. Weisz, McCarty, & Valeri, 2006). First, Weisz and colleagues (2006) reviewed a total of 35 studies and found a small to moderate ($d = 0.34$; range $= –0.66$ to 2.02) overall effect size in depression treatments for children. The vast majority ($N = 31$) of these studies were CBT or included a component targeting youth cognitions.

More recently, Watanabe and colleagues (2007) found similar smaller effects ($RR = 1.39$) in favor of psychotherapy for depression in youth. The authors also tested for the individual effects of various treatment modalities (e.g., IPT) versus control conditions, and found that CBT ($RR = 1.38$), IPT ($RR = 1.68$), and behavioral therapy ($RR = 6.76$) were superior at posttreatment to control groups. However, other modalities such as cognitive therapy and problem-solving therapy did not produce significantly superior outcomes to control groups. None of the individual modalities maintained their effects versus control groups at 6- and 12-month follow-up.

The meta-analytic literature has also provided synthesized information on the efficacy of specific components of CBT with children and adolescents. J. R. Weisz and colleagues (2006) examined whether treatments focusing on restructuring cognitions were more effective than those lacking a cognitive component. The results of their review concluded that treatments employing cognitive restructuring did not produce any significantly greater effects than treatments that did not use cognitive restructuring as a part of their protocol. Similarly, Chu and Harrison (2007) found that CBT treatments only produced a small mean effect size (0.35) on positive cognitive processes while having no significant outcome effects on behavioral (0.01) or coping (0.05) processes. In addition, CBT treatments that involved add-on components (e.g., parent training) did not produce more significant effects than stand-alone CBT (Spielmans, Pasek, & McFall, 2007).

A recent meta-analysis conducted by Horowitz and Garber (2006) focused on selective and universal prevention studies for depression in children and adolescents. *Selective* studies were those in which children at risk for

depressive symptoms were identified by the investigators prior to the implementation of the prevention program. *Universal* programs were those in which a sample of children or adolescents was administered a prevention program regardless of their risk status. The overall weighted mean effect size for all 30 studies in the meta-analytic review was modest ($d = 0.16$); however, type of program moderated the effect size in that selective prevention programs produced a small to moderate effect size ($d = 0.30$), whereas universal programs resulted in a negligible to small effect size ($d = 0 .12$). The results of the selective prevention programs were more aligned with the results found by J. R. Weisz et al.'s (2006) meta-analysis of interventions for depression in children and adolescents. Universal studies were not included in either the J. R. Weisz et al. (2006) or the Watanabe et al. (2007) meta-analyses described previously.

Finally, one meta-analysis specifically examined a CBT group treatment protocol, the *Penn Resiliency Program* (PRP; Brunwasser, Gillham, & Kim, 2009). Other names for PRP protocols include: *Penn Prevention Program*, *Penn Optimism Program*, *Penn Program*, and *Depression Prevention Program*. The acronym PRP will be used to refer to any of the aforementioned programs. Effects for PRP when compared to nonintervention control groups were found to be small and modest (0.11) at posttreatment follow-up; however, when PRP was compared to active treatments, effects were not significantly better than the comparison group at posttreatment (–0.02).

In summary, meta-analyses have indicated small to moderate effects of psychosocial intervention and prevention programs targeting depression in children and adolescents. The treatment orientations of CBT and IPT have been found to be more effective than studies employing other treatment orientations (e.g., cognitive therapy). In particular, CBT displayed more moderate effects when examined against other psychosocial treatments; however, the literature is unclear as to which components of

CBT are effective. Only one meta-analysis has been completed on a specific protocol for depression, the Penn Resiliency Program, which found that effects were small when compared to no treatment control groups and not significant when compared to other active treatments. Further research is needed to clarify some of the discrepancies in findings across the meta-analyses, better understand the components of CBT that are producing efficacious results, and examine the components of IPT since such a review has yet to be completed.

MOVING BEYOND EFFICACY

In the previous section, both IPT and CBT were identified as efficacious interventions for depressed youth. The established criteria for determining the efficacy of psychosocial treatments delineated by Chambless and her colleagues (Chambless et al., 1998; Chambless & Hollon, 1998; Chambless & Ollendick, 2001) focuses primarily on efficacy. Treatment effects under highly controlled conditions, however, may say little about the viability of CBT or IPT in practice settings, including community mental health clinics, primary health clinics, and schools. According to the Institute of Medicine (2001), the definition of *evidence-based practice* is the integration of research evidence, clinical expertise, and patient values. In terms of psychosocial interventions, much of the research evidence has come from highly selected samples in research settings with conditions designed to optimize the impact of receiving a particular intervention, thus maximizing internal validity. Glasgow, Vogt, and Boles (1999) have proposed an alternative model that identifies several key dimensions to recognize an intervention's potential for public health impact. The model, called RE-AIM, includes a greater emphasis on external validity considerations, which are critical to narrowing the science to practice gap. Each of the initials in RE-AIM represents a significant dimension to consider when

evaluating a given program. They include: Reach (R), Efficacy/Effectiveness (E), Adoptability (A), Implementation (I), and Maintenance (M). The focus for this section will be on highlighting some strengths and areas of need along each of these five dimensions for IPT and CBT for youth depression.

The *Reach* dimension in RE-AIM refers to the extent to which interventions are available to those in need. Evidence-based treatments, therefore, are considered to have low Reach if they are designed and tested only in research settings and not disseminated broadly. It is difficult to estimate the number of youth who have received some form of IPT or CBT to alleviate or prevent depression; however, the Reach of these interventions can be evaluated by considering the representativeness of the samples enrolled across studies using these protocols. This evaluation can be viewed in terms of key demographic and clinical characteristics, such as the sex, ethnicity, socioeconomic background, and comorbidity of youth who take part in these trials.

In a review of 18 treatment outcome studies targeting youth depression, J. R. Weisz, Jensen-Doss, and Hawley (2005) found that 100% of the studies reported the age and gender of the youth treated. In contrast, 66% reported the ethnicity of the sample and only 11% reported the socioeconomic characteristics of the sample. Most CBT and IPT studies of depressed youth include samples with both males and females, and several have used block randomization to ensure equal gender representation (e.g., Brent et al., 1997; TADS Team, 2004; J. Weisz et al., 2009) across treatment groups. Overall, depression studies have included slightly larger proportions of females (J. R. Weisz et al., 2005). Some have focused exclusively on treating depression among girls (Miller, Gur, Shanok, & Weissman, 2008; Stark, Streusand, Krumholz, & Patel, 2010), in part due to the well-established rise in prevalence of depressive disorders found for females beginning in adolescence. Several studies have found that gender does not moderate treatment effects (Curry et al., 2006; Rohde et al., 2004). On the other hand, it is not known if socio-economic disadvantage influences the effects of CBT and IPT interventions, mainly because income and education have not been systematically documented in treatment outcome studies focusing on psychosocial interventions (Huey & Polo, 2008). In TADS, family income moderated response to treatment (Curry et al., 2006). Relative to those in the placebo group, the moderate- to low-income group (less than $75,000 per year) who received CBT had an effect size of –0.18. The effect size for their counterparts from high incomes ($75,000 per year or more) was 0.72.

A few IPT and CBT treatment outcome studies of youth depression have focused on ethnic minority youth or enrolled significant numbers of ethnic minority youth. Roselló, Bernal, and colleagues, for example, conducted two RCTs comparing IPT and CBT among Puerto Rican youth in Puerto Rico (Rosselló & Bernal, 1999; Rosselló et al., 2008). In a depression prevention trial, Cardemil, Reivich, and Seligman (2002) evaluated CBT among school samples of both African American and Latino students and presented the results separately for each ethnic group. Additionally, recent IPT trials conducted in New York City have included samples from schools enrolling predominately Latino youth of Caribbean backgrounds (Young, Mufson, & Davies, 2006b). In TADS (2004), a large multisite study, participants included 13% African Americans and 9% Latinos, which authors compared to the 2002 U.S. Census population (16% for each group). In that study, ethnicity did not moderate treatment outcomes (Curry et al., 2006), but sample size limitations across the four conditions prevented separate analyses for each ethnic group represented. A recent study reported secondary analyses of a school-based prevention randomized controlled trial that included Asian Americans, Latinos, and European Americans. CBT was equally efficacious for all three ethnic groups (Marchand,

Ng, Rohde, & Stice, 2010). On the other hand, other CBT studies have found differential effects for ethnicity. Ngo et al. (2009) found that ethnic minority youth treated for depression received more benefit from the intervention than European American youth. Cardemil et al. (2002) compared African American and Latino youth and found that, relative to the control condition, CBT was superior, but only for the Latino group. A few CBT trials focused on depression have reported the inclusion of Asian Americans (e.g., Asarnow et al., 2002; Gillham et al., 2006; Vostanis, Feehan, Grattan, & Bickerton, 1996); however, with the exception of the Marchand et al. (2010) study, the sample sizes have been small and intervention outcomes have not been separately presented for these youth. To date, IPT trials have not included substantial numbers of youth of African American or Asian American backgrounds. No CBT or IPT studies focusing on American Indian youth who met criteria for depression were located.

Exclusionary criteria for clinical trials of youth depression have been based on a number of participant characteristics. These include low reading abilities, lack of English proficiency, risk for self-harm, the presence of psychotic symptoms, and substance abuse (e.g., Rosselló & Bernal, 1999). Some recent studies have minimized the number of youth excluded and instead consistently monitored comorbidity or even focused on populations with comorbid conditions (Vostanis et al., 1996). Rohde et al. (2004) studied the effects of the CWD-A program on adolescents with depressive disorders and comorbid conduct disorder. At posttreatment, compared to those who received life skills/tutoring, significant effects in favor of CWD-A were found for depression but not for externalizing problems. A study of IPT evaluated the impact of anxiety disorders on treatment effects and found that the presence of an anxiety disorder such as social anxiety disorder, generalized anxiety disorder, or panic disorder predicted poorer treatment response, and IPT was associated with a more favorable response in terms of depressive, but not anxious, symptoms (Young et al., 2006b). These findings are somewhat consistent with J. R. Weisz, McCarty, and Valeri's (2006) meta-analytic conclusions, who found that, among 44 treatment outcome studies, the effects of youth depression interventions were greater on anxiety than externalizing symptoms. The skills taught in these interventions, most of which were CBT, are specific to depression and to those conditions most closely associated to depression (i.e., anxiety).

The *Effectiveness* dimension within RE-AIM focuses not only on traditional indicators of program effects (i.e., symptom change) but also on the extent to which the interventions evaluate quality of life indicators. Effectiveness trials are carried out in practice settings rather than in traditional research settings. Moreover, the protocols are delivered by providers already on staff, instead of university research teams or providers hired as part of the study. There is evidence that youth affected with depression seen in community mental health agencies fare poorly using standard care procedures. In a benchmarking study, Weersing and Weisz (2002) noted that the effects of being treated in these settings were small or nonexistent, and were especially poor for African American and Latino youth. Therefore, training clinicians to deliver evidence-based interventions and documenting positive outcomes in these settings is a priority, given the well-documented success found for these interventions when delivered by research groups.

Across all youth depression treatments, meta-analytic results do not suggest that efficacy studies have a decided advantage in terms of effect sizes compared to effectiveness studies (J. R. Weisz et al., 2006); however, data on effectiveness trials thus far have not been consistently favorable for CBT interventions. For example, Kerfoot, Harrington, Harrington, Rogers, and Verduyn (2004) randomized clinicians to deliver either a brief CBT intervention or routine care and found that the majority of youth across both conditions continued to have depressive disorders at the end of treatment. Methodological shortcomings in this study included a small sample size, which meant that most clinicians saw only one case. In a much larger trial, J. Weisz et al. (2009) trained and supervised clinicians of various disciplines and backgrounds from several community mental health clinics on a CBT intervention for depression called Primary and Secondary Control Enhancement (PASCET). Clinicians were randomized to deliver usual care or PASCET. In this study, the majority of youth across both conditions were diagnosis free at posttreatment. Those receiving CBT were found to require fewer sessions and have less need for psychotropic medication compared to usual care; however, receiving CBT was not associated with larger symptom reductions or fewer depressive disorder diagnoses at posttreatment.

IPT effectiveness trials have been conducted in school settings instead of community mental health centers. In a randomized controlled trial, school counselors were trained to deliver IPT (Mufson et al., 2004). Compared to those receiving usual care (individual supportive therapy), youth who received IPT had fewer depressive symptoms, higher social adjustment, and better overall functioning. Most recently, two school-based open trials were conducted using IPT with pregnant adolescent girls (Miller et al., 2008). The sessions were held during the students' health classes and the setting was a public high school in a large metropolitan area, rather than in a research university. Although some elements of effectiveness trials were incorporated, the intervention was delivered by a research team and not by school counselors.

Adoption refers to the acceptability of the program across individuals (both participants and providers), and settings (e.g., clinics). The refusal rate among those approached for participation is often provided as an indicator of acceptability, along with the attrition rate. Additionally, the representativeness of the individuals enrolled relative to the sample targeted for the intervention can serve to determine adoption. These individuals may include providers who are being trained to deliver the program as well as the participants who are being treated.

RCTs carried out in school settings have reported particularly high refusal rates. In one study that included a CBT condition, G. N. Clarke et al. (1995) identified youth at risk for depression using a symptom checklist and reported that over 50% of the participants did not consent to a second interview to determine eligibility into the study. The authors did not find significant clinical and demographic differences between those who agreed and those who did not. Mufson et al. (2004) similarly report low enrollment figures in a randomized trial that included IPT. Most recently, in a study comparing IPT to usual care carried out in several high schools, Young, Mufson, and Gallop (2010) report that only one third of youth with moderate to severe depressive symptoms agreed to participate in a screening evaluation and prevention program. The authors reported that a large number of refusals were because participants did not perceive a need for the intervention. Educational campaigns and improved outreach to help families become aware of depression and treatment options may address these perceptions. Additionally, studies comparing strategies to increase the engagement and enrollment of participants into evidence-based programs are much needed.

Fewer studies have reported on the acceptability of CBT or IPT across provider and agency levels. Kerfoot et al. (2004) reported that over 100 providers who had never been delivered CBT expressed interest in receiving training; however, it is not clear how many were approached, and thus the level of provider acceptability cannot be evaluated. J. Weisz et al. (2009) similarly trained large numbers of providers across several community mental health agencies, but the number of providers and agencies who were approached was also not reported.

Cost-effectiveness and academic outcomes (e.g., grades) are notably missing from the youth treatment outcome literature, including trials of youth depression utilizing IPT and CBT (Watanabe et al., 2007). Evidence of differential success in these indicators is particularly relevant to adoption, since these are central to helping administrators, policymakers, and others make decisions about whether or not to incorporate these state-of-the-art programs.

Patient satisfaction and preferences are important indicators of high adoption potential at the individual participant level. Jaycox et al. (2006) evaluated preferences among adolescents with high levels of depressive symptoms attending a primary health center. The majority of youth preferred psychotherapy over medication, and African American youth were even more likely than European American youth to indicate this preference. In a quality of care study called Youth Partners in Care (Asarnow et al., 2005), youth with depressive disorders or elevated symptoms who received psychotherapy, which consisted of a brief CBT intervention, were more satisfied with their care than those who did not receive this service and also had significantly larger reductions in depressive symptomatology than those receiving usual care. In another study, those receiving CBT reported a stronger therapist alliance than those receiving usual care in community mental health agencies (J. Weisz et al., 2009).

Implementation is also measured across multiple levels according to the RE-AIM guidelines. At the provider level, treatment fidelity is an indicator of how closely the therapist follows a given protocol while delivering the intervention. Most CBT and IPT protocols are manualized, which can assist therapists with both the content and the sequence of specific skills and strategies. Monitoring of fidelity has been documented in a number of RCTs for youth depression (e.g., Garber et al., 2009; Rohde et al., 2004; Stice et al., 2008). For example, Garber et al. (2009)

report therapist fidelity ratings between 88% and 95%, based on an integrity checklist that was completed on a random sample of audio recordings taken from sessions early and late in treatment. Rosselló et al. (2008) found that, in their RCT comparing IPT and CBT, fidelity ratings were lower for IPT (78%–82%) compared to CBT (90%–92%) and suggest that lower fidelity may have impacted the results of the trial; however, they do not provide analyses directly evaluating fidelity and outcome. Similarly, G. Clarke (1998) reviews the treatment fidelity of four RCTs that used CWD-A or a modified version of this protocol. All four studies, one of which was an effectiveness trial, had high mean fidelity scores ranging from 78% to 94%; however, a relationship between fidelity and outcomes was not evaluated, apparently because of the limited variance in the fidelity scores (which were positively skewed) and the difficulty of evaluating fidelity in group protocols. Interpersonal psychotherapy studies conducted on adolescents have also evaluated treatment fidelity (Mufson et al., 2004; Mufson et al., 1999). For example, Mufson et al. (2004) report a mean adherence level of 3.3 on a scale ranging from 1 (poor) to 5 (excellent). No studies were identified that linked therapists' implementation of IPT to treatment outcomes. Therefore, future research on both IPT and CBT protocols should examine the relationship between therapist competence, treatment fidelity, and treatment outcomes. Establishing guidelines for fidelity is critical, given that authors have argued that following a manual with too much rigidity or too little attention to the adaptation needs (e.g., developmental or cultural) of a specific population may result in a poor fit and yield and turn away participants and providers (Bernal & Scharrón-del-Río, 2001; Hollon, Garber, & Shelton, 2005).

Maintenance, in the RE-AIM framework, can be measured at two levels. At the individual level, maintenance refers to the durability of program effects after the treatment is completed. For example, it is not uncommon for RCTs to present follow-up data on participants across treatment groups. The second indicator of maintenance is at the agency level and refers to the sustainability of programs in the schools, mental health agencies, primary care clinics, and other settings where it was originally delivered.

Watanabe et al.'s (2007) meta-analysis evaluated the long-term effects of interventions designed to address youth depression. The results indicate that, in general, psychosocial interventions are efficacious at posttreatment; however, these effects are no longer found 6 months after the intervention or beyond. Recent IPT and CBT studies substantiate that conclusion. For example, Young, Mufson, and Gallop (2010) found that, compared to youth who received routine care from school counselors, those receiving IPT made significantly larger improvements posttreatment; however, the authors report that those in the usual care condition demonstrated a faster rate of improvement during the follow-up period, enough that IPT was no longer superior at the 12-month follow-up assessment. Adaptations to standard CBT and IPT protocols have recently emerged, and several have included a reduced number of sessions. The diminished effects seen in follow-up evaluations suggest that an examination of the benefits of increasing the number of sessions may also be warranted, particularly with selected populations (e.g., comorbid) and in effectiveness research carried out in community settings.

Similarly, there is a dearth of data on whether or not programs delivered in schools, mental health agencies, and other settings are maintained beyond the duration of the studies. Several authors report training usual care providers and offering these trainings to therapists who were originally randomized into a control condition (e.g., Kerfoot et al., 2004); however, studies have not followed these practitioners over time to evaluate the extent to which CBT or IPT protocols are used by these providers or even disseminated to others.

EVIDENCE-BASED PRACTICE

Depressive disorders are highly prevalent and chronic among youth. The course of these disorders is associated with the presence of other psychiatric disorders, health problems, suicidal behavior, and occupational difficulties. Data from national epidemiological studies are not yet available in the United States, but studies consistently show that higher risk for depression is found among adolescent girls and Latino youth. Due to the significant impact and prevalence of depression in youth, data regarding appropriate treatment is of critical importance.

Therapists and other providers can select from several treatment orientations when treating children and adolescents who present with moderate to severe symptoms of depression and may meet criteria for a depressive disorder; however, the data thus far suggest that intervention effect sizes for depression treatment in youth are not as large as for other youth conditions, and there is evidence that these effects do not last beyond the duration of the treatment. This chapter outlines the most widely studied treatment orientations and the only two that have received the highest classification available regarding their efficacy in RCTs. Both IPT and CBT orientations have met the criteria needed to be classified as *well-established* treatments. Beyond that, no individual protocol has reached this classification, primarily because an independent group has not established their efficacy. More evidence is available for some specific modalities of treatment than for others. For example, substantial evidence has been collected regarding the effects of individual treatment using IPT-A for adolescents. In contrast, there is almost no evidence for group or individual IPT for children. Similarly, group CBT interventions (Self-Control Therapy and the Penn Resiliency Program) have been studied and show promising results; however, more studies have been conducted with the Coping with Depression Course for Adolescents, including TADS, the largest clinical trial of youth with severe and chronic depression. Overall, more support exists for the efficacy of group interventions in treating youth depression, but it is likely that the majority of service providers in community mental health agencies will provide individual treatment. Thus, further research is needed to establish the efficacy of such an approach.

Several studies evaluating IPT and CBT against other treatments including medications, usual care, and each other have been conducted; yet, more evidence is needed for definitive conclusions to be drawn regarding their comparative effects. Existing research does, however, indicate that add-on components such as parent involvement may not increase the efficacy of CBT and IPT protocols. In addition, studies regarding the cost-effectiveness of CBT and IPT treatment for depression have not been completed. At this point, there is no evidence that IPT or CBT are better suited for boys or girls. Furthermore, both CBT and IPT studies have included ethnic minority youth (primarily African American and Latinos); however, it is not known if factors such as ethnicity, socioeconomic status, comorbidity, and clinical severity consistently moderate treatment effects.

Effectiveness research is emerging for both CBT and IPT, and studies have increasingly focused on training providers who practice in community settings, schools, and primary care clinics. IPT has shown evidence that school counselors can deliver this intervention effectively, whereas studies of CBT for youth depression have focused on primary care settings and community mental health agencies. On the other hand, there are no established guidelines for the appropriate length of treatment for depression using IPT or CBT, and relapse prevention strategies have not been informed by research for either treatment orientation. Similarly, research is lacking regarding the best practices for training and supporting therapists in these settings.

The evidence available thus supports the use of CBT and IPT in treating depression in children and adolescents; however, much of this support is qualified based on modality, demographic characteristics of the client (e.g., age, ethnicity, socioeconomic status), and/or treatment setting. In order to develop a comprehensive set of guidelines for evidence-based practice with respect to youth depression treatment, research is needed to better understand which treatments are effective for particular clients and settings. Additionally, future treatment development and implementation should be informed by data regarding active ingredients (e.g., cognitive restructuring) and other mediators of treatment outcome.

REFERENCES

Abela, J., & Hankin, B. (2007). *Handbook of depression in children and adolescents.* New York, NY: Guilford Press.

Accordino, D., Accordino, M., & Slaney, R. (2000). An investigation of perfectionism, mental health, achievement, and achievement motivation in adolescents. *Psychology in the Schools, 37,* 535–545.

Ackerson, J., Scogin, F., McKendree-Smith, N., & Lyman, R. (1998). Cognitive bibliotherapy for mild and moderate adolescent depressive symptomatology. *Journal of Consulting and Clinical Psychology, 66,* 685–690.

Allgood-Merten, B., Lewinsohn, P., & Hops, H. (1990). Sex differences and adolescent depression. *Journal of Abnormal Psychology, 99,* 55–63.

American Psychiatric Association. (2000). *Diagnostic and statistical manual of mental disorders* (4th ed., text rev.) (*DSM-IV-TR*). Washington, DC: Author.

Asarnow, J. R., Jaycox, L. H., Duan, N., LaBorde, A. P., Rea, M. M., Murray, P., . . . Wells, K. B. (2005). Effectiveness of a quality improvement intervention for adolescent depression in primary care clinics: A randomized controlled trial. *Journal of the American Medical Association, 293,* 311.

Asarnow, J. R., Scott, C. V., & Mintz, J. (2002). A combined cognitive-behavioral family education intervention for depression in children: A treatment development study. *Cognitive Therapy and Research, 26,* 221–229.

Beck, A. T., Rush, A. J., Shaw, B. F., & Emery, G. (1979). *Cognitive therapy of depression.* New York, NY: Guilford Press.

Bernal, G., & Scharrón-del-Río, M. (2001). Are empirically supported treatments valid for ethnic minorities? Toward an alternative approach for treatment research. *Cultural Diversity & Ethnic Minority Psychology, 7,* 328–342.

Bowlby, J. (1978). Attachment theory and its therapeutic implications. *Adolescent Psychiatry, 6,* 5–33.

Brent, D., Emslie, G., Clarke, G., Wagner, K., Asarnow, J., Keller, M., . . . Abebe, K. (2008). Switching to another SSRI or to venlafaxine with or without cognitive behavioral therapy for adolescents with SSRI-resistant depression: The TORDIA randomized controlled trial. *Journal of the American Medical Association, 299,* 901–913.

Brent, D., Holder, D., Kolko, D., Birmaher, B., Baugher, M., Roth, C., . . . Johnson, B. (1997). A clinical psychotherapy trial for adolescent depression comparing cognitive, family, and supportive therapy. *Archives of General Psychiatry, 54,* 877–885.

Brunwasser, S., Gillham, J., & Kim, E. (2009). A meta-analytic review of the Penn Resiliency Program. *Journal of Consulting and Clinical Psychology, 77,* 1042–1054.

Cardemil, E. V., Reivich, K. J., & Seligman, M. E. P. (2002). The prevention of depressive symptoms in low-income minority middle school students. *Prevention & Treatment, 5.* doi: 10.1037/1522-3736.5.1.58a

Chambless, D. L., Baker, M. J., Baucom, D. H., Beutler, L. E., Calhoun, K. S., Crits-Christoph, P., . . . Haaga, D. F. (1998). Update on empirically validated therapies, II. *Clinical Psychologist, 51,* 3–16.

Chambless, D. L., & Hollon, S. D. (1998). Defining empirically supported therapies. *Journal of Consulting and Clinical Psychology, 66,* 7–18.

Chambless, D. L., & Ollendick, T. H. (2001). Empirically supported psychological interventions: Controversies and evidence. *Annual Review of Psychology, 52,* 685–716.

Chu, B. C., & Harrison, T. L. (2007). Disorder-specific effects of CBT for anxious and depressed youth: A meta-analysis of candidate mediators of change. *Clinical Child and Family Psychology Review, 10,* 352–372.

Clarke, G. (1998). Intervention fidelity in adolescent depression prevention and treatment. *Journal of Prevention and Intervention in the Community, 17,* 19–33.

Clarke, G., Debar, L., Lynch, F., Powell, J., Gale, J., O'Connor, E., . . . von Korff, M. (2005). A randomized effectiveness trial of brief cognitive-behavioral therapy for depressed adolescents receiving antidepressant medication. *Journal of the American Academy of Child & Adolescent Psychiatry, 44,* 888–898.

Clarke, G. N., Hawkins, W., Murphy, M., Sheeber, L., Lewinsohn, P., & Seeley, J. R. (1995). Targeted prevention of unipolar depressive disorder in an at risk sample of high school adolescents: A randomized trial of a group cognitive intervention. *American Academy of Child and Adolescent Psychiatry, 34*, 312–321.

Clarke, G. N., Hornbrook, M., Lynch, F., Polen, M., Gale, J., Beardslee, W., . . . Seeley, J. R. (2001). A randomized trial of a group cognitive intervention for preventing depression in adolescent offspring of depressed parents. *Archives of General Psychiatry, 58*, 1127–1134.

Clarke, G. N., Rohde, P., Lewinsohn, P. M., Hops, H., & Seeley, J. R. (1999). Cognitive-behavioral treatment of adolescent depression: Efficacy of acute group treatment and booster sessions. *Journal of the American Academy of Child and Adolescent Psychiatry, 38*, 272–279.

Costello, E., Angold, A., Burns, B., Stangl, D., Tweed, D., Erkanli, A., & Worthman, C. (1996). The Great Smoky Mountains Study of Youth: Goals, design, methods, and the prevalence of *DSM-III-R* disorders. *Archives of General Psychiatry, 53*, 1129–1136.

Costello, E., Erkanli, A., & Angold, A. (2006). Is there an epidemic of child or adolescent depression? *Journal of Child Psychology and Psychiatry, 47*, 1263–1271.

Cuijpers, P., Van Straten, A., & Warmerdam, L. (2007). Behavioral activation treatments of depression: A meta-analysis. *Clinical Psychology Review, 27*, 318–326.

Curry, J., Rohde, P., Simons, A., Silva, S., Vitiello, B., Kratochvil, C., . . . Pathak, S. (2006). Predictors and moderators of acute outcome in the Treatment for Adolescents with Depression Study (TADS). *Journal of the American Academy of Child & Adolescent Psychiatry, 45*, 1427–1439.

David-Ferdon, C., & Kaslow, N. J. (2008). Evidence-based psychosocial treatments for child and adolescent depression. *Journal of Clinical Child & Adolescent Psychology, 37*, 62–104.

Dimidjian, S., & Davis, K. (2009). Newer variations of cognitive-behavioral therapy: Behavioral activation and mindfulness-based cognitive therapy. *Current Psychiatry Reports, 11*, 453–458.

Garber, J., Clarke, G. N., Weersing, V. R., Beardslee, W. R., Brent, D. A., Gladstone, T. G., . . . Hollon, S. D. (2009). Prevention of depression in at-risk adolescents: A randomized controlled trial. *Journal of the American Medical Association, 301*, 2215–2224.

Gillham, J. E., Hamilton, J., Freres, D. R., Patton, K., & Gallop, R. (2006). Preventing depression among early adolescents in the primary care setting: A randomized controlled study of the Penn Resiliency Program. *Journal of Abnormal Child Psychology, 34*, 195–211.

Gillham, J. E., Reivich, K. J., Jaycox, L. H., & Seligman, M. E. (1995). Prevention of depressive symptoms in school children: Two-year follow-up. *Psychological Science, 6*, 343–351.

Glasgow, R., Vogt, T., & Boles, S. (1999). Evaluating the public health impact of health promotion interventions: The RE-AIM framework. *American Journal of Public Health, 89*, 1322–1327.

Goodyer, I., Dubicka, B., Wilkinson, P., Kelvin, R., Roberts, C., Byford, S., . . . Leech, A. (2007). Selective serotonin reuptake inhibitors (SSRIs) and routine specialist care with and without cognitive behaviour therapy in adolescents with major depression: Randomised controlled trial. *British Medical Journal, 335*(7611), 142–146.

Gunlicks-Stoessel, M., Mufson, L., Jekal, A., & Turner, J. B. (2010). The impact of perceived interpersonal functioning on treatment for adolescent depression: IPT-A versus treatment as usual in school-based health clinics. *Journal of Consulting and Clinical Psychology, 78*, 260–267.

Harrington, R., Whittaker, J., Shoebridge, P., & Campbell, F. (1998). Systematic review of efficacy of cognitive behaviour therapies in childhood and adolescent depressive disorder. *British Medical Journal, 316*(7144), 1559–1563.

Hoek, W., Schuurmans, J., Koot, H., & Cuijpers, P. (2009). Prevention of depression and anxiety in adolescents: A randomized controlled trial testing the efficacy and mechanisms of Internet-based self-help problem-solving therapy. *Trials, 10*(98). Retrieved from www.trialsjournal.com/content/10/1/93

Hollon, S., Garber, J., & Shelton, R. (2005). Treatment of depression in adolescents with cognitive behavior therapy and medications: A commentary on the TADS project. *Cognitive and Behavioral Practice, 12*, 149–155.

Horowitz, J. L., & Garber, J. (2006). The prevention of depressive symptoms in children and adolescents: A meta-analytic review. *Journal of Consulting and Clinical Psychology, 74*, 401–415.

Huey, S. J., & Polo, A. J. (2008). Evidence-based psychosocial treatments for ethnic minority youth. *Journal of Clinical Child & Adolescent Psychology, 37*, 262–301.

Ialongo, N., Edelsohn, G., & Kellam, S. (2001). A further look at the prognostic power of young children's reports of depressed mood and feelings. *Child Development, 72*, 736–747.

Institute of Medicine. (2001). *Crossing the quality chasm: A new health system for the 21st century*. Washington, DC: National Academies Press.

Jacobson, N. S., & Truax, P. (1991). Clinical significance: A statistical approach to defining meaningful change in psychotherapy research. *Journal of Consulting and Clinical Psychology, 59*, 12–19.

Jaycox, L. H., Asarnow, J. R., Sherbourne, C. D., Rea, M. M., LaBorde, A. P., & Wells, K. B. (2006). Adolescent primary care patients' preferences for depression treatment. *Administration and Policy in Mental Health and Mental Health Services Research, 33*, 198–207.

Jaycox, L. H., Reivich, K. J., Gillham, J., & Seligman, M. E. (1994). Prevention of depressive symptoms in school children. *Behaviour Research and Therapy, 32*, 801–816.

Jungbluth, N. J., & Shirk, S. R. (2009). Therapist strategies for building involvement in cognitive-behavioral therapy for adolescent depression. *Journal of Consulting and Clinical Psychology, 77*, 1179–1184.

Kahn, J. S., Kehle, T. J., Jenson, W. R., & Clark, E. (1990). Comparison of cognitive-behavioral, relaxation, and self-modeling interventions for depression among middle-school students. *School Psychology Review, 19*, 196–211.

Kaslow, N. J., & Thompson, M. P. (1998). Applying the criteria for empirically supported treatments to studies of psychosocial interventions for child and adolescent depression. *Journal of Clinical Child & Adolescent Psychology, 27*, 146–155.

Kerfoot, M., Harrington, R., Harrington, V., Rogers, J., & Verduyn, C. (2004). A step too far? Randomized trial of cognitive-behaviour therapy delivered by social workers to depressed adolescents. *European Child & Adolescent Psychiatry, 13*, 92–99.

Kessler, R. C., Avenevoli, S., & Merikangas, K. R. (2001). Mood disorders in children and adolescents: An epidemiologic perspective. *Biological Psychiatry, 49*, 1002–1014.

Kessler, R. C., Berglund, P., Demler, O., Jin, R., Koretz, D., Merikangas, K. R., . . . Wang, P. S. (2003). The epidemiology of major depressive disorder: Results from the National Comorbidity Survey Replication (NCS-R). *Journal of the American Medical Association, 289*, 3095–3105.

Kessler, R. C., McGonagle, K. A., Zhao, S., Nelson, C. B., Hughes, M., Eshleman, S., . . . Kendler, K. S. (1994). Lifetime and 12-month prevalence of *DSM-III-R* psychiatric disorders in the United States: Results from the National Comorbidity Survey. *Archives of General Psychiatry, 51*, 8–19.

Kovacs, M. (1996). Presentation and course of major depressive disorder during childhood and later years of the life span. *Journal of the American Academy of Child & Adolescent Psychiatry, 35*, 705–715.

Kowalenko, N., Rapee, R. M., Simmons, J., Wignall, A., Hoge, R., Whitefield, K., . . . Baillie, A. J. (2005). Short-term effectiveness of a school-based early intervention program for adolescent depression. *Clinical Child Psychology and Psychiatry, 10*, 493–507.

Lavigne, J., LeBailly, S., Hopkins, J., Gouze, K., & Binns, H. (2009). The prevalence of ADHD, ODD, depression, and anxiety in a community sample of 4-year-olds. *Journal of Clinical Child & Adolescent Psychology, 3*, 315–328.

Lewinsohn, P. M., & Clarke, G. N. (1999). Psychosocial treatments for adolescent depression. *Clinical Psychology Review, 19*, 329–342.

Lewinsohn, P. M., Clarke, G. N., Hops, H., & Andrews, J. (1990). Cognitive-behavioral treatment for depressed adolescents. *Behavior Therapy, 21*, 385–401.

Lewinsohn, P. M., Clarke, G. N., Rohde, P., Hops, H., & Seeley, J. R. (1996). A course in coping: A cognitive-behavioral approach to the treatment of adolescent depression. In E. D. Hibbs & P. S. Jensen (Eds.), *Psychosocial treatments for child and adolescent disorders: Empirically based strategies for clinical practice* (pp. 109–135). Washington, DC: American Psychiatric Association.

Lewinsohn, P. M., Pettit, J., Joiner, T. Jr., & Seeley, J. (2003). The symptomatic expression of major depressive disorder in adolescents and young adults. *Journal of Abnormal Psychology, 112*, 244–252.

Lewinsohn, P. M., Roberts, R., Seeley, J., Rohde, P., Gotlib, I., & Hops, H. (1994). Adolescent psychopathology: II. Psychosocial risk factors for depression. *Journal of Abnormal Psychology, 103*, 302–315.

Lewinsohn, P. M., Rohde, P., & Seeley, J. (1998). Major depressive disorder in older adolescents: Prevalence, risk factors, and clinical implications. *Clinical Psychology Review, 18*, 765–794.

Lewinsohn, P. M., Seeley, J., Hibbard, J., Rohde, P., & Sack, W. (1996). Cross-sectional and prospective relationships between physical morbidity and depression in older adolescents. *Journal of American Academy of Child & Adolescent Psychiatry, 35*, 1120–1129.

Marchand, E., Ng, J., Rohde, P., & Stice, E. (2010). Effects of an indicated cognitive-behavioral depression prevention program are similar for Asian American, Latino, and European American adolescents. *Behaviour Research and Therapy, 48*, 821–825.

Mazzucchelli, T., Kane, R., & Rees, C. (2009). Behavioral activation treatments for depression in adults: A meta-analysis and review. *Clinical Psychology: Science and Practice, 16*, 383–411.

Melvin, G. A., Tonge, B. J., King, N. J., Heyne, D., Gordon, M. S., & Klimkeit, E. (2006). A comparison of cognitive-behavioral therapy, sertraline, and their combination for adolescent depression. *Journal of the American Academy of Child & Adolescent Psychiatry, 45*, 1151–1161.

Meyer, A. (1957). *Psychobiology: A science of man.* Springfield, IL: Charles C. Thomas.

Michael, K. D., & Crowley, S. L. (2002). How effective are treatments for child and adolescent depression? A meta-analytic review. *Clinical Psychology Review, 22*, 247–269.

Miller, L., Gur, M., Shanok, A., & Weissman, M. (2008). Interpersonal psychotherapy with pregnant adolescents: Two pilot studies. *Journal of Child Psychology and Psychiatry, 49*, 733–742.

Mufson, L., & Dorta, K. P. (2003). Interpersonal psychotherapy for depressed adolescents. In A. E. Kazdin & J. R. Weisz (Eds.), *Evidence-based psychotherapies for children and adolescents* (pp. 148–164). New York, NY: Guilford Press.

Mufson, L., Dorta, K. P., Wickramaratne, P., Nomura, Y., Olfson, M., & Weissman, M. M. (2004).

A randomized effectiveness trial of interpersonal psychotherapy for depressed adolescents. *Archives of General Psychiatry, 61*, 577–584.

Mufson, L., Weissman, M. M., Moreau, D., & Garfinkel, R. (1999). Efficacy of interpersonal psychotherapy for depressed adolescents. *Archives of General Psychiatry, 56*, 573–579.

Muris, P. (2002). Relationships between self-efficacy and symptoms of anxiety disorders and depression in a normal adolescent sample. *Personality and Individual Differences, 32*, 337–348.

Nelson, E., Barnard, M., & Cain, S. (2003). Treating childhood depression over videoconferencing. *Telemedicine Journal and e-Health, 9*, 49–55.

Ngo, V. K., Asarnow, J. R., Lange, J., Jaycox, L. H., Rea, M. M., Landon, C., . . . Miranda, J. (2009). Outcomes for youths from racial-ethnic minority groups in a quality improvement intervention for depression treatment. *Psychiatric Services, 60*, 1357–1364.

Reinecke, M. A., Ryan, N. E., & DuBois, D. L. (1998). Cognitive-behavioral therapy of depression and depressive symptoms during adolescence: A review and meta-analysis. *Journal of American Academy of Child & Adolescent Psychiatry, 37*, 26–34.

Reynolds, W., & Coats, K. (1986). A comparison of cognitive-behavioral therapy and relaxation training for the treatment of depression in adolescents. *Journal of Consulting and Clinical Psychology, 54*, 653–660.

Rice, F., Lifford, K., Thomas, H., & Thapar, A. (2007). Mental health and functional outcomes of maternal and adolescent reports of adolescent depressive symptoms. *Journal of American Academy of Child & Adolescent Psychiatry, 46*, 1162–1170.

Richardson, L., McCauley, E., & Katon, W. (2009). Collaborative care for adolescent depression: A pilot study. *General Hospital Psychiatry, 31*, 36–45.

Roberts, C., Kane, R., Thomson, H., Bishop, B., & Hart, B. (2003). The prevention of depressive symptoms in rural school children: A randomized controlled trial. *Journal of Consulting and Clinical Psychology, 71*, 622–628.

Roberts, R. E., Lewinsohn, P. M., & Seeley, J. R. (1995). Symptoms of DSM-III-R major depression in adolescence: Evidence from an epidemiological survey. *Journal of the American Academy of Child & Adolescent Psychiatry, 34*, 1608–1617.

Roberts, R., Roberts, C., & Chen, Y. (1997). Ethnocultural differences in prevalence of adolescent depression. *American Journal of Community Psychology, 25*, 95–110.

Roberts, R., & Sobhan, M. (1992). Symptoms of depression in adolescence: A comparison of Anglo, African, and Hispanic Americans. *Journal of Youth and Adolescence, 21*, 639–651.

Rohde, P., Clarke, G. N., Mace, D. E., Jorgensen, J. S., & Seeley, J. R. (2004). An efficacy/effectiveness study of cognitive-behavioral treatment for adolescents with comorbid major depression and conduct disorder. *Journal of the American Academy of Child & Adolescent Psychiatry, 43*, 660–668.

Rosselló, J., & Bernal, G. (1999). Treatment of depression in Puerto Rican adolescents. The efficacy of cognitive-behavioral and interpersonal treatments. *Journal of Consulting and Clinical Psychology, 67*, 734–745.

Rosselló, J., Bernal, G., & Rivera-Medina, C. (2008). Individual and group CBT and IPT for Puerto Rican adolescents with depressive symptoms. *Cultural Diversity and Ethnic Minority Psychology, 14*, 234–245.

Siegel, J., Yancey, A., Aneshensel, C., & Schuler, R. (1999). Body image, perceived pubertal timing, and adolescent mental health. *Journal of Adolescent Health, 25*, 155–165.

Silverman, W. K., & Hinshaw, S. P. (2008). The second special issue on evidence-based psychosocial treatments for children and adolescents: A 10-year update. *Journal of Clinical Child & Adolescent Psychology, 37*, 1–7.

Spielmans, G. I., Pasek, L. F., & McFall, J. P. (2007). What are the active ingredients in cognitive and behavioral psychotherapy for anxious and depressed children? A meta-analytic review. *Clinical Psychology Review, 27*, 642–654.

Stark, K. D., Reynolds, W. M., & Kaslow, N. J. (1987). A comparison of the relative efficacy of self-control therapy and a behavioral problem-solving therapy for depression in children. *Journal of Abnormal Child Psychology, 15*, 91–113.

Stark, K. D., Rouse, L., & Livingston, R. (1991). Treatment of depression during childhood and adolescence. In P. Kendall (Ed.), *Child and adolescent therapy* (pp. 165–206). New York, NY: Guilford Press.

Stark, K. D., Streusand, W., Krumholz, L. S., & Patel, P. (2010). Cognitive-behavioral therapy for depression: The ACTION treatment program for girls. In J. R. Weisz & A. E. Kazdin (Eds.), *Evidence-based psychotherapies for children and adolescents, second edition* (pp. 93–109). New York, NY: Guilford Press.

Stice, E., Burton, E., Bearman, S. K., & Rohde, P. (2007). Randomized trial of a brief depression prevention program: An elusive search for a psychosocial placebo control condition. *Behaviour Research and Therapy, 45*, 863–876.

Stice, E., Rohde, P., Seeley, J. R., & Gau, J. M. (2008). Brief cognitive-behavioral depression prevention program for high-risk adolescents outperforms two alternative interventions: A randomized efficacy trial. *Journal of Consulting and Clinical Psychology, 76*, 595–606.

Sullivan, H. S. (1953). *The interpersonal theory of psychiatry.* New York, NY: W. W. Norton.

Treatment for Adolescents with Depression Study (TADS) Team. (2004). Fluoxetine, cognitive-behavioral therapy, and their combination for adolescents with depression:

Treatment for Adolescents With Depression Study (TADS) randomized controlled trial. *Journal of the American Medical Association, 292*, 807–820.

Twenge, J., & Nolen-Hoeksema, S. (2002). Age, gender, race, socioeconomic status, and birth cohort difference on the children's depression inventory: A meta-analysis. *Journal of Abnormal Psychology, 111*, 578–588.

Vostanis, P., Feehan, C., Grattan, E., & Bickerton, W.-L. (1996). Treatment for children and adolescents with depression: Lessons from a controlled trial. *Clinical Child Psychology and Psychiatry, 1*, 199–212.

Watanabe, N., Hunot, V., Omori, I. M., Churchhill, R., & Furukawa, T. A. (2007). Psychotherapy for depression among children and adolescents: A systematic review. *Acta Psychiatrica Scandinavica, 116*, 84–95.

Weersing, R. V., & Weisz, J. R. (2002). Community clinic treatment of depressed youth: Benchmarking usual care against CBT clinical trials. *Journal of Consulting and Clinical Psychology, 70*, 299–310.

Weissman, M. M., Markowitz, J. C., & Klerman, G. L. (2000). *Comprehensive guide to interpersonal psychotherapy*. New York, NY: Basic Books.

Weisz, J. R., Jensen-Doss, A., & Hawley, K. M. (2005). Youth psychotherapy outcome research: A review and critique of the evidence base. *Annual Review of Psychology, 56*, 337–363.

Weisz, J. R., McCarty, C. A., & Valeri, S. M. (2006). Effects of psychotherapy for depression in children and adolescents: A meta-analysis. *Psychological Bulletin, 132*, 132–149.

Weisz, J., Southam-Gerow, M., Gordis, E., Connor-Smith, J., Chu, B., Langer, D., . . . Weiss, B. (2009). Cognitive-behavioral therapy versus usual clinical care for youth depression: An initial test of transportability to community clinics and clinicians. *Journal of Consulting and Clinical Psychology, 77*, 383–396.

Weisz, J. R., Thurber, C. A., Sweeney, L., Proffitt, V. D., & LeGagnoux, G. L. (1997). Brief treatment of mild-to-moderate child depression using primary and secondary control enhancement training. *Journal of Consulting and Clinical Psychology, 65*, 703–707.

Weisz, J. R., Weiss, B., Han, S. S., Granger, D. A., & Morton, T. (1995). Effects of psychotherapy with children and adolescents revisited: A meta-analysis of treatment outcome studies. *Psychological Bulletin, 117*, 450–468.

Wood, A., Harrington, R., & Moore, A. (1996). Controlled trial of a brief cognitive–behavioural intervention in adolescent patients with depressive disorders. *Journal of Child Psychology and Psychiatry, 37*, 737–746.

Young, J. F., Mufson, L., & Davies, M. (2006a). Efficacy of interpersonal psychotherapy-adolescent skills training: An indicated preventive intervention for depression. *Journal of Child Psychology and Psychiatry, 47*, 1254–1262.

Young, J. F., Mufson, L., & Davies, M. (2006b). Impact of comorbid anxiety in an effectiveness study of interpersonal psychotherapy for depressed adolescents. *Journal of the American Academy of Child and Adolescent Psychiatry, 45*, 904–912.

Young, J. F., Mufson, L., & Gallop, R. (2010). Preventing depression: A randomized trial of Interpersonal Psychotherapy—adolescent skills training. *Depression and Anxiety, 27*, 426–433.

Yu, D., & Seligman, M. (2002). Preventing depressive symptoms in Chinese children. *Prevention and Treatment, 5*(1). doi: 10.1037/1522-3736.5.1.59a

23

Anxiety Disorders in Children and Adolescents

ANTHONY JAMES, FELICITY COWDREY, AND CHRISTINE JAMES

INTRODUCTION

This article focuses on the etiology, assessment, and treatment of the major anxiety disorders—separation anxiety disorder (SAD), generalized anxiety disorder (GAD), social phobia, specific phobias, and panic disorder—diagnosed according to the *Diagnostic and Statistical Manual of Mental Disorders*, 4th edition (*DSM-IV-TR*) (American Psychiatric Association, 2000) criteria, but excludes selective mutism, posttraumatic stress disorder, and obsessive-compulsive disorder, which may involve specific etiologies and treatments.

While *The ICD-10 Classification of Mental and Behavioral Disorders* (World Health Organization, 1992) and *DSM-IV-TR* approaches are widely used, some advocate a more parsimonious approach of including major depressive disorder (MDD) and anxiety into distress disorders and separating fear disorders (Clark & Watson, 2006).

Normal Developmental Fears and Worries

It is crucial that clinicians distinguish normal, developmentally appropriate worries, fears, and shyness from anxiety disorders. Distinguishing features of pathological anxiety include severity, persistence, and associated impairment. An understanding of the developmental patterns of various anxieties is important. For instance, separation anxiety is not evident in young infants due to developmental changes until 6 months when it becomes the norm. School-age children commonly have worries about injury and natural events, whereas older children and adolescents typically have worries and fears related to school performance, social competence, and health issues. Social anxiety occurs more frequently after puberty. Genetic effects on fear are developmentally dynamic from middle childhood to young adulthood, and as children age, familial-environmental influences on fears decline in importance (Kendall, Hudson, Flannery-Schroeder, & Gosch, 2008).

Clinical Presentation

The presentation of anxiety disorders varies with age. Often the young child can present with undifferentiated worries, fears, and multiple somatic complaints—muscle tension, headaches, or stomachaches—and sometimes angry outbursts. The latter may be misdiagnosed as oppositional defiant disorder, as the child tries to avoid anxiety-provoking situations.

Generalized Anxiety Disorder (GAD)

GAD is characterized by chronic, excessive worry about family, health/safety, school, social interactions, world events, and natural disasters with at least one associated somatic symptom. Children with GAD are often perfectionistic, and frequently seek reassurance.

Social Anxiety Disorders (SAD)

SAD is characterized by excessive and developmentally inappropriate fear and distress occurring during separation or threats of separation from significant attachment figures or home. These children worry excessively about their own or their parents' safety and health when separated, have difficulty sleeping alone, experience nightmares with themes of separation, and frequently they have somatic complaints. SAD may be associated with school refusal.

Specific Phobia

Specific phobia is fear of a particular object or situation that is avoided or endured with great distress. A specific fear can develop into a specific phobia if symptoms are significant enough to result in extreme distress or impairment related to the fear, and multiple phobias occur.

Social Phobia

Social phobia is characterized by worry or extreme discomfort in one or more social settings, often with a fear of performing or speaking in public. Social phobia can be so disabling the young person remains isolated in class or is housebound.

Panic Disorder

Panic disorder is characterized by recurrent episodes of intense fear accompanied by at least 4 of 13 symptoms from DSM-IV-TR such as pounding heart, sweating, shaking, difficulty breathing, chest pressure/pain, feeling of choking, nausea, chills, or dizziness. Children and adolescents with panic disorder fear recurrent panic attacks and their consequences, and they can become avoidant and develop agoraphobia.

Epidemiology

Anxiety disorders are among the most common psychiatric conditions diagnosed in children in the community, with between 8% and 21%

affected during childhood or adolescence (*DSM-III* criteria) (Anderson, Williams, McGee, & Silva, 1987), although a recent study in the United Kingdom produced point prevalence estimates of just 3.1% for any anxiety disorder (Meltzer, Gatward, Goodman, & Ford, 2000). The system of diagnostic classification is important (see review, Cartwright-Hatton, McNicol, & Doubleday, 2006). For instance, studies where impairment was required for diagnosis—as per *DSM-IV* or *DSM-II-R* rather than *DSM-III* (Almqvist et al., 1999; Costello, Mustillo, Erkanli, Keeler, & Angold, 2003; Ford, Goodman, & Meltzer, 2003)—found a lower prevalence of anxiety rates. In these studies the rates of anxiety in children under age 12 varies between 2.6% and 5.2%, with separation anxiety being the most common.

Anxiety disorders with an onset in childhood frequently persist into adolescence (Last, Perrin, Hersen, & Kazdin, 1996) and early adulthood (Last, Hansen, & Franco, 1997), and yet often remain untreated, with many cases of social phobia first diagnosed more than 20 years after onset (Schneier, Johnson, Hornig, Liebowitz, & Weissman, 1992).

SAD peaks in adolescence with a standardized person-years of incidence for SAD of 0.72% (Beesdo et al., 2007). SAD is consistently associated with subsequent depression, independent of age at onset for SAD. SAD is associated with a more malignant course and character of depression, hence the need for preventative measures (Beesdo et al., 2007). The Dunedin longitudinal study has shown strong correlations across time from late adolescence to early adulthood and between various anxiety disorders and major depressive disorder (MDD) (Fergusson, Boden, & Horwood, 2007).

Etiology

Biology

Threat interpretation bias appears to be a cognitive factor associated with ongoing childhood anxiety (Waters, Wharton, Zimmer-

Gembeck, & Craske, 2008). Currently, there are two primary hypotheses based on functional MRI data collected during fear acquisition and extinction processes. During fear acquisition, presentation of a conditioned stimulus paired (CS+) with an unconditioned stimulus (UCS) is hypothesized to engage greater amygdala responses than presentation of a conditioned stimulus unpaired (CS–) with the UCS in all adolescents. However, the difference in reactivity to the CS+ relative to the CS– is thought to be greater among anxious adolescents compared to their healthy peers, manifesting as a group-by-stimulus interaction. During fear extinction, greater recruitment of prefrontal regions is seen during presentation of the CS+ relative to the CS– in all adolescents. Work is under way to test whether a group-by-stimulus interaction is likely so that greater differential activity to the CS+ than the CS– characterizes healthy compared to anxious adolescents (Lau, Gregory, Goldwin, Pine, & Eley, 2007; personal communication).

The intrinsic circuit involved in anxiety disorders involves prefrontal cortex inhibition of the amygdala. According to Berkowitz, Coplan, Reddy, and Gorman (2007) there is a distinction between two classes of anxiety disorders. Those disorders involving intense fear and panic—panic disorder, posttraumatic stress disorder, and phobias—that seem to be characterized by an underactivity of the prefrontal cortex, thus disinhibiting the amygdala. Disorders such as GAD and OCD, which involve worry and rumination, on the other hand, seem to be characterized by an overactivity of the prefrontal cortex. The dorsal anterior cingulate is also involved in the fear response (Milad et al., 2007). Functional MRI studies have confirmed that adolescents with GAD, but not controls, show greater activation to fearful faces than to happy faces in a distributed network including the amygdala, ventral prefrontal cortex, and anterior cingulate cortex (McClure et al., 2007). The resulting amygdala hyperactivity appears to be due to a lack of compensatory increase in

modulation by the ventrolateral prefrontal cortex (Monk et al., 2008).

Family and Environment

The relationship between attachment patterns and anxiety disorders is relatively weak, although ambivalent attachment has been found to be associated with later social phobia (Bar-Haim, Dan, Eshel, & Sagi-Schwartz, 2007). Temperamental factors and life events, however, are important in the genesis of anxiety disorders. Preschool-age behavioral inhibition (BI) predicts social anxiety disorder in childhood and early adolescence and anxiety sensitivity (AS) increases the vulnerability for the onset of panic disorder (D. R. Hirshfeld-Becker et al., 2007). Recent prospective studies have also confirmed a link between life events and anxiety (Kroes et al., 2002; Phillips, Hammen, Brennan, Najman, & Bor, 2005), while peer rejection is associated with the development of social anxiety (Storch, Crisp, Roberti, Bagner, & Masia-Warner, 2005). In a review, D. R. Hirshfeld-Becker and colleagues (2007) noted that as most studies have focused on only one factor without controlling for others, these associations cannot be assumed to be additive.

There is strong familiality of anxiety disorders, especially between mother and child (Cooper, Fearn, Willetts, Seabrook, & Parkinson, 2006; Creswell, Willetts, Murray, Singhal, & Cooper, 2008). This applies particularly to social phobia and separation anxiety disorder. The risk of an anxiety disorder in the offspring of a mother with social anxiety disorder is increased with an earlier onset and greater severity of maternal anxiety (Schreier, Wittchen, Höfler, & Lieb, 2008). Shared environmental influences on fear symptoms are important, and are seen in children as young as 4 years. These shared environmental factors correlate highly across anxiety disorders (Eley, Bolton, O'Connor, Perrin, Sith, & Plomin, 2003).

The genetic twin studies of anxiety disorders show unique or nonshared environmental factors are more salient than shared environmental factors; a possible exception being low SES (Moffitt et al., 2007). The influence of family factors is not large—an Australian longitudinal population study of families attending a well-child clinic found that internalizing behaviors were predicted by small family size, parent distress, and parenting, although these factors only predicted 17% of the variance (Bayer, Hiscock, Ukoumunne, Price, & Wake, 2008).

A meta-analysis of 47 cross-sectional studies of parenting and child anxiety examined two general parenting dimensions—warmth versus criticism/rejection, and overcontrol versus autonomy granting (McLeod, Wood, & Weisz, 2007). Lower warmth and responsiveness are hypothesized to foster poorer emotional regulation, whereas overprotection and high parental control are hypothesized to lead to lower self-efficacy (D. R. Hirshfeld-Becker et al., 2007). The findings suggest that parents of anxious children tend to be more over-protective and less granting of autonomy or less warm and accepting than parents of non-anxious children. However, there are important caveats: The effects sizes were extremely modest (–0.21, with parenting behaviors accounting for only 4% of the total variance in measures of child anxiety symptoms or disorders); the directionality is not clear; the question of parental control as either a cause of the child's anxiety, a response by parents to the child's anxiety, or an expression of the parents' own anxiety; the parenting dimensions studied are maybe too broad—some parenting subdimensions (e.g., autonomy-granting, 18% of the variance) demonstrated a significantly stronger association with childhood anxiety than others (e.g., warmth, < 1% of the variance). Also, lower levels of autonomy-granting and excessive overinvolvement were more strongly associated with childhood anxiety than rejection (McLeod et al., 2007).

For internalizing disorders there is evidence for moderate contribution of genetic factors (20%–40% heritability for anxiety disorders; Eley et al., 2003), with most of the variance attributable to unique or nonshared environmental factors. In the case of GAD, however, shared environment does play an important role (Ehringer, Rhee, Young, Corley, & Hewitt, 2006). The interplay of genetic and environmental influences on fears is dynamic. Genetic factors influencing fear intensity at age 8 to 9 years decline substantially in importance. However, new sets of genetic risk factors impacting fear intensity "come on line" in early adolescence, late adolescence, and early adulthood. With age, the influence of the shared environment declines and unique environment increases (Kendler, Gardner, Annas, Neale, Eaves, & Lichtenstein, 2008). Genetic studies indicate a common fear factor early on that becomes more differentiated in adolescence, with, for example, social fears arising in adolescence (Kendler et al., 2008). Differing genes may play a role in mediating SAD in males and females, with heritability of SAD being greater for girls than for boys (L. J. Eaves et al., 1997; Feigon, Waldman, Levy, & Hay, 2001).

There is evidence for a gene x environment (G x E) interaction in pediatric anxiety (Lau, et al., 2008). Twin analyses have shown that the presence of genetic risk for anxiety symptoms enhanced sensitivity toward negative life events in adolescent females (L. Eaves, Silberg, & Erkanli, 2003; Silberg, Rutter, Neale, & Eaves, 2001). Lau et al. (2008) found age-related G x E effects with the genetic variance on separation anxiety symptoms in childhood and panic anxiety symptoms in adolescence increased across higher levels of negative events. However, no such relationship was found for general anxiety or social anxiety. No clear biological mechanisms have been demonstrated yet for G x E effects (Lau et al., 2008), although the association of the 5-HTTLPR polymorphism, which accounts for up to 10% of phenotypic variance in amygdala activation, may be a candidate (Munafò, Brown, & Hariri, 2008).

Overall, these findings point the way to possible preventative interventions with genetic at-risk individuals being taught how to cope with stress prior to the onset of symptoms. The G x E effects also apply to resilience, as environmental factors such as social support (Fox et al., 2005) reduce anxiety symptoms.

Assessment and Diagnosis

A clinical assessment must be able to differentiate normal worries from pathological anxiety. Consideration of the developmental aspects is important and requires experience in various clinical techniques, including observation of play in younger children. Multiple informants—the family, peers if available, and school—are essential. A judgment of the number, type, and severity of symptoms alongside the level of impairment will be necessary. Standardized semistructured interviews such as the K-SADS-PL (Kaufman et al., 1997); Anxiety Disorders Interview Schedule for *DSM-IV* Child Version (ADIS; Silverman & Albano, 1996); or a checklist based on *DSM-IV* criteria may assist diagnosis. Rating scales can be used to measure symptom severity (Myers & Winters, 2002).

Treatment

A number of treatment modalities are advocated for the treatment of pediatric anxiety, including, among others: CBT, pharmacotherapy, family therapy, and psychodynamic therapy (see Practice Parameter JAACAP, 2007). This chapter focuses on CBT and drug treatments, which have a larger evidence-base.

BACKGROUND

The initial trials of cognitive behavior therapy (CBT) (Barrett, Dadds, & Rapee, 1996; Kendall, 1994; Kendall et al., 1997) were positive. Since then, there have been further randomized controlled trials of CBT in various formats: individual, group, and with parent involvement. A number of these studies have shown a statistically significant benefit for CBT versus controls.

Cognitive Behavior Therapy (CBT)

The aim of CBT is to help the child to identify possible cognitive deficits and distortions, to reality-test them, and then to teach new skills or challenge irrational thoughts and beliefs, and replace them with more rational thinking (Kendall, Reber, McLeer, Epps, & Ronan, 1990). CBT is usually delivered over 10 to 20 weekly sessions. More specifically, CBT is a psychological model that involves helping the child to: (a) recognize anxious feelings and bodily or somatic reactions to anxiety, (b) clarify thoughts or cognitions in anxiety-provoking situations (i.e., unrealistic or negative attributions and expectations), (c) develop coping skills (i.e., modifying anxious self-talk into coping self-talk, problem solving), and (d) evaluate outcomes. Emphasis is also put on relapse prevention and maintenance skills (Waters, Wharton, et al., 2008). The behavioral training strategies include: modeling, reality exposure (in vivo exposure), role-playing, social skills (i.e., assertiveness), and relaxation training (i.e., breathing exercises, progressive muscle relaxation). The behavioral treatment is based on the premise that fear or anxiety are learned responses (classically conditioned) that can be "unlearned." An element of treatment known as systematic desensitization involves pairing anxiety stimuli, in vivo or in imagination, in a gradually increasing hierarchy with competing relaxing stimuli such as pleasant images or muscle relaxation. While suitable for older children and adolescents, younger children find it difficult to pair imagined stimuli and use muscle relaxation. A crucial component and maintaining factor in anxiety disorders is avoidance (a negative reinforcer). Exposure in vivo or in imagination, usually in a gradual, hierarchical manner, is therefore considered an important element of treatment. Another symptom that is often addressed using CBT, especially in children, is the disproportionate attention to threat cues (Waters, Wharton, et al., 2008). Threat interpretation bias is a relevant target because CBT encourages the restructuring of anxiety-promoting cognitions and the search for additional information before responding to the situation as if threatening (Muris, Merckelbach, & Damsma, 2000).

Research has highlighted the importance of family factors in the aetiology and maintenance of anxiety disorders (as previously shown), hence a number of studies have actively included family or parents in the treatment package. The involvement can vary from psychoeducation to conjoint therapy, or parental or family groups often run alongside treatment for the child or adolescent.

The application of CBT requires a certain level of cognitive development. Kendall and colleagues (1990) argued that the ability to measure a thought or belief against the notion of a rational standard, and the ability to understand that a thought or belief can cause a person to behave and feel in a certain way, were central to its proper use. The question then arises: At what age does a child have the cognitive capacities to undertake these cognitive operations? Young children under the age of 6 years, preoperational in Piagetian terms, are egocentric and therefore may be able to use decentering techniques such as narrative or stories. An example has been tried, seemingly successfully, although not subject to component analysis, in the treatment of childhood obsessive-compulsive disorder (March, Franklin, Nelson, & Foa, 2001). A recent study of CBT for young children has shown benefit, but this was not an RCT (D. Hirshfeld-Becker, Micco, Simoes, & Henin, 2008).

A systematic review of CBT for the treatment of childhood (> 6 years) and adolescent (< 19 years) anxiety disorders (Cartwright-Hatton, Roberts, Chitsabesan, Fothergill, & Harrington, 2004) in comparison to waiting-list controls, identified 10 studies. Using conservative criteria in a meta-analysis, the remission rate of diagnosed anxiety disorders was 56.5% in the CBT group compared to 34.8% in the controls, with an odds ratio of 3.3 (95% CI 1.9 to 5.6), suggesting a significant benefit for CBT. The review did not examine continuous measures. The authors noted that the reporting of many aspects of the trials was weak, and many of the studies were efficacy trials, therefore of limited generalizability. A further review of the treatment of childhood and adolescent anxiety disorders using CBT (Compton et al., 2004) identified 21 RCTs with waiting-list and/or active treatment controls. A meta-analysis was not undertaken, however, standardized effect size estimates for a variety of anxiety symptom measures showed a medium to large effect for CBT in reducing symptoms in comparison to waiting-list, inactive control, and active control conditions. The authors concluded that a substantial evidence base supported the efficacy of problem-specific cognitive behavioral interventions for a variety of childhood anxiety disorders (Compton et al., 2004). All recent reviews and meta analyses (Hudson, 2005; Ishikawa, Okajima, Matsuoka, & Sakano, 2007; In-Albon & Schneider, 2007; James, Soler, & Weatherall, 2005; Scott, Mughelli, & Deas, 2005) have also shown positive effects for CBT versus controls, with effects sizes (Cohen's d, Cohen, 1988) varying from 0.56 (James, Solar, & Weatherall, 2005) to 0.86 (In-Albon & Scheider, 2007). There is some evidence that shorter treatment trials are as effective as longer trials (Ishikawa et al., 2007). There is little evidence, however, to suggest family or group treatments are more effective than individual treatment (Hudson, 2005; James et al., 2005; Ishikawa et al., 2007). As perhaps anecdotally thought, treatment in a university research center yields better results (effects size university 0.77 vs. routine clinics 0.37) (Ishikawa et al., 2007).

Durability of the treatment effects is a crucial question when evaluating any intervention. Although more difficult to analyze due to dropouts and often changing methodology during the trial follow-up period, the results look very encouraging. Positive effects were found up to several years posttreatment (James et al., 2005; Ishikawa et al., 2007).

An important point is consideration of those children often not included in meta-analyses—that is, children with learning disabilities. Indeed, this group of children deserves more focused treatment research, particularly as the prevalence of psychiatric disorders is high in this population. One diagnostic group where there has been some research is those with autistic spectrum disorder (ASD) or Asperger's syndrome. There are two reported RCTs—one showed family-based CBT was effective in children with high-functioning ASD (71% no longer meting diagnostic criteria) (Chalfant, Rapee, & Carroll, 2007); and another with child only and parental involvement showed a reduction in anxiety symptoms in children with Asperger's syndrome (Sofronoff, Attwood, & Hinton, 2005).

Search Methods

We searched the Cochrane Register of Controlled Trials and the Cochrane Depression, Anxiety, and Neurosis Group Register, which includes relevant randomized controlled trials from the bibliographic databases—the Cochrane Library (to July 2008), EMBASE (1970–July, 2008), MEDLINE (1970–July 2008), and PsycINFO (1970–July 2008). We also searched the references of all included studies and relevant textbooks, and contacted authors in order to identify further trials.

Selection Criteria

Each identified study was assessed for possible inclusion by two reviewers independently. Inclusion criteria consisted of randomized controlled trials of CBT versus waiting-list/attention controls in children (more than 6 years of age) and adolescents (under the age of 19 years) with a *DSM* (*Diagnostic Statistical Manual*) or *ICD* (*International Classification of Diseases*) anxiety diagnosis; and excluding simple phobia, obsessive-compulsive disorder, and posttraumatic stress disorder. Each study was required to conform to the principles of

CBT through use of a protocol and comprised at least eight sessions of CBT.

Data Collection and Analysis

The methodological quality of included trials was assessed by two reviewers independently. The dichotomous outcome of remission of anxiety diagnosis was pooled using relative risk (RR) with 95% confidence intervals (CI). Means and standard deviations of anxiety symptom continuous scores were pooled using the standardized mean difference (SMD). Heterogeneity was assessed and intention-to-treat (ITT) analyses undertaken. The presence of publication bias was assessed using funnel plots.

Results

Seventeen studies with 630 subjects and 393 controls met the inclusion criteria and were included in the analyses. The studies involved community or outpatient subjects only, with anxiety of only mild to moderate severity. The intention-to-treat (ITT) analyses showed a response rate for remission of any anxiety diagnosis of 56% for CBT versus 28.2% for controls (relative risk 0.56 (95% CI, 0.50–0.62), with a positive treatment effect $z = 10.9$, $p < 0.001$ (Figure 23.1). There was no evidence of heterogeneity $\chi^2 = 19.16$ (d.f. = 16) $p = 0.24$, I^2 (variation in relative risk attributable to heterogeneity), 17.5%. The number needed to treat (NNT) was 3.0 (95% CI, 2.5–3.4). There was no evidence of publication bias—Egger's test $t = 0.8$, $p = 0.43$, with a symmetrical Begg's funnel plot (Figure 23.2). For reduction in anxiety symptoms, the standard mean difference (SMD) was –0.58 (95% CI, –0.76 to –0.40) with, again, no significant heterogeneity indicated. Post hoc analyses suggest that individual, group, and family/parental formats of CBT produced fairly similar outcomes.

CBT compared to active controls again showed a positive effect (relative risk 0.56 [95% CI, 0.40–0.67], $Z = 5.07$, $p < 0.001$, with a trend toward heterogeneity [$\chi^2 = 5.7$,

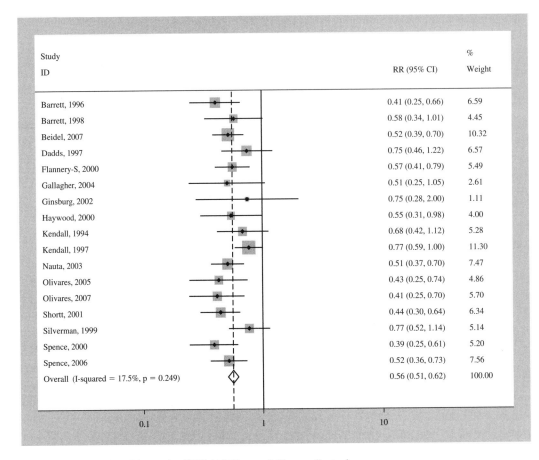

Figure 23.1   Anxiety Diagnosis: CBT (All Formats) Versus Control

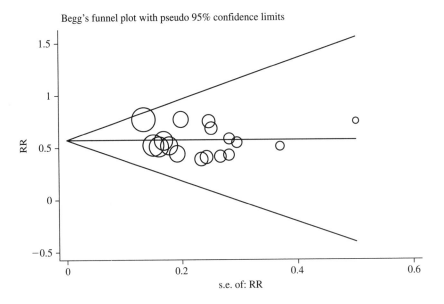

Figure 23.2   Begg's Funnel Plot With Pseudo 95% Confidence Limits

d.f. $= 2$, $p = 0.056$, $I^2 = 65\%$]). There were, however, only three studies (Kendall, Hudson, Flannery-Schroeder, & Gosch, 2008; Masia, Fisher, Shrout, Rathor, & Klein, 2007; P. Olivares-Olivares, Rosa-Alcazar, & Olivares, 2007) involved in this analysis.

Studies employing active controls— relaxation and education—highlight the importance of CBT as the active treatment, although the exact mechanism is not yet clear.

CBT can be readily delivered in schools and via a computer, which makes this treatment potentially attractive for treating the large numbers of young people suffering from anxiety disorders. Preliminary work suggests CBT can be successfully applied to preschool children (D. Hirshfeld-Becker et al., 2008), which may open new avenues for treating targeted groups such as affected children of parents with anxiety disorders.

CONCLUSION

CBT appears an effective treatment for childhood and adolescent anxiety disorders in comparison to waiting list or attention control. There is no evidence for a difference between an individual, group, or parental/family format. CBT can, therefore, be recommended for the treatment of childhood and anxiety disorders, although with only just over half improving, there is a need for further therapeutic developments. Further work is needed to understand the precise mechanisms underlying the effectiveness of CBT. Most studies only use questionnaires or diagnostic interviews of symptoms, which are clearly important. However, that leaves open the issue of the underlying shifts, if any, in cognitions. Clearly, rote learning of rules would not equate to a cognitive therapy (Grave & Blissett, 2004). Unfortunately, few studies of CBT, and only one RCT in the field of childhood anxiety disorders (Chalfant et al., 2007), include measures of cognitive change. Recent work has shown that threat interpretation bias, a

cognitive factor associated with ongoing childhood anxiety (Waters, Wharton, et al., 2008), is specifically reduced with CBT (Waters, Craske, Bergman, & Treanor, 2008).

As noted before, even in research trials, only half of subjects improve with CBT. A possible way, as shown by Fairburn and colleagues in their treatment trials of bulimia nervosa, might be to systematically review all treatment failures and use the results to devise a more targeted and effective treatment package (Wade, Bergin, Martin, Gillespie, & Fairburn, 2006).

Pharmacology

A meta-analysis (Bridge et al., 2007) of the treatment of non-OCD anxiety disorders with serotonin reuptake inhibitors (SSRIs) revealed a pooled rate of response of 69% (95% CI, 65% to 73%) versus 39% (95% CI, 35% to 43%) in those receiving placebo. This gave the numbers needed to treat (NNT) as 3 (95% CI, 2 to 5), which is very reasonable. There appeared to be an age-related response, with adolescents responding better than children. One of the important side effects of SSRIs is the small but definite increased risk of suicidal ideation or self-harm. The pooled absolute rates of suicidal ideation/suicide attempt were low at 1% (95% CI, 0.2% to 2%) in antidepressant-treated participants versus 0.2% (95% CI, −0.2% to 0.5%) in those receiving placebo, yielding a number need to harm (NNH) of 143. Overall, SSRIs are effective at treating non-OCD anxiety. Furthermore, SSRIs appear safe. Neither tricyclic antidepressants (TCAs) nor benzodiazepines appear more effective than placebo in treating childhood anxiety disorders (Dieleman & Ferdinand, 2008), and they are not recommended.

A meta-analysis (Hofmann, Sawyer, Korte, & Smits, 2009) has indicated the beneficial effect of adding psychopharmacology to CBT in the treatment of some anxiety disorders. In children and adolescents the evidence is limited to two studies (Beidel, Turner, Sallee, Ammerman, Crosby, & Pathak, 2007; Walkup et al., 2008) that compared CBT and SSRIs (selective serotonin reuptake inhibitor) antidepressants (fluoxetine and sertraline), The large multi-center study (Walkup et al., 2008) with 488 participants found the combination of CBT with medication was more effective than CBT or medication alone. A leveling off of the effects of medication, but not CBT, on symptom severity after 8 weeks, suggested possible differences in efficacy, with longer-term treatment with CBT possibly being more effective (Beidel et al., 2007; Walkup et al., 2009). There is an intriguing suggestion from fMRI studies (McClure et al., 2007) that those with amygdala hyperactivation, which is the case in pediatric GAD, may be more responsive to SSRIs and CBT. Further work in this area is warranted.

Summary

Anxiety disorders are an active area of clinical and research interest. It is becoming clear that genetic and environmental factors and their interaction play an important but differential role in the aetiology and presentation of the anxiety disorders over the childhood years. Pediatric anxiety disorders are common and associated with considerable morbidity. Comorbities are important as are later associations: SAD, in particular, presages mood disorders in early adulthood. Meta-analyses confirm the efficacy of CBT and SSRIs in treating child and adolescent anxiety disorders; however, further work is needed in identifying suitable targets for prevention, and developing the application of therapeutic techniques such as CBT in schools and via computers. Strategies for understanding and enhancing the therapeutic mechanisms and effectiveness of CBT and drugs and their use in combination treatments are awaited.

REFERENCES

Almqvist, F., Puura, K., Kumpulainen, K., Tuompo-Johansson, E., Henttonen, I., Huikko, E., . . . Tamminen, T. (1999). Psychiatric disorders in 8–9-year-old children based on a diagnostic interview with the parents. *European Child Adolescent Psychiatry*, 8, 17–28.

American Psychiatric Association. (2000). *Diagnostic and statistical manual of mental disorders (DSM-IV-TR)* (4th ed., text revision). Washington, DC: Author.

Anderson, J., Williams, S., McGee, R., & Silva, P. (1987). *DSM-III* disorders in preadolescent children. Prevalence in a large sample from the general population. *Archives General Psychiatry*, 44, 69–76.

Bar-Haim, Y., Dan, O., Eshel, Y., & Sagi-Schwartz, A. (2007). Predicting children's anxiety from early attachment relationships. *Journal of Anxiety Disorders*, 21, 1061–1068.

Barrett, P. M., Dadds, M. R., & Rapee, R. M., (1996). Family treatment of childhood anxiety: A controlled trial. *Journal of Consulting and Clinical Psychology*, 64, 333–342.

Bayer, J. K., Hiscock, H., Ukoumunne, O. C., Price, A., & Wake, M. (2008). Early childhood aetiology of mental health problems: A longitudinal population-based study. *Journal of Child Psychology and Psychiatry*, 49, 116–174.

Beesdo, K., Bitner, A., Pine, D., Stein, M., Höfler, M., Lieb, R., & Wittchen, H. (2007). Incidence of social anxiety disorder and the consistent risk for secondary depression in the first three decades of life. *Archives General Psychiatry*, 64, 903–912.

Beidel, D. C., Turner, S. M., Sallee, F. R., Ammerman, R. T., Crosby, L. A., & Pathak, S. (2007). SET-C versus fluoxetine in the treatment of childhood social phobia. *Journal of the American Academy of Child and Adolescent Psychiatry*, 46, 1622–1632.

Berkowitz, R., Coplan, J., Reddy, D., & Gorman, J. (2007). The human dimension: How the prefrontal cortex modulates the subcortical fear response. *Review Neuroscience*, 18, 191–207.

Bridge, J., Iyengar, S., Salalry, C., Barbe, R., Birmaher, B., Pincus, H., Ren, L., & Brent, D. (2007). Clinical response and risk for reported suicidal ideation and suicide attempts in pediatric antidepressant treatment: A meta-analysis of randomized controlled trials. *Journal of the American Medical Academy*, 297, 1683–1696.

Cartwright-Hatton, S., McNicol, K., & Doubleday, E. (2006). Anxiety in a neglected population: Prevalence of anxiety disorders in pre-adolescent children. *Clinical Psychology Review*, 26, 817–833.

Cartwright-Hatton, S., Roberts, C., Chitsabesan, P., Fothergill, C., & Harrington, R. (2004). Systematic review of the efficacy of cognitive-behaviour therapies for childhood and adolescent anxiety disorders. *British Journal of Clinical Psychology*, 43, 421–436.

Chalfant, A., Rapee, R., & Carroll, L. (2007). Treating anxiety disorders in children with high functioning autistic spectrum disorders: A controlled trial. *Journal of Autism Developmental Disorders*, 37, 1842–1857.

Clark, L., & Watson, D. (2006). Distress and fear disorders: An alternative empirically based taxonomy of the "mood" and "anxiety" disorders. *British Journal of Psychiatry, 189*, 481–483.

Cohen, J. (1988). *Statistical power analysis for the behavioral sciences* (2nd ed.). Hillsdale, NJ: Earlbaum.

Compton, S. N., March, J. S., Brent, D., Albano, A. M., Weering, R., & Curry, J. (2004). Cognitive-behavioral psychotherapy for anxiety and depressive disorders in children and adolescents: An evidence-based medicine review. *Journal of American Academy Child and Adolescent Psychiatry, 43*, 930–959.

Cooper, P., Fearn, V., Willetts, L., Seabrook, H., & Parkinson, M. (2006). Affective disorder in the parents of a clinic sample of children with anxiety disorders. *Journal of Affective Disorders, 93*, 205–212.

Costello, E. J., Mustillo, S., Erkanli, A., Keeler, G., & Angold, A. (2003) Prevalence and development of psychiatric disorders in childhood and adolescence. *Archives of General Psychiatry, 60*, 837–844.

Creswell, C., Willetts, L., Murray, L., Singhal, M., Cooper, P. (2008). Treatment of child anxiety: An exploratory study of the role of maternal anxiety and behaviours in treatment outcome. *Clinical Psychology and Psychotherapy, 15*, 38–44.

Dieleman, G., & Ferdinand, R. (2008). Pharmacotherapy for social phobia, generalized anxiety disorder and separation anxiety disorder in children and adolescents: An overview. *Dutch Journal of Psychiatry, 50*, 43–53.

Eaves, L. J., Silberg, J. L., Meyer, J. M., Maes, H. H., Simonoff, E., Pickles, A., . . . Hewitt, J. K. (1997). Genetics and developmental psychopathology: 2. The main effects of genes and environment on behavioral problems in the Virginia Twin Study of Adolescent Behavioral Development. *Journal of Child Psychology and Psychiatry, 38*, 965–980.

Eaves, L., Silberg, J., & Erkanli, A. (2003). Resolving multiple epigenetic pathways to adolescent depression. *Journal of Child Psychology and Psychiatry, 44*, 1006–1014.

Eley, T., Bolton, D., O'Connor, T., Perrin, S., Smith, P., & Plomin, R. (2003). A twin study of anxiety-related behaviours in pre-school children. *Journal of Child Psychology and Psychiatry, 44*, 945–960.

Ehringer, M., Rhee, S., Young, S., Corley, R., & Hewitt, J. (2006). Genetic and environmental contributions to common psychopathologies of childhood and adolescence: A study of twins and their siblings. *Journal of Abnormal Child Psychiatry, 34*, 1–17.

Feigon, S. A., Waldman, I. D., Levy, F., & Hay, D. A. (2001). Genetic and environmental influences on separation anxiety disorder symptoms and their moderation by age and sex. *Behaviour Genetics, 31*, 403–411.

Fergusson, D. M., Boden, J. M., & Horwood, L. J. (2007). Recurrence of major depression in adolescence and early adulthood, and later mental health educational and economic outcomes. *British Journal of Psychiatry, 191*, 335–342.

Ford, T., Goodman, R., & Meltzer, H. (2003). The British Child and Adolescent Mental Health Survey 1999: The prevalence of DSM-IV disorders. *Journal of the American Academy of Child and Adolescent Psychiatry, 42*, 1203–1211.

Fox, N. A., Nichols, K. E., Henderson, H. A., Rubin, K., Schmidt, L., Hamer, D., . . . Pine, D. S. (2005). Evidence for a gene-environment interaction in predicting behavioral inhibition in middle childhood. *Psychological Science, 16*, 921–926.

Grave, J., & Blissett, J. (2004). Is cognitive behavioral therapy developmentally appropriate for young children? A critical review of the evidence. *Clinical Psychology Review, 24*, 399–420.

Hirshfeld-Becker, D. R., Biederman, J., Henin, A., Faraone, S. V., Micco, J. A., van Grondelle, A., . . . Rosenbaum, J. F. (2007). Clinical outcomes of laboratory-observed preschool behavioral disinhibition at five-year follow-up. *Biological Psychiatry, 62*, 565–572.

Hirshfeld-Becker, D., Masek, B., Henin, A., Raezer Blakely, L., Rettew, D., Dufton, L., . . . Biederman, J. (2008). Cognitive-behavioral intervention with young anxious children. *Harvard Review of Psychiatry, 16*, 113–125.

Hirshfeld-Becker, D., Micco, J., Simoes, N., & Henin, A. (2008). High risk studies and developmental antecedents of anxiety disorders. *American Journal of Medical Genetics, Part C, Seminars in Medical Genetics, 148*, 99–117.

Hofmann, S., Sawyer, A., Korte, K., & Smits, J. (2009). Is it beneficial to add pharmacotherapy to cognitive-behavioral therapy when treating anxiety disorders? A meta-analytic review. *International Journal of Cognitive Therapy, 2*, 160–175.

Hudson, J. (2005). Efficacy of cognitive-behavioral therapy for children and adolescents with anxiety disorders. *Behavioural Change, 22*, 55–70.

In-Albon, T., & Schneider, S. (2007). Psychotherapy of childhood anxiety disorders: A meta-analysis. *Psychotherapy Psychosomatics, 76*, 15–24.

Ishikawa, S., Okajima, I., Matsuoka, H., & Sakano, Y. (2007). Cognitive behavioral therapy for anxiety disorders in children and adolescents: A meta-analysis. *Child Adolescent Mental Health, 12*, 164–172.

James, A., Soler. A., & Weatherall, R. (2005). Cognitive behavioral therapy for anxiety disorders in children and adolescents. *The Cochrane Library, Issue 4*. Chichester, England: John Wiley & Sons (CD004690).

Kaufman, J., Birmaher, B., Brent, D., Rao, U., Flynn, C., Moreci, P., Williamson D. and Ryan, N. (1997). Schedule for Affective Disorders and Schizophrenia for School-Age Children-Present and Lifetime

Version (K-SADS-PL): initial reliability and validity data. *Journal of the American Academy of Child and Adolescent Psychiatry, 36,* 980–988.

Kendall, P. C. (1994). Treating anxiety disorders in youth: Results of a randomized clinical trial. *Journal of Consulting and Clinical Psychology, 62,* 100–110.

Kendall, P. C., Flannery-Schroeder, E., Panichelli-Mindel, S. M., Southam-Gerow, M., Henin, A., & Warman, M. (1997). Therapy for youths with anxiety disorders: A second randomized clinical trial. *Journal of Consulting and Clinical Psychology, 65,* 366–380.

Kendall, P. C., Hudson, J. L., Flannery-Schroeder, E., & Gosch, E. (2008). Cognitive-behavioral therapy for anxiety disordered youth. *Journal of Counseling and Clinical Psychology, 76,* 282–297.

Kendall, P. C., Reber, M., McLeer, S., Epps, J., & Ronan, K. R. (1990) Cognitive-behavioral treatment of conduct-disordered children. *Cognitive Therapy and Research, 14,* 279–297.

Kendler, K., Gardner, C., Annas, P., Neale, M., Eaves, L., & Lichtenstein, P. (2008). A longitudinal twin study of fears from middle childhood to early adulthood: Evidence for a developmentally dynamic genome. *Archives of General Psychiatry, 65,* 421–429.

Kroes, M., Kalff, A. C., Steyaert, J., Kessels, A. G., Feron, F. J., Hendriksen, J. G., . . . Vles, J. S. (2002). A longitudinal community study: do psychosocial risk factors and child behavior checklist scores at 5 years of age predict psychiatric diagnoses at a later age? *Journal of the American Academy of Child and Adolescent Psychiatry, 41,* 955–963.

Last, C. G., Perrin, S., Hersen, M., & Kazdin, A. E. (1996). A prospective study of childhood anxiety disorders. *Journal of the American Academy of Child and Adolescent Psychiatry, 35,* 1502–1510.

Last, C. G., Hansen, C., & Franco, N. (1997). Anxious children in adulthood: A prospective study of adjustment. *Journal of the American Academy of Child and Adolescent Psychiatry, 36,* 645–652.

Lau, J., Gregory, A., Goldwin, M., Pine, D., & Eley, T. (2007). Assessing gene–environment interactions on anxiety symptom subtypes across childhood and adolescence. *Development and Psychopathology, 19,* 1129–1146.

Lau, J., Lissek, S., Nelson, E., Lee, Y., Roberson-Nay, R., Poeth, K., . . . Pine, D. (2008). Fear conditioning in adolescents with anxiety disorders: Results from a novel experimental paradigm. *Journal of the American Academy of Child and Adolescent Psychiatry, 47,* 94–102.

March, J. S., Franklin, M., Nelson, A., & Foa, E. (2001). Cognitive-behavioral psychotherapy for pediatric obsessive-compulsive disorder. *Journal of Child Psychology and Psychiatry, 30,* 8–18.

Masia, C. W., Fisher, H. F., Shrout, P. E., Rathor, S., & Klein, R. G. (2007). Treating adolescents with social anxiety disorder in school: An attention control study.

Journal of Child Psychology and Psychiatry, 48, 676–686.

McClure, E., Adler, A., Monk, C., Cameron, J., Smith, S., Nelson, E., . . . Pine, D. (2007). fMRI predictors of treatment outcome in pediatric anxiety disorders. *Psychopharmacology, 191,* 97–105.

McLeod, B., Wood, J., & Weisz, J. (2007). Examining the association between parenting and childhood anxiety. A meta-analysis. *Clinical Psychology Review, 27,* 155–172.

Meltzer, H., Gatward, R., Goodman, R., & Ford, T. (2000). The mental health of children and adolescents: Great Britain Summary report. *National Statistics.* (Online) Available at www.statistics.gov.uk/downloads/theme_health/KidsMentalHealth.pdf

Milad, M., Quirk, G., Pitman, R., Orr, S., Fischl, B., & Rauch, S. (2007). A role for the human dorsal anterior cingulate cortex in fear expression. *Biological Psychiatry, 62,* 1191–1194.

Moffitt, T., Caspi, A., Harrington, H., Milne, B., Melchior, M., Goldberg, D., & Poulton, R. (2007). Generalized anxiety disorder and depression: Childhood risk factors in a birth cohort followed to age 32. *Psychology Medicine, 37,* 441–452.

Monk, C. S., Telzer, E. H., Moog, K., Bradley, B. P., Mai, X., Louro, H. M., . . . Pine, D. S. (2008). Amygdala and ventrolateral prefrontal cortex activation to masked angry faces in children and adolescents with generalized anxiety disorder. *Archive General Psychiatry, 65,* 568–576.

Munafò, M., Brown, S., & Hariri, A. (2008). Serotonin transporter (%-HTTLPR) genotype and amygdala activation: A meta-analysis. *Biological Psychiatry, 63,* 852–857.

Muris, P., Merckelbach, H., & Damsma, E. (2000). Threat perception bias in nonreferred, socially anxious children. *Journal of Clinical Child Psychology, 29,* 348–359.

Myers, K., & Winters, N. (2002). Ten-year review of rating scales. II: Scales for internalizing disorders. *Journal of the American Academy of Child and Adolescent Psychiatry, 41,* 634–659.

Olivares-Olivares, P., Rosa-Alcazar, A. I., & Olivares, R. J. (2007). Social validity of adolescent intervention in social phobia: Parents vs. teachers [Validez social de la intervencion en adolescentes con fobia social: padres frente a profesores]. *Terapia Psicológica, 25,* 63–72.

Phillips, N. K., Hammen, C. L., Brennan, P. A., Najman, J. M., & Bor, W. (2005). Early adversity and the prospective prediction of depressive and anxiety disorders in adolescents. *Journal of Abnormal Child Psychology, 33,* 13–24.

Practice Parameter JAACAP. (2007). Practice parameter for the assessment and treatment of children and adolescents with anxiety disorders. *Journal of the American Academy of Child and Adolescent Psychiatry, 46,* 267–283.

Schneier, F. R., Johnson, J., Hornig, C. D., Liebowitz, M. R., & Weissman, M. M. (1992) Social phobia: Comorbidity and morbidity in an epidemiologic sample. *Archives of General Psychiatry, 49*, 282–288.

Schreier, A., Wittchen, H., Höfler, M., & Lieb, R. (2008). Anxiety disorders in mothers and their children: Prospective longitudinal community study. *British Journal of Psychiatry, 192*, 308–309.

Scott, R. W., Mughelli, K., & Deas, D. (2005). An overview of controlled studies of anxiety disorders treatment in children and adolescents. *Journal of the National Medical Association, 97*, 13–24.

Silberg, J., Rutter, M., Neale, M., & Eaves, L. (2001). Genetic moderation of environmental risk for depression and anxiety in adolescent girls. *The British Journal of Psychiatry, 179*, 116–121.

Silverman, W., & Albano, A. (1996). *Manual for the Anxiety Disorders Interview Schedule for DSM-IV: Child and parent versions.* San Antonio, TX: The Psychological Corporation.

Sofronoff, K., Attwood, T., & Hinton, S. (2005). A randomized controlled trial of a CBT intervention for anxiety in children with Asperger syndrome. *Journal of Child Psychology and Psychiatry, 46*, 1152–1160.

Storch, E. A., Crisp, H., Roberti, J. W., Bagner, D. M., & Masia-Warner, C. (2005). Psychometric evalution of the social experience questionnaire in adolescents: Descriptive data, reliability and factorial validity. *Child Psychiatry and Human Development, 36*, 167–176.

Wade, T., Bergin, J., Martin, N., Gillespie, N., & Fairburn, C. (2006). A transdiagnostic approach to understanding eating disorders. *Journal of Nervous Mental Disorders, 194*, 510–517.

Walkup, J. T., Albano, A. M., Piacentini, J., Birmaher, B., Compton, S. N., Sherrill, J. T., . . . Kendall, P. C. (2008). Cognitive behavioural therapy, sertraline or a combination in childhood anxiety. *The New England Journal of Medicine, 359*, 2753–2766.

Waters, A., Craske, M., Bergman, R., & Treanor, M. (2008). Threat interpretation bias as a vulnerability factor in childhood anxiety disorders. *Behaviour Research and Therapy, 46*, 39–47.

Waters, A., Wharton, T., Zimmer-Gembeck, M., & Craske, M. (2008). Threat-based cognitive biases in anxious children: Comparison with non-anxious children before and after cognitive behavioral treatment. *Behaviour Research and Therapy, 46*, 358–374.

World Health Organization. (1992). *The ICD-10 classification of mental and behavioral disorders: Clinical description and diagnostic guidelines.* Geneva, Switzerland: Author.

24

School Refusal

GLENN A. MELVIN AND BRUCE J. TONGE

OVERVIEW OF DISORDER

Attendance at school to gain an education is a key developmental task of childhood and adolescence. School refusal is usually a sign of underlying psychopathology and has a broad impact on the young person's social, academic, and emotional development, while also disrupting family functioning. Refusal to attend school therefore represents an urgent problem for families, clinicians, school staff, and of course, the young person. Of the available treatments, cognitive behavioral treatments have the largest evidence base in managing school refusal. There may be a role for medication to supplement psychological treatment; however, further evidence is required.

Diagnostic Criteria

The definition of "school refusal" lacks clarity and multiple definitions exist (Brandibas, Jeunier, Clanet, & Fourasté, 2004; Kearney, 2003). This confusion might impact on a clinician's ability to communicate clearly about children in their care. Berg (1992) provides a useful definition of school refusal as severe emotional upset, such as anxiety or depressive disorders, that precipitates persistent difficulty attending school and an extended school absence. Children remain at home with parental knowledge while defying their best attempts to enforce school attendance.

Children may be extremely oppositional, verbally abusive, and even aggressive toward their parents and others, such as school staff and relatives who try to enforce school attendance; however, these children typically lack antisocial behavior problems. Berg's definition has been used in treatment outcome studies (e.g., Heyne, King, Tonge, & Rollings, 2002).

Truancy, in contrast to school refusal, is school nonattendance characterized by an attempt to *conceal* the absence from school (Berg, 1997). Truants typically spend time during the school day at places other than home, such as parks and shopping malls. Truants have oppositional defiant disorder and conduct disorder in greater proportions than school refusers (Bools, Foster, Brown, & Berg, 1990; Egger, Costello, & Angold, 2003). Overlap may exist between school refusal and truancy; for example, school-refusing children may also stay home from school without parent's knowledge (Bools, Foster, Brown, & Berg, 1990; Berg, Butler, Franklin, Hayes, Lucas, & Sims, 1993). Egger and colleagues (2003) found that a quarter of school refusers were also truants.

School refusal also differs from *school withdrawal*, which is characterized by parental acceptance or even endorsement of the child's school nonattendance (Kearney, 2001b). For example, parents may not value their child's education or may require that the child withdraw from school, for example, to help with a family business. Alternatively, the young person might be withdrawn from school following parental disagreement with the school education program or philosophy.

Kearney (2003) developed criteria for defining when absenteeism including school refusal becomes a clinically relevant problem regardless of the cause. Problematic absenteeism was defined as missing more than 50% of school time for at least 2 weeks and/or experience of difficulty attending school for at least 2 weeks such that significant interference occurs in the child's or family's daily life. These criteria are aimed at capturing clinically relevant cases and acknowledge that anxious refusal behavior may disturb family life while the young person is still actually attending school.

Presentation

School refusal is not a diagnosis in either the *Diagnostic and Statistical Manual of Mental Disorders* (*DSM-IV-TR*) (American Psychiatric Association [APA], 2000) or the *International Classification of Diseases* (*ICD-10*) (World Health Organization, 2004) but is associated with a heterogeneous diagnostic group that typically experiences elevated rates of anxiety and depressive disorders (Borchardt, Giesler, Bernstein, & Crosby, 1994; Egger et al., 2003; N. J. King & Bernstein, 2001; Martin, Cabrol, Bouvard, Lepine, & Mouren-Simeoni, 1999). Given this varied presentation, an overview of the diagnostic findings of school refusal and phenomenology is relevant prior to discussing treatments.

N. J. King and Bernstein (2001) concluded from their review that while school-refusing children typically present with complex and variable psychopathology, there are three main diagnostic profiles, characterized by separation anxiety disorder, phobic anxiety, and a combination of anxiety and mood disorder.

Separation anxiety disorder is the most common psychiatric disorder experienced by school refusers (Borchardt, Giesler, Bernstein, & Crosby, 1994; Last & Strauss, 1990; Martin

et al., 1999). According to the *DSM-IV-TR* (APA, 2000) separation anxiety disorder is characterized by excessive anxiety regarding separation from the person to whom the individual is attached, typically mother or father, or the home. Children with separation anxiety disorder may refuse to attend school because they fear that something bad will happen to their parents or that they will never be reunited (APA, 2000). Consistent with this diagnostic presentation, Last and Strauss (1990) found school refusers to be excessively dependent and experience maternal overprotection.

School refusers also commonly suffer phobic anxiety to a specific situation or aspect of school, such as the classroom, teachers, or playground (Last & Stauss, 1990). More commonly, the young person experiences social phobia focused on the classroom and school yard, such as fear of critical or mean comments from other students or potential embarrassment in social situations (Last & Stauss, 1990; Martin et al., 1999). Phobic school refusers are likely to have more severe problems with school refusal and to be older than separation anxious school refusers (Last & Strauss, 1990).

The other common form of psychopathology associated with school refusal is depressive disorder or a combination of anxiety and depressive disorders (Borchardt et al., 1994; Egger et al., 2003). Experience of an anxiety disorder along with stressors such as social isolation, family conflict, and lack of success returning to school might increase the risk of depressive disorder. School refusers with comorbid anxiety and depressive disorders have been found to experience more severe internalizing symptoms compared with those with anxiety or depression alone (Bernstein & Borchardt, 1991). Moreover, school refusers with depressive disorder were more likely to receive inpatient treatment than outpatient treatment in a matched sample study, suggesting a greater severity of disorder (Borchardt, Giesler, Bernstein, & Crosby, 1994).

While these three types of diagnostic presentation are most common, school refusers can also experience other disorders, such as panic disorder and posttraumatic stress disorder (Last & Strauss, 1990), substance abuse disorder, and learning disorder (McShane, Walter, & Rey, 2001). While Berg's (1997) definition suggests that school refusers generally do not engage in antisocial behavior unless forced to go to school, findings from some studies have found elevated rates of oppositional defiant disorder (Borchardt et al., 1994) and conduct disorder (Egger et al., 2003). Comorbidity is common in clinic-referred school refusers (e.g., Borchardt et al., 1994; Last & Strauss, 1990; McShane et al., 2001).

As well as often experiencing internalizing disorders, school refusers are also likely to have learning disorders and academic problems. For example, Naylor, Staskowski, Kenney, and King (1994) compared inpatient-treated school refusers to psychiatric controls. School refusers had poorer academic performance in reading, math, and written language and more frequently experienced learning disabilities and language impairments than the psychiatric controls.

While most school refusers have a psychiatric diagnosis, studies have shown that not all have a diagnosis. Kearney and Albano (2004) found 33% had no diagnosis, while Egger et al. (2003) found 75% did not have a diagnosis. These differences may be at least partially accounted for by the criteria used for defining school refusal and the sample composition (for example, inpatient vs. community samples). In addition, Kearney (2008) posits that some young people without a diagnosis may in fact be experiencing some symptoms of several disorders; therefore, they do not fall neatly into a single diagnostic category.

Functional Classification of School Refusal

An alternative method of conceptualizing school refusal, proposed by Kearney and Silverman (1990), is to analyze the function of the behavior in an effort to determine the underlying motivating and maintaining factors of the school refusal (Kearney, 2001a). This approach is considered useful given the heterogeneous diagnostic profile of school refusal and is used to inform targets for intervention. The categories include: (a) avoidance of specific fearful situations such as the school bus, classroom, or general overanxiousness in the school setting, for example, while in a certain class or school activity; (b) escape from aversive social situations associated with social anxiety, or a specific situation such as fear of public speaking; (c) attention-getting or separation anxiety behavior in which attention-seeking behaviors are performed with the aim of gaining permission to stay at home; (d) tangible reinforcement as a consequence of pleasant activities other than school such as television, computer games, and time with friends. These four categories of school refusal are either examples of negative reinforcement (escape from aversive stimuli) or positive reinforcement (gaining of a reward for refusal) (Kearney, 2001a). The function(s) of the school-refusing behavior can then be matched to appropriate treatment strategies (Kearney, Pursell, & Alvarez, 2001). However, most research, particularly treatment outcome studies to date follow criteria similar to Berg's.

DEMOGRAPHIC VARIABLES

While limited contemporary data exists on the prevalence of school refusal, it has been estimated that severe school refusal has a point prevalence of about 5% of all clinic-referred children and 0.4% of all school-aged children (N. J. King, Ollendick, & Tonge, 1995). Egger and colleagues (2003) found a 3-month prevalence of 2.0% in a representative community sample; however, this required only a half day missed due to refusal. School refusal may peak in the early teenage years, as it can be harder for parents to enforce attendance at this age (Last & Stauss, 1990). Part of the reason for the lack of data might be the difficulty in distinguishing and classifying school refusal from other types of school attendance problems. School refusal may be mistaken for truancy or school withdrawal and overlap with these presentations. School refusal has been found to occur equally in males and females in clinical (Heyne, King, Tonge, & Rollings, 2002) and community samples (Egger et al., 2003; Granell de Aldaz, Vivas, Gelfand, & Feldman, 1984).

Course

Onset of school refusal may vary from a sudden refusal to attend—for example, refusal after school holidays—to a gradual refusal that builds over weeks or months beginning with vague statements about not liking school, followed by difficult mornings that require persistence from parents to help the young person out of bed prior to refusal to attend. While onset of school refusal can occur at any point during schooling, Ollendick and Mayer (1984) reported that school refusal commonly had an onset at ages 5–6 years (commencement of school) and 10–11 years (transition from elementary to middle school) (N. J. King & Bernstein, 2001). In a community sample, Egger et al. (2003) found school refusers (mean age = 12.3 years) to be younger than truants (14.7 years). Common precipitants to school refusal in adolescents include family and peer conflict, academic issues, changing school or moving, and physical illness (McShane, Walter, & Rey, 2001). In a sample of 168 school refusers, Heyne, King, Tonge, and Rollings (2002) found the most common precipitants of school refusal to be bullying/teasing (35%), social exclusion (26%), transition from primary to secondary schooling (21%), fear of or difficulties with a teacher (21%), illness (19%), academic problems (17%), and separation problems (16%).

IMPACT OF DISORDER

School refusal creates legal problems because school attendance is mandated up to a minimum age of approximately 16 years in Western countries, but the greater problems and consequences are psychological, social, and academic, as well as causing family distress. School refusal significantly increases the risk of poorer educational achievement, social problems, and family disruption (Kearney, 2001a). Some studies have found risk of ongoing psychiatric disorder into adulthood. For example, Buitelaar, van Andel, Duyx, and van Strien (1994) found more than half of a sample of 25 school refusers were still experiencing a psychiatric disorder after an average of 5 years. School refusers are likely to continue to access mental health services (Berg & Jackson, 1985; Flakierska-Praquin, Lindström, & Gillberg, 1997) and are particularly at risk of agoraphobia, anxiety, and depression. Experience of school refusal appears to be associated with ongoing social problems. One study found that a higher proportion of school refusers continued to live at home with their parents 5 years after treatment (Buitelaar et al., 1994). Fewer adult, former refusers were found to have children than the normal population (Flakierska-Praquin et al., 1997).

ASSESSMENT

Assessment of school refusal requires a comprehensive psychiatric interview of the young person and parents to determine the precipitating and maintaining factors of school refusal, including any underlying psychopathology such as separation anxiety disorder and major depressive disorder. In terms of clinical interviews, the Anxiety Disorders Interview Schedule for Children (ADIS-C, Silverman & Albano, 1996) may be useful to determine anxiety and other diagnoses. In addition to administering self-report measures for anxiety (e.g., Revised Children's Manifest Anxiety Scale [Reynolds & Richmond, 1985]; Screen for Child Anxiety Related Emotional Disorders-Revised [Muris & Steerneman, 2001]; Multidimensional Anxiety Scale for Children [March, Parker, Sullivan, Stallings, & Conners,

1997]) and depression (e.g., Reynolds Adolescent Depression Scale–2 [W. M. Reynolds, 2002]; Children's Depression Inventory [Kovacs, 1985]), two school refusal specific measures are worth considering. The School Refusal Assessment Scale–Revised (SRAS-R) is a self-report measure that aims to assess four variables that are hypothesized to maintain school refusal behavior, namely: (1) avoidance of specific fearfulness or generalized anxiety related to school, (2) escape from aversive social situations, (3) attention-getting or separation anxiety, and (4) tangible reinforcement (Kearney, 2002). There are child and parent versions of this instrument. The measure has good psychometric properties (Kearney, 2002, 2006). The Self-Efficacy Questionnaire for School Situations was designed to assess young persons' perceived ability to cope with everyday and challenging school situations that might arise and has satisfactory psychometric properties (Heyne et al., 1998). Cognitive assessment and academic achievement testing (e.g., Wide Range Achievement Test; Wilkinson, 1993) may also be useful to determine the student's profile of strengths and difficulties and achievement level, both of which may contribute to understanding of school refusal behavior.

TREATMENT

At present, there are no national treatment guidelines to assist clinicians in the management of school refusal. Clinical practice is informed by findings from a small body of clinical trials and clinical reviews as well as clinical judgment (N. J. King et al., 1995). The clinician may be challenged by school refusal behavior presenting with a variety of disorders or, in rare cases, no underlying psychopathology.

Treatment Setting

While the majority of clinical trials has investigated outpatient CBT-based treatments for school refusal, some refusers are treated in an inpatient setting (e.g., Flakeierska-Praquin et al., 1997). Inpatient treatment may be justified by the severity of the underlying psychiatric diagnosis, failure of less intensive treatments, or to gain insight into the child's functioning when removed from the family environment. Other than for some diagnostic differences, inpatient and outpatient treated school refusers have been found to be similar (Borchardt et al., 1994; McShane et al., 2001). For example, McShane and colleagues (2001) found that inpatient-treated school refusers had more *DSM-IV* Axis I diagnoses but found no measurable difference between outpatients and inpatients on demographic, psychopathological, and functioning measures; however, they conceded that other unmeasured variables might have influenced the decision to admit. Borchardt et al. (1994) found that in a matched sample of inpatient and outpatient treated school refusers, those treated in an inpatient setting were more likely to be depressed (89%) compared to the outpatient (54%).

Distance education or home schooling is not a recommended treatment, considered as the last option as it promotes avoidance that can cause or maintain anxiety (McShane, Walter, & Rey, 2004). An uncontrolled comparison of treatments found home schooling to result in 0% returning to school (N. R. Blagg & Yule, 1984). Similarly, change in school is rarely considered as a solution to the problem because the young person's difficulties, such as social anxiety and depression, often remain with them at the new school (Elliott, 1999). Change of school may be considered when the working relationship between the family and school has broken down or where a lack of support or exasperation is evident in the school staff.

COGNITIVE AND BEHAVIORAL THERAPIES

Cognitive behavior therapy (CBT) is currently the most empirically validated treatment for school refusal. Early cognitive and behavioral treatment research investigated treatments such as systematic desensitization, relaxation training, and cognitive restructuring (N. J. King et al., 1995). These treatments showed promise in addressing the underlying internalizing disorders. Recent empirical evaluation of CBT for school refusal has focused on comprehensive multicomponent CBT approaches to management rather than evaluation of specific cognitive or behavioral components. Justification for the investigation of this approach partially also comes from the success of CBT in the treatment of disorders that often underlie school refusal, such as social phobia (e.g., Beidel, Turner, & Morris, 2000; Spence, Donovan, & Brechman-Toussant, 2000), separation anxiety disorders (e.g., Kendall, 1994), and depression (e.g., Clarke, Rohde, Lewinsohn, Hops, & Seeley, 1999; Brent et al., 1998). However, treatment for school refusal is not the same as treatment for anxiety or depressive disorder. Additional treatment components to specifically address school return are required. Empirical studies evaluating school refusal are reviewed after the components of a comprehensive treatment program for anxious school refusal is described.

Overview of a Cognitive Behavior Therapy Treatment Program

Cognitive behavioral treatment components are required to be individualized to the young person's diagnosis, the function of the school refusal behavior, and the needs of the family. The following is a summary of a CBT program for anxious school refusers based on a program developed by N. J. King, Ollendick, & Tonge (1995) and then empirically tested (Heyne, King, et al., 2002; Heyne, Rollings, King, & Tonge, 2002; N. J. King et al., 1998).

Psychoeducation

Psychoeducation about the etiology, impact, maintaining factors, and course of school refusal behavior, as well as any psychiatric disorder(s) experienced, is considered universally appropriate. Explanation of the flight and fight response may be useful to contextualize and normalize any physiological symptoms of anxiety, such as palpitations, stomachaches, and shortness of breath. Exploration of hypothesized maintaining factors of school refusal may also be of value to the young person and parents alike.

Relaxation Training

Relaxation strategies such as breathing retraining and progressive muscle relaxation help with the management of anxious symptoms. Relaxation may be indicated particularly if the school refuser expresses anxiety somatically. Relaxation can be used to manage anxious symptoms in times of arousal, for example, the night before school, prior to entering the classroom.

Cognitive Restructuring

Maladaptive thinking patterns such as exaggerated danger or threat about school attendance in phobic youth, underrating capacity to cope with social situations in socially anxious youth, or overestimation of chances of harm befalling parents in separation anxious children are examples of targets for cognitive restructuring.

Social Skills Training

Social skills training can be used to address deficits in social skills and social withdrawal. Preparing responses to questions, as well as insults from other students about school absence, can be a very useful component of preparing for school return, even for socially competent children. Instruction from the therapist, modeling, and in-session practice may be employed to develop social skills. In session practice, using role-plays provides an opportunity for reinforcement of new, adaptive skills. Use of role-plays also provides a model from which the child can imitate.

Exposure

Exposure is a central component of treatment for anxious school refusers. Last, Hansen, and Franco's (1998) justification for use of exposure-based treatment for school refusal comes from the extensive use of these treatments for adult anxiety disorders and phobias in particular. The aim of graded exposure is for the student to work through a hierarchy of successively more difficulty steps toward full-time attendance. A graded return to school is less confronting probably for both the young person and parents. However, this approach takes longer than an immediate return (flooding), which means that the young person continues to miss school during the graded process. Exposure-based tasks can commence prior to the planned return to school. For example, separation anxious children can spend time away from their parents prior to school attendance, such as with friends or relatives. Phobic youth can expose themselves to their school on the weekend or after school hours and familiarize themselves with the environment.

A forced rapid return to school follows the behavioral principle of in vivo flooding, whereby the young person is exposed to the feared stimulus until the fear response has been extinguished. It is important that the young person stay at school long enough for the anxiety and protests to settle down (N. R. Blagg & Yule, 1984). While considered to be a more challenging recommencement at school, some young people may express a preference for attending school for full days, to avoid embarrassment or appearing to be different caused by leaving school early. Moreover, this approach limits time spent at home uninvolved with schoolwork and socializing and opportunities for positive reinforcement involved with staying at home. N. R. Blagg and Yule (1984) recommended considering the need for both parents to be present to escort the young person back to school. Further, if the parents lack the capacity to cope with resistive and hostile behavior, enlisting help first from relatives and then from school or welfare staff should be considered.

Parent Involvement

While family therapy approaches are of unknown efficacy in the treatment of school refusal, parent involvement during cognitive behavioral treatment is considered critical to the success of treatment. A firm nonnegotiable stance is needed from parents regarding the child's return to school despite any protests (Elliott, 1999). This sends a clear message that school return is inevitable and may reduce some resistive behavior. The parent's approach needs to be unified to clearly demonstrate to the young person that school attendance is required and to prevent the young person from seeking leniency from one parent. Parenting style may contribute to the maintenance of school refusal behavior. For example, positive attention given to somatic complaints may reinforce school non-attendance (Granell de Aldaz et al., 1984). Parental reinforcement of school refusal needs to be extinguished (Doobay, 2008). For example, for an attention-seeking child, parents should avoid providing attention to the child during school hours, helping with chores that help parents. Leisure activities such as television and video games that may reinforce nonattendance should also be restricted during school hours. Parents can also play a role in encouraging and supervising the practice of coping skills learned during treatment sessions. Parents will need to support each other in the initial stages of school return to deal with highly resistive and oppositional behavior exhibited by anxious young people when faced with school return. Be aware, young people may have the best of intentions in the days or night before school, which may quickly shift as the school day becomes closer and anxiety increases. For these reasons it is particularly important that fathers are included in treatment, which may require the offering of "after hours" appointment times.

School Return Plan

School and welfare staff, therapist(s), the young person, and parents are required to be involved in the plan for the young person's return to school, along with anyone else that may be involved, such as a physician or relative. For example, it is helpful for the GP to understand the approach to school return to prevent conflicting management strategies such as permission for a day off school in response to somatic complaints. The plan is based around a set date for school return. This date is typically after the young person and parents have had a number of treatment sessions and is negotiated by the young person, parents, school, and therapist. The plan may include details of preparations required for school return; for example, organizing school books and uniform, what time the young person has to get up in the morning, who will escort the young person to school, whether a teacher or student welfare staff member will escort the young person into the classroom, and where the young person can go to settle down if highly distressed. Discussion between all relevant adults regarding the treatment plan is required. An agreed-upon plan is required so that all involved can give clear and consistent messages to the child. When speaking about the young person's return to school, therapists are advised to use "when" rather than "if" to create a sense of inevitability. Strategies for school return are discussed. Shifting parental focus to praise for attendance and avoidance of attention for somatic complaints is emphasized in order to promote extinction of these undesirable behaviors. Following these preparations, the child is escorted back to school by parents or others strong enough to cope with the child's tantrums. The process of escorting typically lasts a few days while fears and distress subside, but may take longer in more severe cases (N. R. Blagg & Yule, 1984). Close contact is kept with the family and school until the child has established a consistent pattern of full-time attendance.

School Involvement

Liaison with school staff is important not only in the development of the return to school plan, but also in providing education about school refusal and preparing strategies to facilitate school attendance. Educating school staff

about the symptoms experienced by the young person and their likely impact may be helpful. Parent strategies for managing illness complaints and reinforcing coping behavior would also be useful for school staff. Teachers may also familiarize the child with current work prior to returning to school, announcing to the class that the child will be returning, and organizing a "buddy" to assist and support the child in settling back into working and playing at school (N. Blagg, 1987). Preparation for the child's school return might also involve school staff understanding how to best greet a child returning to school and the child preparing for questions from peers about where he or she has been. Contingencies also ought to be planned in the event that the child runs away from school. Enlisting parents' help to return the child to school is suggested to avoid the child learning that running away is an effective school avoidance strategy.

Empirical Evidence of Efficacy

School refusal is a condition that has an easily defined and operationalized treatment outcome criterion—attendance at school. However, comparison between studies is limited by the use of varying definitions of school refusal and different thresholds of nonattendance or severity. In the following, recent studies with varying methodologies are reviewed.

Case Studies

School refusal case studies demonstrate treatment techniques and the challenges of treating young people with this presentation, while providing justification for further investigation. A selection of case studies that describe varying approaches to the behavioral and cognitive behavior therapy of school refusal is presented.

Chorpita, Albano, Heimberg, and Barlow (1996) used behavioral treatment guided by a functional assessment to treat school refusal behavior in a 10-year-old girl with separation anxiety disorder and social phobia. The function of the behavior was determined by the School Refusal Assessment Scale to be attention seeking and separation anxious. Parents monitored multiple anxious problem behaviors (somatic complaints, anger and tantrums, tears, and other complaints) from baseline onwards that became the targets of treatment. The young person would not engage in monitoring of anxious behavior. Differential reinforcement schedules were then implemented by the parents. Target behaviors were sequentially ignored, leading to extinction, and a child-selected activity (cooking) was reinforced by the family using praise. Parental ignoring of target behaviors was practiced in session, which also gave the young person feedback on the nature of the reinforcement contingencies. Improvement in target behaviors was evident during treatment and maintained at 24 month follow-up, demonstrating the success of a functional approach to treatment of school refusal.

Rollings, King, Tonge, Heyne, and Young (1998) presented a case study of a 13-year-old girl who was experiencing major depressive disorder, oppositional defiant disorder, and had a 3-week history of refusing to attend school following 2 years of school attendance problems. A 10-session program of child-focused CBT was implemented, comprising problem solving, relaxation training, social skills training, positive reinforcement contingencies, and exposure to school. A graded return to school was used (successively increasing attendance) after a plan for immediate full-time return failed. Near full-time school attendance (95%) was achieved by the end of treatment; however, repeating the eighth grade was necessary. Scores on self-, parent-, and teacher-reported measures of internalizing and externalizing symptoms declined following treatment.

Gosschalk (2004) treated a 5-year-old preschool girl with separation anxiety disorder who presented with excessive crying, clinging to her mother, and resisting attendance at school, requiring parent or teacher support.

The resistive behavior was conceptualized as having an attention-seeking function. Behavioral treatment was used with parent- and teacher-focused strategies. A graded return to school was used. Treatment comprised progressive muscle relaxation to assist with sleeping and relaxation, parents and teachers were taught to ignore of complaints about school attendance and crying to promote extinction. Free play during class time was used as a positive reinforcer for school attendance and to promote social interaction with students other than close friends. Shaping was used to address separation distress with food rewards given to positively reinforce successively longer periods spent at home without the mother or calling after her. After 5 weeks of treatment, full-time school attendance without resistive or anxious behavior was achieved, demonstrating the utility of a parent and teacher model of treatment.

Open Trials

N. R. Blagg and Yule (1984) compared a series of school refusers treated with a behavioral treatment approach: those who received inpatient treatment and those who received home schooling with psychotherapy. Subjects were mostly between 11–16 years and were experiencing extreme difficulty attending school. They were absent for at least 3 days, while accompanied by emotional distress. Children remained home with parental knowledge and antisocial behavior was not evident. Participants were not randomly allocated to treatment.

Behavioral treatment commenced after ruling out school nonattendance due to a legitimate medical illness. Treatment was completed by educational psychologists as a part of their regular duties. Hospital treatment comprised separation from parents via hospitalization, therapeutic milieu, educational and occupational therapy, possible drug treatment, and a discharge plan. Home tuition with psychotherapy was implemented when an immediate return to school was considered to be too difficult for the child. A child psychiatrist provided sessions every 2 weeks to the child, and a psychiatric social worker would see the parents, followed by a family discussion.

The study found that the behavioral treatment led to 93.3% of cases successfully returning to school. "Success" was defined as full-time return to school during the following year with a prompt return to school if relapse occurred. Hospitalization led to 31% successfully returning, and none of the home school and psychotherapy group met the success criteria. Behavioral treatment was also found to be the most time efficient treatment for therapists. Mean length of hospitalization was 45.3 weeks, which is at odds with current practice, whereby hospitalization is often used for stabilization and review rather than long-term treatment (Balkin, 2006). The advantages of the real world naturalistic setting of this trial are probably overshadowed by the limitation of nonrandom allocation to treatment and a lack of a manualized treatment approach.

Kearney and Silverman (1990) used the School Refusal Assessment Scale score to inform treatment of school refusal to eight case studies. Highest score on one of four School Refusal Assessment Scale categories directed the treatment approach. Specific fears and overanxiousness was treated with systematic desensitization and relaxation training; those escaping socially aversive situations were treated with modeling and cognitive restructuring; attention seekers or separation anxious received shaping and differential reinforcement of other behavior; and those gaining tangible reinforcement from school nonattendance received contingency contracting. Treatment duration was 3 to 9 weeks. Seven of eight participants met response criteria of 2 weeks' full-time attendance at the end of treatment and maintained this level of attendance 6 months later. The nonresponding participant left school and got a job. Self- and parent-report measures generally demonstrated improvement on internalizing symptoms. While response to treatment was

encouraging, the conclusions that can be made are limited, as this was an open trial.

Randomized Clinical Trials

Last, Hansen, and Franco (1998) conducted the first randomized controlled trial of an exposure-based treatment for school refusal. Participants were 56 children aged 6 to 17 years with anxiety disorders who had missed at least 10% of school for at least 1 month and were not depressed. The active CBT treatment, a modified adult treatment approach for agoraphobia, was compared to an attentional control treatment known as educational-support (E-S) therapy. The CBT comprised stepwise exposure to school using a hierarchy of feared events developed by the child and cognitive self-statement training, which are designed to help children identify and replace unhelpful thoughts. Educational-Support Therapy is a structured supportive psychotherapy with educational presentations on topics such as anxiety, maladaptive thinking, and fears. Of 56 anxiety disordered participants, 16 dropped out during treatment, all of whom were treated with CBT. Both groups showed significant improvement in the mean percentage of school attendance over time and no difference was detected between groups. By posttreatment, average school attendance was 60% in the E-S therapy group and 67% in the CBT group. This study may have included a narrow group of school refusers by excluding those with depression.

In our group's first treatment investigation we demonstrated the efficacy of a manual-based CBT program on multiple outcome measures (school attendance, self-reported anxiety, and depression), relative to waiting list controls (N. J. King et al., 1998). Participants were aged between 5 and 15 years ($N = 34$), most were experiencing a primary diagnosis of anxiety disorder ($N = 20$; 58.8%), and were either attending school with substantial difficulties, or attending partially or not at all.

The manualized CBT treatment comprised coping skills training, exposure/school return, and contingency management. In contrast to N. R. Blagg and Yule (1984), exposure to school was a graded rather than a flooding approach. Two clinicians were involved in each case, one providing child therapy and the other parent/teacher training. Child therapy comprised six sessions that addressed identification of anxiety-provoking situations, cue-controlled and differential relaxation training, teaching of identification of self-talk and development of coping statements, and imaginal and in vivo exposure to anxiety-provoking situations including school. Treatment sessions were conducted twice a week to enable a prompt return to school. Parents received five sessions that focused on child behavior management using antecedent stimulus control and contingency management procedures. Parents were taught to ignore somatic complaints associated with anxiety and negative comments about school. Positive reinforcement contingencies for positive coping and school attendance were set up. A meeting was held with teachers prior to school return to discuss the treatment progress and plan for school attendance. Strategies including a warm greeting for the student and a buddy system for social support were discussed. Treatment was flexibly delivered, with consideration given to child's age, home situation, and school factors. The CBT group from this sample was followed up via a structured telephone interview 3 to 5 years after treatment (N. King et al., 2001). Of the 15 (94% response) participants who were involved, 13 (87%) demonstrated normal school attendance and received no further psychiatric assistance. Mean school attendance during the 2 weeks prior to the assessment was 86.4%. Mean academic performance was rated as "average" by parents. While diagnostic interviews were not conducted, the study indicated that school refusers who receive CBT generally had a good outcome.

The CBT group displayed significant improvement in school attendance over time and significantly greater school attendance than the wait-list group. Similarly, scores on outcome measures of anxiety (Fear Survey Schedule for Children-II [Gullone & King, 1992]; Revised Children's Manifest Anxiety Scale [C. R. Reynolds & Richmond, 1978]; Child Behavior Checklist Internalizing Scale [Achenbach, 1991]) and self-efficacy (Self Efficacy Questionnaire for School Situations; Heyne et al., 1998) showed significantly greater improvement in the treatment group. Three times as many children attained 90% attendance in the CBT group (15/17) compared with the wait-list (5/17)—a significantly different amount. While the effect of nonspecific effects of therapy cannot be ruled out, the authors concluded that CBT was an efficacious treatment for school refusal.

In our group's second study, Heyne, King, and colleagues (2002) conducted a treatment components analysis of CBT for school refusal. Young people aged 7 to 14 years were randomly allocated to a CBT child therapy, parent and teacher training, or a combination of both these interventions. Participants were of greater severity than those in the N. J. King et al. (1998) study, and met Berg's criteria for school refusal, with all experiencing an anxiety disorder and having missed more than 85% of school. Those with conduct disorder were excluded. Treatment comprised eight sessions. Child therapy included relaxation skills, social skills training, graded desensitization to school attendance, and cognitive therapy. Parent and teacher therapy centered on behavior management skills, including planned escorting of the child to school. School personnel were visited to discuss the student's return to school, strategies to help the child adjust, the planned ignoring of undesirable behaviors, and any measures required to accommodate the child's needs. Further details of this treatment are available in Heyne, Rollings, King, and Tonge (2002).

After 4 weeks and eight sessions, parent/school treatment was found to be superior to child therapy, and the combined treatment was superior to child therapy. By the time of follow-up (after school holidays; mean duration = 4.5 months), no difference between treatments was evident. While the difference between treatments was not maintained, the study findings point to the crucial nature of involving parents and school personnel in treatment to ensure the early success of treatment. Teenagers were found to be less responsive to CBT than children and this might have been due to the presence of a depressive illness (Heyne, King, et al., 2002). Greater understanding is hence required about how best to manage adolescent school refusers, who may be stronger, more verbally or physically abusive, and less fearful of any consequences their parents might impose.

PHARMACOLOGICAL TREATMENT

Case Studies

A small number of studies has been conducted on the pharmacological treatment of school refusal. Early findings demonstrated mixed outcomes of tricyclic antidepressants treatment for school refusal (Berney et al., 1981; Bernstein, Garfinkel, & Borchardt, 1990; Gittelman-Klein & Klein, 1973; Klein, Mannuzza, Chapman, & Fyer, 1992). Durkin (2002) reported on two case studies of the successful use of the antiepileptic gabapentin to treat school refusal. Both teens had missed several years of schooling and had failed multiple previous psychopharmacological drugs. Gabapentin was associated with improvement in school attendance, anxiety, social isolation, and irritability. Further examination of gabapentin is required before meaningful statements can be made about its use for school refusal.

Randomized Controlled Trials

Bernstein et al. (2000) compared an eight-session CBT treatment combined with imipramine to CBT combined with placebo in a sample of 63 school-refusing, depressed, and anxious adolescents (12–18 years). This trial is in step with a recent trend toward the evaluation of combined psychotherapy and pharmacological treatments in an effort to identify treatments that boost treatment response beyond that of a monotherapeutic approach (Melvin et al., 2006; Treatment for Adolescents with Depression Study Team, 2004; Walkup et al., 2008).

To qualify for the study adolescents had to have missed at least 20% of school over the previous 4 weeks and to experience both an anxiety and depressive disorder. Anxiety disorders were primarily overanxious disorder, social phobia, and avoidant disorder. After 8 weeks of treatment, 54% of the CBT and imipramine group were classified as attending school ($\geq$ 75% attendance) compared with 17% of CBT and placebo group. No comment is made about side effects of imipramine apart from the withdrawal of one participant due to manic symptoms. This study was of older adolescents who suffered both anxiety and depressive disorders prior to treatment, which may account for the poorer outcomes.

Sixty-four percent of this sample was followed up 1 year later and mental health problems were found to be common. No significant difference existed between groups in terms of prevalence of anxiety and depressive diagnosis, perhaps due to the high level of additional treatment (psychopharmacological, 67.2%; or outpatient therapy treatment, 62.5%) during the follow-up phase (Bernstein, Mannuzza, Chapman, & Fyer, 2001). Separation anxiety disorder and agoraphobia had the best remission rates (71% and 73%, respectively).

While the impact of adding imipramine to CBT is clear from the significant difference in attendance between groups, the current utility of imipramine is limited for treatment of school refusal. Tricyclic antidepressants are potentially cardiotoxic and can also be lethal in overdose. Tricyclic antidepressants have been demonstrated to be no more effective than placebo in the treatment of depressive disorders in young people (Hazell, O'Connell, Heathcote, & Henry, 2002). A current medication algorithm for treatment of youth depression does not include tricyclic antidepressants (Hughes et al., 2007) and warns of the lack of efficacy and potentially harmful side effects.

In the absence of comprehensive data on pharmacological treatment of school refusal, consideration of the evidence from controlled trials of newer antidepressants, particularly fluoxetine and sertraline, demonstrating their efficacy for the treatment of childhood anxiety and depressive disorders is warranted (e.g., Black & Uhde, 1994; Birmaher et al., 2003; Emslie et al., 2002; Rynn, Siqueland, & Rickels, 2001; Treatment for Adolescents with Depression Study, 2004; Walkup et al., 2008). However, consideration of the use of these medications is only justified for school refusers who have anxiety or depressive disorders, as alleviation of these disorders might lead to improved school attendance.

To address this lack of research on the role of SSRIs in the treatment of school refusal, our team has designed a randomized controlled trial to evaluate the efficacy of augmenting CBT with fluoxetine in the treatment of adolescent school refusal. Adolescents aged 11–15.5 years are randomly allocated to CBT + fluoxetine, CBT + placebo, or CBT alone. Recruitment is currently under way. It was hypothesized that CBT + fluoxetine will be superior to either of the control treatments. Primary outcome measure of the trial is school attendance.

Follow-Up of Treated School Refusers and Predictors of Outcome

Few quality follow-up studies of school refusers have been conducted. In naturalistic follow-up of a clinical population, McShane, Walters, and Rey (2004) found that comorbidity predicted poorer functional outcome 6 months after treatment (but not 3 years after treatment). Social phobia was also identified to predict more impaired functioning 3 years after treatment but not 6 months after (McShane et al., 2004). Interestingly, affective disorder did not predict poorer educational or employment outcomes, and the experience of being bullied was associated with a greater response to treatment, suggesting that this issue is amenable to intervention. Layne, Bernstein, Egan, and Kushner (2003) examined predictors of outcome in a sample receiving CBT with imipramine or placebo (i.e., Bernstein et al., 2000). Poorer outcome was predicted by diagnosis of separation anxiety disorder, avoidant disorder, and lower rate of attendance at baseline.

CONCLUSIONS

School refusal is a psychiatric problem usually associated with anxiety and/or depression that requires timely treatment to alleviate mental illness, ensure prompt return to school, and perhaps prevents longer-term mental health problems. CBT is currently the most effective evidence-based treatment for school refusal. However, the heterogeneity of this group means that a "one size fits all" treatment approach is not the answer. Additional research is required to describe the school refusing population and reach agreement about definitions of school refusal. Questions also remain unanswered about the longer-term efficacy of treatment and the benefit of psychopharmacological agents in the management of school refusal or as an augmentation of CBT and other psychological treatment.

REFERENCES

Achenbach, T. M. (1991). *Manual for the Child Behavior Checklist/4–18 and 1991 profile.* Burlington: University of Vermont Department of Psychiatry.

American Psychiatric Association. (2000). *Diagnostic and statistical manual of mental disorders* (4th ed., text rev.). Washington, DC: Author.

Balkin, R. S. (2006). A reexamination of trends in acute care psychiatric hospitalization for adolescents: Ethnicity, payment, length of stay. *Journal of Professional Counseling, Practice, Theory, & Research, 34*, 49–59.

Beidel, D. C., Turner, S. M., & Morris, T. L. (2000). Behavioral treatment of childhood social phobia. *Journal of Consulting and Clinical Psychology, 68*, 1072–1080.

Berg, I. (1992). Absence from school and mental health. *British Journal of Psychiatry, 161*, 154–166.

Berg, I. (1997). School refusal and truancy. *Archives of Disease in Childhood, 76*, 90–91.

Berg, I., Butler, A., Franklin, J., Hayes, H., Lucas, C., & Sims, R. (1993). DSM-III-R disorders, social factors and management of school attendance problems in the normal population. *Journal of Child Psychology and Psychiatry, 34*, 1187–1203.

Berg, I., & Jackson, A. (1985). Teenage school refusers grow-up. *British Journal of Psychiatry, 147*, 366–370.

Bernstein, G. A., & Borchardt, C. M. (1991). Anxiety disorders of childhood and adolescence: A critical review. *Journal of the American Academy of Child & Adolescent Psychiatry, 30*, 519–532.

Bernstein, G. A., Borchardt, C. M., Perwien, A. R., Crosby, R. D., Kushner, M. G., Thuras, P. D., & Last, C. G. (2000). Imipramine plus cognitive behavioral therapy in the treatment of school refusal. *Journal of the American Academy of Child & Adolescent Psychiatry, 39*, 276–283.

Bernstein, G. A., Garfinkel, B. D., & Borchardt, C. M. (1990). Comparative studies of pharmacotherapy for school refusal. *Journal of the American Academy of Child & Adolescent Psychiatry, 29*, 773–781.

Bernstein, G. A., Mannuzza, S., Chapman, T., & Fyer, M. H. (2001). Treatment of school refusal: One year follow-up. *Journal of the American Academy of Child & Adolescent Psychiatry, 40*, 206–213.

Berney, T., Kolvin, I., Bhate, S. R., Garside, R. F., Jeans, J., Kay, B., & Scarth, L. (1981). School phobia: A therapeutic trial with clomipramine and short-term outcome. *British Journal of Psychiatry, 138*, 110–118.

Birmaher, B., Axelson, D. A., Monk, K., Kalas, C., Clark, D. B., Ehmann, M., . . . Brent, D. A. (2003). Fluoxetine for the treatment of childhood anxiety disorders. *Journal of the American Academy of Child & Adolescent Psychiatry, 42*, 415–423.

Black, B., & Uhde, T. W. (1994). Treatment of elective mutism with fluoxetine: A double-blind, placebo-controlled study. *Journal of the American Academy of Child & Adolescent Psychiatry, 33*, 1000–1006.

Blagg, N. (1987). *School phobia and its treatment*. New York, NY: Croom Helm.

Blagg, N. R., & Yule, W. (1984). The behavioural treatment of school refusal—A comparative study. *Behaviour Research and Therapy, 22*, 119–127.

Bools, C., Foster, J., Brown, I., & Berg, I. (1990). The identification of psychiatric disorders in children who fail to attend school: A cluster analysis of a nonclinical population. *Psychological Medicine, 20*, 171–178.

Borchardt, C. M., Giesler, J., Bernstein, G. A., & Crosby, R. D. (1994). A comparison of inpatient and outpatient school refusers. *Child Psychiatry and Human Development, 24*, 255–264.

Brandibas, G., Jeunier, B., Clanet, C., & Fourasté, R. (2004). Truancy, school refusal and anxiety. *School Psychology International, 25*, 117–126.

Brent, D. A., Kolko, D. J., Birmaher, B., Baugher, M., Bridge, J., Roth, C., & Holder, D. (1998). Predictors of treatment efficacy in a clinical trial of three psychosocial treatments for adolescent depression. *Journal of the American Academy of Child & Adolescent Psychiatry, 37*, 906–914.

Buitelaar, J. K., van Andel, H., Duyx, J. H. M., & van Strien, D. C. (1994). Depressive and anxiety disorders in adolescence: A follow-up study of adolescents with school refusal. *Acta Paedopsychiatrica, 56*, 249–253.

Chorpita, B. F., Albano, A. M., Heimberg, R. G., & Barlow, D. H. (1996). A systematic replication of the prescriptive treatment of school refusal behaviour in a single subject. *Journal of Behavior Therapy & Experimental Psychiatry, 27*, 281–290.

Clarke, G. N., Rohde, P., Lewinsohn, P. M., Hops, H., & Seeley, J. R. (1999). Cognitive-behavioral treatment of adolescent depression: Efficacy of acute group treatment and booster sessions. *Journal of the American Academy of Child and Adolescent Psychiatry, 38*, 272–279.

Doobay, A. F. (2008). School refusal behavior associated with separation anxiety disorder: A cognitive-behavioral approach to treatment. *Psychology in the Schools, 45*, 261–272.

Durkin, J. P. (2002). Gabapentin in complicated school refusal. *Journal of the American Academy of Child & Adolescent Psychiatry, 41*, 632–633.

Egger, H. L., Costello, E. J., & Angold, A. (2003). School refusal and psychiatric disorders: A community study. *Journal of the American Academy of Child & Adolescent Psychiatry, 42*, 797–807.

Elliott, J. G. (1999). Practitioner review: School refusal: Issues of conceptualisation, assessment, and treatment. *Journal of Child Psychology and Psychiatry, 40*, 1001–1012.

Emslie, G. J., Heiligenstin, J. H., Wagner, K. D., Hoog, S. L., Ernest, D. E., Brown, E., . . . Jacobson, J. G. (2002). Fluoxetine for acute treatment of depression in children and adolescents: A placebo-controlled, randomized clinical trial. *Journal of the American Academy of Child & Adolescent Psychiatry, 41*, 1205–1215.

Flakierska-Praquin, N., Lindström, M., & Gillberg, C. (1997). School phobia with separation anxiety disorder: A comparative 20- to 29-year follow up study of 35 school refusers. *Comprehensive Psychiatry, 38*, 17–22.

Gittelman-Klein, R., & Klein, D. F. (1973). School phobia: Diagnostic considerations in the light of imipramine effects. *Journal of Nervous & Mental Disease, 156*, 199–215.

Gosschalk, P. O. (2004). Behavioral treatment of acute onset school refusal in a 5-year-old girl with separation anxiety disorder. *Education and Treatment of Children, 27*, 150–160.

Granell de Aldaz, E., Vivas, E., Gelfand, D. M., & Feldman, L. (1984). Estimating the prevalence of school refusal and school-related fears: A Venezuelan sample. *Journal of Nervous and Mental Disease, 172*, 722–729.

Gullone, E., & King, N. J. (1992). Psychometric evaluation of a revised fear survey schedule for children and adolescents. *Journal of Child Psychology and Psychiatry, 33*, 987–998.

Hazell, P., O'Connell, D., Heathcote, D., & Henry, D. (2002). Tricyclic drugs for depression in children and adolescents. *Cochrane Database of Systematic Reviews*, Issue 2. Art. No. CD002317.

Heyne, D., King, N. J., Tonge, B. J., & Rollings, S. (2002). Precipitants of school refusal. Unpublished raw data.

Heyne, D., King, N. J., Tonge, B., Rollings, S., Pritchard, M., Young, D., & Myerson, N. (1998). The Self-Efficacy Questionnaire for School Situations: Development and psychometric evaluation. *Behaviour Change, 15*, 31–40.

Heyne, D., King, N. J., Tonge, B. J., Rollings, S., Young, D., Pritchard, M., & Ollendick, T. H. (2002). Evaluation of child therapy and caregiver training in the treatment of school refusal. *Journal of the American Academy of Child & Adolescent Psychiatry, 41*, 687–695.

Heyne, D., Rollings, S., King, N., & Tonge, B. (2002). *School refusal*. Oxford, England: British Psychological Society; Blackwell Publishing.

Hughes, C. W., Emslie, G. J., Crismon, M. L., Posner, K., Birmaher, B., Ryan, N., . . . the Texas Consensus Conference Panel on Medication Treatment of Childhood Major Depressive Disorder (2007). Texas Children's Medication Algorithm Project: Update from Texas Consensus Conference Panel on medication treatment of Childhood Major Depressive Disorder. *Journal of the American Academy of Child & Adolescent Psychiatry, 46*, 667–686.

Kearney, C. A. (2001a). Understanding the functions. In *School refusal behavior in youth: A functional approach to assessment and treatment* (pp. 87–98). Washington, DC: American Psychological Association.

Kearney, C. A. (2001b). What is school refusal? In *School refusal behavior in youth: A functional approach to assessment and treatment* (pp. 3–24). Washington, DC: American Psychological Association.

Kearney, C. A. (2002). Identifying the function of school refusal behavior: A revision of the School Refusal Assessment Scale. *Journal of Psychopathology and Behavioral Assessment, 24*, 235–245.

Kearney, C. A. (2003). Bridging the gap among professionals who address youths with school absenteeism: Overview and suggestions for consensus. *Professional Psychology: Research and Practice, 34*, 57–65.

Kearney, C. A. (2006). Confirmatory factor analysis of the School Refusal Assessment Scale-Revised: Child and parent versions. *Journal of Psychopathology and Behavioral Assessment, 28*, 139–144.

Kearney, C. A. (2008). School absenteeism and school refusal in youth: A contemporary review. *Clinical Psychology Review, 28*, 451–471.

Kearney, C. A., & Albano, A. M. (2004). The functional profiles of school refusal behavior: Diagnostic aspects. *Behavior Modification, 28*, 147–161.

Kearney, C. A., Pursell, C., & Alvarez, K. (2001). Treatment of school refusal behavior in children with mixed functional profiles. *Cognitive and Behavioral Practice, 8*, 3–11.

Kearney, C. A., & Silverman, W. K. (1990). A preliminary analysis of a functional model of assessment and treatment for school refusal behavior. *Behavior Modification, 14*, 340–366.

Kendall, P. C. (1994). Treating anxiety disorders in children: Results of a randomized clinical trial. *Journal of Consulting and Clinical Psychology, 62*, 100–110.

King, N., Tonge, B. J., Heyne, D., Turner, S., Pritchard, M., Young, D., & Ollendick, T. (2001). Cognitive-behavioural treatment of school-refusing children: Maintenance of improvement at 3- to 5-year follow up. *Scandinavian Journal of Behaviour Therapy, 30*, 85–89.

King, N. J., & Bernstein, G. A. (2001). School refusal in children and adolescents: A review of the past 10 years. *Journal of the American Academy of Child & Adolescent Psychiatry, 40*, 197–205.

King, N. J., Ollendick, T. H., & Tonge, B. J. (1995). *School refusal: Assessment and treatment*. Needham Heights, MA: Allyn & Bacon.

King, N. J., Tonge, B. J., Heyne, D., Pritchard, M., Rollings, S., Young, D., . . . Ollendick, T. H. (1998). Cognitive-behavioral treatment of school refusing children: A controlled evaluation. *Journal of the American Academy of Child & Adolescent Psychiatry, 37*, 395–403.

Klein, D. F., Mannuzza, S., Chapman, T., & Fyer, A. J. (1992). Child panic revisited. *Journal of the American Academy of Child & Adolescent Psychiatry, 31*, 112–116.

Kovacs, M. (1985). The Children's Depression Inventory. *Psychopharmacology Bulletin, 21*, 995–998.

Last, C. G., Hansen, C., & Franco, N. (1998). Cognitive-behavioral treatment of school phobia. *Journal of the American Academy of Child & Adolescent Psychiatry, 37*, 404–411.

Last, C. G., & Strauss, C. C. (1990). School refusal in anxiety-disordered children and adolescents. *Journal of the American Academy of Child & Adolescent Psychiatry, 29*, 31–35.

Layne, A. E., Bernstein, G. A., Egan, E. A., & Kushner, M. G. (2003). Predictors of treatment response in anxious-depressed adolescents with school refusal. *Journal of the American Academy of Child & Adolescent Psychiatry, 42*, 319–326.

March, J. S., Parker, J. D., Sullivan, K., Stallings, P., & Conners, K. (1997). Multidimensional Anxiety Scale for Children (MASC): Factor structure reliability, and validity. *Journal of the American Academy of Child & Adolescent Psychiatry, 36*, 554–565.

Martin, C., Cabrol, S., Bouvard, M. P., Lepine J. P., & Mouren-Simeoni, M. C. (1999). Anxiety and depressive disorders in fathers and mothers of anxious school refusing children. *Journal of the American Academy of Child & Adolescent Psychiatry, 38*, 916–922.

McShane, G., Walter, G., & Rey, J. M. (2001). Characteristics of adolescents with school refusal. *Australian and New Zealand Journal of Psychiatry, 35*, 822–826.

McShane, G., Walter, G., & Rey, J. M. (2004). Functional outcome of adolescents with "school refusal." *Clinical Child Psychology and Psychiatry, 9*, 53–60.

Melvin, G. A., Tonge, B. J., King, N. J., Heyne, D. A., Gordon, M. S., & Klimkeit, E. K. (2006). A comparison of cognitive behavioural therapy, sertraline and their combination for adolescent depression. *Journal of the American Academy of Child & Adolescent Psychiatry, 45*, 1151–1161.

Muris, P., & Steerneman, P. (2001). The revised version of the Screen for Child Anxiety Related Emotional Disorders (SCARED-R): First evidence for its reliability and validity in a clinical sample. *British Journal of Clinical Psychology, 40*, 35–44.

Naylor, M. W., Staskowski, M., Kenney, M. C., & King, C. A. (1994). Language disorders and learning disabilities in school-refusing adolescents. *Journal of the American Academy of Child & Adolescent Psychiatry, 33*, 1331–1337.

Ollendick, T. H., & Mayer, J. A. (1984). School phobia. In S. M. Turner (Ed.), *Behavioral theories and treatment of anxiety* (pp. 367–411). New York, NY: Plenum Press.

Reynolds, C. R., & Richmond, B. O. (1985). *Revised Children's Manifest Anxiety Scale (RCMAS) manual.* Los Angeles, CA: Western Psychological Services.

Reynolds, W. M. (2002). *Reynold's adolescent depression scale* (2nd ed.). Lutz, FL: Psychological Assessment Resources.

Reynolds, C. R., & Richmond, B. O. (1978). What I Think and Feel: A revised measure of children's manifest anxiety. *Journal of Abnormal Child Psychology, 6*, 271–280.

Rollings, S., King, N., Tonge, B., Heyne, D., & Young, D. (1998). Cognitive behavioural intervention with a depressed adolescent experiencing school attendance difficulties. *Behaviour Change, 15*, 87–97.

Rynn, M. A., Siqueland, L., & Rickels, K. (2001). Placebo-controlled trial of sertraline in the treatment of children with generalized anxiety disorder. *American Journal of Psychiatry, 158*, 2008–2014.

Silverman, W. K., & Albano, A. M. (1996). *The Anxiety disorders interview schedule for DSM-IV: Child and parent versions.* San Antonio, TX: Graywind.

Spence, S. H., Donovan, C., & Brechman-Toussaint, M. (2000). The treatment of childhood social phobia: The effectiveness of a social skills training-based, cognitive-behavioural intervention, with and without parental involvement. *Journal of Child Psychology and Psychiatry, 41*, 713–726.

Treatment for Adolescents with Depression Study (TADS) Team. (2004). Fluoxetine, cognitive behavioral therapy and their combination for adolescents with depression. *Journal of the American Medical Association, 292*, 807–820.

Walkup, J., Albano, A. M., Piacentini, J., Birmaher, B., Compton, S. N., Sherrill, J. T., . . . Kendall, P. C. (2008). Cognitive behavioral therapy, sertraline, or a combination in childhood anxiety. *New England Journal of Medicine, 359*, 1–14.

Wilkinson, G. S. (1993). *Wide range achievement test—Revision 3.* Wilmington, DE: Jastak Association.

World Health Organization. (2004). *International classification of diseases* (10th rev.). Geneva, Switzerland: Author.

25

Anorexia Nervosa

CYNTHIA M. BULIK, KIMBERLY A. BROWNLEY, JENNIFER R. SHAPIRO, AND NANCY D. BERKMAN

OVERVIEW OF THE DISORDER

Anorexia nervosa (AN) is a serious psychiatric illness characterized by an inability to maintain a normal healthy body weight ($< 85\%$ of ideal body weight [IBW]). By virtue of its toll on physical health and body composition, in particular, it is the most recognizable eating disorder. Younger individuals who are still growing fail to make expected increases in weight (and often height) and bone density. Somewhat remarkable, despite increasing emaciation, individuals with AN continue to desire additional weight loss, may see themselves as fat even when severely underweight, and often engage in unhealthy behaviors to lose weight (e.g., purging, dieting, excessive exercise, fasting). Psychologically, AN is marked by shape and weight playing a central role in self-evaluation. Amenorrhea of at least 3 months is a diagnostic criterion; however, there do not appear to be meaningful differences between individuals with AN who do and do not menstruate (Attia & Roberto, 2009; Gendall et al., 2006; Watson & Andersen, 2003). AN presents either as the restricting subtype in

which low weight is achieved and maintained through caloric restriction and increased physical activity only, as well as the binge-purge subtype in which the individual regularly engages in binge eating or purging behavior (i.e., self-induced vomiting or the misuse of laxatives, diuretics, or enemas). Associated personality features, many of which exist premorbidly, include perfectionism, obsessionality, anxiety, harm avoidance, and low self-esteem (Wonderlich, Lilenfeld, Riso, Engel, & Mitchell, 2005).

AN is commonly comorbid with major depression (Halmi et al., 1991; Walters & Kendler, 1995) and anxiety disorders (C. Bulik, Sullivan, Fear, & Joyce, 1997; Kaye et al., 2004). Several studies have shown that anxiety disorders often predate onset of the eating disorder (C. Bulik et al., 1997; Kaye et al., 2004), and depression often persists postrecovery (Sullivan, Bulik, Fear, & Pickering, 1998).

Diagnostic Criteria and Clinical Characteristics

Two sets of diagnostic criteria for AN are presented in Table 25.1. These criteria, from the *Diagnostic and Statistical Manual for Mental Disorders III-R* and *IV* (American Psychiatric Association [APA], 1987, 1994), represent the most common criteria used in recent randomized clinical trials (RCT) of AN.

Acknowledgments: This research was supported by the contract 290-02-0016 from the Agency for Healthcare Research and Quality. We also thank Xiaofei Mo, MD, and Anne Cercone, BA, for their assistance with the literature review.

TABLE 25.1   *DSM-IV-TR* **Diagnostic Criteria for Anorexia Nervosa**

Source	Diagnostic Criteria
DSM-III-R Criteria for Anorexia Nervosa (307.10)	A. Refusal to maintain body weight over a minimal normal weight for age and height (e.g., weight loss leading to maintenance of body weight 15% below that expected or failure to make expected weight gain during period of growth, leading to body weight 15% below that expected). B. Intense fear of gaining weight or becoming fat, even though underweight. C. Disturbance in the way in which one's body weight, size, or shape is experienced (e.g., the person claims to "feel fat" even when emaciated, believes that one area of the body is "too fat" even when obviously underweight). D. In females, absence of at least three consecutive menstrual cycles when otherwise expected to occur (primary and secondary amenorrhea). (A woman is considered to have amenorrhea if her periods occur only following hormone, e.g., estrogen, administration.)
DSM-IV Criteria for Anorexia Nervosa (307.10)	A. Refusal to maintain body weight at or above a minimally normal weight for age and height (e.g., weight loss leading to maintenance of body weight less than 85% of that expected or failure to make expected weight gain during period of growth, leading to body weight less than 85% of that expected). B. Intense fear of gaining weight or becoming fat, even though underweight. C. Disturbance in the way in which one's body weight or shape is experienced, undue influence of body weight or shape on self-evaluation, or denial of the seriousness of the current low body weight. D. In postmenarchal females, amenorrhea (i.e., the absence of at least three consecutive cycles). (A woman is considered to have amenorrhea if her periods occur only following hormone, e.g., estrogen, administration.) *Specify Type:* **Restricting Type:** During the current episode of anorexia nervosa, the person has not regularly engaged in binge-eating or purging behavior (i.e., self-induced vomiting or the misuse of laxatives, diuretics, or enemas). **Binge Eating/Purging Type:** During the current episode of anorexia nervosa, the person has regularly engaged in binge eating or purging behavior (i.e., self-induced vomiting or the misuse of laxatives, diuretics, or enemas).

Source: Reprinted with permission from the *Diagnostic and Statistical Manual of Mental Disorders, Fourth Edition, Text Revision* (Copyright © 2000). American Psychiatric Association.

Demographic Variables

Based on data from the National Comorbidity Study-Replication, the mean prevalence of AN in adults (ages 18 and older) living in the United States is 0.9% among women and 0.3% among men (Hudson, Hiripi, Pope, & Kessler, 2007). Prevalence of subthreshold AN, defined as one criterion short of threshold, is greater—ranging from 0.37% to 1.3% (McKnight Investigators, 2003; Wittchen, Nelson, & Lachner, 1998). Estimates do not exist for the prevalence of AN or subthreshold AN in children under age 18 living in the United States.

There is some controversy regarding the incidence of AN, with some studies suggesting an increased incidence of AN in recent years (Eagles, Johnston, Hunter, Lobban, & Millar, 1995; Jones, Fox, Babigan, & Hutton, 1980; Lucas, Beard, O'Fallon, & Kurland, 1988; Milos et al., 2004; Møller-Madsen & Nystrup, 1992; Szmukler, 1985; Willi & Grossman, 1983) and others reporting stable rates (Hall & Hay, 1991; Hoek, 1991; Jorgensen, 1992; Nielsen, 1990). The most common age of onset is between 15 and 19 years (Lucas, Beard, O'Fallon, & Kurland, 1991), although anecdotal reports suggest an increase in the prepubertal period (S. Gowers, Crisp, Joughin, & Bhat, 1991) and in older adults (Beck, Casper, & Andersen, 1996; Inagaki et al., 2002). AN afflicts females disproportionately, with a sex ratio of approximately 9:1 (American Psychiatric Association, 2000).

Impact of Anorexia Nervosa

Psychiatric and medical consequences. AN carries with it multiple medical and psychological sequelae, including depression, anxiety, social withdrawal, fatigue, and multiple medical complications (Halmi et al., 1991; Kaplan, 1993; Katzman, 2005; Sharp & Freeman, 1993). AN takes a social toll as well. Due to the prolonged and all-encompassing nature of the illness, many individuals miss out on the normal developmental milestones associated with adolescence (C. M. Bulik, 2002). The most detailed longitudinal cohort study followed individuals with AN and their age-matched peers for 20 years in Göteborg, Sweden. After 5 years, those who had had AN were more likely to have personality disorders (especially avoidant, dependent, obsessive-compulsive, or passive-aggressive) as well as higher rates of obsessive-compulsive disorder, Asperger's syndrome, any autism-like condition, and empathy disorder (I. Gillberg, Råstam, & Gillberg, 1995). At 10 years these observations persisted (Råstam, Gillberg, & Wentz, 2003; Wentz, Gillberg, Gillberg, & Råstam, 2001; Wentz, Gillberg, Gillberg, & Råstam, 2000), and the AN group had a higher lifetime prevalence of depression (Ivarsson, Råstam, Wentz, Gillberg, & Gillberg, 2000).

A history of AN has also been associated with subsequent problems with reproduction (C. Bulik, Sullivan, Fear, Pickering, & Dawn, 1999), osteoporosis (Rigotti, Neer, Skates, Herzog, & Nussbaum, 1991), and continued low body mass index (BMI).

Recovery. A common question is whether individuals can recover from AN. In the aforementioned Swedish follow-up study (C. Gillberg, Råstam, & Gillberg, 1994a; C. Gillberg, Råstam, & Gillberg, 1994b; Råstam, Gillberg, & Gillberg, 1995), at 5 years, approximately one half of individuals with AN were considered to be recovered. A full 59% had no eating disorder diagnosis and 41% had a good outcome, according to the commonly used Morgan-Russell general outcome scale. Six percent continued to meet diagnostic criteria for AN, 22% had bulimia nervosa, and 14% met criteria for eating disorder not otherwise specified. At 10 years (Nilsson, Gillberg, Gillberg, & Råstam, 1999; Råstam, Gillberg, & Wentz, 2003; Wentz, Gillberg, Gillberg, & Råstam, 2001), 27% of individuals met criteria for some eating disorder diagnosis. Thus, within 10 years of study entry, recovery occurred in the majority of patients, but a significant minority continued to struggle with active symptoms of the disorder.

These results were mirrored in a New Zealand study that contacted patients after 12 years for follow-up assessments and compared their outcomes with age-matched individuals from the same community (C. Bulik, Sullivan, Fear, & Pickering, 2000; Sullivan, Bulik, Fear, & Pickering, 1998). Of the AN patients, 30% were fully recovered at follow-up; 21% continued to have an eating disorder, including 10% who continued to meet diagnostic criteria for AN. Women with histories of AN continued to have lower BMIs, higher scores on scales of disordered eating, and the desire to be at a lower weight.

Relapse is a common problem for individuals with AN. A Danish study assessed relapse in 121 patients 4 to 22 years posttreatment. Using life-table methods, 14% of the population relapsed in the first year. For those left to evaluate in subsequent years, the relapse rate declined below 4% per year (Isager, Brinch, Kreiner, & Tolstrup, 1985). In a separate study that defined relapse as meeting full criteria for AN for at least 1 week following full recovery, 40% of patients experienced a relapse after a median of 8 years (Herzog et al., 1999).

Mortality. AN has the highest mortality rate of any psychiatric illness (Sullivan, 1995). The standardized mortality ratio ranges from 1.36 (among females 20 years following treatment) to 30.5 (among females less than 1 year following treatment) (Birmingham, Su, Hlynsky, Goldner, & Gao, 2005; Eckert, Halmi, Marchi, Grove, & Crosby, 1995; Herzog et al., 2000; Keel et al., 2003; Lee, Chan, & Hsu, 2003;

Møller-Madsen, Nystrup, & Nielsen, 1996). Based on an analysis of studies published between 1966 and 1995, premature all-cause death risk in individuals with AN was 5 times higher than expected, due to increased rates of premature death from both natural (4 times higher than expected) and unnatural (11 times higher than expected) causes (Harris & Barraclough, 1998). Notably, premature death risk due to suicide was 32 times higher than expected, and approximately 65% of deaths due to natural causes were directly attributed to starvation. Thus, AN is a pernicious disorder with serious and sometimes life-threatening consequences.

SOURCES OF INFORMATION FOR THIS REPORT

The evidence base for treatments for AN is limited. In order to present the evidence base for AN treatment, we draw from three sources of information. No meta-analyses are available combining results from psychosocial interventions for AN.

1. Consensus Panel Recommendations from the American Psychiatric Association (APA) and the American Academy for Pediatrics (AAP) on the treatment of AN.
2. The Agency for Healthcare Research and Quality (AHRQ) evidence-based report on treatments for AN. On behalf of the National Institutes of Health (NIH) Office of Research on Women's Health, the National Institute of Mental Health, and the Health Resources and Services Administration, AHRQ commissioned the RTI International-University of North Carolina Evidence-Based Practice Center (RTI-UNC EPC) to conduct an extensive systematic review of the literature on treatment and outcomes of AN, bulimia nervosa, and binge eating disorder (Berkman et al., 2006). We draw on the results of this review of RCTs of

behavioral interventions for AN in order to present the core evidence base for treatment of this disorder.
3. For purposes of this chapter, we conducted an evidence report update, employing the identical search process of the initial AHRQ evidence-based review to identify all studies published between 2005 and March 2008.

The AHRQ evidence-based report was developed with ongoing consultation with a Technical Expert Panel (TEP) comprised of 10 individuals (researchers, practitioners, and a patient advocate). Four key questions guided the evidence-based review and are relevant to the present chapter.

1. What is the evidence for the efficacy of treatments or combinations of treatments for AN?
2. What is the evidence of harms associated with the treatment or combination of treatments for AN?
3. What factors are associated with efficacy of treatment among patients with AN?
4. Does the efficacy of treatment for AN differ by sex, gender, age, race, ethnicity, or cultural group?

Complete methods of the review can be found in the evidence report (Berkman et al., 2006). In this chapter, we focus only on psychosocial interventions for AN; outcome categories included eating, psychiatric and psychological, and biomarker measures.

In order to identify all relevant literature, we searched six major databases: AGRICOLA (National AGRICultural OnLine Access), CINAHL (Cumulative Index to Nursing and Applied Health), Cochrane Collaborative libraries, ERIC (Educational Resources Information Center), MEDLINE (National Library of Medicine's premier bibliographic database covering the fields of medicine, nursing, dentistry, veterinary medicine, the health-care system, and the preclinical sciences), and

PsycINFO (the American Psychological Association abstract database of psychological literature from the 1800s to the present). We generated Medical Subject Heading (MeSH) search terms for MEDLINE searches and used comparable terms for other databases. MeSH terms included *anorexia* and *anorexia nervosa*. We limited our searches by type of study, including RCT, single-blind, double-blind, and cross-over designs. We also asked experts in the field and the TEP for additional articles that our searches may not have captured. Table 25.2 summarizes the inclusion criteria for selected abstracts.

We reviewed each abstract systematically against the a priori criteria presented in Table 25.2 to determine inclusion. Procedurally, a first reviewer evaluated abstracts for inclusion. If that reviewer decided the article was worthy of inclusion, it was retained. If an article was judged not to meet inclusion criteria, it was reevaluated by a senior reviewer who could reverse the decision. Each exclusion decision was given a coded reason for exclusion.

For the studies included in the initial report, criteria adapted from West et al. (2002) were used to rate the quality of individual studies. The quality rating reflected a cumulative scoring of 25 items in 11 categories: (1) research aim/study question, (2) study population, (3) randomization, (4) blinding, (5) interventions, (6) outcomes, (7) statistical analysis, (8) results, (9) discussion, (10) external validity, and (11) funding/sponsorship. Each item was weighted equally and a score was calculated out of 100%, excluding items not applicable based on study design. In the next step, the scores were collapsed into three categories: poor (0%–59%), fair (60%–74%), and good

TABLE 25.2   Inclusion Criteria for AHRQ Report and Updated Review

Category	Criteria
Study population	Humans All races, ethnicities, and cultural groups 10 years of age or older
Study settings and geography	All nations
Time period	Published from 1980 to the present
Publication criteria	All languages Articles in print Articles in the "gray literature," published in nonpeer-reviewed journals, or unobtainable during the review period were excluded.

Admissible evidence (study design and other criteria)	Original research studies that provide sufficient detail regarding methods and results to enable use and adjustment of the data and results.
	Anorexia nervosa must be diagnosed according to *DSM-III, DSM III-R, DSM-IV, ICD-10*, Feighner, or Russell criteria.
	Relevant outcomes: eating related, psychiatric or psychological, and biomarker measures must be able to be abstracted from data presented in the papers.
	Eligible study designs include:
	  Randomized controlled trials:
	  Double-blinded, single-blinded, and cross-over designs (data from prior to the first cross-over).
	  Anorexia nervosa studies: initiated with 10 or more participants and followed for any length of time.
	  Outcomes studies:
	  Observational studies, including prospective and retrospective cohort studies and case series studies, with and without comparison populations.
	  Disease population must be followed for a minimum of 1 year.
	  Disease population must include 50 or more participants at the time of the analysis.

(75%–100%). Studies rated as poor were excluded from the summary review (see Berkman et al., 2006, for details).

For the updated review, we did not evaluate the quality of newly published individual studies or reevaluate the quality of the evidence base as a whole. We did, however, expand the review in one important way. Clinical consensus agrees that the initial and critical step in the treatment of AN is weight restoration (also called renutrition or refeeding). However, very little empirical evidence exists to evaluate the optimal approach to refeeding. Here, we include weight restoration as one of our target treatments for discussion, and we present findings from the clinical consensus panel recommendations that are available, as well as the few relevant published studies in the area. Consensus panel recommendations are also included for other psychosocial interventions presented in this review.

WEIGHT RESTORATION/ NUTRITIONAL REHABILITATION

Restoring healthy eating patterns and healthy weight are the critical first steps in the clinical management of AN (American Psychiatric Association, 2006; Yager & Andersen, 2005). Although this is a common approach, strikingly, this is the aspect of treatment that is least studied to date. This is, in part, due to the logistic difficulties of randomization in inpatient treatment settings, the potential cost of funding studies of inpatient weight restoration in the United States, and the complexities of adequate insurance coverage for the refeeding phase of treatment.

Consensus Panel Recommendations

American Psychiatric Association. The APA practice guidelines specify eight aims of treatment for AN (Table 25.3).

With reference to nutritional rehabilitation, the APA practice guidelines emphasize the importance of restoring weight, normalizing eating patterns, achieving normal perceptions of hunger and satiety, and correcting biological and psychological sequelae of malnutrition (Golden & Meyer, 2004; Kaye, Gwirtsman, Obarzanek, & George, 1988). According to APA guidelines, inpatient weight restoration is recommended for individuals at 75% of IBW or lower. In addition, APA guidelines emphasize determining targeted weights and working toward expected rates of controlled weight gain (i.e., 2–3 pounds/week for individuals who are in the hospital, 0.5–1 pounds/week for outpatient, and between those two amounts for partial hospitalization or intensive

---

TABLE 25.3   APA Practice Guidelines for the Treatment of Anorexia Nervosa

Aim 1. Restore the patient to a healthy weight (associated with the return of menses and normal ovulation in female patients, normal sexual drive and hormone levels in male patients, and normal physical and sexual development in children and adolescents).

Aim 2. Treat the patient's physical complications.

Aim 3. Enhance the patient's motivation to cooperate in the restoration of healthy eating patterns and participate in treatment.

Aim 4. Educate the patient regarding healthy nutrition and eating patterns.

Aim 5. Help the patient reassess and change core dysfunctional cognitions, attitudes, motives, conflicts, and feelings related to the eating disorder.

Aim 6. Treat the patient's associated psychiatric conditions, including deficits in mood and impulse regulation, self-esteem, and behavior.

Aim 7. Enlist family support and provide family counseling and therapy where appropriate.

Aim 8. Prevent the patient from relapsing.

Source: Reprinted with permission from *APA Practice Guidelines for the Treatment of Patients with Eating Disorders, Third Edition* (Copyright © 2006). American Psychiatric Association.

outpatient approaches). The guidelines caution against rapid refeeding, which can lead to fluid retention and a condition known as "refeeding syndrome" (Solomon & Kirby, 1990). Refeeding syndrome is characterized by cardiovascular, neurologic, and hematologic complications due to shifts in phosphate from extracellular to intracellular spaces. This occurs in patients who have total body phosphorus depletion as a result of malnutrition and can occur in response to oral, parenteral, or enteral nutrition (Birmingham, Alothman, & Goldner, 1996; Birmingham, Puddicombe, & Hlynsky, 2004; Solomon & Kirby, 1990). The APA guidelines do not provide direction regarding how best to attain these targeted weight gains.

American Academy of Pediatrics. The practice guidelines for the AAP focus heavily on the role of the pediatrician during the refeeding process, but also provide some guidance as to the pace and approach to refeeding. The AAP states that the pediatrician involved in the treatment of a hospitalized patient with AN should be prepared to provide nutrition via a nasogastric tube or intravenously when necessary. The guidelines also alert physicians to possible metabolic, cardiac, and neurologic complications associated with malnourishment and refeeding, and explicitly warn against refeeding syndrome in severely malnourished patients (Solomon & Kirby, 1990). The guidelines encourage the pediatrician to focus on slow refeeding, possibly with phosphorus supplementation in order to achieve adequate weight gain and avoid refeeding syndrome.

Evidence Base

One recent inpatient study suggests that the addition of cycle enteral nutrition to usual meals and snacks increases energy intake, improves short-term weight and fat-free mass gains, and is associated with a longer relapse-free period postdischarge (Rigaud, Brondel, Poupard, Talonneau, & Brun, 2007). Although

inpatient weight restoration is common, especially in severely malnourished individuals, the evidence does not yet exist to compare this approach to an intensive outpatient or partial hospitalization approach for reasons mentioned earlier; these include logistical issues related to inpatient randomization, and funding and insurance coverage limitations for inpatient weight restoration studies in the United States. Such comparisons are critical, however, given the high relapse rate posthospitalization (Herzog et al., 1999). Presumably, the high posthospitalization relapse rate reflects the fact that the tightly controlled conditions under which supervised weight gain occurs simply cannot generalize to noninstitutional settings. At this time, there are no validated methods for improving generalizability that directly reduce relapse.

One published study compared strict and lenient operant conditioning approaches to refeeding and found that the lenient approach was more economical of nursing time and more acceptable to the patients, but not more beneficial in promoting weight gain (Touyz, Beumont, Glaun, Phillips, & Cowie, 1984). A recent study compared specialist outpatient treatment with general child and adolescent outpatient treatment and with inpatient treatment and found no differences on any biological, eating, or psychological outcome measures. However, those who refused randomization to inpatient treatment, but then continued with outpatient treatment, showed a greater increase in Morgan-Russell average outcome scores after 1 year of treatment (S. G. Gowers et al., 2007).

Refeeding is a challenging and anxiety-provoking part of treatment for the patient with AN. Though the APA and AAP guidelines provide some assistance for the physician who is directing or assisting with the refeeding process, there is less guidance for managing the psychological aspects of treatment during this very difficult time. Studies are desperately needed in order to determine the optimal approach to weight restoration: one that achieves adequate weight gain and addresses the psychological challenges of refeeding in a manner that is acceptable to the patient and family.

Conclusions

The consensus opinion is that the restoration of healthy eating and resumption of healthy weight are necessary and critical first steps in the treatment of AN. Indeed, most other elements of treatment and recovery are contingent upon achieving these objectives. However, to date, few studies have evaluated refeeding to determine optimal conditions or key individual difference factors that influence or predict successful refeeding. RCTs are needed to establish an evidence base for refeeding paradigms that maximize weight gain and establish healthy eating behavior while also addressing important emotional and family issues that may interfere with meeting these goals.

COGNITIVE BEHAVIOR THERAPY

Consensus Panel Recommendations

APA. The APA recommends a comprehensive treatment plan that evolves from the foundation of a strong therapeutic alliance between patient and provider (American Psychiatric Association, 2006). Awareness of the patient's cultural background and trauma history can be important in establishing these connections. A team approach to treatment is the preferred model of care. The team approach targets not only the patient's eating symptoms and behaviors but also his/her general medical condition and psychiatric status/safety. The treatment team ideally consists of clinicians who can provide nutritional counseling, rehabilitation, and pharmacological interventions, as needed. The APA recommends that family involvement and education be considered on a case-by-case basis.

The APA stipulates four primary goals of treatment to help patients:

1. Understand and cooperate with their nutritional and physical rehabilitation.
2. Understand and change behaviors and dysfunctional attitudes related to their AN.
3. Improve their interpersonal and social functioning.
4. Address coexisting psychopathology and psychological conflicts that reinforce or maintain their dysfunctional eating behaviors.

The practitioner is advised to develop and express empathy toward the patient, educate the patient about AN, provide positive reinforcement for meeting treatment goals, and help the patient develop his or her own sense of motivation to recover. These elements may be particularly critical in the early stages of treatment of the acutely ill patient, when more formal psychotherapy is often difficult due to high levels of patient negativism and mild cognitive impairment.

The APA emphasizes that all successful treatments are built on a working knowledge of the patient and his/her salient issues in key areas related to psychodynamic conflicts, cognitive development, psychological defenses, family dynamics, and comorbid psychological diagnoses. In addition, the APA states that psychotherapy alone is insufficient to treat the medically compromised patient with AN, and recommends that every patient receives individual psychotherapy after initial weight restoration for a minimum of 1 year.

After weight restoration, the focus of psychotherapy is to help patients understand the roles that cognitive distortions, developmental factors and familial influences, and poor emotion regulation played in their illness. Improving coping skills and developing strategies to avoid or minimize risk of relapse are also important goals during this phase of treatment. The APA makes no specific recommendations about which forms of psychotherapy to pursue, but rather acknowledges that cognitive behavior therapy (CBT) is the most widely studied and substantiated approach to date, despite conflicting opinions about CBT's effectiveness among experienced clinicians. For the chronically ill patient who shows a suboptimal response to psychotherapy, nonverbal therapeutic methods (creative arts, movement therapy, occupational therapy) can be useful.

AAP. The AAP makes no specific recommendations regarding the utility of CBT in the treatment of children with AN (*Pediatrics*, 2003). Rather the AAP's position statement on the treatment of eating disorders in children emphasizes the pediatrician's role in screening, education, and advocacy.

Evidence Base

CBT studies generally used a form of therapy specifically tailored to AN to include cognitive and behavioral features associated with maintaining eating pathology. Of the three CBT studies reviewed, one followed inpatient weight restoration and compared CBT to nutritional counseling (Pike, Walsh, Vitousek, Wilson, & Bauer, 2003), while two followed outpatients in the underweight state and compared CBT to interpersonal therapy (IPT), nonspecific supportive clinical management (NCSM) (V. McIntosh et al., 2005) (later renamed Specialist Supportive Clinical Management [SSCM]; V. V. McIntosh et al., 2006), or behavioral therapy (BT) (Channon, De Silva, Hemsley, & Perkins, 1989) (Table 25.4). Interpersonal therapy for AN derives from IPT previously used for depression (Klerman, Weissman, Rounsaville, & Chevron, 1984) and bulimia nervosa (Fairburn, 1993), and targets one interpersonal problem area; interpersonal disputes, role transitions, grief, or interpersonal deficits. In the McIntosh study (V. McIntosh et al., 2005), SSCM reflected a treatment similar to community-based treatments from a clinician familiar with the treatment of eating disorders; it incorporated elements of sound clinical management and supportive psychotherapy and in this instance was delivered in manualized form.

Compared to nutritional counseling (which included both nutrition education and food exchanges), CBT significantly reduced relapse risk and increased the likelihood of good outcomes (Pike, Walsh, Vitousek, Wilson, & Bauer, 2003). Notably, good outcomes were more common in those who received antidepressant medication in addition to CBT compared to those who were treated with CBT but did not receive medication. Global outcome ratings were highest in the group receiving SSCM, followed by CBT and then IPT, but SSCM differed significantly from IPT only (V. McIntosh et al., 2005). When compared to a control treatment that consisted of routine outpatient management, CBT and BT were both associated with greater improvements in nutritional functioning but lesser improvements in ratings of drive for thinness (Channon, De Silva, Hemsley, & Perkins, 1989).

Conclusions

Based on the limited evidence base available for CBT, one can tentatively conclude that CBT reduces relapse risk for adults with AN after weight restoration, but it is not clear whether CBT is more helpful than other approaches in the acutely underweight state. Strong conclusions about the efficacy of CBT for treatment of AN cannot be drawn until these studies are replicated and extended to include adolescent as well as adult patients.

FAMILY-BASED THERAPY

Consensus Panel Recommendations

APA. The APA endorses family and couples therapy to address the impact of the illness on the patient's social network (and vice versa) as well as group therapy for patients who are emotionally stable enough to tolerate hearing about and seeing the progress and shortcomings of other group members. The APA guidelines underscore that family therapy is

TABLE 25.4 Results From Behavioral Intervention Trials in Adults: Anorexia Nervosa

Source, Treatment, and Setting	Major Outcome Measures	Significant Change Over Time Within Groups	Significant Differences Between Groups at Endpoint	Significant Differences Between Groups in Change Over Time
Channon et al., 1989 CBT vs. BT vs. "Usual care" control Outpatient	Eating: • EDI • M-R scale Biomarker: • BMI • M-R scale Psych: • BDI • MOCI • M-R scale	No statistics reported.	At 6-month FU, CBT associated with better psychosexual functioning than BT and BT was associated with greater improvement in menstrual functioning than CBT. At 1-year FU, the BT group scored better than the CBT group on preferred weight. CBT and BT combined were associated with greater improvements on nutritional functioning than the control group. The control group showed greater improvements on drive for thinness than the combined CBT and BT groups.	No statistics reported.
V. McIntosh et al., 2005 CBT vs. IPT vs. NSCM Outpatient	Eating: • EDE • EDI Biomarker: • BMI • Percent body fat • Weight Psych: • GAF • HDRS		Compared to IPT, NSCM associated with higher likelihood of "good" global outcome.	NSCM superior to IPT in improving global functioning and eating restraint over 20 weeks. NSCM superior to CBT in improving global functioning over 20 weeks. CBT superior to IPT in improving eating restraint over 20 weeks.
Pike et al., 2003 CBT vs. nutritional counseling Outpatient	Eating: • Recovery • Relapse • Tx failure • M-R scale	No statistics reported.	Compared to nutrition counseling, CBT associated with lower percentage tx failures, higher percentage "good" outcome, and longer time (weeks) to relapse.	No statistics reported.
Dare et al., 2001 CAT vs. focal vs. family vs. "routine" therapy	Eating: • M-R scale • Recovery	No statistics reported.	At 1-year FU, compared to routine tx, focal and family tx associated with higher weight; also, higher percentage of patients in focal and family tx were recovered or	No statistics reported.

Study / Setting	Measures	Findings	Statistics
Outpatient	Biomarker: • BMI • Percent ABW • M-R scale Psych: • M-R scale	significantly improved (i.e., > 85% IBW, no/few menstrual or BN symptoms).	No statistics reported.
Treasure et al., 1995 CAT vs. EBT Outpatient	Eating: • M-R scales Biomarker: • BMI • Weight Psych: • M-R scales • Self progress scale	Compared to EBT, CAT associated with higher self-rating of improvement.	No statistics reported.
Crisp et al., 1991; and S. Gowers et al., 1994 Inpatient tx vs. outpatient individual and family therapy and dietary counseling vs. group therapy vs. no formal tx Inpatient and outpatient	Eating: • M-R scale • Remission Biomarker: • BMI • M-R scale • Weight Psych: • M-R scale	At 1-year FU, global score and menstruation improved in all 4 groups, nutrition score improved in 3 active tx groups, and mental state improved in outpatient family/diet counseling group. At 2-year FU, mental state improved in outpatient family/diet counseling; global score, menstruation, and nutrition improved in groups that received outpatient family/diet counseling and no formal tx.	Compared to "no formal tx," outpatient family/diet counseling associated with higher weight and BMI at 1- and 2-year FU. Compared to "no formal tx," weight increased more at 1-year FU in all 3 active groups. Weight increased more at 2-year FU in outpatient family/diet counseling compared to "no formal tx" group.

Note: ABW, average body weight; BDI, Beck Depression Inventory; BMI, body mass index; BT, behavioral therapy; CAT, cognitive-analytic therapy; CBT, cognitive behavior therapy; EBT, educational behavioral therapy; EDE, Eating Disorders Examination; EDI, Eating Disorders Inventory (EDI-2, Garner, 1991); FU, follow-up; GAF, Global Assessment of Functioning (*DSM-IV*); HDRS, Hamilton Depression Rating Scale; IBW, ideal body weight; IPT, interpersonal therapy; MOCI, Maudsley Obsessional Compulsive Index; M-R, Morgan and Russell; NSCM, nonspecific supported clinical management; Psych, psychiatric and psychological; pt, patients; Tx, treatment; vs., versus more beneficial than individual therapy for patients who are younger than age 19 years, have been ill for no more than 3 years, and are weight restored. Therefore, family therapy for children and adolescents is strongly endorsed both during acute illness and after weight restoration. Family therapy has several components but begins with helping the parents to develop a consistent approach to refeeding, sympathizing with their situation, and explicitly refuting the belief that they caused the disordered eating. Siblings are often engaged to support the affected sibling. Parents use the therapist as a source of support and consultation to help them determine how best to refeed and weight restore their child.

AAP. The AAP guidelines similarly underscore the importance of the pediatrician collaborating closely with mental health experts to provide the necessary psychological, social, and psychiatric care (Powers, 1996; A. L. Robin, Gilroy, & Dennis, 1998; Yager, 1994). One role of the pediatrician is to help monitor psychotropic medication side effects, such as drowsiness, that can interfere with cognitive function and with treatment engagement. The AAP guidelines note that multidisciplinary teams often find it helpful to divide the treatment, with mental health clinicians providing individual, family, and group therapy. The AAP highlights that family therapy is especially helpful for younger children and adolescents and is imperative for improving long-term prognosis (Eisler et al., 1997; Geist, Heinmaa, Stephens, Davis, & Katzman, 2000; Russell, Szmukler, Dare, & Eisler, 1987). The guidelines acknowledge that optimal gains are achieved via family therapy only after proper nutritional status has been restored because malnourished patients often experience cognitive impairment that interferes with the learning and application of concepts taught in family therapy sessions.

Evidence Base

The evidence for family-based studies includes two studies that incorporated various

forms of family therapy with adults (Crisp et al., 1991; Dare, Eisler, Russell, Treasure, & Dodge, 2001; S. Gowers, Norton, Halek, & Crisp, 1994); five family therapy studies focused exclusively on adolescents (Eisler et al., 2000; Eisler, Simic, Russell, & Dare, 2007; Geist, Heinmaa, Stephens, Davis, & Katzman, 2000; Lock, Agras, Bryson, & Kraemer, 2005; Lock, Couturier, & Agras, 2006; Lock, Le Grange, Agras, & Dare, 2001; A. Robin, Siegel, Koepke, Moye, & Tice, 1994; A. L. Robin, Siegel, & Moye, 1995); and one that combined adolescent and adult patients (Eisler et al., 1997; Russell et al., 1987) (Table 25.5).

Focal therapy is a standardized form of time-limited psychoanalytic psychotherapy in which the therapist takes a nondirective stance and intentionally withholds advice about the eating-related problems or symptoms. Instead, he or she addresses: (a) the conscious and unconscious meanings of the symptoms in terms of the patient's history and of their experience with their family, (b) the effects of the symptom and its influence upon the patient's current relationships, and (c) the manifestation of those influences in the patient's relationship with the therapist in the present and as it controls the patient's desire to get benefit from therapy (a focus on the transference; Dare et al., 2001). Dare et al. (2001) compared focal family therapy to standard family therapy and routine treatment. In this instance, family therapy focused on the child's eating disorder as a problem of family life affecting all family members, helping parents to take a very active role to oppose the anorectic eating habits and eliminating the eating disorder, as far as is possible, from its controlling role in family relationships. Routine treatment involved low contact outpatient management consisting of 30-minute sessions with a trainee psychiatrist who provided specific information about the nature and consequences of AN, supportive encouragement toward a more regular, sustainable, and healthy diet, and regular monitoring of weight and physical status. In this setting, focal family therapy was superior to

TABLE 25.5   Results From Behavioral Intervention Trials in Adolescents Only and Adolescents and Adults Combined: Anorexia Nervosa

Source, Treatment, Setting, and Quality Score	Major Outcome Measures	Significant Change Over Time Within Groups	Significant Differences Between Groups at Endpoint	Significant Differences Between Groups in Change Over Time
Eisler et al., 2000; and Eisler et al., 2007 CFT vs. SFT Outpatient	Eating: • Bulimic symptoms • EAT • EDI Biomarker: • Percent ABW • BMI • Weight Psych: • MOCI • SMFQ • Depression • Obsessionality	No statistics reported.	No statistics reported.	CFT superior to SFT in reducing ED-related traits, depression, and obsessionality after 1 year of tx. At 5-year FU, no differences between SFT and CFT on major outcomes; however, SFT superior to CFT in rate of menstrual functioning return, and in percent average weight gain within subgroup defined as having high levels of "expressed emotion."
Geist et al., 2000 Family therapy vs. family group psychoeducation Inpatient	Eating: • EDI Biomarker: • Percent IBW Psych: • BSI • CDI • FAM III	No statistics reported.	No differences on any measures.	No differences on any measures.

(Continued)

TABLE 25.5 Results From Behavioral Intervention Trials in Adolescents Only and Adolescents and Adults Combined: Anorexia Nervosa (*Continued*)

Source, Treatment, Setting, and Quality Score	Major Outcome Measures	Significant Change Over Time Within Groups	Significant Differences Between Groups at Endpoint	Significant Differences Between Groups in Change Over Time
Russell et al., 1987; and Eisler et al., 1997 Family therapy vs. individual therapy Outpatient	Eating: • M-R scales • Readmit rate Biomarker: • Percent ABW • M-R scales • Weight Psych: • M-R scales	No statistics reported.	No statistics reported.	Among early onset, less chronic AN patients, family therapy superior to individual therapy in improving nutritional status, menstrual and psychosexual function, and weight over 1-year tx; family therapy also more likely associated with a "good" outcome over 1-year tx and 5-year FU.
A. L. Robin et al., 1994; and A. L. Robin et al., 1995 BFST vs. EOIT Outpatient and inpatient	Eating: • EAT • EDI • Eating conflict Biomarker: • BMI • Weight • Menstruation Psych: • BDI • BSQ • PARQ • IBC	No statistics reported.	No differences on any measures.	BFST superior to EOIT in increasing BMI to post-tx and 1-year FU, and in improving mother's positive communication at FU.
Lock et al., 2005; and Lock et al., 2006	Eating: • EDE • YBC-EDS	No differences on any measures.	No differences on any measures.	No differences on any measures among those with most severe YBC-EDS symptoms. At 1 year, longer-term tx associated with better BMI outcome in those with most severe ED symptoms, and with

Long-term (12 months) vs. short-term (6 months) family therapy Outpatient	Biomarker: • BMI • Weight		better EDE global outcome in those with nonintact families. An average of 4 years after tx, no differences between groups in BMI or EDE measures.
S. G. Gowers et al., 2007; Byford et al., 2007 Specialist outpatient vs. General child and adolescent mental health service vs. in patient Outpatient and inpatient	Eating: • EDI • M-R food intake Biomarker: • BMI • Weight • Menstruation Psych: • M-R scales • FAD • MFQ • HoNOSCA	No statistics reported.	No statistics reported, except in subanalysis among those randomized to inpatient: refusing admission and continuing outpatient associated with greater increase in M-R average outcome after 1 year of tx. Treatments did not differ significantly in cost-effectiveness. No differences on any measures.

Note: ABW, average body weight; AN, anorexia nervosa; BDI, Beck Depression Inventory; BFST, behavioral family systems therapy; BMI, body mass index; BSI, Brief Symptom Inventory; BSQ, Body Shape Questionnaire; CDI, Children's Depression Inventory; CFT, conjoint family therapy; EAT, Eating Attitudes Test; ED, eating disorders; EDE, Eating Disorders Examination; EDI, Eating Disorders Inventory; EOIT, ego-oriented individual therapy; FAD, Family Assessment Device; FAM-III, Family Assessment Measure; FU, follow-up; HoNOSCA, Health of the Nation Outcome Scale for Children and Adolescents; IBC, Interaction Behavior Code; IBW, ideal body weight; MFQ, Mood and Feelings Questionnaire; MOCI, Maudsley Obsessional Compulsive Index; M-R, Morgan and Russell; PARQ, Parent Adolescent Relationship Questionnaire; Psych, psychiatric and psychological; SFT, separated family therapy; SMFQ, Short Mood and Feeling Questionnaire; tx, treatment; vs., versus; YBC-EDS, Yale-Brown-Cornell Eating Disorders Scale routine treatment in increasing percentage of adult body weight, restoring menstruation, and decreasing bulimic symptoms; overall clinical improvement was rated as modest (Dare et al., 2001).

A second RCT compared outcomes in adults with AN assigned to one of four treatment options: (1) inpatient treatment, (2) outpatient individual and family therapy, (3) outpatient group therapy, and (4) referral back to family physician. At 1-year follow-up, outpatient therapy involving the family (as well as inpatient and outpatient group therapy) was superior to family physician referral in terms of weight gain, return of menstruation, and various aspects of sexual and social adjustment. At 2-year follow-up, only the outpatient family and physician referral groups were compared, confirming superiority of the individual plus family therapy approach to family physician referral for weight and BMI gain (Crisp et al., 1991; S. Gowers et al., 1994).

Other forms of family-based psychotherapy, including conjoint family therapy (CFT), separated family therapy (SFT), behavioral family systems therapy (BFST), and family psychoeducation, have been investigated in the treatment of adolescents with AN. In CFT the family is treated as a unit, whereas in SFT the parents and the patient are seen separately. BFST combines cognitive restructuring and problem-solving communication training. Eisler and colleagues (Eisler et al., 2000) compared family therapy focusing on parental control of renutrition and found that CFT provided a significant advantage over SFT on eating and mood outcomes, but not on weight outcomes. At 5-year follow-up, there were no differences between the groups on weight, eating, or mood; however, SFT was superior to CFT in promoting return of menstruation. In addition, SFT was superior to CFT in weight gain in the subgroup of participants from families with high levels of maternal expressed emotion (Eisler, Simic, Russell, & Dare, 2007). Robin and colleagues (A. Robin et al., 1994;

A. L. Robin et al., 1995) compared BFST to ego-oriented individual therapy, which emphasized building ego strength, adolescent autonomy, and insight into the emotional blocks to eating. In terms of increasing BMI and restoring menstruation, BFST was superior to ego-oriented individual therapy; however, there were no differences between treatments in terms of eating or mood outcomes. Notably, Geist et al. (2000) compared the effects of 4 months of family therapy versus family psychoeducation on outcomes in 25 female adolescents with newly diagnosed restrictive eating disorders. At the end of treatment, the groups achieved similar average levels of IBW (95% vs. 91%) and did not differ on any measures of eating disorder pathology (Geist et al., 2000).

A limited number of studies have addressed concerns of optimal duration and timing of family therapy. Adolescents randomized to short (10 sessions over 6 months) versus long (20 sessions over 12 months) family therapy employing a manual-based model of initial parental control of refeeding did not differ on eating, psychiatric, or biomarker outcomes (Lock et al., 2005; Lock et al., 2001). However, longer-term therapy was more effective for those with either nonintact families or those with more severe eating-related obsessions. At 4-year follow-up, there were no differences between the short versus long family therapy on outcomes such as BMI and global functioning assessed with the Eating Disorders Examination (Lock, Couturier, & Agras, 2006). Finally, family therapy was more effective for younger patients with earlier onset of AN than for older patients with a more chronic course (Eisler et al., 1997; Russell, Szmukler, Dare, & Eisler, 1987).

Conclusions

Overall, family therapy focusing on parental control of renutrition is efficacious in treating younger patients with AN, especially those treated in the earlier stages of their illness.

Although few differences were observed when comparing different models of family therapy, each approach led to clinically meaningful weight gain and psychological improvement. Moreover, two studies produced results suggesting that family therapy was superior to individual therapy for adolescent patients with shorter duration of illness. In contrast, there is no evidence supporting family therapy (as currently practiced) as an effective treatment for adults with AN and a comparatively long duration of illness.

COGNITIVE ANALYTIC THERAPY

Cognitive analytic therapy (CAT) is a treatment that borrows from both psychodynamic and behavioral approaches, combining elements of cognitive therapy and brief, focused, psychodynamic psychotherapy (Treasure et al., 1995). CAT assists patients in developing a formal multifaceted conceptualization (in diagram form) of anorexia in their experience of themselves and their early and current relationships, and helps them to use this insight to manage their feelings and relationships rather than rely on AN to function in this capacity.

Consensus Panel Recommendations

Neither the APA nor the AAP make specific recommendations regarding the use of CAT in adult or adolescent patients with AN.

Evidence Base

Two studies using CAT failed to find any advantage of CAT over educational behavioral therapy or focal family therapy in eating, mood, or weight outcomes (Dare et al., 2001; Treasure et al., 1995) (Table 25.4). Dare and colleagues (2001) found CAT to be equivalent to focal family therapy in increasing percentage of adult body weight, restoring menstruation, and decreasing bulimic symptoms;

overall clinical improvement was modest. In a small pilot study of adult patients with AN, weight and Morgan-Russell outcomes (nutritional, menstrual, mental state, psychosexual functioning, social functioning) were evaluated in a group assigned to CAT versus a group assigned to educational behavioral treatment in which patients monitored their daily intake using diaries. At the end of the study, the CAT group reported higher self-ratings of improvement compared to the group assigned to educational behavioral treatment (Treasure et al., 1995).

Conclusions

Compared with other forms of psychotherapy used in the treatment of AN, CAT has received less attention and systematic evaluation. Limited findings suggest that patients who undergo CAT achieve similar gains (weight restoration, clinical improvement) compared to those undergoing family therapy; however, the evidence base is insufficient at this time to conclude that CAT is an efficacious treatment strategy for adults or adolescents with AN.

SUMMARY

Anorexia nervosa is a pernicious illness and successful treatment requires involvement of a multidisciplinary team of practitioners with expertise in the management of medical, psychological, and family issues that impact the course of recovery (American Psychiatric Association, 2006). Refeeding and weight restoration are pivotal first steps in treatment; individuals at 75% of IBW or lower usually require inpatient hospitalization to initially address these crucial issues, although many other factors influence level of care decisions. Hospitalization can be very costly, both in terms of financial and emotional stress incurred by the patient and family. Therefore, when facilities are available, hospitalization can be followed by various levels of step-down care that allow for increasing autonomy and exposure to real-life eating and emotional situations. The APA and AAP provide practice guidelines for physicians treating patients with AN. Despite its importance, no RCTs for AN have established the optimal approach to inpatient weight restoration and postdischarge weight gain maintenance. Standards are lacking regarding the appropriateness of the recommendation for hospitalization at 75% IBW, methods and milestones of renutrition, and transitions from inpatient treatment to less structured environments. Further studies are clearly needed to address these important aspects of treatment toward the goal of maximizing treatment gains and minimizing financial and psychological burdens on patients and their families.

Various forms of psychotherapy have been used in the treatment of AN, and a select few have been evaluated in the context of an RCT. These include CBT, family therapy, and CAT delivered in both hospital and outpatient settings. At the time of our 2006 review, the evidence base for psychotherapy treatment efficacy in adults was weak and for treatment efficacy in adolescents was modest (Berkman et al., 2006).

For adults with AN, tentative evidence suggests that CBT reduces relapse risk after weight has been restored, especially among those who also are treated with antidepressant medication; however, the extent to which CBT is helpful in those who are acutely underweight remains unclear. When provided as outpatient treatment for underweight patients, CBT was similar to other forms of psychotherapy (e.g., IPT or SSCM) in improving weight, mood, or eating behavior. None of the CBT findings have been replicated, and no CBT-focused RCTs have been conducted in younger patients.

Efficacy of family therapy and CAT, as they are currently practiced, has yet to be determined. For younger patients, family therapy focusing on parental control of refeeding results in clinically meaningful weight gain and psychological improvement and may be superior to individual therapy for adolescent patients with shorter duration of illness. For adults, family therapy may be more effective than medical management by a family physician. Generally, there is a need for studies that include the adult patient's family of insertion (spouse and offspring of the patient) and that incorporate life span-appropriate and family constellation modifications to the therapy model. Until then, the potential efficacy of family therapy for adults cannot be ruled out. Likewise, more studies are needed to establish the efficacy of CAT and to compare CAT to other cognitive and behavioral treatment modalities.

Critiquing the Literature

Overall, the literature on psychotherapy treatments for AN is lacking in several key areas (Berkman et al., 2006).

1. Generally, studies have been underpowered. Samples have been too small to examine important questions about differential efficacy as a function of race/ethnicity, sex, or age; or worse yet, subgroup analyses exploring difference based on these factors have been performed on outcome variables in the absence of a priori hypotheses, possibly resulting in inflated error rates of discovery and misleading conclusions.

2. Studies have also been ill-conceived with respect to participant drop out (attrition), which has been quite high (up to 43%) and often unbalanced across treatment groups. Some studies only analyzed outcomes among participants who actually completed the study, ignoring potentially important information gained through intent-to-treat analyses that incorporate data obtained from participants before they drop out of the trial. Beyond these most basic issues, the overall quality of the literature has suffered due to inattention to study design details and inadequate follow-up to assess long-term

outcomes (such as osteoporosis, dental health, cardiovascular health, etc.). Addressing these problems will require researchers and clinicians to (a) identify means of increasing motivation for treatment and treatment retention for individuals with AN who enroll in clinical studies; and (b) increase scientific rigor by adhering to stricter methods of randomization, measurement, and statistical design.

3. Consensus definitions for stage of illness, remission, recovery, and relapse do not exist. As a result, it is difficult to interpret results within and across studies. Standardized definitions of these terms for AN along with standardized methods to measure them will facilitate cross-study comparisons and meta-analytic approaches. Ultimately, these improvements will enable researchers and clinicians to interpret and appreciate statistically significant and clinically meaningful differences in treatment outcomes.

4. Males and persons of racial/ethnic minorities are grossly underrepresented in clinical trials involving patients with AN. As a result, we have a poor understanding of the prevalence of AN in these important subgroups and have no knowledge of their unique treatment needs or responses to treatment. Accumulating this information must become a priority in future RCTs; this will not only improve recruitment and retention of participants in treatment trials but also advance our ability to tailor treatment strategies to meet the needs of these diverse individuals.

5. Clinical trials for AN do not adequately reflect the type of treatment typically available and delivered in the community and, thus, are unable to address the key challenges facing many clinicians who treat patients with this disorder. Often, insurance coverage limitations present a major stumbling block to diversifying treatment studies into the community. Working in partnership with insurance companies (in order to increase access to trials given the current reimbursement milieu) may be critical to success and to transitioning from efficacy to effectiveness studies.

6. Studies to date have not been forthcoming about adverse events, specifically, the degree of medical compromise experienced by study participants or strategies developed to monitor for potential harm. Given the high attrition from AN trials, behavioral interventions should pay greater attention to both physical and psychological harms associated with interventions that may impact the decision to continue treatment. All studies should report adverse events associated with interventions and whether adverse events differ between underweight and weight-restored patients.

Future Research Needs

Discovering new interventions that target the core biological and psychological features of AN, address adverse medical sequelae such as osteoporosis, and enhance motivation and retention in medication trials are critically needed steps. Research on innovative medications and behavioral treatments are warranted. These innovative approaches can include adapting interventions that are efficacious for other disorders as well as identifying new interventions for increasing motivation, acceptability, and retention in treatment. In addition, further dismantling of complex therapies such as CBT to determine the active therapeutic components is also warranted.

Application of new information technologies has shown promise in the treatment of eating disorders. Preliminary studies have found good treatment acceptability in the use of the Internet and text messaging for bulimia nervosa and binge eating disorder (Bauer, Hagel, Okon,

Meermann, & Kordy, 2006; Bauer, Percevic, Okon, Meermann, & Kordy, 2003; Shapiro et al., 2007; Shapiro et al., 2010). Adequately powered clinical trials that include the use of e-mail, the Internet, personal digital assistants, text messaging, and other technological advances to enhance treatment will add to future treatment development and should be the next steps for testing technological approaches. Given the high rates of shame, denial, and interpersonal deficits experienced by patients with AN, these approaches (which provide a higher degree of privacy than is afforded by direct patient–therapist contact in a public health-care setting) may be particularly helpful. These approaches also provide improved access to outpatient treatment for patients who live in remote/rural areas, which are likely underserved by psychotherapists and doctors with expertise in AN. Finally, these approaches may promote treatment retention and relapse prevention by increasing the frequency of patient–provider contact.

In sum, our working knowledge of effective psychotherapy treatments for AN is limited on many fronts. Larger, multisite RCTs that include more diverse patient samples, employ more rigorous methodological and analytical approaches, and address the core pathology and long-term medical and psychological sequelae of AN are needed. Ultimately, knowledge gained from future studies will clarify the role of psychotherapy within the multidisciplinary treatment framework as well as improve delivery of treatments tailored to meet the specific needs of individual patients and their families.

REFERENCES

American Psychiatric Association. (1987). *Diagnostic and statistical manual of mental disorders. Edition III-R* (3rd, rev. ed.). Washington, DC: Author.

American Psychiatric Association. (1994). *Diagnostic and statistical manual for psychiatric disorders: Fourth edition*. Washington, DC: Author.

American Psychiatric Association. (2000). *Diagnostic and statistical manual of mental disorders. Fourth edition text revision*. Washington, DC: Author.

American Psychiatric Association. (2006). Practice guideline for the treatment of patients with eating disorders, third edition. Retrieved from www .psychiatryonline.com/pracGuide/loadGuidelinePdf .aspx?file=EatingDisorders3ePG_04-28-06

Attia, E., & Roberto, C. A. (2009). Should amenorrhea be a diagnostic criterion for anorexia nervosa? *International Journal of Eating Disorders, 42*, 581–589.

Bauer, S., Hagel, J., Okon, E., Meermann, R., & Kordy, H. (2006). Erfahrungen mit dem Einsatz des Short Message Service (SMS) in der nachstationären Betreuung von Patientinnen mit Bulimia nervosa. *Psychodynamische Psychotherapie, 3*, 127–136.

Bauer, S., Percevic, R., Okon, E., Meermann, R., & Kordy, H. (2003). Use of text messaging in the aftercare of patients with bulimia nervosa. *European Eating Disorders Review, 11*, 279–290.

Beck, D., Casper, R., & Andersen, A. (1996). Truly late onset of eating disorders: A study of 11 cases averaging 60 years of age at presentation. *International Journal of Eating Disorders, 20*, 389–395.

Berkman, N., Bulik, C., Brownley, K., Lohr, K., Sedway, J., Rooks, A., & Gartlehner, G. (2006). *Management of eating disorders. Evidence Report/Technology Assessment No. 135*. Rockville, MD: AHRQ Publication No. 06-E010. (Prepared by the RTI International-University of North Carolina Evidence-Based Practice Center under Contract No. 290-02-0016).

Birmingham, C. L., Alothman, A. F., & Goldner, E. M. (1996). Anorexia nervosa: Refeeding and hypophosphatemia. *International Journal of Eating Disorders, 20*, 211–213.

Birmingham, C. L., Su, J., Hlynsky, J., Goldner, E., & Gao, M. (2005). The mortality rate from anorexia nervosa. *International Journal of Eating Disorders, 38*, 143–146.

Birmingham, C. L., Puddicombe, D., & Hlynsky, J. (2004). Hypomagnesemia during refeeding in anorexia nervosa. *Eating and Weight Disorders, 9*, 236–237.

Bulik, C., Sullivan, P., Fear, J., & Joyce, P. (1997). Eating disorders and antecedent anxiety disorders: A controlled study. *Acta Psychiatrica Scandinavica, 96*, 101–107.

Bulik, C., Sullivan, P., Fear, J., & Pickering, A. (2000). Outcome of anorexia nervosa: Eating attitudes, personality, and parental bonding. *International Journal of Eating Disorders, 28*, 139–147.

Bulik, C., Sullivan, P., Fear, J., Pickering, A., & Dawn, A. (1999). Fertility and reproduction in women with anorexia nervosa: A controlled study. *Journal of Clinical Psychiatry, 2*, 130–135.

Bulik, C. M. (2002). Eating disorders in adolescents and young adults. *Child and Adolescent Psychiatric Clinics of North America, 11*, 201–218.

Byford, S., Barrett, B., Roberts, C., Clark, A., Edwards, V., Smethurst, N., & Gowers, S. G. (2007). Economic evaluation of a randomised controlled trial for anorexia nervosa in adolescents. *British Journal of Psychiatry, 191*, 436–440.

Channon, S., De Silva, P., Hemsley, D., & Perkins, R. (1989). A controlled trial of cognitive-behavioural and behavioural treatment of anorexia nervosa. *Behaviour Research and Therapy, 27*, 529–535.

Crisp, A., Norton, K., Gowers, S., Halek, C., Bowyer, C., Yeldham, D., . . . Bhat, A. (1991). A controlled study of the effect of therapies aimed at adolescent and family psychopathology in anorexia nervosa. *British Journal of Psychiatry, 159*, 325–333.

Dare, C., Eisler, I., Russell, G., Treasure, J., & Dodge, L. (2001). Psychological therapies for adults with anorexia nervosa: Randomised controlled trial of outpatient treatments. *British Journal of Psychiatry, 178*, 727–736.

Eagles, J., Johnston, M., Hunter, D., Lobban, M., & Millar, H. (1995). Increasing incidence of anorexia nervosa in the female population of northeast Scotland. *American Journal of Psychiatry, 152*, 1266–1271.

Eckert, E. D., Halmi, K. A., Marchi, P., Grove, W., & Crosby, R. (1995). Ten-year follow-up of anorexia nervosa: Clinical course and outcome. *Psychological Medicine, 25*, 143–156.

Eisler, I., Dare, C., Hodes, M., Russell, G., Dodge, E., & Le Grange, D. (2000). Family therapy for adolescent anorexia nervosa: The results of a controlled comparison of two family interventions. *Journal of Child Psychology and Psychiatry, 41*, 727–736.

Eisler, I., Dare, C., Russell, G., Szmukler, G., le Grange, D., & Dodge, E. (1997). Family and individual therapy in anorexia nervosa. A 5-year follow-up. *Archives of General Psychiatry, 54*, 1025–1030.

Eisler, I., Simic, M., Russell, G. F., & Dare, C. (2007). A randomised controlled treatment trial of two forms of family therapy in adolescent anorexia nervosa: A five-year follow-up. *Journal of Child Psychology and Psychiatry, 48*, 552–560.

Fairburn, C. G. (1993). Interpersonal psychotherapy for bulimia nervosa. In G. Klerman & M. Weissman (Eds.), *New applications of interpersonal psychotherapy* (pp. 355–378). Washington, DC: American Psychiatric Press.

Geist, R., Heinmaa, M., Stephens, D., Davis, R., & Katzman, D. (2000). Comparison of family therapy and family group psychoeducation in adolescents with anorexia nervosa. *Canadian Journal of Psychiatry, 45*, 173–178.

Gendall, K., Joyce, P., Carter, F., McIntosh, V., Jordan, J., & Bulik, C. M. (2006). The psychobiology and diagnostic significance of amenorrhea in anorexia nervosa. *Fertility Sterility, 85*, 1531–1535.

Gillberg, C., Råstam, M., & Gillberg, I. (1994a). Anorexia nervosa: Physical health and neurodevelopment at 16 and 21 years. *Developmental Medicine and Child Neurology, 36*, 567–575.

Gillberg, I. C., Råstam, M., & Gillberg, C. (1994b). Anorexia nervosa outcome: Six-year controlled longitudinal study of 51 cases including a population cohort. *Journal of the American Academy of Child and Adolescent Psychiatry, 33*, 729–739.

Gillberg, I., Råstam, M., & Gillberg, C. (1995). Anorexia nervosa 6 years after onset: Part. Personality disorders. *Comprehensive Psychiatry, 36*, 61–69.

Golden, N. H., & Meyer, W. (2004). Nutritional rehabilitation of anorexia nervosa. Goals and dangers. *International Journal Adolescent Medical Health, 16*(2), 131–144.

Gowers, S., Crisp, A., Joughin, N., & Bhat, A. (1991). Premenarcheal anorexia nervosa. *Journal of Child Psychology Psychiatry, 32*, 515–524.

Gowers, S., Norton, K., Halek, C., & Crisp, A. (1994). Outcome of outpatient psychotherapy in a random allocation treatment study of anorexia nervosa. *International Journal of Eating Disorders, 15*, 165–177.

Gowers, S. G., Clark, A., Roberts, C., Griffiths, A., Edwards, V., Bryan, C., . . . Barrett, B. (2007). Clinical effectiveness of treatments for anorexia nervosa in adolescents: Randomised controlled trial. *British Journal of Psychiatry, 191*, 427–435.

Hall, A., & Hay, P. J. (1991). Eating disorder patient referrals from a population region 1977–1986. *Psychological Medicine, 21*, 697–701.

Halmi, K., Eckert, E., Marchi, P., Sampugnaro, V., Apple, R., & Cohen, J. (1991). Comorbidity of psychiatric diagnoses in anorexia nervosa. *Archives of General Psychiatry, 48*, 712–718.

Harris, E. C., & Barraclough, B. (1998). Excess mortality of mental disorder. *British Journal of Psychiatry, 173*, 11–53.

Herzog, D., Dorer, D., Keel, P., Selwyn, S., Ekeblad, E., Flores, A., . . . Keller, M. B. (1999). Recovery and relapse in anorexia and bulimia nervosa: A 7.5-year follow-up study. *Journal of the American Academy of Child and Adolescent Psychiatry, 38*, 829–837.

Herzog, D., Greenwood, D., Dorer, D., Flores, A., Ekeblad, E., Richards, A., . . . Keller, M. B. (2000). Mortality in eating disorders: A descriptive study. *International Journal of Eating Disorders, 28*, 20–26.

Hoek, H. W. (1991). The incidence and prevalence of anorexia nervosa and bulimia nervosa in primary care. *Psychological Medicine, 21*, 455–460.

Hudson, J. I., Hiripi, E., Pope, H. G., Jr., & Kessler, R. C. (2007). The prevalence and correlates of eating disorders in the National Comorbidity Survey Replication. *Biology Psychiatry, 61*, 348–358.

Inagaki, T., Horiguchi, J., Tsubouchi, K., Miyaoka, T., Uegaki, J., & Seno, H. (2002). Late onset anorexia nervosa: Two case reports. *International Journal of Psychiatry Medicine, 32*, 91–95.

Isager, T., Brinch, M., Kreiner, S., & Tolstrup, K. (1985). Death and relapse in anorexia nervosa: Survival analysis of 151 cases. *Journal of Psychiatric Research, 19*, 515–521.

Ivarsson, T., Råstam, M., Wentz, E., Gillberg, I. C., & Gillberg, C. (2000). Depressive disorders in teenage-onset anorexia nervosa: A controlled longitudinal, partly community-based study. *Comprehensive Psychiatry, 41*, 398–403.

Jones, D., Fox, M., Babigan, H., & Hutton, H. (1980). Epidemiology of anorexia nervosa in Monroe County, New York: 1960–76. *Psychosomatic Medicine, 42*, 551–558.

Jorgensen, J. (1992). The epidemiology of eating disorders in Fyn County Denmark, 1977–1986. *Acta Psychiatrica Scandinavica, 85*, 30–34.

Kaplan, A. (1993). Medical aspects of Anorexia Nervosa and Bulimia Nervosa. In S. H. Kennedy (Ed.), *Handbook of eating disorders* (pp. 22–29). Toronto, Canada: University of Toronto.

Katzman, D. (2005). Medical complications in adolescents with anorexia nervosa: A review of the literature. *International Journal of Eating Disorders, 37*, S52–S59.

Kaye, W., Bulik, C., Thornton, L., Barbarich, B. S., Masters, K., & Group, P. F. C. (2004). Comorbidity of anxiety disorders with anorexia and bulimia nervosa. *American Journal of Psychiatry, 161*, 2215–2221.

Kaye, W., Gwirtsman, H., Obarzanek, E., & George, D. (1988). Relative importance of calorie intake needed to gain weight and level of physical activity in anorexia nervosa. *American Journal of Clinical Nutrition, 47*, 989–994.

Keel, P., Dorer, D., Eddy, K., Franko, D., Charatan, D., & Herzog, D. (2003). Predictors of mortality in eating disorders. *Archives of General Psychiatry, 60*, 179–183.

Lee, S., Chan, Y., & Hsu, L. (2003). The intermediate-term outcome of Chinese patients with anorexia nervosa in Hong Kong. *American Journal of Psychiatry, 160*, 967–972.

Lock, J., Agras, W. S., Bryson, S., & Kraemer, H. C. (2005). A comparison of short- and long-term family therapy for adolescent anorexia nervosa. *Journal of the American Academy of Child Adolescent Psychiatry, 44*, 632–639.

Lock, J., Couturier, J., & Agras, W. S. (2006). Comparison of long-term outcomes in adolescents with anorexia nervosa treated with family therapy. *Journal of the American Academy of Child Adolescent Psychiatry, 45*, 666–672.

Lock, J., Le Grange, D., Agras, W., & Dare, C. (2001). *Treatment manual for anorexia nervosa: A family-based approach.* New York, NY: Guilford Press.

Lucas, A. R., Beard, C. M., O'Fallon, W. M., & Kurland, L. T. (1988). Anorexia nervosa in Rochester, Minnesota: A 45-year study. *Mayo Clinic Proceedings, 63*, 433–442.

Lucas, A. R., Beard, C. M., O'Fallon, W. M., & Kurland, L. T. (1991). 50-year trends in the incidence of anorexia nervosa in Rochester, Minn.: A population-based study. *American Journal of Psychiatry, 148*, 917–922.

McIntosh, V., Jordan, J., Carter, F., Luty, S., McKenzie, J., Bulik, C., . . . Joyce, P. R. (2005). Three psychotherapies for anorexia nervosa: A randomized controlled trial. *American Journal of Psychiatry, 162*, 741–747.

McIntosh, V. V., Jordan, J., Luty, S. E., Carter, F. A., McKenzie, J. M., Bulik, C. M., & Joyce, P. R. (2006). Specialist supportive clinical management for anorexia nervosa. *International Journal of Eating Disorders, 39*, 625–632.

McKnight Investigators. (2003). Risk factors for the onset of eating disorders in adolescent girls: results of the McKnight longitudinal risk factor study. *American Journal of Psychiatry, 160*, 248–254.

Milos, G., Spindler, A., Schnyder, U., Martz, J., Hoek, H., & Willi, J. (2004). Incidence of severe anorexia nervosa in Switzerland: 40 years of development. *International Journal of Eating Disorders, 36*, 118–119.

Møller-Madsen, S. & Nystrup, J. (1992). Incidence of anorexia nervosa in Denmark. *Acta Psychiatrica Scandinavica, 86*, 187–200.

Møller-Madsen, S., Nystrup, J., & Nielsen, S. (1996). Mortality in anorexia nervosa in Denmark during the period 1970–1987. *Acta Psychiatrica Scandanavica, 94*, 454–459.

Nielsen, S. (1990). The epidemiology of anorexia nervosa in Denmark from 1973–1987: A nationwide register study of psychiatric admission. *Acta Psychiatrica Scandinavica, 81*, 507–514.

Nilsson, E. W., Gillberg, C., Gillberg, I. C., & Råstam, M. (1999). Ten-year follow-up of adolescent-onset anorexia nervosa: Personality disorders. *Journal of the American Academy of Child Adolescent Psychiatry, 38*, 1389–1395.

Pike, K., Walsh, B., Vitousek, K., Wilson, G., & Bauer, J. (2003). Cognitive behavior therapy in the post-hospitalization treatment of anorexia nervosa. *American Journal of Psychiatry, 160*, 2046–2049.

Powers, P. S. (1996). Initial assessment and early treatment options for anorexia nervosa and bulimia nervosa. *Psychiatric Clinics of North America, 19*, 639–655.

Råstam, M., Gillberg, C., & Wentz, E. (2003). Outcome of teenage-onset anorexia nervosa in a Swedish community-based sample. *European Journal of Child Adolescent Psychiatry, 12*(Suppl. 1), I78–I90.

Råstam, M., Gillberg, I., & Gillberg, C. (1995). Anorexia nervosa 6 years after onset: Part II. Comorbid psychiatric problems. *Comprehensive Psychiatry, 36*, 70–76.

Rigaud, D., Brondel, L., Poupard, A. T., Talonneau, I., & Brun, J. M. (2007). A randomized trial on the efficacy of a 2-month tube feeding regimen in anorexia nervosa: A 1-year follow-up study. *Clinical Nutrition, 26*, 421–429.

Rigotti, N., Neer, R., Skates, S., Herzog, D., & Nussbaum, S. (1991). The clinical course of osteoporosis in anorexia nervosa: A longitudinal study of cortical bone mass. *Journal of the American Medical Association, 265*, 1133–1137.

Robin, A., Siegel, P., Koepke, T., Moye, A., & Tice, S. (1994). Family therapy versus individual therapy for adolescent females with anorexia nervosa. *Developmental and Behavioral Pediatrics, 15*, 111–116.

Robin, A. L., Gilroy, M., & Dennis, A. B. (1998). Treatment of eating disorders in children and adolescents. *Clinical Psychology Review, 18*, 421–446.

Robin, A. L., Siegel, P. T., & Moye, A. (1995). Family versus individual therapy for anorexia: Impact on family conflict. *International Journal of Eating Disorders, 17*, 313–322.

Russell, G. F. M., Szmukler, G. I., Dare, C., & Eisler, I. (1987). An evaluation of family therapy in anorexia and bulimia nervosa. *Archives of General Psychiatry, 44*, 1047–1056.

Shapiro, J. R., Reba-Harrelson, L., Dymek-Valentine, M., Woolson, S. L., Hamer, R. M., & Bulik, C. M. (2007). Feasibility and acceptability of CD-ROM-based cognitive-behavioural treatment for binge-eating disorder. *European Eating Disorders Review, 15*, 175–184.

Shapiro, J. R., Bauer, S., Andrews, E., Pisetsky, E., Bulik-Sullivan, B., Hamer, R. M., & Bulik, C. M. (2010). Mobile therapy: Use of text-messaging in the treatment of bulimia nervosa. *International Journal of Eating Disorders, 43*, 513–519.

Sharp, C., & Freeman, C. (1993). The medical complications of anorexia nervosa. *British Journal of Psychiatry, 162*, 452–462.

Solomon, S. & Kirby, D. (1990). The refeeding syndrome: A review. *Journal of Parenteral and Enteral Nutrition, 14*, 90–97.

Sullivan, P. F. (1995). Mortality in anorexia nervosa. *American Journal of Psychiatry, 152*, 1073–1074.

Sullivan, P. F., Bulik, C. M., Fear, J. L., & Pickering, A. (1998). Outcome of anorexia nervosa. *American Journal of Psychiatry, 155*, 939–946.

Szmukler, G. (1985). The epidemiology of anorexia nervosa and bulimia. *Journal of Psychiatric Research, 19*, 143–153.

Touyz, S., Beumont, P., Glaun, D., Phillips, T., & Cowie, I. (1984). A comparison of lenient and strict operant conditioning programmes in refeeding patients with anorexia nervosa. *British Journal of Psychiatry, 144*, 517–520.

Treasure, J., Todd, G., Brolly, M., Tiller, J., Nehmed, A., & Denman, F. (1995). A pilot study of a randomised trial of cognitive analytical therapy vs. educational behavioral therapy for adult anorexia nervosa. *Behaviour Research and Therapy, 33*, 363–367.

Walters, E. E., & Kendler, K. S. (1995). Anorexia nervosa and anorexic-like syndromes in a population-based female twin sample. *American Journal of Psychiatry, 152*, 64–71.

Watson, T., & Andersen, A. (2003). A critical examination of the amenorrhea and weight criteria for diagnosing anorexia nervosa. *Acta Psychiatrica Scandinavica, 108*, 175–182.

Wentz, E., Gillberg, C., Gillberg, I. C., & Råstam, M. (2001). Ten-year follow-up of adolescent-onset anorexia nervosa: Psychiatric disorders and overall functioning scales. *Journal of Child Psychology and Psychiatry, 42*, 613–622.

Wentz, E., Gillberg, I. C., Gillberg, C., & Råstam, M. (2000). Ten-year follow-up of adolescent-onset anorexia nervosa: Physical health and neurodevelopment. *Developmental Medicine and Child Neurology, 42*, 328–333.

West, S., King, V., Carey, T., Lohr, K., McKoy, N., Sutton, S., & Lux, L. (2002). *Systems to rate the strength of scientific evidence. Evidence report*. Rockville, MD: Agency for Healthcare Research and Quality.

Willi, J., & Grossman, S. (1983). Epidemiology of anorexia nervosa in a defined region of Switzerland. *American Journal of Psychiatry, 140*, 564–567.

Wittchen, H. U., Nelson, C. B., & Lachner, G. (1998). Prevalence of mental disorders and psychosocial impairments in adolescents and young adults. *Psychological Medicine, 28*, 109–126.

Wonderlich, S., Lilenfeld, L., Riso, L., Engel, S., & Mitchell, J. (2005). Personality and anorexia nervosa. *International Journal of Eating Disorders, 37*(Suppl.), S68–S71.

Yager, J. (1994). Psychosocial treatments for eating disorders. *Psychiatry, 57*, 153–164.

Yager, J., & Andersen, A. E. (2005). Clinical practice. Anorexia nervosa. *New England Journal of Medicine, 353*, 1481–1488.

26

Bulimia

ATA GHADERI

OVERVIEW OF DISORDER

Almost 30 years ago, British psychiatrist and professor Gerald Russell described what, at that time, was considered an apparently new psychiatric condition called *bulimia nervosa* (BN) as a variant of anorexia nervosa (Russell, 1979). BN is characterized by recurrent episodes of binge eating and inappropriate compensatory behavior, such as self-induced vomiting or abusing laxatives. Binge eating is defined as the consumption of excessively large amounts of food within a short period of time accompanied by a sense of lack of control during the binge episode.

Russell's observation and description set the context for early community research (e.g., P. J. Cooper & Fairburn, 1983) and studies of its clinical features (e.g., Fairburn et al., 1982), as well as epidemiological research showing that a significant number of young women in Western societies were affected by BN (Fairburn, 1984; Hsu, 1996; Rand & Kuldau, 1992).

Diagnostic Criteria

BN was soon entered in the *Diagnostic and Statistical Manual of Mental Disorders* (*DSM*)

in 1980 (American Psychiatric Association [APA], 1980) under the name of "bulimia." Limitations of the *DSM-III* description of bulimia soon became apparent and were followed by years of research and vigorous debates. The current version of the *DSM* (i.e., *DSM-IV-TR*) describes bulimia now in terms of BN from a phenomenological perspective, including the patient's characteristic psychopathology, according to the following criteria:[1]

A. Recurrent episodes of binge eating. An episode of binge eating is characterized by both of the following:
  1. Eating, in a discrete period of time (e.g., within any 2-hour period), an amount of food that is definitely larger than what most people would eat during a similar period of time and under similar circumstances.
  2. A sense of lack of control over what one is eating during the episode (e.g., a feeling that one cannot stop eating or control what or how much one is eating).
B. Recurrent inappropriate compensatory behavior in order to prevent weight gain,

Acknowledgment: During the preparation of this chapter, the author was supported by a research grant from Swedish Research Council (grant no. 421-2004-2614).

[1]The following list is reprinted with permission from the *Diagnostic and Statistical Manual of Mental Disorders, Fourth Edition, Text Revision* (Copyright © 2000). American Psychiatric Association.

such as self-induced vomiting; misuse of laxatives, diuretics, enemas, or other medications; fasting or excessive exercise.

C. Binge eating and inappropriate compensatory behaviors both occur, on average, at least twice a week for 3 months.

D. Self-evaluation is unduly influenced by body shape and weight.

E. The disturbance does not occur exclusively during episodes of anorexia nervosa.

Specify type:

*   *Purging type*: During the current episode of bulimia nervosa, the person has regularly engaged in self-induced vomiting or the misuse of laxatives, diuretics, or enemas.
*   *Nonpurging type*: During the current episode of bulimia nervosa, the person has used inappropriate compensatory behaviors, such as fasting or excessive exercise, but has not regularly engaged in self-induced vomiting or the misuse of laxatives, diuretics, or enemas.

BN is defined in a similar way in the current version of the most widely used European classification system, the *International Classification of Diseases (ICD-10)* (World Health Organization [WHO], 1993).

Demographic Variables

Gender, Prevalence, Incidence, and Ethnicity

BN is more common among women (about 90% women and 10% men) and affects 1% to 2% of young adults and sometimes adolescents (usually between the ages of 16 and 35). Although estimation of prevalence of BN is complicated by factors such as uncertainty of the result of studies based on self-report and the bias in studies using patient records—due to the fact that most individuals with BN are not in treatment (Fairburn, Welch, Norman, O'Connor, & Doll, 1996; Whitehouse, Cooper, Vize, Hill, & Vogel, 1992)—there is some

reliable evidence of an increase in the prevalence of BN during the last few decades (Kendler et al., 1991; Soundy, Lucas, Suman, & Melton, 1995). Yearly incidence of BN has been estimated as 29 women and 1 man per 100,000/year (Fairburn & Harrison, 2003). It occurs more often among Caucasians and mainly in Western societies.

Age of Onset, Subsequent Course, and Prognosis

BN starts in much the same way as anorexia nervosa, usually between mid- and late teenage years. Among a substantial portion of the patients with BN, the diagnostic criteria of anorexia nervosa are met for a time (Sullivan, Bulik, Carter, Gendall, & Joyce, 1996), and there are clear indications of a substantial migration between BN, anorexia nervosa, and eating disorders not otherwise specified (EDNOS) (Fairburn, Cooper, & Shafran, 2003). In a review of a large number of studies among patients who have been followed-up for 5–10 years, 50% fully recovered, while almost 20% still met the full criteria for BN (Keel & Mitchell, 1997). In addition, the same authors found that around 30% experienced relapse into bulimic symptoms. In another study, Keel and colleagues (Keel, Mitchell, Miller, Davis, & Crow, 1999) invited women with a diagnosis of BN to participate in a follow-up assessment more than 10 years after the presentation. They found that 11% from that sample still met the full criteria for BN and 18.5% were diagnosed with EDNOS, while almost 70% were in full or partial remission (Keel et al., 1999). Using different definitions of outcome, full recovery ranged from 38% to 47%, 10 years after the presentation (Keel, Mitchell, Davis, Fieselman, & Crow, 2000). In another study, the probability of remission at 24 months was 40% (Grilo et al., 2003), and it increased to 74% at the 60-month follow-up (Grilo et al., 2007). In conclusion, the longer the duration of the follow-up, the fewer amount of patients who meet the full criteria for BN.

Genetic and Environmental Risk Factors

Although empirical research shows that inter-action of genetics and a range of environ-mental risk factors are the best explanations for emergence and maintenance of BN, we know virtually nothing about how these risk factors operate at the individual level. Different combinations of various risk factors (i.e., a multifactorial model) seem to be the best explanation for different patients with BN. Potential patterns of familial transmission are unclear or nonexistent, although the preva-lence of depression and substance abuse among the relatives of the bulimic probands is increased. Proband-wise concordance for BN has been shown to be around 23% in mono-zygotic twins and 9% in dizygotic twins (Kendler et al., 1991). Research on the genetics of clinical cases of BN does not suggest her-itability, but data from the general population (Bulik, Sullivan, & Kendler, 1998; Wade et al., 1999) indicate a clear genetic contribution to BN. The knowledge gained from the extensive studies dealing with the neurobiology of BN is quite limited, as many of the reported abnor-malities might be secondary to the chaotic eating habits of the patients and a long history of dieting.

Environmental risk factors for BN include family history of any eating disorder; depres-sion and obesity; experiences such as family dieting or being teased; premorbid character-istics such as low self-esteem, early menarche, and low perceived social support from the family; as well as a narrow repertoire of cop-ing. These factors have been shown in a large number of studies (Fairburn & Harrison, 2003; Ghaderi, 2001). Much more research is needed on the pathogenesis of BN before any firm conclusions can be made.

Impact of Bulimia Nervosa

Bulimia nervosa is a severe and relatively chronic condition that is associated with a poorer quality of life (P. Hay, 2003), comorbid psychopathology (Kaye, Bulik, Thornton, Barbarich, & Masters, 2004; O'Brien & Vin-cent, 2003), and serious medical complications such as electrolyte disturbance (Wolfe, Metz-ger, Levine, & Jimerson, 2001) and dental damage in cases with frequent vomiting, laxative, or diuretic abuse (Ashcroft & Milosevic, 2007).

As mentioned earlier, no more than 50% achieve full and lasting recovery 10 years after the presentation of the disorders (Keel et al., 2000). However, despite its negative psycho-logical, social, and medical consequences, only a small portion of those suffering from BN seek professional treatment (Fairburn, Cooper, Doll, Norman, & O'Connor, 2000), which might be due to the fear of stigma, low mental health literacy, shame, fear of change, or cost (Hepworth & Paxton, 2007). Longer duration of BN, defined as the time between the onset of symptoms and the first treatment intervention, might lead to a less favorable treatment outcome (Reas, Williamson, Martin, & Zucker, 2000). Successful treatment of BN is not easily achieved. We need to enhance awareness of the available empirically sup-ported treatments to increase the number of patients who seek help as early as possible.

EMPIRICALLY SUPPORTED TREATMENTS FOR BULIMIA NERVOSA

Unlike anorexia nervosa, where the current state of research on its treatment is character-ized by paucity and methodological limitations in available studies, there are a substantial number of studies comparing pharmacological, psychosocial, and combination treatments for BN to wait-list controls or placebo treatments; in some cases to each other. To date, 73 ran-domized controlled trials (RCTs) have been conducted on the treatment of BN. In addition, several meta-analysis (Ghaderi & Andersson, 1999; Hartmann, Herzog, & Drinkmann, 1992; Lewandowski, Gebing, Anthony, & O'Brien, 1997; Nakash-Eisikovits, Dierberger, &

Westen, 2002; Whittal, Agras, & Gould, 1999), systematic reviews (Bacaltchuk & Hay, 2003; Bacaltchuk, Hay, & Mari, 2000; Bacaltchuk, Trefiglio, de-Oliveira, Lima, & Mari, 1999; Bacaltchuk et al., 2000b; P. J. Hay, Bacaltchuk, & Stefano, 2004), and practice guidelines (American Psychiatric Association Work Group on Eating Disorders Washington, 2000; National Institute for Clinical Excellence [NICE], 2004) are also available.

Before reviewing the current body of knowledge on the treatment of BN to suggest guidelines for evidence-based practice, we need to briefly reconsider what is suggested to be an empirically supported treatment and how we should weigh different types of studies (e.g., RCTs vs. single-subject experiments) in deciding whether a treatment meets the criteria for being empirically supported.

Defining Evidence

Chambless and Hollon (1998) suggest that efficacy trials should be given the greatest weight in evaluating benefits of a given treatment. However, they also noted that such trials should be followed by effectiveness research in clinical settings and with various populations. They also suggested that for a treatment to be considered efficacious, it has to meet the criteria for efficacy (i.e., significantly better than a wait-list or no-treatment control group) in at least two RCTs, which are conducted by two independent research groups. If the treatment in this same manner is compared to placebo or another bona fide treatment, then it might be considered efficacious and specific in its mechanisms of action. Treatments that are found to be superior to other rival alternative interventions are more highly valued. Similarly, treatments that show efficacy in three or more independently conducted single-subject designs, with at least three participants in each study, are considered efficacious.

The next, lower level of evidence (i.e., possibly efficacious) is assigned when only one study supports a treatment's efficacy, or when all the available studies are performed by only one research group. The parallel of this level of evidence based on studies with single-subject design is when only one such study, with at least three participants, has been conducted.

A large number of clinicians and scientists have criticized the definitions, procedures, or underlying assumptions in identifying empirically supported treatments and highlighted the limitations of this approach (Garfield, 1998; Westen, Novotny, & Thompson-Brenner, 2004). In addition, the actual interpretation and use of this set of criteria as well as the resulting conclusions in developing clinical guidelines for the treatment of eating disorders has also been criticized (Wilson & Shafran, 2005). An alternative set of definitions for different levels of evidence and formulating clinical guidelines has been used by the Guideline Development Group, convened by the National Collaborating Center for Mental Health for Developing Clinical Guidelines, commissioned by the National Institute for Clinical Excellence (NICE) in the United Kingdom (NICE, 2004). There are four levels of evidence, and recommendations are assigned a grade from A (strong empirical support from well-conducted randomized trials) to C (expert opinion without strong empirical data). The first level of evidence that is obtained from a single, high-quality RCT or a meta-analysis of RCTs receives the highest grade (A). The NICE guidelines are methodologically rigorous and are in contrast with the Practice Guideline for Eating Disorders of the American Psychiatric Association, which does not detail criteria for evaluating supporting research (Wilson & Shafran, 2005). There are different opinions about what kinds of studies should comprise the basis for different levels of evidence, and to what extent. Likewise, the transparency in evaluating the research varies substantially. Given the rigor of the methodology used in forming the NICE guidelines and the inclusive and ambitious work in collecting and evaluating research on the treatment of BN in a transparent way, the focus of this chapter will be on identifying and evaluating the more recent research that has been produced after the studies considered in the NICE guidelines. Its focus will also be to weigh, as well as to synthesize, the evidence from research in total to suggest guidelines for evidence-based treatment of BN. Consequently, although the NICE review included studies until early 2004, electronic searches were made using major bibliographic databases (MEDLINE and PsycINFO) from January 2003 to August 2008, in addition to Cochrane Database for Systematic Reviews for treatment studies of BN. The same search filters that were used in the NICE review search strategy were used in this research, though restricted to BN and related items (for a detailed description, see Appendix 8 in complete NICE guidelines; NICE, 2004). Studies already included in the NICE review were excluded.

Thus, evidence-based practice for the treatment of BN suggested here will take into account the number and quality of studies conducted after the NICE review in order to decide whether any new conclusions can be reached by considering factors such as independence of studies and allegiance effect when the design of the study permits its evaluation; the magnitude, generalization, and maintenance of treatment effects in terms of effect size of both specific and general psychopathology of BN; the proportion of patients in full and partial remission at follow-ups; and the proportion of patients who relapse. Furthermore, costs of the treatment, the generalization of outcomes from treatment trials to clinical practice, as well as the ease of dissemination, will be briefly discussed.

In the following text, available evidence for specific psychological, pharmacological, and combinational treatment of BN will be presented along with the aforementioned dimensions (i.e., rate of remission, relapse, cost, dissemination, etc.). Treatments with a substantial number of experimental trials of their efficacy (i.e., RCTs and single-subject design), quasi-experimental or other studies with weaker designs, and consensus/expert panel recommendations are not considered. Studies comparing the efficacy and effectiveness of different treatments to each other will also be reviewed. After a critical review of the current body of knowledge on treatment of BN, guidelines for evidence-based practice in the treatment of BN will be presented.

PSYCHOLOGICAL TREATMENTS

Cognitive Behavior Therapy for Bulimia Nervosa (CBT-BN)

Given the large number of RCTs comparing CBT-BN with no treatment (wait-list), placebo, medication, other forms of psychotherapy, the combination of medication and CBT-BN, as well as dismantling studies of CBT included and evaluated in the NICE review, only the outcome of RCTs, meta-analysis, and systematic reviews of the studies completed after the NICE review (i.e., not included in NICE) will be considered in the following. There are almost no studies using single-subject design methodology for investigating the efficacy of CBT-BN.

NICE Guidelines and Later Developments

CBT-BN Versus Wait-List Control or Placebo

Review of evidence in the NICE guidelines concludes CBT-BN to be clinically and significantly superior to wait-list control in terms of remission from binge eating (i.e., cessation of binge eating) and reduction in mean frequency of binge eating and purging by the end of treatment. CBT-BN is also clinically and significantly superior to wait-list control with regard to the mean depression score by the end of the treatment. In a large number of studies, CBT-BN has been shown to be effective in reducing both the specific and the general psychopathology of BN. The effect sizes are large, and at least three methodologically sound RCTs have been identified and included in the review of each of the core symptoms or general psychopathology of BN. Given the current state of our knowledge on the course of BN and efficacy of CBT-BN, therapist-delivered CBT-BN has not been compared to a wait-list or placebo condition since the NICE review, with one exception (Fairburn et al., 2009). Logically, the later studies have been designed to move our knowledge forward by addressing questions raised from previous research, focusing on ways of improving CBT-BN (Fairburn et al., 2009; Ghaderi, 2006b), comparing its efficacy in group versus individual format (Chen et al., 2003), its efficacy in a sequential treatment in group versus individual format (Nevonen & Broberg, 2006), and the efficacy of face-to-face therapy versus telemedicine (Mitchell et al., 2008).

Other studies have addressed important issues, such as whether a graded dose of CBT-BN can be useful with pharmacotherapy in a stepped care format (Schmidt et al., 2004), or how effective pure and guided self-help is in different settings such as primary care (Banasiak, Paxton, & Hay, 2005; F. A. Carter, McIntosh, Joyce, Sullivan, & Bulik, 2003; Ghaderi & Scott, 2003; Robinson & Serfaty, 2008; Walsh, Fairburn, Mickley, Sysko, & Parides, 2004). Some such studies have compared CBT-based self-help to family therapy for adolescents (Schmidt et al., 2007). Studies on the self-help version of CBT-BN will be described in the section of CBT-based self-help later in this chapter.

When CBT fails, given the lack of additional effects of other therapies (e.g., interpersonal psychotherapy or pharmacotherapy) delivered after CBT (Mitchell et al., 2002), a viable option to improve the outcome of CBT would be to enhance CBT-BN—an effort that was made by the Oxford group and resulted in an enhanced version of CBT-BN, named CBT-E (enhanced), and that increased levels of individualization as tested by Ghaderi (2006a). Outcome of the recently completed Oxford-Liecester trial testing the efficacy of CBT-E is very encouraging. One hundred and fifty-four patients with any eating disorders, excluding patients with a BMI below 17.5, were randomized into the broad or focused version of CBT-E, or into an 8-week long waiting list. Those in the wait-list condition were, after reevaluation, randomized to receive CBT-E in either broad or focused form. Data were then analyzed using intention to treat and closed follow-ups were conducted up to 60 weeks after the end of treatment. Given heterogeneity of the sample, with not all the patients reporting binge eating or purging, global changes in eating disorder severity was used as the main outcome measure. It was defined as a reduction in mean global Eating Disorders Examination (EDE) score and a normative categorical outcome variable in terms of achieving a level of eating disorder feature less than one standard deviation (SD) above the community mean, which is a highly conservative standard. At the end of the 20 weeks of treatment, 52.7% of those with BN and 53.3% of those with EDNOS had an EDE score within one SD above the community mean. The corresponding figures at the 60-week follow-up were 61.4% and 45.7%, respectively; which, if compared to earlier trials of CBT-BN (e.g., the largest and the most rigorous one) (Agras, Walsh, Fairburn, Wilson, & Kraemer, 2000), is a considerably better outcome. However, direct comparisons between the new and old treatment manual is necessary to substantiate this conclusion. Furthermore, there were no overall significant differences between the broad and the focused version of CBT-E, with exception of patients with substantial additional psychopathology of the type treated in the broad version (i.e., clinical perfectionism, mood intolerance, etc.) achieving better outcome. The opposite was the case among the remaining patients. The authors conclude that the simpler focused form of CBT-E should be viewed as the default form, since it is easier to learn and implement, and that the broader form is reserved for marked additional psychopathology that are addressed in that form of CBT-E.

Increased level of individualization (Ghaderi, 2006b) compared to standard CBT-BN, that in itself includes some level of individualization, resulted in some significant differences at the end of the treatment by favoring the individualized condition. However, the 18-month follow-up analyses showed only slight differences between the conditions. This trial proved to be similar to the comparison between the focused and extended version of the CBT-E in the Oxford-Leicester trial (Fairburn et al., 2009), with only a few differences between the conditions for more complex cases. Independent replications with larger samples than the one in Ghaderi (2006b) ($N = 50$) and blind assessments are needed before any firm conclusions can be drawn.

Another interesting and new study in this context is the one conducted by Mitchell et al. (2004) on the prevention of relapse among patients who might feel or fear a recurrence of symptoms after a course of CBT-BN. They were invited to receive additional therapy visits whenever they felt or feared such recurrence of symptoms. None of the 30 subjects who relapsed during the follow-up sought additional treatment visits. Although many of these relapses are not of clinical severity, some are. More research on potent relapse strategies is needed.

Chen and colleagues (2003) compared the efficacy of CBT-BN in group versus individual format. Forty-four of the 60 patients who were randomized into group or individual CBT completed the treatment with no statistical differences between the outcome of the two conditions. Methodological shortcomings such as low power and the lack of independent (blind) assessment limit the generalizability of the conclusions from that study. Hopefully, future research will address these limitations.

Another interesting study, which was completed after the publication of the NICE guidelines, investigated the effect of sequenced individual versus group treatment of patients with BN (Nevonen & Broberg, 2006). Eighty-six patients were matched and randomized into group or individual treatment and received

10 sessions of CBT, followed by 13 sessions of IPT. The percentage of patients who remitted and recovered was equivalent between the conditions, although some significant differences were found favoring the individual treatment, similar to the study by Chen and colleagues (2003). This is a novel approach, in need of further replication. The significance of interpersonal difficulties among patients with BN has been considered in the latest version of CBT-BN; that is, CBT-E. It contains a module for work on interpersonal difficulties when the analyses and observations in the early course of the therapy indicate that interpersonal issues might maintain BN.

It should be noted that, despite being the most studied and the most effective treatment of BN thus far (see comparisons between CBT-BN and other psychotherapies or pharmacotherapy later in the text), less than 50% of patients achieve a full and lasting recovery following CBT-BN. The treatment of BN needs to be enhanced substantially. CBT-E is a promising development, but further evaluations and improvements are needed. In addition, a considerable number of the patients relapse during the first 6 months following the end of psychological treatments, although the relapse rate is markedly lower in CBT-BN compared to medication (Bacaltchuk, Hay, & Trefiglio, 2001; P. J. Hay et al., 2004; NICE, 2004). On the other hand, a good number of patients improve from posttreatment to follow-ups. The mechanisms underlying relapse need to be studied and further improvements need to be made in order to increase the total rate of response to CBT-BN.

CBT-BN Versus Other Psychological Treatments

Based on meta-analyses and systematic reviews, there is insufficient evidence to conclude whether there is a clinically significant difference between CBT-BN on one hand and behavior therapy (BT)—CBT combined with exposure and response prevention, psychodynamic psychotherapy, or focal supportive psychotherapy—on the other hand, regarding the main outcome variables (i.e., remission from or reduction in mean frequency of binge eating and purging) by the end of the treatment or at the follow-up. However, there is some evidence that CBT-BN is superior to psychodynamic psychotherapy on mean depression scores and general psychiatric symptoms by the end of treatment. A more interesting finding is the strong evidence showing CBT-BN to be superior to Interpersonal Psychotherapy (IPT) on remission from binge eating and purging by the end of treatment, as well as the fact that no such difference exists at the 1-year follow-up. CBT has not been compared to other psychological treatments during the last few years following the NICE review.

CBT-BN Versus Pharmacological Treatments

Taken together, the meta-analyses and reviews of RCTs comparing CBT-BN to antidepressant medication provide some evidence, albeit limited, of the superiority of CBT-BN (i.e., clinically significant difference in favor of CBT-BN) with regard to remission from binge eating and purging (for details, see NICE guidelines). On the other hand, there is insufficient evidence to determine whether there is a clinically significant difference between the two treatments in terms of reduction in mean frequency of binge eating or purging, mean depression score, or general psychiatric symptoms at the end of treatment. Likewise, there is insufficient evidence to determine whether differences are maintained at the follow-up, and if more sophisticated studies with longer-term closed follow-ups are needed. However, available evidence shows that the number of patients remitting is significantly higher for CBT-BN than for antidepressant treatment (see NICE guidelines). The systematic review also showed that the relative risk of no remission by antidepressant treatment versus CBT was 1.28 (NICE, 2004). Over the last 5 years since the publication of the NICE guidelines in 2004, no studies have

been conducted on the relative efficacy of CBT-BN versus antidepressants, nor have there been any systematic efforts to investigate the long-term outcomes and dropout rates in closed follow-ups. Lack of long-term follow-up is one of the major shortcomings in the research literature, and such studies are yet to be conducted and reported. The studies published between 2003 and 2008 have focused on more sophisticated questions, such as short- and long-term pharmacotherapy combined with a stepped care approach to psychotherapy (Schmidt et al., 2004). They have also been focusing on some more clinically important questions such as the efficacy of pharmacotherapy and CBT-based self-help in primary care (Walsh et al., 2004), as well as the efficacy of different types of selective serotonin reuptake inhibitors (SSRI) compared to placebo or each other (Erzegovesi et al., 2004; Hedges et al., 2003; Leombruni et al., 2006; Nickel et al., 2005).

CBT-BN in Combination With Medication Versus CBT-BN or Medication Alone

More research is needed to determine if CBT-BN in combination with medication might be superior to CBT-BN or medication alone. Although there is limited evidence from a couple of studies showing that the combination might be statistically superior to CBT-BN alone with regard to the frequency of binge eating at the end of the treatment, the results are unlikely to be clinically significant, according to the NICE review. Interestingly, accumulated knowledge from the conducted studies thus far suggests that it is unlikely that there is a clinically significant difference between CBT-BN alone and the combination of CBT-BN and medication with regard to mean depression score at the end of the treatment.

CBT-Based Self-Help of BN

The NICE review included four studies using pure or guided self-help in the analysis of its efficacy and effectiveness. The evidence suggested that a clinically significant difference between pure self-help and wait-list, in terms of remission from binge eating and purging, was unlikely. Evidence for determining whether guided self-help could have an impact on the remission rate was insufficient. Likewise, evidence was insufficient or non-existent to determine whether pure or guided self-help could have any impact on frequency of binge eating and purging, as well as an impact on severity of depression symptoms or interpersonal functioning by the end of treatment. From the available studies, it could not be concluded whether guided self-help differs from pure self-help on remission of binge eating by the end of treatment. However, guided self-help was superior to pure self-help in terms of reduction in mean frequency of binge eating at posttreatment. Since the NICE review, another trial has been conducted to investigate the efficacy of guided self-help for BN in primary care (Banasiak et al., 2005), with promising outcomes in contrast to the results of the study by Walsh and colleagues (2004) included in NICE. Two studies with small samples have been conducted to compare pure and guided self-help for BN (Ghaderi, 2006a; Ghaderi & Scott, 2003). One study has tested efficacy of CBT-based self-help by combining self-help with guidance and use of a discussion forum via the Internet (Ljotsson et al., 2007), while another study investigated the use of e-mail as the support channel in combination with self-help (Robinson & Serfaty, 2008). Initial results from a European multicenter study to determine the effectiveness and feasibility of an online self-help treatment support program for BN has also been reported (Carrard et al., 2006). In addition, another study focused on the feasibility and efficacy of a CD-ROM-based CBT self-help (Bara-Carril et al., 2004), and one recently completed trial (Steele & Wade, 2008) evaluated the effect of reducing perfectionism through self-help as a potential treatment target for individuals with BN. Finally, a study by Schmidt and colleagues

(2006) investigated whether personalized feedback would improve the outcome of CBT-based self-help for BN.

Banasiak et al. (2005) investigated efficacy of guided self-help delivered by general practitioners in the normal course of their practice by comparing it to a delayed treatment control condition among 109 patients with full or subthreshold BN who were randomized to one of the conditions. Patients in the treatment condition received support and guidance during 17 weeks. Both groups were then reassessed 1 week later, as well as 3 and 6 months after the end of the self-help intervention. A 60% reduction in mean frequency of binge eating was observed in the guided self-help group, and 28% achieved remission from binge eating and purging. The corresponding values in the delayed treatment group were 6% and 11%. Furthermore, treatment gains were maintained at the 3- and 6-month follow-ups.

Ghaderi (2006a) and Ghaderi and Scott (2003) compared efficacy of pure and guided CBT-based self-help in two different (but small) samples of patients with full or subthreshold BN and binge eating disorder ($N = 31$ and 29, respectively). No significant differences were found between pure and guided self-help in these studies, which might be due to lack of power. Treatment completers reported improvements that were similar in magnitude to those seen in CBT-BN, but the intention to treat analyses showed modest improvements that were sustained at the 6-month follow-up.

In the study by Ljótsson et al. (2007), 73 patients with full or subthreshold BN and binge eating disorder were randomized to either a wait-list control condition or to receive 12 weeks of CBT-based self-help in combination with support via the Internet and use of an Internet discussion forum. Patients reported marked improvement after 12 weeks of self-help compared to the control group on both primary and secondary outcome measures. Intent-to-treat analyses revealed that 37%

(46% among completers) had no binge eating or purging at the end of the treatment, and a considerable number of patients achieved clinically significant improvements on most of the other measures as well. Results were maintained at the 6-month follow-up and provide evidence to support the continued use and development of self-help programs. Analyses of outcome for patients with full diagnosis of BN showed similar outcome (i.e., 43% full recovery at the 6-month follow-up assessment). Interestingly, the corresponding level of recovery for patients with subthreshold BN was 40% at the 6-month follow-up, which lends some support to the transdiagnostic perspective on eating disorders (Fairburn et al., 2003).

In the study by Robinson and Serfaty (2008), 97 patients with BN, binge eating disorders, or EDNOS were randomized to therapist-administered e-mail therapy for BN, unsupported self-directed writing, or a waiting list control condition. Posttreatment data were available for only 63% of the patients, with significantly fewer of those who received an active treatment meeting the criteria for an eating disorder at the follow-up compared to the wait-list condition. The study was unfortunately compromised by its limited power, the use of less stringent methods of assessment of eating disorders, and the high dropout rate.

Initial results (i.e., the Swiss sample $N = 41$) from the multicenter European study of self-help (Carrard et al., 2006) are positive, but preliminary. Patients were supported through three face-to-face interviews with a therapist and weekly e-mail contact. By the end of treatment, patients reported significant improvements in overall symptomatology according to Symptom Checklist-90 and on all the subscales of the Eating Disorders Inventory. Given the difficulties in measuring the core symptoms of BN through self-report measures and the preliminary nature of the results, the outcome of the study should be interpreted with caution. The potential of the delivery of self-help and support via the

Internet; the possibilities to use simple, but highly illustrative techniques such as graphs based on patients' self-report showing the relation between the level of regular eating and the frequency of binge eating during the course of the self-help treatment; and other interactive means of providing guidance to the patients makes the delivery of self-help through the Internet an area worth much more attention and research.

Bara-Carril et al. (2004) investigated the feasibility and efficacy of a CD-ROM-based CBT self-help among 47 patients with full or subthreshold BN. Unfortunately, the study was compromised by the lack of a suitable control group and the use of self-report only to measure the core symptoms of eating disorders. Due to ease of delivery and preliminary encouraging results, the efficacy of CBT-based self-help via CD-ROM should be further investigated.

A recent study focusing on young patients compared family therapy with CBT-based self-help to treat full or subthreshold BN among adolescents (Schmidt et al., 2007). Although there were no differences between the treatments at the 12-month follow-up, the adolescents receiving self-help achieved a significantly greater reduction in binge eating compared to those in the family therapy condition. Guided self-help was perceived as more acceptable, had lower costs, and resulted in a more rapid reduction in core symptoms of BN and EDNOS compared to family therapy, which lends additional support to the efficacy of guided self-help as a first-step treatment of BN.

Finally, Schmidt et al. (2006) investigated the potential additional effect of personalized feedback to CBT-based self-help in an RCT where 61 patients received 14 sessions of self-help with or without added personalized feedback on current physical and psychological status, risk and problems, and variables facilitating or hindering change. The personalized feedback was delivered in a number of ways to maximize the outcome. The added feedback improved the outcome by reducing self-induced vomiting and dietary restriction more effectively by the end of the treatment; however, the differences were less salient at the 6-month follow-up, with no changes concerning the frequency of binge eating or excessive exercising. Although this was a pilot study with low power, considerable drop out, and use of self-report measures instead of investigator-based measures of eating pathology, it targets a very important question in the era of evidence-based practice. More studies are needed to help us know whether further individualization improves the outcome of our (currently) most effective treatments.

In a recently completed trial (Steele & Wade, 2008), 48 patients with full or subthreshold BN were randomly assigned to receive eight sessions of support for using CBT-based self-help focusing on either CBT for perfectionism, CBT for BN, or a placebo (mindfulness-based cognitive therapy for depression). The authors used a baseline period (6 weeks) prior to pretreatment assessment to evaluate potential changes in the absence of any treatment. No significant changes were found during the baseline period, and no significant changes were observed between the treatment conditions or time × condition interactions by the end of treatment or at the 6-month follow-up assessment. However, all of the conditions resulted in significant time effects and improvements on core psychopathology of BN. Despite some limitations such as low power and short duration of the self-help treatment, this is the first study to investigate nonspecific factors involved in guided self-help for BN and the first study to target only perfectionism in the treatment of whole symptomatology BN. It warrants future dismantling studies, investigating therapy processes and the association between perfectionism, mindfulness, and bulimic symptoms.

In addition to the aforementioned studies, the result of a systematic review of self-help treatments for recurrent binge eating (i.e., for BN and binge eating disorder) indicated that patients treated with self-help had a reduced number of binge eating episodes at the end of treatment (Stefano, Bacaltchuk, Blay, & Hay, 2006). However, this review only included studies between 1994 and 2004, most of which have been evaluated in the NICE review.

Conclusions

The current body of knowledge supports efficacy of CBT-BN for the treatment of BN. Since the NICE review, a good number of self-help studies have been conducted, and the more recent data corroborates the conclusions made in NICE. CBT-based self-help is suggested to be a viable first step in the treatment of BN.

INTERPERSONAL PSYCHOTHERAPY FOR BN (IPT-BN)

Interpersonal Psychotherapy (IPT; Klerman, Weissman, Rounsaville, & Chevron, 1995) is an evidence-based treatment for depression. The IPT was adapted for the treatment of BN by Chris Fairburn (Fairburn, 1997), initially as a control condition in a trial of CBT-BN (Fairburn et al., 1991). It proved to be as effective as CBT-BN at the 1-year follow-up, although it did significantly worse than CBT-BN directly at posttreatment. The IPT-BN has been compared to a wait-list control condition in one study (Wilfley et al., 1993), to CBT-BN in a few, very well-conducted studies (Agras et al., 2000; Fairburn et al., 1991), and in a sequential treatment of CBT and IPT (Nevonen & Broberg, 2006). IPT-BN should also be compared to pharmacotherapy and a placebo control condition in future studies. The relatively recent study by Nevonen and Broberg (2006), where the effect of CBT-BN followed by IPT-BN was investigated in individual versus group format, does not permit any conclusions as to efficacy of IPT-BN in itself. More research is needed on the efficacy, effectiveness, and mechanisms of change in IPT for BN, as it produces similar outcomes as CBT-BN at the 1-year follow-up, but it seems to operate through other pathways and mechanisms than those targeted in CBT-BN.

The NICE Guidelines conclude that IPT-BN could be viewed as an alternative to CBT-BN (Evidence level B), but the patients should be informed that it takes up to 12 months to achieve results comparable to CBT-BN.

Conclusions

More research has been conducted on CBT-BN than IPT-BN, both before and after the NICE review. The IPT has been combined with CBT in a sequential study, and their combination showed promising results both in individual and group format. Paucity of research on IPT for BN during the last 5 years and the lack of studies showing higher efficacy of other psychological treatments besides CBT and IPT for BN (see the following section) makes it plausible to retain the conclusions made by NICE.

OTHER PSYCHOLOGICAL TREATMENTS

There is insufficient evidence to consider other psychological treatments as clinically and significantly efficacious in the treatment of BN. Most of the studies investigating the outcome of such treatments (e.g., psychodynamically or psychoanalytically oriented psychotherapies, symbol drama, and body awareness therapies) are case reports, uncontrolled trials, or in a few cases, RCTs (e.g., Garner et al., 1993) with methodological shortcomings such as low power, high selection of patients, and lack of long-term follow-ups that significantly limit the conclusions that can be made.

An interesting new development that warrants further research is the positive effects of a very brief intervention called Healthy Dieting for BN (Burton & Stice, 2006). In this study, 85 patients with full or subthreshold BN were randomized into a six session healthy dieting intervention or a wait list condition, and were assessed through a 3-month follow-up. Those receiving the healthy dieting program, in comparison to the wait-list condition, showed significant improvements with regards to BN symptoms, and the results were maintained at the 20-week follow-up assessment. By the 3-month follow-up, 35% of the intervention participants were in remission, versus 10% of the controls. The effect sizes with regard to decrease in binge eating and purging in this study were large to average and are almost comparable to those found in the full CBT trials of BN (Ghaderi & Andersson, 1999). Consequently, given the outcome and the short duration of the treatment, independent and further research with larger samples and longer follow-ups is definitely warranted.

Conclusions Regarding Psychological Treatments

The current body of knowledge supports efficacy of CBT-BN and IPT for the treatment of BN. There is currently insufficient evidence to recommend any other psychosocial interventions for the treatment of BN. Since the NICE review, a good number of self-help studies has been conducted, and the more recent data corroborate conclusions made in NICE. The CBT-based self-help is suggested to be a viable first step in the treatment of BN.

PSYCHOPHARMACOLOGICAL TREATMENTS

Antidepressants are often prescribed for patients with BN, as they are more easily administered than psychotherapy in primary care (Fairburn, 2006).

According to the NICE review of empirical studies, until early 2004 there is some evidence, albeit limited, suggesting that anti-depressants (i.e., regardless of being SSRI, tricyclics, etc.) are superior to placebo (i.e., clinically significant different) in terms of remission from binge eating and purging by the end of the treatment. On the other hand, evidence for efficacy of antidepressants (SSRI and tricyclics) compared to placebo in terms of the clinical improvement (i.e., at least a 50% reduction in the frequency of binge eating or purging) is strong. Interestingly, although the review team found limited evidence for the superiority of tricyclics on mean depression score by the end of the treatment, there was insufficient evidence to determine whether SSRIs reduce the symptoms of depression by the end of treatment among patients with BN.

During the last few years, several studies have further investigated efficacy of SSRIs compared to placebo within the frame of more complex hypotheses, such as the relationship between 5-HTTLPR Polymorphism (showing no clear relationship) and treatment response to SSRI (Erzegovesi et al., 2004), or the efficacy of SSRI in primary care (Walsh et al., 2004). Unfortunately, the methodological shortcomings, such as the lack of a double-blind procedure in the study by Erzegovesi et al. (2004) and high drop out rate in the study by Walsh and colleagues (2004), limit the reliability of the potential conclusions based on the outcome of these studies. In another single-blind study, two slightly different kinds of SSRI (Fluoxetine vs. Citalopram) were compared to each other (Leombruni et al., 2006), both resulting in significant improve-ments in eating psychopathology and both resulting in similar drop out rates. By mea-suring different aspects of the eating and general psychopathology, the researchers observed that the efficacy profiles of the two drugs were not overlapping. They concluded that Citalopram might be more useful in depressed patients with BN, whereas Fluox-etine showed more specific effects on the core symptoms of bulimia. The relative efficacy of drugs should be investigated in more depth to consider potential specific effects of each drug on specific psychopathology of BN.

In a small RCT, one with 20 patients and only short-term evaluation, Sertraline proved to be superior to placebo in terms of reducing binge eating and purging (Milano, Petrella, Sabatino, & Capece, 2004). The magnitude of effects was similar to other antidepressant medications evaluated thus far.

Given the modest and, at best, moderate long-term outcome of antidepressants on BN, the efficacy of other drugs such as anticonvul-sants (e.g., Topiramate) has been investigated in a couple of studies (Hedges et al., 2003; Nickel et al., 2005). Both of these studies report promising results in terms of significant reduction in binge eating and purging (more than 50% reduction in dichotomous terms, not continuous) as well as improvement on meas-ures of quality of life, anxiety, body image, and depression. Notably, duration of treatment was short (10 weeks); no long-term follow-up data were reported; the sample size was small; and in both studies, the investigators chose to use less stringent measures than what is considered to be the gold standard in the assessment of eating disorders (i.e., the Eating Disorders Examination). More research is needed to determine whether Topiramate might be con-sidered a viable option in the pharmacological treatment of BN, as the magnitude of effects are similar to those found in SSRI treatment of BN.

In an ambitious and interesting study, Schmidt and colleagues (2004) investigated the short- and long-term outcome of Fluvox-amine (an SSRI) combined with a stepped care approach to psychotherapy. This was a 1-year, prospectively randomized, double-blind, placebo-controlled, three-way parallel-group multicenter study. The author concluded that the use of Fluvoxamine in the treatment of patients with BN could not be recommended due to the limited evidence of benefit, problems of toleration, and doubts about the safety of the drug among patients with BN. Interestingly, Erzegovesi and colleagues (2004) concluded that Fluvoxamine showed significant efficacy in the short-term treatment of BN, a finding that might be related more to the measures used than to the clinically significant changes among the patients compared to placebo.

Conclusions

Research on pharmacotherapy has mostly been focused on further improvement of SSRI as well as investigation of the effect of some other therapeutic agents such as Topiramate, which is an antiepiletptic drug. The findings regarding Fluvoxamine are mixed. The findings regarding Citalopram and Sertraline are encouraging and in need of further evaluation. Most of the studies conducted after the NICE review have considerable methodological shortcomings, and the result of the most rigorous one (Schmidt et al., 2004) is negative (i.e., Fluvoxamine cannot be recommended in the treatment of patients with BN).

Other Treatments (New Developments)

In a case report, Hausmann and colleagues (2004) described use of Repetitive Transcranial Magnetic Stimulation (rTMS) with a depressed patient with BN. After 10 sessions of rTMS, the patient recovered completely from binge and purge symptoms as assessed by the Binge-Purge Diary. The same research group reported on the outcome of rTMS in a single-center, randomized, double-blind, sham-controlled trial with 14 patients suffering from BN (Walpoth et al., 2007). The average number of binge episodes declined significantly in both groups, showing that rTMS does not exert additional benefit over placebo.

RELATIVE EFFICACY OF PSYCHOSOCIAL TREATMENTS TO PHARMACOLOGICAL TREATMENTS

As described earlier, there is evidence suggesting a clinically significant difference between CBT-BN and pharmacological treatments, favoring CBT-BN with regard to remission from binge eating and purging. Further studies are needed to investigate the long-term outcome and relative efficacy of CBT-BN compared to drugs. Another important conclusion in NICE is that drugs are not as acceptable or as well-tolerated as psychological treatments. Furthermore, due to increased risk of self-harm among patients with BN, the safety and risk of overdose should be considered thoroughly before drugs are prescribed. Other variables, such as terminating the treatment early due to adverse effects of the drug and the need to switch medication in an effort to sustain a remission of symptoms, a lack of data on long-term outcome of medication on core symptoms of BN, as well as high rate of relapse when medication is terminated, lead to rather tentative and unfavorable conclusions. Taking all the aforementioned points into account, CBT-BN was given the highest grade of evidence (grade A) compared to SSRI—specifically Fluoxetine (grade C)—in the NICE evaluation of the treatment of BN. Current research does not provide any data that lead to revision of these recommendations.

The Maintenance of Treatment Effects

Only a few studies of the treatment of BN include long-term follow-ups, and an even smaller number have used closed follow-ups. Relapse rates between 30% and 50% have been reported for successfully treated patients after 6 months to 6 years of follow-up (American Psychiatric Association Work Group on Eating Disorders Washington, 2000), although the relapse rates of well-conducted CBT-BN trials are substantially smaller (Agras et al., 2000). The results are markedly better maintained in CBT-BN compared to medication as concluded in the NICE review, and there is still no evidence of superiority or cost-effectiveness of combined psychotherapy and medication. More studies are needed to compare IPT with Fluoxetine or other antidepressant medications in terms of maintenance of treatment effects;

although the natural course of action in IPT, as shown in trials of CBT and IPT, would probably show a steady improvement from post-treatment to the 1-year follow-up, while a significant rate of relapse is expected in the medication condition. However, the initial level of improvement (i.e., posttreatment) is expected to be higher in the medication condition, and longer follow-ups than 1 year are needed to make a balanced and informed evaluation of the comparative maintenance of outcome in these treatments.

The Generalization of Outcomes From Treatment Trials to Clinical Practice

In a review of several meta-analysis (Butler, Chapman, Forman, & Beck, 2006), the mean effect size of efficacy studies of BN was 1.27 (Cohen's d) with a standard deviation of 0.11, but very few studies of the effectiveness of psychological treatments of BN have been conducted thus far—mostly the simplified versions of CBT (e.g., J. C. Carter & Fairburn, 1998; Durand & King, 2003). The mean effect of these few effectiveness studies shows a slightly smaller effect size (Cohen's d around 0.8) than efficacy studies summarized by Öst (2008) (mean effect size: 1.2). One study using data from naturalistic samples where clinicians with various theoretical orientations treat patients with bulimic symptoms (Thompson-Brenner & Westen, 2005) shows that the treatment in the community is substantially longer than what is prescribed in manuals, due to substantial comorbidity. Unfortunately, the study was compromised due to lack of systematic observations, diversity in the methods and modes of assessment and evaluation, as well as insufficient information regarding treatment integrity, quality, and fidelity.

Some systematic studies of the clinical effectiveness of psychological treatments have been conducted with regard to other psychiatric disorders such as social phobia (Gaston, Abbott, Rapee, & Neary, 2006), showing that treatments that have been tested in RCTs are potentially transportable to private practice settings. The review of CBT effectiveness in clinical settings for other psychiatric disorders show comparable effects as in efficacy studies, and in some cases show higher effect sizes in clinical settings (e.g., for conduct disorder) than in efficacy studies (Öst, 2008). Much more research is needed before any reliable conclusions can be made regarding the generalization of outcome from treatment trials of BN to clinical practice. With regards to antidepressant medication, the NICE review concluded that clinical effectiveness of antidepressants does not depend on the qualification of the prescribing doctor.

The Ease of Dissemination of Effective Treatments

In the treatment of BN, medication has the advantage of being easier to disseminate compared to psychological treatments (Fairburn, 2006). However, given the modest effect of SSRI in primary care, as shown by Walsh and colleagues (2004), and the uncertain long-term outcomes, high rate of relapse, as well as the higher acceptability of psychological treatments compared to medication, the dissemination of CBT-BN and IPT-BN needs to be investigated. Guided self-help based on CBT is a promising treatment, not only because of its outcome according to efficacy trials, but also because it allows for more adequate dissemination in areas lacking specialty resources (Agras & Robinson, 2008). The CBT is underutilized in clinical practice (Wilson, 2005), and methods for a wider dissemination of evidence-based treatments should be developed and studied (Wilfley & Cohen, 1997).

Cost-Effectiveness

Cost of the treatments in relation to the outcome and the relapse rate is an important issue. CBT-BN is more costly than antidepressant treatment. The NICE review estimated the incremental cost per successfully treated patient with BN to be somewhere between £4,126.41 and £4,942.23 (or between $6,631.43 and $7,939.55), depending on whether the medication is prescribed in primary care or in secondary care by physicians with different levels of expertise and cost. The analyses showed that the cost-effectiveness of CBT-BN would be high if the decision makers are willing to pay the incremental cost for an additional successfully treated individual. Cost-effectiveness would be even higher than what the current calculations suggest if the broader health service costs could be included in the analyses. Furthermore, the review team concluded that the combination therapy of CBT-BN and antidepressants is unlikely to be cost-effective. Mitchell, Peterson, and Agras (1999) explored the cost-effectiveness of BN treatment using hypothetical data and concluded that psychological treatments were likely to be cost-effective (Mitchell, Peterson, & Agras, 1999).

Research during recent years has, unfortunately, not added significantly to better the estimation of the cost-effectiveness analysis of psychotherapy versus pharmacotherapy or their combination. The NICE conclusions remain as they are, based on the best estimations thus far.

Use of Empirically Supported Treatments

A large survey among clinicians ($N = 698$) who specialize in the treatment of eating disorders and who were members of a large eating disorders organization showed that the majority identified other treatments than CBT or IPT as their primary approach to treatment (Simmons, Milnes, & Anderson, 2008). This finding is in line with an earlier study (Mussell et al., 2000), in which 60 psychologists, who reported that at least 5% of their typical psychotherapy caseload included patients with eating disorders, responded to a questionnaire. These psychologists were a subset of 500 randomly selected, doctoral level psychologists

(response rate $= 55\%$). Although CBT techniques are reported to be used frequently, the majority of the psychologists indicated they had not received training in the CBT or IPT for eating disorders (Mussell et al., 2000). This is in contrast with the findings in the Simmons et al. (2008) study, where the majority of respondents had received prior training in use of manual-based treatments. Other studies show that one of the major obstacles to the use of evidence-based treatments for BN and a stepped-care approach is that few therapists are trained in CBT or IPT (Dalle Grave, Ricca, & Todesco, 2001). Future research is needed to investigate the quality of the training and its relation to the use of evidence-based training. Evidence-based treatments are unavailable in most clinical service settings, and addressing the problems of increasing the dissemination of these treatments should be a priority (Wilson, Grilo, & Vitousek, 2007).

A NOTE ON THE META-ANALYSES OF GROUP DESIGNS

The results of meta-analysis of RCTs and practice guidelines that heavily focus on efficacy trials have been criticized for not being generalizable to the way psychotherapy is conducted in the real world (Goldfried & Wolfe, 1998; Westen & Morrison, 2001). The proposed constructive alternatives such as studying theoretically integrated interventions or using process research findings to improve treatment manuals for making therapy research more clinically valid (Goldfried & Wolfe, 1998) have barely been tested, with very few exceptions, such as the basic process that might guide the treatment of generalized anxiety disorders (Borkovec & Inz, 1990; Critchfield, Henry, Castonguay, & Borkovec, 2007). A good number of solutions to bridge the gap between clinical research and practice have been suggested by experienced psychotherapy researchers (Kazdin, 2008). Studying the mechanism of change in psychotherapy, investigating moderators and translating the results to clinical care, conducting qualitative studies in addition to quantitative investigations, use of systematic measure to evaluate patient progress in daily clinical practice, and direct collaborations between researchers and clinicians are among the suggestions to enhance the knowledge base and improve patient care. These suggestions also help to build the groundwork for forming evidence-base treatment. Many of these suggestions are in line with the true essence of the scientist-practitioner model (Hayes, Barlow, & Nelson-Gray, 1999), incorporating new insights from research and practice. More studies need to be conducted before this line of research can significantly inform evidence-based practice.

EVIDENCE-BASED PRACTICES

Results of studies after the NICE review corroborate the recommendations made in NICE (NICE, 2004). Data suggest that CBT-BN should be considered the first-line treatment of choice for BN. An alternative to CBT-BN is IPT. However, the patients should be informed that it takes 8 to 12 months for IPT to achieve results comparable with CBT. Self-help based on CBT in combination with professional guidance has also been shown to be a viable first step in the treatment of BN. Patients with BN should be encouraged to follow such a program, combined with support and guidance as a first step.

As an alternative to self-help, patients can also be offered a trial of an antidepressant drug. They should be informed that the long-term effects are unknown, that the risk of relapse is higher in medication compared to psychological treatments, and that any beneficial effects will be rapidly apparent. Topiramate, Citalopram, and Sertraline are potential candidates to Fluoxetine, but more research is needed before they can be established as safe and efficacious in the treatment of BN.

The treatment of the majority of patients with BN should be conducted in an outpatient setting. The NICE recommendations, in this regard (NICE, 2004) remain unchanged. Medical management of most patients with BN falls within routine medical care. In the case of patients with a high level of purging behavior (frequent self-induced vomiting and taking large quantities of laxatives), especially if they are also underweight, fluid and electrolyte balance should be checked routinely. The NICE recommendations in this regard should be followed.

The patients should be informed about what treatments are evidence-based with regard to BN. If a patient wishes to receive another kind of treatment with insufficient knowledge on its efficacy and effectiveness, then such a treatment (psychological or pharmacological) should be conducted in light of rigorous and continuous clinical assessment. A lack of significant progress, defined in terms of reliable change (Jacobson & Truax, 1991) after about 20 sessions of psychotherapy and 12 weeks of pharmacotherapy, should be a marker for shifting to an evidence-based treatment. Well-established measures such as the Eating Disorder Examination (Z. Cooper, Cooper, & Fairburn, 1989), which is a semistructured interview, and its equivalent questionnaire (i.e., EDE-Q; Fairburn & Beglin, 1994), combined with some measure of quality of life, assessment of impairment due to BN, social adjustment, as well as depression and anxiety, should be routinely used in the treatment of BN in clinical practice.

Excellent books and treatment manuals are available for conducting CBT or IPT for BN (Fairburn, 1997, 2008; Fairburn, Marcus, & Wilson, 1993; Waller et al., 2007; Wilson & Pike, 1993), and several CBT-based self-help books can be used in combination with guidance and support as a first-step treatment of BN (P. J. Cooper, 1995; Fairburn, 1995b; Schmidt & Treasure, 1993). Accompanying these self-help books, guides for clinicians on how to provide support are also available (Fairburn,

1995a; Treasure & Schmidt, 1997). Finally, a very good resource on the assessment of eating disorders can be found in Mitchell and Peterson (2007), as well as in Fairburn (2008).

REFERENCES

Agras, W. S., & Robinson, A. H. (2008). Forty years of progress in the treatment of the eating disorders. *Nordic Journal of Psychiatry, 62*(Suppl. 47), 19–24.

Agras, W. S., Walsh, T., Fairburn, C. G., Wilson, G. T., & Kraemer, H. C. (2000). A multicenter comparison of cognitive-behavioral therapy and interpersonal psychotherapy for bulimia nervosa. *Archives of General Psychiatry, 57*, 459–466.

American Psychiatric Association. (1980). *Diagnostic and statistical manual of mental disorders* (3rd ed.). Washington, DC: Author.

American Psychiatric Association. (2000). *Diagnostic and statistical manual of mental disorders* (4th ed., text rev.). Washington, DC: Author.

American Psychiatric Association Work Group on Eating Disorders Washington, DC, U.S. (2000). Practice guideline for the treatment of patients with eating disorders (Revision). *American Journal of Psychiatry, 157*(Suppl. 1), 1–39.

Ashcroft, A., & Milosevic, A. (2007). The eating disorders: 1. Current scientific understanding and dental implications. *Dental Update, 34*, 544–546, 549–550, 553–554.

Bacaltchuk, J., & Hay, P. (2003). Antidepressants versus placebo for people with bulimia nervosa. *Cochrane Database of Systematic Reviews, 4*, Art. No. CD003391.

Bacaltchuk, J., Hay, P., & Mari, J. J. (2000). Antidepressants versus placebo for the treatment of bulimia nervosa: A systematic review. *Australian and New Zealand Journal of Psychiatry, 34*, 310–317.

Bacaltchuk, J., Hay, P., & Trefiglio, R. (2001). Antidepressants versus psychological treatments and their combination for bulimia nervosa. *Cochrane Database of Systematic Reviews, 4*, Art. No. CD003385. doi:003310.001002/14651858.CD14003385

Bacaltchuk, J., Trefiglio, R. P., de-Oliveira, I. R., Lima, M. S., & Mari, J. J. (1999). Antidepressants versus psychotherapy for bulimia nervosa: A systematic review. *Journal of Clinical Pharmacy and Therapeutics, 24*, 23–31.

Bacaltchuk, J., Trefiglio, R. P., de-Oliveira, I. R., Hay, P., Lima, M. S., & Mari, J. J. (2000). Combination of antidepressants and psychological treatments for bulimia nervosa: A systematic review. *Acta Psychiatrica Scandinavica, 101*, 256–264.

Banasiak, S. J., Paxton, S. J., & Hay, P. (2005). Guided self-help for bulimia nervosa in primary care: A randomized controlled trial. *Psychological Medicine, 35*, 1283–1294.

Bara-Carril, N., Williams, C. J., Pombo-Carril, M. G., Reid, Y., Murray, K., Aubin, S., . . . Schmidt, U. (2004). A preliminary investigation into the feasibility and efficacy of a CD-ROM-based cognitive-behavioral self-help intervention for bulimia nervosa. *International Journal of Eating Disorders, 35*, 538–548.

Borkovec, T. D., & Inz, J. (1990). The nature of worry in generalized anxiety disorder: A predominance of thought activity. *Behaviour Research and Therapy, 28*, 153–158.

Bulik, C. M., Sullivan, P. F., & Kendler, K. S. (1998). Heritability of binge-eating and broadly defined bulimia nervosa. *Biological Psychiatry, 44*, 1210–1218.

Burton, E., & Stice, E. (2006). Evaluation of a healthy-weight treatment program for bulimia nervosa: A preliminary randomized trial. *Behaviour Research and Therapy, 44*, 1727–1738.

Butler, A. C., Chapman, J. E., Forman, E. M., & Beck, A. T. (2006). The empirical status of cognitive-behavioral therapy: A review of meta-analyses. *Clinical Psychology Review, 26*, 17–31.

Carrard, I., Rouget, P., Fernandez-Aranda, F., Volkart, A. C., Damoiseau, M., & Lam, T. (2006). Evaluation and deployment of evidence based patient self-management support program for Bulimia Nervosa. *International Journal of Medical Information, 75*, 101–109.

Carter, F. A., McIntosh, V. V., Joyce, P. R., Sullivan, P. F., & Bulik, C. M. (2003). Role of exposure with response prevention in cognitive-behavioral therapy for bulimia nervosa: Three-year follow-up results. *International Journal of Eating Disorders, 33*, 127–135.

Carter, J. C., & Fairburn, C. G. (1998). Cognitive-behavioral self-help for binge eating disorder: A controlled effectiveness study. *Journal of Consulting and Clinical Psychology, 66*, 616–623.

Chambless, D. L., & Hollon, S. D. (1998). Defining empirically supported therapies. *Journal of Consulting and Clinical Psychology, 66*, 7–18.

Chen, E., Touyz, S. W., Beumont, P. J., Fairburn, C. G., Griffiths, R., Butow, P., . . . Basten, C. (2003). Comparison of group and individual cognitive-behavioral therapy for patients with bulimia nervosa. *International Journal of Eating Disorders, 33*, 241–254.

Cooper, P. J. (1995). *Bulimia nervosa and binge-eating. A guide to recovery.* New York, NY: University Press.

Cooper, P. J., & Fairburn, C. G. (1983). Binge-eating and self-induced vomiting in the community. A preliminary study. *British Journal of Psychiatry, 142*, 139–144.

Cooper, Z., Cooper, P. J., & Fairburn, C. G. (1989). The validity of the eating disorder examination and its subscales. *British Journal of Psychiatry, 154*, 807–812.

Critchfield, K. L., Henry, W. P., Castonguay, L. G., & Borkovec, T. D. (2007). Interpersonal process and outcome in variants of cognitive-behavioral psychotherapy. *Journal of Clinical Psychology, 63*, 31–51.

Dalle Grave, R., Ricca, V., & Todesco, T. (2001). The stepped-care approach in anorexia nervosa and bulimia nervosa: Progress and problems. *Eating and Weight Disorders, 6*, 81–89.

Durand, M. A., & King, M. (2003). Specialist treatment versus self-help for bulimia nervosa: A randomised controlled trial in general practice. *British Journal of General Practice, 53*(490), 371–377.

Erzegovesi, S., Riboldi, C., Di Bella, D., Di Molfetta, D., Mapelli, F., Negri, B., . . . Bellodi, L. (2004). Bulimia Nervosa, 5-HTTLPR polymorphism and treatment response to four SSRIs: A single-blind study. *Journal of Clinical Psychopharmacology, 24*, 680–682.

Fairburn, C. G. (1984). Bulimia: Its epidemiology and management. *Research Publications- Association for Research on Nervous and Mental Disorders, 62*, 235–258.

Fairburn, C. G. (1995a). *Guided self-help for bulimia nervosa. Therapist's manual for use in conjunction with Overcoming Binge Eating.* Oxford, England: Department of Psychiatry, Warneford Hospital.

Fairburn, C. G. (1995b). *Overcoming binge eating.* New York, NY: Guilford Press.

Fairburn, C. G. (1997). Interpersonal psychotherapy for bulimia nervosa. In D. M. Garner & P. E. Garfinkel (Eds.), *Handbook of treatment for eating disorders* (pp. 278–294). New York, NY: Guilford Press.

Fairburn, C. G. (2006). Treatment of bulimia nervosa. In S. Wonderlich, J. E. Mitchell, M. de Zwaan, & H. Steiger (Eds.), *Annual review of eating disorders: Part 2-2006.* Abingdon, United Kingdom: Radcliffe Publishing Ltd.

Fairburn, C. G. (2008). *Cognitive behavior therapy and eating disorders.* New York, NY: Guilford Press.

Fairburn, C. G., & Beglin, S. J. (1994). Assessment of eating disorders: Interview or self-report questionnaire? *International Journal of Eating Disorders, 16*, 363–370.

Fairburn, C. G., Cooper, Z., Doll, H. A., Norman, P., & O'Connor, M. (2000). The natural course of bulimia nervosa and binge eating disorder in young women. *Archives of General Psychiatry, 57*, 659–665.

Fairburn, C. G., Cooper, Z., Doll, H. A., O'Conner, M. E., Bohn, K., Hawker, D. M., . . . Palmer, R. L. (2009). Transdiagnostic cognitive-behavioral therapy for patients with eating disorders: A two-site trial with 60 week follow-up. *American Journal of Psychiatry, 166*, 311–319.

Fairburn, C. G., Cooper, Z., & Shafran, R. (2003). Cognitive behaviour therapy for eating disorders: A "transdiagnostic" theory and treatment. *Behaviour Research and Therapy, 41*, 509–528.

Fairburn, C. G., & Harrison, P. J. (2003). Eating disorders. *Lancet, 361*, 406–417.

Fairburn, C. G., Jones, R., Peveler, R. C., Carr, S. J., Solomon, R. A., O'Connor, M. E., . . . Hope, R. A. (1991). Three psychological treatments for bulimia nervosa. A comparative trial. *Archives of General Psychiatry, 48*, 463–469.

Fairburn, C. G., Marcus, M. D., & Wilson, G. T. (1993). Cognitive behaviour therapy for binge eating and bulimia nervosa: A comprehensive treatment manual. In C. G. Fairburn & G. T. Wilson (Eds.), *Binge eating: Nature, assessment and treatment* (pp. 361–404). New York, NY: Guilford Press.

Fairburn, C. G., Welch, S. L., Norman, P. A., O'Connor, M. E., & Doll, H. A. (1996). Bias and bulimia nervosa: How typical are clinic cases? *American Journal of Psychiatry, 153*, 386–391.

Fairburn, C. G., Wu, F. C., McCulloch, D. K., Borsey, D. Q., Ewing, D. J., Clarke, B. F., & Bancroft, J. H. (1982). The clinical features of diabetic impotence: A preliminary study. *British Journal of Psychiatry, 140*, 447–452.

Garfield, S. L. (1998). Some comments on empirically supported treatments. *Journal of Consulting and Clinical Psychology, 66*, 121–125.

Garner, D. M., Rockert, W., Davis, R., Garner, M. V., Olmsted, M. P., & Eagle, M. (1993). Comparison of cognitive-behavioral and supportive-expressive therapy for bulimia nervosa. *American Journal of Psychiatry, 150*, 37–46.

Gaston, J. E., Abbott, M. J., Rapee, R. M., & Neary, S. A. (2006). Do empirically supported treatments generalize to private practice? A benchmark study of a cognitive-behavioural group treatment programme for social phobia. *British Journal of Clinical Psychology, 45*(Pt. 1), 33–48.

Ghaderi, A. (2001). Review of risk factors for eating disorders: Implications for primary prevention and cognitive behavioural therapy. *Scandinavian Journal of Psychology, 30*, 57–74.

Ghaderi, A. (2006a). Attrition and outcome in self-help treatment for bulimia nervosa and binge eating disorder: A constructive replication. *Eating Behaviors, 7*, 300–308.

Ghaderi, A. (2006b). Does individualization matter? A randomized trial of standardized (focused) versus individualized (broad) cognitive behavior therapy for bulimia nervosa. *Behaviour Research and Therapy, 44*, 273–288.

Ghaderi, A., & Andersson, G. (1999). Meta-analysis of CBT for bulimia nervosa: Investigating the effects using *DSM-III-R* and *DSM-IV* criteria. *Scandinavian Journal of Behaviour Therapy, 28*, 79–87.

Ghaderi, A., & Scott, B. (2003). Pure and guided self-help for full and sub-threshold bulimia nervosa and binge eating disorder. *British Journal of Clinical Psychology, 42*, 257–269.

Goldfried, M. R., & Wolfe, B. E. (1998). Toward a more clinically valid approach to therapy research. *Journal of Consulting and Clinical Psychology, 66,* 143–150.

Grilo, C. M., Pagano, M. E., Skodol, A. E., Sanislow, C. A., McGlashan, T. H., Gunderson, J. G., & Stout, R. L. (2007). Natural course of bulimia nervosa and of eating disorder not otherwise specified: 5-year prospective study of remissions, relapses, and the effects of personality disorder psychopathology. *Journal of Clinical Psychiatry, 68,* 738–746.

Grilo, C. M., Sanislow, C. A., Shea, M. T., Skodol, A. E., Stout, R. L., Pagano, M. E., . . . McGlashan, T. H. (2003). The natural course of bulimia nervosa and eating disorder not otherwise specified is not influenced by personality disorders. *International Journal of Eating Disorders, 34,* 319–330.

Hartmann, A., Herzog, T., & Drinkmann, A. (1992). Psychotherapy of bulimia nervosa: What is effective? A meta-analysis. *Journal of Psychosomatic Research, 36,* 159–167.

Hausmann, A., Mangweth, B., Walpoth, M., Hoertnagel, C., Kramer-Reinstadler, K., Rupp, C. I., & Hinterhuber, H. (2004). Repetitive transcranial magnetic stimulation (rTMS) in the double-blind treatment of a depressed patient suffering from bulimia nervosa: A case report. *International Journal of Neuropsychopharmacology, 7,* 371–373.

Hay, P. (2003). Quality of life and bulimic eating disorder behaviors: Findings from a community-based sample. *International Journal of Eating Disorders, 33,* 434–442.

Hay, P. J., Bacaltchuk, J., & Stefano, S. (2004). Psychotherapy for bulimia nervosa and binging. *Cochrane Database of Systematic Reviews, 3,* Art. No. CD000562. doi:000510.001002/14651858. CD14000562.pub14651852

Hayes, S. C., Barlow, D. H., & Nelson-Gray, R. O. (1999). *The scientist practitioner. Research and accountability in the age of managed care.* Boston, MA: Allyn & Bacon.

Hedges, D. W., Reimherr, F. W., Hoopes, S. P., Rosenthal, N. R., Kamin, M., Karim, R., & Capece, J. A. (2003). Treatment of bulimia nervosa with topiramate in a randomized, double-blind, placebo-controlled trial, Part 2: Improvement in psychiatric measures. *Journal of Clinical Psychiatry, 64,* 1449–1454.

Hepworth, N., & Paxton, S. J. (2007). Pathways to help-seeking in bulimia nervosa and binge eating problems: A concept mapping approach. *International Journal of Eating Disorders, 40,* 493–504.

Hsu, L. K. G. (1996). Epidemiology of the eating disorders. *The Psychiatric Clinics of North America, 19,* 681–700.

Jacobson, N. S., & Truax, P. (1991). Clinical significance: A statistical approach to defining meaningful change in psychotherapy research. *Journal of Consulting and Clinical Psychology, 59,* 12–19.

Kaye, W. H., Bulik, C. M., Thornton, L., Barbarich, N., & Masters, K. (2004). Comorbidity of anxiety disorders with anorexia and bulimia nervosa. *American Journal of Psychiatry, 161,* 2215–2221.

Kazdin, A. E. (2008). Evidence-based treatment and practice: New opportunities to bridge clinical research and practice, enhance the knowledge base, and improve patient care. *American Psychologist, 63,* 146–159.

Keel, P. K., & Mitchell, J. E. (1997). Outcome in bulimia nervosa. *American Journal of Psychiatry, 154,* 313–321.

Keel, P. K., Mitchell, J. E., Davis, T. L., Fieselman, S., & Crow, S. J. (2000). Impact of definitions on the description and prediction of bulimia nervosa outcome. *International Journal of Eating Disorders, 28,* 377–386.

Keel, P. K., Mitchell, J. E., Miller, K. B., Davis, T. L., & Crow, S. J. (1999). Long-term outcome of bulimia nervosa. *Archives of General Psychiatry, 56,* 63–69.

Kendler, K. S., MacLean, C., Neale, M., Kessler, R., Heath, A., & Eaves, L. (1991). The genetic epidemiology of bulimia nervosa. *American Journal of Psychiatry, 148,* 1627–1637.

Klerman, G. L., Weissman, M. M., Rounsaville, B. J., & Chevron, E. S. (1995). *Interpersonal psychotherapy of depression: A brief, focused, specific strategy.* New York, NY: Jason Aronson.

Leombruni, P., Amianto, F., Delsedime, N., Gramaglia, C., Abbate-Daga, G., & Fassino, S. (2006). Citalopram versus Fluoxetine for the treatment of patients with bulimia nervosa: A single-blind randomized controlled trial. *Advances in Therapy, 23,* 481–494.

Lewandowski, L. M., Gebing, T. A., Anthony, J. L., & O'Brien, W. H. (1997). Meta-analysis of cognitive-behavioral treatment studies for bulimia. *Clinical Psychology Review, 17,* 703–718.

Ljotsson, B., Lundin, C., Mitsell, K., Carlbring, P., Ramklint, M., & Ghaderi, A. (2007). Remote treatment of bulimia nervosa and binge eating disorder: A randomized trial of Internet-assisted cognitive behavioural therapy. *Behaviour Research and Therapy, 45,* 649–661.

Milano, W., Petrella, C., Sabatino, C., & Capece, J. A. (2004). Treatment of bulimia nervosa with Sertraline: A randomized controlled trial. *Advances in Therapy, 21,* 232–237.

Mitchell, J. E., Agras, W., Wilson, G., Halmi, K., Kraemer, H., & Crow, S. (2004). A trial of a relapse prevention strategy in women with bulimia nervosa who respond to cognitive-behavior therapy. *International Journal of Eating Disorders, 35,* 549–555.

Mitchell, J. E., Crosby, R. D., Wonderlich, S. A., Crow, S., Lancaster, K., Simonich, H., . . . Myers, T. C. (2008). A randomized trial comparing the efficacy of cognitive-behavioral therapy for bulimia nervosa delivered via telemedicine versus face-to-face. *Behaviour Research and Therapy, 46,* 581–592.

Mitchell, J. E., Halmi, K., Wilson, G. T., Agras, W. S., Kraemer, H., & Crow, S. (2002). A randomized secondary treatment study of women with bulimia nervosa who fail to respond to CBT. *International Journal of Eating Disorders, 32*, 271–281.

Mitchell, J. E., & Peterson, C. B. (2007). *Assessment of eating disorders.* New York, NY: Guilford Press.

Mitchell, J. E., Peterson, C. B., & Agras, S. (1999). Cost-effectiveness of psychotherapy for eating disorders. In N. E. Miller & K. M. Magruder (Eds.), *The cost-effectiveness of psychotherapy: A guide for practitioners, researchers and policymakers.* New York, NY: Oxford University Press.

Mussell, M. P., Crosby, R. D., Crow, S. J., Knopke, A. J., Peterson, C. B., Wonderlich, S. A., & Mitchell, J. E. (2000). Utilization of empirically supported psychotherapy treatments for individuals with eating disorders: A survey of psychologists. *International Journal of Eating Disorders, 27*, 230–237.

Nakash-Eisikovits, O., Dierberger, A., & Westen, D. (2002). A multidimensional meta-analysis of pharmacotherapy for bulimia nervosa: Summarizing the range of outcomes in controlled clinical trials. *Harvard Review of Psychiatry, 10*, 193–211.

National Institute for Clinical Excellence (NICE). (2004). *Eating disorders: Core interventions in the treatment and management of anorexia nervosa, bulimia nervosa and related eating disorders.* Developed by the National Collaborating Centre for Mental Health (No. Clinical Guideline 9). London, England.

Nevonen, L., & Broberg, A. G. (2006). A comparison of sequenced individual and group psychotherapy for patients with bulimia nervosa. *International Journal of Eating Disorders, 39*, 117–127.

Nickel, C., Tritt, K., Muehlbacher, M., Gil, F. P., Mitterlehner, F. O., Kaplan, P., . . . Nickel, M. K. (2005). Topiramate treatment in bulimia nervosa patients: A randomized, double-blind, placebo-controlled trial. *International Journal of Eating Disorders, 38*, 295–300.

O'Brien, K. M., & Vincent, N. K. (2003). Psychiatric comorbidity in anorexia and bulimia nervosa: Nature, prevalence, and causal relationships. *Clinical Psychology Review, 23*, 57–74.

Öst, L. G. (2008). *Does CBT work in routine clinical practice, or only in the ivory towers of the researchers?* Paper presented at the 38th EABCT Annual Congress (European Association for Behavioral and Cognitive Therapies), 10–13 September.

Rand, C. S., & Kuldau, J. M. (1992). Epidemiology of bulimia and symptoms in a general population: Sex, age, race, and socioeconomic status. *International Journal of Eating Disorders, 11*, 37–44.

Reas, D. L., Williamson, D. A., Martin, C. K., & Zucker, N. L. (2000). Duration of illness predicts outcome for bulimia nervosa: A long-term follow-up study. *International Journal of Eating Disorders, 27*, 428–434.

Robinson, P., & Serfaty, M. (2008). Getting better byte by byte: A pilot randomised controlled trial of email therapy for bulimia nervosa and binge eating disorder. *European Eating Disorders Review, 16*, 84–93.

Russell, G. F. M. (1979). Bulimia nervosa: An ominous variant of anorexia nervosa. *Psychological Medicine, 9*, 429–448.

Schmidt, U., Cooper, P. J., Essers, H., Freeman, C. P., Holland, R. L., Palmer, R. L., . . . Webster, J. (2004). Fluvoxamine and graded psychotherapy in the treatment of bulimia nervosa: A randomized, double-blind, placebo-controlled, multicenter study of short-term and long-term pharmacotherapy combined with a stepped care approach to psychotherapy. *Journal of Clinical Psychopharmacology, 24*, 549–552.

Schmidt, U., Landau, S., Pombo-Carril, M. G., Bara-Carril, N., Reid, Y., Murray, K., . . . Katzman, M. (2006). Does personalized feedback improve the outcome of cognitive-behavioural guided self-care in bulimia nervosa? A preliminary randomized controlled trial. *British Journal of Clinical Psychology, 45*, 111–121.

Schmidt, U., Lee, S., Beecham, J., Perkins, S., Treasure, J., Yi, I., . . . Eisler, I. (2007). A randomized controlled trial of family therapy and cognitive behavior therapy guided self-care for adolescents with bulimia nervosa and related disorders. *American Journal of Psychiatry, 164*, 591–598.

Schmidt, U., & Treasure, J. (1993). *Getting better bit(e) by bit(e): A survival kit for sufferers of bulimia nervosa and binge eating disorders.* Hove, England: Psychology Press.

Simmons, A. M., Milnes, S. M., & Anderson, D. A. (2008). Factors influencing the utilization of empirically supported treatments for eating disorders. *Eating Disorders, 16*, 342–354.

Soundy, T. J., Lucas, A. R., Suman, V. J., & Melton, L. J. III. (1995). Bulimia nervosa in Rochester, Minnesota from 1980 to 1990. *Psychological Medicine, 25*, 1065–1071.

Steele, A. L., & Wade, T. D. (2008). A randomised trial investigating guided self-help to reduce perfectionism and its impact on bulimia nervosa: A pilot study. *Behaviour Research and Therapy, 46*, 1316–1323.

Stefano, S. C., Bacaltchuk, J., Blay, S. L., & Hay, P. (2006). Self-help treatments for disorders of recurrent binge eating: A systematic review. *Acta Psychiatrica Scandinavica, 113*, 452–459.

Sullivan, P. F., Bulik, C. M., Carter, F. A., Gendall, K. A., & Joyce, P. R. (1996). The significance of a prior history of anorexia in bulimia nervosa. *International Journal of Eating Disorders, 20*, 253–261.

Thompson-Brenner, H., & Westen, D. (2005). A naturalistic study of psychotherapy for bulimia nervosa, part 1: Comorbidity and therapeutic outcome. *Journal of the Nervous and Mental Diseases, 193,* 573–584.

Treasure, J., & Schmidt, U. (1997). *A clinician's guide to getting better bit(e) by bit(e).* Hove, England: Psychology Press.

Wade, T., Martin, N. G., Neale, M. C., Tiggemann, M., Treloar, S. A., Bucholz, K. K., . . . Heath, A. C. (1999). The structure of genetic and environmental risk factors for three measures of disordered eating. *Psychological Medicine, 29,* 925–934.

Waller, G., Cordery, H., Corstorphine, E., Hinrichsen, H., Lawson, R., . . . Russel, K. (2007). *Cognitive behavioral therapy for eating disorders: A comprehensive treatment guide.* Cambridge, England: Cambridge University Press.

Walpoth, M., Hoertnagl, C., Mangweth-Matzek, B., Kemmler, G., Hinterholzl, J., Conca, A., & Hausmann, A. (2007). Repetitive transcranial magnetic stimulation in bulimia nervosa: Preliminary results of a single-centre, randomised, double-blind, sham-controlled trial in female outpatients. *Psychotherapy and Psychosomatics, 77,* 57–60.

Walsh, B., Fairburn, C. G., Mickley, D., Sysko, R., & Parides, M. K. (2004). Treatment of Bulimia Nervosa in a primary care setting. *American Journal of Psychiatry, 161,* 556–561.

Westen, D., & Morrison, K. (2001). A multidimensional meta-analysis of treatments for depression, panic, and generalized anxiety disorder: An empirical examination of the status of empirically supported therapies. *Journal of Consulting and Clinical Psychology, 69,* 875–899.

Westen, D., Novotny, C. M., & Thompson-Brenner, H. (2004). The empirical status of empirically supported psychotherapies: Assumptions, findings, and reporting in controlled clinical trials. *Psychological Bulletin, 130,* 631–663.

Whitehouse, A. M., Cooper, P. J., Vize, C. V., Hill, C., & Vogel, L. (1992). Prevalence of eating disorders in three Cambridge general practices: Hidden and conspicuous morbidity. *British Journal of General Practice, 42*(355), 57–60.

Whittal, M. L., Agras, W. S., & Gould, R. A. (1999). Bulimia nervosa: A meta-analysis of psychosocial and pharmacological treatments. *Behavior Therapy, 30,* 117–135.

Wilfley, D. E., Agras, W. S., Telch, C. F., Rossiter, E. M., Schneider, J. A., Cole, A. G., . . . Raeburn, S. D. (1993). Group cognitive-behavioral therapy and group interpersonal psychotherapy for the nonpurging bulimic individual: A controlled comparison. *Journal of Consulting and Clinical Psychology, 61,* 296–305.

Wilfley, D. E., & Cohen, L. R. (1997). Psychological treatment of bulimia nervosa and binge eating disorder. *Psychopharmacology Bulletin, 33,* 437–454.

Wilson, G. T. (2005). Psychological treatment of eating disorders. *Annual Review of Clinical Psychology, 1,* 439–465.

Wilson, G. T., Grilo, C. M., & Vitousek, K. M. (2007). Psychological treatment of eating disorders. *American Psychologist, 62,* 199–216.

Wilson, G. T., & Pike, K. M. (1993). Eating disorders. In D. H. Barlow (Ed.), *Clinical handbook of psychological disorders: A step-by-step treatment manual.* New York, NY: Guilford Press.

Wilson, G. T., & Shafran, R. (2005). Eating disorders guidelines from NICE. *Lancet, 365*(9453), 79–81.

Wolfe, B. E., Metzger, E. D., Levine, J. M., & Jimerson, D. C. (2001). Laboratory screening for electrolyte abnormalities and anemia in bulimia nervosa: A controlled study. *International Journal of Eating Disorders, 30,* 288–293.

World Health Organization (WHO) (Ed.). (1993). *International classification of diseases and related health problems* (10th rev.). Geneva, Switzerland: Author.

27

Sleep Disorders in Children

KURT A. FREEMAN, TONYA M. PALERMO, AND MEGAN SCOTT

OVERVIEW OF DISORDER

While many behavioral patterns are concerning to parents, sleep disturbance in some form is one of the most common complaints raised by parents to pediatricians; in fact, behind oppositional behavior, sleep disturbance is the second-most common complaint raised by parents (Christophersen & Mortweet, 2001). This is likely due to the high prevalence rates of pediatric sleep disturbances. Specifically, between 15% and 40% of infants, toddlers, and preschoolers and approximately 15%–25% of school-aged children in the United States demonstrate some qualitative and/or quantitative disturbance in sleep onset, sleep quality, and/or sleep maintenance (for reviews, see Mindell, Kuhn, Lewin, Meltzer, & Sadeh, 2006; Owens, Palermo, & Rosen, 2002; Ramchandani, Wiggs, Webb, & Stores, 2000).

Pediatric sleep problems include a variety of difficulties. Some have a physiological basis (e.g., obstructive sleep apnea, restless legs syndrome; Kotagal, 2003), for which a critical component of treatment resides with the medical sciences. However, most pediatric sleep disturbances, particularly the most common pediatric sleep disturbances of bedtime refusal and frequent night waking (Blum & Carey, 1996), have minimal to no underlying physiological disturbance. Instead, these difficulties are largely or exclusively behaviorally based (Brown & Piazza, 1999; Kuhn & Elliott, 2003;

Mindell, 1993, 1999). While the etiology of bedtime refusal and night waking includes a combination of biological, circadian, and developmental variables interacting with environmental and behavioral factors (Mindell et al., 2006), research highlights the importance of disruptions in parent management or parent–child interactions as influential in their development and/or maintenance (Lozoff, Wolf, & Davis, 1985; also see Mindell, 1999).

Emphasis of this chapter will be on sleep disorders with minimal to no underlying pathophysiology, as these are most likely to be treated directly by psychologists and other mental health professionals. Note, however, that many children may have more than one sleep disorder, including possibly a biologically based and behaviorally based disorder (e.g., obstructive sleep apnea and a behavioral sleep disorder; Mindell, Owens, & Carskadon, 1999). As such, careful attention to comprehensive assessment and intervention is critical for successfully ameliorating sleep disturbances in children.

Further, this chapter focuses exclusively on the treatment literature for bedtime resistance and night waking, and primarily on those problems when presented by children ages 5 years and younger. Although school-aged children and adolescents display difficulties initiating and maintaining sleep (e.g., Abdel-Khalek, 2004; Morrison, McGee, & Stanton, 1992; Price, Coates, Thoresen, & Grinstead,

1978) and there is increasing attention to the co-occurrence of sleep disturbance and adverse health consequences among older youth (e.g., Fallone, Owens, & Deane, 2002; Wolfson & Carskadon, 1998), only a small number of treatment studies exist with older children and adolescents without developmental disorders. As a result, existing practice parameters focus on sleep disturbances in younger children (Morgenthaler et al., 2006).

Diagnostic Criteria

Sleep disorders in children can be classified based on criteria from three sources: the *Diagnostic and Statistical Manual* (4th edition, text revision) (*DSM-IV-TR*) of the American Psychiatric Association (APA, 2000), the *International Classification of Diseases* (*ICD*) of the World Health Organization (WHO, 2007), and the *International Classification of Sleep Disorders* (2nd edition) (*ICSD-2*; American Academy of Sleep Medicine [AASM], 2005). Of these systems, the *ICSD-2* provides the greatest specificity of sleep disorders, followed by the *DSM-IV-TR*. The *ICD* provides the least specificity of different sleep disorders and may be least frequently used by psychologists for classification purposes; as such, the remainder of this section focuses primarily on the classifications available through the *ICSD-2* and *DSM-IV-TR*.

Each of the available diagnostic systems differentiates between parasomnias and dyssomnias. Parasomnias are sleep disturbances that are characterized as abnormal behavioral or physiological events that occur while one is asleep, during specific sleep stages, or during sleep–wake transitions. Examples of parasomnias include but are not limited to sleep terrors, confusional arousals, and sleepwalking. These disorders involve the activation of physiological systems at inappropriate times during the sleep–wake sequence.

In contrast, dyssomnias are characterized by disturbances in one's ability to initiate and/or sustain sleep or excessive sleepiness.

Dyssomnias can be further divided into *intrinsic* and *extrinsic* forms (AASM, 2005). Intrinsic dyssomnias are exclusively or largely the result of physiological disturbances. Examples include breathing-related sleep disorders (e.g., sleep apnea), narcolepsy, and circadian rhythm sleep disorder. Intrinsic dyssomnias are likely to be most successfully treated through pharmacological intervention, though certainly some may benefit from behavioral strategies as well. Extrinsic dyssomnias, on the other hand, are largely or exclusively influenced by environmental/contextual variables. Examples for children include bedtime refusal/bedtime settling problems and frequent night waking. Extrinsic dyssomnias are the most common sleep disorders among child/pediatric populations (see Mindell et al., 2006). Further, they are most successfully treated through behavioral interventions.

As just noted, the most prevalent sleep disturbances in children are bedtime refusal/resistance and frequent night waking (Blum & Carey, 1996). As such, these sleep disturbances will be the primary focus of this chapter. Bedtime refusal involves child behavioral patterns that interrupt or delay the process of a child settling into bed at night when expected to do so. Bedtime refusal can be passive (e.g., nonresponse to parental request for child to go to bed). However, more commonly it is active in form and includes behaviors such as "stalling, verbal protests, crying, clinging, refusing to go to bed, getting out of bed, attention-seeking behaviors, and multiple requests for food, drinks, and stories" (Mindell et al., 2006, p. 1263).

Bedtime refusal within existing diagnostic systems is classified somewhat differently depending on the system used. Within the *ICSD-2*, bedtime refusal is classified as a behavioral insomnia of childhood, limit-setting type. The *DSM-IV-TR* does not provide a diagnostic classification that specifically captures bedtime refusal. As such, professionals using this system must determine whether classification of the bedtime refusal is best characterized as dyssomnia not otherwise specified, separation anxiety disorder, or some other related diagnosis typically used with youth. For example, a child's presentation that includes bedtime refusal, but also pervasive noncompliance, disruptive behavior, and other behavioral difficulties may be best classified as some form of disruptive behavior disorder. Behavioral patterns characteristic of a child hesitant to be alone at bedtime who also demonstrates difficulties being apart from parents at other times may be described best as separation anxiety disorder.

Frequent night waking is typically characterized as a dyssomnia in available diagnostic classification systems. Within the *ICSD-2*, night waking would be classified as Behavioral Insomnia of Childhood, Sleep Onset Association Type (AASM, 2005; Mindell et al., 2006). This is because most children presenting with frequent night-waking problems rely on some type of sleep association to fall asleep at bedtime, either through activities (e.g., rocking, being fed) or the presence of others (i.e., a parent/care providers). Consequently, when children experience normal nighttime arousals, they have difficulty putting themselves back to sleep. Night waking is typically viewed as problematic when it involves "signaling" by the child (e.g., crying out, getting out of bed) and is frequent and/or prolonged (Mindell et al., 2006). When night waking co-occurs with bedtime refusal, the most appropriate diagnosis within the *ICSD-2* would be Behavioral Insomnia of Childhood, Mixed Type. Again, within the *DSM-IV-TR*, no specific diagnostic category captures frequent night waking. The professional relying on this system must determine how to best characterize this problematic behavioral pattern (e.g., Dyssomnia NOS).

As Mindell and colleagues (2006) pointed out in their review of treatments for bedtime refusal and night waking, these behavioral patterns are typically defined as problematic by care providers rather than the child him/herself.

As such, they do not necessarily represent a complaint of subjective sleep disturbance by the child. This is in contrast to adult sleep disorders, which usually have a significant component of subjective distress by the person. Further, the definition of "sleep problems" in young children is greatly influenced by the "developmental, environmental, and cultural context in which they occur" (Mindell et al., 2006, p. 1278). For example, one family may be very comfortable in the family bed with their 4-year-old child, while another may be frustrated by their child's inability to sleep in his/her own room. Finally, because of the potential influence of bedtime and sleep disturbances on not just the child but also the family, it is important that one consider not only child daytime functioning, but also parental, marital, and family functioning variables as relevant outcomes in need of attention.

Demographic Variables

To date, research has not adequately and extensively investigated the association between traditionally defined demographic variables such as intraparticipant features (e.g., age, gender), family variables (e.g., family constellation, number of siblings), parental variables (e.g., parental stress, maternal depression), and increased risk of displaying sleep disturbances, particularly bedtime resistance and night waking. Thus, the clinician working with children presenting with sleep disturbances must extrapolate from other potentially relevant research that may help inform understanding of factors influencing presentation of sleep disturbances (e.g., effects of maternal depression on child functioning).

Variables other than traditionally defined demographic variables have been shown to be associated with sleep disturbances in children generally, and bedtime refusal and night waking specifically. Data clearly shows that a significant portion of children who experience sleep disturbances at earlier ages continue to do so over time. For instance, sleep problems are more likely in school-aged children if disturbances were present before the age of 6 months (Pollock, 1992, 1994). Further, Kataria, Swanson, and Trevathon (1987) found that 84% of their sample of children 15 to 48 months of age who had bedtime settling and night waking difficulties at initial assessment demonstrated similar disturbances 3 years later. Thus, while evidence shows that most children will likely outgrow behavioral sleep disturbances by mid-adolescence (Gregory & O'Connor, 2002), for a significant portion of children sleep disturbances persist for extended periods of time without treatment.

While sleep disturbance is common in the general population, presence of chronic medical or developmental conditions is associated with increased prevalence. Children with developmental disorders (e.g., Couturier et al., 2005; Honomichl, Goodlin-Jones, Burnham, Gaylor, & Anders, 2002; Krakowiak, Goodlin-Jones, Hertz-Picciotto, Croen, & Hansen, 2008), chronic medical conditions (e.g., Maganti et al., 2006; Miller, Palermo, Powers, Scher, & Hershey, 2003), and blindness/visual impairment (Stores & Ramchandani, 1999), for example, may experience a greater frequency and/or severity of sleep disturbances than similar aged healthy peers.

Impact of Disorder

At first glance bedtime refusal and/or frequent night waking may seem relatively benign behavioral patterns. This may be true for transient and infrequent episodes of these behavioral patterns. In contrast, frequent and/or persistent disturbances of this nature may predispose children to a host of challenges. Children who experience excessive daytime sleepiness due to insufficient or interrupted sleep are at greater risk for mood disturbances, behavioral disruption, and impaired cognitive functioning. Specifically, mood problems are common in children with sleep disturbances, with an exacerbation of negative mood and a decrease in positive mood and affect (Ali,

Pitson, & Stradling, 1993; Lewin, England, & Rosen, 1995). Amount of sleep obtained by children and their presentation of externalizing behavior problems are negatively associated based on classroom teacher report (Paavonen et al., 2002; Paaavonen, Solantaus, Almqvist, & Aronen, 2003), parent report (Smedje, Broman, & Hetta, 2001), and self-report (Liu & Zhou, 2002). Further, decreased amount of sleep has been associated with peer problems in adolescents (Smedje et al., 2001). Cognitive functioning and memory problems may also exist in children with sleep disturbances (Steenari et al., 2003), creating the potential for negatively affected academic performance. Higher order cognitive processes mediated by the prefrontal cortex (e.g., abstract reasoning, cognitive flexibility) are particularly suspect to the influence of disruptions in the quality or quantity of sleep (see Mindell et al., 2006). Further, children who have excessive daytime sleepiness due to disturbed sleep have a greater risk for increased daytime accidental injuries and a greater risk for negative effects on cardiovascular, immune, and metabolic systems (Mindell & Owens, 2003).

Sleep disturbances also affect parent and parent–child functioning. Mothers of children with sleep disturbances show heightened distress, which improves with effective treatment (France, Blampied, & Wilkinson, 1991; Hiscock, Bayer, Hampton, Ukoumunne, & Wake, 2008). Persistent bedtime problems result in parents becoming fatigued, reducing tolerance for bedtime problems, and affecting general family satisfaction (Gelman & King, 2001; Owens, Spirito, McGuinn, & Nobile, 2000). They have also been linked to maternal psychiatric symptoms (Lozoff et al., 1985; Minde et al., 1993), parental stress (Doo & Wing, 2006), and marital discord (Cortesi, Giannotti, Sebastiani, Vagnoni, & Marioni, 2008). Finally, sleep disturbances adversely affect parent–child interactions while improvements produce positive changes in daytime parent–child interactions (see Kuhn & Weidinger, 2000), improve family satisfaction (Mindell &

Durand, 1993), reduce parental stress (Reid, Walter, & O'Leary, 1999), and result in improvements in paternal depressive symptoms (Leeson, Barbour, Romaniuk, & Warr, 1994).

Collectively, these data demonstrate the importance of addressing sleep disruptions demonstrated by children. Fortunately, there is a foundational and growing body of literature addressing interventions for bedtime refusal and night waking.

CONSENSUS PANEL RECOMMENDATIONS

A solid body of literature now exists supporting the use of empirically based behavioral management strategies to treat bedtime problems and night wakings in infants, toddlers, and preschoolers up to the age of 5 (Mindell, 1999; Mindell et al., 2006). Most recently, practice parameters have been developed for the use of behavioral treatments for bedtime problems and night wakings in young children (Morgenthaler et al., 2006). A companion review paper summarizes the most up-to-date peer-reviewed scientific literature on this topic (Mindell et al., 2006). These practice parameters were developed by the AASM, a professional organization that has developed evidence-based practice parameters to provide health-care professionals with recommendations for the evaluation and management of pediatric and adult patients with sleep disorders.

The AASM has convened several task forces of experts to develop parameters that are based on an exhaustive review of the scientific literature. The AASM develops these practice parameters according to the recommendations of the Agency for Healthcare Research and Quality and the National Guideline Clearinghouse. Separate review and practice parameters papers undergo a peer-review process by outside reviewers before they are submitted to the AASM Board of Directors for approval. After approval, the review and practice parameters papers are published in the journal

Sleep. Every 3 to 5 years, the AASM reevaluates the practice parameters and publishes updates when necessary. Currently, only one practice parameter available for pediatrics exists, which is on the topic of bedtime resistance and night wakings.

The experts developing the practice parameters used a system for classifying the evidence in support of particular interventions that is adapted from Sackett (1993), and includes five levels of evidence ranging from the highest level (I), represented by randomized, well-designed trials with low alpha and beta error to the lowest level (V), represented by case series. A system of three terms (*Standard, Guideline, Option*) is also used to refer to the level of recommendation adapted from Eddy (1992). At the highest level, the term *Standard* is used, which generally implies the use of Level I evidence; a *Guideline* reflects a moderate degree of clinical certainty corresponding to use of Level II or Level III evidence; and an *Option* reflects uncertain clinical use and implies either inconclusive or conflicting evidence.

Mindell (1999) and Kuhn and Elliott (2003) also evaluated the treatment research for bedtime resistance and night waking, both using the criteria established by Chambless and colleagues (Chambless & Hollon, 1998; Chambless et al., 1996) to categorize the research on psychological treatments. Using the criteria to determine whether interventions are empirically validated, interventions are categorized as "well-established," "probably efficacious," or "promising" based on the quality and quantity of research.

Several specific recommendations are made in the practice parameters for the treatment of bedtime problems and night waking (Morgenthaler et al., 2006), as well as in the critical reviews of research using the Chambless criteria (Kuhn & Elliott, 2003; Mindell, 1999). Behavioral interventions are considered to be effective in the treatment of these behavioral difficulties in young children, producing reliable and significant clinical improvement in children's sleep and in parent and family well-being. Further, six specific behavioral treatments have been identified with sufficient evidence for classification using established criteria for evaluating research. Those interventions include unmodified extinction, extinction with parental presence, parent education, graduated extinction, bedtime fading/positive routines, and scheduled awakenings.

Description of Treatments

Unmodified extinction, sometimes referred to as *planned parental ignoring*, involves establishing a regular bedtime routine and bedtime and wake time, and avoiding any response to the child who displays resistance (e.g., crying/whining) after being put to bed. If children leave the bedroom, parents are instructed to physically return them to bed with little to no verbal interaction. The only difference in the modified version with parental presence is that parents are allowed to remain in the child's room but they are still to avoid any response to the child.

Preventive education involves specific educational interventions that are designed to prevent the occurrence or the development of sleep problems in children. Focus of the information provided is typically on behavioral interventions of positive routines and extinction. Many of the studies in this line of research emphasize providing written material to parents regarding child sleep habits and methods of promoting those habits as the source of intervention.

Graduated extinction is similar to unmodified extinction, with the difference being that parents ignore bedtime resistance for predetermined periods before briefly checking on the child. Either a progressive (e.g., every 5 minutes, then 10 minutes) or a fixed (e.g., every 5 minutes) checking schedule can be used. Similar to unmodified extinction, the goal is to enable a child to develop the ability to soothe him or herself to sleep independently.

Positive routines involve parents developing a set bedtime routine that is characterized by pleasant and quiet activities that are done in a consistent manner each night. The goal is to establish a link between bedtime behaviors and sleep onset. This intervention may be done alone or in combination with faded bedtime and response cost. Faded bedtime refers to temporarily delaying the child's bedtime to more closely coincide with the sleep onset time that the child is currently able to achieve and then fading the bedtime earlier on subsequent nights as the child is successful with falling asleep quickly. When response cost is added, this involves taking the child out of bed for a brief period of time should the child not fall asleep quickly. The goal behind these strategies is to strengthen the connection between being in bed and falling asleep quickly as well as reducing affective and physiological arousal at bedtime.

The last intervention is scheduled awakenings, which involves having parents determine the typical time of night waking for their child and then set an alarm to preemptively awaken their child at a set time each night that is 15 to 30 minutes prior to the child's typical spontaneous awakening. In addition, the parent is to provide their typical response to the awakening such as feeding, rocking, or soothing, just as if the child had awakened spontaneously. Some protocols recommend that parents not wake their children completely, but instead simply gently arouse them to ensure that their eyes open and allow them to fall back to sleep.

EXTINCTION

Based on the AASM-sponsored analysis of existing research (Mindell et al., 2006), unmodified extinction and extinction with parental presence are interventions considered as Standards for bedtime settling and/or night-waking problems in young children (Morgenthaler et al., 2006). Using criteria to determine whether psychological interventions are empirically validated (Chambless & Hollon, 1998; Chambless et al., 1996), unmodified extinction is considered a "well-established" intervention, whereas extinction with parental presence is considered a "promising" intervention (Kuhn & Elliott, 2003). Researchers have also made slight changes/additions to unmodified extinction to address concerns about worsening of problems early in treatment. Although not included as standard recommended treatments, research on these modifications is reviewed in this section. Additionally, we review available research on the use of extinction with special populations, demonstrating the effectiveness of variations of unmodified extinction with diverse populations.

Randomized Controlled Trials

Unmodified Extinction

Four RCTs including a total of 172 children ages 6 to 60 months have been conducted to examine the effect of unmodified extinction on pediatric sleep disturbances (France et al., 1991; Reid et al., 1999; Rickert & Johnson, 1988; Seymour, Brock, During, & Poole, 1989). In order to assess its effectiveness as a treatment for infants and young children, unmodified extinction has been compared to the use of a combination of sedative medication and extinction, graduated extinction, scheduled awakening, and a control or wait-list group. One study compared the effectiveness of two different methods of treatment delivery, therapist-guided extinction and written instructions for extinction, and a wait-list control (Seymour et al., 1989). Across all studies, unmodified extinction was found to significantly improve bedtime refusal and/or nighttime waking. Additionally, completion of secondary analysis (Kuhn & Elliott, 2003) when available data permitted (i.e., Reid et al., 1999; Rickert & Johnson, 1998; Seymour et al., 1989) showed effect sizes ranging from $d = 0.68$–2.63, depending on the variable assessed.

France et al. (1991) compared the effectiveness of standard extinction in treating nighttime waking in infants and young children against extinction + medication placebo, and extinction + sedative medication, trimeprazine. All three groups experienced significant reductions in the frequency and duration of their nighttime waking and maintained these reductions over an 18-month follow-up period. Those participants who received the extinction + trimeprazine achieved improvements more quickly than those in the other groups. These researchers also examined parental stress over the course of the study and, contrary to previous findings (Rickert & Johnson, 1988), found no significant increases in parental anxiety during the implementation of standard extinction or extinction + medication placebo or sedative medication.

Two RCTs compared the effectiveness of unmodified extinction to other interventions, graduated extinction and scheduled awakening, and a wait-list control group (Reid et al., 1999; Rickert & Johnson, 1988). Rickert and Johnson (1988) showed that unmodified extinction procedures and scheduled awakening were significantly more effective in treating nocturnal waking/crying than no treatment over an 8-week intervention, gains that maintained at 3- and 6-week follow-up visits. Note that five families refused to participate in this study because they were unwilling to ignore their child's crying. Unmodified extinction produced greater improvements than scheduled awakening during the first week of treatment, though between-group differences disappeared over the course of the study. Although unmodified extinction led to rapid, significant reductions in nocturnal waking, crying increased twofold in the first 2 days of treatment prior to significantly declining over the course of the 8-week treatment.

Reid and colleagues (1999) found that unmodified extinction and graduated extinction were both effective in significantly reducing bedtime refusal and nighttime waking of children ages 16–48 months as compared to no treatment. There were no significant differences in the effectiveness of the treatment methods, and the gains of both treatment approaches were maintained over the 2-month follow-up period. No differences in maternal distress were evident between groups, indicating that mothers who implemented unmodified extinction did not experience significantly greater stress due to the implementation of this treatment, as has been suggested in other research (Rickert & Johnson, 1988; Owens et al., 2002). Mothers reported satisfaction with both unmodified and graduated extinction procedures and indicated that they would recommend both treatments (Reid et al., 1999).

One RCT examined the method of delivering intervention and the impact of different approaches to the implementation of extinction procedures in the treatment of sleep disturbances (Seymour et al., 1989). Both providing written instructions and therapist-guided unmodified extinction led to significant improvements in bedtime behaviors and night waking when compared to a wait-list control group, suggesting effectiveness of unmodified extinction may not be dependent on the assistance of a therapist.

Extinction With Parental Presence

Using a randomized controlled design, France and Blampied (2005) compared the effectiveness of unmodified extinction against two modified extinction interventions: extinction with minimal parental checks (a version of graduated extinction) and extinction with parental presence, as intervention for night waking and bedtime crying in infants. Parents in the extinction with minimal parent checks group were instructed to check on their infant every 10 minutes during night-settling and night-waking difficulties. Parents in the extinction with parental presence group were told to lie in a separate bed in the infant's room, pretend to sleep, and to refrain from attending to the infant during the first week of treatment. After the first week, parents in the parental presence group returned to their own beds and followed the unmodified extinction procedures. All three groups demonstrated significant

decreases in the frequency of night waking. The unmodified extinction group showed crying bursts during the first period of the intervention but demonstrated rapid decreases in awakening and crying over the course of the treatment. The extinction with minimal checks intervention resulted in gradual declines in the duration of bedtime crying over the first 2 weeks of treatment and then recovery of crying during the third and fourth week. In contrast, the parental presence group demonstrated decreased level of crying after the first week of treatment, which generally remained at low levels for the duration of treatment with the exception of some spontaneous recovery by two participants in the fourth week.

Modified Extinction

Although unmodified extinction has been shown to be effective, researchers have tested slight modifications and/or additions to this procedure to increase effectiveness, address possible limitations of unmodified extinction, and/or both. Moore, Friman, Fruzzetti, and MacAleese (2007) completed an RCT of the Bedtime Pass Program to treat bedtime resistance displayed by 3- to 6-year-old children. This procedure provides children with a card exchangeable for one trip out of the room or a visit with their parent each night after bedtime. After using the pass, the child must relinquish it and parents are expected to use unmodified extinction procedures for the rest of the night. When compared to a monitoring control group, young children demonstrated significant decreases in their bedtime refusal, specifically a decrease in the frequency of leaving the room and the time to quiet, when compared to the control group.

Meta-Analyses of RCTs

To date, no meta-analytic studies have been conducted to investigate the effects of group-based research on unmodified extinction, extinction with parental presence, or other modifications to extinction.

Single-Subject Experimental Analyses

Unmodified Extinction

France and Hudson (1990) used a multiple-baseline across participants design to investigate use of unmodified extinction for night waking exhibited by seven infants. Significant declines in the frequency and duration of night waking were observed following introduction of the intervention, improvements that maintained at a 3-month and 2-year follow-up assessment.

Modified Extinction

Four single-subject analyses have investigated the use of modified extinction procedures. Chadez and Nurius (1987) showed that extinction combined with cognitive restructuring (addressing parental beliefs regarding their effectiveness as parents), effectively treated bedtime crying exhibited by a 7-month-old female. Using a multiple-baseline across participants design Rapoff, Christophersen, and Rapoff (1982) showed that unmodified extinction plus bedtime routines and mild punishment effectively reduced rates of crying and whining at bedtime for three of their six participants.

Two single-subject studies have examined the use of the Bedtime Pass Program as an intervention for bedtime problems. Both studies found that the Bedtime Pass Program was effective in eliminating bedtime resistance (Friman et al., 1999; Freeman, 2006); furthermore, the treatment was rated as more acceptable than other treatment options by parents and pediatricians (Friman et al., 1999). An initial component analysis suggested that both treatment components (i.e., the "pass" exchangeable for one free trip out of the room + unmodified extinction) lead to the best outcome as compared to access to the pass alone (Freeman, 2006).

Special Populations

Single-subject analyses have been conducted to investigate the effectiveness of modified and unmodified extinction procedures in treating night waking and bedtime refusal in specific populations (Didden, De Moor, & Kruit, 1999; Thackeray & Richdale, 2002; Weiskop, Richdale, & Matthews, 2005). Unmodified extinction procedures have been found to be effective in eliminating nighttime crying with a young child with physical disabilities (Didden et al., 1999). Modified extinction procedures were demonstrated to be effective in children with learning disabilities, Fragile X syndrome, and intellectual disabilities.

The implementation of the 5 Step Sleep Programme, a manualized intervention that combines reinforcement strategies, teaching on instruction giving, implementation of a bedtime routine, partner support strategies, and standard extinction, with three boys ages 5 to 10 with intellectual disabilities and sleeping difficulties was investigated using a multiple-baseline across participants design (Thackeray & Richdale, 2002). All participants showed improvement in their sleep difficulties posttreatment based on family-identified pretreatment target goals. Two weeks following the implementation of extinction, all participants were able to fall asleep independently, difficulties with sleeping in their own bed were improved in two children, and one child's night waking was improved. All gains were maintained at a 3-month follow-up and additional improvements were seen in one child's night waking.

A similar intervention approach was investigated as a treatment for sleep problems in 13 children with autism and Fragile X syndrome (Weiskop et al., 2005) using a multiple-baseline across participants design. Pre-sleep disturbances improved for all participants, gains that maintained at follow-up. The frequency with which participants fell asleep in their own bed improved for eight participants and these gains were maintained for most participants. Sleep latency was improved for six of the children, with most of these children maintaining these gains at the follow-up. Night waking improved for seven children at both the end of intervention and the follow-up.

For the six participants who demonstrated difficulties with cosleeping (i.e., child sleeping in parental bed) at baseline, all demonstrated improvements following treatment. It should be noted that the majority of the participants demonstrated an extinction burst during treatment. All the mothers indicated that they would recommend this treatment and the average satisfaction score indicated an overall high satisfaction with the treatment program.

Bramble (1996, 1997) tested the effects of a modified extinction procedure for night settling and night waking displayed by 15 children ages 3.5 to 12 years with severe intellectual disabilities with an uncontrolled, within-subjects design. The intervention, which included the establishment of a bedtime routine, rapid bedtime settling, extinction, and positive reinforcement in the morning contingent on improvement in the child's nighttime behavior, was rated by parents to be effective in decreasing the severity of sleep problems at the end of the treatment phase and at a 4-month and 18-month follow-up. Parents indicated that improvements in sleep problems were seen within several nights of the start of treatment, and they reported generally high satisfaction with the intervention (Bramble, 1997). The majority of the participants rated the approach to be "just right" for their child, with a minority indicating it was "rather difficult," but all the participants continued with the treatment (Bramble, 1996).

Meta-Analyses of Single-Subject Experimental Analyses

To date, no meta-analytic studies have been conducted of studies using single-subject designs to summarize the effects of unmodified extinction, extinction with parental presence, or other modifications to extinction.

Conclusions

Unmodified extinction is considered a well-established treatment and a Standard intervention for sleep difficulties for children up to age 5 years (Kuhn & Elliott, 2003; Mindell, 1999; Morgenthaler et al., 2006; Owens et al., 2002). Importantly, unmodified extinction produces faster results than graduated extinction or scheduled waking (Rickert & Johnson, 1988), and concerns about parental dissatisfaction with the treatment (Rickert & Johnson, 1988; Owens et al., 2002) are not always supported (France et al., 1991; Reid et al., 1999). Note, however, that reported satisfaction ratings are provided by parents following the successful completion of unmodified extinction. To date, researchers have not investigated pretreatment expectations and how they may be associated with both treatment outcome and ultimate satisfaction. Furthermore, data are not available from parents who attempt extinction but are unable or unwilling to continue its use. Given that parental refusal to use unmodified extinction has been indicated as a reason for nonparticipation (Rickert & Johnson, 1988), parental opinion about this treatment remains important. Careful attention to the match between unmodified extinction and parental willingness is important, particularly given that unsuccessful attempts to implement extinction make bedtime settling problems more resistant to future attempts at treatment (Lawton, France, & Blampied, 1991).

Relatively minor additions or modifications have been developed to mitigate potentially aversive aspects of unmodified extinction, notably the presence of worsening of targeted behavior early in treatment. Importantly, the Bedtime Pass Program has been shown to reduce nighttime settling problems for children ages 3 to 10 years without worsening of behavior (Friman et al., 1999; Freeman, 2006) and is rated as very acceptable by parents and pediatricians alike (Friman et al., 1999). As such, this may be more appropriate for parents who express distress or concern about the use of standard extinction, and for children over the age of 5 years. Single-subject analyses also suggest that modified extinction procedures are appropriate for and effective in the treatment of sleep difficulties exhibited by children with developmental and physical disabilities (Bramble, 1996, 1997; Didden et al., 1999; Thackeray & Richdale, 2002; Weiskop et al., 2005), including for children over the chronological age of 5 years.

Although the term *extinction* is used in existing research, none of the studies reviewed utilized preintervention assessment procedures necessary to establish that extinction is the operative behavioral process in described interventions. Extinction involves breaking the contingency between a behavioral event and its reinforcing consequence. To do this, one must first identify the consequence maintaining a behavior and then arrange the environment such that the reinforcing consequence does not follow the behavior. That is, in order to determine that removal of adult attention in response to crying out from the room is in fact extinction, one must first demonstrate that adult attention maintains the crying out. Calls for increased emphasis on the function of bedtime resistance have occurred (Brown & Piazza, 1999), and demonstrations exist showing the ability to identify contingencies impacting bedtime resistance (O'Reilly, Lancioni, & Sigafoos, 2004). While procedures labeled as extinction are generally effective, it is possible that treatment failures may occur because the functional reinforcer(s) have not been identified for the targeted resistance, thus the prescribed intervention strategy is not targeting the correct variable(s). We concur with Brown and Piazza (1999) that increased emphasis on functional assessment of bedtime resistance would be beneficial. We also submit that the high success rate of described interventions suggests that it is reasonable to presume that for most children, bedtime resistance is operant, and as such, unmodified extinction addresses the most likely candidate reinforcement contingencies by eliminating access to parental attention, escape from the room, and engagement in preferred activities. Increased emphasis on pretreatment assessment to identify specific reinforcement contingencies may be most important in response to treatment failures and/or for special populations.

PREVENTATIVE PARENTAL EDUCATION

Based on the expert panel review convened by the AASM, preventative parental education received support at the level of a Standard (Morgenthaler et al., 2006). This is consistent with earlier reviews (Kuhn & Elliott, 2003; Mindell, 1999) that found these interventions to be in the category of a "well-established" intervention, using criteria from clinical psychology.

Randomized Controlled Trials

To date, a total of five RCTs including a total of 1,157 infants from birth to 3 months of age at enrollment have been conducted investigating the effects of providing parents/caregivers with information about infant and child sleep habits and methods of addressing sleep problems (Adair, Zuckerman, Bauchner, Phillip, & Levenson, 1992; Kerr, Jowett, & Smith, 1996; Pinilla & Birch, 1993; St. James-Roberts, Sleep, Morris, Owen, & Gillham, 2001; Wolfson, Lacks, & Futterman, 1992). Preventative interventions typically involve expectant parents (Pinilla & Birch, 1993; Wolfson et al., 1992) or parents of newborns (Adair et al., 1992; Kerr et al., 1996; St. James-Roberts et al., 2001). Three studies (Kerr et al., 1996; Pinilla & Birch, 1993; Wolfson et al., 1992) compared the effects of providing parents with information about infant sleeping habits and methods for promoting self-sleeping against a wait-list control. St. James-Roberts et al. (2001) compared educational support in the form of providing a 10-page guide about infant sleeping and crying against a more prescriptive behavioral program that included written and verbal information about infant sleep habits and methods of promoting positive sleeping skills. Adair and colleagues (1992) used historical controls in their study of preventative education, and thus presumably these children received "treatment as usual."

Results of studies testing preventative methods in the form of educational programs demonstrate significant positive effects. All studies showed that infants in the treatment condition demonstrated fewer disturbances in targeted bedtime and sleep (e.g., increased sleep duration, number of sleep waking) variables as compared to control groups. Further, when assessed, targeted parent behaviors also improved (St. James-Roberts et al., 2001; Wolfson et al., 1992). The written educational intervention offered by St. James-Roberts and colleagues (2001) was not as effective as their behavioral program, though the behavioral program implemented by these researchers was more analogous to the preventative informational program offered by Wolfson et al. (1992).

Meta-Analyses of RCTs

No meta-analytic studies of group designs of parent education as an intervention are available.

Single-Subject Experimental Analyses

To date, only one single-subject analysis of parent education as an intervention for bedtime resistance and/or night waking has been completed (Weymouth, Hudson, & King, 1987). Researchers investigated the effects of providing an advice booklet to treat the amount of time children between the ages of 13 and 42 months spent in their own beds and nighttime disruptions (instances of night waking and calling out) using a multiple-baseline across participants design. In a series of three separate analyses varying primarily by the amount of therapist contact offered, they found promising support that providing an advice booklet on strategies for addressing bedtime resistance and/or night waking helped reduce these

presenting problems, even with relatively minimal therapist guidance. Further, they offered social validity data documenting that the vast majority of participants found the advice booklet helpful and indicated that they would refer it to a friend.

Meta-Analyses of Single-Subject Experiments

To date, there have been no meta-analytic studies conducted regarding single-subject analyses of preventative educational treatments.

Conclusions

Parent education is effective in preventing the development of bedtime settling and/or waking problems in infants. In fact, available evidence has led to parent education/prevention to be considered a Standard treatment (Morgenthaler et al., 2006). The format of treatment delivery has varied markedly across treatment studies (e.g., written material only vs. written and oral material). Insufficient evidence exists to determine which information delivery system(s) is most advantageous. Further, while positive effects have generally been seen, to date there have been no investigations of the child, family, or other characteristics that may influence effects of parent education as a preventative option. More work is needed in order to identify a priori which children and families are likely to benefit from brief educational preventative approaches and those who may require more support to address nighttime difficulties.

Only Wolfson et al. (1992) provide data sufficient for calculating effect sizes. Specifically, for sleep variables measured, effect sizes at follow-up ranged from a small effect ($d = 0.232$) for the number of night wakings to a large effect ($d = 0.728$) for "number of sleep episodes." Further, they showed that their treatment produced a large effect on parental efficacy in managing sleep in their infants ($d = 0.928$). Wolfson et al. (1992)

also evaluated the clinical significance of their findings by comparing between groups the percentage of children meeting defined criteria for independently sleeping through the night. They found that a significantly greater number of children in the intervention group met criteria for successfully sleeping through the night on their own as compared to those in the control group. While these data offer preliminary evidence of large and clinically significant effects of parent education, more careful scrutiny of the effects of this type of intervention is needed.

GRADUATED EXTINCTION

Graduated extinction as an intervention is considered at the Guideline level for bedtime resistance and/or night waking (Morgenthaler et al., 2006), based on available AASM-sponsored analysis of the research (Mindell et al., 2006). While Mindell (1999) originally categorized this treatment as "probably efficacious," additional positive findings published after that review result in it being considered "well-established" (Kuhn & Elliott, 2003), based on criteria for considering empirical validation of psychological treatments.

Randomized Controlled Trials

Eight RCTs including a total of 745 children ages 4 to 48 months have been conducted investigating graduated extinction to treat child sleep disturbances (Adams & Rickert, 1989; Eckerberg, 2002, 2004; Hiscock & Wake, 2002; Hiscock et al., 2008; Pritchard & Appleton, 1988; Reid et al., 1999; Sadeh, 1994). Graduated extinction has been compared against unmodified extinction and positive bedtime routines (Adams & Rickert, 1989; Reid et al., 1999), as well as against cosleeping with parents (Sadeh, 1994). Eckerberg (2002, 2004) compared the effectiveness of two variations of graduated extinction. In addition, two RCTs compared

graduated extinction against psychoeducation to treat pediatric sleep disturbances and the impact of treatment on maternal depression (Hiscock & Wake, 2002; Hiscock et al., 2008). An additional study compared graduated extinction with and without support visits from a therapist (Pritchard & Appleton, 1988). Collectively these studies demonstrate that graduated extinction effectively reduces bedtime settling and/or night-waking problems. Secondary analysis of effect sizes completed by Kuhn and Elliott (2003) showed large effects for variables of bedtime tantrum frequency ($d = 0.75$) and duration ($d = 1.50$) in the Adams and Rickert (1989) study and for good bedtimes ($d = 1.93$) and good nighttimes ($d = 2.03$) in the Reid et al. (1999) study.

Two well-designed RCTs compared the effectiveness of graduated extinction to two other well-researched behavioral interventions for nighttime waking and bedtime resistance. Adams and Rickert (1989) compared the success of graduated extinction, the establishment of a positive bedtime routine, and a control condition in reducing bedtime tantrums in 36 toddlers and preschool-age children. Children in both treatment groups experienced significant decreases in the frequency and duration of tantrums during the initial weeks of treatment and at the 3- and 6-week follow-up evaluations as compared to the control group. Generally, there was minimal to no differences between the two treatment groups. However, marital satisfaction improved most significantly in the group that used the positive routines intervention.

As previously discussed, Reid et al. (1999) found that both graduated extinction and unmodified extinction significantly reduced bedtime refusal and nighttime waking as compared to no treatment; furthermore, there were no differences across treatment groups and treatment gains maintained over the 2-month follow-up period. There were no significant differences between the groups on measures of maternal stress, and mothers reported satisfaction with both unmodified and graduated extinction procedures.

Pritchard and Appleton (1988) provided one of the first analyses of a modified version of standard extinction consistent with what is now termed *graduated extinction*. They required parents to use standard extinction procedures with regular checks on their child's safety with minimal interaction every 20 minutes until their child's problematic behavior ceased (Pritchard & Appleton, 1988). Families were randomly assigned to one of two groups; one group received additional support visits with a therapist over the course of treatment while the other did not. Participants in both groups demonstrated significant reductions in night waking. There were no significant differences between the two groups, indicating that additional support is not necessary in the implementation of treatment.

Eckerberg (2002) investigated the effectiveness of two variations of a two-step graduated extinction program in the treatment of spontaneous awakening and nighttime crying in infants under 18 months of age. In the two-step program, children were first taught to fall asleep alone and then taught to go back to sleep alone when they wake during the night. Versions of the treatment varied based on whether treatment recommendations were offered in writing or directly by a trained professional. Both versions provide support from a trained professional during the second step of the intervention. Results showed significant improvement in sleep latency and night waking following the intervention, with no differences between groups. With the exception of one participant, sleep problems were completely solved or had improved at the 1- and 3-month follow-ups.

In a follow-up study, Eckerberg (2004) investigated the same interventions with 95 infants and young children between 4 and 45 months of age, by adding 28 additional participants to their initial study. The new participants were assigned to a written information group. Both groups experienced significant improvement in the number of signaled awakenings, time awake during the

night, nighttime sleep time, and total sleep time as registered on the participants' sleep diaries. Parents reported significant improvements in daytime behavior and family well-being.

Sadeh (1994) randomly assigned 50 infants ages 9 to 12 months with sleep disturbances to receive either graduated extinction or cosleeping interventions. Sleep disturbances were measured using two methods: parental report via a sleep log and actigraphy. An actigraph is a watch-like device that measures motion and uses pattern of motion to determine wakefulness and immobility to define sleep. Movement is sensed by an omni-directional mercury switch that is open when there is no movement and closed when movement is detected. Sleep–wake patterns are analyzed using a validated computer-based automatic sleep-scoring algorithm. No between-group differences in treatment outcome were found, so their data were pooled for data analyses. Percent of time asleep while in bed, the number of night wakings, and the percent of active sleep improved from pre- to posttreatment as measured by actigraphy and parental report. No significant differences were found for changes in the time of sleep onset based on either measure.

Two RCTs have compared the effect of graduated extinction to a control group in the treatment of infant sleep problems and the impact on maternal depression (Hiscock & Wake, 2002; Hiscock et al., 2008). Hiscock and Wake (2002) investigated the effect of graduated extinction as compared to a control group who received psychoeducational information about typical sleep behaviors in infants. An unspecified number of parents in the graduated extinction condition chose to use "adult fading," whereby parents remained in the room until the infant fell asleep and gradually removed their presence over a period of several weeks. After 2 months, infants in the intervention group experienced greater improvements in their sleep problems than the control group and significantly more mothers in the control group had sought out additional help. Maternal depression improved in both groups at 2 months, with mothers in the intervention group experiencing greater improvement, but by 4 months there was no longer a significant difference between groups. Mothers in the intervention group rated their amount and quality of sleep more positively than the control group; further, they reported significantly higher satisfaction with the sleep strategies than mothers in the control group. Hiscock and colleagues (2008) used similar procedures to analyze the long-term effects of a population-based application of behavioral treatment for infant sleep problems by training public health nurses to offer specific behavioral interventions, including graduated extinction. However, while treatment benefits were noted for maternal depression and parent–child interaction variables, analysis does not allow for a specific determination of the effects of graduated extinction against either no treatment or other treatments.

Nonrandomized Between-Groups and Within-Subjects Design Studies

A between-groups design was used by Minde, Faucon, and Falkner (1994) to investigate the effect of graduated extinction on sleep disturbances in 50 infants between the ages of 12 and 36 months and their daytime interactions with their mothers. Twenty-eight infants were assigned to treatment based on preintervention Composite Sleep scores (derived from sleep diaries and including sleep latency, frequency and duration of night waking, sleep and wake time, and amount of time child spent in parents' bed over a 2-week period) in the moderate or higher range; 30 were assigned to the control group, given that Composite Sleep scores on measures of sleep behavior were indicative of minimal to no sleep disturbance. Of the 28 families participating in the treatment group, five families refused to implement graduated extinction and instead were taught to use a fading intervention (i.e., parents told to remain

in the room, but gradually move away from their child by lying next to the child, then sitting up next to the child, to sitting in a chair next to the bed, and so on). After 6 weeks of treatment, the participants in the intervention group demonstrated a 30% decrease in their Composite Sleep score. Gains made following the intervention period were maintained 3 months later. At the 3-month follow-up evaluation, the treatment group continued to have significantly higher Composite Sleep scores as compared to the control group, indicating that they still exhibited significantly more sleep difficulties than the control group, who had never had difficulties with sleep behaviors. Participants in the intervention group showed significant improvement in their behavioral ratings and improved mother–child interaction during feedings. No significant changes were found for mother–child interaction during playtime. However, it is unclear to what extent that intervention was effective because the two treatment interventions were not analyzed separately and the number of participants in the parental presence group was only five.

A within-subjects group design was used by Leeson and colleagues (1994) to investigate the effectiveness of graduated extinction combined with wrapping, termination of night feedings after 10:00 P.M., and the establishment of daytime routine in decreasing the frequency and duration of night waking in infants between 8 and 12 months of age. Twenty families were enrolled in a 5-day residential treatment program at Torrens House in Australia. Parents were instructed to settle their child to sleep in their preferred way and use graduated extinction procedures to respond to night waking. Parents responded at 2-, 4-, 6-, 8-, and then 10-minute intervals and continued to respond at 10-minute intervals until their infant fell asleep. If the infant was still crying after an hour, the parents were instructed to start the graduated extinction procedures over. Beyond the graduated extinction procedure, parents were instructed to wrap their child in a sheet prior to putting them to sleep, cease night feeds after 10:00 P.M., and to establish a regular daytime routine with regular patterns of feeding, playtime, and sleeping. At the end of treatment, 48% of the infants slept through the last 2 nights without difficulty, and the rest woke briefly at one or two points but were able to settle with minimal parental interaction. At the 1-month follow-up evaluation, the frequency and duration of night waking had significantly decreased. Three-month post-treatment gains were maintained for the majority of participants (86%); parents of three participants who showed no improvement indicated they did not continue to use the treatment. Leeson et al. (1994) also demonstrated that there was a significant decrease in the number of mothers and fathers who met criteria for depression on a standardized evaluation tool from baseline to 1-month follow-up.

Meta-Analyses of Group Design Research

To date, no meta-analytic studies have been conducted to investigate the effects of group-based research on graduated extinction or its modifications.

Single-Subject Experimental Analyses

Three single-subject, multiple-baseline studies have been conducted to investigate the effectiveness of standard graduated extinction and adapted graduated extinction as a treatment for sleep disturbances in infants and young children (Durand & Mindell, 1990; Lawton et al., 1991; Mindell & Durand, 1993) and parental sleep, maternal and paternal depression, and mothers' ratings of marital satisfaction (Mindell & Durand, 1993).

Lawton et al. (1991) tested the effects of graduated extinction with six children between the ages of 6 and 14 months using a multiple-baseline across participants design. Three infants showed improvements of 80% or more, whereas the other three showed a reduction in sleep problems of 50% or less. Three showed

clinically significant reductions in the frequency and duration of night waking. One participant showed clinically significant reduction in the duration, but not frequency, of night waking. Five participants who had baseline difficulties with bedtime delays all demonstrated statistically significant reductions. The participants who displayed sleep-onset problems during the baseline phase demonstrated improvements in this behavior, although improvements did not reach clinical significance.

Durand and colleagues (Durand & Mindell, 1990; Mindell & Durand, 1993) tested graduated extinction procedures using single-subject designs with infants and young children. In the first study, they demonstrated that graduated extinction produced rapid improvements in the bedtime refusal and night waking of a 14-month-old female (Durand & Mindell, 1990). In a follow-up investigation, Mindell and Durand (1993) showed that graduated extinction combined with positive bedtime routines both improved bedtime and waking problems in six children ages 18 to 52 months and led to significant improvements in parental sleep. Further, parents reported being satisfied with the treatment at a posttreatment and 1-month follow-up appointment. In addition, mothers and fathers reported significant decreases in depressive symptoms and mothers reported significant increases in marital satisfaction over the course of treatment.

Special Populations

Single-subject analyses have been conducted to investigate the effectiveness of graduated extinction procedures in treating night waking and bedtime refusal in several special populations (Durand, Gernert-Dott, & Mapston, 1996; Vervloed, Hoevenaars, & Maas, 2003). Graduated extinction has been found to be effective in eliminating sleep latency and night waking in a 4½-year-old child with visual impairment (Vervloed et al., 2003). Modified graduated extinction procedures were demonstrated to be effective in treating bedtime disturbances and night waking in children with developmental disabilities (Durand et al., 1996).

Conclusions

Research using both RCTs and single-subject analyses suggest that graduated extinction is an established treatment for sleep difficulties in typically developing infants, toddlers, and young children (Mindell, 1999; Mindell et al., 2006; Morgenthaler et al., 2006; Owens et al., 2002). Further, single-subject analyses suggest that unmodified and modified graduated extinction procedures are appropriate for and effective in the treatment of sleep difficulties exhibited by children with visual impairments and developmental disabilities (Durand et al., 1996; Vervloed et al., 2003). More studies using RCT designs have been conducted on graduated extinction with a larger number of total participants as compared to unmodified extinction. However, limitations in methodology temper the support for this intervention, thus resulting in it being considered a "guideline" (Morgenthaler et al., 2006).

The effects of graduated extinction may be equivocal to unmodified extinction and positive routines, although it may produce more gradual results (Adams & Rickert, 1989; Reid et al., 1999). Graduated extinction appears to lead to positive secondary outcomes, including decreased levels of maternal and paternal depression and improvements in parental sleep (Eckerberg, 2004; Hiscock & Wake, 2002; Hiscock et al., 2008; Leeson et al., 1994; Mindell & Durand, 1993). Interestingly, mothers using positive routines reported significantly higher marital satisfaction than those in the graduated extinction group despite both treatments producing equivocal results (Adams & Rickert, 1989). Developing a more complete understanding of the determinants of secondary benefits to graduated extinction will help explain such findings.

When assessed, the majority of parents report being satisfied with graduated extinction (Mindell & Durand, 1993; Reid et al., 1999);

however, satisfaction ratings have been provided by parents following the successful completion of graduated extinction. Similar to the data with unmodified extinction, researchers have not investigated pretreatment expectations and how they may be associated with both treatment outcome and ultimate satisfaction. In existing studies, researchers have indicated that some parents refused to use extinction procedures (Hiscock & Wake, 2002) or were given the option between graduated extinction or other interventions due to clinical experience indicating that some families are uncomfortable with this treatment (Hiscock et al., 2008). These reports continue to temper the viability of extinction-based procedures, in this case graduated extinction, as feasible with all families. Treatment fidelity has rarely been directly investigated and is an important determinant of the success of a given treatment, potentially relating to its satisfaction as well. Leeson et al. (1994) noted that the participants who demonstrated no improvement at the follow-up evaluation had all discontinued the intervention following the treatment phase of the study, suggesting that treatment fidelity may be important in maintaining long-term improvements in sleep disturbances.

FADED BEDTIME/POSITIVE ROUTINES

Bedtime fading and positive routines received support in the AASM consensus panel recommendations at the level of a Guideline (Morgenthaler et al., 2006). This is consistent with earlier reviews (Kuhn & Elliott, 2003; Mindell, 1999) that found these interventions to be in the category of a "promising intervention," using criteria from clinical psychology.

Randomized Controlled Trials

Only one RCT has been reported on the use of positive routines. Adams and Rickert (1989) randomly assigned 36 children age 18 to 48 months who were exhibiting bedtime tantrums to one of three groups: positive routines, extinction, or control. Children who received either active treatment, positive routines, or extinction had fewer tantrums and for shorter periods than children in the control group during 6 weeks of treatment and at 3 and 6 weeks after treatment. Although both treatments were more effective than the control condition, parents of the positive routine group reported significantly improved marital satisfaction, suggesting additional benefits of this treatment strategy. In their review of treatment efficacy in pediatric sleep medicine, Kuhn and Elliott (2003) computed effect sizes for Adams and Rickert's (1989) study. They report large effect sizes for both the frequency of bedtime tantrums ($d = 0.75$) and duration of bedtime tantrums ($d = 1.50$) during treatment and at follow-up (frequency: $d = 0.88$; duration: $d = 1.83$).

Within-Subject Group Studies

One within-subject group study also found beneficial results with positive routines and/or bedtime fading. Specifically, Galbraith and Hewitt (1993) showed that the positive routines procedure produced rapid effects in 45 typically developing children ages 5 to 72 months.

Meta-Analysis of Group Design Research

To date, there has been no meta-analysis of research on the effects of positive routines/faded bedtime using either RCT or other group designs.

Single-Subject Experimental Analyses

Positive routines were first used by Milan, Mitchell, Berger, and Pierson (1981) in three children ages 2 to 15 years who were severely handicapped and demonstrating bedtime tantrums. A within-subject, A–B–C design was used, and the intervention was effective in gaining voluntary bedtime compliance in all three cases. Piazza and Fisher (1991a, 1991b) used positive routines with faded bedtime to eliminate severe sleep disturbances and increase appropriate sleep in a total of five children ages 3 to 19 years across the two studies. Two other treatment outcome studies have evaluated faded bedtime, both with and without response cost, in a total of 17 children ages 4 to 14 years with developmental disabilities (Piazza, Fisher, & Moser, 1991; Piazza, Fisher, & Sherer, 1997), finding improvements in sleep behaviors. Ashbaugh and Peck (1998) replicated the study by Piazza and Fisher (1991a) using faded bedtime with response to treat on a typically developing 2-year-old, demonstrating positive results.

Meta-Analyses of Single-Subject Experiments

To date, no meta-analytic studies have been conducted on single-subject experiments testing positive routines/faded bedtime interventions.

Conclusions

Although the literature base on positive routines and bedtime fading is small, there are some promising findings. These techniques provide alternatives to extinction-based protocols for treatment of bedtime tantrums in both typically developing children and in children with developmental disabilities. In several recent reviews (Kuhn & Elliott, 2003; Mindell, 1999), the authors have pointed out similarities between positive routines and faded bedtime procedures with two very effective behavioral interventions for adult insomnia, sleep restriction, and stimulus-control instructions. Further evaluation of these interventions is needed, especially in controlled studies.

SCHEDULED WAKING

Based on available reviews of the research, scheduled waking as an intervention is considered at the level of a Guideline according to the AASM taskforce (Morgenthaler et al., 2006) and "probably efficacious" using guidelines specified by the American Psychological Association (Kuhn & Elliott, 2003; Mindell, 1999).

Randomized Controlled Trials

Only one RCT has been completed investigating the effects of scheduled awakenings. As described earlier, Rickert and Johnson (1988) randomly assigned 36 infants and toddlers to one of three experimental groups to evaluate the effects of scheduled awakenings and systematic ignoring against a control. While both treatments were effective in reducing targeted behavior, extinction produced more rapid effects. Kuhn and Elliott's (2003) secondary analysis demonstrated a large effect size ($d = 1.11$) for the number of awakenings.

Meta-Analysis of RCTs

To date, there has been no meta-analysis of research on the use of scheduled night waking to treat spontaneous night waking.

Single-Subject Experimental Analyses

The remaining three studies investigating scheduled awakening utilized single-subject design procedures. McGarr and Hovell (1980) were the first to describe this intervention. Using an ABAB withdrawal design, they demonstrated the benefits of scheduled awakening with a 3-month-old female; furthermore, they successfully faded out the waking schedule while maintaining effects. Subsequently, Johnson and colleagues (Johnson, Bradley-Johnson, & Stack, 1981; Johnson & Lerner, 1985) completed two single-subject analyses of this intervention, with a total of 15 children between the ages of 6 months and 30 months. Again, using a multiple-baseline design across participants, with an embedded ABAB withdrawal design for four participants

in the Johnson and Lerner (1985) study, findings indicated significant decreases in night waking using scheduled awakening.

Meta-Analysis of Single-Subject Experiments

To date, no meta-analyses have been completed to investigate the demonstrated effects of scheduled night waking as a treatment for night waking.

Conclusions

The small body of research on scheduled awakenings suggests that it is an effective treatment for frequent night waking. This treatment may be particularly useful for children who have become resistant to extinction-based procedures due to its inconsistent implementation, for children who engage in behavior patterns (e.g., self-injury, vomiting) that are extremely difficult or unsafe to ignore (Kuhn & Weidinger, 2000), or in situations when parents are resistant to use extinction-based procedures for whatever reason.

The primary limitation of treatment appears to be the length of time needed to produce complete cessation of night waking/crying (Kuhn & Weidinger, 2000; Mindell, 1999). Available literature suggests that parents can expect to implement the treatment for 7 or more weeks before seeing satisfactory results. Further, this treatment does not address bedtime struggles. Given the high co-occurrence between bedtime and night waking difficulties, it may be a limited treatment for many children presenting with sleep disturbances.

EVIDENCE-BASED PRACTICES

Existing literature provides support for behavioral interventions for the most common sleep problems in young children: bedtime resistance and night waking. While medications are prescribed with some regularity for these issues (Mindell, Moline, Zendell, Brown, & Fry, 1994), despite discouragement of such practices by sleep experts (e.g., Sheldon, Spire, & Levy, 1992), it is increasingly recognized that behavioral treatments are effective. Further, behavioral treatments produce better long-term outcomes than medications (Ramchandani et al., 2000). Using rigorous criteria, evaluations of existing studies offer primary support for the use of unmodified extinction, graduated extinction, and parental education as the most established interventions (Kuhn & Elliott, 2003; Mindell, 1999; Morgenthaler et al., 2006). Available information supports extinction with parental presence, scheduled waking, and positive routines/ faded bedtime as viable treatments for consideration. Thus, professionals providing support to families with concerns about their infant or young child's bedtime and sleep habits have available a host of treatments with varying degrees of support from which to choose. Further, while the majority of research involves typically developing children, growing support exists for the use of behavioral interventions to address bedtime and sleep disturbances in children with developmental or physical conditions. These preliminary data offer evidence for selecting behaviorally based interventions when working with children with special health-care and/or developmental needs as well.

Operational definitions have been developed to evaluate whether psychological treatments are empirically validated (Chambless & Hollon, 1998; Chambless et al., 1996) and practice parameters for the treatment of sleep problems in young children have been published (i.e., Morgenthaler et al., 2006). However, evidence-based practice goes beyond analysis of extant literature on a specific intervention or problem area and includes considering both research on the clinical problem with research on related concepts/ issues. Taking the example of research on extinction-based procedures, one's knowledge base about the effects of parental mental health status on treatment outcomes for children, and

clinical decision making based on professional experience are important to blend with the known research base. Thus, professionals working with children with sleep difficulties must have a strong working knowledge of research reviewed in this chapter, but also a grasp on the literature regarding biologically-based sleep disorders, early child development (particularly normative vs. nonnormative behavioral patterns), parent–child interactions, and effects of variables such as socioeconomic status, family constellation, and parental mental health status on treatment outcome, to name a few other areas.

Making clinical decisions regarding how to proceed with treatment must also include determining how to best deliver information about empirically supported treatments. To date, the format of treatment delivery has varied widely across studies. Although most studies rely on well-trained clinicians or researchers to deliver treatment, others have relied on self-help strategies through use of booklets or pamphlets. Provision of treatment recommendations via written presentation is generally as effective as treatment information delivered through clinician contact (Eckerberg, 2002; Scott & Richards, 1990; Seymour et al., 1989), though some evidence suggests that having both written material and clinician contact results in faster improvements (Seymour et al., 1989). Weymouth et al. (1987) suggested that their results indicated that some families could successfully self-implement interventions with written material, whereas others benefited from the assistance of a clinician. In a telephone survey of 229 parents of children 12 to 35 months (Johnson, 1991), many parents indicated using treatments based on information provided through typical mass media outlets (e.g., books, television) with high rates of success. Findings from this survey, coupled with those of the research reviewed in this chapter, suggests that many parents are likely to be able to implement behavioral treatments for infant and young child sleep disturbances with minimal to no support from trained professionals. However, it is likely that variables such as chronicity of presenting bedtime/sleep problems, presence of other emotional or behavioral challenges on the part of the child or parent, and parent variables affect whether providing brief written descriptions is sufficient to ameliorate presenting problems or if therapist-guided assistance is needed. Clinicians must therefore decide the best mode of treatment delivery based on their context (e.g., private practice vs. working within a hospital setting) and assessment of family and child presentation.

Cultural context and variables should also be included when making empirically-informed decisions about problem definition and treatment selection. For example, race and socio-economic status have been shown to be independently associated with sleep behaviors in young children within the United States (Crabtree et al., 2005). Furthermore, cross-cultural investigations comparing individuals living in Western and non-Western countries suggest notable differences in sleep habits, sleeping arrangements, and prevalence of sleep disorders (e.g., Chng, 2008; Jenni & O'Connor, 2005; Liu, Liu, Owens, & Kaplan, 2005). Thus, evaluation and treatment of sleep disorders, particularly behaviorally based sleep problems, require careful consideration of the cultural context in which bedtime and sleep behaviors are exhibited (Owens, 2005).

A significant number of published studies rely on multifaceted interventions rather than a single treatment. In fact, of the studies reviewed by Mindell et al. (2006), which served as the foundation for developing practice parameters (Morgenthaler et al., 2006), 58% employed more than one treatment. Most commonly, some type of reinforcement procedure and standardized bedtime routine was paired with either unmodified or graduated extinction. This points to the fact that addressing bedtime resistance and night waking problems may be best achieved by addressing not only specific interactions at the point of difficulty (i.e., attempting to put the child in bed), but also routines that prepare a child for bedtime and increase motivation on the part of the child to adhere to parental expectations. Evidence-based practice for treating bedtime settling and night waking problems, therefore, involves decision making regarding the constellation of treatments that may be combined to address presenting concerns. Doing so must take into account specifics about the presenting problems, but also the capacity of a child's care providers to implement treatment components in intended ways. In fact, some studies have purposefully provided parents with treatment options for their consideration (Hiscock et al., 2008; Scott & Richards, 1990).

There are a variety of strengths apparent in the literature base on treatment of behavioral sleep problems in infants and children. A range of designs have been used to evaluate the effectiveness of several different intervention strategies for treatment of bedtime resistance and night waking and across study designs, generally research is supportive. Several comprehensive review articles summarize the literature base (Kuhn & Elliott, 2003; Mindell et al., 2006). In addition, practice parameters have been developed to guide clinicians in the use of specific recommended treatments when working with these populations (Morgenthaler et al., 2006). Strengths of individual treatment studies include elements of trial design such as the consideration of extended follow-up/maintenance of treatment effects in many studies, and the comparison of two active treatments, which reduces risk of bias.

A variety of weaknesses are also apparent in the treatment literature. The evidence base is reliant upon a relatively small total pool of child subjects, particularly compared to the adult literature on insomnia/sleep disturbance (Kuhn & Ellliott, 2003). For many of the interventions there are only a few, and sometimes only one, available RCTs. While some suggest that it is important to consider the entire range of evidence when evaluating the extant literature, including single-subject designs (Horner et al., 2005), current convention is to consider RCTs as the most rigorous evidence of support. Moreover, studies were not generally powered to examine therapeutic processes or individual differences in treatment response. While there is some suggestion that marital discord and maternal depression affect success of behavioral treatment for sleep problems in young children (see Mindell et al., 2006, for a review), available research provides minimal to no guidance regarding child or family differences that may predict success of one treatment over another.

Other limitations in the treatment research concern the lack of consistency in outcome measures used among studies. Primarily, behavioral outcome measures (e.g., number of tantrums, frequency of night wakings) have demonstrated change, while few measures of sleep have demonstrated change with intervention. There are weaknesses apparent across the majority of the treatment studies conducted to address bedtime resistance and night waking in children in aspects of trial design and reporting. Insufficient details are provided about treatment fidelity, and thus in the majority of the studies whether or not parents adhered to and/or implemented treatment recommendation is unknown. Finally, treatment expectations were also rarely reported, a notable limitation given that others have demonstrated the importance of expectations about an intervention when investigating treatment outcome (Goosens, Vlaeyen, Hidding, Kole-Snijders, & Evers, 2005).

Beyond limitations of the reviewed research is the relative dearth of attention to the treatment of sleep problems in older children and adolescents. Evidence supports a high comorbidity between sleep disturbances in adolescents and psychiatric issues (Goldstein, Bridge, & Brent, 2008; Ivanenko, Barnes, Crabtree, & Gozal, 2004; Johnson, Roth, Schultz, & Breslau, 2006). Because of this, clinicians are beginning to develop and implement sleep interventions for these adolescents. As one example, Bootzin and Stevens (2005)

describe the development of a six-session group treatment of sleep disturbances in adolescents who have received treatment for substance abuse that uses cognitive behavioral interventions. Similarly, there have been several sleep educational interventions developed and tested in youth with physical health conditions, including migraine headaches (Bruni, Galli, & Guidetti, 1999) and juvenile fibromyalgia (Degotardi et al., 2006). Despite these recent examples of attention sleep problems in older children and adolescents, much remains to be done to address this gap in the literature.

Despite these limitations, sufficient evidence exists supporting the use of behavioral treatments for bedtime and sleep problems in infants and children. Thus, clinical child and pediatric psychologists are encouraged to recognize the significant negative impact these sleep disturbances can have on the child and family, and as a result implement best practices in their treatment. Evidence-based practice in this area involves drawing from specific research on the treatment of these difficulties, while also using other available evidence and clinical decision making to determine best practices for any given client.

REFERENCES

Abdel-Khalek, A. M. (2004). Prevalence of reported insomnia and its consequences in a survey of 5,044 adolescents in Kuwait. *Sleep, 27*, 726–731.

Adair, R., Zuckerman, B., Bauchner, H., Phillipp, B., & Levenson, S. (1992). Reducing night waking in infancy: A primary care intervention. *Pediatrics, 89*, 585–588.

Adams, L. A., & Rickert, V. I. (1989). Reducing bedtime tantrums: Comparison between positive routines and graduated extinction. *Pediatrics, 84*, 756–761.

Ali, N. J., Pitson, D. J., & Stradling, D. J. (1993). Snoring, sleep disturbance, and behaviour in 4–5 year olds. *Archives of Disabled Children, 68*, 360–366.

American Academy of Sleep Medicine. (2005). *International classification of sleep disorders* (2nd ed.). Westchester, IL: Author.

American Psychiatric Association (APA). (2000). *Diagnostic and statistical manual of mental disorders* (4th ed., text rev.). Washington, DC: Author.

Ashbaugh, R., & Peck, S. M. (1998). Treatment of sleep problems in a toddler: A replication of the faded bedtime with response cost protocol. *Journal of Applied Behavior Analysis, 31,* 127–129.

Blum, N. J., & Carey, W. B. (1996). Sleep problems among infants and young children. *Pediatric Review, 17,* 88–93.

Bootzin, R. R., & Stevens, S. J. (2005). Adolescents, substance abuse, and the treatment of insomnia and daytime sleepiness. *Clinical Psychology Reviews, 25,* 629–644.

Bramble, D. (1996). Consumer opinion concerning the treatment of a common sleep problem. *Child: Care, Health, and Development, 22,* 355–366.

Bramble, D. (1997). Rapid-acting treatment for a common sleep problem. *Developmental Medicine & Child Neurology, 39,* 543–547.

Brown, K. A., & Piazza, C. C. (1999). Enhancing the effectiveness of sleep treatments: Developing a functional approach: Commentary. *Journal of Pediatric Psychology, 24,* 487–489.

Bruni, O., Galli, F., & Guidetti, V. (1999). Sleep hygiene and migraine in children and adolescents. *Cephalalgia, 19*(Suppl. 25), 57–59.

Chadez, L. H., & Nurius, P. S. (1987). Stopping bedtime crying: Treating the child and the parents. *Journal of Clinical Child Psychology, 16,* 212–217.

Chambless, D. L., & Hollon, S. D. (1998). Defining empirically supported therapies. *Journal of Consulting and Clinical Psychology, 66,* 7–18.

Chambless, D. L., Sanderson, W. C., Shoham, V., Johnson, S. B., Pope, K. S., Crits-Christoph, P., . . . McCurry, S. (1996). An update on empirically validated therapies. *The Clinical Psychologist, 49,* 5–14.

Chng, S. Y. (2008). Sleep disorders in children: The Singapore perspective. *Annals of the Academy of Medicine, Singapore, 37,* 706–709.

Christophersen, E. R., & Mortweet, S. L. (2001). *Treatments that work with children: Empirically supported strategies for managing childhood problems.* Washington, DC: American Psychological Association.

Cortesi, F., Giannotti, F., Sebastiani, T., Vagnoni, C., & Marioni, P. (2008). Cosleeping versus solitary sleeping in children with bedtime problems: Child emotional problems and parental distress. *Behavioral Sleep Medicine, 6,* 89–105.

Couturier, J. L., Speechley, K. N., Steele, M., Norman, R., Stringer, B., & Nicolson, R. (2005). Parental perception of sleep problems in children of normal intelligence with pervasive developmental disorders: Prevalence, severity, and pattern. *Journal of the American Academy of Child & Adolescent Psychiatry, 44,* 815–822.

Crabtree, V. M., Korhonen, J. B., Montgomery-Downs, H. E., Jones, V. F., O'Brien, L. M., & Gozal, M. (2005). Cultural influences on the bedtime behaviors of young children. *Sleep Medicine, 6,* 319–324.

Degotardi, P. J., Klass, E. S., Rosenberg, B. S., Fox, D. G., Gallelli, K. A., & Gottlieb, B. S. (2006). Development and evaluation of a cognitive-behavioral intervention for juvenile fibromyalgia. *Journal of Pediatric Psychology, 31,* 714–723.

Didden, R., De Moor, J., & Kruit, I. W. (1999). The effects of extinction in the treatment of sleep problems with a child with a physical disability. *International Journal of Disability, 46,* 247–252.

Doo, S., & Wing, Y. K. (2006). Sleep problems of children with pervasive developmental disorders: Correlation with parental stress. *Developmental Medicine & Child Neurology, 48,* 650–655.

Durand, V. M., Gernert-Dott, P., & Mapston, E. (1996). Treatment of sleep disorder in children with developmental disabilities. *The Journal of the Association for Persons with Developmental Disability, 21,* 114–122.

Durand, V. M., & Mindell, J. A. (1990). Behavioral treatment of multiple childhood sleep disorders: Effects on child and family. *Behavior Modification, 14,* 37–49.

Eckerberg, B. (2002). Treatment of sleep problems in families with small children: Is written information enough? *Acta Paediatrica, 91,* 952–959.

Eckerberg, B. (2004). Treatment of sleep problems in families with young children: Effects of treatment on family well-being. *Acta Paediatrica, 93,* 126–134

Eddy, D. (1992). *A manual for assessing health practices and designing practice policies: The explicit approach.* Philadelphia, PA: American College of Physicians.

Fallone, G., Owens, J. A., & Deane, J. (2002). Sleepiness in children and adolescents: Clinical implications. *Sleep Medicine Review, 6,* 287–306.

France, K. G., & Blampied, N. M. (2005). Modification of systematic ignoring in the management of infant sleep disturbance: Efficacy and distress. *Child & Family Behavior Therapy, 27,* 1–16.

France, K. G., Blampied, N. M., & Wilkinson, P. (1991). Treatment of infant sleep by trimeprazine in combination with extinction. *Journal of Developmental Behavior and Pediatrics, 12,* 308–314.

France, K. G., & Hudson, S. M. (1990). Behavior management of infant sleep disturbance. *Journal of Applied Behavior Analysis, 23,* 91–98.

Freeman, K. A. (2006). Treating bedtime resistance with the bedtime pass: A systematic replication and component analysis with 3-year-olds. *Journal of Applied Behavior Analysis, 39,* 423–428.

Friman, P. C., Hoff, K. E., Schnoes, C., Freeman, K. A., Woods, D. W., & Blum, N. (1999). The bedtime pass: An approach to bedtime crying and leaving the room. *Archives of Pediatric and Adolescent Medicine, 153,* 1027–1029.

Galbraith, L., & Hewitt, K. E. (1993). Behavioural treatment for sleep disturbance. *Health Visitor, 66,* 169–171.

Gelman, V. S., & King, N. J. (2001). Wellbeing of mothers with children exhibiting sleep disturbance. *Australian Journal of Psychology, 53*, 18–22.

Goldstein, T. R., Bridge, J. A., & Brent, D. A. (2008). Sleep disturbance preceding completed suicide in adolescents. *Journal of Consulting and Clinical Psychology, 76*, 84–91.

Goossens, M. E. J. B, Vlaeyen, J. W. S., Hidding, A., Kole-Snijders, A., & Evers, S. M. A. A. (2005). Treatment expectancy affects the outcome of cognitive-behavioral interventions in chronic pain. *Clinical Journal of Pain, 21*, 18–26.

Gregory, A. M., & O'Connor, T. G. (2002). Sleep problems in childhood: A longitudinal study of developmental change and association with behavior problems. *Journal of the American Academy of Child and Adolescent Psychiatry, 41*, 964–971.

Hiscock, H., Bayer, J. K., Hampton, A., Ukoumunne, O. C., & Wake, M. (2008). Long-term mother and child mental health effects of a population-based infant sleep intervention: Cluster-randomized, controlled trial. *Pediatrics, 122*, 621–627.

Hiscock, H., & Wake, M. (2002). Randomised controlled trial of behavioural infant sleep intervention to improve infant sleep and maternal mood. *British Medical Journal, 324*, 1062–1067.

Honomichl, R. D., Goodlin-Jones, B. L., Burnham, M., Gaylor, E., & Anders, T. F. (2002). Sleep patterns of children with pervasive developmental disorders. *Journal of Autism & Developmental Disorders, 32*, 553–561.

Horner, R. H., Carr, E. G., Halle, J., McGee, G., Odom, S., & Wolery, S. (2005). The use of single-subject research to identify evidence-based practice in special education. *Exceptional Children, 71*, 165–179.

Ivanenko, A., Barnes, M. E., Crabtree, V. M., & Gozal, D. (2004). Psychiatric symptoms in children with insomnia referred to a pediatric sleep medicine center. *Sleep Medicine, 5*, 253–259.

Jenni, O. G., & O'Connor, B. B. (2005). Children's sleep: An interplay between culture and biology. *Pediatrics, 115*, 204–216.

Johnson, C. M. (1991). Infant and toddler sleep: A telephone survey of parents in one community. *Journal of Developmental and Behavioral Pediatrics, 12*, 108–114.

Johnson, C. M., Bradley-Johnson, S., & Stack, J. M. (1981). Decreasing the frequency of infants' nocturnal crying with the use of scheduled awakenings. *Family Practice Research Journal, 1*, 98–104.

Johnson, C. M., & Lerner, M. (1985). Amelioration of infant sleep disturbances: II. Effects of scheduled awakenings by compliant parents. *Infant Mental Health Journal, 6*, 21–30.

Johnson, E. O., Roth, T., Schultz, L., & Breslau, N. (2006). Epidemiology of *DSM-IV* insomnia in adolescence: Lifetime prevalence, chronicity, and an emergent gender difference. *Pediatrics, 117*, e247–e256.

Kataria, S., Swanson, M. S., & Trevathon, G. E. (1987). Persistence of sleep disturbances in preschool children. *Behavioral Pediatrics, 110*, 642–646.

Kerr, S. M., Jowett, S. A., & Smith, L. N. (1996). Preventing sleep problems in infants: A randomized controlled trial. *Journal of Advanced Nursing, 24*, 938–942.

Kotagal, S. (2003). Sleep disorders in childhood. *Neurological Clinics of North America, 21*, 961–981.

Krakowiak, P., Goodlin-Jones, B., Hertz-Picciotto, I., Croen, L., & Hansen, R. (2008). Sleep problems in children with autism spectrum disorders, developmental delays, and typical development: A population-based study. *Journal of Sleep Research, 17*, 197–206.

Kuhn, B. R., & Elliott, A. J. (2003). Treatment efficacy in behavioral pediatric sleep medicine. *Journal of Psychosomatic Research, 54*, 587–597.

Kuhn, B. R., & Weidinger, D. (2000). Interventions for infant and toddler sleep disturbances: A review. *Child & Family Behavior Therapy, 22*, 33–50.

Lawton, C., France, K. G., & Blampied, N. M. (1991). Treatment of infant sleep disturbance by graduated extinction. *Child & Family Behavior Therapy, 13*, 39–56.

Leeson, R., Barbour, J., Romaniuk, D., & Warr, R. (1994). Management of infant sleep problems in a residential unit. *Child: Care, Health, and Development, 20*, 89–100.

Lewin, D. S., England, S. J., & Rosen, R. C. (1995). Neuropsychological sequelae of obstructive sleep apnea in children. *Sleep Research, 25*, 304–310.

Liu, X., Liu, L., Owens, J. A., & Kaplan, D. L. (2005). Sleep patterns and sleep problems among school-children in the United States and China. *Pediatrics, 115*, 241–249.

Liu, X., & Zhou, H. (2002). Sleep duration, insomnia and behavioral problems among Chinese adolescents. *Psychiatry Research, 111*, 75–85.

Lozoff, B., Wolf, A. W., & Davis, N. S. (1985). Sleep problems seen in pediatric practice. *Pediatrics, 75*, 477–483.

Maganti, R., Hausman, N., Koehn, M., Sandok, E., Glurich, I., & Mukesh, B. N. (2006). Excessive daytime sleepiness and sleep complaints among children with epilepsy. *Epilepsy & Behavior, 8*, 272–277.

McGarr, R. J., & Hovell, M. F. (1980). In search of the sand man: Shaping an infant to sleep. *Education and Treatment of Children, 3*, 173–182.

Milan, M. A., Mitchell, Z. P., Berger, M. I., & Pierson, D. F. (1981). Positive routines: A rapid alternative to extinction for elimination of bedtime tantrum behavior. *Child Behavior Therapy, 3*, 13–25.

Miller, V. A., Palermo, T. M., Powers, S. W., Scher, M. S., & Hershey, A. D. (2003). Migraine headaches and sleep disturbances in children. *Headache: The Journal of Head and Face Pain, 43*, 362–368.

Minde, K., Faucon, A., & Falkner, S. (1994). Sleep problems in toddlers: Effects of treatment on their daytime behavior. *Journal of the American Academy on Child and Adolescent Psychiatry, 33*, 1114–1121.

Minde, K., Popiel, K., Leos, N., Falkner, S., Parker, K., & Handly-Derry, M. (1993). The evaluation and treatment of sleep disturbances in young children. *Journal of Child Psychology and Psychiatry, 34*, 521–533.

Mindell, J. A. (1993). Sleep disorders in children. *Health Psychology, 12*, 151–162.

Mindell, J. A. (1999). Empirically supported treatments in pediatric psychology: Bedtime refusal and night wakings in young children. *Journal of Pediatric Psychology, 24*, 465–481.

Mindell, J. A., & Durand, V. M. (1993). Treatment of childhood sleep disorders: Generalization across disorders and effects on family members. *Journal of Pediatric Psychology, 18*, 731–750.

Mindell, J. A., Kuhn, B., Lewin, D. S., Meltzer, L. J., & Sadeh, A. (2006). Behavioral treatment of bedtime problems and night wakings in infants and young children. *Sleep, 29*, 1263–1276.

Mindell, J. A., Moline, M. L., Zendell, S. M., Brown, L. W., & Fry, J. M. (1994). Pediatricians and sleep disorders: Training and practice. *Pediatrics, 94*, 194–200.

Mindell, J. A., & Owens, J. A. (2003). *A clinical guide to pediatric sleep: Diagnosis and management of sleep problems.* Philadelphia, PA: Lippincott Williams & Wilkins.

Mindell, J. A., Owens, J. A., & Carskadon, M. A. (1999). Developmental features of sleep. *Child and Adolescent Psychiatry Clinics of North America, 8*, 695–725.

Moore, B. A., Friman, P. C., Fruzzetti, A. E., & MacAleese, K. (2007). Brief report: Evaluating the Bedtime Pass Program for child resistance to bedtime—A randomized, controlled trial. *Journal of Pediatric Psychology, 32*, 283–287.

Morgenthaler, T. I., Owens, J., Alessi, C., Boehlecke, B., Brown, T. M., Coleman, J., Jr., . . . Swick, T. J. (2006). Practice parameters for behavioral treatment of bedtime problems and night wakings in infants and young children. *Sleep, 29*, 1277–1281.

Morrison, D. N., McGee, R., & Stanton, W. R. (1992). Sleep problems in adolescence. *Journal of the American Academy of Child and Adolescent Psychiatry, 31*, 94–99.

O'Reilly, M. F., Lancioni, G. E., & Sigafoos, J. (2004). Using paired-choice assessment to identify variables maintaining sleep problems in a child with severe disabilities. *Journal of Applied Behavior Analysis, 37*, 209–212.

Owens, J. A. (2005). Introduction: Culture and sleep in children. *Pediatrics, 115*(1 Suppl.), 201–203.

Owens, J. A., Palermo, T. M., & Rosen, C. L. (2002). Overview of current management of sleep disturbances in children: II-Behavioral interventions. *Current Therapeutic Research, 63*(Suppl. B), B38–B53.

Owens, J. A., Spirito, A., McGuinn, M., & Nobile, C. (2000). Sleep habits and sleep disturbances in elementary school-aged children. *Journal of Developmental and Behavioral Pediatrics, 21*, 27–36.

Paavonen, E. J., Almqvist, F., Tamminen, T., Moilanen, I., Piha, J., Räsänen, E., & Aronen, E. T. (2002). Poor sleep and psychiatric symptoms at school: An epidemiological study. *European Child & Adolescent Psychiatry, 17*, 10–17.

Paavonen, E. J., Solantaus, T., Almqvist, F. E., & Aronen, E. T. (2003). Four-year follow-up study of sleep and psychiatric symptoms in preadolescents: Relationship of persistent and temporary sleep problems to psychiatric symptoms. *Developmental and Behavioral Pediatrics, 24*, 307–314.

Piazza, C. C., & Fisher, W. (1991a). A faded bedtime with response cost protocol for treatment of multiple sleep problems in children. *Journal of Applied Behavior Analysis, 24*, 129–140.

Piazza, C. C., & Fisher, W. W. (1991b). Bedtime fading in the treatment of pediatric insomnia. *Journal of Behavior Therapy and Experimental Psychiatry, 22*, 53–56.

Piazza, C. C., Fisher, W., & Moser, H. (1991). Behavioral treatment of sleep dysfunction in patients with the Rett syndrome. *Brain & Development, 13*, 232–237.

Piazza, C. C., Fisher, W. W., & Sherer, M. (1997). Treatment of multiple sleep problems in children with developmental disabilities: Faded bedtime with response cost versus bedtime scheduling. *Developmental Medicine & Child Neurology, 39*, 414–418.

Pinilla, T., & Birch, L. L. (1993). Help me make it through the night: Behavioral entrainment of breast-fed infants' sleep patterns. *Pediatrics, 91*, 436–444.

Pollock, J. I. (1992). Predictors and long-term associations of reported sleep difficulties in infancy. *Journal of Reproductive and Infant Psychology, 10*, 151–168.

Pollock, J. I. (1994). Night wakings at five years of age: Predictors and prognosis. *Journal of Child Psychology and Child Psychiatry and Allied Disciplines, 35*, 699–708.

Price, V. A., Coates, T. J., Thoresen, C. E., & Grinstead, O. A. (1978). Prevalence and correlates of poor sleep among adolescents. *American Journal of the Disabled Child, 132*, 583–586.

Pritchard, A., & Appleton, P. (1988). Management of sleep problems in pre-school children. *Early Child Development and Care, 34*, 227–240.

Ramchandani, P., Wiggs, L., Webb, V., & Stores, G. (2000). A systematic review of treatments for settling problems and night waking in young children. *British Medical Journal, 320*, 209–213.

Rapoff, M. A., Christophersen, E. R., & Rapoff, K. E. (1982). The management of common childhood bedtime problems by pediatric nurse practitioners. *Journal of Pediatric Psychology, 7*, 179–196.

Reid, M. J., Walter, A. L., & O'Leary, S. G. (1999). Treatment of young children's bedtime refusal and nighttime waking: A comparison of "standard" and graduated ignoring procedures. *Journal of Abnormal Child Psychology, 27,* 5–16.

Rickert, V. I., & Johnson, C. M. (1988). Reducing nocturnal awakening and crying episodes in infants and young children: A comparison between scheduled awakenings and systematic ignoring. *Pediatrics, 81,* 203–212.

Sackett, D. L. (1993). Rules of evidence and clinical recommendations for the management of patients. *Canadian Journal of Cardiology, 9,* 487–489.

Sadeh, A. (1994). Assessment of intervention for infant night waking: Parental reports and activity-based home monitoring. *Journal of Consulting and Clinical Psychology, 62,* 63–68.

Scott, G., & Richards, M. P. M. (1990). Night waking in infants: Effects of providing advice and support for parents. *Journal of Child Psychology and Psychiatry, 31,* 551–567.

Seymour, F. W., Brock, P., During, M., & Poole, G. (1989). Reducing sleep disruptions in young children: Evaluation of therapist-guided and written information approaches: A brief report. *Journal of Child Psychiatry and Allied Disciplines, 30,* 913–918.

Sheldon, S. H., Spire, J. P., & Levy, H. B. (1992). *Pediatric sleep medicine.* Philadelphia, PA: Saunders.

Smedje, J., Broman, J.-E., & Hetta, J. (2001). Associations between disturbed sleep and behavioural difficulties in 635 children aged six to eight years: A study based on parents' perceptions. *European Child and Adolescent Psychiatry, 10,* 1–9.

Steenari, J. R., Vountela, V., Paavonen, E. J., Carlson, S., Fjällberg, M., & Aronen, E. T. (2003). Working memory and sleep in 6- to 13-year-old schoolchildren. *Journal of the American Academy of Child and Adolescent Psychiatry, 42,* 85–92.

St. James-Roberts, I., Sleep, J., Morris, S., Owen, C., & Gillham, P. (2001). Use of a behavioural programme in the first 3 months to prevent infant crying and sleep problems. *Journal of Paediatric Child Health, 37,* 289–297.

Stores, G., & Ramchandani, P. (1999). Sleep disorders in visually impaired children. *Developmental Medicine and Child Neurology, 41,* 348–352.

Thackeray, E. J., & Richdale, A. L. (2002). The behavioral treatment of sleep difficulties in children with an intellectual disability. *Behavioral Interventions, 17,* 211–213.

Vervloed, M. P. J., Hoevenaars, E., & Maas, A. (2003). Behavioral treatment of sleep problems in a child with a visual impairment. *Journal of Visual Impairment & Blindness, 97,* 28–37.

Weiskop, S., Richdale, A., & Matthews, J. (2005). Behavioral treatment to reduce sleep problems in children with autism or fragile X syndrome. *Developmental Medicine & Child Neurology, 47,* 94–104.

Weymouth, J., Hudson, A., & King, N. (1987). The management of children's nighttime behavior problems: Evaluation of an advice booklet. *Behavioural Psychotherapy, 15,* 123–133.

Wolfson, A. R., Carskadon, M. A. (1998). Sleep schedules and daytime functioning in adolescents. *Child Development, 69,* 875–878.

Wolfson, A., Lacks, P., & Futterman, A. (1992). Effects of parent training on infant sleeping patterns, parents' stress, and perceived parental competence. *Journal of Consulting and Clinical Psychology, 60,* 41–48.

World Health Organization (WHO). (2007). *International classification of diseases* (10th rev.). Geneva, Switzerland: Author.

28

Child Abuse and Neglect

AMY L. DAMASHEK AND MARK J. CHAFFIN

OVERVIEW OF DISORDER

Child maltreatment is not a disorder but rather is a set of behaviors and experiences. The phenomenon of child maltreatment is comprised of two elements, maltreating behaviors and maltreatment experiences, that together constitute a socially defined problem with mental health relevance. Maltreatment experiences are associated with increased risk for a range of internalizing and externalizing mental health disorders (Mannarino & Cohen, 1996; Maughan & Cicchetti, 2002; Tyler, Johnson, & Brownridge, 2008) and can have a negative impact on educational, behavioral, interpersonal, social, and health status (Anda et al., 2006; Eckenrode, Rowe, Laird, & Brathwaite, 1995; Erickson & Egeland, 2002; Kinard, 1999; Rogosch, Cicchetti, & Aber, 1995). Maltreated children form a considerable portion of clinical child psychologists' caseloads in traditional mental health services settings and are commonly seen in health care, behavioral medicine, juvenile or criminal justice, substance abuse, public health, and special education services. Individuals who engage in maltreating behavior, including physical abuse, sexual abuse, or neglect, also are seen in mental health and related social services systems.

Experiencing maltreatment creates no specific symptom profile or set of needs, and there are no simple clinical treatments for maltreatment experiences per se. In clinical practice, interventions for maltreated children are matched to the primary presenting symptoms and functional impairments. These can vary widely from child to child. For example, a young maltreated child with separation anxiety would likely need a completely different treatment than an older maltreated child with oppositional and aggressive behavior. In other words, clinical treatments selected for maltreated children are assessment driven, rather than based primarily on the child's status as a victim of maltreatment. There are some intervention models that have been developed with maltreatment-related conditions in mind, or that include maltreatment-focused content when this is believed to be directly relevant to the presenting symptomatic problem. For example, trauma-focused cognitive behavior therapy (TF-CBT) for abuse-related posttraumatic stress disorder (PTSD) includes a substantial and integral content focus on sexual or physical abuse as part of the model (Cohen, Mannarino, & Deblinger, 2006). In addition, some models have been specifically designed for children in child welfare foster care (e.g., Chamberlain, Price, et al., 2008). What distinguishes these models from their more general counterparts is that they have been adapted to include specific maltreatment content or adapted for use in a child welfare context.

Services delivered to children who have experienced maltreatment can extend beyond the confines of formal mental health treatments to include supportive services. Some maltreated children and their caregivers may receive supportive services or self-help materials that promote coping. Such services are designed to help children and their families sort out potential confusion surrounding the maltreatment experience, understand their own reactions to the experience, or guide them through their involvement in social services and judicial systems. These services include support groups for foster or kinship care parents (Barth, Yeaton, & Winterfelt, 1994) or court testimony preparation programs for sexually abused children (Lipovsky & Stern, 1997). Many of these services are designed or delivered by mental health professionals. Maltreatment-focused supportive or psychoeducational content may be delivered in the absence of a disorder or impairment, or clinicians may blend these supportive materials with more disorder-specific evidence-based treatments as part of an overall intervention approach with maltreated children.

Similar to maltreatment experiences, maltreating behavior per se is not a mental disorder. It is a set of behaviors. However, it has a more direct link to intervention model selection. Maltreating behavior *is* the primary presenting problem in these cases, and usually indicates the need for some action to change the behavior or prevent its recurrence. Maltreating behavior may also suggest the need for a more comprehensive assessment of the family's concrete and mental health service needs. There are several intervention models that focus directly on changing and preventing recurrence of maltreating behaviors. The behaviors targeted by these programs can be simple or complex, and the intervention models can differ considerably depending on the type of maltreating behavior or even the subcategory of maltreating behavior involved. The range of models can include parenting skills programs aimed at changing harsh and violent child discipline methods, programs designed for adult child molesters, programs for youth who commit juvenile-on-juvenile sexual abuse, and comprehensive programs addressing the broad range of caregiving problems and environmental circumstances comprising child neglect.

Diagnostic Criteria

Like many other social problems, child maltreatment is defined socially or legally, rather than by psychodiagnostic nosology. It is to some extent a culturally and historically relative construct, although definitions may be reasonably consensual and temporally stable within a given culture. Designating behavior or situations as child maltreatment serves a social-regulatory function. It is the basis on which society may step in where a child's care or circumstances are viewed as intolerable. Child abuse is a relatively modern idea that first appeared in the United States around the end of the 19th century. The concept was originally applied by legal and social advocates to children living in the most abject states of deprivation and cruelty (MacMillan, 1996; Radbill, 1987). In 1935, the U.S. government provided the first federal funding and guidelines to states to address the issue of child maltreatment. Later, in 1962, Kempe's description of the Battered Child Syndrome (Kempe, Silverman, Steele, Droegemueller, & Silver, 1962) laid out some of the earliest diagnostic criteria for medical identification of child physical abuse. Clinical psychology's interest in child abuse surged beginning in the early 1980s and was strongly focused on sexual abuse; however, the focus has gradually started to reflect interest in other and more prevalent subtypes (Chaffin, 2006).

The U.S. Department of Health and Human Services defines maltreatment as "any recent act or failure to act on the part of a parent or caretaker, which results in death, serious physical or emotional harm, sexual abuse, or exploitation, or an act or failure to act which presents an imminent risk of serious harm" (USDHHS, 2010, p. 19). However, broader criteria may be applied in epidemiologic and social science research, as well as in clinical practice. For example, the U.S. National Incidence Study and many state laws identify maltreatment on the basis of an endangerment standard rather than a harm or imminent harm standard (Sedlack & Broadhurst, 1996). Although definitions of physical abuse and neglect are usually limited to behavior by parents and caregivers, most researchers and practitioners place no such limit on definitions of sexual abuse.

Most definitions of maltreatment recognize four major subcategories: (1) physical abuse or nonaccidental physical injury to a child; (2) sexual abuse, which is often defined similarly to sex crime statutes; (3) child neglect, which is often vaguely defined; and (4) psychological abuse, also often vaguely defined. Neglect is by far the most prevalent subcategory, accounting for 78% of all reports of maltreatment, compared to around 18% for physical abuse and 10% for sexual abuse (USDHHS, 2010). Although subcategories of maltreatment may overlap in a given case, each may present a set of distinctive etiologies, contexts, and intervention needs. For example, physical abuse most often occurs in the context of child discipline; therefore, many physical abuse interventions focus on teaching parents alternative child discipline and behavior management skills. In child neglect and sexual abuse cases, discipline issues are less likely to be involved. A substantial minority of sexual abuse cases arise from pedophilia, and in these cases intervention needs can be fairly unique. But pedophilia does not characterize most sexual abuse cases, so even within the subcategory of sexual abuse, there are fairly important treatment-relevant distinctions. For example, juvenile-on-juvenile sexual abuse may be driven by experimentation or opportunity, suggesting considerably different intervention needs than sexual abuse driven by pedophilia.

Neglect is a particularly complex subcategory of maltreatment because it encompasses such a broad range of caregiver behaviors and environmental circumstances. Neglect includes acts of caregiver commission and omission that may or may not involve caregiver culpability. It can include environmental circumstances such as dangerous housing or inadequate clothing, or caregiver inability to shield a child from the harmful actions of others. Neglect is itself comprised of a number of subcategories (e.g., environmental, supervisory, educational, medical, or emotional neglect) for which no universally accepted taxonomy or clear criteria exist. Differing forms of neglect may arise from different pathways and result in different child outcomes, suggest differing intervention needs (Dubowitz et al., 2005).

Impact of Disorder

The mental health impact of child maltreatment can vary widely from child to child. Depending upon the case, maltreatment may not produce any measurable adverse mental health effects. In other cases, it may produce mild and transitory problems. In still others, it can produce lasting and serious impairments across multiple major life domains. Functional impairment on broadband measures such as the Child Behavior Checklist is reported in around half of all children in child welfare. Receipt of mental health services lags well behind the service need suggested by these figures, except for children who have been sexually abused. Less than 20% of physically abused and neglected children receive some mental health services, although around 50% show functional impairment. Approximately 80% of sexually abused children in child welfare receive some sort of mental health service, higher than their approximately 50% rate of functional impairment (Hurlburt et al., 2004).

Because maltreatment is comprised of such diverse experiences, impact pathways are correspondingly numerous. Trauma frameworks are commonly applied to understand maltreatment impact, but are probably overly narrow. For example, a variety of event characteristics may impact whether maltreatment is experienced as traumatic or results in PTSD symptoms (Hanson et al., 2001). Not all maltreatment is experienced as traumatic, and not all child trauma constitutes maltreatment. For example, neglect of very young children is one of the most common forms of maltreatment, yet may carry little risk for being experienced as traumatic. Not only do experiences vary, but so does children's resilience to adversity. Resilience to serious adversity is both common and shows significant individual variability (Bonanno, 2004). For example, the downstream impact of maltreatment on mental health and behavioral status may differ depending on certain genetic polymorphisms (e.g., Caspi et al., 2002). Moreover, the social and relational context, particularly responses of significant others to the child after the abuse are important protective factors (e.g., Chaffin, Wherry, & Dykman, 1997; Cohen & Mannarino, 2000).

It is also important to note that maltreatment rarely occurs in isolation from other life adversities. Because maltreatment is often bundled with other adversities, such as exposure to intimate partner violence, poverty, and family dysfunction, the contribution of maltreatment to mental health problems is difficult to isolate. The overall cumulative burden of adversity, rather than the particular type of adversity, may best determine the extent of mental health impact (Finkelhor, Ormrod, & Turner, 2007). However, the idea of cumulative burden does not imply that maltreatment impact is an artifact of global family dysfunction or some other broad adversity. Evidence favoring a direct causal connection between maltreatment and disorders is supported by prospective findings from community samples (Boney-McCoy & Finkelhor, 1996), and findings that there is a sharp increase in disorder risk that is temporally concordant with the onset of the maltreatment experience (Chaffin, Silovsky, & Vaughn, 2005). In clinical practice, the causal strength of the connection between maltreatment and mental health problems may be less important than the nature of the problems themselves, and the social or psychological factors that mediate maintenance

of these problems. For example, the mediating role of stigma, shame, and attributions in the relationship between child sexual abuse and adverse outcomes has been well-documented (Feiring & Taska, 2005), and many treatment models directly target these mediating attributions.

One particular mental health impact deserves mention because the link with serious abuse is intrinsic. Posttraumatic stress disorder is a prevalent condition among abused children, particularly sexually abused children. Lifetime prevalence of PTSD among adults who were sexually assaulted as children has been estimated to be as high as one in three (Hanson et al., 2001). More importantly, PTSD is one of the few disorders that includes abuse as a proximal cause of the disorder among its diagnostic criteria (i.e., having experienced trauma, in this case traumatic abuse). This is one reason why abuse-focused treatments for PTSD are among the most developed of all child maltreatment-oriented psychotherapies. These treatments include abuse-focused content as an integral part of the treatment model. Another disorder with a direct link to maltreatment is reactive attachment disorder (RAD), which includes seriously pathogenic early care among its diagnostic criteria. In contrast to PTSD, RAD appears to be a very uncommon disorder, even among seriously abused children, although the diagnosis has become popular in some foster care and adoption communities (Chaffin et al., 2006).

In this chapter, we will discuss two groups of intervention models: (1) treatments for maltreated children that include integral maltreatment content and focus, including interventions designed primarily for use in child welfare-related systems; and (2) treatments to change maltreating behavior that have been evaluated for this outcome. We will include interventions related to experiencing or committing physical abuse, sexual abuse, and neglect. In keeping with a treatment rather than a prevention focus, we will not review primary or targeted prevention programs unless they also include a treatment version. We will not include supportive services, service delivery, or purely case management and service coordination models (e.g., Systems of Care or Family Group Conferencing). We also will not include treatments designed for children exposed to family violence because it is controversial whether exposure to family violence constitutes child maltreatment.

The California Evidence-Based Clearinghouse for Child Welfare (CEBC)

Most of the evidentiary reviews in this chapter are drawn from the ongoing work done by the California Evidence-Based Clearinghouse for Child Welfare (CEBC). The CEBC is sponsored by the California Department of Social Services in cooperation with the Chadwick Center on Children and Families/Rady Children's Hospital, and the Child and Family Services Research Center in San Diego. The CEBC was commissioned to identify and disseminate information about evidence-based practices to child welfare agencies and their service delivery partners. The CEBC currently includes reviews covering 31 topic areas and over 100 individual programs. Each program is reviewed by a group of topical experts and scored on two dimensions: (1) scientific evidence of effectiveness and (2) relevance to child welfare. These ratings are updated periodically as new evidence is identified. The full set of reviews is available at www .cachildwelfareclearinghouse.org/. Evidentiary ratings for programs are made on a scale of 1 (Well-Supported) to 6 (Concerning), according to the criteria shown in Table 28.1. Programs lacking enough evidence on which to base a rating also are described, but are not rated. Clearinghouse ratings of child welfare relevance reflect the extent to which programs were designed for maltreatment populations and evaluated directly for maltreatment related outcomes. For purposes of this chapter, we will select more prevalent and higher rated models within the three major maltreatment subtypes.

Where there is a potentially highly rated model that has not yet been reviewed by the Clearinghouse, we will attempt to estimate where it might fall under the CEBC rating system. Where new published findings have emerged in the interim between CEBC rating and this chapter, we will note the possible implications of the new findings.

INTERVENTIONS FOR MALTREATING BEHAVIOR

Child Neglect

Homebuilders

Overview. Homebuilders is an intensive, short-term, home-based program to prevent out-of-home child placement or help reunify children in the foster care system with their biological parents (Fraser, Walton, Lewis, Pecora, & Walton, 1996; Kinney, Dittmar, & Firth, 1991; Kinney, Haapala, Booth, & Leavitt, 1990). The model has been used for a number of years as a response to family crisis situations where a child is at risk of being placed out of the home (i.e., in foster care or psychiatric treatment). Like other crisis intervention models designed for a level of problem (imminent child removal or family dissolution), rather than a type of problem (e.g., a particular condition or behavior), the intervention framework is fairly general, and the specific content of the intervention is individualized for each family. We are including it in the neglect section because that is the most common scenario resulting in out-of-home placement. Homebuilders employs a problem-solving framework to manage crises. Home visitors teach specific communication skills designed to diffuse conflict, and guide the family through problem-solving steps by identifying and weighing alternative solutions to current crises. The family's concrete needs are assessed and plans for meeting these needs are developed. Common examples include help in getting food stamps, cleaning

TABLE 28.1   California Evidence-Based Clearinghouse for Child Welfare Scientific Rating Scale and Criteria

Rating	Criteria
1 Well-Supported	• There is no clinical or empirical evidence or theoretical basis indicating that the practice constitutes a substantial risk of harm to those receiving it, compared to its likely benefits.
	• The practice has a book, manual, and/or other available writings that specify components of the service and describes how to administer it.
	• Multiple Site Replication: At least two rigorous randomized controlled trials (RCTs) in different usual care or practice settings have found the practice to be superior to an appropriate comparison practice. The RCTs have been reported in published, peer-reviewed literature.
	• In at least one RCT, the practice has shown to have a sustained effect at least 1 year beyond the end of treatment.
	• Outcome measures must be reliable and valid, and administered consistently and accurately across all subjects.
	• If multiple outcome studies have been conducted, the overall weight of the evidence supports the benefit of the practice.
2 Supported	• There is no clinical, empirical evidence, or theoretical basis indicating that the practice constitutes a substantial risk of harm to those receiving it, compared to its likely benefits.
	• The practice has a book, manual, and/or other available writings that specifies the components of the practice protocol and describes how to administer it.
	• At least one rigorous randomized controlled trial (RCT) in usual care or a practice setting has found the practice to be superior to an appropriate comparison practice. The RCT has been reported in published, peer-reviewed literature.
	• In at least one RCT, the practice has shown to have a sustained effect of at least 6 months beyond the end of treatment.
	• Outcome measures must be reliable and valid, and administered consistently and accurately across all subjects.
	• If multiple outcome studies have been conducted, the overall weight of evidence supports the benefit of the practice.
3 Promising	• There is no clinical, empirical evidence, or theoretical basis indicating that the practice constitutes a substantial risk of harm to those receiving it, compared to its likely benefits.
	• The practice has a book, manual, and/or other available writings that specifies the components of the practice protocol and describes how to administer it.
	• At least one study utilizing some form of control (e.g., untreated group, placebo group, matched wait list) has established the practice's benefit over the placebo, or found it to be comparable to or better than an appropriate comparison practice. The study has been reported in published, peer-reviewed literature.
	• If multiple outcome studies have been conducted, the overall weight of evidence supports the benefit of the practice.
4 Fails to Demonstrate Effect	• Two or more randomized controlled trials (RCTs) have found the practice has not resulted in improved outcomes when compared to usual care. The studies have been reported in published, peer-reviewed literature.
	• If multiple outcome studies have been conducted, the overall weight of evidence does not support the benefit of the practice.
5 Concerning	• If multiple outcome studies have been conducted, the overall weight of evidence suggests the intervention has a negative effect on clients served.
	• There is a reasonable theoretical, clinical, empirical, or legal basis suggesting that the practice constitutes a risk of harm to those receiving it, compared to its likely benefits.
Not Rated	• Insufficient evidence on which to base a rating.

the home, finding employment, and securing appointments with community agencies. In recent years, developers have focused on importing elements from parenting skills training models. The program is delivered by Bachelor's or Master's level providers who carry low caseloads and meet with families for 2-hour sessions, three to five times per week, for a period of 1 to 3 months. After stabilization is achieved, families are referred to noncrisis services to address remaining problems that were not fully addressed by Homebuilders.

CEBC recommendations. Homebuilders was rated as 2, or "Supported," by the CEBC in February 2009. There have not been published interim studies that would alter that rating.

RCTs. Homebuilders has been compared to usual care reunification services in an RCT with child welfare clients (Fraser et al., 1996). Families in the Homebuilders program had higher rates of reunification at the end of services (96.5%) than did the control group (32.1%). During a 1-year follow-up period, an additional 20.8% of children in the control group returned home. Reunification times for families in the Homebuilders program were shorter than in the control group (21 vs. 45 days). Among children who were returned home, there was no significant difference in the amount of time that children remained at home between the treatment group (351.3 days) and the control group (310.3 days). A 6-year follow-up of the families from the original trial found that more families in the treatment (65%) than in the control group (35%) discontinued services due to family stabilization (Walton, 1998). However, the two groups did not differ on days of future child welfare involvement, number of future child welfare referrals, and the amount of future out-of-home placements.

Cost analysis. In a quasi-experimental study, costs due to out-of-home placements have been found to be lower for participants in the Homebuilders program (average of $1,913 per family) than for families in typical reunification programs (average of $7,334 per family;

Wood, Baron, & Schroeder, 1988). An independent meta-analytic cost study conducted by the Washington State Institute for Public Policy estimated the benefit-to-cost ratio of Homebuilders as 2.54, with a total benefits minus costs of $4,775 per participant (Lee, Aos, & Miller, 2008).

Conclusions. Homebuilders is a model that has been in existence for several years, and was originally applied to prevent psychiatric rather than child welfare placements. Applied to child welfare, the model has been demonstrated to prevent placement and accelerate reunification, both of which are key benchmarks for child welfare systems. It is less clear that the model is superior to other services for reducing future maltreating behavior or improving longer-term family functioning. To some extent, these longer-term outcomes may depend on the type and quality of services to which families are linked after the crisis intervention is completed, complicating evaluation of the model for ultimate child maltreatment outcomes. One critique of Homebuilders and other crisis intervention models is that the conceptual fit may be questionable with child welfare families, whose problems are often more chronic than acute (Staudt & Drake, 2002). The strongest fit for child welfare populations would appear to be in circumstances where averting imminent placement or where pursuing rapid reunification is the goal, and these are the outcomes for which the model is best supported.

Family Connections

Overview. Family Connections (DePanfilis & Dubowitz, 2005) is a community-based home-visiting program delivered within the context of participants' neighborhoods (typically inner city). The program is designed to help families meet their children's basic needs and prevent or treat neglect. The program is based on an ecological model in which children's development is considered within the context of their home and neighborhood. The model emphasizes social support as a central theme in child neglect and uses activities that embed families within community and neighborhood social networks. For example, multifamily recreational activities are held several times per year. Parents are connected with social supports at local community centers, churches, or social service organizations. Links are also arranged to external treatment programs (e.g., substance abuse treatment) or social programs (e.g., tutoring or jobs programs). Families in the program meet with a home visitor (graduate student therapists in the studies to date) for approximately 1 hour per week.

CEBC recommendations. Family Connections was rated 3, or "Promising," by the CEBC in May 2008. There have not been published interim findings that would likely alter that rating.

RCTs. There has been one randomized dose study (3 months vs. 9 months) of 154 parents referred for child neglect, with or without formal child welfare involvement (DePanfilis & Dubowitz, 2005). Improvement over time was noted for parenting attitudes, parenting competence, social support, and parenting stress. Parents were noted to improve their physical and psychological care of their children and the children showed lower levels of Child Behavior Checklist (CBCL) internalizing and externalizing problems. No significant differences were found between the two dose conditions for child welfare or maltreatment variables, although there were greater improvements in CBCL scores for the 9-month condition (–15 raw score points) versus the 3-month condition (–5 raw score points). Lower dose clients were 7.35 times more likely to complete their assigned program (Girvin, DePanfilis, & Daining, 2007). A follow-up secondary analysis found that boys' CBCL internalizing and externalizing scores decreased more than girls' scores (Lindsey, Hayward, & DePanfilis, 2010).

Cost studies. In the absence of dose differences for most major outcomes, cost-effect analyses favored the lower cost 3-month dose condition with regard to improvements in

maltreating behavior, risk factors, protective factors, and child safety (DePanfilis & Dubowitz, 2005; DePanfilis et al., 2008). Cost per CBCL raw score unit of change was somewhat lower for the 9-month condition (DePanfilis, Dubowitz, & Kunz, 2008).

Conclusions. This is a promising program requiring additional controlled trial study. There has been one published RCT comparing dose levels, which provides limited information to inform conclusions about model efficacy. There appears to be little advantage of the 9-month over the 3-month service dose. It remains unclear clear how the within-subjects improvements over time noted in both conditions would compare to some alternate service condition or to no intervention.

SafeCare

Overview. SafeCare is a streamlined version of the original Project 12-Ways or Ecobehavioral Model, one of the earliest interventions evaluated for child neglect (J. R. Lutzker, Frame, & Rice, 1982; Lutzer & Rice, 1987). SafeCare is a set of practical, concrete skill modules designed for use by paraprofessional home visitors. The modules use behavioral techniques (i.e., role play, modeling, coaching, behavioral feedback) to teach basic caregiving and home management skills to parents of young children. The three modules of the model are home safety, child health, and parent–child interaction. In the home safety module, home visitors and caregivers evaluate the home to identify child safety hazards and eliminate them (e.g., removing hazardous objects, installing cabinet latches, eliminating clutter, etc.). In the child health module, caregivers are educated about how to respond appropriately to various child injuries and illness by using a health manual and a basic health supplies. The third module trains caregivers of young children in basic parent–child interaction and caregiving skills, such as use of labeled praise. The third module also teaches parents how to establish a planned set of daily routines and activities, such as a bedtime, mealtime, and playtime routines (J. Lutzker & Bigelow, 2002). The program is targeted for parents of children ages 5 and below, which is the most common child age group for neglect. SafeCare can be delivered as one part of a more comprehensive home-based program that includes case management, supportive services, and assistance in meeting basic needs.

CEBC recommendations. SafeCare was rated as 3, or "Promising," by the CEBC in December 2007. In the interim, three new RCTs and a field implementation study have been nearing completion, but published findings are currently unavailable. As these findings become available, the CEBC rating may be revised.

RCTs. The model has been tested in over 60 published studies, most of which were descriptive, single-subject, multiple-baseline, within-subjects, or quasi-experimental comparison group designs. There is one published RCT, but outcome analyses were limited to completers only. Single-subject studies have documented expected behavioral and home environment changes corresponding to each content module (Bigelow & Lutzker, 1998; J. R. Lutzker et al., 1998; Rosenfield-Schlichter et al., 1983; Tertinger, Greene, & Lutzker, 1984). Group within-subjects studies have reported similar findings in the aggregate (Campbell, Lutzker, & Cuvo, 1982; Campbell et al., 1983; J. R. Lutzker et al., 1998; Tertinger et al., 1984). In the largest quasi-experimental trial, Wesch and Lutzker (1991) compared 232 families served by 12-Ways with a matched comparison receiving services as usual. The 12-Ways families had fewer re-reports (42% vs. 56%) and future out-of-home child placements (13% vs. 25%). Another quasi-experimental study compared recidivism rates for families receiving SafeCare services to those of families receiving standard in-home family preservation services (Gershater-Molko et al., 2002). SafeCare completers had a 15% cumulative failure rate, compared to 44% for services as usual. Finally, a recent RCT compared the effectiveness of a modified version of

SafeCare (SC+) for rural high-risk parents (i.e., those with depression, substance abuse, or domestic violence) to standard home-based mental health services (SAU) in preventing child maltreatment. The modification included therapist training in Motivational Interviewing as well as ways to respond appropriately to interpersonal violence and substance abuse. Families in SC+ were more likely to enroll in and remain in services than those in SAU. The number of days posttreatment to a child welfare report was longer for those in the SC+ (200.5 days) group than those in SAU (103 days), although the difference was not statistically significant. However, families in SC+ had fewer reports that were related to domestic violence than did those in SAU. Families in SC+ also reported greater improvements in the parenting behaviors that were targeted than those in SAU (Silovsky et al., 2011).

Conclusions. SafeCare addresses several of the most common needs seen in child neglect cases. Practical and behaviorally specific needs are targeted in a structured and systematic way. Neglect cases have proven to be a difficult maltreatment population to affect, and intervention outcomes have historically been disappointing (USDHHS, 1995). SafeCare has perhaps the largest overall body of research among child neglect-focused interventions. The total body of evidence supports the program's logic model, although the individual published studies have design limitations from a strict efficacy perspective. The model has recently seen increased research and practice interest, with several RCTs under way, as well as development and implementation studies. A new national implementation and dissemination center has been developed at Georgia State University.

Physical Abuse Behavior

Parent–Child Interaction Therapy

Overview. Parent–child interaction therapy (PCIT) is a treatment originally designed for children ages 3–7 with disruptive behavior disorders (Eyberg & Boggs, 1998). The concept of applying PCIT as a treatment for parents' physically abusive behavior was originally described by Urquiza and McNeil (1996). The program teaches caregivers to engage in positive interactions with their children, use contingent praise, avoid coercive or negative parenting behavior, and apply a consistent behavioral time-out discipline strategy. A defining feature of PCIT is that it is delivered via direct skill coaching of parent behaviors over a wireless earphone during live parent–child interactions. There are two treatment phases. In the first phase of treatment, parents learn positive interaction skills including labeled praise, reflection of child speech, behavioral description, imitation, and ignoring of minor misbehavior. In the second phase, parents learn to give effective commands and consistently apply a structured time-out procedure for young children, or logical consequences for older children. The treatment is typically delivered in a clinic in which parents are observed and coached through a one-way mirror, but adaptations to home-based settings have been described (Nixon et al., 2003, 2004; Ware, 2008).

CEBC recommendations. The PCIT was rated as "Well-Supported" by the CEBC in December 2009.

RCTs. Several RCTs have demonstrated the effectiveness of PCIT for reducing behavior problems and increasing compliance in children with disruptive behavior disorders (Eyberg, Boggs, & Algina, 1995; McNeil, Capage, Bahl, & Blanc, 1999; Nixon, 2001; Nixon et al., 2003, 2004; Shuhman, Foote, Eyberg, Boggs, & Algina, 1998). Benefits include risk factors for child physical abuse, such as lowered levels of parenting stress (Shuhman et al., 1998). Gains from PCIT have been found to maintain at up to 6 years in follow-up studies (Hood & Eyberg, 2003). Cultural adaptations of PCIT have been developed and a Hispanic cultural adaptation is undergoing RCT testing (McCabe et al., 2005). One RCT with physically abusive parents has examined future child physical abuse outcomes

(Chaffin et al. 2004), finding significantly better survival for future physical abuse reports among parents randomized to PCIT (19%) versus a standard didactic parenting group (49%), which represents an effect size of 0.85. Adaptations of PCIT for use with physically abusive parents included the addition of self-control coaching and extension of the model to parents of children ages 4–12. The reduction in future abuse rates was mediated by observed within-treatment changes in negative parent–child interactions, supporting the logic model. As expected, the effect was specific for physical abuse behavior, not neglect behavior. Another RCT tested program retention outcomes for chronic child welfare cases. Cases randomized to PCIT with a motivational enhancement component showed improved retention (85%) compared to those randomized to standard parenting groups with or without motivational enhancement (61%; Chaffin et al., 2009). A follow-up RCT delivered in a field agency found that PCIT in combination with a motivational enhancement was superior to services as usual or PCIT only in reducing child welfare reports for parents with chronic and severe child welfare histories (Chaffin, Funderburk, Bard, Valle, & Gurwitch, 2011). Another RCT compared standard PCIT to a wait-list control for mothers who had a history of child maltreatment or were considered high-risk for maltreatment. The investigators found that the families in the PCIT condition had greater decreases in child behavior problems, caregiver stress, and child abuse potential than the wait-list group. Moreover, the PCIT group participants were observed to have more positive parent–child interactions and were less likely to be reported to child welfare post-treatment than the wait-list group (Thomas & Zimmer-Gembeck, 2011).

A quasi-experimental trial compared PCIT with foster parent–child dyads to PCIT with regular parent–child dyads. Comparable gains were noted in both groups, suggesting that established PCIT benefits generalize to foster care settings (Timmer, Urquiza, & Zebel,

2006). Finally, another quasi-experimental study found that PCIT was equally effective in reducing child behavior problems and caregiver psychological distress for clinic-referred mother-child dyads with exposure to interpersonal violence in comparison to those without exposure to interpersonal violence (Timmer, Ware, Urquiza, & Zebell, 2010).

Meta-analysis. A systematic review of 24 PCIT studies found child behavior change improvements with effect sizes of 0.55 to 1.3, depending on the type of measure. The study also reported parenting improvements with effect sizes of 0.68 to 3.1, depending on the type of measure (Thomas & Zimmer-Gembeck, 2007). Most studies contributing data to the meta-analysis were from outside a child welfare context.

Cost analysis. PCIT for physically abusive parents was evaluated by Lee et al. (2008) as part of their meta-analytic review of child abuse-related program costs and benefits conducted by the Washington State Institute for Public Policy. The calculated benefit-to-cost ratio was 5.93, representing a benefit-cost difference of $4,962 per participant. These were the most favorable figures among the child abuse intervention programs evaluated in the review, but should be interpreted cautiously given that effect sizes for these specific outcomes were drawn from a single RCT with abusive parents.

Conclusions. PCIT has strong support for reducing child behavior problems, increasing parental warmth, and decreasing negative parenting practices, with long-term gains posttreatment. Feasibility for extension to behavior problems in foster care context has been demonstrated. A major application of the model is as a treatment for changing physically abusive parent behavior. PCIT is one of only a few interventions with RCT support for reducing future physical abuse reports. PCIT shares parenting skill content with several other parent training models, described later. The live coached dyadic delivery format of PCIT has been identified in parenting program

component meta-analyses to be associated with larger parent and child behavior change effect sizes (Kaminski, Valle, Filene, & Boyle, 2008). This suggests that PCIT might be particularly appropriate for child welfare cases where large effects are needed and where adequate resources for the dyadic delivery format are available.

The Incredible Years

Overview. The Incredible Years (IY) is a parenting and child behavior management skill training program comprised of three curricula for parents, teachers, and children. The IY shares common roots with Project KEEP, PCIT, and other behavioral parent training programs influenced by the work of Patterson and colleagues (Patterson, Reid, & Eddy, 2002). The IY has just begun to be adapted and evaluated in the context of child maltreatment but, like the PCIT and Triple-P parenting models reviewed in this chapter, has a rich empirical literature in related areas. The IY has previously been delivered as a treatment for child behavior disorders as well as a school-based behavior problem prevention program for high-risk populations. This has included studies among parents from high-risk contexts, such as Head Start, that sometimes have high rates of future child welfare involvement. The program is delivered in 12 weekly 2-hour group sessions by a trained facilitator who leads group discussions about parenting and child behavior management issues. Materials include video vignettes that cover a range of parenting issues and feature real parents modeling effective parenting techniques. Group discussions follow the viewing of vignettes and behavioral rehearsal of skills is encouraged. Vignettes cover topics including child-led play, encouraging child learning, use of praise and rewards, effective limit setting, handling noncompliance, and problem solving. Parents are given weekly homework assignments to generalize skills learned in the group (Gross et al., 2003; Reid, Webster-Stratton, & Beauchaine, 2001).

CEBC recommendations. Incredible Years was rated as "Well-Supported" by the CEBC in February 2008. There have been no interim published studies that might alter that rating.

RCTs. Several randomized clinical trials have shown IY to be effective for child behavior problems and parenting outcomes outside of a child welfare context. The IY has been found to reduce harsh, critical, and ineffective parenting and to increase supportive, consistent, and positive parenting in samples of mothers in Head Start programs in the United States (Baydar, Reid, & Webster-Stratton, 2003; Reid, Webster-Stratton, & Baydar, 2004; Reid et al., 2001). A trial of the program in low-income urban communities found that the parents in the program demonstrated higher self-efficacy (ES = 0.40), less coercive discipline (ES = 0.42 at baseline; ES = 0.34 at 1-year follow-up), and more positive parenting (ES = 0.30; Gross et al., 2003) than those in the control group. Randomized clinical trials with socially disadvantaged families in the United Kingdom have also found significant reductions in child behavior problems (ES = 0.48–0.78) and negative parenting (ES = –0.38) as well as increases in positive parenting (ES = 0.38), compared to control groups (Gardner, Burton, & Klimes, 2006; Hutchings et al., 2007).

In a child welfare context, IY has been evaluated in one RCT with biological and foster parents, compared to services as usual. Parents randomized to the IY condition showed greater improvement on a parenting practices interview in areas of positive parenting, with 3-month follow-up effect sizes as high as 0.59 (Linares, Montalto, Li, & Oza, 2006). No studies to date have measured future physical abuse behavior outcomes.

Conclusions. There is considerable evidence supporting IY for improving and preventing child behavior problems. Trials have included higher risk segments of the population, and one randomized trial has been conducted specifically with parents and foster parents in a child welfare context, suggesting that standard IY benefits generalize to these populations and

contexts. To date, maltreatment behavior outcomes have not been directly measured in a IY trial, but interview and questionnaire outcome measures support changes in domains potentially related to physical abuse with caregivers of maltreated children. The IY offers potential advantages in a number of areas including the efficiency of the group delivery format, ready availability of videotaped vignettes for modeling parenting skills, an established training and dissemination infrastructure, and materials that are available in multiple languages.

Triple-P Positive Parenting Program

Overview. The Triple-P Positive Parenting Program was originally developed and tested in Australia. The program was designed to prevent and treat behavior problems in children by promoting positive parenting skills. The program has recently been adapted to treat parents at risk for physical abuse (Sanders et al., 2004). Parenting materials address five developmental periods from infancy through adolescence, across five levels of intensity. The lower intensity levels correspond to a general population audience, and higher levels are designed for progressively higher risk populations. Parenting skill content is compatible across levels, so that Triple-P can be applied as a comprehensive parenting, behavior management, and child abuse prevention model, saturating a community with information about parenting skills.

Level 1 Triple-P is a social marketing campaign aimed at educating communities about available parenting resources and modeling skill-based approaches to common child management problems. Level 2 is a brief anticipatory guidance intervention provided in primary care settings (e.g., doctor's office, day care centers, schools). Primary care providers give information to caregivers about managing common childrearing challenges in brief one to two 10-minute sessions and use tips sheets and short illustrative videos for modeling. Level 3 is a four-session program, provided in a primary care setting to parents of children with mild to moderate behavior problems. In level 3, four brief (15–30 minutes) behavioral counseling sessions are used to address identified problems. Sessions include practical advice on managing behavior problems and use of tip sheets or videos. The sessions may also include behavioral rehearsal, skill modeling, coaching, and feedback on skills. Level 4 Triple-P is an 8- to 10-session intensive parenting program designed for parents of children with more serious behavior problems. It can be delivered in either individual, group, or self-help modes. It also provides parents with information and uses active skills training strategies. Level 5, or enhanced Triple-P, is designed for families that face additional difficulties that may interfere with their parenting (such as depression or relationship conflict) and includes up to 11 sessions of home-based skills training, parental mood management, stress coping, and marital communication skills. Maltreatment-focused enhancements used in level 5 or sometimes in level 4 services can include attributional retraining and anger management, a combined package that is also called Pathways Triple-P.

CEBC recommendations. The Triple-P Positive Parenting Program was rated as "Well-Supported" by the CEBC in February 2008. In the interim, an additional meta-analysis has been published that reported effect sizes that reinforce the current CEBC rating.

RCTs. Over 90 intervention outcome studies, including multiple RCTs of Triple-P programs outside the child maltreatment area, have been published. The studies demonstrate significant core improvements in child behavior problems, lower levels of dysfunctional parenting, and increased sense of parental competence (e.g., Bor, Sanders, & Markie-Dadds, 2002; Leung, Sanders, Leung, Mak, & Lau, 2003; Martin & Sanders, 2003; Sanders, Markie-Dadds, Tully, & Bor, 2000). Studies have also reported positive changes in parental mental health status and marital or relationship adjustment (Zubrick et al., 2005), although these benefits may be found less consistently

than core program benefits. The program has been adapted for children with developmental disabilities and for use internationally. In addition, Triple-P has been successfully adapted for indigenous Australian families (Turner, Richards, & Sanders, 2007). An RCT conducted with parents engaging in or at high risk for child maltreatment compared standard Triple-P with Triple-P including the maltreatment focused Pathways enhancements. Both groups showed improvement across a range of parenting and risk measures, with caregivers in the enhanced version of Triple-P showing more positive change in negative parental attributions, demonstrating the intended incremental benefit of the Pathways additions (Sanders et al., 2004).

Recently, maltreatment outcomes were examined in a cluster-randomized trial in the United States. The trial compared population child maltreatment outcomes among 18 counties, nine randomly assigned to receive multi-level Triple-P versus nine randomized to services as usual (Prinz, Sanders, Shapiro, Whitaker, & Lutzker, 2009). The experimental condition involved efforts to saturate treatment counties with the model at multiple levels. Treatment and control counties did not differ demographically or with respect to pretreatment child welfare statistics. A total of 649 service providers across an array of service sectors was trained, and up to 13,000 families received some form of Triple-P services beyond level 1 (approximately 25% received level 4 or 5 services). Impressively large and statistically significant effect sizes were reported in favor of the treatment counties for rates of substantiated child maltreatment (ES = 1.09), out-of-home placements (ES = 1.22) and child abuse-related injuries seen in hospitals and emergency rooms (ES = 1.14). Demonstrating effects at a population level might be viewed as especially impressive given that not all at-risk individuals in the treatment county population received direct services.

Meta-analyses of group designs. Three meta-analytic studies have found positive effects of Triple-P programs for child behavior problems and parenting. One study specifically examined the effects of the intensive level 4 program on parenting styles and competencies. The metaanalysis included studies that targeted a range of children from those with mild behavior problems to those with more severe problems in several countries. The study found large effects for reducing dysfunctional parenting styles at posttest (mean effect size = 0.68 at posttest and 0.80 at follow-up) and increased parental competency (0.65 at posttest and 0.67 at follow-up), regardless of the delivery modality (i.e., group, individual, or self-help format; De Graaf, Speetjens, Smit, de Wolff, & Tavecchio, 2008). A second meta-analysis of different parenting programs found that Triple-P had small to large effects for parent-reported child behavior problems (ES ranged from 0.45 to 1.26) and parenting outcomes (ES ranged from 0.36 to 1.44; Thomas & Zimmer-Gembeck, 2007). The study compared Triple-P and PCIT effect sizes, reporting some advantages for PCIT in some areas, but equivalence in others. Finally, Nowak and Heinrichs (2008) combined over 50 studies in a random effects meta-analysis, examining several effect domains and moderators. Level 4 and 5 Triple-P yielded the largest effects. Larger effects were also noted among parents of younger children and parents reporting initially greater child behavior management problems. These findings suggest good effectiveness for the more treatment-oriented levels of Triple-P.

Conclusions. Triple-P is well-supported for reducing child behavior problems and improving parenting in general. Adaptations for high-risk and abusive parents have been developed and large population level maltreatment reduction effects have been found for populations receiving multilevel Triple-P. Effects by maltreatment subtype have not yet been reported. Pathways Triple-P augmented with anger management and attributional retraining was designed specifically for parents engaging in coercive or harsh parenting, suggesting that physical abuse might be the main

maltreatment subtype affected. The cluster randomized trial in the United States combined primary prevention, targeted prevention, and treatment services to saturate treatment counties. It is currently unclear how much each of these service levels might have contributed to the net countywide effect or whether an overall synergy among prevention intervention service levels was involved. In addition, it is not known exactly how many active child welfare cases were served in the treatment counties. To date, no RCT of Pathways Triple-P evaluating abuse behavior outcomes has been conducted. Regardless of this limitation, the size of the population level maltreatment reduction effect in the U.S. trial justifies considerable enthusiasm for the model as a combined child maltreatment prevention and treatment program.

Abuse-Focused Cognitive Behavior Therapy

Overview. Abuse-focused cognitive behavior therapy (AF-CBT) is designed to treat parents of school-age children who have physically abused children as well as those who frequently use harsh punishment, have high levels of negative interactions with their children, or have poor child behavior management skills. The program is based on principles from learning and behavior theory, family systems, and cognitive therapy. The goal of AF-CBT is to train parents in noncoercive and nonviolent parenting strategies and to promote prosocial behavior among parents and children (D. J. Kolko & Swenson, 2002). Specifically, treatment providers establish an agreement with caregivers to refrain from violence, educate caregivers about the cognitive behavioral model, provide information about the effects of abusive experiences on children, and correct cognitive errors or misattributions that may lead to abusive behavior. The program also teaches parents cognitive self-control and affect management techniques, child behavior management skills, and communication and problem-solving skills. The treatment is typically delivered by a licensed mental health professional, either in home or in a clinic. Families participate for a minimum of one session per week for a period of 3–6 months (D. J. Kolko & Swenson, 2002).

CEBC recommendations. Abuse-focused cognitive behavior therapy was rated 3, or "Promising," by the CEBC in June 2008. There have been no interim published studies that might alter that rating.

RCTs. Abuse-focused cognitive behavior therapy has been evaluated in one RCT. The study compared AF-CBT to family therapy and to a small nonrandomized group receiving routine community services. In this study, there was a trend for parents in both the AF-CBT (10% of families) and family therapy (12% of families) conditions to have fewer future reports of maltreatment compared to routine community services (30% of families), but the difference did not reach statistical significance (D. Kolko, 1996), and study power was modest ($N = 47$). In addition, parents in AF-CBT and Family Therapy self-reported significantly lower levels of risk factors than did the control group, and children in AF-CBT and family therapy had lower levels of child internalizing and externalizing symptoms compared to routine community care.

Conclusions. Parents receiving AF-CBT showed positive changes on most risk and outcome indicators. These changes were similar to those found with a less clearly defined family therapy study arm delivered in the laboratory setting, and both were superior to usual services. Interpretation of study comparisons is limited by the unknown effectiveness of the family therapy comparison and by the nonrandom allocation to usual services. The AF-CBT model includes familiar cognitive behavioral techniques, which have been shown to reduce physical abuse behavior in a primary prevention context (Bugental et al., 2002). Additional controlled tests of the model, using larger samples and randomized usual services or no treatment conditions, might clarify model efficacy.

Sexually Abusive Behavior

Cognitive Behavior/Relapse-Prevention (CBT/RP) Therapy for Adult Sex Offenders

Overview. Group-based CBT/RP therapy (Pithers and Cumming, 1995) is a core approach commonly used with adult sex offenders. Clinical practices across different programs are unstandardized, but tend to share many common elements, consistent with published treatment guidelines (ATSA, 2005). A number of manuals and workbooks exist and are in use, with many similarities among them (e.g., Steen, 2000). CBT/RP programs commonly require approximately 2 years of weekly sessions. Techniques involve identification and avoidance of sex offense risk situations, resolution of thinking errors associated with the behavior, planning alternative behavioral or cognitive responses to counter the progression from risk to behavior, and increasing self-monitoring and self-control. Creating external behavioral constraints and imposing high levels of supervisory monitoring are usually included as a collateral component of RP. Other elements common in these programs include exercises to develop victim empathy, full disclosure of sexually deviant thoughts and behaviors, and an emphasis on accepting personal responsibility for the behavior. Regular polygraph interrogations are used by some treatment providers. Classical conditioning techniques or antiandrogen drugs are sometimes used as adjunctive treatments to change paraphilic arousal patterns if these are present. Programs may be delivered in correctional institutions or in community settings in collaboration with criminal justice system oversight. Alternatives to CBT/RP treatment models based on intimate relationship enhancement and general life-course improvement have been developed, but are only beginning to be tested (Ward & Marshall, 2004).

CEBC Recommendations. CBT/RP treatment was not rated by the CEBC. It was rated in 2004 by a consensus panel developing guidelines for child physical and sexual abuse interventions, sponsored by the U.S. Office for Victims of Crime (Saunders, Berliner, & Hanson, 2004). Under that system, it was given an evidentiary rating designated for programs having two or more studies using comparison groups, but without randomization, approximately equivalent to a 3, or "Promising," under the CEBC system. In the interim, a large RCT was published finding no treatment effect for ultimate outcomes (Marques, Wiederanders, Day, Nelson, & van Ommeren, 2005).

RCTs. There has been one RCT of CBT/RP for adult sex offenders. The study compared sexual abuse recidivism outcomes for prison volunteers randomized to CBT/RP treatment ($N = 259$) versus no-treatment controls ($N = 225$), along with a comparison group of nonvolunteers ($N = 220$). No significant differences in sexual recidivism were found among the groups at up to 8-year follow-up (19%–21%) (Marques et al., 2005).

Meta-analyses of group designs. Several narrative and meta-analytic reviews of non-randomized and single-group studies have been published, often summarizing upwards of 60 studies, but the results are controversial and in places contradictory. Most have concluded that there is lower recidivism among treated groups, with aggregate reductions of around 6 percentage points, or approximately a one-third reduction. Considerable debate has ensued about the methodological adequacy of the component studies in these meta-analyses, given that many involved group allocations based on self-selection or clinician decision. Much of the debate has centered around the relative weight that should be given to the aggregate findings across multiple relatively weak studies versus the findings of the RCT.

Conclusions. There is a large volume of studies on this topic, but little clarity. It is difficult to draw a clear conclusion about treatment effectiveness given the design limitations of most outcome studies. Publication of the lone RCT conducted, which yielded null findings, has led to considerable controversy in the field about the role of randomized trials

(Marshall & Marshall, 2007). For those embracing an evidence-based practice perspective, additional RCTs are plainly needed to clarify the effectiveness of this model, and to test plausible alternative models. Given the public safety implications of this treatment area, null findings from the lone RCT are cause for concern.

Multisystemic Therapy (MST) for Youth With Problem Sexual Behaviors (MST-PSB)

Overview. Up to half of all child sexual abuse is committed by other juveniles. Age 13 is the peak age at which individuals commit sexual abuse of a young child. MST is a well-known intervention for delinquent adolescents that has been tested and adapted for this population. MST has roots in family therapy and social-ecological perspectives, and emphasizes working with and through primary caregivers and other important figures in an adolescent's social ecology to change delinquent behavior. Services are delivered by licensed mental health professionals who carry very small caseloads and work with parents and youth in their homes, schools, neighborhoods, and communities. Services are short term (i.e., between 4 and 6 months) and involve frequent contact. Individualized assessment-driven case plans are developed with families, and the assessed needs are guided by an understanding of empirically demonstrated delinquency risk factors. The main factors assessed and targeted include affiliation with delinquent peers, low parental monitoring and engagement, school drop out, and weak prosocial affiliations. MST does not have fixed content or use a set of treatment techniques that are applied uniformly across cases. Rather, it is more of a comprehensive assessment-driven system. Known delinquency risk factors are assessed, a set of tailored ecologically oriented goals are matched to the assessed needs, practical and action-oriented activities and techniques to achieve the goals are executed, progress toward goal attainment and service quality control are strictly monitored, and obstacles are quickly identified and subjected to further problem solving. Provider agencies, provider staff, and supervisors must be licensed to deliver MST and meet ongoing quality assurance criteria monitored by the developer. In contrast to other comprehensive models, such as wrap-around or service coordination models, all service needs except psychotropic medication are addressed directly by the MST team rather than by referral to outside programs. The overarching philosophy of MST delivery is that providers directly provide whatever it takes to help families meet goals.

CEBC recommendations. MST for adolescent sexual abusers was reviewed in June 2011 and was given a provisional rating of "1" or "Established." MST for general delinquency has been listed as a model program by the Blueprints for Violence Prevention Project (Mihalic, Irwin, Elliott, Fagan, & Hansen, 2001), and was one of three best supported models identified by the U.S. Surgeon General's report on youth violence (USDHHS, 2001).

RCTs. MST for general delinquency and other problems has been evaluated in over 15 RCTs across various populations, contrasted with alternative services of different types. When implemented faithfully, MST appears to be effective in reducing delinquent and related behaviors among seriously delinquent youth. Three RCTs have focused specifically on adolescent sexual abusers. In the first small efficacy trial with juvenile sexual offenders ($N = 16$), Borduin, Henggeler, Blaske, and Stein (1990) reported that significantly fewer youth in a standard MST condition (12.5%) than in a probation counseling condition (75%) were rearrested for sexual crimes over a 3-year follow-up. A second study included 48 juvenile sexual offenders randomized to standard MST or usual services (a combination of cognitive behavioral group therapy and individual treatment administered in a juvenile court setting) conditions. At 8.9 years posttreatment, MST participants were significantly less likely than their usual services counterparts to be

rearrested for sexual (8% vs. 46%) and non-sexual (29% vs. 58%) offenses (Borduin, Schaeffer, & Heiblum, 2009). Both of these studies were conducted with youth who had extensive prior delinquent backgrounds. The future sex offense rates in the usual care conditions are considerably higher than what is typically found in most studies (Chaffin, 2005), suggesting that benefits were obtained with an unusually severe population. A more recent RCT with a broader and more typical juvenile sexual abuser population ($N = 127$) compared an adapted version of MST to usual treatment, which was a version of RP/CBT. One-year follow-up outcomes showed that MST was more effective than usual services for changing sex offense risk behaviors, delinquent and substance use behaviors, externalizing problems, and reducing out-of-home placement trajectories (Letourneau et al., 2009). Consistent with the MST logic model, these advantages were mediated by increasing parental consistency in limiting delinquent peer affiliations and responding to teen misbehavior (Henggeler et al., 2009).

Meta-analyses. Curtis, Ronan, and Borduin (2004) conducted a meta-analysis of MST trials with seriously delinquent youth, where fidelity to the model was assessed as good. The estimated mean effect size was 0.51. An alternate meta-analysis conducted by Littell (2006) reported only nonsignificant trends in favor of MST, discrepant from earlier narrative reviews and from the Curtis, Ronan, and Borduin (2004) meta-analysis. Examining the two meta-analyses, different studies with somewhat different populations were included in each. In particular, the Littell (2006) findings may have been influenced by results from a very large unpublished Canadian field trial, where uncertain model fidelity, high comparison condition quality, and inclusion of less severe youth may have attenuated the outcome differences between the groups. The discrepancy may reflect the sensitivity of MST to variations in fidelity, or the possibility that while MST offers advantages among the most serious delinquency cases, less intensive models deliver equivalent benefits among lower severity cases or for other types of problems.

Cost studies. The Washington State Institute for Public Policy evaluated the cost benefit for MST as a treatment for reducing general criminal recidivism and its substantial associated costs. Although MST is a moderately expensive intervention, costing over $4,000 per case, and is complicated to implement, the long-term benefit-to-cost ratio was estimated at a very impressive 28:1, based on an estimated effect size of 0.31 (Aos, Phipps, Barnoski, & Leib, 2001). A more recent study, using re-arrest data from a 13.7-year follow-up of a randomized controlled trial for serious juvenile offenders, examined the value of MST for taxpayers and crime victims. The investigators found that cumulative benefits to taxpayers and crime victims ranged from $75,000 to $199,000 per MST participant (Klietz, Borduin, & Schaeffer, 2010). Costs within a child welfare context have not been calculated.

Conclusions. MST is the only treatment model for juvenile sex offenders with any RCT support. Most alternative models are adaptations of adult sex offender CBT/RP treatment models that have not been subjected to controlled outcome testing with adolescents, although they are in far wider use than MST. MST may be particularly suited for those sexually abusive youth who also have serious general antisocial and delinquent problems, and the model may be more intensive than necessary for youth with more limited problems (Chaffin, 2005). The model has a very well-organized and specified implementation infrastructure with international reach.

Interventions for Maltreated Children

Attachment and Biobehavioral Catch-Up (ABC)

Overview. The ABC program is designed to help young child welfare foster care or adoptive children, ages 3 and under, regulate their emotional and physiological responses by training caregivers to respond to them in nurturing and predictable ways (Dozier et al., 2006; Dozier, Dozier, & Manni, 2002). The program is delivered in 10 individual home-based sessions with caregivers and children. The sessions are designed to facilitate attachment to the caregiver and to create an environment that promotes emotion regulation. Parents are instructed in how to provide patient nurturance to children, even if the children appear to push the caregivers away. The program also teaches parents how to create a safe, predictable, and stable environment. Specific skills include teaching parents to follow the child's lead in play, avoiding behaviors that young foster children might interpret as frightening, and creating conditions in which children can learn to identify feelings and safely express their emotions.

CEBC recommendations. The ABC program was rated 3, or "Promising," by the CEBC in December 2009. There have not been interim published studies that might alter that rating.

RCTs. The ABC program has been evaluated in three randomized controlled trials. One study compared ABC to developmental education and found that children in the ABC group had lower postintervention cortisol levels (mean difference = 0.38); however, parents' reports of child behavior problems did not differ (Dozier et al., 2006). In a second study, parents kept diaries about children's attachment-related behaviors, and those children in the ABC group showed less avoidant behavior (i.e., anger, inability to be soothed) than the children in the comparison group (Dozier, Lindhiem, Lewis, Bick, Bernard, & Peloso, 2009). A third randomized trial compared ABC with an educational intervention for foster children and a control group, examining changes in children's cortisol levels after being exposed to the Strange Situation. Cortisol levels were higher for the educational intervention group prior to exposure, and decreased after exposure, while levels for the ABC group were low at both points, suggesting somewhat lower stress levels for the ABC group (Dozier, Peloso, Lewis, Laurenceau, & Levine, 2008).

Meta-analyses. There have been no meta-analyses of ABC. There has been a meta-analysis of over 70 studies evaluating attachment interventions broadly (Bakermans-Kranenburg, van IJzendoorn, & Juffer, 2003), and examining elements associated with larger effect sizes. The ABC program is consistent with several of the characteristics noted in the meta-analysis as associated with larger effect sizes (e.g., behaviorally targeted, time limited, focused primarily on increasing parental sensitivity, and including fathers as well as mothers).

Conclusions. Evidence supporting the potential positive effects of the ABC program are encouraging; however, the most consistent effects have been found with biological markers and diary entries, and these may not be straightforward to interpret. The program appears promising for improving children's stress levels and emotion regulation skills, areas that could have positive downstream implications for children's development, parenting success, and placement stabilization. The program has not demonstrated symptomatic reductions in child behavior problems, although this is not its core intended target and may not be the most salient mental health construct for infants and toddlers. The model may have particular relevance for foster care or adoptive contexts with very young children, where achieving permanency and placement success is the goal, although these specific outcomes have not yet been tested. The content of the ABC model is a good example of the general type of program recommended by an attachment intervention task force (Chaffin et al., 2006). It is one of the only attachment promotion models with RCT support among foster children. The promising status of the ABC model is especially relevant considering that there have been concerning and potentially harmful attachment therapy models marketed to child welfare foster and adoptive parents (Chaffin et al., 2006; Lilienfeld, 2007). The ABC would appear to be a sound and safer alternative to these concerning attachment therapy models.

Trauma-Focused Cognitive Behavior Therapy (TF-CBT)

Overview. TF-CBT is a treatment for children with abuse-related posttraumatic stress disorder (PTSD) or significant PTSD symptoms (Cohen et al., 2006). Developmental variations of the model are available for children ranging in age from 3 to 18. Parents are included in the treatment, although most core model elements are delivered by a licensed mental health professional in direct psychotherapy sessions with the child. Model content is organized around sexual abuse trauma and most outcome data is with sexually abused children, but the framework can be expanded to other types of abuse trauma. Foundations of the model are in exposure therapy and extinction techniques to decondition anxiety or fear responses to abuse-related thoughts or stimuli. In the exposure component, children are taught emotion regulation and coping skills (e.g., relaxation skills), which is followed by gradual exposure conducted by developing a narrative account of the traumatic experiences. A hallmark of exposure techniques in TF-CBT is that they are gradual rather than the prolonged exposure or flooding techniques sometimes used in exposure therapies with adults. Exposure in TF-CBT is not intended to involve catharsis or unmanageable distress. When distress occurs, children are encouraged to use coping and emotion regulation skills. Cognitive therapy techniques to correct any distorted cognitions and attributions are the second component of the model. The cognitive component aims to destigmatize the abuse experience, correct misattributions, reduce shame or guilt, and provide facts about sexual abuse and its causes. Parents are educated about trauma, understanding their child's reactions, and taught parenting techniques for managing problem behaviors sometimes seen among sexually abused children (e.g., sexual behavior problems, separation anxiety). Parents are encouraged to respond to issues around the child's trauma in a calm and matter-of-fact way. In sexual abuse cases, victimization prevention skills are also taught. Children and caregivers participate in treatment weekly for 12–18 sessions. The treatment is typically provided in an outpatient clinic or community agency and delivered by a licensed mental health professional.

CEBC recommendations. TF-CBT was rated 1, or "Well-Supported," by the CEBC in June 2008. In the interim, there have been no new published studies that might change this rating. A randomized dismantling trial varying the amount of gradual exposure was recently completed but is not yet published.

RCTs. Ten published studies from seven RCTs, including one international trial and one multisite trial, have demonstrated positive effects for abused and traumatized children receiving TF-CBT (Cohen & Mannarino, 1996, 1997, 1998; Cohen, Deblinger, Mannarino, & Steer, 2004; Cohen, Mannarino, & Knudsen, 2005; Deblinger, Lippmann, & Steer, 1996; Deblinger, Steer, & Lippmann, 1999; Deblinger, Stauffer, & Steer, 2001; King et al., 2000; Smith et al., 2007). TF-CBT has been found to be superior to nondirective supportive therapy in reducing internalizing symptoms as measured by the Child Behavior Checklist (ES = 0.81) and inappropriate sexual behaviors as measured by the Children's Sexual Behavior Inventory (ES = 0.61) among sexually abused preschoolers (Cohen & Mannarino, 1996). Benefits were maintained at a 1-year follow-up (Cohen & Mannarino, 1997). A dismantling trial examining parent- and child-delivered components has supported the importance of the child component for PTSD symptom improvement and the parent component for behavior problem improvement (Deblinger et al., 1996; King et al., 2000). Other studies have found that TF-CBT is more effective than comparison treatments in increasing children's coping skills and knowledge, decreasing non-offending mothers' intrusive thoughts and emotional reactivity regarding their child's abuse, and increasing mothers' effective parenting skills (Deblinger et al., 1996; Deblinger et al., 2001). These benefits were maintained at a 2-year follow-up (Deblinger et al., 1999). A multisite trial found that TF-CBT was more effective than Child Centered Therapy in reducing children's symptoms of depression, PTSD symptoms, behavior problems, feelings of shame, interpersonal mistrust, and parents' depression (Cohen et al., 2004). A follow-up of the children from this study found that decreases in anxiety, sexual problems, and dissociation were maintained at a 6-month follow-up, and PTSD symptoms and dissociation symptom improvements were maintained at 12-month follow-up (Cohen et al., 2005). In another study incorporating a wider range of trauma causes (e.g., car accidents), 92% of patients who received TF-CBT in comparison to 42% of those who were wait-listed no longer met criteria for PTSD. Effects maintained at a 6-month follow-up, and effects of TF-CBT were mediated by changes in maladaptive cognitions (Smith et al., 2007), consistent with the CBT model. Finally, the model has been successfully disseminated to several community agencies with positive results (i.e., reduction in child symptoms, fewer placement disruptions; Cohen & Mannarino, 2008).

Conclusions. Effectiveness of TF-CBT is supported by multiple RCTs conducted specifically with abused children, by independent investigators, and including reasonable follow-up. It is correctly considered one of the best supported models in the child maltreatment field. TF-CBT was the first abuse-oriented child therapies model designated as well-supported by a consensus review panel (Saunders, Berliner, & Hanson, 2004), and retained that designation when rated by the CEBC. Versions of the model have been found to reduce trauma symptoms and behavior problems across a range of ages, from preschoolers to adolescents. The model has most often been tested for children with sexual abuse-related PTSD, but has been tested for

PTSD symptoms related to other types of trauma (Smith et al., 2007). A clear treatment manual is available (Cohen et al., 2006), and free introductory interactive training is available online (http://tfcbt.musc.edu). Widespread dissemination of the model has been promoted by the Substance Abuse and Mental Health Services Administration (SAMHSA)'s National Child Traumatic Stress Network. The TF-CBT should be considered a first-line treatment for children with abuse-related PTSD or significant PTSD symptoms. It is important to remember that the focus of the model is quite specific—abused children with PTSD symptoms. Because child abuse is not invariably traumatic, nor does it always produce lasting trauma symptoms, application of exposure-based treatments outside this symptomatic area should be considered cautiously.

Cognitive Behavior Therapy for Childhood Sexual Behavior Problems (CBT-CSBP)

Overview. Aggressive or persistently inappropriate child sexual behavior problems can occur among young children who have been maltreated. They can become a significant problem when they occur in foster care. Half or more of children with sexual behavior problems have a history of sexual abuse, and many others have experienced physical abuse or neglect (Friedrich, 1993; Merrick, Litrownik, Everson, & Cox, 2008). CBT-CSBP is a treatment for these types of behavior problems and can be delivered in a group or individual format. Treatment is short term and typically lasts from 12 to 16 sessions. Treatment is conducted in an outpatient clinic setting and is delivered by a licensed mental health professional. CBT-CSBP programs focus on teaching children clear and specific rules about sexual behavior, teaching self-control skills to promote stopping and thinking before acting, and teaching children sexual abuse prevention skills. Caregiver involvement is considered crucial in these programs, and all CBT-CSBP programs tested in the literature include an active caregiver component. Caregivers are taught how to monitor their children's interactions with other children and how to monitor and eliminate evocative environmental stimuli. Caregivers are also educated about developmentally normal versus concerning childhood sexual behaviors, and instructed in basic child behavior management skills. These skills include use of selective attention, use of labeled praise and reinforcements, and application of consistent time-out consequences. Homework and skill practice assignments are commonly involved. Trauma-focused cognitive behavior therapy (TF-CBT) protocols for young sexually abused children with PTSD symptoms, described in the preceding section of this chapter, have included many of these same CBT-CSBP elements for cases where both PTSD symptoms and sexual behavior problems co-occur.

CEBC recommendations. Cognitive behavioral treatment for school-aged children with sexual behavior problems has received a rating of "2" or "Supported" as of April 2011. Treatment for preschool-aged children has not been rated. A consensus panel focused on childhood sexual behavior problems recognized outpatient CBT-CSBP, either freestanding or as a part of TF-CBT, as the first-line treatment for aggressive or persistent inappropriate sexual behavior problems (Chaffin et al., 2008). Given that there are multiple RCTs by independent groups supporting this treatment, it might be rated as "Well-Supported" under CEBC criteria.

RCTs. Two RCTs have examined freestanding group CBT-CSBP programs. Carpentier, Silovsky, & Chaffin (2006) compared short-term CBT-CSBP to psychodynamic play therapy with a 10-year follow-up for reports of future sexually abusive behavior and sex crimes as the main outcome of interest. A contrast group of general clinic children with no sexual behavior problems also was included. At 10-year follow-up, the CBT-CSBP group had lower rates of future sexual abuse reports compared to the psychodynamic play therapy group, and did not differ from the general clinic children without sexual behavior problems (2% vs. 10%, vs. 3%, respectively). Pithers, Gray, Busconi, and Houchens (1998) compared two CBT-CSBP models, one with and one without a modified relapse prevention component, which taught children to recognize risk signals and avoid them. Both models included parents and had parent education components. There was some early advantage of the incremental component with some subgroups of children but not others. At follow-up, both groups had improved significantly and there was no incremental impact of the added relapse prevention component on sexual behavior outcomes. Two other RCTs have examined blended TF-CBT + CBT-CSBP treatments delivered using an individual parent–child format to cases where children had both PTSD symptoms and sexual behavior problems. Cohen & Mannarino (1996, 1997) compared TF-CBT to nonspecific supportive therapy for scores on a sexual behavior problem checklist. The TF-CBT group demonstrated a significant reduction in problem sexual behaviors, while the nonspecific group did not. Several children in the nonspecific group had to be removed from that condition due to persistent and serious sexual behavior problems, and were subsequently provided TF-CBT, after which their sexual behavior problems improved. Additional reasonably good quality, but nonrandomized, trials have supported findings from the RCTs. Silovsky, Niec, Bard, and Hecht (2007) used a wait-list control design with preschool-aged children receiving group-based CBT-CSBP. Multiple baseline and treatment period measures were obtained. Improvement trajectories were found to accelerate significantly when children entered treatment. Similar wait-list findings were reported for blended TF-CBT + CBT-CSBP treatments (Stauffer & Deblinger, 1996).

Meta-analysis. St. Amand, Bard, and Silovsky (2008) combined within-subjects results from 11 outcome studies and examined how component elements across treatments corresponded with effect sizes. The overall degree of change in sexual behavior problems across the course of treatment was estimated at 0.46–0.49 standard deviations. Treatments that included elements focused on teaching child behavior management skills to parents and abuse prevention skills to children were found to yield larger effect sizes. Programs that included elements derived from adolescent or adult sex offender models yielded reduced benefits in terms of nonsexual behavior problems. There was no difference in effect sizes for studies using group as opposed to individual modalities, or where CBT-CSBP treatment was freestanding versus blended with TF-CBT for co-occurring PTSD symptoms.

Conclusions. Childhood sexual behavior problems appear to respond well to CBT-CSBP treatment. Substantial reductions can be obtained in a short amount of time. Meta-analysis points to teaching behavior management skills to caregivers as a key component. In the only RCT with long-term follow-up, improvements yielded by CBT-CSBP translate into reduced rates of future sex crime and sexual abuse perpetration reports. After receiving CBT-CSBP, future rates of committing sex crimes or sexual abuse are very low, and no different from those of general clinic children without sexual behavior problems.

Keeping Foster and Kin Parents Supported and Trained (KEEP)

Overview. KEEP is a program designed to help maintain placement stability for foster care children, ages 5–12, by teaching foster and kinship caregivers effective behavioral parenting skills. The model is a less intensive adaptation of Multidimensional Treatment Foster Care (MTFC), a program originally developed for delinquent youth in juvenile justice foster homes (Chamberlain, 2003). In KEEP, foster parents learn to encourage child cooperation, use behavioral contingencies emphasizing positive reinforcement, balance encouragement with limits, promote school engagement, and encourage positive peer relationships. Foster parents also learn stress reduction skills. Skills are taught using active learning strategies, such as role plays. Foster caregivers in the program attend weekly parent support groups and training groups. In addition, each foster parent receives weekly calls from the group facilitator to discuss problems the caregiver might have in implementing homework assignments from the group and to collect data on the child's behaviors (Chamberlain, Moreland, & Reid, 1992).

CEBC recommendations. KEEP was rated as 3, or "Promising," by the CEBC in November 2009 based on evidence with the related MTFC model in other populations, and findings from a small early child welfare foster care trial. A multicounty implementation project is recently under way (Chamberlain, Brown, et al., 2008), but there are no published outcome findings.

RCTs. The Multidimensional Treatment Foster Care model, on which KEEP is based, has substantial RCT support in the delinquency literature. Among both delinquent boys and girls, significant reductions in future antisocial behavior, school performance, and psychosocial outcomes have been found, relative to group care (e.g., Eddy, Whaley, & Chamberlain, 2004; Leve, Chamberlain, & Reid, 2005). There have been two RCTs of the KEEP model specifically in a child welfare context. In the first trial, 72 foster families were assigned to KEEP or two usual foster care control conditions (one with and one without supplemental compensation). Fewer (29%) of the Project KEEP placements failed than those in the usual foster care control group (53%), and KEEP children showed a greater decrease in behavior problems (Chamberlain, Moreland, & Reid, 1992). In the second RCT, 700 foster/kinship parents and 700 children were randomized to either standard foster care or Project KEEP conditions. Compared to regular foster care, children in Project KEEP were about twice as likely to experience a positive exit from care at 6-months follow-up (17% vs. 9%). In regular foster care, negative exits or foster care disruptions were strongly

related to the child's number of previous disruptions in standard foster care, but this was not the case in the KEEP condition. Among higher risk children, up to half or more in standard foster care disrupted by 6 months, compared to 10%–20% in KEEP foster homes, regardless of risk level. In other words, the benefits of KEEP for reducing disruptions were largest among those children at the highest risk for disruption and among children with more disruptive behavior problems (Price et al., 2008). Behavior problem improvements were mediated by increases in the proportion of positive reinforcement skills used by foster parents, consistent with the logic model of the intervention (Chamberlain, Price, et al., 2008).

Conclusions. Foster care disruption and behavior problems in foster care are major concerns in child welfare. Accumulated foster care disruptions appear to be both reflections of and causes of poor child behavior outcomes, describing a downward trajectory for many children in the system. Interrupting this trajectory is important. Among models tested for these outcomes, KEEP has perhaps the best current RCT support. Enthusiasm for this model is legitimately high.

CONCLUSIONS

The dominant theme for evidence-based practice in child maltreatment over the past decade has been "borrowing." Many supported models are adaptations of evidence-based models developed in other mental health and behavior change areas. The CEBC has identified well over 100 child maltreatment treatment and prevention models. Of these, only four treatment models, plus an additional three treatment models we have added in this chapter, meet or are currently likely to meet CEBC criteria as "Well-Supported." Of these seven total models, five are direct adaptations of models originally designed for other populations and problems, adapted for use with abused children or abusive parents. This includes PCIT, Triple-P, the Incredible Years, MST, and KEEP. The remaining two well-supported models are cognitive behavior therapy models developed specifically for abused children (i.e., TF-CBT and CBT-CSBP). Although these are not adaptations of existing brand-name models, they are drawn from a well-established family of CBT treatment models and techniques. The TF-CBT is drawn primarily from established exposure therapy or desensitization models, and CBT-CSBP draws heavily from established behavioral parent training and CBT approaches.

The borrowed status of these seven treatments is encouraging in two respects. First, models borrowed from related fields can potentially deliver multiple types of benefits with one treatment—both the originally designed benefits, and the adapted benefits. For example, behavioral parent training delivered to abusive parents (e.g., PCIT, IY, Pathways Triple-P) can yield both reduced risk for engaging in physical abuse and improvements in child behavior problems. Similarly, MST for adolescent sex offenders can deliver both reductions in risk for future sexual abuse behavior and reductions in risk for general delinquency. It is not necessary to identify separate treatments in order to realize both types of outcomes. Second, it is encouraging that evidence-based treatment models are proving robust to adaptation and extension. This suggests that we do not necessarily need to develop specialized models de novo for every practice niche or unique population. In many cases, effectiveness in one outcome domain or population can generalize to related outcome domains and populations. A sort of cross-cultural exchange among evidence-based models seems feasible. Cross-cultural exchange might lead to much faster progress than practice silos, each with their separate and slowly developing clinical sciences. We have yet to fully define the edges of the envelope for many models. We presume that models have envelopes of effectiveness, within which fairly simple adaptations continue to

yield good results. Establishing outer boundaries, beyond which more than simple adaptations may be required, requires additional research. Once enough adaptations have been established, it is unlikely that subsequent adaptations of similar models for similar purposes need to be evaluated to full criteria in order to be considered reasonably supported. For example, given that MTFC has demonstrated effectiveness with teen delinquents, and an adapted version (Project KEEP) also improves outcomes for young child welfare foster children, it might be unreasonable to require an adaptation for teen child welfare foster children to produce two independent RCTs before treating that adaptation as a well-supported treatment. A similar point might be made within a family of models. For example, if a group of very similar behavioral parent training models are supported to reduce risk for physical abuse, this evidence might add support to other models from the same closely related family.

Not all areas of child maltreatment practice have benefitted equally from model borrowing. Interventions for child neglect, in particular, have seen little progress toward identifying well-supported practice models or cross-cultural exchange with other areas. What limited adaptation work has been done suggests that neglect outcomes may fall outside the envelope for many established models. For example, PCIT benefits appear limited to reducing future physical abuse reports, not neglect reports. There might be several reasons why developing effective models for neglect is especially challenging. There are no obvious related mental health treatment fields from which to borrow. Neglect is often embedded in a context of deep poverty and social disadvantage, and in some cases can represent a chronic life situation. Compared to physical abuse and sexual abuse, it can be difficult to identify which specific behaviors or circumstances need to change. An almost unlimited number of potential change targets is common in neglect cases including unemployment, isolation, drug or alcohol problems, domestic violence, low education, limited caregiving skills, basic needs, low neighborhood cohesiveness, exposure to violence, marginalization, and discrimination. All of these are formidable problems in their own right, and it is difficult to know which to prioritize or where service efforts might have much impact within a time frame that matches the child's needs for safety and permanency. Although it might be tempting to prescribe a service for every problem in an effort to be comprehensive, this is not feasible and is probably ultimately counterproductive. Stacking multiple services may be well-intentioned, but often impairs outcomes rather than enhancing them (Kaminski et al., 2008), and the analogy to polypharmacy in psychiatry is apt. There is simply insufficient scientific knowledge about neglect, and interventions for neglect, to guide prescriptive processes. Recently, a consortium of federal agencies, including the National Institute of Health (NIH), the Administration on Children, Youth, and Families (ACYF), and the Centers for Disease Control (CDC), have coordinated funding efforts to increase both basic science and intervention research focusing on child neglect. These efforts need to continue. Among existing models, The SafeCare model is viewed as especially promising and is currently the subject of considerable development research.

Among treatments for physical abuse behavior, most of the better supported models are adapted from behavioral parent training programs originally developed to treat child behavior problems. These models share considerable curriculum content in common, although they differ in delivery approach. This suggests that other and similar behavioral parent training models might be similarly effective, and that selection from among these models might depend on which delivery approach best fits the service context and population needs. For example, parenting skill content could be embedded in an existing home visiting program or delivered in a clinic using live dyadic coaching. Alternatively, it could be delivered using modeling in a community-based group. Given similarity in curriculum content between parenting programs for abusive parents and programs for foster parents who are working to manage child behavior problems in foster care, joint or parallel services for both sets of parents might be suggested.

Treatments for sexually abusive behavior present a mixed picture. Treatment response appears to vary considerably across developmental levels. Sexual behavior problems among preteen children appear very responsive to limited and focused treatments, and the envelope for these treatment techniques appears flexible (i.e., group or individual formats appear equally effective, and content can be delivered in either freestanding programs or blended with TF-CBT). At the opposite end of the continuum, the effectiveness of even very intensive, restrictive, and long-term treatment for adult sexual abusers remains controversial and, in our opinion, the current evidence is inconclusive. Findings with adolescent abusers occupy a middle ground between children and adults. It is clear that treatment *can* work very well with this population. All three RCTs of MST with the population have demonstrated sizable effects. But MST has not been widely adopted in programs serving these youth, and the effectiveness of more widely used adaptations of adult sex offender models with this population have not been subjected to any controlled testing. MST is costly, and might be a more intensive treatment than some of these youth require.

Treatments designed specifically for maltreated children are fairly few, and for reasons discussed at the beginning of this chapter, this is to be expected. Maltreatment has diverse sequelae, and it is the severity and form of symptoms that should most directly determine treatment model selection, not the child's status as maltreated. Maltreated children can often be served using regular evidence-based models matched to their main problems or impairments. Educational materials to help children and caregivers understand their abuse experiences might be incorporated into regular treatments as needed or used with asymptomatic children. These sorts of educational materials have not been subjected to controlled trial testing, and so were not reviewed here. In cases of abuse-related PTSD, the main problems or impairments are inherently intertwined with aspects of the maltreatment itself, and there is a well-supported model for these cases that is specifically designed for abused children. The TF-CBT model should be considered the first-line treatment for abuse-related PTSD. It is perhaps the best supported of all psychotherapy models developed for abused children. However, it is important to bear in mind that TF-CBT is intended for children with significant PTSD symptoms, and not all abused children evidence these symptoms.

Attachment problems are another area with a direct link to early maltreatment. Treatment for attachment problems is a controversial area. A set of very concerning treatments have sprung up for children described as attachment disordered, who are usually foster or adoptive children. Most of these models have developed outside mainstream practice and science. The models go under different and changing names, but are commonly known as holding therapy, corrective attachment therapy, rage reduction therapy, or the Evergreen Model. A series of adverse events related to these therapies, including child death, have been reported. Despite multiple cautions (see Chaffin et al., 2006; Lilienfeld, 2007) these concerning attachment therapies continue to flourish in some sectors of foster care and child welfare practice. Although these treatments often advertise themselves to foster or adoptive parents and to case workers as the only effective models for maltreated children with attachment problems, and assert that normal treatments are ineffective, this claim is contrary to the available evidence. In this chapter, we have reviewed an attachment promotion model (attachment and behavioral catch-up, or ABC) that does not use these concerning techniques, is based on a more sound scientific

foundation, and has RCT support in a foster care context.

In 2004, the Kauffman Foundation sponsored a project designed to identify the best supported child abuse treatment models. An advisory panel of over 30 experts was able to identify only three models with more than limited scientific support that were ready for dissemination (Kauffman Foundation, 2004). That same year, the Office for Victims of Crime sponsored a guidelines project. A panel of over a dozen experts reviewed and rated scientific support for 24 child abuse treatments (Saunders, Berliner, & Hanson, 2004). Only one met criteria as well-supported. In this chapter, we have identified seven models that have either been designated as well-supported by the CEBC or likely will be when they are reviewed or their reviews are updated. This is not a large number, but it represents considerable progress in the interim between the 2004 reviews and the present.

REFERENCES

Anda, R. F., Felitti, V. J., Bremmer, J. D., Walker, J. D., Whitfield, C., & Perry, B. D. (2006). The enduring effects of abuse and related adverse experiences in childhood. *European Archives of Psychiatry & Clinical Neuroscience, 256*, 174–186.

Aos, S., Phipps, P., Barnoski, R., & Leib, R. (2001). *The comparative costs and benefits of programs to reduce crime*. Olympia, WA: Washington State Institute for Public Policy. Document 01-05-1201.

Association for the Treatment of Sexual Abusers (ATSA). (2005). *Practice standards and guidelines for members of the Association for the Treatment of Sexual Abusers*. Beaverton, OR: Author.

Bakermans-Kranenburg, M. J., van Ijzendoorn, M. H., & Juffer, F. (2003). Less is more: Meta-analysis of sensitivity and attachment interventions in early childhood. *Psychological Bulletin, 129*, 195–215.

Barth, R. P., Yeaton, J., & Winterfelt, N. (1994). Psychoeducational groups with foster parents of sexually abused children. *Child & Adolescent Social Work Journal, 11*, 405–424.

Baydar, N., Reid, M. J., & Webster-Stratton, C. (2003). The role of mental health factors and program engagement in the effectiveness of a preventive parenting program for Head Start mothers. *Child Development, 74*, 1433–1453.

Bigelow, K. M., & Lutzker, J. R. (1998). Using video to teach planned activities to parents reported for child abuse. *Child & Family Behavior Therapy, 20,* 1–14.

Bonanno, G. A., Wortman, C. B., & Nesse, R. M. (2004). Prospective patterns of resilience and maladjustment during widowhood. *Psychology and Aging, 19,* 260–271.

Boney-McCoy, S., & Finkelhor, D. (1996). Is youth victimization related to trauma symptoms and depression after controlling for prior symptoms and family relationships? A longitudinal, prospective study. *Journal of Consulting and Clinical Psychology, 64,* 1406–1416.

Bor, W., Sanders, M. R., & Markie-Dadds, C. (2002). The effects of the Triple P-Positive Parenting Program on preschool children with co-occurring disruptive behavior and attentional/hyperactive difficulties. *Journal of Abnormal Child Psychology, 30,* 571–587.

Borduin, C. M., Henggeler, S. W., Blaske, D. M., & Stein, R. J. (1990). Multisystemic treatment of adolescent sexual offenders. *International Journal of Offender Therapy & Comparative Criminology, 34,* 105–113.

Borduin, C. M., Schaeffer, C. M., & Heiblum, N. (2009). A randomized clinical trial of multisystemic therapy with juvenile sexual offenders: Effects on youth social ecology and criminal activity. *Journal of Consulting and Clinical Psychology. 77,* 26–37.

Bugental, D. B., Ellerson, P. C., Lin, E. K., Rainey, B., Kokotovic, A., & O'Hara, N. (2002). A cognitive approach to child abuse prevention. *Journal of Family Psychology, 16,* 243–258.

Campbell, R. V., Lutzker, J. R., & Cuvo, A. J. (1982, May). *Comparision study of affection in low socioeconomic families across status of abuse, neglect, and non-abuse neglect.* Paper presented at the Eighth Annual Convention of the Association for Behavior Analysis, Milwaukee, WI.

Campbell, R. V., O'Brien, S., Bickett, A. D., & Lutzker, J. R. (1983). In-home parent training, treatment of migraine headaches, and marital counseling as an ecobehavioral approach to prevent child abuse. *Journal of Behavior Therapy and Experimental Psychiatry, 14,* 147–154.

Carpentier, M. Y., Silovsky, J. F., & Chaffin, M. (2006). Randomized trial of treatment for children with sexual behavior problems: Ten-year follow-up. *Journal of Consulting and Clinical Psychology, 74,* 482–488.

Caspi, A., McClay, J., Moffitt, T., Mill, J., Martin, J., Craig, I. W., . . . Poulton, R. (2002). Role of genotype in the cycle of violence in maltreated children. *Science, 297,* 851–854.

Chaffin, M. (2005). Can we develop evidence based practice for adolescent sex offenders? In R. E. Longo & D. Prescott (Eds.), *Current perspectives: Working with sexually aggressive youth and youth with sexual behavior problems* (pp. 661–681). Holyoke, MA: NEARI Press.

Chaffin, M. (2006). The changing focus of child maltreatment research and practice within psychology. *Journal of Social Issues, 62,* 663–684.

Chaffin, M., Berliner, L., Block, R., Cavanaugh Johnson, T., Friedrich, W. N., Garza Lewis, D., . . . Silovsky, J. (2008). Report of the ATSA Task Force on Children with Sexual Behavior Problems. *Child Maltreatment, 13,* 199–218.

Chaffin, M., Funderburk, B., Bard, D., Valle, L. H., & Gurwitch, R. (2011). A combined motivation and Parent-Child Interaction Therapy package reduces child welfare recidivism in a randomized dismantling field trial. *Journal of Consulting and Clinical Psychology, 79,* 84–95.

Chaffin, M., Hanson, R., Saunders, B. E., Nichols, T., Barnett, D., Zeanah, C., . . . Miller-Perrin, C. (2006). Report of the APSAC Task Force on attachment therapy, reactive attachment disorder, and attachment problems. *Child Maltreatment, 11,* 76–89.

Chaffin, M., Silovsky, J. F., Funderburk, B., Valle, L. A., Brestan, E. V., Balachova, T., . . . Bonner, B. (2004). Parent-Child Interaction Therapy with physically abusive parents: Efficacy for reducing further abuse reports. *Journal of Consulting and Clinical Psychology, 72,* 500–510.

Chaffin, M., Silovsky, J. F., & Vaughn, C. (2005). Temporal concordance of anxiety disorders and child sexual abuse: Implications for direct vs. artifactual effects of sexual abuse. *Journal of Clinical Child and Adolescent Psychology, 34,* 210–222.

Chaffin, M., Valle, L. A., Funderburk, B., Silovsky, J., Gurwitch, R., McCoy, C., . . . Kees, M. (2009). A motivational intervention can improve retention in PCIT for low-motivation child welfare clients. *Child Maltreatment, 14,* 356–368.

Chaffin, M., Wherry, J. N., & Dykman, R. (1997). School age children's coping with sexual abuse: Abuse stresses and symptoms associated with four coping strategies. *Child Abuse & Neglect, 21,* 227–240.

Chamberlain, P. (2003). The Oregon Multidimensional Treatment Foster Care model: Features, outcomes, and progress in dissemination. *Cognitive and Behavioral Practice, 10,* 303–312.

Chamberlain, P., Brown, C. H., Saldana, L., Reid, J., Wang, W., Marsenich, L., . . . Bouwman, G. (2008). Engaging and recruiting counties in an experiment on implementing evidence-based practice in California. *Administration and Policy in Mental Health and Mental Health Services Research, 35,* 250–260.

Chamberlain, P., Moreland, S., & Reid, K. (1992). Enhanced services and stipends for foster parents: Effects on retention rates and outcomes for children. *Child Welfare, 71,* 387–401.

Chamberlain, P., Price, J., Leve, L. D., Laurent, H., Landsverk, J., & Reid, J. B. (2008). Prevention of behavior problems for children in foster care: Outcomes and mediation effects. *Prevention Science, 9,* 17–27.

Chamberlain, P., Price, J., Reid, J. B., & Landsverk, J. (2008). Cascading implementation of a foster and kinship parent intervention. *Child Welfare, 87,* 27–48.

Cohen, J. A., Deblinger, E., Mannarino, A. P., & Steer, R. A. (2004). A multisite, randomized controlled trial for children with sexual abuse-related PTSD symptoms. *Journal of the American Academy of Child and Adolescent Psychiatry, 43,* 393–402.

Cohen, J. A., & Mannarino, A. P. (1998). Interventions for sexually abused children: Initial treatment outcome findings. *Child Maltreatment, 3,* 17–26.

Cohen, J. A., & Mannarino, A. P. (1996). A treatment outcome study for sexually abused preschool children: Initial findings. *Journal of the American Academy of Child and Adolescent Psychiatry, 35,* 42–50.

Cohen, J. A., & Mannarino, A. P. (1997). A treatment study for sexually abused preschool children: Outcome during a one-year follow-up. *Journal of the American Academy of Child and Adolescent Psychiatry, 36,* 1228–1235.

Cohen, J. A., & Mannarino, A. P. (2000). Predictors of treatment outcome in sexually abused children. *Child Abuse & Neglect, 24,* 983–994.

Cohen, J. A., & Mannarino, A. P. (2008). Disseminating and implementing trauma-focused CBT in community settings. *Trauma Violence Abuse, 9,* 214–226.

Cohen, J. A., Mannarino, A. P., & Deblinger, E. (2006). *Treating trauma and traumatic grief in children and adolescents.* New York, NY: Guilford.

Cohen, J. A., Mannarino, A. P., & Knudsen, K. (2005). Treating sexually abused children: One year follow-up of a randomized controlled trial. *Child Abuse & Neglect, 29,* 135–146.

Curtis, N. M., Ronan, K. R., & Borduin, C. M. (2004). Multisystemic treatment: A meta-analysis of outcome studies. *Journal of Family Psychology, 18,* 411–419.

Deblinger, E., Lippmann, J., & Steer, R. (1996). Sexually abused children suffering posttraumatic stress symptoms: Initial treatment outcome findings. *Child Maltreatment, 1,* 310–321.

Deblinger, E., Stauffer, L. B., & Steer, R. A. (2001). Comparitive efficacies of supportive and cognitive behavioral group therapies for young children who have been sexually abused and their non-offending mothers. *Child Maltreatment, 6,* 332–343.

Deblinger, E., Steer, R. A., & Lippmann, J. (1999). Two-year follow-up study of cognitive behavioral therapy for sexually abused children suffering from post-traumatic stress symptoms. *Child Abuse & Neglect, 23,* 1371–1378.

De Graaf, I., Speetjens, P., Smit, F., de Wolff, M., & Tavecchio, L. (2008). Effectiveness of the Triple P Positive Parenting Program on parenting: A meta-analysis. *Family Relations, 57,* 553–566.

DePanfilis, D., & Dubowitz, H. (2005). Family Connections: A program for preventing child neglect. *Child Maltreatment, 10,* 108–123.

DePanfilis, D., Dubowitz, H., & Kunz, J. (2008). Assessing the cost-effectiveness of Family Connections. *Child Abuse & Neglect, 32,* 335–351.

Dozier, M., Lindhiem, O., Lewis, E., Bick, J., Bernard, K., Brohawn, D., . . . Peloso, E. (2009). Effects of a foster parent training program on young children's attachment behaviors: Preliminary evidence from a randomized clinical trial. *Child and Adolescent Social Work Journal, 26,* 321–332.

Dozier, M., Dozier, D., & Manni, M. (2002). Recognizing the special needs of infants' and toddlers' foster parents: Development of a relational intervention. *Zero to Three Bulletin, 22,* 7–13.

Dozier, M., Peloso, E., Lewis, E., Laurenceau, J., & Levine, S. (2008). Effects of an attachment based intervention on the cortisol production of infants and toddlers in foster care. *Development and Psychopathology, 20,* 845–859.

Dozier, M., Peloso, E., Lindheim, O., Gordon, M. K., Manni, M., Sepulveda, S., . . . Levine, S. (2006). Developing evidence-based interventions for foster children: An example of a randomized clinical trial with infants and toddlers. *Journal of Social Issues, 62,* 767–785.

Dubowitz, H., Newton, R. R., Litrownik, A. J., Lewis, T., Briggs, E. C., Thompson, R., . . . Feerick, M. M. (2005). Examination of a conceptual model of child neglect. *Child Maltreatment, 10,* 173–189.

Eckenrode, J., Rowe, E., Laird, M., & Brathwaite, J. (1995). Mobility as a mediator of the effects of child maltreatment on academic performance. *Child Development, 66,* 1130–1142.

Eddy, J. M., Whaley, R. B., & Chamberlain, P. (2004). The prevention of violent behavior by chronic and serious male juvenile offenders: A 2-year follow-up of a randomized clinical trial. *Journal of Emotional and Behavioral Disorders, 12,* 2–8.

Erickson, M. F., & Egeland, B. (2002). Child neglect. In J. E. B. Myers, L. Berliner, J. Briere, C. T. Hendrix, C. Jenny, & T. A. Reid (Eds.), *The APSAC handbook on child maltreatment: Second edition* (pp. 3–20). Thousand Oaks, CA: Sage.

Eyberg, S. M., & Boggs, S. R. (1998). Parent-child interaction therapy: A psychosocial intervention for the treatment of young conduct-disordered children. In J. M. Briesmeister & C. E. Schaefer (Eds.), *Handbook of parent training: Parents as co-therapists for children's behavior problems* (2nd ed., pp. 61–97). Hoboken, NJ: Wiley.

Eyberg, S. M., Boggs, S. R., & Algina, J. (1995). Parent-child interaction therapy: A psychosocial model for the treatment of young children with conduct problem behavior and their families. *Psychopharmacology Bulletin, 31,* 83–91.

Feiring, C., & Taska, L. S. (2005). The persistence of shame following sexual abuse: A longitudinal look at risk and recovery. *Child Maltreatment, 10,* 337–349.

Finkelhor, D., Ormrod, R. K., & Turner, H. A. (2007). Polyvictimization and trauma in a national longitudinal cohort. *Development and Psychopathology, 19,* 149–166.

Fraser, M. W., Walton, E., Lewis, R. E., Pecora, P. J., & Walton, W. K. (1996). An experiment in family reunification: Correlates of outcomes at one-year follow-up. *Children and Youth Services Review, 18,* 335–361.

Friedrich, W. N. (1993). Sexual victimization and sexual behavior in children: A review of recent literature. *Child Abuse & Neglect, 17,* 59–66.

Gardner, F., Burton, J., & Klimes, I. (2006). Randomised controlled trial of a parenting intervention in the voluntary sector for reducing child conduct problems: Outcomes and mechanisms of change. *Journal of Child Psychology and Psychiatry, 47,* 1123–1132.

Gershater-Molko, R. M., Lutzker, J. R., & Wesch, D. (2002). Using recidivism data to evaluate Project Safecare: Teaching bonding, safety and healthcare skills to parents. *Child Maltreatment, 7,* 277–285.

Girvin, H., DePanfilis, D., & Daining, C. (2007). Predicting program completion among families enrolled in a child neglect prevention intervention. *Research on Social Work Practice, 17,* 674–685.

Gross, D., Fogg, L., Webster-Stratton, C., Garvey, C., Julion, W., & Grady, J. (2003). Parent training of toddlers in day care in low-income urban communities. *Journal of Consulting and Clinical Psychology, 71,* 261–278.

Hanson, R. F., Saunders, B., Kilpatrick, D., Resnick, H., Crouch, J. A., & Duncan, R. (2001). Impact of childhood rape and aggravated assault on adult mental health. *American Journal of Orthopsychiatry, 71,* 108–119.

Henggeler, S. W., Letourneau, E. J., Chapman, J. E., Borduin, C. M., Schewe, P. A., & McCart, M. R. (2009). Mediators of change for multisystemic therapy with juvenile sexual offenders. *Journal of Consulting and Clinical Psychology, 77,* 451–462.

Hood, K. K., & Eyberg, S. M. (2003). Outcomes of Parent-Child Interaction Therapy: Mothers' reports of maintenance three to six years after treatment. *Journal of Clinical Child and Adolescent Psychology, 32,* 419–429.

Hurlburt, M. S., Leslie, L. K., Landsverk, J., Barth, R.P., Burns, B. J., Gibbons, R. D., . . . Zhang, J. (2004). Contextual predictors of mental health service use among children open to child welfare. *Archives of General Psychiatry, 61,* 1217–1224.

Hutchings, J., Bywater, T., Daley, D., Gardner, F., Whitaker, C., Jones, K., . . . Edward, R. T. (2007). Parenting intervention in Sure Start services for children at risk of developing conduct disorder: Pragmatic randomized controlled trial. *British Medical Journal, 334*(7595), 678.

Kaminski, J. W., Valle, L. A., Filene, J. H., & Boyle, C. L. (2008). A meta-analytic review of components associated with parent training program effectiveness. *Journal of Abnormal Child Psychology, 36,* 567–589.

Kauffman Foundation. (2004). *Closing the quality chasm in child abuse treatment: Identifying and disseminating best practices. The findings of the Kauffman Best Practices Project to help children heal from child abuse.* Kansas City, MO: Kauffman Foundation.

Kempe, C. H., Silverman F. N., Steele, B. F., Droegemueller, W., & Silver, H. K. (1962). The battered-child syndrome. *Journal of the American Medical Association, 181,* 17–24.

Kinard, E. M. (1999). Perceived social skills and social competence in maltreated children. *American Journal of Orthopsychiatry, 69,* 465–481.

King, N. J., Tonge, B. J., Mullen, P., Myerson, N., Heyne, D., Rollings, S., . . . Ollendick, T. H. (2000). Treating sexually abused children with posttraumatic stress symptoms: A randomized clinical trial. *Journal of the American Academy of Child and Adolescent Psychiatry, 39,* 1347–1355.

Kinney, J., Dittmar, K., & Firth, W. (1991). Keeping families together: The Homebuilders model. *Children Today, 9,* 14–19.

Kinney, J., Haapala, D., Booth, C., & Leavitt, S. (1990). The Homebuilders model. In J. K. Whittaker, J. Kinnery, E. M. Tracy, & C. Booth (Eds.), *Reaching high-risk families: Intensive family preservation in human services* (pp. 31–64). Hawthorne, NY: Aldine de Gruyter.

Klietz, S. J., Borduin, C. M., & Schaeffer, C. M. (2010). Cost–benefit analysis of multisystemic therapy with serious and violent juvenile offenders. *Journal of Family Psychology, 24,* 657–666.

Kolko, D. (1996). Individual cognitive behavioral treatment and family therapy for physically abused children and their offending parents: A comparison of clinical outcomes. *Child Maltreatment, 1,* 322–342.

Kolko, D. J., & Swenson, C. C. (2002). *Assessing and treating physically abused children and their families: A cognitive behavioral approach.* Thousand Oaks, CA: Sage Publications.

Lee, S., Aos, S., & Miller, M. (2008). *Evidence-based programs to prevent children from entering and remaining in the child welfare system: Benefits and costs for Washington.* Olympia, WA: Washington State Institute for Public Policy, Document No. 08-07-3901.

Letourneau, E. J., Henggeler, S. W., Borduin, C. M., Schewe, P. A., McCart, M. R., Chapman, J. E., & Saldana, L. (2009). Multisystemic therapy for juvenile sexual offenders: 1-year results from a randomized effectiveness trial. *Journal of Family Psychology, 23,* 89–102.

Leung, C., Sanders, M. R., Leung, S., Mak, R., & Lau, J. (2003). An outcome evaluation of the implementation of the Triple P-Positive Parenting Program in Hong Kong. *Family Process, 42*, 531–544.

Leve, L. D., Chamberlain, P., & Reid, J. B. (2005). Intervention outcomes for girls referred from juvenile justice: Effects on delinquency. *Journal of Consulting and Clinical Psychology, 73*, 1181–1185.

Lilienfeld, S. O. (2007). Psychological treatments that cause harm. *Perspectives on Psychological Science, 2*, 53–70.

Linares, L. O., Montalto, D., Li, M. M., & Oza, V. S. (2006). A promising parenting intervention in foster care. *Journal of Consulting and Clinical Psychology, 74*, 32–41.

Lindsey, M. A., Hayward, R. A., & DePanfilis, D. (2010). Gender differences in behavioral outcomes among children at risk of neglect: Findings from a family-focused prevention intervention. *Research on Social Work Practice, 20*, 572–581.

Lipovsky, J., & Stern, P. (1997). Preparing children for court: An interdisciplinary view. *Child Maltreatment, 2*, 150–163.

Littell, J. (2006). The case for multisystemic therapy: Evidence or orthodoxy. *Children and Youth Services Review, 27*, 445–463.

Lutzker, J., & Bigelow, K. (2002). *Reducing child maltreatment: A guidebook for parent services*. New York, NY: Guilford Press.

Lutzker, J. R., Bigelow, K. M., Doctor, R. M., & Kessler, M. L. (1998). Safety, health care, and bonding within an ecobehavioral approach to treating and preventing child abuse and neglect. *Journal of Family Violence, 13*, 163–185.

Lutzker, J. R., Frame, R. E., & Rice, J. M. (1982). Project 12-Ways: An ecobehavioral approach to the treatment and prevention of child abuse and neglect. *Education & Treatment of Children, 5*, 141–155.

Lutzker, J. R., & Rice, J. M. (1987). Using recidivism data to evaluate Project 12-Ways: An ecobehavioral approach to the treatment and prevention of child abuse and neglect. *Journal of Family Violence, 2*, 283–290.

MacMillan, H. L. (1996). History of child protection services. *Canadian Journal of Psychiatry, 45*, 702–710.

Mannariono, A. P., & Cohen, J. A. (1996). Abuse-related attributions and perceptions, general attributions, and locus of control in sexually abused girls. *Journal of Interpersonal Violence, 11*, 162–180.

Marques, J. K., Wiederanders, M., Day, D. M., Nelson, C., & van Ommeren, A. (2005). Effects of a relapse prevention program on sexual recidivism: Final results from California's Sex Offender Treatment and Evaluation Project (SOTEP). *Sexual Abuse: Journal of Research and Treatment, 17*, 79–107.

Marshall, W. L., & Marshall, L. E. (2007). The utility of the random controlled trial for evaluating sexual offender treatment: The gold standard or an inappropriate strategy. *Sexual Abuse: A Journal of Research and Treatment, 19*, 175–191.

Martin, A. J., & Sanders, M. R. (2003). Balancing work and family: A controlled evaluation of the Triple-P Positive Parenting Program as a work-site intervention. *Child and Adolescent Mental Health, 8*, 161–169.

Maughan, A., & Cicchetti, D. (2002). Impact of child maltreatment and interadult violence on children's emotion regulation abilities and socioemotional adjustment. *Child Development, 73*, 1525–1542.

McCabe, K. M., Yeh, M., Garland, A. F., Lau, A. S., & Chavez, C. (2005). The GANA Program: A tailoring approach to adapting parent-child interaction therapy for Mexican Americans. *Education and Treatment of Children, 28*, 111–129.

McNeil, C. B., Capage, L. C., Bahl, A., & Blanc, H. (1999). Importance of early intervention for disruptive behavior problems: Comparison of treatment and waitlist-control groups. *Early Education and Development, 10*, 445–454.

Merrick, M. T., Litrownik, A. J., Everson, M. D., & Cox, C. E. (2008). Beyond sexual abuse: The impact of other maltreatment experiences on sexualized behaviors. *Child Maltreatment, 13*, 122–132.

Mihalic, S., Irwin, K., Elliott, D., Fagan, A., & Hansen, D. (2001, July). *Blueprints for violence prevention. Juvenile Justice Bulletin*. Washington, DC: U.S. Office for Juvenile Justice and Violence Prevention (pp. 1–15).

Nixon, R. D. V. (2001). Changes in hyperactivity and temperament in behaviourally disturbed preschoolers after parent-child interaction therapy (PCIT). *Behaviour Change, 18*, 168–176.

Nixon, R. D. V., Sweeney, L., Erickson, D. B., & Touyz, S. W. (2003). Parent-child interaction therapy: A comparison of standard and abbreviated treatments for oppositional defiant preschoolers. *Journal of Community and Clinical Psychology, 71*, 251–260.

Nixon, R. D. V., Sweeney, L., Erickson, D. B., & Touyz, S. W. (2004). Parent-child interaction therapy: One- and two-year follow-up of standard and abbreviated treatments for oppositional preschoolers. *Journal of Abnormal Child Psychology, 32*, 263–271.

Nowak, C., & Heinrichs, N. (2008). A comprehensive meta-analysis of Triple P-Positive Parenting Program using hierarchical linear modeling: Effectiveness and moderating variables. *Clinical Child and Family Psychology Review, 11*, 114–144.

Patterson, G. R., Reid, J. B., & Eddy, J. M. (2002). A brief history of the Oregon model. In J. B. Reid, G. R. Patterson, & J. Snyder (Eds.), *Antisocial behavior in children and adolescents: A developmental analysis and model for intervention* (pp. 3–20). Washington, DC: American Psychological Association.

Pithers, W. D., & Cumming, G. F. (1995). Relapse prevention: A method for enhancing behavioral self-management and external supervision of the sexual aggressor. In H. R. Cellini (Ed.), *The sex offender: Corrections, treatment and legal practice* (pp. 20–32). Kingston, NJ: Civic Research Institute.

Pithers, W. D., Gray, A., Busconi, A., & Houchens, P. (1998). Children with sexual behavior problems: Identification of five distinct child types and related treatment considerations. *Child Maltreatment, 3,* 384–406.

Price, J. M., Chamberlain, P., Landsverk, J., Reid, J. B., Leve, L. D., & Laurent, H. (2008). Effects of a foster parent training intervention on placement changes of children in foster care. *Child Maltreatment, 13,* 64–75.

Prinz, R. J., Sanders, M. R., Shapiro, C. J., Whitaker, D. J., & Lutzker, J. R. (2009). Population-based prevention of child maltreatment: The U.S. triple P system population trial. *Prevention Science, 10,* 1–12.

Radbill, S. X. (1987). Children in a world of violence: A history of child abuse. In R. E. Helfer & R. S. Kempe (Eds.), *The battered child* (4th rev. & exp. ed., pp. 3–22). Chicago, IL: University of Chicago Press.

Reid, M. J., Webster-Stratton, C., & Baydar, N. (2004). Halting the development of conduct problems in Head Start children: The effect of parent training. *Journal of Clinical Child and Adolescent Psychology, 33,* 279–291.

Reid, M. J., Webster-Stratton, C., & Beauchaine, T. P. (2001). Parent training in Head Start: A comparison of program response among African American, Asian American, Caucasian, and Hispanic mothers. *Prevention Science, 2,* 209–227.

Rogosch, F. A., Cicchetti, D., & Aber, J. L. (1995). The role of child maltreatment in early deviations in cognitive and affective processing abilities and later peer relationship problems. *Development and Psychopathology, 7,* 591–609.

Rosenfield-Schlichter, M. D., Sarber, R. E., Bueno, G., Greene, B. F., & Lutzker, J. R. (1983). Maintaining accountability for an ecobehavioral treatment of one aspect of child neglect: Personal cleanliness. *Education & Treatment of Children, 6,* 153–164.

Sanders, M. R., Markie-Dadds, C., Tully, L. A., & Bor, W. (2000). The Triple P-Positive Parent Program: A comparison of enhanced, standard, and behavioral family intervention for parents of children with early onset conduct problems. *Journal of Consulting and Clinical Psychology, 68,* 624–640.

Sanders, M. R., Pidgeon, A., Gravestock, F., Connors, M. D., Brown, S., & Young, R. M. (2004). Does parental attributional retraining and anger management enhance the effects of the Triple P-Positive Parenting Program with parents at-risk of child maltreatment? *Behavior Therapy, 35,* 513–535.

Saunders, B. E., Berliner, L., & Hanson, R. F. (Eds.). (2004). *Child physical and sexual abuse: Guidelines for treatment* (revised report, April 26, 2004). Charleston, SC: National Crime Victims Research and Treatment Center.

Sedlack, A. J., & Broadhurst, D. D. (1996). *Executive summary of the Third National Incidence Study of Child Abuse and Neglect.* Washington, DC: U.S. Department of Health and Human Services.

Shuhman, E. M., Foote, R. C., Eyberg, S. M., Boggs, S., & Algina, J. (1998). Efficacy of Parent Child Interaction Therapy: Interim report of a randomized trial with short term maintenance. *Journal of Clinical Child Psychology, 27,* 34–45.

Silovsky, J. F., Bard, D., Chaffin, M., Hecht, D., Burris, L., Owora, A., . . . Lutzker, J. (2011). Prevention of child maltreatment in high-risk rural families: A randomized clinical trial with child welfare outcomes. *Children and Youth Services Review, 33,* 1435–1444.

Silovsky, J. F., Niec, L., Bard, D., & Hecht, D. B. (2007). Treatment for preschool children with interpersonal sexual behavior problems: A pilot study. *Journal of Clinical Child and Adolescent Psychology, 36,* 378–391.

Smith, P., Yule, W., Perrin, S., Tranah, T., Dalgleish, T., & Clark, D. M. (2007). Cognitive-behavioral therapy for PTSD in children and adolescents: A preliminary randomized controlled trial. *Journal of the American Academy of Child and Adolescent Psychiatry, 46,* 1051–1061.

St. Amand, A., Bard, D. E., & Silovsky, J. F. Meta-analysis of treatment for child sexual behavior problems: Practice elements and outcomes. *Child Maltreatment. Special Issue: Children with Sexual Behavior Problems, 13,* 145–116.

Staudt, M., & Drake, B. (2002). Intensive family preservation services: Where's the crisis? *Children and Youth Services Review, 24,* 777–795.

Stauffer, L. B., & Deblinger, E. (1996). Cognitive behavioral groups for nonoffending mothers and their young sexually abused children: A preliminary treatment outcome study. *Child Maltreatment, 1,* 65–76.

Steen, C. (2000). *The adult relapse prevention workbook.* Brandon, VT: Safer Society Press.

Tertinger, D. A., Greene, B. F., & Lutzker, J. R. (1984). Home safety: Development and validation of one component of an ecobehavioral treatment program for abused and neglected children. *Journal of Applied Behavior Analysis, 17,* 159–174.

Thomas, R., & Zimmer-Gembeck, M. J. (2011). Accumulating evidence for Parent-Child Interaction Therapy in the prevention of child maltreatment. *Child Development, 82,* 177–192.

Thomas, R., & Zimmer-Gembeck, M. J. (2007). Behavioral outcomes of Parent-Child Interaction Therapy and Triple P-Positive Parenting Program: A review and meta-analysis. *Journal of Abnormal Child Psychology, 35,* 475–495.

Timmer, S. G., Urquiza, A. J., & Zebell, N. (2006). Challenging foster caregiver-maltreated child relationships: The effectiveness of parent-child interaction therapy. *Children and Youth Services Review, 28,* 1–19.

Timmer, S. G., Ware, L. M., Urquiza, A. J., & Zebell, N. M. (2010). The effectiveness of Parent-Child Interaction Therapy for victims of interparental violence. *Violence and Victims, 25,* 486–503.

Turner, K. M. T., Richards, M., & Sanders, M. R. (2007). Randomized clinical trial of a group parent education programme for Australian indigenous families. *Journal of Paediatrics and Child Health, 43,* 429–437.

Tyler, K. A., Johnson, K. A., & Brownridge, D. A. (2008). A longitudinal study of the effects of child maltreatment on later outcomes among high-risk adolescents. *Journal of Youth and Adolescence, 37,* 506–521.

Urquiza, A. J., & McNeil, C. B. (1996). Parent-child interaction therapy: An intensive dyadic intervention for physically abusive families. *Child Maltreatment, 1,* 134–144.

U.S. Department of Health and Human Services. (1995). *A review of family preservation and family reunification programs.* James Bell & Associates, Inc. and the Chapin Hall Center for Children at the University of Chicago. Washington, DC: Author.

U.S. Department of Health and Human Services. (2001). *Youth violence: A report of the Surgeon General.* Rockville, MD: National Center for Injury Prevention and Control; Substance Abuse and Mental Health Services Administration, Center for Mental Health Services; and National Institutes of Health, National Institute of Mental Health.

U.S. Department of Health and Human Services, Administration on Children, Youth and Families, Children's Bureau (2010). *Child maltreatment 2009.* Retrieved from www.acf.hhs.gov/programs/cb/pubs/cm09/cm09.pdf

Walton, E. (1998). In-home family-focused reunification: A six-year follow-up of a successful experiment. *Social Work Research, 22,* 205–214.

Ward, T., & Marshall, W. L. (2004). Good lives, aetiology and the rehabilitation of sex offenders: A bridging theory. *Journal of Sexual Aggression, 10,* 153–169.

Ware, L. M. (2008). Efficacy of in-home parent-child interaction therapy. *Dissertation Abstracts International: Section B: Sciences and Engineering, 68*(8-B), 5598.

Wesch, D., & Lutzker, J. R. (1991). A comprehensive 5-year evaluation of Project 12-Ways: An ecobehavioral program for treating and preventing child abuse and neglect. *Journal of Family Violence, 6,* 17–35.

Wood, S., Baron, K., & Schroeder, C. (1988). In-home treatment of abusive families: Cost and placement at one year. *Psychotherapy, 25,* 409–414.

Zubrick, S. R., Ward, K. A., Silburn, S. R., Lawrence, D., Williams, A. A., Blair, E., . . . Sanders, M. R. (2005). Prevention of child behavior problems through universal implementation of a group behavioral family intervention. *Prevention Science, 6,* 287–304.

Author Index

Subject Index